1943 Abraham Maslow (1908–1970) publishes *A Theory of Motivation*, establishing the hierarchy of needs.

1950 Erik Erikson (1902–1994) expands on Freud's theory to include social aspects of personality development with the publication of *Childhood and Society*.

©2016 MACMILLAN

1951 John Bowlby (1907–1990) publishes *Maternal Care and Mental Health*, one of his first works on the importance of parent–child attachment.

MONKEY BUSINESS IMAGES/SHUTTERSTOCK

1953 Publication of the first papers describing DNA, our genetic blueprint.

DIGITAL VISION VECTORS/GETTY IMAGES

1957 Harry Harlow (1905–1981) publishes *Love in Infant Monkeys*, describing his research on attachment in rhesus monkeys.

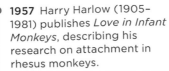

MARTIN ROGERS/GETTY IMAGES

1961 The morning sickness drug thalidomide is banned after children are born with serious birth defects, calling attention to the problem of teratogens during pregnancy.

1961 Alfred Bandura (b. 1925) conducts the Bobo Doll experiments, leading to the development of social learning theory.

1979 Urie Bronfenbrenner (1917–2005) publishes his work on ecological systems theory

1986 John Gottman (b. 1942) founded the "Love Lab" at the University of Washington to study what makes relationships work.

1987 Carolyn Rovee-Collier (1942–2014) shows that even young infants can remember in her classic mobile experiments.

FOTOSEARCH/FOTOSEARCH/SUPERSTOCK

1990 The United Nations treaty *Convention on the Rights of the Child* children are no longer considered solely the possession of their parents. Currently all UN nations have signed on, except Somalia, South Sudan, and the United States.

TONGRO/GETTY IMAGES

1993 Howard Gardner (b. 1943) publishes *Multiple Intelligences*, a major new understanding of the diversity of human intellectual abilities. Gardner has since revised and expanded his ideas in many ways.

| | | | |
| 1800 | | 1900 | 2000 |

ANYAIVANOVA/ISTOCK/THINKSTOCK

1953 B.F. Skinner (1904–1990) conducts experiments on rats and establishes operant conditioning.

1955 Emmy Werner (b. 1929) begins her Kauai study, which focuses on the power of resilience.

DONNA DAY/EXACTOSTOCK-1598/SUPERSTOCK

1956 K. Warner Schaie's (b. 1928) Seattle Longitudinal Study of Adult Intelligence begins.

1965 Head Start, an early-childhood-education program, launched in the United States.

1965 Mary Ainsworth (1913–1999) starts using the "Strange Situation" to measure attachment.

1966 Diana Baumrind (b. 1928) publishes her first work on parenting styles.

1972 Beginning of the Dunedin, New Zealand, study—one of the first longitudinal studies to include genetic markers.

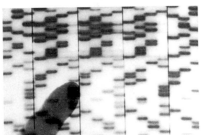
TETRA IMAGES/GETTY IMAGES

1990–Present New brain imaging technology allows pinpointing of brain areas involved in everything from executive function to Alzheimer's disease.

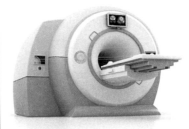
©2016 MACMILLAN
BARIS SIMSEK/GETTY IMAGES

1990 Barbara Rogoff (b. 1950) publishes *Apprenticeship in Thinking*, making developmentalists more aware of the significance of culture and context. Rogoff provided new insights and appreciation of child-rearing in Latin America.

1994 Steven Pinker (b. 1954) publishes *The Language Instinct*, focusing attention on the interaction between neuroscience and behavior, helping developmentalists understand the need for physiological understanding as part of human growth. These themes continue in his later work, such as *How the Mind Works* in 1997.

1995–Present Onward. There are many more discoveries and research chronicled in this book.

BLEND IMAGES/BLEND IMAGES/SUPERSTOCK

The Developing Person Through Childhood and Adolescence

New Visualizing Development

Also new to this edition are full-page illustrations of key topics in development. Every chapter now includes an infographic display of data on key issues ranging from the biology of twin births to the milestones in the journey to emerging adulthood across the world. These illustrations combine global statistics, maps, charts, and photographs. Aware of the many modalities of learning, I have worked closely with noted designer Charles Yuen to use these infographics to reinforce key ideas.

New Online Data Connections Activities

Understanding how we use data as developmentalists is an important part of what students learn in their courses. Data is a crucial part of understanding that developmental science is a science—and not just common sense. In this edition, I have created interactive activities based on important data from rates of breast-feeding to risk taking in adolescence. These are designed for students to be able to practice interpreting data.

For example, how do rates of breast-feeding differ by state across the United States and around the world, or how do rates of various risk-taking behaviors differ by gender or age during adolescence? These interactive activities are designed to engage students, make them more active learners, help them retain important material, and develop a deeper understanding of the quantitative data that we use in development. Instructors can assign these activities in the online LaunchPad that accompanies this book.

Child Development and Nursing Career Correlation Guides

Many students taking this course will be interested in future careers in nursing or early child development. This book and accompanying testing material are fully correlated to the NAEYC (National Association for the Education of Young Children) career preparation goals and the NCLEX (nursing) licensure exams.

Content Changes in the Tenth Edition

Child and adolescent development, like all sciences, builds on past learning. Many facts and concepts are scaffolds that remain strong over time: stages and ages, norms and variations, dangers and diversities, classic theories and fascinating applications. However, the study of development is continually changed by

Bonded That fathers enjoy their sons is not surprising, but notice the infant reaching for Dad's face. At this age, infants show their trust in adults by grabbing and reaching.

Family Pride Grandpa Charilaos is proud of his tavern in northern Greece (central Macedonia), but he is even more proud of his talented grandchildren, including Maria Soni (shown here). Note her expert fingering. Her father and mother also play instruments; is that nature or nurture?

discoveries and experiences, so no paragraph in this tenth edition is exactly what it was in the first edition, and only a few are exactly like the ninth.

Highlights of updates in the text appear below.

Part I. The Beginnings
1. Introduction

- New chapter opener on Professor Berger's experience at the birth of her grandson, Caleb, illustrates some of the reasons for the study of human development
- Discussion of the three domains of development brought forward in the chapter
- Differential susceptibility illustrated with example of children with a particular version of the serotonin transporter gene 5-HTTPLR
- Rationale for the shift by developmentalists from studying only the period of birth through adolescence to studying the entire life span explained in full
- The difference-equals-deficit error defined and discussed
- Expanded section on sexual orientation
- New *Opposing Perspectives* box considers use of the word *race*
- Plasticity now discussed in the context of the dynamic-systems approach
- New *A View from Science* box discusses the fear of a vaccination–autism link
- *Visualizing Development: Diverse Complexities*

2. Theories

- New chapter opener illustrates three aspects shared by all theories: (1) behavior can be surprising, (2) humans develop theories to explain everything, and (3) experience and culture matter
- A separate major section now devoted to discussion of each theory
- Classical conditioning illustrated by example of *white coat syndrome*
- Discussion of information processing expanded with inclusion of new insights from neuroscience, including photos comparing brain scans of healthy adults with those of adults who were diagnosed with ADHD as children
- Physical therapists' tailoring of treatment regimes to each patient used as an example of guiding someone through the zone of proximal development
- The introduction to the universal perspective (humanism and evolutionary theory) has been expanded
- In discussion of humanism: long-term effects on children whose parents did not have unconditional positive regard for them
- In discussion of evolutionary theory: a new subsection on evolution and culture
- *Visualizing Development: Breast-feeding Diversity*

3. The New Genetics

- Major sections reorganized for smoother information flow
- Expanded explanation of genes includes discussion of epigenetics
- In discussion of genetic variations: a new paragraph on *jumping* discusses transfer of some genetic material from one chromosome to the other when sperm and ova pair up
- New section on male/female differences in infertility
- Expanded section on IVF
- *Visualizing Development: One Baby or More*

4. Prenatal Development and Birth

- New chapter opener about the birth of Professor Berger's grandson illustrates constancies in prenatal development and birth as well changes in culture and context over time

- Section on the final three months of pregnancy reorganized to include subsections on organ maturation and the mother–child relationship
- Expanded section on cesarean delivery, including a paragraph on negative factors that appear months to years after birth
- Behavioral teratogens now discussed in a separate subsection
- New *A View from Science* box discusses conflicting advice given to pregnant women about their health and potential teratogens
- New subsection *What Do We Know?* raises questions about the state of our knowledge of teratogens and their effects
- Discussion of low birthweight now a separate major section
- New subsection on family bonding
- *Visualizing Development: A Healthy Newborn*

Part II. The First Two Years
5. The First Two Years: Biosocial Development
- *Failure to thrive* now discussed early in the chapter in explanation of percentile rankings
- New comparison of infants' sleep patterns in various cultures
- New figure (5.3) indicates percentage of co-sleeping infants in 14 countries
- New subsection on specialization of brain areas
- In section on brain development: a significantly expanded subsection on transient exuberance of dendrites and pruning
- Expanded introduction to the section on motor skills
- New subsection on dynamic sensory motor systems in discussion of motor skills
- New *A Case to Study* box on SIDS
- *Visualizing Development: Nature, Nurture, and the Brain*

6. The First Two Years: Cognitive Development
- New chapter opener about Professor Berger's conversation with a dentist parallels steps in the development of infant cognition
- New *A View from Science* box explores insights from modern research about Piaget's stage theory
- fNIRS (functional near infrared spectroscopy) has been added to the list (and illustration) of techniques used by neuroscientists to understand brain function
- Revised and expanded introduction to information-processing theory
- In section on information processing: discussion of memory has been substantially reorganized and revised
- Research on the ability of infants of bilingual mothers ability to distinguish between the two languages has been added
- New research on cultural differences in what sounds infants prefer
- Discussion of *mean length of utterance (MLU)* as a measure of a child's language progress
- *Visualizing Development: Early Communication and Language Development*

7. The First Two Years: Psychosocial Development
- Chapter substantially reorganized: new major section *Brain and Emotions; The Development of Social Bonds* major section brought forward and now precedes the major section *Theories of Infant Psychosocial Development*
- Expanded discussion of infants' experience of fear
- *Growth of the Brain* section significantly revised: now includes discussion of how cultural differences are encoded in the brain as well as revised subsections on development of social impulses and on stress

Proud Peruvian In rural Peru, an early-education program (Pronoei) encourages community involvement and traditional culture. Preschoolers, like this girl in a holiday parade, are proud to be themselves, and that helps them become healthy and strong.

Bliss for Boys But not for moms. Finger painting develops fine motor skills, which is part of the preschool curriculum in early childhood. This boy shows why most stay-home 3-year-olds miss out on this joy.

- Section on behaviorism and social learning now includes research showing that variations in proximal and distal parenting lead to variations in toddler behavior
- New sections on how humanism and evolutionary theory explain infant psychosocial development
- Section on infant day care substantially revised and reorganized; now includes a new *A View from Science: The Mixed Realities of Infant Day Care*
- *Visualizing Development: Developing Attachment*

Part III. Early Childhood
8. Early Childhood: Biosocial Development
- *Child Maltreatment* now a major section
- New research on nutrition, including long-term effects of childhood obesity
- Section on nutritional deficiencies revised and expanded
- Intellectual disability as a result of failure of the corpus callosum to develop
- Expanded section on stress hormones and their impact
- New *A View from Science: Eliminating Lead* includes illustration of the effects of lead exposure on the brain
- New subhead *Accuracy of State Data* discusses inconsistencies in how different states report child maltreatment
- New subsection presents new research on long-term impact of child maltreatment on development of social skills
- *Visualizing Development: Developing Motor Skills*

9. Early Childhood: Cognitive Development
- New chapter opener presents cognitive characteristics of a young child as exemplified in Professor Berger's conversation with her young grandson when he tried to convince her to play an imaginary basketball game
- Section on conservation and logic significantly revised with insights from recent research
- New *A Case to Study: Stones in the Belly* illustrates preoperational cognition
- New subsection *Overimitation* expands discussion in previous edition
- New subsection *STEM Learning* looks at Vygotsky's theory as it is applies to the current emphasis on STEM education
- Recent research on the naming explosion and fast-mapping
- *Visualizing Development: Early-Childhood Schooling*

10. Early Childhood: Psychosocial Development
- Section on protective optimism revised
- Introduction to major section *Play* revised and expanded
- Section on *Culture and Cohort* revised and expanded; includes figure showing time spent in various activities by children from four cultures/ethnicities
- Section on drama and pretending revised with new data on how much "screen time" young children have each day
- Section on gender development brought forward
- Section on moral development significantly reorganized and expanded
- *Visualizing Development: Less Play, Less Safe?*

Part IV. Middle Childhood
11. Middle Childhood: Biosocial Development
- *Special Education* now a major section
- New chapter opener highlights questions about parents' impact on a child's physical development
- New section on children's health habits
- New *A View from Science: What Causes Childhood Obesity?*

No Toys Boys in middle childhood are happiest playing outside with equipment designed for work. This wheelbarrow is perfect, especially because at any moment the pusher might tip it.

- New major section *Developmental Psychopathology* is a revised and reorganized treatment of issues around children with special needs, including a revised section on ADHD and drug treatments for children
- New *A Case to Study: Lynda Is Getting Worse* illustrates the difficulty in diagnosing psychopathologies
- New Figure 11.4 shows percentage of 6- to 17-year-olds medicated for emotional or behavioral difficulties during the last six months
- Dysgraphia added to the discussion of specific learning disorders
- New Figure 11.5 shows percentage of 3- to 21-year-olds with special educational needs in 1981, 2001, 2012
- *Visualizing Development: Childhood Obesity Around the Globe*

12. Middle Childhood: Cognitive Development
- Recent research added to the *Information Processing* section detailing how the ability to estimate magnitude (such as understanding the relative size of fractions) predicts later math proficiency
- Section on bilingual education brought forward
- Recent research on academic achievement that shows children have to internalize the positive expectations of teachers and parents for those expectations to motivate learning
- Recent research about the provision (or lack of provision) of arts education
- Section on international testing revised and expanded
- New research on changes in teachers' and state legislators' attitudes toward the Common Core (more negative)
- Second-language learning as an example of how policy affects education
- New section on ethnic diversity in U.S. schools
- *Visualizing Development: Education in Middle Childhood Around the World*

13. Middle Childhood: Psychosocial Development
- Social rejection as a cause and a consequence of feeling inferior
- Revised section on self-concept includes focus on the importance of social comparison
- New section *Culture and Self-Esteem* discusses what healthy self-esteem means in different cultures
- Revised section on two-parent families
- *Visualizing Development: A Wedding, or Not? Family Structures Around the World*

Part V. Adolescence
14. Adolescence: Biosocial Development
- Chapter reorganized: section on growth brought forward under new major heading *Growth and Nutrition;* sections on *Brain Development* and *Sexual Maturation* each now a major heading
- New *A View from Science: Stress and Puberty*
- Section *Body Fat and Chemicals* combines sections *Body Fat* and *Hormones* from previous edition
- Discussion of brain development brought forward
- *Visualizing Development: The Timing of Puberty*

15. Adolescence: Cognitive Development
- Discussion of the imaginary audience revised and updated to include impact of social media
- Three short problems have been added for students to test themselves on intuitive and analytical reasoning

Don't Worry Contemporary teenagers, like this couple, are more likely to be seen in public hugging and kissing but are less likely to be sexually active than similar couples were 20 years ago.

- Major section on technology and cognition reorganized and substantially revised under the heading *Digital Natives*
- New section on the dangers of sexting
- *Visualizing Development: Thinking in Adolescence*

16. Adolescence: Psychosocial Development

- Significantly revised introduction to the section on peer pressure
- New section on social networking in discussion of peers
- New *Opposing Perspectives: E-cigarettes: Path to Addiction or Healthy Choice?*
- *Visualizing Development: How Many Adolescents Are in School?*

Epilogue: Emerging Adulthood

- Section on biosocial development substantially revised; now includes discussion of organ reserve, homeostasis, allostasis
- New *A Case to Study: An Adrenaline Junkie*
- Revised and expanded section on current contexts of college
- Revised section *Identity Achieved*

Ongoing Features

Many characteristics of this book have been acclaimed in every edition and continue to shine.

Writing That Communicates the Excitement and Challenge of the Field

An overview of the science of human development should be lively, just as real people are. Each sentence conveys tone as well as content. Chapter-opening vignettes bring student readers into the immediacy of development. Examples and explanations abound, helping students connect theory, research, and their own experiences.

Coverage of Brain Research

Inclusion of the exciting results from neuroscience is a familiar feature of this book. Brain development is the most obvious example: Every chapter includes a section on the brain, often enhanced with charts and photos. The following list highlights some of this material:

PET scans of brains of a depressed and a non-depressed person, p. 6; illustrated, p. 6

The three domains of development, p. 7; illustrated, p. 7

Critical periods of development, p. 16

Neuroscience and the limits of Piaget's developmental theory, pp. 48–49

Brain scans of adults with ADHD, pp. 49–50; illustrated, p. 49

Influence of copy number variations on basic brain structures, p. 84

Genetic counseling and psychological disorders, pp. 92–93

Prenatal growth of the brain, pp. 103–104; illustrated, p. 105

Teratogenic effects on brain development, pp, 113–114; illustrated, p. 114

Brain development in the first two years, pp. 142–147; illustrated, p. 144; p. 146

Experience-expectant and experience-dependent brain development, pp. 146–147

Coverage of Diversity

Multicultural, international, multiethnic, sexual orientation, wealth, age, gender— all these words and ideas are vital to appreciating how people develop. Research uncovers surprising similarities and notable differences: We have much in common, yet each human is unique. From the discussion of social contexts in Chapter 1 to the coverage of cultural differences in emerging adulthood in the Epilogue, each chapter highlights possibilities and variations.

New research on family structures, immigrants, bilingualism, and ethnic differences in health are among the many topics that illustrate human diversity. Listed here is a smattering of the discussions of culture and diversity in this new edition. Respect for human differences is evident throughout. You will note that examples and research findings from many parts of the world are included, not as add-on highlights but as integral parts of the description of each age.

Inclusion of all kinds of people in the study of development, pp. 9–15
Multicontextual considerations in development (SES, cohort, family configuration, etc.), pp. 11–15
Culture defined; the need to include people of many cultures in developmental study, p. 11
Race and ethnic group defined and discussed (includes *Opposing Perspectives*), pp. 12–13
Changes to ethnic make-up of the United States, illustrated, p. 31
Learning within a culture; cultural transmission, pp. 52–54
Vygotsky's sociocultural theory, pp. 52–54
Humanism and Maslow's hierarchy, pp. 55–57, illustrated, p. 56
Developmental theories reflecting historical and cultural influences of their time, pp. 57–61
Variations in breast-feeding practices around the world, illustrated, p. 63
Genetic variations among people: alleles, p. 68
Male and female sex chromosomes, pp. 71–72, illustrated, p. 71
Opposing Perspectives: international differences in sex selection, pp. 72–73
Methods of labor and birth in England, Peru, and the United States, illustrated, p. 106
Rates of cesarean births in selected countries, pp. 108–109, illustrated, p. 108
Birthing practices in various cultures, pp. 110–111
Ethnic differences in the allele that causes low folic acid, p. 115
A View from Science: Conflicting advice about teratogens in the United States, United Kingdom, and Canada, pp. 117–118
Immigrant paradox, p. 123
Rates of low birthweight in various countries, pp. 123–125, illustrated, p. 124
Postpartum depression, p. 128
The father's role in supporting the mother, pp. 128–129
Opposing Perspectives: cultural differences in co-sleeping, pp. 140–141; rates in various countries, p. 140
Cultural commitment to certain foods and tastes, p. 154
Cultural variations in the time at which walking occurs, pp. 159–160
Cultural variations in infant mortality rates, pp. 161–162
A Case to Study: cultural variations in SIDS rates, pp. 162–163, illustrated, p. 162
Breast-feeding and HIV-positive women in Africa, pp. 165–166

Family Unity Thinking about any family—even a happy, wealthy family like this one—makes it apparent that each child's family experiences differ. For instance, would you expect this 5-year-old boy to be treated the same way as his two older sisters? And how about each child's feelings toward the parents? Even though the 12-year-olds are twins, one may favor her mother while the other favors her father.

RADIUS IMAGES/MASTERFILE

Not Victims An outsider might worry that these two boys would be bullied, one because he is African American and the other because he appears to be disabled. But both are well liked for the characteristics shown here: friendliness and willingness to help and be helped.

Up-to-Date Coverage

My mentors welcomed curiosity, creativity, and skepticism; as a result, I am eager to read and analyze thousands of articles and books on everything from autism to zygosity. The recent explosion of research in neuroscience and genetics has challenged me, once again, first to understand and then to explain many complex findings and speculative leaps. My students continue to ask questions and share their experiences, always providing new perspectives and concerns.

Topical Organization Within a Chronological Framework

The book's basic organization has endured. Four chapters begin the book with coverage of definitions, theories, genetics, and prenatal development. These chapters provide a developmental foundation and explain the life-span perspective, plasticity, nature and nurture, multicultural awareness, risk analysis, gains and losses, family bonding, and many other basic concepts.

The other four parts correspond to the major periods of development. Each part contains three chapters, one for each of three domains: biosocial, cognitive, and psychosocial. The topical organization within a chronological framework is a useful scaffold for students' understanding of the interplay between age and domain. The chapters are color-coded with tabs on the right-hand margins. The pages of the biosocial chapters have turquoise tabs, the cognitive chapters have blue tabs, and the psychosocial chapters have lime-green tabs.

Three Series of Integrated Features

Three series of deeper discussions appear as integral parts of the text where they are relevant. Readers of earlier editions will remember *A Case to Study* and *A View from Science;* new to this edition is the *Opposing Perspectives* feature. It is my belief that these features belong as part of the text, and hence they are placed exactly where they are relevant. I chose not to have separate chapters or boxes on diversity or abnormal development, because these topics are not discrete: They are integral to understanding every child.

End-of-Chapter Summary

Each chapter ends with a summary, a list of key terms (with page numbers indicating where the word is introduced and defined), and three or four application exercises designed to help students apply concepts to everyday life. Key Terms appear in boldface type in the text and are defined in the margins and again in a glossary at the back of the book. The outline on the first page of each chapter, the new learning objectives, and the system of major and minor subheads facilitate the survey-question-read-write-review (SQ3R) approach.

A "Summing Up" feature at the end of each section provides an opportunity for students to pause and reflect on what they've just read. Observation Quizzes inspire readers to look more closely at certain photographs, tables, and figures. The "Especially for . . ." questions in the margins, many of which are new to this edition, apply concepts to real-life careers and social roles.

©2016 MACMILLAN

Didn't Want to Marry This couple were happily cohabiting and strongly committed to each other but didn't wed until they learned that her health insurance would not cover him unless they were legally married.

Photographs, Tables, and Graphs That Are Integral to the Text

Students learn a great deal from this book's illustrations because Worth Publishers encourages authors to choose the photographs, tables, and graphs and to write captions that extend the content. The Online Data Connections further this process by presenting numerous charts and tables that contain detailed data for further study.

Supplements

After teaching every semester for many years, I know well that supplements can make or break a class. Students are now media savvy and instructors use many new tools. Many supplements are available for both students and professors.

LaunchPad

A comprehensive web resource for teaching and learning, Worth Publishers' online course space offers:

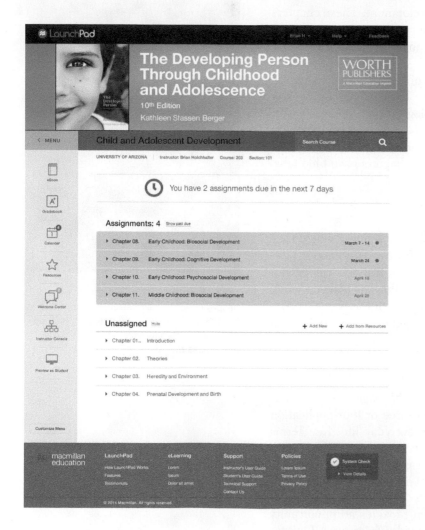

- Prebuilt units for each chapter, curated by experienced educators, with relevant media organized and ready to be assigned or customized to suit your course
- One location for all online resources, including an interactive e-Book, LearningCurve's adaptive quizzing (see below), videos, activities, and more
- Intuitive and useful analytics, with a gradebook that lets you track how students in the class are performing individually and as a whole
- A streamlined and intuitive interface that lets you build an entire course in minutes

The LaunchPad can be previewed at www.macmillanhighered.com/launchpad/bergerca10e

LearningCurve

The **LearningCurve** quizzing system reflects the latest findings from learning and memory research. LearningCurve's adaptive and formative quizzing provides an effective way to get students involved in the coursework. It combines:

- A unique learning path for each student, with quizzes shaped by each individual's correct and incorrect answers
- A personalized study plan, to guide students' preparation for class and for exams
- Feedback for each question with live links to relevant e-Book pages, guiding students to the resources they need to improve their areas of weakness

The LearningCurve system combines adaptive question selection, immediate feedback, and an interactive interface to engage students in a learning experience that is unique to them. Each LearningCurve quiz is fully integrated with other resources in LaunchPad, so students will be able to review using Worth's extensive library of videos and activities. And state-of-the-art question-analysis reports allow instructors to track the progress of individual students as well as their class as a whole.

A team of dedicated instructors—including Diana Riser, Columbus State University, Carolyn Ensley, Wilfrid Laurier University, Jim Cuellar, Indiana University, Bloomington; Lisa Hager, Spring Hill College; Jessica Herrick, Mesa State College; Sara Lapsley, Simon Fraser University; Rosemary McCullough, Ave Maria University; Wendy Morrison, Montana State University; Emily Newton, University of California, Davis; Curtis Visca, Saddleback College; and Devon Werble, East Los Angeles Community College—have worked closely to develop more than 5,000 quizzing questions developed specifically for this book.

You'll find the following in our LaunchPad:

Human Development Videos

In collaboration with dozens of instructors and researchers, Worth has developed an extensive archive of video clips. This collection covers the full range of the course, from classic experiments (like the Strange Situation and Piaget's conservation tasks) to investigations of children's play to adolescent risk-taking. Instructors can assign these videos to students through LaunchPad or choose one of 50 popular video activities that combine videos with short-answer and multiple-choice questions. For presentation purposes, our videos are available in a variety of formats to suit your needs, and highlights of the series appear periodically in the text's margin.

Instructor's Resources

Now fully integrated with LaunchPad, this collection of resources written by Richard O. Straub (University of Michigan, Dearborn) has been hailed as the richest collection of instructor's resources in developmental psychology. The resources include learning objectives, springboard topics for discussion and debate, handouts for student projects, course-planning suggestions, ideas for term projects, and a guide to audiovisual and online materials.

Interactive Presentation Slides

A new, extraordinary series of "next-generation" interactive presentation lectures gives instructors a dynamic yet easy-to-use new way to engage students during classroom presentations of core developmental psychology topics. Each lecture provides opportunities for discussion and interaction and enlivens the psychology classroom with an unprecedented number of embedded video clips and animations from Worth's library of videos. In addition to these animated presentations, Worth also offers a set of prebuilt slide sets with all chapter art and illustrations. These slides can be used as is, or they can be customized to fit individual needs.

Test Bank and Computerized Test Bank

The test bank, prepared by Jillene Seiver (Bellevue College) includes at least 100 multiple-choice and 70 fill-in-the-blank, true-false, and essay questions for each chapter. Good test questions are critical to every course, and we have gone through each and every one of these test questions with care. We have added more challenging questions, and questions are keyed to the textbook by topic, page number, and level of difficulty. Questions are also organized by NCLEX, NAEYC, and APA goals and Bloom's taxonomy. We have also written rubrics for grading all of the short-answer and essay questions in the test bank.

The Diploma computerized test bank guides instructors step by step through the process of creating a test. It also allows them to quickly add an unlimited number of questions; edit, scramble, or resequence items; format a test; and include pictures, equations, and media links. The accompanying gradebook enables instructors to record students' grades throughout the course and includes the capacity to sort student records, view detailed analyses of test items, curve tests, generate reports, and add weights to grades.

Thanks

I'd like to thank the academic reviewers who have read this book in every edition and who have provided suggestions, criticisms, references, and encouragement. They have all made this a better book. I want to mention especially those who have reviewed this edition:

Phyllis Acadia, *Capella University*

Sandra Barrueco, *The Catholic University of America*

Tracy Bartel, *Chatham University*

Patricia Bellas, *Irvine Valley College*

Joanne Benjamin, *San Diego City College*

Kate Byerwalter, *Grand Rapids Community College*

Katherine Cloutier, *Michigan State University*

Julia Conrad, *Colorado Mountain College-West Garfield Campus*

Bret Cormier, *Kentucky State University*

Jennifer Cuddapah, *Hood College*

Linda Fayard, *Mississippi Gulf Coast Community College*

Christine Feeley, *Suffolk County Community College*

Phil Freneau, *College of the Redwoods*

Megan Geerdts, *Rutgers University*

Kim Glackin, *Metropolitan Community College-Blue River*

April Grace, *Madisonville Community College*

Misty Hicks, *Missouri State University*

Christine Hodges, *Coastal Carolina University*

Erica Holt, *Germanna Community College*

Christie Kaaland, *Antioch University*

Carol Kessler, *Cabrini College*

Donna Lutz, *Hofstra University*

Elisa Magidoff, *Canada College and Skyline College*

Christopher Magnuson, *Ottawa University*

Martha Mendez-Baldwin, *Manhattan College*

Mary Beth Miller, *Fresno City College*

Mary O'Boyle, *Northeast Community College*

Krista Paduchowski, *University of Massachusetts-Lowell*

Doug Pearson, *Normandale Community College*

John Prange, *Irvine Valley College*

Robert Sasse, *Palomar College*

Joseph Schroer, *Miami University-Ohio*

Alex Schwartz, *Santa Monica College*

Delar K. Singh, *Eastern Connecticut State University*

Jay Slosar, *Chapman University*

Sheila Smith, *Foothill College*

Randall Stiles, *University of Nevada-Las Vegas*

Michael Streppa, *Montreat College*

Michelle Wright, *DePaul University*

In addition, I wish to thank the instructors who participated in our survey. We've tried to apply the insights gained from their experiences with the last edition to make this new edition even better.

Andreea DiLorenzo, *Monmouth University*

Linda Fayard, *Mississippi Gulf Coast Community College*

Kim Glackin, *Metropolitan Community College-Blue River*

Misty Hicks, *Missouri State University*

Deborah Lewis, *Miramar College*

Christine Hughes Pontier, *University of Miami*

Lynn Shelley, *Westfield State University*

Glenda L. Smith, *University of Alabama at Birmingham School of Nursing*

Beth Bigler White, *University of Tennessee*

The editorial, production, and marketing people at Worth Publishers are dedicated to meeting the highest standards of excellence. Their devotion of time, effort, and talent to every aspect of publishing is a model for the industry. I particularly would like to thank Stacey Alexander, Jessica Bayne, Tom Churchill, Betsy Draper, Lisa Kinne, Blake Logan, Bianca Moscatelli, Andrea Musick Page, Tracey Kuehn, Catherine Michaelsen, Katherine Nurre, Felicia Ruocco, Lauren Samuelson, Barbara Seixas, and Cecilia Varas.

Kathleen Stassen Berger

New York, January 2015

Dedication

Finally, I wish to dedicate this edition to my brother, Glen Harold Stassen, a dedicated professor and author, as well as my beloved only sibling. My plan was to reach old age with him, but he died in 2014.

the beginnings

The science of human development includes many beginnings. Each of the first four chapters of this text forms one corner of a solid foundation for our study.

Chapter 1 introduces definitions and dimensions, explaining research strategies and methods that help us understand how people develop. The need for science, the power of culture, and the necessity of an ecological approach are all explained.

Without ideas, our study would be only a jumble of observations. Chapter 2 provides organizing guideposts: Five major theories, each leading to many other theories and hypotheses, are described.

Chapter 3 explains heredity. Genes never act alone, yet no development—whether in body or brain, at any time, in anyone—is unaffected by DNA.

Chapter 4 details the prenatal growth of each developing person from a single cell to a breathing, grasping, crying newborn. Many circumstances—from the mother's diet to the father's care to the culture's values—affect development every day of embryonic and fetal growth.

As you see, the science and the wonder of human life begin long before the first breath. Understanding the beginnings described in each of these chapters prepares us to understand each developing child, and each of us.

CHAPTER 1

Introduction

What Will You Know?*

1. How can the study of children, each one unique, be a science?
2. Does his or her ethnic group make any difference in a child's development?
3. Is childhood today different from childhood fifty years ago?
4. How can we know what changes between one year of life and the next?
5. Do scientists always investigate the crucial questions?

At 6:11 A.M. I am holding my daughter's bent right leg in place with all my strength. A nurse holds her left leg while the midwife commands, "Push . . . push . . . push." Finally, a head is visible, small and wet, but perfect. In a moment, body and limbs emerge—all 4,139 grams of Caleb, perfect as well. Every number on the monitor is good, and my new grandson breathes and moves as a healthy newborn should. Bethany, smiling, begins to nurse.

This miracle makes celestial music ring in my ears. The ringing grows louder. Bethany shimmers, then the room grows dark. Suddenly, I am on the floor, looking up at six medical professionals: I have fainted.

"I am fine," I insist, scrambling back onto the couch where I spent the night. Six people stare down at me.

"You need to go to triage," one says.

"No, I am fine. Sorry I fainted."

"We must send you to triage, in a wheelchair."

What can I say to make them ignore me and focus on Bethany and Caleb?

"You can refuse treatment," a nurse tells me.

Oh yes, thank you, the law now requires patient consent.

I am wheeled down to Admitting; I explain that I was with my laboring daughter all night with no food or sleep. I refuse treatment.

The admitting nurse takes my blood pressure—normal—and checks with her supervisor. She lets me return before the placenta is delivered.

I am thankful, but puzzled. As a developmental scholar and author, I understand birth, numbers, jargon, monitors, body language, medical competence, hospital cleanliness, hall noises, and more. I do not panic. I knew that Bethany was strong and

---

*"What will you know?" questions start each chapter, one question for each major heading. These questions are intended to highlight provocative, memorable issues within the chapter. More specific questions ("What have you learned?") follow each section summary.

Born Blissful One of us rests after an arduous journey, and the other rejoices after crying and fainting.

healthy, and every prenatal visit confirmed a healthy fetus. I was grateful, but not surprised, that all was well.

I told the triage nurse that I had not slept or eaten all night—true, but I had done that before, never fainting. Why this time?

This incident is a fitting introduction for Chapter 1, which begins to explain what we know, what we don't know, and how we learn about human development. For me and other scientists, and also for you and everyone else, unexpected moments occur as each life is lived. Emotions mix with intellect, family bonds with professional competence, contexts with cultures, personal experiences with academic knowledge, generalities with exceptions.

Many details of Caleb's arrival were unlike birth in other cultures and eras. Yet other aspects have always been part of the human experience. This chapter, and those that follow, will help you understand the specifics and the universals of development.

Understanding How and Why

science of human development The science that seeks to understand how and why people of all ages and circumstances change or remain the same over time.

The **science of human development** *seeks to understand how and why people—all kinds of people, everywhere, of every age—change over time.* The goal of this science is to help Earth's 7 billion people fulfill their potential.

Each aspect of this definition above merits explanation.

The Need for Science

Developmental study is a *science*. It depends on theories, data, analysis, critical thinking, and sound methodology, just like every other science. All scientists ask questions and seek answers in order to ascertain "how and why." In this process, scientists gather evidence on whatever they are studying, be it chemical elements, rays of light, or, here, child behavior.

One hallmark of the science of human development is that it is interdisciplinary; that is, scientists from many academic disciplines (biology, psychology, sociology, anthropology, economics, and history among them) contribute to our understanding of how and why people grow.

Science is especially useful when we study children: Lives depend on it. What should pregnant women eat and drink? How much should babies cry? When and how should children be punished? What should 5-year-olds learn? Should they learn in school or at home? Through required memorization or free play? About God or about algebra?

People have disagreed about almost every question in child development—often vehemently, sometimes violently. Some parents beat their children; others imprison such parents. Some parents sacrifice vast sums to send their children to schools that others abhor. Science informs, guides, and redirects those on all sides of every dispute.

The Scientific Method

scientific method A way to answer questions using empirical research and data-based conclusions.

theory A comprehensive set of ideas.

hypothesis A specific prediction that can be tested.

empirical Based on observation, experience, or experiment; not theoretical.

To discard unexamined opinions and to rein in personal biases, we follow the five steps of the **scientific method** (see Figure 1.1):

1. *Begin with curiosity.* On the basis of **theory,** prior research, or personal observation, pose a question.
2. *Develop a hypothesis.* Shape the question into a **hypothesis,** a specific prediction to be examined.
3. *Test the hypothesis.* Design and conduct research to gather **empirical** evidence (data).

| 1. Curiosity | 2. Hypothesis | 3. Test | 4. Analyze data and draw conclusions | 5. Report the results |

4. *Analyze data and draw conclusions.* Determine whether the evidence supports the hypothesis.
5. *Report the results.* Share the data, procedures, statistics, conclusions, and alternative explanations.

FIGURE 1.1
Process, Not Proof Built into the scientific method—in questions, hypotheses, tests, and replication—is a passion for possibilities, especially unexpected ones.

The Need for Replication

As you see, scientists begin with curiosity and then seek the facts, drawing conclusions only after careful research. **Replication**—repeating the procedures and methods of a study with different participants—may be a final step (Jasny et al., 2011). Scientists learn from each other, building on what has gone before. They hesitate to draw conclusions or to believe the results of others' research until replication has occurred—although often the media broadcast surprising findings before replication.

This method is not foolproof. Scientists sometimes draw conclusions too quickly, misinterpret data, or ignore alternative perspectives, as discussed at the end of this chapter. Something that is valid for one group of children in one time and place may not be valid elsewhere or in another time. Scientists continually refine methods, question the conclusions drawn by others, and occasionally discover—to their shock and horror—that another scientist has not followed the procedures outlined above. Replication is needed to verify conclusions.

Always, however, asking questions and testing hypotheses by gathering data is the foundation of science; always, scientists seek facts, not untested assumptions.

replication Repeating a study, usually using different participants.

The Nature–Nurture Controversy

A great puzzle of development—the *nature–nurture debate*—is an easy example of the need for science. **Nature** refers to the influence of the genes that people inherit. **Nurture** refers to environmental influences, which begin with the health and diet of the embryo's mother and continue lifelong, including the impacts of family, school, community, and culture.

The nature–nurture debate has many other names, among them *heredity–environment* and *maturation–learning*. Under whatever name, the basic question is: *How much of any characteristic, behavior, or emotion is the result of genes, and how much is the result of experience?*

Some people believe that most traits are inborn, that children are innately good ("an innocent child") or bad ("beat the devil out of them"). Others stress nurture, crediting or blaming parents, neighborhoods, drugs, or even food when someone is good or bad, a hero or a criminal.

Neither belief is accurate. The question is "how much," not "which," because both genes and the environment affect every characteristic: Nature always affects nurture, and then nurture affects nature. Even "how much" is misleading if it implies that nature and nurture each contribute a fixed amount (Eagly & Wood, 2013; Lock, 2013).

nature In development, nature refers to the traits, capacities, and limitations that each individual inherits genetically from his or her parents at the moment of conception.

nurture In development, nurture includes all the environmental influences that affect the individual after conception. This includes everything from the mother's nutrition while pregnant to the implicit values of the nation.

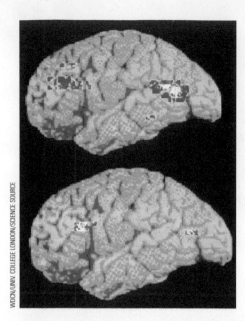

Red Means Stop At top, the red areas on this PET scan show abnormally low metabolic activity and blood flow in a depressed person's brain, in contrast to the normal brain at bottom. Neuroscience confirms that depression is biological, not just psychological.

differential susceptibility The idea that people vary in how sensitive they are to particular experiences. Often such differences are genetic, which makes some people affected "for better *and* for worse" by life events. (Also called *differential sensitivity*.)

A complex nature–nurture interaction is apparent in every moment of our lives, as is evident in the opening vignette of this chapter. I fainted at Caleb's birth because of at least ten factors (age, air quality, exhaustion, exertion, gender, hormones, joy, low blood sugar, memory, relief), each influenced by both nature and nurture. The combination, and no single factor, landed me on the floor.

Some People Are Vulnerable

Each aspect of nature and nurture depends on other aspects of nature and nurture, in ways that vary for each individual (Manuck & McCaffery, 2014). For instance, the negative impact of a beating, or of any other experience, might be magnified because of the particular versions of genes that a person has. The opposite is true as well: Some genes are protective, making people less vulnerable to difficult or traumatic experiences. Similarly, differences in nurture can either protect against or worsen the impact of a person's genetic make-up.

For example, some people inherit genes (nature) for diabetes but never get that disease because nurture (in this case, diet and exercise) protects them. Or a person could be overweight and sedentary (both risk factors for diabetes and many other ailments) but never become diabetic because their genes buffer the effects of their habits.

Sometimes protective factors, in either nature or nurture, outweigh liabilities. As one review explains, "there are, indeed, individuals whose genetics indicate exceptionally high risk of disease, yet they never show any signs of the disorder" (Friend & Schadt, 2014, p. 970).

This is called **differential susceptibility** (or differential sensitivity)—that is, how sensitive a person is to any particular environmental experience differs from one person to another because of the particular genes each person has inherited. Some people are like dandelions—hardy, growing and thriving in good soil or bad, with or without ample sun and rain. Other people are like orchids—quite wonderful, but only when ideal growing conditions are met (Ellis & Boyce, 2008; Laurent, 2014).

For example, in one study, depression in pregnant women was assessed and then the emotional maturity of their children was measured. Those children who had a particular version of the serotonin transporter gene (5-HTTLPR) were likely to be emotionally immature if their mothers had been depressed, but *more* mature than average if their mothers had not been depressed (Babineau et al., 2014).

The Baby with Colic

An example of differential susceptibility comes from the 10 to 20 percent of all infants who cry for hours at a time in the first 3 months of life, presumably as a result of genes. They are said to have colic, and their frustrated parents cannot comfort them (J.S. Kim, 2011).

A colicky baby is like an orchid, and future development depends on nurture. For some, their inconsolable crying makes the parents unusually responsive. Then the children become better than average (more outgoing, generous, high-achieving) when they outgrow their early difficulties. Other naturally difficult orchids provoke parental anger, or even rejection, the effects of which last long after the colic has subsided. They become low-achieving, unhappy children.

One study of colicky babies confirms that parents react in many ways (Landgren et al., 2012). One mother said:

> There were moments . . . when she was apoplectic and howling so much that I almost got this thought, 'now I'll take a pillow and put it over her face just until she quietens down, until the screaming stops.'

By contrast, another mother said:

> In some way, it made me stronger, and made my relationship with my son stronger. . . . Because I felt that he had no one else but me. 'If I can't manage, no one can.' So I had to cope.

As two developmental experts explain:

> Differential susceptibility implies . . . that it may be mistaken to regard some children—like highly negative infants—as simply more vulnerable to the negative effects of adversity. And this is because such children may also benefit more than others from environmental support and enrichment.
>
> *[Belsky & Pluess, 2012, p. 3]*

These experts find that genetic vulnerability (in this case, the DRD4 gene) does not disappear. During adolescence even well-nurtured orchids are more rebellious and impulsive than the less temperamental dandelions, but nurture always affects nature.

The specifics of differential susceptibility require complex and extensive empirical data, as thousands of scientists seeks to understand exactly how nature and nurture interact to produce each particular human trait with each version of each gene. But the simple conclusion remains: Neither genes nor upbringing alone make a child amazingly good or incredibly bad (Masten, 2014). Both nature and nurture matter.

The Three Domains

Obviously, it is impossible to examine nature and nurture on every aspect of human development at once. Typically therefore, individual scientists study one characteristic at a time. A century ago, physical development (such as tooth eruption or running speed) was the main focus of developmental research, but scientists now realize that not only the body but also the intellect and emotions develop throughout life. To understand the whole person, an interdisciplinary approach to human development has replaced the old silo approach of the past.

To make it easier to study, development is often considered in three domains—*biosocial, cognitive,* and *psychosocial.* (Figure 1.2 describes each domain.) Each domain includes several academic disciplines: The biosocial includes biology,

FIGURE 1.2

The Three Domains The division of human development into three domains makes it easier to study, but remember that very few factors belong exclusively to one domain or another. Development is not piecemeal but holistic: Each aspect of development is related to all three domains.

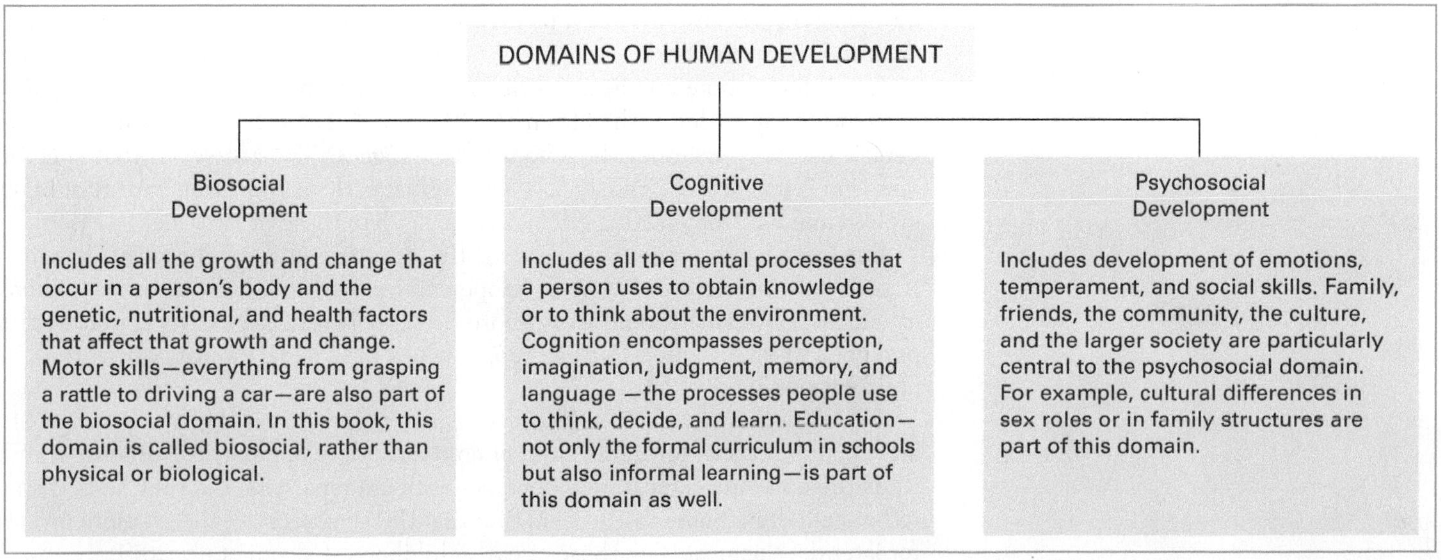

DOMAINS OF HUMAN DEVELOPMENT		
Biosocial Development	**Cognitive Development**	**Psychosocial Development**
Includes all the growth and change that occur in a person's body and the genetic, nutritional, and health factors that affect that growth and change. Motor skills—everything from grasping a rattle to driving a car—are also part of the biosocial domain. In this book, this domain is called biosocial, rather than physical or biological.	Includes all the mental processes that a person uses to obtain knowledge or to think about the environment. Cognition encompasses perception, imagination, judgment, memory, and language —the processes people use to think, decide, and learn. Education—not only the formal curriculum in schools but also informal learning—is part of this domain as well.	Includes development of emotions, temperament, and social skills. Family, friends, the community, the culture, and the larger society are particularly central to the psychosocial domain. For example, cultural differences in sex roles or in family structures are part of this domain.

neuroscience, and medicine; the cognitive includes psychology, linguistics, and education; and the psychosocial includes economics, sociology, and history. Typically, each scholar follows a particular thread within one domain, using clues and conclusions from other scientists who have concentrated on that same thread.

However, since every person is a whole tapestry of multi-colored threads, every aspect of growth is biopsychosocial, touching on all three domains. For example, babies start speaking because of maturation of the brain, mouth, and vocal cords (*biological*), which allows them to express connections between objects and words (*cognitive*), which could not occur unless people talked to them (*psychosocial*).

This constant interaction of domains presents a problem: Words and pages follow in sequence and the mind thinks one thought at a time. That makes it impossible to describe or grasp all domains simultaneously. The scientific method weaves disparate threads together, as evidence-based conclusions from many sources advance our understanding of the whole person.

Childhood and Adulthood

Are children more important than adults? For decades, because the focus of developmentalists was on physical growth, the answer to this question was yes. Consequently, the study of human development was the study of child development, with a nod to the physical declines of old age. That produced, as a famous critic described, "a curiously broken trajectory of knowledge . . . [with] a brave beginning, a sad ending, and an empty middle (Bronfenbrenner, 1977, p. 525).

Since people were not thought to develop over the years of adulthood, developmentalists did not study adults. The opposing giants of developmental theory, Sigmund Freud and Jean Piaget, agreed on one thing: The final stage of development began in early adolescence and then continued without significant change until death.

Recently, however, that empty middle has been filled. Scientists now gather data about adulthood, discovering many developmental changes. For example, sexual appetites, cognitive perspectives, and employment attitudes all change markedly from ages 15 to 65.

No one now thinks that development stops at age 15. Although many scholars still focus on one part of the lifespan, every developmentalist considers what happened before, and what will happen after, each particular period. For instance, one influential scholar believes infancy is "the foundation and catalyst of human development" (Bornstein, 2014, p. 121). In other words, he studies infancy to understand the rest of life.

Is childhood more important, influential, and determinative than adulthood? If a person is, say, malnourished from age 30 to 33, is that as harmful as if that same person had been malnourished from birth to age 3? The answer to that specific question is no. Neuroscientists have proven that early malnutrition can stunt brain growth and have long-lasting effects far worse than those of later malnutrition.

But scientists are not certain about the cognitive and psychosocial domains. If you had to choose only one developmental period in which to invest billions of education dollars, should you choose preschools or colleges? Or if you were a psychologist who wanted to treat people who would benefit most, would they be children or adults?

The answer is not obvious. Some research suggests that the first years of life are the most crucial for intellectual or emotional development, but other research finds the opposite: Educating parents, or even grandparents, may be the best way to help children. Some researchers find that the adolescent years are more pivotal for later development than those of early childhood (Falconi et al., 2014).

Political debates need solid data. Should the U.S. Congress protect fetuses and infants (e.g., WIC, mother/infant food supplements), or preschoolers (e.g. Head Start), or older children (e.g., public schools), or emerging adults (e.g., college subsidies), or employees (e.g., raising the minimum wage) or seniors (e.g., Social Security and Medicare)?

All of these age groups need help, but government programs are expensive. If we knew that a particular investment in one age group would have greater impact overall than the same money invested at another age, that would guide policy. But developmentalists disagree, even on who needs financial support most, much more on who most needs education, or family support. More science is needed. This leads us to the second phase of our definition.

SUMMING UP   The scientific study of human development follows five steps: curiosity, hypothesis, data collection, conclusions, and reporting. Scientists build on prior studies, examining procedures and replicating results—thus confirming or refuting conclusions. This research method is designed to avoid wishful thinking, untested assumptions, and prejudice.

For instance, scientists no longer assume that development is either totally genetic or totally environmental. Instead, nature and nurture always interact, with variations between one person and another, as highlighted by differential susceptibility. Colic is one example.

The scientific method is followed within many disciplines and in all three domains—biosocial, cognitive, and psychosocial. Although each researcher typically concentrates on one aspect of development in one domain, no one stays in their own silo because science connects everyone's data and conclusions.

Once developmental scientists focused almost exclusively on children. Then adult development was recognized. Now researchers seek to understand which interventions at what ages are most effective for optimal development.

WHAT HAVE YOU LEARNED?
1. What makes the study of human development a science?
2. Why is replication sometimes considered an essential follow-up to the five steps of the scientific method?
3. Why is it a mistake to ask whether a human behavior stems from nature or nurture?
4. Why are some children more affected by their environment than others?
5. What is the difference between each of the three domains—biosocial, cognitive, and psychosocial?
6. Why do some people believe that the years of childhood are more crucial for development than the years of adulthood? ●

Including All Kinds of People

Developmentalists study everyone—young and old, rich and poor, of every ethnicity, background, sexual orientation, culture, and nation.

Difference or Deficit?

One reason to study people of all kinds is to combat the human inclination to think that anyone who is different is also deficient, i.e., lacking in something that is important for a good life. We are amused when young girls say, "Boys stink," or their male classmates say, "Girls are stupid," but adults have the same tendency: to judge people unlike themselves as inferior.

Family Pride Grandpa Charilaos is proud of his tavern in northern Greece (central Macedonia), but he is even more proud of his talented grandchildren, including Maria Soni (shown here). Note her expert fingering. Her father and mother also play instruments—is that nature or nurture?

KUTTIG/RF KIDS/ALAMY

For example, although males and females are similar in almost every trait, humans tend to look for sex differences, not similarities, and then to make sexist judgments. Most research finds far more similarities than differences between the sexes. One of the very few proven gender differences is that women are more tenderhearted and men more sexually driven (Hyde, 2014). If you are male, do you think that women are weak because they are too emotional; if you are female, do you think men are too obsessed with sex? If you answer yes, how human of you. And how wrong.

Negative judgments are too readily made about people who raise their children differently or who believe in an unfamiliar religion. Have you heard people criticize teenagers, middle-aged adults, or senior citizens? People tend to be critical of whatever age group is not their own.

The human tendency to observe differences and then conclude that people are inferior if they are unlike the observer is called the **difference-equals-deficit error.** Too quickly and without thought, differences are assumed to be problems (Akhtar & Jaswal, 2013).

difference-equals-deficit error The mistaken belief that a deviation from some norm is necessarily inferior to behavior or characteristics that meet the standard. Often the "norm" is the standard for the observer, and difference is anyone unlike oneself.

Sexual Orientation

The importance of accepting diversity is apparent when considering sexual orientation. Most teenagers are powerfully attracted to members of the other sex, but some—fewer than 1 teenager in 20—are attracted to people of their own sex (Brakefield et al., 2014). Same-sex attraction does not necessarily become sexual behavior, and even attraction is in dispute, as explained in Chapter 16. Here we use sexual orientation to illustrate a difference that was once assumed to be a deficit.

This perceived deficit led school bullies to target classmates thought to be lesbian, gay, bisexual, or transgender (LGBT) (Juvonen & Graham, 2014), and many LGBT teenagers themselves felt inferior. As a result, LGBT teenagers committed suicide at a much higher rate than did their heterosexual peers (Herek, 2010).

Over time, however, activism, scientific data, and other factors combined to cause a dramatic change in the culture. In the 1970s, psychiatrists and psychologists declared, "Homosexuality per se implies no impairment in judgment, stability, reliability" (Conger, 1975, p. 633), and by 2014, same-sex marriage—forbidden

Video: Research of Geoffrey Saxe
http://qrs.ly/9c4eoxh

FOOTAGE BY GEOFFREY SAXE

in every U.S. state before 2004—became legal in more than 30 U.S. states and in 17 other nations.

As this difference is less assumed to be a deficit, serious depression and crippling anxiety among LGBT youth has become less common. This is true generally, as well as within each family and community, although certainly there are some areas and families that reject such teens. Their rate of psychological problems is half as high in jurisdictions with policies that indicate acceptance (e.g., laws against hate crimes) compared to communities where same-sex attraction is still considered a deficit (Hatzenbuehler, 2014).

Culture, Ethnicity, and Race

To include "all kinds of people" requires that researchers study children of many cultures, ethnicities, and races. Yet each of these three terms is often confused, by scientists as well as non-scientists.

Culture, ethnicity, and *race* are **social constructions,** which means that they are created by society. Social constructions are powerful, affecting thoughts and behavior (as evident with people's ideas regarding sexual orientation), but since they arise from society, they can be changed by society. Because the study of development focuses on change over time, it is crucial that the fluidity and distinct meaning of each of these words be understood.

A System of Shared Beliefs

For social scientists, **culture** is "the system of shared beliefs, conventions, norms, behaviors, expectations and symbolic representations that persist over time and prescribe social rules of conduct" (Bornstein et al., 2011, p. 30). Culture is far more than eating certain foods or practicing certain rituals; it is a powerful social construction.

Each family, community, and college has a particular culture. For instance, Jamaicans in the United States are said to be tri-cultural (Jamaican, Black, American) (Ferguson et al., 2014). In any one person several cultures may clash.

Furthermore, individuals within each culture sometimes rebel against their culture's expected "beliefs, conventions, norms, behaviors." Cultural influences must be recognized, but not slavishly: Culture is powerful, but also fluid and changing.

social construction An idea that is built on shared perceptions, not on objective reality. Many age-related terms (such as *childhood, adolescence, yuppie,* and *senior citizen*) are social constructions, strongly influenced by social assumptions.

culture A system of shared beliefs, norms, behaviors, and expectations that persist over time and prescribe social behavior and assumptions.

Hard Floor, Hard Life These are among the thousands of unaccompanied children who fled Latin America and arrived in Arizona and Texas in 2014. Developmentalists predict that the effects of their hazardous journey will stay with them, unless sources of resilience—such as a caring family and supportive community—are quickly found. Culture and context make a difference for every childhood experience.

OBSERVATION QUIZ How many children are sleeping here in this photograph? (see answer, page 12)

POLARIS/NEWSCOM

Watch **Video: Interview with Barbara Rogoff** to learn more about the role of culture in the development of Mayan children in Guatemala.

To appreciate that culture is a matter of beliefs and values, not superficial differences, consider language. Of course, people speak distinct languages, but that in itself is not a cultural difference. However, among some English-speaking groups in the United States, linguistic proficiency and independent thinking are encouraged. In families in those groups, children are encouraged to talk freely, and when they do, the adults listen approvingly. In other groups, a prime value is that each child learn respect for parents, and, by extension, for every adult: Children should never interrupt an adult conversation.

One of my East Indian students remembered:

> My mom was outside on the porch talking to my aunt. I decided to go outside; I guess I was being nosey. While they were talking I jumped into their conversation which was very rude. When I realized what I did it was too late. My mother slapped me in my face so hard that it took a couple of seconds to feel my face again.

> *[C., personal communication]*

Notice that my student continues to reflect her culture; she labels her own behavior "nosey" and "very rude." She later wrote that she expects children to be seen but not heard and that her own son makes her "very angry" when he interrupts.

As in this case, cultural values, learned in childhood, tend to persist even when the overall culture has shifted. Culture is not a straightjacket, however. In fact, many parents (including many of Asian ancestry) allow their children more freedom of expression than their parents allowed them. And many parents who have been in North America all their lives nonetheless teach their children not to interrupt adults.

Heritage

People of an **ethnic group** share certain attributes, almost always including ancestral heritage and usually national origin, religion, and language (Whitfield & McClearn, 2005). Ethnic group is not the same as cultural group: People of a particular ethnicity need not share a culture (compare people of Irish descent in Ireland and in Illinois), and some cultures include people of several ethnic groups (consider British culture).

Ethnicity is a social construction, affected by the social context. For everyone, ethnic identity is strengthened if (1) other members of the same group are nearby, and (2) other groups consider the person an outsider. Thus, ethnicity depends partly on context.

For example, people born in Africa who are longtime residents of North America typically consider themselves African, unless they are with many other African-born people. Then they might consider themselves by region (e.g. West African) or nation (Nigerian). However, African-born people living in their home country usually identify with a more specific ethnic group, such as the Ibo, Hausa, or Yoruba in Nigeria or the Kikuyo, Luhya, and Luo in Kenya.

Similar particular identities are evident everywhere: Ethnic identity becomes more specific and more salient (Sicilian, not just Italian; South Korean, not just East Asian) under certain circumstances. Many Americans are puzzled by distant civil wars (e.g., in Syria, or Sri Lanka, or the Ukraine) because people who look alike seem to be bitter enemies. However, those on opposing sides see many ethnic differences between them.

Physical appearance is sometimes a marker for ethnicity. The most visible example is skin color, often taken to indicate race. However, race is also a social construction—and a misleading one. There are reasons to abandon the term as well as reasons to keep it, as the following explains.

ethnic group People whose ancestors were born in the same region and who often share a language, culture, and religion.

// ANSWER TO OBSERVATION QUIZ
(from page 11) Nine—not counting the standing boy or the possible tenth one whose head is under the blanket. Rumpled blankets suggest that eight more are elsewhere at the moment. Each night hundreds of children sleep in this Border Protection Processing Facility in Brownsville, Texas. They are detained while authorities decide whether to send them back to the countries they fled or to a safe place in the United States.

opposing perspectives*

Using the Word *Race*

The term **race** is used to categorize people via physical markers, particularly outward appearance. Historically, most North Americans believed that race was the outward manifestation of inborn biological differences. Fifty years ago, races were categorized by skin color: white, black, red, and yellow (Coon, 1962).

It is obvious now, but was not a few decades ago, that no one's skin is really white or black or red or yellow. Social scientists are convinced that race is a social construction, that society used color terms to exaggerate differences in skin tones.

Genetic analysis confirms that the biological concept of race is inaccurate. Although most genes are identical in every human, those few genetic differences that distinguish one person from another are poorly indexed by appearance (Race, Ethnicity, and Genetics Working Group of the American Society of Human Genetics, 2005).

Skin color is particularly misleading because dark-skinned people with African ancestors have "high levels of genetic population diversity" (Tishkoff et al., 2009, p. 1035) and dark-skinned people with non-African ancestors (such as indigenous Australians or Maori in New Zealand) share neither culture nor ethnicity with Africans.

Race is more than a flawed concept; it is a destructive one. It is used to justify racism: Slavery, lynching, and segregation were directly connected to the conviction that race was inborn. Racism continues today in less obvious ways (some highlighted later in this book), impeding the goal of our study—to help all kinds of people fulfill their potential.

Since race is a social construction that leads to racism and distracts us from recognizing other social problems, some social scientists believe that the term should be abandoned (Gilroy, 2000). It is no longer used in many nations.

A study of 141 nations found that 85 percent never use the word *race* on their census forms (Morning, 2008). Only in the United States does the census still distinguish between race and ethnicity, stating that Hispanics "may be of any race."

Because of the way human cognition works, such labels encourage stereotyping (Kelly et al., 2010). As one scholar explains:

> The United States' unique conceptual distinction between race and ethnicity may unwittingly support the longstanding belief that race reflects biological difference and ethnicity stems from cultural difference. In this scheme, ethnicity is socially produced but race is an immutable fact of nature. Consequently, walling off race from ethnicity on the census may reinforce essentialist interpretations of race and preclude understanding of the ways in which racial categories are also socially constructed.

> [Morning, 2008, p. 255]

Perhaps to avoid racism, the word *race* should not be used.

But consider the opposite perspective (Bliss, 2012). In a society with a history of racial discrimination, reversing that cultural

race A group of people who are regarded by themselves or by others as distinct from other groups on the basis of physical appearance, typically skin color. Social scientists think race is a misleading concept, as biological differences are not signified by outward appearance.

Young Laughter Friendship across ethnic lines is common at every age, when schools, workplaces, and neighborhoods are not segregated. However, past history has an impact: These two girls share so much that they spontaneously laugh together, unaware that this scene in a restaurant could not have happened 50 years ago. Many of the youngest cohorts have trouble understanding lynching, poll taxes, separate swimming pools, or even the historic March on Washington in 1963.

heritage may require recognizing race. Although race is a social construction, not a biological distinction, it is powerful nonetheless. Particularly in adolescence, people who are proud of their racial identity are likely to achieve academically, resist drug addiction, and feel better about themselves (Crosnoe & Johnson, 2011; Zimmerman et al., 2013).

Many medical, educational, and economic conditions—from low birthweight to college graduation, from family income to health insurance—reflect racial disparities. To overcome such disparities, race may first need to be recognized.

Indeed, many social scientists argue that pretending that race does not exist allows racism to thrive (e.g., sociologists Marvasti & McKinney, 2011; anthropologist McCabe, 2011). Two political scientists studying criminal justice found that people who claim to be color-blind display "an extraordinary level of naiveté" (Peffley & Hurwitz, 2010, p. 113).

According to some scholars the election of President Obama revealed racial prejudice, and uninformed anti-racism unearths new forms of racism (Sullivan, 2014; Hughey & Parks, 2014). Perhaps race must be named and recognized before it can fade.

---

*Every page of this text includes information that requires critical thinking and evaluation. In addition, almost every chapter contains an Opposing Perspectives feature that highlights conflicting views of a developmental issue.

Socioeconomic Status

Some social scientists believe that when studying "all kinds of people," differences in **socioeconomic status (SES)** are more potent than cultural or ethnic differences. SES affects every moment of development, from whether or not a zygote is conceived (rates of sexual activity and contraception vary by SES) to when a person dies (wealthy people live longer).

socioeconomic status (SES) A person's position in society as determined by income, occupation, education, and place of residence. (Sometimes called *social class*.)

Like culture, ethnicity, and race, SES is a complicated category. Income is part of socioeconomic status, but only part: For children, their neighborhood and their parents' level of education is often more influential. This is reflected when people speak of social class, as in "the shrinking middle class" or "working class values." Such phrases imply habits and attitudes as much as income (Stephens et al., 2012).

Consider a U.S. family comprised of an infant, an unemployed mother, and a father who earns $18,000 a year. Their SES would be low if the wage earner were an illiterate dishwasher living in an urban slum, but it would be high if the wage earner were a PhD student living on campus and teaching part-time.

However, when governments categorize people they rely almost exclusively on income. The U.S. federal poverty line is based primarily on food cost and family size. That standard was set in 1965 and is still used, although economists find that shelter and medical costs are better indicators of income adequacy than food.

According to 2014 federal cutoffs, a household of three people with a combined annual income under $19,790 (in Alaska, $24,730) is officially poor.

Policies and practices regarding poverty vary from nation to nation. In the United States, the gap between rich and poor, and between young and old, has increased in the past three decades (Lowrey, 2014) (see Figure 1.3). That has resulted in increased disparities in health, education, and neighborhood between those at the top and bottom.

For example, the life expectancy gap between the rich and poor has widened in the United States. Wealthy people live about six years longer than they did thirty years ago, but poor people die at almost the same age, on average, as their parents did.

FIGURE 1.3

The Rich Get Richer The Gini index is a measure of income equality, ranging from zero (everyone equal) to one (one person has all the money). Values here are after taxes, which shows that the gap between rich and poor is widening in the United States and Finland but not in other countries. Worldwide, the gap between the richest people and the poorest is even wider, estimated at about 0.63 on the Gini.

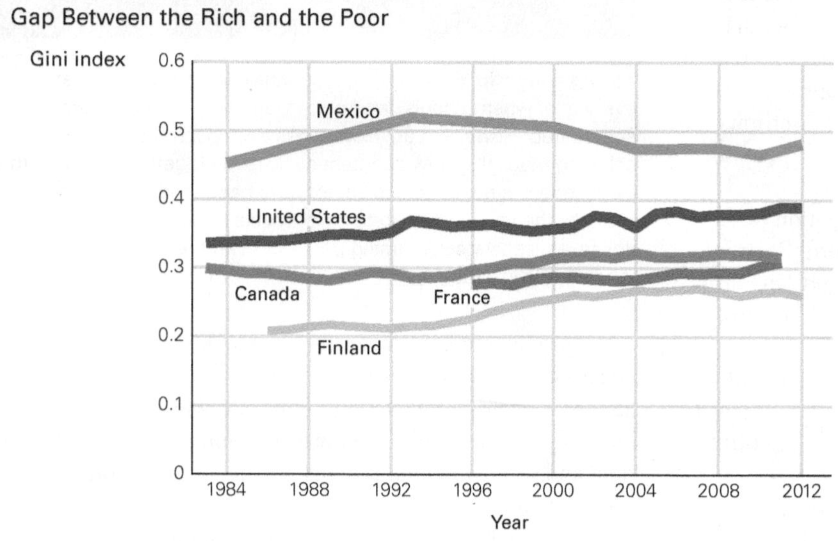

Gap Between the Rich and the Poor

Source: Lowrey, 2014.

SES affects almost every aspect of life in every nation and in every region of each nation, as illustrated in Visualizing Development (see the inside cover). That fact is known to everyone who examines the data, although not everyone agrees about the specifics or the implications (Chambers et al., 2014).

Finding the Balance

All humans are the same. Yet as sex, culture, ethnicity, and SES make clear, every group is different. Furthermore, genetically each individual is unique. Is that a paradox, a dilemma, or a challenge? How general, and how specific, should developmentalists be? A leading scholar wrote:

> Psychologists and psychiatrists are fond of writing sentences such as "individuals with the short allele of the serotonin transporter [the 5-HTTLPR gene mentioned

earlier] are vulnerable to depression if they experience past stressors." . . . I suggest that they should more often write sentences such as "women with a European pedigree possessing the short allele of the serotonin transporter who live in a large city far from their family, and grew up as a later born child in an economically disadvantaged family are at risk for depression."

[Kagan, 2011, p. 111]

Kagan's suggestion is meant to be an exaggeration: The right balance between generalizations and specifics is not obvious, but Kagan insists that developmental conclusions should never be "contextually naked" (2011, p. 112). In other words, variations in background and circumstances should always be considered. Not only are neither nature nor nurture determinative, but also making simple predictions, across or within groups, is a mistake.

Both dismissing the impact of SES, culture, and so on, and taking it too much to heart, are mistakes. One of my students did the former, saying, "That's just a statistic, it doesn't apply to me," and another did the latter, saying "Now that I know all the risks for a woman like me, I will never have children." I tried to dissuade them both.

Remember that differences are not necessarily deficits, racial and ethnic categories are social constructions, and income does not trump education. Yet all differences, categories, and incomes have an effect on everyone, an effect that is neither intractable nor irrelevant. Effects change over time. This leads to the third aspect of our definition.

Fresh Fruit Many religious groups provide food for low-income families. Lisa Arsa is fortunate to have found this Seventh Day Adventist food pantry for herself and her son, Isaac. Unfortunately, the food donated to low-income families is usually high in salt, sugar, and fat—among the reasons why the U.S. rates of obesity and diabetes rise as income falls.

SUMMING UP Persons of every age, culture, and background teach us what is universal and what is unique in human development. Differences among people are not necessarily deficits, although some people mistakenly assume that their own path and choices are best for everyone.

Each person grows up with an ethnic identity and within several cultures. As social constructions, culture and ethnicity can change, but they have an impact. Race is no longer considered a biological category, but it is nonetheless a potent factor in development. Finally, socioeconomic status, which includes parents' income and education, powerfully affects the development of a child: SES affects medical care, schooling, and neighborhood, each shaping every child's body and brain. Taking all the contextual influences on child development into account, while recognizing that each child is unique, not determined by their SES or any social construction, is a challenge for developmentalists.

As Time Goes On

The effects of time are the heartbeat of human development, the essence of what we study. As already explained, an earlier idea—that development advances gradually until about age 18, steadies, and then declines—has been refuted by life-span research. We now know, though, that aspects of change appear and disappear, with increases, decreases, and zigzags (see Figure 1.4).

The pace of change differs as well. Sometimes *discontinuity* is evident: Change can occur rapidly and dramatically, as when caterpillars become butterflies. Sometimes *continuity* is found: Growth can be gradual, as when redwoods add rings over hundreds of years. And sometimes no change seems to occur: Stability itself is remarkable.

Humans experience simple growth, radical transformation, improvement, and decline as well as stability, change, and continuity—day to day, year to year, and generation to generation.

No matter what the pattern, age is always significant, and that is the focus of our study. Is it normal for a boy to throw himself down, kicking and screaming, when he is frustrated? Yes, if he is 2 years old; no, if he is 12. Is it normal for a girl to be interested in boys? Yes, at age 16; no, at age 6. More broadly, children think, play, and learn differently depending partly on their age.

Critical Periods

Some changes are sudden and profound because of a **critical period,** a time when something *must* occur for normal development or the only time when an abnormality can occur. For instance, the critical period for humans to grow arms and legs, hands and feet, fingers and toes, is between 28 and 54 days after conception. After that, it is too late: Unlike some insects, humans never grow replacement limbs or digits.

critical period A time when a particular type of developmental growth (in body or behavior) must happen for normal development to occur.

FIGURE 1.4
Patterns of Developmental Growth Many patterns of developmental growth have been discovered by careful research. Although linear progress seems most common, scientists now find that almost no aspect of human change follows the linear pattern exactly.

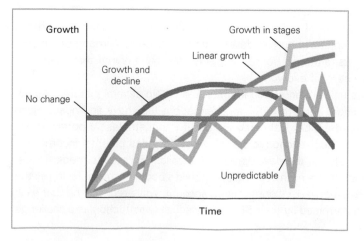

Thalidomide

We know the critical period for limb formation because of a tragic occurrence. Between 1957 and 1961, thousands of newly pregnant women in 30 nations took *thalidomide,* an anti-nausea drug. This change in nurture (via the mother's blood-stream) disrupted nature (the embryo's genetic program).

If an expectant woman ingested thalidomide during the 26 days of the critical period for limb formation, her newborn's arms or legs were malformed or absent (Moore & Persaud, 2007). Whether all four limbs, or just arms, or only hands were missing depended on exactly when the drug was taken. If thalidomide was ingested only after day 54, the newborn had normal body structures.

Sensitive Periods

Life has few critical periods. Often, however, a particular development occurs more eas-ily—not exclusively—at a certain time. Such a time is called a **sensitive period.**

An example is found in language acqui-sition. If children do not communicate in their first language between ages 1 and 3, they might do so later (hence, these years are not critical), but their grammar is impaired (hence, these years are sensitive).

Similarly, childhood is a sensitive period for learning to pronounce a second or third language with a native accent. Many adults master a new language, but strangers might ask, "Where are you from?" Native speakers can detect an accent that reveals that the second language was learned after childhood.

Often in development, individual exceptions to general patterns occur. Sweep-ing generalizations, like those in the language example, do not hold true in every case. Accent-free speech *usually* must be learned before puberty, but exceptional nature and nurture (a person naturally adept at hearing and then immersed in a new language) can result in flawless second-language pronunciation (Birdsong, 2006; Muñoz & Singleton, 2011).

Because of sensitive periods, however, such exceptions are rare. According to a study of native Dutch speakers who become fluent in English, only 1 in 20 such adults masters native pronunciation (Schmid et al., 2014).

Your Child's Teacher This 19-year-old attending Oang Ninh College in Hanoi, Vietnam, is studying to be a teacher. Emerging adulthood worldwide is a period of exploration and change: He may change professions and locations in the next six years.

sensitive period A time when a certain type of development is most likely, although it may still happen later with more difficulty. For example, early childhood is considered a sensitive period for language learning.

Ecological Systems

A leading developmentalist, Urie Bronfenbrenner (1917–2005), led the way to de-velopmentalists considering all the contextual influences on the developing child as time goes on. Just as a naturalist studying an organism examines the ecology (the relationship between the organism and its environment) of a tiger, tree, or trout, Bronfenbrenner recommended that developmentalists take an **ecological-systems approach** (Bronfenbrenner & Morris, 2006) to understand humans.

Systems Within Systems Within Systems

The ecological-systems approach recognizes three nested levels of factors that surround individuals and affect them (see Figure 1.5). Most obvious are *micro-systems*—each person's immediate surroundings, such as family and peer group.

ecological-systems approach A perspective on human development that considers all the influences from the various contexts of development. (Later renamed *bioecological theory*.)

FIGURE 1.5

The Ecological Model According to developmental researcher Urie Bronfenbrenner, each person is significantly affected by interactions among a number of overlapping systems, which provide the context of development. *Microsystems*—family, peer groups, classroom, neighborhood, house of worship—intimately and immediately shape human development. Surrounding and supporting the microsystems are the *exosystems*, which include all the external networks, such as community structures and local educational, medical, employment, and communications systems, that influence the microsystems. Influencing both of these systems is the *macrosystem,* which includes cultural patterns, political philosophies, economic policies, and social conditions. *Mesosystems* refer to interactions among systems, as when parents and teachers coordinate to educate a child. Bronfenbrenner eventually added a fifth system, the *chrono system,* to emphasize the importance of historical time.

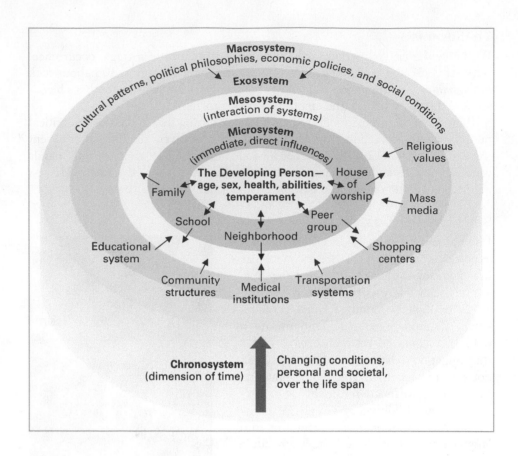

The impact of each microsystem depends partly on timing. For instance, peers are far more important in adolescence than in infancy.

Also important are *exosystems* (local institutions such as school and church) and *macrosystems* (the larger social setting, including cultural values, economic policies, and political processes).

Two more systems are related to these three. One is the *mesosystem,* consisting of the connections among the other systems. The other is the *chronosystem* (liter-

Breathe, Don't Sink Ben Schwenker is learning "drown-proofing," important for a skinny 8-year-old, since his low body fat (a physiological system) makes floating harder. Ecological systems also make this skill vital, since Ben is in Marietta, a city with thousands of pools, in Georgia, a state bordered by the Atlantic. Another system is relevant: Ben was diagnosed with autism at age 1; for him, a sense of body strength and autonomy is particularly important.

ally, "time system"); it is the historical context that allows developmentalists to focus specifically on the influence of changing historical circumstances.

Bronfenbrenner believed that people need to be studied in their natural contexts repeatedly over time (Bronfenbrenner, 1977; 1986). He looked at children playing, or mothers putting babies to sleep, or nurses in hospitals—never asking people to come to a scientist's laboratory for a contrived experiment.

Toward the end of his life, Bronfrenbrenner renamed his approach *bioecological theory* to highlight the role of biology, recognizing that systems within the body (e.g., the sexual-reproductive system, the cardiovascular system) affect the external systems as time goes on (Bronfenbrenner & Morris, 2006).

Historical Change

In studying development, it matters, of course, how old a child is, but it also matters what the political and medical conditions are when a child reaches a particular age. Both generational and cohort effects need to be considered. This needs some explanation.

All persons born within a few years of one another are called a **cohort.** Cohorts travel through life together, affected by the interaction between their chronological age and the values, events, technologies, and culture of the era. From the moment of birth, when parents decide the name of their baby, historical context is crucial (see Table 1.1).

Consider attitudes and data about marijuana. In the United States in the 1930s, marijuana was declared illegal, but enforcement was erratic. Then in the 1980s, marijuana was labeled a "gateway drug," likely to lead to drug abuse and addiction (Kandel, 2002). People were arrested and jailed for possession of even a few ounces of the drug.

From 1990 on, attitudes gradually changed. By 2014, general marijuana use became legal in two states, and medical use was permitted in several others. According to a Gallup poll, more than half (54 percent) of Americans approve making marijuana use legal, as long as it is used by adults and not in public (Motel, 2014).

These historical shifts have had a notable effect on high school students (Johnston et al., 2014 and previous years). In 1978, only 12 percent thought experimental use of marijuana was harmful, and more than half had tried the drug. In 1991, when the gateway drug message became widespread, 80 percent thought there was "great risk" in regular use and only 21 percent ever smoked the drug. Since then, marijuana use has increased as attitudes have become more accepting: Approximately one-third of high school seniors used it in 2013.

Thus cohort, more than generation, influences attitudes and behavior toward marijuana. The same is true for adults' attitudes and behavior: It matters more

"Hey! Elbows off the table."

Twenty-First-Century Manners If he obeyed his father but kept texting, would Emily Post be pleased?

cohort People born within the same historical period who therefore move through life together, experiencing the same events, new technologies, and cultural shifts at the same ages. For example, the effect of the Internet varies depending on what cohort a person belongs to.

TABLE 1.1	Popular First Names Since 1933
Girls:	**Boys:**
2013: Sophia, Emma, Olivia, Isabella, Ava	2013: Noah, Liam, Jacob, Mason, William
1993: Jessica, Ashley, Sarah, Samantha, Emily	1993: Michael, Christopher, Matthew, Joshua, Tyler
1973: Jennifer, Amy, Michelle, Kimberly, Lisa	1973: Michael, Christopher, Jason, James, David
1953: Mary, Linda, Deborah, Patricia, Susan	1953: Robert, James, Michael, John, David
1933: Mary, Betty, Barbara, Dorothy, Joan	1933: Robert, James, John, William, Richard

Source: U.S. Social Security Administration

when an adult was born than how old that adult is. It is wiser, for example, to seek generalities about people born in 1950 rather than about people who are in their 60s, or 70s, or whatever (see Figure 1.6).

FIGURE 1.6

Not Generation Sometimes people praise (or criticize) young adults for their attitudes or behavior, but perhaps people should credit (or blame) history instead. Note that even when they were young, the oldest generations did not think that marijuana should be legal, nor were they likely to endorse same-sex marriage or even mothers of young children working outside the home. On many issues, personal experience matters more than age.

OBSERVATION QUIZ Why is the line for Millennials much shorter than the line for the Silent Generation? (see answer, p. 25)

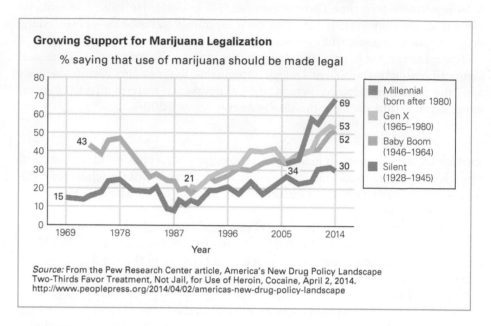

Growing Support for Marijuana Legalization

% saying that use of marijuana should be made legal

Legend:
- Millennial (born after 1980)
- Gen X (1965–1980)
- Baby Boom (1946–1964)
- Silent (1928–1945)

Source: From the Pew Research Center article, America's New Drug Policy Landscape Two-Thirds Favor Treatment, Not Jail, for Use of Heroin, Cocaine, April 2, 2014. http://www.peoplepress.org/2014/04/02/americas-new-drug-policy-landscape

Plasticity

plasticity The idea that abilities, personality, and other human characteristics can change over time. Plasticity is particularly evident during childhood, but even older adults are not always "set in their ways."

dynamic-systems approach A view of human development as an ongoing, ever-changing interaction between the physical, cognitive, and psychosocial influences. The crucial understanding is that development is never static but is always affected by, and affects, many systems of development.

The term **plasticity** denotes two complementary aspects of development: Human traits can be molded (as plastic can be), and yet people maintain a certain durability (as plastic does). This provides both hope and realism—hope because change is possible and realism because development builds on what has come before.

Plasticity is basic to our contemporary understanding of human development because it simultaneously incorporates two facts: People can change over time, and new behavior depends partly on what has already happened.

This is evident in one of the newer approaches to development, the **dynamic-systems approach.** The idea behind this approach is that human development is an ongoing, ever-changing interaction between the individual and all the systems described above. This approach began with nature:

> [S]easons change in ordered measure, clouds assemble and disperse, trees grow to a certain shape and size, snowflakes form and melt, minute plants and animals pass through elaborate life cycles that are invisible to us, and social groups come together and disband.
>
> [Thelen & Smith, 2006, p. 271]

Especially for Future Teachers Does the classroom furniture shown in the photograph to the right affect instruction? (see response, page 22)

Dynamic Interaction A dynamic-systems approach highlights the ever-changing impact that each part of a system has on all the other parts. This classroom scene reflects the eagerness for education felt by many immigrants, the reticence of some boys in an academic context, and a global perspective (as demonstrated by the world map). These facets emerge from various systems—family, gender, and culture—and they have interacted to produce this moment.

OBSERVATION QUIZ What country is this? (see answer, page 22)

Note the word *dynamic:* Physical contexts, emotional influences, the passage of time, each person, and every aspect of the ecosystem are always interacting, always in flux, always in motion. For instance, a new approach to developing the motor skills of children with autism spectrum disorder stresses the dynamic systems that undergird movement—the changing aspects of the physical and social contexts (Lee & Porretta, 2013). Using those systems may help the autistic child—not to make the autism disappear (plasticity implies that past conditions are always influential) but to make the child function more smoothly.

Plasticity is especially useful in understanding the potential of a particular person: Everyone is constrained by past circumstances but not confined by them. David is an example.

a case to study

Plasticity and David

My sister-in-law had rubella (called German measles) early in her third pregnancy, a fact not recognized until David was born, blind and dying. Heart surgery two days after birth saved his life, but surgery at 6 months to remove a cataract destroyed that eye. Malformations of his thumbs, ankles, teeth, feet, spine, and brain became evident. He was skinny; he cried a lot. Predictions were dire. Some people wondered why his parents did not place him in an institution. He did not walk or talk for years.

He was born in 1967, just when parents and educators successfully advocated that "every child can learn." Plasticity meant there was hope for David, and my brother and his wife sought out specialists who believed David could defy early predictions.

For example, most 9-month-olds can crawl but David did not, because his parents kept him safe in their arms or in his crib. Then a consultant from the Kentucky School for the Blind put him on a large rug, teaching him to feel the boundaries and crawl safely.

At age 1 David did not talk, but an audiologist found that he could hear, and teachers encouraged my brother and his wife to sing and read to him. At age 2½ he did not chew, but a nutritionist showed his parents how to force him to eat food that was not pureed. In middle childhood, doctors repaired his heart, removed the remaining cataract, realigned his jaw, replaced the dead eye with a glass one, and straightened his spine with a brace.

Dozens of educators taught him. David attended three specialized preschools, then a mainstreamed public school, then a special high school, then the University of Louisville.

Remember, plasticity cannot erase genes, childhood experiences, or permanent damage. David's disabilities are always with him. But the interaction of nature and nurture meant that, by age 10, David had skipped a year of school and was a fifth-grader, reading at the eleventh-grade level with thick glasses. He learned German and Russian, with some Spanish and Korean, and how to circumvent his handicaps. For example, he walks

My Brother's Children Michael, Bill, and David (left to right) are adults now, with quite different personalities, abilities, and offspring (4, 2, and none), and contexts (in Massachusetts, Pennsylvania, and California). Yet despite genes, prenatal life, and contexts, I see the shared influence of Glen and Dot, my brother and sister-in-law—evident here in their similar, friendly smiles.

and swims for exercise, since he could not play basketball (as his brothers did).

David now works as a translator of German texts. He enjoys that because, as he told me, "I like providing a service to scholars, giving them access to something they would otherwise not have." He uses a computer to read and write.

Family members continue to be crucial to his well-being. They still remind him to wash his hair, guide him in social situations, and accompany him to medical appointments. David now has two sisters-in-law who telephone him weekly, discussing politics, religion, sports, and so on. The baby whose birth was a reason for despair has become an adult who contributes to his family and his community. Plasticity is possible; David proves that.

SUMMING UP A critical period is a time when something *must* occur to ensure normal development or the *only* time when an abnormality might occur. Critical periods are common in fetal development, but rare later on. A sensitive period is a time when a specific development can occur most easily, with genes as well as experiences affecting what occurs in each sensitive time.

Urie Bronfenbrenner's bioecological approach notes that each person is situated within larger systems of family, school, community, and culture, all of which are constantly changing as time goes on. Each person is affected by the particular context of their society at the time: Attitudes and habits are influenced more by cohort than by age.

Although many constraints affect development, people alter and transcend their contexts and conditions, demonstrating plasticity, as evident in the dynamic-systems approach. Change is possible lifelong, although early developments never disappear completely.

WHAT HAVE YOU LEARNED?

1. What is the difference between a critical period and a sensitive period?
2. How is the drug thalidomide an example of a critical period?
3. What did Bronfenbrenner emphasize in his ecological-systems approach?
4. Why does it matter what cohort a particular person belongs to?
5. How is the concept of plasticity both hopeful and discouraging?

Using the Scientific Method

There are hundreds of ways to design scientific studies and analyze results. Scientists are aware that no design is absolutely perfect, which is one reason researchers hope for replication of their studies and confirmation from other researchers who use a different design. In addition, statistics and calculations help scientists interpret their data. (Some statistical perspectives are presented in Table 1.2.)

TABLE 1.2	Statistical Measures Often Used to Analyze Research Results
Measure	**Use**
Effect size	Indicates how much one variable affects another. Effect size ranges from 0 to 1: An effect size of 0.2 is small, 0.5 moderate, and 0.8 large.
Significance	Indicates whether the results might have occurred by chance. If the results would occur by chance fewer than 5 times in 100, that is considered significant at the 0.05 level, once in 100 is significant at 0.01; once in 1,000 is significant at 0.001.
Cost-benefit analysis	Calculates how much an intervention costs versus how much it saves. This is particularly useful to analyze spending on children, since expensive interventions (e.g. preschool) often save money later on.
Odds ratio	Indicates how a particular variable compares to a standard, set at 1. For example, one study found that, although less than 1 percent of all child homicides occurred at school, the odds were similar for public and private schools. The odds of such deaths occurring in high schools, however, were 18.47 times that of elementary or middle schools (set at 1.0) (MMWR, January 18, 2008).
Factor analysis	Hundreds of variables could affect any given behavior. In addition, many variables (such as family income and parental education) may overlap. Factor analysis clusters variables together to form a factor. For example, SES combines income and education.
Meta-analysis	A "study of studies." Researchers use statistical tools to synthesize the results of previous, separate studies. Then they analyze the accumulated results, using criteria that weight each study fairly.

Who Participates? For all these measures, the characteristics of the people who participate in the study (formerly called the subjects, now called the participants) are important, as is the number of people who are studied.

Every research design, method, and statistical measure has strengths as well as weaknesses. It is impossible to describe them all here; there are so many that colleges offer year-long courses in research design and other courses in statistics. Here we describe three basic research strategies—observation, the experiment, and the survey—and then three ways developmentalists study change over time.

Observation

Scientific observation requires researchers to record behavior systematically and objectively. Observations often occur in a naturalistic setting such as a home, where people behave normally. Scientific observation can also occur in a laboratory where scientists record human reactions in various situations, often with wall-mounted video cameras and the scientist in another room.

Observation is crucial to the development of hypotheses. However, observation provides issues to explore, not proof.

For example, one study of how long parents lingered when dropping off their children in preschool found that children were slower to engage with toys or friends when their parents stayed longer (Grady et al., 2012). This could mean that parental hesitancy to leave made children less social with friends. However, the opposite interpretation is also possible. Perhaps shy children cause parents to linger. Thus this study led to two alternative hypotheses: More research is needed to ascertain which one is more accurate.

The Experiment

The **experiment** establishes what causes what. In the social sciences, experimenters typically impose a particular treatment on a group of volunteer participants or expose them to a specific condition and then note whether their behavior changes.

LaunchPad

Video Activity: What's Wrong with This Study explores some of the major pitfalls of the process of designing a research study.

scientific observation A method of testing a hypothesis by unobtrusively watching and recording participants' behavior in a systematic and objective manner—in a natural setting, in a laboratory, or in searches of archival data.

experiment A method to determine cause and effect. Researchers control the participants and the interventions, which makes it easier to understand what causes what, for whom.

SERGIY BYCHUNENKO/ SHUTTERSTOCK

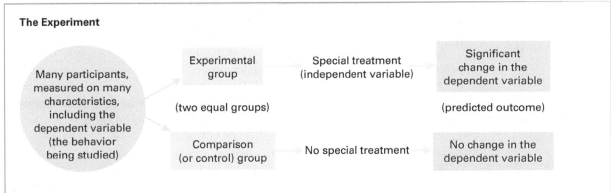

The Experiment

Many participants, measured on many characteristics, including the dependent variable (the behavior being studied)

→ Experimental group — Special treatment (independent variable) → Significant change in the dependent variable

(two equal groups) — (predicted outcome)

→ Comparison (or control) group — No special treatment → No change in the dependent variable

Procedure:

1. Divide participants into two groups that are matched on important characteristics, especially the behavior that is the dependent variable on which this study is focused.

2. Give special treatment, or intervention (the independent variable), to one group (the experimental group).

3. Compare the groups on the dependent variable. If they now differ, the cause of the difference was probably the independent variable.

4. Publish the results.

FIGURE 1.7

How to Conduct an Experiment The basic sequence diagrammed here applies to all experiments. Many additional features, especially the statistical measures listed in Table 1.2 and various ways of reducing experimenter bias, affect whether publication occurs. (Scientific journals reject reports of experiments that were not rigorous in method and analysis.)

independent variable In an experiment, the variable that is introduced to see what effect it has on the dependent variable. (Also called *experimental variable*.)

dependent variable In an experiment, the variable that may change as a result of whatever new condition or situation the experimenter adds. In other words, the dependent variable *depends* on the independent variable.

survey A research method in which information is collected from a large number of people by interviews, written questionnaires, or some other means.

case study An in-depth study of one person, usually requiring personal interviews to collect background information and various follow-up discussions, tests, questionnaires, and so on.

Especially for Nurses In the field of medicine, why are experiments conducted to test new drugs and treatments? (see response, page 26)

FIGURE 1.8

I Forgot? If this were the only data available, you might conclude that ninth-graders have suddenly become more sexually active than twelfth-graders. But we have 20 years of data—ninth-graders always answer differently by twelfth grade.

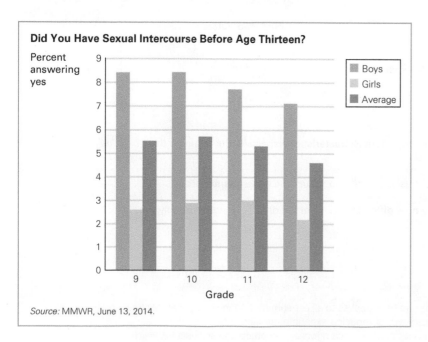

Did You Have Sexual Intercourse Before Age Thirteen?

Source: MMWR, June 13, 2014.

In technical terms, the experimenters manipulate an **independent variable,** which is the imposed treatment or special condition (also called the *experimental variable*; a *variable* is anything that can vary). They note whether this independent variable affects whatever they are studying, called the **dependent variable** (which *depends* on the independent variable).

Thus, the independent variable is the new, special treatment; any change in the dependent variable is the result. The purpose of an experiment is to find out whether an independent variable affects the dependent variable. In a typical experiment (as diagrammed in Figure 1.7), two groups of participants are studied. One group, the *experimental group,* is subjected to the particular treatment or condition (the independent variable); the other group, the *comparison group* (also called the *control group*), is not.

The Survey

A third research method is the **survey,** in which information is collected from a large number of people by interview, questionnaire, or some other means. This is a quick, direct way to obtain data.

Unfortunately, although surveys may be quick and direct, they are not necessarily accurate. When pollsters try to predict elections, they survey thousands of potential voters. They hope that the people they survey will vote as they say they will, that undecided people will follow the trends, and that people who refuse to give their opinion, or who are not included, will be similar to those surveyed. None of this is certain. Some people lie, some change their minds, some (especially those who don't have phones or who never talk to strangers) are never counted.

Furthermore, survey answers are influenced by the wording and the sequence of the questions. For instance, according to many scientists, "climate change" and "global warming" are two ways to describe the same phenomenon, yet many people believe in climate change but not in global warming (McCright & Dunlap, 2011). For that reason, surveys that seem to be about the same issue may reach opposite conclusions.

Additionally, survey respondents present themselves as they would like to be perceived. For instance, every two years since 1991, high school students in the United States have been surveyed. The participants are carefully chosen to be representative of all students in the nation. The most recent survey included 13,633 students from all 50 states and from schools large and small, public and private (MMWR, June 13, 2014).

Students are asked whether they had sexual intercourse *before* age 13. Every year, compared to the twelfth-grade boys, far more ninth-grade boys say they had sex before age 13 (see Figure 1.8). Do seniors forget or do ninth-graders lie? Or are some 13-year-olds proud of early sexual experience but ashamed by age 17? Or have all the sexually experienced boys left school by twelfth grade? These are all possibilities; surveys cannot tell us.

To understand responses in more depth, another method can be used—the **case study,** which is an in-depth study of one person. Case studies usually require personal interviews, background information, test or questionnaire results, and more.

Although case studies seem more accurate than more superficial measures, the assumptions and interpretations of the researcher may bias the results.

Even if accurate, the case study applies only to one person, who may be quite unlike other people. For instance, my report on my nephew David is a case study, but David is unique: Other embryos exposed to rubella may have quite different lives than David's.

Studying Development over the Life Span

In addition to conducting observations, experiments, and surveys, developmentalists must be mindful of the last part of our definition of the science of human development—they measure how people *change (or remain the same) over time*. To do this they use one of three basic research designs: cross-sectional, longitudinal, or cross-sequential (see Figure 1.9).

// ANSWER TO OBSERVATION QUIZ
(from page 20) Because surveys rarely ask children their opinions, and the Millennials did not reach adulthood until about 2005.

FIGURE 1.9

Which Approach Is Best? Cross-sequential research is the most time-consuming and complex, but it yields the best information. One reason that hundreds of scientists conduct research on the same topics, replicating one another's work, is to gain some advantages of cross-sequential research without waiting for decades.

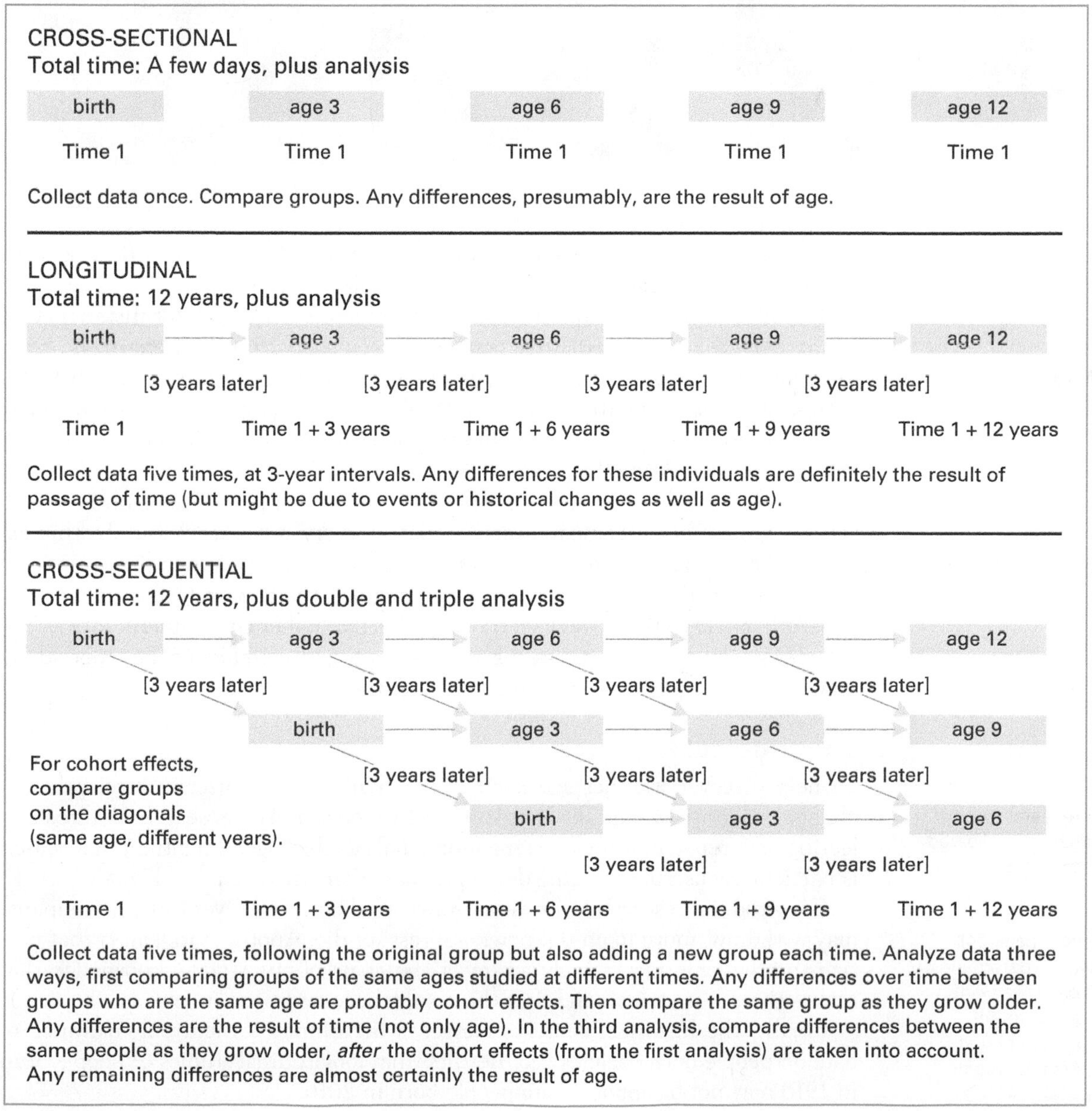

CROSS-SECTIONAL
Total time: A few days, plus analysis

birth	age 3	age 6	age 9	age 12
Time 1	Time 1	Time 1	Time 1	Time 1

Collect data once. Compare groups. Any differences, presumably, are the result of age.

LONGITUDINAL
Total time: 12 years, plus analysis

| birth | → | age 3 | → | age 6 | → | age 9 | → | age 12 |

[3 years later]   [3 years later]   [3 years later]   [3 years later]

| Time 1 | Time 1 + 3 years | Time 1 + 6 years | Time 1 + 9 years | Time 1 + 12 years |

Collect data five times, at 3-year intervals. Any differences for these individuals are definitely the result of passage of time (but might be due to events or historical changes as well as age).

CROSS-SEQUENTIAL
Total time: 12 years, plus double and triple analysis

birth → age 3 → age 6 → age 9 → age 12

[3 years later]   [3 years later]   [3 years later]   [3 years later]

birth → age 3 → age 6 → age 9

For cohort effects, compare groups on the diagonals (same age, different years).

[3 years later]   [3 years later]   [3 years later]

birth → age 3 → age 6

[3 years later]   [3 years later]

| Time 1 | Time 1 + 3 years | Time 1 + 6 years | Time 1 + 9 years | Time 1 + 12 years |

Collect data five times, following the original group but also adding a new group each time. Analyze data three ways, first comparing groups of the same ages studied at different times. Any differences over time between groups who are the same age are probably cohort effects. Then compare the same group as they grow older. Any differences are the result of time (not only age). In the third analysis, compare differences between the same people as they grow older, *after* the cohort effects (from the first analysis) are taken into account. Any remaining differences are almost certainly the result of age.

Six Stages of Life These photos show Sarah-Maria, born in 1980 in Switzerland, at six stages of her life: infancy (age 1), early childhood (age 3), middle childhood (age 8), adolescence (age 15), emerging adulthood (age 19), and adulthood (age 30).

OBSERVATION QUIZ Longitudinal research best illustrates continuity and discontinuity. For Sarah-Maria, what changed over 30 years and what didn't? (see answer, page 28)

cross-sectional research A research design that compares groups of people who differ in age but are similar in other important characteristics.

longitudinal research A research design in which the same individuals are followed over time, as their development is repeatedly assessed.

// Response for Nurses (from page 24) Experiments are the only way to determine cause-and-effect relationships. If we want to be sure that a new drug or treatment is safe and effective, an experiment must be conducted to establish that the drug or treatment improves health.

Cross-Sectional Research

The quickest and least expensive way to study development over time is with **cross-sectional research,** in which groups of people of one age are compared with groups of people of another age. Such research has found, for instance, that in the United States in 2012, 74 percent of men aged 25 to 29 were in the labor force, but only 52 percent of those aged 60 to 64 were (U.S. Bureau of Labor Statistics, 2011). It seems that about one-third of all men stop working between age 30 and age 60. Younger adults might imagine them golfing in the sun, happy with their pensions and free time.

Cross-sectional design seems simple. However, it is difficult to ensure that the various groups being compared are similar in every way except age. In this example, the younger U.S. men, on average, had more education than the older ones. Thus, what seems to be the result of age might actually have to do with schooling: Perhaps education, not age, accounted for the higher employment rates of the younger adults. Or perhaps age discrimination was the problem: The older adults may have wanted jobs but been unable to get them.

Longitudinal Research

To help discover whether age itself rather than cohort causes a developmental change, scientists undertake **longitudinal research.** This research requires collecting data repeatedly on the same individuals as they age. Longitudinal research is particularly useful in tracing development over many years.

Longitudinal research has several drawbacks, however. Over time, participants may withdraw, move to an unknown address, or die. Another problem is that participants become increasingly aware of the goals of the study—knowledge that makes them less typical, and thus the results become less valid.

Finally, the historical context changes, which limits the current relevance of data on people born decades ago. Results from longitudinal studies of people born in 1910 may not be applicable to people born in 2010.

Longitudinal research requires years of data. For example, alarm about possible future harm caused by ingesting *phthalates* and *bisphenol A* (BPA) (chemicals used in manufacturing) from plastic baby bottles and infant toys leads many parents to use glass baby bottles. But perhaps the risk of occasional shattered glass causes more harm than the chemicals in plastic, or perhaps the mother's use of cosmetics, which puts phthalates in breast milk, is a much greater source of the chemicals than any bottles (Wittassek et al., 2011).

Could breast-feeding harm infants? Virtually every scientist and pediatrician is convinced that the benefits of breast milk outweigh any dangers. However, we need accurate predictions about the future for infants who are breast- or bottle-fed now.

Another issue is whether e-cigarettes will entice more teenagers to become addicted to nicotine. Those who profit from vaping say no; public health doctors fear yes. Only longitudinal research can answer for certain, but then it might be too late (Hajek et al., 2014; Bhatnagar et al., 2014; Dutra & Glantz, 2014).

Cross-Sequential Research

Scientists have found a third strategy, called **cross-sequential research,** which combines cross-sectional and longitudinal research. (It is also referred to as *cohort-sequential* or *time-sequential research*.) With this design, researchers study several groups of people of different ages (a cross-sectional approach) and follow them over the years (a longitudinal approach).

With cross-sequential design, researchers compare a group of, say, 6-year-olds, with data on the same individuals at birth and age 3 (a longitudinal approach); they also compare this data with data from another group at birth and at age 3 and with data on a group of newborns (a cross-sectional approach) (see Figure 1.9).

If those 6-year-olds were similar at birth to the new babies and the 3-year-olds, then the newborns will probably develop as the 6-year-old did. But if historical changes have made the new babies healthier, or heavier, or different in any other notable way, then some data on the 6-year-olds may not apply.

Here is one example. Cross-sequential research discovered that when a father is absent or unemployed, his children suffer more in middle childhood than infancy (Sanson et al., 2011). That conclusion could not have been reached by cross-sectional or longitudinal research alone.

Especially for Future Researchers What is the best method for collecting data? (see response, page 29)

cross-sequential research A research design in which researchers first study several groups of people of different ages (a cross-sectional approach) and then follow those groups over the years (a longitudinal approach). (Also called *cohort-sequential research* or *time-sequential research*.)

Compare These With Those These children seem ideal for cross-sectional research—they are school children of both sexes and many ethnicities. Their only difference seems to be age, so a study might conclude that 6-year-olds raise their hands but 16-year-olds do not. But any two groups in cross-sectional research may differ in ways that are not obvious—perhaps income, national origin, or culture—and that may be the underlying reason for any observed age differences.

SUMMING UP Scientists use many methods and research designs to investigate development. Ideally, conclusions from one type of study are confirmed by other types. For example, careful and systematic observation can discover phenomena that were previously unnoticed, and then experiments can uncover causes. Surveys are quick but vulnerable to bias in the questions asked, the answers given, and the interpretation of those answers. Case studies are detailed, but it is folly to draw general conclusions from the details of any one individual.

To study change over time, cross-sectional, longitudinal, and cross-sequential designs are used, each with advantages and disadvantages. Cross-sectional is quickest, longitudinal may be more accurate, and cross-sequential combines the two, reaching conclusions that neither cross-sectional nor longitudinal research could find in isolation.

WHAT HAVE YOU LEARNED?
1. How do scientific observation and experimentation differ?
2. Why do experimenters use a control (or comparison) group as well as an experimental group?
3. What are the strengths and weaknesses of the survey method?
4. What are the advantages and disadvantages of cross-sectional research?
5. What are the advantages and disadvantages of longitudinal research?
6. What are the advantages and disadvantages of cross-sequential research?

Cautions and Challenges from Science

The scientific method illuminates and illustrates human development as nothing else does. Facts, hypotheses, and possibilities have all emerged that would not be known without science—and people of all ages are healthier, happier, and more capable than people of previous generations because of it.

For example, infectious diseases in children, illiteracy in adults, depression in late adulthood, and racism and sexism at every age are much less prevalent today than a century ago. Science deserves credit for all these advances. Even violent death is less likely, with scientific discoveries and universal education considered likely reasons (Pinker, 2011).

Developmental scientists have also discovered unexpected sources of harm. Video games, cigarettes, television, shift work, and asbestos are all less benign than people first thought. Although the benefits of science are many, so are the pitfalls. We now discuss three potential hazards: misinterpreting correlation, depending too heavily on numbers, and ignoring ethics.

Correlation and Causation

Probably the most common mistake in interpreting research is confusing correlation with causation. A **correlation** exists between two variables if one variable is more—or less—likely to occur when the other does. A correlation is *positive* if both variables tend to increase together or decrease together, *negative* if one variable tends to increase while the other decreases, and *zero* if no connection is evident.

To illustrate: From birth to age 9, there is a positive correlation between age and height (children grow taller as they grow older), a negative correlation between age and napping (children nap less often as they grow older), and zero correlation between age and number of toes (children do not grow new toes with age). (Now try the quiz on correlation in Table 1.3.)

correlation A number between +1.0 and −1.0 that indicates the degree of relationship between two variables, expressed in terms of the likelihood that one variable will (or will not) occur when the other variable does (or does not). A correlation indicates only that two variables are somehow related, not that one variable causes the other to occur.

TABLE 1.3	Quiz on Correlation	
Two Variables	Positive, Negative, or Zero Correlation?	Why? (Third Variable)
1. Ice cream sales and murder rate	_____	_____
2. Reading ability and number of baby teeth	_____	_____
3. Sex of adult and his or her average number of offspring	_____	_____

For each of these three pairs of variables, indicate whether the correlation between them is positive, negative, or nonexistent. Then try to think of a third variable that might determine the direction of the correlation. The correct answers are printed upside down at right.

Many correlations are unexpected. For instance, first-born children are more likely to develop asthma than are later-born children, teenage girls have higher rates of mental health problems than do teenage boys, and newborns of immigrants weigh more than do newborns of nonimmigrants. All these surprising correlations are discussed later.

However, *correlation is not causation*. Just because two variables are correlated does not mean that one causes the other—even if it seems logical that it does. Correlation proves only that the variables may be connected. Indeed, sometimes two variables follow the same pattern but are not connected at all (see Visualizing Development on p. 31).

Many mistaken and even dangerous conclusions are drawn because people misunderstand correlation, as the following A View from Science explains.

Answers:
1. Positive; third variable: heat
2. Negative; third variable: age
3. Zero; each child must have a parent of each sex; no third variable

// Response for Future Researchers
(from page 27) There is no best method for collecting data. The method used depends on many factors, such as the age of participants (infants can't complete questionnaires), the question being researched, and the time frame.

⚗ a view from science

Vaccination and Autism

The most recent confusion of correlation and causation regards autism spectrum disorders. Generally, the first signs of autism occur early in life, when a parent notices something wrong with how their baby responds to people. For instance, the infant might not smile, laugh, or even listen to voices or look at faces the way most babies do. Then talking is delayed, abnormal, or even absent, and the baby cries at sensations that don't bother most infants.

Thirty years ago some psychologists blamed mothers' child care for autism (the "refrigerator mom") but now most experts believe something genetic or prenatal disrupted normal social connections in the brain. That implies either that the parents carry the genes for autism or that the mother harmed the fetal brain when she was pregnant, or both (Persico & Merelli, 2014). Understandably, some parents seek a cause elsewhere. Among the possibilities are pollution, pesticides, or drugs administered during birth. But the easiest target has been immunization.

From birth to 18 months, the United States Centers for Disease Control recommends that babies get 25 doses of vaccine,

sometimes in combination such as MMR (mumps, measles, and rubella) and DTaP (diphtheria, tetanus, and pertussis). As a result, when a parent first notices symptoms of autism, almost always she or he will remember a recent immunization.

Another correlation is evident: The rate of children diagnosed with autism spectrum disorders has risen dramatically over the past two decades, from about one child in a thousand to one in 88, and the number of vaccines has risen as well. Many parents are convinced that this proves causation.

No scientist who has examined the evidence agrees. But a decade ago, state legislators heeded the fears of their constituents to allow some parents to enroll their children in school without required immunization. Every U.S. state allows some parents to refuse to vaccinate their children for medical reasons (two states), for medical or religious reasons (29 states), or for medical, religious, or personal belief reasons (19 states).

Colorado and California have the most unvaccinated children (about 20 percent) and the highest rates of childhood diseases. In 2010, California had an epidemic of whooping cough (pertussis). Ten babies died (Seppa, 2014).

That horrifies some doctors and scientists (Offit, 2011). Immunization is a major reason that 99 percent of all infants in developed nations survive at least until adolescence, compared to the nineteenth century when half of all babies died. That also illustrates why the scientific method is so important.

Fearful parents do not deserve all the blame. Almost twenty years ago, the leading medical journal in England (the *Lancet*) published a study of 12 children by a British doctor, linking the MMR to autism (Wakefield et al., 1998). A flurry of research followed, but his results were not replicated—quite the opposite.

By 2005, longitudinal, prospective, and retrospective studies of thousands of children in the United States, the United Kingdom, and Denmark found no correlation between vaccination and autism or any other disease (Andrews et al., 2004; Madsen et al., 2003; Institute of Medicine (U.S). Safety Review Committee, 2004). Since then, researchers confirmed that unvaccinated children are more likely to become seriously ill. The Wakefield study was "retracted," which means that the editors of the *Lancet* found such faulty data collection that the conclusions are invalid.

Sadly, that does not convince all the parents. Suspicion of science and of the federal government has led to suspicion of vaccination. Fortunately, infectious diseases spread slowly if most children are immunized, a phenomena called "herd immunity." As a result, even non-immunized children rarely contract diseases.

Unfortunately, if immunization rates fall lower than about 90 percent, social protection wanes. That explains why five times as many U.S. children had measles in 2014 than in the average of the previous 15 years. As fewer children are immunized, more will contract measles, chickenpox, mumps, or other preventable diseases. Even some immunized children will get sick, because no vaccine is always effective.

The other tragedy is that fewer research dollars will be spent on finding the genes and toxins that cause autism. Too many parents misunderstand correlation and causation, and then try to protect their own child while increasing the risk for everyone.

Truth or Dare Swine flu is rare but real, not a hoax. But if a vaccine prevents disease so people have no personal experience with it, and if people suspect anything from their federal government, then some individuals (like this man in Scotland, 2009) avoid the truth and take the dare—risking illness. Sadly, at Glasgow University in 2012, 39 students contracted mumps, which two doses of MMR for all babies would have prevented. Recent mumps epidemics in Scotland, England, California, and Iowa had doctors scrambling to find enough vaccine to immunize the children and young adults who were most vulnerable.

Ethics

The most important caution for all scientists, especially for those studying humans, is to uphold ethical standards in their research. Each academic discipline and every professional society involved in the study of human development has a **code of ethics** (a set of moral principles) delineating specific practices to protect the integrity of research.

Ethical standards and codes are increasingly stringent. In the United States, most educational and medical institutions have an *Institutional Review Board*

code of ethics A set of moral principles or guidelines that members of a profession or group are expected to follow.

Diverse Complexities

It is often repeated that "the United States is becominwg more diverse," a phrase that usually refers only to ethnic diversity and not to economic and religious diversity (which are also increasing and merit attention). From a developmental perspective, two other diversities are also important—age and region, as shown below. What are the implications for schools, colleges, employment, health care, and nursing homes in the notable differences in the ages of people of various groups? And are attitudes about immigration, or segregation, or multiracial identity affected by the ethnicity of one's neighbors?

THE ETHNIC MAKE-UP OF THE UNITED STATES IS CHANGING DATA FROM 2000-2009

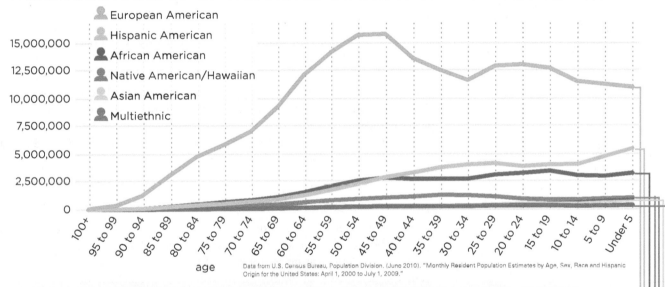

Data from U.S. Census Bureau, Population Division. (June 2010). "Monthly Resident Population Estimates by Age, Sex, Race and Hispanic Origin for the United States: April 1, 2000 to July 1, 2009."

REGIONAL DIFFERENCES IN ETHNICITY ACROSS THE UNITED STATES

In the United States, there are regional as well as age differences in ethnicity. This map shows which counties have an ethnic population greater than the national average. Counties where more than one ethnicity or race is greater than the national average are shown as multiethnic. Areas for which data are unavailable are left unshaded.

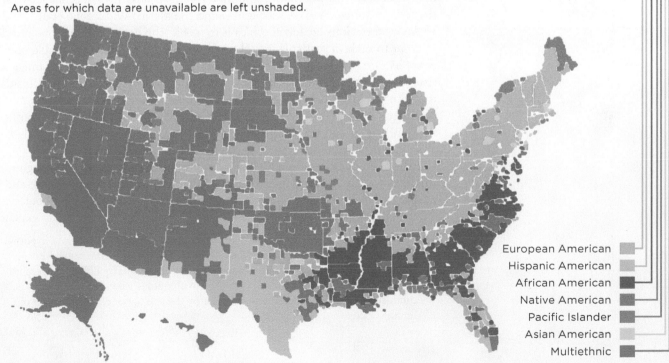

Video Activity: Eugenics and the Feebleminded: A Shameful History illustrates what can happen when scientists fail to follow a code of ethics.

Especially for Future Researchers and Science Writers Do any ethical guidelines apply when an author writes about the experiences of family members, friends, or research participants? (see response, page 34)

(IRB), a group that permits only research that follows certain guidelines. IRBs often slow down scientific study, but they are necessary: Some research conducted more than 50 years ago, before IRBs were established, was clearly unethical, especially when the participants were children, members of minority groups, prisoners, or animals (Blum, 2002; Washington, 2006).

Scientists—and everyone else—are horrified to learn about the Tuskegee study that did not treat people who had syphilis or the Little Albert research that taught an infant to fear white furry things. Details of these studies, and several others, continue to haunt current scientists, who follow many safeguards to make sure such moral lapses never happen again.

Protection of Research Participants

The most important safeguards are those that ensure no one is harmed by the study. Participation must be voluntary and confidential. This entails the *informed consent* of the participants—that is, they must understand and agree to the research procedures, knowing what risks are involved. For children, consent must be obtained from the parents as well, and the children must be allowed to end their participation at any time.

When the study is over, the participants must be "debriefed"—told what the study was about and what the results were.

Integrity of Scientific Study

Scientists are obligated to "promote accuracy, honesty, and truthfulness" (American Psychological Association, 2010) in their methods and conclusions.

Deliberate falsification is unusual. When it does occur, it leads to ostracism from the scientific community, dismissal from a teaching or research position, and, sometimes, criminal prosecution. This occurred recently with Diederik Stapel, a Dutch social psychologist. He created data that was not actually collected. Unfortunately, he is one of several prominent scientists, in both the physical and the social sciences, who have committed fraud. Almost always, other scientists are the first to notice the deception and sound the alarm (W. Stroebe et al., 2012).

Another obvious breach of ethics is to "cook" the data, or distort one's findings, in order to make a particular conclusion seem to be the only reasonable one. This is not as rare as it should be. Tenure, promotion, and funding all encourage scientists to publish, and publishers seek remarkable findings. Awareness of this danger is leading to increased calls for replication (Carpenter, 2012).

Scientists are rewarded for publishing surprising results. When a hypothesis is not confirmed, that may lead to the "file drawer problem"; that is, a study is filed away and never published because the results are not exciting.

Ethical standards cannot be taken for granted. As stressed in the beginning of this chapter, researchers, like all other humans, have strong opinions, and they expect research to confirm their opinions. Therefore, sometimes without even realizing it, they might try to achieve the results they want. As one team explains:

> Our job as scientists is to discover truths about the world. We generate hypotheses, collect data, and examine whether or not the data are consistent with those hypotheses. . . . [But we] often lose sight of this goal, yielding to pressure to do whatever is justifiable to compile a set of studies we can publish. This is not driven by a willingness to deceive but by the self-serving interpretation of ambiguity. . . .
>
> [Simmons et al., 2011, pp. 1359, 1365]

Obviously, collaboration, replication, and transparency are essential ethical safeguards for all scientists.

Science as a Way to Help Humankind

Science can be a catalyst for social change, improving the lives of millions of people, as you will see often in this text. For example, the spread of preschool education, or the acceptance of children with disabilities, arose directly from research in child development.

In this chapter, changed attitudes about sexual orientation (page 22) and about marijuana (page 21) have followed new research on those topics. For both of these issues, and many others, the passions of people on opposite sides make evidence-based, unbiased studies especially needed—but these studies are not always available. For example, partly because marijuana has been illegal, two leaders fear that the current debates "are missing an essential piece of information: scientific evidence about the effects of marijuana on the adolescent brain" (DuPont & Lieberman, 2014, p. 557).

The ultimate purpose of the science of human development is to help "all kinds of people, everywhere, of every age" live satisfying and productive lives. Consider these questions:

- Do we know enough about prenatal drug use to protect every fetus?
- Do we know enough about poverty to enable everyone to be healthy?
- Do we know enough about various family structures to understand the impact on children of marriage, or divorce, or single parenthood?
- Do we know enough about television, video games, the Internet, and cell phones to use these to enhance learning, not harm children?

The answer to all these questions is a resounding *NO*. Few funders are eager to support scientific studies of drug abuse, poverty, nonstandard families, or technology, partly because people have strong opinions and economic motives that may conflict with scientific findings and conclusions.

The next cohort of developmental scientists will build on what is known, mindful of what needs to be explored, answering the questions just posed and many more. Remember that the goal is to help all 7 billion people on Earth fulfill their potential. Much more needs to be learned. The rest of this book is a start.

SUMMING UP Although science has improved human development in many ways, caution is needed in interpreting results and in designing research. Sometimes people think that correlation indicates cause. It does not.

Research on human development must subscribe to high ethical standards. Participants must be respected and must give informed consent. Political and publishing concerns can interfere with objective research. Scientists must study and report data on issues that affect the development of all people.

WHAT HAVE YOU LEARNED?
1. Why does correlation not prove causation?
2. Why do most colleges and hospitals have an IRB?
3. What are the primary ethical principles used when scientists study humans?
4. Why are some important questions about human development not yet answered?

SUMMARY

Understanding How and Why

1. The study of human development is a science that seeks to understand how people change or remain the same over time. As a science, it begins with questions and hypotheses and then uses various methods to gather empirical data.

2. Science needed to help humans thrive, although human judgment is always part of the process. For that reason, researchers draw conclusions based on empirical data. Then replication confirms, modifies, or refutes the conclusions of a scientific study.

3. The universality of human development and the uniqueness of each individual's development are both evident in nature (the genes) and nurture (the environment); no person is quite like another. Nature and nurture always interact, and each human characteristic is affected by that interaction.

4. Crucial to the study of nature and nurture is the concept of differential susceptibility—the idea that certain genes increase or decrease the likelihood that a child will be affected by the environment.

5. Within each person, every aspect of development interacts with the others, but it is useful to divide development into three domains – biosocial, cognitive, and psychosocial.

Including All Kinds of People

6. All kinds of people, of every age, culture, and background, are studied by developmental scientists. In studying human variations, one pitfall to avoid is the difference-equals-deficit error. Sexual orientation is an example of a difference that is assumed by some to be a deficit.

7. *Culture, ethnicity,* and *race* are social constructions, concepts created by society, that nonetheless have an impact on human development. Culture includes beliefs and patterns; ethnicity refers to ancestral heritage. Many social scientists prefer not to use that term "race" because it has been destructive.

8. Socioeconomic status (SES) is an important influence on human development, affecting a person's opportunities, health, and even abilities at every age. As with other differences among people, developmentalists seek to find the balance between recognizing similarities and respecting differences.

As Time Goes On

9. Time is a crucial variable in studying human development. A critical period is a time when something *must* occur to ensure normal development or the only time when an abnormality might occur. Many developments can occur more easily—but not exclusively—at a particular time, called a sensitive period.

10. Urie Bronfenbrenner's ecological-systems or bioecological approach notes that each child is situated within larger systems of family, school, community, and culture. Changes within a person, or changes in the context, affect all other aspects of the system.

11. Certain experiences or innovations shape people of each cohort because they are members of a particular generation who share the experience of significant historical events.

12. Throughout life, human development is plastic. *Plasticity* emphasizes that it is possible for individuals to change their characteristics and behavior as they develop, although it is also true that their childhood experiences affect later development.

13. A dynamic-systems approach to development emphasizes that change is ongoing, with each part of development affecting every other part. Continuity (sameness) and discontinuity (sudden shifts) are part of every life.

Using the Scientific Method

14. Commonly used research methods when studying people are scientific observation, the experiment, and the survey. Each can provide insight and discoveries, yet none are without flaws. Replication, or using another method to study the same topic is needed.

15. An additional challenge for developmentalists is to study change over time. Two traditional research designs are often used: cross-sectional research (comparing people of different ages) and longitudinal research (studying the same people over time).

16. Both traditional methods to study human develop have limitations. A better method may be cross-sequential research (combining the two other methods).

Cautions and Challenges from Science

17. A correlation shows that two variables are related. However, it does not prove that one variable *causes* the other: The relationship of variables may be opposite to the one expected, or both may be the result of a third variable.

18. Ethical behavior is crucial in all the sciences. Not only must participants be protected and data kept confidential (primary concerns of IRBs), but results must be fairly reported and honestly interpreted. Scientists must be mindful of the implications of their research.

19. Appropriate application of scientific research depends partly on the training and integrity of the scientists. The most important ethical question is whether scientists are designing, conducting, analyzing, publishing, and applying the research that is most critically needed.

// **Response for Future Researchers and Science Writers** (from page 32) Yes. Anyone you write about must give consent and be fully informed about your intentions. They can be identified by name only if they give permission. For example, family members gave permission before anecdotes about them were included in this text. My nephew David read the first draft of his story (see page 21) and is proud to have his experiences used to teach others.

KEY TERMS

science of human development (p. 4)

scientific method (p. 4)

theory (p. 4)

hypothesis (p. 4)

empirical (p. 4)

replication (p. 5)

nature (p. 5)

nurture (p. 5)

differential sensitivity (p. 6)

difference-equals-deficit error (p. 10)

social construction (p. 11)

culture (p. 11)

ethnic group (p. 12)

race (p. 13)

socioeconomic status (SES) (p. 14)

critical period (p. 16)

sensitive period (p. 17)

ecological-systems approach (p. 17)

cohort (p. 19)

plasticity (p. 20)

dynamic-systems approach (p. 20)

scientific observation (p. 23)

experiment (p. 23)

independent variable (p. 23)

dependent variable (p. 24)

survey (p. 24)

case study (p. 24)

cross-sectional research (p. 26)

longitudinal research (p. 26)

cross-sequential research (p. 27)

correlation (p. 28)

code of ethics (p. 30)

APPLICATIONS

1. It is said that culture is pervasive but that people are unaware of it. List 30 things you did *today* that you might have done differently in another culture. Begin with how, when, and where you woke up.

2. How would your life be different if your parents were much higher or lower in SES than they are? Consider all three domains.

3. Design an experiment to answer a question you have about human development. Specify the question and the hypothesis and then describe the experiment. How would you prevent your conclusions from being biased and subjective?

4. A longitudinal case study can be insightful but is also limited in generality. Describe the life of one of your older relatives, explaining what aspects of their development are unique and what aspects might be relevant for everyone.

Theories

According to many news reports (Goodman, 2012; Pearce, 2012), Larry De-Primo, a 25-year-old police officer on duty in Times Square, saw a barefoot man on a frigid November night, asked his shoe size (12), and bought him all-weather boots and thermal socks. As DePrimo bent down to help the man don his gift, a tourist from Arizona snapped his photo. Days later, the tourist wrote to the New York Police Department, who put the image on their website. It went viral.

Then came theories.

Commentators asked: Was this real or a hoax? Was DiPrimo's act typical ("most cops are honorable, decent people"), atypical ("truly exceptional"), or in between ("not all NYC cops are short-tempered, profiling, or xenophobic")? Is the officer young and naïve, are his parents proud and wonderful, was his assignment (anti-terrorism patrol) neglected or boring?

These questions reflect not science but "folk theories," which arise from preconceptions and everyday experience (Bazinger & Kühberger, 2012). Nonetheless, this anecdote illustrates three aspects shared by all theories, scientific as well as folk: (1) behavior can be surprising, (2) humans develop theories to explain everything, and (3) experience and culture matter.

Regarding theories of this incident, past experience is particularly apparent: An advocate for the homeless suspected that the photo was staged; the tourist was reminded of her father, also a police officer; many commentators used this event to criticize someone, among them New York City's mayor (for not helping the poor), the police (for harassing the homeless), journalists (for focusing "on murder and mayhem"), or the barefoot man himself (for choosing his plight). A year later, DePrimo was promoted; his father, responding to more speculation, said his service record was the reason, not the boots (Antenucci, 2013).

Badge and Boots This is Larry DePrimo, a police officer in Manhattan, who astonished everyone when he bought boots for a barefoot man on a cold afternoon.

developmental theory A group of ideas, assumptions, and generalizations that interpret and illuminate the thousands of observations that have been made about human growth. A developmental theory provides a framework for explaining the patterns and problems of development.

In this chapter, we explain several of the most insightful theories of human development. Because they are comprehensive and complex, they propel science forward, inspiring thousands of scientists to experiment and explain. These theories share with all theories the three characteristics just listed, but unlike folk theories, they lead to new insights and alternate interpretations.

Simple pronouncements regarding one incident are relatively easy to prove or disprove. DePrimo is from my local precinct; I know his commanding officer, who praised him. This was not a hoax.

What Theories Do

Every theory is an explanation of facts and observations, a set of concepts and ideas that organize the confusing mass of experiences that each of us encounters every minute. Some theories are idiosyncratic, narrow, and useless to anyone except the people who thought of them. Others are much more elaborate and insightful, such as the major theories described in this chapter.

A **developmental theory** is a systematic statement of general principles that provides a framework for understanding how and why people change as they grow older. Facts and observations are connected to patterns of change and explanations, weaving the details into a meaningful whole. A developmental theory is more than a hunch or a hypothesis, and is far more comprehensive than a folk theory. Developmental theories provide insights that are both broad and deep.

Kurt Lewin (1943) once quipped, "Nothing is as practical as a good theory." Like many other scientists, he knew that theories can be insightful. Of course, theories differ; some are less comprehensive or adequate than others, some are no longer useful, and some reflect one culture but not another.

Questions and Answers

As we saw in Chapter 1, the first step in the science of human development is to pose a question, which often springs from a developmental theory. Among the thousands of important questions are the following, each central to one of the five theories described in this chapter:

1. Does the impact of early experience—of breast-feeding or attachment or abuse—linger into adulthood, even if the experience seems to be forgotten?
2. Does learning depend on specific encouragement, punishment, and/or role models?
3. Do children develop morals, even if they are not taught right from wrong?
4. Does culture guide parents' behavior, such as how they react to a child's cry?
5. Is survival an inborn instinct, underlying all personal and social decisions?

Each of these five questions is answered "yes" by, in order, psychoanalytic theory, behaviorism, cognitive theory, sociocultural theory, and the two universal theories, humanism and evolutionary theory. Each question is answered "no" or "not necessarily" by several others. For every answer, more questions arise: Why or why not? When and how? So what? This last question is crucial; the implications and applications of the answers affect everyone's daily life.

To be more specific about what theories do:

- Theories produce *hypotheses*.
- Theories generate *discoveries*.
- Theories offer *practical guidance*.

Facts and Norms

A **norm** is an average or usual event or experience. It is related to the word "normal," although it has a slightly different meaning. Something can be outside the norm, but that does not make it abnormal.

To be abnormal implies that something is wrong, but norms are neither right nor wrong. A norm is an average—not an arithmetical mean or median, but a mode, a common behavior. Thus, norms can be calculated (such as the norm for the age at which babies walk or children read), but, as you learned in Chapter 1, differences from the norm are not necessarily deficits.

For example, it is not the norm for police officers to spend their own money to buy boots for strangers, which is why DePrimo's act generated headlines. But his act would not be called abnormal.

Do not confuse theories with norms or facts. Theories raise questions and suggest hypotheses, and they lead to research to gather empirical data. Those data are facts that suggest conclusions, which may verify or refute some aspect of the theory; however, other interpretations of the data and new research to investigate the theory are always possible.

Obviously, the scientific method is needed because "each theory of developmental psychology always has a view of humans that reflects philosophical, economic, and political beliefs" (Miller, 2011, p. 17). A theory can begin the process, but then scientists develop hypotheses, design studies, and collect and analyze data that lead to conclusions that undercut some theories and modify others. (**Developmental Link:** These five steps are explained in Chapter 1.)

Humans spontaneously develop theories about everything they observe. Some theories are better than others. Developmental theories are very useful: Without them, we would be merely reactive and bewildered, adrift and increasingly befuddled, blindly following our culture and our prejudices, less able to help anyone with a developmental problem.

> **norm** An average, or typical, standard of behavior or accomplishment, such as the norm for age of walking or the norm for greeting a stranger.

EMILY ROSE BENNETT/STAFF/THE AUGUSTA CHRONICLE/ZUMAPRESS.COM

ASTAPKOVICH VLADIMIR ITAR-TASS PHOTOS/NEWSCOM

Backpacks or Bouquets? Children worldwide are nervous on the first day of school, but their coping reflects implicit cultural theories. Kindergartener Madelyn Ricker in Georgia shows her new backpack to her teacher, and elementary school children in Russia bring flowers to their teachers.

SUMMING UP Theories provide a framework for organizing and understanding the thousands of observations we make and the daily behaviors that occur in every aspect of development. Theories are not facts, but they allow us to question norms, suggest hypotheses, and provide guidance. Thus, theories are practical and applied: They help us frame and organize our millions of experiences.

WHAT HAVE YOU LEARNED?

1. What three things do theories do?
2. What is the difference between a theory and a norm?
3. What is the relationship between theories and facts?

Psychoanalytic Theory: Freud and Erikson

Inner drives, deep motives, and unconscious needs rooted in childhood—especially in experiences in the first six years—form the foundation of **psychoanalytic theory.** These basic underlying forces are thought to influence every aspect of thinking and behavior, from the smallest details of daily life to the crucial choices of a lifetime.

psychoanalytic theory A grand theory of human development that holds that irrational, unconscious drives and motives, often originating in childhood, underlie human behavior.

Freud's Ideas

Psychoanalytic theory originated with Sigmund Freud (1856–1939), an Austrian physician who treated patients suffering from mental illness. He listened to their remembered dreams and to their uncensored streams of thought, and he constructed an elaborate, multifaceted theory. Much of it concerns child development.

According to Freud, development in the first six years of life occurs in three stages, each characterized by sexual interest and pleasure arising from a particular part of the body. In infancy the erotic body part is the mouth (the *oral stage*). In early childhood it is the anus (the *anal stage*). In the preschool years it is the penis (the *phallic stage*), a source of pride and fear among boys and a reason for sadness and envy among girls. Then, after a quiet period (*latency*), the *genital stage* arrives at puberty, lasting throughout adulthood. (Table 2.1 describes stages in Freud's theory.)

Freud maintained that sensual pleasure (from stimulation of the mouth, anus, or penis) is linked to major developmental stages, needs, and challenges. During the oral stage, for example, sucking provides not only nourishment but also erotic joy and attachment to the mother. Kissing in adulthood is a vestige of the oral stage. Next, during the anal stage, pleasures arise from self-control, initially with toileting.

One of Freud's most influential ideas was that each stage includes its own struggles. Conflict occurs, for instance, when mothers try to wean their babies (oral stage), toilet train their toddlers (anal stage), deflect the sexual curiosity and fantasies of their 5-year-olds (phallic stage), and limit the sexual interests of adolescents (genital stage). According to Freud, how children experience and resolve

Freud at Work In addition to being the world's first psychoanalyst, Sigmund Freud was a prolific writer. His many papers and case histories, primarily descriptions of his patients' symptoms and sexual urges, helped make the psychoanalytic perspective a dominant force for much of the twentieth century.

SCIENCE SOURCE

©2016 MACMILLAN

No Choking During the oral stage, children put everything in their mouths, as Freud recognized and as 12-month-old Harper Vasquez does here. Toy manufacturers and lawyers know this too, which is why many toy packages say "Choking hazard: small parts, not appropriate for children under age 3."

TABLE 2.1	Comparison of Freud's Psychosexual and Erikson's Psychosocial Stages	
Approximate Age	Freud (Psychosexual)	Erikson (Psychosocial)
Birth to 1 year	*Oral Stage* The lips, tongue, and gums are the focus of pleasurable sensations in the baby's body, and sucking and feeding are the most stimulating activities.	*Trust vs. Mistrust* Babies either trust that others will satisfy their basic needs, including nourishment, warmth, cleanliness, and physical contact, **or** develop mistrust about the care of others.
1–3 years	*Anal Stage* The anus is the source of pleasure in the baby's body, and toilet training is the most important activity.	*Autonomy vs. Shame and Doubt* Children either become self-sufficient in many activities, including toileting, feeding, walking, exploring, and talking, **or** doubt their own abilities.
3–6 years	*Phallic Stage* The phallus, or penis, is the most important body part, and pleasure comes from genital stimulation. Boys are proud of their penises; girls wonder why they don't have them.	*Initiative vs. Guilt* Children either try to undertake many adultlike activities **or** internalize the limits and prohibitions set by parents. They feel either adventurous **or** guilty.
6–11 years	*Latency* Not really a stage, latency is an interlude. Sexual needs are quiet; psychic energy flows into sports, schoolwork, and friendship.	*Industry vs. Inferiority* Children busily practice and then master new skills **or** feel inferior, unable to do anything well.
Adolescence	*Genital Stage* The genitals provide pleasurable sensations. The young person seeks sexual stimulation and satisfaction in heterosexual relationships.	*Identity vs. Role Confusion* Adolescents ask themselves "Who am I?" They establish sexual, political, religious, and vocational identities **or** are confused about their roles.
Adulthood	Freud believed that the genital stage lasts throughout adulthood. He also said that the goal of a healthy life is "to love and to work."	*Intimacy vs. Isolation* Young adults seek companionship and love **or** become isolated from others, fearing rejection. *Generativity vs. Stagnation* Adults contribute to future generations through work, creative activities, and parenthood **or** they stagnate. *Integrity vs. Despair* Older adults try to make sense of their lives, either seeing life as a meaningful whole **or** despairing at goals never reached.

these conflicts determines personality lifelong because "the early stages provide the foundation for adult behavior" (Salkind, 2004, p. 125).

Freud did not believe that new stages occurred after puberty; rather, he believed that adult personalities and habits were influenced by what happened in childhood. Unconscious conflicts rooted in early life may be evident in adult behavior—for instance, smoking cigarettes (oral) or keeping a clean and orderly house (anal) or falling in love with a much older partner (phallic).

Erikson's Ideas

Many of Freud's followers became famous theorists themselves, Carl Jung, Alfred Adler, and Karen Horney among them. They acknowledged the importance of the unconscious and of early childhood experience, but each of them expanded and modified Freud's ideas. For scholars in child development, one neo-Freudian, Erik Erikson (1902–1994), is the most insightful. He proposed a comprehensive developmental theory.

Erikson described eight developmental stages, each characterized by a particular challenge, or *developmental crisis* (summarized in Table 2.1). Although Erikson named two polarities at each crisis, he recognized a wide range of outcomes

A Legendary Couple In his first 30 years, Erikson never fit into a particular local community, since he frequently changed nations, schools, and professions. Then he met Joan. In their first five decades of marriage, they raised a family and wrote several books. If he had published his theory at age 73 (when this photograph was taken) instead of in his 40s, would he still have described life as a series of crises?

Especially for Teachers Your kindergartners are talkative and always moving. They almost never sit quietly and listen to you. What would Erik Erikson recommend? (see response, page 44)

between those opposites. Typically, development at each stage leads to neither extreme but to something in between.

In the stage of *initiative versus guilt,* for example, 3- to 6-year-olds undertake activities that exceed the limits set by their parents and culture. They jump into swimming pools, pull their pants on backwards, make cakes according to their own recipes, and wander off alone. Efforts to act independently produce the child's feelings of pride or failure and then lifelong guilt if adults are too critical or if social norms are too strict. Decades later, most adults fall somewhere between unbridled initiative and crushing guilt, depending on their early childhood experiences.

As you can see from Table 2.1, Erikson's first five stages are closely related to Freud's stages. Erikson, like Freud, believed that problems of adult life echo unresolved childhood conflicts. He thought the first stage, *trust versus mistrust,* was particularly crucial. For example, an adult who has difficulty establishing a secure, mutual relationship with a life partner may never have resolved that first crisis of early infancy, trust versus mistrust.

Every stage echoes throughout life. For instance, in late adulthood, one older person may be outspoken while another avoids saying anything because each resolved the initiative-versus-guilt stage in opposite ways.

In two crucial aspects, Erikson's stages differ significantly from Freud's:

1. Erikson's stages emphasized family and culture, not sexual urges.
2. Erikson recognized adult development, with three stages after adolescence.

SUMMING UP Both Freud and Erikson thought unconscious drives and early experiences form later personality and behavior, but they differed on the origins of those drives and experiences. Freud believed development depended on three psychosexual stages that impacted later habits and personality, not only in the next two periods (latency and genital) but lifelong. Conflict between the child's impulses and the parents' restrictions was inevitable, forming personality. On the other hand, Erikson's eight psychosocial stages were characterized by developmental crises resolved through the individual's relationship to family, and culture, a process that continued lifelong.

WHAT HAVE YOU LEARNED?

1. What is the basic idea of psychoanalytic theory?
2. What body parts are connected to the oral, anal, and phallic stages?
3. Which psychosocial stage did Erikson believe was a foundation for all later relationships?
4. In what two ways does Erikson's theory differ from Freud's?

Behaviorism: Conditioning and Social Learning

Another comprehensive theory arose in direct opposition to the psychoanalytic notion of the unconscious. John B. Watson (1878–1958) argued that if psychology was to be a true science, psychologists should examine only what they could see and measure: behavior, not irrational thoughts and hidden urges. In his words:

A Conventional Couple The identity crisis looks like a rejection of social norms, from her multicolored hair to his two-color pants. But Erikson noted that underlying the crisis is the wish to find another teenager who shares the same identity— as these two have done.

Why don't we make what we can *observe* the real field of psychology? Let us limit ourselves to things that can be observed, and formulate laws concerned only with those things. . . . We can observe behavior—what the organism does or says.

[Watson, 1998, p. 6]

According to Watson, if psychologists focus on behavior, they will realize that everything can be learned. He wrote:

Give me a dozen healthy infants, well-formed, and my own specified world to bring them up in and I'll guarantee to take any one at random and train him to become any type of specialist I might select—doctor, lawyer, artist, merchant-chief, and yes, even beggar-man and thief, regardless of his talents, penchants, tendencies, abilities, vocations, and race of his ancestors.

[Watson, 1998, p. 82]

Other psychologists, especially in the United States, agreed. They developed **behaviorism** to study observable behavior, objectively and scientifically. Behaviorism is also called *learning theory* because it describes the learning process.

For everyone at every age, behaviorists believe there are natural laws of human behavior. Those laws allow simple actions to become complex competencies, as various forces in the environment affect each action. Learning is far more than an academic skill, such as learning to read. It includes learning to suck on a nipple, learning to smile at a caregiver, learning to hold hands when crossing the street, and so on.

Learning theorists believe that development occurs not in stages but bit by bit. A person learns to talk, read, or anything else one tiny step at a time. Behaviorists study **conditioning,** the processes by which responses link to particular stimuli. In the first half of the twentieth century, behaviorists described only two types of conditioning: classical and operant. Both are still described in parenting-advice books.

Classical Conditioning

A century ago, Russian scientist Ivan Pavlov (1849–1936), after winning the Nobel Prize for his work on animal digestion, examined the link between stimulus and response. While studying salivation, Pavlov noted that his experimental dogs drooled not only at the smell of food but also, eventually, at the sound of the footsteps of the people bringing food. This observation led Pavlov to perform a famous experiment: He conditioned dogs to salivate when hearing a particular noise.

Pavlov began by sounding a tone just before presenting food. After a number of repetitions of the tone-then-food sequence, dogs began salivating at the sound even when there was no food. This simple experiment demonstrated **classical conditioning** (also called *respondent conditioning*).

In classical conditioning, a person or animal learns to associate a neutral stimulus with a meaningful stimulus, gradually responding to the neutral stimulus in the same way as to the meaningful one. In Pavlov's original experiment, the dog associated the tone (the neutral stimulus) with food (the meaningful stimulus) and eventually responded to the tone as if it were the food itself. The conditioned response to the tone, no longer neutral but now a conditioned stimulus, was evidence that learning had occurred.

Behaviorists see dozens of examples of classical conditioning in child development. Infants learn to smile at their parents because they associate them with food and play; toddlers become afraid of busy streets if the noise of traffic repeatedly frightens them; students enjoy—or fear—school, depending on what happened in kindergarten.

An Early Behaviorist John Watson was an early proponent of learning theory. His ideas are still influential and controversial today.

behaviorism A grand theory of human development that studies observable behavior. Behaviorism is also called *learning theory* because it describes the laws and processes by which behavior is learned.

conditioning According to behaviorism, the processes by which responses become linked to particular stimuli and learning takes place. The word *conditioning* is used to emphasize the importance of repeated practice, as when an athlete *conditions* his or her body.

classical conditioning The learning process in which a meaningful stimulus (such as the smell of food to a hungry animal) is connected with a neutral stimulus (such as the sound of a tone) that had no special meaning before conditioning. (Also called *respondent conditioning*.)

A Contemporary of Freud Ivan Pavlov was a physiologist who received the Nobel Prize in 1904 for his research on digestive processes. It was this line of study that led to his discovery of classical conditioning, when his research on dog saliva led to insight about learning.

OBSERVATION QUIZ In appearance, how is Pavlov similar to Freud, and how do both look different from the other theorists pictured? (see answer, page 46)

operant conditioning The learning process by which a particular action is followed by something desired (which makes the person or animal more likely to repeat the action) or by something unwanted (which makes the action less likely to be repeated). (Also called *instrumental conditioning.*)

// Response for Teachers (from page 42) Erikson would note that the behavior of 5-year-olds is affected by their developmental stage and by their culture. Therefore, you might design your curriculum to accommodate active, noisy children.

One specific example of classical conditioning is called the *white coat syndrome,* which occurs in people for whom past experiences with medical professionals (who wore white coats) conditioned anxiety. For that reason, when someone dressed in white takes their blood pressure, it is higher than it would be under normal circumstances.

White coat syndrome is apparent in about half of the U.S. population over age 80 (Bulpitt et al., 2013). It began when those elders were children. Today many nurses, especially in pediatrics, wear colorful blouses and many doctors wear street clothes: They dress to prevent conditioned anxiety.

Operant Conditioning

The most influential North American proponent of behaviorism was B. F. Skinner (1904–1990). Skinner agreed that psychology should focus on the science of behavior. He did not dispute Pavlov's classical conditioning, but, as a good scientist, he built on Pavlov's conclusions with his own experiments. His most famous contribution was to recognize another type of conditioning—**operant conditioning** (also called *instrumental conditioning*)—in which animals (including people) act and then something follows that action.

In other words, he went beyond observation of learning by association, in which one stimulus is paired with another stimulus (in Pavlov's experiment, the tone with the food). He focused instead on what happens *after* a behavior elicits a particular response. If the consequence that follows is enjoyable, the animal tends to repeat the behavior; if the consequence is unpleasant, the animal might not. Usually, operant conditioning occurs only after several repetitions of an action that result in similar consequences.

Pleasant consequences are sometimes called *rewards,* but behaviorists do not call them that because what some people consider a reward may actually be a punishment, an unpleasant consequence. For instance, some teachers think they are rewarding children by giving them more recess time, but some children may hate the social pressures of recess.

The opposite is true as well: Something thought to be a punishment may actually be a positive consequence. For example, parents think they punish their children by withholding dessert. But a particular child might dislike the dessert, so being deprived of it is no punishment.

Sometimes teachers send misbehaving children out of the classroom and principals suspend them from school. However, if a child hates the teacher, leaving class is rewarding, and if a child hates school, suspension is a reward. Indeed, research on school discipline finds that some measures, including school suspension, *increase* later misbehavior (Osher et al., 2010).

Rats, Pigeons, and People B. F. Skinner is best known for his experiments with rats and pigeons, but he also applied his knowledge to human behavior. For his daughter, he designed a glass-enclosed crib in which temperature, humidity, and perceptual stimulation could be controlled to make her time in the crib enjoyable and educational. He encouraged her first attempts to talk by smiling and responding with words, affection, or other positive reinforcement.

In order to stop misbehavior, it is more effective to encourage good behavior, to "catch them being good." Three times as many African American children are suspended as European American children, even though white children are the majority in schools. The statistics on school discipline raise a troubling question: Is suspension a punishment for the child, or is it a reward for the teacher? Or even a sanctioned expression of racism (Tajalli & Garba, 2014; Shah, 2011)?

The true test is the *effect* a consequence has on the individual's future actions, not whether it is intended to be a reward or a punishment. A child, or an adult, who repeats an offense may have been reinforced, not punished, for the first infraction.

Consequences that increase the frequency or strength of a particular action are called reinforcers, in a process called **reinforcement** (Skinner, 1953). According to behaviorism, almost all of our daily behavior, from saying "Good morning" to earning a paycheck, can be explained as the result of past reinforcement.

Social Learning

At first, behaviorists thought all behavior arose from a chain of learned responses, the result of either the association between one stimulus and another (classical conditioning) or of past reinforcement (operant conditioning). Thousands of experiments inspired by learning theory have demonstrated that both classical conditioning and operant conditioning occur often as children grow.

However, research finds that people at every age are social and active, not just reactive. Instead of responding merely to their own direct experiences, "people act on the environment. They create it, preserve it, transform it, and even destroy it . . . in a socially embedded interplay" (Bandura, 2006, p. 167).

That social interplay is the foundation of **social learning theory** (see Table 2.2), which holds that humans sometimes learn without personal reinforcement. This learning often occurs through **modeling,** when people copy what they see others do (also called *observational learning*). However, modeling is not simple imitation, and some people are more likely to be followed as roles models than others. Indeed, people model only some actions, of some individuals, in some contexts, and sometimes they do the opposite of what they have observed.

Generally, modeling is most likely to occur when the observer is uncertain or inexperienced (which explains why modeling is especially powerful in childhood) and when the model is admired, powerful, nurturing, or similar to the observer (Bandura, 1986, 1997).

Especially for Teachers Same problem as previously (talkative kindergartners), but what would a behaviorist recommend? (see response, page 47)

Still Social Learning This photo shows Bandura in middle age, but even in his 80s, he is on the faculty at Stanford University. As a proponent of social learning, he believes he still can influence students and faculty.

reinforcement When a behavior is followed by something desired, such as food for a hungry animal or a welcoming smile for a lonely person.

social learning theory An extension of behaviorism that emphasizes the influence that other people have over a person's behavior. Even without specific reinforcement, every individual learns through observation and imitation of other people. (Also called *observational learning*.)

modeling The central process of social learning, by which a person observes the actions of others and then copies them.

TABLE 2.2	Three Types of Learning	
Behaviorism is also called *learning theory* because it emphasizes the learning process, as shown here.		
Type of Learning	**Learning Process**	**Result**
Classical Conditioning	Learning occurs through association.	Neutral stimulus becomes conditioned response.
Operant Conditioning	Learning occurs through reinforcement and punishment.	Weak or rare responses become strong, frequent responses. Or, with punishment, unwanted responses become extinct.
Social Learning	Learning occurs through modeling what others do.	Observed behaviors become copied behaviors.

Learning to Be a Dad Note how the 2-year-old angles the bottle and the doll's body, just as his father does. Even his left hand, gentle on the head, shows that he is learning how to be a good father from watching his dad.

Video Activity: Modeling: Learning by Observation features the original footage of Bandura's famous experiment.

Social learning is particularly noticeable in early adolescence, when children want to be similar to their peers despite their parents' wishes. That impulse may continue into adulthood. Is your speech, hairstyle, or choice of shoes similar to those of your peers, or of an entertainer, or a sports hero? Why?

SUMMING UP Unlike Freud and Erikson, behaviorists emphasize that psychologists should study what can be observed and measured, not the unconscious. Behaviorists also thought that every behavior is the product of learning, and they set out to understand the laws of learning. Pavlov's experiment with dogs (classical conditioning) and Skinner's experiments with rats and pigeons (operant conditioning) demonstrated that learning is a lifelong process that guides human behavior. Social learning theorists extended behaviorism to include learning through the observation and imitation (modeling) of other people.

WHAT HAVE YOU LEARNED?
1. What is the basic idea of behaviorism?
2. How does the way a nurse or doctor dress illustrate classical conditioning?
3. In operant conditioning, why is a reinforcement different from what people often call a reward?
4. According to social learning, how do people choose their role models?

Cognitive Theory: Piaget and Information Processing

Social scientists sometimes write about the "cognitive revolution," which occurred in about 1980 when psychoanalytic and behaviorist research and therapy were overtaken by a focus on cognition. That does not mean that behaviorism and psychoanalysis are no longer relevant: The cognitive revolution adds another aspect to our understanding of children without demolishing previous conceptions of development (Watrin & Darwich, 2012).

// ANSWER TO OBSERVATION QUIZ
(from page 44) Both are balding, with white beards. Note also that none of the other theorists in this chapter have beards—a cohort difference, not an ideological one.

According to **cognitive theory,** thoughts and expectations profoundly affect attitudes, beliefs, values, assumptions, and actions. This revolution was the result of an increasing awareness of the power of the mind. Cognitive theory dominated psychology for decades, becoming a grand theory.

cognitive theory A grand theory of human development that focuses on changes in how people think over time. According to this theory, our thoughts shape our attitudes, beliefs, and behaviors.

Piaget's Stages of Development

The first major cognitive theorist was the Swiss scientist Jean Piaget (1896–1980), considered by many "the greatest developmental psychologist of all time" (Haidt, 2013, p. 6). Piaget's academic training was in biology, with a focus on shellfish—a background that taught him to look very closely at small details. He became interested in human thought when he was hired to standardize an IQ test by noting at what age children answered each question correctly.

Although he did his job, noting when children knew, for example, that a bicycle had two wheels and a hand had five fingers, it was the children's wrong answers that intrigued him. *How* children think is much more revealing, Piaget concluded, than *what* they know.

In the 1920s, most scientists believed that babies could not yet think. But Piaget used scientific observation with his own three infants, finding them curious and thoughtful.

Later he studied hundreds of schoolchildren. From this work, Piaget formed the central thesis of cognitive theory: How children think changes with time and experience, and their thought processes affect their behavior. According to cognitive theory, to understand humans of any age, one must understand intellectual processes.

Would You Talk to This Man? Children loved talking to Jean Piaget, and he learned by listening carefully—especially to their incorrect explanations, which no one before Piaget had paid much attention to. All his life, Piaget studied the way children think.

Piaget maintained that cognitive development occurs in four age-related periods, or stages: *sensorimotor, preoperational, concrete operational,* and *formal operational* (see Table 2.3). Each period fosters certain cognitive processes: Infants

How to Think About Flowers A person's stage of cognitive growth influences how he or she thinks about everything, including flowers. (a) To an infant, in the sensorimotor stage, flowers are "known" through pulling, smelling, and even biting. (b) At the concrete operational stage, children become more logical. This boy can understand that flowers need sunlight, water, and time to grow. (c) At the adult's formal operational stage, flowers can be part of a larger, logical scheme—for instance, to earn money while cultivating beauty. As illustrated by all three photos, thinking is an active process from the beginning of life until the end.

// Response for Teachers (from page 45) Behaviorists believe that anyone can learn anything. If your goal is quiet, attentive children, begin by reinforcing a moment's quiet or a quiet child, and soon all the children will be trying to remain quietly attentive for several minutes at a time.

(a)

(b)

(c)

think via their senses, preschoolers have language but not logic, school-age children have simple logic. Finally, formal, abstract reasoning becomes possible at puberty (Inhelder & Piaget, 1958/2013b; Piaget, 1952/2011).

Piaget found that intellectual advancement occurs because humans at every age seek **cognitive equilibrium**—a state of mental balance. The easiest way to achieve this balance is to interpret new experiences through the lens of preexisting ideas. For example, infants grab new objects in the same way that they grasp familiar objects, a child's first concept of God is as a loving—or punishing—parent, and at every age, children interpret their parents' behavior by assuming everyone thinks in the same way that they themselves do.

Achieving equilibrium is not always easy, however. Sometimes a new experience or question is jarring or incomprehensible. Then the individual experiences *cognitive disequilibrium,* an imbalance that creates confusion. As Figure 2.1 illustrates, disequilibrium can cause cognitive growth if people adapt their thinking. Piaget describes two types of cognitive adaptation:

- **Assimilation:** New experiences are reinterpreted to fit, or *assimilate,* into old ideas.
- **Accommodation:** Old ideas are restructured to include, or *accommodate,* new experiences.

Accommodation is more difficult than assimilation, but it advances thought. Children—and everyone else—actively develop new concepts. In Piagetian terms, they *construct* ideas based on their experiences.

Ideally, when two people disagree, or when they surprise each other by what they say, adaptation is mutual. For example, when parents are startled by their children's opinions, the parents may revise their concepts of their children and even of reality, accommodating to new perceptions. If an honest discussion occurs, the children, too, might accommodate. Cognitive growth is an active process; clashing concepts require new thought.

Information Processing

Piaget is credited with discovering that people's assumptions and perceptions affect their development, an idea now accepted by most social scientists. However, many think Piaget's theories were limited. Neuroscience, cross-cultural studies, and step-by-step understanding of cognition have revealed the limitations of Piaget's theory.

As one admirer explains, Piaget's "claims were too narrow and too broad" (Hopkins, 2011, p. 35). The narrowness comes from his focus on science, ignoring that people can be advanced in their understanding of physics and biology but not in other aspects of thought. The broadness is in his description of stages. Contrary to Piaget's ideas, "intelligence is now viewed more as a modular system than as a unified system of general intelligence" (Hopkins, 2011, p. 35).

Now consider a newer version of cognitive theory, **information-processing theory,** inspired by the input, programming, memory, and output of a sophisti-

cognitive equilibrium In cognitive theory, a state of mental balance in which people are not confused because they can use their existing thought processes to understand current experiences and ideas.

assimilation The reinterpretation of new experiences to fit into old ideas.

accommodation The restructuring of old ideas to include new experiences.

information-processing theory A perspective that compares human thinking processes, by analogy, to computer analysis of data, including sensory input, connections, stored memories, and output.

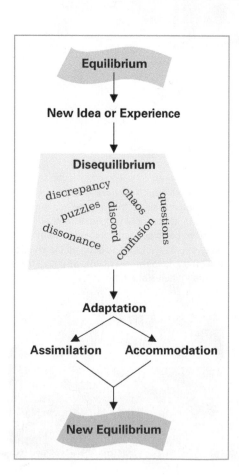

FIGURE 2.1

Challenge Me Most of us, most of the time, prefer the comfort of our conventional conclusions. According to Piaget, however, when new ideas disturb our thinking, we have an opportunity to expand our cognition with a broader and deeper understanding. Living in another country, attending college far from home, or even a deep conversation with someone who disagrees with you—all these advance intelligence via disequilibrium.

TABLE 2.3	Piaget's Periods of Cognitive Development		
	Name of Period	Characteristics of the Period	Major Gains During the Period
Birth to 2 years	Sensorimotor	Infants use senses and motor abilities to understand the world. Learning is active, without reflection.	Infants learn that objects still exist when out of sight (*object permanence*) and begin to think through mental actions.
2–6 years	Preoperational	Children think symbolically, with language, yet children are *egocentric*, perceiving from their own perspective.	The imagination flourishes, and language becomes a significant means of self-expression and social influence.
6–11 years	Concrete operational	Children understand and apply logic. Thinking is limited by direct experience.	By applying logic, children grasp concepts of conservation, number, classification, and many other scientific ideas.
12 years through adulthood	Formal operational	Adolescents and adults use abstract and hypothetical concepts. They can use analysis, not only emotion.	Ethics, politics, and social and moral issues become fascinating as adolescents and adults use abstract, theoretical reasoning.

cated computer. When conceptualized in that way, thinking is affected by changes in the activity of the brain.

Information processing is "a framework characterizing a large number of research programs" (Miller, 2011, p. 266). Instead of interpreting *responses* by infants and children, as Piaget did, this cognitive theory focuses on the *processes* of thought—that is, how minds work before a response.

Information-processing theorists note that responses can occur in many ways, including through the senses and bodily activity, which in turn affect thinking (Glenberg et al., 2013). The underlying theoretical basis of information processing is that the details of process shed light on the specifics of outcome.

According to this perspective, cognition begins when input is picked up by the five senses. It proceeds to brain reactions, connections, and stored memories, and it concludes with some form of output. For infants, output consists of moving a hand, making a sound, or staring a split second longer at one stimulus than at another. As a person develops, information-processing scientists study not only words but also hesitations, neuronal activity, and bodily reactions (heartbeat, blood pressure, and the like).

The latest techniques to study the brain have produced insights from neuroscience on the sequence and strength of neuronal communication and have discovered patterns beyond those traced by early information-processing theory. With the aid of sensitive technology, information-processing research has also overturned some of Piaget's findings, as explained in later chapters.

However, the basic tenet of cognitive theory is true for neuroscience, information processing, and for Piaget: Ideas matter. For example, how children interpret a future social situation, such as whether they anticipate welcome or rejection, affects the quality of their actual friendships. Positive information processing correlates with positive friendships.

This approach to understanding cognition has many applications. For instance, it has long been recognized

We Try Harder Details of brain scans require interpretation from neurologists, but even the novice can see that adults who have been diagnosed with ADHD (second line of images) reacted differently in this experiment when they were required to push a button only if certain letters appeared on a screen. Sustained attention to this task required more brain power (the lit areas) for those with ADHD. Notice also that certain parts of the brain were activated by the healthy adults and not by the ADHD ones. Apparently adults who had problems paying attention when they were children have learned to focus when they need to, but they do it in their own way and with more effort.

CUBILLO ET AL. (2012). A REVIEW OF FRONTO-STRIATAL AND FRONTO-CORTICAL BRAIN ABNORMALITIES IN CHILDREN AND ADULTS WITH ATTENTION DEFICIT HYPERACTIVITY DISORDER (ADHD) AND NEW EVIDENCE FOR DYSFUNCTION IN ADULTS WITH ADHD DURING MOTIVATION AND ATTENTION. CORTEX, 48(2), 194–215. DOI: 10.1016/J.CORTEX.2011.04.007 WITH PERMISSION FROM ELSEVIER

Healthy Control Adults

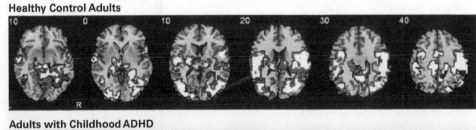

Adults with Childhood ADHD

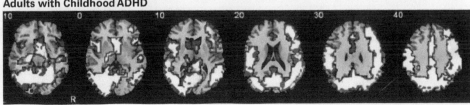

that children with ADHD (attention-deficit/hyperactivity disorder) tend to have difficulty learning in school, obeying their parents, and making friends (whether or not they are excessively active). Information-processing research has led to the discovery that certain brain circuits (called *fronto-striatal systems*) do not function normally in children with ADHD. Consequently, it is hard for them to read facial expressions and interpret voice tones in order to understand others' emotions (Uekermann et al., 2010).

This means that children with ADHD may not know whether their father's "Come here" is an angry command or a loving suggestion. Nor do they immediately know if a classmate is hostile or friendly. Information processing helps in remediation: If a specific brain function can be improved, children may learn more, obey more, and gain friends.

Remember that all theories are designed to be useful. The Opposing Perspectives feature is one illustration of the way psychoanalytic, behaviorist, and cognitive theory might apply to common parental concerns—how and when to respond to a baby's cry, and how and when to toilet train their child.

opposing perspectives

Toilet Training—How and When?

Parents hear opposite advice about when to respond to an infant's cry. Some experts tell them that ignoring the cry will reduce the infant's future happiness (psychoanalytic theory—advocating attachment parenting), while others tell them that responding to every cry will teach the child to be demanding and spoiled (behaviorist theory—advocating strong character). Neither theory directly predicts dire results, but each underlies one side or the other of this debate.

Meanwhile, cognitive theory seeks to understand the reason for the cry. Is it a reflexive wail of hurt and hunger, or is it an expression of social pain? According to this theory, when people understand what a particular action means to the actor, then effective response is possible. Thus all three theories have led to advice for parents—although the advice is conflicting.

Another practical example is toilet training. In the nineteenth century, many parents believed that bodily functions should be controlled as soon as possible in order to distinguish humans from lower animals. Consequently, they began toilet training in the first months of life (Accardo, 2006). Then psychoanalytic theory

pegged the first year as the oral stage (Freud) or the time when trust was crucial (Erikson), before the toddler's anal stage (Freud) began or autonomy needs (Erikson) emerged.

Consequently, psychoanalytic theory led to postponing toilet training to avoid serious personality problems later on. Soon this was part of many manuals on child rearing. For example, a leading pediatrician, Barry Brazelton, wrote a popular book for parents advising that toilet training should not begin until the child is cognitively, emotionally, and biologically ready—around age 2 for daytime training and age 3 for nighttime dryness.

What to Do? Books on infant care give contradictory advice. Even in this photo one can see that these modern mothers follow divergent parenting practices. One is breast-feeding a one-year-old, another has toilet-trained her toddler, one sits cross-legged so her baby can be on her lap, which would be impossible for another—and so on.

ANDREA MOHIN/THE NEW YORK TIMES/REDUX PICTURES

SUMMING UP Cognitive theory holds that to understand a person, one must learn how that person thinks. According to Piaget, cognition develops in four distinct, age-related stages: sensorimotor, preoperational, concrete operational, and formal operational. According to information-processing theory, the human mind is similar to a sophisticated computer: a multiplicity of components are processed by particular programs within the brain, eventually resulting in learning new skills, perceptions, and actions.

WHAT HAVE YOU LEARNED?

1. What is the basic idea of cognitive theory?
2. How do the processes of assimilation and accommodation lead to more advanced thinking?
3. In what ways are assimilation and accommodation similar?
4. How does information processing connect to neuroscience, the study of the brain?
5. What do all the cognitive theories have in common?

> As a society, we are far too concerned about pushing children to be toilet trained early. I don't even like the phrase "toilet training." It really should be toilet learning.
>
> *[Brazelton & Sparrow, 2006, p. 193]*

By the middle of the twentieth century, many U.S. psychologists had rejected psychoanalytic theory and become behaviorists. Since they believed that learning depends primarily on conditioning, some suggested that toilet training occur whenever the parent wished, not at a particular age. In one application of behaviorism, children drank quantities of their favorite juice, sat on the potty with a parent nearby to keep them entertained, and then, when the inevitable occurred, the parent praised and rewarded them—a powerful reinforcement. Children were conditioned (in one day, according to some behaviorists) to head for the potty whenever the need arose (Azrin & Foxx, 1974).

Rejecting both of these theories, some Western parents prefer to start potty training very early. One U.S. mother began training her baby just 33 days after birth. She noticed when her son was about to defecate, held him above the toilet, and had trained him by 6 months (Sun & Rugolotto, 2004). Such early training is criticized by all of the grand theories, although each theory has a particular critique, as now explained.

Psychoanalysts would wonder what made her such an anal person, with a need for cleanliness and order that did not consider the child's needs. Behaviorists would say that the mother was trained, not the son. She taught herself to be sensitive to his body; she was reinforced when she read his clues correctly. Cognitive theory would wonder what the mother was thinking. For instance, did she have an odd fear of normal body functions?

What is best? Dueling theories and diverse parental practices have led the authors of an article for pediatricians to conclude that "despite families and physicians having addressed this issue for generations, there still is no consensus regarding the best method or even a standard definition of toilet training" (Howell et al., 2010, p. 262). One comparison study of toilet-training methods found that the behaviorist approach was best for older children with serious disabilities but that almost every method succeeded with the average young child. No method seemed to result in marked negative emotional consequences (Klassen et al., 2006). Many sources explain that because each child is different, there is no "right" way, "the best strategy for implementing training is still unknown" (Colaco et al., 2013, p. 49).

That conclusion arises from cognitive theory, which holds that each person's assumptions and ideas determine their actions. Therefore, since North American parents are from many cultures with diverse assumptions, marked variation is evident in beliefs regarding toilet training.

Contemporary child-rearing advice also considers the child's own cognitive development. If the child is at the sensorimotor stage, then body sensations and reflexive actions are central to training. Later on, when language has been added to the mix, the child's intellectual awareness (as evidenced by wanting "big boy" underpants and so on) is crucial.

What values are embedded in each practice? Psychoanalytic theory focuses on later personality, behaviorism stresses conditioning of body impulses, and cognitive theory considers variation in the child's intellectual capacity and in adult values. Even the idea that each child is different, making no one method best, is the outgrowth of a theory. There is no easy answer, but many parents are firm believers in one approach or another. That confirms the statement at the beginning of this chapter: We all have theories, sometimes strongly held, whether we know it or not.

DR. JAMES WERTSCH

Affection for Children Vygotsky lived in Russia from 1896 to 1934, when war, starvation, and revolution led to the deaths of millions. Throughout this turmoil, Vygotsky focused on learning. His love of children is suggested by this portrait: He and his daughter have their arms around each other.

sociocultural theory A newer theory that holds that development results from the dynamic interaction of each person with the surrounding social and cultural forces.

apprenticeship in thinking Vygotsky's term for how cognition is stimulated and developed in people by more skilled members of their community.

guided participation The process by which people learn from others who guide their experiences and explorations. This learning is direct and interactive.

zone of proximal development In sociocultural theory, a metaphorical area, or "zone," surrounding a learner that includes all the skills, knowledge, and concepts that the person is close ("proximal") to acquiring but cannot yet master without help.

Sociocultural Theory: Vygotsky and Beyond

New theories have emerged that are multicultural and multidisciplinary, unlike the first three theories. These theories are "new" in that their applications to human development are relatively recent, although their roots are ancient.

The central thesis of **sociocultural theory** is that human development results from the dynamic interaction between developing persons and their surrounding society. Culture is viewed not as something external that impinges on developing persons but as integral to their development every day via the social context (all the dynamic systems described in Chapter 1).

Social Interaction

The pioneer of the sociocultural perspective was Lev Vygotsky (1896–1934), a psychologist from the former Soviet Union. In the United States, Urie Bronfrenbrenner (1917-2005), an American also born in the Soviet Union, was an early advocate of this approach: His ecological approach emphasizes the social context of development. (The basics of the ecological approach are accepted by virtually all contemporary developmentalists, and therefore were described in Chapter 1.)

Vygotsky noted that each community in his native land (comprising Asians and Europeans of many faiths and many languages) taught children whatever beliefs and habits they valued. For example, his research included how farmers used tools, how illiterate people thought of abstract ideas, and how children learned in school.

In his view, each person, schooled or not, develops with the guidance of more skilled members of his or her society, who are tutors or mentors in an **apprenticeship in thinking** (Vygotsky, 2012). Just as, in earlier centuries, a young person might become an apprentice to an experienced artisan, learning the trade, Vygotsky believed that adults teach children how to think by explaining ideas, asking questions, and repeating values.

To describe this process, Vygotsky developed the concept of **guided participation,** the method used by parents, teachers, and entire societies to teach novices the skills and habits expected within their culture. Tutors engage learners (also called *apprentices*) in joint activities, offering instruction and "mutual involvement in several widespread cultural practices with great importance for learning: narratives, routines, and play" (Rogoff, 2003, p. 285). Active apprenticeship and sensitive guidance are central to sociocultural theory because each person depends on others to learn. This process is informal, pervasive, and social.

All cultural patterns and beliefs are social constructions, not natural laws, according to sociocultural theorists. These theorists find customs to be powerful, shaping the development of every person, and they contend that some assumptions need to shift to allow healthier development. Vygotsky stressed this point, arguing that disabled children should be educated (Vygotsky, 1994b). This is a cultural belief that has become law in the United States but is not yet accepted in many other nations.

The Zone of Proximal Development

According to sociocultural theory, all learning is social, whether people are learning a manual skill, a social custom, or a language. As part of the apprenticeship of thinking, a mentor (parent, peer, or professional) finds the learner's **zone of proximal development,** an imaginary area surrounding the child, which contains the skills, knowledge, and concepts that the learner is close (proximal) to acquiring but cannot yet master without help.

Through sensitive assessment of each learner, mentors engage mentees within that zone. Together, in a "process of joint construction," new knowledge is attained (Valsiner, 2006). The mentor must avoid two opposite dangers: boredom and failure. Some frustration is permitted, but the learner must be actively engaged, never passive or overwhelmed (see Figure 2.2).

To make this seemingly abstract process more concrete, consider an example: a father teaching his daughter to ride a bicycle. He begins by rolling her along, supporting her weight while telling her to keep her hands on the handlebars, to push the right and left pedals in rhythm, and to look straight ahead. As she becomes more comfortable and confident, he begins to roll her along more quickly, praising her for steadily pumping. Within a few lessons, he is jogging beside her, holding only the handlebars.

When the father senses that his daughter can balance, he urges her to pedal faster while he loosens his grip. Without realizing it, she rides on her own.

Note that this is not instruction by preset rules or reinforcement. Sociocultural learning is active: No one learns to ride a bike by reading and memorizing written instructions, and no good teacher merely repeats a prepared lesson. Also note that the father is not the only teacher here. The culture also teaches, via the child having seen other people on bikes, and via special bikes for young children. All such bikes are smaller, of course, but some have no pedals and some have training wheels, both of which are cultural artifacts that can help guide participation in bike riding.

Because each learner has personal traits and experiences, education must be individualized. Learning styles vary: Some people need more assurance; some learn best by looking, others by hearing.

A mentor must sense when support or freedom is needed and how peers can help (they may be the best mentors). Skilled teachers know when the zone of proximal development expands and shifts.

Excursions into and through the zone of proximal development are everywhere. At the thousand or so science museums in the United States, children ask numerous questions, and adults guide their scientific knowledge (Haden, 2010). Physical therapists tailor exercises to the particular patient and the surrounding context. For example, when physical therapists provide exercise for patients in intensive care, they not only take into account the illness but also the culture of the ICU (Pawlik & Kress, 2013).

In another example that occurs for every Western child, learning to sit at the table and eat with a knife and fork is a long process, with many steps of guided participation. Parents do not "spoon-feed" their 3-year-olds

Home-Schooling Academic achievement tests in reading and math class may crowd out practical skills, such as how to apply proper pressure with a rolling pin. This boy is fortunate that his mother guides him in mastering the domestic arts. He also is learning other skills in regular school.

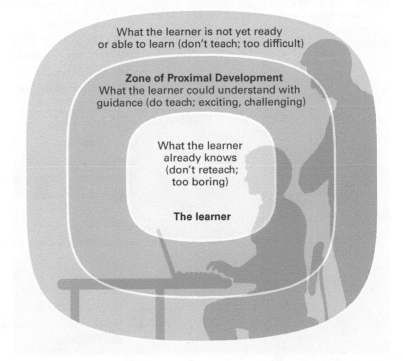

What the learner is not yet ready or able to learn (don't teach; too difficult)

Zone of Proximal Development
What the learner could understand with guidance (do teach; exciting, challenging)

What the learner already knows (don't reteach; too boring)

The learner

FIGURE 2.2

The Magic Middle Somewhere between the boring and the impossible is the zone of proximal development, where interaction between teacher and learner results in knowledge never before grasped or skills not already mastered. The intellectual excitement of that zone is the origin of the joy that both instruction and study can bring.

or expect them to cut their own meat. Instead they find the proper zone of proximal development, and provide appropriate tools and experiences.

In general, mentors, attuned to ever-shifting abilities and motivation, continually urge a new competence—the next level, not the moon. For their part, learners ask questions, show interest, and demonstrate progress, which guides and inspires the mentors. When education goes well, both are fully engaged and productive within the zone of proximal development. Particular skills and processes vary enormously, but the overall interaction is the same.

Taking Culture into Account

The sociocultural perspective has led contemporary scientists to consider social context in every study. Earlier theorists and researchers are criticized for failing to do so. This newer approach considers not only differences between one nation and another, but also differences between one region and another, between one cohort and another, between one ethnic group and another, and so on.

This approach has led to a wealth of provocative findings, many of which are described later. A sociocultural perspective has been particularly helpful in early childhood education (Woodrow, 2014), as children have diverse cultural experiences by the time they enter preschool.

Culture is not a monolith, with every child in a particular community, or even a particular family, experiencing the same influences. Instead, culture needs to be considered person by person: Each individual participates in some aspects of the community culture while rejecting or modifying others.

Consider two sisters:

> When the local constables knocked on Chona's parents' door with their wooden staffs, searching for children to send to the school, her parents hid their children under the wooden bed just inside the door and told the constables that the children did not exist. But Chona's sister Susana, ever rebellious, leaped out from under the bed and yelled . . . "I want to go to school."
>
> *[Rogoff, 2011, p. 5]*

Especially for Adoptive Families Does the importance of attachment mean that adopted children will not bond securely with nonbiological caregivers? (see response, page 56)

These two sisters, both speaking a local language, raised in the same tribal culture (Mayan, in San Pedro, Guatemala), nevertheless followed distinct cultural paths. Later Susana refused an arranged marriage and moved to a nearby town, unlike her unschooled sister who married a man she did not like and stayed close to her childhood home all her life. Culture shapes everyone, but each person experiences it differently.

SUMMING UP   Sociocultural theory is more multicultural than the theories described earlier in this chapter. The pioneer of sociocultural theory was Lev Vygotsky, who said that each learner is an apprentice, guided by a more skilled or knowledgeable person. Learning occurs within a zone a proximal development, that region that the learner is almost able to learn—neither too advanced nor too simple—via sensitive collaboration between a teacher (who could be a parent or a peer) and a learner who is ready to master the next step. Cultural differences are crucial in both what is learned and how it is learned.

WHAT HAVE YOU LEARNED?

1. How is "apprenticeship in thinking" an example of sociocultural theory?
2. How does the teacher encourage learning in the zone of proximal development?
3. What is an example of a cultural difference in the expectations a child might have about school?

The Universal Perspective: Humanism and Evolution

No developmentalist doubts that each person is unique, yet many social scientists contend that the sociocultural focus on differences (cultural, ethnic, sexual, economic) depicts a fractured understanding of development.

Moreover, no developmentalist doubts that nonhuman animals can help us understand humans. However, many think that the psychoanalytic emphasis on sexual needs, and the behaviorist stress on laws of behavior, ignore aspects of development that characterize all humans but not all animals.

Universal theories hold that people share impulses and motivations, which they express in ways most other animals cannot. A universal perspective has been articulated in many developmental theories, each expressed in particular ways but always contending that humans have much in common with each other.

Here we describe two of the most prominent of such perspectives: humanism and evolutionary theory. These two may seem to be opposite, in that humanism emphasizes the heights of human striving and evolutionary theory begins with consideration of quite simple instincts, but several recent scholars have found many similarities in these theories, contending that the "hierarchy of human motives" (humanism) can be anchored "firmly in the bedrock of modern evolutionary theory" (Kenrick et al., 2010, p. 292).

Humanism

Many scientists are convinced that there is something hopeful, unifying, and noble in the human spirit, something ignored by psychoanalytic theory (which envisions self-centered, childhood sexuality) and by behaviorism (which seems to ignore free will). The limits of those two theories were apparent to two Americans: Abraham Maslow (1908–1970) and Carl Rogers (1902–1987), both deeply religious men.

Maslow and Rogers had witnessed the Great Depression and two world wars and concluded that traditional psychological theories underrated human potential by focusing on evil, not good. They founded a theory called **humanism** that became prominent after World War II, as millions read Maslow's *Toward a Psychology of Being* (1999) and Rogers's *On Becoming a Person* (2004).

Maslow believed that all people—no matter what their culture, gender, or history—have the same basic needs. He arranged these needs in a hierarchy, often illustrated as a pyramid (see Figure 2.3):

1. Physiological: needing food, water, warmth, and air
2. Safety: feeling protected from injury and death
3. Love and belonging: having friends, family, and a community (often religious)
4. Esteem: being respected by the wider community as well as by oneself
5. Self-actualization: becoming truly oneself, fulfilling one's unique potential while appreciating all of humanity

Hope and Laughter Maslow studied law before psychology, and he enjoyed deep discussions with many psychoanalytic theorists who escaped Nazi-dominated Europe. He believed the human spirit could overcome oppression and reach self-actualization, where faith, hope, and humor abound.

humanism A theory that stresses the potential of all humans for good and the belief that all people have the same basic needs, regardless of culture, gender, or background.

// **Response for Adoptive Families** (from page 54) Not at all. Attachment is the result of responsiveness, not biology. In some cultures, many children are adopted from infancy, and the emotional ties to their caregivers are no less strong than for other children.

This pyramid caught on almost immediately; it was one of the most "contagious ideas of behavioral science" because it seemed insightful about human psychology (Kenrick et al., 2010, p. 292). This theory is not a developmental theory in the traditional sense, in that Maslow did not believe that the levels were connected to a particular stage or age. However, his levels are sequential: Lower levels need to be satisfied before the higher levels.

Thus meeting a child's needs for basic care, for safety, and for friendship was a prerequisite for self-esteem and self-actualization. At the highest level, when basic needs have been met, people can be fully themselves—creative, spiritual, curious, appreciative of nature, able to respect everyone else.

Rogers also stressed the need to accept and respect one's own personhood as well as that of everyone else. He thought that people should give each other *unconditional positive regard,* which means that they should see (regard) each other with appreciation (positive) without conditions (unconditional). This is what parents often do for their children: they love and cherish them even when the child cries, disobeys, or encounters trouble.

If parents do not have unconditional positive regard for their children, the danger is that the children will have long-lasting problems with intimacy and self-acceptance (Roth & Assor, 2012). Rogers spent the last years of his life trying to reconcile opposing factions in Northern Ireland, South Africa, and Russia; he believed all sides need to listen to each other.

As you can see, humanists emphasize what all people have in common, not their national, ethnic, or cultural divisions. Maslow contended that everyone, universally, must satisfy each lower level of the hierarchy of needs before moving higher. A starving man, for instance, may not be concerned for his own safety when he seeks food (level 1 precedes level 2), or an unloved woman might not care about self-respect because she needs love (level 3 precedes level 4).

Maslow thus was more accepting of people who others see as hostile to their nation, or religion, or group. Destructive and inhumane actions may be the conse-

FIGURE 2.3

Moving Up, Not Looking Back Maslow's hierarchy is like a ladder: Once a person stands firmly on a higher rung, the lower rungs are no longer needed. Thus, someone who has arrived at step 4 might devalue safety (step 2) and risk personal safety to gain respect.

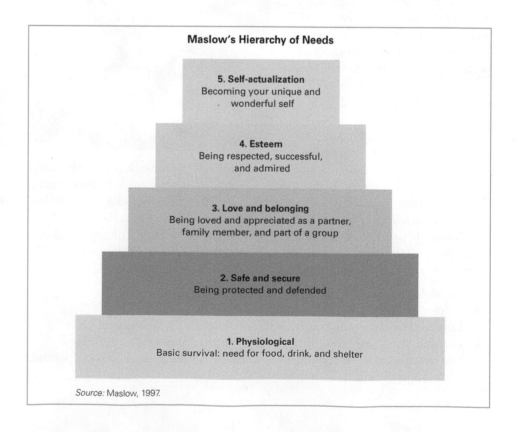

Maslow's Hierarchy of Needs

5. Self-actualization
Becoming your unique and wonderful self

4. Esteem
Being respected, successful, and admired

3. Love and belonging
Being loved and appreciated as a partner, family member, and part of a group

2. Safe and secure
Being protected and defended

1. Physiological
Basic survival: need for food, drink, and shelter

Source: Maslow, 1997.

quence of unmet lower needs, which may be met later if a child was neglected or abused. Recovery is possible.

Notice the relevance for child development. Babies seek food and comfort, children seek approval, and not until adulthood can a person focus wholeheartedly on success and esteem, beyond the immediate approval of friends and family. Satisfaction of early needs is crucial for later self-acceptance, according to Maslow. People may become thieves or even killers, unable to reach their potential, to self-actualize, if they were unsafe or unloved as children.

Rogers agreed that adults who were deprived of unconditional positive regard in childhood might become selfish and antisocial. He developed a method of psychological therapy widely used to help people become more accepting of themselves and therefore of other people, overcoming early deprivation.

Humanism is still prominent among medical professionals because they recognize that pain is not always physical (the first two levels) but can also be social (the next two) (Majercsik, 2005; Zalenski & Raspa, 2006). Even the very sick need love and belonging (friends and family) and esteem (the dying need respect).

Evolutionary Theory

You are familiar with Charles Darwin and his ideas, first published 150 years ago: Essentially he showed that plants, insects, birds, and animals developed over billions of years, as life evolved from primitive cells to humans (Darwin, 1859).

But you may not realize that serious research on human development inspired by this theory does not focus on lower creatures, but instead studies the history of human characteristics. Evolutionary psychology is quite recent (Simpson & Kenrick, 2013). As two leaders in this field write:

> During the last two decades, the study of the evolutionary foundations of human nature has grown at an exponential rate. In fact, it is now a booming interdisciplinary scientific enterprise, one that sits at the cutting edge of the social and behavioral sciences.
>
> [Gangestad & Simpson, 2007, p. 2]

Why Adults Protect Their Children

Evolutionary theory has intriguing explanations for many issues in human development, including a pregnant woman's nausea, 1-year-olds' attachment to their parents, and obesity in childhood and beyond. According to this theory, many impulses, needs, and behaviors evolved to help children survive and thrive many millennia ago (Konner, 2010).

To understand human development, this theory contends that humans should understand the lives of our early ancestors. For example, many people are terrified of snakes; they scream and break into a cold sweat upon seeing one. However, virtually no one is terrified of automobiles. Yet for current deaths in the United States, the ratio of snake to car deaths is 1 to 10,000. In 2014, only two people died from snake bites: a Kentucky man in a snake-handling religious service, and a Missouri man who picked up a copperhead to show his son (Otto, 2014). The extreme reaction to snakes derives from instinctive fears that evolved over millennia, when snakes were common killers. Thus,

> evolutionarily, ancient dangers such as snakes, spiders, heights, and strangers appear on lists of common phobias far more often than do evolutionarily modern dangers such as cars and guns, even though cars and guns are more dangerous to survival in the modern environment.
>
> [Confer et al., 2010, p. 111]

Since our fears have not caught up to modern inventions, we use our minds to pass laws regarding infant seats, child safety restraints, seat belts, red lights, and

Especially for Nurses Maslow's hierarchy is often taught in health sciences because it alerts medical staff to the needs of patients. What specific hospital procedures might help? (see response, page 59)

Especially for Teachers and Counselors of Teenagers Teen pregnancy is destructive of adolescent education, family life, and sometimes even health. According to evolutionary theory, what can be done about this? (see response, page 60)

speed limits. Humanity is succeeding in such measures: The U.S. motor-vehicle death rate has been cut in half over the past 20 years.

Other modern killers—climate change, drug addiction, obesity, pollution—also require social management because instincts are contrary to what we now know about the dangers of each of these. Evolutionary theory contends that recognizing the ancient origins of destructive urges—such as the deadly desire to eat calorie-dense chocolate cake—is the first step in controlling them (King, 2013).

According to evolutionary theory, every species has two long-standing, biologically based drives: survival and reproduction. Understanding these two drives provides insight into protective parenthood, the death of newborns, infant dependency, child immaturity, the onset of puberty, and much more (Konner, 2010).

Later chapters will explain these, but here is one example. Adults consider babies cute—despite the reality that babies have little hair, no chins, stubby legs, and round stomachs—all of which are considered unattractive in adults. The reason, evolutionary theory contends, is that adults are instinctually attuned to protect and cherish the young of the species.

A competing instinct is to perpetuate one's progeny, even at the expense of other people's children. That might lead to infanticide, again explained by evolutionary theory. Chimpanzee males who take over a troop kill babies of the deposed male; humans, of course, have created laws against such practices (Hrdy, 2009).

Genetic Links

A basic idea from evolutionary theory—**selective adaptation**—proposes that humans today react in ways that helped promote survival and reproduction long ago. According to one version of selective adaptation, genes for traits that aid survival and reproduction are selected over time to allow the species to thrive (see Figure 2.4).

Some of the best qualities of people—cooperation, spirituality, and self-sacrifice—may have originated thousands of years ago when people survived because they took care of one another. Childhood itself, particularly the long period when children depend on their parents, can be explained via evolution (Konner, 2010).

The process of selective adaptation works as follows: If one person happens to have a trait that makes survival more likely, the gene (or combination of genes) responsible for that trait is likely to be passed on to the next generation because that person is likely to survive long enough to reproduce. Anyone who inherits a beneficial gene (or combination of genes) has an increased chance of growing up, finding a mate, and bearing children—some of whom would inherit that gene (or genes) and the resultant desirable trait.

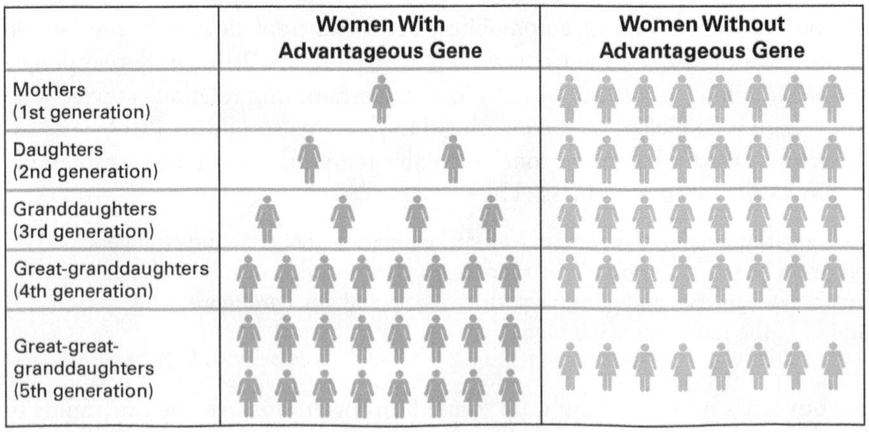

selective adaptation The process by which living creatures (including people) adjust to their environment. Genes that enhance survival and reproductive ability are selected, over the generations, to become more prevalent.

FIGURE 2.4

Selective Adaptation Illustrated Suppose only one of nine mothers happened to have a gene that improved survival. The average woman had only one surviving daughter but this gene mutation might mean more births and more surviving children, such that each woman who had the gene bore two girls who survived to womanhood instead of one. As you see, in 100 years, the "odd" gene becomes more common, making it a new normal.

	Women With Advantageous Gene	Women Without Advantageous Gene
Mothers (1st generation)	👤	👤👤👤👤👤👤👤👤
Daughters (2nd generation)	👤 👤	👤👤👤👤👤👤👤👤
Granddaughters (3rd generation)	👤 👤 👤 👤	👤👤👤👤👤👤👤
Great-granddaughters (4th generation)	👤👤👤👤👤👤👤👤	👤👤👤👤👤👤
Great-great-granddaughters (5th generation)	👤👤👤👤👤👤👤👤👤👤👤👤👤👤👤👤	👤👤👤👤👤👤

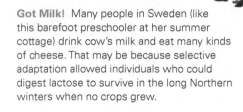

For example, originally almost all human babies could digest lactose in their mother's milk but probably became *lactose intolerant* as they grew older, and therefore unable to digest too much cow's milk (Suchy et al., 2010). In a few regions thousands of years ago cattle were domesticated and raised for their meat. In those places, "killing the fatted calf" provided a rare feast for the entire community when a major celebration occurred.

In cattle-raising regions, if a young woman chanced to have an aberrant gene for the enzyme that allows digestion of cow's milk and drank milk intended for a calf, she was likely to avoid malnutrition, experience early puberty, sustain many pregnancies, and breast-feed her thriving babies. For all those reasons, she would raise many children. In that way, the next generation would include more people who inherited that gene. Interestingly, there are several distinct versions of lactose tolerance: Apparently different odd genes appeared in several cattle-raising regions, and in each area selective adaptation increased the prevalence of the gene (Mattar et al., 2012).

This process of selective adaptation continues over many generations. The fact that the odd gene for lactose tolerance became more common, providing survival in cattle-raising communities, explains why few Scandinavians are lactose-intolerant but many Africans are—a useful fact for Wisconsin dairy farmers who want to ship milk to starving children in Senegal.

Once it was understood that milk might make some children sick, better ways to relieve hunger were found. Although malnutrition is still a global problem, about a third fewer children are malnourished than was the case in 1990 (UNICEF, 2012). One reason is that nutritionists now know which foods are digestible, nourishing, and tasty for whom. Evolutionary psychology has helped with that.

For groups as well as individuals, evolutionary theory notices how the interaction of genes and environment affects survival and reproduction. Genetic variations are particularly beneficial when the environment changes, which is one reason genetic diversity benefits humanity as a whole.

If a species' gene pool does not include variants that allow survival in difficult circumstances (such as exposure to a new disease or to an environmental toxin), the entire species becomes extinct. One recent example is HIV/AIDS, deadly in most untreated people but not in a few who are genetically spared. No wonder biologists worry when a particular species becomes inbred—diversity is protective.

Evolution and Culture

Genetic variation among humans, differential sensitivity, and plasticity (explained in Chapter 1) enable humans to survive and multiply. This variation applies not only to biological traits (such as digestion of milk) but also to psychological traits that originate in the brain and then are shaped by culture (Confer et al., 2010; Tomasello, 2009).

Evolutionary theory contends that certain epigenetic factors foster socialization, parenthood, communication, and language, all of which helped humans a hundred thousand years ago and allowed societies a few thousand years ago to develop writing, then books, and then universities. As a result, humans learn from history

Got Milk! Many people in Sweden (like this barefoot preschooler at her summer cottage) drink cow's milk and eat many kinds of cheese. That may be because selective adaptation allowed individuals who could digest lactose to survive in the long Northern winters when no crops grew.

// **Response for Nurses** (from page 57) Reassurance from nurses (explaining procedures, including specifics and reasons) helps with the first two, and visitors, cards, and calls might help with the next two. Obviously, specifics depend on the patient, but everyone needs respect as well as physical care.

// **Response for Teachers and Counselors of Teenagers** (from page 58)
Evolutionary theory stresses the basic human drive for reproduction, which gives teenagers a powerful sex drive. Thus, merely informing teenagers of the difficulty of caring for a newborn (some high school sex-education programs simply give teenagers a chicken egg to nurture) is not likely to work. A better method would be to structure teenagers' lives so that pregnancy is impossible—for instance, with careful supervision or readily available contraception.

and from strangers in distant continents. The fact that you are reading this book, accepting some ideas and rejecting others, is part of the human heritage that will aid future generations, according to evolutionary theory.

In recent years, "evolutionary psychology has grown from being viewed as a fringe theoretical perspective to occupying a central place within psychological science" (Confer et al., 2010). This theory is insightful and intriguing, but some interpretations are hotly disputed.

For instance, an evolutionary account of mental disorders suggests that some symptoms (such as an overactive imagination or crushing anxiety) are normal extremes of adaptive traits, and that few people should be considered mentally ill. In this view, depression particularly can be seen to have been adaptive in ancient times, and now is seen as a mood that needs to be treated with respect and by making changes in life circumstances rather than treating it with drugs (Rothenberg, 2014).

This perspective is rejected by many psychologists and by neuroscientists who consider many forms of mental illness to be caused by an imbalance of neurotransmitters or a deficit in some particular parts of the brain. Also controversial are explanations of sex differences, as the following explains.

⚗️ a view from science

If Your Mate Were Unfaithful

Men seek more sexual partners than women do. Brides are younger, on average, than grooms. These are norms, not followed in every case, but apparent in every culture. Why?

An evolutionary explanation begins with biology. Since females, not males, become pregnant and breast-feed, in most of human history mothers needed mature, strong men to keep predators away. That helped women fulfill their evolutionary destiny, to bear children who would live long enough to reproduce. Consequently, women chose men who were big and strong, and then kept them nearby with home cooking and sex.

A man was more able to father many children if he removed his rivals and had multiple sexual partners—all young, curvaceous, and healthy—who would birth many surviving babies with that man's genes. This theory explains why powerful kings had many young wives and concubines. Those ancient needs may have led to male/female hormonal differences, so that even today many men are attracted to younger women, while many women seek one steady marriage partner.

The evolutionary reasons for men to become faithful partners to one woman despite their impulse included the fact that men needed to keep other men away in order to protect their children (Lukas & Clutton-Brock, 2013). Men tried to show women that they were powerful mates, displaying impulses that now fuel gang wars and dangerous driving. For their part, women tried to show men that they were sexually exciting. In other words, useful evolutionary traits may have gone awry in today's circumstances, fueling risk-taking in adolescents that is destructive (Ellis et al., 2012).

Does this interpretation have empirical research support? Evolutionary scientists have asked people of many ages, nationalities, and religions to imagine their romantic partner either "forming a deep emotional attachment" or "enjoying passionate sexual intercourse" with another man or woman. Then the participants are asked which of those two possibilities is more distressing. The men generally are more upset at sexual infidelity while the women are more upset with emotional infidelity (Buss et al., 2001).

For example, one study involved 212 college students, all U.S. citizens, whose parents were born in Mexico (Cramer et al., 2009). As with other populations, more women (60 percent) were distressed at the emotional infidelity and more men (66 percent) at the sexual infidelity.

A meta-analysis of 47 independent samples—sometimes reported by skeptics who doubted evolution—confirms that men are more sexually jealous than women are (Sagarin et al., 2012). Of course, this does not prove the evolutionary explanation, but that particular sex difference does seem universal.

Evolutionary theory explains this oft-replicated result by noting that for centuries a woman has needed a soul mate to be emotionally committed, to ensure that he will provide for her and her children, whereas a man has needed a woman to be sexually faithful to ensure that her children are also his. (She knows her children are hers, because she birthed them; he is sure only if he is positive she never had another lover.)

Many women reject the evolutionary explanation for sex differences. They contend that hypothetical scenarios do not reflect actual experience and that patriarchy and sexism, not genes, produce mating attitudes and patterns (Vandermassen, 2005; Varga et al., 2011).

Similar controversies arise with other applications of evolutionary theory. People do not always act as evolutionary theory predicts: Parents sometimes abandon their newborns, adults sometimes handle snakes, and so on. In the survey of Mexican American college students that was cited in A View from Science, more than one-third did not follow the typical pattern for their gender (Cramer et al., 2009).

Nonetheless, evolutionary theorists contend that humans need to understand the universal, biological impulses within our species in order to control destructive reactions (e.g., we need to make "crimes of passion" illegal) and to promote constructive ones (to protect against newer dangers by manufacturing safer cars and guns).

SUMMING UP   Universal theories include humanism and evolutionary theory, both of which stress that all people have the same underlying needs. Humanism holds that everyone merits respect and positive regard in order to become self-actualized. Evolutionary theory contends that thousands of years of selective adaptation have led humans to experience emotions and impulses that have satisfied two universal needs of every species: to survive and to reproduce.

WHAT HAVE YOU LEARNED?
1. Why is humanism considered a hopeful theory?
2. How does Maslow's hierarchy of needs differ from Erikson's stages?
3. How does evolutionary psychology explain human instincts?
4. What is the evolutionary explanation of why parents protect their children?
5. What does the idea of selective adaptation imply about genetics?
6. Why do many women disagree with the evolutionary explanation of sex differences?

What Theories Contribute

Each major theory discussed in this chapter has contributed to our understanding of human development (see Table 2.4):

- *Psychoanalytic theories* make us aware of the impact of early-childhood experiences, remembered or not, on subsequent development.
- *Behaviorism* shows the effect that immediate responses, associations, and examples have on learning, moment by moment and over time.
- *Cognitive theories* bring an understanding of intellectual processes, including the fact that thoughts and beliefs affect every aspect of our development.
- *Sociocultural theories* remind us that development is embedded in a rich and multifaceted cultural context, evident in every social interaction.
- *Universal theories* stress that human differences are less significant than characteristics that are shared by all humans, in every place and era.

No comprehensive view of development can ignore any of these theories, yet each has encountered severe criticism. Psychoanalytic theory has been faulted for being too subjective; behaviorism, for being too mechanistic; cognitive theory, for undervaluing emotions; sociocultural theory, for neglecting individuals; and universal theories, for slighting cultural, gender, and economic variations. Most developmentalists prefer an **eclectic perspective,** choosing what they consider

eclectic perspective The approach taken by most developmentalists, in which they apply aspects of each of the various theories of development rather than adhering exclusively to one theory.

TABLE 2.4	Five Perspectives on Human Development		
Theory	Area of Focus	Fundamental Depiction of What People Do	Relative Emphasis on Nature or Nurture?
Psychoanalytic theory	Psychosexual (Freud) or psychosocial (Erikson) stages	Battle unconscious impulses and overcome major crises.	More nature (biological, sexual impulses, and parent–child bonds)
Behaviorism	Conditioning through stimulus and response	Respond to stimuli, reinforcement, and models.	More nurture (direct environment produces various behaviors)
Cognitive theory	Thinking, remembering, analyzing	Seek to understand experiences while forming concepts.	More nature (mental activity and motivation are key)
Sociocultural theory	Social context, expressed through people, language, customs	Learn the tools, skills, and values of society through apprenticeships.	More nurture (interaction of mentor and learner, within contexts)
Universal perspective	Needs and impulses that all humans share as a species	Develop impulses, interests, and patterns to survive and reproduce.	More nature (needs and impulses apply to all humans)

the best aspects of each theory. Rather than adopt any one of these theories exclusively, they make selective use of all of them.

Obviously, all theories reflect the personal background of the theorist (Demorest, 2004), as do all criticisms of theories. Being eclectic, not tied to any one theory, is beneficial because everyone, scientist as well as layperson, tends to be biased. It is easy to dismiss alternative points of view, but using all five theories opens our eyes and minds to aspects of development that we might otherwise ignore. As one overview of seven developmental theories (including those explained here) concludes, "Because no one theory satisfactorily explains development, it is critical that developmentalists be able to draw on the content, methods, and theoretical concepts of many theories" (Miller, 2011, p. 437).

As you will see in many later chapters, theories provide a fresh look at behavior. Imagine a parent and a teacher discussing a child's actions. Each suggests a possible explanation that makes the other say, "I never thought of that." If they listen to each other with an open mind, together they understand the child better.

Having five theories is like having five perceptive observers. All five are not always on target, but it is better to use theory to expand perception than to stay in one narrow groove. A hand functions best with five fingers, although each finger is different and some fingers are more useful than others.

SUMMING UP Theories are needed to suggest hypotheses, to spur investigation, and, finally, to collect data and form conclusions so that empirical evidence can replace untested assumptions. All five of the major theories have met with valid criticism, but each has also advanced our understanding. Most developmentalists are eclectic, making selective use of all these theories and others. This helps guard against bias and keeps scientists, parents, students, and everyone else open to alternative explanations for the complexity of human life.

WHAT HAVE YOU LEARNED?

1. What is the key criticism and key contribution of psychoanalytic theory?
2. What is the key criticism and key contribution of behaviorism?
3. What is the key criticism and key contribution of cognitive theory?
4. What is the key criticism and key contribution of sociocultural theory?
5. What is the key criticism and key contribution of universal theories?
6. What are the advantages and disadvantages of an eclectic perspective?

Breast-feeding Diversity

Breast-feeding is an interesting example of cultural variations in child development practices around the world. In some parts of the world, and in some cohorts in each country, mothers breast-feed for years—in other places and in other cultural groups, mothers see formula-feeding as safer and more modern. Rates of breast-feeding seem to vary by cohort and culture. Virtually every scientist and pediatrician is convinced that the benefits of breast milk outweigh any dangers, with numerous advantages evident years after infancy. However, the experiences of each cohort differ from earlier cohorts.

U.S. HISTORICAL BREAST-FEEDING STATISTICS

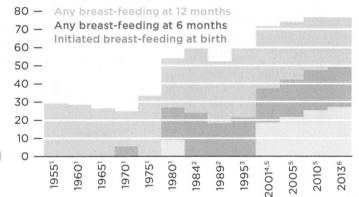

Any breast-feeding at 12 months
Any breast-feeding at 6 months
Initiated breast-feeding at birth

80 —
70 —
60 —
50 —
40 —
30 —
20 —
10 —
0 —

1955[1] 1960[1] 1965[1] 1970[1] 1975[1] 1980[1] 1984[2] 1989[2] 1995[3] 2001[4,5] 2005[5] 2010[5] 2013[6]

Source: (1) Martinez, Gilbert A.; Dodd, David, A. & Samartgedes, Jo Ann. (1981). Milk feeding patterns in the United States during the first 12 months of life. *Pediatrics, 68*(6), 863–868.
(2) Ryan, Alan S.; Rush, David; Krieger, Fritz W. & Lewandowski, Gregory E. (1991). Recent declines in breast-feeding in the United States, 1984 through 1989. *Pediatrics, 88*(4), 719–727.
(3) Ryan, Alan S. (1997). The resurgence of breastfeeding in the United States. *Pediatrics, 99*(4), E12.
(4) Ryan, Alan S.; Zhou, Wenjun & Acosta, Andrew. (2002). Breastfeeding continues to increase into the new millennium. *Pediatrics, 110*(6), 1103–1109. doi: 10.1542/peds.110.6.1103
(5) Centers for Disease Control and Prevention. (2014). *Breastfeeding Among U.S. Children Born 2001–2011, CDC National Immunization Survey.* Atlanta, GA: National Center for Chronic Disease Prevention and Health Promotion, Centers for Disease Control and Prevention.
(6) Centers for Disease Control and Prevention. (2013, July). *Breastfeeding Report Card—United States, 2013.* Atlanta, GA: National Center for Chronic Disease Prevention and Health Promotion, Centers for Disease Control and Prevention.

RATES OF BREAST-FEEDING AROUND THE WORLD

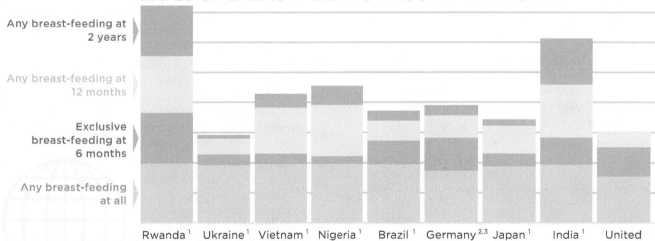

Any breast-feeding at 2 years
Any breast-feeding at 12 months
Exclusive breast-feeding at 6 months
Any breast-feeding at all

Rwanda[1] Ukraine[1] Vietnam[1] Nigeria[1] Brazil[1] Germany[2,3] Japan[1] India[1] United States[4]

Source: (1) World Health Organization. (2014). Infant and young child feeding data by country. Retrieved from: http://www.who.int/nutrition/databases/infantfeeding/countries/en/
(2) UNICEF. (2014). *Infant and Young Child Feeding Indicators.* New York, NY: United Nations.
(3) Banks, Jane W. (2003). Ka'nisténhsera Teiakotihsnie's: A native community rekindles the tradition of breastfeeding. *AWHONN Lifelines, 7*(4), 340–347. doi: 10.1177/1091592303257828
(4) Centers for Disease Control and Prevention. (2013, July). *Breastfeeding Report Card—United States, 2013.* Atlanta, GA: National Center for Chronic Disease Prevention and Health Promotion, Centers for Disease Control and Prevention.

WHAT AN OBSERVER INFLUENCED BY EACH OF THE FIVE PERSPECTIVES MIGHT SAY ABOUT THESE STATISTICS

① **Psychoanalytic.** The close mother–infant bond is crucial for the child's psychological development. Nations with lower rates of breast-feeding are likely to have higher rates of anxiety and depression among adults.

② **Behaviorist.** Breast-feeding becomes habitual and reinforcing to both mother and child. That is why, among mothers who are breast-feeding at 6 months, many continue—even when nutritionally it is no longer needed.

③ **Cognitive.** Whether or not a woman breast-feeds depends on what she believes. That is why rates of breast-feeding have increased in Western nations over the past few decades.

④ **Sociocultural.** Cultural variations are apparent. All infants need to be fed, but the wide differences from place to place show that how babies are fed depends more on culture than on other factors.

⑤ **Evolutionary (a universal perspective).** Evolutionary needs have always required breast-feeding, but women who wanted to be more "modern" moved away from it. As evolutionary factors have become better understood in the United States, breast-feeding is increasing.

**Many hypotheses spring from each theory. These are possible interpretations—not accepted by everyone or guided by any of these theories.

SUMMARY

What Theories Do

1. A theory provides a framework of general principles to guide research and to explain observations. Each of the five major developmental theories—psychoanalytic, behaviorist, cognitive, sociocultural, and universal—interprets human development from a distinct perspective and organizes observation and research to aid comprehension of human experience and behavior.

2. Theories are neither true nor false. They are not facts; they suggest hypotheses to be tested. Good theories are practical: They aid inquiry, interpretation, and daily life.

3. A norm is a usual standard of behavior. Norms are not theories, although they may result from theories if a theory suggests that a certain behavior is proper. Norms are not necessarily good or bad, although sometimes differences from the norm are falsely considered deficits.

Psychoanalytic Theory: Freud and Erikson

4. Psychoanalytic theory emphasizes that human actions and thoughts originate from unconscious impulses and childhood conflicts. Freud theorized that sexual urges arise during three stages of childhood development—oral, anal, and phallic—and continue, after latency, in the genital stage. Conflict is inevitable in every stage.

5. Erikson described psychosocial, not psychosexual, stages. He described eight successive stages of development, each involving a crisis that must be resolved as people mature within their context. Societies, cultures, and family members shape each person's development.

6. All psychoanalytic theories stress the legacy of childhood. According to Freud, conflicts associated with children's erotic impulses have a lasting impact on adult personality. Erikson thought that the resolution of each crisis affects adult development.

Behaviorism: Conditioning and Social Learning

7. Behaviorists, or learning theorists, believe that scientists should study observable and measurable behavior. Behaviorism emphasizes conditioning—a lifelong learning process.

8. In classical behaviorism, there are two basic kinds of learning. One is classical conditioning, which describes the learning that occurs when one stimulus is linked to another. The other kind is operant conditioning, when the reinforcement or punishment that follows an action guides future behavior.

9. Social learning theory recognizes that people learn by observing others. Children are particularly susceptible to social learning, as they model their behavior, first after their parents and then after popular peers and famous people.

Cognitive Theory: Piaget and Information Processing

10. Cognitive theorists believe that thoughts and beliefs powerfully affect attitudes, actions, and perceptions.

11. Piaget proposed four age-related periods of cognition, each propelled by an active search for cognitive equilibrium. At every stage, assimilation and accommodation advance thinking.

12. Information processing focuses on each aspect of cognitive input, processing, and output. Neuroscience discoveries about how the brain functions have been particularly interesting for information processing theories.

Sociocultural Theory: Vygotsky and Beyond

13. Sociocultural theory explains human development in terms of the guidance, support, and structure provided by knowledgeable members of the society through culture and mentoring.

14. Vygotsky described how learning occurs through social interactions, in which mentors guide learners through their zone of proximal development.

The Universal Perspective: Humanism and Evolution

15. The universal perspective focuses on the shared impulses and common needs of all humanity. At their core, all humans are far more alike than different.

16. The two leaders of humanism—both Americans from the same cohort—were Maslow and Rogers. Maslow described five basic needs of all humans, following a sequence beginning with survival and ending with self-actualization. Rogers stressed the dignity of each person, who needs respect and appreciation (unconditional positive regard).

17. Evolutionary theory contends that contemporary humans inherit genetic tendencies that have fostered survival and reproduction of the human species for tens of thousands of years. Through selective adaptation, human genes are the underlying reason for many human behaviors, including gender differences, mental illness, and family bonds.

What Theories Contribute

18. Psychoanalytic, behavioral, cognitive, sociocultural, and universal theories have aided our understanding of human development, yet no single theory describes the full complexity and diversity of human experience. Most developmentalists are eclectic, drawing upon many theories.

KEY TERMS

developmental theory (p. 38)
norm (p. 39)
psychoanalytic theory (p. 40)
behaviorism (p. 43)
conditioning (p. 43)
classical conditioning (p. 43)

operant conditioning (p. 44)
reinforcement (p. 45)
social learning theory (p. 45)
modeling (p. 45)
cognitive theory (p. 47)
cognitive equilibrium (p. 48)

assimilation (p. 48)
accommodation (p. 48)
information-processing theory
  (p. 48)
sociocultural theory (p. 52)
apprenticeship in thinking
  (p. 52)

guided participation (p. 52)
zone of proximal development
  (p. 52)
humanism (p. 55)
selective adaptation (p. 58)
eclectic perspective (p. 61)

APPLICATIONS

1. Developmentalists sometimes talk about "folk theories," which are theories developed by ordinary people, who may not know that they are theorizing. Choose three sayings commonly used in your culture, such as (from the dominant U.S. culture) "A penny saved is a penny earned" or "As the twig is bent, so grows the tree." Explain the underlying assumptions, or theory, that each saying reflects.

2. Behaviorism has been used to change personal habits. Think of a habit you'd like to change (e.g., stop smoking, exercise more, watch less TV). Count the frequency of that behavior for a week, noting the reinforcers for each instance. Then, and only then, develop a substitute behavior, reinforcing yourself for it. Keep careful data for several days. What did you learn?

3. Ask three people to tell you their theories about male–female differences in mating and sexual behaviors. Which of the theories described in this chapter is closest to each explanation, and which theory is not mentioned?

CHAPTER 3

The New Genetics

What Will You Know?

1. What is the relationship between genes and chromosomes?
2. Is twinning genetic or can a person choose to have twins?
3. How could a person have the gene for something that is never apparent?
4. If both parents have alcoholism, will their children have alcoholism, too?
5. Why are some children born with Down syndrome?

"She needs a special school. She cannot come back next year," Elissa's middle school principal told us.

We were stunned. Apparently the school staff thought that our wonderful daughter, bright and bubbly (Martin called her "frothy"), was learning disabled. They had a label for it: "severely spatially disorganized." We had noticed that she misplaced homework, got lost, left books at school, forgot where each class met on which day—but that seemed insignificant compared to her strengths in reading, analyzing, and friendship.

I knew the first lesson from genetics: Genes affect everything, not just physical appearance, intellect, and predisposition to specific diseases, so it dawned on me that Elissa had inherited our behavior patterns. Our desks were covered with papers; our home had assorted objects everywhere. If we needed masking tape, or working scissors, or silver candle sticks, we had to search in several places. Was that why we were unaware of Elissa's failings?

The second lesson from genetics is that nurture always matters. My husband and I had both learned to compensate for innate organizational weaknesses. Since he often got lost, Martin did not hesitate to ask strangers for directions; since I was prone to mislaying important documents, I kept my students' papers in clearly marked folders at my office. Despite our genes, we both were successful; we thought Elissa would be fine.

There is a third lesson. Whether or not a gene is expressed, that is, whether or not it actively affects a person, depends partly on the social context of that person's life. We determined not to let Elissa's genes impair her future. Because we now paid attention, we called our friends who gave us advice about how to help Elissa overcome her disability, including finding a professional tutor to teach spatial skills. Elissa began to list her homework assignments, check them off when done, put them carefully in her bag (not crumpled in the bottom), and then take her backpack to school.

We did our part: Martin attached her bus pass to her backpack; I wrote an impassioned letter telling the principal it would be unethical to expel her, we bought another

The Moment of Conception This ovum is about to become a zygote. It has been penetrated by a single sperm, whose nucleus now lies next to the nucleus of the ovum. Soon, the two nuclei will fuse, bringing together about 20,000 genes to guide development.

gamete A reproductive cell; that is, a sperm or ovum that can produce a new individual if it combines with a gamete from the other sex to make a zygote.

zygote The single cell formed from the union of two gametes, a sperm and an ovum.

deoxyribonucleic acid (DNA) The chemical composition of the molecules that contain the genes, which are the chemical instructions for cells to manufacture various proteins.

chromosome One of the 46 structures made of DNA (in 23 pairs) that almost every cell of the human body contains and that, together, contain all the genes. Other species have more or fewer chromosomes.

gene A small section of a chromosome; the basic unit for the transmission of heredity. A gene consists of a string of chemicals that provide instructions for the cell to manufacture certain proteins.

allele A variation that makes a gene different in some way from other genes for the same characteristics. Many genes never vary; others have several possible alleles.

Especially for Scientists A hundred years ago, it was believed that humans had 48 chromosomes, not 46; 20 years ago, it was thought that humans had 100,000 genes, not 20,000 or so. Why? (see response, page 70)

set of textbooks so she would have one at school and one at home. The three of us also toured other schools—aware that we needed to heed her school's principal, not simply disagree. Elissa understood that she might need a different school, so she studied diligently, hoping she would not need to leave her friends.

Success! Elissa aced her final exams, and the principal, somewhat reluctantly, allowed her to return. She became a good student all through high school and college, and is now a gifted strategist, a master organizer, an accomplished professional.

This chapter explains these three lessons. New scientific discoveries about genetics are published every day, leading to many ethical dilemmas and practical choices. I hope the implications of this chapter mean that you will never be stunned by what the school tells you about your middle-school child.

The Genetic Code

A reproductive cell is called a **gamete.** Every person begins life as a single cell, called a **zygote;** the zygote is the combination of two gametes, one sperm and one ovum. The zygote contains all a person's genes, which affect every aspect of development lifelong. Many people have misconceptions about heredity, so the beginning of this chapter is crucial to understanding human development.

What Genes Are

First, we review some biology. All living things are composed of cells. The work of cells is done by *proteins*. Each cell manufactures certain proteins according to a code of instructions stored by molecules of **deoxyribonucleic acid (DNA)** at the heart of the cell. These coding DNA molecules are on a **chromosome.**

Humans have 23 pairs of chromosomes (46 in all), which contain the instructions to make all the proteins that a person needs for life and growth (see Figure 3.1). The instructions in the 46 chromosomes are organized into genes, with each **gene** usually at a precise location on a particular chromosome. Humans have about 20,000 genes, each directing the formation of specific proteins, which are made from a string of 20 amino acids.

The instructions for making those amino acids are located on about 3 billion pairs of chemicals, called base pairs, arranged in precise order. A small variation—such as repeated pairs, or one missing pair—changes the gene a tiny bit. Although all humans have most of the same genes with identical codes, those tiny variations of certain genes make each person unique. Each variation of a particular gene is called an **allele** of that gene.

RNA (ribonucleic acid, another molecule) and additional DNA surround each gene. In a process called *methylation,* this additional material enhances, transcribes, connects, empowers, silences, and alters genetic instructions. This noncoding material used to be called *junk*—but no longer. The influences of this surrounding material "alter not the gene itself, but rather the regulatory elements that control the process of gene expression" (Furey & Sethupathy, 2013, p. 705). Methylation continues throughout life, from conception until death.

Obviously, genes are crucial, but even more crucial is whether or not a gene is expressed. The RNA regulates and transcribes genetic instructions, turning some genes and alleles on or off. In other words, a person can have the genetic tendency for a particular trait, disease, or behavior, but that tendency might never appear in that person's life because it was never turned on. Think of a light switch: A lamp might have a new bulb and an electricity source, but the room stays dark unless the switch is flipped.

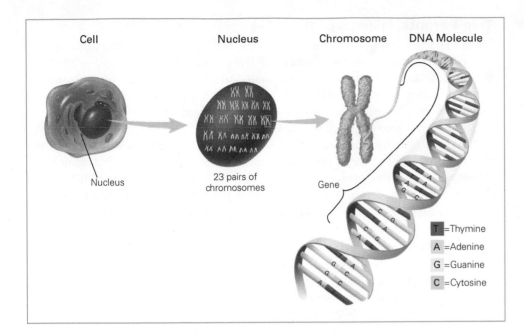

FIGURE 3.1

How Proteins Are Made The genes on the chromosomes in the nucleus of each cell instruct the cell to manufacture the proteins needed to sustain life and development. The code for a protein is the particular combination of four bases, T-A-G-C (thymine, adenine, guanine, and cytosine).

Cell

Nucleus

Nucleus

23 pairs of chromosomes

Chromosome

Gene

DNA Molecule

T =Thymine
A =Adenine
G =Guanine
C =Cytosine

Some genetic activation occurs because of prenatal RNA, but some occurs because of later factors, biological (such as pollution) and psychological (as with social rejection). The study of exactly how genes change in form and expression is called **epigenetics,** with *epi* a Greek root meaning "around, above, below."

Researchers who sought a single gene for, say, schizophrenia, or homosexuality, or even something quite specific such as memory for math formulas, have been disappointed: No such genes exist. Instead, almost every trait arises from a combination of genes, each with a small potential impact. Then epigenetics is crucial: Events and circumstances surrounding the genes determine whether or not genes are expressed or stay silent (Ayyanathan, 2014).

epigenetics The study of how environmental factors affect genes and genetic expression—enhancing, halting, shaping, or altering the expression of genes and resulting in a phenotype that may differ markedly from the genotype.

Variations

It is human nature for people to notice differences more than commonalities. All people are the same in many ways, not only with two eyes, hands, and feet, but also with the ability to communicate in language, the capacity to love and hate, and the wish for a meaningful life.

Alternate Forms

Nonetheless, each of us is distinct in small ways, not only because of our experiences but also because of our genes. Many scientists seek genetic causes for dissimilarities. Differences begin with alleles, some of which reflect transpositions, deletions, or repetitions of those 3 billion base pairs. Some genes are *polymorphic* (literally, "many forms") or, more formally, *single-nucleotide polymorphisms* (abbreviated SNPs, pronounced "snips"). Studying the impact of those SNPs is crucial for understanding why one person is unlike another.

Polymorphic genes can have two, three, or more versions. Most alleles seem inconsequential; some cause minor differences, such as the shape of an eyebrow or the shade of skin; a few rare ones are devastating. Several destructive alleles in combination with specific epigenetic conditions make a person develop schizophrenia, or diabetes, or some other serious problem (Plomin et al., 2013).

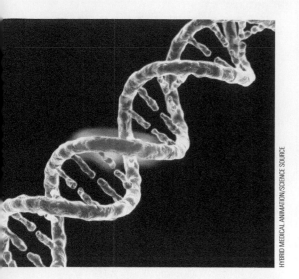

Twelve of 3 Billion Pairs This is a computer illustration of a small segment of one gene. Even a small difference in one gene can cause major changes in a person's phenotype.

HYBRID MEDICAL ANIMATION/SCIENCE SOURCE

genome The full set of genes that are the instructions to make an individual member of a certain species.

// Response for Scientists (from page 68):
There was some scientific evidence for the wrong numbers (e.g., chimpanzees have 48 chromosomes), but the reality is that humans tend to overestimate many things, from the number of genes to their grade on the next test. Scientists are very human: They tend to overestimate until the data prove them wrong.

genotype An organism's entire genetic inheritance, or genetic potential.

homozygous Referring to two genes of one pair that are exactly the same in every letter of their code. Most gene pairs are homozygous.

Two Parents, Millions of Gametes

Some variation springs from the simple fact that it takes two people to make one new person. Each parent contributes half the genetic material. Thus the 23 chromosomes from one parent, with their thousands of genes, match up with the 23 from the other, forming identical or nearly identical pairs. Chromosome 1 from the sperm matches with chromosome 1 from the ovum, chromosome 2 with chromosome 2, and so on through the 22nd pair.

On those chromosomes, each gene from one parent connects with its counterpart from the other parent, and the interaction between the two determines the inherited traits of the future person. Since some alleles from the father differ from the alleles from the mother, their combination produces a zygote unlike either parent. Thus each new person is a product of two parents but unlike either one.

Diversity at conception is increased by another fact: When a man or woman makes sperm or ova, and then their chromosomes pair up when they join, some genetic material is transferred from one chromosome to the other, a phenomena called jumping. As a result, "even if two siblings get the same chromosome from their mother, their chromosomes aren't identical" (Zimmer, 2009, p. 1254).

All these kinds of genetic diversity help societies, because creativity, prosperity, and even species survival is enhanced when one person is unlike another, although there are benefits when genes are shared as well. There is an optimal level of diversity and similarity: Human societies are close to that level (Ashraf & Galor, 2013).

The entire packet of instructions to make a living organism is called the **genome.** There is a genome for every species and variety of plant and animal—even for every bacterium and virus. Knowing the genome of *homo sapiens,* which was decoded in 2001, is only a start at understanding human genetics, since each individual has a slightly different set of those 3 billion base pairs.

The particular member of each chromosome pair from each parent on a given gamete is randomly selected. A man or woman can produce 2^{23} different gametes—more than 8 million versions of his or her own 46 chromosomes. If a given couple conceived a billion zygotes, each would be genetically unique because of the chromosomes of the particular sperm that fertilized that particular ovum. Interacting alleles, methylation, and other genetic forces add more variations to the zygote. Epigenetic influences silence some genes and allow expression of others. Nurture creates even more variations.

Matching Genes and Chromosomes

The genes on the chromosomes constitute the organism's genetic inheritance, or **genotype,** which endures throughout life. Growth requires duplication of the code of the original cell again and again.

Matching Autosomes

In 22 of the 23 pairs of chromosomes, both members of the pair are closely matched. As already explained, some of the specific genes have alternate alleles, but at least each of these 44 chromosomes finds its comparable chromosome, making a pair. Those 44 chromosomes are called *autosomes,* which means that they are independent (*auto* means "self") of the sex chromosomes (the 23rd pair).

Each autosome, from number 1 to number 22, contains hundreds of genes in the same positions and sequence. If the code of the gene from one parent is exactly like the code on the same gene from the other parent, the gene pair is **homozygous** (literally, "same-zygote").

However, the match is not always letter perfect because the mother might have a different allele of a particular gene than the father has. If a gene's code differs from that of its counterpart, the two genes still pair up, but the zygote (and, later, the person) is **heterozygous.** This can occur with any of the gene pairs, on any of the autosomes. Which particular homozygous or heterozygous genes my brother and I inherited from our parents was purely a matter of chance, and had no connection to the fact that I am a younger sister, not an older brother.

Sex Chromosomes

However, for the **23rd pair** of chromosomes, my sex reveals a marked difference between my brother and me. My 23rd pair matched, but his did not. In that he was like all males: When gametes combine to form the zygote, half of the time a dramatic mismatch occurs. In males, the 23rd pair has one X-shaped chromosome and one Y-shaped chromosome. It is called **XY.** In females, the 23rd pair is composed of two X-shaped chromosomes. Accordingly, it is called **XX.**

Because a female's 23rd pair is XX, all of a mother's ova contain either one X or the other—but always an X. And because a male's 23rd pair is XY, half of a father's sperm carry an X chromosome and half a Y. The X chromosome is bigger and has more genes, but the Y chromosome has a crucial gene, called *SRY*, that directs the embryo to make male hormones and organs. Thus, sex depends on which sperm penetrates the ovum—a Y sperm with the SRY gene, creating a boy (XY), or an X sperm, creating a girl (XX) (see Figure 3.2).

Uncertain Sex Every now and then, a baby is born with "ambiguous genitals," meaning that the child's sex is not abundantly clear. When this happens, a quick analysis of the chromosomes is needed, to make sure there are exactly 46 and to see whether the 23rd pair is XY or XX. The karyotypes shown below indicate a normal baby boy (*left*) and girl (*right*).

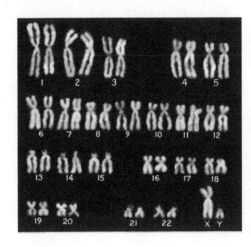
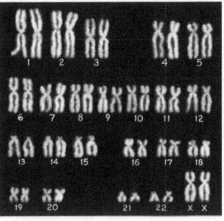

BIOPHOTO ASSOCIATES/SCIENCE SOURCE

heterozygous Referring to two genes of one pair that differ in some way. Typically one allele has only a few base pairs that differ from the other member of the pair.

23rd pair The chromosome pair that, in humans, determines sex. The other 22 pairs are autosomes, inherited equally by males and females.

XY A 23rd chromosome pair that consists of an X-shaped chromosome from the mother and a Y-shaped chromosome from the father. XY zygotes become males.

XX A 23rd chromosome pair that consists of two X-shaped chromosomes, one each from the mother and the father. XX zygotes become females.

Possible Combinations of Sex Chromosomes

Father's chromosomes
44+XY

Mother's chromosomes
44+XX

Sperm
22+ Y 22+ Y 22+ X 22+ X   22+ X 22+ X 22+ X 22+ X   Ova

Zygotes
44+ XY   44+ XY   44+ XX   44+ XX

Male   Male   Female   Female

FIGURE 3.2

Determining a Zygote's Sex Any given couple can produce four possible combinations of sex chromosomes; two lead to female children and two to male. In terms of the future person's sex, it does not matter which of the mother's Xs the zygote inherited. All that matters is whether the father's Y sperm or X sperm fertilized the ovum. However, for X-linked conditions it matters a great deal because typically one, but not both, of the mother's Xs carries the trait.

In some other species, sex is not determined at conception. In certain reptiles, for instance, temperature during incubation of the fertilized egg affects the sex of the embryo (Hare & Cree, 2010). However, for humans, the zygote is either XX or XY, a fact that in the past was not revealed to anyone until the baby was born. Pregnant women ate special foods, slept in a particular way, or repeated certain prayers, all in a vain attempt to control the sex of their fetus—who had been male or female at conception.

Today, sex can be known much earlier: Parents choose names, decorate nurseries, and bond with the future boy or girl—or reject him or her, as the Opposing Perspectives explains. A zygote's sex cannot be changed.

SUMMING UP The normal human genome contains approximately 20,000 genes on exactly 46 chromosomes, using an estimated 3 billion base pairs of code to make a person. Some genes, called alleles, are polymorphic. Because of small differences

opposing perspectives

Too Many Boys?

Parents can choose the sex of their newborn. Millions of couples have done this. Is this a problem?

The birth of a child of unwanted sex can be prevented long before birth in three ways: (1) by inactivating X or Y sperm before conception, (2) by inserting only the male or female zygotes after in vitro conception, or (3) by aborting XX or XY fetuses. Should all or some of these three methods be banned? In at least 36 nations, prenatal sex selection is illegal, but not in the United States (Murray, 2014).

One nation that forbids prenatal sex selection is China. This was not always so. In about 1979, China began a "one-child" policy, urging and sometimes forcing couples to have only one child. That may have helped achieve the intended goal: reduction of poverty caused by too many dependent children. But the Chinese government did not anticipate advances in prenatal testing, nor realize the strength of the tradition that sons, not daughters, should care for aged parents. An unintended consequence was that many parents chose to have their only child be a boy. Among the unanticipated results over several decades were: (1) almost a million abortions of female fetuses, (2) thousands of newborn girls available for adoption, and, currently (3) far more unmarried young men than women.

In 1993, the Chinese government forbade prenatal testing for sex selection. Many couples broke the law. In 2013, China rescinded the one-child policy. Yet from 2015–2020, according to the best projections from the population division of United Nations secretariat, 115 males will be born for every 100 females. Since the natural sex ratio at birth is 104:100, it is evident that selective abortion is expected to continue.

Indeed, sex preferences are apparent in every nation. One elderly Indian man said, "We should have at least four children per family, three of them boys" (quoted in Khanna, 2010, p. 66).

MANISH SWARUP/AP PHOTO

My Strength, My Daughter That's the slogan these girls in New Delhi are shouting at a demonstration against abortion of female fetuses in India. The current sex ratio of children in India suggests that this campaign has not convinced every couple.

in their genetic codes, those alleles make each person unlike any other. The result is that each person is unique yet similar to all other humans. The entire instruction code is the genome, contained in a single cell called the zygote. Each person's genetic code (their genotype) is expressed because of many environmental influences, an interaction called epigenetics, which produces the phenotype. This is true even for one's sex, which is determined by a pair of chromosomes, but maleness and femaleness are expressed in many ways.

WHAT HAVE YOU LEARNED?

1. How many pairs of chromosomes and how many genes does a person usually have?
2. What causes the similarities of all humans?
3. Why do two sisters or two brothers in the same family differ genetically?
4. Which is more important for a person's daily life, the phenotype or genotype, and why?
5. What determines whether a baby will be a boy or a girl?

Couples of Asian ancestry in the United States also have a disproportionate number of boys (Puri et al., 2011). In some Western nations, including Germany, girls are preferred—both as newborns and as caregivers of the old (Wilhelm et al., 2013).

The argument in favor of sex selection is freedom to choose. Some fertility doctors in the United States believe that reproductive rights include that each couple be able to decide how many children to have, and what sex they should be (Murray, 2014). Some people who themselves would not abort a fetus nonetheless favor personal freedom—in this case, freedom to "balance" the family.

Why would anyone object to freedom? The Chinese experience shows that sex selection can have unanticipated consequences. For instance, now many more young Chinese men than women die prematurely. The developmental explanation is that unmarried young men in every culture take risks to attract women and become depressed if they remain single when they want marriage and fatherhood.

Other problems may occur. Males are more likely to be learning disabled, drug addicted, and criminal; they're also more likely to start wars, commit suicide, and suffer heart attacks. Any nation with more men than women may experience increases in all these problems.

But wait: Chromosomes and genes do not determine behavior. Every sex difference is a product of culture. Even traits that originate with biology, such as the propensity to heart attacks, are affected more by environment (in this case, diet and cigarettes) than by XX or XY chromosomes. Perhaps nurture could change

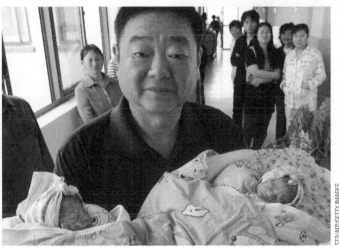

Mama Is 60 Wu Jingzhou holds his newborn twin daughters, born to his 60-year-old wife after in vitro fertilization. Ordinarily, it is illegal in China, as in most other nations, for women to have children after menopause. But an exception was made for this couple since the death of their only child, a young woman named Tingling, was partly the government's fault.

if nature produced more males than females, and then societies would not suffer. The frequency of sex selection is influenced by national policy and cultural values (Parker, 2012).

Might laws against prenatal sex choices be unnecessary if culture could shift? "Might" . . . "if" . . . Critical thinking needed.

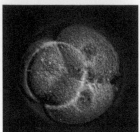

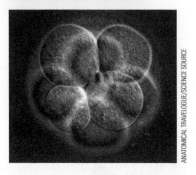

ANATOMICAL TRAVELOGUE/SCIENCE SOURCE

Still Stems But not much longer. These three photos show early cell duplication and division, with each new cell exactly like the others, with all the genetic instructions to make a whole person, or any cell of a person's body. A technician could remove one cell and test it for defects, and the remaining cells would still grow into a fetus as if nothing had happened. But in another 24 hours, that is impossible—the stem cells would begin to differentiate and any removal might be lethal.

stem cells Cells from which any other specialized type of cell can form.

New Cells, New Functions

Within hours after conception, the zygote begins *duplication* and *division*. First, the 23 pairs of chromosomes carrying all the genes duplicate to form two complete sets of the genome. These two sets move toward opposite sides of the zygote, and the single cell splits neatly down the middle into two cells, each containing the original genetic code. These two cells duplicate and divide, becoming four, which duplicate and divide, becoming eight, and so on.

The name of the developing mass of cells changes as it multiplies—from morula to blastocyst, from embryo to fetus—and finally, at birth, baby. (**Developmental Link:** Prenatal growth is detailed in Chapter 4.)

Every Cell the Same

Nine months after conception, a newborn has about 26 billion cells, all influenced by whatever nutrients, drugs, hormones, viruses, and so on came from the pregnant woman. Almost every human cell carries a complete copy of the genetic instructions of the one-celled zygote.

Adults have about 37 trillion cells, each with the same 46 chromosomes and the same thousands of genes of the original zygote (Bianconi, et al., 2013). This explains why DNA testing of any body cell, even from a drop of blood or a snip of hair, can identify "the real father," "the guilty criminal," "the long-lost brother." DNA lingers long after death. Some living African Americans claimed Thomas Jefferson as an ancestor: DNA testing proved some of them right and some of them wrong (Foster et al., 1998).

Indeed, because the Y chromosome is passed down to every male descendant, and because the genes on the Y typically do not change much from one generation to another, men have the Y of a male ancestor who died thousands of years ago.

Tracing the Y chromosome suggests that thousands of East Asian men may be descendants of Genghis Khan—although that twelfth-century leader's bones and thus his DNA have never been found (Stoneking & Delfin, 2010). Such genetic sleuthing is not totally reliable: It is quite possible to trace ancestry for several generations; it is much more complex to go back for hundreds of years. But history suggests Khan may have impregnated many women.

Stem Cells

The cells that result from the early duplication and division are called **stem cells;** these cells are able to produce any other cell and thus to become a complete person. Indeed, as later described, sometimes these cells split apart and each becomes an identical twin.

After about the eight-cell stage, although duplication and division continue, a third process, *differentiation,* begins. In differentiation, cells specialize, taking different forms and reproducing at various rates depending on where they are located. For instance, some cells become part of an eye, others part of a finger, still others part of the brain. They are no longer stem cells. Blood cells in the umbilical cord, however, may act like stem cells.

Scientists have discovered ways to add genes to certain differentiated cells in a laboratory process that reprograms those cells, making them like stem cells again. However, scientists do not yet know how to use reprogrammed stem cells to cure genetic conditions without harming other cells. In fact, there are many kinds of stem cells, and thousands of potential uses (Slack, 2012).

One use of reprogrammed cells has been found: to test drugs to treat diseases caused by genes, either directly (such as sickle-cell anemia) or indirectly (such as heart disease, diabetes, and dementia) (Zhu & Huangfu, 2013; Vogel, 2010).

Some restrictions on stem cell research in the United States were lifted in 2009, and some states (e.g., California) and nations (e.g., South Korea) allow more extensive research, but everywhere many ethical and practical issues remain (Nguyen et al., 2013). As the head of the Michael J. Fox Foundation for Parkinson's Research said, "All my exposure was pop media. I thought it was all about stem cells. I have not totally lost hope on cell replacement, I just don't think it's a near-term hope" (Hood, quoted in Holden, 2009).

The Placenta

One of the first signs of differentiation is the formation of the placenta, the organ that sustains the developing person throughout pregnancy. The outer cells of the blastocyst surround the inner cells, even before differentiation of body cells has begun, soon creating tiny blood vessels called villi that will connect the mother to the embryo via the umbilical cord. Those blood vessels exchange waste products from the fetus and nourishment from the mother to enable growth and life.

In some cultures, the placenta is revered and ceremoniously buried once the baby is born. In the United States it is usually discarded, "a throwaway organ" that deserves more respect (Kaiser, 2014, p. 1073).

The fact that the placenta is formed from the early duplicating cells allows early genetic testing. In chorionic villus sample (CVS), a sample of the placental blood is removed and analyzed. Many chromosomal and genetic disorders can be detected at this early stage.

Later in pregnancy, cells from the fetus are sloughed off and circulate in the amniotic fluid, and these can also be removed and analyzed in a process called amniocentesis. (**Developmental Link:** Chromosomal and genetic disorders are discussed at the end of this chapter.)

Twins

Thus far we have described conception as if one sperm fertilized one ovum, beginning the process of duplication and differentiation. But that is not always the case. To understand multiple conceptions, you need to know the difference between monozygotic and dizygotic twins (see Visualizing Development, p. 76).

Monozygotic Twins

Although every zygote is genetically unique, about once in 250 human conceptions duplication results in one or more complete splits, creating two, or four, or even eight separate zygotes, each identical to the first single cell. This creation of identical embryos has been done experimentally for lower animals, but it is illegal for humans in a laboratory. However, nature does it occasionally in the first hours after conception. (An incomplete split creates *conjoined twins,* formerly called Siamese twins.)

If each of those separated cells from one zygote then duplicates, divides, differentiates, implants, grows, and survives, multiple births occur. One separation results in **monozygotic (MZ) twins,** from one (*mono*) zygote (also called *identical twins*). Two or three separations create monozygotic quadruplets or octuplets.

Because monozygotic multiples originate from the same zygote, they have virtually identical genetic instructions for appearance, psychological traits, disease vulnerability, and everything else genetic. Remember, however, that epigenetic influences begin as soon as conception occurs: Monozygotic twins look very much alike, but their environment can influence their development in many ways that distinguish one from the other.

Monozygotic twins are blessed in some ways: They can donate a kidney or other organ to their twin with no organ rejection, thus avoiding major complications

Video Activity: Identical Twins: Growing Up Apart gives a real-life example of how genes play a significant role in people's physical, emotional, social, and mental development.

monozygotic (MZ) twins Twins who originate from one zygote that splits apart very early in development. (Also called *identical twins.*) Other monozygotic multiple births (such as triplets and quadruplets) can occur as well.

VISUALIZING DEVELOPMENT

One Baby or More

Humans usually have one baby at a time, but sometimes twins are born. Most often they are from two ova fertilized by two sperm (*lower left*), resulting in dizygotic twins. Sometimes, however, one zygote splits in two (*lower right*), resulting in monozygotic twins; if each of these zygotes splits again, the result is monozygotic quadruplets.

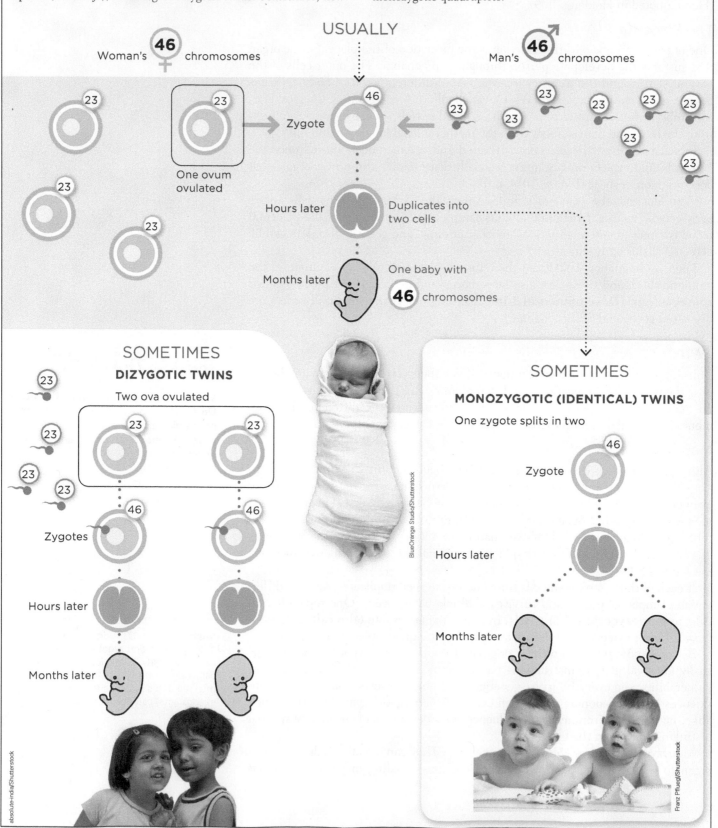

USUALLY

Woman's **46** chromosomes   Man's **46** chromosomes

23   23   46   Zygote   23   23   23   23   23   23   23   23

One ovum ovulated

Hours later   Duplicates into two cells

Months later   One baby with **46** chromosomes

SOMETIMES
DIZYGOTIC TWINS

Two ova ovulated

23   23   23

23   23

Zygotes   46   46

Hours later

Months later

absolute-india/Shutterstock

BlueOrange Studio/Shutterstock

SOMETIMES
MONOZYGOTIC (IDENTICAL) TWINS

One zygote splits in two

46   Zygote

Hours later

Months later

Franz Pfluegl/Shutterstock

with surgical transplants. On a lighter note, they can also befuddle their parents and teachers, who may use special signs (such as different earrings) to tell them apart. Usually, the twins themselves find their own identities while enjoying twinship. They might enjoy inherited athletic ability, for instance, with one playing basketball and the other soccer.

As one monozygotic twin writes:

> Twins put into high relief *the* central challenge for all of us: self-definition. How do we each plant our stake in the ground, decide how sensitive, callous, ambitious, cautious, or conciliatory we want to be every day? . . . Twins come with a built-in constant comparison, but defining oneself against one's twin is just an amped-up version of every person's life-long challenge: to individuate, to create a distinctive persona in the world.
>
> *[Pogrebin, 2010, p. 9]*

Dizygotic Twins

Among naturally conceived twins, only about one in five pairs is monozygotic. About once in 60 conceptions, **dizygotic (DZ) twins** are conceived. They are also called *fraternal twins,* although since *fraternal* means "brotherly" (as in fraternity), the term is inaccurate. DZ twins are as likely to be two girls, or a boy and a girl, as two boys. In every case, dizygotic twins began life as two separate zygotes created by two ova fertilized by two sperm at the same time. (Usually, women release only one ovum per month, but sometimes double or triple ovulation occurs, a tendency that is affected by genes.)

People sometimes say that twinning "skips a generation" but that also is not accurate. What it skips is fathers—but not exactly. Since dizygotic twinning depends on multiple ovulation, the likelihood of a woman bearing twins depends on her genes, not her husband's. However, a man has half his genes from his mother. If multiple ovulation is in his family, he will not produce twins, but if the X he inherited from his mother is the one that encouraged multiple ovulation, his daughters (who always get his X) might.

When dizygotic twinning occurs naturally, the incidence varies by ethnicity. For example, about 1 in 11 Yorubas in Nigeria is a twin, as are about 1 in 45 European Americans, 1 in 75 Japanese and Koreans, and 1 in 150 Chinese. Age matters, too: Older women more often double-ovulate and thus have more twins.

After twins are conceived, their chance of survival until birth depends on the prenatal circumstances. An early sonogram might reveal two developing organisms, but later only one embryo continues to grow. This *vanishing twin* phenomenon may occur in about 12 percent of pregnancies (Giuffrè et al., 2012).

Like all full siblings, DZ twins have about half of their genes in common. They can differ markedly in appearance, or they can look so much alike that only genetic tests can determine whether they are monozygotic or dizygotic.

Chance determines which sperm fertilizes each ovum, so about half are same-sex pairs and half are boy–girl pairs. Of course, in the rare incidence that a woman releases two ova at once and also has sex with two different men over a short period, it is possible for fraternal twins to have different fathers and thus share only a fourth of the same genes.

Assisted Reproduction

The statistic above—twins born about once in 60 pregnancies—refers to natural conception. However, the twin birth rate has increased by 50 percent in the past two decades, and the triplet birth rate has doubled. The primary reason is that

dizygotic (DZ) twins Twins who are formed when two separate ova are fertilized by two separate sperm at roughly the same time. (Also called *fraternal* twins.)

when couples want children but are infertile (a condition affecting about 12 percent of U.S. couples), about half of them choose **assisted reproductive technology (ART).**

Infertility

Infertility is defined as failure to conceive a child after a year of trying. Rates vary by nation, primarily because of the quality of medical care and the incidence of sexually transmitted infections, many of which cause infertility. About one-third of all fertility problems originate in the woman, about one-third in the man, and in about one-third, the cause is unknown.

Some couples are subfertile, that is, less fertile than ideal but not sterile. It is not unusual for a couple to believe they are infertile, begin ART or adoption, and then spontaneously conceive. For subfertile couples, one developmental factor falls more heavily on women. Although both sexes become less fertile every year beginning at about age 18, for women the decline is steeper. Pregnancy after age 40 is unusual, and menopause (naturally at about age 50) makes ovulation impossible. By contrast, men produce sperm lifelong.

Since age is a factor, if a couple have trouble conceiving, they should consult a fertility specialist as soon as they can. The simplest cause is that the ovaries do not release ova. In that case, a woman can take a drug (usually Clomid) to cause ovulation. The drug may cause release of several ova at once, causing multiple births and risking preterm birth—a risk many are willing to take.

Another relatively simple solution appears when the man produces no viable sperm. In that case, the woman can be inseminated with another man's sperm, a procedure that usually does not include any personal contact between the man who donates sperm (stored in a laboratory) and the woman. Doctors have used this method of fertilizing an ovum for more than 100 years.

In Vitro Fertilization

In the twenty-first century, the most common ART method is **in vitro fertilization (IVF),** "a relatively routine way to have children, with an estimated 5 million babies born to date" (Thompson, 2014, p. 361). In this method, ova are surgically removed from an ovary, fertilized in a lab dish (*in vitro* means "in glass"), and then inserted into the uterus.

Often, a sperm is inserted directly into each ovum to improve the odds of fertilization, in a procedure called **intra-cytoplasmic sperm injection (ICSI).** Zygotes that fail to duplicate, or blastocysts tested positive for serious genetic diseases, are rejected. Many women ask that several fertilized ova be inserted: twins or even triplets seem like a bonus when a couple has been infertile for years.

Doctors have refined this procedure since the first IVF baby, Louise Brown, was born in England in 1978. Now they wait two to six days after conception, making sure division and duplication occur smoothly, before inserting the developing cells into the uterus. Between 1 and 3 percent of all newborns in developed nations and thousands more in developing nations are the result of IVF, making one scholar call IVF "a new norm of family life" (Franklin, 2013, p. 30).

Those numbers allow careful, longitudinal research. In general, IVF children develop as well as other children. A slightly higher risk of birth complications is evident, but that might not be directly from the IVF procedure but rather from other conditions common in such pregnancies: older parents and low birthweight (Fauser et al., 2014).

ART has enabled millions of couples to have children. Indeed, some parents have children who are not genetically or biologically theirs if others donate the

---

assisted reproductive technology (ART) A general term for the techniques designed to help infertile couples conceive and then sustain a pregnancy.

in vitro fertilization (IVF) Fertilization that takes place outside a woman's body (as in a glass laboratory dish). The procedure involves mixing sperm with ova that have been surgically removed from the woman's ovary. If a zygote is produced, it is inserted into a woman's uterus, where it may implant and develop into a baby.

intra-cytoplasmic sperm injection (ICSI) An in vitro fertilization technique in which a single sperm cell is injected directly into an ovum.

sperm, the ova, and/or the womb. The word *donate* may be misleading, since most donors—often college students—are paid for their sperm, ova, or pregnancy.

The reality that three people could contribute to the birth of a baby before someone else becomes the child's parent evokes moral issues. Increasingly, the "real" parents are thought to be those who raise a child, not those who conceive it, although not everyone agrees with this view (Franklin, 2013). Whether with their own gametes or someone else's, most people who become parents via IVF are married heterosexuals, but ART makes parenthood possible for many others, including single parents and same-sex couples.

Some nations forbid IVF to many who wish it, asking not only for proof of marriage but sometimes proof of financial and emotional health (as in Switzerland). Several European nations limit the numbers of blastocysts inserted into the uterus at one time, partly because national health care pays for both IVF and newborn care. According to research in seven nations, inserting just one blastocyst results in as many successful pregnancies as inserting multiple blastocysts, with fewer low-birthweight newborns (7 percent compared to 30 percent), primarily because each fetus develops alone (Grady et al., 2012).

The United States has no legal restrictions on IVF, although the procedure is expensive (about $20,000 for all the drugs and monitoring as well as the procedure itself) and not covered by insurance, which makes it beyond the reach of many couples. Medical societies provide some oversight. For example, the California Medical Board removed his license to practice medicine from the physician who inserted 12 blastocysts in Nadya Suleman. She gave birth to eight surviving babies in 2009, a medical miracle but a developmental disaster.

SUMMING UP The genes of the zygote duplicate themselves again and again. Although the first cells are stem cells, and therefore each could become a whole person, soon the cells differentiate as they multiply. Each cell becomes a particular type, traveling to the location on the body where it will perform whatever is needed, becoming skin, blood, bone, part of the brain, and so on.

Twins are monozygotic (one zygote, from the same stem cells) or dizygotic (two zygotes). Dizygotic twins occur if a woman ovulates two ova at once, but many couples have the opposite problem—no conception at all. Fertility measures help about half of such couples to conceive, via assisted reproductive technology (ART). The best-known measure of ART currently is in vitro fertilization, which can help when either the male or the female is subfertile. ART raises many ethical issues, especially when the donors of the sperm and/or ovum are not the parents of the offspring. An additional issue is that the rate of preterm and low-birthweight births increases if two or more zygotes are implanted.

WHAT HAVE YOU LEARNED?

1. How does differentiation affect stem cells?
2. What are the advantages and disadvantages of being a monozygotic twin?
3. What are the genetic similarities between monozygotic and dizygotic twins?
4. What ART measures help a woman who is infertile?
5. What ART measures help a man who is infertile?
6. What international differences are apparent in IVF?

From Genotype to Phenotype

As already explained, when a sperm and ovum create a zygote, they establish the *genotype*: all the genes of the developing person. That begins several complex processes that combine to form the **phenotype**—the person's appearance, behavior, and brain and body functions. Nothing is totally genetic, not even such obvious traits as height or hair color, but nothing is untouched by genes, including working overtime or not at all, wanting or refusing a divorce, or becoming a devoted or a rejecting parent (Plomin et al., 2013).

The genotype instigates body and brain formation, but the phenotype depends on many genes and on the environment. The phenotype is influenced from the moment of conception until the moment of death, sometimes directly (epigenetic) and sometime via cultural and familial circumstances.

Almost every trait is **polygenic** (affected by many genes) and **multifactorial** (influenced by many factors). A zygote might have the alleles for becoming, say, a musical genius, but that potential may never be expressed. Accurate prediction of the phenotype is impossible, even if the genotype is entirely known (Lehner, 2013).

Almost daily, researchers describe additional complexities in polygenic and multifactorial interaction. It is apparent that "phenotypic variation . . . results from multiple interactions among numerous genetic and environmental factors." To describe this "fundamental problem of interrelating genotype and phenotype in complex traits" (Nadeau & Dudley, 2011, p. 1015), we begin with epigenetics.

phenotype The observable characteristics of a person, including appearance, personality, intelligence, and all other traits.

polygenic Referring to a trait that is influenced by many genes.

multifactorial Referring to a trait that is affected by many factors, both genetic and environmental, that enhance, halt, shape, or alter the expression of genes, resulting in a phenotype that may differ markedly from the genotype.

Epigenetics

All important human characteristics are *epigenetic;* this applies also to diseases that are known to be inherited, such as cancer, schizophrenia, and autism (Kundu, 2013; Plomin et al., 2013).

Type 2 diabetes is a notable example. People who inherit genes that put them at risk do not always become diabetic. However, lifestyle factors might activate that genetic risk. If that happens, epigenetic changes to the genes make diabetes irreversible: Diet and insulin may control the disease, but the pre-diabetic state never returns (Reddy & Natarajan, 2013).

One intervention—bariatric surgery to dramatically reduce weight—leads to remission of diabetes in most (72 percent) patients, but over the years full diabetes returns for more than half of them. Crucial is conscientious diet and exercise for decades; remission is possible, but the disease is latent, never disappearing because genetic changes cannot be erased (Sjöström et al., 2014).

The same may be true for other developmental changes over the life span. Drug use—cocaine, cigarettes, alcohol, and so on—may produce epigenetic changes that make addiction likely, even if a person has stopped using the drug for years (Bannon et al., 2014). Treatment and other factors help, of course, but the addict can never use the drug again as an unaffected person would.

In general, environmental influences (such as injury, temperature extremes, drug abuse, and crowding) can impede healthy development, whereas others (nourishing food, loving care, play) can facilitate it, all because of differential susceptibility and epigenetic change. A recent discovery is that some environmental factors that suppress or release genes are cognitive, not biological.

For example, if a person feels lonely and rejected, that feeling can affect the RNA, which allows genetic potential for heart disease or social anxiety to be expressed (Slavich & Cole, 2013). Note that the *feeling* of loneliness, not the objective number of friends or social contacts, has significant epigenetic influence.

No trait—even one with strong, proven genetic origins, such as blood pressure or severe depression—is determined by genes alone because "development is an epigenetic process that entails cascades of interactions across multiple levels of causation, from genes to environments" (Spencer et al., 2009, p. 80). Because epigenetic influences occur lifelong, latent genes can become activated at any point.

Sisters, But Not Twins, In Iowa From their phenotype, it is obvious that these two girls share many of the same genes, as their blond hair and facial features are strikingly similar. And you can see that they are not twins; Lucy is 7 years old and Ellie is only 4. It may not be obvious that they have the same parents, but they do—and they are both very bright and happy because of it. This photo also shows that their genotypes differ in one crucial way: One of them has a dominant gene for a serious condition.

OBSERVATION QUIZ Who has that genetic condition? (see answer, page 82)

A surprising example might be political ideology: Several researchers report that a particular allele of a dopamine receptor gene (DRD4-R7) correlates with being liberal, but only if a person has many friends. Loners, even with the liberal-leaning allele, are more conservative (Settle et al., 2010). Genotype alone does not determine phenotype for any psychological trait, but the double whammy—genes and environment—does.

Gene–Gene Interactions

Many discoveries have followed the completion of the **Human Genome Project** in 2001. One of the first surprises was that humans have far fewer than 100,000 genes, the number often cited in the twentieth century. A person has a total of about 20,000 genes.

The precise number is elusive because—another surprise—it is not always easy to figure out where one gene starts and another ends, or if a particular stretch of DNA is actually a gene (Rouchka & Cha, 2009). Nor is it always easy to predict exactly how the genes from one parent will interact with the genes from the other. We do, however, know some basics of genetic interaction, as described now.

Additive Heredity

Some genes and alleles are *additive* because their effects *add up* to influence the phenotype. When genes interact additively, the phenotype usually reflects the contributions of every gene that is involved. Height, hair curliness, and skin color, for instance, are usually the result of additive genes. Indeed, height is probably influenced by 180 genes, each contributing a very small amount (Enserink, 2011).

Most people have ancestors of varied height, hair curliness, skin color, and so on, so their children's phenotype does not mirror the parents' phenotypes (although the phenotype always reflects the genotype). I see this in my family: Our daughter Rachel is of average height, shorter than her father or me, but taller than either of our mothers. She apparently inherited some of her grandmothers' height genes via our gametes. And none of my children have exactly my skin color—

Human Genome Project An international effort to map the complete human genetic code. This effort was essentially completed in 2001, though analysis is ongoing.

Especially for Future Parents Suppose you wanted your daughters to be short and your sons to be tall. Could you achieve that? (see response, page 83)

Genetic Mix Dizygotic twins Olivia and Harrison have half their genes in common, as do all siblings from the same parents. If the parents are close relatives, who themselves share most alleles, the non-shared half is likely to include many similar genes. That is not the case here, as mother (Nicola) is from Wales and father (Gleb) is from the nation of Georgia, which includes many people of Asian ancestry. Their phenotypes, and the family photos on the wall, show many additive genetic influences.

©2016 MACMILLAN

// ANSWER TO OBSERVATION QUIZ
(from page 80) Ellie has a gene for achondroplasia, the most common form of dwarfism, which affects her limb growth, making her a little person. Because of her parents and her sister, she is likely to have a long and accomplished life: Her problems are less likely to come from her genotype than from how other people perceive her phenotype.

dominant–recessive pattern The interaction of a heterozygous pair of alleles in such a way that the phenotype reflects one allele (the dominant gene) more than the other (the recessive gene).

carrier A person whose genotype includes a gene that is not expressed in the phenotype. The carried gene occurs in half of the carrier's gametes and thus is passed on to half of the carrier's children. If such a gene is inherited from both parents, the characteristic appears in the phenotype.

FIGURE 3.3

Changeling? No. If two brown-eyed parents both carry the blue-eye gene, they have one chance in four of having a blue-eyed child. Other recessive genes include the genes for red hair, Rh negative blood, and many genetic diseases.

OBSERVATION QUIZ Why do these four offspring look identical except for eye color? (see answer, page 84)

apparent when we borrow clothes from each other and are distressed that a particular shade is attractive on one but ugly on another.

How any additive trait turns out depends partly on all the genes a child happens to inherit (half from each parent, which means one-fourth from each grandparent). Some genes amplify or dampen the effects of other genes, aided by all the other DNA and RNA (not junk!) in the zygote (Pauler et al., 2012).

Dominant–Recessive Heredity

Not all genes are additive. In one non-additive form, alleles interact in a **dominant–recessive pattern,** when one allele, the *dominant gene,* is more influential than the other, the *recessive gene.* The dominant gene controls the expression of a characteristic even when a recessive gene is the other half of a pair.

Everyone has recessive genes that are not apparent in the phenotype. For instance, no one would guess, simply by looking at me, that my mother had to stretch to reach 5'4." But Rachel has half of her genes from me, and one of my height genes may be recessive. Every person is a **carrier** of recessive genes, *carried* on the genotype but not expressed in the phenotype.

Most recessive genes are harmless. For example, blue eyes are determined by a recessive allele and brown eyes by a dominant one, so a child conceived by a blue-eyed parent (who always has two recessive blue-eye genes) and a brown-eyed parent will usually have brown eyes. No harm in that.

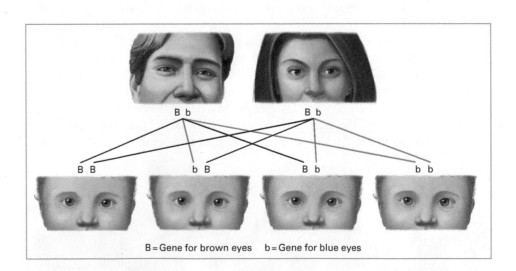

B = Gene for brown eyes   b = Gene for blue eyes

"Usually have brown eyes" but not always. Sometimes a brown-eyed person is a carrier of the blue-eye gene. In that case, in a blue-eye/brown-eye couple, every child has at least one blue-eye gene (from the blue-eyed parent) and half of them will have a blue-eye recessive gene (from the brown-eyed parent). That half will have blue eyes because they have no dominant brown-eye gene. The other half will have a brown-eye dominant gene and thus have brown eyes but be carriers of the blue-eye gene, like their brown-eyed parent.

This gets tricky if both parents are carriers. Thus if two brown-eyed parents both have the blue-eye recessive gene, the chances are one in four that their child will have blue eyes (see Figure 3.3). This example is simple, because one pair of genes is the main determinant of eye color. However, as with almost every trait, eye color is polygenic, with other genes having some influence. Eyes are various shades of blue and brown, sometimes hazel, sometimes greenish.

TABLE 3.1	The 23rd Pair and X-Linked Color Blindness		
23rd Pair	Phenotype	Genotype	Next Generation
1. XX	Normal woman	Not a carrier	No color blindness from mother
2. XY	Normal man	Normal X from mother	No color blindness from father
3. XX	Normal woman	Carrier from father	Half her children will inherit her X. The girls with her X will be carriers; the boys with her X will be color-blind.
4. XX	Normal woman	Carrier from mother	Half her children will inherit her X. The girls with her X will be carriers; the boys with her X will be color-blind.
5. XY	Color-blind man	Inherited from mother	All his daughters will have his X. None of his sons will have his X. All his children will have normal vision, unless their mother also had an X for color blindness.
6. XX	Color-blind woman (rare)	Inherited from both parents	Every child will have one X from her. Therefore, every son will be color-blind. Daughters will be only carriers, unless they also inherit an X from the father, as their mother did.

The crucial fact is that a recessive gene is carried, but not apparent, unless a child happens to inherit the same recessive gene from both parents. Most recessive genes are harmless (like the genes for blue eyes) but some are lethal (like those that cause serious diseases, discussed at the end of this chapter). It is important to understand the double recessive, so parents do not blame each other when their child has a recessive disease, and husbands do not suspect infidelity if his child is unexpectedly blue-eyed or red-haired.

A special case of the dominant–recessive pattern occurs with genes that are **X-linked** (located on the X chromosome). If an X-linked gene is recessive—as are the genes for most forms of color blindness, many allergies, several diseases, and some learning disabilities—the fact that it is on the X chromosome is critical in determining whether it will be expressed in the phenotype (see Table 3.1). Boys will have the trait; girls will usually be carriers.

To understand this, remember that the Y chromosome is much smaller than the X, containing far fewer genes. For that reason, genes on the X almost never have a match on the Y. Therefore, recessive traits carried on the X have no dominant gene on the Y.

A boy, XY, with a recessive gene on his X, has no gene on his Y to counteract it, so his phenotype is affected. A girl will be affected only if she has the recessive trait on both her X chromosomes, which is rare. This explains why males with an X-linked disorder inherited it from their mothers, not their fathers. Because of their mothers, 20 times more men than women are color-blind (McIntyre, 2002).

Copy Number Variations

For any living creature, the outcomes of all the interactions involved in heredity are difficult to predict. A small deletion, repetition, or transposition in any of the 3 billion base pairs may be inconsequential, deadly, or something in between.

When the human genome was first mapped in 2001, it was hoped that a specific additive, recessive, or dominant gene could be located for each genetic disorder. Then a cure would soon follow. That "one gene/one disorder" expectation proved to be fantasy, disappointing many doctors who hoped that personalized medicine was imminent (Marshall, 2011). Molecular analysis found, instead, that thousands of seemingly minor variations in base pairs turn out to be influential—

X-linked A gene carried on the X chromosome. If a male inherits an X-linked recessive trait from his mother, he expresses that trait because the Y from his father has no counteracting gene. Females are more likely to be carriers of X-linked traits but are less likely to express them.

// Response for Future Parents (from page 81): Possibly, but you wouldn't want to. You would have to choose one mate for your sons and another for your daughters, and you would have to use sex-selection methods. Even so, it might not work, given all the genes on your genotype. More important, the effort would be unethical, unnatural, and possibly illegal.

each in small ways. Since there are 3 billion base pairs, all the small variations can add up to have a notable impact.

Attention has focused on **copy number variations,** which are genes with repeats (from one to hundreds) or deletions of base pairs. Copy number variations correlate with almost every disease and condition, including heart disease, impaired intellectual abilities, mental illness, and many cancers.

We all have copy number variations: There is no person who is completely normal, genetically. One team, looking specifically at genes for neurons in the brain, says "dysfunctions abound . . . with a large number of functional variants in every genome" (Macosko & McCarroll, 2013, p. 564).

Researchers are just beginning to understand the implications of copy number variations, although many hope that soon such genetic information will help target drugs and other medical measures, such as which cocktail of chemotherapy will stop which cancer. Even that may be a hopeful fantasy. Since epigenetics shows that environmental influences can actually change genetic expression, personalized medicine must consider each individual's habits of mind and life at least as much as their genes (Horwitz et al., 2013).

To further complicate matters, sometimes one-half of a gene pair switches off completely, allowing the other free rein but potentially causing a problem if that remaining gene has a deleterious variation, recessive or not. For girls, one X of the 23rd pair is deactivated early in prenatal life. The implications of that shut-off are not well understood, but it is known that sometimes that X is from the ovum, sometimes from the sperm. Boys, of course, have only one X, so it always is activated.

Parental Imprinting

X deactivation in girls but not boys is not the only case that is affected by a person's sex. Sometimes the same allele affects male and female embryos differently. It also matters whether a gene came from the mother or the father, a phenomenon called *parental imprinting.*

The best-known example of parental imprinting occurs with a small deletion on chromosome 15. If that deletion came from the father's chromosome 15, the child may develop Prader-Willi syndrome and be obese, slow-moving, and stubborn. If that deletion came from the mother's chromosome 15, the child will have Angelman syndrome and be thin, hyperactive, and happy—sometimes too happy, laugh-

---

copy number variations Genes with various repeats or deletions of base pairs.

// ANSWER TO OBSERVATION QUIZ
(from page 82): This is a figure, drawn to illustrate the recessive inheritance of blue eyes, and thus eyes are the only difference shown. If this were a real family, each child would have a distinct appearance.

Especially For Medical Doctors
Can you look at a person and then write a prescription that will personalize medicine to their particular genetic susceptibility? (see response, page 86)

She Laughs Too Much No, not the smiling sister, but the 10-year-old on the right, who has Angelman syndrome. She inherited it from her mother's chromosome 15. Fortunately, her two siblings inherited the mother's other chromosome 15 and are normal. If she had inherited the identical deletion on her father's chromosome 15, she would have developed Prader-Willi syndrome, which would cause her to be overweight as well as always hungry and often angry. With Angelman syndrome, however, laughing, even at someone's pain, is a symptom.

MARIA PLATT-EVANS/SCIENCE SOURCE

ing when no one else does. In both cases, intellectual development is impaired, though in somewhat distinct ways.

Parental imprinting is quite common. Early in prenatal development (day 15), an estimated 553 genes act differently depending on whether they come from the mother or from the father—a much higher number than previously thought (Gregg, 2010). Imprinting may be affected by the sex of the embryo as well as the sex of the parent. For instance, women develop multiple sclerosis more often than men, and they usually inherit it from their mothers, not their fathers, probably for genetic as well as epigenetic reasons (Huynh & Casaccia, 2013).

SUMMING UP   The distinction between genotype (heredity) and phenotype (manifest appearance and observed behavior) is one of the many complexities in genetics and human development. All traits are epigenetic, the product of genetic and nongenetic influences, beginning with methylation at conception and continuing life-long. Furthermore, most traits are polygenic, the result of many genes that interact—some additively and some in a dominant–recessive pattern—with thousands of minor variations in base pairs, many of which may be affected by the sex of the parent and the zygote.

WHAT HAVE YOU LEARNED?

1. Why is a person's genotype not apparent in the phenotype?
2. What is the difference between an epigenetic characteristic and a multifactorial one?
3. What are the main patterns of genetic interaction?
4. Why do polygenic traits suggest that additive genes are more common than dominant–recessive ones?
5. How does parental imprinting affect the genotype and phenotype?   ●

Nature and Nurture

The goal of this chapter is to help every reader grasp the complex interaction between genotype and phenotype. This is not easy. For decades, in many nations, millions of scientists have struggled to understand this complexity. Each year brings advances in statistics and molecular analysis, new data to uncover various patterns, all resulting in hypotheses to be explored.

Now we examine two complex traits: addiction and visual acuity, in two specific manifestations, alcoholism and nearsightedness. As you will see, understanding the progression from genotype to phenotype has many practical implications.

Alcoholism

At various times throughout history, people have considered the abuse of drugs to be a moral weakness, a social scourge, or a personality defect. Historically and internationally, the focus has been on alcohol, since people everywhere discovered fermentation thousands of years ago. Alcohol has been declared illegal (as in the United States from 1919 to 1933) or considered sacred (as in many Judeo-Christian rituals), and people with alcoholism have been jailed, jeered, or even burned at the stake.

We now know that inherited biochemistry affects alcohol metabolism; punishing those with the genes does not stop addiction. There is no single "alcoholic gene," but alleles that make alcoholism more likely have been identified on every chromosome except the Y (Epps & Holt, 2011).

Welcome Home For many women in the United States, white wine is part of the celebration and joy of a house party, as shown here. Most people can drink alcohol harmlessly; there is no sign that these women are problem drinkers. However, danger lurks. Women get drunk on less alcohol than men, and females with alcoholism tend to drink more privately and secretly, often at home, feeling more shame than bravado. All that makes their addiction more difficult to recognize.

Especially for Drug Counselors Is the wish for excitement likely to lead to addiction? (see response, page 88)

// Response for Medical Doctors (from page 84) No. Personalized medicine is the hope of many physicians, but appearance (the phenotype) does not indicate alleles, recessive genes, copy number variations, and other genetic factors that affect drug reactions. Many medical researchers seek to personalize chemotherapy for cancer, but although this is urgently needed, success is still experimental, even when the genotype is known.

To be more specific, genes create an addictive pull that can be overpowering, extremely weak, or somewhere in between, as each person's biochemistry reacts to alcohol by causing sleep, nausea, aggression, joy, relaxation, forgetfulness, sex urges, or tears. Metabolism allows some people to "hold their liquor" and therefore drink too much, whereas others (including many East Asians) sweat and become red-faced after just a few sips, an embarrassing response that may lead to abstinence. This inherited "flushing" tendency not only makes alcohol addiction rare, but it also improves metabolism of alcohol (Kuwahara et al., 2014).

Although the emphasis at first was on the genes that cause biological addiction, we now know that genes that affect personality traits may be pivotal (Macgregor et al., 2009). Temperamental traits known to be inherited, among them a quick temper, sensation-seeking, and high anxiety, all encourage drinking.

Moreover, some contexts (such as fraternity parties) make it hard to avoid alcohol. Other contexts (such as a church social in a "dry" county) make it difficult to swallow anything stronger than lemonade.

Sex (biological—either XX or XY) and gender (cultural) also affect the risk of alcoholism. For biological reasons (body size, fat composition, metabolism), women become drunk on less alcohol than men, and women who are heavy drinkers double their risk of mortality compared to men (Wang et al., 2014).

Many cultures encourage men to drink but not women (Chartier et al., 2014). For example, in Japan, both sexes have the same genes for metabolizing alcohol, yet women drink only about one-tenth as much as men. When women of Japanese ancestry live in the United States, their alcohol consumption increases. Apparently, Americans of Asian decent try to adopt the drinking patterns of their new culture (Makimoto, 1998).

Nearsightedness

Age, genes, and culture affect vision as well. The effects of age are easy to notice. Newborns focus only on things within 1 to 3 feet of their eyes; vision improves steadily until about age 10. The eyeball changes shape at puberty, increasing nearsightedness (myopia), and again in middle age, decreasing myopia. The effects of genes and culture on eyesight are more complex, as you will see.

Heritable?

A study of British twins found that the Pax6 gene, which governs eye formation, has many alleles that make people somewhat nearsighted (Hammond et al., 2004). Heritability was almost 90 percent, which means that if one monozygotic twin was nearsighted, the other twin was almost always nearsighted, too.

However, **heritability** indicates only how much of the variation in a particular trait, *within a particular population, and in a particular context and era* can be traced to genes. For example, the heritability of height is very high (about 95 percent) when children receive good medical care and nutrition, but low (about 20 percent) when children are malnourished. Thus, the 90 percent heritability of nearsightedness among the British may not apply elsewhere.

Indeed, it does not. In some African communities, vision heritability is close to zero because severe vitamin A deficiency makes vision depend much more on diet than on genes. If a child has no vitamin A, that child may become blind, even if the genotype is programmed for great vision. Scientists are working to develop a strain of maize (the local staple) that is high in vitamin A. If they succeed, heritability will increase and overall vision will improve (Harjes et al., 2008).

What about children who are well-nourished? Is their vision entirely inherited? Cross-cultural research suggests that it is not (Seppa, 2013).

One report claimed that "myopia is increasing at an 'epidemic' rate, particularly in East Asia" (Park & Congdon, 2004, p. 21). The first published research on this phenomenon appeared in 1992, when scholars noticed that, in army-mandated medical exams of all 17-year-old males in Singapore, 26 percent were nearsighted in 1980 but 43 percent were nearsighted in 1990 (Tay et al., 1992). A recent article in the leading British medical journal suggests that, although genes are to blame for most cases of severe myopia, "any genetic differences may be small" for the common nearsightedness of Asian school children (I. Morgan et al., 2012, p. 1739). Nurture must somehow be involved. But how?

> **heritability** A statistic that indicates what percentage of the variation in a particular trait within a particular population, in a particular context and era, can be traced to genes.

Outdoor Play?

One possible culprit is homework. As Chapter 12 describes, contemporary East Asian children are amazingly proficient in math and science. Fifty years ago, most Asian children were laborers; now almost all are diligent students. As their developing eyes focus on their books, those with a genetic vulnerability to myopia may lose acuity for objects far away—which is exactly what nearsightedness means.

A study of Singaporean 10- to 12-year-olds found a positive correlation between nearsightedness (measured by optometric exams) and high achievement, especially in language proficiency (presumably reflecting more reading). Correlation is not proof, but the odds ratio was 2.5 and the significance was 0.001, which makes this data impossible to ignore (Saw et al., 2007).

Data from the United States on children playing sports has led some ophthalmologists to suggest that the underlying cause of myopia among Americans is too little exposure to daylight (I. Morgan et al., 2012). Perhaps if children spent more time outside playing, fewer would need glasses.

Between the early 1970s and the early 2000s, nearsightedness in the U.S. population increased from 25 to 42 percent (Vitale et al., 2009). Urbanization, television, and fear of strangers have kept many U.S. children indoors most of the time, unlike children of earlier generations who played outside for hours each day. One

No Time for Play Chinese children spend most of their time in school, at home doing school work, or in school activities, such as this parade in Wan Chai.

OBSERVATION QUIZ Focus on education is one reason for China's economic success, but these children wear one of the negative consequences. (see answer, page 89)

// Response for Drug Counselors (from page 86): Maybe. Some people who love risk become addicts; others develop a healthy lifestyle that includes adventure, new people, and exotic places. Any trait can lead in various directions. You need to be aware of the connections so that you can steer your clients toward healthy adventures.

ophthalmologist comments that "we're kind of a dim indoors people nowadays" (Mutti quoted in Holden, 2010, p. 17). Formerly, genetically vulnerable children did not necessarily become nearsighted; now they do.

Practical Applications

Since genes affect every disorder, no one should be blamed or punished for inherited problems. However, knowing that genes never act in isolation allows prevention after birth. For instance, if alcoholism is in the genes, parents can keep alcohol out of their home, hoping their children become cognitively and socially mature before imbibing. If nearsightedness runs in the family, parents can play outdoors with their children every day.

Of course, outdoor play and abstention from alcohol are recommended for all children, as are dozens of other behaviors, such as flossing, saying "please," getting enough sleep, eating vegetables, and writing thank-you notes. No parent can enforce every recommendation, but awareness of genetic risks can guide priorities.

 # a case to study

Mickey Mantle

Ignoring the nature–nurture interaction can be lethal. Consider baseball superstar Mickey Mantle, who hit more home runs in World Series baseball (18) than any other player before or since. Most of his male relatives suffered from alcoholism and died before middle age, including his father, who died of Hodgkin disease (a form of cancer) at age 39. Mantle became "a notorious alcoholic [because he] believed a family history of early mortality meant he would die young" (Jaffe, 2004, p. 37). He ignored his genetic predisposition to alcoholism.

At age 46, Mantle said, "If I knew I was going to live this long, I would have taken better care of myself." He never developed

Hodgkin disease, and if he had, chemotherapy that was discovered and developed since his father's death would likely have saved him—an example of environment prevailing over genes.

However, drinking destroyed Mantle's liver. He understood too late what he had done. When he was dying, he told his fans at Yankee Stadium: "Please don't do drugs and alcohol. God gave us only one body, keep it healthy. If you want to do something great, be an organ donor" (quoted in Begos, 2010). Despite a last-minute liver transplant, he died at age 63—15 years younger than most men of his time.

SUMMING UP Genes affect every trait—whether it is something wonderful, such as a wacky sense of humor; something fearful, such as a violent temper; or something quite ordinary, such as a tendency to be bored. The environment affects every trait as well, in ways that change as maturational, cultural, and historical processes unfold. Genes themselves can be modified through epigenetic factors, not only biological ones but also psychological ones. This is apparent in height, alcoholism, nearsightedness, and almost every other physical and psychological condition. All have genetic roots, developmental patterns, and environmental triggers.

WHAT HAVE YOU LEARNED?

1. Regarding heritability, why is it important to know which population at what historical time provided the data?
2. What nature and nurture reasons make one person develop alcoholism and another not?

3. What nature and nurture reasons make one person nearsighted and another not?
4. What is the practical application resulting from understanding the relationship between nature and nurture? •

Chromosomal and Genetic Problems

Video: Genetic Disorders
http://qrs.ly/pg4eoxw

We now focus on conditions caused by an extra chromosome or a single destructive gene. Three factors make these conditions relevant to human development:

1. They provide insight into the complexities of nature and nurture.
2. Knowing their origins helps limit their effects.
3. Information combats prejudice: Difference is not always deficit.

Not Exactly 46

As you know, each sperm or ovum usually has 23 chromosomes, creating a zygote with 46 chromosomes and eventually a person. However, cells do not always split exactly in half to make those reproductive cells.

One variable known to correlate with chromosomal abnormalities is the parents' age, particularly the age of the mother. A suggested explanation is that, since ova begin to form before a girl is born, older mothers have older ova. When the 46 chromosomes of the mother make ova, usually the split is even, 23/23. But older women are more likely to have some ova that have 22 or 24 chromosomes. Sperm also are diminished in quantity and normality as men age.

Miscounts are not rare. One estimate is that 5 to 10 percent of all zygotes have more or fewer than 46 chromosomes (Brooker, 2009); another estimate suggests that the rate is as high as 50 percent (Fragouli & Wells, 2011). Estimates vary because no one knows for certain. Almost all abnormal zygotes fail to duplicate, divide, differentiate, and implant, or are spontaneously aborted before a woman even knows she is pregnant. Thus an accurate count of zygotes with extra chromosomes is impossible to obtain.

If implantation does occur, many zygotes with chromosomal miscounts are aborted, either spontaneously (miscarried) or by choice. It is estimated that the abortion rate for such zygotes is about 5 percent. Ninety-nine percent of newborns have the usual 46 chromosomes, but for those who do not, birth is hazardous.

About 5 percent of stillborn (dead at birth) babies have 47 chromosomes (Miller & Therman, 2001), and many other babies with 47 chromosomes die within the first few days. Only once in about every 200 births does a newborn survive with 45, 47, or, rarely, 48 or 49 chromosomes.

Survival is much more common if some of the cells have 46 chromosomes and some 47, a condition called *mosaicism*, or if the problem does not involve a whole chromosome but only a missing or extra piece of a chromosome. Overall, advanced analysis suggests mosaicism "may represent the rule rather than the exception" (Lupski, 2013, p. 358). We may all be mosaics, some more than others. Usually this has no detectable effect on development, although it seems as if cancer is more likely if a person has extra or missing genetic material.

Down Syndrome

If an entire chromosome is missing or added, that leads to a recognizable *syndrome,* a cluster of distinct characteristics that tend to occur together. Usually the cause is three chromosomes at a particular location instead of the usual two (a condition called a *trisomy*). The most common extra-chromosome condition that

// **ANSWER TO OBSERVATION QUIZ**
(from page 87): Not the boy/girl uniforms, which some research says may increase attention, but three of the four have glasses. Did the lad in front forget his?

results in a surviving child is **Down syndrome,** also called *trisomy-21* because the person has three copies of chromosome 21.

Some 300 distinct characteristics can result from that third chromosome 21. No individual with Down syndrome is identical to another, but trisomy-21 usually produces specific physical characteristics—a thick tongue, round face, and slanted eyes as well as distinctive hands, feet, and fingerprints.

Many people with Down syndrome also have hearing problems, heart abnormalities, muscle weakness, and short stature. They are usually slower to develop intellectually, especially in language, and they reach their maximum intellectual potential at about age 15 (Rondal, 2010). Some are severely intellectually disabled; others are of average or above-average intelligence. That extra chromosome affects the person lifelong, but family context, educational efforts, and possibly medication can decrease the harm (Kuehn, 2011).

Down syndrome A condition in which a person has 47 chromosomes instead of the usual 46, with 3 rather than 2 chromosomes at the 21st site. People with Down syndrome typically have distinctive characteristics, including unusual facial features, heart abnormalities, and language difficulties. (Also called *trisomy-21*.)

Universal Happiness All young children delight in painting brightly colored pictures on a big canvas, but this scene is unusual for two reasons: Daniel has trisomy-21, and this photograph was taken at the only school in Chile where normal and special-needs children share classrooms.

OBSERVATION QUIZ How many characteristics can you see that indicate that Daniel has Down syndrome? (see answer, page 92)

REUTERS/CLAUDIA DAUT/LANDOV

Problems of the 23rd Pair

Every human has at least 44 autosomes and one X chromosome; an embryo cannot develop without those 45. However, about 1 in every 500 infants is born with only one sex chromosome (no Y) or with three or more (not just two) (Hamerton & Evans, 2005); the particular combination of sex chromosomes results in specific syndromes (see Table 3.2).

TABLE 3.2	Common Abnormalities Involving the Sex Chromosomes		
Chromosomal Pattern	**Physical Appearance**	**Psychological Characteristics**	**Incidence***
XXY (Klinefelter Syndrome)	Male. Usual male characteristics at puberty do not develop—penis does not grow, voice does not deepen. Usually sterile. Breasts may develop.	Can have some learning disabilities, especially in language skills.	1 in 700 males
XYY (Jacob's Syndrome)	Male. Typically tall.	Risk of intellectual impairment, especially in language skills.	1 in 1,000 males
XXX (Triple X Syndrome)	Female. Normal Appearance.	Impaired in most intellectual skills.	1 in 500 females
XO (only one sex chromosome) (Turner Syndrome)	Female. Short, often "webbed," neck. Secondary sex characteristics (breasts, menstruation) do not develop.	Some learning disabilities, especially related to math and spatial understanding; difficulty recognizing facial expressions of emotion.	1 in 2,000 females

*Incidence is approximate at birth.

Source: Hamerton & Evans, 2005; Aksglaede et al., 2013; Powell, 2013

Having an odd number of sex chromosomes impairs cognition and sexual maturation, with varied specifics depending on epigenetics (Hong & Reiss, 2014). It is not unusual for an affected person to seem to be developing normally until they find they are infertile. Then diagnosis reveals the undetected problem.

Gene Disorders

Everyone carries alleles that *could* produce serious diseases or handicaps in the next generation. Most such genes have no serious consequences because they are recessive. The phenotype is affected only when the inherited gene is dominant or when a zygote is homozygous for a particular recessive condition, that is, when the zygote has received the recessive gene from both parents.

Dominant Disorders

Most of the 7,000 *known* single-gene disorders are dominant (always expressed) (Milunsky, 2011). Severe dominant disorders are rare because people with such disorders usually die in childhood and thus do not pass the gene on to children.

Severe dominant disorders become common only when they are latent in childhood, manifest in adulthood. That is the case with *Huntington disease,* a fatal central nervous system disorder caused by a copy number variation—more than 35 repetitions of a particular set of three base pairs. The symptoms first appear in middle age, when some people have had several children, as did the original Mr. Huntington. Half of them inherited his dominant gene, which is why the disease is named after him.

Another exception to the general rule that serious dominant diseases are not inherited is a rare but severe form of Alzheimer's disease. It causes dementia before age 60. Most forms of Alzheimer's, which begin after age 70, are not dominant.

Recessive Disorders

Severe recessive diseases are more numerous because they are passed down from one generation to the next by carriers who do not know they carry the recessive gene. Some such recessive conditions are X-linked, including hemophilia and Duchenne muscular dystrophy.

Fragile X syndrome is caused by more than 200 repetitions on one gene (Plomin et al., 2013). (Some repetitions are normal, but not this many.) The cognitive deficits caused by fragile X syndrome are the most common form of *inherited* intellectual disability (many other forms, such as trisomy-21, are not usually inherited). Boys are much more often impaired by fragile X than are girls.

Most recessive disorders are on the autosomes, not the X or Y (Milunsky, 2011). Carrier detection is possible for about 500 of them, and diagnosis of the actual disorder is possible for thousands of them, creating an ethical dilemma. Should someone be told about a genetic disorder if no treatment is available and if the knowledge will not change anything?

The Most Common Disorders

Some recessive diseases are very common, and that has led to research and effective treatment. About 1 in 12 North American men and women carries an allele for cystic fibrosis, thalassemia, or sickle-cell disease, all devastating in children of both sexes. That high incidence occurs because carriers have benefited from the gene, although the double recessive is harmful.

Especially for Teachers Suppose you know that one of your students has a sibling who has Down syndrome. What special actions should you take? (see response, page 93)

Especially for Future Doctors Might a patient who is worried about his or her sexuality have an undiagnosed abnormality of the sex chromosome? (see response, page 93)

fragile X syndrome A genetic disorder in which part of the X chromosome seems to be attached to the rest of it by a very thin string of molecules. The cause is a single gene that has more than 200 repetitions of one triplet.

To explain this benefit, consider the most studied example: sickle-cell anemia. Carriers of the sickle-cell gene die less often from malaria, which is prevalent in parts of Africa. Indeed, four distinct alleles cause sickle-cell anemia, each originating in a malaria-prone region.

Selective adaptation allowed the gene to become widespread because it protected more people (the carriers) than it killed (those who inherited the recessive gene from both parents). Odds were that if a couple were both carriers and had four children, one would die of sickle cell, one would not be a carrier and thus might die of malaria, but two would be carriers. These carriers would not only develop normally but they would also have added protection against a common, fatal disease, and thus they would be likely to become parents themselves. In that way, the recessive trait became widespread.

Almost every disease and risk of death is more common in one ethnic group than in another (Weiss & Koepsell, 2014). About 11 percent of Americans with African ancestors are carriers of the sickle-cell gene; cystic fibrosis is more common among Americans with ancestors from northern Europe because carriers may have been protected from cholera. Dark skin is protective against skin cancer, and light skin allows more vitamin D to be absorbed from the sun—a benefit if a baby lives where sunlight is scarce.

Furthermore, almost every infectious disease is more or less common because of particular alleles (McLaren et al., 2013). For example, an allele provides protection against HIV. That allele is not yet common because, unlike malaria and cholera, HIV has become widespread only in the past decades. However, many scientists are working to artificially provide exactly the chemical protection that a few people have naturally.

Video: Genetic Testing explores the pros and cons of knowing what diseases may eventually harm us or our unborn children.

Genetic Counseling and Testing

Until recently, after the birth of a child with a severe disorder, couples blamed witches or fate, not genes or chromosomes. That has changed, with many young adults concerned about their genes long before parenthood. Virtually everyone has a relative with a serious condition and wonders what their children will inherit. People are also curious about their own future health. Many pay for commercial genetic testing, which often provides misleading information.

Psychological Disorders

Misinformation and mistaken fears are particularly destructive for psychological disorders, such as depression, schizophrenia, and autism. No doubt genes are a factor in all of these conditions (Plomin et al., 2013). Yet, as with addiction and vision, the environment is crucial for every disorder—not only what the parents do but also what the community and governments do.

This was confirmed by a study of the entire population of Denmark, where good medical records and decades of free public health allow accurate research on mental health. If both Danish parents developed schizophrenia, 27 percent of their children developed it; if one parent had it, 7 percent of their children developed it. These same statistics can be presented another way: Even if both parents developed the disease, almost three-fourths (73 percent) of their children never did (Gottesman et al., 2010). (Some of them developed other psychological disorders, again providing evidence for epigenetics.)

Even more persuasive is evidence pertaining to monozygotic twins. If one identical twin develops schizophrenia, often—but not always—the other twin also develops a psychological disorder. Obviously, genes are powerful, but also obviously, schizophrenia is not entirely genetic. Epigenetics, and prenatal and childhood experiences, are crucial.

Numerous studies have identified environmental influences on schizophrenia, including fetal malnutrition, birth in the summer, adolescent use of psychoactive drugs, emigration in young adulthood, and family emotionality during adulthood. Because environment is crucial, few scientists advocate genetic testing for schizophrenia or any mental condition. They fear that a positive test would lead to depression and stress, factors that might cause a disorder that would not have appeared without the test. Further, a positive genetic diagnosis might add to the prejudice against people who become mentally ill (Mitchell et al., 2010).

The Need for Counseling

The problems with testing for genes that cause mental disorders are only one of several complications that might emerge from a societal uptick in genetic testing. Scientists—and the general public—have many opinions about genetic testing, and nations have varying policies (Plows, 2011).

One complication is that science has revealed much more than anyone imagined a decade ago. Laws and ethics have not kept up with the possibilities, and very few prospective parents can interpret their own genetic history or laboratory results without help. Some seek abortion or sterilization without needing such a drastic step; others blithely give birth to one impaired child after another.

Professionals trained to provide **genetic counseling** help prospective parents understand their genetic risk so that they can make informed decisions. The genetic counselor's task is complicated, for many reasons. One is that testing is now possible for hundreds of conditions, but it is not always accurate.

Moreover, a particular gene might increase the risk of a problem by only a tiny amount, perhaps 0.1 percent. Further, every adult is a carrier for something. It is crucial to explain test results carefully, since many people misinterpret words such as *risks* and *probability,* especially when considering personal and emotionally charged information (O'Doherty, 2006).

// **Response for Teachers** (from page 91):
As the text says, "information combats prejudice." Your first step would be to read about Down syndrome. You would learn, among other things, that it is not usually inherited (your student need not worry about his or her progeny) and that some children with Down syndrome need extra medical and educational attention. You might need to pay special attention to your student, whose parents might focus on the sibling.

// **Response for Future Doctors**
(from page 91): That is highly unlikely. Chromosomal abnormalities are evident long before adulthood. It is quite normal for adults to be worried about sexuality for social, not biological, reasons. You could test the karyotype, but that may be needlessly alarmist.

genetic counseling Consultation and testing by trained experts that enables individuals to learn about their genetic heritage, including harmful conditions that they might pass along to any children they may conceive.

NATHAN MORGAN/THE NEW YORK TIMES/REDUX

Who Has the Fatal Dominant Disease?
The mother, but not the children. Unless a cure is found, Amanda Kalinsky will grow weak and suffer from dementia, dying before age 60. She and her husband, Bradley, wanted children without Amanda's dominant gene for a rare disorder, Gerstmann-Straussler-Scheinker disease. Accordingly, they used IVF and pre-implantation testing. Only zygotes without the dominant gene were implanted. This photo shows the happy result.

Even doctors do not always understand genetics. Consider the experience of one of my students. A month before she became pregnant, Jeannette was required to have a rubella vaccination for her job. Hearing that she had had the shot, her prenatal care doctor gave her the following prognosis:

> My baby would be born with many defects, his ears would not be normal, he would be intellectually disabled. . . . I went home and cried for hours and hours. . . .
> I finally went to see a genetic counselor. Everything was fine, thank the Lord, thank you, my beautiful baby is okay.

[Jeannette, personal communication]

It is possible that Jeannette misunderstood what she was told, but that is exactly why the doctor should not have spoken. Genetic counselors are trained to make information clear. If sensitive counseling is available, then preconception, prenatal, or even prenuptial (before marriage) testing is especially useful for:

- individuals who have a parent, sibling, or child with a serious genetic condition
- couples who have had several spontaneous abortions or stillbirths
- couples who are infertile
- couples from the same ethnic group, particularly if they are relatives
- women over age 35 and men over age 40

Genetic counselors follow two ethical rules: (1) tests are confidential, beyond the reach of insurance companies and public records, and (2) decisions are made by the clients, not by the counselors.

However, these guidelines are not always easy to follow (Parker, 2012). One quandary arises when parents already have a child with a recessive disease, but tests reveal that the husband does not carry that gene. Should the counselor tell the couple that their next child will not have this disease because the husband is not the biological father of the first?

Another quandary arises when DNA is collected for one purpose—say, to assess the risk of sickle-cell disease—and analysis reveals another quite different problem, such as an extra sex chromosome or a high risk of breast cancer. This problem is new: Even a few years ago, testing was so expensive that research did not discover any conditions except those for which they were testing. Now, because of genome sequencing, many counselors learn about thousands of conditions that were not suspected and are not treatable (Kaiser, 2013). Must they inform the person? Must they tell blood relatives?

The current consensus is that information should be shared if:

1. the person wants to hear it
2. the risk is severe and verified
3. an experienced counselor explains the data
4. treatment is available (Couzin-Frankel, 2011)

But not everyone accepts that consensus. Scientists and physicians disagree about severity, certainty, and treatment. A group of experts recently advocated informing patients of any serious genetic disorder, even when the person does not want to know, and when the information might be harmful (Couzin-Frankel, 2013).

An added complication is that individuals differ in their willingness to hear bad news. What if one person wants to know, but other family members—perhaps a parent or a monozygotic twin who has the same condition—do not. We all are carriers. Do we all want to know of what?

Sometimes couples make a decision (such as to begin or to abort a pregnancy) that reflects a mistaken calculation of the risk, at least as the professional interprets it (Parker, 2012). Even with careful counseling, people with identical genetic conditions often make opposite choices.

For instance, 108 women who already had one child with fragile X syndrome were told they had a 50 percent chance of having another such child. Most (77 percent) decided to avoid pregnancy with sterilization or excellent contraception, but some (20 percent) deliberately had another child (Raspberry & Skinner, 2011). Always the professional explains facts and probabilities; always the clients decide.

Many developmentalists stress that changes in the environment, not in the genes, are more likely to improve health. In fact, some believe that the twenty-first-century emphasis on genes is a way to avoid focusing on poverty, pollution, pesticides, and so on, even though such factors cause more health problems than genes do (Plows, 2011). Instead of genetic counseling, should we advocate health counseling?

As you have read many times in this chapter, genes are part of the human story, influencing every page, but they do not determine the plot or the final paragraph. The remaining chapters describe the rest of the story.

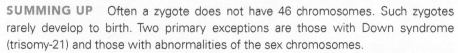

Reach for the Sky Gavin and Jake Barker both have cystic fibrosis, which would have meant early death had they been born 50 years ago. Now their parents pound on their chests twice a day to loosen phlegm—and they can enjoy jumping on the trampoline while wearing special pneumatic vests under their shirts.

SUMMING UP Often a zygote does not have 46 chromosomes. Such zygotes rarely develop to birth. Two primary exceptions are those with Down syndrome (trisomy-21) and those with abnormalities of the sex chromosomes.

Every person is a carrier for some serious genetic conditions. Most of these conditions are rare and polygenetic. A few recessive-gene diseases, such as sickle-cell disease, are comparatively common because the recessive gene protected against some common lethal conditions, and thus carriers were likely to survive. Serious dominant diseases are rare because the affected person has no children. However, a few dominant conditions, such as Huntington's, continue because their effects are not evident until middle adulthood. Most inherited psychological conditions are additive and multifactorial, thus difficult to predict. .

For all chromosomal and genetic problems, counseling helps couples clarify their values and understand probabilities and consequences. However, the decision to conceive or abort involves personal and ethical values, so the final decision is made by those directly involved.

WHAT HAVE YOU LEARNED?
1. Why does this textbook on normal development include abnormal development?
2. What usually happens when a zygote has fewer or more than 46 chromosomes?
3. What are the consequences if a baby is born with trisomy-21?
4. Why are a few recessive traits (such as sickle-cell) quite common?
5. Why are relatively few genetic conditions dominant?
6. Why do people need counselors, not merely fact sheets about genetic conditions?

SUMMARY

The Genetic Code

1. Genes are the foundation for all development, first instructing the living creature to form the body and brain and then influencing thought and behavior. Human conception occurs when two gametes (an ovum and a sperm, each with 23 chromosomes) combine to form a zygote, 46 chromosomes in a single cell.

2. Genes and chromosomes from each parent match up to make the zygote. The match is not always perfect because of genetic variations called alleles.

3. The sex of an embryo depends on the sperm: A Y sperm creates an XY (male) embryo; an X sperm creates an XX (female) embryo. Virtually every cell of every living creature has the unique genetic code of the zygote that began that life. The human genome contains about 20,000 genes in all.

New Cells, New Functions

4. Early duplication of the original one-celled zygote creates stem cells, each of which could become a person. Soon differentiation occurs, and cells develop into the placenta or part of the developing body.

5. Twins occur if a zygote splits into two separate beings (monozygotic, or identical, twins) or if two ova are fertilized in the same cycle by two sperm (dizygotic, or fraternal, twins).

6. Monozygotic multiples are genetically the same. Dizygotic multiples have only half of their genes in common, as do all siblings who have the same parents.

7. Assisted reproductive technology (ART), including drugs and in vitro fertilization (IVF), has led not only to millions of much-wanted babies but also to an increase in multiple births, who have a higher rate of medical problems. Several aspects of ART raise ethical and medical questions.

From Genotype to Phenotype

8. Genes interact in various ways—sometimes additively, with each gene contributing to development, and sometimes in a dominant–recessive pattern. Environmental factors influence the phenotype as well. Epigenetics is the study of all the environmental factors that affect the expression of genes, beginning at conception.

9. The environment interacts with the genetic instructions for every trait. Almost every aspect of a person is multifactorial and polygenic.

10. The first few divisions of a zygote are stem cells, capable of becoming any part of a person. Then cells differentiate, specializing in a particular function.

11. Combinations of chromosomes, interactions among genes, and myriad influences from the environment all ensure both similarity and diversity within and between species. This aids health and survival.

Nature and Nurture

12. Environmental influences are crucial for almost every complex trait, with each person experiencing different environments. Customs and contexts differ markedly.

13. Genetic makeup can make a person susceptible to a variety of conditions; nongenetic factors also affect susceptibility. Examples include alcoholism and nearsightedness. Cultural and familial differences affecting both of these problems are dramatic evidence for the role of nurture.

14. Knowing the impact of genes and the environment can be helpful. People are less likely to blame someone for a characteristic that is inherited; realizing that a child is at risk of a serious condition may help with prevention.

Chromosomal and Genetic Problems

15. Often a gamete has fewer or more than 23 chromosomes. Usually such zygotes do not implant, grow, or survive.

16. Infants may survive if they have three chromosomes at the 21st location (Down syndrome, or trisomy-21) or one, three, or more sex chromosomes instead of two. Affected individuals have lifelong physical and cognitive impairment but can live a nearly normal life.

17. Everyone is a carrier for genetic abnormalities. Genetic disorders are usually recessive (not affecting the phenotype unless inherited from both parents). If a disorder is dominant, the trait is usually mild, varied, or inconsequential until middle adulthood.

18. Genetic testing and counseling can help many couples. Testing usually provides information about possibilities, not actualities. Couples, counselors, and cultures differ in the decisions they make when risks are known.

KEY TERMS

gamete (p. 68)

zygote (p. 68)

deoxyribonucleic acid (DNA) (p. 68)

chromosome (p. 68)

gene (p. 68)

allele (p. 68)

epigenetic (p.69)

genome (p. 70)

genotype (p. 70)

homozygous (p. 70)

heterozygous (p. 71)

23rd pair (p. 71)

XY (p. 71)

XX (p. 71)

stem cells (p. 74)

monozygotic (MN) twins (p. 75)

dizygotic (DZ) twins (p. 75)

assisted reproductive technology (ART) (p. 78)

in vitro fertilization (IVF) (p. 78)

intra-cytoplasmic sperm injection (ICSI) (p. 78)

phenotype (p. 79)

polygenic (p. 80)

multifactorial (p. 80)

Human Genome Project (p. 81)

dominant-recessive pattern (p. 82)

carrier (p. 82)

X-linked (p. 83)

copy number variations (p. 84)

heritability (p. 87)

Down syndrome (p. 90)

fragile X syndrome (p. 91)

genetic counseling (p. 93)

APPLICATIONS

1. Pick one of your traits, and explain the influences that both nature *and* nurture have on it. For example, if you have a short temper, explain its origins in your genetics, your culture, and your childhood experiences.

2. Many adults have a preference for having a son or a daughter. Interview adults of several ages and backgrounds about their preferences. If they give the socially preferable answer ("It does not matter"), ask how they think the two sexes differ. Listen and take notes—don't debate. Analyze the implications of the responses you get.

3. Draw a genetic chart of your biological relatives, going back as many generations as you can, listing all serious illnesses and causes of death. Include ancestors who died in infancy. Do you see any genetic susceptibility? If so, how can you overcome it?

4. List a dozen people you know who need glasses (or other corrective lenses) and a dozen who do not. Are there any patterns? Is this correlation or causation?

CHAPTER 4

Prenatal Development and Birth

The scientific study of human development is not only about how individuals change over time, it is about how contexts and cultures change over time. Historical change—Bronfenbrenner's chronosystem—is dramatically apparent in prenatal development and childbirth. If your knowledge of these comes from a high school biology class, or from your mother's experience with you, get ready for surprises.

My daughter Elissa recently had her second child. She and her husband were together with the midwife in the labor room of the Birthing Center; I was with Asa, age 5, in the family room. Periodically Asa ran down the hall to see his parents. Usually the midwife let us come in, and Elissa smiled and asked him how he was doing. Sometimes we had to wait for a minute. Then, contraction over, mother and son smiled at each other again.

When the baby was born, the nurse came to tell us, "There's a new person who wants to meet you." Asa said, "Let me put this last Lego piece in." He did, and brought his new creation to show his parents, who introduced him to his brother, sucking on his mother's breast. Six hours later, the whole family was home.

The contrast between this 2014 birth and Elissa's own arrival is stark. Back then, midwives were banned from my New York City hospital. Fathers were relegated to waiting rooms, as my husband, Martin, had been for our first two babies. Newly empowered by feminism, I convinced my board-certified obstetrician to let Martin witness birth. He wept when he held her, wet and wide-eyed, moments old. Then she was wiped, weighed, wrapped, and wheeled away. The nurses did not let me hold my daughter until she was 24 hours old. They said that I had no milk, that I needed rest, that my baby was tired, too. Wrong, wrong, wrong.

On day two, Martin brought our older children to visit. They were not permitted on the maternity floor, so they could not view their sister through the nursery glass. But I could hobble down to a special room to greet them. That was an innovation: Formerly no visitors under age 12 could set foot in the hospital.

On day three, I was breast-feeding and talking on the phone when an aide came to take Elissa back to the nursery. She scolded me.

"Hang up that phone. When you nurse, you must give your baby undivided attention."

Wrong. She was old-fashioned; I knew better. I had nursed Bethany and Rachel while setting the table, stirring a pot, turning pages, and, of course, holding a phone. I was a pioneer, unlike that aide. I was riding the wave of liberation that was moving millions of women forward toward a brighter, fairer, unisex future.

Now I am the old-fashioned one. My daughter and her husband made dozens of decisions about this pregnancy and birth that I never imagined possible.

This chapter describes what we now know about prenatal growth and birth, and some of the vast differences from one era, one culture, even one family to another. Possible harm is noted: causes and consequences of diseases, malnutrition, drugs, pollution, stress, and so on, from the earliest days of life. Fathers, particularly, have become more active partners, while all of us—medical professionals, governments, and family members—affect the early life of each developing person. This chapter will help us do our part.

germinal period The first two weeks of prenatal development after conception, characterized by rapid cell division and the beginning of cell differentiation.

embryonic period The stage of prenatal development from approximately the third through the eighth week after conception, during which the basic forms of all body structures, including internal organs, develop.

fetal period The stage of prenatal development from the ninth week after conception until birth, during which the fetus gains about 7 pounds (more than 3,000 grams) and organs become more mature, gradually able to function on their own.

Prenatal Development

The most dramatic and extensive transformation of life occurs before birth. To make it easier to study, prenatal development is often divided into three main periods. The first two weeks are called the **germinal period;** the third through the eighth week is the **embryonic period;** from then until birth is the **fetal period.** (Alternative terms are presented in Table 4.1.)

TABLE 4.1	Timing and Terminology

Popular and professional books use various phrases to segment the stages of pregnancy. The following comments may help to clarify the phrases used.

- *Beginning of pregnancy:* Pregnancy begins at conception, which is also the starting point of *gestational age.* However, the organism does not become an *embryo* until about two weeks later, and pregnancy does not affect the woman (and is not confirmed by blood or urine testing) until implantation. Perhaps because the exact date of conception is usually unknown, some obstetricians and publications count from the woman's last menstrual period (LMP), usually about 14 days *before* conception.

- *Length of pregnancy:* Full-term pregnancies last 266 days, or 38 weeks, or 9 months. If the LMP is used as the starting time, pregnancy lasts 40 weeks, sometimes expressed as 10 lunar months. (A lunar month is 28 days long.)

- *Trimesters:* Instead of *germinal period, embryonic period,* and *fetal period,* as used in this text, some writers divide pregnancy into three-month periods called *trimesters.* Months 1, 2, and 3 are called the *first trimester;* months 4, 5, and 6, the *second trimester;* and months 7, 8, and 9, the *third trimester.*

- *Due date:* Although a specific due date based on the LMP is calculated, only 5 percent of babies are born on that exact day. Babies born between two weeks before and one week after that date are considered *full term.* (This is recent; until 2012, three weeks before and two weeks after were considered full term.) Because of increased risks for post-mature babies, labor is often induced if the baby has not arrived within 7 days after the due date, although many midwives and doctors prefer to wait to see if labor begins spontaneously.

Germinal: The First 14 Days

You learned in Chapter 3 that the one-celled zygote duplicates, divides, and multiplies. Soon after the 16-cell stage, differentiation begins as those early cells take on distinct characteristics and gravitate toward particular locations.

About a week after conception, the cell mass, now called a *blastocyst,* forms two distinct parts—a shell that will become the *placenta* and a nucleus that will become the embryo.

The first task of the outer cells is to achieve **implantation**—that is, to embed themselves in the nurturing lining of the uterus (see Figure 4.1). This process is far from automatic; about half of natural conceptions and an even larger proportion of in vitro conceptions never implant (see Table 4.2). Most new life ends before an embryo begins (Sadler, 2012).

implantation The process, beginning about 10 days after conception, in which the developing organism burrows into the placenta that lines the uterus, where it can be nourished and protected as it continues to develop.

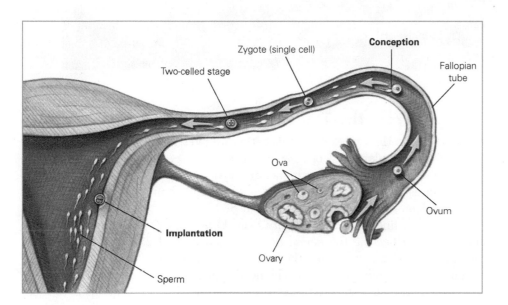

FIGURE 4.1

The Most Dangerous Journey In the first 10 days after conception, the organism does not increase in size because it is not yet nourished by the mother. However, the number of cells increases rapidly as the organism prepares for implantation, which occurs successfully not quite half of the time.

TABLE 4.2	Vulnerability During Prenatal Development

The Germinal Period

An estimated 60 percent of all zygotes do not grow or implant properly and thus do not survive the germinal period. Many of these organisms are abnormal; few women realize they were pregnant.

The Embryonic Period

About 20 percent of all embryos are aborted spontaneously. This is usually called an early *miscarriage,* a term that implies something wrong with the woman, when in fact the most common reason for a spontaneous abortion is a chromosomal abnormality.

The Fetal Period

About 5 percent of all fetuses are aborted spontaneously before viability at 22 weeks or are *stillborn,* defined as born dead after 22 weeks. This is much more common in poor nations.

Birth

Because of all these factors, only about 31 percent of all zygotes grow and survive to become living newborn babies. Age of the mother is crucial. One estimate is that less than 3 percent of all conceptions after age 40 result in live births.

Sources: Bentley & Mascie-Taylor, 2000; Corda et al., 2012; Laurino et al., 2005.

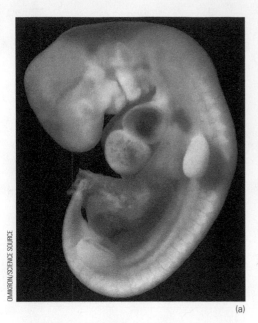

OMIKRON/SCIENCE SOURCE

(a)

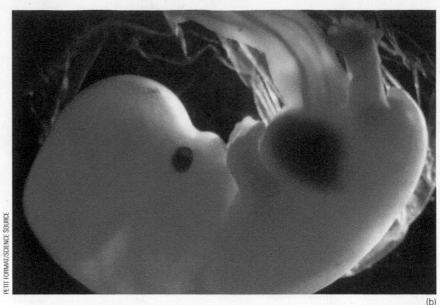

PETIT FORMAT/SCIENCE SOURCE

(b)

The Embryonic Period (*a*) At 4 weeks past conception, the embryo is only about 1/8 inch (3 millimeters) long, but already the head has taken shape. (*b*) By 7 weeks, the organism is somewhat less than an inch (2 centimeters) long. Eyes, nose, the digestive system, and even the first stage of toe formation can be seen.

embryo The name for a developing human organism from about the third through the eighth week after conception.

fetus The name for a developing human organism from the start of the ninth week after conception until birth.

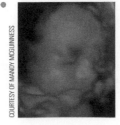

COURTESY OF MANDY MCGUINNESS

Meet Your Baby This is Elisa Clare McGuinness at 22 weeks post-conception. She continued to develop well for the next 4 months, becoming a healthy, 3,572-gram newborn, finally able to meet her family—two parents and an older brother.

Embryo: From the Third Through the Eighth Week

The start of the third week after conception initiates the *embryonic period,* during which the formless mass of cells becomes a distinct being—not yet recognizably human but worthy of a new name, **embryo.** (The word *embryo* is often used loosely, but each stage of development has a particular name; here, embryo refers to the developing human from day 14 to day 56.)

First, a thin line (called the *primitive streak*) appears down the middle of the embryo; it will become the *neural tube* between 20 and 27 days after conception and eventually develop into the central nervous system (the brain and spinal column) (Stiles & Jernigan, 2010). The head appears in the fourth week, as eyes, ears, nose, and mouth start to form. Also in the fourth week, a minuscule blood vessel that will become the heart begins to pulsate.

By the fifth week, buds that will become arms and legs emerge. The upper arms and then forearms, palms, and webbed fingers grow. Legs, knees, feet, and webbed toes, in that order, emerge a few days later, each having the beginning of a skeletal structure. Then, 52 and 54 days after conception, respectively, the fingers and toes separate (Sadler, 2012).

As you can see, prenatally, the head develops first, in a *cephalo-caudal* (literally, "head-to-tail") pattern, and the extremities form last, in a *proximo-distal* (literally, "near-to-far") pattern. At the end of the eighth week after conception (56 days), the embryo weighs just one-thirtieth of an ounce (1 gram) and is about 1 inch (2½ centimeters) long. It has all the basic organs and body parts (except sex organs) of a human being, including elbows and knees. It moves frequently, about 150 times per hour, but this movement is imperceptible and random; it will be many months before deliberate movement occurs.

Fetus: From the Ninth Week Until Birth

The organism is called a **fetus** from the beginning of the ninth week after conception until birth. The fetal period encompasses dramatic change, from a tiny, sexless creature smaller than the final joint of your thumb to a boy or girl about 20 inches (51 centimeters) long.

The Third Month

If the 23rd chromosomes are XY, the SRY gene on the Y triggers the development of male sexual organs. Otherwise, female organs develop. The male fetus experiences a rush of the hormone testosterone, affecting many structures and connections in the brain (Filová et al., 2013).

Of course, the range of brain and behavioral variations *among* males and *among* females is greater than the variations *between* the average man and woman. Nonetheless, neurological sex differences begin early in prenatal development.

By the end of the third month, the sex organs may be visible via **ultrasound** (in a *sonogram*), which is similar to an X-ray but uses sound waves instead of radiation. The 3-month-old fetus weighs about 3 ounces (87 grams) and is about 3 inches (7.5 centimeters) long. Early prenatal growth is very rapid, with considerable variation, especially in body weight. The numbers just given—3 months, 3 ounces, 3 inches—are rounded off for easy recollection. (Metric measures—100 days, 100 grams, 100 millimeters—are similarly imprecise yet useful.)

The Middle Three Months

In the fourth, fifth, and sixth months, the heartbeat becomes stronger. Digestive and excretory systems develop. Fingernails, toenails, and buds for teeth form, and hair grows (including eyelashes).

The brain increases about six times in size and develops many new neurons (*neurogenesis*) and synapses (*synaptogenesis*). Indeed, mid-pregnancy is the peak time for creation of new brain cells. Before this, the cortex had been smooth, but now the brain begins to have the folds and wrinkles that allow a human brain to be far larger and more complex than the brains of other animals (Stiles & Jernigan, 2010). Following the proximo-distal sequence, first the brain stem above the back of the neck, then the midbrain, and finally the cortex develop and connect.

Brain development occurs in every prenatal month, but these middle three months are especially crucial (Johnson, 2011). The entire central nervous system becomes responsive during mid-pregnancy, beginning to regulate basic body functions such as breathing and sucking. Advances in neurological functioning at the end of this trimester allow the fetus to reach the **age of viability,** the point of development when a fetus born far too early can become a baby who is able to survive.

Survival is far from automatic; almost all 22-week-old newborns who were born a few decades ago died. Currently, if the fetus has been developing well, the mother is healthy, and birth occurs in an advanced neonatal unit, some very immature babies survive.

In Japan, with excellent neonatal care, 20 percent of 22-week-old newborns survive without major neurological impairment (Ishii et al., 2013). In developing nations, such small babies never live, and even in developed nations, many hospitals do not routinely initiate intensive care unless the fetus is at least 25 weeks old.

The Final Three Months

Reaching viability simply means that life outside the womb is *possible.* Many babies born between 22 and 24 weeks die, and survivors born before 27 weeks often develop slowly because they have missed some essential brain development in the uterus (Månsson & Stjernqvist, 2014). Each day of the final three months improves the odds not only of survival but also of a healthy life and normal cognition. (More on preterm birth appears later in this chapter.) Many aspects of prenatal life are awe-inspiring; the fact that an ordinary woman provides a far better home for a fetus than the most advanced medical technology can attain is one of them.

 **LaunchPad**

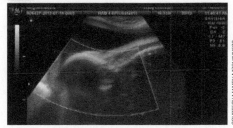

Video: Prenatal Period: 3D Ultrasound shows a real-life ultrasound of a developing fetus.

ultrasound An image of a fetus (or an internal organ) produced by using high-frequency sound waves. (Also called *sonogram*.)

Especially for Biologists Many people believe that the differences between the sexes are sociocultural, not biological. Is there any prenatal support for that view? (see response, page 105)

age of viability The age (about 22 weeks after conception) at which a fetus might survive outside the mother's uterus if specialized medical care is available.

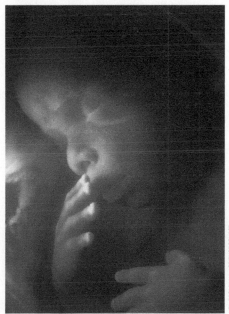

Almost Viable If this fetus were born, he might survive, although given his age (5 months) and sex (male), probably not. Much better would be to stay in the uterus another four months, when his eyes would be open, ready to see.

One of the Tiniest Rumaisa Rahman was born after 26 weeks and 6 days, weighing only 8.6 ounces (244 grams). Nevertheless, at age 5 she became a normal kindergartner. Rumaisa gained 5 pounds (2,270 grams) in the hospital and then, 6 months after her birth, went home. Her twin sister, Hiba, who weighed 1.3 pounds (590 grams) at birth, had gone home two months earlier and, ironically, was diagnosed with cerebral palsy at age 1 (Muraskas et al., 2012).

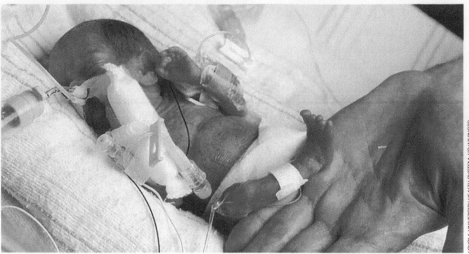

LOYOLA UNIVERSITY HEALTH SYSTEM, HO/AP PHOTO

Video: Brain Development Animation: Prenatal
http://qrs.ly/j34eoyp

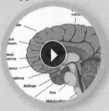

AULA MEDICAL MEDIA/SHUTTERSTOCK

Organ Maturation Even at 26 weeks, a preterm infant is a tiny creature requiring intensive care for each gram of nourishment and every shallow breath. Breathing tubes and feeding tubes are needed, and often other special equipment as well. By contrast, after 37 weeks or more, the typical full-term newborn is ready to thrive at home on mother's milk—no expert help, oxygenated air, or special feeding required. For thousands of years, that is how humans survived: We would not be alive if any of our ancestors had required intense newborn care.

The critical difference between life and death, or between a fragile preterm newborn and a robust one, is maturation of the neurological, respiratory, and cardiovascular systems. As the brain matures, the organs of the body begin to work in harmony. The heart beats faster during activity; fetal movement as well as heart rate quiet down during rest (not necessarily when the mother wants to sleep).

In the final three months of prenatal life, the lungs begin to expand and contract, and breathing muscles are exercised as the fetus swallows (into the lungs, not the stomach) and spits out amniotic fluid. The valves of the heart go through a final maturation, as do the arteries and veins throughout the body.

In those final prenatal months, the brain not only develops more neurons, but also connects them to each other, destroying neurons that are not functioning. As the body matures, the skin of the skull thickens. That prevents "brain bleeds," one of the hazards of preterm birth in which paper-thin blood vessels in the skull collapse.

The fetus usually gains at least 4½ pounds (2.1 kilograms) in the third trimester, increasing to an average of about 7½ pounds (about 3.4 kilograms) at birth. By full term, human brain growth is so extensive that the *cortex* (the brain's advanced outer layers) has formed several folds in order to fit into the skull (see Figure 4.2). Although some large mammals (whales, for instance) have bigger brains than humans, no other creature needs as many folds because, relative to size, the human cortex contains much more material than the brains of non-humans.

The Mother–Child Relationship The relationship between mother and child intensifies during the final three months as the fetus's size and movement make the pregnant woman very aware of it. In turn, her sounds, the tastes of her food (via amniotic fluid), and her behavior patterns become part of fetal consciousness. If she is up at dawn, her newborn infant is likely to be wide-awake then as well.

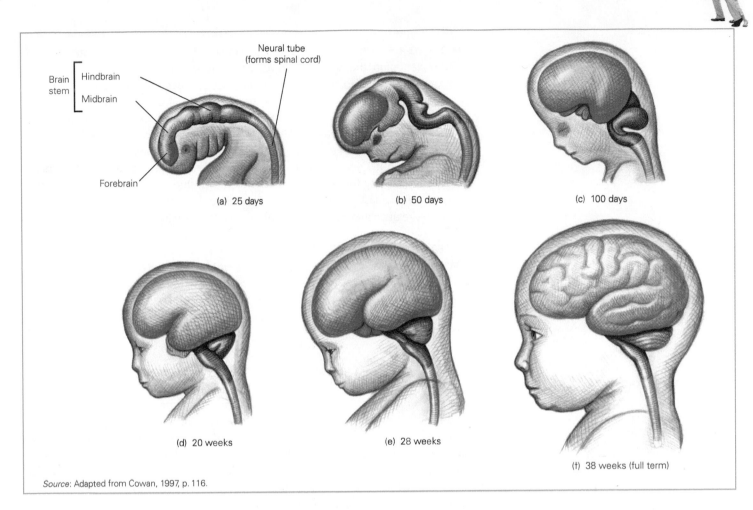

Brain stem [Hindbrain / Midbrain]

Neural tube (forms spinal cord)

Forebrain

(a) 25 days

(b) 50 days

(c) 100 days

(d) 20 weeks

(e) 28 weeks

(f) 38 weeks (full term)

Source: Adapted from Cowan, 1997, p. 116.

FIGURE 4.2

Prenatal Growth of the Brain Just 25 days after conception *(a)*, the central nervous system is already evident. The brain looks distinctly human by day 100 *(c)*. By 200 days after gestation *(e)*, at the very time brain activity begins, the various sections of the brain are recognizable. When the fetus is full term (266 days) *(f)*, all the parts of the brain, including the cortex (the outer layers), are formed, folding over one another and becoming more convoluted, or wrinkled, as the number of brain cells increases.

// **Response for Biologists** (from page 103): Only one of the 46 human chromosomes determines sex, and the genitals develop last in the prenatal sequence, suggesting that dramatic male–female differences are cultural. On the other hand, several sex differences develop before birth.

Auditory communication from mother to child begins at the 28th week and improves each week as fetal hearing (or newborn hearing if a baby is born early) becomes more acute (Bisiacchi et al., 2009). The fetus startles and kicks at loud noises, listens to the mother's heartbeat and voice, and is comforted by rhythmic music and movement, such as when the mother sings as she walks. Other voices are also heard, and many men begin to relate to their future child by stroking the mother's abdomen and talking to the fetus, thrilling to feel the kick.

If the mother is fearful or anxious, the fetal heart beats faster and body movements increase, and later, the infant is likely to startle at noises and unexpected sights. Maternal stress in pregnancy affects the fetus, infant, and child in many ways—although scientists do not agree on exactly how stress should be measured and what all the effects of prenatal anxiety are (Graignic-Philippe et al., 2014). Fathers can mitigate stress, and many do, not only with reassuring words but also with massage, provisioning, and so on.

N. BROMHALL/SCIENCE SOURCE

Can He Hear? A fetus, just about at the age of viability, is shown fingering his ear. Such gestures are probably random; but yes, he can hear.

SUMMING UP In the first two weeks of rapid cell duplication, differentiation, and finally implantation, the newly conceived organism is transformed from a one-celled zygote to a many-celled embryo. The embryo soon develops the beginning of the central nervous system (3 weeks), a heart and a face (4 weeks), arms and legs (5 weeks), hands and feet (6 weeks), and fingers and toes (7 weeks), while the inner organs take shape. By 8 weeks, all the body structures except the male and female sex organs are in place. Fetal growth then proceeds rapidly, including mid-trimester weight gain (about 2 pounds, almost 1,000 grams) and brain maturation, which make viability possible. By full term (38 to 40 weeks), all the organs function well in the newborn, who usually weighs between 6 and 9 pounds, or between 2,700 and 4,000 grams. The relationship between parents and child intensifies as birth approaches.

WHAT HAVE YOU LEARNED?

1. What are three major developments in the germinal period?
2. What body parts develop during the period of the embryo?
3. How much weight does the fetus gain, and when?
4. How does brain development affect survival?
5. What occurs between age of viability and full-term development?

Birth

About 38 weeks (266 days) after conception, the fetal brain signals the release of hormones, specifically *oxytocin,* to prepare the fetus and mother for labor. The average baby is born after 12 hours of active labor for first births and 7 hours for subsequent births, although often birth takes twice or half as long, with biological, psychological, and social circumstances all significant. The definition of "active" labor varies, which is one reason some women believe they are in active labor for days and others say 10 minutes.

Choice, Culture, or Cohort? Why do it that way? Both of these women (in Peru, on the *left,* in England, on the *right*) chose methods of labor that are unusual in the United States, where birth stools and birthing pools are uncommon. However, in all three nations, most births occur in hospitals—a rare choice a century ago.

REUTERS/ENRIQUE CASTRO-MENDIVIL/LANDOV

FRANK HERHOLDT/GETTY IMAGES

Birthing positions also vary—sitting, squatting, lying down. Some women give birth while immersed in warm water, which helps the woman relax; some cultures expect women to be upright, supported by family members during birth; some doctors insist that a woman must lie down on her back. Figure 4.3 shows the universal stages of birth.

The Newborn's First Minutes

Newborns usually breathe and cry on their own. Between spontaneous cries, the first breaths of air bring oxygen to the lungs and blood, and the infant's color changes from bluish to pinkish. (Pinkish refers to blood color, visible beneath the skin, and applies to newborns of all hues.) Eyes open wide; tiny fingers grab; even tinier toes stretch and retract. The newborn is instantly, zestfully, ready for life.

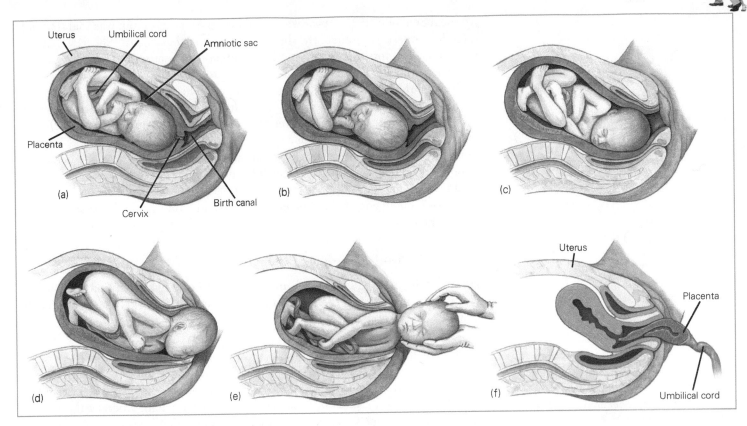

FIGURE 4.3

A Normal, Uncomplicated Birth *(a)* The baby's position as the birth process begins. *(b)* The first stage of labor: The cervix dilates to allow passage of the baby's head. *(c)* Transition: The baby's head moves into the "birth canal," the vagina. *(d)* The second stage of labor: The baby's head moves through the opening of the vagina (the baby's head "crowns") and *(e)* emerges completely. *(f)* The third stage of labor is the expulsion of the placenta. This usually occurs naturally, but the entire placenta must be expelled, so birth attendants check carefully. In some cultures, the placenta is ceremonially buried, to commemorate its life-giving role.

Nevertheless, there is much to be done. If birth occurs with a trained professional, mucus in the baby's throat is removed, especially if the first breaths seem shallow or strained. The umbilical cord is cut to detach the placenta, leaving an inch or so of the cord, which dries up and falls off several days later to leave the belly button. The infant is often given to the mother to preserve its body heat and to breast-feed a first meal of colostrum, a thick substance that helps the newborn's digestive and immune systems. Either before or after the mother holds the baby, the attending doctor or midwife weighs and examines the newborn, making sure that lungs, heart, legs, spine and so on are all as they should be.

One widely used assessment of infant health is the **Apgar scale** (see Table 4.3), first developed by Dr. Virginia Apgar. When she earned her MD from Columbia

> **Apgar scale** A quick assessment of a newborn's health. The baby's color, heart rate, reflexes, muscle tone, and respiratory effort are given a score of 0, 1, or 2 twice—at one minute and five minutes after birth—and each time the total of all five scores is compared with the maximum score of 10 (rarely attained).

TABLE 4.3	Criteria and Scoring of the Apgar Scale				
Five Vital Signs					
Score	Color	Heartbeat	Reflex Irritability	Muscle Tone	Respiratory Effort
0	Blue, pale	Absent	No response	Flaccid, limp	Absent
1	Body pink, extremities blue	Slow (below 100)	Grimace	Weak, inactive	Irregular, slow
2	Entirely pink	Rapid (over 100)	Coughing, sneezing, crying	Strong, active	Good; baby is crying

Source: Apgar, 1953.

Medical School in 1933, Apgar wanted to become a surgeon but was told that only men did surgery. Consequently, she became an anesthesiologist. She saw that "delivery room doctors focused on mothers and paid little attention to babies. Those who were small and struggling were often left to die" (Beck, 2009, p. D-1).

To save those young lives, Apgar developed a simple rating scale of five vital signs—color, heart rate, cry, muscle tone, and breathing—to alert doctors to newborn health. Since 1950, birth attendants worldwide have used the Apgar (often remembering the acronym "Appearance, Pulse, Grimace, Activity, and Respiration") at one minute and again at five minutes after birth, assigning each vital sign a score of 0, 1, or 2. (See also Visualizing Development, p. 126.)

If the five-minute Apgar is 7 or higher, the baby is okay. If the five-minute total is below 7, emergency help is needed (the hospital loudspeaker may say, "Paging Dr. Apgar").

Medical Assistance

How closely any particular birth matches the foregoing description depends on the parents' preparation, the position and size of the fetus, and the customs of the culture.

The Cesarean

cesarean section (c-section) A surgical birth, in which incisions through the mother's abdomen and uterus allow the fetus to be removed quickly, instead of being delivered through the vagina. (Also called simply *section*.)

Midwives are as skilled at delivering babies as physicians, but in the United States only medical doctors are licensed to perform surgery. One-third of U.S. births occur via **cesarean section** (**c-section,** or simply *section*), whereby the fetus is removed through incisions in the mother's abdomen. Cesareans are controversial: The World Health Organization suggested that c-sections are medically indicated in only 15 percent of births. In some nations, cesareans are less than 5 percent of births, and birth is hazardous for both mother and child.

Most nations have fewer cesareans than the United States, but some—especially in Latin America—have more (see Figure 4.4). The rate has stabilized in the United States, but in many countries the rate is increasing. The most dramatic increases are in China, where the rate in 1991 was 5 percent, by 2001, 20 percent,

FIGURE 4.4

Too Many Cesareans or Too Few? Rates of cesarean deliveries vary widely from nation to nation. Latin America has the highest rates in the world (note that 45 percent of all births in Brazil are by cesarean), and sub-Saharan Africa has the lowest (the rate in Chad is less than half of 1 percent). The underlying issue is whether some women who should have cesareans do not get them, while other women have unnecessary cesareans. This data, from the United Nations, is an estimate as of 2010—rates may change every year.

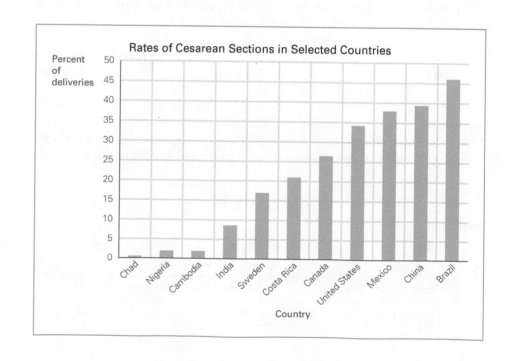

and in 2008 40 percent nationwide with 64 percent in major cities (Feng et al., 2014; Juan, 2010).

In the United States, the rate rose between 1996 and 2008 (from 21 percent to 34 percent) before stabilizing. Variation is dramatic from one hospital to another—from 7 to 70 percent (Kozhimannil et al., 2013). Cesareans have many advantages for doctors and hospitals (easier to schedule, quicker, and more profitable).

One reason for the rise in c-sections is that modern medicine can eliminate pain in the lower half of the body while keeping the mother awake. One woman, named Resch, had a cesarean because her fetus was in a breech position (buttocks first, not head first).

> Resch felt "a lot of rough pushing and pulling" and "a painless suction sensation" as if her body were "a tar pit the baby was wrestled from." She heard the doctor say to the resident: "Hold her up by the hips," and Resch peered down. She saw her daughter for the first time, wet and squirming… Resch's husband held the baby next to Resch's cheek. Resch felt "overwhelmed by emotions . . . joy, awe, anxiety, relief, surprise." She gave thanks for her healthy baby, and for modern obstetrical care.
>
> *[Lake, 2012, p. 23]*

The disadvantages appear later. C-sections increase medical complications after birth and reduce breast-feeding (Malloy, 2009). By age 3, children born by cesarean have double the rate of childhood obesity: 16 percent compared to 8 percent (Huh et al., 2012). The reason may be that babies delivered vaginally have beneficial bacteria in their gut but those delivered surgically do not (Wallis, 2014).

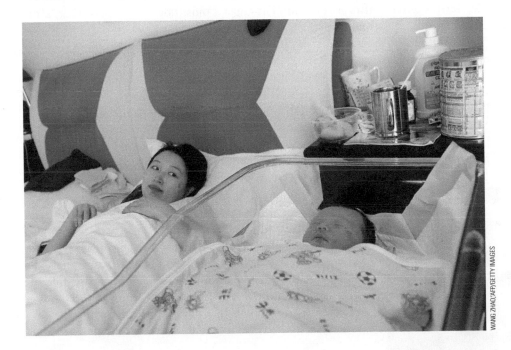

Pick Up Your Baby! Probably she can't. In this maternity ward in Beijing, China, most patients are recovering from cesarean sections, making it difficult to cradle, breast-feed, or carry a newborn until the incision heals.

WANG ZHAO/AFP/GETTY IMAGES

Newborn Survival

A century ago, at least 5 of every 100 newborns in the United States died (De Lee, 1938), as did more than half of newborns in developing nations. In the least developed nations, the rate of newborn death is now about 1 in 20, although an accurate count is not available as some rural newborn deaths are not tallied. One estimate is that worldwide almost 2 million newborns (1 in 70) die each year (Rajaratnam et al., 2010).

Every year, an estimated 273,500 women die in pregnancy or birth, almost all of them in nations with very poor medical care (Alkire et al., 2012). A suggested solution is to increase training of doctors or midwives so that cesarean sections could be more available when women were unable to deliver vaginally.

Currently in the United States, newborn mortality (when a baby is born alive but dies in the first day) is about 1 in 250—a statistic that includes very fragile newborns weighing less than 1 pound. That rate is far too high; about forty nations do better. Nonetheless, in the United States and elsewhere, medical measures have saved millions of babies and thousands of women. Almost never does a woman in the United States die of complications of pregnancy, abortion, or birth—the rate is about 1 in 50,000, although some indications are that the rate is rising slightly, as more pregnancies are unintended (Finer & Zolna, 2014).

Critics point out, however, that survival should not be the only measure of success. Several aspects of birth arise from custom or politics, not from necessity.

A particular issue in medically-advanced nations concerns the attention lavished on "miracle babies" who require intensive care, microsurgery, and weeks in the hospital (Longo, 2013). Those who survive often, but not always, need special care all their lives. Only happy outcomes are published; the public cost and the family burden are not publicized.

Questions of costs—emotional as well as financial—abound. All types of medical intervention vary more by doctor, hospital, day of the week, and region than by the circumstances of the birth—even in Sweden, where obstetric care is paid for by the government (Schytt & Waldenström, 2010).

A rare complication (uterine rupture), which sometimes happens when women give birth vaginally after a cesarean, has caused most doctors to insist that, after one cesarean, subsequent births must be cesarean. Many women and some experts think this is too cautious, but juries blame doctors for inaction more than for action. To avoid lawsuits, doctors intervene (Schifrin & Cohen, 2013).

Most U.S. births now take place in hospital labor rooms with high-tech operating rooms nearby in case they are needed. Another 5 percent of U.S. births occur in *birthing centers* (not in a hospital), and less than 1 percent occur at home (home births are illegal in some jurisdictions). About half of the home births are planned and half not, because of unexpectedly rapid labor. The unplanned ones are hazardous if no one is nearby to rescue a newborn in distress.

Compared with the United States, *planned* home births are more common in many other developed nations (2 percent in England, 30 percent in the Netherlands) where midwives are paid by the government. In the Netherlands, special ambulances called *flying storks* speed mother and newborn to a hospital if needed. Dutch research finds home births better for mothers and no worse for infants than hospital births (de Jonge et al., 2013).

A crucial question is how supportive the medical professionals are. One committee of obstetricians decided that

Especially for Conservatives and Liberals Do people's attitudes about medical intervention at birth reflect their attitudes about medicine at other points in their life span, in such areas as assisted reproductive technology (ART), immunization, and life support? (see response, page 112)

Mother Laboring, Doula Working In many nations, doulas work to help the birth process, providing massage, timing contractions, and preparing for birth. In the United States, doulas typically help couples decide when to leave home, avoiding long waits between hospital admittance and birth. Here, in Budapest, this expectant mother will have her baby with a licensed midwife at home. Nora Schimcsig is her doula; the two women will be together from this moment in early labor to the first breast-feeding of the newborn.

planned home births are acceptable because women have "a right to make a medically informed decision about delivery," but they also insisted that a trained midwife or doctor be present, that the woman not be high-risk (e.g., no previous cesarean), and that speedy transportation to a hospital be possible (American College of Obstetricians and Gynecologists Committee on Obstetric Practice, 2011).

Historically, women in hospitals labored by themselves until birth was imminent; fathers and other family members were kept away. No longer, as the opening anecdote illustrates. Almost everyone now agrees that a laboring woman should never be alone.

Many women have a **doula,** a person trained to support the laboring woman. Doulas time contractions, use massage, provide encouragement, and do whatever else is helpful. Every comparison study finds that the rate of medical intervention is lower when doulas are part of the birth team. Doulas have proven to be particularly helpful for immigrant, low-income, or unpartnered women who may be intimidated by doctors (Kang, 2014; Vonderheid et al., 2011).

doula Someone who helps with the birth process. Traditionally in Latin America, a doula was the only professional who attended childbirth. Now doulas are likely to arrive at the woman's home during early labor and later work alongside a hospital's staff.

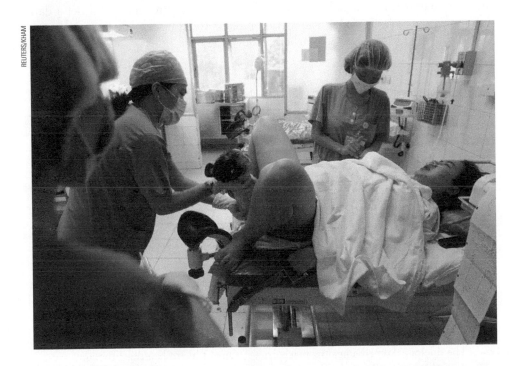

REUTERS/KHAM

Everyone Healthy and Happy A few decades ago in the developing world and a century ago in advanced nations, hospital births were only for birthing women who were near death, and only half of the fetuses survived. That has changed, particularly in Asia, where women prefer to give birth in hospitals. Hospital births themselves are not what they were. Most new mothers participate in the process: Here Le Thi Nga is about to greet her newborn after pulling with all her strength on the belt that helped her push out the head.

OBSERVATION QUIZ What evidence shows that even in Hanoi, technology is part of this birth? (see answer, page 113)

SUMMING UP   Most newborns score at least 7 out of 10 on the Apgar scale and thrive without medical assistance. If necessary, neonatal surgery and intensive care save lives. Although modern medicine has reduced maternal and newborn deaths, many critics deplore treating birth as a medical crisis rather than a natural event. Responses to this critique include women choosing to give birth in hospital labor rooms rather than operating rooms, in birthing centers instead of hospitals, or even at home. The assistance of a doula is another recent practice that reduces medical intervention.

WHAT HAVE YOU LEARNED?

1. Why has the Apgar scale increased newborns' survival rate?
2. Why has the rate of cesarean sections increased?
3. Why are developmentalists concerned that surgery is often part of birth?
4. Why are home births more common in some nations than others?
5. Why do women choose to have a doula in addition to a midwife or doctor?

// Response for Conservatives and Liberals (from page 110): Yes, some people are much more likely to want nature to take its course. However, personal experience often trumps political attitudes about birth and death; several of those who advocate hospital births are also in favor of spending one's final days at home.

teratogen An agent or condition, including viruses, drugs, and chemicals, that can impair prenatal development and result in birth defects or even death.

behavioral teratogens Agents and conditions that can harm the prenatal brain, impairing the future child's intellectual and emotional functioning.

GILLES MINGASSON/GETTY IMAGES

Swing High and Low Adopted by loving parents but born with fetal alcohol syndrome, Philip, shown here at age 11, sometimes threatened to kill his family members. His parents sent him to this residential ranch in Eureka, Montana (nonprofit, tuition $3,500 a month) for children like him. This moment during recess is a happy one; it is not known whether he learned to control his fury.

Especially for Judges and Juries How much protection, if any, should the legal system provide for fetuses? Should pregnant women with alcoholism be jailed to prevent them from drinking? What about people who enable them to drink, such as their partners, their parents, bar owners, and bartenders? (see response, page 115)

Harm to the Fetus

The early days of life place the developing human on the path toward health and success—or not. Fortunately, healthy newborns are the norm, not the exception. However, if something is amiss, it is often part of a cascade that may become overwhelming (Rossignol et al., 2014).

Harmful Substances

A cascade may begin before a woman realizes she is pregnant, as many toxins, illnesses, and experiences can cause harm early in pregnancy. Every week, scientists discover an unexpected **teratogen,** which is anything—drugs, viruses, pollutants, malnutrition, stress, and more—that increases the risk of prenatal abnormalities and birth complications.

One of my students told me that she now knew all the things that can go wrong, so she never wanted to have a baby. As I explained to her and as you will now read, most problems can be avoided, mitigated, or remedied. Prenatal life is not a dangerous period to be feared; it is a natural process to be protected. The outcome is usually a wonderfully formed newborn.

Behavioral Teratogens

Some teratogens cause no physical defects but affect the brain, making a child hyperactive, antisocial, or learning-disabled. These are **behavioral teratogens.** About 20 percent of all children have difficulties that *could* be connected to behavioral teratogens, although the link is not straightforward: The cascade is murky. One of my students wrote:

> I was nine years old when my mother announced she was pregnant. I was the one who was most excited. . . . My mother was a heavy smoker, Colt 45 beer drinker and a strong caffeine coffee drinker.
>
> One day my mother was sitting at the dining room table smoking cigarettes one after the other. I asked "Isn't smoking bad for the baby? She made a face and said "Yes, so what?"
>
> I said " So why are you doing it?"
>
> She said, "I don't know.". . .
>
> During this time I was in the fifth grade and we saw a film about birth defects. My biggest fear was that my mother was going to give birth to a fetal alcohol syndrome (FAS) infant. . . . My baby brother was born right on schedule. The doctors claimed a healthy newborn. . . . Once I heard healthy, I thought everything was going to be fine. I was wrong, then again I was just a child. . . .
>
> My baby brother never showed any interest in toys. . . . [H]e just cannot get the right words out of his mouth. . . . [H]e has no common sense. . . .
>
> Why hurt those who cannot defend themselves?

> *[J., personal communication]*

As you remember from Chapter 1, one case proves nothing. J. blames her mother, although genes, postnatal experiences, and lack of preventive information and services may be part of the cascade as well. Nonetheless, J. rightly wonders why her mother took a chance.

Behavioral teratogens can be subtle, yet their effects may last a lifetime. That is one conclusion from research on the babies born to pregnant women exposed to flu during the pandemic of 1918. By middle age, although some of these babies became wealthy, happy, and brilliant, on average those born in flu-ravaged regions had less education, employment, and income than those born a year earlier (Almond, 2006). They are almost all dead now, dying a few years earlier than if their prenatal life had begun in 1917 or 1919.

Risk Analysis

Life requires risks: We analyze which chances to take and how to minimize harm. To pick an easy example: Crossing the street is risky. Knowing that, we cross carefully; it would be much more harmful to stay on our block.

Risk analysis is crucial throughout human development (Sheeran et al., 2014). You read in Chapter 3 that pregnancy after age 35 increases the chance of many disorders, but mature parents are more likely to have many assets, psychological as well as material, that benefit their children. Depending on many aspects of the social context, it may be wise to have a baby at age 18 or 42 or any other age. Always, risk analysis is needed; many problems can be prevented or overcome.

Although all teratogens increase the *risk* of harm, none *always* causes damage; risk analysis involves probabilities, not certainties, and resilient and protective influences are relevant (Aven, 2011). The impact of teratogens depends on the interplay of many factors, both destructive and constructive, an example of the dynamic-systems perspective described in Chapter 1.

// ANSWER TO OBSERVATION QUIZ
(from page 111): The computer print-out on the far right. Monitors during labor track contractions, fetal heart rate, and sometimes more, printing out the record minute-by-minute, so medical staff can judge whether to speed up labor or birth. In this case, no medical help was required.

The Critical Time

Timing is crucial. Some teratogens cause damage only during a *critical period* (see Figure 4.5). (**Developmental Link:** Critical and sensitive periods are described in Chapter 1.) Obstetricians recommend that *before* pregnancy occurs, women should avoid drugs (especially alcohol), supplement a balanced diet with extra folic acid and iron, update their immunizations, and gain or lose weight if needed. Indeed, pre-conception health is at least as important as post-conception health (see Table 4.4).

The first days and weeks after conception (the germinal and embryonic periods) are critical for body formation, but health during the entire fetal period affects the brain, and thus behavioral teratogens affect the fetus at any time. Some teratogens that cause preterm birth or low birthweight are particularly harmful in the second half of pregnancy.

TABLE 4.4	Before Pregnancy	
What Prospective Mothers Should Do	**What Prospective Mothers Really Do (U.S. Data)**
1. Plan the pregnancy.	1. At least a third of all pregnancies are not intended.
2. Take a daily multivitamin with folic acid.	2. About 60 percent of women aged 18 to 45 do not take multivitamins.
3. Avoid binge-drinking (defined as four or more drinks in a row).	3. One in seven women in their childbearing years binge-drink.
4. Update immunizations against all teratogenic viruses, especially rubella.	4. Unlike in many developing nations, relatively few pregnant women in the United States lack basic immunizations.
5. Gain or lose weight, as appropriate.	5. About one-third of all U.S. women of childbearing age are obese, and about 5 percent are underweight. Both extremes increase complications.
6. Reassess use of prescription drugs.	6. Ninety percent of pregnant women take prescription drugs (not counting vitamins).
7. Develop daily exercise habits.	7. More than half of women of childbearing age do not exercise.

Sources: Bombard et al., 2013; MMWR, (July 20, 2012); Brody, 2013; Mosher et al., 2012; U.S. Department of Health and Human Services, 2012.

In fact, one study found that although smoking cigarettes throughout prenatal development can harm the fetus, smokers who quit early in pregnancy had no higher risks of birth complications than did women who never smoked (McCowan et al., 2009). Another longitudinal study of 7-year-olds found that, although alcohol is a teratogen at every period of pregnancy, binge drinking in the last trimester was more harmful to the brain (Niclasen et al., 2014).

How Much Is Too Much?

A second factor affecting the harm from teratogens is the dose and/or frequency of exposure. Some teratogens have a **threshold effect;** they are virtually harmless

threshold effect In prenatal development, when a teratogen is relatively harmless in small doses but becomes harmful once exposure reaches a certain level (the threshold).

FIGURE 4.5

The embryonic period (from the third to the eight week) is the most sensitive time for causing structural birth defects. Organs have different periods of sensitivity to birth defects: Some are vulnerable for a long time (e.g., the brain), others for a shorter time (e.g., the arms). The embryonic period (weeks 3 to 8) is the most sensitive time for structural birth defects. During the fetal period, the brain is the most at risk for defects. Sometimes teratogens can affect multiple organs at the same time. Individual differences in susceptibility to teratogens may be caused by a fetus's genetic makeup or peculiarities of the mother, including the effectiveness of her placenta or her overall health. The dose and timing of the exposure are both important.

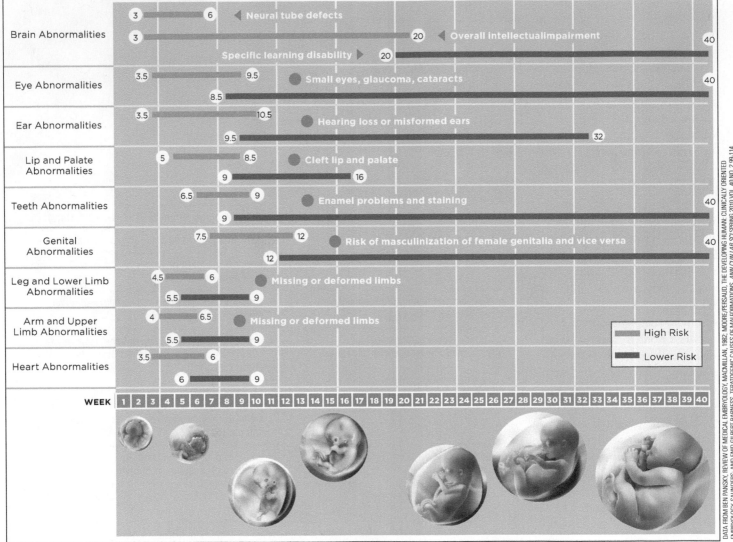

DATA FROM BEN PANSKY, REVIEW OF MEDICAL EMBRYOLOGY, MACMILLAN, 1982; MOORE/PERSAUD, THE DEVELOPING HUMAN: CLINICALLY ORIENTED EMBRYOLOGY, SAUNDERS; AND ENID GILBERT-BARNESS, TERATOGENIC CAUSES OF MALFORMATIONS, ANN CLIN LAB SCI SPRING 2010 VOL. 40 NO. 2 99-114.

until exposure reaches a certain level, at which point they "cross the threshold" and become damaging. This threshold is not a fixed boundary: Dose, timing, frequency, and other teratogens affect when the threshold is crossed (O'Leary et al., 2010).

A few substances are beneficial in small amounts but fiercely teratogenic in large quantities. Vitamin A, for instance, is essential for healthy development but causes abnormalities if the dose is 50,000 units per day or higher (obtained only in pills, don't worry about eating carrots) (Naudé et al., 2007). Experts rarely specify thresholds, partly because one teratogen may affect the threshold of another. Alcohol, tobacco, and marijuana are more teratogenic, with a lower threshold for each, when all three are combined.

Is there a safe dose for psychoactive drugs? Consider alcohol. During the period of the embryo, a mother's heavy drinking can cause **fetal alcohol syndrome (FAS),**

fetal alcohol syndrome (FAS) A cluster of birth defects, including abnormal facial characteristics, slow physical growth, and reduced intellectual ability, that may occur in the fetus of a woman who drinks alcohol while pregnant.

which distorts the facial features of a child (especially the eyes, ears, and upper lip). Later in pregnancy, alcohol is a behavioral teratogen.

However, alcohol during pregnancy does not always result in evident harm. If it did, almost everyone born in Europe before 1980 would be affected, since wine or beer was part of most Europeans' daily diet.

Currently, pregnant women are advised to avoid alcohol, but women in the United Kingdom receive conflicting advice about drinking an occasional glass of wine (Raymond et al., 2009). French women are told to abstain, but many (between 12 and 63 percent, depending on specifics of the research) do not heed that message (Dumas et al., 2014). Should all women who might become pregnant refuse a legal substance that men use routinely? Wise? Probably. Necessary? Maybe not.

Innate Vulnerability

Genes are a third factor that influence the effects of teratogens. When a woman carrying dizygotic twins drinks alcohol, for example, the twins' blood alcohol levels are equal; yet one twin may be more severely affected than the other because their alleles for the enzyme that metabolizes alcohol differ. Differential susceptibility is evident for fetal alcohol disorders, and probably for many other problems as well (McCarthy & Eberhart, 2014).

The Y chromosome may make male fetuses more vulnerable to many problems. Boys are more likely to be spontaneously aborted or stillborn and also more likely to be harmed by teratogens than female fetuses are. This is true overall, but the male/female hazard rate differs from one teratogen to another (Lewis & Kestler, 2012).

Genes are important not only at conception but also during pregnancy. One maternal allele results in low levels of folic acid in a woman's bloodstream and hence in the embryo, which can produce *neural-tube defects*—either *spina bifida,* in which the tail of the spine is not enclosed properly (enclosure normally occurs at about week 7), or *anencephaly,* when part of the brain is missing. Neural-tube defects are more common in certain ethnic groups (Irish, English, and Egyptian), but the crucial maternal allele is rare among Asians and sub-Saharan Africans (Mills et al., 1995).

Since 1998 in the United States, manufacturers have had to add folic acid to every packaged cereal, an intervention that reduced neural-tube defects by 26 percent in the first three years after the law went into effect (MMWR, September 13, 2002). But some women rarely eat cereal and do not take vitamins. Data by region is not always available, but in 2010 in Appalachia (where many women are of British descent), about 1 newborn in 1,000 had a neural-tube defect.

Applying the Research

Results of teratogenic exposure cannot be predicted precisely in individual cases. However, much is known about destructive and damaging teratogens, including what individuals and society can do to reduce the risks. Table 4.5 lists some teratogens and their possible effects, as well as preventive measures.

General health during pregnancy is at least half the battle. Women who maintain good nutrition and avoid drugs and teratogenic chemicals (which are often found in pesticides, cleaning fluids, and cosmetics) usually have healthy babies. Some medications are necessary (e.g., for women with epilepsy, diabetes, and severe depression), but consultation should begin *before* conception.

Many women assume that herbal medicines or over-the-counter drugs are safe. Not so. As pediatrics professor Allen Mitchell explains, "Many over-the-counter drugs were grandfathered in with no studies of their possible effects during pregnancy" (quoted in Brody, 2013, p. D 5).

Smoke-free Babies Posters such as this one have had an impact. Smoking among adults is only half of what it was thirty years ago, a third of women smokers quit when they know they are pregnant, while the other two-thirds cut their smoking in half. Unfortunately, the heaviest smokers are least likely to quit—they need more than posters to motivate them to break the habit.

Especially for Nutritionists Is it beneficial that most breakfast cereals are fortified with vitamins and minerals? (see response, page 119)

// **Response for Judges and Juries** (from page 112): Some laws punish women who jeopardize the health of their fetuses, but a developmental view would consider the micro-, exo-, and macrosystems.

TABLE 4.5 Teratogens: Effects of Exposure and Prevention of Damage*

Teratogens	Effects of Exposure on Fetus	Measures for Preventing Damage (Laws, doctors, and individuals can all increase prevention)
Diseases		
Rubella (German measles)	In embryonic period, causes blindness and deafness; in first and second trimesters, causes brain damage.	Immunization before becoming pregnant.
Toxoplasmosis	Brain damage, loss of vision, intellectual disabilities.	Avoid eating undercooked meat and handling cat feces or garden dirt during pregnancy.
Measles, chicken pox, influenza	May impair brain functioning.	Immunization of all children and adults.
Syphilis	Baby is born with syphilis, which, untreated, leads to brain and bone damage and eventual death.	Early prenatal diagnosis and treatment with antibiotics.
HIV	Baby may catch the virus. Without treatment, illness and death are likely during childhood.	Prenatal drugs and cesarean birth make HIV transmission rare.
Other sexually transmitted infections, including gonorrhea and chlamydia	Not usually harmful during pregnancy but may cause blindness and infections if transmitted during birth.	Early diagnosis and treatment; if necessary, cesarean section, treatment of newborn.
Infections, including infections of urinary tract, gums, and teeth	May cause premature labor, which increases vulnerability to brain damage.	Good dental and medical care before pregnancy.
Pollutants		
Lead, mercury, PCBs (polychlorinated biphenyls); dioxin; and some pesticides, herbicides, and cleaning compounds	May cause spontaneous abortion, preterm labor, and brain damage.	May be harmless in small doses, but pregnant women should avoid exposure, such as drinking well water, eating unwashed fruits or vegetables, using chemicals, eating fish from polluted waters.
Radiation		
Massive or repeated exposure to radiation, as in medical X-rays	May cause small brains (microcephaly) and intellectual disabilities. Background radiation probably harmless.	Sonograms, not X-rays, during pregnancy. Pregnant women who work directly with radiation need special protection.
Social and Behavioral Factors		
Very high stress	May cause cleft lip or cleft palate, spontaneous abortion, or preterm labor. May affect brain, temperament of newborn.	Adequate relaxation, rest, and sleep; reduce intensity of employment, housework, and child care.
Malnutrition	When severe, interferes with conception, implantation, normal fetal development.	Eat a balanced diet, be of normal weight before pregnancy, gain 25–35 lbs (10–15 kg) during pregnancy. Iron is particularly crucial.
Excessive, exhausting exercise	Can harm fetal growth if it interferes with woman's sleep, digestion, or nutrition.	Regular, moderate exercise is best for everyone.
Medicinal Drugs		
Lithium	Can cause heart abnormalities.	Avoid all medicines, whether prescription or over the counter, during pregnancy unless given by a medical professional who knows recent research on teratogens.
Tetracycline	Can harm teeth.	
Retinoic acid	Can cause limb deformities.	
Streptomycin	Can cause deafness.	
ACE inhibitors	Can harm digestive organs.	
Phenobarbital	Can affect brain development.	
Thalidomide	Can stop ear and limb formation.	

TABLE 4.5 (Continued)

Psychoactive Drugs

Caffeine	Normal, modest use poses no problem.	Avoid excessive use. (Note that coffee, tea, cola drinks, and chocolate all contain caffeine).
Alcohol	May cause fetal alcohol syndrome (FAS) or fetal alcohol effects (FAE).	Stop or severely limit alcohol consumption; especially dangerous are three or more drinks a day or four or more drinks on one occasion.
Tobacco	Reduces birthweight, increases risk of malformations of limbs and urinary tract, and may affect the baby's lungs.	Ideally, stop smoking before pregnancy. Stopping during pregnancy also beneficial.
Marijuana	Heavy exposure affects central nervous system; when smoked, may hinder fetal growth.	Avoid or strictly limit marijuana consumption.
Heroin	Slows fetal growth, increases prematurity. Addicted newborns need treatment to control withdrawal.	Treatment needed before pregnancy but if already pregnant, gradual withdrawal on methadone is better than continued use of heroin.
Cocaine	Slows fetal growth, increases prematurity and then learning problems.	Stop before pregnancy; if not, babies need special medical and educational attention in their early years.
Inhaled solvents (glue or aerosol)	May cause abnormally small head, crossed eyes, and other indications of brain damage.	Stop before becoming pregnant; damage can occur before a woman knows she is pregnant.

* The field of toxicology advances daily. Research on new substances begins with their effects on nonhuman species, which provides suggestive (though not conclusive) evidence. This table is a primer; it is no substitute for careful consultation with a knowledgeable professional. A useful website provided by the Organization of Teratology Specialists (in English and Spanish) that lists many specific teratogenic drugs is http://www.otispregnancy.org.

Sadly, a cascade of teratogens is most likely to begin with women who are already vulnerable. For example, cigarette smokers are more often drinkers (as was J.'s mother), and those whose jobs require exposure to chemicals and pesticides (such as migrant workers) are more often malnourished and lack access to medical care (McLaurin, 2014).

a view from science

Conflicting Advice

Pregnant women want to know about the thousands of drugs, chemicals, and diseases that might harm the fetus, yet, as explained in Chapter 1, the scientific method is designed to be cautious. It takes years for replication, data from alternate designs, and exploration of various hypotheses to reach sound conclusions.

On almost any issue, scientists disagree until the weight of evidence is unmistakable. It took decades before all researchers agreed on such (now obvious) teratogens as rubella and cigarettes.

One current dispute is whether pesticides should be allowed on the large farms that produce most of the fruits and vegetables for consumption in the United States. No biologist doubts that pesticides harm frogs, fish, and bees, but the pesticide industry

insists that careful use (e.g., spraying on plants, not workers) does not harm people. Developmentalists, however, worry that pregnant women who breathe these toxins might have children with brain damage. As one scientist said "pesticides were designed to be neurotoxic. Why should we be surprised if they cause neurotoxicity?" (Lambhear, quote in Mascarelli, 2013, p. 741).

Scientists have convinced the U.S. government to ban one pesticide, chlorpyrifos, from household use (it once was commonly used to kill roaches and ants), but that drug is still widely used in agriculture and is used in homes in other nations. There is evidence from analyzing blood in the umbilical cord that many fetuses are exposed to chlorpyrifos, and longitudinal research finds that these children have lower intelligence and more behavior problems than other children (Horton et al., 2012). However, Dow Chemical Company, which sells the pesticide, argues that the research does not take into account all the confounding factors, such as the living conditions of farm-workers' children (Mascarelli, 2013).

In this dispute, developmentalists choose to protect the fetal brain, which is why this chapter advises pregnant women to avoid pesticides. However, on many other teratogens, developmentalists themselves are conflicted. Fish consumption and exposure to plastics are examples.

Pregnant women in the United States are told to eat less fish, but those in the United Kingdom are told to eat more fish. The reason for these opposite messages is that fish contains mercury (a teratogen) and DHA (an omega-3 fatty acid needed for fetal brain development). Scientists weigh the benefits and risks of fish consumption, and wonder how to teach women how to judge each kind of fish and where it swam, choosing benefits while avoiding risks (Lando & Lo, 2014).

Another dispute involves bisphenol A (commonly used in plastics), banned in Canada but allowed in the United States. Traces of the substance are found in the urine of most pregnant women, but most scientists think that very low amounts are harmless. The question is, where is the threshold?

Many experiments on rodents find bisphenol A teratogenic. For example, when pregnant rats are exposed to bisphenol A, even low doses affect sexual organs (Christiansen et al., 2014).

Confirmation regarding the effects of exposure on humans is difficult. Controlled experiments are unethical: No one would deliberately raise bisphenol A levels in pregnant women to see if it harmed their offspring. Surveys give conflicting results, partly because other key variables—age, education, income—correlate with both urine levels of the chemical and intelligence of children. Should regulations be guided by experiments on mice? The answer depends on a person's attitudes about plastic, pregnancy, and politics.

To make all this more difficult, pregnant women are, ideally, happy and calm: Stress and anxiety affect the fetus. Pregnancy often increases fear and anxiety (Rubertsson et al., 2014); scientists do not want to add to the worry. Prospective parents want clear, immediate answers, yet scientists cannot always provide them.

Advice from Doctors

Although prenatal care is helpful in protecting the developing fetus, even doctors are not always careful. One concern is pain medication. Opioids (narcotics) may do damage to the fetus and aspirin may cause excessive bleeding during birth. Yet a recent study found that 23 percent of pregnant women on Medicaid are given a prescription for a narcotic (Desai et al., 2014).

Worse still is that some doctors do not ask women about harmful life patterns. For example, one Maryland study found that almost one-third of pregnant women were not asked about their alcohol use (Cheng et al., 2011). Those who were over age 35 and college educated were least likely to be queried. Did their doctors assume they knew the dangers? Wrong. This study and other research have found that such women are the most likely to drink during pregnancy.

To learn what medications are safe in pregnancy, women often consult the Internet. However, a study of 25 websites that together listed 235 medications as safe, found that only 103 of those 235 had been assessed by TERIS (a respected national panel of teratologists who evaluate the impact of drugs on prenatal development). Further, of those 103, only 60 were considered safe. The rest were not *proven* harmful, but the experts felt there was not enough evidence to state they were safe (Peters et al., 2013). Many of these 25 Internet sites used unreliable evidence, and sometimes the same drug was on the safe list of one site and the danger list of another.

Video Activity: Teratogens explores the factors that enable or prevent teratogens from harming a developing fetus.

What Do We Know?

Now we know that prenatal teratogens can cause structural problems during the embryonic period and several diseases throughout pregnancy, as well as behavioral problems and reproductive impairment later in life. But it is not easy to know which teratogens, at what doses, when, and for whom. Almost every common disease, almost every food additive, most prescription and nonprescription drugs (even caffeine and aspirin), many minerals and chemicals in the air and water, emotional stress, exhaustion, and poor nutrition *might* impair prenatal development—but only at some times, in some amounts, in some mammals.

Most research is conducted with mice; harm to humans is rarely proven to everyone's satisfaction. That is not surprising, since hundreds of thousands of drugs, diseases, and pollutants are now evident, many of them newly developed or newly diagnosed. It takes careful, replicated research before scientists reach a consensus, and then wide communication before women are aware of risks.

Even for proven risks, as with alcohol and cigarettes, many pregnant women are not convinced. In the United States, from 2006 to 2010, nearly 8 percent of pregnant women drank alcohol, with rates higher (10 percent) among women with a college degree (see Figure 4.6).

Furthermore, even when evidence seems clear, the proper social response is controversial. It is legal to arrest and jail pregnant women who use alcohol or other psychoactive drugs in six states (Minnesota, North Dakota, Oklahoma, South Dakota, Tennessee, and Wisconsin).

If a baby is stillborn and the mother used meth, she may be convicted of murder, as occurred for an Oklahoma woman, Theresa Hernandez, who was sentenced to 15 years (Fentiman, 2009). Alabama jailed several new mothers because their babies had illegal substances in their bloodstream (Eckholm, 2013). Many doctors and developmentalists worry that such penalties make women reluctant to see a doctor when they are pregnant, or even to have the baby in a hospital.

// **Response for Nutritionists** (from page 115): Useful, yes; optimal, no. Some essential vitamins are missing (too expensive), and individual nutritional needs differ, depending on age, sex, health, genes, and eating habits. The reduction in neural-tube defects is good, but many women don't eat cereal or take vitamin supplements before becoming pregnant.

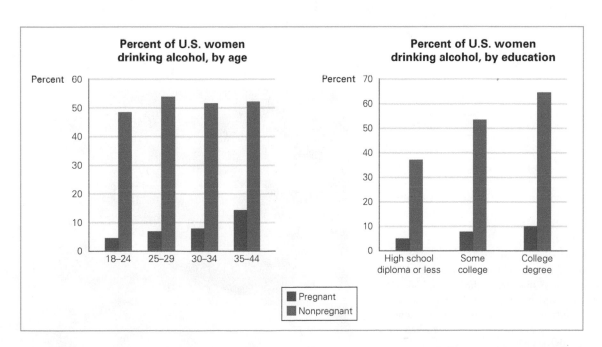

FIGURE 4.6

Trouble Ahead About half of U.S. women drink alcohol. That is not troubling, since occasional drinking in adulthood seems harmless. Most women stop drinking when they are pregnant. This is what almost all experts recommend, since drinking increases the risk of facial abnormalities in the first trimester and of brain damage throughout. The pregnant rates here are of women still reporting "any use" of alcohol in the third trimester. The data is frightening, since most neurons of the prefrontal cortex develop in the final months of pregnancy. Apparently, older is not wiser, and education does not lead to abstinence—quite the opposite. Since alcohol is a proven risk to the fetal brain, do 14 percent of older pregnant women suffer from alcoholism, unable to quit?

Especially for Social Workers When is it most important to convince women to be tested for HIV: before pregnancy, after conception, or immediately after birth? (see response, page 122)

false positive The result of a laboratory test that reports something as true when in fact it is not true. This can occur for pregnancy tests, when a woman might not be pregnant even though the test says she is, or during pregnancy when a problem is reported that actually does not exist.

Prenatal Care

Seeing a medical professional in the first trimester has many benefits: Women learn what to eat, what to do, and what to avoid. Some serious conditions, syphilis and HIV among them, can be diagnosed and treated before they harm the fetus. Prenatal tests (of blood, urine, and fetal heart rate as well as ultrasound) reassure parents, facilitating the crucial parent-child bond, long before fetal movement is apparent.

In general, early care protects fetal growth, makes birth easier, and renders parents better able to cope. When complications (such as twins, gestational diabetes, and infections) arise, early recognition increases the chance of a healthy birth. As birth approaches, prospective parents often attend classes where they learn about the birth process, including what they can do in the final weeks and hours, and that itself reduces confusion and increases the odds of a healthy newborn.

Unfortunately, however, about 20 percent of early pregnancy tests *raise* anxiety instead of reducing it. For instance, the level of alpha-fetoprotein (AFP) may be too high or too low, or ultrasound may indicate multiple fetuses, abnormal growth, Down syndrome, or a mother's narrow pelvis. Many such warnings are **false positives;** that is, they falsely suggest a problem that does not exist. Any warning, whether false or true, requires further testing, worry, and soul-searching. Consider the following.

opposing perspectives

"What Do People Live to Do?"

John and Martha, both under age 35, were expecting their second child. Martha's initial prenatal screening revealed low alpha-fetoprotein, which could indicate Down syndrome.

Another blood test was scheduled. . . . John asked:

"What exactly is the problem?" . . .

"We've got a one in eight hundred and ninety-five shot at a retarded baby."

John smiled, "I can live with those odds."

"I'm still a little scared."

He reached across the table for my hand. "Sure," he said, "that's understandable. But even if there is a problem, we've caught it in time. . . . The worst-case scenario is that you might have to have an abortion, and that's a long shot. Everything's going to be fine." . . .

"I might *have to have* an abortion?" The chill inside me was gone. Instead I could feel my face flushing hot with anger. "Since when do you decide what I *have* to do with my body?"

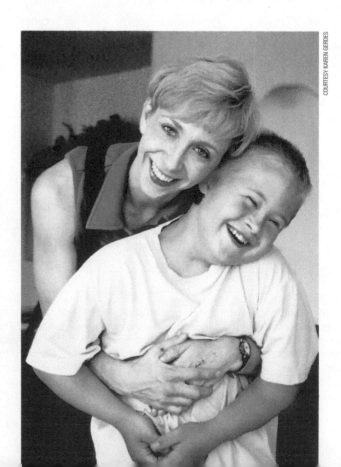

COURTESY KAREN GERDES

Happy Boy Martha Beck not only loves her son Adam (shown here), but she also writes about the special experiences he has brought into the whole family's life—hers, John's, and their other children's. She is "pro-choice"; he is a chosen child.

Complications During Birth

Any birth complication usually has multiple causes: A fetus is low birthweight, preterm, genetically vulnerable, or exposed to teratogens, *and* a mother is unusually young, old, small, stressed, or ill. As an example, **cerebral palsy** (a disease marked by difficulties with movement) was once thought to be caused solely by birth procedures (excessive medication, slow breech birth, or use of forceps to pull the fetal head through the birth canal). However, we now know that cerebral palsy results from genetic sensitivity, teratogens, and maternal infection (Mann et al., 2009), worsened by insufficient oxygen to the fetal brain at birth.

A lack of oxygen is **anoxia.** Anoxia often occurs for a second or two during birth, indicated by a slower fetal heart rate, with no harm done. To prevent prolonged anoxia, the fetal heart rate is monitored during labor and the Apgar is used immediately after birth.

Again, however, anoxia is only part of a cascade. How long anoxia can continue without harming the brain depends on genes, birthweight, gestational age, drugs in the bloodstream (either taken by the mother before birth or given during birth), and many other factors. Thus, anoxia is part of a cascade of factors that may cause cerebral palsy. Almost every birth complication is the result of a similar cascade.

> **cerebral palsy** A disorder that results from damage to the brain's motor centers. People with cerebral palsy have difficulty with muscle control, so their speech and/or body movements are impaired.
>
> **anoxia** A lack of oxygen that, if prolonged, can cause brain damage or death.

John looked surprised. "I never said I was going to decide anything," he protested. "It's just that if the tests show something wrong with the baby, of course we'll abort. We've talked about this."

"What we've talked about," I told John in a low, dangerous voice, "is that I am pro-choice. That means I decide whether or not I'd abort a baby with a birth defect. . . . I'm not so sure of this."

"You used to be," said John.

"I know I used to be." I rubbed my eyes. I felt terribly confused. "But now . . . look, John, it's not as though we're deciding whether or not to have a baby. We're deciding what *kind* of baby we're willing to accept. If it's perfect in every way, we keep it. If it doesn't fit the right specifications, whoosh! Out it goes.". . .

John was looking more and more confused. "Martha, why are you on this soapbox? What's your point?"

"My point is," I said, "that I'm trying to get you to tell me what you think constitutes a 'defective' baby. What about . . . oh, I don't know, a hyperactive baby? Or an ugly one?"

"They can't test for those things and—"

"Well, what if they could?" I said. "Medicine can do all kinds of magical tricks these days. Pretty soon we're going to be aborting babies because they have the gene for alcoholism, or homosexuality, or manic depression. . . . Did you know that in China they abort a lot of fetuses just because they're female?" I growled. "Is being a girl 'defective' enough for you?"

"Look," he said, "I know I can't always see things from your perspective. And I'm sorry about that. But the way I see it, if a baby is going to be deformed or something, abortion is a way to keep everyone from suffering—*especially* the baby. It's like shooting a horse that's broken its leg. . . . A lame horse dies slowly, you know? . . . It dies in terrible pain. And it can't run anymore. So it can't enjoy life even if it doesn't die. Horses live to run; that's what they do. If a baby is born not being able to do what other people do, I think it's better not to prolong its suffering."

". . . And what is it," I said softly, more to myself than to John, "what is it that people do? What do we live to do, the way a horse lives to run?"

[*Beck, 1999, pp. 132–133, 135*]

The second AFP test was in the normal range, "meaning there was no reason to fear . . . Down syndrome" (p. 137).

As you read in Chapter 3, genetic counselors help couples discuss their choices *before* becoming pregnant. John and Martha had had no counseling because the pregnancy was unplanned and their risk for Down syndrome was low. The opposite of a false positive is a *false negative,* a mistaken assurance that all is well. Amniocentesis later revealed that the second AFP was a false negative. Their fetus had Down syndrome after all.

// Response for Social Workers (from page 120): Testing and then treatment are useful at any time because women who know they are HIV-positive are more likely to get treatment, reduce the risk of transmission, or avoid pregnancy. If pregnancy does occur, early diagnosis is best. Getting tested after birth is too late for the baby.

SUMMING UP   Risk analysis is complex but necessary to protect every fetus. Many factors reduce risk, including the mother's health and nourishment before pregnancy, her early prenatal care and drug use, and the father's support. Each teratogen may harm the fetus, although, as risk analysis implies, the impact varies from none at all to very serious. The timing of exposure, the amount of toxin ingested, and the genes of the mother and fetus are crucial factors.

WHAT HAVE YOU LEARNED?

1. Why is risk analysis more crucial than targeting any one teratogen?
2. When are teratogens most harmful to the future baby?
3. Why is it difficult to pin down the impact of behavioral teratogens?
4. What is a specific example of the impact of genes on birth defects?
5. How do doctors protect the fetus, and when might a doctor do harm?
6. How do anoxia and cerebral palsy illustrate the need for risk analysis?

Low Birthweight: Causes and Consequences

Some newborns are small and immature. With modern hospital care, tiny infants usually survive, but it would be better for everyone—mother, father, baby, and society—if all fetuses developed for at least 35 weeks and all newborns weighed more than 2,500 grams (5½ pounds). (Usually, this text gives pounds before grams, but hospitals worldwide report birthweight using the metric system, so grams precede pounds and ounces here.)

The World Health Organization defines **low birthweight (LBW)** as under 2,500 grams. LBW babies are further grouped into **very low birthweight (VLBW),** under 1,500 grams (3 pounds, 5 ounces), and **extremely low birthweight (ELBW),** under 1,000 grams (2 pounds, 3 ounces). It is possible for a newborn to weigh as little as 500 grams, and they are the most vulnerable—about half of them die even with excellent care (Lau et al., 2013).

Remember that fetal weight normally doubles in the last trimester of pregnancy, with 900 grams (about 2 pounds) of that gain occurring in the final three weeks. Thus, a baby born **preterm** (three or more weeks early; no longer called *premature*) is usually, but not always, LBW. In addition, some fetuses gain weight slowly throughout pregnancy and are *small-for-dates,* or **small for gestational age (SGA).** A full-term baby weighing only 2,600 grams and a 30-week-old fetus weighing only 1,000 grams are both SGA, even though the first is not technically low birthweight.

Mothers and Small Babies

Maternal or fetal illness might cause SGA, but maternal drug use is a more common cause. Every psychoactive drug slows fetal growth, with tobacco implicated in 25 percent of all low-birthweight births worldwide.

Another common reason for slow fetal growth as well as preterm birth is malnutrition. Women who begin pregnancy underweight, who eat poorly during pregnancy, or who gain less than 3 pounds (1.3 kilograms) per month in the last six months more often have underweight infants.

Unfortunately, many risk factors—underweight, undereating, underage, and smoking—tend to occur together. To make it worse, many such mothers live in poor neighborhoods, where pollution is high—another risk factor for low birthweight (Stieb et al., 2012).

low birthweight (LBW) A body weight at birth of less than 5½ pounds (2,500 grams).

very low birthweight (VLBW) A body weight at birth of less than 3 pounds, 5 ounces (1,500 grams).

extremely low birthweight (ELBW) A body weight at birth of less than 2 pounds, 3 ounces (1,000 grams).

preterm A birth that occurs 3 or more weeks before the full 38 weeks of the typical pregnancy—that is, at 35 or fewer weeks after conception.

small for gestational age (SGA) (Also called *small-for-dates.*) A term for a baby whose birthweight is significantly lower than expected, given the time since conception. For example, a 5-pound (2,265-gram) newborn is considered SGA if born on time but not SGA if born two months early.

What About the Father?

The causes of low birthweight just mentioned rightly focus on the pregnant woman. However, fathers—and grandmothers, neighbors, and communities—are often crucial. As an editorial in a journal for obstetricians explains: "Fathers' attitudes regarding the pregnancy, fathers' behaviors during the prenatal period, and the relationship between fathers and mothers . . . may indirectly influence risk for adverse birth outcomes" (Misra et al., 2010, p. 99).

As already explained in Chapter 1, each person is embedded in a social network. Since the future mother's behavior impacts the fetus, everyone who affects her also affects the fetus. She may be stressed because of her boss, her mother, her mother-in-law, and especially her partner. One example is that unintended pregnancies increase the incidence of low birthweight (Shah et al., 2011).

Not only fathers but also the entire social network and culture are crucial (Lewallen, 2011). This is most apparent in what is called the **immigrant paradox.** Many immigrants have difficulty getting education and well-paid jobs; their socioeconomic status is low. Low SES correlates with low birthweight. Thus, newborns born to immigrants are expected to be underweight. But, paradoxically, they are generally healthier in every way, including birthweight, than newborns of U.S.-born women of the same gene pool (García Coll & Marks, 2012).

This paradox was first called the *Hispanic paradox,* because, although U.S. residents born in Mexico or South America average lower SES than people of Hispanic descent born in the United States, their newborns have fewer problems. The same discrepancy has now been demonstrated for immigrants from the Caribbean, Africa, Eastern Europe, and Asia. Why? The crucial factor may be fathers and grandmothers, who keep pregnant immigrant women drug-free and healthy, counteracting the stress of poverty (Luecken et al., 2013).

> **immigrant paradox** The surprising, paradoxical fact that low SES immigrant women tend to have fewer birth complications than native-born peers with higher incomes.

Consequences of Low Birthweight

You have already read that life itself is uncertain for the smallest newborns. Ranking worse than most developed nations—and just behind Cuba and Croatia—the infant mortality rate (death in the first year) of the United States is 34th in the world, about 6 deaths per 1,000 live births, according to the United Nations. The main reason is that the United States has more extremely low-birthweight newborns (Lau et al., 2013).

For survivors born very low birthweight, every developmental milestone—smiling, holding a bottle, walking, talking—is later. Low-birthweight babies experience cognitive difficulties as well as visual and hearing impairments. High-risk newborns become infants and children who cry more, pay attention less, disobey, and experience language delays (Aarnoudse-Moens et al., 2009; Stolt et al., 2014).

Longitudinal research from many nations finds that children who were at the extremes of SGA or preterm have many neurological problems in middle childhood, including smaller brain volume, lower IQs, and behavioral difficulties (Clark et al., 2013; Hutchinson et al., 2013; van Soelen et al., 2010). Even in adulthood, risks persist: Adults who were LBW are more likely to develop diabetes and heart disease, partly because they are more often obese.

Longitudinal data provide both hope and caution. Remember that risk analysis gives probabilities, not certainties—averages are not true in every case. By age 4, some ELBW infants are normal in brain and body.

Comparing Nations

In some northern European nations, only 4 percent of newborns weigh under 2,500 grams; in several South Asian nations, including India, Pakistan, and the

Philippines, more than 20 percent do. Worldwide, far fewer low-birthweight babies are born than two decades ago; as a result, neonatal deaths have been reduced by one-third (Rajaratnam et al., 2010).

Some nations, China and Bangladesh among them, have improved markedly. In 1970, an estimated half of Chinese newborns were LBW; recent estimates put that number at 6 percent (Chen et al., 2013). In 1990, half of newborns in Bangladesh were LBW (World Bank, 1994, p. 214); now the rate is 22 percent (UNICEF, 2014). In some nations, community health programs aid the growth of the fetus. That has an effect, according to a study provocatively titled *Low birth weight outcomes: Why better in Cuba than Alabama?* (Neggers & Crowe, 2013).

In some nations, notably in sub-Saharan Africa, the LBW rate is rising because global warming, HIV, food shortages, wars, and other problems affect pregnancy. Another nation with a troubling rate of LBW is the United States, where the rate fell throughout most of the twentieth century, reaching a low of 7.0 percent in 1990. But then it rose again, with the 2012 rate at 7.99 percent, ranging from under 6 percent in Alaska to over 12 percent in Mississippi. The U.S. rate is higher than that of virtually every other developed nation (see Figure 4.7 for a sampling).

Many scientists have developed hypotheses to explain the U.S. rates. One logical possibility is assisted reproduction, since ART often leads to low-birthweight twins and triplets. However, LBW rates rose for naturally conceived babies as well, so ART cannot be the only explanation.

Added to the puzzle is the fact that several changes in maternal ethnicity, age, and health since 1990 should have decreased LBW, not increased it. For example, African Americans have LBW newborns much more often than the national average (almost 13.2 percent compared with 8 percent), and younger teenagers have smaller babies than do women in their 20s. However, since 1990 the birth rate among both groups has decreased markedly, so average LBW should decrease, not increase. Furthermore, maternal obesity and diabetes have increased since 1990; both lead to heavier babies. Nonetheless, more underweight babies are born.

Something must be amiss. One possibility is nutrition. Nations with many small newborns are also nations where hunger is prevalent. In both Chile and China, LBW fell as nutrition improved.

As for the United States, the U.S. Department of Agriculture (2014) reports an increase in the rate of *food insecurity* (measured by skipped meals, use of food stamps, and outright hunger) between the first 7 years of the twenty-first century and the next 7, from about 11 percent to about 15 percent. Hunger directly affects LBW, and food insecurity

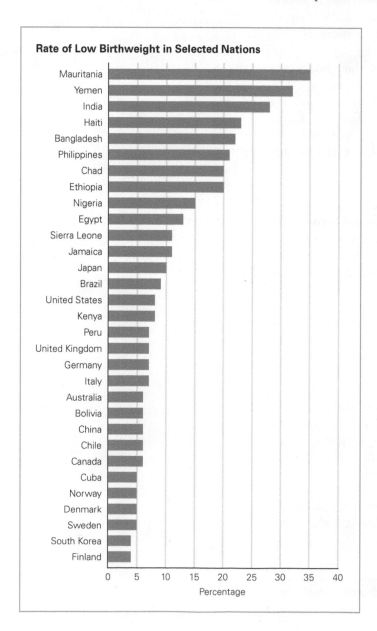

Rate of Low Birthweight in Selected Nations

FIGURE 4.7

Getting Better Some public health experts consider the rate of low birthweight to be indicative of national health, since both are affected by the same causes. If that is true, the world is getting healthier, since the LBW world average was 28 percent in 2009 but 16 percent in 2012. When all nations are included, 47 report LBW at 6 percent or less (United States and United Kingdom are not among them).

SOURCE: UNICEF, 2014

also increases chronic illness, which itself correlates with LBW (Seligman & Schillinger, 2010). Food insecurity rates are higher among women in their prime reproductive years than among middle-aged women or men of any age, and highest of all among single women with children.

Another possibility is drug use. For example, the rate of smoking and drinking among high school girls reached a low in 1992, then increased, then decreased. Most U.S. women giving birth in the first decade of the twenty-first century are in a cohort that experienced rising drug use when they were younger; they may still suffer the effects. If that is the reason, the recent decrease in drug use among teenagers will result in fewer LBW babies soon.

Another possible cause of LBW is pollution. Air pollution is decreasing in the United States. If pollution is the cause, fewer LBW babies will be born. On the other hand, many chemicals are more common in the maternal blood stream than they were. Looking at food, drug, pollution, and chemical trends in various nations will help developmentalists understand how to prevent LBW in the future.

A Growing Trend The rate of first births to women in their 40s tripled from 1990 to 2008, although most newborns (96%) have mothers under age 40. Nonetheless, prenatal testing and medical advances have made late motherhood less risky than it was, with some happy results. This mother is 42.

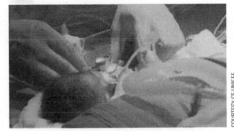

Watch **Video: Low Birthweight in India,** which discusses the causes of low birthweight among babies in India.

SUMMING UP Low birthweight, either because of slow prenatal growth or preterm birth, increases vulnerability and may slow down development lifelong. Causes are many, from drug use to hunger, and vary markedly from nation to nation. The birth process itself can worsen the effects of any prenatal risk, with the smallest newborns at particular risk for early death or lifetime impairment. In general, low SES increases the risk for low birthweight, but some international data as well as the immigrant paradox suggest that it is not simply poverty that causes underweight newborns.

WHAT HAVE YOU LEARNED?

1. What are the differences among LBW, VLBW, and ELBW?
2. What are four reasons a baby might be born LBW?
3. What are the national and international trends in low birthweight?
4. How might the father's role be one reason for immigration paradox?
5. What is the prediction for the future of an ELBW newborn who survives?

The New Family

Humans are social creatures, seeking interaction with their families and their societies. We have already seen how crucial social support is during pregnancy; social interaction may become even more important once the child is born.

The Newborn

Before birth, developing humans already affect their families through fetal movements and hormones that trigger maternal nurturance (food aversions, increased

VISUALIZING DEVELOPMENT

A Healthy Newborn

Just moments after birth, babies are administered their very first test. The APGAR score is an assessment tool used by doctors and nurses to determine whether a newborn requires any medical intervention. It tests five specific criteria of health, and the medical professional assigns a score of 0, 1, or 2 for each category. A perfect score of 10 is rare—most babies will show some minor deficits at the 1 minute mark, and many will still lose points at the 5 minute mark.

GRIMACE RESPONSE/REFLEXES

(2) A healthy baby will indicate his displeasure when his airways are suctioned—he'll grimace, pull away, cough, or sneeze.

(1) Baby will grimace during suctioning.

(0) Baby shows no response to being suctioned and requires immediate medical attention.

RESPIRATION

(2) A good strong cry indicates a normal breathing rate.

(1) Baby has a weak cry or whimper, or slow/irregular breathing.

(0) Baby is not breathing and requires immediate medical intervention.

PULSE

(2) A pulse of 100 or more beats per minute is healthy for a newborn.

(1) Baby's pulse is less than 100 beats per minute.

(0) A baby with no heartbeat requires immediate medical attention.

APPEARANCE/COLOR

(2) Body and extremities should show good color, with pink undertones indicating good circulation.

(1) Baby has some blueness in the palms and soles of the feet. Many babies exhibit some blueness at both the 1 and 5 minute mark; most warm up soon after.

(0) A baby whose entire body is blue, grey, or very pale requires immediate medical intervention.

ACTIVITY AND MUSCLE TONE

(2) Baby exhibits active motion of arms, legs, body.

(1) Baby shows some movement of arms and legs.

(0) A baby who is limp and motionless requires immediate medical attention.

REFLEXES IN INFANTS

Never underestimate the power of a reflex. For developmentalists, newborn reflexes are mechanisms for survival, indicators of brain maturation, and vestiges of evolutionary history. For parents, they are mostly delightful and sometimes amazing.

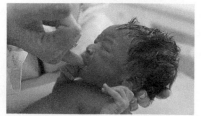

THE SUCKING REFLEX A newborn, just a few minutes old, demonstrates that he is ready to nurse by sucking on a doctor's finger.

ASTIER/BSIP/SCIENCE SOURCE/PHOTO RESEARCHERS, INC.

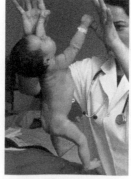

THE GRASPING REFLEX When the doctor places a finger on the palm of a healthy infant, he or she will grasp so tightly that the baby's legs can dangle in space.

PETIT FORMAT/PHOTO RESEARCHERS

THE STEP REFLEX A one-day-old girl steps eagerly forward long on legs too tiny to support her body.

JENNIE WOODCOCK; REFLECTIONS PHOTOLIBRARY/CORBIS

sleep, and more). At birth, a newborn's appearance (big hairless head, tiny toes, and so on) stirs the human heart, evident in adults' brain activity and heart rate. Fathers are often enraptured by their scraggly newborn and protective of the exhausted mothers, who may appreciate their husbands more than before, for hormonal as well as practical reasons.

Newborns are likewise responsive social creatures in the first hours of life (Zeifman, 2013). They listen, stare, cry, stop crying, and cuddle. In the first day or two, a professional might administer the **Brazelton Neonatal Behavioral Assessment Scale (NBAS),** which records 46 behaviors, including 20 reflexes. Parents who watch the NBAS are often amazed—and this fosters early parent–child connection (Hawthorne, 2009).

Technically, a **reflex** is an involuntary response to a particular stimulus. Humans of every age instinctively protect themselves (the eye blink is an example). That definition makes reflexes seem automatic. Not quite true. Actually, the strength and reliability of newborn reflexes varies depending on genes, drugs in the bloodstream, and overall health. (See Visualizing Development, p. 126.)

- *Reflexes that maintain oxygen supply.* The *breathing reflex* begins even before the umbilical cord, with its supply of oxygen, is cut. Additional reflexes that maintain oxygen are reflexive *hiccups* and *sneezes,* as well as *thrashing* (moving the arms and legs about) to escape something that covers the face.
- *Reflexes that maintain constant body temperature.* When infants are cold, they *cry, shiver,* and *tuck their legs* close to their bodies. When they are hot, they try to *push away* blankets and then stay still.
- *Reflexes that manage feeding.* The *sucking reflex* causes newborns to suck anything that touches their lips—fingers, toes, blankets, and rattles, as well as natural and artificial nipples of various textures and shapes. In the *rooting reflex,* babies turn their mouths toward anything that brushes against their cheeks—a reflexive search for a nipple—and start to suck. *Swallowing* also aids feeding, as does *crying* when the stomach is empty and *spitting up* when too much is swallowed quickly.

Other reflexes are not necessary for survival but signify the state of brain and body functions. Among them are the:

- *Babinski reflex.* When a newborn's feet are stroked, the toes fan upward.
- *Stepping reflex.* When newborns are held upright, feet touching a flat surface, they move their legs as if to walk.
- *Swimming reflex.* When held horizontally on their stomachs, newborns stretch out their arms and legs.
- *Palmar grasping reflex.* When something touches newborns' palms, they grip it tightly.
- *Moro reflex.* When someone bangs on the table they are lying on, newborns fling their arms outward and then bring them together on their chests, crying with wide-open eyes.

These reflexes are responses to experiences, not unlike an adult's sudden fear, or lust, or anger.

The senses are also responsive: New babies listen more to voices than to traffic, for instance. Thus, in many ways, newborns connect with the people of their world, who are predisposed to respond (Zeifman, 2013). If the baby performing these actions on the Brazelton NBAS were your own, you would be proud and amazed; that is part of being human.

Brazelton Neonatal Behavioral Assessment Scale (NBAS) A test often administered to newborns that measures responsiveness and records 46 behaviors, including 20 reflexes.

reflex An unlearned, involuntary action or movement in response to a stimulus. A reflex occurs without conscious thought.

Video: Newborn Reflexes shows several infants displaying the reflexes discussed in this section.

New Mothers

About half of all women experience significant physical problems soon after birth, such as healing from a c-section, painfully sore nipples, or problems with urination (Danel et al., 2003). However, worse than any of these physical problems are psychological ones. When the level of birth hormones decreases, between 8 and 15 percent of women experience **postpartum depression,** a sense of inadequacy and sadness (called *baby blues* in the mild version and *postpartum psychosis* in the most severe form) (Perfetti et al., 2004).

With postpartum depression, baby care (feeding, diapering, bathing) feels very burdensome. The newborn's cry may not compel the mother to carry and nurse her infant. Instead, the mother may have thoughts of neglecting or abusing the infant, thoughts so terrifying that she is afraid of herself.

The first sign that something is amiss may be euphoria after birth. A new mother may be unable to sleep, or to stop talking, or to push aside irrational worries. Some of this behavior is normal, but family members and medical personnel need to be alert to the mother's emotions. After the initial high, severe depression may set in, with a long-term impact on the child.

But postpartum depression is not due to hormonal changes alone. From a developmental perspective, some causes of postpartum depression (such as financial stress) predate the pregnancy; others (such as marital problems) occur during pregnancy; others correlate with birth (especially if the mother is alone and imagined a different birth than actually occurred); and still others are specific to the particular infant (such as health, feeding, or sleeping problems). Successful breast-feeding mitigates maternal depression (Figueiredo et al., 2014), one of the many reasons a lactation consultant is an important part of the new mother's support team.

postpartum depression A new mother's feelings of inadequacy and sadness in the days and weeks after giving birth.

Especially for Nurses in Obstetrics Can the father be of any practical help in the birth process? (see response, page 130)

Expecting a Girl She is obviously thrilled and ready, and they bought a crib, but he seems somewhat nervous. Perhaps someone should tell him that his involvement will help his newborn become a happy and accomplished child and adult, a source of paternal pride and joy for the next forty years or more.

101DALMATIANS/GETTY IMAGES

New Fathers

As we have seen, fathers-to-be help mothers-to-be stay healthy, nourished, and drug-free. The father's role in birth may also be crucial.

Being There

At birth, the father's presence reduces complications, in part because he reassures his wife. I observed this when my daughter, Elissa, birthed Asa (now 5, as noted in the opening of this chapter). Asa's birth took much longer than his younger brother's; Elissa's anxiety rose when the doctor and midwife discussed a possible cesarean for "failure to progress" without asking her opinion. Her husband told her, "All you need to do is relax between contractions and push when a contraction comes. I will do the rest." She listened. He did. No cesarean.

Whether or not he is present at the birth, the father's legal acceptance of the birth is important to mother and

newborn. A study of all live, single births in Milwaukee from 1993 to 2006 (151,869 babies!) found that complications correlated with several expected variables (e.g., maternal cigarette smoking) and one unexpected one—no father listed on the birth record. This connection was especially apparent for European Americans: When the mother did not list the father, rates of long labor, cesarean section, and other complications increased (Ngui et al., 2009).

Currently, about half of all U.S. women are not married when their baby is born (Monte & Ellis, 2014), but fathers are usually listed. When fathers acknowledge their role, birth is better for mother and child.

Couvade

Fathers may experience pregnancy and birth biologically, not just psychologically with stress, worry, and so on. Many fathers have symptoms of pregnancy and birth, including weight gain and indigestion during pregnancy and pain during labor (Leavitt, 2009). Among the Papua in New Guinea and the Basques in Spain, husbands used to build a hut when birth was imminent and then lie down to writhe in mock labor (Klein, 1991).

Paternal experiences of pregnancy and birth are called **couvade**— expected in some cultures, normal in many, and considered pathological in others (M. Sloan, 2009). A recent study in India found that most new fathers experienced couvade (Ganapathy, 2014). In the United States, couvade is unnoticed and unstudied, but many fathers are intensely involved with their future child (Brennan et al., 2007; Racburn, 2014).

Fathers are usually the first responders when the mother experiences postpartum depression; they may be instrumental in getting the support the mother and baby need (Cuijpers et al., 2010; Goodman & Gotlib, 2002). But fathers are vulnerable to depression, too; other people need to help. Indeed, sometimes the father experiences more problems than the mother (Bradley & Slade, 2011).

> **couvade** Symptoms of pregnancy and birth experienced by fathers.

Mutual Joy Ignore this dad's tattoo and earring, and the newborn's head wet with amniotic fluid. Instead recognize that, for thousands of years, hormones and instincts propel fathers and babies to reach out to each other, developing lifelong connections.

Parental Alliance

Remember John and Martha, the young couple whose amniocentesis revealed that their fetus had trisomy-21 (Down syndrome)? One night at 3:00 A.M., after about seven months of pregnancy, Martha was crying uncontrollably. She told John she was scared.

> "Scared of what?" he said. "Of a little baby who's not as perfect as you think he ought to be?"

// **Response for Nurses in Obstetrics** (from page 128): Usually not, unless he is experienced, well taught, or has expert guidance. But his presence provides emotional support for the woman, which makes the birth process easier and healthier for mother and baby.

"I didn't say I wanted him to be perfect," I said. "I just want him to be normal. That's all I want. Just normal."

"That is total bullshit. . . . You don't want this baby to be normal. You'd throw him in a dumpster if he just turned out to be normal. What you really want is for him to be superhuman."

"For your information," I said in my most acid tone, "I was the one who decided to keep this baby, even though he's got Down's. You were the one who wanted to throw him in a dumpster."

"How would you know?" John's voice was still gaining volume. "You never asked me what I wanted, did you? No. You never even asked me."

[Beck, 1999, p. 255]

This episode ended well, with a long, warm, and honest conversation between the two prospective parents. Each learned what their fetus meant to the other, a taboo topic until that night. Adam, their future son, became an important part of their relationship.

Their lack of communication up to this point, and the sudden eruption of unexpressed emotions, is not unusual, because pregnancy itself raises memories from childhood and fears about the future. Yet honest and intimate communication is crucial throughout pregnancy, birth, and child rearing. Such early communication between new parents helps to form a **parental alliance,** a commitment by both parents to cooperate in raising their child.

The parental alliance is especially beneficial when the infant is physically vulnerable, such as having a low birthweight. The converse is also true: Family conflict when a newborn needs extra care increases the risk of child maladjustment and parental divorce (Whiteside-Mansell et al., 2009).

parental alliance Cooperation between a mother and a father based on their mutual commitment to their children. In a parental alliance, the parents support each other in their shared parental roles.

Family Bonding

To what extent are the first hours after birth crucial for the **parent–infant bond,** the strong, loving connection that forms as parents hold, examine, and feed their newborn? It has been claimed that this bond develops in the first hours after birth when a mother touches her naked baby, just as sheep and goats must immediately smell and nuzzle their newborns if they are to nurture them (Klaus & Kennell, 1976).

However, the hypothesis that early skin-to-skin contact is *essential* for human nurturance has been proven false (Eyer, 1992; Lamb, 1982). Substantial research on monkeys begins with *cross-fostering,* a strategy in which newborns are removed from their biological mothers in the first days of life and raised by another female or even a male. A strong and beneficial relationship sometimes develops (Suomi, 2002).

This finding does not contradict the generalization that prospective parents' active involvement in pregnancy, birth, and care of the newborn benefits all three. Factors that encourage parents (biological or adoptive) to nurture their newborns may have lifelong benefits (Champagne & Curley, 2010).

The role of early contact has become apparent with **kangaroo care,** in which the newborn lies between the mother's breasts, skin-to-skin, listening to her heartbeat and feeling her body heat. Many studies find that kangaroo-care newborns sleep more deeply, gain weight more quickly, and spend more time alert than do infants with standard care (Feldman et al., 2002; Ferber & Makhoul, 2004; Gathwala et al., 2010). Father involvement may also be important, including father–infant kangaroo care (Feeley et al., 2013).

parent–infant bond The strong, loving connection that forms as parents hold, examine, and feed their newborn.

kangaroo care A form of newborn care in which mothers (and sometimes fathers) rest their babies on their naked chests, like kangaroo mothers that carry their immature newborns in a pouch on their abdomen.

ROLEX DELA PENA/EPA/NEWSCOM

Kangaroo care benefits babies, not only in the hospital but months later, either because of improved infant adjustment to life outside the womb or because of increased parental sensitivity and effectiveness. Which of these two is the explanation? Probably both.

Implementation of many strategies, especially for fragile infants and their parents, is especially needed in developing nations, where kangaroo care and other measures could reduce deaths by 20 to 40 percent (Bhutta et al., 2008). From a developmental perspective, the most difficult time for high-risk infants occurs when they leave the hospital, days or weeks after birth. At this juncture, measures to involve parents in early care are crucial. As we will see in later chapters, the relationship between parent and child develops over months and years, not merely hours. Birth is one step of a lifelong journey.

SUMMING UP   Every member of the new family contributes to their shared connection, enabling them all to thrive. The new baby has responsive senses and many reflexes. Close observation and reflection reveal how much the new baby can do. The father's support increases the likelihood of a healthy, happy newborn and mother. Postpartum depression of the mother is not rare; factors before and after birth affect how serious and long-lasting it is. Family relationships begin before conception, may be strengthened throughout pregnancy and birth, and continue throughout the life span. Bonding at birth is facilitated by early contact between mother, father, and baby, and kangaroo care benefits the baby, but neither are essential for a close parental alliance or for a healthy parent–infant relationship.

WHAT HAVE YOU LEARNED?

1. What do newborns do to aid their survival?
2. What impact do fathers have during and after birth?
3. How do fathers experience pregnancy?
4. What are the signs of postpartum depression?
5. What affects the parent–infant bond?
6. What are the results of kangaroo care?

SUMMARY

Prenatal Development

1. The first two weeks of prenatal growth are called the germinal period. During this time, the single-celled zygote multiplies into more than 100 cells that will eventually form both the placenta and the embryo. The growing organism travels down the fallopian tube to implant in the uterus.

2. The third through eighth weeks after conception make up the embryonic period. The heart begins to beat, and the eyes, ears, nose, and mouth form, the skeletal outline and inner organs form. By the eighth week, the embryo has the basic organs and features of a human, with the exception of the sex organs.

3. The fetal period extends from the ninth week until birth. In the ninth week, the sexual organs develop. By the end of the third month, all the organs and body structures have formed. The fetus attains viability at 22 weeks, when the brain can regulate basic body functions.

4. The average fetus gains approximately 4½ pounds (2,040 grams) from the 6th to the 9th month, weighing 7½ pounds (3,400 grams) at birth. Maturation of brain, lungs, and heart ensures survival of more than 99 percent of all full-term babies born in developed nations.

Birth

5. Birth typically begins with contractions that push the fetus out of the uterus and then through the vagina. The Apgar scale, which rates the newborn at one minute and again at five minutes after birth, provides a quick evaluation of the infant's health.

6. Medical assistance can speed contractions, dull pain, and save lives. However, many aspects of medicalized birth have been criticized as impersonal and unnecessary, including about half the cesareans performed in the United States. Contemporary birthing practices—such a birthing centers and, especially in some European nation, home births—are aimed at finding a balance—protecting the baby but also allowing more parental involvement and control.

Harm to the Fetus

7. Risk analysis is crucial in predicting prenatal development, because no teratogen always causes harm, but many factors affect whether harm will occur and how serious it will be.

8. Some teratogens (diseases, drugs, and pollutants) cause physical impairment, especially during the first weeks of development. Others, called behavioral teratogens, harm the fetal brain and therefore, in later life, impair cognitive abilities and affect personality.

9. Whether a teratogen harms an embryo or fetus depends on timing, dose, and genes. Public and personal health practices can protect against prenatal complications. Support and help from the father and other family members affect the pregnant woman's health.

10. Birth complications, such as unusually long and stressful labor that includes anoxia (a lack of oxygen to the fetus), have many causes, and are made worse by teratogens and other prenatal factors.

Low Birthweight: Causes and Consequences

11. Low birthweight (under 5½ pounds, or 2,500 grams), very low birthweight (VLBW—under 1500 grams), and extremely low birthweight (ELBW under 1000 grams) may arise from multiple births, placental problems, maternal illness, malnutrition, smoking, drinking, illicit drug use, and age.

12. Compared with full-term, normal weight newborns, preterm and underweight babies experience more medical difficulties and psychological problems for many years. Babies that are small for gestational age (SGA) are especially vulnerable.

13. National differences are apparent in the frequency of low birth weight, primarily because of undernourished mothers. In addition, family support may be crucial, and may be one reason for the immigration paradox, that in developed nations, women born in other nations are more likely to have full term newborns than native-born women.

The New Family

14. Humans are social animals, from the moment of birth. The Brazelton Neonatal Behavioral Assessment Scale measures 46 newborn behaviors, 20 of which are reflexes. In many ways newborns contribute to early family bonding.

15. Fathers can be supportive during pregnancy as well as helpful in birth. Paternal support correlates with shorter labor and fewer complications. Some fathers become so involved with the pregnancy and birth that they experience couvade.

16. Many women feel unhappy, incompetent, or unwell after giving birth. This may reach the level of postpartum depression. Fathers may have a crucial influence on the health and welfare of mother and child. Ideally, a parental alliance forms to help the child develop well.

17. Kangaroo care benefits all babies but especially those who are vulnerable. Mother–newborn interaction should be encouraged, although the parent–infant bond depends on many factors in addition to birth practices.

KEY TERMS

germinal period (p. 100)
embryonic period (p. 100)
fetal period (p. 100)
implantation (p. 101)
embryo (p. 102)
fetus (p. 102)
ultrasound (p. 103)
age of viability (p. 103)
Apgar scale (p. 107)

cesarean section (c-section)
 (p. 108)
doula (p. 111)
teratogen (p. 112)
behavioral teratogens (p. 112)
threshold effect (p. 113)
fetal alcohol syndrome (FAS)
 (p. 114)
false positive (p. 120)
cerebral palsy (p. 121)

anoxia (p. 121)
low birthweight (LBW) (p. 122)
very low birthweight (VLBW)
 (p. 122)
extremely low birthweight
 (ELBW) (p. 122)
preterm (p. 122)
small for gestational age (SGA)
 (p. 122)
immigrant paradox (p. 123)

Brazelton Neonatal Behavioral
 Assessment Scale (NBAS)
 (p. 127)
reflex (p. 127)
postpartum depression (p. 128)
couvade (p. 129)
parental alliance (p. 130)
parent–infant bond (p. 130)
kangaroo care (p. 130)

APPLICATIONS

1. Go to a nearby greeting-card store and analyze the cards about pregnancy and birth. Do you see any cultural attitudes (e.g., variations depending on the sex of the newborn or of the parent)? If possible, compare those cards with cards from a store that caters to another economic or ethnic group.

2. Interview three mothers of varied backgrounds about their birth experiences. Make your interviews open-ended—let them choose what to tell you, as long as they give at least a 10-minute description. Then compare and contrast the three accounts, noting especially any influences of culture, personality, circumstances, and cohort.

3. People sometimes wonder how any pregnant woman could jeopardize the health of her fetus. Consider your own health-related behavior in the past month—exercise, sleep, nutrition, drug use, medical and dental care, disease avoidance, and so on. Would you change your behavior if you were pregnant? Would it make a difference if you, your family, and your partner did not want a baby?

the first two years

PART 2

Adults don't change much in a year or two. They might have longer, grayer, or thinner hair; they might gain or lose weight; they might learn something new. But if you saw friends you hadn't seen for a few years, you'd recognize them immediately.

Imagine caring for a newborn 24/7 for a month and then leaving for two years. On your return, you might not recognize him or her. The baby would have quadrupled in weight, grown a foot taller, and sprouted a new head of hair. Behavior and emotions change, too—less crying, but new laughter and fear—including fear of you.

A year or two is not much compared with the 80 or so years of the average life. However, in their first two years, humans reach half their adult height, learn to talk in sentences, and express almost every emotion—not just joy and fear but also love, jealousy, and shame. Invisible changes in the brain are even more crucial, setting the pattern for the life span. The next three chapters describe these radical and awesome changes.

CHAPTER 5

The First Two Years:
Biosocial Development

> **What Will You Know?**
>
> 1. What part of an infant grows most in the first two years?
> 2. Does brain wiring in the first two years depend on genes or experience?
> 3. Which of the five senses develops last: seeing, hearing, tasting, touching, or smelling?
> 4. What happens if a baby does not get his or her vaccinations?

Our first child, Bethany, was born when I was in graduate school. I memorized developmental norms, including walking and talking at 12 months. In her first year, she babbled and said "mama," but at 14 months, Bethany had not yet taken her first step.

To reassure myself, I told my husband that genes were more influential than anything we did. I had read that babies in Paris are among the latest walkers in the world, and my grandmother was French. To my relief, Bethany soon began walking, and by age 5 she was the fastest runner in her kindergarten. My genetic explanation was bolstered when our next two children, Rachel and Elissa, were also slow to walk. My students with ancestors from Guatemala and Ghana bragged about their infants who walked before a year; those from China and France had later walkers. Genetic, I thought.

Fourteen years after Bethany, Sarah was born. I could afford a full-time caregiver, Mrs. Todd, from Jamaica. She thought Sarah was the most advanced baby she had ever known, except for her own daughter, Gillian. I told her that Berger children walk late.

"She'll be walking by a year," Mrs. Todd told me. "Gillian walked at 10 months."

"We'll see," I graciously replied, confident of my genetic explanation.

I underestimated Mrs. Todd. She bounced my delighted baby on her lap, day after day, and spent hours giving her "walking practice." Sarah took her first step at 12 months—late for a Todd, early for a Berger, and a humbling lesson for me.

As a scientist, I know that a single case proves nothing. My genetic explanation might be valid, especially since Sarah shares only half her genes with Bethany and since my daughters are only one-eighth French, a fraction I had ignored when they were infants.

Nonetheless, I now notice how caretakers influence every aspect of biosocial growth. As you read this chapter, you also will see that caregiving enables babies to grow, move, and learn. Development is not as straightforward and automatic, nor as genetically determined, as it once seemed. Genes provide the outline, but every moment of life after birth shapes and guides the young person to become a distinct, and special, human being.

LaunchPad

Video: Physical Development in Infancy and Childhood offers a quick review of the physical changes that occur in a child's first two years.

---

percentile A point on a ranking scale of 0 to 100. The 50th percentile is the midpoint; half the people in the population being studied rank higher and half rank lower.

failure to thrive A serious medical condition in early infancy, when the baby does not gain weight as rapidly as he or she is expected to.

FIGURE 5.1

Eat and Sleep The rate of increasing weight in the first weeks of life makes it obvious why new babies need to be fed day and night.

Body Changes

In infancy, growth is so rapid and the consequences of neglect so severe that gains are closely monitored. Medical checkups, including measurement of height, weight, and head circumference, provide the first clues as to whether an infant is progressing as expected—or not.

Body Size

Newborns lose several ounces in the first three days and then gain an ounce a day for months. Birthweight typically doubles by 4 months and triples by a year. On average, a 7-pound newborn will be 21 pounds at 12 months (9,525 grams, up from 3,400 grams grams at birth). Height increases, too: A typical baby grows 10 inches (24 centimeters) in a year.

Physical growth then slows, but not by much. Most 24-month-old children weigh almost 28 pounds (13 kilograms) and have added another 4 inches (10 centimeters) or so. Typically, 2-year-olds are half their adult height and about one-fifth their adult weight, four times heavier than they were at birth (see Figure 5.1).

At each well-baby checkup (monthly at first), growth is compared to the baby's previous numbers. Often, measurements are expressed as a **percentile,** from 0 to 100, that indicates where an individual ranks on a particular measure. Percentiles are often used for school achievement; here they are used to indicate how an infant's growth compares to other babies of the same age.

Thus, a 3-month-old's weight at the 30th percentile means that 30 percent of 3-month-old babies weigh less and 70 percent weigh more. If the percentile were 60, then 60 percent weigh less and 40 percent weigh more. The fact that the first baby is a little smaller and the second a little bigger than average is not a problem, since humans vary on every dimension. Only one baby in a 100 is exactly average, at the 50th percentile.

For any baby, however, an early sign of trouble occurs when a percentile moves 20 percent or more, either up or down. If an average baby suddenly grows more slowly, that could be the first sign of a medical condition called **failure to thrive.** If weight gain is accelerated, as when a baby at the 30th percentile is at the 60th percentile a month later, that may signal later obesity.

A dramatic shift in percentile in either direction was once blamed solely on parents. For small babies, it was thought that parents made feeding stressful, leading to "nonorganic failure to thrive." Now dozens of medical conditions have been discovered that cause failure to thrive. Thus, organic causes may impede growth. Pediatricians consider it "outmoded" to blame parents (Jaffe, 2011, p. 100).

Sleep

Throughout childhood, regular and ample sleep correlates with normal brain maturation, learning, emotional regulation, academic success, and psychological adjustment (Maski & Kothare, 2013). Lifelong, sleep deprivation can cause poor health, and vice versa. As with many health habits, sleep patterns begin in the first year.

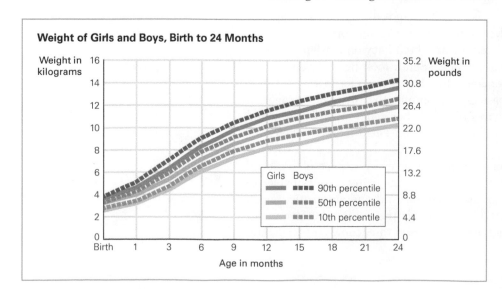

Weight of Girls and Boys, Birth to 24 Months

Same Boy, Much Changed All three photos show Conor: first at 3 months, then at 12 months, and finally at 24 months. Note the rapid growth in the first two years, especially apparent in the changing proportions of the head compared to the body and legs.

Newborns spend most of their time sleeping, about 15 to 17 hours a day. Hours of sleep decrease rapidly with maturity: The norm per day for the first 2 months is 14¼ hours; for the next 3 months, 13¼ hours; for 6 to 17 months, 12¾ hours. Remember that norms are simply averages. Among every 20 newborns in the United States, parents report that one sleeps only nine hours per day and one sleeps 19 hours (Sadeh et al., 2009) (see Figure 5.2).

Cultural differences are apparent. By age 2, the typical toddler in New Zealand sleeps 15 percent more than the typical Japanese one, 13.3 hours a day compared to 11.6 (Sadeh et al., 2010). Everywhere, full-term newborns sleep more than pre-term newborns, who need to eat every two hours.

Infants also vary in how long they sleep at a stretch. If "sleeping through the night" means sleeping from midnight to 5 A.M., half of all babies sleep through the night at least once by 3 months, but if a night is from 10 P.M. to 6 A.M., some 1-year-olds still do not sleep all night long (Russell et al., 2013).

Over the first months, the relative amount of time spent in each type or stage of sleep changes. Babies born preterm may always seem to be dozing. Full-term newborns dream a lot; about half their sleep is **REM sleep** (rapid

REM (rapid eye movement) sleep
A stage of sleep characterized by flickering eyes behind closed lids, dreaming, and rapid brain waves.

FIGURE 5.2

Good Night, Moon Average sleep per 24-hour period is given in percentiles because there is much variation in how many hours a young child normally sleeps. Other charts from this study show nighttime sleep and daytime napping. Most 1-year-olds sleep about 10 hours a night, with about 2 hours of napping, but some sleep much less. By age 3, about 10 percent have given up naps altogether. Note that these data are drawn from reports by U.S. parents, based on an Internet questionnaire. Actual sleep monitors or reports by a more diverse group of parents would show even more variation.

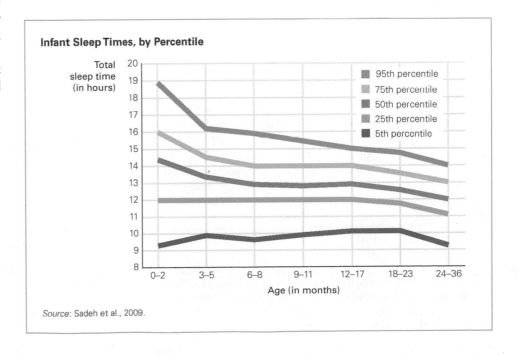

Infant Sleep Times, by Percentile

Source: Sadeh et al., 2009.

eye movement sleep), with flickering eyes and rapid brain waves. That indicates dreaming. REM sleep declines over the early weeks, as does "transitional sleep," the dozing, half-awake stage. At 3 or 4 months, quiet sleep (also called *slow-wave sleep*) increases markedly.

By about 3 months, all the various states of waking and sleeping become more evident. Thus, although newborns often seem half asleep, neither in deep sleep nor wide awake, by 3 months most babies have periods of alertness and periods of deep sleep (when noises do not rouse them).

Sleep varies not only because of biology (age and genes) but also because of caregiver actions. Babies who are fed cow's milk and cereal sleep longer and more soundly—easier for parents but not good for the baby. Social environment matters more directly: If parents respond to predawn cries with food and play, babies learn to wake up early and often, night after night, which may not be good for anyone (Sadeh et al., 2009).

Insufficient sleep may become a serious problem for parents as well as for infants, because "[p]arents are rarely well-prepared for the degree of sleep disruption a newborn infant engenders, and many have unrealistic expectations about

 ## opposing perspectives

Where Should Babies Sleep?

Traditionally, most middle-class U.S. infants slept in cribs in their own rooms; it was feared that they would be traumatized if their parents had sex. By contrast, most infants in Asia, Africa, and Latin America slept near their parents, a practice called **co-sleeping,** and sometimes in their parents' bed, called **bed-sharing.** In those cultures, nighttime parent–child separation was considered cruel.

Even today, at baby's bedtime, Asian and African mothers worry more about separation, whereas European and North American mothers worry more about privacy. A survey found that parents act on these fears: The extremes were 82 percent of Vietnam babies co-sleeping compared with 6 percent in New Zealand (Mindell et al., 2010) (see Figure 5.3). Cohort is also significant. In the United States, bed-sharing doubled from 1993 to 2010, from 6.5 percent to 13.5 percent (Colson et al., 2013).

This difference in practice may seem related to income since low-SES families are less likely to have an extra room and women with less education are more likely to sleep beside their baby (Colson et al., 2013). But even wealthy Japanese families often co-sleep. By contrast, many low-income North American families find a separate bedroom for their children. Co-sleeping results from culture and custom, not merely income, which makes it a difficult practice to change (Ball & Volpe, 2013).

co-sleeping A custom in which parents and their children (usually infants) sleep together in the same room.

bed-sharing When two or more people sleep in the same bed. If one of those people is an infant, some researchers worry that the adult will roll over on the infant.

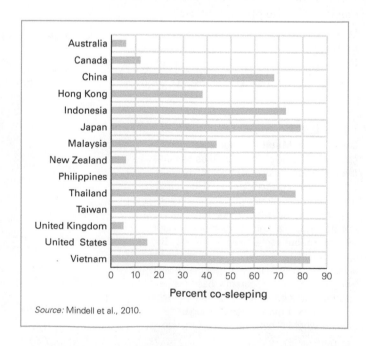

FIGURE 5.3

Awake at Night Why the disparity between Asian and non-Asian rates of co-sleeping? It may be that Western parents use a variety of gadgets and objects—monitors, night lights, pacifiers, cuddle cloths, sound machines—to accomplish the same things Asian parents do by having their infant beside them.

Source: Mindell et al., 2010.

the first few postnatal months." As a result many parents become "desperate" and institute patterns that they may later regret. (Russell et al., 2013, p. 68). This is more common in first-time parents; sleep problems are less often reported for later-born children.

An Internet study of more than 5,000 North American children under age 3 found that, according to their parents, sleep was a problem for 25 percent (Sadeh et al., 2009). Of course, parents are more troubled by their baby's difficulty going to sleep, or staying asleep, than the baby is. This does not render sleep difficulties insignificant; overtired parents are less patient and responsive.

Parents will be frustrated if they expect their infant to conform to the parents' sleep–wake schedule because infant brain patterns and digestion do not allow young babies to sleep quietly all night long. Maternal depression and family dysfunction are more common when infants wake up frequently at night (Piteo et al., 2013).

Parent reactions shape infant sleep patterns, which in turn affect the parents (Sadeh et al., 2010). Ideally, mutual adaptations allow everyone's needs to be met, but, as the Opposing Perspectives feature explains, this is more controversial than it seems.

Especially for New Parents You are aware of cultural differences in sleeping practices, which raises a very practical issue: Should your newborn sleep in bed with you? (see response, page 143)

The argument for bed-sharing is that the parents can quickly respond to a hungry or frightened baby without needing to get up to feed or comfort their infant. Breast-feeding, often done every hour or two at first, is less exhausting when the mother can stay in bed as she nurses.

Yet the argument against bed-sharing rests on a chilling statistic: Sudden infant death is twice as likely when babies sleep beside their parents (Vennemann et al., 2012). (Sudden infant death syndrome is discussed at the end of this chapter.) Many young parents occasionally go to sleep after drinking or drugging. If their baby is beside them, bed-sharing (not merely co-sleeping) is dangerous.

Since many ethnic groups co-sleep as a cultural practice, instead of arguing against it, experts seek ways to make it safe (Ball & Volpe, 2013). One innovation is the creation of a "co-sleeper" (an attachment to the parents' bed), which avoids soft quilts or rollover danger.

One reason for opposite practices is that adults are affected by their own early experiences. This phenomenon is called *ghosts in the nursery* because new parents bring decades-old memories into the bedrooms of their children. Those ghosts can encourage either co-sleeping or separate rooms.

For example, compared with Israeli adults who, as infants, had slept near their parents, those who had slept communally with other infants (as sometimes occurred on kibbutzim) were more likely to interpret their own infants' nighttime cries as distress, requiring comfort (Tikotzky et al., 2010). That is how a ghost affects current behavior: If parents think their crying babies are frightened, lonely, and distressed, they want to respond. Quick responses are easier with co-sleeping.

But remember that infants learn from experience. If babies become accustomed to bed-sharing, they will crawl into their parents' bed long past infancy. Parents might lose sleep for years because they wanted more sleep when their babies were small.

Developmentalists hesitate to declare either co-sleeping or separate bedrooms best because the issue is "tricky and complex" (Gettler & McKenna, 2010, p. 77). Sleeping alone may encourage independence—a trait appreciated in some cultures, abhorred in others. Past experiences (ghosts in the nursery) affect us all: Should some ghosts be welcomed and others banned?

Infant at Risk? Sleeping in the parents' bed is a risk factor for SIDS in the United States, but don't worry about this Japanese girl. In Japan, 97 percent of infants sleep next to their parents, yet infant mortality is only 3 per 1,000—compared with 7 per 1,000 in the United States. Is this bed, or this mother, or this sleeping position protective?

SUMMING UP Birthweight doubles, triples, and quadruples by 4 months, 12 months, and 24 months, respectively. Height increases by about a foot (about 30 centimeters) in the first two years. Such norms are useful as general guidelines, but personal percentile rankings over time are more telling. They indicate whether a particular infant's brain and body are growing appropriately. With maturation, sleep becomes regular, dreaming becomes less common, and distinct sleep–wake patterns develop. The youngest infants sleep more hours in total but for less time at a stretch; by age 1, most babies sleep longer at night, with a nap or two during the day. Cultural and caregiving practices influence norms, schedules, and expectations.

WHAT HAVE YOU LEARNED?

1. What specific facts indicate that infants grow rapidly in the first year?
2. Why are pediatricians not troubled when an infant is consistently small, say at the 20th percentile in height and weight?
3. How much do newborns usually sleep and dream?
4. How do sleep patterns change from birth to 18 months?

Brain Development

head-sparing A biological mechanism that protects the brain when malnutrition disrupts body growth. The brain is the last part of the body to be damaged by malnutrition.

From two weeks after conception to two years after birth, the brain grows more rapidly than any other organ, from about 25 percent of adult weight at birth to 75 percent at age 2 (see Figure 5.4). Prenatal and postnatal brain growth (measured by head circumference) affects later cognition (Gilles & Nelson, 2012). If teething or a stuffed-up nose temporarily slows weight gain, nature slows growth of the body but not the brain, a phenomenon called **head-sparing.**

FIGURE 5.4
Growing Up Two-year-olds are totally dependent on adults, but they have already reached half their adult height and three-fourths of their adult brain size.

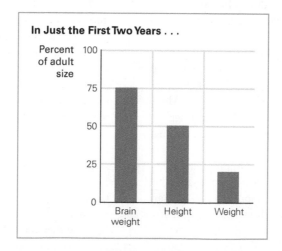

In Just the First Two Years . . .

Connections in the Brain

Head circumference provides a rough idea of how the brain is growing, which is why medical checkups include measurement of skull circumference. The distance around the head typically increases about 38 percent (from 13 to 18 inches, or from 33 to 46 centimeters) in the first year. Much more significant (although harder to measure) are changes in the brain's communication system. To understand this, we review the basics of neurological development (see Visualizing Development, p. 144).

Communication within the central nervous system (CNS)—the brain and spinal cord—begins with nerve cells, called **neurons.** Most neurons are created before birth, at a peak production rate of 250,000 new cells per minute in midpregnancy (Purves et al., 2004). Some of those early brain cells die before birth, as the brain prunes as well as proliferates neurons (Stiles & Jernigan, 2010).

At birth, the human brain has billions of neurons. Some are deep inside the brain in a region called the *brain stem,* which controls automatic responses such as heartbeat, breathing, temperature, and arousal. Others are in the midbrain, in

neuron One of billions of nerve cells in the central nervous system, especially in the brain.

areas that affect emotions and memory. And most neurons (about 70 percent) are in the **cortex,** the brain's six outer layers (sometimes called the *neocortex*). The cortex is crucial: Most thinking, feeling, and sensing occur in the cortex, although parts of the midbrain join in (Johnson, 2011).

The last part of the brain to mature is the **prefrontal cortex,** the area for anticipation, planning, and impulse control. It is not, as once thought, "functionally silent during most of infancy" (Grossmann, 2013, p. 303). Nonetheless, many connections between emotions and logic have not yet formed. The prefrontal cortex gradually becomes more efficient over the next decades (Wahlstrom et al., 2010). (**Developmental Link:** A major discussion of the growth of the prefrontal cortex is in Chapter 14.)

Specialization

All areas of the brain specialize, becoming fully functioning at different ages. Brain stem regions maintain breathing and heartbeat, and thus can sustain life by seven months after conception, or even earlier with advanced medical care. Until the brain stem begins to function, the fetus is not viable outside the womb.

Some particular areas in the midbrain underlie emotions and impulses. These functions are apparent in the first year and are shared with many other animals. For humans, emotional regulation and impulse control continue to develop throughout childhood, as those parts of the brain mature.

Specialized regions in the cortex allow particular kinds of perception and cognition, first cognition of exciting, social interactions and later cognition of more abstract thoughts (Grossmann, 2013). These areas reach final maturation in adulthood, by about age 25.

Many examples of specialization are in the cortex. There is a visual cortex, an auditory cortex, and an area dedicated to the sense of touch for each body part— including each finger of a person and each whisker of a rat (Barnett et al., 2006). These sensory areas require maturation and learning, but all are present at birth.

Humans have a much larger frontal cortex relative to body size than any other animal, and humans have many areas that are activated and coordinated with various experiences. That is why people can plan and create better than any mouse, whale, or chimpanzee.

Dendrites Sprouting

Within and between areas of the central nervous system, neurons are connected to other neurons by intricate networks of nerve fibers called **axons** and **dendrites** (see Figure 5.5). Each neuron has a single axon and numerous dendrites, which spread out like the branches of a tree. The axon of one neuron meets the dendrites of other neurons at intersections called **synapses,** which are critical communication links within the brain.

To be more specific, neurons communicate by sending electrochemical impulses through their axons to synapses, to be picked up by the dendrites of other neurons. The dendrites bring the message to the cell bodies of their neurons, which, in turn, convey the message via their axons to the dendrites of other neurons.

Axons and dendrites do not touch at synapses. Instead, the electrical impulses in axons typically cause the release of chemicals called **neurotransmitters,** which carry information from the axon of the sending neuron, across a pathway called the **synaptic gap,** to the dendrites of the receiving neuron, a process speeded up by myelination (**Developmental Link:** Myelination is discussed in detail in Chapter 8.)

cortex The outer layers of the brain in humans and other mammals. Most thinking, feeling, and sensing involves the cortex.

prefrontal cortex The area of the cortex at the very front of the brain that specializes in anticipation, planning, and impulse control.

// **Response for New Parents** (from page 141): From the psychological and cultural perspectives, babies can sleep anywhere as long as the parents can hear them if they cry. The main consideration is safety: Infants should not sleep on a mattress that is too soft, nor beside an adult who is drunk or drugged. Otherwise, each family should decide for itself.

axon A fiber that extends from a neuron and transmits electrochemical impulses from that neuron to the dendrites of other neurons.

dendrite A fiber that extends from a neuron and receives electrochemical impulses transmitted from other neurons via their axons.

synapse The intersection between the axon of one neuron and the dendrites of other neurons.

neurotransmitter A brain chemical that carries information from the axon of a sending neuron to the dendrites of a receiving neuron.

synaptic gap The pathway across which neurotransmitters carry information from the axon of the sending neuron to the dendrites of the receiving neuron.

Nature, Nurture, and the Brain

The mechanics of neurological functioning are varied and complex; neuroscientists hypothesize, experiment, and discover more each day. Brain development begins with genes and other biological elements, but hundreds of epigenetic factors affect brain development from the first to the final minutes of life. Particularly important in human development are experiences: Plasticity means that dendrites form or atrophy is response to nutrients and events. The effects of early nurturing experiences are lifelong, as proven many times in mice; research on humans suggests similar effects.

NATURE

Human brains are three times as large per body weight and take years longer to mature than the brains of any other creature, but the basics of brains are the same from mouse to elephant. New dendrites form and unused ones die—especially in infancy and adolescence. Brain plasticity is lifelong.

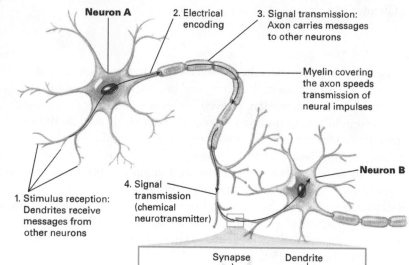

Neuron A

2. Electrical encoding

3. Signal transmission: Axon carries messages to other neurons

Myelin covering the axon speeds transmission of neural impulses

Neuron B

1. Stimulus reception: Dendrites receive messages from other neurons

4. Signal transmission (chemical neurotransmitter)

Synapse   Dendrite

Axon

Neuron B

Neuron A

Neurotransmitters

In the synapse—an intersection between axon and dendrite—neurotransmitters carry information from one neuron to another.

PHOTO: STOCKBYTE / GETTY IMAGES

NURTURE

In the developing brain, connections from axon to dendrite reflect how a baby is treated. In studies of rats, scientists learned that when a mother mouse licks her newborn its methylation of a gene (called Nr3c1) is reduced, allowing increased serotonin to be released by the hypothalamus and reducing stress hormones. Baby mice who were frequently licked and nuzzled by their mothers developed bigger and better brains!

Researchers believe that, just as in rats, the human mothers who cuddle, cradle, and caress their babies shape their brains for decades.

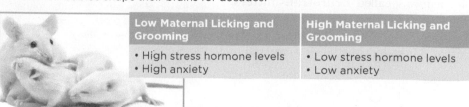

Low Maternal Licking and Grooming	High Maternal Licking and Grooming
• High stress hormone levels • High anxiety	• Low stress hormone levels • Low anxiety

Exuberance and Pruning

At birth, the brain contains at least 100 billion neurons, more than a person needs. Some of these neurons disappear in programmed cell death, and some new neurons will be created, but not as many as were created before birth. By contrast, the newborn's brain has far fewer dendrites and synapses than the person will eventually need. During the first months and years, rapid growth and refinement in axons, dendrites, and synapses occur, especially in the cortex. Dendrite growth is the major reason that brain weight triples from birth to age 2 (Johnson, 2011).

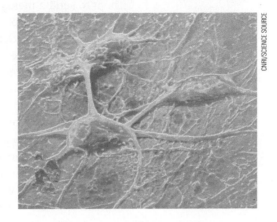

An estimated fivefold increase in dendrites in the cortex occurs in the 24 months after birth, with about 100 trillion synapses being present at age 2. According to one expert, "40,000 new synapses are formed every second in the infant's brain" (Schore & McIntosh, 2011, p. 502).

FIGURE 5.5

How Two Neurons Communicate The infant brain contains billions of neurons, each with one axon and many dendrites. Every electrochemical message causes thousands of neurons to fire, each transmitting the message across the synapse to neighboring neurons. This electron micrograph shows neurons greatly magnified, with their tangled but highly organized and well-coordinated sets of dendrites and axons.

This extensive *postnatal* brain growth is highly unusual for mammals. It occurs in humans because heads cannot grow large enough before birth to contain the brain networks needed to sustain human development. Although prenatal brain development is remarkable, it is limited because the human pelvis is relatively small, so the newborn head must be much smaller than the adult head to make birth possible. For that reason, unlike other mammals, humans must nurture and protect their offspring for more than a decade while the child's brain continues to develop (Konner, 2010).

Early dendrite growth is called **transient exuberance**: *exuberant* because it is so rapid and *transient* because some of it is temporary. The expansive brain growth is followed by **pruning.** Just as a gardener might prune a rose bush by cutting away some growth to enable more, or more beautiful, roses to bloom, unused brain connections atrophy and die.

transient exuberance The great but temporary increase in the number of dendrites that develop in an infant's brain during the first two years of life.

pruning When applied to brain development, the process by which unused connections in the brain atrophy and die.

As one expert explains it, there is an "exuberant overproduction of cells and connections followed by a several year long sculpting of pathways by massive elimination" (Insel, 2014, p. 1727). Notice the word *sculpting,* as if a gifted artist created an intricate sculpture from raw marble or wood. Human infants are gifted and flexible artists, developing their brains as needed for whatever family, culture, or society they happen to be born into.

Thinking and learning require connections among many parts of the brain, a process made more efficient because some potential connections are pruned. For example, to understand any sentence in this text, you need to know the letters, the words, the surrounding text, the ideas they convey, and how they relate to your other thoughts and experiences. You also realize that your understanding differs from that of another, especially if that other person grew up in a home and nation unlike yours. That realization begins long past infancy.

Babies' brains have the same requirements, with pruning first in the sensory cortex (especially if a baby does not hear or see anything) and then in other parts of the brain. No wonder it takes years to learn to read (see the Thinking Critically feature in Chapter 6), and no wonder your brain automatically reads these roman letters, and, for most of you, is befuddled when viewing Arabic, Cyrillic, or Chinese words.

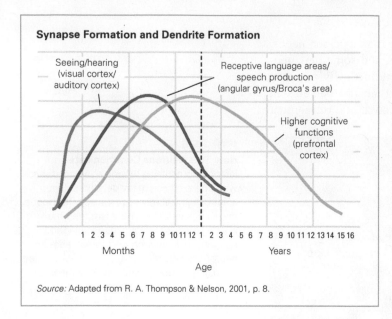

Synapse Formation and Dendrite Formation

Seeing/hearing (visual cortex/auditory cortex)

Receptive language areas/speech production (angular gyrus/Broca's area)

Higher cognitive functions (prefrontal cortex)

1 2 3 4 5 6 7 8 9 10 11 12 | 1 2 3 4 5 6 7 8 9 10 11 12 13 14 15 16
Months | Years

Age

Source: Adapted from R. A. Thompson & Nelson, 2001, p. 8.

FIGURE 5.6

Brain Growth in Response to Experience
These curves show the rapid rate of experience-dependent synapse formation for three functions of the brain (senses, language, and analysis). After the initial increase, the underused neurons are gradually pruned, or inactivated, as no functioning dendrites are formed from them.

experience-expectant brain functions
Brain functions that require certain basic common experiences (which an infant can be expected to have) in order to develop normally.

experience-dependent brain functions
Brain functions that depend on particular, variable experiences and that therefore may or may not develop in a particular infant.

Experience Shapes the Brain

The specifics of brain structure and growth depend not only on genes and maturation: Experience may be even more crucial. Infant brain organization itself depends partly on input, and some dendrites wither away because they are never used—that is, no experiences have caused them to send a message to other neurons.

Expansion and pruning of dendrites occur for every aspect of early experience, from noticing musical rhythms to understanding emotions (Scott et al., 2007). Experience—both expected and varied—shapes the infant brain, as pruning eliminates unused connections.

Strangely enough, this loss of dendrites increases brainpower. The space between neurons in the human brain—especially in regions for advanced, abstract thought—is far greater than the space in chimpanzee brains (Miller, 2010). It may seem logical that the more densely packed neurons of chimps would make them smarter than people, but the opposite is true. The probable explanation is that having more space for dendrite formation allows more connections as well as more pruning, thus fostering complex thinking.

Further evidence of the benefit of cell death comes from one of the sad symptoms of fragile X syndrome (described in Chapter 3), "a persistent failure of normal synapse pruning" (Irwin et al., 2002, p. 194). Affected children experience intellectual slowness without this pruning; their dendrites are too dense and long, making thinking difficult. Similar problems occur for children with autism: their brains are unusually large and full, which makes communication between neurons less efficient (Lewis et al., 2013).

Thus, pruning is essential. Normally, as brains mature, the process of extending and eliminating dendrites is exquisitely attuned to experience, as the appropriate links in the brain are established, protected, and strengthened. As with the rose bush, pruning needs to be done carefully, allowing further growth.

Without certain experiences, some pruning may occur that limits later thought rather than aiding it. One group of scientists speculates that "lack of normative experiences may lead to overpruning of neurons and synapses, both of which may lead to reduction of brain activity" (Moulson et al., 2009, p. 1051).

Necessary and Possible Experiences

What are those needed "normative experiences"? A scientist named William Greenough identified two experience-related aspects of brain development (Greenough et al., 1987):

- **Experience-expectant brain function.** Certain functions require basic experiences in order to develop, just as a tree requires water. Those experiences are part of almost every infant's life, and thus, almost every human brain grows as human genes direct. Brains need and expect such experiences; development would suffer without them.
- **Experience-dependent brain function.** Some brain functions depend on particular experiences. These specific experiences are not essential: They happen to infants in some families and cultures but not in others. Because of experience-dependent experiences, humans can be quite different from one another, yet all fully human.

The basic, expected experiences *must* happen for normal brain maturation to occur, and they almost always do. For example, in deserts and in the Arctic, on isolated farms and in crowded cities, almost all babies have things to see, objects to manipulate, and people to love them. Babies everywhere welcome such experiences: They look around, they grab for objects, they smile at people. As a result, baby brains develop. Without such expected experiences, brains might wither.

In contrast, dependent experiences *might* happen; because of them, one brain differs from another, even though both brains are developing normally. Experiences vary, such as which language babies hear, what faces they see, whether curiosity is encouraged, or how their mother reacts to frustration.

Depending on those particulars, infant brains vary in structure and connections; some dendrites grow and some neurons thrive while others die (Stiles & Jernigan, 2010). Consequently, experience-expectant events make all people similar, yet everyone is unique because each undergoes particular experience-dependent experiences.

An important application of experience-expectant and experience-dependent brain development comes from research on twins (Tucker-Drob et al., 2011). Generally, children who grow up in low-income families tend to have lower intelligence scores than those in higher income families, especially when the family is stressed by having two babies to raise at the same time. Is this difference an experience-expectant or experience-dependent result? It depends.

Until about 10 months, no matter what their SES, families with twins provide adequate experience-expectant circumstances (things to see, people to love). However, once the babies begin walking and talking, those from high-SES families are more likely to be encouraged to explore, talk, and play. Consequently, almost all high-SES toddlers have adequate experience-dependent conditions for intellectual growth. When differences appear in their IQ, they can usually be traced to genetic differences, not experiential ones.

Some low-SES families encourage experience-dependent cognition and some do not, and the results are likely to become evident when the families have toddler twins. Whatever intelligence differences appear between twins in low-SES families are likely attributable to differences in experience-dependent stimulation, but for twins in high-SES families, experience-dependent stimulation is likely to be sufficient (Tucker-Drob et al., 2011).

Examples from Bird Brains

The distinction between essential and variable input to the brain's networks can be made for all mammals. But some of the most persuasive research has been done with songbirds. All male songbirds have a brain region dedicated to listening and reproducing sounds (experience-expectant), but birds of the same species that happen to live in different locations produce slightly different songs (experience-dependent) (Konner, 2010).

These birdsongs are not unlike regional accents, as with English-speaking adults who grew up in Kingston (Jamaica) or Kolkata (India) or Kalamazoo (United States). Indeed, accents vary even by neighborhood in any large city.

Birds inherit genes that produce the brain cells they need, which might be neurons dedicated to learning new songs (canaries) or to finding hidden seeds (chickadees). That is experience-expectant: Songs and seeds are essential. For the dendrites and neurons to connect as needed within the particular ecological niche, birds *depend* on specific experiences with learning songs or finding seeds (Barinaga, 2003).

A human example comes from face recognition: All infants need to see faces (experience-expectant), but which particular face differences they learn to notice depends on who they see, as the following explains.

Especially for Parents of Grown Children Suppose you realize that you seldom talked to your children until they talked to you and that you often put them in cribs and playpens. Did you limit their brain growth and their sensory capacity? (see response, page 149)

⚗️ a view from science

Face Recognition

Unless you have *prosopagnosia* (face blindness, relatively uncommon), the *fusiform face area* of your brain is astonishingly adept at face recognition. This area is primed among newborns, who are quicker to recognize a face they have just seen once than older children and adults (Zeifman, 2013). However, because of experience-expectancies, every face is fascinating early in life: Babies stare at pictures of monkey faces and photos of human ones, at drawings and toys with faces, as well as at live faces.

Soon, experiences refine perception, and experience-dependent learning begins (de Heering et al., 2010). By 3 months, babies smile more readily at familiar people and are more accurate at differentiating faces from their own ethnic group (called the *own-race effect*). Babies are not prejudiced: The own-race effect results from limited multiethnic experience.

Indeed, children of one ethnicity, adopted and raised exclusively among people of another ethnicity, recognize differences among people of their adopted group more readily than differences among people of their biological group (Telzer et al., 2013).

The importance of early experience is confirmed by two studies. In the first study, from 6 to 9 months of age infants were repeatedly shown a book with pictures of six monkey faces, each with a name written on the page (see photo). One-third of the infants' parents read the names while showing the pictures; another one-third said only "monkey" as they turned each page; the final one-third simply turned the pages with no labeling.

At 9 months, infants in all three groups viewed pictures of six *unfamiliar* monkeys. The infants who had heard names of monkeys were better at distinguishing one new monkey from another than were the infants who saw the same picture book but did not hear each monkey's name (Scott & Monesson, 2010).

Now consider the second study. It is known that most people do not notice the individuality of newborns. Some even claim that "all babies look alike." However, one study found that 3-year-olds with younger siblings were much better at recognizing differences between photos of unfamiliar newborns than were 3-year-olds with no younger brothers or sisters (Cassia et al., 2009). This finding shows, again, that experience matters, contributing to development of dendrites in the fusiform face area.

The ability to differentiate faces improves with age—you are now quicker to recognize your best friend than you were as a child. Distinguishing individual faces is best learned via early exposure, but adults can learn to recognize individuals of other ethnic groups or even individual animals of the same species or breed. This recognition takes slightly longer without early experience involving dozens of named individuals from that group, but it is never too late to learn. Infancy is a sensitive period, but plasticity is lifelong.

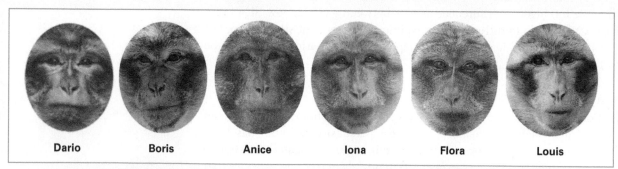

Dario   Boris   Anice   Iona   Flora   Louis

Iona Is Not Flora If you heard that Dario was not Louis or Boris, would you stare at unfamiliar monkey faces more closely in the future? For 6-month-olds, the answer is yes.

Harming the Infant Brain

Thus far, we have focused on the many normal variations that families offer babies; most infants develop well within their culture. For brain development, it does not matter whether a person learns French or Farsi or expresses emotions dramatically or subtly (e.g., throwing themselves to the floor or merely pursing their lips, a cultural difference). However, the research has also found that infant brains do not develop well if they do not have the basic experiences that all humans expect and need.

Lack of Stimulation

To begin with, infants need stimulation. Playing with a young baby, allowing varied sensations, and encouraging movement (arm waving in the early months, walking later on) are all fodder for brain connections. Severe lack of stimulation stunts the brain, as has been shown many times, not only with mice but also with humans. As one review explains, "enrichment and deprivation studies provide powerful evidence of . . . widespread effects of experience on the complexity and function of the developing system" (Stiles & Jernigan, 2010, p. 345).

This does not mean that babies require spinning, buzzing, multitextured, and multicolored toys. In fact, such toys may be a waste of money. Infants are fascinated by simple objects and facial expressions. Fortunately, although elaborate infant toys are not needed, there is no evidence that they harm the brain; babies prevent overstimulation by ignoring them. A simple application of what has been learned about the prefrontal cortex is that hundreds of objects, from the very simple to the quite complex, can capture an infant's attention.

Stress and the Brain

In addition to lack of stimulation, some specific experiences are particularly harmful, especially in the first six months (Jansen et al., 2010). If the brain produces an overabundance of stress hormones (as when an infant is frequently terrified, or when the whole family experiences a massive earthquake and flood), sometimes that damages the brain's later functioning.

If the brain later produces too few stress hormones, that might make the person emotionally flat (never happy, sad, or angry). Note that this is an emotional response. An infant might be terrified (by yelling, frightening faces, witnessed abuse) without directly being hurt.

Exactly how and when this happens is not yet clear; research finds conflicting conclusions (Jansen et al., 2010). Some stress seems part of every infant's life: It may even be experience-expectant, necessary for later emotional development. But there is a limit to how much stress an infant can accommodate, and too much early stress is likely to be maladaptive later on (Propper & Holochwost, 2013).

For example, years later, a kindergarten teacher might notice that one child becomes furious or terrified at a slight provocation and another child seems indifferent to everything. Why? In both cases, the underlying cause could be excessive stress-hormone production in infancy, changing how that child's brain responds to stress.

Shaken Baby Syndrome

Another example is much more direct, the consequence of adults who do not understand the immaturity of the infant brain. Because the prefrontal cortex has not yet developed, telling infants to stop crying is pointless because they cannot *decide* to stop crying. Such decisions require brain maturity not yet present.

Some adults react to crying by shaking a baby. This can cause **shaken baby syndrome,** a life-threatening condition that occurs when infants are shaken back and forth sharply and quickly. That stops the crying because blood vessels in the brain rupture and neural connections break. Pediatricians consider shaken baby syndrome an example of *abusive head trauma* (Christian et al., 2009). Death is the worst consequence; lifelong intellectual impairment is the more likely one.

Not every infant who has neurological symptoms of head trauma is the victim of abuse. In fact, legal experts worry that some caregivers are falsely accused of shaking a baby when other organic causes of brain damage occur (Byard, 2014).

// **Response for Parents of Grown Children** (from page 147): Probably not. Brain development is programmed to occur for all infants, requiring only the stimulation that virtually all families provide—warmth, reassuring touch, overheard conversation, facial expressions, movement. Extras such as baby talk, music, exercise, mobiles, and massage may be beneficial but are not essential.

shaken baby syndrome A life-threatening injury that occurs when an infant is forcefully shaken back and forth, a motion that ruptures blood vessels in the brain and breaks neural connections.

Nonetheless, infant brains are more vulnerable and infant behavior less controllable than adults', so the response to a screaming, frustrating baby should be to comfort or walk away, never to shake, yell, or hit.

Lest you cannot imagine the frustration that some parents feel when their baby cries, consider what one mother in Sweden said about her colicky baby, now age 4.

> There were moments when, both me and my husband… when she was apoplectic and howling so much that I almost got this thought, 'now I'll take a pillow and put over her face just until she quietens down, until the screaming stops' (Landgren et al., 2012).

Severe Social Deprivation

The developmental community was stunned and saddened by the discovery of a girl named Genie, born in 1957. Genie spent most of her childhood tied to a chair, never hearing human speech (her father barked and growled at her) or feeling love, because her parents were severely disturbed. After being discovered at age 13, she eventually responded to affection and learned to talk, but she never spoke or responded as a normal child would. Most developmentalists concluded that her rescue came too late; her brain had already passed the sensitive period for development of many abilities.

But Genie was just one person, and as you remember from Chapter 1, one case is not proof of any general principle. Perhaps Genie had been born with brain damage. Or perhaps her early care after the rescue was itself traumatic (Rymer, 1994).

More research, with more participants, was needed but would be unethical to perform with humans. Consequently, Marian Diamond, William Greenough, and their colleagues studied some "deprived" rats (raised alone in small, barren cages) and compared them with "enriched" rats (raised in large cages with toys and other rats). In this experiment, both deprived and enriched rats were killed and their brains studied. The brains of the enriched rats were larger and heavier, with more dendrites (M. C. Diamond, 1988; Greenough & Volkmar, 1973).

A Fortunate Pair Elaine Himelfarb (shown in the background), of San Diego, California, is shown here in Bucharest about to adopt 22-month-old Maria. This joyous moment may be represented through Maria's childhood— or maybe not.

Much research with other mammals confirms that isolation and sensory deprivation harm the developing brain. Social and emotional development are especially affected by deprivation. This is further explored with longitudinal studies of orphans from Romania, as described in Chapter 7.

Intervention

The fact that infant brains respond to their circumstances suggests that waiting until proof that a young child is mistreated is waiting too long. At birth, babies begin to adapt to their world, becoming withdrawn and quiet if their caregivers are depressed or becoming loud and demanding if that is the best way to get fed.

Such early reactions help babies survive but set patterns that are destructive later on. Thus, understanding development as dynamic and interactive means helping caregivers from the start, not waiting until destructive patterns are established (Tronick & Beegly, 2011).

A program to do this, beginning with high-risk mothers *before* any evidence of problems arose and including individualized support that did not require the mothers to leave their homes, resulted in less stress for the mothers and improved language development in the infants (Lowell et al., 2011). Developmentalists want this for every infant, either formally as in this program, or informally as when a relative or a neighbor helps a new mother with whatever she needs.

Implications for Caregivers

Developmental discoveries about early brain development have many implications for loving, low-risk caregivers as well as those at high risk. First, since each brain region follows a sequence of growing, connecting, and pruning, it helps to know which developmental events are experience-expectant and when those expectations arise.

For example, proliferation and pruning begin at about 4 months in the visual and auditory cortexes, which explains why very young infants are attentive to sights and sounds. Consequently, remedies for blind or deaf infants should occur early in life to prevent atrophy of those brain regions. Hearing-impaired infants whose difficulties are recognized and remediated with cochlear implants before age 2 become more adept at understanding and expressing language than those with the same losses who get implants after 2½ (Tobey et al., 2013). Brain expectancy is the reason.

The language areas of the brain develop most rapidly between the ages of 6 and 24 months; that is when infants most need to hear speech, so they can recognize the characteristics of their local language long before they utter a word (Saffran et al., 2006). At the same time, some experiences are probably meaningless before the brain is ready. A 6-month-old might be indifferent to books, yet book-reading may be a favorite activity at 12 months. Infants respond to whatever their brains need; that's why musical mobiles, cars on the street, and, best of all, animated caregivers, are fascinating.

This preference reflects **self-righting,** the inborn drive to remedy deficits. Infants with few toys develop their brains by using whatever is available. Their brains expect human interaction and whatever objects their parents find to interest them. Neurons are designed to develop dendrites; plasticity is apparent from the beginning of life (Tomalski & Johnson, 2010).

Thus, how people respond to infants echoes lifelong. This means that caressing a newborn, singing to a preverbal infant, and showing affection toward a toddler may be essential to developing the child's full potential. If such experiences are missing, lifelong brain damage may result.

> **self-righting** The inborn drive to remedy a developmental deficit; literally, to return to sitting or standing upright after being tipped over. People of all ages have self-righting impulses, seeking emotional as well as physical balance.

SUMMING UP Brain growth is rapid during the first months of life, when the number of dendrites and synapses within the cortex increases exponentially. By age 2, the brain already weighs three-fourths of its adult weight. Pruning of underused and unconnected dendrites begins in the sensory areas and then occurs in other areas. Although some brain development is maturational, experience is also essential—both the universal experiences that almost every infant has (experience-expectant brain development) and the particular experiences that reflect the child's family or culture (experience-dependent brain development). Infant brains need stimulation—though not so much as to become overwhelming—for dendrites to grow and neurological connections to proliferate. Extreme early stress or social deprivation may permanently harm the person's brain.

WHAT HAVE YOU LEARNED?

1. What is the difference between the cortex and the rest of the brain?
2. How does the brain change from birth to age 2?
3. How can pruning increase brain potential?
4. What is the difference between experience-expectant and experience-dependent brain function?
5. What is the effect of stress or social deprivation on early brain development?
6. What should caregivers remember about brain development when an infant cries? ●

Perceiving and Moving

You learned in Chapter 2 that Piaget called the first period of intelligence the *sensorimotor* stage, emphasizing that cognition develops from the senses and motor skills. The same concept—that infant brain development depends on sensory experiences and early activity—underlies the discussion you have just read. Experience molds the brain, which seeks an array of sensory and motor experiences.

The Senses

Every sense functions at birth. Newborns have open eyes, sensitive ears, and responsive noses, tongues, and skin. Indeed, very young babies use all their senses to attend to everything. For instance, in the first months of life, they smile at strangers and suck almost anything in their mouths.

Why are new infants not more discriminating? Because sensation precedes perception. Then perception leads to cognition. Thus, in order to learn, babies begin by responding to every sensation that might be significant; they will learn which sensations are meaningful.

sensation The response of a sensory system (eyes, ears, skin, tongue, nose) when it detects a stimulus.

Sensation occurs when a sensory system detects a stimulus, as when the inner ear reverberates with sound or the eye's retina and pupil intercept light. Thus, sensations begin when an outer organ (eye, ear, nose, tongue, or skin) meets anything that can be seen, heard, smelled, tasted, or touched.

Genetic selection over more than 100,000 years affects all the senses. Humans cannot hear what mice hear, or see what bats see, or smell what puppies smell; humans do not need those sensory abilities. However, survival requires babies to respond to people, and newborns innately do so with every sense they have (Konner, 2010; Zeifman, 2013).

perception The mental processing of sensory information when the brain interprets a sensation.

Perception occurs when the brain processes a sensation. This happens in the cortex, usually as the result of a message from one of the sensing organs, such as from the eye to the visual cortex. If a particular sensation occurs often, it connects with past experience, making a particular sight worth interpreting (M. E. Diamond, 2007).

Some sensations are beyond a baby's comprehension at first. A newborn has no idea that the letters on a page might have significance, that Sister's face should be distinguished from Brother's, or that the smells of roses and garlic have different connotations. Perceptions require experience.

Infants' brains are especially attuned to their own repeated social experiences. Thus, a newborn named Emily has no concept that *Emily* is her name, but she has the brain and auditory capacity to hear sounds in the usual speech range (not the high sounds that only dogs can hear) and an inborn preference for repeated patterns and human speech, so she attends to people saying her name. At about 4 months, when her auditory cortex is rapidly creating and pruning dendrites, the repeated word *Emily* is perceived as well as sensed, especially because that sound emanates from the people Emily has learned to love. Before 6 months, Emily may open her eyes and turn her head when her name is called. It will take many more months before she tries to say "Emmy" and still longer before she knows that *Emily* is indeed her name.

Thus, perception follows sensation, when sensory stimuli are interpreted in the brain. Then cognition follows perception, when people think about what they have perceived. (Later, cognition no longer depends on sensation: People imagine, fantasize, hypothesize.) The sequence from sensation to perception to cognition requires that an infant's sense organs function. No wonder the parts of the cortex dedicated to hearing, seeing, and so on develop rapidly. Now some specifics.

Hearing

The sense of hearing develops during the last trimester of pregnancy and is already quite acute at birth, when certain sounds trigger reflexes, even without conscious perception. Sudden noises startle newborns, making them cry. Familiar, rhythmic sounds such as a heartbeat are soothing: That is one reason kangaroo care reduces newborn stress, because the infant's ear rests on the mother's chest. (**Developmental Link:** Kangaroo care is explained in Chapter 4.)

A newborn's hearing can be checked with advanced equipment; this is routinely done at most hospitals in North America and Europe, since early remediation benefits deaf infants. Screening is needed later as well because some infants develop hearing losses in the early months (Harlor & Bower, 2009). Normally, even in the first days of life, infants turn their heads at a sound. Soon they can pinpoint the source of the noise.

Because of maturation of the language areas of the cortex, even 4-month-old infants attend to voices, developing expectations of the rhythm, segmentation, and cadence of spoken words long before comprehension (Minagawa-Kawai et al., 2011). Soon, sensitive hearing combines with the maturing brain to distinguish patterns of sounds and syllables.

Infants become accustomed to their native language, such as which syllable is stressed (dialects vary), if changing inflection matters (as in Chinese), whether certain sound combinations are repeated, and so on. All this is based on very careful listening to human speech, including speech not directed toward them with words they do not yet understand (Buttelmann et al., 2013).

Seeing

By contrast, vision is immature at birth. Although in mid-pregnancy the eyes open and are sensitive to bright light (if the pregnant woman is sunbathing in a bikini, for instance), the fetus has nothing much to see. Consequently, newborns are legally blind; they focus only on things between 4 and 30 inches (10 and 75 centimeters) away (Bornstein et al., 2005).

Almost immediately, experience combines with maturation of the visual cortex to improve the ability to see shapes and notice details. Vision improves so rapidly that researchers are hard-pressed to describe the day-by-day improvements (Dobson et al., 2009).

By 2 months, infants not only stare at faces, but also, with perception, smile. (Smiling can occur earlier but not because of perception.) As perception builds, visual scanning improves. Thus, 3-month-olds look closely at the eyes and mouth, smiling more at smiling faces than at angry or expressionless ones. They pay attention to patterns, colors, and motion (Kellman & Arterberry, 2006).

Especially for Nurses and Pediatricians The parents of a 6-month-old have just been told that their child is deaf. They don't believe it because, as they tell you, the baby babbles as much as their other children did. What do you tell them? (see response, page 155)

Who's This? Newborns don't know much, but they look intently at faces. Repeated sensations become perceptions, so in about 6 weeks, this baby will smile at Dad, Mom, a stranger, the dog, and at every other face. If this father in Utah responds like typical fathers everywhere, by 6 months cognition will be apparent: The baby will chortle with joy at seeing him but become wary of unfamiliar faces.

BLEND IMAGES / GETTY IMAGES

binocular vision The ability to focus the two eyes in a coordinated manner in order to see one image.

Because **binocular vision** (coordinating both eyes to see one image) is impossible in the womb (nothing is far enough away), many newborns seem to use their two eyes independently, momentarily appearing wall-eyed or cross-eyed. Normally, experience leads to rapid focus and binocular vision. Usually between 2 and 4 months, both eyes focus on a single thing (Wang & Candy, 2010).

This ability aids in the development of depth perception, which has been demonstrated in 3-month-olds, although it was once thought to develop much later. Toddlers who are experienced crawlers and walkers are very adept at deciding if a given path is safe to cross upright or is best traversed sitting or crawling. This illustrates early coordination of the senses and motor skills (Kretch & Adolph, 2013). (This does not mean that toddlers can be trusted not to fall off tables or out of windows.)

Tasting and Smelling

As with vision and hearing, smell and taste function at birth and rapidly adapt to the social world. Infants learn to appreciate what their mothers eat, first through breast milk and then through smells and spoonfuls of the family dinner.

Some herbs and plants contain natural substances that are medicinal. The foods of a particular culture may aid survival: For example, bitter foods provide some defense against malaria, hot spices help preserve food and thus work against food poisoning, and so on (Krebs, 2009). Thus, for 1-year-olds, developing a taste for their family cuisine may save their lives.

Learning About a Lime As with every other normal infant, Jacqueline's curiosity leads to taste and then to a slow reaction, from puzzlement to tongue-out disgust. Jacqueline's responses demonstrate that the sense of taste is acute in infancy and that quick brain perceptions are still to come.

Families who eat foods that protected their community pass on those preferences to their children throughout childhood. Taste preferences endure when a person migrates to another culture or when historical circumstances change so that a particular food that was once protective is no longer so. Indeed, one reason for the obesity epidemic is that, when starvation was a threat, families sought high-fat foods; now their descendants enjoy French fries, whipped cream, and bacon, jeopardizing their health.

Adaptation also occurs for the sense of smell. When breast-feeding mothers used a chamomile balm to ease cracked nipples during the first days of their babies' lives, those babies preferred that smell almost two years later, compared with babies whose mothers used an odorless ointment (Delaunay-El Allam et al., 2010).

As babies learn to recognize each person's scent, they prefer to sleep next to their caregivers, and they nuzzle into their caregivers' chests—especially when the adults are shirtless. One way to help infants who are frightened of water (some love bathing, some hate it) is for the parent to join the baby in the tub. The smells of the adult's body mix with the smell of soap. The smell, touch, sight, and voice of the caretaker are pleasant, making the entire experience comforting.

Touch and Pain

The sense of touch is acute in infants. Wrapping, rubbing, massaging, and cradling are each soothing to many new babies. Even when their eyes are closed, some infants stop crying and visibly relax when held securely by their caregivers. The newborn's ability to be comforted by touch is tested in the Brazelton NBAS, described in Chapter 4. In the first year of life, their heart rate slows and babies relax when stroked gently and rhythmically on the arm (Fairhurst et al., 2014).

Pain and temperature are not among the traditional five senses, but they are often connected to touch. Some babies cry when being changed, distressed at the sudden coldness on their skin. Some touches are unpleasant—a poke, pinch, or pat—although this varies from one baby to another.

Scientists are not certain about infant pain. Some experiences that are painful to adults (circumcision, setting of a broken bone) are much less so to newborns, although that does not mean that newborns never feel pain (Reavey et al., 2014). For many newborn medical procedures, from a pinprick to minor surgery, a taste of sugar right before the event is an anesthetic. An empirical study conducted with an experimental group and a control group found that newborns typically cry lustily when their heel is pricked (to get a blood sample, routine after birth) but not if they have had a drop of sucrose beforehand (Harrison et al., 2010).

Some people imagine that the fetus feels pain; others say that the sense of pain does not mature until months after birth. Many young infants cry inconsolably, at times; digestive pain is the usual explanation. Often, infants fuss before their first tooth erupts: Teething is said to be painful. However, these explanations are unproven; infant crying may not indicate pain, and absence of crying does not necessarily mean absence of pain (true for adults, too).

Physiological measures, including stress hormones, erratic heartbeats, and rapid brain waves, are studied to assess pain in preterm infants, who typically undergo many procedures that would be painful to an adult (Holsti et al., 2011). Infants' brains are immature: We cannot assume that they do, or do not, feel pain, or feel it in the way that we do.

// **Response for Nurses and Pediatricians** (from page 153): Urge the parents to begin learning sign language and investigate the possibility of cochlear implants. Babbling has a biological basis and begins at a specified time, in deaf as well as hearing babies. If their infant can hear, sign language does no harm. If the child is deaf, however, noncommunication may be destructive.

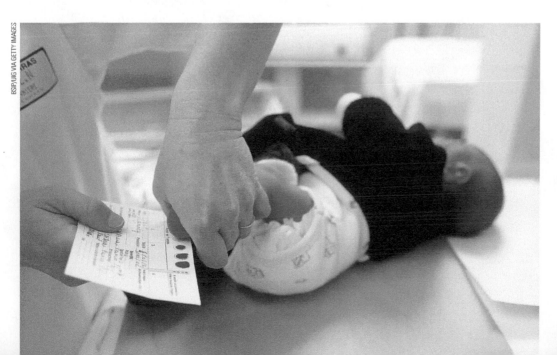

The First Blood Test This baby will cry, but most experts believe the heel prick shown here is well worth it. The drops of blood will reveal the presence of any of several genetic diseases, including sickle cell disease, cystic fibrosis, and phenylketonuria. Early diagnosis allows early treatment, and the cries subside quickly with a drop of sugar water or a suck of breast milk.

Motor Skills

motor skills The learned abilities to move some part of the body, in actions ranging from a large leap to a flicker of the eyelid. (The word *motor* here refers to movement of muscles.)

The most dramatic **motor skill** (any movement ability) is independent walking, which explains why I worried when Bethany did not take a step (as described in the introduction to this chapter). All the basic motor skills, from the newborn's head-lifting to the toddler's stair-climbing, develop over the first two years.

The first evidence of motor skills is in the reflexes, explained in Chapter 4. Although the definition of reflexes implies that they are automatic, their strength and duration vary from one baby to another. Many newborn reflexes disappear by 3 months, but some morph into more advanced motor skills.

Caregiving and culture matter. Reflexes become skills if they are practiced and encouraged. As you saw in the chapter's beginning, Mrs. Todd set the foundation for my fourth child's walking when Sarah was only a few months old. Similarly, some very young babies can swim—if adults have helped them in the water.

Gross Motor Skills

gross motor skills Physical abilities involving large body movements, such as walking and jumping. (The word *gross* here means "big.")

Deliberate actions that coordinate many parts of the body, producing large movements, are called **gross motor skills.** These skills emerge directly from reflexes and proceed in a *cephalocaudal* (head-down) and *proximodistal* (center-out) direction. Infants first control their heads, lifting them up to look around. Then they control their upper bodies, their arms, and finally their legs and feet. (See At About This Time.)

Sitting develops gradually; it requires developing the muscles to steady the top half of the body. By 3 months, most babies can sit propped up in a lap. By 6 months, they can usually sit unsupported. Babies never propped up (as in some institutions for abandoned babies) sit much later.

Crawling is another example of the head-down and center-out direction of skill mastery. When placed on their stomachs, many newborns reflexively try to lift

OBSERVATION QUIZ Which of these skills has the greatest variation in age of acquisition? Why? (see answer, page 158)

at about this time

Age Norms (in Months) for Gross Motor Skills

	When 50% of All Babies Master the Skill	When 90% of All Babies Master the Skill
Sit unsupported	6	7.5
Stands holding on	7.4	9.4
Crawls (creeps)	8	10
Stands not holding	10.8	13.4
Walking well	12.0	14.4
Walk backward	15	17
Run	18	20
Jump up	26	29

Note: As the text explains, age norms are affected by culture and cohort. The first five norms are based on babies in five continents [Brazil, Ghana, Norway, USA, Oman, and India] (World Health Organization, 2006). The next three are from a USA-only source (Coovadia & Wittenberg, 2004; based on Denver II [Frankenburg et al., 1992]). Mastering skills a few weeks earlier or later does not indicate health or intelligence. Being very late, however, is a cause for concern.

their heads and move their arms as if they were swimming. As they gain muscle strength, infants wiggle, attempting to move forward by pushing their arms, shoulders, and upper bodies against whatever surface they are lying on.

Usually by 5 months, infants add their legs to this effort, inching forward (or backward) on their bellies. Exactly when this occurs depends partly on how much "tummy time" the infant has had to develop the muscles, and that, of course, is affected by the caregiver's culture (Zachry & Kitzmann, 2011).

Between 8 and 10 months after birth, most infants can lift their midsections and crawl (or *creep,* as the British call it) on "all fours," coordinating the movements of their hands and knees. Crawling depends on experience as well as maturation. Some normal babies never do it, especially if the floor is cold, hot, or rough, or if they have always lain on their backs (Pin et al., 2007). It is not true that babies *must* crawl to develop normally.

All babies find some way to move before they can walk (inching, bear-walking, scooting, creeping, or crawling), but many resist being placed on their stomachs. Overweight babies master gross motor skills later than thinner ones: Practice and balance is harder when the body is heavy (Slining et al., 2010). As soon as they are able, babies walk (falling frequently but getting up undaunted and trying again), because walking is much quicker than crawling, and it has another advantage—free hands (Adolph et al., 2012).

The dynamic system underlying every motor skill has three interacting elements: strength, maturation, and practice. We illustrate these three here with walking.

1. *Muscle strength.* Newborns with skinny legs and 3-month-olds buoyed by water make stepping movements, but 6-month-olds on dry land do not; their legs are too chubby for their underdeveloped muscles. As they gain strength, they stand and then walk.
2. *Brain maturation.* The first leg movements—kicking (alternating legs at birth and then both legs together or one leg repeatedly at about 3 months)—occur without much thought. As the brain matures, deliberate leg action becomes possible.
3. *Practice.* Unbalanced, wide-legged, short strides become a steady, smooth gait.

This last item, *practice,* is powerfully affected by caregiving before the first independent step. Some adults spend hours helping infants walk (holding their hands or the back of their shirts) or providing walkers (dangerous if not supervised).

Once toddlers are able to walk by themselves, they practice obsessively, barefoot or not, at home or in stores, on sidewalks or streets, on lawns or in mud. They fall often, but that does not stop them; "they average between 500 and 1,500 walking steps per hour so that by the end of each day, they have taken 9,000 walking steps and traveled the length of 29 football fields" (Adolph et al., 2003, p. 494).

Fine Motor Skills

Small body movements are called **fine motor skills.** The most valued fine motor skills are finger movements, enabling humans to write, draw, type, tie, and so on. Movements of the tongue, jaw, lips, and toes are fine movements, too.

Advancing and Advanced At 8 months, she is already an adept crawler, alternating hands and knees, intent on progress. Probably she will be walking before a year.

fine motor skills Physical abilities involving small body movements, especially of the hands and fingers, such as drawing and picking up a coin. (The word *fine* here means "small.")

Video: Fine Motor Skills in Infancy and Toddlerhood
http://qrs.ly/1h4eozr

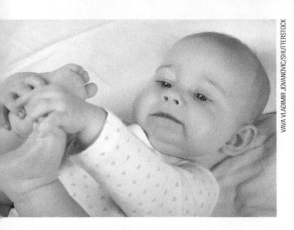

Success At 6 months, this baby is finally able to grab her toes. From a developmental perspective, this achievement is as significant as walking, as it requires coordination of feet and fingers. Note her expression of determination and concentration.

// **ANSWER TO OBSERVATION QUIZ**
(from page 156): Jumping up, with a three-month age range for acquisition. The reason is that the older an infant is, the more impact both nature and nurture have.

Actually, mouth skills precede finger skills by many months (newborns can suck; chewing precedes drawing by a year or more). Since every culture encourages finger dexterity, children practice finger movements, and adults teach how to use spoons, or chopsticks, or markers.

By contrast, mouth skills such as spitting or biting are not praised. (Only other children admire blowing bubbles with gum.) Eventually, most children try to whistle, an advanced skill that some adults have not mastered. One mouth skill, pronunciation, develops gradually without special encouragement, although some older children and bilingual adults need focused practice to say difficult sounds.

Regarding hand skills, newborns have a strong reflexive grasp but lack control. During their first 2 months, babies excitedly stare and wave their arms at objects dangling within reach. By 3 months, they can usually touch such objects, but because of limited eye–hand coordination, they cannot yet grab and hold on unless an object is placed in their hands.

By 4 months, infants sometimes grab, but their timing is off: They close their hands too early or too late. Finally by 6 months, with a concentrated, deliberate stare, most babies can reach, grab, and grasp almost any object that is of the right size. Some can even transfer an object from one hand to the other. Almost all can hold a bottle, shake a rattle, and yank a sister's braids.

Toward the end of the first year and throughout the second, finger skills improve as babies master the pincer movement (using thumb and forefinger to pick up tiny objects). They can feed themselves first with hands, then fingers, then utensils (Ho, 2010). (See At About This Time.)

As with gross motor skills, fine motor skills are shaped by culture and opportunity. For example, when given "sticky mittens" (with Velcro) that allow grabbing, infants master hand skills sooner than usual. Their perception advances as well (Libertus & Needham, 2010; Soska et al., 2010). More generally, all senses and motor skills expand the baby's cognitive awareness, with practice advancing both skill and cognition (Leonard & Hill, 2014).

In the second year, grasping becomes more selective, as experience sculpts the brain. Toddlers learn when *not* to pull at a sister's braids or an adult's earrings or glasses. (Wise adults remove accessories before holding a baby.)

Dynamic Sensory-Motor Systems

Young human infants are, physiologically, an unusual combination of motor ineptness (they cannot walk for many months), sensory acuteness (all senses function at birth), and curiosity (Konner, 2010). What a contrast to kittens, for instance, who are born deaf, with eyes sealed shut, and who stay beside their mother although they can walk.

Human newborns listen and look from day 1, eager to practice every skill as soon as possible. An amusing example is rolling over. At about 3 months, infants can roll over from their stomachs to their backs, but not vice versa because their arms are no help when they are flat on their backs. Once they can roll from stomach to back, many babies do so and then fuss, turtle-like, with limbs flailing. When some kind bystander flips them back on their stomachs, they roll over and then fuss again. The same occurs for stairs: They can crawl up before they dare come down. Instead, they want someone to carry them down so they can crawl up again.

The most important experiences are perceived with interacting senses and skills, in dynamic systems. Breast milk, for instance, is a mild sedative, so the newborn literally feels happier at Mother's breast, connecting that pleasure with taste, touch, smell, and sight. But in order for all those joys to occur, the infant must actively suck at the nipple (an inborn motor skill, which becomes more efficient with practice).

Because of brain immaturity, *cross-modal perception* (using several senses to understand the same experience) is particularly common in young infants. Synesthesia (when a sensation is perceived with more than one sense, as when a sound has a color) is also more common in early infancy, because the various parts of the brain are less distinct (Ozturk et al., 2013).

at about this time

Age Norms (in Months) for Fine Motor Skills

	When 50% of All Babies Master the Skill	When 90% of All Babies Master the Skill
Grasps rattle when placed in hand	3	4
Reaches to hold an object	4.5	6
Thumb and finger grasp	8	10
Stacks two blocks	15	21
Imitates vertical line (drawing)	30	39

Source: World Health Organization, 2006.

Infants respond to motion as well as to sights and sounds. Many new parents soothe their baby's distress by rocking, carrying, or even driving (with the baby in a safety seat) while crooning a lullaby; here again, infant comfort is dynamically connected with social interaction. Massage is especially calming when infants realize that the touch comes from a familiar caregiver who simultaneously provides auditory and visual stimulation. Even vacuuming the carpet with the baby in a sling may quiet a fussy baby because steady noise, changing sights, and carrying combine to soothe distress.

By 6 months, babies have learned to coordinate senses and skills, expecting another person's lip movements to synchronize with speech, for instance (Lewkowicz, 2010). Grabbing, crawling, and walking are dynamic systems that allow exploration, which in turn fosters cognition (Leonard & Hill, 2014).

The time at which walking occurs is a better predictor than age of a child's verbal ability, perhaps because walking children elicit more language from caregivers than crawling ones do (Walle & Campos, 2014). No wonder Piaget linked cognitive and physical development, as Chapter 6 describes.

Cultural Variations

Culture affects every infant move. All healthy infants develop skills in the same sequence, but the age of acquisition varies because each culture encourages certain kinds of practice. When U. S. infants are grouped by ethnicity, generally African American babies are ahead of Latino babies when it comes to walking. In turn, Latino babies are ahead of those of European descent.

Internationally, the earliest walkers are in Africa, where many well-nourished and healthy babies walk at 10 months. The latest walkers may be in rural China (15 months) (Adolph & Robinson, 2013). (Infants prevented from walking, or who are confined to cribs in institutions, walk much later.)

What accounts for normal variation? The power of genes is suggested not only by ethnic differences but also by identical twins, who begin to walk on the same day more often than fraternal twins do. Striking individual differences are apparent in infants' strategies, effort, and concentration in mastering motor skills, again suggesting something inborn (Thelen & Corbetta, 2002).

But much more than genes contribute to variations, as the example that opened this chapter shows. Cultural patterns affect acquisition of every sensory and motor

Bossa Nova Baby? This boy in Brazil demonstrates his joy at acquiring the gross motor skill of walking, which quickly becomes dancing whenever music plays.

skill, with the important of practice evident in hundreds of studies on infant walking (Adolph and Robinson, 2013).

Early reflexes may not fade if culture and conditions allow extensive practice. This has been demonstrated with legs (the stepping reflex), hands (the grasping reflex), and crawling (the swimming reflex). Senses and motor skills are part of a complex and dynamic system in which practice counts (Thelen & Corbetta, 2002). Nutrition makes a difference as well: Both malnourished and overweight children are slower to develop motor skills.

Cross-cultural research finds that some caregivers (including those from Jamaica like Mrs. Todd, who cared for my youngest daughter) provide rhythmic stretching exercises for their infants as part of daily care; their infants are among the world's youngest walkers (Adolph & Berger, 2005). Other cultures discourage or even prevent infants from crawling or walking.

The people of Bali, Indonesia, never let their infants crawl, because babies are considered divine and crawling is for animals (Diener, 2000). Similar reasoning appeared in colonial America, where "standing stools" were designed for children so they could strengthen their legs without sitting or crawling (Calvert, 2003).

By contrast, traditionally the Beng people of the Ivory Coast are proud when their babies start to crawl but do not let them walk until at least 1 year. Although the Beng do not recognize the connection, one reason for this prohibition may be birth control: Beng mothers do not resume sexual relations until their baby takes a first step (Gottlieb, 2000). Another culture with late walkers are the Ache, who live in the jungles of Paraguay, where poisonous snakes could kill a young child. The Ache hold their babies near them day and night; the children first walk on their own at about two years (Adolph & Robinson, 2013).

Although variation in the timing of the development of motor skills is normal, slow development relative to the norm within an infant's culture suggests that attention should be paid: Early visual, auditory, and motor difficulties are much easier to remedy than the same problems discovered later in childhood.

Remember the dynamic systems of senses and motor skills: If one aspect of the system lags behind, the other parts may be affected as well. On the other hand, early walkers are thrilled to have within reach dozens of objects they were unable to explore before—caregivers beware.

SUMMING UP All the senses function at birth, with hearing the most acute sense and vision the least developed. Every sense allows perception to develop and furthers social understanding. Caregivers are soon recognized by sight, touch, smell, and voice. Using both eyes in coordination to understand depth takes several weeks. Pain perception seems less acute for newborns than for older children and adults.

Gross motor skills follow a genetic timetable for maturation; they are also affected by practice and experience. Caregivers and cultures that encourage movement of the infant body in the first months of life are likely to have babies who walk before a year. Fine motor skills also develop with time and experience, combining with the senses as part of dynamic systems. Mouth skills precede finger skills, although both are immature in the early months and years. All the skills are practiced relentlessly as soon as possible, advancing learning and thinking.

WHAT HAVE YOU LEARNED?

1. What is the relationship between perception and sensation?
2. What particular sounds and patterns do infants pay attention to?
3. How does an infant's vision change over the first year?

4. What is universal and what is cultural in the development of gross motor skills in infancy?

5. Why do infants develop fine motor skills using their fingers later than gross motor skills?   ●

Surviving in Good Health

Although precise worldwide statistics are unavailable, the United Nations estimates that more than 8 billion children were born between 1950 and 2015. Almost a billion of them died before age 5.

Although most of those 1 billion deaths could have been prevented, far more would have died without recent public health measures. In 1950 1 young child in 5 died, but only about 1 child in 20 is projected to die in 2014 (United Nations, 2015). In earlier centuries, more than half of all newborns died in infancy. Those are official statistics; probably millions more died without being counted.

Better Days Ahead

In the twenty-first century in developed nations, 99.9 percent of newborns who survive the first month live to adulthood. Even in the poorest nations, where a few decades ago infant mortality was accepted as part of the human experience, 99 percent of newborns who survive those early days live at least until age 15, although the rate of newborn death is much higher than it would be with good medical care. Some nations have seen dramatic improvement. Chile's rate of infant mortality, for instance, was almost 4 times higher than the rate in the United States in 1970; now the two rates are even (see Figure 5.7).

The world death rate in the first five years of life has dropped about 2 percent per year since 1990, (Rajaratnam et al., 2010) with the rate in developed nations less than 1 in 1,000, and in least developed nations about 1 in 200. Public health measures (clean water, nourishing food, immunization) deserve most of the credit.

As children survive, parents focus more effort and income on each child, having fewer children overall. That advances the national economy, which allows for better schools and health care. Infant survival and maternal education are the

FIGURE 5.7

More Babies Are Surviving Improvements in public health—better nutrition, cleaner water, more widespread immunization—over the past three decades have meant millions of survivors. In some of the very least developed nations (e.g., Malawi) rates are still 1 in 100.

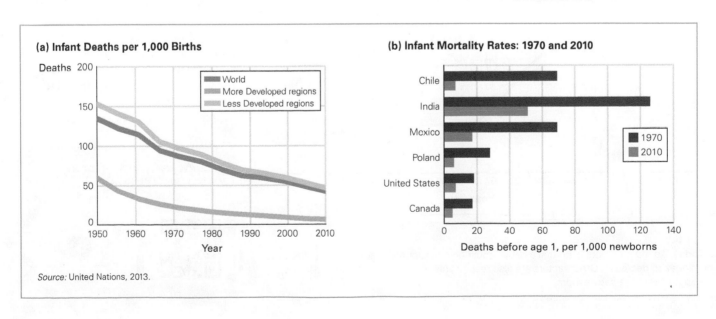

(a) Infant Deaths per 1,000 Births

Deaths
World
More Developed regions
Less Developed regions

(b) Infant Mortality Rates: 1970 and 2010

Chile, India, Mexico, Poland, United States, Canada

1970
2010

Deaths before age 1, per 1,000 newborns

Source: United Nations, 2013.

two main reasons the world's fertility rate in 2010 was half the 1950 rate. This is found in data from numerous nations, especially developing ones, where educated women have far fewer children than those who are uneducated (de la Croix, 2013).

If there were enough public health professionals, the current newborn and child death rate could be cut in half again. Public health measures help parents as well as children, via better food distribution, less violence, more education, cleaner water, and more widespread immunization (Farahani et al., 2009).

Well Protected Disease and early death are common in Africa, where this photo was taken, but neither is likely for 2-year-old Salem. He is protected not only by the nutrition and antibodies in his mother's milk but also by the large blue net that surrounds them. Treated bed nets, like this one provided by the Carter Center and the Ethiopian Health Ministry, are often large enough for families to eat, read, as well as sleep together, without fear of malaria-infected mosquitoes.

a case to study

Scientist at Work

Susan Beal, a young scientist with four children, studied SIDS deaths in Australia for years, responding to phone calls, often at 5 or 6 A.M., that another baby had died. At first she felt embarrassed to question the parents, sometimes arriving before the police or the coroner. But parents were grateful to know that someone was trying to understand the puzzle that had just killed their infant. She realized that parents tended to blame themselves and each other, so she sought to get them talk to each other, as she reassured them that scientists shared their bewilderment. (Scan the QR code below with your smartphone to watch a short interview with Susan Beal.)

As a scientist, she noted dozens of circumstances at each death. Some things did not matter (such as birth order), others increased the risk (maternal smoking and lambskin blankets). A breakthrough came when Beal noticed an ethnic variation: Australian babies of Chinese descent died of SIDS far less often than did those of European descent. Genetic? Most experts thought so. But Beal noticed that almost all SIDS babies were sleeping on their stomachs, contrary to the Chinese custom of placing infants on their backs to sleep. She developed a new hypothesis: Sleeping position mattered.

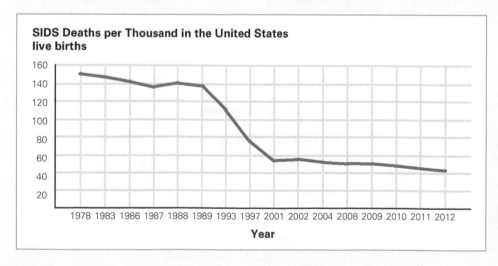

SIDS Deaths per Thousand in the United States live births

http://www.youtube.com/watch?v=ZIPt5q2QJ9I

FIGURE 5.8

Alive Today As more parents learn that a baby should be on his or her "back to sleep," the SIDS rate continues to decrease. Other factors are also responsible for the decline—fewer parents smoke cigarettes in the baby's room.

SOURCES: NATIONAL VITAL STATISTICS REPORTS, *FORTHCOMING*; HOYERT & XU, 2012; MURPHY ET AL., 2012; KOCHANEK ET AL., 2011; MINIÑO ET AL., 2007; HOYERT ET AL., 2005; MATHEWS ET AL., 2003; HOYERT ET AL., 1999; GARDNER & HUDSON, 1996; MACDORMAN & ROSENBERG, 1993; MONTHLY VITAL STATISTICS REPORT, 1980.

Considering Culture

Often cultural variations are noted in infant care. There are many ways to care for a baby, with all the experience-dependent versions of child care designed to raise children who are prepared for their culture. One theme of this book, as introduced in Chapter 1, it that difference is not deficit. Usually variations are simply alternative ways to meet basic infant needs for nutrition, love, and care.

Sometimes, however, one mode of infant care is much better than another, and here a cross-cultural perspective is especially useful, as evidenced in research about **sudden infant death syndrome (SIDS).**

Every year until the mid-1990s, tens of thousands of infants died of SIDS, called *crib death* in North America and *cot death* in England. Tiny infants smiled at their caregivers, waved their arms at rattles that their small fingers could not yet grasp, went to sleep seemingly healthy, and never woke up. As parents mourned, scientists asked why, testing hypotheses (the cat? the quilt? natural honey? homicide? spoiled milk?) to no avail. Sudden infant death was a mystery. To some extent, it still is, but one risk factor—sleeping on the stomach—is now known worldwide, thanks to the work of one scientist, as described in A Case to Study.

> **sudden infant death syndrome (SIDS)**
> A situation in which a seemingly healthy infant, usually between 2 and 6 months old, suddenly stops breathing and dies unexpectedly while asleep.

To test her hypothesis, Beal convinced a large group of non-Chinese parents to put their newborns to sleep on their backs. Almost none of them died suddenly. After several years of gathering data, she drew a surprising conclusion: Back-sleeping protected against SIDS. Her published reports (Beal, 1988) caught the attention of doctors in the Netherlands, where pediatricians had told parents to put their babies to sleep on their stomachs. Two Dutch scientists (Engelberts & de Jonge, 1990) recommended back-sleeping; thousands of parents took heed. SIDS was reduced in Holland by 40 percent in one year—a stunning replication.

Replication and application spread. By 1994, a "Back to Sleep" campaign in nation after nation cut the SIDS rate dramatically (Kinney & Thach, 2009; Mitchell, 2009). In the United States in 1984 SIDS killed 5,245 babies; in 1996, that number was down to 3,050; in 2011 it was 1,910 (see Figure 5.8). Such results indicate that, in the United States alone, about 40,000 children and young adults are alive today who would be dead if they had been born before 1990. The campaign has been so successful

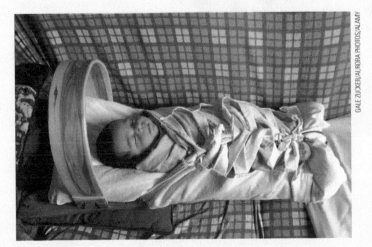

No SIDS Allowed For centuries, Native-American babies, such as this boy in Arizona, slept on their backs in cradle boards. Back-sleeping was also customary among the Navaho's genetic ancestors, in Asia, protecting them from SIDS.

that physical therapists report that babies now crawl later than they used to; they therefore advocate *tummy time*—putting awake infants on their stomachs to develop their muscles (Zachry & Kitzmann, 2011).

Stomach-sleeping is a proven, replicated risk, but it is not the only one: SIDS still occurs. Beyond sleeping position, other risks include low birthweight, being male, parents who smoke cigarettes, soft blankets or pillows, winter, bedsharing, abnormalities in the brainstem, the heart, the mitochondria, and the microbiome (Neary & Breckenridge, 2013; Ostfeld et al., 2010). Most SIDS victims experience several risks, suggesting again a cascade of biological and social circumstances.

That does not surprise Susan Beal, who quickly realized that SIDS victims are found in many kinds of households, rich and poor, native-born and immigrant. She sifted through all the evidence and found the main risk—stomach-sleeping—but she has continued to study other factors. She praises the courage of the hundreds of parents who talked with her hours after their baby died.

Immunization

immunization A process that stimulates the body's immune system by causing production of antibodies to defend against attack by a particular contagious disease. Creation of antibodies may be accomplished either naturally (by having the disease), by injection, by drops that are swallowed, or by a nasal spray. (These imposed methods are also called *vaccination*.)

Immunization primes the body's immune system to resist a particular disease. Immunization (often via *vaccination*) may have had "a greater impact on human mortality reduction and population growth than any other public health intervention besides clean water" (J. P. Baker, 2000, p. 199). Within the past 50 years, immunization eliminated smallpox and dramatically reduced chickenpox, flu, measles, mumps, pneumonia, polio, rotavirus, tetanus, and whooping cough. Now scientists seek to immunize against HIV/AIDS, malaria, Ebola, and other viral diseases.

Immunization protects not only from temporary sickness but also from complications, including deafness, blindness, sterility, and meningitis. Sometimes the damage from illness is not apparent until decades later. Having mumps in childhood, for instance, can cause sterility and doubles the risk of schizophrenia in adulthood (Dalman et al., 2008).

Some people cannot be safely immunized, including the following:

- Embryos, who may be born blind, deaf, and brain-damaged if their pregnant mother contracts rubella (German measles)
- Newborns, who may die from a disease that is mild in older children
- People with impaired immune systems (HIV-positive, aged, or undergoing chemotherapy), who can become deathly ill

Fortunately, each vaccinated child stops transmission of the disease and thus protects others, a phenomenon called *herd immunity* (mentioned in Chapter 1). Although specifics vary by disease, usually if 90 percent of the people in a community (a herd) are immunized, the disease does not spread. Without herd immunity, some community members die of a "childhood" disease.

Everywhere parents can refuse to vaccinate their children for medical reasons, but in 19 states of the United States, parents are able to opt out of vaccination because of "personal belief" (Blad, 2014). In Colorado, for instance, 15 percent of all kindergartners have never been immunized against measles, mumps, rubella, diphtheria, tetanus, or whooping cough. That is below herd immunity, and an epidemic could occur—with infants most likely to suffer.

SCOTT EELLS/REDUX

True Dedication This young Buddhist monk lives in a remote region of Nepal, where, until recently, measles was a fatal disease. Fortunately, a UNICEF porter carried the vaccine over mountain trails for two days so that this boy—and his whole community—could be immunized.

Especially for Nurses and Pediatricians A mother refuses to have her baby immunized because she wants to prevent side effects. She wants your signature for a religious exemption, which in some jurisdictions allows the mother to refuse vaccination. What should you do? (see response, page 167)

Problems with Immunization

Infants may react to immunization by being irritable or even feverish for a day or so, to the distress of their parents. However, parents do not notice if their child does *not* get polio, measles, or so on. Before the varicella (chicken pox) vaccine, more than 100 people in the United States died each year from that disease, and 1 million were itchy and feverish for a week. Now almost no one dies of varicella, and far fewer get chicken pox.

Many parents are concerned about the potential side effects of vaccines. Whenever something seems to go amiss with vaccination, the media broadcast it, which frightens parents. This has occurred particularly as rates of autism have risen. (**Developmental Link:** The link between fear of immunization and increased rates of autism is discussed in A View from Science in Chapter 1.) As a result, the rate of missed vaccinations in the United States has been rising over the past decade. This horrifies public health workers, who, taking a longitudinal and society-wide perspective, realize that the risks of the diseases are far greater than the risks from immunization. The 2014 spike in measles cases was the highest since 1994, one result of increasing numbers of parents objecting to vaccination.

Concerns about safety are greatest for newer vaccines, including the annual flu shot. Pregnant women and young children are particularly likely to be seriously affected by flu, which has led the United States Centers for Disease Control to recommend vaccination. However, most pregnant women and about 30 percent of parents do not follow that recommendation (MMWR, March 7, 2014).

In 2012, two states, Connecticut and New Jersey, required flu vaccination for all 6- to 59-month-olds in licensed day-care centers. Flu immunization rates of young Connecticut children rose from 68 to 84 percent. In the 2012–2013 winter, far fewer young children in Connecticut were hospitalized for flu than in previous years, although rates rose everywhere else. Since most Connecticut children are not in day care, apparently herd immunity, added to the perception of parents that flu vaccination was safe, was protective. Meanwhile, Colorado had the highest rate of flu hospitalizations, an increase from previous years (MMWR, March 7, 2014).

Nutrition

As already explained, infant mortality worldwide has plummeted in recent years for several reasons: fewer sudden infant deaths, advances in prenatal and newborn care, and, as you just read, immunization. One more measure is making a huge difference: better nutrition.

Breast Is Best

Ideally, nutrition starts with *colostrum,* a thick, high-calorie fluid secreted by the mother's breasts at birth. After about three days, the breasts begin to produce milk.

Compared with formula based on cow's milk, human milk is sterile, always at body temperature, and rich in many essential nutrients for brain and body (Wambach & Riordan, 2014; Drover et al., 2009). Babies who are exclusively breast-fed are less often sick, partly because breast milk provides antibodies and decreases allergies and asthma. Disease protection continues lifelong: Babies who are exclusively breast-fed in the early months become obese less often (Huh et al., 2011) and thus have lower rates of diabetes and heart disease.

Breast-feeding is especially protective for preterm babies; if a tiny baby's mother cannot provide breast milk, physicians recommend milk from another woman (Schanler, 2011). (Once a woman has given birth, her breasts can continue to produce milk for decades.)

The specific fats and sugars in breast milk make it more digestible and better for the brain than any substitute (Drover et al., 2009; Wambach & Riordan, 2014). The composition of breast milk adjusts to the age of the baby, with milk for premature babies distinct from that for older infants. Quantity increases to meet the demand: Twins and even triplets can be exclusively breast-fed for months.

Formula is preferable only in unusual cases, such as when the mother is HIV-positive or uses toxic or addictive drugs. Even then, however, breast milk without supplementation may be advised, depending on the alternatives. For example, in some African nations, HIV-positive women are encouraged to breast-feed because infants' risk of catching HIV from their mothers is lower than the risk of dying from infections, diarrhea, or malnutrition as a result of bottle-feeding (Cohen,

Video: Nutritional Needs of Infants and Children: Breast Feeding Promotion shows UNICEF's efforts to educate women on the benefits of breastfeeding.

Same Situation, Far Apart: Breast-Feeding Breast-feeding is universal. None of us would exist if our fore-mothers had not successfully breast-fed their babies for millennia. Currently, breast-feeding is practiced worldwide, but it is no longer the only way to feed infants, and each culture has particular practices.

Do You Believe It?
This table lists so many advantages that some skepticism seems warranted. However, every item on this list arises from research that considers confounding factors, such as the mother's health and education. It may be that breast milk is truly a miracle food.

TABLE 5.1	The Benefits of Breast-Feeding

For the Baby	For the Mother
Balance of nutrition (fat, protein, etc.) adjusts to age of baby	Easier bonding with baby
Breast milk has micronutrients not found in formula	Reduced risk of breast cancer and osteoporosis
Less infant illness, including allergies, ear infections, stomach upsets	Natural contraception (with exclusive breast-feeding, for several months)
Less childhood asthma	Pleasure of breast stimulation
Better childhood vision	Satisfaction of meeting infant's basic need
Less adult illness, including diabetes, cancer, heart disease	No formula to prepare; no sterilization
Protection against many childhood diseases, since breast milk contains antibodies from the mother	Easier travel with the baby
Stronger jaws, fewer cavities, advanced breathing reflexes (less SIDS)	**For the Family**
Higher IQ, less likely to drop out of school, more likely to attend college	Increased survival of other children (because of spacing of births)
Later puberty, fewer teenage pregnancies	Increased family income (because formula and medical care are expensive)
Less likely to become obese or hypertensive by age 12	Less stress on father, especially at night

Sources: Beilin & Huang, 2008; Riordan & Wambach, 2009; Schanler, 2011; U.S. Department of Health and Human Services, 2011.

FIGURE 5.10

A Smart Choice In 1970, educated women were taught that formula was the smart, modern way to provide nutrition—but no longer. Today, more education for women correlates with more breast milk for babies. About half of U.S. women with college degrees now manage three months of *exclusive* breast-feeding—no juice, no water, and certainly no cereal.

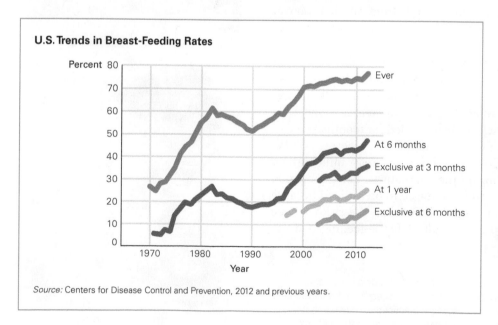

U.S. Trends in Breast-Feeding Rates

Source: Centers for Disease Control and Prevention, 2012 and previous years.

2007; Kuhn et al., 2009). The worst option in that circumstance is a mixture of breast- and formula-feeding.

Doctors worldwide recommend breast-feeding with no other foods—not even juice—for the first months of a newborn's life. (Table 5.1 lists some of the benefits of breast-feeding.) Some pediatricians suggest adding foods (rice cereal and bananas) at 4 months; others want mothers to wait until 6 months (Fewtrell et al., 2011). For breast milk to meet the baby's nutritional needs, the mother must be well fed and hydrated (especially important in hot climates), and avoid alcohol, cigarettes, and other drugs.

Breast-feeding was once universal, but by the mid-twentieth century many mothers thought formula was better. Fortunately, that has changed again. In the United States, 77 percent of infants are breast-fed at birth, 48 percent at 6 months (most with other food as well), and 25 percent at a year (virtually all with other food and drink) (U.S. Department of Health and Human Services, 2011) (see Figure 5.10). Worldwide, about half of all 2-year-olds are still nursing, usually at night.

Encouragement of breast-feeding and help from family members, especially new fathers, are crucial. Ideally, nurses visit new mothers weekly at home; such visits (routine in some nations, rare in others) increase the likelihood that breast-feeding will continue. It is also true that, as with many aspects of child care, "there may be little net benefit to breast-feeding if it results in distressed mothers or marital or family discord" (Brody, 2012). In other words, "breast is best" when compared to formula, but exclusive breast-feeding is not always best when a family's entire life together is considered. In developed nations, sterile formula has nourished millions of infants, who have become happy and healthy children.

Malnutrition

Protein-calorie malnutrition occurs when a person does not consume enough food to sustain normal growth. This form of malnutrition affects roughly one-fourth of the world's children in developing nations: They suffer from **stunting,** being short for their age because chronic malnutrition kept them from growing. Stunting is most common in the poorest nations (see Figure 5.11).

Even worse is **wasting,** when children are severely underweight for their age and height (2 or more standard deviations below average). Many nations, especially in East Asia, Latin America, and central Europe, have seen improvement in child nutrition in the past decades, with an accompanying decrease in wasting and stunting.

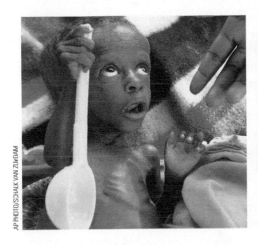

In some other nations, however, primarily in Africa, wasting has increased. And in several nations in South Asia, about one-third of young children are stunted (World Health Organization, 2014). In some nations, the traditional diet for young children or their mothers does not provide sufficient vitamins, fat, and protein for robust health (Martorell & Young, 2012). As a result, the infant's energy is reduced and normal curiosity is absent (Osorio, 2011). Young children naturally want to do whatever they can: A child with no energy is a child who is not learning.

Chronically malnourished infants and children suffer in three additional ways:

1. Their brains may not develop normally. If malnutrition has continued long enough to affect height, it may also have affected the brain.
2. Malnourished children have no body reserves to protect them against common diseases. About half of all childhood deaths occur because malnutrition makes a childhood disease lethal.
3. Some diseases result directly from malnutrition—both **marasmus** during the first year, when body tissues waste away, and **kwashiorkor** after age 1, when growth slows down, hair becomes thin, skin becomes splotchy, and the face, legs, and abdomen swell with fluid (edema).

Prevention, more than treatment, is needed. Sadly, some children hospitalized for marasmus or kwashiorkor die even after feeding because their digestive systems

protein-calorie malnutrition A condition in which a person does not consume sufficient food of any kind. This deprivation can result in several illnesses, severe weight loss, and even death.

stunting The failure of children to grow to a normal height for their age due to severe and chronic malnutrition.

wasting The tendency for children to be severely underweight for their age as a result of malnutrition.

Same Situation, Far Apart: Children Still Malnourished Infant malnutrition is common in refugees (like this baby now living in Thailand, *right*) or in countries with conflict or crop failure (like Niger, at *left*). Relief programs reach only some of the children in need around the world. The children in these photographs are among the lucky ones who are being fed.

// Response for Nurses and Pediatricians (from page 164): It is difficult to convince people that their method of child rearing is wrong, although you should try. In this case, listen respectfully and then describe specific instances of serious illness or death from a childhood disease. Suggest that the mother ask her grandparents if they knew anyone who had polio, tuberculosis, or tetanus (they probably did). If you cannot convince this mother, do not despair: Vaccination of 95 percent of toddlers helps protect the other 5 percent. If the mother has genuine religious reasons, talk to her clergy adviser.

marasmus A disease of severe protein-calorie malnutrition during early infancy, in which growth stops, body tissues waste away, and the infant eventually dies.

kwashiorkor A disease of chronic malnutrition during childhood, in which a protein deficiency makes the child more vulnerable to other diseases, such as measles, diarrhea, and influenza.

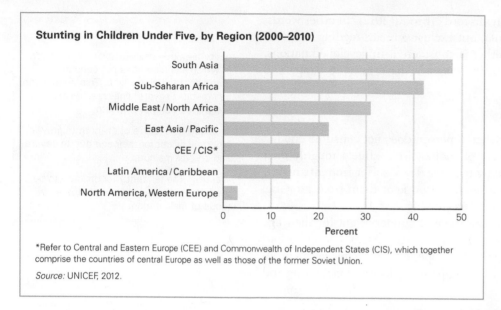

Stunting in Children Under Five, by Region (2000–2010)

*Refer to Central and Eastern Europe (CEE) and Commonwealth of Independent States (CIS), which together comprise the countries of central Europe as well as those of the former Soviet Union.

Source: UNICEF, 2012.

FIGURE 5.11

Genetic? The data show that basic nutrition is still unavailable to many children in the developing world. Some critics contend that Asian children are genetically small and therefore that Western norms make it appear as if India and Africa have more stunted children than they really do. However, children of Asian and African descent born and nurtured in North America are as tall as those of European descent. Thus, malnutrition, not genes, accounts for most stunting worldwide.

Video: Malnutrition and Children in Nepal shows the plight of children in Nepal who suffer from protein energy malnutrition (PEM).

are already failing (M. Smith et al., 2013). Ideally, prenatal nutrition, then breast-feeding, and then supplemental iron and vitamin A stop malnutrition before it starts. Once malnutrition is apparent, highly nutritious formula (usually fortified peanut butter) often restores weight—but not always.

Some severely malnourished children still die. Researchers believe that for them, a combination of factors—genetic susceptibility, poor nutrition, infection, and abnormal bacteria in the digestive system (the microbiome)—is fatal (M. Smith et al., 2013). Giving severely ill children an antibiotic to stop infection saves lives—but always, prevention is best (Gough et al., 2014).

A study of two very poor African nations (Niger and Gambia) found several specific factors that reduced the likelihood of wasting and stunting: breast-feeding, both parents at home, water piped to the house, a tile (not dirt) floor, a toilet, electricity, immunization, a radio, and the mother's secondary education (Oyekale & Oyekale, 2009). Overall, "a mother's education is key in determining whether her children will survive their first five years of life" (United Nations, 2011, p. 26).

Several items on this list are taken for granted by readers of this book. However, two themes apply to everyone at any age: (1) Prevention is better than treatment, and (2) people with some knowledge tend to protect their health and that of their family. The next chapters continue these themes.

SUMMING UP Various public health measures have saved billions of infants in the past century. Immunization protects those who are inoculated and also halts the spread of contagious diseases (via herd immunity). Smallpox has been eliminated, and many other diseases are rare except in regions of the world where public health professionals have not been able to establish best practices. In the United States, success at reducing childhood diseases have led some parents to refuse immunization completely, which may lead to an epidemic if herd immunity falls too low.

Breast milk is the ideal infant food, improving development for decades and reducing infant malnutrition and death. Fortunately, rates of breast-feeding are increasing in developing nations; most underdeveloped nations have always had high rates of breast-feeding. Malnutrition has not been eliminated, however. If a breast-feeding mother is severely malnourished, or if a toddler does not get sufficient nourishment, diseases flourish and learning diminishes. In some parts of the world, children still suffer from stunting and wasting, which are the most visible results of malnutrition.

WHAT HAVE YOU LEARNED?

1. Why are immunization rates low in some African and South Asian nations?
2. Why do doctors worry about immunization rates in the United States?
3. What are the reasons for and against breast-feeding until a child is at least 1 year old?
4. What is the relationship between malnutrition and disease?
5. As an indication of malnutrition, which is better, stunting or wasting? Why?

SUMMARY

Body Changes

1. In the first two years of life, infants grow taller, gain weight, and increase in head circumference—all indicative of development. Birthweight doubles by 4 months, triples by 1 year, and quadruples by 2 years.

2. Medical checkups in the first months of a child's life focus especially on weight, height, and head circumference, because early detection of slow growth can halt later problems.

3. The amount of time a child sleeps gradually decreases over the first two years. Bed-sharing is the norm in many developing nations, and co-sleeping is increasingly common in developed ones.

Brain Development

4. Brain size increases dramatically, from about 25 to 75 percent of the adult brain's weight in the first two years. Complexity increases as well, with cell growth, development of dendrites, and formation of synapses. Both growth and pruning aid cognition.

5. Experience is vital for brain development. An infant who is socially isolated, over-stressed, or deprived of stimulation may be impaired lifelong.

Perceiving and Moving

6. At birth, the senses already respond to stimuli. Prenatal experience makes hearing the most mature sense. Vision is the least mature sense at birth, but it improves quickly. Infants use all their senses to strengthen their early social interactions.

7. Infants gradually improve their motor skills as they begin to grow and brain maturation continues. Gross motor skills are soon evident, from rolling over to sitting up (at about 6 months), from standing to walking (at about 1 year), from climbing to running (before age 2).

8. Babies gradually develop the fine motor skills to grab, aim, and manipulate almost anything within reach. Experience, time, motivation, and practice allow infants to advance in all their motor skills.

Surviving in Good Health

9. About 2 billion infant deaths have been prevented in the past half-century because of improved health care. One major innovation is immunization, which has eradicated smallpox and virtually eliminated polio and measles. More medical professionals are needed to prevent, diagnose, and treat the diseases that still cause many infant deaths in poor nations.

10. Breast-feeding is best for infants, partly because breast milk helps them resist disease and promotes growth of every kind. Most babies are breast-fed at birth, but in North America only half are breast-fed at six months, and few of those are exclusively breast-fed, as doctors worldwide recommend.

11. Severe malnutrition stunts growth and can cause death, both directly through marasmus or kwashiorkor and indirectly through vulnerability if a child catches measles, an intestinal virus, or some other illness.

KEY TERMS

percentile (p. 138)
failure to thrive (p. 138)
REM (rapid eye movement) sleep (p. 139)
co-sleeping (p. 140)
bed-sharing (p. 140)
head-sparing (p. 142)
neuron (p. 142)
cortex (p. 143)

prefrontal cortex (p. 143)
axon (p. 143)
dendrite (p. 143)
synapse (p. 143)
neurotransmitter (p. 143)
synaptic gap (p. 143)
transient exuberance (p. 145)
pruning (p. 145)
experience-expectant (p. 146)

experience-dependent (p. 146)
shaken baby syndrome (p. 149)
self-righting (p. 151)
sensation (p. 152)
perception (p. 152)
binocular vision (p. 154)
motor skills (p. 156)
gross motor skills (p. 156)
fine motor skills (p. 157)

sudden infant death syndrome (SIDS) (p. 163)
immunization (p. 164)
protein-calorie malnutrition (p. 167)
stunting (p. 167)
wasting (p. 167)
marasmus (p. 167)
kwashiorkor (p. 167)

APPLICATIONS

1. Immunization regulations and practices vary, often for social and political reasons. Ask at least two faculty or administrative staff members what immunizations the students at your college must have and why. If you hear, "It's a law," ask why.

2. Observe three infants (whom you do not know) in public places such as a store, playground, or bus. Look closely at body size and motor skills. From that, estimate the age in months, and then ask the caregiver how old the infant is.

3. Ask three to ten adults whether they were bottle-fed or breast-fed and, if breast-fed, for how long. Any correlation with body size, health?

CHAPTER 6

The First Two Years:
Cognitive Development

What Will You Know?

1. Why did Piaget compare 1-year-olds to scientists?
2. Why isn't Piaget's theory of sensorimotor intelligence universally recognized as insightful?
3. What factors influence whether infants remember what happens to them before they can talk?
4. When and how do infants learn to talk?

"You've been flossing more," the hygienist told me approvingly after she cleaned my teeth. Hurray, I am happy that she noticed. I never flossed as a child (did flossing exist then?) and I have rarely flossed in adulthood (I had no time, I rationalized) but for the past two months I have been flossing every morning. This change of behavior was primarily cognitive. First I read research that found a negative correlation between flossing and heart disease. Then I applied several techniques of behavior modification to myself. I am glad this new daily action accumulated to something remarkable.

But then she made excessive demands.

"You need to brush three minutes each time, and floss twice a day."

"Why?"

"You will have less tartar."

"What is wrong with tartar?"

"It causes gingivitis."

"What is wrong with gingivitis?"

"It causes periodontitis."

"What is wrong with periodontitis?"

She looked at me as if I were incredibly stupid, and said, "It is terrible, it is expensive, it is time-consuming. You could lose a tooth."

I could have asked what's wrong with losing a tooth. Instead I was quiet.

How does this apply to infant cognitive development? The cascade of events, from another minute of daily brushing to a tooth lost forever, is not unlike the cascade that transforms a newborn into a talking, goal-directed 2-year-old. Infants learn each day, from their first attempt to suck and swallow to their comprehension of some laws of physics, from recognition of Mother's voice to memory for action sequences they have witnessed, from a reflexive cry to deliberate sentences.

Each day of looking and learning seems insignificant, yet responses accumulate to develop a toddler who thinks, understands, pretends, and explains. This chapter describes in detail those early days and months, which build the intellectual foundation for later thinking and talking. Nurture is not the only influence, of course; maturation is crucial too, but nurture is crucial.

Newborns seem to know nothing. Two years later they can make a wish, say it out loud, and blow out their birthday candles. Thousands of developmentalists have traced this rapid progression, finding that preverbal infants understand much more than adults once realized and that every day brings new cognitive development, guided by experience.

This chapter begins with Piaget, specifically his six stages of intellectual progression over the first two years. We then describe another approach to understanding infant cognition, information processing, with some intriguing research that uses methods such as habituation and brain scans and reveals preverbal memory and communication. The most dramatic evidence of early intellectual growth—talking fluently or haltingly in whatever language the caregivers choose—is then described.

The final topic of this chapter may be most important: What is the best way to nurture early cognition? Do developmentalists know answers that other people need to know?

Sensorimotor Intelligence

As you remember from Chapter 2, Jean Piaget was a Swiss scientist who earned his doctorate in 1918, when most scientists thought infants ate, cried, and slept but did not yet learn. When Piaget became a father, he used his scientific observa-

---

TABLE 6.1   The Six Stages of Sensorimotor Intelligence

For an overview of the stages of sensorimotor thought, it helps to group the six stages into pairs.

The first two stages involve the infant's responses to its own body.

Primary Circular Reactions

Stage One (birth to 1 month)	*Reflexes:* sucking, grasping, staring, listening
Stage Two (1–4 months)	*The first acquired adaptations:* accommodation and coordination of reflexes *Examples:* sucking a pacifier differently from a nipple; attempting to hold a bottle to suck it

The next two stages involve the infant's responses to objects and people.

Secondary Circular Reactions

Stage Three (4–8 months)	*Making interesting sights last:* responding to people and objects *Example:* clapping hands when mother says "patty-cake"
Stage Four (8–12 months)	*New adaptation and anticipation:* becoming more deliberate and purposeful in responding to people and objects *Example:* putting mother's hands together in order to make her start playing patty-cake

The last two stages are the most creative, first with action and then with ideas.

Tertiary Circular Reactions

Stage Five (12–18 months)	*New means through active experimentation:* experimentation and creativity in the actions of the "little scientist" *Example:* putting a teddy bear in the toilet and flushing it
Stage Six (18–24 months)	*New means through mental combinations:* thinking before doing, new ways of achieving a goal without resorting to trial and error. *Example:* before flushing the teddy bear, hesitating because of the memory of the toilet overflowing and mother's anger

tion skills with his own babies. Contrary to conventional wisdom, he realized that infants are active learners, adapting to experience. His theories and observations have earned Piaget the admiration of developmentalists ever since. (**Developmental Link:** Piaget's theory of cognitive development is introduced in Chapter 2.)

Piaget called cognition in the first two years **sensorimotor intelligence,** named about the early senses and motor skills described in Chapters 4 and 5. Those early reflexes and body movements are used by infants to develop their minds, adapting to experience. Sensorimotor intelligence is subdivided into six stages (see Table 6.1).

Stages One and Two: Primary Circular Reactions

In every aspect of sensorimotor intelligence, the brain and the senses interact with experiences, each shaping the other as part of a dynamic system (Ambady & Bharucha, 2009). Piaget described the interplay of sensation, perception, and cognition as *circular reactions,* emphasizing that, as in a circle, there is no beginning and no end. Each experience leads to the next, which loops back (see Figure 6.1). The first two stages of sensorimotor intelligence are **primary circular reactions,** involving the infant's body.

Stage one, called the *stage of reflexes,* lasts only a month. It includes senses as well as motor reflexes, the foundations of sensorimotor thought. Soon reflexes become deliberate actions; sensation leads to perception, perception leads to cognition, and then cognition leads back to sensation.

Stage two, *first acquired adaptations* (also called *stage of first habits*), begins because reflexes adjust to whatever responses they elicit. Adaptation is cognitive; it includes both assimilation and accommodation. (**Developmental Link:** Assimilation and accommodation are explained in Chapter 2.) Infants adapt their reflexes as their responses teach them about what the body does and how each action feels.

Here is one example. In a powerful reflex, full-term newborns suck anything that touches their lips. Their first learning challenge is to suck, swallow, and suck

---

Video: Sensorimotor Intelligence in Infancy and Toddlerhood
http://qrs.ly/lj4ep00

©2016 MACMILLAN

sensorimotor intelligence Piaget's term for the way infants think—by using their senses and motor skills—during the first period of cognitive development.

primary circular reactions The first of three types of feedback loops in sensorimotor intelligence, this one involving the infant's own body. The infant senses motion, sucking, noise, and other stimuli and tries to understand them.

FIGURE 6.1

Never Ending Circular reactions keep going because each action produces pleasure that encourages more action.

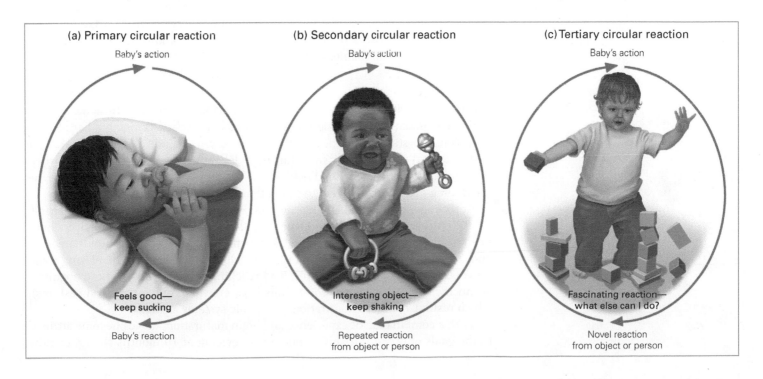

(a) Primary circular reaction
Baby's action
Feels good— keep sucking
Baby's reaction

(b) Secondary circular reaction
Baby's action
Interesting object— keep shaking
Repeated reaction from object or person

(c) Tertiary circular reaction
Baby's action
Fascinating reaction— what else can I do?
Novel reaction from object or person

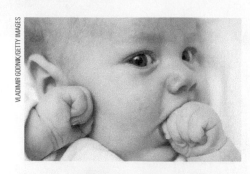

Time for Adaptation Sucking is a reflex at first, but adaptation begins as soon as an infant differentiates a pacifier from her mother's breast or realizes that her hand has grown too big to fit into her mouth. This infant's expression of concentration suggests that she is about to make that adaptation and suck just her thumb from now on.

secondary circular reactions The second of three types of feedback loops in sensorimotor intelligence, this one involving people and objects. Infants respond to other people, to toys, and to any other object they can touch or move.

Especially for Parents When should parents decide whether to feed their baby only by breast, only by bottle, or using some combination of the two? When should they decide whether or not to let their baby use a pacifier? (see response, page 176)

again without spitting up too much—a major task that often takes a few days, with the mother learning how to help her baby latch, suck, and swallow.

During the first stage, in the first month, infants *adapt* their sucking reflex to bottles or breasts, pacifiers or fingers, each requiring specific types of tongue pushing. This adaptation signifies that infants have begun to interpret sensations; as they accommodate, they are "thinking."

During stage two, which Piaget pegged from about 1 to 4 months of age, additional adaptation of the sucking reflex begins. Infant cognition leads babies to suck in some ways for hunger, in other ways for comfort—and not to suck fuzzy blankets or hard plastic. Once adaptation occurs, it sticks.

Adaptation is quite specific. For instance, 4-month-old breast-fed babies may reject milk from the nipple of a bottle if they have never experienced it. Or suppose 4-month-olds have discovered how to suck their thumbs, and have practiced thumb-sucking to their joy and satisfaction. Then suppose the parents decide that a pacifier is better—cleaner, perhaps, or healthier for teeth. That may be too late. Their baby may refuse to readapt, spitting out the pacifier and finding the thumb instead. Piaget believed that people of all ages tend to be stuck in their ways for cognitive reasons; early adaptation is one example.

Stages Three and Four: Secondary Circular Reactions

In stages three and four, development advances from primary to **secondary circular reactions.** Those reactions extend beyond the infant's body; this circular reaction is between the baby and something else.

During stage three (4 to 8 months), infants attempt to produce exciting experiences, *making interesting sights last.* Realizing that rattles make noise, for example, they wave their arms and laugh whenever someone puts a rattle in their hand. The sight of something delightful—a favorite squeaky toy, a smiling parent—can trigger active efforts for interaction.

Next comes stage four (8 months to 1 year), *new adaptation and anticipation* (also called the *means to the end*). Babies may ask for help (fussing, pointing, gesturing) to accomplish what they want. Thinking is more innovative because adaptation is more complex. For instance, instead of always smiling at Grandpa, an infant might first assess his mood. Stage-three babies know how to continue an experience; stage-four babies initiate and anticipate.

Pursuing a Goal

An impressive attribute of stage four is that babies work hard to achieve their goals. A 10-month-old girl might crawl over to her mother, bringing a bar of soap as a signal to start her bath, and then start to remove her clothes to make her wishes crystal clear—finally squealing with delight when the bath water is turned on. Similarly, if a 10-month-old boy sees his father putting on his coat to leave, he might drag over his own jacket to signal that he wants to go along.

At that age, babies indicate that they are hungry—and keep their mouths firmly shut if the food on the spoon is something they do not like. If the caregivers have been using sign language, among the first signs learned by 10-month-olds are "eat" and "more." Even without parental signing, babies this age begin displaying some universal signs—pointing, pushing, and reaching up to be held. These cognitive advances benefit from new motor skills (e.g., crawling, grabbing, hand gestures), which result from brain maturation—dynamic systems again.

With a combination of experience and brain maturation, babies become attuned to the goals of others, an ability much more evident at 10 months than 8 months

(Brandone et al., 2014). It seems that at Piaget's fourth stage of sensorimotor intelligence, personal understanding begins to extend to social understanding.

Object Permanence

Piaget thought that, at about 8 months, babies first understand the concept of **object permanence**—the realization that objects or people continue to exist when they are no longer in sight. As Piaget discovered, not until about 8 months do infants search for toys that have fallen from the crib, rolled under a couch, or disappeared under a blanket. Blind babies also acquire object permanence toward the end of their first year, reaching for an object that they hear nearby (Fazzi et al., 2011).

As a recent statement of this phenomenon explains:

> Many parents in our typical American middle-class households have tried out Piaget's experiment in situ: Take an adorable, drooling 7-month-old baby, show her a toy she loves to play with, then cover it with a piece of cloth right in front of her eyes. What do you observe next? The baby does not know what to do to get the toy! She looks around, oblivious to the object's continuing existence under the cloth cover, and turns her attention to something else interesting in her environment. A few months later, the same baby will readily reach out and yank away the cloth cover to retrieve the highly desirable toy. This experiment has been done thousands of times and the phenomenon remains one of the most compelling in all of developmental psychology.
>
> *[Xu, 2013, p. 167]*

This excerpt describes Piaget's classic experiment to measure object permanence: An adult shows an infant an interesting toy, covers it with a lightweight cloth, and observes the response. The results:

- Infants younger than 8 months do not search for the object by removing the cloth.
- At about 8 months, infants search removing the cloth immediately after the object is covered but not if they have to wait a few seconds.
- At 18 months, they search quite well, even after a wait, but not if they have seen the object put first in one place and then moved to another. They search in the first place, not the second, a mistake called the *A-not-B error*. Thus they search where they remember seeing it put (A), somehow not understanding that they saw it moved (to B). When a healthy, bright toddler exhibits this obvious failing, observers usually agree with Piaget: A-not-B is a sign of immature brain development, not a lack of innate intelligence.
- By 2 years, children fully understand object permanence, progressing through several stages of ever-advanced cognition (Piaget, 1954/2013).

This research provides many practical suggestions. If young infants fuss because they see something they cannot have (keys, a cell phone, candy), caregivers are advised to put that coveted object out of sight. Fussing stops if object permanence has not yet appeared.

By contrast, for toddlers, hiding a forbidden object is not enough. It must be securely locked up or discarded, lest the child later retrieve it, climbing onto the kitchen counter or under the bathroom sink to do so. Since object permanence develops gradually, peek-a-boo is too advanced in the first months, but it is fun just about the time that object permanence is new. As comprehension of hidden objects matures, peek-a-boo becomes boring, but hide-and-seek becomes fun. Again, take into account the age of the child: At first

object permanence The realization that objects (including people) still exist when they can no longer be seen, touched, or heard.

Family Fun Peek-a-boo makes all three happy, each for cognitive reasons. The 9-month-old is discovering object permanence, his sister (at the concrete operational stage) enjoys making her brother laugh, and their mother understands more abstract ideas—such as family bonding.

// **Response for Parents** (from page 174): Both decisions should be made within the first month, during the stage of reflexes. If parents wait until the infant is 4 months or older, they may discover that they are too late. It is difficult to introduce a bottle to a 4-month-old who has never sucked on an artificial nipple or a pacifier to a baby who has already adapted the sucking reflex to a thumb.

Especially for Parents One parent wants to put all the breakable or dangerous objects away when the toddler is able to move around independently. The other parent says that the baby should learn not to touch certain things. Who is right? (see response, page 179)

tertiary circular reactions The third of three types of feedback loops in sensorimotor intelligence, this one involving active exploration and experimentation. Infants explore a range of new activities, varying their responses as a way of learning about the world.

"little scientist" The stage-five toddler (age 12 to 18 months) who experiments without anticipating the results, using trial and error in active and creative exploration.

Exploration at 15 Months One of the best ways to investigate food is to squish it in your hands, observe changes in color and texture, and listen for sounds. Taste and smell are primary senses for adults when eating, but it looks as if Jonathan has already had his fill of those.

hide-and-seek must be quick and simple, with the giggling child hiding in the same obvious place again and again. After a few years, the game can become more elaborate (longer waiting, more imaginative hiding).

Piaget believed that failure to search before 8 months meant that infants had no concept of object permanence—that "out of sight" literally means "out of mind." That belief has been questioned. As one researcher points out, "Amid his acute observation and brilliant theorizing, Piaget . . . mistook infants' motor incompetence for conceptual incompetence" (Mandler, 2004, p. 17).

A series of clever experiments in which objects seemed to disappear behind a screen while researchers traced babies' eye movements and brain activity revealed that long before 8 months, infants are surprised if an object vanishes (Baillargeon & DeVos, 1991; Spelke, 1993). The idea that such surprise indicates object permanence is accepted by some scientists, who believe that "infants as young as 2 and 3 months of age can represent fully hidden objects" (Cohen & Cashon, 2006, p. 224). Other scientists are not convinced (Mareschal & Kaufman, 2012).

Further research on object permanence continues to raise questions and produce surprises. For instance, many other creatures (cats, monkeys, dogs, birds) develop object permanence at younger ages than Piaget found. The animal ability seems to be innate, not learned, as wolves can develop it as well as dogs—but neither is adept at "invisible" displacement, as when an object is moved by a hand underneath a cloth that covers it (Fiset & Plourde, 2013). At a certain age, children figure this out, but dogs do not.

Stages Five and Six: Tertiary Circular Reactions

In their second year, infants start experimenting in thought and deed—or, rather, in the opposite sequence, deed and thought. They act first (stage five) and think later (stage six).

Tertiary circular reactions begin when 1-year-olds take independent actions to discover the properties of other people, animals, and things. Infants no longer respond only to their own bodies (primary reactions) or to other people or objects (secondary reactions). Their cognition is more like a spiral than a closed circle, increasingly creative with each discovery.

Piaget's stage five (ages 12 to 18 months), *new means through active experimentation,* builds on the accomplishments of stage four. Now goal-directed and purposeful activities become more expansive.

Toddlers delight in squeezing all the toothpaste out of the tube, drawing on the wall, or uncovering an anthill—activities they have never seen an adult do. Piaget referred to the stage-five toddler as a "**little scientist**" who "experiments in order to see." Their research method is trial and error. Their devotion to discovery is familiar to every adult scientist—and to every parent. Protection needed.

Finally, in the sixth stage (ages 18 to 24 months), toddlers use *mental combinations,* intellectual experimentation via imagination that can supersede the active experimentation of stage five. Because they combine ideas, stage-six toddlers think

ARIEL SKELLEY/AGE FOTOSTOCK

about consequences, hesitating a moment before yanking the cat's tail or dropping a raw egg on the floor.

Thus, the stage-six sequence may begin with thought followed by action. Of course, the urge to explore may overtake caution: Things that are truly dangerous (cleaning fluids, swimming pools, open windows) need to be locked and gated.

The ability to combine ideas allows stage six toddlers to pretend. For instance, they know that a doll is not a real baby, but they can belt it into a stroller and take it for a walk. At 22 months, my grandson gave me imaginary "shoe ice cream" and laughed when I pretended to eat it.

Piaget describes another stage-six intellectual accomplishment involving both thinking and memory. **Deferred imitation** occurs when infants copy behavior they noticed hours or even days earlier (Piaget, 1962/2013). Piaget described his daughter, Jacqueline, who observed another child

> who got into a terrible temper. He screamed as he tried to get out of a playpen and pushed it backward, stamping his feet. Jacqueline stood watching him in amazement, never having witnessed such a scene before. The next day, she herself screamed in her playpen and tried to move it, stamping her foot lightly several times in succession.

[Piaget, 1962, p. 63].

Push Another Button Little scientists "experiment in order to see" as this 14-month-old does. Many parents realize, to their distress, that their infant has deleted a crucial file, or called a distant relative on a cell phone, because the toddler wants to see what happens.

deferred imitation A sequence in which an infant first perceives something done by someone else and then performs the same action hours or even days later.

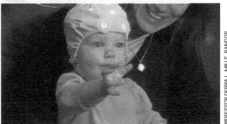

Video: Event-Related Potential (ERP) Research shows a procedure in which the electrical activity of an infant's brain is recorded to see if the brain responds differently to familiar versus unfamiliar words.

a view from science

Piaget and Modern Research

As detailed by hundreds of developmentalists, many infants reach the stages of sensorimotor intelligence earlier than Piaget predicted (Oakes et al., 2011). Not only do 5-month-olds show surprise when objects seem to disappear (evidence of object permanence before 8 months) but babies younger than 1 year pretend and defer imitation (both stage-six abilities, according to Piaget) (Teiser et al., 2014; Slater, 2012; Meltzoff & Moore, 1999). How could a gifted scientist be so wrong? There are at least three reasons.

First, Piaget's original insights were based on his own infants. Direct observation of three children is a start, and Piaget was an extraordinarily meticulous and creative observer, but no contemporary researcher would stop there. Given the immaturity and variability of babies, dozens of infants must be studied.

For instance, as evidence for early object permanence, Renée Baillargeon (2000) listed 30 studies involving more than a thousand infants younger than 6 months old. She and her collaborators continued to study object permanence with hundreds of infants, learning when and in what circumstances babies understand the concept, based not on one infant but on many infants of various backgrounds (e.g., Baillargeon et al., 2012).

Second, infants are not easy to study; there are problems with "fidelity and credibility" (Bornstein et al., 2005, p. 287). To overcome these problems, modern researchers use innovative statistics, research designs, sample sizes, and strategies that were not available to Piaget. As a result, contemporary scientists often find that object permanence, deferred imitation, and other sensorimotor accomplishments occur earlier, and with more variation, than

TABLE 6.2 Some Techniques Used by Neuroscientists to Understand Brain Function

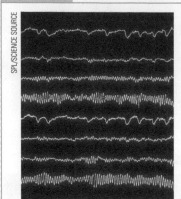

EEG, normal brain

Technique

EEG (electroencephalogram)

Use

Measures electrical activity in the top layers of the brain, where the cortex is.

Limitations

Especially in infancy, much brain activity of interest occurs below the cortex.

ERP when listening

Technique

ERP (event-related potential)

Use

Notes the amplitude and frequency of electrical activity (as shown by brain waves) in specific parts of the cortex in reaction to various stimuli.

Limitations

Reaction within the cortex signifies perception, but interpretation of the amplitude and timing of brain waves is not straightforward.

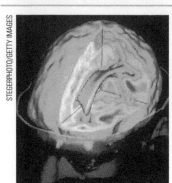

fMRI when talking

Technique

fMRI (functional magnetic resonance imaging)

Use

Measures changes in blood flow anywhere in the brain (not just the outer layers).

Limitations

Signifies brain activity, but infants are notoriously active, which can make fMRIs useless.

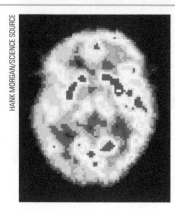

PET scan of sleep

Technique

PET (positron emission tomography)

Use

PET (like fMRI) reveals activity in various parts of the brain. Locations can be pinpointed with precision, but PET requires injection of radioactive dye to light up the active parts of the brain.

Limitations

Many parents and researchers hesitate to inject radioactive dye into an infant's brain unless a serious abnormality is suspected.

fNIRS of a college student

Technique

fNIRS (functional near-infrared spectroscopy)

Use

Via light waves that indicate blood flow, the fNIRS measures activity in the cortex and beyond. The device is portable and non-invasive: no need for expensive equipment, electrodes, or special dye. This is especially useful for infants who do not stay still or for sports players who might have concussions.

Limitations

Does not show activity deep in the brain, so the amygdala and hippocampus, among other crucial areas, cannot be measured.

For both practical and ethical reasons, it is difficult to use these techniques on large, representative samples. One of the challenges of neuroscience is to develop methods that are harmless, quick, acceptable to parents and babies, and comprehensive. A more immediate challenge is to depict the data in ways that are easy to interpret and understand.

More to Come Hundreds of neuroscientists are developing new ways to perceive and analyze infant brain activity, as part of a $300 million dollar investment President Obama announced in 2014 as part of BRAIN (**B**rain **R**esearch through **A**dvancing **I**nnovative **N**eurotechnologies).

Piaget had assumed (Carey, 2009). For instance, if an infant looks a few milliseconds longer when an object seems to have vanished, is that evidence of object permanence? Many researchers believe the answer is yes—but only advanced cameras, programmed by computers, can measure it.

One particular research strategy has been a boon to scientists, confirming the powerful curiosity of very young babies. That research method is called **habituation** (from the word *habit*). Habituation refers to getting accustomed to an experience after repeated exposure, as when the school cafeteria serves macaroni day after day or when infants repeatedly encounter the same sound, sight, toy, or so on. Evidence of habituation is loss of interest (or, for macaroni, loss of appetite).

Using habituation as a research strategy with infants involves repeating one stimulus until babies lose interest and then presenting another, slightly different stimulus (a new sound, sight, or other sensation). Babies indicate that they detect a difference between the two stimuli with a longer or more focused gaze; a faster or slower heart rate; more or less muscle tension around the lips; a change in the rate, rhythm, or pressure of suction on a nipple. Such subtle indicators are recorded by technology that was unavailable to Piaget (such as eye-gaze cameras and heart monitors).

By inducing habituation and then presenting a new stimulus, scientists have learned that even 1-month-olds can detect the difference between a *pah* sound and a *bah* sound, between a circle with two dots inside it and a circle without any dots, and much more. Babies younger than 6 months perceive far more than Piaget imagined, in part because he depended on observable actions (removing that cloth), not subtle signs.

Third, several ways of measuring brain activity now allow scientists to record infant cognition before even subtle observable evidence is found (see Table 6.2) (Johnson, 2011). In **fMRI** (functional magnetic resonance imaging), a burst of electrical activity measured by blood flow within the brain is recorded, indicating that neurons are firing. This leads researchers to conclude that a particular stimulus has been noticed and processed. Scientists now know exactly which parts of the brain signify what

sensations or thoughts, so electrical activity in the face area, for instance, means that the infants is processing a face. The current push to map the brain will make such discoveries more precise, allowing us to understand when the infant sees one face as rewarding and another as merely interesting.

Conclusions about early cognition are not accepted by every scientist, in part because brain imagery of normal infants is difficult and expensive. Brain scans may provide crucial information if an infant is seriously ill or injured, but many parents refuse to allow such measures on healthy infants. Further, infants fuss or move when neurological tests are underway, and hundreds of scans are needed for accurate conclusions. All this slows down neurological confirmation of infant cognition.

Nonetheless, as detailed in Chapter 5, early brain growth is rapid and wide-ranging: Dendrites proliferate, and pruning is extensive. The first months and years of life are filled with mental activity, prime time for cognitive development, as neurological research attests. Brain scans can document cognitive advances in ways that Piaget never imagined.

For instance, one experiment found that when infants hear speech, their brains begin to react more notably (registered on ERPs, or event-related potentials) at the same time that their gaze tends to focus on the mouth more than the eyes (Kushnerenko et al., 2013). The experimenters suggested that, in the last half of the first year, brain maturation more than chronological age is crucial for language development.

---

habituation The process of becoming accustomed to an object or event through repeated exposure to it, and thus becoming less interested in it.

fMRI Functional magnetic resonance imaging, a measuring technique in which the brain's electrical excitement indicates activation anywhere in the brain; fMRI helps researchers locate neurological responses to stimuli.

Despite several valid criticisms of Piaget's work, he was correct in many ways. Infancy is a time for several distinct advances in cognition, and each new stage described by Piaget coincides with significant new connections in brain networks and functions. Piaget was right to describe babies as avid and active learners who "learn so fast and so well" (Xu & Kushnir, 2013, p. 28). His main mistake was underestimating how rapidly their learning occurs.

// Response for Parents (from page 176): It is easier and safer to babyproof the house because toddlers, being "little scientists," want to explore. However, it is important for both parents to encourage and guide the baby. If having untouchable items prevents a major conflict between the adults, that might be the best choice.

SUMMING UP Piaget discovered, studied, and then celebrated active infant learning, which he described in six stages of sensorimotor intelligence. Babies use senses and motor skills to understand their world, first with reflexes and then by adapting through assimilation and accommodation. Piaget's detailed descriptions contrasted with earlier assumptions that babies did not think until they could talk. Thousands of researchers followed his lead, using advanced technology to demonstrate cognitive development of the early months.

We now know that object permanence, pursuit of goals, and deferred imitation all develop before the ages that Piaget assigned to his stages. The infant is a "little scientist" not only at 1 year, as Piaget described, but months earlier. Thinking develops before infants have the motor skills to demonstrate their thoughts; eye movements and brain scans find that babies have active minds. Nonetheless, the avid curiosity of the toddler, with the ability to imagine, pretend, and remember, is as notable and impressive today as it was for Piaget with his own children almost a century ago.

WHAT HAVE YOU LEARNED?

1. Why did Piaget call his first stage of cognition *sensorimotor* intelligence?
2. How do the first two sensorimotor stages illustrate primary circular reactions?
3. What is one example of how a stage-three infant might make interesting events last?
4. How is object permanence an example of stage four of sensorimotor intelligence?
5. In sensorimotor intelligence, what is the difference between stages five and six?
6. What is now known about the sequence of object permanence, from before 6 months to after 2 years?

Information Processing

information-processing theory A perspective that compares human thinking processes, by analogy, to computer analysis of data, including sensory input connections, stored memories, and output.

As explained in Chapter 2, Piaget's sweeping overview of four periods of cognition contrasts with **information-processing theory,** a perspective analogous to computer functioning, including input, memory, programs, analysis, and output. Just as input connects with a program and then leads to output on a computer, sensation leads to perception, which may produce cognition. Those links are described and traced in detail by information-processing theorists.

For infants, output might be moving a hand to uncover a toy (object permanence), saying a word to signify recognition (e.g., *mama*), or looking at one photo longer than another (habituation). Some recent studies examine changes in brain waves when infants see a picture (Kouider et al., 2013); such research both confirms and refutes Piaget's theory.

To understand the many aspects of information processing in infancy, consider the baby's reaction to an empty stomach. A newborn simply cries as a reflex to hunger pangs, but an older hungry infant hears Mother's voice, looks for her, reaches to be picked up, and then nuzzles at her breast. Or, at an even older age, the toddler signs or says something to indicate hunger.

Each step of this process requires information to be processed. Older infants are more thoughtful and effective because of advanced information processing. Advances occur weekly or even day-by-day in the first year, with no sudden leaps, contrary to Piaget's notion of six discrete stages (Cohen & Cashon, 2006).

The information-processing perspective, aided by modern technology, has uncovered many aspects of infant cognition. As one researcher summarizes, "Rather than bumbling babies, they are individuals who . . . can learn surprisingly fast about the patterns of nature" (Keil, 2011, p. 1023). Concepts and categories seem to develop in infants' brains by 6 months or earlier (Mandler & DeLoach, 2012).

GILKIS · EMELKE VAN WYK/GALLO IMAGES/GETTY IMAGES

What Next? Information-processing research asks what these babies are thinking as they both pull on the same block. Will those thoughts lead to hitting, crying, or sharing?

This perspective helps tie together many aspects of infant cognition. In earlier decades, infant intelligence was measured via age of sitting up, grasping, and so on, but we now know that age of achieving motor skills does not predict later intellectual achievement, although when an infant is way behind schedule (e.g., not sitting up at 8 months) that may indicate cognitive delay.

However, information-processing research has found perceptual measures that do predict later intelligence. For example, early attention and relatively rapid habituation correlate with later cognitive ability. Babies who focus intently on new stimuli, and then quickly become bored, may be more intelligent than babies who stare aimlessly (Bornstein & Colombo, 2012). Rapid habituation is an encouraging sign; smart babies like novelty.

Now let us look at two specific aspects of infant cognition that illustrate the information-processing approach: affordances and memory. Affordances concern perception or, by analogy, input. Memory concerns brain organization and output—that is, storage and retrieval.

Affordances

Perception, remember, is the processing of information that arrives at the brain from the sense organs. Decades of thought and research led Eleanor and James Gibson to conclude that perception is far from automatic (E. J. Gibson, 1969; J. J. Gibson, 1979). Perception—for infants, as for the rest of us—is a cognitive accomplishment that requires selectivity: "Perceiving is active, a process of obtaining information about the world. . . . We don't simply see, we look" (E. J. Gibson, 1988, p. 5). Or, as one neuroscientist said, "You see what you expect or are trained to see, not what is there" (Freeman, quoted in Bower, 2007, p. 106).

The environment (people, places, and objects) *affords,* or offers, many opportunities to interact with whatever is perceived (E. J. Gibson, 1997). Each of these opportunities is called an **affordance.** Which particular affordance is perceived and acted on depends on four factors: sensory awareness, immediate motivation, current level of development, and past experience.

As an example, imagine that you are lost in an unfamiliar city. You need to ask directions. Of whom? Not the first person you see. You want someone knowledgeable and approachable. Affordance is what you seek, and you scan the facial expression, body language, gender, dress, etc. of passersby (Miles, 2009). They, in turn, assess the affordance of your request. Are you genuinely lost, and do they know how to direct you? If they judge that your request is a scam, or they decide that your question is beyond them, their judgment of the affordance will force you to find another person.

Developmentalists studying children emphasize that age of the perceiver affects what affordances are perceived. For example, since toddlers enjoy running as soon as their legs allow it, every open space affords running: a meadow, a building's long hall, a highway. To adults, affordance of running is much more limited: They worry about a bull grazing in the meadow, neighbors behind the hallway doors, or traffic on the road. Furthermore, because motivation is pivotal in affordances, toddlers move when most adults prefer to stay put.

Selective perception of affordances depends not only on age, motivation, and context but also on culture. Just as a baby might be oblivious to something adults consider crucial—or vice versa—an American in, say, Cambodia might miss an important sign of the social network. In every nation, foreigners behave in ways considered rude, but their behavior may simply indicate different affordances from those of the natives.

Variation in affordance is also apparent within cultures. City-dwellers complain that visitors from rural areas walk too slowly, yet visitors complain that urbanites

Especially for Computer Experts In what way is the human mind *not* like a computer? (see response, page 183)

affordance An opportunity for perception and interaction that is offered by a person, place, or object in the environment.

Depth Perception This toddler in a laboratory in Berkeley, California, is crawling on the experimental apparatus called a visual cliff. She stops at the edge of what she perceives as a drop-off.

visual cliff An experimental apparatus that gives the illusion of a sudden drop-off between one horizontal surface and another.

Especially for Parents of Infants When should you be particularly worried that your baby will fall off the bed or down the stairs? (see response, page 184)

dynamic perception Perception that is primed to focus on movement and change.

are always in a hurry. Sidewalks afford either fast travel or views of architecture, depending on the perceiver.

Research on Early Affordances

Experience affects which affordances are perceived. This is obvious in studies of depth perception. Research demonstrating this began with an apparatus called the **visual cliff,** designed to provide the illusion of a sudden drop-off between one horizontal surface and another (see photo). In a classic research study, 6-month-olds, urged forward by their mothers, wiggled toward Mom over the supposed edge of the cliff, but 10-month-olds, even with Mother's encouragement, fearfully refused to budge (E. J. Gibson & Walk, 1960).

Scientists once thought that a visual deficit—specifically, inadequate depth perception—prevented 6-month-olds from seeing the drop, which was why they moved forward. According to this hypothesis, as the visual cortex matured, 10-month-olds perceived that crawling over a cliff afforded falling.

Later research (using advanced technology) disproved that interpretation. Some 3-month-olds notice the drop: Their heart rate slows and their eyes open wide when they are placed over the cliff. Depth perception is in place, but until they can crawl, they do not realize that crawling over an edge affords falling.

Reaction to the visual-cliff hazard depends not only on vision but also on experience with crawling and on other specifics, such as the particular texture and depth of the supposed cliff. The difference is in *processing,* not input—in affordance, not sensory ability. Those conclusions were drawn by Eleanor Gibson herself, the scientist who did the early visual-cliff research and who explained the concept of affordance (Adolph & Kretch, 2012). Further research on the visual cliff includes the social context, with the tone of the mother's encouragement indicating whether or not the cliff affords crawling (Kim et al., 2010).

A similar sequence happens with fear of many objects. By 9 months, infants attend to snakes and spiders more readily than to other similar images, but they do not yet fear them. A few months later, perhaps because they have learned from others, they are afraid of such creatures. Thus, perception is a prerequisite, but it does not always lead to affordance (LoBue, 2013).

Movement and People

Despite the variations from one infant to another in the particular affordances they perceive, all babies are attracted to two kinds of affordances. Babies pay close attention to things that move and to people.

Dynamic perception focuses on movement. Infants love motion. As soon as they can, they move their bodies—grabbing, scooting, crawling, and walking. To their delight, such motion changes what the world affords, an early example of dynamic perception. As a result, infants strive to master the next motor accomplishment, and repeat whatever ability they already have (Adolph et al., 2012). They love to watch things that move—passing cars, flickering images on a screen, mobiles.

It's almost impossible to teach a baby not to chase and grab any moving creature, including a dog, a cat, or even a cockroach. Infants' interest in motion was the inspiration for another experiment that sought to learn what affordances were perceived by babies too young to talk or walk (van Hof et al., 2008). A ball was moved at various speeds in front of infants aged 3 to 9 months. Most tried to touch or catch the ball as it passed within reach. However, marked differences appeared in their perception of the affordance of "catchableness."

Sometimes younger infants did not reach for slow-moving balls yet tried to grasp the faster balls. They tried but failed, touching the ball only about 20 percent of the time. By contrast, the 9-month-olds knew when a ball afforded catching. They grabbed the slower balls and did not try to catch the fastest ones; their success rate was almost 100 percent. This "follows directly from one of the key concepts of ecological psychology, that animals perceive the environment in terms of action possibilities or affordances" (van Hof et al., 2008, p. 193).

Another universal principle of infant perception is **people preference.** This follows from evolutionary psychology: Over the millennia, humans survived by learning to attend to, and rely on, one another. You just read that the affordance of the visual cliff depends partly on the tone of the mother's voice. Infants soon recognize their caregivers and expect certain affordances (comfort, food, entertainment) from them.

Very young babies are particularly interested in emotional affordances, using their limited perceptual abilities and intellectual understanding to respond to smiles, shouts, and so on. Indeed, in one study, babies watched a three-second video demonstration by an actor whose face was covered (so no visual expression could be seen) as he acted out happiness, anger, or indifference. The results: 6-month-olds can distinguish whether a person is happy or angry by body moments alone (Zieber et al., 2014). Hundreds of experiments have shown that infants are able to connect movements, facial expressions, and tone of voice long before they understand language. This ability led to an interesting hypothesis:

> Given that infants are frequently exposed to their caregivers' emotional displays and further presented with opportunities to view the affordances (Gibson, 1959, 1979) of those emotional expressions, we propose that the expressions of familiar persons are meaningful to infants very early in life.
>
> [Kahana-Kalman & Walker-Andrews, 2001, p. 366]

Building on earlier research design, these researchers tested their hypothesis by presenting infants with two moving images side by side on one video screen (Kahana-Kalman & Walker-Andrews, 2001). Both images were of the same woman, either the infant's own mother or a stranger. In one image, the woman was joyful; in the other, sad. Each presentation was accompanied by an audiotape of that woman's happy *or* sad talk.

Previous studies had found that 7-month-olds could match emotional words with facial expressions, but younger babies could not. In that research, at 7 months, but not earlier, infants looked longer at strangers whose voice matched the emotion on their face and less long at strangers whose face did not match the tone.

These researchers first replicated the earlier experiments, again finding that 3½-month-old babies could not match a stranger's voice and facial expression. Then the 3½-month-olds saw two images of their *own* mother and heard her happy or her sad voice. They correctly matched visual and vocal emotions. They looked longest when their smiling mother talked happily; but, when their mother sounded sad, they stared more at the video of their sad-faced mother than at the video of their happy mother—thus connecting sound and sight, presumably based on their past experience with that person.

The researchers noticed something else as well. When infants saw and heard their happy mothers, they smiled twice as fast, seven times as long, and much more brightly (cheeks raised and lips upturned) than for the happy strangers. Experience had taught them that a smiling mother affords joy. The affordances of a smiling stranger are more difficult to judge.

Memory

Information-processing research, with detailed behavioral and neurological measures, finds that memory is evident in very young babies. Within the first weeks after birth, infants recognize their caregivers by face, voice, and smell. Memory

Grab Him As with most babies, she loves grabbing any creature, hoping for a reaction. To recognize that people change over time, imagine these two a few years or decades older. She would not grab him, and if she did, he would not be placid.

// **Response for Computer Experts** (from page 181): In dozens of ways, including speed of calculation, ability to network across the world, and vulnerability to viruses. In at least one crucial way, the human mind is better: Computers become obsolete or fail within a few years, while human minds keep advancing for decades.

// **Response for Parents of Infants** (from page 182): Constant vigilance is necessary for the first few years of a child's life, but the most dangerous age is from about 4 to 8 months, when infants can move but do not yet fear falling over an edge.

LaunchPad

Video: Contingency Learning in Young Infants shows Carolyn Rovee-Collier's procedure for studying instrumental learning in young infants.

improves month by month. In one study, after 6-month-olds had had only two half-hour sessions with a novel puppet, a month later they remembered the experience—an amazing feat of memory for babies who could not talk or even stand up (Giles & Rovee-Collier, 2011).

There are several distinct types of memories, each in a particular part of the brain that is developing in its own way. That means that, even though infants already remember some things, other kinds of memory build and emerge throughout childhood. Instead of noting the many "faults and shortcomings relative to an adult standard," it may be more appropriate to realize that children of all ages remember what they need to remember (Bjorklund & Sellers, 2014, p. 142). Sensory and caregiver memories are apparent in the first month, motor memories by 3 months, and then, at about 9 months, more complex memories (Mullally & Maguire, 2014).

Forget About Infant Amnesia

The evidence suggests that *infant amnesia,* which is the belief that infants remember nothing, is mistaken. It is true that adults rarely remember events that occurred before they were 3. Children do somewhat better, remembering what happened at age 2. But the fact that memories fade with time does not mean that memory is absent.

If you forgot your third grade teacher's name, for example, that does not mean that you had no memory when you were 9; it just means that you do not now remember what you could easily remember many years ago. And memory itself may be inaccessible, but not completely gone. If you saw a photo of your third grade teacher, and a list of four possible names for her or him, you probably could choose correctly.

No doubt memory is fragile in the first months of life and improves with age over the first months and years. Apparently a certain amount of experience and a certain amount of brain maturation are required in order to process and recall what happens (Bauer et al., 2010). But some of that experience happens on day one—or even in the womb—and some memories may begin long before a baby can say them.

Selective Amnesia As we grow older, we forget about spitting up, nursing, crying, and almost everything else from our early years. However, strong emotions (love, fear, mistrust) may leave lifelong traces.

One reason for the apparent fragility is linguistic: People use words to store (and sometimes distort) memories, so preverbal children have difficulty with recall (Richardson & Hayne, 2007), while adults cannot access their infant memories because they did not yet have words to solidify them. Another probable reason is that memories fade over time: Adults cannot remember what happened when they were 1, but 2-year-olds can, because the memory traces in the brain have not yet been degraded (Mullally & Maguire 2014).

Conditions of Memory

Many studies seek to understand what infants *can* remember, even if they cannot later put memories into words. Memories are particularly evident if:

- Motivation and emotion are high.
- Retrieval is strengthened by reminders and repetition.

The most dramatic proof of infant memory comes from innovative experiments in which 3-month-olds learned to move a mobile by kicking their legs (Rovee-Collier, 1987, 1990). The infants lay on their backs connected to a mobile by means of a ribbon tied to one foot (see photo). Virtually every baby began making occasional kicks (as well as random arm movements and noises) and realized that kicking made the mobile move. They then kicked more vigorously and frequently, sometimes laughing at their accomplishment. So far, this is no surprise—observing self-activated movement is highly reinforcing to infants, a dynamic perception.

When some infants had the mobile-and-ribbon apparatus reinstalled and reconnected *one week later,* most started to kick immediately. Their reaction indicated that they remembered their previous experience. But when other 3-month-old infants were retested *two weeks later,* they began with only random kicks. Apparently they had forgotten what they had learned—evidence that memory is fragile early in life. But that conclusion needs revision, or at least qualification.

Reminders and Repetition

The lead researcher in the mobile experiments, Carolyn Rovee-Collier, developed another experiment demonstrating that 3-month-old infants *could* remember after two weeks *if* they had a brief reminder session before being retested (Rovee-Collier & Hayne, 1987). A **reminder session** is any experience that helps people recollect an idea, a thing, or an event.

In this particular reminder session, *two weeks* after the initial training, the infants watched the mobile move but were *not* tied to it and were positioned so that they could *not* kick. The next day, when they were again connected to the mobile and positioned so that they could move their legs, they kicked as they had learned to do two weeks earlier.

Apparently, watching the mobile move on the previous day had revived their faded memory. The information about making the mobile move was stored in their brains, but they needed processing time to retrieve it. The reminder session provided that time. Other research similarly finds that repeated reminders are more powerful than single reminders and that context is crucial, especially for infants younger than 9 months old: Being tested in the same room as the initial experience aids memory (Rovee-Collier & Cuevas, 2009).

A Little Older, a Little More Memory

After about 6 months of age, infants retain information for a longer time than younger babies do, with less training or reminding. Many researchers find that by 9 months, memory markedly improves, although it is not clear if this is purely maturational or if it is the result of locomotion, since 9-month-olds can usually crawl (Mullally & Maguire, 2014).

Memory researchers now believe that several kinds of memory, lodged in various parts of the brain, reach an important level of maturation at about 9 months. For example, linguistic memory is evident when a baby's vocalizations begin to sound like the speech he or she has heard. Motor memory is evident when an infant first watches someone else play with a new toy and, the next day, plays with it in the same way as he or she had observed. Infants younger than 9 months do not usually do this.

He Remembers! In Rovee-Collier's experiment, a young infant immediately remembers how to make the familiar mobile move. (Unfamiliar mobiles do not provoke the same reaction.) He kicks his right leg and flails both arms, just as he learned to do several weeks ago.

reminder session A perceptual experience that helps a person recollect an idea, a thing, or an experience.

Who Is Thinking? They all are. Julie is stretching her sensorimotor intelligence as she rotates a piece to make it fit, while her mother notices that her 2-year-old is ready for a puzzle with 20 cardboard pieces. But the champion thinker may be baby Samara; babies learn a lot by watching.

Many experiments show that 1-year-olds can transfer learning from one object or experience to another. They learn from various people and events—from parents and strangers, from other babies and older siblings, from picture books and family photographs (Hayne & Simcock, 2009).

The dendrites and neurons of the brain change to reflect remembered experiences during infancy. (**Developmental Link:** Experience-related brain growth is described in Chapter 5.) Note that these experiments are further evidence of several facts already mentioned: Babies observe affordances carefully, and they are especially attuned to movement, people, and emotions.

The crucial insight from information processing is that the brain is a very active organ, changing with each day's events. Therefore, the particulars of early experiences and memory are critically important in determining what a child knows or does not know.

Generalization becomes possible. At every age "people perceive more of a visual scene than was presented to them." Even infants develop expectancies for what they observe and fill in the unseen parts (Mullally & Maguire, 2014).

Many studies show that infants remember not only specific events and objects but also patterns and general goals (Keil, 2011). Some examples come from research, such as memory of what syllables and rhythms are heard and how objects move in relation to other objects. Additional examples arise from close observations of babies at home, such as what they expect from a parent or a babysitter, or what details indicate bedtime. Every day of their young lives, infants are processing information and storing conclusions.

Especially for Teachers People of every age remember best when they are active learners. If you had to teach fractions to a class of 8-year-olds, how would you do it? (see response, page 188)

SUMMING UP Information processing analyzes each component of how thoughts begin: how they are organized, remembered, and expressed, and how cognition builds, day by day. Infants' perception is powerfully influenced by particular experiences and motivation; affordances perceived by one infant differ from those perceived by another. Memory depends on brain maturation and on experience. For that reason, memory is fragile in the first year (though it can be triggered by reminders) and becomes more robust, although still somewhat fragile, in the second year. In both perception and memory, babies are similar to adults in many ways—infant amnesia is a myth. On the other hand, information-processing research confirms that experience and maturation both advance cognition: Infants do not process information as well as older children or adults do.

WHAT HAVE YOU LEARNED?

1. How do the affordances of this book, for instance, differ for someone at 1 month, 12 months, and 20 years of age?
2. What are several hypotheses to explain why infants refuse to crawl over visual cliffs?
3. What two preferences show that infants are selective in early perception?
4. What conditions help 3-month-olds remember something?
5. How is infant memory similar to, and unlike, adult memory?

Language: What Develops in the First Two Years?

The brains of other species have nothing like the neurons and networks that support the 6,000 or so human languages. Many other animals communicate, but their language is primitive. The human linguistic ability at age 2 far surpasses that of full-grown adults from every other species. How do babies do it? Part of the answer is that learning language is a priority; babies listen intensely, figuring out speech. One scholar explains "infants are acquiring much of their native language before they utter their first word" (Aslin, 2012, p. 191).

The Universal Sequence

The sequence of language development is the same worldwide (see At About This Time). Some children learn several languages, some only one; some learn rapidly and others slowly, but they all follow the same path. Even deaf infants who become able to hear (thanks to cochlear implants) follow the sequence, catching up to their age-mates unless they have multiple disabilities (Fazzi et al., 2011). Those who learn sign language also begin with one word at a time, and then sign sentences of increasing length and complexity.

Who Is Babbling? Probably both the 6-month-old and the 27-year-old are. During every day of infancy, mothers and babies communicate with noises, movements (notice the hands), and expressions.

Listening and Responding

Newborns prefer to listen to the language their mother spoke when they were in the womb, not because they understand the words, of course, but because they are familiar with the rhythm, the sounds, and the cadence.

Surprisingly, newborns of bilingual mothers differentiate between both languages (Byers-Heinlein et al., 2010). Data were collected on 94 newborns (age 0 to 5 days) in a large hospital in Vancouver, Canada. Half were born to mothers who spoke both English and Tagalog (a native language of the Philippines), one-third to mothers who spoke only English, and one-sixth to mothers who spoke English

at about this time

The Development of Language in the First Two Years

Age*	Means of Communication
Newborn	Reflexive communication—cries, movements, facial expressions.
2 months	A range of meaningful noises—cooing, fussing, crying, laughing.
3–6 months	New sounds, including squeals, growls, croons, trills, vowel sounds.
6–10 months	Babbling, including both consonant and vowel sounds repeated in syllables.
10–12 months	Comprehension of simple words; speech-like intonations; specific vocalizations that have meaning to those who know the infant well. Deaf babies express their first signs; hearing babies also use specific gestures (e.g., pointing) to communicate.
12 months	First spoken words that are recognizably part of the native language.
13–18 months	Slow growth of vocabulary, up to about 50 words.
18 months	Naming explosion—three or more words learned per day. Much variation.
21 months	First two-word sentence.
24 months	Multiword sentences. Half the toddler's utterances are two or more words long.

*The ages in this table reflect norms. Many healthy, intelligent children attain each linguistic accomplishment earlier or later than indicated here.

// **Response for Teachers** (from page 186):
Remember the three principles of infant
memory: real life, motivation, and repetition.
Find something children already enjoy that
involves fractions—even if they don't realize
it. Perhaps get a pizza and ask them to
divide it in half, quarters, eighths, sixteenths,
and so on.

child-directed speech The high-pitched,
simplified, and repetitive way adults speak
to infants and children. (Also called *baby
talk* or *motherese*.)

babbling An infant's repetition of
certain syllables, such as *ba-ba-ba*, that
begins when babies are between 6 and
9 months old.

Especially for Nurses and Pediatricians The
parents of a 6-month-old have just been told
that their child is deaf. They don't believe it
because, as they tell you, the baby babbles
as much as their other children did. What do
you tell them? (see response, page 190)

Are You Hungry? Pronunciation is far more
difficult than hand skills, but parents want to
know when their baby wants more to eat.
One solution is evident here. This mother is
teaching her 12-month-old daughter the sign
for "more," a word most toddlers say several
months later.

and Chinese. The bilingual mothers used English in more formal contexts and
non-English with family.

The infants in all three groups sucked on a pacifier connected to a recording
of 10 minutes of English or Tagalog matched for pitch, duration, and number of
syllables. As evident in the frequency and strength of their sucking, most of the infants with bilingual mothers preferred Tagalog, presumably because their mothers
were likely to speak English in formal settings but Tagalog when with family and
friends, whereas those with monolingual mothers preferred English.

The Chinese bilingual babies (who had never heard Tagalog) nonetheless preferred it. The researchers believe that they liked Tagalog because the rhythm of that
language is more similar to Chinese than to English (Byers-Heinlein et al., 2010).

Similar results, showing that babies like to hear familiar language, come from
everyday life. Young infants attend to voices more than to mechanical sounds (a
clock ticking) and look closely at the facial expressions of someone talking to them
(Minagawa-Kawai et al., 2011). By 6 months, by observing mouth movements
alone (no sound), they can decipher whether or not that person is speaking their
native language (Weikum et al., 2007). By 1 year, they are more likely to imitate
the actions of a stranger speaking their native language than those of a person who
speaks another language (Buttelmann et al., 2013).

Infants' ability to distinguish sounds they hear improves, whereas the ability to
hear sounds never spoken in their native language (such as how an "r" or an "l" is
pronounced) deteriorates (Narayan et al., 2010). If parents want a child to be fluent in two languages, they should speak both of them to their baby.

In every language, adults use higher pitch, simple words, repetition, varied
speed, and exaggerated emotional tone when talking to infants (Bryant & Barrett,
2007). This special language form is sometimes called *baby talk,* since it is directed to babies, and sometimes called *motherese,* since mothers universally speak
it. Nonmothers speak it as well. For that reason, scientists prefer the more formal
term, **child-directed speech.**

No matter what term is used, child-directed speech fosters learning, and babies
communicate as best they can. By 4 months, they squeal, growl, gurgle, grunt,
croon, and yell, telling everyone what is on their minds in response to both their
own internal state and their caregivers' words. At 7 months, infants begin to recognize words that are highly distinctive (Singh, 2008): *Bottle, dog,* and *mama,* for
instance, might be differentiated, but words that sound alike (*baby, Bobbie,* and
Barbie) are not.

Not only do infants prefer child-directed speech; they also like alliteration,
rhymes, repetition, melody, rhythm, and varied pitch (Hayes & Slater, 2008; Schön
et al., 2008). Think of your favorite lullaby (itself an alliterative word); obviously,
babies prefer sounds over content.

Babbling and Gesturing

Between 6 and 9 months, babies repeat certain syllables
(*ma-ma-ma, da-da-da, ba-ba-ba*), a vocalization called **babbling** because of the way it sounds. Babbling is experience-
expectant; all babies babble, even deaf ones. Since babies like
to make interesting sights last, as Piaget found, babbling increases in response to child-directed speech. Deaf babies stop
babbling but increasingly engage in responsive gesturing.

Toward the end of the first year, babbling begins to sound
like the infant's native language; infants imitate accents, cadence, consonants, and so on. Videos of deaf infants whose

parents sign to them show that 10-month-olds use about a dozen distinct hand gestures in a repetitive manner similar to babbling.

Many caregivers, recognizing the power of gestures, teach "baby signs" to their 6- to 12-month-olds, who communicate with hand signs months before they move their tongues, lips, and jaws to make specific words. There is no evidence that baby signing accelerates talking (as had been claimed), but it may make parents more responsive, which itself is an advantage (Kirk et al., 2013).

One early gesture is pointing, an advanced social gesture that requires understanding another person's perspective. Most animals cannot interpret pointing; most 10-month-old humans look toward wherever someone else points and can already use a tiny index finger (not just a full hand) to point themselves, even to a place where an object belongs but is not yet there (Liszkowski et al., 2009; Liszkowski & Tomasello, 2011). Pointing is well developed by 12 months, especially when the person who is pointing also speaks (e.g., "look at that") (Daum et al., 2013).

Babbling and gesturing before speech vary from infant to infant—sometimes for biological reasons, sometimes for social ones. Developmentalists can detect early signs of autism, attention-deficit/hyperactivity disorder, hearing impairment, and dyslexia by examining videos of the communication patterns of young infants. However, definitive diagnosis is not possible simply by observation in the early months.

Show Me Where Pointing is one of the earliest forms of communication, emerging at about 10 months. As you see here, pointing is useful lifelong for humans.

First Words

Finally, at about 1 year, the average baby utters a few words, understood by caregivers if not by strangers. For example at 13 months, a child named Kyle knew standard words such as *mama,* but he also knew *da, ba, tam, opma,* and *daes,* which his parents knew to be, respectively, "downstairs," "bottle," "tummy," "oatmeal," and "starfish." He also had a special sound that he used to call squirrels (Lewis et al., 1999).

Gradual Beginnings

In the first months of the second year, spoken vocabulary increases gradually (perhaps one new word a week). A 12-month-old who speaks two words might not speak eight words until several weeks later. However, meanings are learned rapidly; babies understand about 10 times more words than they can say.

Initially, the first words are merely labels for familiar things (*mama* and *dada* are common), but early words are soon accompanied by gestures, facial expressions, and nuances of tone, loudness, and cadence (Saxton, 2010). Imagine meaningful communication in "Dada," "Dada?," and "Dada!" Each is a **holophrase,** a single word that expresses an entire thought.

Intonation (variation in tone and pitch) is extensive in both babbling and holophrases, but there sometimes is a lull between the age of babbling and the age of recognizable words. Apparently at about 1 year, infants reorganize their vocalization from universal to language-specific. They are no longer just making noises; they are trying to communicate in a specific language.

Uttering meaningful words takes all their attention—none is left over for intonation. Careful tracing of early language finds other times when vocalization slows before a burst of new talking; perception affects action (Pulvermüller & Fadiga, 2010), and neurological advances may temporarily inhibit speech (Parladé & Iverson, 2011).

holophrase A single word that is used to express a complete, meaningful thought.

The Naming Explosion

Spoken vocabulary builds rapidly once the first 50 words are mastered, with 21-month-olds typically saying twice as many words as 18-month-olds (Adamson & Bakeman, 2006). This language spurt is called the **naming explosion** because many early words are nouns, that is, names of persons, places, or things.

Between 12 and 18 months, almost every infant learns the name of each significant caregiver (often *dada, mama, nana, papa, baba, tata*) and sibling (and sometimes each pet). Other frequently uttered words refer to the child's favorite foods (*nana* can mean "banana" as well as "grandma") and to elimination (*pee-pee, wee-wee, poo-poo, ka-ka, doo-doo*).

Notice that all these words have two identical syllables, each a consonant followed by a vowel. Many words follow that pattern—not just baba but also bobo, bebe, bubu, bibi. Other early words are only slightly more complicated—ma-me, ama, and so on. The meaning of these words varies by language, but every baby says such words, and everywhere culture assigns meaning to them.

Cultural Differences

Cultures and families vary in how much child-directed speech children hear. Some parents read to their infants, teach them signs, and respond to every burp or fart as if it were an attempt to talk. Other parents are much less verbal. They use gestures and touch; they say "hush" and "no" instead of expanding vocabulary.

By 5 months, babies prefer adults who often use child-directed speech, even when those talkative adults are temporarily silent. Apparently, just as infants seek to master motor skills as soon as they can, they seek to learn language from the best teachers available (Schachner & Hannon, 2011).

Cultural differences are readily apparent in what linguistic sounds capture attention. Infants soon favor the words, accents, and linguistic patterns of their home language. For instance, a study of preverbal Japanese and French infants found that words with the first consonant at the front of the mouth and the second consonant at the back (as in "bat") was preferred by infants in France, but the opposite (as in "tap") was true in Japan. This was the case because of the language (French or Japanese) the babies had heard (Gonzalez-Gomez et al., 2014).

The traditional idea that children should be "seen but not heard" is contrary to what developmentalists recommend and many contemporary families do—encourage talking. By contrast, many other families value children who listen respectfully without talking. Everywhere, however, infants listen to whatever speech

naming explosion A sudden increase in an infant's vocabulary, especially in the number of nouns, that begins at about 18 months of age.

Especially for Caregivers A toddler calls two people "Mama." Is this a sign of confusion? (see response, page 193)

// Response for Nurses and Pediatricians (from page 188): Urge the parents to learn sign language and investigate cochlear implants. Babbling has a biological basis and begins at a specified time, in deaf as well as in hearing babies. However, deaf babies eventually begin to use gestures more and to vocalize less than hearing babies. If their infant can hear, sign language does no harm. If the child is deaf, however, lack of communication may be devastating.

Universal or Culture-Specific? Both. All children enjoy music and like to bang on everything, from furniture to people. Making noise is fun, but even infants prefer the noises of their community and do their best to repeat them. This boy has learned to play the bongo drums (notice the skilled angle of his hands) thanks to his grandfather.

they hear and appreciate the sounds of their culture. Even musical tempo is culture-specific: 4- to 8-month-olds seem to like their own native music best (Soley & Hannon, 2010).

Parts of Speech

Although all new talkers say names, use similar sounds, and prefer nouns more than other parts of speech, the ratio of nouns to verbs and adjectives varies from place to place (Waxman et al., 2013). For example, by 18 months, English-speaking infants speak far more nouns than verbs compared to Chinese or Korean infants. Why?

One explanation goes back to the language itself. The Chinese and Korean languages are "verb-friendly" in that verbs are placed at the beginning or end of sentences. That facilitates learning. By contrast, English verbs occur anywhere in a sentence, and their forms change in illogical ways (e.g., *go, gone, will go, went*). This irregularity may make English verbs harder to learn, although the fact that English verbs often have distinctive suffixes (*-ing, -ed*) and helper words (*was, did, had*) may make it easier (Waxman et al., 2013).

An alternative explanation considers the entire social context: Playing with a variety of toys and learning about dozens of objects are routine in North America, whereas East Asian cultures emphasize human interactions—specifically, how one person responds to another. Accordingly, North American infants are expected to name many objects, whereas Asian infants are expected to act on objects and respond to people.

Thus, Chinese toddlers might learn the equivalent of *come, play, love, carry, run,* and so on earlier. Indeed, 14-month-olds in Chinese-speaking families learn some new words more readily than do their English-speaking peers, with the Chinese infants better able to learn action words than object labels (Chan et al., 2011).

A simpler explanation is that young children are sensitive to sounds. Verbs are learned more easily if they sound like the action (Imai et al., 2008), and such verbs are more common in some languages than others.

English does not have many onomatopoeic verbs, which makes verb-learning difficult. (*Jump, kiss,* and *poop*—all learned early on—are exceptions.) When the same word could be a noun or a verb, English-speaking mothers say them differently: *Kiss,* for instance, is spoken with more emphasis as a noun than a verb, so babies learn the noun before the verb (Conwell & Morgan, 2012). The infant's focus on sounds explains why many toddlers who have never been on a farm know that cows "moo" and ducks "quack."

Every language has some words and concepts that are difficult. English-speaking infants confuse *before* and *after*; Dutch-speaking infants misuse *out* when it refers to taking off clothes; Korean-speaking infants need to learn two meanings of *in* (Mandler, 2004). Learning adjectives is easier in Italian and Spanish than in English or French because of patterns in those languages (Waxman & Lidz, 2006). Specifically, adjectives can stand by themselves without the nouns. If I want a blue cup from a group of multicolored cups, I would ask for "a blue cup" or "a blue one" in English but simply "uno azul" (a blue) in Spanish. Despite such variations, in every language, infants rapidly acquire both vocabulary and grammar.

Putting Words Together

Grammar includes all the methods that languages use to communicate meaning. Word order, prefixes, suffixes, intonation, verb forms, pronouns and negations, prepositions and articles—all of these are aspects of grammar. Grammar can be discerned in holophrases, as one word can be spoken differently depending on

grammar All the methods—word order, verb forms, and so on—that languages use to communicate meaning, apart from the words themselves.

Early Communication and Language Development

A COMMUNICATION MILESTONES: THE FIRST TWO YEARS

These are norms. Many intelligent and healthy babies vary in the age at which they reach these milestones.

Months	Communication Milestone
0	Reflexive communication—cries, movements, facial expressions
1	Recognizes some sounds Makes several different cries and sounds Turns toward familiar sounds
3	A range of meaningful noises—cooing, fussing, crying, laughing Social smile well established Laughter begins Imitates movements Enjoys interaction with others
6	New sounds, including squeals, growls, croons, trills, vowel sounds Meaningful gestures including showing excitement (waving arms and legs) Deaf babies express their first signs Expresses negative feelings (with face and arms) Capable of distinguishing emotion by tone of voice Responds to noises by making sounds Uses noise to express joy and unhappiness Babbles, including both consonant and vowel sounds repeated in syllables
10	Makes simple gestures, like raising arms for "pick me up" Recognizes pointing Makes a sound (not in recognizable language) to indicate a particular thing Responds to simple requests
12	More gestures, such as shaking head for "no" Babbles with inflection, intonation Names familiar people (like "mama," "dada," "nana") Uses exclamations, such as "uh-oh!" Tries to imitate words Points and responds to pointing First spoken words
18	Combines two words (like "Daddy bye-bye") Slow growth of vocabulary, up to about 50 words Language use focuses on 10–30 holophrases Uses nouns and verbs Uses movement, including running and throwing, to indicate emotion Naming explosion may begin, three or more words learned per day Much variation: Some toddlers do not yet speak
24	Combines three or four words together; half the toddler's utterances are two or more words long Uses adjectives and adverbs ("blue," "big," "gentle") Sings simple songs

SOURCES & CREDITS LISTED ON P. SC-1

SOURCE: AMERICAN ACADEMY OF PEDIATRICS

B UNIVERSAL FIRST WORDS

Across cultures, babies' first words are remarkably similar. The words for mother and father are recognizable in almost any language. Most children will learn to name their immediate family and caregivers between the ages of 12 and 18 months.

Language	Mother	Father
English	mama, mommy	dada. daddy
Spanish	mama	papa
French	maman, mama	papa
Italian	mamma	bebbo, papa
Latvian	mama	te-te
Syrian Arabic	mama	babe
Bantu	be-mama	taata
Swahili	mama	baba
Sanskrit	nana	tata
Hebrew	ema	abba
Korean	oma	apa

PHOTO: R. EKO BINTORO/THINKSTOCK

C MASTERING LANGUAGE (MLU)

Children's use of language becomes more complex as they acquire more words and begin to master grammar and usage. A child's spoken words or sounds (utterances) are broken down into the smallest units of language to determine their length and complexity:

SAMPLES OF UTTERANCES

"Doggie!" = 1

"Doggie + Sleep" = 2

"Doggie + Sleep + ing" = 3

"Shh! + Doggie + Sleep + ing" = 4

"Shh! + Doggie + is + Sleep + ing" = 5

"Shh! + The + Doggie + is + Sleep + ing" = 6

SOURCE: COURTESY OF MONICA KALFUR, SLP

meaning. However, grammar becomes essential when babies begin to use two-word combinations (Bremner & Wachs, 2010). That typically happens between 18 and 24 months.

For example, "Baby cry" and "More juice" follow grammatical word order. No child asks, "Juice more," and even toddlers know that "cry baby" is not the same as "baby cry." By age 2, children combine three words. English grammar uses subject–verb–object order. For example, toddlers say "Mommy read book," rather than any of the five other possible sequences of those three words.

Children's proficiency in grammar correlates with the length of their sentences, which is why in every language **mean length of utterance (MLU)** is considered an accurate way to measure a child's language progress (e.g., Miyata et al., 2013). The child who says "Baby is crying" is advanced compared with the child who says "Baby crying" or simply the holophrase "Baby." (See Visualizing Development, p. 192.)

Young children can master two languages, not just one. Children are statisticians: They implicitly track the number of words and phrases and learn those expressed most often, in one, two, or more languages (Johnson & Tyler, 2010). (**Developmental Link:** Bilingual learning is discussed in detail in Chapter 9.) The toddler who often hears two languages will soon speak two languages.

Theories of Language Learning

Worldwide, people who are not yet 2 years old already speak their native language, or two or three languages if that is what they hear. They can express hopes, fears, and memories, and they continue to learn rapidly: All teenagers communicate with nuanced words and gestures, and some compose lyrics or deliver orations that move thousands of their co-linguists. These impressive accomplishments raise the question: How is language learned so easily and so well?

Answers come from three schools of thought, each connected to a theory introduced in Chapter 2: behaviorism, sociocultural theory, and evolutionary psychology. The first theory says that infants are directly taught, the second that social impulses propel infants to communicate, and the third that infants understand language because of brain advances several millennia ago that allowed survival of our species.

Theory One: Infants Need to Be Taught

The seeds of the first perspective were planted more than 50 years ago, when the dominant theory in North American psychology was behaviorism, or learning theory. The essential idea was that all learning is acquired, step-by-step, through association and reinforcement. Just as Pavlov's dogs learned to associate sound with food, infants may associate objects with words, especially if reinforcement occurs.

B. F. Skinner (1957) noticed that spontaneous babbling is usually reinforced. Typically, every time the baby says "ma-ma-ma-ma," a grinning mother appears, repeating the sound and showering the baby with attention, praise, and perhaps food. The baby learns affordances and repeats "ma-ma-ma-ma" when lonely or hungry; through operant conditioning, talking begins.

Skinner believed that most parents are excellent instructors, responding to their infants' gestures and sounds, thus reinforcing speech (Saxton, 2010). Even in preliterate societies, parents use child-directed speech, responding quickly with high pitch, short sentences, stressed nouns, and simple grammar—exactly the techniques that behaviorists would recommend. In every culture that has been studied, those infants who learn language faster have parents who speak to them often. Few parents know the theory of behaviorism, but many use behaviorist

mean length of utterance (MLU) The average number of words and meaningful sounds (such as *-ing* and *huh?*) in a typical sentence (called utterance, because children may not talk in complete sentences). MLU is often used to indicate how advanced a child's language development is.

// **Response for Caregivers** (from page 190): Not at all. Toddlers hear several people called "Mama" (their own mother, their grandmothers, their cousins' and friends' mothers) and experience mothering from several people, so it is not surprising if they use "Mama" too broadly. They will eventually narrow the label down to one person, unless both their parents are women. Usually such parents differentiate, with one called Mama and the other Mom, or both by their first names.

techniques that Skinner would recommend, because these methods succeed (Tamis-LeMonda et al., 2014).

The core ideas of this theory are the following:

- Parents are expert teachers, although other caregivers help.
- Frequent repetition is instructive, especially when linked to daily life.
- Well-taught infants become well-spoken children.

Behaviorists note that some 3-year-olds converse in elaborate sentences; others just barely put one simple word with another. Such variations correlate with the amount of language each child has heard. Parents of the most verbal children teach language throughout infancy—singing, explaining, listening, responding, and reading to their children every day, even before age 1 (Forget-Dubois et al., 2009) (see Figure 6.2).

FIGURE 6.2

Maternal Responsiveness and Infants' Language Acquisition Learning the first 50 words is a milestone in early language acquisition, as it predicts the arrival of the naming explosion and multiword sentences a few weeks later. Researchers found that half the 9-month-old infants of highly responsive mothers (top 10 percent) reached this milestone at 15 months. The infants of nonresponsive mothers (bottom 10 percent) lagged significantly behind.

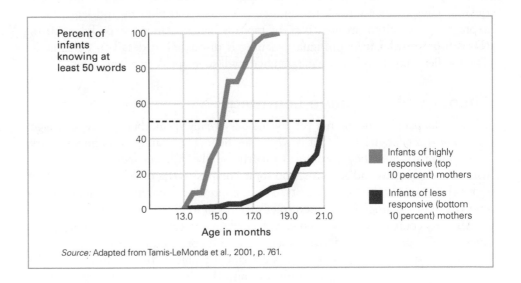

Source: Adapted from Tamis-LeMonda et al., 2001, p. 761.

In one detailed U.S. study, researchers analyzed a 10-minute sample of the language that mothers used with their 9-month-old infants (Tamis-LeMonda et al., 2001). All the mothers were middle class, from the same nation (to control for SES and culture). One mother never imitated her infant's babbling; another mother imitated 21 times, babbling back in conversation. All mothers described things or actions (e.g., "That is a spoon you are holding—spoon"), but one offered only 4 descriptions while another gave 33 in the 10-minute segment.

The frequency of maternal responsiveness at 9 months predicted language acquisition at 17 months. It was not that noisy infants, whose genes might soon make them verbal, elicited more talk. Some quiet infants had mothers who frequently suggested play activities, described things, and asked questions. Quiet infants with talkative mothers usually became more verbal toddlers than their peers.

According to behaviorists, if adults want children who speak, understand, and (later) read well, they must talk to their infants. A recent application of this theory comes from commercial videos, designed to advance toddlers' vocabulary. Typically, such videos use repetition and attention-grabbing measures (sound, tone, color) to encourage babies to learn new words (Vaala et al., 2010). Such videos, and Skinner's theories, have come under attack from many developmentalists, as explained in the following Opposing Perspectives feature.

Especially for Educators An infant daycare center has a new child whose parents speak a language other than the one the teachers speak. Should the teachers learn basic words in the new language, or should they expect the baby to learn the majority language? (see response, page 196)

opposing perspectives

Language and Video

Toddlers can learn to swim in the ocean, throw a ball into a basket, walk on a narrow path beside a precipice, call on a cell phone, cut with a sharp knife, play a guitar, say a word on a flashcard, recite a poem, utter a curse, and much more—if provided appropriate opportunity, encouragement, and practice. Indeed, toddlers in some parts of the world do each of these things—sometimes to the dismay, disapproval, and even shock of adults from elsewhere. Infants do what others do, a trait that fosters rapid learning and challenges caregivers, who try to keep "little scientists" safe. Since language is crucial, many North American parents hope to accelerate talking and understanding.

Commercial companies recognize that toddlers love learning and that parents are eager to teach. Infants are fascinated by dynamic activity, especially when it includes movement, sound, and people. This explains the popularity of child-directed videos— "like crack for babies," as one mother said (quoted in DeLoache et al., 2010, p. 1572). Such products are named to appeal to parents, such as *Baby Einstein, Brainy Baby,* and *Mozart for Mommies and Daddies—Jumpstart Your Newborn's I.Q.*

They are advertised with testimonials. Scientists consider such advertisement deceptive, since one case proves nothing and only controlled experiments prove cause and effect.

In fact, many scientists believe the truth is opposite the commercial claims. A famous study found that infants watching *Baby Einstein* were delayed in language compared to other infants (Zimmerman et al., 2007). The American Association of Pediatricians suggests no screen time (including television, tablets, smartphones, and commercial videos) for children under age 2.

These conclusions are not "robust." That means that some interpretations of the evidence endorse prohibition, but others do not. Some scientists argue that the data are open to many conclusions, depending on the particular statistical analysis used (Ferguson & Donnellan, 2014).

An author of the original critique defended the anti-video findings, arguing that "a reanalysis rooted in dissatisfaction with previous results will necessarily be biased and can only obscure scientific discoveries" (Zimmerman, 2014, p. 138).

Overall, most developmentalists find that, although some educational videos may help older children, videos during infancy are no "substitute for loving, face-to-face relationships" (Lemish &

Kolucki, 2013, p. 335). The crucial factor for intellectual growth seems to be caregiver responsiveness to the individual child, face to face (Richert et al., 2011).

More specifically, there is a "transfer deficit" when infants learn from books and video screens, meaning they are less likely to understand and apply what they have learned than if they learned directly from another person (Barr, 2013). One solution is for caregivers to interact more with their infants and ban or limit videos. Another solution, if the parents want the child to learn vocabulary or other material from a book or video, is to let the child see the same two-dimensional presentation again and again. Toddlers often choose to repeat exposure long past the time the parents are bored, a sign that learning at that age requires more repetitions than later on (Barr, 2013).

One product, *My Baby Can Read,* was pulled off the market in 2012 because experts repeatedly attacked its claims, and the cost of defending lawsuits was too high (Ryan, 2012). But many such products are still sold, and new ones appear continually. The owners of *Baby Einstein* lost a lawsuit in 2009, promised not to claim it was educational, and offered a refund, yet, as one critic notes:

> The bottom line is that this industry exists to capitalize on the national preoccupation with creating intelligent children as early as possible, and it has become a multi-million dollar enterprise. Even after . . . the Baby Einstein Company itself admitted its products are not educational, Baby Einstein products continue to fly off of the shelves.
>
> *[Ryan, 2012, p. 784]*

Another study gave videos to one group of parents and none to a control group. They found no evidence that videos could actually teach young babies to read, or even recognize letters, although many parents in this study were enthusiastic about the videos (Neuman et al., 2014).

Is science too cautious or are parents too quick to be swayed by commercial testimony? If a video-watching toddler becomes more verbal, perhaps the timing was a coincidence: All normal babies burst forth with new words at a certain point.

What is your opinion? More importantly, how does your opinion connect to your bias about scientists, or about corporations, or about parents?

Theory Two: Social Impulses Foster Infant Language

The second theory is called *social-pragmatic.* It arises from the sociocultural reason for language: communication. According to this perspective, infants communicate because humans are social beings, dependent on one another for survival and joy. Each culture has practices that further social interaction; talking is one

Same Situation, Far Apart: Before Words
The Polish babies learning sign language (*top*) and the New York infant interpreting a smile (*bottom*) are all doing what babies do: trying to understand communication long before they are able to talk.

// **Response for Educators** (from page 194): Probably both. Infants love to communicate, and they seek every possible way to do so. Therefore, the teachers should try to understand the baby and the baby's parents, but they should also start teaching the baby the majority language of the first school.

such practice. Thus, all infants (and no chimpanzees) master words and grammar to join the social world in which they find themselves (Tomasello & Herrmann, 2010).

According to this perspective, it is the emotional messages of speech, not the words, that propel communication. In one study, people who had never heard English (Shuar hunter-gatherers living in isolation near the Andes Mountains) listened to tapes of North American mothers talking to their babies. The Shuar successfully distinguished speech conveying comfort, approval, attention, and prohibition, without knowing any of the words (Bryant & Barrett, 2007). This study suggests that the social content of speech is universal; therefore, since babies are social creatures, they learn whatever specifics their culture provides.

Suppose an 18-month-old is playing with an unnamed toy and an adult utters a word. Does the child connect that word to the toy? A behaviorist, learning-by-association prediction would be yes, but the answer is no. In an experiment, when toddlers played with a fascinating toy and adults said a word, the toddlers looked up, figured out what the adult was looking at, and assigned the new word to that, not to the fascinating toy (Baldwin, 1993). This supports theory two: The toddlers wanted to know what the adults intended.

Evidence for social learning comes from educational programs for children. Many 1-year-olds enjoy watching television and videos, as the Opposing Perspectives feature on page 195 explains, but they learn best when adults are actively involved in teaching. In a controlled experiment, 1-year-olds learned vocabulary much better when someone taught them directly than when the same person gave the same lesson on video (Roseberry et al., 2009).

According to theory two, then, social impulses, not explicit teaching, lead infants to learn language. According to this theory, people differ from the great apes in that they are social, driven to communicate (Tomasello & Herrmann, 2010).

Theory Three: Infants Teach Themselves

A third theory holds that language learning is genetically programmed to begin at a certain age; adults need not teach it (theory one), nor is it a by-product of social interaction (theory two). Instead, it arises from the universal genetic impulse to imitate. Languages have been developed to take advantage of this maturation process. For example, English has articles (*the, an, a*) that signal to the baby that the next word will be the name of an object, and since babies have "an innate base" that primes them to learn, such articles facilitate learning nouns (Shi, 2014, p. 9).

As already explained in the research on memory, infants and toddlers observe what they see and they apply it—not slavishly but according to their own concepts and intentions, which develop as the brain matures. Theory three proposes that this is exactly what they do with the language they hear (Saxton, 2010).

This theory is buttressed by research that finds that variations in children's language ability correlate with differences in brain activity and perceptual ability, evident months before the first words are spoken and apart from the particulars of parental input (Cristia et al., 2014). Some 5-year-olds are far more verbal than others because they were born to be so.

This perspective began soon after Skinner proposed his theory of verbal learning. Noam Chomsky (1968, 1980) and his followers felt that language is too complex to be mastered merely through step-by-step conditioning. Although behaviorists focus on variations among children in vocabulary size, Chomsky focused on similarities in language acquisition—the universals, not the differences.

Noting that all young children master basic grammar according to a schedule, Chomsky cited this *universal grammar* as evidence that humans are born with a mental structure that prepares them to seek some elements of human language. For example, everywhere, a raised tone indicates a question, and infants prefer questions to declarative statements (Soderstrom et al., 2011). This suggests that infants are wired to have conversations, and caregivers universally ask them questions long before they can answer back.

Chomsky labeled this hypothesized mental structure the **language acquisition device (LAD)**. The LAD enables children, as their brains develop, to derive the rules of grammar quickly and effectively from the speech they hear every day, regardless of whether their native language is English, Thai, or Urdu. On their part, adults, because of their own LAD, instinctively help children learn whatever superficial differences appear between one language and another.

Other scholars agree with Chomsky that all infants are primed, naturally, to understand and speak whatever language they hear. They are eager learners, and speech becomes one more manifestation of neurological maturation (Wagner & Lakusta, 2009). This idea does not strip languages and cultures of their differences in sounds, grammar, and almost everything else, but the basic idea is that "language is a window on human nature, exposing deep and universal features of our thoughts and feelings" (Pinker, 2007, p. 148).

According to theory three, language is experience-expectant, as the developing brain quickly and efficiently connects neurons to support whichever language the infant hears. Because of this experience expectancy, the various languages of the world are all logical, coherent, and systematic. Then some experience-dependent learning occurs as each brain adjusts to a particular language.

Research supports this perspective as well. As you remember, newborns are primed to listen to speech (Vouloumanos & Werker, 2007), and all infants babble *ma-ma* and *da-da* sounds (not yet referring to mother or father). No reinforcement or teaching is required; all a baby needs is time, and that will allow dendrites to grow, mouth muscles to strengthen, neurons to connect, and speech to be heard. This theory might explain why poets put together phrases that they have never heard to produce novel understanding, and why people hear words in their dreams that make no sense. Thus, the language impulse may arise from the brain, not from other people.

Nature even provides for deaf infants. All 6-month-olds, hearing or not, prefer to look at sign language over nonlinguistic pantomime. For hearing infants, this preference disappears by 10 months because their affinity for gestural language is not necessary for communication (Krentz & Corina, 2008). Deaf infants are signing by then, which is their particular expression of LAD, a universal impulse.

A Hybrid Theory

Which of these three perspectives is correct? Perhaps all of them are true, to some extent. In one monograph that included details and results of 12 experiments, the authors presented a hybrid (which literally means "a new creature, formed by combining other living things") of previous theories (Hollich et al., 2000). Since infants learn language to do numerous things—to indicate intention, call objects by name, put words together, talk to family members, sing to themselves, express

Especially for Nurses and Pediatricians
Eric and Jennifer have been reading about language development in children. They are convinced that because language develops naturally, they need not talk to their 6-month-old son. How do you respond? (see response, page 199)

language acquisition device (LAD) Chomsky's term for a hypothesized mental structure that enables humans to learn language, including the basic aspects of grammar, vocabulary, and intonation.

wishes, remember the past, and much more—some aspects of language learning are best explained by one theory at one age and other aspects by another theory at another age.

Although originally developed to explain acquisition of first words, mostly nouns, this theory also explains learning verbs: Perceptual, social, and linguistic abilities combine to make that possible (Golinkoff & Hirsh-Pasek, 2008). Linguists seek to understand how most children acquire more than one language; it seems that many strategies help (Canagarajah & Wurr, 2011).

One study supporting the hybrid theory began, as did the study previously mentioned, with infants looking at pairs of objects that they had never seen and never heard named. One of each pair was fascinating to babies and the other was boring, specifically "a blue sparkle wand . . . [paired with] a white cabinet latch . . . a red, green, and pink party clacker . . . [paired with] a beige bottle opener" (Pruden et al., 2006, p. 267). The experimenter said a made-up name (not an actual word), and then the infants were tested to see whether they assigned the new word to the object that had the experimenter's attention (the dull one) or to the one that was interesting to them.

Unlike the similar study already described, which involved 18-month-olds, the participants in this one were 10-month-olds. They responded differently than the older infants did. The 10-month-olds seemed to assign the word to the fascinating object, not the dull one. These researchers' interpretation was that *how* language is learned depends on the age of the child as well as on the particular circumstances. Behaviorism may work for young children, social learning for slightly older ones: "The perceptually driven 10-month-old becomes the socially aware 19-month-old" (Pruden et al., 2006, p. 278).

Current thinking is that children are not exclusively social learners or behaviorists and that learning a new word or grammar form is not an all-or-none accomplishment. Instead, partial learning occurs: A lack of evident mastery of a word makes it easier to learn that word or a related word later on (Yurovsky et al., 2014).

This may be easier to understand with an example. Suppose a 1-year-old meets an unfamiliar child named Tom and fails to say his name or wave "bye-bye Tom" when asked. That might be considered failure—Chomsky might say the child was not ready, Skinner might say the child was not sufficiently reinforced, social learning theorists might say that Tom was not socially important.

But then, a week later, the child might see Tom again, hear that his name is Tom, and immediately say "Tom." The likely explanation is that partial learning occurred the first time, so the second time it became evident. Such experiences are common: A toddler might surprise everyone by saying a word that was heard earlier. Learning is more likely if all three factors (reinforcement, social impulses, maturation) combine.

After intensive study, yet another group of scientists also endorsed a hybrid theory, concluding that "multiple attentional, social, and linguistic cues" contribute to early language (Tsao et al., 2004, p. 1081). It makes logical and practical sense for nature to provide several paths toward language learning and for various theorists to emphasize one or another of them (Sebastián-Gallés, 2007).

It also seems that some children learn better one way and others another way (Goodman et al., 2008), and that families and cultures vary in how they teach. Since every human must learn language, nature allows diversity in specifics so that the goal is always attained. Ideally, parents talk often to their infants (theory one), encourage social interaction (theory two), and appreciate the innate abilities of the child (theory three).

As one expert concludes:

> our best hope for unraveling some of the mysteries of language acquisition rests with approaches that incorporate multiple factors, that is, with approaches that incorporate not only some explicit linguistic model, but also the full range of biological, cultural, and psycholinguistic processes involved.
>
> *[Tomasello, 2006, pp. 292–293]*

The idea that every theory is correct may seem idealistic. However, many scientists who are working on extending and interpreting research on language acquisition arrive at a similar conclusion. They contend that language learning is neither the direct product of repeated input (behaviorism) nor the result of a specific human neurological capacity (LAD). Rather, from an evolutionary perspective, "different elements of the language apparatus may have evolved in different ways," and thus, a "piecemeal and empirical" approach is needed (Marcus & Rabagliati, 2009, p. 281). In other words, no single theory explains how babies learn language: Humans accomplish this feat in many ways.

What conclusion can we draw from all the research on infant cognition? It is clear that infants are active learners of language and concepts and that they seek to experiment with objects and find ways to achieve their goals. This is the cognitive version of the biosocial developments noted in Chapter 5, that babies strive to roll over, crawl, walk, and so on as soon as they can. (See Visualizing Development, p. 192.)

// **Response for Nurses and Pediatricians** (from page 197): Although humans may be naturally inclined to communicate with words, exposure to language is necessary. You may not convince Eric and Jennifer, but at least convince them that their baby will be happier if they talk to him.

SUMMING UP From the first days of life, babies attend to words and expressions, responding as well as their limited abilities allow—crying, cooing, and soon babbling. Before age 1, they understand simple words and communicate with gestures. At 1 year, most infants speak a few words in their native language. Vocabulary builds slowly at first but then more rapidly as the holophrase, the naming explosion, and then the two-word sentence appear.

The impressive language learning of the first two years can be explained in many ways: that caregivers must teach language, that infants learn because they are social beings, that inborn cognitive capacity propels infants to acquire language as soon as maturation makes that possible. Because infants vary in culture, learning style, and social context, a hybrid theory contends that each theory may be valid for explaining some aspects of language learning at some ages.

WHAT HAVE YOU LEARNED?

1. What communication abilities do infants have before they talk?
2. What aspects of early language development are universal, apparent in every culture?
3. What is typical of the first words that infants speak and the rate at which they acquire them?
4. What are the early signs of grammar in infant speech?
5. According to behaviorism, how do adults teach infants to talk?
6. According to sociocultural theory, why do infants try to communicate?
7. What does the idea that child speech results from brain maturation imply for caregivers?

SUMMARY

Sensorimotor Intelligence

1. Piaget realized that very young infants are active learners who seek to understand their complex observations and experiences. The six stages of sensorimotor intelligence involve early adaptation to experience.

2. Sensorimotor intelligence begins with reflexes and ends with mental combinations. The six stages occur in pairs, with each pair characterized by a circular reaction; infants first react to their own bodies (primary), then respond to other people and things (secondary), and finally, in the stage of tertiary circular reactions, infants become more goal-oriented, creative, and experimental as "little scientists."

3. Infants gradually develop an understanding of objects. According to Piaget's classic experiments, infants understand object permanence and begin to search for hidden objects at about 8 months.

4. Newer research, using brain scans and other methods, finds that Piaget underestimated infant cognition. His conclusions about when infants understand object permanence and when they defer imitation have been revised.

Information Processing

5. Another approach to understanding infant cognition involves information-processing theory, which looks at each step of the thinking process, from input to output. The perceptions of a young infant are attuned to the particular affordances, or opportunities for action, that are present in the infant's world.

6. Objects, creatures, and especially people that move are particularly interesting to infants because they afford many possibilities for interaction and perception. From a baby's perspective, the world is filled with exciting opportunities for learning; adults may be more cautious.

7. Infant memory is fragile but not completely absent. Reminder sessions help trigger memories, and young brains learn motor sequences and respond to repeated emotions (their own and those of other people) long before they can remember with words.

8. Memory is multifaceted; infant amnesia is a myth. At about 9 months, infant memories improve. Repetition is especially important for infant memory.

Language: What Develops in the First Two Years?

9. Language learning, which distinguishes the human species from other animals, is an amazing infant accomplishment. By age 2, babies are talking to express wishes and memory, as well as what they experience at the moment.

10. Attempts to communicate are apparent in the first weeks and months. Infants babble at about 6 months, understand words and gestures by 10 months, and speak their first words at about 1 year. Deaf infants make their first signs before 1 year.

11. Vocabulary builds slowly until the infant knows approximately 50 words. Then the naming explosion begins.

12. Toward the end of the second year, toddlers put words together in short sentences. The tone of holophrases is evidence of grammar, but putting two or three words together in proper sequence is proof.

13. Various theories explain how infants learn language as quickly as they do. The three main theories emphasize different aspects of early language learning: that infants must be taught, that their social impulses foster language learning, and that their brains are genetically attuned to language as soon as the requisite maturation has occurred.

14. Each theory of language learning is confirmed by some research. The challenge for developmental scientists has been to formulate a hybrid theory that uses all the insights and research on early language learning. The challenge for caregivers is to respond to the infant's early attempts to communicate, expecting neither too much nor too little.

KEY TERMS

sensorimotor intelligence
(p. 173)

primary circular reactions
(p. 173)

secondary circular reactions
(p. 174)

object permanence (p. 175)

tertiary circular reactions
(p. 176)

"little scientist" (p. 176)

deferred imitation (p. 177)

habituation (p. 179)

fMRI (p. 179)

information-processing theory
(p. 180)

affordance (p. 181)

visual cliff (p. 182)

dynamic perception (p. 182)

people preference (p. 183)

reminder session (p. 185)

child-directed speech (p. 188)

babbling (p. 188)

holophrase (p. 189)

naming explosion (p. 190)

grammar (p. 191)

mean length of utterance
(MLU) (p. 193)

language acquisition device
(LAD) (p. 197)

APPLICATIONS

1. Elicit vocalizations from an infant—babbling if the baby is under age 1, words if the baby is older. Write down all the baby's communication for 10 minutes. Then ask the primary caregiver to elicit vocalizations for 10 minutes, and write these down. What differences are apparent between the baby's two attempts at communication? Compare your findings with the norms described in the chapter.

2. Piaget's definition of *intelligence* is "adaptation." Others consider a good memory or an extensive vocabulary to be a sign of intelligence. How would you define intelligence? Give examples.

3. Many educators recommend that parents read to babies every day, even before 1 year of age. What theory of language development does this reflect and why? Ask several parents if they did so, and why or why not.

4. Test an infant's ability to search for a hidden object. Ideally, the infant should be about 7 or 8 months old, and you should retest over a period of weeks. If the infant can immediately find the object, make the task harder by pausing between hiding and searching or by moving the object from one hiding place to another.

The First Two Years:
Psychosocial Development

What Will You Know?

1. How do smiles, tears, anger, and fear change from birth to age 2?
2. Does a baby's temperament predict lifelong personality?
3. What are the signs of a secure attachment between parent and infant?
4. What are opposing theories about the development of infant emotions?
5. Do babies benefit or suffer when they are placed in infant day care?

My 1-week-old grandson cried. Often. Again and again. Day and night. For a long time. Again. He and his parents were staying with me for a few months. I was not the caregiver, so I didn't mind the crying for myself. But I did mind for my sleep-deprived daughter.

And I worried about her husband. He spent many hours, day and night, carrying my grandson while my daughter slept.

"It seems to me that you do most of the baby-comforting," I told him.

"That's because Elissa does most of the breast-feeding," he answered with a smile.

This chapter opens by tracing infants' emotions as their brains mature and their experiences accumulate, and it notes temperamental and cultural differences. All babies cry early on, but soon their emotions take many forms. This discussion leads to an exploration of caregiver–infant interaction, particularly *synchrony, attachment,* and *social referencing.* For every aspect of caregiving, fathers as well as mothers are included, a change from a few decades ago.

Then we apply each of the five theories introduced in Chapter 2, not only to understand infant emotions but also to consider a controversial topic: Who should be the caregivers? Families and cultures answer this question in many ways. Fortunately, as this chapter explains, although temperaments and caregivers vary, most infants (including my now-happy grandson) thrive, as long as their basic physical and emotional needs are met.

Now Happy Asa How does a crying baby become a happy toddler? A clue is here: devoted father and grandfather.

COURTESY OF KATHLEEN BERGER

Emotional Development

In their first two years, infants progress from reactive pain and pleasure to complex patterns of social awareness (see At About This Time), a movement from basic instinctual emotions to learned and then thoughtful ones (Panksepp & Watt, 2011). Infant emotions arise more from the body than from thought, so speedy, uncensored reactions—crying, startling, laughing, raging—are common.

Early Emotions

At first there is pleasure and pain. Newborns are happy and relaxed when fed and drifting off to sleep. They cry when they are hurt or hungry, tired or frightened (as by a loud noise or a sudden loss of support).

Some infants have bouts of uncontrollable crying, called *colic,* probably from immature digestion; some have *reflux,* probably from immature swallowing. About 20 percent of babies cry "excessively," more than three hours a day, for more than three days a week, for more than three weeks (J. S. Kim, 2011).

Smiling and Laughing

Soon, additional emotions become recognizable. Curiosity is evident as infants (and people of all ages) respond to objects and experiences that are new but not too novel. Happiness is expressed by the **social smile,** evoked by a human face at about 6 weeks. Preterm babies smile a few weeks later because the social smile is affected by age since conception, not age since birth.

Infants worldwide express social joy, even laughter, between 2 and 4 months (Konner, 2007; Lewis, 2010). Laughter builds as curiosity does; a typical 6-month-old laughs loudly upon discovering new things, particularly social experiences that balance familiarity and surprise, such as Daddy making a funny face. They prefer looking at happy faces over sad ones, even if the happy faces are not looking at them (Kim & Johnson, 2013).

Anger and Sadness

The positive emotions of joy and contentment are soon joined by negative emotions, which are expressed more often in infancy than later on (Izard, 2009). Anger is evident at 6 months, usually triggered by frustration, such as when infants are prevented from moving or grabbing.

To investigate infants' response to frustration, researchers "crouched behind the child and gently restrained his or her arms for 2 minutes or until 20 seconds of hard crying ensued" (Mills-Koonce et al., 2011, p. 390). "Hard crying" was not infrequent: Infants hate to be strapped in, caged in, closed in, or even just held in place when they want to explore. In that study, frustrated infants whose fathers were less nurturant tended to be quicker to react with elevated **cortisol,** the stress hormone—an indication that the infants were already developing learned emotional reactions.

In infancy, anger is generally a healthy response to frustration, unlike sadness, which also appears in the first months. Sadness indicates withdrawal and is accompanied by a greater increase in the body's production of cortisol.

at about this time

Developing Emotions

Birth	Distress; contentment
6 weeks	Social smile
3 months	Laughter; curiosity
4 months	Full, responsive smiles
4–8 months	Anger
9–14 months	Fear of social events (strangers, separation from caregiver)
12 months	Fear of unexpected sights and sounds
18 months	Self-awareness; pride; shame; embarrassment

As always, culture and experience influence the norms of development. This is especially true for emotional development after the first eight months.

social smile A smile evoked by a human face, normally first evident in infants about 6 weeks after birth.

cortisol The primary stress hormone; fluctuations in the body's cortisol level affect human emotions.

CHRISTOPHER HERWIG/GETTY IMAGES

Smiles All Around Joy is universal when an infant smiles at her beaming grandparents—a smile made even better when the tongue joins in. This particular scene took place in Kazakhstan in central Asia.

This is one conclusion from experiments in which 4-month-olds were taught to pull a string to see a picture, which they enjoyed—not unlike the leg-kicking study to move the mobile, described in Chapter 6. Then the string was disconnected. Most babies reacted by angrily jerking the string. Some, however, quit trying and looked sad (Lewis & Ramsay, 2005); their cortisol rose markedly. This suggests that some babies learn, to their sorrow, to repress their anger.

Since sadness produces physiological stress (measured by cortisol levels), sorrow negatively impacts the infant. All social emotions, particularly sadness and fear, probably shape the brain (Fries & Pollak, 2007; M. H. Johnson, 2011). As you learned in Chapter 5, experience matters. Sad and angry infants whose mothers are depressed become fearful toddlers (Dix & Yan, 2014). Too much sadness early in life correlates with depression later on.

Fear

Fear in response to some person, thing, or situation (not just being startled in surprise) is evident at about 9 months and soon becomes more frequent and obvious. Two kinds of social fear are typical:

> **Separation anxiety**—clinging and crying when a familiar caregiver is about to leave
>
> **Stranger wariness**—fear of unfamiliar people, especially when they move too close, too quickly

Separation anxiety is normal at age 1, intensifies by age 2, and usually subsides after that. Fear of separation interferes with infant sleep. For example, infants who fall asleep next to familiar people may wake up frightened if they are alone (Sadeh et al., 2010). The solution is not necessarily to sleep with the baby, but neither is it to ignore the child's natural fear of separation. (**Developmental Link:** Co-sleeping and bed-sharing are discussed in Chapter 5.)

Some babies are comforted by a "transitional object," such as a teddy bear or blanket beside them, as they transition from sleeping in their parents' arms to sleeping alone. Music, a night light, an open door, may all ease the fear.

Transitional objects are not pathological; they are the infant's way of coping with anxiety. However, if separation anxiety remains strong after age 3 and impairs the child's ability to leave home, go to school, or play with friends, it is considered an emotional disorder. Separation anxiety as a disorder can be diagnosed at any age and is quite different from the "strong interdependence among family members," which is normative in some cultures (American Psychiatric Association, 2013, p. 193).

Separation anxiety may be apparent outside the home. Strangers—especially those who do not resemble or move like familiar caregivers—merit stares, not smiles, at age 1. This is a good sign: Infant memory is active and engaged. Fear of strangers is normative, which means that every toddler typically manifests it, but genes and parents make it stronger (with tears and hiding) or weaker (with a wary look). Children whose parents are themselves anxious are likely to fear new people throughout childhood (Brooker et al., 2013).

Many normal 1-year-olds fear anything unexpected, from the flush of the toilet to the pop of a jack-in-the-box, from closing elevator doors to the tail-wagging approach of a dog. With repeated experience and reassurance, older infants might enjoy flushing the toilet (again and again) or calling the dog (and might cry if the dog does *not* come). Note the transition from instinct to learning to thought (Panksepp & Watt, 2011).

Every aspect of early emotional development interacts with cultural beliefs, expressed in parental actions. There seems to be more separation anxiety and

separation anxiety An infant's distress when a familiar caregiver leaves; most obvious between 9 and 14 months.

stranger wariness An infant's expression of concern—a quiet stare while clinging to a familiar person, or a look of fear—when a stranger appears.

Developmentally Correct Both Santa's smile and Olivia's grimace are appropriate reactions for people of their age. Adults playing Santa must smile no matter what, and if Olivia smiled, that would be troubling to anyone who knows about 7-month-olds. Yet every Christmas, thousands of parents wait in line to put their infants on the lap of oddly dressed, bearded strangers.

Especially for Nurses and Pediatricians Parents come to you concerned that their 1-year-old hides her face and holds onto them tightly whenever a stranger appears. What do you tell them? (see response, page 207)

stranger wariness in Japan than in Germany because Japanese infants "have very few experiences with separation from the mother," whereas in German towns, "infants are frequently left alone outside of stores or supermarkets" while their mothers shop (Saarni et al., 2006, p. 237).

Toddlers' Emotions

Emotions take on new strength during toddlerhood, as both memory and mobility advance (Izard, 2009). For example, throughout the second year and beyond, anger and fear become less frequent but more focused, targeted toward infuriating or terrifying experiences. Similarly, laughing and crying are louder and more discriminating.

The new strength of emotions is apparent in temper tantrums. Toddlers are famous for fury. When something angers them they might yell, scream, cry, hit, and throw themselves on the floor. Logic is beyond them; if adults respond with anger or teasing, that makes it worse.

One child was angry at her feet and said she did not want them. When a parent offered to get scissors and cut them off, a new wail of tantrum erupted. With temper tantrums, soon sadness comes to the fore, at which time comfort—rather than acquiescence or punishment—is helpful (Green et al., 2011).

Social Awareness

Temper can be seen as an expression of selfhood. So can new toddler emotions: pride, shame, jealousy, embarrassment, disgust, and guilt. These emotions require social awareness, which typically emerges from family interactions. For instance, in a study of infant jealousy, when mothers deliberately paid attention to another infant, babies moved closer to their mothers, bidding for attention. Brain activity also registered social awareness (Mize et al., 2014).

Culture is crucial here, with independence a value in some families but not in others. Many North American parents encourage toddler pride (saying, "You did it yourself"—even when that is untrue), but Asian families typically cultivate modesty and shame. Such differences may still be apparent in adult personality and judgment. Are you more likely to be annoyed at people who brag or who say they failed? Probably family values taught you that reaction.

Disgust is also strongly influenced by other people as well as by maturation. According to a study that involved many children of various ages, many 18-month-olds (but not younger infants) express disgust at touching a dead animal. None, however, are yet disgusted when a teenager curses at an elderly person—something that parents and older children often find disgusting (Stevenson et al., 2010).

Self-Awareness

self-awareness A person's realization that he or she is a distinct individual whose body, mind, and actions are separate from those of other people.

In addition to social awareness, another foundation for emotional growth is **self-awareness**, the realization that one's body, mind, and activities are distinct from those of other people (Kopp, 2011). Closely following the new mobility that results from walking is an emerging sense of "me" and "mine" that leads the infant to develop a new consciousness of others at about age 1.

Very young infants have no sense of self—at least of *self* as most people define it, but self-awareness grows during toddlerhood with

> self-referential emotions . . . . By the end of the second year [about 20 months] and increasingly in the third [after 24 months], the simple joy of success becomes accompanied by looking and smiling to an adult and calling attention to the feat; the simple sadness of failure becomes accompanied either by avoidance of eye contact with the adult and turning away or by reparative activity and confession.
>
> [Thompson, 2006, p. 79]

In a classic experiment (Lewis & Brooks, 1978), 9- to 24-month-olds looked into a mirror after a dot of rouge had been surreptitiously put on their noses. If they reacted by touching the red dot on their noses, that meant they knew the mirror showed their own faces. None of the babies younger than 12 months did that, although they sometimes smiled and touched the dot on the "other" baby in the mirror.

However, at some time between 15 and 24 months, babies become self-aware, touching their noses with curiosity and puzzlement. Self-recognition in the mirror/ rouge test (and in photographs) usually emerges at about 18 months, along with two other advances: pretending and using first-person pronouns (*I, me, mine, my-self, my*) (Lewis, 2010).

As another scholar explains it, "an explicit and hence reflective conception of the self is apparent at the early stage of language acquisition at around the same age that infants begin to recognize themselves in mirrors" (Rochat, 2013, p. 388). This is yet another example of the interplay of all the infant abilities—walking, talking, and emotional self-understanding all work together to make the 18-month-old a quite different person from the 8-month-old.

My finger, my body, and me Mirror self-recognition is particularly important in her case, as this 2-year-old has a twin sister. Parents need to make sure each child develops his or her own identity. Parents may enjoy dressing twins alike, and giving them rhyming names, but each baby needs to forge an identity.

SUMMING UP   A newborn's emotions are distress and contentment, expressed by crying or looking relaxed. The social smile is evident at about 6 weeks. Curiosity, laughter, anger (when infants are kept from something they want), and fear (when something unexpected occurs) soon appear, becoming evident in the latter half of the first year. At about a year, separation anxiety and stranger wariness peak, gradually fading as the child grows older. Toddlers become conscious that they are individuals apart from other individuals sometime after 15 months, and that allows them to experience and express many emotions that indicate self-awareness and awareness of other people's reactions to them. Throughout infancy, cultural expectations and parental actions shape emotions.

WHAT HAVE YOU LEARNED?
1.   What are the first emotions to appear in infants?
2.   What experiences trigger anger and sadness in infants?
3.   What do typical 1-year-olds fear?
4.   How do emotions differ between the first and second year of life?
5.   What is the significance of the toddler's reaction to seeing herself in the mirror? ●

 LaunchPad

Video Activity: Self-Awareness and the Rouge Test shows the Rouge Test, which assesses how and when self-awareness appears in infancy.

Brain and Emotions

Brain maturation is involved in the developments just described because all reactions begin in the brain (Johnson, 2011). Experience promotes specific connections between neurons and emotions.

Links between expressed emotions and brain growth are complex and thus difficult to assess and describe (Lewis, 2010). Compared with the emotions of adults, discrete emotions during early infancy are murky and unpredictable. The growth of synapses and dendrites is a likely explanation for the gradual refinement and expression of discrete emotions, the result of past experiences and ongoing maturation.

Growth of the Brain

Many specific aspects of brain development support social emotions (Lloyd-Fox et al., 2009). For instance, the social smile and laughter appear as the cortex matures

// Response for Nurses and Pediatricians (from page 205): Stranger wariness is normal up to about 14 months. This baby's behavior actually might indicate secure attachment!

(Konner, 2010). The same is probably true for fear, self-awareness, and anger. The brains of 8-month-olds respond to other people who look or act afraid, and that probably enhances the infant's own expression of fear (Missana et al., 2014).

Cultural differences become encoded in the infant brain, called "a cultural sponge" by one group of scientists (Ambady & Bharucha, 2009, p. 342). It is difficult to measure exactly how infant brains are molded by their context, in part because parents are reluctant to allow the brains of their normally developing infants to be scanned.

One study (Zhu et al., 2007) of adults—half born in the United States and half in China—found that a particular area of the brain (the medial prefrontal cortex) was activated for both groups when the adults judged whether certain adjectives applied to them. However, when asked whether those adjectives applied to their mothers, that brain area was activated only for the Chinese participants.

Researchers consider this United States-versus-China finding to be "neuroimaging evidence that culture shapes the functional anatomy of self-representation" (Zhu et al., 2007, p. 1310). They speculate that brain activation occurs because the Chinese participants learned, as babies, that they are closely aligned with their mothers, whereas the Americans learned to be independent.

Beyond culture, an infant's brain activity interacts with caregiver responses, probably in the first months of life as well as through the years of childhood (Nelson et al., 2014). Highly reactive 15-month-olds (who were quick to cry) with responsive caregivers (not hostile or neglectful) became less fearful, less angry, and so on. By age 4, they were able to regulate their emotions, presumably because they had developed neurological links between brain excitement and emotional response. In contrast, highly reactive toddlers whose caregivers were less responsive were often overwhelmed by emotions later on (Ursache, et al., 2013). Differential susceptibility is apparent: Innate reactions and caregiver actions together sculpt the brain.

Learning About Others

The tentative social smile of 2-month-old infants to any face soon becomes a quicker and fuller smile when they see a familiar, loving caregiver. This occurs because, with repeated experience, the neurons that fire together become more closely and quickly connected to each other (via dendrites).

Social preferences form in the early months, connected not only with a person's face, but also with voice, touch, and smell. Early social awareness is one reason adopted children ideally join their new parents in the first days of life (a marked change from 100 years ago, when adoptions began after age 1).

Social awareness is also a reason to respect an infant's reaction to a babysitter: If a 6-month-old screams and clings to the parent when the sitter arrives, another caregiver probably needs to be found. (Do not confuse this reaction with separation anxiety at 12 months—a normal, expected reaction to everyone.)

Every experience that a person has—especially in the early days and months—activates and prunes neurons, such that the firing patterns from one axon to a dendrite reflect past learning. As illustrated in Visualizing Development in Chapter 5, p. 144, this was first shown dramatically with baby mice: Some were licked and nuzzled by their mothers almost constantly, and some were neglected. A mother mouse's licking of her newborn babies reduced methylation of a gene (Nr3c1), which allowed more serotonin (a neurotransmitter) to be released by the hypothalamus (a region of the brain discussed in Chapter 8).

Serotonin not only increased momentary pleasure (mice love being licked) but also started a chain of epigenetic responses to reduce cortisol from many parts of the brain and body, including the adrenal glands. The effects on both brain and behavior are lifelong for mice and probably for humans as well.

For many humans, social anxiety is stronger than any other anxieties. Certainly to some extent this is genetic. But epigenetic research finds environmental influences important as well. This was clearly shown in a longitudinal study of 1,300 adolescents (twins and siblings): Their genetic tendency toward anxiety was evident at every age, but life events affected how strong that anxiety was felt (Zavos et al., 2012).

A smaller study likewise found that if the infant of an anxious biological mother is raised by a responsive adoptive mother who is not anxious, the inherited anxiety does not materialize (Natsuaki et al., 2013). Parents need to be comforting (as with the nuzzled baby mice) but not overprotective. Fearful mothers tend to raise fearful children, but fathers who offer their infants exciting but not dangerous challenges (such as a game of chase, crawling on the floor) reduce later anxiety (Majdandžić et al., 2013).

Stress

Emotions are connected to brain activity and hormones, but the connections are complicated; they are affected by genes, past experiences, hormones, and neurotransmitters not yet understood (Lewis, 2010). One link is clear: Excessive fear and stress harms the developing brain. The hypothalamus (discussed further in Chapter 8), in particular, grows more slowly if an infant is often frightened.

Brain scans of children who were maltreated in infancy show abnormal responses to stress, anger, and other emotions later on, including to photographs of frightened people. Some children seem resilient, but many areas of the brain (the hypothalamus, the amygdala, the HPA axis, the hippocampus, and the prefrontal cortex—all explained in later chapters) are affected by abuse, especially if the maltreatment begins in infancy (Bernard et al., 2014; Cicchetti, 2013a).

Since early caregiving affects the brain lifelong, caregivers need to be consistent and reassuring. This is not always easy. Remember that some infants cry inconsolably in the early weeks. As one researcher notes:

> An infant's crying has 2 possible consequences: it may elicit tenderness and desire to soothe, or helplessness and rage. It can be a signal that encourages attachment or one that jeopardizes the early relationship by triggering depression and, in some cases, even neglect or abuse.
>
> [J. S. Kim, 2011, p. 229]

Sometimes mothers are blamed, or blame themselves, when an infant cries. This attitude is not helpful: A mother who feels guilty or incompetent may become angry at her baby, which leads to unresponsive parenting, an unhappy child, and then hostile interactions. Presumably the results would be the same if the father, or grandmother, were the primary caregiver, although extensive research on those infant-caregiver relationships has not yet been published. Years later, first-grade classmates and teachers are likely to consider children of unresponsive mothers disruptive and aggressive (Lorber & Egeland, 2011).

But the opposite may occur if early crying produces solicitous parenting. Then, when the baby outgrows the crying, the parent–child bond may be exceptionally strong.

No Tears Needed In the first weeks of life, babies produce no tears. However, sadness is obvious—unlike adults who might smile while tears betray them. Given what is known about the infant brain, we hope photography did not postpone baby-comforting.

Synesthesia

Brain maturation may affect an infant's ability to differentiate emotions—for instance, distinguishing between fear and joy. Some infants seem to cry at everything.

Early emotional confusion seems similar to *synesthesia,* a phenomenon in which one sense triggers another in the brain. For older children and adults, the most common form of synesthesia is when a number or letter evokes a vivid color. Among adults, synesthesia is unusual; often, it is partly genetic and indicates artistic creativity (K. J. Barnett et al., 2008).

Synesthesia seems more common in infants because the boundaries between the sensory parts of the cortex are still forming (Walker et al., 2010). Textures seem associated with vision, sounds with smells, and the infant's own body seems connected to the bodies of others.

These sensory connections allow *cross-modal perception,* when a sensation from one mode (such as a sound) is also experienced in another mode (such as sight). A caregiver's smell and voice may evoke a vision of that person, for instance, or a sound may be connected with a shape. For example, when 4-month-old infants hear words that seem more staccato—such as "kiki"—they are more likely to look at an angular shape than a round one (Ozturk et al., 2013).

The tendency of one part of the brain to activate another may also occur for emotions. An infant's cry can be triggered by pain, fear, tiredness, surprise, or excitement; laughter can turn to tears. Discrete emotions during early infancy are more difficult to recognize, differentiate, or predict than the same emotions in adulthood; infant emotions erupt, increase, or disappear for unknown reasons (Camras & Shutter, 2010). Brain immaturity is a likely explanation.

Temperament

Temperament is defined as the "biologically based core of individual differences in style of approach and response to the environment that is stable across time and situations" (van den Akker et al., 2010, p. 485). "Biologically based" means that these traits originate with nature, not nurture.

Confirmation that temperament arises from the inborn brain comes from an analysis of the tone, duration, and intensity of infant cries after the first inoculation, before much experience outside the womb. Cry variations at this very early stage correlate with later temperament (Jong et al., 2010).

Temperament is *not* the same as personality, although temperamental inclinations may lead to personality differences. Generally, personality traits (e.g., honesty and humility) are learned, whereas temperamental traits (e.g., shyness and aggression) are genetic. Of course, for every trait, nature and nurture interact.

The New York Longitudinal Study

In laboratory studies of temperament, infants are exposed to events that are frightening or attractive. Four-month-olds might see spinning mobiles or hear unusual sounds. Older babies might confront a noisy, moving robot or a clown who quickly moves close to them. During such experiences, some children laugh, some cry, others are quiet, and still others exhibit some combination of these reactions that might be signs of one of four types of babies: easy (40%), difficult (10%), slow-to-warm-up (15%), and hard-to-classify (35%).

These categories originate from the *New York Longitudinal Study* (NYLS). Begun in the 1960s, the NYLS was the first large study to recognize that each newborn has distinct inborn traits (Thomas & Chess, 1977). According to the NYLS, by 3 months, infants manifest nine traits that cluster into the four categories just listed.

temperament Inborn differences between one person and another in emotions, activity, and self-regulation. It is measured by the person's typical responses to the environment.

©2016 MACMILLAN

Video: Temperament in Infancy and Toddlerhood
http://qrs.ly/j44ep09

BILL BACHMANN/DANITADELIMONT.COM

Stranger Danger Some parents teach their children to be respectful of any adult; others teach them to fear any stranger. No matter what their culture or parents say, each of these two sisters in Nepal reacts according to her inborn temperament.

Although the NYLS began a rich research endeavor, its nine dimensions have not held up in later studies. Generally, only three (not nine) dimensions of temperament are found (Hirvonen et al., 2013; van den Akker et al., 2010; Degnan et al., 2011), each of which affects later personality and school performance. The following three dimensions of temperament are apparent:

Effortful control (able to regulate attention and emotion, to self-soothe)
Negative mood (fearful, angry, unhappy)
Exuberant (active, social, not shy)

Each of these dimensions is associated with distinctive brain patterns as well as behavior, with the last of these (exuberance versus shyness) most strongly traced to genes (Wolfe et al., 2014).

Since these temperamental traits are apparent at birth, some developmentalists seek to discover which alleles affect specific emotions (M. H. Johnson & Fearon, 2011). For example, researchers have found that the 7-repeat allele of the DRD4 VNTR gene, when combined with the 5-HTTLPR genotype, results in 6-month-olds who are difficult—they cry often, are hard to distract, and are slow to laugh (Holmboe et al., 2011). Infants with a particular allele of the MOA gene are quick to anger. You need not remember the letters of these alleles, but remember that infant emotions vary, partly for genetic reasons.

One longitudinal study analyzed temperament in the same children at 4, 9, 14, 24, and 48 months and in middle childhood, adolescence, and adulthood. The scientists designed laboratory experiments with specifics appropriate for the age of the children; collected detailed reports from the mothers and later from the participants themselves; and gathered observational data and physiological evidence, including brain scans. Past data were reevaluated each time, and cross-sectional and international studies were considered (Fox et al., 2001, 2005, 2013; Hane et al., 2008; L. R. Williams et al., 2010; Jarcho et al., 2013).

Half of the participants did not change much over time, reacting the same way and having similar brain-wave patterns when confronted with frightening experiences. Curiously, the participants most likely to change from infancy to age 4 were the inhibited, fearful ones. Least likely to change were the exuberant babies (see Figure 7.1). Apparently, adults coax frightened infants to be brave but let exuberant children stay happy.

The researchers found unexpected gender differences. As teenagers, the formerly inhibited boys were more likely than the average adolescent to use drugs, but the inhibited girls were less likely to do so (L. R. Williams et al., 2010). The most likely explanation is cultural: Shy boys seek to become less anxious by drinking alcohol, smoking marijuana, or snorting cocaine, but shy girls may be more accepted as they are, or more likely to obey their parents.

Examination of these children in adulthood found intriguing differences between brain and behavior. Those who were inhibited in childhood still showed, in brain scans, evidence of their infant temperament. That confirms that biology affected their traits. However, learning (specifically cognitive control) was evident: Their behavior was similar to those with a more outgoing temperament, unless other factors caused serious emotional problems. Apparently, most of them had learned to override their initial temperamental reactions—not to erase their innate impulses, but to keep them from impairing adult action (Jarcho et al., 2013).

Continuity and change were also evident in another study that found that angry infants were likely to make their mothers hostile toward them, and, if that happened, such infants became antisocial children. However, if the mothers were loving and patient, despite the difficult temperament of the children, hostile traits were not evident later on (Pickles et al., 2013).

Especially for Nurses Parents come to you with their fussy 3-month-old. They say they have read that temperament is "fixed" before birth, and they are worried that their child will always be difficult. What do you tell them? (see response, page 213)

FIGURE 7.1

Do Babies' Temperaments Change? It is possible—especially if they were fearful babies. Adults who are reassuring help children overcome fearfulness. If fearful children do not change, it is not known whether that's because their parents are not sufficiently reassuring (nurture) or because the babies themselves are temperamentally more fearful (nature).

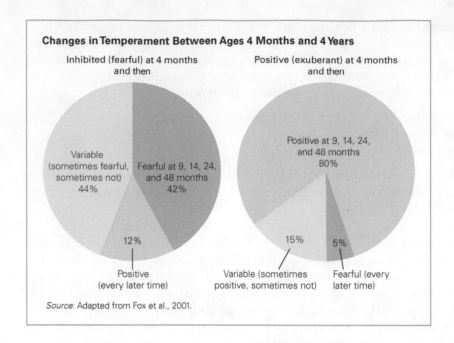

Changes in Temperament Between Ages 4 Months and 4 Years

Inhibited (fearful) at 4 months and then

Variable (sometimes fearful, sometimes not) 44%

Fearful at 9, 14, 24, and 48 months 42%

12%

Positive (every later time)

Positive (exuberant) at 4 months and then

Positive at 9, 14, 24, and 48 months 80%

15%

5%

Variable (sometimes positive, sometimes not)

Fearful (every later time)

Source: Adapted from Fox et al., 2001.

Other studies confirm that difficult infants often become easier—*if* their parents provide excellent, patient care (Belsky & Pluess, 2009). How could this be? Some scientists suggest that, since fussy and scared children often come to the parents for comfort or reassurance, they are particularly likely to flourish with responsive parenting, but they wither if their parents are rejecting (Stupica et al., 2011). This is differential susceptibility again.

The two patterns evident in all these studies—continuity and improvement—have been replicated in many longitudinal studies of infant temperament, especially for antisocial personality traits. Difficult babies tend to become difficult children, but family and culture sometimes mitigate negative outcomes.

Goodness of Fit

All the research finds that traces of childhood temperament endure, blossoming into adult personality, but all the research also confirms that innate tendencies are only part of the story. Context always shapes behavior. Ideally, parents find a **goodness of fit**—that is, meshing infant temperament and parent personality to allow smooth infant–caregiver interactions. With a good fit, parents of difficult babies build a close and affectionate relationship; parents of exuberant infants learn to protect them from harm; parents of slow-to-warm-up toddlers encourage them while giving them time to adjust.

However, not only does infant temperament vary, parental temperament varies as well. One study found that parents who claimed goodness of fit between themselves and their infant were likely to be better parents, even when such obvious correlates as education were taken into account (Seifer et al., 2014). Obviously, adults need to adjust to babies more than vice-versa, but even in infancy, a person's temperament affects how people treat him or her.

Childhood temperament is linked to the parents' genes and their personalities, which often are assessed using five dimensions, called the **Big Five**—openness, conscientiousness, extroversion, agreeableness, and neuroticism. Adults who are high in extroversion (surgency), high in agreeableness (effortful control), and low in neuroticism (negative mood) tend to be warmer and more competent parents (de Haan et al., 2009).

goodness of fit A similarity of temperament and values that produces a smooth interaction between an individual and his or her social context, including family, school, and community.

Big Five The five basic clusters of personality traits that remain quite stable throughout life: openness, conscientiousness, extroversion, agreeableness, and neuroticism.

SUMMING UP   Brain maturation underlies much of emotional development in the first two years. The circumstances of an infant's life affect emotions and sculpt the brain, with long-lasting effects. Early maltreatment can be particularly devastating to later emotional expression, because extreme early fear increases cortisol, which may damage the hippocampus. Some babies are more difficult, which can begin a cascade of hostile relationships or can eventually increase the mutual responsiveness of caregiver and child.

Temperament is inborn, with some babies much easier and others more difficult, some more social and others more shy. Such differences are partly genetic and therefore lifelong, but caregiver responses channel temperament into useful or destructive traits.

WHAT HAVE YOU LEARNED?

1. What is known and unknown about the impact of brain maturation on emotions?
2. How does stress affect early brain development?
3. Why is synesthesia more common in infancy than later on?
4. What happens to traits of temperament as development continues?
5. How do parents and cultures affect temperament?

The Development of Social Bonds

As you see, the social context has a powerful impact on development. So does the infant's age, via brain maturation. With regard to emotional development, the age of the baby determines specific social interactions that lead to growth—first synchrony, then attachment, and finally social referencing (see Visualizing Development, p. 216).

Synchrony

Early parent–child interactions are described as **synchrony,** a mutual exchange that requires split-second timing. Metaphors for synchrony are often musical—a waltz, a jazz duet—to emphasize that each partner must be attuned to the other, with moment-by-moment responses. Synchrony is evident in the first three months, becoming more frequent and elaborate as the infant matures (Feldman, 2007).

synchrony A coordinated, rapid, and smooth exchange of responses between a caregiver and an infant.

Both Partners Active

Detailed research reveals the symbiosis of adult–infant partnerships. Adults rarely smile at young infants until the infants smile at them, several weeks after birth. That tentative baby smile is like a switch that turns on the adults, who usually grin broadly and talk animatedly (Lavelli & Fogel, 2005).

Direct observation reveals synchrony; anyone can see it when watching a caregiver play with an infant who is too young to talk. It is also evident in computer measurement of the millisecond timing of smiles, arched eyebrows, and so on (Messinger et al., 2010). Synchrony is a powerful learning experience for the new human. In every interaction, infants read others' emotions and develop social skills, such as taking turns and watching expressions.

Synchrony usually begins with adults imitating infants (not vice versa), with tone and rhythm (Van Puyvelde et al., 2010). Adults respond to barely perceptible infant facial expressions and body motions. This helps infants connect their internal state with behaviors that are understood within their culture. Synchrony

Four Happy People Synchrony lets infants and caregivers communicate crucial messages: "I love you," or "How delightful!," or simply "Let's have fun."

is particularly apparent in Asian cultures, perhaps because of a cultural focus on interpersonal sensitivity (Morelli & Rothbaum, 2007).

In Western cultures as well, parents and infants become partners. This relationship is crucial when the infant is at medical risk. The necessity of time-consuming physical care might overwhelm concern about psychosocial needs, yet those needs are as important for long-term health as are the biological ones (Newnham et al., 2009). Responsiveness to the individual, not simply to the impaired human, leads to a strong, mutual love between parents and child (Solomon, 2012).

Neglected Synchrony

Is synchrony necessary? If no one plays with an infant, what will happen? Experiments involving the **still-face technique** have addressed these questions (Tronick, 1989; Tronick & Weinberg, 1997).

still-face technique An experimental practice in which an adult keeps his or her face unmoving and expressionless in face-to-face interaction with an infant.

In still-face studies, an infant faces an adult who responds normally while two video cameras simultaneously record their interpersonal reactions. Frame-by-frame analysis reveals that parents instinctively synchronize their responses to the infants' movements, with exaggerated tone and expression. Babies reciprocate with smiles and flailing limbs.

To be specific, long before they can reach out and grab, infants respond excitedly to caregiver attention by waving their arms. They are delighted if the adult moves closer so that a waving arm can touch the face or, even better, a hand can grab hair. You read about this eagerness for interaction (when infants try to "make interesting events last") in Chapter 6.

In response, adults open their eyes wide, raise their eyebrows, smack their lips, and emit nonsense sounds. Hair-grabbing might make adults bob their head back and forth, in a playful attempt to shake off the grab, to the infants' delight, or might cause a sudden angry expression, with a loud "No" making the infant burst into tears. Even that is better than no response at all.

In still-face experiments, the adult stops all expression on cue, staring quietly with a "still face" for a minute or two. Sometimes by 2 months, and clearly by 6 months, infants are upset when their parents are unresponsive. Babies frown, fuss, drool, look away, kick, cry, or suck their fingers. By 5 months, they also vocalize, as if to say, "React to me" (Goldstein et al., 2009).

Many studies of still faces and other reactions reach the same conclusion: Babies need synchrony. Responsiveness aids psychosocial and biological development, evident in heart rate, weight gain, and brain maturation. Particularly in the first year, depressed and anxious mothers are less likely to respond with synchrony to their infants, and then babies become less able to respond to social cues (Atzil et al., 2014).

Attachment

Toward the end of the first year, face-to-face synchrony almost disappears. Once infants can walk, they are no longer content to respond, moment by moment, to adult facial expressions and vocalizations.

Instead **attachment** becomes evident. Actually, attachment is lifelong, beginning before birth and influencing relationships throughout life (see At About This Time). Thousands of researchers on every continent have studied attachment.

Researchers were inspired by John Bowlby (1982, 1983) and by Mary Ainsworth, who described mother–infant relationships in central Africa 60 years ago (Ainsworth, 1967). Attachment studies have occurred in every nation, with extensive research on atypical population (e.g., infants with Down syndrom, with autism, and so on) and on adult relationships with other adults and with their own children (Simpson & Rholes, 2015; Grossmann et al., 2014).

> **attachment** According to Ainsworth, "an affectional tie" that an infant forms with a caregiver—a tie that binds them together in space and endures over time.

Signs of Attachment

Infants show their attachment through *proximity-seeking* (such as approaching and following their caregivers) and through *contact-maintaining* (such as touching, snuggling, and holding). Those attachment expressions are evident when a baby

---

🗓 at about this time

Stages of Attachment

Birth to 6 weeks	*Preattachment.* Newborns signal, via crying and body movements, that they need others. When people respond positively, the newborn is comforted and learns to seek more interaction. Newborns are also primed by brain patterns to recognize familiar voices and faces.
6 weeks to 8 months	*Attachment in the making.* Infants respond preferentially to familiar people by smiling, laughing, babbling. Their caregivers' voices, touch, expressions, and gestures are comforting, often overriding the infant's impulse to cry. Trust (Erikson) develops.
8 months to 2 years	*Classic secure attachment.* Infants greet the primary caregiver, play happily when he or she is present, show separation anxiety when the caregiver leaves. Both infant and caregiver seek to be close to each other (proximity) and frequently look at each other (contact). In many caregiver–infant pairs, physical touch (patting, holding, caressing) is frequent.
2 to 6 years	*Attachment as launching pad.* Young children seek their caregiver's praise and reassurance as their social world expands. Interactive conversations and games (hide-and-seek, object play, reading, pretending) are common. Children expect caregivers to comfort and entertain.
6 to 12 years	*Cultural attachment.* Children seek to make their caregivers proud by learning whatever adults want them to learn, and adults reciprocate. In concrete operational thought (Piaget), specific accomplishments are valued by adults and children. Children develop loyalty to family, community, nation.
12 to 18 years	*New attachment figures.* Teenagers explore and make friendships independent from parents, using their working models of earlier attachments as a base. With formal operational thinking (Piaget), shared ideals and goals become influential.
18 years on	*Attachment reinvented.* Adults develop relationships with others, especially relationships with romantic partners and their own children, influenced by earlier attachment patterns. Past insecure attachments from childhood can be repaired rather than repeated, although this does not always happen.

Source: Adapted from Grobman, 2008.

VISUALIZING DEVELOPMENT

Developing Attachment

Attachment begins at birth and continues lifelong. Much depends not only on the ways in which parents and babies bond, but also on the quality and consistency of caregiv- ing, the safety and security of the home environment, and individual and family experience. While the patterns set in infancy may echo in later life, they are not determinative.

HOW MANY CHILDREN ARE SECURELY ATTACHED?

The specific percentages of children who are secure and insecure vary by culture, parent responsiveness, and specific temperament and needs of both the child and the care- giver. Generally, about a third of all 1-year-olds seem insecure.

50-70%	10-20%	10-20%	5-10%
Securely Attached (Type B)	Avoidant Attachment (Type A)	Ambivalent Attachment (Type C)	Disorganized Attachment (Type D)

ATTACHMENT IN THE STRANGE SITUATION MAY INFLUENCE RELATIONSHIPS THROUGH THE LIFE SPAN

Attachment patterns formed early affect adults lifelong, but later experiences of love and rejection may change early patterns. Researchers measure attachment by examining children's behaviors in the Strange Situation where they are separated from their parent and play in a room with an unfamiliar caregiver. These early patterns can influence later adult relationships. As life goes on, people become more or less secure, avoidant, or disorganized.

Securely Attached [Type B]

In the Strange Situation, children are able to separate from caregiver but prefer caregiver to strangers.

> Later in life, they tend to have good relationships and good self-esteem.

Avoidant [Type A]

In the Strange Situation, children avoid caregiver.

> Later in life, they tend to be aloof in personal relationships.

Resistant/Ambivalent [Type C]

In the Strange Situation, children appear upset and wor- ried when separated from caregiver; they may hit or cling.

> Later in life, their relationships may be angry, stormy, unpredictable.

Disorganized [Type D]

In the Strange Situation, children appear angry, confused, erratic, or fearful.

> Later in life, they can demonstrate odd behavior—including sudden emotions.

THE CONTINUUM OF ATTACHMENT

Avoidance and anxiety occur along a continuum. Neither genes nor cultural varia- tions were understood when the Strange Situation was first developed (in 1965). Some contemporary reseachers believe the link between childhood attachment and adult personality is less straightforward.

Low Avoidance

Secure   Resistant

Low Anxiety   High Anxiety

Avoidant   Disorganized

High Avoidance

cries if the caregiver closes the door when going to the bathroom or fusses if a back-facing car seat prevents the baby from seeing the parent.

To maintain contact when driving in a car and to reassure the baby, some caregivers in the front seat reach back to give a hand, or install a mirror so they can see the baby and the baby can see them as they drive. Some caregivers take the baby into the bathroom, leading to one's mother's complaint that she hadn't been alone in the bathroom for two years (Senior, 2014). As in this example, maintaining contact need not be physical: Visual or verbal connections are often sufficient.

Caregivers also are attached. They keep a watchful eye on their baby, and they initiate interactions with expressions, gestures, and sounds. Before going to sleep at midnight they might tiptoe to the crib to gaze at their sleeping infant, or, in daytime, absentmindedly smooth their toddler's hair.

Attachment is universal, being part of the inborn social nature of the human species, but specific manifestations depend on the culture as well as the age of the people who are attached to each other. For instance, Ugandan mothers never kiss their infants, but they often massage them, contrary to Westerners, who rarely massage except when they are putting on lotion.

Some American adults remain in contact with each other via daily phone calls, e-mails, or texts and keep in proximity by sitting in the same room as each reads quietly. In other cultures, adults often hold hands, hug, touch each others' faces, shoulders, buttocks. Some scholars believe that attachment to infants, not only from mothers but also fathers, grandparents, and nonrelatives, is the reason that *Homo sapiens* thrived when other species became extinct (Hrdy, 2009).

Secure and Insecure Attachment

Attachment is classified into four types: A, B, C, and D (see Table 7.1). Infants with **secure attachment** (type B) feel comfortable and confident. The caregiver is a *base for exploration*, providing assurance and enabling discovery. A toddler might, for example, scramble down from the caregiver's lap to play with an intriguing toy but periodically look back and vocalize (contact-maintaining) or bring the toy to the caregiver for inspection (proximity-seeking).

By contrast, insecure attachment (types A and C) is characterized by fear, anxiety, anger, or indifference. Some insecure children play independently without maintaining contact; this is **insecure-avoidant attachment** (type A). The

Video Activity: Mother Love and the Work of Harry Harlow features classic footage of Harlow's research, showing the setup and results of his famous experiment.

secure attachment A relationship in which an infant obtains both comfort and confidence from the presence of his or her caregiver.

insecure-avoidant attachment A pattern of attachment in which an infant avoids connection with the caregiver. The infant seems not to care about the caregiver's presence, departure, or return.

TABLE 7.1	Patterns of Infant Attachment				
Type	Name of Pattern	In Play Room	Mother Leaves	Mother Returns	Toddlers in Category (%)
A	Insecure-avoidant	Child plays happily.	Child continues playing.	Child ignores her.	10–20
B	Secure	Child plays happily.	Child pauses, is not as happy.	Child welcomes her, returns to play.	50–70
C	Insecure-resistant/ambivalent	Child clings, is preoccupied with mother.	Child is unhappy, may stop playing.	Child is angry; may cry, hit mother, cling.	10–20
D	Disorganized	Child is cautious.	Child may stare or yell; looks scared, confused.	Child acts oddly—may scream, hit self, throw things.	5–10

insecure-resistant/ambivalent attachment A pattern of attachment in which an infant's anxiety and uncertainty are evident, as when the infant becomes very upset at separation from the caregiver and both resists and seeks contact on reunion.

disorganized attachment A type of attachment that is marked by an infant's inconsistent reactions to the caregiver's departure and return.

opposite reaction is **insecure-resistant/ambivalent attachment** (type C). Children with this type of attachment cling to caregiver and are angry at being left.

Ainsworth's original schema differentiated only types A, B, and C. Later researchers discovered a fourth category (type D), **disorganized attachment.** Type D infants may shift suddenly from hitting to kissing their mothers, from staring blankly to crying hysterically, from pinching themselves to freezing in place.

Among the general population, about two-thirds of infants are secure (type B). Their mothers' presence gives them courage to explore; her departure causes distress; her return elicits positive social contact (such as smiling or hugging) and then more playing. The infant's balanced reaction—being concerned but not overwhelmed by comings and goings—indicates security. Early research was only on mothers; later, fathers and other caregivers were included, since they also could have secure or insecure attachments to an infant.

About one-third of infants are insecure, either indifferent (type A) or unduly anxious (type C). About 5 to 10 percent of infants fit into none of these categories; they are disorganized (type D), with no consistent strategy for social interaction, even avoidance or resistance. Sometimes they become hostile and aggressive, difficult for anyone to relate to (Lyons-Ruth et al., 1999). Unlike the first three types, disorganized infants have elevated levels of cortisol in reaction to stress (Bernard & Dozier, 2010).

Measuring Attachment

Ainsworth (1973) developed a now-classic laboratory procedure called the **Strange Situation** to measure attachment. In a well-equipped playroom, an infant is observed for eight episodes, each lasting three minutes. First, the child and mother are together. Next, according to a set sequence, the mother and then a stranger come and go. Infants' responses to their mother indicate which type of attachment they have formed.

Researchers are trained to distinguish types A, B, C, and D. They focus on the following:

Strange Situation A laboratory procedure for measuring attachment by evoking infants' reactions to the stress of various adults' comings and goings in an unfamiliar playroom.

> *Exploration of the toys.* A secure toddler plays happily.
> *Reaction to the caregiver's departure.* A secure toddler notices when the caregiver leaves and shows some sign of missing him or her.
> *Reaction to the caregiver's return.* A secure toddler welcomes the caregiver's reappearance, usually seeking contact, and then plays again.

Excited, Troubled, Comforted This sequence is repeated daily for 1-year-olds, which is why the same sequence is replicated to measure attachment. As you see, toys are no substitute for mother's comfort if the infant or toddler is secure, as this one seems to be. Some, however, cry inconsolably or throw toys angrily when left alone.

Attachment is not always measured via the Strange Situation; surveys and interviews are also used. Sometimes parents answer 90 questions about their children's characteristics, and sometimes adults are interviewed extensively (according to a detailed protocol) about their relationships with their own parents, again with various specific measurements (Fortuna & Roisman, 2008).

Research measuring attachment has revealed that some behaviors that might seem normal are, in fact, a sign of insecurity. For instance, an infant who clings to the caregiver and refuses to explore the toys might be type A. Likewise, adults who say their childhood was happy and their mother was a saint, especially if they provide few specific memories, might be insecure. And young children who are immediately friendly to strangers may never have formed a secure attachment (Tarullo et al., 2011).

Assessments of attachment that were developed and validated for middle-class North Americans may be less useful in other cultures. Infants who seem dismissive or clingy may not necessarily be insecure. Everywhere, however, parents and infants are attached to each other, and everywhere secure attachment predicts academic success and emotional stability (Erdman & Ng, 2010; Otto & Keller, 2014; Drake et al., 2014).

Insecure Attachment and the Social Setting

At first, developmentalists expected secure attachment to "predict all the outcomes reasonably expected from a well-functioning personality" (R. A. Thompson & Raikes, 2003, p. 708). But this expectation turned out to be naive.

Securely attached infants *are* more likely to become secure toddlers, socially competent preschoolers, high-achieving schoolchildren, and capable parents. Attachment affects early brain development, one reason these later outcomes occur (Diamond & Fagundes, 2010). But insecure infants are not doomed to later failure.

Although attachment patterns form in infancy (see Table 7.2), they are not set in stone; they may change when the family context changes, such as new abuse or income loss. Poverty increases the likelihood of insecure attachment, and insecure attachment correlates with later learning problems, but a third variable may be the reason for this correlation. For instance, many aspects of low SES increase the risk of low school achievement, hostile children, fearful adults, all also increased with insecure infant attachment.

The underlying premise—that responsive early parenting leads to secure attachment, which buffers stress and encourages exploration—seems valid. However, attachment behaviors in the Strange Situation provide only one sign of the quality of the parent–child relationship. Linking early attachment and later problems directly may not be warranted (Keller, 2014).

Insights from Romania

No scholar doubts that close human relationships should develop in the first

TABLE 7.2	Predictors of Attachment Type

Secure attachment (type B) is more likely if:

- The parent is usually sensitive and responsive to the infant's needs.
- The infant–parent relationship is high in synchrony.
- The infant's temperament is "easy."
- The parents are not stressed about income, other children, or their marriage.
- The parents have a working model of secure attachment to their own parents.

Insecure attachment is more likely if:

- The parent mistreats the child. (Neglect increases type A; abuse increases types C and D.)
- The mother is mentally ill. (Paranoia increases type D; depression increases type C.)
- The parents are highly stressed about income, other children, or their marriage. (Parental stress increases types A and D.)
- The parents are intrusive and controlling. (Parental domination increases type A.)
- The parents actively suffer from alcoholism. (Father with alcoholism increases type A; mother with alcoholism increases type D.)
- The child's temperament is "difficult." (Difficult children tend to be type C.)
- The child's temperament is "slow to warm up." (This correlates with type A.)

year of life and that the lack of such relationships risks dire consequences. Unfortunately, thousands of children born in Romania are proof.

When Romanian dictator Nicolae Ceausescu forbade birth control and abortions in the 1980s, illegal abortions became the leading cause of death for Romanian women aged 15 to 45 (Verona, 2003), and more than 100,000 children were abandoned to crowded, impersonal, state-run orphanages. The children experienced severe deprivation, including virtually no normal interaction, play, or conversation.

In the two years after Ceausescu was ousted and killed in 1989, thousands of those children were adopted by North American, western European, and Australian families. Those who were adopted before 6 months of age fared best; the adoptive parents established synchrony via play and caregiving. Most of the children developed normally.

For those adopted after 6 months, and especially after 12 months, early signs were encouraging: Skinny infants gained weight and grew faster than other 1-year-olds, developing motor skills they had lacked (H. Park et al., 2011). However, their early social deprivation soon became evident in their emotions and intellect. Many were overly friendly to strangers throughout childhood, a sign of insecure attachment (Tarullo et al., 2011). At age 11, their average IQ was only 85, 15 points below normal (Rutter et al., 2010).

Even among those who were well nourished, or who caught up to normal growth, many became impulsive, angry teenagers. Apparently, the stresses of adolescence and emerging adulthood have exacerbated the cognitive and social strains on these young people and their families (Merz & McCall, 2011).

These children are now adults, many with serious emotional or conduct problems. The cause is more social than biological. Research on children adopted nationally and internationally finds that many develop into normal adults, but every stress—from rejection in infancy to early institutionalization to the circumstances of the adoption process—makes it more difficult for the infant to become a happy, well-functioning adult (Grotevant & McDermott, 2014).

Romanian infants are no longer available for international adoption, even though some remain abandoned. Research confirms that early emotional deprivation, not genes or nutrition, is their greatest problem. Romanian infants develop best in their own families, second best in foster families, and worst in institutions (Nelson et al., 2007). As best we know, this applies to infants everywhere: Families usually nurture their babies better than strangers who care for many infants at once, and the more years children spend in an impersonal institution, the more likely it is they will become socially and intellectually impaired (Julian, 2013).

Fortunately, in Eastern Europe and elsewhere, institutions have improved or been shuttered; more-recent adoptees are not as impaired as those Romanian orphans (Grotevant & McDermott, 2014). However, some infants in every nation are deprived of healthy interaction, sometimes within their own families. Ideally, no infant is institutionalized, but if that ideal is not reached, institutions need to change so that psychological health is as important as physical health (McCall, 2013). Children need responsive caregivers from early infancy on, biological relatives or not.

Preventing Problems

All infants need love and stimulation; all seek synchrony and then attachment—secure if possible, insecure if not. Without some adult support, infants become disorganized and adrift, emotionally troubled. Extreme early social deprivation is difficult to overcome.

Danger Ongoing Look closely and you can see danger. That bent crib bar could strangle an infant, and that chipped paint could contain lead. (Lead tastes sweet; is that why two of the children are biting it?) Fortunately, these three Romanian infants (photographed in 1990) escaped those dangers to be raised in loving adoptive homes. Unfortunately, the damage of social isolation (note the sheet around the crib) could not be completely overcome: Some young adults who spent their first year in an institution like this still carry emotional scars.

Since synchrony and attachment develop over the first year, and since a third of all parents have difficulty establishing secure attachments, many developmentalists have sought to discover what particularly impairs these parents and what can be done to improve their parenting.

Secure attachment is more difficult to achieve when the parents were abused as children, when families are socially isolated, when mothers are young adolescents, or when infants are unusually difficult (Zeanah et al., 2011). If biological parents do not care for their newborns, foster or adoptive parents need to be found quickly so that synchrony and attachment can develop (McCall, 2013).

Some birth parents, fearing that they cannot provide responsive parenting, choose adoptive parents for their newborns. If high-risk birth parents believe they can provide good care, early support may prevent later problems. Success has been reported when skilled professionals come to the home to nurture relationships between infant and caregiver (Lowell et al., 2011). If a professional helps parents in the first days after birth, perhaps by using the Brazelton Neonatal Behavioral Assessment Scale (mentioned in Chapter 4) to encourage bonding, then problems need never start (e.g., Nugent et al., 2009).

Social Referencing

Social referencing refers to seeking emotional responses or information from other people, much as a student might consult a dictionary or other reference work. Someone's reassuring glance, cautionary words, or a facial expression of alarm, pleasure, or dismay—those are social references.

Even at 8 months, infants notice where other people are looking and use that information to look in the same direction themselves (Tummeltshammer et al., 2014). After age 1, when infants can walk and are "little scientists," their need to consult others becomes urgent as well as more accurate.

Toddlers search for clues in gazes, faces, and body position, paying close attention to emotions and intentions. They focus on their familiar caregivers, but they also use relatives, other children, and even strangers to help them assess objects and events. They are remarkably selective, noticing that some strangers are reliable references and others are not (Fusaro & Harris, 2013).

Social referencing has many practical applications. Consider mealtime. Caregivers the world over smack their lips, pretend to taste, and say "yum-yum," encouraging toddlers to eat their first beets, liver, or spinach. For their part, toddlers become astute at reading expressions, insisting on the foods that the adults *really* like. If mother likes it, and presents it on the spoon, then they eat it—otherwise not (Shutts et al., 2013).

Through this process, some children develop a taste for raw fish or curried goat or smelly cheese—foods that children in other cultures refuse. Similarly, toddlers use social cues to understand the difference between real and pretend eating, as well as to learn which objects, emotions, and activities are forbidden.

Fathers as Social Partners

Fathers enhance their children's social and emotional development in many ways (Lamb, 2010). Synchrony, attachment, and social referencing are sometimes more apparent with fathers than with mothers. Furthermore, fathers typically elicit more smiles and laughter from their infants than mothers do, probably because they play more exciting games, while mothers do more caregiving and comforting (Fletcher et al., 2013).

social referencing Seeking information about how to react to an unfamiliar or ambiguous object or event by observing someone else's expressions and reactions. That other person becomes a social reference.

Rotini Pasta? Look again. Every family teaches their children to relish delicacies that other people avoid. Examples are bacon (not in Arab nations), hamburgers (not in India), and, as shown here, a witchetty grub. This aboriginal Australian boy is about to swallow an insect larva.

Although gender, cultural, and age differences emerge fathers and mothers often work together to raise the children. One researcher reports "mothers and fathers showed patterns of striking similarity: they touched, looked, vocalized, rocked, and kissed their newborns equally" (Parke, 2013, p. 121). Differences are obvious from one couple to another, but not from one gender to another—except for smiling (women do it more).

It is a stereotype that African American, Latin American, and Asian American fathers are less nurturing and more strict than other men (Parke, 2013). Within the United States, the trend toward more father–infant interaction than in previous cohorts is apparent among all ethnic groups, although income and place of residence play a role (Roopnarine & Hossain, 2013; Qin & Chang, 2013).

Close father–infant relationships can teach infants (especially boys) appropriate expressions of emotion, particularly anger. The results may endure: Teenagers are less likely to lash out at friends and authorities if, as infants, they experienced a warm, responsive relationship with their father (Hoeve et al., 2011).

Same Situation, Far Apart: Bonded That fathers enjoy their sons is not surprising, but notice the infants' hands—one clutching Dad's hair tightly and the other reaching for Dad's face. At this age, infants show their trust in adults by grabbing and reaching. Synchrony and attachment are mutual, in Ireland *(left)*, Kenya *(right)*, and in your own neighborhood.

Less rigid gender roles seem to be developing in every nation, allowing a greater caregiving role for fathers within every nation (Lamb, 2013). One U.S. example of historical change is the number of married women with children under age 6 who are employed. In 1970, 30 percent of married mothers of young children earned paychecks; in 2012, 60 percent did (U.S. Bureau of Labor Statistics, 2013). These statistics include many mothers of infants, who often rely on the baby's father for child care.

Note the reference to "married" mothers: About half the mothers of infants in the United States are not married, and their employment rates are higher than their married counterparts. Often, the fathers of their infants are active in child care, whether or not they cohabit. As detailed later in this chapter, fathers—not necessarily married—often care for infants when mothers are at work.

Nonetheless, in most cultures and ethnic groups, fathers of every marital status still spend less time with infants than mothers do (Parke, 2013; Tudge, 2008). National cultures and parental attitudes are influential: Some women are gatekeepers, believing that child care is their special domain. They exclude fathers (perhaps indirectly, saying, "You're not holding her right").

When mothers engage the fathers in child care, they must not imply that he cannot do it properly. For example, she may lay out the clothes the baby is to wear, as if he could not find clothes (Pedersen & Kilzer, 2014). Both parents, ideally, are infant caregivers.

One male/female difference seems to persist: When asked to play with their baby, mothers typically caress, read, sing, or play traditional games such as peek-a-boo. Fathers are more exciting: They move their infant's limbs in imitation of walking, kicking, or climbing, or they swing the baby through the air, sideways, or even upside down. Mothers might say, "Don't drop him"; fathers and babies laugh with joy. In this way, fathers tend to help children become less fearful.

Over the past 20 years, father–infant research has tried to answer three questions:

1. Can men provide the same care as women?
2. Is father–infant interaction different from mother–infant interaction?
3. How do fathers and mothers cooperate to provide infant care?

Many studies over the past two decades have answered yes to the first two questions. A baby fed, bathed, and diapered by Dad is just as happy and clean as when Mom does it. Gender differences are sometimes found in specifics, but they are not harmful.

On the third question, the answer depends on the family (Bretherton, 2010). Usually, mothers are caregivers and fathers are playmates, but not always. Each couple, given their circumstances (which might include being immigrant, low-income, or same-sex), finds their own way to complement each other to help their infant thrive (Lamb, 2010). Traditional mother–father roles may be switched, with no harm to the baby (Parke, 2013).

A constructive *parental alliance* can take many forms, but it cannot be taken for granted, no matter what the family configuration. Single-parent families, or grandparent families, are not necessarily better or worse than nuclear families. (**Developmental Link:** Family forms are discussed in Chapter 13.)

Sometimes no one is happy with the infant, and then the baby suffers. Father care can be quite wonderful, but it is not always so. One study reported that 7 percent of fathers of 1-year-olds were depressed, and they were four times as likely to spank as were nondepressed fathers (40 percent versus 10 percent) (Davis et al., 2011) (see Figure 7.2). (**Developmental Link:** Punishment is discussed in Chapter 10.)

Family members affect each other. Paternal depression correlates with maternal depression and with sad, angry, disobedient toddlers. Cause and consequence are intertwined. When anyone is depressed or hostile, everyone (mother, father, baby, sibling) needs help.

FIGURE 7.2

Shame on Who? Not on the toddlers, who are naturally curious and careless, but maybe not on the fathers, either. Both depression and spanking are affected by financial stress, marital conflict, and cultural norms; who is responsible for those?

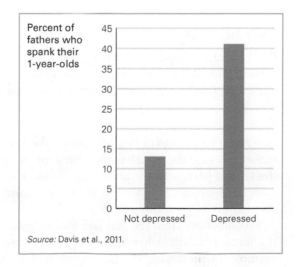

Source: Davis et al., 2011.

SUMMING UP Caregivers and young infants engage in split-second interaction, which is evidence of synchrony. Still-face research has found that infants depend on such responsiveness and try to elicit it. Attachment between people is universal; it is apparent in infancy with contact-maintaining and proximity-seeking behaviors as 1-year-olds explore their world. Such early patterns may persist, affecting how adults respond to their own infants. Without responsive caregivers, as happened to some institutionalized Romanian infants, the child may be impaired socially lifelong.

Toddlers use other people as social references to guide them in their exploration. Fathers are as capable as mothers in social partnerships with infants, although they may favor physical, creative play more than mothers do. Every family member affects all the others; ideally, they cooperate to create a caregivers' alliance to support the baby's development.

WHAT HAVE YOU LEARNED?

1. How might synchrony affect early emotional development?
2. How might an infant demonstrate proximity-seeking and contact-maintaining attachment?
3. How might each of the four types of attachment be expressed in adulthood?
4. What has been learned from the research on Romanian infants?
5. How is social referencing important in toddlerhood?
6. How do fathers contribute to infant development?

Video: Theories of Emotional Development in Infancy and Toddlerhood summarizes the theories of personality development described in this section.

Theories of Infant Psychosocial Development

Consider again the theories discussed in Chapter 2. As you will see, theories lead to insight and applications that are relevant for the final topic of this chapter, infant day care.

You will notice that the two universal theories, humanism and evolution, are discussed separately. That is because the implications of each for infants diverge, and thus they should not be lumped together.

You will also see that sociocultural theory is *not* described as a separate theory. From that omission do not conclude that it is irrelevant—quite the opposite. In every topic of this chapter, cultural differences are highlighted: A sociocultural approach is needed throughout the study of infant psychosocial development. Thus a separate section devoted to it would seem peculiar.

Psychoanalytic Theory

Psychoanalytic theory connects biosocial and psychosocial development. Sigmund Freud and Erik Erikson each described two distinct stages of early development, one in the first year and one beginning in the second.

Freud: Oral and Anal Stages

According to Freud (1935/1989, 2001), the first year of life is the *oral stage*, so named because the mouth is the young infant's primary source of gratification. In the second year, with the *anal stage*, pleasure comes from the anus—particularly from the sensual satisfaction of bowel movements and, eventually, the psychological pleasure of controlling them.

Freud believed that the oral and anal stages are fraught with potential conflicts. If a mother frustrates her infant's urge to suck—weaning too early or too late, for example, or preventing the baby from sucking a thumb or a pacifier—that may

Especially for Nursing Mothers You have heard that if you wean your child too early he or she will overeat or develop alcoholism. Is it true? (see response, page 227)

later lead to an *oral fixation*. A person with an oral fixation is stuck (fixated) at the oral stage, and therefore, as an adult, he or she eats, drinks, chews, bites, or talks excessively, still seeking the mouth-related pleasures of infancy.

Similarly, if toilet training is overly strict or if it begins before the infant is mature enough, then the toddler's refusal—or inability—to comply will clash with the wishes of the adult, who denies the infant normal anal pleasures. That may lead to an anal personality—an adult who seeks self-control, with an unusually strong need for regularity and cleanliness in all aspects of life. (**Developmental Link:** Theory of toilet training is discussed in Chapter 2.)

Erikson: Trust and Autonomy

According to Erikson, the first crisis of life is **trust versus mistrust,** when infants learn whether or not the world can be trusted to satisfy basic needs. Babies feel secure when food and comfort are provided with "consistency, continuity, and sameness of experience" (Erikson, 1963, p. 247). If social interaction inspires trust, the child (later the adult) confidently explores the social world.

The second crisis is **autonomy versus shame and doubt,** beginning at about 18 months, when self-awareness emerges. Toddlers want autonomy (self-rule) over their own actions and bodies. Without it, they feel ashamed and doubtful. Like Freud, Erikson believed that problems in early infancy could last a lifetime, creating adults who are suspicious and pessimistic (mistrusting) or easily shamed (lacking autonomy).

Erikson was aware of cultural variations. He knew that mistrust and shame could be destructive or not, depending on local norms and expectations. Westerners expect toddlers to go through the stubborn and defiant "terrible twos"; that is a sign of the urge for autonomy. Parents in some other places expect toddlers to be more responsive to parent demands, using shame to control misbehavior.

A study of children in three nations found that the Japanese were highest in shame, the Koreans highest in guilt, and the U.S. children highest in pride (Furukawa et al., 2012). As a result, U.S. children are less fearful and less obedient.

Behaviorism

From the perspective of behaviorism, emotions and personality are molded as parents reinforce or punish a child. Behaviorists believe that parents who respond joyously to every glimmer of a grin will have children with a sunny disposition. The opposite is also true:

> Failure to bring up a happy child, a well-adjusted child—assuming bodily health—falls squarely upon the parents' shoulders. [By the time the child is 3] parents have already determined . . . [whether the child] is to grow into a happy person, wholesome and good-natured, whether he is to be a whining, complaining neurotic, an anger-driven, vindictive, over-bearing slave driver, or one whose every move in life is definitely controlled by fear.
>
> [Watson, 1928, pp. 7, 45]

Later behaviorists recognized that infant behavior also has an element of **social learning,** as infants learn from other people. You already saw an example, social referencing. Social learning occurs throughout life (Morris et al., 2007; Rendell et al., 2011). Toddlers express emotions in various ways—from giggling to cursing—just as their parents or older siblings do.

For example, a boy might develop a hot temper if his father's outbursts seem to win his mother's respect; a girl might be coy, or passive-aggressive, if that is what she has seen at home. These examples are deliberately sexist: Gender roles, in particular, are learned, according to social learning.

All Together Now Toddlers in an employees' day-care program at a flower farm in Colombia learn to use the potty on a schedule. Will this experience lead to later personality problems? Probably not.

trust versus mistrust Erikson's first crisis of psychosocial development. Infants learn basic trust if the world is a secure place where their basic needs (for food, comfort, attention, and so on) are met.

autonomy versus shame and doubt Erikson's second crisis of psychosocial development. Toddlers either succeed or fail in gaining a sense of self-rule over their actions and their bodies.

social learning The acquisition of behavior patterns by observing the behavior of others.

Only in America Toddlers in every nation of the world sometimes cry when emotions overwhelm them, but in the United States young children are encouraged to express emotions and Halloween is a national custom, unlike in other nations. Candy, dress-up, ghosts, witches, and ringing doorbells after sunset—no wonder many young children are overwhelmed.

Parents often unwittingly encourage certain traits in their children. This is evident in the effects of proximal versus distal parenting. Should parents carry infants most of the time, or will that spoil them? Should babies have many toys, or will that make them too materialistic?

Answers to these questions refer to the distinction between **proximal parenting** (being physically close to a baby, often holding and touching) and **distal parenting** (keeping some distance—providing toys, encouraging self-feeding, talking face-to-face instead of communicating by touch). Caregivers tend to behave in proximal or distal ways very early, when infants are only 2 months old (Kärtner et al., 2010).

Variations in proximal and distal parenting lead to variations in toddler behavior. For instance, toddlers who, as infants, were often held, patted, and hushed (proximal) become toddlers who are more obedient to their parents but less likely to recognize themselves in a mirror (Keller et al., 2010; Keller et al., 2004). Cultural differences in personality are apparent when researchers compared the Nso people of Cameroon (very proximal) with the Greeks in Athens (very distal). Further research in other nations confirms that caregiving styles affect later behavior (Borke et al., 2007; Kärtner et al., 2011).

Should you pick up your crying baby (proximal) or give her a pacifier (distal)? Should you breast-feed until age 2 or longer (proximal) or switch to bottle-feeding before 6 months (distal)? Of course, many factors influence parental actions, and breast-feeding is only one example of parental behavior. But every parental response is influenced by whatever assumptions the culture holds. According to behaviorism, each action reinforces a lesson that the baby learns, in this case about people and objects.

Cognitive Theory

Cognitive theory holds that thoughts determine a person's perspective. Early experiences are important because beliefs, perceptions, and memories make them so, not because they are buried in the unconscious (psychoanalytic theory) or burned into the brain's patterns (behaviorism).

According to many cognitive theorists, early experiences help infants develop a **working model,** which is a set of assumptions that becomes a frame of reference for later life (Johnson et al., 2010). It is a "model" because early relationships form a prototype, or blueprint; it is "working" because it is a work in progress, not fixed or final.

Ideally, infants develop "a working model of the self as lovable, and competent" because the parents are "emotionally available, loving, and supportive of mastery efforts" (Harter and Bukowski, 2012, p. 12). However, reality does not always conform to this ideal. A 1-year-old girl might develop a model, based on her parents' inconsistent responses to her, that people are unpredictable. She will continue to apply that model to everyone: Her childhood friendships will be insecure, and her adult relationships will be guarded.

The crucial idea, according to cognitive theory, is that an infant's early experiences themselves are not necessarily pivotal, but the interpretation of those experiences is (Olson & Dweck, 2009). Children may misinterpret their experiences, or parents may offer inaccurate explanations, and these form ideas that affect later thinking and behavior.

In this way, working models formed in childhood echo lifelong. A hopeful message from cognitive theory is that

proximal parenting Caregiving practices that involve being physically close to the baby, with frequent holding and touching.

distal parenting Caregiving practices that involve remaining distant from the baby, providing toys, food, and face-to-face communication with minimal holding and touching.

Especially for Pediatricians A mother complains that her toddler refuses to stay in the car seat, spits out disliked foods, and almost never does what she says. How should you respond? (see response, page 228)

working model In cognitive theory, a set of assumptions that the individual uses to organize perceptions and experiences. For example, a person might assume that other people are trustworthy and be surprised by an incident in which this working model of human behavior is erroneous.

The Best Baby Transport Stroller or sling, carriage or carrier, leave babies at home or bring them to work? Such decisions are strongly influenced by culture, with long-lasting implications. Mothers compare particular brands and designs of strollers, trying to decide on the best one, but it rarely occurs to them that taking the baby outside is, itself, a major decision.

Hush Babies cry and parents soothe them the world over, while contexts shape both crying and soothing. The little girl (*left*) will probably quiet soon, as she is held snuggly next to her father's body. The boy (*right*) is less likely to settle down, as he is surrounded by strangers in a Ukrainian contest to see which baby can crawl fastest. What level is this on Maslow's hierachy?

people can rethink and reorganize their thoughts, developing new models. Our mistrustful girl might marry a faithful and loving man and gradually develop a new working model. The form of psychotherapy that seems most successful at the moment is called cognitive-behavioral, in which new thoughts about how to behave are developed. In other words, a new working model is developed.

Humanism

Remember from Chapter 2 that Maslow described a hierarchy of needs (physiological, safety/security, love/belonging, success/esteem, and self-actualization), with the lower levels being prerequisites for higher ones. Infants begin at the first level: Their emotions serve to ensure that physiological needs are met. That's why babies cry when they are hungry or hurt, as adults usually do not. Basic survival needs must be satisfied to enable the person to reach higher levels (Silton et al., 2011).

Humanism reminds us that caregivers also have needs and that their needs influence how they respond to infants. Self-actualized people (level 5) no longer demand their children's love and respect, so they can guide an infant well even if the child is momentarily angry (as when getting the child immunized). But most young parents are at level 3 or 4, seeking love or respect. They may be troubled by "ghosts in the nursery" (first mentioned in Chapter 5 in the discussion of infant sleep). Their own babyhood experience includes unmet needs, and their early distress interferes with their ability to nurture the next generation.

For example, while all experts endorse breast-feeding as the best way to meet infants' physiological needs, many mothers quit breast-feeding after trying for a few days, and many fathers feel excluded if the mother spends most of her time and attention on nursing. This may puzzle some experts but not the humanist theorists, who realize that a parent's needs may clash with an infant's needs (Mulder & Johnson, 2010).

For example, one mother of a 1-year-old said:

> My son couldn't latch so I was pumping and my breasts were massive and I'm a pretty small woman with big breasts and they were enormous during pregnancy. It has always been a sore spot for me and I've never loved my breasts. And that has been hard for me in not feeling good about myself. And I stopped pumping in January and slowly they are going back and I'm beginning to feel some confidence again and that definitely helps. Because I felt overweight, your boobs are not your own and you are exhausted and your body is strange it's just really hard to want to share that with someone. They think you are beautiful, they love it and love you the way you are but it is not necessarily what you feel.
>
> *[quoted in Shapiro, 2011, p. 18]*

// **Response for Nursing Mothers** (from page 224): Freud thought so, but there is no experimental evidence that weaning, even when ill-timed, has such dire long-term effects.

// **Response for Pediatricians** (from page 226): Consider the origins of the misbehavior—probably a combination of the child's inborn temperament and the mother's distal parenting. Acceptance and consistent responses (e.g., avoiding disliked foods but always using the car seat) is more warranted than anger. Perhaps this mother is expressing hostility toward the child—a sign that intervention may be needed. Find out.

This woman's need for self-respect was overwhelming, causing her to stop breast-feeding in order to feel some confidence about her shape. Neither her husband's love of her body nor her son's need for breast milk helped because she was not past level 3 (love and belonging). Her "strange" body attacked her self-esteem (level 4).

Her personal needs may have been unmet since puberty (she says, "I've never loved my breasts"). She blames her husband for not understanding her feelings and her son who "couldn't latch." Since all babies learn to latch with time and help, this woman's saying that her son couldn't latch suggests something amiss in synchrony and attachment—unmet baby needs because of unmet mother needs.

By contrast, some parents understand their baby's need for safety and security (level 2) even if they themselves are far beyond that stage. Kevin is an example.

> Kevin is a very active, outgoing person who loves to try new things. Today he takes his 11-month-old daughter, Tyra, to the park for the first time. Tyra is playing alone in the sandbox, when a group of toddlers joins her. At first, Tyra smiles and eagerly watches them play. But as the toddlers become more active and noisy, Tyra's smiles turn quickly to tears. She . . . reaches for Kevin, who picks her up and comforts her. But then Kevin goes a step further. After Tyra calms down, Kevin gently encourages her to play near the other children. He sits at her side, talking and playing with her. Soon Tyra is slowly creeping closer to the group of toddlers, curiously watching their moves.
>
> *[Lerner & Dombro, 2004, p. 42]*

Evolutionary Theory

Remember that evolutionary theory stresses two needs: survival and reproduction. Human brains are extraordinarily adept at those tasks. However, not until about two decades of maturation is the human brain fully functioning. A child must be nourished, protected, and taught much longer than offspring of any other species. Infant and parent emotions ensure this lengthy protection (Hrdy, 2009).

Emotions for Survival

Infant emotions are part of this evolutionary mandate. All the reactions described in the first part of this chapter—from the hunger cry to the temper tantrum—can be seen from this perspective (Konner, 2010).

For example, newborns are extraordinarily dependent, unable to walk or talk or even sit up and feed themselves for months after birth. They must attract adult devotion—and they do. That first smile, the sound of infant laughter, and their role in synchrony are all powerfully attractive to adults—especially to parents.

Adults call their hairless, chinless, round-faced, small-limbed creatures "cute," "handsome," "beautiful," "adorable," and willingly devote hours to carrying, feeding, changing, and cleaning them. Adaptation is evident: Mothers and fathers have the genetic potential to be caregivers, and grandparents have done it before, but, according to evolutionary psychology, whether or not that potential is expressed, turning busy adults into devoted caregivers, depends on the particular survival needs of infants in that community.

If humans were motivated merely by financial reward, no one would have children. Yet evolution has created adults who find parenting worth every sacrifice. The costs are substantial: Food (even breast milk requires the mother to eat more), diapers, clothes, furniture, medical bills, toys, and child care (whether paid or unpaid) are just a start.

Before a child becomes independent, many parents have bought a bigger residence, and spent thousands on education, vacations, and much more. These are

only the financial costs; the emotional costs are greater. A recent book about parenting titled *"All Joy and No Fun"* highlights the paradox: People choose to sacrifice time, money, and fun because they find parenting deeply satisfying (Senior, 2014).

Indeed, successful reproduction depends on years of self-sacrificing; humans have evolved to provide it. Hormones—specifically, oxytocin—do much more than trigger birth and promote breast-feeding; they increase the impulse to bond with others, especially one's children (Feldman et al., 2011). Both men and women have oxytocin in their blood and saliva, and this hormone continues to be produced as needed for caregiving. For fathers, oxytocin increases and testosterone decreases as they care for their infants, a biological adaptation to an evolutionary need (Weisman et al., 2014).

Evolutionary theory holds that over human history, attachment, with proximity-seeking and contact-maintaining, promoted species survival by keeping toddlers near caregivers and keeping caregivers vigilant. Infants fuss at still faces, they express fear of separation, and they laugh when adults play with them, all of which sustain parent–child interdependence. We inherited these emotional reactions from our great-great-grandparents, who would have died without them.

As explained in Chapter 4, human bonding is unlike that of goats and sheep—a mother does not need to nuzzle her newborn immediately. Bonding, followed by synchrony and then attachment, is enhanced by experiences at birth, but the caregiver–infant relationship is strengthened in many other ways. Social connections are stronger and more flexible for humans than for other animals. Toddlers attend to adult expressions (social referencing) as one more way to establish the bond between themselves and others.

Allocare

Evolutionary social scientists note that if mothers were exclusive caregivers of each child until adulthood, a given woman could rear only one or two offspring—not enough for the species to survive. Instead, before the introduction of reliable birth control, the average interval between births for humans was two to four years.

Humans birth children at relatively short intervals and raise them successfully because of **allocare**—the care of children by people other than the biological parents (Hrdy, 2009). Allocare is essential for *Homo sapiens'* survival.

Compared with many other species (for instance, mother chimpanzees never let another chimp hold their babies), human mothers have evolved to let other people help with child care, and other people are usually eager to do so (Kachel et al., 2011). Throughout the centuries, the particular person to provide allocare has varied by culture and ecological conditions.

Same Situation, Far Apart: Safekeeping
Historically, grandmothers were sometimes crucial for child survival. Now, even though medical care has reduced child mortality, grandmothers still do their part to keep children safe, as shown by these two—in the eastern United States *(left)* and western China *(right)*.

allocare Literally, "other-care"; the care of children by people other than the biological parents.

Often fathers helped but not always: Some men were far away, fighting, hunting, or seeking work, while some had several wives and a dozen or more children. In those situations, other women (daughters, grandmothers, sisters, friends) and sometimes other men provided allocare (Hrdy, 2009).

SUMMING UP All theories recognize that infant care is crucial: Psychosocial development depends on it. Psychoanalytic theory stresses the effects of early caregiving routines—with Freud stressing the lifelong impact of the oral and anal stages and Erikson focusing on the development of trust and autonomy. Behaviorists emphasize early learning, with parents reinforcing or punishing infant reactions. Cognitive theories emphasize working models. In all these theories, lifelong patterns are said to begin in infancy, but later change is possible. Culture is crucial.

Humanists consider the basic needs of adults as well as infants. Consequently, they acknowledge the parental side of the parent–infant interaction. According to evolutionary theory, inborn impulses provide the interdependence that humans have always needed. Since human brains and thoughts take many years to mature, allocare has been essential for the survival of the species. All adults—especially fathers and grandmothers—are primed to care for infants, but the particular survival and reproductive needs of the community determine whether or not they do so.

WHAT HAVE YOU LEARNED?

1. According to Freud, what might happen if a baby's oral needs are not met?
2. How might Erikson's crisis of "trust versus mistrust" affect later life?
3. What cultural differences are apparent in Erikson's crisis of "autonomy versus shame and doubt"?
4. How do behaviorists explain the development of emotions and personality?
5. What does a "working model" mean within cognitive theory?
6. According to humanism, how might caregivers' own needs affect their response to an infant?
7. How does evolution explain the parent–child bond?
8. Why is allocare necessary for survival of the human species?

Infant Day Care

Cultural variations in allocare are vast. Each theory just described can be used to justify or criticize variations. No theory directly endorses any particular position. Nonetheless, theories are made to be useful, so we include some implications of various theories in our discussion.

Many Choices

It is estimated that about 134 million babies will be born each year from 2010 to 2021 (United Nations, 2013). Most newborns are cared for primarily or exclusively by their mothers; allocare increases as the baby gets older. Fathers and grandmothers typically provide care as well. Daily care by a non-relative, trained and paid to provide it, occurs for only about 15 percent of infants worldwide, a statistic that obscures the vast range from one culture to another.

For instance, virtually no infant in some of the poorest nations receives regular non-maternal care unless the mother is dead, and then a close relative takes over. By contrast, 90 percent of the infants of the wealthiest families within some developed nations are cared for regularly by a nanny or babysitter at home, a family day-care provider in her (almost never his) home, or a trained professional in a day-care center, where there are separate rooms for infants, toddlers, and so on.

Same Situation, Far Apart: Instead of Mothers Casper, Wyoming *(left)*, is on the opposite side of the Earth from Dhaka, Bangladesh *(right)*, but day care is needed in both places, as shown here.

OBSERVATION QUIZ What three cultural differences do you see in the pictures above? (see answer, page 233)

As discussed previously, fathers worldwide increasingly take part in baby care. However, some cultures still expect fathers to stay at a distance and others favor equality (Lamb, 2013).

Most nations provide some paid leave for mothers who are in the workforce. Some also provide paid leave for fathers, and several nations provide paid family leave that can be taken by either parent or shared between them. The length of paid leave varies from a few days to about 15 months (see Figure 7.3). Laws in many nations guarantee that a mother's job will be open to her when her leave is over.

Some concern about job security and shared care arises from humanism, which values the well-being of every family member. As found by a group of family physicians, mothers are more likely to become depressed if they are sole caregivers without employment or outside support (Gjerdingen et al., 2014).

Since behaviorists emphasize learning, they seek to ensure that every baby has the proper experiences, whether provided by the mother or by someone else. One popular effort to ensure this is to send trained visitors to mothers of infants at home. They provide toys, books, and advice, encouraging caregiver–infant relationships—a practice that reduces child abuse and other physical and psychological problems (Olds, 2006).

Uncertainty About What is Best

There is no agreed-on best practice. As one review explained: "This evidence now indicates that early nonparental care environments sometimes pose risks to young children and sometimes confer benefits" (Phillips et al., 2011). The same can be said for parents: Some provide excellent care; some do not.

Many people believe that the practices of their own family or culture are best and that other patterns harm either the infant or the mother. This is another example of the difference-equals-deficit error. Without evidence, assumptions flourish. Some people advocate professional care for children of all ages; others disagree. For ideological as well a economic reasons, center-based infant care is common in France, Israel, China, Norway, and Sweden, where it is heavily subsidized by the governments and many families take it for granted as a valuable public right.

Center care is scarce in South Asia, Africa, and Latin America. Many parents believe it is harmful. (Table 7.3 lists five essential characteristics of high-quality infant day care, wherever it may be located.)

TABLE 7.3	**High-Quality Day Care**

High-quality day care during infancy has five essential characteristics:

1. *Adequate attention to each infant.* A small group of infants (no more than five) needs two reliable, familiar, loving caregivers. Continuity of care is crucial.

2. *Encouragement of language and sensorimotor development.* Infants need language—songs, conversations, and positive talk—and easily manipulated toys.

3. *Attention to health and safety.* Cleanliness routines (e.g., handwashing), accident prevention (e.g., no small objects), and safe areas to explore are essential.

4. *Professional caregivers.* Caregivers should have experience and degrees/certificates in early-childhood education. Turnover should be low, morale high, and enthusiasm evident.

5. *Warm and responsive caregivers.* Providers should engage the children in active play and guide them in problem solving. Quiet, obedient children may indicate unresponsive care.

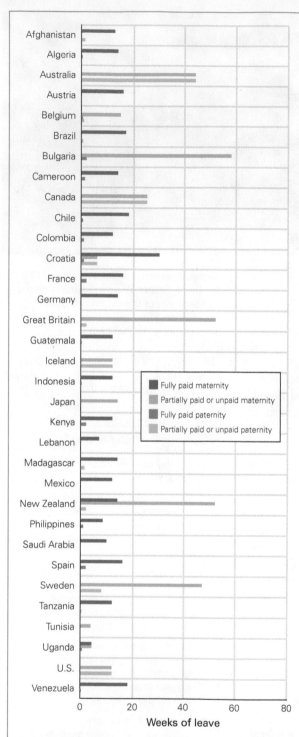

Afghanistan
Algeria
Australia
Austria
Belgium
Brazil
Bulgaria
Cameroon
Canada
Chile
Colombia
Croatia
France
Germany
Great Britain
Guatemala
Iceland
Indonesia
Japan
Kenya
Lebanon
Madagascar
Mexico
New Zealand
Philippines
Saudi Arabia
Spain
Sweden
Tanzania
Tunisia
Uganda
U.S.
Venezuela

■ Fully paid maternity
■ Partially paid or unpaid maternity
■ Fully paid paternity
■ Partially paid or unpaid paternity

0   20   40   60   80
Weeks of leave

Source: ILO Database on Conditions of Work and Employment Laws, 2011.

Note: In some cases, leave can be shared between parents or other family members. Many nations have increased leave in the past three years.

Especially for Day-Care Providers A mother who brings her child to you for day care says that she knows she is harming her baby, but economic necessity compels her to work. What do you say? (see response, page 234)

FIGURE 7.3

A Changing World No one was offered maternity leave a century ago because the only jobs that mothers had were unregulated. Now, virtually every nation has a maternity leave policy, revised every decade or so. As of 2012, only Australia, Iceland, and Canada offered policies reflecting gender equality. That may be the next innovation in many nations.

Most nations are between those two extremes. One example comes from Australia, where the government has recently attempted to increase the birth rate. Parents are given $5,000 for each new-born, parental leave is paid, and public subsidies provide child-care centers. The law endorses the concept that young children benefit from interactions with other children, yet many Australians contend that babies need exclusive maternal care (Harrison et al., 2014). As you might imagine, each side claims support from psychological theory: sociocultural versus Freud.

Parents are caught in the middle. For example, one Australian mother of a 12-month-old boy chose center care, but said:

> I spend a lot of time talking with them about his day and what he's been doing and how he's feeling and they just seem to have time to do that, to make the effort to communicate. Yeah they've really bonded with him and he's got close to them. But I still don't like leaving him there. And he doesn't, to be honest. . . . Because he's used to sort of having, you know, parents.
>
> [quoted in Boyd et al., 2013]

Underlying every policy and practice are theories about what is best. In the United States, marked variations are apparent by state and by employer, with some employers far more generous than the law requires. Almost no company pays for paternal leave, with one exception: The U.S. military allows 10 days of paid leave for fathers.

In the United States, only 20 percent of infants are cared for *exclusively* by their mothers (i.e., no other relatives or babysitters) throughout their first year. This is in contrast to Canada, which is similar to the United States in ethnic diversity but has far more generous maternal leave and lower rates of maternal employment. In the first year of life, most Canadians are cared for only by their mothers (Babchishin et al., 2013). Obviously, these differences are affected by culture, economics, and politics more than by any universal needs of babies.

The home visiting programs that help some novice mothers do not always have the desired effects (Paulsell et al., 2014), and grandmother care, informal care, and center care have each sometimes been destructive. For example, in most nations and centuries, infants were more likely to survive if their grandmothers were nearby, especially when they were newly weaned (Sear & Mace, 2008). The hypothesis is that grandmothers provided essential nourishment and protection. But in one era (northern Germany, 1720–1874), living with a grandmother, especially a paternal grandmother, had a negative effect on infant survival (Beise & Voland, 2002).

Mixed evidence can also be found for center care, as the following A View from Science explains.

a view from science

The Mixed Realities of Center Day Care

A professional organization, the National Association for the Education of Young Children, recently revised its standards for care of babies from birth to 15 months, based on current research (NAEYC, 2014). Breast-feeding is encouraged (via bottles of breast milk that mothers have expressed earlier), babies are always put to sleep on their backs, group size is small (no more than eight infants), and the ratio of adults to babies is 1:4 or fewer.

Many specific practices are recommended to keep infant minds growing and bodies healthy. For instance, "before walking on surfaces that infants use specifically for play, adults and children remove, replace, or cover with clean foot coverings any shoes they have worn outside that play area. If children or staff are barefoot in such areas, their feet are visibly clean." Another recommendation is to "engage infants in frequent face-to-face social interactions"—including talking, singing, smiling, touching (NAEYC, 2014).

Such responsive care, unfortunately, has not been routine for infants, especially those not cared for by their mothers. A large study in Canada (Côté et al., 2008) found that infant girls seemed to develop equally well in various care arrangements. However, boys from high-income families with allocare fared less well than similar boys whose mothers provided all their care. By age 4, those who had been in day care were slightly more assertive or aggressive, with more emotional problems (e.g., a teacher might note that a kindergarten boy "seems unhappy").

The opposite was true for boys from low-income families: On average, they benefited from nonmaternal care, again according to teacher reports. The researchers insist that no policy implications can be derived from this study, partly because care varied so much in quality, location, and provider (Côté et al., 2008).

Research in the United States has also found that center care benefits infants of low-income families (Peng & Robins, 2010). For less impoverished children, questions arise. An ongoing longitudinal study by the Early Child Care Network of the National Institute of Child Health and Human Development (NICHD) has followed the development of more than 1,300 children from birth to age 11. Early day care correlated with many cognitive advances, especially in language.

The social consequences were less stellar, however. Most analyses find that secure attachment to the mother was as common among infants in center care as among infants cared for at home. Like other, smaller studies, the NICHD research confirms that the mother–child relationship is pivotal.

However, infant day care seemed detrimental when the mother was insensitive *and* the infant spent more than 20 hours a week in a poor-quality program with too many children (McCartney et al., 2010). Again, boys in such circumstances had more conflicts with their teachers than did the girls or other boys with a different mix of maternal traits and day-care experiences.

More recent work finds that high quality care in infancy benefits the cognitive skills of children of both sexes and all income groups, with no evidences of emotional harm, especially when it is followed by good preschool care (Li et al., 2013). This raises another question: Might changing attitudes and female employment, and centers that reflect new research on infant development (as expressed in the NAEYC standards above) produce more positive results from center care? Or is there something about the connection between mother and baby that evolved over the millennia, as evolutionary theory might posit, that makes mother care better for infants than allocare?

A Stable, Familiar Pattern

No matter what form of care is chosen or what theory is endorsed, individualized care with stable caregivers seems best (Morrissey, 2009). Caregiver change is especially problematic for infants because each simple gesture or sound that a baby makes not only merits an encouraging response but also requires interpretation by someone who knows that particular baby well.

For example, "baba" could mean bottle, baby, blanket, banana, or some other word that does not even begin with *b*. This example is an easy one, but similar communication efforts—requiring individualized emotional responses, preferably from a familiar caregiver—are evident even in the first smiles and cries.

A related issue is the diversity of baby care providers. Especially when the home language is not the majority language, parents hesitate to let people of another linguistic background care for their infants. That is one reason that, in the United

// **ANSWER TO OBSERVATION QUIZ**
(from page 231): The Bangladeshi children are dressed alike, are the same age, and are all seated around toy balls in a net—there's not a book in sight, unlike in the Wyoming setting.

// **Response for Day-Care Providers** (from page 232): Reassure the mother that you will keep her baby safe and will help to develop the baby's mind and social skills by fostering synchrony and attachment. Also tell her that the quality of mother–infant interaction at home is more important than anything else for psychosocial development; mothers who are employed full time usually have wonderful, secure relationships with their infants. If the mother wishes, you can discuss ways to be a responsive mother.

States, immigrant parents often prefer care by relatives instead of by professionals (Miller et al., 2014). Relationships are crucial, not only between caregiver and infant, but also between caregiver and parent (Elicker et al., 2014).

Particularly problematic is instability of non-maternal care, as when an infant is cared for by a neighbor, a grandmother, a center, and then another grandmother, each for only a month or two. By age 3, children with unstable care histories are likely to be more aggressive than those with stable non-maternal care, such as being at the same center with the same caregiver for years (Pilarz & Hill, 2014).

As is true of many topics in child development, questions remain. But one fact is without question: Each infant needs personal responsiveness. Someone should serve as a partner in the synchrony duet, a base for secure attachment, and a social reference who encourages exploration. Then infant emotions and experiences—cries and laughter, fears and joys—will ensure that psychosocial development goes well.

SUMMING UP   The psychosocial impact of infant day care depends on many factors, including the culture. Although many nations pay mothers of infants to stay home with their babies, maternal employment does not seem harmful if someone else provides responsive care. Continuity is crucial; mothers, fathers, and others can all be good caregivers.

Cultures vary greatly not only in whether they provide paid child care, but whether they approve of such care. The United States tends to favor maternal care over center care but makes it difficult for families to survive without maternal employment.

WHAT HAVE YOU LEARNED?

1. What are the advantages of nonmaternal infant care?
2. What are the disadvantages of nonmaternal care?
3. What are gender and social class differences in the effects of nonmaternal care?
4. Why is it difficult to draw conclusions about the effects of infant day care?

SUMMARY

Emotional Development

1. Two emotions, contentment and distress, appear as soon as an infant is born. Smiles and laughter are evident in the early months. Between 4 and 8 months of age, anger emerges in reaction to restriction and frustration, and it becomes stronger by age 1.

2. Reflexive fear is apparent in very young infants. Fear of something specific, including fear of strangers and of separation, is typically strong toward the end of the first year.

3. In the second year, social awareness produces more selective fear, anger, and joy. As infants become increasingly self-aware, emotions emerge that encourage an interface between the self and others—specifically, pride, shame, and affection. Self-recognition (measured by the mirror/rouge test) emerges at about 18 months.

Brain and Emotions

4. Stress impedes early brain and emotional development. Some infants are particularly vulnerable to the effects of early maltreatment.

5. Temperament is a set of genetic traits whose expression is influenced by the context. Inborn temperament is linked to later personality, although plasticity is also evident. At least in the United States, parents tend to encourage exuberance and discourage fear.

The Development of Social Bonds

6. Often by 2 months, and clearly by 6 months, infants become more responsive and social, and synchrony is evident. Infants are disturbed by a still face because they expect and need social interaction.

7. Attachment, measured by the baby's reaction to the caregiver's presence, departure, and return in the Strange Situation, is crucial. Some infants seem indifferent (type A attachment—insecure-avoidant) or overly dependent (type C—insecure-resistant/ambivalent), instead of secure (type B). Disorganized attachment (type D) is the most worrisome. Secure attachment provides encouragement for infant exploration and may influence the person lifelong.

8. As they play, toddlers engage in social referencing, looking to other people's facial expressions and body language to detect what is safe, frightening, or fun. Fathers tend to help toddlers become more adventuresome.

9. Infants frequently use fathers as partners in synchrony, as attachment figures, and as social references, developing emotions and exploring their world via father caregiving.

Theories of Infant Psychosocial Development

10. According to all major theories, caregiver behavior is especially influential in the first two years. Freud stressed the mother's impact on oral and anal pleasure; Erikson emphasized trust and autonomy. Both believed that the impact of these is lifelong.

11. Behaviorists focus on learning; parents teach their babies many things, including when to be fearful or joyful. Cognitive theory holds that infants develop working models based on their experiences. Both these theories suggest that later developments can modify early experiences.

12. Humanism notes that some adults are stuck in their own unfinished development, which impairs their ability to give infants the loving responses they need.

13. Evolutionary theorists recognize that both infants and caregivers have impulses and emotions, developed over millennia, that foster the survival of each new member of the human species.

Infant Day Care

14. The impact of non-maternal care depends on many factors; it varies from one nation, one family, and even one child to another. Girls and infants from low-income households are more likely than boys from high-income households to benefit.

15. Although each theory and each culture has a somewhat different emphasis, all agree that quality of care (responsive, individualized, stable) is crucial, particularly in infancy, no matter who provides that care.

KEY TERMS

social smile (p. 204)
cortisol (p. 204)
separation anxiety (p. 205)
stranger wariness (p. 205)
self-awareness (p. 206)
temperament (p. 210)
goodness of fit (p. 212)
Big Five (p. 212)

synchrony (p. 213)
still-face technique (p. 214)
attachment (p. 215)
secure attachment (p. 217)
insecure-avoidant attachment
   (p. 217)
insecure-resistant/ambivalent
   attachment (p. 218)

disorganized attachment
   (p. 218)
Strange Situation (p. 218)
social referencing (p. 221)
trust versus mistrust (p. 225)
autonomy versus shame and
   doubt (p. 225)
social learning (p. 225)

proximal parenting (p. 226)
distal parenting (p. 226)
working model (p. 226)
allocare (p. 229)

APPLICATIONS

1. One cultural factor influencing infant development is how infants are carried from place to place. Ask four mothers whose infants were born in each of the past four decades how they transported them—front or back carriers, facing out or in, strollers or carriages, in car seats or on mother's laps, and so on. Why did they choose the mode(s) they chose? What are their opinions and yours on how such cultural practices might affect infants' development?

2. Observe synchrony for three minutes. Ideally, ask the parent of an infant under 8 months of age to play with the infant. If no infant is available, observe a pair of lovers as they converse. Note the sequence and timing of every facial expression, sound, and gesture of both partners.

3. Telephone several day-care centers to try to assess the quality of care they provide. Ask about factors such as adult/child ratio, group size, and training for caregivers of children of various ages. Is there a minimum age? Why or why not? Analyze the answers, using Table 7.3 as a guide.

PART 2

The Developing Person So Far:
The First Two Years

BIOSOCIAL

Body Changes and Brain Development Over the first two years, body weight quadruples and brain weight triples. Connections between brain cells grow dense, with complex networks of dendrites and axons. Neurons become coated with myelin, sending messages more efficiently. Experiences that are universal (experience-expectant) and culture-bound (experience-dependent) aid brain growth, partly by pruning unused connections between neurons.

Perceiving and Moving Brain maturation underlies the development of all the senses. Seeing, hearing, and moving progress from reflexes to coordinated voluntary actions, including focusing, grasping, and walking. Culture is evident in sensory and motor development: Brain networks respond to the particular experiences of each infant's life.

Surviving in Good Health Infant health depends on immunization, parental practices (including "back to sleep"), and nutrition. Breast milk protects health and has so many other benefits that the World Health Organization recommends exclusive breast-feeding for the first four to six months. Survival rates are much higher today than even a few decades ago, with less marasmus and kwashiorkor, yet in some regions, infant growth is still stunted because of malnutrition.

COGNITIVE

Sensorimotor Intelligence and Information Processing As Piaget describes it, in their first two years infants progress from knowing their world through immediate sensory experiences to "experimenting" on their world through actions and mental images. Information-processing theory stresses the links between sensory experiences and perception. Research finds traces of memory at 3 months, of object permanence at 4 months, and of deferred imitation at 9 months—all much younger ages than Piaget described.

Language Interaction with responsive adults exposes infants to the structures of communication and language. By age 1, infants usually speak a word or two. By age 2, language has exploded: Toddlers talk in short sentences and add vocabulary each day. Language develops through reinforcement, neurological maturation, and social motivation; all three processes combine to create a very conversational toddler.

PSYCHOSOCIAL

Emotions Emotions are a newborn's simple reactions, but by age 2 a toddler's emotions have developed into complex, self-conscious responses. Infants' self-awareness and independence are shaped by parents and the culture. Much of basic temperament is inborn and apparent throughout life.

The Development of Social Bonds Parents and infants respond to each other by synchronizing their behavior. Toward the end of the first year, secure attachment to the parent sets the stage for the child's increasingly independent exploration of the world. Insecure attachment—avoidant, resistant, or disorganized—signifies a parent–child relationship that hinders learning. The effects may endure, although children and adults may develop new attachment patterns. Infants actively participate socially, using social referencing to interpret their experiences. Every theory has a somewhat different understanding of how early emotions develop. Mothers, fathers, and day-care providers encourage infants' social confidence, yet cultures differ markedly on how much allocare infants experience.

early childhood

PART 3

From ages 2 to 6, children spend most of their waking hours discovering, creating, laughing, and imagining—all the while acquiring the skills they need. They chase each other and attempt new challenges (developing their bodies); they play with sounds, words, and ideas (developing their minds); they invent games and dramatize fantasies (learning social skills and morals).

These were once called the *preschool years* because school started in first grade. But first grade is no longer first; most children begin school before age 6. Therefore, we use the term *early childhood*.

These could also be called the play years, since young children love to play, whether quietly tracking a beetle through the grass or riotously turning a bedroom into a shambles. Their words and minds are playful, too; They explain that "a bald man has a barefoot head" or that "the sun shines so children can go outside to play."

Early childhood—by whatever name—is a time of extraordinary growth, impressive learning, and spontaneous play, joyful not only for young children but also for anyone who knows them.

CHAPTER 8

Early Childhood:
Biosocial Development

What Will You Know?

1. Do children eat too much, too little, or just the right amount?
2. Does brain maturation make children laugh or cry too quickly?
3. If children never climb up trees or wade in water, do they suffer?
4. Are accidents accidental?
5. Which is worse, neglect or abuse?

When I was 4, I jumped off the back of our couch again and again, trying to fly. I did it many times because I tried it with and without a cape, with and without flapping my arms. My laughing mother wondered whether she had made a mistake in letting me see *Peter Pan*. An older woman warned that jumping would hurt my uterus. I didn't know what a uterus was, I didn't heed that lady, and I didn't stop until I decided I could not fly because I had no pixie dust.

When you were 4, I hope you also wanted to fly and someone laughed while keeping you safe. Protection, appreciation, and fantasy are all needed in early childhood. Do you remember trying to skip, climb a tree, or write your name? Young children try, fail, and try again. They become skilled and wise, eventually understanding some of life's limitations, including that humans have no wings. Advances in body and brain, and the need for adult protection, are themes of this chapter. Amazing growth, unexpected injury, and sobering maltreatment are all described.

Body Changes

In early childhood as in infancy, the body and brain develop according to powerful epigenetic forces—biologically driven and socially guided, experience-expectant and experience-dependent. (**Developmental Link:** Experience-expectant and experience-dependent brain development are explained in Chapter 5.) During this period, bodies and brains mature in size and function.

Growth Patterns

Compare an unsteady 24-month-old with a cartwheeling 6-year-old. Body differences are obvious. Height and weight increase greatly in those four years (by about a foot and 16 pounds, or almost 30 centimeters and 8 kilograms), but that is not the most remarkable change. During early childhood, proportions shift radically: Children slim down as the lower body lengthens and fat turns to muscle.

Size and Balance These cousins are only four years apart, but note the doubling in leg length and marked improvement in balance. The 2-year-old needs to plant both legs on the sand, while the 6-year-old cavorts on one foot.

Victory! He's on his way. This boy participates in a British effort to combat childhood obesity; mother and son exercising in Liverpool Park is part of the solution. Harder to implement are dietary changes: Many parents let children eat as much as they want.

In fact, the average body mass index (BMI, a ratio of weight to height) is lower at ages 5 and 6 than at any other time of life. (**Developmental Link:** Body mass index is defined in Chapter 11.) Gone are the infant's protruding belly, round face, short limbs, and large head. The center of gravity moves from the breast to the belly, enabling cartwheels, somersaults, and many other motor skills. The joys of dancing, gymnastics, and pumping a swing become possible; changing proportions enable new achievements.

New shape and ability occur as weight and height increase. Over each year of early childhood, well-nourished children grow about 3 inches (about 7½ centimeters) and gain almost 4½ pounds (2 kilograms). By age 6, the average child in a developed nation:

- Is at least 3½ feet tall (more than 110 centimeters)
- Weighs between 40 and 50 pounds (between 18 and 23 kilograms)
- Looks lean, not chubby
- Has adult-like body proportions (legs constitute about half the total height)

When many ethnic groups live together in a nation with abundant food and adequate medical care, children of African descent tend to be tallest, followed by those of European, then Asian, and then Latino descent. However, height differences are greater *within* ethnic groups than *between* groups, evidence again that ethnic differences are not primarily biological.

Nutrition

Although they rarely starve, preschool children sometimes are malnourished, even in nations with abundant food. The main reason is that small appetites are often satiated by unhealthy foods, crowding out needed vitamins.

Adults often encourage children to eat, protecting them against famine that was common a century ago. Unfortunately, that encouragement is destructive in almost every nation. For example 30 years ago in Brazil, the most common nutritional problem was undernutrition; now it is overeating (Monteiro et al., 2004). Low-income Brazilians are particularly vulnerable, but even wealthy Brazilians eat a less nutritious, higher calorie diet than they did a few decades ago (Monteiro et al., 2011).

In developed nations, children or grandchildren of immigrants are more likely to ingest inadequate amounts of healthy food than their elders who were born elsewhere (de Hoog et al., 2014). Further, the rate of poor nutrition increases as family income decreases; the same is true of obesity. Childhood obesity is not simply a problem in itself, it is also a marker of poor nutrition, and likely to reduce the functioning of the immune system lifelong (Rook et al., 2014).

There are many explanations of the increasing obesity as income falls. One is that many low-income children live with grandmothers who knew firsthand the dangers of malnutrition. They reward children with sweets, and they foster other eating patterns that combat starvation that no longer is a problem. They do not realize that traditional diets in Latin America or Africa are healthier than current foods advertised to children on television (de Hoog et al., 2014).

Of course, mothers and fathers also contribute to childhood obesity. Many family habits—less exercise, more television watching, fewer vegetables, more fast food—are more common in low-SES families than in those with wealthier, more educated parents (Cespedes et al., 2013).

Caregivers need to realize that appetite decreases between ages 2 and 6 because young children grow more slowly and need fewer calories per pound than they did as infants. This is especially true for the current generation, who burn fewer calories because they are less active compared to children fifty years ago. Once most children lived in rural areas where they played outside all day. Instead of adjusting to this ecological change, many adults fret, threaten, and cajole children to overeat ("Eat all your dinner and you can have ice cream").

Many developmentalists promote more exercise in children. Such efforts are not always successful, as is evident from a study of many Latin American nations (Barboza, 2013). (**Developmental Link:** Obesity and exercise are discussed in Chapter 11.) There is good news in the United States, however. Obesity among preschoolers has declined slightly in recent years. It still is far too high (about 12 percent) but a combination of public education and parental action has led to improvement (MMWR, January 18, 2013; MMWR, August 9, 2013).

Nutritional Deficiencies

Although many young children consume more than enough calories, they do not always obtain adequate iron, zinc, and calcium. For example, North American children now drink less milk than formerly, which means they ingest less calcium and will have weaker bones later on.

Eating a wide variety of fresh foods may be essential for optimal health. Compared with the average child, those preschoolers who eat more dark-green and orange vegetables and less fried food benefit in many ways. They gain bone mass but not fat, according to a study that controlled for other factors that might correlate with body fat, such as gender (girls have more), ethnicity (people of some ethnic groups are genetically thinner), and income (poor children have worse diets) (Wosje et al., 2010).

Sugar is a major problem. Many customs entice children to eat sweets—in birthday cake, holiday candy, desserts, and other treats. Sweetened cereals and drinks (advertised as containing 100 percent of daily vitamins) are a poor substitute for a balanced, varied diet, partly because some nutrients have not yet been identified, much less listed on food labels. The lack of micronutrients is severe among people in poor nations, but vitamin pills and added supplements do not always help (Ramakrishnan et al., 2011).

Within the United States, children of all ethnicities drink more sweetened beverages than they once did, a problem particularly common among African Americans (de Hoog et al., 2014). They have a higher incidence of lactose intolerance, so they may avoid drinking milk. However, that may needlessly reduce nutrition. Most African Americans can digest some milk, and yogurt is a good calcium source if children are truly upset by lactose (Marette & Picard-Deland, 2014). However, yogurt is expensive and non-traditional, so parents need to be aware that yogurt drinks are far better for children than drinks with sugar or corn syrup.

An added complication is that an estimated 3 to 8 percent of all young children are allergic to a specific food, almost always a common, healthy one: Cow's milk, eggs, peanuts, tree nuts (such as almonds, walnuts, etc.), soy, wheat, fish, and shellfish are the usual culprits. Diagnostic standards for allergies vary (which explains the range of estimates), and treatment varies even more (Chafen et al., 2010).

Some experts advocate total avoidance of the offending food—there are peanut-free schools, where no one is allowed to bring a peanut butter sandwich for lunch—but other experts suggest that tolerance should be gradually increased, beginning by giving babies a tiny bit of peanut butter (Reche et al., 2011). Indeed, exposure to peanuts can begin before birth: A study of pregnant women who

Especially for Nutritionists A parent complains that she prepares a variety of vegetables and fruits, but her 4-year-old wants only French fries and cake. What should you advise? (see response, page 245)

JO UNRUH/GETTY IMAGES

Apples, Blueberries, or Oranges Preschoolers love having a choice, so it is the adults' task to offer good options. Which book before bed? Which striped shirt before school? Which healthy snack before going out to play?

Eat Your Veggies On their own, children do not always eat wisely.

VAHAN SHIRVANIAN/CARTOONSTOCK.COM

"I'm not hungry, I ate with Rover."

Especially for Early-Childhood Teachers You know that young children are upset if forced to eat a food they hate, but you have eight 3-year-olds with eight different preferences. What do you do? (see response, page 246)

ingested peanuts found that their children were less likely to be allergic (Frazier et al., 2014). Fortunately, many childhood food allergies are outgrown, but since young children are already at nutritional risk, allergies make a balanced diet even harder.

Yet another complication is that many young children are compulsive about daily routines, insisting that bedtime be preceded by tooth-brushing, a book, and prayers—or by a snack, sitting on the toilet, and a song, in that order. My grandson always wanted a story, but not just any story. He told me it had to be a made-up story about an animal that has a problem that is solved by the end of the story. Thankfully, despite such very specific criteria, his literary standards were low, so I could comply. Whatever the routine, children expect it and are upset if someone puts them to bed without it.

Fortunately, as a team of experts contends, "Most, if not all, children exhibit normal age-dependent obsessive-compulsive behaviors [that are] usually gone by middle childhood" (March et al., 2004, p. 216). Parents need to balance their concern for good nutrition with the child's normal wish for sameness. This is another reason a variety of healthy foods, including some that may not be the family's usual fare, need to be fed early in life, before the child develops antipathy to particular fruits or vegetables.

Oral Health

Not surprisingly, tooth decay correlates with obesity; both result from a diet with too much sugar and too little fiber (Hayden et al., 2013). More than one-third of all U.S. children under age 6 already have at least one cavity (Brickhouse et al., 2008). Sugary fruit drinks and soda are prime causes, and sugar-free soda contains acid that makes decay more likely (Holtzman, 2009).

"Baby" teeth are replaced naturally at about ages 6 to 10. The schedule is primarily genetic, with girls a few months ahead of boys. However, tooth care should begin years before the permanent teeth erupt. Severe tooth decay in early childhood harms those permanent teeth (which form below the first teeth) and can cause jaw malformation, chewing difficulties, and speech problems. The United States Preventive Services Task Force (a panel of experts in evidence-based medicine) urges pediatricians to add fluoride coats to the teeth of preschoolers who have no other source of fluoride, as that is proven to reduce cavities (Moyer, 2014).

Teeth are affected by diet and illness, which means that the state of a young child's teeth can alert the doctor or dentist to other health problems. The process works in reverse as well: Infected teeth can affect the rest of the child's body.

Most preschoolers visit the dentist if they have U.S.-born, middle-class parents; however, the less education parents have, the less likely they are to know the importance of early dental care (Horowitz et al., 2013).

If the parent was raised in a nation with inadequate dental care (sometimes evident in the number of toothless elders), they may not schedule dentist visits for their children or insist on tooth brushing. However, in many countries ignorance is not the problem; access and income are. In the United States, free dentistry is not available to most poor parents, who "want to do better" for their children's teeth than they did for their own (Lewis et al., 2010).

SUMMING UP   Between ages 2 and 6, children's body proportions change as they grow taller and thinner, with variations depending on genes, nutrition, income, and ethnicity. Young children usually have small appetites and picky eating habits. Unfortunately, many adults encourage overeating, not realizing that being overweight leads to life-threatening illness. Obesity increases as education and income fall. Oral health is a serious problem: Many children eat unhealthy foods, especially too much sugar, developing cavities. If adults grew up in nations with few dentists, they may not realize that young children need to develop tooth-brushing habits and that seeing the dentist in early childhood is important for later health.

WHAT HAVE YOU LEARNED?

1. About how much does a well-nourished child grow in height and weight from ages 2 to 6?
2. Why do many adults overfeed children?
3. How do childhood allergies affect nutrition?
4. Why are today's children more at risk of obesity than children 50 years ago?
5. What specific measures should be part of oral health in early childhood?

Brain Development

Brains grow rapidly before birth and throughout infancy, as you saw in Chapter 5. By age 2, most neurons have connected to other neurons and substantial pruning has occurred. The 2-year-old's brain already weighs 75 percent of what it will weigh in adulthood; the 6-year-old's brain is 90 percent of adult weight. (The major structures of the brain are diagrammed in Figure 8.1)

Since most of the brain is already present and functioning by age 2, what remains to develop? The most important parts!

Although the brains and bodies of other primates seem better than humans in some ways (they climb trees earlier and faster, for instance) and although many animals have abilities humans lack (smell in dogs, for instance), humans have intellectual capacities far beyond any other animal. Considered from an evolutionary perspective, our brains allowed the human species to develop "a mode of living built on social cohesion, cooperation and efficient planning . . . survival of the smartest" seems more accurate than survival of the fittest" (Corballis, 2011, p. 194).

As the prefrontal cortex matures, social understanding develops, distinguishing humans from other primates. For example, a careful series of tests given to 106 chimpanzees, 32 orangutans, and 105 human 2½-year-olds found that young children were "equivalent . . . to chimpanzees on tasks of physical cognition but far outstripped both chimpanzees and orangutans on tasks of social cognition" such as pointing or following someone's gaze (Herrmann et al., 2007, p. 1365).

Children become better at controlling their emotions when they are with other people, no longer wailing, hitting, or laughing out loud on impulse. This is directly connected to brain development as time passes and family experiences continue, although how much of such control is brain-based and how much is a matter of earlier parenting is disputed (DeLisi, 2014; Kochanska et al., 2009). Nonetheless, gradual self-control is apparent.

For example, when a stranger greets them, many 2-year-olds are speechless, hiding behind their mothers if possible. By age 5, a kindergartner who hides is unusual. Adults may still feel shy, but they bravely respond. Brain scans of the prefrontal cortex and amygdala (soon described) taken at age 18 may show inhibition,

// Response for Nutritionists (from page 243): The nutritionally wise advice would be to offer only fruits, vegetables, and other nourishing, low-fat foods, counting on the child's eventual hunger to drive him or her to eat them. However, centuries of cultural custom make such wisdom difficult. A physical checkup, with a blood test, may be warranted to make sure the child is healthy.

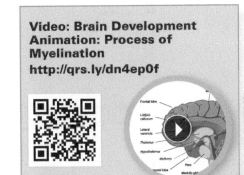

Video: Brain Development Animation: Process of Myelination
http://qrs.ly/dn4ep0f

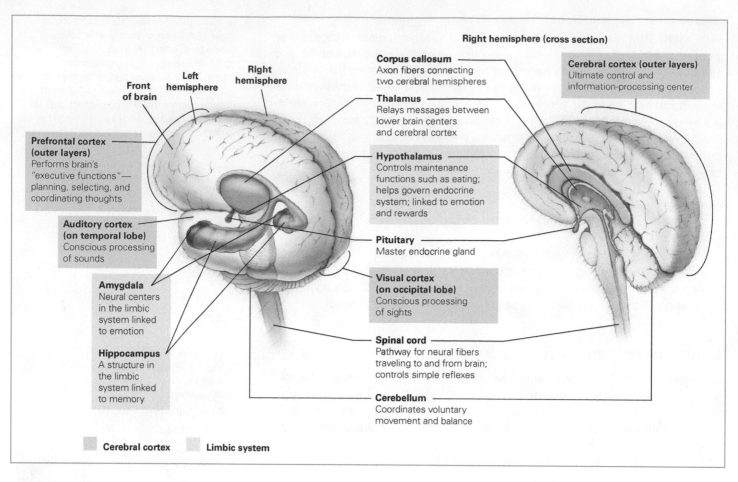

Right hemisphere (cross section)

Corpus callosum
Axon fibers connecting
two cerebral hemispheres

Cerebral cortex (outer layers)
Ultimate control and
information-processing center

**Front
of brain**

**Left
hemisphere**

**Right
hemisphere**

Thalamus
Relays messages between
lower brain centers
and cerebral cortex

**Prefrontal cortex
(outer layers)**
Performs brain's
"executive functions"—
planning, selecting, and
coordinating thoughts

Hypothalamus
Controls maintenance
functions such as eating;
helps govern endocrine
system; linked to emotion
and rewards

**Auditory cortex
(on temporal lobe)**
Conscious processing
of sounds

Pituitary
Master endocrine gland

Amygdala
Neural centers
in the limbic
system linked
to emotion

**Visual cortex
(on occipital lobe)**
Conscious processing
of sights

Hippocampus
A structure in
the limbic
system linked
to memory

Spinal cord
Pathway for neural fibers
traveling to and from brain;
controls simple reflexes

Cerebellum
Coordinates voluntary
movement and balance

Cerebral cortex   Limbic system

FIGURE 8.1

Connections A few of the dozens of named parts of the brain are shown here. Although each area has particular functions, the entire brain is interconnected. The processing of emotions, for example, occurs primarily in the limbic system, where many brain areas are involved, including the amygdala, hippocampus, and hypothalamus.

myelination The process by which axons become coated with myelin, a fatty substance that speeds the transmission of nerve impulses from neuron to neuron.

// Response for Early-Childhood Teachers (from page 244): Remember to keep food simple and familiar. Offer every child the same food, allowing refusal but no substitutes—unless for all eight. Children do not expect school and home routines to be identical; they eventually taste whatever other children enjoy.

but most inhibited people no longer act in extremely anxious ways (Schwartz et al., 2010). (**Developmental Link:** Emotional regulation is further discussed in Chapter 10.)

Speed of Thought

After infancy, some brain growth is the result of proliferation of the communication pathways (dendrites and axons). However, most increased brain weight occurs because of **myelination.** *Myelin* (sometimes called the *white matter* of the brain) is a fatty coating on the axons that speeds signals between neurons (see Figure 8.2).

Although myelination continues for decades, the effects are especially apparent in early childhood (Silk & Wood, 2011). The areas of the brain that show greatest early myelination are the motor and sensory areas (Kolb & Whishaw, 2013), so preschoolers react more quickly to sounds and sights with every passing year.

Speed of thought from axon to neuron becomes pivotal when several thoughts must occur in rapid succession. By age 6, most children can see an object and immediately name it, catch a ball and throw it, write their ABCs in proper sequence, and so on. In fact, rapid naming of letters and objects—possible only when myelination is extensive—is a crucial indicator of later reading ability (Shanahan & Lonigan, 2010).

Of course, adults must be patient when listening to young children talk, helping them get dressed, or watching them write each letter of their names. Everything is done more slowly by 6-year-olds than by 16-year-olds because the younger children's brains have less myelination, which slows information processing. However, thanks to myelination, older preschoolers are faster than toddlers, who sometimes forget what they were doing before they finish.

The Brain's Connected Hemispheres

One part of the brain that grows and myelinates rapidly during early childhood is the **corpus callosum,** a long, thick band of nerve fibers that connects the left and right sides of the brain. Growth of the corpus callosum makes communication between the hemispheres more efficient, allowing children to coordinate the two sides of their brains and hence, both sides of their bodies.

Serious disorders result when the corpus callosum fails to develop: This failure is one of several possible causes of autism (Frazier et al., 2012; Floris et al., 2013). Such failures lead to a variety of symptoms, always including intellectual disability (Cavalari & Donovick, 2014).

To understand the significance of the corpus callosum, note that each side of the body and brain specializes and is therefore dominant for certain functions. This is **lateralization,** literally, "sidedness." The entire human body is lateralized, apparent not only in right- or left-handedness but also in the feet, the eyes, the ears, and the brain itself. People prefer to kick a ball, wink an eye, or listen on the phone with their preferred foot, eye, or ear. Genes, prenatal hormones, and early experiences all affect which side does what. Lateralization advances with development of the corpus callosum (Kolb & Whishaw, 2013). The strength of lateralization varies—some people are more ambidextrous than others.

Left-handed people tend to have thicker corpus callosa than right-handed people do, perhaps because they need to readjust the interaction between the two sides of their bodies, depending on the task. For example, most left-handed people brush their teeth with their left hand because using their dominant hand is more natural, but they shake hands with their right hand because that is what the social convention requires.

The Left-Handed Child

Infants and toddlers usually prefer one hand to the other for grabbing spoons and rattles. Indeed, there is evidence that lateralization begins in the womb, so some newborns are already left- or right-handed (Ratnarajah et al., 2013). By age 2 most children have a dominant hand for scribbling and throwing. Preschool teachers notice that about 1 child in 10 prefers the left hand.

Many cultures try to make every child right-handed, with some success. When left-handed children are forced to use their right hands, most learn to write right-handedly. But neurologically, success is incomplete: Their brains are only partly reprogrammed, as evidenced when they choose their left hand to comb their hair, throw a ball, or wield a hammer.

Many cultures imply that being right-handed is best, an example of the *difference-equals-deficit error,* explained in Chapter 1. Consider language: In English, a "left-handed compliment" is insincere, and no one wants to have "two left feet" or to be "out in left field." In Latin, *dexter* (as in *dexterity*) means "right" and *sinister* means "left" (and also "evil"). *Gauche,* the French word for *left,* means "socially awkward" in English. Many languages are written from left to right, which is easier for right-handed people.

The design of doorknobs, scissors, baseball mitts, instrument panels, and other objects favor the right hand. (Some manufacturers have special versions for lefties, but few young children know to ask for them.) In many Asian and African

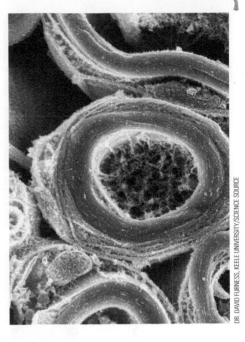

FIGURE 8.2

Faster and Faster Myelination is a lifelong process. Shown here is a cross section of an axon (dark middle) coated with many layers of Schwann cells, as more and more myelin wraps around the axon throughout childhood. Age-related slowdowns in late adulthood are caused by the gradual disappearance of myelin layers.

corpus callosum A long, thick band of nerve fibers that connects the left and right hemispheres of the brain and allows communication between them.

lateralization Literally, "sidedness," referring to the specialization in certain functions by each side of the brain, with one side dominant for each activity. The left side of the brain controls the right side of the body, and vice versa.

Especially for Early-Childhood Teachers You know you should be patient, but frustration rises when your young charges dawdle on the walk to the playground a block away. What should you do? (see response, page 249)

DR. DAVID FURNESS, KEELE UNIVERSITY/SCIENCE SOURCE

Smarter than Most? Beware of stereotypes. Obviously, this student is a girl, Asian, left-handed, and attending a structured school (note the uniform). Each of these four characteristics leads some to conclude that she is more intelligent than other 7-year-olds. But all children have brains with the potential to learn: Specific teaching, not innate characteristics, is crucial.

cultures, only the left hand is used for wiping after defecation; it is an insult to give someone anything with that "dirty" hand.

Developmentalists advise against switching a child's handedness, not only because this causes adult–child conflicts and may create neurological confusion but also because left lateralization is an advantage in some professions, especially those involving creativity and split-second actions.

A disproportionate number of artists, musicians, and sports stars were/are left-handed, including Pele, Babe Ruth, Monica Seles, Bill Gates, Oprah Winfrey, Jimi Hendrix, Lady Gaga, and Justin Bieber. Using both sides of the body is an advantage: LeBron James writes left-handed but plays basketball right-handed. Five of the past six presidents of the United States were/are lefties: Gerald Ford, Ronald Reagan, George H.W. Bush, Bill Clinton, and Barack Obama.

Acceptance of left-handedness is more widespread now than a century ago. More adults in Great Britain and the United States claim to be left-handed today (about 10 percent) than in 1900 (about 3 percent) (McManus et al., 2010). There seem to be more left-handed men than women, as well as more left-handers in North America than elsewhere. Whether this is cultural or genetic is not known.

The Whole Brain

Astonishing studies of humans whose corpus callosa were severed to relieve severe epilepsy, as well as research on humans and other vertebrates with intact corpus callosa, have revealed how the brain's hemispheres specialize. Typically, the brain's left half controls the body's right side as well as areas dedicated to logical reasoning, detailed analysis, and the basics of language. The brain's right half controls the body's left side and areas dedicated to emotional and creative impulses, including appreciation of music, art, and poetry. Thus, the left side notices details and the right side grasps the big picture.

This left–right distinction has been exaggerated, especially when broadly applied to people (Hugdahl & Westerhausen, 2010). No one is exclusively left-brained or right-brained (except severely brain-damaged individuals). Moreover, the brain is plastic, especially in childhood, so a lost function in one hemisphere is sometimes replaced in the other hemisphere. (**Developmental Link:** Brain plasticity is discussed in Chapter 1.)

Both sides of the brain are usually involved in every skill. That is why the corpus callosum is crucial. As myelination progresses, signals between the two hemispheres become quicker and clearer, enabling children to become better thinkers and less clumsy. For example, no 2-year-old can hop on one foot, but most 6-year-olds can—an example of brain balancing. Many songs, dances, and games that young children love involve moving their bodies in some coordinated way—difficult, but fun because of that. Logic (left brain) without emotion (right brain) is a severe impairment, as is the opposite (Damasio, 2012).

Maturation of the Prefrontal Cortex

The entire frontal lobe continues to develop for many years after early childhood; dendrite density and myelination are still increasing in emerging adulthood. Nonetheless, neurological control advances significantly every year between ages 2 and 6, as is evident in several ways:

- Sleep becomes more regular.
- Emotions become more nuanced and responsive.
- Temper tantrums subside.
- Uncontrollable laughter and tears are less common.

One example of the maturing brain is in the game Simon Says. Players are supposed to follow the leader *only* when orders are preceded by the words "Simon says." Thus, if leaders touch their noses and say, "Simon says touch your nose," players are supposed to touch their noses, but when leaders touch their noses and say, "Touch your nose," no one is supposed to follow the example. Young children lose at this game because they impulsively do what they see and hear. Older children can think before acting. The prefrontal cortex works!

Such advances can be observed in every child, but might personal experience rather than brain maturation be the reason? A convincing demonstration that something neurological, not experiential, is the primary reason for these changes comes from a series of experiments with shapes and colors.

These experiments begin with young children given a set of cards with clear outlines of trucks or flowers, some red and some blue. They are asked to "play the shape game," putting trucks in one pile and flowers in another. Three-year-olds (and even some 2-year-olds) can do this correctly.

Then children are asked to "play the color game," sorting the cards by color. Most children under age 4 fail. Instead, they sort by shape, as they had done before. This basic test has been replicated in many nations; 3-year-olds usually get stuck in their initial sorting pattern. By age 5 (and sometimes age 4), most children make the switch.

When this result was first obtained, experimenters thought perhaps the children didn't have enough experience to know their colors; so the scientists switched the order, first playing "the color game." Most 3-year-olds did that correctly, because most 3-year-olds know the difference between red and blue. Then, when asked to play "the shape game," they sorted by color! Even with a new set of cards, such as yellow and green or rabbits and boats, 3-year-olds still tend to sort however they did originally, either by color or shape.

Researchers are looking into many possible explanations for this result (Müller et al., 2006; Marcovitch et al., 2010; Ramscar et al., 2013). All agree, however, that something in the brain must mature before children are able to switch from one way of sorting objects to another. (**Developmental Link:** Maturation of the prefrontal cortex is also discussed in Chapters 5, 11, and 14.)

Impulsiveness and Perseveration

Neurons have only two kinds of impulses: on–off or activate–inhibit. Each is signaled by biochemical messages from dendrites to axons to neurons. Both activation and inhibition are necessary for thoughtful adults, who neither leap too quickly nor hesitate too long. A balanced brain is best throughout life: One sign of cognitive loss in late adulthood is that some of the elderly become too cautious or too impulsive.

Many young children are notably unbalanced. They are impulsive, flitting from one activity to another. That explains why many 3-year-olds cannot stay quietly on one task, even in "circle time" in preschool, where each child is supposed to sit in place, not talking or touching anyone. Poor **impulse control** signfies a personality disorder in aduthood but not in early childhood. Few 3-year-olds are capable of sustained attention, which is required in primary school.

For some preschoolers, the see-saw tips in the opposite direction, when children play with a single toy for hours. **Perseveration** refers to the tendency to persevere in, or stick to, one thought or action, as evident in the card-sorting study just described (Hanania, 2010).

Many explanations for perseveration are plausible, and the tendency is unmistakable. Often young children repeat one phrase or question again and again, and

// Response for Early-Childhood Teachers (from page 247): One solution is to remind yourself that the children's brains are not yet myelinated enough to enable them to quickly walk, talk, or even button their jackets. Maturation has a major effect, as you will observe if you can schedule excursions in September and again in November. Progress, while still slow, will be a few seconds faster.

impulse control The ability to postpone or deny the immediate response to an idea or behavior.

perseveration The tendency to persevere in, or stick to, one thought or action for a long time.

often once they start giggling they find it hard to stop. Another example of perseveration occurs when a child has a tantrum when told to end an activity. (Wise teachers give a warning—"Cleanup in 5 minutes"—which may help.) The tantrum itself may perseverate. Crying may become uncontrollable because the child is stuck in the emotion that triggered the tantrum.

Impulsiveness and perseveration are opposite manifestations of the same underlying cause: immaturity of the prefrontal cortex. No young child is perfect at regulating attention; impulsiveness and perseveration are evident in every young child.

A longitudinal study of children from ages 3 to 6 found their ability to pay attention increased steadily, and that led to academic learning and behavioral control (fewer outbursts or tears) (Metcalfe et al., 2013). That development continues in middle childhood as brain maturation (innate) and emotional regulation (learned) allow most children to pay attention and switch activities as needed. By adolescence, teenagers change tasks at the sound of the bell.

Ashes to Ashes, Dust to Dust Many religious rituals have sustained humans of all ages for centuries, including listening quietly in church on Ash Wednesday—as Nailah Pierre tries to do. Sitting quietly is developmentally difficult for young children, but for three reasons she may succeed: (1) gender (girls mature earlier than boys), (2) experience (she has been in church many times), and (3) social context (she is one of 750 students in her school attending a special service at Nativity Catholic church).

Exceptions include children with attention-deficit/hyperactivity disorder (ADHD), who are too impulsive for their age. An imbalance between the left and right sides of the prefrontal cortex and abnormal growth of the corpus callosum seem to underlie (and perhaps cause) ADHD (Gilliam et al., 2011).

As with all biological maturation, development of impulse control and behavioral flexibility is related to upbringing. A study of Korean preschoolers found that they developed impulse control and reduced perseveration sooner than a comparable group of English children. This study included the shape–color task: At age 3, 40 percent of Korean children but only 14 percent of British ones successfully shifted from sorting by shape to color. The researchers considered many possible reasons and concluded that "a cultural explanation is more likely" (Oh & Lewis, 2008, p. 96).

Emotions and the Brain

Now that we have considered the prefrontal cortex, we turn to another region of the brain, sometimes called the *limbic system,* the major system for emotions. Emotional expression and emotional regulation advance during early childhood. (**Developmental Link:** Emotional regulation is discussed further in Chapters 10 and 15.) Crucial to that advance are three parts of the brain—the amygdala, the hippocampus, and the hypothalamus.

The Limbic System

The **amygdala** is a tiny structure deep in the brain. It registers emotions, both positive and negative, especially fear (Kolb & Whishaw, 2013). Increased amygdala activity is one reason some young children have terrifying nightmares or sudden terrors, overwhelming the prefrontal cortex. Similarly, a child may refuse to enter an elevator or may be hysterical at a nightmare.

The amygdala responds to comfort but not to logic. If a child is terrified of, say, a dream of a lion in the closet, an adult should not laugh but might open the closet door and command the lion to go home.

Another structure in the emotional network is the **hippocampus,** located next to the amygdala. A central processor of memory, especially memory for locations, the hippocampus responds to the anxieties of the amygdala by summoning memory. A child can remember, for instance, whether previous elevator riding was scary or fun.

Early memories of location are fragile because the hippocampus is still developing. Nonetheless, emotional memories from early childhood can interfere with expressed, rational thinking: An adult might have a panic attack but not know why.

The interaction of the amygdala and the hippocampus is sometimes helpful, sometimes not; fear can be constructive or destructive (LaBar, 2007). Studies of animals find that when the amygdala is surgically removed, the animals are fearless in situations that should scare them. For instance, a cat without an amygdala will stroll nonchalantly past monkeys—something no normal cat would do (Kolb & Whishaw, 2013).

A third part of the limbic system, the **hypothalamus,** responds to signals from the amygdala (arousing) and from the hippocampus (usually dampening) by producing cortisol, oxytocin, and other hormones that activate parts of the brain and body (see Figure 8.3). Ideally, this hormone production occurs in moderation. Both temperamental inhibition and parental responses affect whether or not the hypothalamus will overreact, making the preschooler too anxious—as about 20 percent of 4- to 7-year-olds are (Paulus et al., 2014).

As the limbic system develops, young children watch their parents' emotions closely. If a parent looks worried when entering an elevator, the child may fearfully cling to the parent when the elevator moves. If this sequence recurs often enough, the child may become hypersensitive to elevators, as fear from the amygdala joins memories from the hippocampus, increasing cortisol production via the hypothalamus. If, instead, the parent makes elevator riding fun (letting the child push the buttons, for instance), initial fears subside, and the child's brain will be aroused to enjoy elevators—even when there is no need to go from floor to floor.

Knowing the varieties of fears and joys is helpful when a teacher takes a group of young children on a trip. To stick with the elevator example, one child might be terrified while another child might rush forward, pushing the close button before the teacher enters. Every experience (elevators, fire engines, train rides, animals at the zoo, a police officer) is likely to trigger a range of emotions, without much reflection, in a group of 3-year-olds: A class trip needs several adults, ready to respond to whatever reactions the children have.

Stress Hormones

During infancy and early childhood, extreme stress may cause cortisol to flood the brain and destroy part of the hippocampus. There is "extensive evidence of the

amygdala A tiny brain structure that registers emotions, particularly fear and anxiety.

hippocampus A brain structure that is a central processor of memory, especially memory for locations.

hypothalamus A brain area that responds to the amygdala and the hippocampus to produce hormones that activate other parts of the brain and body.

Especially for Neurologists Why do many experts think the limbic system is an oversimplified explanation of brain function? (see response, page 253)

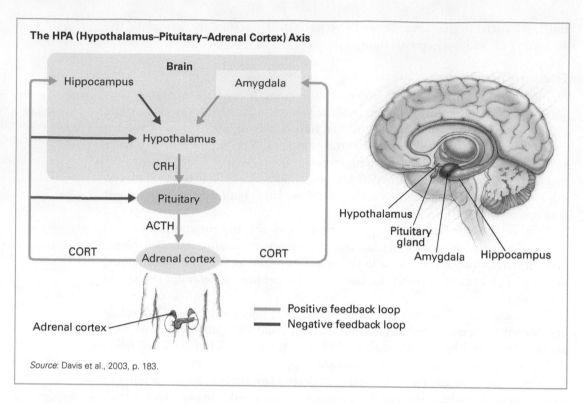

FIGURE 8.3

A Hormonal Feedback Loop This diagram simplifies a hormonal linkage, the HPA (hypothalamus–pituitary–adrenal) axis. Both the hippocampus and the amygdala stimulate the hypothalamus to produce CRH (corticotropin-releasing hormone), which in turn signals the pituitary gland to produce ACTH (adrenocorticotropic hormone). ACTH then triggers the production of CORT (glucocorticoids) by the adrenal cortex (the outer layers of the adrenal glands, atop the kidneys). Fear may either build or disappear, depending on other factors, including how the various parts of the brain interpret that first alert from the amygdala.

Video Activity: The Childhood Stress-Cortisol Connection examines how high cortisol levels can negatively impact a child's overall health.

disruptive impacts of toxic stress" (Shonkoff et al., 2012). Too much of that hormone early in life may lead to permanent deficits in learning and health, causing major depression, post-traumatic stress disorder, and attention-deficit/hyperactivity disorder in childhood and adolescence.

Yet some stress is needed for normal brain growth. Emotionally arousing experiences—meeting new friends, entering school, visiting a strange place—seem beneficial if a young child has someone or something to moderate the stress. Parental support and child temperament at age 3 are crucial moderators. When past support and experience are in place, cortisol will not be overwhelming. A study of 5- and 6-year-olds exposed to a stressful experience found that cortisol rose dramatically in some children but not at all in others, probably because of individual variations in genes and early childhood experiences (de Weerth et al., 2013).

In an experiment, brain scans and hormone measurements were taken of 4- to 6-year-olds immediately after a fire alarm. (Teoh & Lamb, 2013). As measured by their cortisol levels, some children were upset and some were not. Two weeks later, they were questioned about the event. Those with higher cortisol reactions to the alarm remembered more details than did those with less stress, which suggests that some stress aided memory. There are good evolutionary reasons for that: People need to remember experiences that arouse their emotions, so they can avoid, or adjust to, similar experiences in the future.

Generally, a balance between arousal and reassurance is needed. For instance, if children are witnesses to a crime (a stressful experience), a child's memory is

"I would share, but I'm not there developmentally."

Good Excuse It is true that emotional control of selfish instincts is difficult for young children because the prefrontal cortex is not yet mature enough to regulate some emotions. However, family practices can advance social understanding.

more accurate when an interviewer is warm and attentive, listening carefully but not suggesting some answers instead of others (Teoh & Lamb, 2013).

Studies of maltreated children suggest that excessive stress hormone levels in early childhood permanently damage the brain. The impaired hypothalamus produces hormones that affect emotions lifelong (Evans & Kim, 2013; Wilson et al., 2011).

Sadly, this topic leads again to those adopted Romanian children mentioned in Chapter 7. When some of them (presumably those who experienced more stress) saw pictures of happy, sad, frightened, or angry faces, their limbic systems were less reactive than were those of Romanian children who were living with their biological parents. The adopted children's brains were also less lateralized, suggesting less specialized, less efficient thinking (Nelson et al., 2014). Thus, early stress had probably impaired their brains.

Romania no longer permits wholesale international adoptions. Nonetheless, as mentioned earlier, some children are raised in institutions. They are confined to cribs most of the time, and are severely impaired in motor skills, as well as language and social bonding. As you remember, adoption (local or international) should occur before age 1 for the best outcomes.

That is not always possible, however. In one study, at about age 2 some institutionalized Romanian children were randomly assigned to well-paid and trained foster parents. By age 4, they were smarter (by about 10 IQ points) than those who remained institutionalized (Nelson et al., 2007). This research suggests that ages 2 to 4 constitute a sensitive time for learning because families are able to balance challenge and comfort for each individual, allowing normal brain maturation.

Unfortunately, although these children did better than those who remained in institutions, they lagged behind another group who were with their parents the whole time. That group did not receive excellent physical and medical care, as the foster children did, but they were loved and stimulated by growing up in their families. In neurological development, that made all the difference (Marshall, 2014).

// **Response for Neurologists** (from page 251): The more we discover about the brain, the more complex we realize it is. Each part has specific functions and is connected to every other part.

SUMMING UP   The brain continues to mature during early childhood. Myelination is notable in several crucial areas. One is the corpus callosum, which connects the two sides of the brain and therefore allows control of the two sides of the body. The human brain and body are lateralized, which means left-handed children are so because of their brain functioning. Many cultures and parents have tried to make them right-handed, a practice that developmentalists discourage.

Increased myelination speeds up actions and reactions. Furthermore, the prefrontal cortex enables the balancing of action and inhibition, allowing children to think before they act and to stop one action to begin another. As impulsiveness and perseveration decrease, children become better able to learn.

Several key areas of the brain—including the amygdala, the hippocampus, and the hypothalamus—are involved in emotions. Children whose early experiences are highly stressful and who lack nurturing caregivers may be impaired in emotional regulation and expression.

WHAT HAVE YOU LEARNED?

1.   How much does the brain grow from ages 2 to 6?
2.   Why is myelination important for thinking and motor skills?
3.   What is the function of the corpus callosum?
4.   What should parents do if their toddler seems left-handed?
5.   How does the prefrontal cortex affect impulsivity and perseveration?
6.   What is the function of each of the three areas of the brain that are part of the limbic system?
7.   Is stress beneficial or harmful to young children?

Improving Motor Skills

Maturation of the prefrontal cortex allows impulse control, and myelination of the corpus callosum and lateralization of the brain permit better physical coordination. No wonder children move with greater speed, agility, and grace as they age (see Visualizing Development, p. 255).

Mastery of gross and fine motor skills results not only from maturation but also from extensive, active play. A study in Brazil, Kenya, and the United States tracked how young children spend their time. Cultural variations and differences based on socioeconomic status (SES) emerged, but at every income level in all three nations, children spent more time playing than doing anything else—including chores, lessons, and conversations (Tudge et al., 2006).

Gross Motor Skills

Gross motor skills improve dramatically. When playing, many 2-year-olds fall down and bump clumsily into each other. By contrast, some 5-year-olds are skilled and graceful, performing coordinated dance steps or sports moves.

There remains much for them to learn, especially in the ability to adjust to other people and circumstances. Thus a 5-year-old can sometimes kick a ball with precision, but it is much harder for that child to be a good team player on a soccer team. At every age and skill, physical maturity precedes social maturity.

Specific Skills

Many North American 5-year-olds can ride a tricycle, climb a ladder, and pump a swing, as well as throw, catch, and kick a ball. A few can do these things by age 3,

Developing Motor Skills

Every child can do more with each passing year. These examples detail what one child might be expected to accomplish from ages 2 to 6. But each child is unique, and much depends on culture, practice, and maturity.

SKILLS

AVERAGE HEIGHT IN INCHES
BOYS 45.5   GIRLS 45.0

Draw and paint recognizable images
Write simple words
Read a page of print   **6 years**
Tie shoes
Catch a small ball

BOYS 43.0   GIRLS 42.5

Skip and gallop in rhythm
Clap, bang, sing in rhythm
Copy difficult shapes and letters
Climb trees, jump over things   **5 years**
Use a knife to cut
Wash face, comb hair

Catch a beach ball
Use scissors
Hop on either foot
Feed self with fork
Dress self   **4 years**
Copy most letters
Pour juice without spilling
Brush teeth

BOYS 40.5   GIRLS 40.0

Kick and throw a ball
Jump with both feet
Pedal a tricycle
Copy simple shapes   **3 years**
Walk down stairs
Climb ladders

BOYS 37.5   GIRLS 37.0

Run without falling
Climb out of crib
Walk up stairs   **2 years**
Feed self with spoon
Draw spirals

BOYS 34.1   GIRLS 33.5

and some 5-year-olds can already skate, dive, and ride a bike—activities that demand balanced coordination and use of both brain hemispheres. Elsewhere, some 5-year-olds swim in oceans or climb cliffs. Brain maturation, motivation, and guided practice undergird all motor skills.

Adults need to make sure children have a safe space to play, with time, appropriate equipment, and playmates. Children learn best from peers who demonstrate whatever the child is ready to try, from catching a ball to climbing a tree. Of course, culture and locale influence particulars: Some small children learn to ski, others to sail.

Practice with the Big Kids Ava is unable to stand as Carlyann can (*left*) but she is thrilled to be wearing her tutu in Central Park, New York, with 230 other dancers in a highly organized attempt to break a record for the most ballerinas on pointe at the same moment. Motor skills are developing in exactly the same way on the other side of the world (*right*) despite superficial opposites (boys, Japan, soccer, pick-up game).

Recent urbanization concerns many developmentalists. A century ago, children with varied skill levels played together in empty lots or fields without adult supervision, but now more than half the world's children live in cities. Many of these are "megacities . . . overwhelmed with burgeoning slums and environmental problems" (Ash et al., 2008, p. 739).

Crowded, violent streets not only impede development of gross motor skills but also add to the natural fears of the immature amygdala, compounded by the learned fears of adults. Gone are the days when parents told their children to go out and play, to return when hunger, rain, or nightfall brought them home. Now many parents fear strangers and traffic, keeping their 3- to 5-year-olds inside (Taylor et al., 2009).

That worries many childhood educators, who believe that children need space and freedom to play in order to develop well. Indeed, many agree that "Environment is the Third Teacher . . . because the environment is viewed as another teacher having the power to enhance children's sense of wonder and capacity for learning" (Stremmel, 2012, p. 136).

Environmental Hazards

Observable dangers are not the only reason children are slower to develop skilled gross motor skills. Such skills require practice to develop, but children who breathe heavily polluted air tend to be impaired in brain development as well as to exercise less. Often they also live in crowded neighborhoods and attend poor schools. They

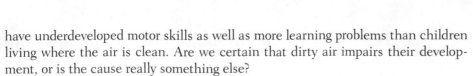

have underdeveloped motor skills as well as more learning problems than children living where the air is clean. Are we certain that dirty air impairs their development, or is the cause really something else?

Scientists have grappled with this question and and found that environmental substances impair brain development in young children at every SES level, especially those in lower-income families. This conclusion is easiest to demonstrate with asthma, which reduces oxygen to the brain. In the United States, asthma is far more prevalent among children who live in poverty than among those who do not (U.S. Department of Health and Human Services, 2012, November). (**Developmental Link:** Asthma is discussed in Chapter 11.)

As you already know, the dynamic-systems approach to development means that every impairment has many causes, both in the immediate context and in past genetic and environmental factors. Nonetheless, a recent study conducted in British Columbia, where universal public health care and detailed birth records allow solid research, showed that air pollution from traffic and industry early in life was a cause, not just a correlate, of asthma (Clark et al., 2010).

This study began with all births in 1999 and 2000 in southwest British Columbia (which includes a major city, Vancouver). For three years, 37,401 children were studied, 3,482 of whom were diagnosed with asthma by age 3. Each of those 3,482 was matched on SES, gender, and so on with five other children from the same group. Exposure to air pollution (including carbon monoxide, nitric oxide, nitrogen dioxide, particulate matter, ozone, sulfur dioxide, black carbon, wood smoke, car exhaust, and smoke from parents' cigarettes) was carefully measured.

One finding was that parents could not always protect their children, partly because they did not know when substances caused poor health. For example, although carbon monoxide emissions are not visible, when compared to their five matched peers, those children who were diagnosed with asthma were more likely to live near major highways, where carbon monoxide is prevalent. Conversely, because wood smoke is easy to see and smell, some parents tried to avoid it, but burning wood did not increase asthma.

Respiratory problems are not the only early-childhood complications caused by pollution. Research on lower animals suggests that hundreds of substances in the air, food, and water affect the brain and thus impede balance, motor skills, and motivation. Many substances have not been tested, but some—including lead in the water and air, pesticides in the soil or on clothing, bisphenol A (BPA) in plastic, and secondhand cigarette smoke—are proven harmful.

One recent concern is the contamination from *e-waste,* a term that includes discarded computers, cell phones, and other outmoded electronic devices. E-waste may spew pollutants that affect the brains of infants and children, although not all scientists are convinced. As one group of researchers explains: "Although data suggest that exposure to e-waste is harmful to health, more well designed epidemiological investigations in vulnerable populations, especially pregnant women and children, are needed to confirm these associations" (Grant et al., 2013, p. e357).

The administrator of environmental public health for the state of Oregon said, "We simply do not know—as scientists, as regulators, as health professionals—the health impacts of the soup of chemicals to which we expose human beings" (Shibley, quoted in T. D. Johnson, 2011). Whether you think Shibley is needlessly alarmist or is simply stating the obvious depends on your own perspective—and maybe on your amygdala.

Lead, however, has been thoroughly researched. There is no doubt that lead is severely toxic. The history of lead exposure in the following A View from Science illustrates the long path from science to practice.

⚗ a view from science

Eliminating Lead

Lead was recognized as a poison a century ago (Hamilton, 1914). The symptoms of *plumbism,* as lead poisoning is called, were obvious—intellectual disability, hyperactivity, and even death if the level reached 70 micrograms per deciliter of blood.

The lead industry defended the heavy metal. Manufacturers argued that low levels were harmless, and blamed parents for letting their children eat flaking chips of lead paint (which tastes sweet). Further, since children with high levels of lead in their blood were often from low-SES families, some argued that malnutrition, inadequate schools, family conditions, or a host of other causes were the reasons for their reduced IQ (Scarr, 1985). This seemed plausible to many developmentalists. I am chagrined to confess that explanation made sense to me when I wrote the first edition of this textbook (Berger, 1980).

Consequently, lead remained a major ingredient in paint (it speeds drying) and in gasoline (it raises octane) for most of the twentieth century. The fact that babies in lead-painted cribs, that preschoolers playing near traffic, and that children living beside industrial waste were intellectually impaired and hyperactive was claimed to be correlation, not causation.

Finally, chemical analysis of blood and teeth, with careful longitudinal and replicated research, proved that lead was indeed a poison for all children (Needleman et al., 1990; Needleman & Gatsonis, 1990). The United States banned lead in paint (in 1978) and automobile fuel (in 1996). The blood level that caused plumbism was set at 40 micrograms per deciliter, then 20, then 10, (and recently, danger is thought to begin at 5 micrograms), but no level has been proven to be risk-free (MMWR, April 5, 2013).

Regulation has made a difference: The percentage of U.S. 1- to 5-year-olds with more than 5 micrograms of lead per deciliter of blood was 8.6 percent in 1999–2001, 4.1% in 2003–2006, and 2.6 percent in 2007–2010 (see Figure 8.4). Children who are young, low-SES, and/or living in old housing tend to have higher levels (MMWR, April 5, 2013) and lower IQs.

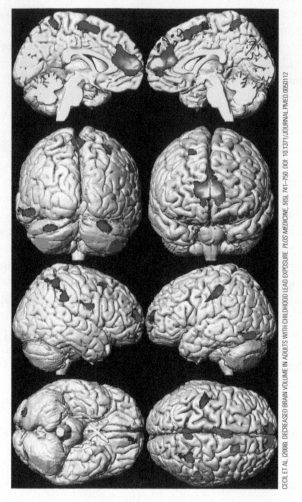

CECIL ET AL. (2008) DECREASED BRAIN VOLUME IN ADULTS WITH CHILDHOOD LEAD EXPOSURE. *PLOS MEDICINE,* 5(5), 741–750. DOI: 10.1371/JOURNAL.PMED.0050112

Toxic Shrinkage A composite of 157 brains of adults—who, as children, had high lead levels in their blood—shows reduced volume. The red and yellow hot spots are all areas that are smaller than areas in a normal brain. No wonder lead-exposed children have multiple intellectual and behavioral problems.

Fine Motor Skills

Fine motor skills are harder to master than gross motor skills. Whistling, winking, and especially writing are difficult. Pouring juice into a glass, cutting food with a knife, and achieving anything more artful than a scribble with a pencil all require a level of muscular control, patience, and judgment that is beyond most 2-year-olds.

Many fine motor skills involve two hands and thus both sides of the brain: The fork stabs the meat while the knife cuts it; one hand steadies the paper while the

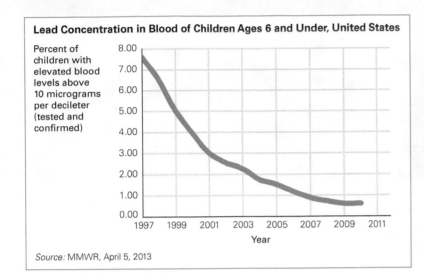

Lead Concentration in Blood of Children Ages 6 and Under, United States

Percent of children with elevated blood levels above 10 micrograms per deciliter (tested and confirmed)

Source: MMWR, April 5, 2013

FIGURE 8.4

Dramatic Improvement in a Decade Once researchers established the perils of high lead levels in children's blood, the percentage of children suffering from plumbism fell by more than 300 percent. Levels are higher in states that once had heavy manufacturing and lower in mountain and Pacific states.

Parents now take precautions. They are increasing their children's calcium intake, wiping window ledges clean, testing drinking water, avoiding lead-based medicines and crockery (available in some other nations), and making sure children never eat chips of lead-based paint.

In some states (e.g., Colorado and Wyoming), average lead levels for young children are close to zero. In other states that once had extensive lead-based manufacturing, young children are still at risk, probably because of lead in the soil and dust. In 2010, Pennsylvania documented 509 children under age 6 with more than 20 micrograms per deciliter in their blood; Ohio had 417; and Michigan had 254 (National Center for Environmental Health, 2012).

Remember from Chapter 1 that scientists sometimes use data collected for other reasons to draw new conclusions. This is the case with lead. About 15 years after the sharp decline in blood lead levels in preschool children, the rate of violent crime committed by teenagers and young adults fell sharply. Coincidence? Some scientists decided to test it. As it happened, some nations reduced lead in the environment sooner or later than others, and crime rates plummeted 15 years later in each nation. Teenagers with less lead in their blood as infants committed fewer crimes. Again this could be correlation, not causation, but this time researchers hesitate to make that argument.

A scientist comparing these trends concluded that some teenagers commit impulsive, violent crimes because their brains were poisoned by lead years ago. The correlation is found not only in the United States but also in every nation that has reliable data on lead and crime—Canada, Germany, Italy, Australia, New Zealand, France, and Finland (Nevin, 2007). In the past decade, many researchers have found that lead levels in early childhood predict later attention deficits, school suspensions (Amato et al., 2013; Goodlad et al., 2013), and juvenile delinquency.

There is now no doubt that lead, even at quite low levels in the blood of a young child, harms the brain. That raises many other questions about the effects of brain damage, and about the long-term effects of hundreds, perhaps thousands, of new chemicals in the air, water, and soil.

other writes; tying shoes, buttoning shirts, cutting paper, and zipping zippers require both hands.

Limited myelination of the corpus callosum may be the underlying reason that shoelaces get knotted, paper gets ripped, and zippers get stuck. Short, stubby fingers add to the problem. As with gross motor skills, practice and maturation are key; using glue, markers, and scraps of cloth are part of the preschool curriculum.

Same Situation, Far Apart: Finger Skills Children learn whatever motor skills their culture teaches. Some master chopsticks, with fingers to spare; others cut sausage with a knife and fork. Unlike these children in Japan (*left*) and Germany (*right*), some never master either, because about one-third of adults worldwide eat directly with their hands.

Especially for Immigrant Parents You and your family eat with chopsticks at home, but you want your children to feel comfortable in Western culture. Should you change your family's eating customs? (see response, page 262)

Puzzles—with large pieces of splinter-proof wood or heavy, smooth cardboard—are essential supplies.

Traditional academic learning depends on fine motor skills and body control. Writing requires finger control, reading a line of print requires eye control, classroom schedules require bladder control, and so on. These are beyond most young children, so even the brightest 3-year-old is not allowed in first grade.

Slow maturation is one reason many 6-year-olds are frustrated if their teachers demand that they write neatly and cut straight. Some educators suggest waiting until a child is "ready" for school; some suggest that preschools should focus on readiness; still others suggest that schools should adjust to the immaturity of the child, instead of trying to make the child adjust. This controversy is explored in the next chapter.

Fine motor skills—like many other biological characteristics, such as bones, brains, and teeth—mature on average about six months earlier in girls than in boys. By contrast, boys often are ahead of girls in gross motor skills.

Many studies find that fine motor skills correlate with later school performance, which may be one reason that primary school girls typically outperform boys on tests of reading and writing. Although these gender differences seem to be biological, they may be the result of motivation and practice, as young girls are more likely to dress up and play with dolls (fine motor skills), while boys are more likely to climb and kick (gross motor skills) (Saraiva et al., 2013).

Artistic Expression

Young children are imaginative, creative, and not yet self-critical. They love to express themselves, especially if their parents applaud their performances, display their artwork, and otherwise communicate approval. The fact that their fine motor skills are immature, and thus their drawings lack precision, is irrelevant. Perhaps the immaturity of the prefrontal cortex is a blessing, allowing the creativity without self-criticism.

All forms of artistic expression blossom during early childhood; 2- to 6-year-olds love to dance around the room, build an elaborate tower of blocks, make music by pounding in rhythm, and put bright marks on shiny paper. In every artistic domain, skill takes both practice and maturation.

For example when drawing a person, 2- to 3-year-olds usually draw a "tadpole"—a circle head, dots for eyes, sometimes a smiling mouth, and then a line or two beneath to indicate the rest of the body. Gradually, tadpoles get torsos, limbs, hair, and so on. Children's artwork is not intended to be realistic: It communicates thoughts and self-expression (Papandreou, 2014). It is a mistake for adults to say "that looks like a . . ." or worse, "you forgot the feet."

Cultural and cohort differences are apparent in all artistic skills. For the most part, Chinese culture incorporates the idea that drawing benefits from instruction, so young children are guided in how best to draw a person, a house, and—most important for the Chinese—a word.

Consequently, by age 9, Chinese children draw more advanced pictures than children of other cultures. Adult encouragement, child practice, and developing technical skill correlate with more mature, creative drawings a few years later (Chan & Zhao, 2010; Huntsinger et al., 2011).

Some parents enroll their preschool children in music lessons, hoping they will learn to play. As a result, those preschoolers become better at listening to sounds, evident in listening to speech as well as music. Neurological evidence finds that their brains reflect their new auditory abilities, a remarkable testimony to the role of family and cultural encouragement of preschool art (Strait et al., 2013).

Bliss for Boys But not for moms. Finger painting develops fine motor skills, which is part of the preschool curriculum in early childhood. This boy shows why most stay-at-home 3-year-olds miss out on this joy.

SUMMING UP   Maturation of the brain leads to better hand and body control. Gross motor skills advance every year as long as young children have space to play, older children to emulate, and freedom from environmental toxins. Sadly, crowding, fear of strangers, and pollution reduce the opportunities many contemporary children have to develop gross motor skills and may affect their overall learning, as well.

Young children also develop their fine motor skills, which prepares them for formal education. They love to dance, draw, and build, all encouraging the gradual mastery of arm and finger movements, which will be essential when they start to write. Gender differences, with girls ahead on average in fine motor skills and boys ahead in gross motor skills, may be biological or cultural.

WHAT HAVE YOU LEARNED?

1.   What three factors help children develop their motor skills?
2.   How have cohort changes affected the development of gross motor skills?
3.   What is known and unknown about the effects on young children of chemicals in food, air, and water?
4.   How does brain maturation affect children's artistic expression?
5.   What are conflicting interpretations of gender differences in motor skills?   ●

Injuries and Abuse

In almost all families of every income, ethnicity, and nation, parents want to protect their children while fostering their growth. Yet far more children die from violence—either accidental or deliberate—than from any specific disease.

The contrast between disease and accidental death is most obvious in developed nations, where medical prevention, diagnosis, and treatment make fatal illness rare until late adulthood. In the United States, four times as many 1- to 4-year-olds die of accidents than of cancer, which is the leading cause of disease death during these years (National Center for Health Statistics, 2013). Indeed, in 2010, more young U.S. children were murdered (385) than died of cancer (346). This was not always true, but cancer deaths have decreased over the past half century, while child homicide has increased.

// **Response for Immigrant Parents** (from page 260): Children develop the motor skills that they see and practice. They will soon learn to use forks, spoons, and knives. Do not abandon chopsticks completely, because young children can learn several ways of doing things, and the ability to eat with chopsticks is a social asset.

Avoidable Injury

Worldwide, injuries cause millions of premature deaths among adults as well as children: Not until age 40 does any specific disease overtake accidents as a cause of mortality, and 14 percent of all life-years lost worldwide are caused by injury (World Health Organization, 2010).

In some nations, malnutrition, malaria, and other infectious diseases *combined* cause more infant and child deaths than injuries do, but those nations also have high rates of child injury. India, for example, has one of the highest rates worldwide of child motor-vehicle deaths; most children who die in such accidents are pedestrians (Naci et al., 2009). Everywhere, young children are at greater risk than slightly older ones. In the United States, 2- to 6-year-olds are more than twice as likely to be seriously hurt than 6- to 10-year-olds.

Age-Related Dangers

Why are young children so vulnerable? Some reasons have just been explained. Immaturity of the prefrontal cortex makes young children impulsive; they plunge into danger. Unlike infants, their motor skills allow them to run, leap, scramble, and grab in a flash, before a watching adult can stop them. Their curiosity is boundless; their impulses uninhibited. Then, if they do something that becomes dangerous, such as lighting a fire while playing with matches, fear and stress might make them slow to get help.

Age-related trends are apparent in particulars. Falls are more often fatal for the youngest (under 24 months) and oldest (over 80 years); preschoolers have high rates of poisoning and drowning; motor vehicle deaths peak from ages 15 to 25. Specific statistics reveal reasons for vulnerabilities. For instance, not only are 1- to 4-year-olds more likely to die of drowning than any other age group, they drown

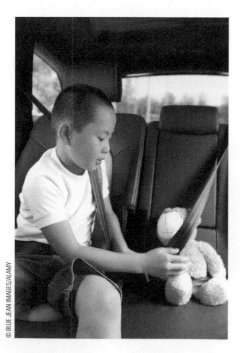

Same Situation, Far Apart: Keeping Everyone Safe Preventing child accidents requires action by both adults and children. In the United States (*left*), adults passed laws and taught children—including this boy who buckles in his stuffed companion. In France (*right*), teachers stop cars while children hold hands to cross the street—each child keeping his or her partner moving ahead.

in swimming pools six times more often but in boating accidents only one-twelfth as often as older children and adults (MMWR, May 16, 2014). Usually the deadly swimming pool is in their own back yard, with their parents unaware that their preschooler was outside.

Injury Control

Instead of using the term *accident prevention,* public health experts prefer **injury control** (or **harm reduction**). Consider the implications. *Accident* implies that an injury is random, unpredictable; if anyone is at fault, it's a careless parent or an accident-prone child. This is called the "accident paradigm"—as if "injuries will occur despite our best efforts," allowing the public to feel blameless (Benjamin, 2004, p. 521).

Injury control suggests that the impact of an injury can be limited if appropriate controls are in place, and *harm reduction* implies that harm can be minimized. Minor mishaps (scratches and bruises) are bound to occur, but serious injury is unlikely if a child falls on a safety surface instead of on concrete, if a car seat protects the body in a crash, if a bicycle helmet cracks instead of a skull, or if swallowed pills come from a tiny bottle. Reducing harm from childhood behavior can be accomplished by a concerted effort of professionals and parents, as I know too well from my own experience described in the following A Case to Study.

> **injury control/harm reduction** Practices that are aimed at anticipating, controlling, and preventing dangerous activities. These practices reflect the beliefs that accidents are not random and that injuries can be made less harmful if proper controls are in place.

a case to study

"My Baby Swallowed Poison"

The first strategy that most people think of to prevent injury to young children is to educate the parents. However, public health research finds that laws that apply to everyone are more effective than education, especially if parents are so overwhelmed by the daily demands of child care and money management that they do not realize they need to learn.

For example, infant car seats have saved thousands of lives. However, use of car seats is much less common when it is voluntary than when it is mandated. For that reason, car seats are now legally required.

Parents often consider safety a lower priority than everyday concerns. That explains two findings from the research: (1) The best time to convince parents to use a car seat is before they take their newborn home from the hospital, and (2) the best way to make sure a car seat is correctly used is to have an expert show the parents how it works—not simply tell them or make them watch a video (Tessier, 2010).

Motivation and education are crucial, yet in real life, everyone has moments of foolish indifference. Then automatic safety measures save lives (Damashek & Kuhn, 2014).

I know this firsthand. Our daughter Bethany, at age 2, climbed onto the kitchen counter to find, open, and swallow most of a bottle of baby aspirin. Where was I? In the next room, nursing our second child and watching television. I did not notice what Bethany was doing until I checked on her during a commercial.

Bethany is alive and well today, protected not by her foolish mother but by all three levels of prevention explained on the next page. Primary prevention included laws limiting the number of baby aspirin per container, secondary prevention included my pediatrician's written directions when Bethany was a week old to buy syrup of ipecac, and tertiary prevention was my phone call to Poison Control.

I told the helpful stranger who answered the phone, "My baby swallowed poison." He calmly asked me a few questions and then advised me to give Bethany ipecac to make her throw up. I did, and she did.

In retrospect, I realize I had bought that ipecac two years before, when I was a brand-new mother and ready to follow every word of my pediatrician's advice. I might not have done so if the doctor had waited until Bethany was able to climb before he recommended it, because by then I might have had more confidence in my own ability to prevent harm.

I still blame myself, but I am grateful for all three levels of prevention that protected my child. In some ways, my own education helped avert a tragedy. I had chosen a wise pediatrician; I knew the number for Poison Control (FYI: 1-800-222-1222). As I remember all the mistakes I made in parenting (only a few mentioned in this book), I am grateful for every level of prevention. Without protective laws and a national network to help parents, the results might have been tragic.

Less than half as many 1- to 5-year-olds in the United States were fatally injured in 2012 as in 1982, thanks to laws that limit poisons, prevent fires, and regulate cars. Control has not yet caught up with newer hazards, however. For instance, many homes in California, Florida, Texas, and Arizona now have swimming pools: In those states drowning is a leading cause of child death. One result: Although overall rates of accidental death increase as income falls, for pool drowning before age 5, rates of more affluent ethnic groups are higher than for poorer groups (MMWR, May 16, 2014).

Prevention

Prevention begins long before any particular child, parent, or legislator does something foolish. Unfortunately, no one notices injuries and deaths that did not happen. For developmentalists, two types of analysis are useful to predict danger and prevent it.

One is to look at all the systems that led to a serious injury. Causes can be found in the child, the microsystem, the exosystem, and the macrosystem, and thus measures can be taken to protect children in the future.

For example, when a child is hit by a car, it might be because the child was impulsive, the parents were neglectful (microsystem), the community was not child-friendly (no parks, traffic lights, sidewalks, or curbs—all exosystem), and/or because the culture valued fast cars over slow pedestrians (macrosystem). Once all those factors are recognized, preventive measures become clear, from holding the hand of young children when crossing the street all the way to national speed limits.

The second type of analysis involves understanding statistics. For example, the rate of childhood poisoning decreased markedly when pill manufacturers adopted bottles with safety caps that are difficult for children to open; such a statistic goes a long way in countering individual complaints about inconvenience. New statistics show a rise in the number of children being poisoned by taking adult recreational drugs, such as cocaine, alcohol, or marijuana, and that has led to new strategies for prevention (Fine et al., 2012).

Levels of Prevention

Three levels of prevention apply to every health and safety issue.

- In **primary prevention**, the overall situation is structured to make harm less likely. Primary prevention fosters conditions that reduce everyone's chance of injury.
- **Secondary prevention** is more specific, averting harm in high-risk situations or for vulnerable individuals.
- **Tertiary prevention** begins after an injury has already occurred, limiting damage.

In general, tertiary prevention is the most visible of the three levels, but primary prevention is the most effective (Cohen et al., 2010). An example comes from data on pedestrian deaths. As compared with 20 years ago, fewer children in the United States today die after being hit by a motor vehicle (see Figure 8.5). How does each level of prevention contribute?

Primary prevention includes sidewalks, pedestrian overpasses, streetlights, and traffic circles. Cars have been redesigned (e.g., better headlights, windows, and brakes), and drivers' competence has improved (e.g., stronger penalties keep many drunk drivers off the road). Reduction of traffic via improved mass transit provides additional primary prevention.

Secondary prevention reduces danger in high-risk situations. School crossing guards and flashing lights on stopped school buses are secondary prevention, as

primary prevention Actions that change overall background conditions to prevent harm.

secondary prevention Actions that avert harm in a high-risk situation, such as holding a child's hand while crossing the street.

tertiary prevention Actions, such as immediate and effective medical treatment, that reduce harm or prevent disability after injury.

Especially for Urban Planners Describe a neighborhood park that would benefit 2- to 5-year-olds. (see response, page 266)

are salt on icy roads, warning signs before blind curves, speed bumps, and walk/don't walk signals at busy intersections.

Finally, *tertiary prevention* reduces damage after an accident. Examples include laws against hit-and-run drivers, speedy ambulances, efficient emergency room procedures, and effective follow-up care, all of which have been improved from decades ago.

Medical personnel speak of the *golden hour,* the hour following an accident, when a victim should be treated. Of course, there is nothing magical about 60 minutes in contrast to 61 minutes, but the faster an injury victim reaches a trauma center, the better the chance of survival (Dinh et al., 2013).

Culture and Injury Prevention: Baby on the Plane

I once was the director of a small preschool. I was struck by the diversity of fears and prevention measures, some helpful and some not. Some parents were thrilled that our children painted, but others worried about the ingredients of the paint, for instance. We had an outdoor sandbox; some parents thought that could give the children worms.

I knew that all children need to grab, run, and explore to develop their motor skills as well as their minds, yet they also need to be prevented from falling down stairs, eating pebbles, or running into the street—as many are inclined to do. That meant that teachers needed to balance freedom and prohibition. Yet the specifics of that balance are understood differently by various cultures.

Adults do not agree on the best strategies to prevent injury. Consider what one mother wrote about her flight from Australia to California:

> I travelled with my 10-month-old daughter and was absolutely and thoroughly disappointed in the treatment we received from the flight crew captain at the time. I was told or more like instructed that I was to "restrain" my child for the whole flight, which was 13 hours.
>
> I said that other people were able to move around the plane freely, why wasn't she? I was told that due to turbulence she would have to be restrained for the whole trip. On several occasions the flight crew captain would make a point of going out of his way to almost scold me for not listening to him when I would put her down to crawl around.

[Retrieved April 3, 2011, from Complaints.com]

This same mother praised her treatment on other long flights, specifically on Asian airlines, when her child was allowed to move more freely and the crew was helpful. Which culture is better at protecting children without needlessly restraining them?

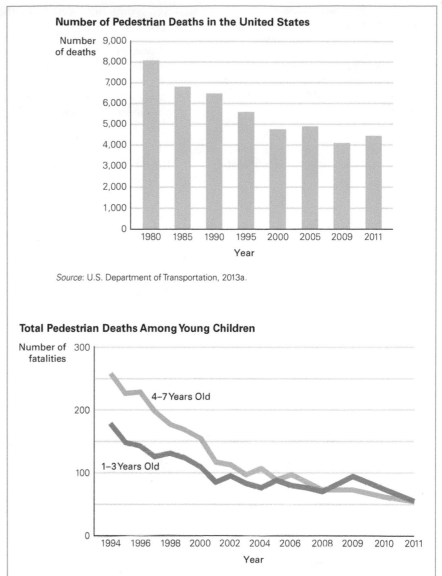

Number of Pedestrian Deaths in the United States

Source: U.S. Department of Transportation, 2013a.

Total Pedestrian Deaths Among Young Children

Source: U.S. Department of Transportation, 2013b.

FIGURE 8.5

While the Population Grew This chart shows dramatic evidence that prevention measures are succeeding in the United States. Over the same time period, the total population has increased by about one-third, making these results even more impressive.

// **Response for Urban Planners** (from page 264): The adult idea of a park—a large, grassy, open place—is not best for young children. For them, you would design an enclosed area, small enough and with adequate seating to allow caregivers to socialize while watching their children. The playground surface would have to be protective (since young children are clumsy), with equipment that encourages motor skills. Teenagers and dogs should have their own designated area, far from the youngest children.

My sympathies were with the mother, and I praised the Asian crews, until I read this response:

> Consider the laws in the U.S. regarding child safety in an automobile. Nobody thinks a child should be free to crawl around in a car. No parent thinks their rights have been violated because their child is prevented from free flight inside a car when it impacts. Why not just put the child in the bed of a truck and drive around? . . . Her child could get stepped on, slammed against a seat leg, wedged under a seat, fallen on, etc.
>
> *[Retrieved April 3, 2011, from Complaints.com]*

Both sides in this dispute make sense, yet both cannot be right. The data prove that safety seats in cars save lives, but "impact" in planes is unlike that in a car crash. Statistical analysis is needed, or at least studies of injured children on airplanes, considering all the systems involved. Do passengers on planes step on crawling children? If so, is that controllable harm or a serious hazard?

SUMMING UP Worldwide, young children are more likely to be seriously hurt or killed accidently than they are to suffer from any specific disease. However, most such harm can prevented, which is why developmentalists prefer the term "injury control" rather than "accident prevention." The contrast between death from disease and death from unintentional injury is particularly stark in the United States. Nonetheless, rates of such deaths have fallen since prevention is better understood. Three levels of prevention are crucial: primary (in the entire culture), secondary (for high-risk situations), and tertiary (after the injury, to reduce the harm).

WHAT HAVE YOU LEARNED?
1. What can be concluded from the data on rates of childhood injury?
2. How do injury deaths compare in developed and developing nations?
3. What are some examples of primary prevention?
4. What are some examples of secondary prevention?
5. Why and how do cultures differ in determining acceptable risk?

Especially for Criminal Justice Professionals Over the past decade, the rate of sexual abuse has gone down by almost 20 percent. What are three possible explanations? (see response, page 268)

child maltreatment Intentional harm to, or avoidable endangerment of, anyone under 18 years of age.

child abuse Deliberate action that impairs a child's physical, emotional, or sexual well-being.

child neglect Failure to meet a child's basic physical, educational, or emotional needs.

Child Maltreatment

Until about 1960, people thought child maltreatment was rare and consisted of a sudden attack by a disturbed stranger. Today we know better, thanks to a careful observation in one Boston hospital (Kempe & Kempe, 1978).

Maltreatment is neither rare nor sudden, and 82 percent of the time the perpetrators are the child's parents (U.S. Department of Health and Human Services, 2013, December). That makes it much worse: Ongoing maltreatment, with no protector, is much more damaging than a single incident, however injurious.

Definitions and Statistics

Child maltreatment now refers to all intentional harm to, or avoidable endangerment of, anyone under 18 years of age. Thus, child maltreatment includes both **child abuse,** which is deliberate action that is harmful to a child's physical, emotional, or sexual well-being, and **child neglect,** which is failure to meet essential physical or emotional needs. Neglect may be worse than abuse. It also is "the most common and most frequently fatal form of child maltreatment" (Proctor & Dubowitz, 2014, p. 27). About three times as many neglect as abuse cases occur in the United States, a ratio probably found in many other nations.

To be specific, data on cases of *substantiated* maltreatment in the United States in 2012 indicate that 78 percent were cases of neglect, 18 percent of physical abuse, and 9 percent of sexual abuse. (A few were tallied in two categories) (U.S. Department of Health and Human Services, 2013, December). Yet neglect is too often ignored by the public, who are "stuck in an overwhelming and debilitating" concept of maltreatment that focuses only on immediate bodily harm (Kendall-Taylor et al., 2014, p. 810).

Substantiated maltreatment means that a case has been reported, investigated, and verified (see Figure 8.6). In 2012, almost 700,000 children suffered substantiated abuse in the United States. Substantiated maltreatment harms about 1 in every 90 children aged 2 to 5 annually.

Reported maltreatment means simply that the authorities have been informed. Since 1993, the number of children *reported* as maltreated in the United States has ranged from about 2.7 million to 3.6 million per year, with 3.2 million in 2012 (U.S. Department of Health and Human Services, 2013, December).

The 4.5-to-1 ratio of reported versus substantiated cases occurs because:

1. Each child is counted only once, so five verified reports about a single child result in one substantiated case.
2. Substantiation requires proof. Not every investigation finds unmistakable harm or a witness willing to testify. Sometimes reports provide too little information, and the child cannot be located.
3. Many professionals are *mandated reporters,* required to report any signs of possible maltreatment. Often signs could be maltreatment, but investigation finds that no harm occurred (Pietrantonio et al., 2013).
4. Some reports are "screened out," which means that the agency decides the case does not come under their jurisdiction, such as when a case belongs under the jurisdiction of the military or of a Native American tribe (who have their own systems).
5. A report may be false or deliberately misleading (though few are) (Sedlak & Ellis, 2014).

Abuse Victim? Fair-skinned Anna, age 5, told the school nurse she was sunburned because her mommy, Patricia, took her to a tanning salon. Patricia said Anna was gardening in the sun; Anna's father and brother (shown here) said all three waited outside the salon while Patricia tanned inside. The story led to an arrest for child endangerment, a court trial, and a media frenzy. Was the media abusive, the nurse intrusive, or the opposite? If your child is sunburned, is it your fault?

substantiated maltreatment Harm or endangerment that has been reported, investigated, and verified.

reported maltreatment Harm or endangerment about which someone has notified the authorities.

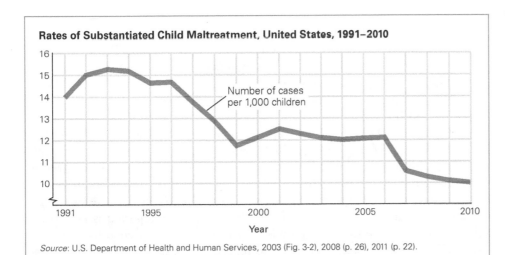

Rates of Substantiated Child Maltreatment, United States, 1991–2010

Number of cases per 1,000 children

Source: U.S. Department of Health and Human Services, 2003 (Fig. 3-2), 2008 (p. 26), 2011 (p. 22).

OBSERVATION QUIZ The data point for 2010 is close to the bottom of the graph. Does that mean it is close to zero? (see answer, page 269)

FIGURE 8.6

Still Far Too Many The number of substantiated cases of maltreatment of children under age 18 in the United States is too high, but there is some good news: The rate has declined significantly from its peak in 1993.

Especially for Nurses While weighing a 4-year-old, you notice several bruises on the child's legs. When you ask about them, the child says nothing and the parent says the child bumps into things. What should you do? (see response, page 270)

OBSERVATION QUIZ Have all types of maltreatment declined since 2000? (see answer, page 270)

FIGURE 8.7

Getting Better? As you can see, the number of victims of child maltreatment in the United States has declined in the past decade. The legal and social-work responses to serious maltreatment have improved over the years, which is a likely explanation for the decline. Other, less sanguine explanations are possible, however.

// Response for Criminal Justice Professionals (from page 266): Hopefully, more adults or children are aware of sexual abuse and stop it before it starts. A second possibility is that sexual abuse is less often reported and substantiated because the culture is more accepting of teenage sex (most victims of sexual abuse are between ages 10 and 18). A third possible explanation is that the increase in the number of single mothers means that fathers have less access to children (fathers are the most frequent sexual abusers).

Frequency of Maltreatment

How often does maltreatment actually occur? No one knows. Not all cases are noticed, not all that are noticed are reported, and not all reports are substantiated. Part of the problem is drawing the line between harsh discipline and abuse, and between momentary and ongoing neglect. Similar issues apply in every nation, city, and town, with marked variations in reports and confirmations. In general, only the most severe cases are tallied.

If we rely on official U.S. statistics, trends are apparent. Officially, substantiated child maltreatment increased from about 1960 to 1990 but decreased thereafter (see Figure 8.7). Physical and sexual abuse declined, but neglect did not. Other sources also report declines, particularly in sexual abuse, over the past two decades. That seems to be good news; perhaps national awareness has led to better reporting and then better prevention.

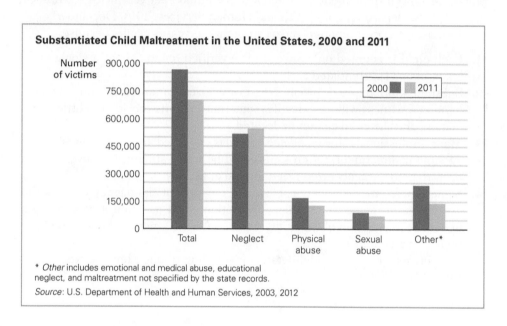

Substantiated Child Maltreatment in the United States, 2000 and 2011

* *Other* includes emotional and medical abuse, educational neglect, and maltreatment not specified by the state records.

Source: U.S. Department of Health and Human Services, 2003, 2012

Accuracy of State Data

Unfortunately, official reports leave room for doubt. For example, Pennsylvania reports fewer victims of child maltreatment than Maine (3,416 compared to 3,781 in 2010), but the child population of Pennsylvania is ten times that of Maine. Why? It's not lack of personnel: Pennsylvania has twenty times as many professionals screening and investigating (2831 to 145). Maybe it's the definition of maltreatment: Less than 10 percent of the Pennsylvania victims are said to be neglected, but 66 percent are considered victims of sexual abuse, although nationwide only 9 percent of maltreated children are. Does that mean that the Pennsylvania laws ignore most children who would be considered victims if they lived in another state? Or are the overworked investigators in Maine too quick to confirm maltreatment?

How maltreatment is defined and whether or not it is reported is powerfully influenced by culture (one of my students asked, "When is a child too old to be beaten?") and by personal willingness to report. The United States has become more culturally diverse; could that be why reports are down?

For developmentalists, a particular problem is that maltreatment is most common early in life, when children are too young to be required to go to school (where teachers would notice a problem) and too young to ask for help. In fact, infants have the highest rates of maltreatment, and 28 percent of all cases occur during early childhood (U.S. Department of Health and Human Services, 2013, December). Those are reported and substantiated cases; probably many more never reach outsiders' attention.

Warning Signs

Instead of relying just on official statistics, every reader of this book can recognize developmental problems. Often the first sign of maltreatment is delayed development, such as slow growth, immature communication, lack of curiosity, or unusual social interactions. All these difficulties may be evident even at age 1, when they could be noticed by a relative or a neighbor. Unfortunately, many people do not know what is normal for infants (crying, clinging, smiling) and what is not (fear of caregiver, gaining less than a pound a month).

By early childhood, maltreated children may seem fearful, startled by noise, defensive and quick to attack, and confused between fantasy and reality. These are symptoms of **post-traumatic stress disorder (PTSD).** PTSD was first identified in combat veterans, then in adults who had experienced some emotional injury or shock (after a serious accident, natural disaster, or violent crime), and more recently in some maltreated children, who suffer neurologically, emotionally, and behaviorally (Neigh et al., 2009; Weiss et al., 2013).

Table 8.1 lists signs of child maltreatment, both neglect and abuse. None of these signs is *proof* of abuse, but whenever any of them occurs, something is amiss.

Consequences of Maltreatment

The consequences of maltreatment involve not only the child but also the entire community. Regarding specifics, much depends on the community culture.

Customs and Maltreatment

The impact of any child-rearing practice is affected by the cultural context. Certain customs (such as circumcision, pierced ears, and spanking) are considered abusive among some groups but not in others; their effects vary accordingly. Children suffer if their parents seem to love them less than most parents in their

post-traumatic stress disorder (PTSD)
An anxiety disorder that develops after a profoundly shocking or frightening event, such as rape, severe beating, war, or natural disaster. Symptoms may include flashbacks to the event, hyperactivity and hypervigilance, displaced anger, sleeplessness, nightmares, sudden terror or anxiety, and confusion between fantasy and reality.

TABLE 8.1	Signs of Maltreatment in Children Aged 2 to 10

Injuries that are unlikely to be accidents, such as bruises on both sides of the face or body; burns with a clear line between burned and unburned skin

Repeated injuries, especially broken bones not properly tended (visible on X-ray)

Fantasy play, with dominant themes of violence or sex

Slow physical growth

Unusual appetite or lack of appetite

Ongoing physical complaints, such as stomachaches, headaches, genital pain, sleepiness

Reluctance to talk, play, or move, especially if development is slow

No close friendships; hostility toward others; bullying of smaller children

Hypervigilance, with quick, impulsive reactions, such as cringing, startling, or hitting

Frequent absence from school

Frequent change of address

Frequent change in caregivers

Fearfulness, rather than joy, on seeing caregiver

// **Response for Nurses** (from page 268): Any suspicion of child maltreatment must be reported, and these bruises are suspicious. Someone in authority must find out what is happening so that the parent as well as the child can be helped.

// **ANSWER TO OBSERVATION QUIZ** (from page 268) Most types of abuse are declining, but not neglect. This kind of maltreatment may be the most harmful because the psychological wounds last for decades.

neighborhood. If parents forbid something most other children have (from candy to cell phones) or punishes more severely or not at all, a child might feel unloved.

However, although culture is always relevant, the impact of maltreatment is multifaceted and long-lasting. The effects on adults of past maltreatment depend partly on the current relationship between the adult and the parent. If they manage to have a good relationship (more common if abuse was not chronic), then effects are less pervasive because the adult feels loved despite the mistreatment (Schafer et al., 2014).

Body and Brain

Developmentalists realize that the consequences of maltreatment include much more than the immediate harm. The biological and academic impairment resulting from maltreatment is obvious, as when a child is bruised, broken, afraid to talk, or failing in school.

However, when researchers follow maltreated children over the years, deficits in social skills seem more crippling than physical or intellectual damage. Maltreated children tend to hate themselves and then hate everyone else. Even if the child was mistreated early on and then not after age 5, emotional problems (externalizing for the boys and internalizing for the girls) linger (Godinet et al., 2014). The effects (drug abuse, social isolation, poor health) of maltreatment are still evident in adulthood (Sperry & Widom, 2013; Mersky et al., 2013).

Hate is corrosive. A warm and enduring friendship might repair some damage, but maltreatment makes friendship unlikely. Many studies have found that mistreated children typically regard other people as hostile and exploitative; hence, they are less friendly, more aggressive, and more isolated than other children. The earlier abuse starts and the longer it continues, the worse their relationships are, with physically and sexually abused children likely to be irrationally angry and neglected children often withdrawn (Petrenko et al., 2013).

Finding and keeping a job is a critical aspect of adult well-being, yet adults who were maltreated suffer in this way as well. One study carefully matched 807 children who had experienced substantiated abuse with other children who were of the same sex, ethnicity, and family SES. About 35 years later, long after maltreatment had stopped, those who had been mistreated were 14 percent less likely to be employed than those who had not been abused. The researchers concluded: "abused and neglected children experience large and enduring economic consequences" (Currie & Widom, 2010, p. 111). In this study, women were more impaired than men: It may be that self-esteem, emotional stability, and social skills are even more important for female than for male workers.

This study is just one of hundreds of longitudinal studies, all of which find that maltreatment affects people decades after broken bones, or skinny bodies, or medical neglect disappear. To protect the health of the entire society in the future, prevention of child maltreatment is crucial.

Prevention

To halt child abuse and neglect, many measures of prevention are needed. Changes in the entire culture may be the most effective, but they also are the most difficult to implement.

Three Levels of Prevention

Just as with injury control, the ultimate goal with regard to child maltreatment is *primary prevention,* a social network of customs and supports that make parents, neighbors, and professionals protect every child. Neighborhood stability, parental education, income support, and fewer unwanted children all reduce maltreatment.

Secondary prevention involves spotting warning signs and intervening to keep a risky situation from getting worse. For example, insecure attachment, especially of the disorganized type, is a sign of a disrupted parent–child relationship, which is a risk factor for maltreatment. Many researchers have found ways to repair insecure attachment before it becomes harmful. (**Developmental Link:** Attachment types are explained in detail in Chapter 7.) Critics argue that primary prevention is more effective in the long run, but projects are more likely to be funded and implemented if they focus on high-risk families (Nelson & Caplan, 2014).

An important aspect of secondary prevention is reporting the first signs of maltreatment so that families can be helped before a child is damaged for life. Every parent and child interacts with several other people, who can notice signs of normal and abnormal development.

Some people are *mandated reporters,* professionals who are legally required to report signs of abuse. Together, they provide more than half of all reports in the United States; teachers and law enforcement personnel each provide about 17 percent of reports (U.S. Department of Health and Human Services, 2013, December). It is not their responsibility to be certain that abuse has occurred; that is the job of social workers who, as already mentioned, investigate.

Sometimes reports come from neighbors (5 percent) or relatives (7 percent). You might wonder why more lay people do not report abuse. One reason is ignorance: Many abusers deliberately change residences and break off contact with relatives. That in itself is a sign of trouble. Another reason is that people fear the anger of the abuser or worry that the officials will makes things worse.

Tertiary prevention limits harm after maltreatment has occurred. Reporting and substantiating abuse are the first steps. Often the caregiver needs help in providing better care. Sometimes the child needs another home.

Permanency Planning

All levels of prevention require helping caregivers provide a safe, nurturing, and stable home. This is true for biological parents, a foster family, or an adoptive family. Whenever a child is removed from an abusive or neglectful home, **permanency planning** is needed: That means that plans need to be made to nurture the child until adulthood—either by supporting the original family or finding another home (Scott et al., 2013).

permanency planning An effort by child-welfare authorities to find a long-term living situation that will provide stability and support for a maltreated child. A goal is to avoid repeated changes of caregiver or school, which can be harmful to the child.

Family Protection Relatives are a safety net. Ideally, they feed and play with the young members of the family (as these grandfathers do). This is secondary prevention, allowing parents to provide good care. Rarely tertiary prevention is needed. About 2 percent of all U.S. grandparents are foster or adoptive parents of their grandchildren. This does not benefit the adults, but it may be the best solution for mistreated children.

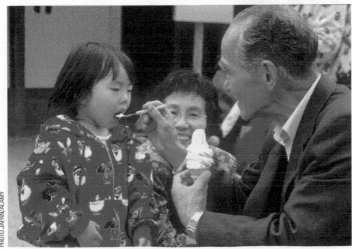

foster care A legal, publicly supported system in which a maltreated child is removed from the parents' custody and entrusted to another adult or family. Foster care providers are reimbursed for expenses incurred in meeting the child's needs.

kinship care A form of foster care in which a relative of a maltreated child, usually a grandparent, becomes the approved caregiver.

adoption A legal proceeding in which an adult or couple is granted the joys and obligations of being a child's parent(s).

In **foster care,** children are officially taken from their parents and entrusted to another adult or family; foster parents are reimbursed for the expenses they incur in meeting the children's needs. In every year from 2000 to 2014, almost half a million children in the United States were in foster care. Many of them were in a special version of foster care called **kinship care,** in which a relative—usually a grandmother—becomes the caregiver. This estimate is for official kinship care; three times as many children are unofficially cared for by relatives.

In every nation, most foster children are from low-income, ethnic-minority families—a statistic that reveals problems in the macrosystem as well as the microsystem. In the United States, children in foster care often have experienced severe maltreatment and have multiple physical, intellectual, and emotional problems (Jones & Morris, 2012). Most develop better in foster care (including kinship care) than with their original abusive families if a supervising agency provides ongoing financial support and counseling (Oosterman et al., 2007).

Adequate support is not typical, however. One obvious failing is that many children move from one foster home to another for reasons that are unrelated to the child's behavior or wishes (Jones & Morris, 2012). Each move increases the risk of a poor outcome. Another problem is that kinship care is sometimes used as an easy, less expensive solution.

Supportive services are especially needed in kinship care, since the grandparent typically lives in the same community of poverty, racism, and/or violence that contributed to the original problems. All of this affects the foster child as well (Hong et al., 2011).

Most adults, even in the most troubled communities, want success for children and do their best to provide it. Many adults raised by grandparents fare well, but grandparents need even more help from friends, relatives, and agencies than parents, yet they are less likely to get it.

Adoptive Homes

Adoption (when an adult or couple is legally granted parenthood) is the best permanent option when a child should not be returned to a parent (Scott et al., 2013).

Mother–Daughter Love, Finally After a difficult childhood, 7-year-old Alexia is now safe and happy in her mother's arms. Maria Luz Martinez was her foster parent and has now become her adoptive mother.

However, adoption is difficult for many reasons, including the following:

- Judges and biological parents are reluctant to release children for adoption.
- Most adoptive parents prefer infants, so it is harder to find adoptive homes for older children.
- Some agencies screen out families not headed by a heterosexual married couple.
- Some professionals insist that adoptive parents be of the same ethnicity and religion as the child.
- Kinship caregivers are reluctant to sever the parental rights of their child or other relative.

As detailed many times in this chapter, caring for young children is not easy, whether it involves making them brush their teeth or keeping them safe from harm. Parents shoulder most of the burden, and their love and protection usually result in strong and happy children. Beyond the microsystem, however, complications abound. Adults are failing many young children, as statistics throughout this chapter reveal. The entire community benefits from well-nurtured children; how to achieve that goal is the question we all must answer.

SUMMING UP   Although abuse seems to have decreased in the United States as more of the public has become aware of it, still about 700,000 children are tallied each year as maltreated—more often neglected than abused. Maltreatment has life-long consequences. Neglect is often worse than abuse, as social and emotional deficits are harder to remedy than physical harm.

In primary prevention, laws and customs need to protect every child, with measures to reduce poverty, to strengthen families, and to nurture all children. In secondary prevention, supervision, forethought, and protective care can prevent harm to those at risk, with signs of neglect and abuse apparent in the first months of life, and obvious by early childhood. In tertiary prevention, quick and effective medical and psychosocial intervention is needed when injury or maltreatment occurs. Foster care and adoption are sometimes best for children, but these options are not as available as they need to be. Putting an end to maltreatment of all kinds is urgent, but this goal is difficult to achieve because changes are needed in families, cultures, communities, and laws.

WHAT HAVE YOU LEARNED?

1. Why did few people recognize childhood maltreatment 50 years ago?
2. Why is neglect in childhood considered more harmful than abuse in the long term?
3. Why is it difficult to know exactly how often child maltreatment occurs?
4. What are the common signs that indicate a child may be maltreated?
5. What are the long-term consequences of childhood maltreatment?
6. What are the advantages and disadvantages of foster care?
7. Why does permanency planning rarely result in adoption?

SUMMARY

Body Changes

1. Well-nourished children continue to gain weight and add height during early childhood. Unfortunately, however, many adults overfeed children, not realizing that young children are naturally quite thin.

2. Culture, income, and family customs all affect children's growth. In contrast to past decades, children of low-income families are twice as likely to be overweight as their wealthier counterparts. Worldwide, an increasing number of children are eating too much, which puts them at risk for multiple health problems and diseases.

3. Many young children consume too much sugar and too little calcium and other nutrients. One consequence is poor oral health. Children need to brush their teeth and visit the dentist years before their permanent teeth erupt.

Brain Development

4. The brain continues to grow in early childhood, reaching 75 percent of its adult weight at age 2 and 90 percent by age 6. Lateralization helps the brain specialize and allows left-right coordination.

5. During early childhood myelination is substantial and speeds transmission of messages from one part of the brain to another; the corpus callosum becomes thicker and functions much more effectively; and the prefrontal cortex, known as the executive of the brain, is strengthened as well.

6. Brain changes enable more reflective, coordinated thought and memory, better planning, and quicker responses. Left–right specialization is apparent in the brain as well as in the body, although the entire brain and the entire body work together to perform most skills.

7. The expression and regulation of emotions are fostered by several brain areas, including the amygdala, the hippocampus, and the hypothalamus. Childhood trauma may create a flood of stress hormones (especially cortisol) that damage the brain and interfere with learning. However, some stress aids learning if reassurance is also present.

Improving Motor Skills

8. Gross motor skills continue to develop; clumsy 2-year-olds become 6-year-olds who move their bodies well, guided by their peers, practice, motivation, and opportunity—all of which vary by culture. Children's main activity is play. Playing with other children in safe places helps develop skills that benefit children's physical, intellectual, and social development.

9. Urbanization and chemical pollutants are two factors that hamper development. More research is needed, but it is already apparent that high lead levels in the blood can impair the brain.

10. Fine motor skills are difficult to master during early childhood. Young children enjoy expressing themselves artistically, which helps them develop their body and finger control. Fortunately, self-criticism is not yet strong.

Injuries and Abuse

11. Accidents cause more child deaths than diseases in early childhood, with young children more likely to suffer a serious injury or premature death than older children. Close supervision and public safeguards can protect young children from their own eager, impulsive curiosity.

12. In the United States, various preventive measures have reduced the rate of serious injury, but medical measures have reduced disease deaths even faster. Four times as many young children die of injuries than of the leading cause of disease death.

13. Injury control occurs on many levels, including long before and immediately after each harmful incident. Primary prevention protects everyone, secondary prevention focuses on high-risk conditions and people, and tertiary prevention occurs after an injury. All are needed.

Child Maltreatment

14. Child maltreatment includes ongoing abuse and neglect, usually by a child's own parents. Each year, about 3 million cases of child maltreatment are reported in the United States; about 700,000 of these are substantiated. Rates have been decreasing in recent years.

15. Physical abuse is the most obvious form of maltreatment, but neglect is more common and more harmful. Health, learning, and social skills are all impeded by abuse and neglect, not only during childhood but also decades later.

16. Tertiary prevention may include placement of a child in foster care, including kinship care. In any case, families, whether biological or foster, need supportive services to prevent maltreatment.

17. Permanency planning is required because frequent changes of home environment are harmful to children. Adoption is much less common than returning the child to the biological parents, although adoption is a permanent solution that may be the best solution for the child.

KEY TERMS

myelination (p. 246)
corpus callosum (p. 247)
lateralization (p. 247)
impulse control (p. 249)
perseveration (p. 249)
amygdala (p. 251)
hippocampus (p. 251)

hypothalamus (p. 251)
injury control/harm reduction
  (p. 263)
primary prevention (p. 264)
secondary prevention (p. 264)
tertiary prevention (p. 264)
child maltreatment (p. 266)

child abuse (p. 266)
child neglect (p. 266)
substantiated maltreatment
  (p. 267)
reported maltreatment (p. 267)
post-traumatic stress disorder
  (PTSD) (p. 269)

permanency planning (p. 271)
foster care (p. 272)
kinship care (p. 272)
adoption (p. 272)

APPLICATIONS

1. Keep a food diary for 24 hours, writing down what you eat, how much, when, how, and why. Then think about nutrition and eating habits in early childhood. Do you see any evidence in yourself of imbalance (e.g., not enough fruits and vegetables, too much sugar or fat, eating when you are not really hungry)? Did your food habits originate in early childhood, in adolescence, or at some other time?

2. Go to a playground or other place where young children play. Note the motor skills that the children demonstrate, including abilities and inabilities, and keep track of age and gender. What differences do you see among the children?

3. Ask several parents to describe each accidental injury of each of their children, particularly how it happened and what the consequences were. What primary, secondary, or tertiary prevention measures would have made a difference?

4. Think back to your childhood and the children you knew at that time. Was there any maltreatment? Considering what you have learned in this chapter, why or why not?

CHAPTER 9

Early Childhood:
Cognitive Development

What Will You Know?

1. Are young children selfish or just self-centered?
2. Do children get confused if they hear two languages?
3. Is preschool for play or learning?

Asa, not yet 3 feet tall, held a large rubber ball. He wanted me to play basketball with him.

"We can't play basketball; we don't have a hoop," I said.

"We can imagine a hoop," he answered, throwing up the ball.

"I got it in," he said happily. "You try."

I did.

"You got it in, too," he announced and did a little dance.

Soon I was tired and sat down.

"I want to sit and think my thoughts," I told him.

"Get up," he urged. "You can play basketball and think your thoughts."

Asa is typical. Imagination comes easily to him, and he aspires to the skills of older, taller people in his culture. He thinks by doing, and his vocabulary is impressive, but he does not yet understand that my feelings differ from his, that I would rather sit than throw a ball at an imaginary basket. He does know, however, that I usually respond to his requests.

This chapter describes these characteristics of the young child—imagination, active learning, vocabulary, and some difficulty understanding another person's perspective. I hope it also conveys the joy of understanding the thinking of young children. When that happens, you might do what I did: Get up and play.

Thinking During Early Childhood

You have just learned in Chapter 8 that every year of early childhood advances motor skills, brain development, and impulse control. In Chapter 6, you learned about the impressive development of memory and language in the first two years of life. Each of these developmental advances affects cognition. Thinking during early childhood is multi-faceted, creative, and remarkable.

Piaget: Preoperational Thought

Early childhood is the time of **preoperational intelligence,** the second of Piaget's four periods of cognitive development (described in Table 2.3 on p. 49). He called

> **preoperational intelligence** Piaget's term for cognitive development between the ages of about 2 and 6; it includes language and imagination (which involve symbolic thought), but logical, operational thinking is not yet possible at this stage.

early-childhood thinking *preoperational* because children do not yet use logical operations (reasoning processes) (Inhelder & Piaget, 1964/2013).

Preoperational children are no longer in the stage of sensorimotor intelligence because they can think in symbols, not just via senses and motor skills. In **symbolic thought,** an object or word can stand for something else, including something out of sight or imagined. Language is the most apparent example of symbolic thought, because using words makes it possible to think about many more things at once. However, although vocabulary and imagination can soar in early childhood, logical connections between ideas are not yet active, not yet *operational*.

The word *dog*, for instance, is at first only the family dog sniffing at the child, not yet a symbol (Callaghan, 2013). By age 2, the word becomes a symbol: It can refer to a remembered dog, or a plastic dog, or an imagined dog. Symbolic thought allows for the language explosion (detailed later in this chapter), which enables children to talk about thoughts and memories. However, since thought during these years is *preoperational*, it is hard for young children to understand the historical connections, similarities, and differences between dogs and wolves, or even between a Labrador retriever and a poodle.

Symbolic thought helps explain **animism,** the belief of many young children that natural objects (such as a tree or a cloud) are alive and that non-human animals have the same characteristics as the child.

Many children's stories include animals or objects that talk and listen (Aesop's fables, *Winnie-the-Pooh, Goodnight Moon, The Day the Crayons Quit*). Preoperational thought is symbolic and magical, not logical and realistic. Childish animism gradually disappears with maturation (Kesselring & Müller, 2011).

symbolic thought A major accomplishment of preoperational intelligence that allows a child to think symbolically, including understanding that words can refer to things not seen and that an item, such as a flag, can symbolize something else (in this case, a country).

Can Fish Talk? Of course they can. As every preschooler who watches Finding Nemo knows, some fish talk and help each other, just like egocentric children do.

© WALT DISNEY/COURTESY EVERETT COLLECTION

Obstacles to Logic

Piaget described symbolic thought as characteristic of preoperational thought. He noted four limitations that make logic difficult until about age 6: centration, focus on appearance, static reasoning, and irreversibility.

Centration is the tendency to focus on one aspect of a situation to the exclusion of all others. Young children may, for example, insist that Daddy is a father, not a brother, because they center on the role that he fills for them. The daddy example illustrates a particular type of centration that Piaget called **egocentrism**— literally, "self-centeredness." Egocentric children contemplate the world exclusively from their personal perspective.

Egocentrism is not selfishness. One 3-year-old chose to buy a model car as a birthday present for his mother: His "behavior was not selfish or greedy; he carefully wrapped the present and gave it to his mother with an expression that clearly showed that he expected her to love it" (Crain, 2005, p. 108).

A second characteristic of preoperational thought is a **focus on appearance** to the exclusion of other attributes. For instance, a girl given a short haircut might worry that she has turned into a boy. In preoperational thought, a thing is whatever it appears to be—evident in the joy young children have in wearing the hats or shoes of a grown-up, clomping noisily and unsteadily around the living room.

Third, preoperational children use **static reasoning.** They believe that the world is stable, unchanging, always in the state in which they currently encounter it.

animism The belief that natural objects and phenomena are alive.

centration A characteristic of preoperational thought in which a young child focuses (centers) on one idea, excluding all others.

egocentrism Piaget's term for children's tendency to think about the world entirely from their own personal perspective.

focus on appearance A characteristic of preoperational thought in which a young child ignores all attributes that are not apparent.

static reasoning A characteristic of preoperational thought in which a young child thinks that nothing changes. Whatever is now has always been and always will be.

Many children cannot imagine that their own parents were ever children. If they are told that Grandma is their mother's mother, they still do not understand how people change with maturation.

One preschooler wanted his grandmother to tell his mother to never spank him because "she has to do what her mother says." Often a preschooler whose baby brother or sister sucks a bottle wants a bottle, too. The answer, "You had a bottle when you were little, now you are a big kid," is not convincing.

The fourth characteristic of preoperational thought is **irreversibility.** Preoperational thinkers fail to recognize that reversing a process sometimes restores whatever existed before. A young girl might cry because her mother put lettuce on her sandwich. Overwhelmed by her desire to have things "just right," she might reject the food even after the lettuce is removed because she believes that what is done cannot be undone.

Conservation and Logic

Piaget highlighted several ways in which preoperational intelligence disregards logic. A famous set of experiments involved **conservation,** the notion that the amount of something remains the same (is conserved) despite changes in its appearance.

Suppose two identical glasses contain the same amount of pink lemonade, and the liquid from one of these glasses is poured into a taller, narrower glass. If young children are asked whether one glass contains more or, alternatively, both glasses contain the same amount, they will insist that the narrower glass (with the higher level) has more. (See Figure 9.1 for other examples.)

All four characteristics of preoperational thought are evident in this mistake. Young children fail to understand conservation because they focus (*center*) on what they see (*appearance*), noticing only the immediate (*static*) condition. It does not occur to them that they could reverse the process and recreate the level of a moment earlier (*irreversibility*).

Piaget's original tests of conservation required children to respond verbally to an adult's questions. Later research has found that when the tests of logic are simplified or made playful, young children may succeed. In many ways, children indicate via eye movements or gestures that they know something before they can say it in words (Goldin-Meadow & Alibali, 2013). Further, conservation and many more logical ideas are understood bit by bit, with active, guided experience, and glimmers of understanding are apparent even at age 4 (Sophian, 2013).

Especially for Nutritionists How can Piaget's theory help you encourage children to eat healthy foods? (see response, page 281)

irreversibility A characteristic of preoperational thought in which a young child thinks that nothing can be undone. A thing cannot be restored to the way it was before a change occurred.

conservation The principle that the amount of a substance remains the same (i.e., is conserved) even when its appearance changes.

Easy Question; Obvious Answer (*below, left*) Sadie, age 5, carefully makes sure both glasses contain the same amount. (*below, right*). When one glass of pink lemonade is poured into a wide jar, she triumphantly points to the tall glass as having more. Sadie is like all 5-year-olds; only a developmental psychologist or a 7-year-old child knows better.

Tests of Various Types of Conservation

Type of Conservation	Initial Presentation	Transformation	Question	Preoperational Child's Answer
Volume 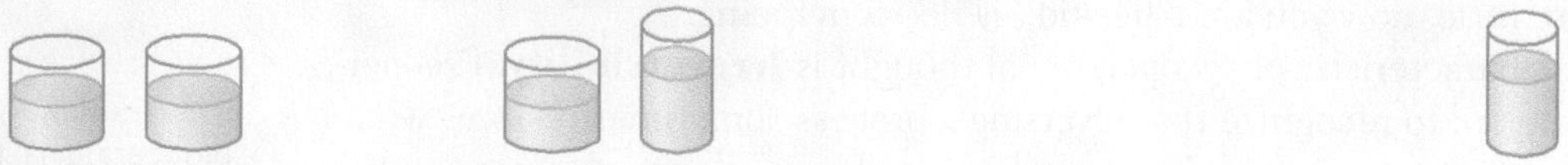	Two equal glasses of liquid.	Pour one into a taller, narrower glass.	Which glass contains more?	The taller one.
Number	Two equal lines of checkers.	Increase spacing of checkers in one line.	Which line has more checkers?	The longer one.
Matter 	Two equal balls of clay.	Squeeze one ball into a long, thin shape.	Which piece has more clay?	The long one.
Length	Two sticks of equal length.	Move one stick.	Which stick is longer?	The one that is farther to the right.

FIGURE 9.1

Conservation, Please According to Piaget, until children grasp the concept of conservation at (he believed) about age 6 or 7, they cannot understand that the transformations shown here do not change the total amount of liquid, checkers, clay, and wood.

Video Activity: Achieving Conservation focuses on the changes in thinking that make it possible for older children to pass Piaget's conservation-of-liquid task.

As with sensorimotor intelligence in infancy, Piaget underestimated what preoperational children could understand. Piaget was right that young children are not as logical as older children, but he did not realize how much they could learn.

Brain scans, video responses measured in milliseconds, and the computer programs that developmentalists now use were not available to him. Studies from the past 20 years show intellectual activity before age 6 that was not previously understood; they also show that Piaget was perceptive about many aspects of cognition (Crone & Ridderinkhof, 2011).

Given the new data, it is easy to criticize Piaget. However, many adults make the same mistakes. For instance, the shapes of boxes and bottles in the grocery store make it hard to compare volume visually and so undermine adults' sense of conservation—that's why laws require that ounces or grams be listed on the containers. Animism is evident in many religious and cultural myths that include talking, thinking animals.

Indeed, many adults in the United States encourage children to believe in Santa Claus, the Tooth Fairy, and so on. If we consider preschoolers foolish to imagine that animals and plants have human traits, how should we judge ourselves if we talk to our pets or mourn the death of a tree? When adults say, "Nothing ever changes," or, "He can never be trusted," is that static reasoning?

A review of the research finds that children are "naïve skeptics . . . as likely to doubt as to believe" (Woolley & Ghossainy, 2013, p. 1496). They use their best judgment and most reliable sources to decide what is true. Adults are often more skeptical than young children because they have more experience, but they also believe in things not seen (from germs to heaven) because other adults whom they trust (scientists or clergy, depending on specifics) say such unseen things exist.

Preschoolers also rely on their own experience and on trusted sources, but their social network is more limited. Consequently, they rely heavily on their parents and on rules governing behavior (Lane & Harris, 2014). Because of their cognitive limits, smart 3-year-olds sometimes are foolish, as Caleb is. (See below.)

a case to study

Stones in the Belly

As we were reading a book about dinosaurs, 3-year-old Caleb told me that some dinosaurs (*sauropods*) have stones in their bellies. It helps them digest their food and then poop and pee.

I was amazed, never having known this before.

"I didn't know that dinosaurs ate stones," I said.

"They don't eat them."

"Then how do they get the stones in their bellies? They must swallow them."

"They don't eat them."

"Then how do they get in their bellies?"

"They are just there."

"How did they get there?"

"They don't eat them," said Caleb. "Stones are dirty. We don't eat them."

I dropped it, but my question apparently puzzled him. Later he asked his mother, "Do dinosaurs eat stones?"

"Yes, they eat stones so they can grind their food," she answered.

At that, Caleb was quiet.

In all of this, preoperational cognition is evident. Caleb is bright; he can name several kinds of dinosaurs, as can many young children.

But logic eludes Caleb. He is preoperational, not operational.

It seemed obvious to me that dinosaurs must have swallowed the stones. However, in his static thinking, Caleb said the stones "are just there." In thinking that is typical of egocentrism, he rejects the thought that they ate them, because he has been told that stones are too dirty to eat.

He is egocentric, reasoning from his own experience, and animistic, in that he thinks animals would not eat stones because he does not. Caleb has no personal experience with dinosaurs, but my question made him think. He trusts his mother, who told him never to eat stones, or, for that matter, sand from the sandbox, or food that fell on the floor. If anyone told him he could eat those things they would seem foolish, as I seemed when I said dinosaurs might eat stones. He did not accept my authority: The implications of the fact that I am his mother's mother are beyond his static thinking.

But, like many young children, Caleb is curious, and my question raised his curiosity. He consulted his authority, my daughter.

Should I have expected him to tell me that I was right, when his mother agreed with me? No. That would have required far more understanding of reversibility and far less egocentrism than most young children can muster.

Vygotsky: Social Learning

For decades, the magical, illogical, and self-centered aspects of cognition dominated our concepts of early-childhood thought. Scientists were understandably awed by Piaget. His description of egocentrism and magical thinking was confirmed daily by anecdotes of young children's behavior.

Vygotsky emphasized another side of early cognition—that each person's thinking is shaped by other people's wishes and goals. He emphasized the social aspects of development, a contrast to Piaget's emphasis on the individual. That led Vygotsky to notice the power of culture, acknowledging that "the culturally specific nature of experience is an integral part of how the person thinks and acts," as several developmentalists explain (Gauvain et al., 2011). Learning is not done in isolation; according to many contemporary educators, it depends on joint engagement.

// **Response for Nutritionists** (from page 279): Take each of the four characteristics of preoperational thought into account. Because of egocentrism, having a special place and plate might assure the child that this food is exclusively his or hers. Since appearance is important, food should look tasty. Since static thinking dominates, if something healthy is added (e.g., grate carrots into the cake, add milk to the soup), do it before the food is given to the child. In the reversibility example in the text, the lettuce should be removed out of the child's sight and the "new" hamburger presented.

Words Fail Me Could you describe how to tie shoes? The limitations of verbal tests of cognitive understanding are apparent in the explanation of many skills.

OBSERVATION QUIZ What three sociocultural factors make it likely that the child pictured above will learn? (see answer, page 284)

scaffolding Temporary support that is tailored to a learner's needs and abilities and aimed at helping the learner master the next task in a given learning process.

OBSERVATION QUIZ Is the girl below right- or left-handed? (see answer, page 284)

Mentors

Vygotsky believed that cognitive development is embedded in a social context at every age (Vygotsky, 1934/1987). He stressed that children are curious and observant. They ask questions—about how machines work, why weather changes, where the sky ends—and seek answers from more knowledgeable mentors, who might be their parents, teachers, older siblings, or just a stranger. The answers they get are affected by the mentors' perceptions and assumptions—that is, their culture—which shapes their thought.

As you remember from Chapter 2, children learn through *guided participation,* as mentors teach them. Parents are their first guides, although children are guided by many others, too.

According to Vygotsky, children learn because their mentors do the following:

- Present challenges.
- Offer assistance (without taking over).
- Add crucial information.
- Encourage motivation.

Overall, the ability to learn from mentors indicates intelligence; according to Vygotsky, "What children can do with the assistance of others might be in some sense even more indicative of their mental development than what they can do alone" (Vygotsky, 1980, p. 85).

Scaffolding

Vygotsky believed that all individuals learn within their *zone of proximal development (ZPD),* an intellectual arena in which new ideas and skills can be mastered. *Proximal* means "near," so the ZPD includes the ideas children are close to understanding and the skills they can almost master, but are not yet able to demonstrate independently. How and when children learn depends, in part, on the wisdom and willingness of mentors to provide **scaffolding,** or temporary sensitive support, to help them within their developmental zone. (**Developmental Link:** The ZPD is discussed in Chapter 2.)

Good mentors provide plenty of scaffolding, encouraging children to look both ways before crossing the street (while holding the child's hand) or letting them stir the cake batter (perhaps while covering the child's hand on the spoon handle, in guided participation). Crucial in every activity is joint engagement, when both learner and mentor are actively involved together in the learning zone (Adamson et al., 2014).

As always, cultural differences are crucial. Consider book reading, for instance, an activity parents worldwide do with their young children, in part because it fosters language,

Count by Tens A large, attractive abacus could be a scaffold. However in this toy store, the position of the balls suggests that no mentor is nearby. Children are unlikely to grasp the number system without a motivating guide.

Same or Different? Which do you see? Most people focus on differences, such as ethnicity or sex. But a developmental perspective appreciates similarities: book reading to a pre-literate child cradled on a parent's lap.

reading, and moral development. When an adult reads to children, the adult scaffolds—explaining, pointing, listening, describing—within the child's zone of development. Middle-class American adults do not tell the child to be quiet, but often prolong the session by expanding on the child's questions and asking questions of their own, so that the book reading becomes a scaffold for dialogue.

By contrast, book reading in low-income families tends to emphasize content over conversation, with parents telling children what is happening in the story and expecting the child to listen and learn. Comparative research finds that parents scaffold whatever is important in their culture, with Chinese American parents more likely to point out problems encountered by the book's characters because of misbehavior and the Mexican Americans more likely to highlight emotions that the characters might feel (Luo et al., 2014).

Overimitation

Sometimes scaffolding is inadvertent, as when children observe something said or done and then try to do likewise—including things that adults would rather the child not do. Young children curse, kick, and worse because someone else showed them how. One of the ominous behaviors that preschool teachers sometimes witness is a young child trying to get another child to engage in sex. The child must have seen something most adults think children should not see. (This is quite different from the normal curiosity that children have about each other's bodies.)

More benignly, children imitate habits and customs that are meaningless, a trait called **overimitation,** evident in humans but rare in other animals. This stems from the child's eagerness to learn from mentors, allowing "rapid, high-fidelity intergenerational transmission of cultural forms" (Nielsen & Tomaselli, 2010, p. 735).

Overimitation was demonstrated in a series of experiments with 3- to 6-year-olds, 64 of them from Bushman communities in South Africa and Botswana and, for comparison, 64 from cities in Australia and 19 from aboriginal communities within Australia. Australian middle-class adults often scaffold for children with words and actions, but Bushman adults rarely do. The researchers expected the urban Australian children to follow adult demonstrations, since they were accustomed to learning in that way. They did not expect the Bushman children to do so (Nielsen et al., 2014).

overimitation When a person imitates an action that is not a relevant part of the behavior to be learned. Overimitation is common among 2- to 6-year-olds when they imitate adult actions that are unnecessary.

Especially for Driving Instructors
Sometimes your students cry, curse, or quit. How would Vygotsky advise you to proceed? (see response, page 286)

// **ANSWER TO OBSERVATION QUIZ**
(from page 282): Motivation (this father and son are from Spain, where yellow running shoes are popular), human relationships (note the physical touching of father and son), and materials (the long laces make tying them easier).

In part of the study, some children one-by-one from each cultural group observed an adult perform irrelevant actions, such as waving a red stick above a box three times and then using that stick to push down a knob to open the box, which could be easily and more efficiently opened by merely pulling down the same knob by hand. Then children were given the stick and the box. No matter what their cultural background, the children followed the adult example, waving the stick three times and not using their hands directly on the knob.

Other children did not see the demonstration. When they were given the stick and asked to open the box, they simply pulled the knob. Then they observed an adult do the stick-waving opening—and they did something odd: They copied those inefficient actions, even though they already knew the easy way to open the box (Nielsen & Tomaselli, 2010).

Apparently, children everywhere learn from others through observation, even if they have not been taught to do so. They even learn to do things contrary to their prior learning. Thus, scaffolding occurs through observation as well as explicit guidance. Across cultures, overimitation is striking and even generalizes to other similar situations. Children everywhere are strongly inclined to learn whatever adults from their culture do (Nielsen et al., 2014).

That is exactly what Vygotsky expected and explained. Curiously, young children are not adept at figuring out new ways to use various tools (Nielsen et al., 2014). Young children's minds are quick to imitate what adults do, but slow to figure out creative ways to accomplish their goals. That innovative ability, apparently, must wait until more cognitive maturation has occurred.

Language as a Tool

Although all the objects of a culture guide children, Vygotsky believed that words are especially pivotal. He thought language advances thinking in two ways (Fernyhough, 2010). The first way is with internal dialogue, or **private speech,** in which people talk to themselves (Vygotsky, 2012). Young children use private speech often. They talk aloud to review, decide, and explain events to themselves (and, incidentally, to anyone else within earshot) (Al-Namlah et al., 2012).

private speech The internal dialogue that occurs when people talk to themselves (either silently or out loud).

Older preschoolers are more selective, effective, and circumspect, sometimes whispering. Audible or not, private speech aids cognition and self-reflection; adults should encourage it (Perels et al., 2009; Benigno et al., 2011). Many people of all ages talk to themselves when alone or write down ideas to help them think. That is private speech as well. Preschool curricula based on Vygotsky's ideas use games, play, social interaction, and private speech to develop executive functioning (Winsler et al., 2009).

The second way in which language advances thinking, according to Vygotsky, is by mediating the social interaction that is vital to learning (Vygotsky, 2012). This **social mediation** function of speech occurs during both formal instruction (when teachers explain things) and casual conversation.

social mediation Human interaction that expands and advances understanding, often through words that one person uses to explain something to another.

Words entice people into the zone of proximal development, as mentors guide children to learn numbers, recall memories, and follow routines. Indeed, children who count out loud and use other aspects of private speech to help them with numbers are likely to advance in mathematical understanding.

STEM Learning

// **ANSWER TO OBSERVATION QUIZ**
(from page 282): Right-handed. Her dominant hand is engaged in something more comforting than exploring the abacus.

A practical use of Vygotsky's theory concerns the current emphasis on STEM (Science, Technology, Engineering, Math) education. Because finding more young people to specialize in those fields is crucial for economic growth, educators and political leaders are continually seeking ways to make STEM fields attractive to adolescents and young adults of all ethnicities (Rogers-Chapman, 2013; Wang, 2013).

Research on early childhood suggests that STEM education actually begins long before high school. This is increasingly recognized by experts, who note that most parents and teachers have much to learn about math and science if they wish to teach these subjects to young children (Hong et al., 2013; Bers et al., 2013).

For example, learning about numbers is possible very early in life. Even babies have a sense of whether one, two, or three objects are in a display, although exactly what infants understand about numbers is controversial (Varga et al., 2010). If Vygotsky is correct that words are tools, toddlers need to hear number words and science concepts early (not just counting and shapes, but fractions and science principles, such as the laws of motion) so that other knowledge becomes accessible. In math understanding, it is evident that preschoolers gradually learn to

- Count objects, with one number per item (called *one-to-one correspondence*).
- Remember times and ages (bedtime at 8, a child is 4 years old, and so on).
- Understand sequence (first child wins, last child loses).
- Know what numbers are higher than others. (It is not obvious to young children that 7 is greater than 4.)

These and many other cognitive accomplishments of young children have been the subject of extensive research: Mentoring and language are always found to be pivotal.

Especially in math, computers can promote a dialogue that helps contemporary young children learn. Educational software becomes "a conduit for collaborative learning" (Cicconi, 2014, p. 58) as Web 2.0 programs respond to the particular abilities and needs of the learner.

Often in preschool classrooms with interactive education, two or three children work together, each mentoring the other, talking aloud as the computer prompts them. This can occur at home, too: Educators frown on using a computer screen as a substitute for human interaction, but they sometimes consider it an adjunct to promote learning, just as a book might be (Alper, 2013).

Culture affects language, which in turn fosters math knowledge. For example, English-speaking and Chinese-speaking preschoolers seem to have equal comprehension of 1 to 10, but the Chinese are ahead in their understanding of 11 to 19. Among the many possible explanations is a linguistic one: In all the Chinese dialects, the names for 11 to 19 are logical and direct, the equivalent of ten-one, ten-two, ten-three, and so on. This system is easier for young children to understand than eleven, twelve, thirteen, and so on.

German-speaking children may be slower to master numbers from 20 to 99, since they say the equivalent of one-and-twenty, two-and-twenty, and so on, not twenty-one, twenty-two, and so on. In these and many other ways, cultural restraints and routines affect young children's understanding of math (Göbel et al., 2011).

By age 3 or 4, children's brains are mature enough to comprehend numbers, store memories, and recognize routines. Whether or not children actually demonstrate such understanding depends on what they hear and how they participate in various activities within their families, schools, and cultures.

Some 2-year-olds hear sentences such as "One, two, three, takeoff," and "Here are two cookies," and "Dinner in five minutes" several times a day. They are shown an interesting

OBSERVATION QUIZ Could this photo have been taken 10 years ago? (see answer, page 287)

Learning or Playing? Teachers once demanded that each child sit at his or her desk, hands folded, mouth shut, too far from other children to touch them or even pass a note. Despite their divergent perspectives, both Piaget and Vygotsky studied how children actually learn—and the classroom you see here is a result.

HERO IMAGES/GETTY IMAGES

// **Response for Driving Instructors** (from page 284): Use guided participation to scaffold the instruction so that your students are not overwhelmed. Be sure to provide lots of praise and days of practice. If emotion erupts, do not take it as an attack on you.

theory-theory The idea that children attempt to explain everything they see and hear by constructing theories.

bit of moss, or are alerted to the phases of the moon, or learn about the relationship between pace, breathing, and the steepness of a hill. Others never hear such comments—and they have a harder time with math in first grade, with science in the third grade, and with STEM subjects when they are older. According to Vygotsky, words mediate between brain potential and comprehension, and this process begins long before formal education.

Children's Theories

Piaget and Vygotsky both recognized that children work to understand their world. No contemporary developmental scientist doubts that. How do children acquire their impressive knowledge? Part of the answer is that children do more than gain words and concepts; they develop theories to help them understand and remember—theories that arise from both brain maturation and personal experience (Baron-Cohen et al., 2013).

Theory-Theory

Humans of all ages want explanations. **Theory-theory** refers to the idea that children naturally construct theories to explain whatever they see and hear. In other words, the theory about how children think is that they construct a theory. All people

> search for causal regularities in the world around us. We are perpetually driven to look for deeper explanations of our experience, and broader and more reliable predictions about it. . . . Children seem, quite literally, to be born with . . . the desire to understand the world and the desire to discover how to behave in it.
>
> [*Gopnik, 2001, p. 66*]

According to theory-theory, the explanation for cognition is that humans seek reasons, causes, and underlying principles to make sense of their experience. That requires curiosity and thought, connecting bits of knowledge and observations, which is what young children do. Humans always want theories (even false ones, sometimes) to help them understand the world. Especially in childhood, theories are subject to change as new evidence accumulates (Meltzoff & Gopnik, 2013).

Exactly how do children seek explanations? They ask questions, and, if they are not satisfied with the answers, they develop their own theories. This is particularly evident in children's understanding of God and religion. One child thought his grandpa died because God was lonely; another thought thunder occurred because God was rearranging the furniture.

Theories do not appear randomly. Children wonder about the underlying purpose of whatever they observe, and in order to develop a theory about what causes what and why, they note how often a particular event occurs. They follow the same processes that scientists do: asking questions, developing hypotheses, gathering data, and drawing conclusions.

Of course, a child's method of understanding and interpreting experience lacks the rigor of scientific experiments, but questions of physics, biology, and the social sciences are explored: "infants and young children not only detect statistical patterns, they use those patterns to test hypotheses about people and things" (Gopnik, 2012, p. 1625). Their conclusions are not always correct: Like all good scientists, they allow new data to promote revision.

For instance, when I was a young child, I noticed that my father never carried an umbrella. Since I looked up to him, I assumed he must have had a good reason. Neither did my brother, which confirmed for me that my father was right. Consequently, throughout all my adult years, I never carried an umbrella.

Over time I developed many reasons for my father's behavior. He must have realized, I decided, that umbrellas poke people in the eye, get forgotten, blow away, and are lost. Then, when Dad was in his 80s, my brother asked him why he didn't like umbrellas. The answer stunned me: "Chamberlain."

Neville Chamberlain was famous for carrying an umbrella when he was prime minister of England from 1937 to 1940. He was photographed with his black umbrella after signing the Munich Agreement in 1938, when he mistakenly and naively announced that Hitler would not attack England. For Dad, umbrellas symbolized foolish trust and he said that no political leader would dare carry an umbrella. I had constructed a theory to justify something I observed. That is theory-theory.

In the egocentrism of early childhood, preschoolers theorize that everyone operates as they themselves do, which makes them more aware of situational differences than personality differences. For instance, each child knows that he or she acts differently, say, in a familiar playground on a sunny day than on an unfamiliar street in a thunderstorm. Context is crucial, but the child is the same person in both situations.

That explains the results of a series of experiments in which children observe that one puppet refuses to play on a trampoline or ride a bicycle and another puppet does both. Four-year-olds theorize that the playing puppet must know that the trampoline is safe, not that one puppet is brave and the other fearful. By age 6, children are more able to explain behavior based on temperament, not situation (Seiver et al., 2013).

One common theory-theory is that everyone intends to do things correctly. For that reason, when asked to repeat something ungrammatical that an adult says, children often correct the grammar. They theorize that the adult intended to speak grammatically but failed to do so (Over & Gattis, 2010).

This is an example of a general principle: Children theorize about intentions before they imitate what they see. As you have read, when children saw an adult wave a stick before opening a box, the children theorized that, since the adult did it deliberately, stick-waving must somehow be important.

Theory of Mind

Mental processes—thoughts, emotions, beliefs, motives, and intentions—are among the most complicated and puzzling phenomena that humans encounter every day. Adults wonder why people fall in love with the particular persons they do, why they vote for the candidates they do, or why they make foolish choices—from signing for a huge mortgage to buying an overripe cucumber. Children are likewise puzzled about a playmate's unexpected anger, a sibling's generosity, or an aunt's too-wet kiss.

To know what goes on in another's mind, people develop a *folk psychology*, which includes ideas about other people's thinking, called **theory of mind.** Theory

// **ANSWER TO OBSERVATION QUIZ**
(from page 285) No. Each child has a tablet-
-not used in schools until 2010. In the next
five years, some school systems purchased
tablets for every child, as is apparent here.

theory of mind A person's theory of what other people might be thinking. In order to have a theory of mind, children must realize that other people are not necessarily thinking the same thoughts that they themselves are. That realization seldom occurs before age 4.

Candies in the Crayon Box Anyone would expect crayons in a crayon box, but once a child sees that candy is inside, he expects that everyone else will also know that candies are inside!

©2016 MACMILLAN

Especially for Social Scientists Can you think of any connection between Piaget's theory of preoperational thought and 3-year-olds' errors in this theory-of-mind task? (see response, page 290)

Video: Theory of Mind: False-Belief Tasks
http://qrs.ly/ba4ep0i

AMI PARIKH/SHUTTERSTOCK

of mind is an emergent ability, slow to develop but typically beginning in most children at about age 4 (Carlson et al., 2013). Some aspects of theory of mind develop sooner than age 4, and some later. However, longitudinal research finds that the preschool years typically begin with 2-year-olds not knowing that other people think differently than they do but end with 6-year-olds having a well-developed theory of mind (Wellman et al., 2011).

Generally, realizing that thoughts do not mirror reality is beyond very young children, but that realization dawns on them sometime after age 3. It then occurs to them that people can be deliberately deceived or fooled—an idea that requires some theory of mind.

In one of dozens of false-belief tests that researchers have developed, a child watches a puppet named Max put a toy dog into a red box. Then Max leaves and the child sees the dog taken out of the red box and put in a blue box. When Max returns, the child is asked, "Where will Max look for the dog?" Most 3-year-olds confidently say, "In the blue box"; most 6-year-olds correctly say, "In the red box," a pattern found in more than a dozen nations. Interestingly, although some cultural differences appear, the most notable differences are neurological, not cultural: Deaf or autistic children are remarkably slow to develop theory of mind (Carlson et al., 2013).

The development of theory of mind can be seen when young children try to escape punishment by lying. Their face often betrays them: worried or shifting eyes, pursed lips, and so on. Parents sometimes say, "I know when you are lying," and, to the consternation of most 3-year-olds, parents are usually right.

In one experiment, 247 children, aged 3 to 5, were left alone at a table that had an upside-down cup covering dozens of candies (Evans et al., 2011). The children were told *not* to peek, and the experimenter left the room. For 142 children (57 percent), curiosity overcame obedience. They peeked, spilling so many candies onto the table that they could not put them back under the cup. The examiner returned, asking how the candies got on the table. Only one-fourth of the participants (more often the younger ones) told the truth.

The rest lied, and their skill increased with their age. The 3-year-olds typically told hopeless lies (e.g., "The candies got out by themselves"); the 4-year-olds told unlikely lies (e.g., "Other children came in and knocked over the cup"). Some of the 5-year-olds, however, told plausible lies (e.g., "My elbow knocked over the cup accidentally").

This particular study was done in Beijing, China, but the results seem universal: Older children are better liars. Beyond the age differences, the experimenters found that the more logical liars were also more advanced in theory of mind and executive functioning (Evans et al., 2011), which indicates a more mature prefrontal cortex (see Figure 9.2).

Of course, many egocentric children convince themselves that something is true when it is not—as do some adults. This does not mean that they are unable to recount what they see and hear, but it does mean that what they say should be evaluated, not swallowed whole. (See A View From Science.)

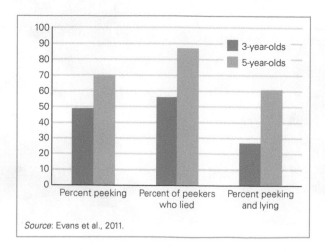

Source: Evans et al., 2011.

FIGURE 9.2

Better with Age? Could an obedient and honest 3-year-old become a disobedient and lying 5-year-old? Apparently yes, as the proportion of peekers and liars in this study more than doubled over those two years. Does maturation make children more able to think for themselves or less trustworthy?

⚗ a view from science

Witness to a Crime

One application of early cognitive competency has received attention among lawyers and judges. Children may be the only witnesses to crimes, especially of sexual abuse or domestic violence. Can a young child's words be trusted? Adults have gone to both extremes in answering this question. As one legal discussion begins:

> Perhaps as a result of the collective guilt caused by disbelieving the true victims of this abuse, in recent years the pendulum has swung in the opposite direction, to an unwavering conviction that a young child is incapable of fabricating a story of abuse, even when the tale of mistreatment is inherently incredible.
>
> *[Shanks, 2011]*

The answer to the question, "Is child testimony accurate?" is: "Sometimes." In recent years, psychologists have shown that people of all ages misremember (Frenda et al., 2011; Lyons et al., 2010) and that each age group misremembers in particular ways.

Younger children, not yet imbued with stereotypes, are sometimes more accurate than older witnesses who are influenced by prejudice (Brainerd et al., 2008), but they may confuse time, place, person, and action—even though they may describe each accurately. Further, young children want to please adults and themselves, and they may lie to do so. Developmental psychologists have developed many research-based suggestions to improve the accuracy of child witnesses (Lamb, 2014).

Words and expressions can plant false ideas in young children's minds, either deliberately (as an abuser might) or inadvertently (as a fearful parent might). Children's shaky grasp of reality makes them vulnerable to scaffolding memories that are imagined, not experienced (Bruck et al., 2006). This happened tragically 35 years ago in many jurisdictions, when adults suddenly realized that small children could be sexually abused and then decided that sexual abuse was rampant in preschools.

For instance, 3-year-olds at Wee Care nursery school in New Jersey convinced a judge that a teacher had sexually abused them in bizarre ways (including making them lick peanut butter off her genitals) (Ceci & Bruck, 1995) when, in fact, no abuse had occurred. In retrospect, one wonders why any adult believed what they heard. Since then, much has been learned about witnesses of all ages.

Young children are not necessarily worse than adults at recounting experiences if they are interviewed with open-ended questions by someone who does not indicate what the preferred answers are (Brainerd et al., 2008; Feltis et al., 2010). Children who have already learned to tell coherent narratives provide more accurate accounts of what happened (Kulkofsky & Klemfuss, 2008). Whether or not a child understands the difference between truth and falsehood is irrelevant to accuracy; the crucial factor is whether the interviewer is straightforward or suggestive (Lyon et al., 2008).

With sexual abuse in particular, a child might believe that some lewd act is OK if an adult says so. Only years later does the victim realize that it was abuse. Research on adult memory finds that sometimes adults reinterpret what happened to them, with genuine memories of experiences that were criminal. However, people of all ages sometimes believe that an event, including abuse, occurred when it did not (Geraerts et al., 2009).

This knowledge provides guidelines for police officers, social workers, judges, teachers, and parents. When children are witnesses, they should simply be asked to tell what happened, perhaps with eyes closed to reduce their natural attempt to please (Kyriakidou et al., 2014). If, instead, an adult says, "Did he touch you there?" a child might say yes if he thinks that is what the adult wants to hear. Preschoolers' cognition is a mix of egocentric fantasy, social influence, and innocent honesty—care must be taken to neither automatically believe nor disbelieve what children say.

Brain and Context

Many studies have found that a child's ability to develop theories correlates with neurological maturation, which also correlates with advances in executive processing—the reflective, anticipatory capacity of the mind (Mar, 2011; Baron-Cohen et al., 2013). Detailed brain studies find that theory of mind activates several areas of the brain (Koster-Hale & Saxe, 2014). This makes sense, as theory of mind is a complex ability that humans develop in social contexts, and thus is not likely to reside in just one neurological region.

Evidence for the crucial role of brain maturation comes from the other research on the same 3- to 5-year-olds whose lying was studied. The experimenters asked the children to say "day" when they saw a picture of the moon and "night" when they saw a picture of the sun.

Brothers and Sisters When every family had many children, as in this Western Australian family, even 3-year-olds had to learn when a brother was to be trusted not to move the chair.

The children needed to inhibit their automatic reaction, and the ability to do this indicates advanced executive function, which correlates with maturation of the prefrontal cortex. Even when compared to other children who were the same age, those who failed the day–night tests typically told impossible lies, whereas their age-mates who were high in executive function told more plausible lies (Evans et al., 2011).

Does the crucial role of neurological maturation make context irrelevant? No: Nurture is always important. For instance, research finds that language development fosters theory of mind, especially when mother–child conversations involve thoughts and wishes. Similarly, social interactions with other children advance a child's thinking process, especially when the other children are siblings of about the same age (McAlister & Peterson, 2013). As one expert quipped, "Two older siblings are worth about a year of chronological age" (Perner, 2000, p. 383).

As brothers and sisters argue, agree, compete, and cooperate, and as older siblings fool younger ones, it dawns on 3-year-olds that not everyone thinks as they do. Theory of mind advances. By age 5, siblings have learned to persuade their younger siblings to give them a toy, and they've learned how to gain parental sympathy by acting as if their older brothers and sisters have victimized them. Parents, beware: Asking, "Who started it?" may be irrelevant.

SUMMING UP Preoperational children, according to Piaget, can use symbolic thought but are illogical and egocentric, limited by the appearance of things and by their immediate experience. Their egocentrism occurs not because they are selfish, but because their minds are immature. Vygotsky realized that children are powerfully influenced by their social contexts, including their mentors and the cultures in which they live. In their zone of proximal development, children are ready to move beyond their current understanding, especially if deliberate or inadvertent scaffolding occurs.

Children use their cognitive abilities to develop theories about their experiences, as is evident in theory-theory and in theory of mind, which appears between ages 3 and 5. Humans of all ages seek to explain their observations and become more adept at understanding the thoughts and goals of other people. This seems to be the result of both brain maturation and experience.

WHAT HAVE YOU LEARNED?

1. What are the strengths of preoperational thought?
2. What is the difference between egocentrism in a child and selfishness in an adult?
3. How does guided participation increase a child's zone of proximal development?
4. Why did Vygotsky think that talking to oneself is not a sign of illness but an aid to cognition?
5. What factors spur the development of theory of mind?

// **Response for Social Scientists** (from page 288): According to Piaget, preschool children focus on appearance and on static conditions (so they cannot mentally reverse a process). Furthermore, they are egocentric, believing that everyone shares their point of view. No wonder they believe that they had always known the puppy was in the blue box and that Max would know that, too.

Language Learning

Learning language is the premier cognitive accomplishment of early childhood. Two-year-olds use short, telegraphic sentences ("Want cookie," "Where Daddy go?"), omitting adjectives, adverbs, and articles. By contrast, 5-year-olds seem able to say almost anything (see At About This Time).

at about this time

Language in Early Childhood*

Approximate Age	Characteristic or Achievement in First Language
2 years	*Vocabulary:* 100–2,000 words *Sentence length:* 2–6 words *Grammar:* Plurals; pronouns; many nouns, verbs, adjectives *Questions:* Many "What's that?" questions
3 years	*Vocabulary:* 1,000–5,000 words *Sentence length:* 3–8 words *Grammar:* Conjunctions, adverbs, articles *Questions:* Many "Why?" questions
4 years	*Vocabulary:* 3,000–10,000 words *Sentence length:* 5–20 words *Grammar:* Dependent clauses, tags at sentence end ("...didn't I?" "...won't you?") *Questions:* Peak of "Why?" questions; many "How?" and "When?" questions
6 years	*Vocabulary:* 5,000–30,000 words *Sentence length:* Some seem unending ("...and...who...and...that...and...") *Grammar:* Complex, depending on what the child has heard, with some children correctly using the passive voice ("Man bitten by dog") and subjunctive ("If I were...") *Questions:* Some about social differences (male–female, old–young, rich–poor) and many other issues

*These norms are based on middle-class children in the United States. Children of diverse backgrounds and contexts will differ, and even many middle-class U.S. children are slower or faster to reach these norms.

A Sensitive Time

Brain maturation, myelination, scaffolding, and social interaction make early childhood ideal for learning language. As you remember from Chapter 1, scientists once thought that early childhood was a *critical period* for language learning—the *only* time when a first language could be mastered and the best time to learn a second or third one.

It is easy to understand why they thought so. Young children have powerful motivation and ability to sort words and sounds into meaning (theory-theory), which makes them impressive language learners. For that reason, teachers and parents should converse with children many hours each day. However, the critical-period hypothesis is false: Many people learn a new language after age 6.

Instead, early childhood is a *sensitive period* for language learning—for rapidly and easily mastering vocabulary, grammar, and pronunciation. Young children are language sponges; they soak up every verbal drop they encounter.

Exactly how sensitive the preschool years are is still disputed (DeKeyser, 2013). There is no doubt that it is easier to learn a first or second language earlier than later, nor is there any doubt that some people learn a second language in adulthood. Adult language learning is harder, but not impossible.

Preoperational thinking—which is not logical—helps with language. For example, in a conversation I had with Asa, he said a toy lion was a mother. I said it couldn't be a mother because it had a mane. Rather than realizing that I might know something about male and female lions, and rather than asking about the

Video Activity: Language Acquisition in Young Children features video clips of a new sign language created by deaf Nicaraguan children and provides insights into how language evolves.

new word (mane), he confidently insisted that this particular lion was a mother with a mane.

Asa is not alone. One of the valuable (and sometimes frustrating) traits of young children is that they talk about many things to adults, to each other, to themselves, to their toys—unfazed by misuse, mispronunciation, ignorance, stuttering, and so on (Marazita & Merriman, 2010). Language comes easily partly because preoperational children are not self-critical about what they say. Egocentrism has advantages; this is one of them.

The Vocabulary Explosion

The average child knows about 500 words at age 2 and more than 10,000 at age 6 (Herschensohn, 2007). That's more than six new words a day. These are averages. Estimates of vocabulary size at age 6 vary from 5,000 to 30,000: Some children learn six times as many words as others. Always, however, vocabulary builds quickly, and comprehension is more extensive than speech.

It is not always easy to know how many words a child understands, in part because some tests of vocabulary are more stringent than others (Hoffman et al., 2013). For example, after children listened to a book about a raccoon that saw its reflection in the water, they were asked what "reflection" means. Here are five answers:

1. "It means that your reflection is yourself. It means that there is another person that looks just like you."
2. "Means if you see yourself in stuff and you see your reflection."
3. "Is like when you look in something, like water, you can see yourself."
4. "It mean your face go in the water."
5. "That means if you the same skin as him, you blend in." (Hoffman et al., 2013, pp. 13–14)

Which of these five children knows the vocabulary word? The correct answer to that question could be none, all, or some number in between.

In another example, when a story included "a chill ran down his spine," children were asked what chill meant. One child answered, "When you want to lay down and watch TV—and eat nachos" (Hoffman et al., 2013, p. 15). Correct?

Fast-Mapping

After painstakingly learning one word at a time between 12 and 18 months of age, children develop interconnected categories for words, a kind of grid or mental map that makes speedy vocabulary acquisition possible. Each of the children above answered the question: They thought they knew the word, and they sort of did.

Learning a word after one exposure is called **fast-mapping** (Woodward & Markman, 1998). Rather than figuring out the exact definition after hearing it in several contexts, children hear a word once and quickly stick it into a category in their mental language grid. They think they understand it.

Language mapping is not precise. For example, children rapidly connect new animal names close to already-known animal names, without knowing all the details. Thus, *tiger* is easy to map if you know *lion*, but a leopard might be called a tiger. A trip to the zoo facilitates fast-mapping of animal names because zoos scaffold learning by placing similar animals near each other.

All preschoolers can fast map words, but some children are quicker than others, and some words are easier than others. A study that tested young children's ability to fast-map two made-up words (koob and tade) found that it was easier to remem-

fast-mapping The speedy and sometimes imprecise way in which children learn new words by tentatively placing them in mental categories according to their perceived meaning.

ber the unusual word (koob) because it was less likely to be confused with other similar-sounding words (Weismer et al., 2013).

Picture books offer many opportunities to advance vocabulary through scaffolding and fast-mapping. A mentor might encourage the next steps in the child's zone of proximal development, such as that tigers have stripes and leopards spots, or, for an older child, that calico cats are almost always female and that lions with manes are always male.

This process explains children's learning of color words. Generally, 2-year-olds already know some color words, but they fast-map them (K. Wagner et al., 2013). For instance, "blue" could be used for some greens or grays. It is not that children cannot see the hues. Instead, they apply words they know to broad categories, and they have not yet learned the boundaries that adults use.

Thus, all women may be called mothers, all cats can be kitties, and all bright colors red. As one team of scientists explains, adult color words are the result of slow-mapping (K. Wagner et al., 2013), which is not what young children do.

Words and the Limits of Logic

Closely related to fast-mapping is a phenomenon called *logical extension*: After learning a word, children use it to describe other objects in the same category. One child told her father she had seen some "Dalmatian cows" on a school trip to a farm. Instead of criticizing her foolishness, he remembered the Dalmatian dog she had petted the weekend before and realized that she saw Holstein cows, not Jersey ones.

Bilingual children who don't know a word in the language they are speaking often insert a word from the other language, code-switching in the middle of a sentence instead of the usual code-switching that occurs when the context changes. That mid-sentence switch may be considered wrong, but actually that is evidence of the child's drive to communicate.

To call it "Spanglish" when a Spanish-speaking person uses some English words deprecates a logical way to explain something (Otheguy & Stern, 2010). Soon, children realize who understands which language, and they avoid substitutions when speaking to a monolingual person. That illustrates theory of mind.

Some English words are particularly difficult for every child to use correctly—*who/whom, have been/had been, here/there, yesterday/tomorrow*. More than one child has awakened on Christmas morning and asked, "Is it tomorrow yet?" A child told to "stay there" or "come here" may not follow instructions because the terms are confusing. It might be better to say, "Stay there on that bench" or "Come here to hold my hand." Every language has difficult concepts that are expressed in words; children everywhere learn them eventually.

Extensive study of children's language abilities finds that fast-mapping is only one of many techniques that children use to learn language. When a word does not refer to an object on the mental map, children find other ways to master it (Carey, 2010). If a word does not refer to anything the child can see or otherwise sense or act on, it may be ignored. Always, however, action helps. A hole is to dig; love is hugging; hearts beat.

Acquiring Grammar

Remember from Chapter 6 that *grammar* includes structures, techniques, and rules that communicate meaning. Knowledge of grammar is essential for learning to speak, read, and write. A large vocabulary is useless unless a person knows how to put words together. Each language has its own grammar rules; that's one reason children speak in one-word sentences first.

Brain and Basics

By age 2, children understand the basics. For example, English-speaking children know word order (subject/verb/object), saying, "I eat apple," rather than any of the five other possible sequences of those three words. They use plurals, tenses (past, present, and future), and nominative, objective, and possessive pronouns (*I, me,* and *mine* or *my*).

Children apply rules of grammar as soon as they figure them out, using their own theories about how language works and their experience regarding when and how often various rules apply (Meltzoff & Gopnik, 2013). For example, English-speaking children quickly learn to add an *s* to form the plural: Toddlers follow that rule when they ask for two cookies or more blocks.

Soon they add an *s* to make the plural of words they have never heard before, even nonsense words. If preschoolers are shown a drawing of an abstract shape, told it is called a *wug,* and are then shown two of these shapes, they say there are two *wugs.* Children realize words have a singular and a plural before they use that grammar form themselves (Zapf & Smith, 2007).

One reason for variation in particulars of language learning is that several parts of the brain are involved, each myelinating at a distinct rate. Furthermore, many genes and alleles affect comprehension and expression. In general, genes affect *expressive* (spoken or written) language more than *receptive* (heard or read) language. Thus, some children are relatively talkative or quiet because they inherit that tendency, but experience (not genes) determines what they understand. For that, parents and teachers are crucial.

Grammar Mistakes

Sometimes children apply the rules of grammar when they should not. This error is called **overregularization.** By age 4, many children overregularize that final *s,* talking about *foots, tooths,* and *mouses.* This signifies knowledge, not stupidity: Many children first say words correctly (*feet, teeth, mice*), repeating what they have heard. Later, they are smart enough to apply the rules of grammar, and overregularize, assuming that all constructions follow the rules (Ramscar & Dye, 2011). The child who says, "I goed to the store" needs to hear, "Oh, you went to the store?" rather than criticism.

More difficult to learn is an aspect of language called **pragmatics**—knowing which words, tones, and grammatical forms to use with whom (Siegal & Surian, 2012). In some languages, it is essential to know which set of words to use when a person is older or not a close friend or family member.

For example, French children learn the difference between *tu* and *vous* in early childhood. Although both words mean "you," *tu* is used with familiar people, while *vous* is the more formal expression (as well as the plural expression). In other languages, children learn that there are two words for grandmother, depending on whose mother she is.

English does not make those distinctions, but pragmatics is important for early-childhood learning nonetheless. Children learn that there are many practical differences in vocabulary and tone depending on the context and, once theory of mind is established, on the audience.

Knowledge of pragmatics is evident when a 4-year-old pretends to be a doctor, a teacher, or a parent. Each role requires different speech. On the other hand, children often blurt out questions that embarrass their parents ("Why is that lady so fat?" or "I don't want to kiss grandpa because his breath smells"): The pragmatics of polite speech require more social understanding than many young children possess.

overregularization The application of rules of grammar even when exceptions occur, making the language seem more "regular" than it actually is.

pragmatics The practical use of language that includes the ability to adjust language communication according to audience and context.

Learning Two Languages

Language-minority people (those who speak a language that is not their nation's dominant one) suffer if they do not also speak the majority language. In the United States, those who are not proficient in English have lower school achievement, diminished self-esteem, and inadequate employment, as well as many other problems. Fluency in English can erase these liabilities; fluency in another language then becomes an asset.

In the United States in 2011, 22 percent of schoolchildren spoke a language other than English at home, with most of them (77 percent) also speaking English well, according to their parents (U.S. Census Bureau, 2011) (see Figure 9.3). The percentage of bilingual children is higher in many other nations. In many African, Asian, and European nations, by sixth grade most schoolchildren are bilingual, and some are trilingual.

How and Why

Unlike a century ago, everyone now seeking U.S. citizenship must be able to speak English. Some people believe that national unity is threatened by language-minority speakers. By contrast, other people emphasize that international understanding is crucial and that ideally, everyone should speak several languages.

Should a nation have one official language, several, or none? Individuals and nations have divergent answers. Switzerland has three official languages; Canada has two; India has one national language (Hindi), but many states of India also have their own, for a total of 28 official languages; the United States has none.

Some adults fear that young children who are taught two languages might become semilingual, not bilingual, "at risk for delayed, incomplete, and possibly even impaired language development" (Genesee, 2008, p. 17). Others have used their own experience to argue the opposite, that "there is absolutely no evidence that children get confused if they learn two languages" (Genesee, 2008, p. 18).

This second position has much more research support. Soon after the vocabulary explosion, children who have heard two languages since birth usually master two distinct sets of words and grammar, along with each language's pauses, pronunciations, intonations, and gestures. Proficiency is directly related to how much language they hear (Hoff et al., 2012).

Early childhood is the best time to learn languages. Neuroscience finds that for adults who mastered two languages when they were young, both languages are located in the same areas of the brain with no impact on the cortex structure (Klein et al., 2014). They manage to keep the two languages separate, activating one and temporarily inhibiting the other when speaking to a monolingual person. They may

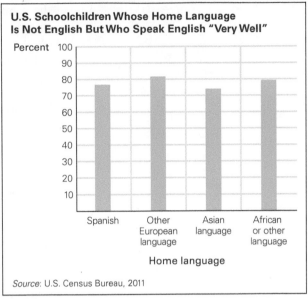

U.S. Schoolchildren Whose Home Language Is Not English But Who Speak English "Very Well"

Source: U.S. Census Bureau, 2011

FIGURE 9.3

Mastering English: The Younger, the Better Of all the schoolchildren whose home language is not English, this is the proportion who, according to their parents, speak English well. Immigrant children who attend school almost always master English within five years.

Camels Protected, People Confused Why the contrasting signs? Does everyone read English at the international airport in Chicago (O'Hare) but not on the main road in Tunisia?

be a millisecond slower to respond when they must switch languages, but their brains function better overall. Being bilingual benefits the brain lifelong, further evidence for plasticity. Indeed, the bilingual brain may provide some resistance to Alzheimer's dementia in old age (Costa & Sebastián-Gallés, 2014).

Learning a "foreign" language in high school or college, as required of most U.S. children, is too late for fluency. After childhood, the logic of language is possible to grasp, so adults can learn the rules of forming the past tense, for instance. However, pronunciation, idioms, and exceptions to the rules are confusing and rarely mastered after puberty. The human brain is designed to learn language best in childhood.

Do not equate pronunciation and spoken fluency with comprehension and reading ability. Many adults who speak the majority language with an accent are nonetheless proficient in the language and culture (difference is not deficit). From infancy on, hearing is more acute than vocalization. Almost all young children mispronounce whatever language they speak, blithely unaware of their mistakes.

For example, almost all young children transpose sounds (*magazine* becomes *mazagine*), drop consonants (*truck* becomes *ruck*), convert difficult sounds to easier ones (*father* becomes *fadder*), and drop complex sounds (*cherry* become *terry*). Mispronunciation does not impair fluency primarily because young children are more receptive than expressive—they hear better than they talk. For instance, when 4-year-old Rachel asked for a "yeyo yayipop," her father repeated, "You want a yeyo yayipop?" She replied, "Daddy, sometimes you talk funny."

Language Loss and Gains

Schools in all nations stress the dominant language, sometimes exclusively. Consequently, language-minority parents fear that their children will make a *language shift,* becoming more fluent in the school language than in their home language, which might be forgotten. Language shift occurs everywhere if theory-theory leads children to conclude that their first language is inferior to the new one (Bhatia & Ritchie, 2013).

Some language-minority children in Mexico shift to Spanish, some children of Canada's First Nations (as native peoples are called there) shift to French, some children in the United States shift to English. In China, all speak some form of Chinese, but some shift occurs from Mandarin, Cantonese, and so on to another.

No shift is inevitable: The attitudes and practices of parents and the community are crucial. Another crucial aspect is cohort, as shown by a multi-faceted study of children who switched from Bangla to English when they entered primary school in London. Those children, now adult, often no longer teach their children the language and the customs of their parents (Rasinger et al., 2013).

Remember that young children are preoperational: They center on the immediate status of their language (not on future usefulness or past glory), on appearance more than substance. No wonder many shift toward the language of the dominant culture.

Since language is integral to culture, if a child is to become fluently bilingual, everyone who speaks with the child should show appreciation of both cultures, and children need to hear twice as much talk as usual (Hoff et al., 2012). If the parents do not speak the majority language, they benefit their child's learning by talking, listening, and playing with the child extensively in the home language. Learning one language well makes it easier to learn another (Hoff et al., 2014).

Bilingual Learners These are Chinese children learning a second language. Could this be in the United States? No, this is a class in the first Chinese-Hungarian school in Budapest. There are three clues: the spacious classroom, the trees outside, and the letters on the book.

ATTILA KISBENEDEK/AFP/GETTY IMAGES

The same practices can make a child fluently trilingual, as some 5-year-olds are. One parent might spend hours each day talking and reading to a child in French, for instance, the other parent in English, and that child might play with friends and learn from teachers at a Spanish-speaking preschool.

The extent of exposure is crucial: Unfortunately it is typical for one parent to speak with the child much less than the other, and the child's language learning reflects that deficit (MacLeod et al., 2013). If a young child is immersed in three languages, he or she may speak all three without an accent—except whatever accent their mother, father, and friends have.

Listening, Talking, and Reading

Because understanding the printed word is crucial, a meta-analysis of about 300 studies analyzed which activities in early childhood aided reading later on. Both vocabulary and phonics (precise awareness of the sounds of words) predicted literacy (Shanahan & Lonigan, 2010). Five specific strategies and experiences were particularly effective for children of all income levels, languages, and ethnicities.

1. *Code-focused teaching.* In order for children to read, they must "break the code" from spoken to written words. It helps if they learn the letters and sounds of the alphabet (e.g., "A, alligators all around" or, conventionally, "B is for baby").
2. *Book reading.* Vocabulary as well as familiarity with pages and print will increase when adults read to children, allowing questions and conversation.
3. *Parent education.* When teachers and other professionals teach parents how to stimulate cognition (as in book reading), children become better readers. Adults need to use words to expand vocabulary. Unfortunately, too often adults use words primarily to control ("don't touch"; "stop that"), not to teach.
4. *Language enhancement.* Within each child's zone of proximal development, mentors can expand vocabulary and grammar, based on the child's knowledge and experience.
5. *Preschool programs.* Children learn from teachers, songs, excursions, and other children. (We discuss variations of early education next, but every study finds that preschools advance language acquisition.)

SUMMING UP   Children learn language rapidly and well during early childhood, with an explosion of vocabulary and mastery of many grammatical constructions. Fast-mapping is one way children learn. Overregularization, mispronunciation, and errors in precision are common and are not problematic at this age. Instead, practical communication skills advance.

Young children can learn two languages almost as easily as one if adults talk frequently, listen carefully, and value both languages. In brain development, children benefit from learning two languages. However, some children whose parents speak a minority language undergo a language shift, abandoning their first language. Others never master a second language because they were not exposed to one during the sensitive time for language learning.

WHAT HAVE YOU LEARNED?

1. What is the evidence that early childhood is a sensitive time for learning language?
2. How does fast-mapping aid the language explosion?
3. How does overregularization signify a cognitive advance?
4. What in language learning shows the limitations of logic in early childhood?
5. What are the advantages of teaching a child two languages?
6. How can the language shift be avoided?

Especially for Immigrant Parents You want your children to be fluent in the language of your family's new country, even though you do not speak that language well. Should you speak to your children in your native tongue or in the new language? (see response, page 300)

Early-Childhood Schooling

Today, every nation provides early-childhood education. It may be financed by the government or privately. It may be for a privileged few or for almost every child (Georgeson & Payler, 2013).

In France, Denmark, Norway, and Sweden, more than 95 percent of all 3- to 5-year-olds are enrolled in government-sponsored schools. Norway also pays for education for 1- and 2-year-olds, and 80 percent of them attend (Ellingsaeter, 2014). The reasons for the international variations are historical, economic, and political, but one message from child development research has reached almost every parent and politician worldwide—young children are amazingly capable and eager to learn.

Homes and Schools

Developmental research does not translate directly into specific practices in early education, so no program can legitimately claim to be exactly what Piaget or Vygotsky would prescribe (Hatch, 2012). It seems fair to say that developmental theories and understanding of children can inspire educators, suggest hypotheses, and advance ideas, but applications to each child depend on analysis and reflection.

Beyond the amazing potential of young children to learn, another robust conclusion from research on children's learning seems not yet universally understood: Quality matters (Gambaro et al., 2014). If the home learning environment is poor, a good preschool program aids health, cognition, and social skills. If, instead, a family provides excellent education, children still may benefit from attending a high-quality preschool, but not as much as less fortunate children.

Indeed, it is better for children to be in excellent home care than in a low-quality, overcrowded day-care center. One expert criticizes inadequate subsidies that result in low-quality care: "Parents can find cheap babysitting that's bad for their kids on their own. They don't need government help with that (Barnett, quoted in Samuels & Klein, 2013, p. 21).

Quality is difficult to judge, and competition does not necessarily improve it: "[B]ecause quality is hard for parents to observe, competition seems dominated by price." To save money and make a profit, programs hire fewer teachers—so saving money may reduce quality (Gambaro et al., 2014, p. 22).

The United States has some excellent early-childhood programs, but most are not that good (Magnuson & Waldfogel, 2014). It is a mistake to conclude that mother care is better than care by another relative or nonrelative, or vice versa. Some mothers are fabulous, others disastrous. The same is true for fathers, grandmothers, day-care centers (unless strictly regulated by the government), and so on.

Quality cannot be judged by the name of a program or by its sponsorship. Educational institutions for 3- to 5-year-olds are called preschools, nursery schools, day-care centers, pre-primary programs, pre-K classes, and kindergartens. Sponsors can be public (federal, state, or city), private, religious, or corporate. Further, children, parents, and cultures differ, so an excellent program for one child might be less effective for another.

Professional assessment of quality also seems inadequate, if the goal of preschool is to further math, reading, and social skills (Sabol et al., 2013). However, one aspect—child-teacher interaction—does correlate with more learning. A bad sign is a teacher who sits and watches; look for teachers who talk, laugh, guide, and play with the children.

In order to sort through this variety, we review here some of the distinctions among types of programs. One broad distinction concerns the program goals. Is it designed to encourage creative individuality, in which case it may be called *child-centered*; or is it to prepare the child for formal education, in which case it may be called *teacher-directed*; or is it to give skills to low-SES children so they can learn in school, in which case it is an intervention program (such as *Head Start*).

Child-Centered Programs

Many programs are called *child-centered*, or *developmental*, because they stress each child's development and growth. Teachers in such programs believe children need to follow their own interests rather than adult directions. For example, they agree that "children should be allowed to select many of their own activities from a variety of learning areas that the teacher has prepared" (Lara-Cinisomo et al., 2011). The physical space and the materials (such as dress-up clothes, art supplies, puzzles, blocks, and other toys) are arranged to allow exploration.

Most child-centered programs encourage artistic expression. Some educators argue that young children are gifted in seeing the world more imaginatively than older people do. According to advocates of child-centered programs, this peak of creative vision should be encouraged; children need many opportunities to tell stories, draw pictures, dance, and make music for their own delight.

That does not mean that academics are ignored. Advocates of math learning, for instance, believe that children have a natural interest in numbers and that child-centered schools can guide those interests as children grow (Stipek, 2013).

Child-centered programs are often influenced by Piaget, who emphasized that each child will discover new ideas if given a chance, or by Vygotsky, who thought that children learn from other children, with adult guidance. Some childhood educators believe that Piaget and Vygotsky advocate opposite approaches, with Piaget less likely to want the teacher to guide and instruct the child. Both, however, seek to bring out the child's inner strengths, so both can be considered child-centered.

"We teach them that the world can be an unpredictable, dangerous, and sometimes frightening place, while being careful not to spoil their lovely innocence. It's tricky."

Tricky Indeed Young children are omnivorous learners, picking up habits, curses, and attitudes that adults would rather not transmit. Deciding what to teach—by actions more than words—is essential.

Especially for Teachers In trying to find a preschool program, what should parents look for? (see response, page 301)

Especially for Unemployed Early-Childhood Teachers You are offered a job in a program that has ten 3-year-olds for every one adult. You know that is too many, but you want a job. What should you do? (see response, page 301)

Tibet, China, India, and . . . Italy? Over the past half-century, as China increased its control of Tibet, thousands of refugees fled to northern India. Tibet traditionally had no preschools, but young children adapt quickly, as in this preschool program in Ladakh, India. This Tibetan boy is working on a classic Montessori board.

Montessori Schools

One type of child-centered school began in the slums of Rome in 1907, when Maria Montessori opened a nursery school (Standing, 1998). She believed that children needed structured, individualized projects to give them a sense of accomplishment. Her students completed puzzles, used sponges and water to clean tables, traced shapes, and so on.

Contemporary **Montessori schools** still emphasize individual pride and achievement, presenting many literacy-related tasks (e.g., outlining letters and looking at books) to young children. Specific materials differ from those that Montessori developed, but the underlying philosophy is the same. Children seek out learning tasks; they do not sit quietly in groups while a teacher instructs them. That makes Montessori programs child-centered (Lillard, 2013).

This philosophy seems to work. A study of 5-year-olds in inner-city Milwaukee who were chosen by lottery to attend Montessori programs found that the children were advanced in prereading (such as recognizing letters), math, and theory of mind, compared with their peers in other schools (Lillard & Else-Quest, 2006).

Some benefits became more apparent by middle school (a phenomenon called a *sleeper effect,* because the benefits seem to hibernate for a while) (Lillard, 2013). The probable explanation: Montessori tasks lead to self-confidence, curiosity, and exploration, which eventually motivate children to learn to read, calculate, and so on.

Reggio Emilia

Another form of early-childhood education is **Reggio Emilia,** named after the town in Italy where it began. In Reggio Emilia, children are encouraged to master skills that are not usually taught in North American schools until age 7 or so, such as writing and using tools (hammers, knives, and so on).

Reggio schools do not provide large-group instruction, with lessons in, say, forming letters or cutting paper. Instead, "Every child is a creative child, full of potential" (Gandini et al., 2005, p. 1), with personal learning needs and artistic drives. Measurement of achievement, such as standardized testing to see whether children recognize the 26 letters of the alphabet, is antithetical to the conviction that each child should explore and learn in his or her own way. Each child's learning is documented via scrapbooks, photos, and daily notes—not to measure progress, but to help the child and the parent take pride in accomplishments (Caruso, 2013).

Appreciation of the arts is evident. Every Reggio Emilia school originally had a studio, an artist, and space to encourage creativity (Forbes, 2012). Consequently, as more schools in many nations follow the Reggio Emilia model, they all should have a large central room with many hubs of activity and a low child/adult ratio. Children's art is displayed on white walls and hung from high ceilings, and floor-

Montessori schools Schools that offer early-childhood education based on the philosophy of Maria Montessori, which emphasizes careful work and tasks that each young child can do.

Reggio Emilia A program of early-childhood education that originated in the town of Reggio Emilia, Italy, and that encourages each child's creativity in a carefully designed setting.

// **Response for Immigrant Parents** (from page 297): Children learn by listening, so it is important to speak with them often. Depending on how comfortable you are with the new language, you might prefer to read to your children, sing to them, and converse with them primarily in your native language and find a good preschool where they will learn the new language. The worst thing you could do would be to restrict speech in either tongue.

ELIZABETH FLORES KRT/NEWSCOM

Child-Centered Pride How could Rachel Koepke, a 3-year-old from a Wisconsin town called Pleasant Prairie, seem so pleased that her hands (and cuffs) are blue? The answer arises from northern Italy—Rachel attended a Reggio Emilia preschool that encourages creative expression.

to-ceiling windows open to a spacious, plant-filled playground. Big mirrors are part of the schools' décor—again, with the idea of fostering individuality and self-expression. However, individuality does not mean that children do not work together. On the contrary, group projects are encouraged.

Often those group projects include exploring some aspect of the natural world. One analysis of Reggio Emilia in the United States found "a science-rich context that triggered and supported preschoolers' inquiries and effectively engaged preschoolers' hands, heads, and hearts with science" (Inan et al., 2010, p. 1186).

Teacher-Directed Programs

Teacher-directed preschools stress academics, often taught by one adult to the entire group. The curriculum includes learning the names of letters, numbers, shapes, and colors according to a set timetable; every child naps, snacks, and goes to the bathroom on schedule as well. Children learn to sit quietly and listen to the teacher. Praise and other reinforcements are given for good behavior, and time-outs (brief separation from activities) are imposed to punish misbehavior.

In teacher-directed programs, the serious work of schooling is distinguished from the unstructured play of home. According to a study of preschool educators, some teachers endorse ideas that indicate their teacher-directed philosophy, such as that children should form letters correctly before they are allowed to write a story (Lara-Cinisomo et al., 2011).

The goal of teacher-directed programs is to make all children "ready to learn" when they enter elementary school. For that reason, basic skills are stressed, including precursors to reading, writing, and arithmetic, perhaps through teachers asking questions that children answer together in unison. Behavior is also taught, as children learn to respect adults, to follow schedules, to hold hands when they go on outings, and so on.

Children practice forming letters, sounding out words, counting objects, and writing their names. If a 4-year-old learns to read, that is success. (In a child-centered program, that might arouse suspicion that there was too little time to play

// Response for Teachers (from page 299): Tell parents to look at the people more than the program. Parents should see the children in action and note whether the teachers show warmth and respect for each child.

// Response for Unemployed Early-Childhood Teachers (from page 299): It would be best for you to wait for a job in a program where children learn well, organized along the lines explained in this chapter. You would be happier, as well as learn more, in a workplace that is good for children. Realistically, though, you might feel compelled to take the job. If you do, change the child/adult ratio—find a helper, perhaps a college intern or a volunteer grandmother. But choose carefully—some adults are not helpful at all. Before you take the job, remember that children need continuity: You can't leave simply because you find something better.

Learning from One Another Every nation creates its own version of early education. In this scene at a nursery school in Kuala Lumpur, Malaysia, note the head coverings, uniforms, and distance between the sexes. None of these elements would be found in most early-childhood-education classrooms in North America or Europe.

or socialize.) Good behavior, not informal social interaction, is rewarded—leading one critic to suggest that "readiness" is too narrowly defined (Winter, 2011).

Many teacher-directed programs were inspired by behaviorism, which emphasizes step-by-step learning and repetition, with reinforcement (praise, gold stars, prizes) for accomplishment. Another inspiration for teacher-directed programs comes from information-processing research indicating that children who have not learned basic vocabulary and listening skills by kindergarten often fall behind in primary school. Many state legislatures mandate that preschoolers master specific concepts, an outcome best achieved by teacher-directed learning (Bracken & Crawford, 2010).

Comparing Child-Centered and Teacher-Directed Programs

Most developmentalists advocate child-centered programs. They fear that the child's joy and creativity will be squashed if there are specific goals set for all children. As Penelope Leach wrote: "Goals come from the outside. . . . It is important that people see early learning as coming from inside children because that's what makes clear its interconnectedness with play, and therefore the inappropriateness of many 'learning goals'" (Leach, 2011, p. 17).

Many developmentalists resist legislative standards and academic tests for young children, arguing that social skills and creative play are essential for healthy development but difficult to measure. (**Developmental Link:** Children's play is discussed in Chapter 10.) Finding the right balance between formal and informal assessment, and between child-centered and teacher-directed learning, is a goal of many educators as they try to ensure that each child has the learning environment that works best for him or her (Fuligni et al., 2012).

Teachers' classroom behaviors do not necessarily follow what developmentalists recommend (Tonyan et al., 2013). Even teachers who say they are child-centered—especially if they are novice teachers—tend to be quite teacher-directed. They might tell children what to do instead of asking them their ideas. Teachers with more experience or training are more often consistent in belief and behavior—and teacher-directed (Wen et al., 2011).

The pressure for teachers to instruct, not facilitate, also comes from many parents. Those who are immigrants from Africa, Asia, and Latin America are particularly likely to want their children to learn academic skills and respect adult authority. Thus, they often seek teacher-directed preschools instead of child-centered ones. That may explain enrollment statistics from Norwegian preschools, which tend to be child-centered. Although Norwegian schools are free beginning at age 1, among immigrants, 92 percent of Western European, North American, and Australian 1- to 5-year-olds attend, compared to only 70 percent of those from other continents (Ellingsaeter, 2014).

Cultural differences may be crucial. Historically in China, teacher-directed curricula were the norm, with expectations for basic skills that every child should learn. Preschool children still wear uniforms, follow schedules, and so on, all set by the teachers and higher authorities, in accord with the culture. Recently, the Chinese government decided that young children needed to be more creative (Vong, 2013). However, implementation of creativity in China is not what a North American teacher would expect.

One teacher thought she was following that new directive by allowing the children to draw their own pictures. First, she fried an egg in view of the class and asked the children to draw an egg. "Most children drew a big one and colored the centre of the egg a bright yellow color. Some drew several small ones. When a child mixed yellow with white colors, the teacher corrected her" (Vong, 2013, p. 185).

Preparing for School

Several programs designed for children from low-SES families were established in the United States decades ago. Some solid research on the results of these programs is now available.

Head Start

In the early 1960s, millions of young children in the United States were thought to need a "head start" on their formal education to foster better health and cognition before first grade. Consequently since 1965, the federal government has funded a massive program for 4-year-olds called **Head Start.**

The goals for Head Start have changed over the decades, from lifting families out of poverty to promoting literacy, from providing dental care and immunizations to teaching Standard English. Although initially most Head Start programs were child-centered, they have become increasingly teacher-directed as waves of legislators have approved and shaped them. Children learn whatever their Head Start teachers and curricula emphasize. Not surprisingly, specific results vary by program and cohort.

For example, many low-income 3- and 4-year-olds in the United States are not normally exposed to math. After one Head Start program engaged children in a board game with numbers, their mathematical understanding advanced significantly (Siegler, 2009).

A 2007 congressional reauthorization of funding for Head Start included a requirement for extensive evaluation to answer two questions:

1. What difference does Head Start make to key outcomes of development and learning (in particular, school readiness) for low-income children? How does Head Start affect parental practices?
2. Under what circumstances and for whom does Head Start achieve the greatest impact?

The answers were not as dramatic as either advocates or detractors had hoped (U.S. Department of Health and Human Services, 2010). Head Start improved literacy and math skills, oral health, and parental responsiveness during early childhood. However, many academic benefits faded by first grade.

One explanation is that, unlike when Head Start began, many children in the comparison group were enrolled in other early-childhood programs—sometimes excellent ones, sometimes not. Another explanation is the elementary schools for low-SES children were of low quality, so the Head Start children sank back to the norm.

The research found that benefits were strongest for children with the lowest family incomes, for those living in rural areas, and for those with disabilities (U.S. Department of Health and Human Services, 2010). These children were least likely to find other sources of early education. Most Head

> **Head Start** A federally funded early-childhood intervention program for low-income children of preschool age.

Disaster Recovery The success of Head Start led to Early Head Start for children such as this 2-year-old in Biloxi, Mississippi. When Hurricane Katrina destroyed most of the community, it was the first educational program to reopen. Since a family is a system, not just a collection of individuals, this Head Start program is helping parents as well as entire families recover.

Start children advanced in language and social skills, but by elementary school, the comparison children often caught up, with one exception: Head Start children were still ahead in vocabulary.

That finding also supports what you know about language development. Any good preschool will introduce children to words they would not learn at home. Children will fast-map those words, gaining a linguistic knowledge base that facilitates expanded vocabulary throughout life.

A recent study of children born in 2001 found that those who went to Head Start were advanced in math and language, but, compared to similar children who had only their mother's care, they had more behavior problems, according to their teachers (R. Lee et al., 2014). Of course, one interpretation of that result is that the teachers reacted negatively to the self-assertion of the Head Start children, rating the children's attitude a problem when really it was the teachers who had the problem.

National data have discovered something that even defenders of Head Start find problematic. Many Hispanic children are from low-income families and hence eligible for Head Start. However, relatively few of them participate.

There are many plausible reasons for this. One reason is fear of deportation. Although almost all young Latinos are citizens, their parents might be afraid that enrolling them would jeopardize other members of the family. Another reason is that the parents may be unaware of the educational benefits of preschool education. A third reason may be that, since few Head Start teachers speak Spanish, parents and teachers have difficulty communicating, so parents stay away. For whatever reason, many children from Spanish-speaking homes avoid preschool and enter kindergarten with poor English language skills, creating problems that are discussed in Chapters 12 and 15.

Long-Term Gains from Intensive Programs

This discussion of philosophies, practices, and programs may give the impression that the research on early-childhood cognition is contradictory. That is not true. Specifics are debatable, but empirical evidence and longitudinal evaluation find that preschool education advances learning. Ideally, each program has a curriculum that guides practice, all the adults collaborate, and experienced teachers respond to each child.

The best evidence comes from three longitudinal programs that enrolled children for years, sometimes beginning with home visits in infancy, sometimes continuing in after-school programs through first grade. One program, called *Perry* (or *High/Scope*), was spearheaded in Michigan (Schweinhart & Weikart, 1997); another, called *Abecedarian,* got its start in North Carolina (Campbell et al., 2001); a third, called *Child–Parent Centers,* began in Chicago (Reynolds, 2000). Because of the political context that existed when these programs began, all were focused on children from low-SES families.

All three programs compared experimental groups of children with matched control groups and reached the same conclusion: Early education has substantial long-term benefits that become most apparent when children are in the third grade or later. By age 10, children who had been enrolled in any one of these three programs scored higher on math and reading achievement tests than did other children from the same backgrounds, schools, and neighborhoods. They were less likely to be placed in special classes for children with special needs or to repeat a year of school.

An advantage of decades of longitudinal research is that teenagers and adults who received early education can be compared with those who did not. For all three programs, early investment paid off. In adolescence, the children who had

undergone intensive preschool education had higher aspirations, possessed a greater sense of achievement, and were less likely to have been abused. As young adults, they were more likely to attend college and less likely to go to jail. As middle-aged adults, they were more often employed, paying taxes, healthy, and not needing government subsidies (Reynolds & Ou, 2011; Schweinhart et al., 2005; Campbell et al., 2014).

All three research projects found that providing direct cognitive training, with specific instruction in various school-readiness skills, was useful. Each child's needs and talents were considered—a circumstance made possible because the child/adult ratio was low. This combined child-centered and teacher-directed programs, with all the teachers trained together and cooperating, so children were not confused. Teachers involved parents in their children's education, and each program included strategies to enhance the home–school connection.

These programs were expensive (ranging from $6,000 to $18,000 annually per child in 2014 dollars). From a developmental perspective, the decreased need for special education and other social services later on made early education a "wise investment" (Duncan & Magnuson, 2013, p. 128). Additional benefits to society over the child's lifetime, including increased employment and tax revenues, as well as reduced crime, are worth much more than the cost of the programs.

The greatest lifetime return came from boys from high-poverty neighborhoods in the Chicago preschool program: The social benefit over their lifetime was more than 12 times the cost (Reynolds et al., 2011). Unfortunately costs are immediate and benefits are long-term. Consequently, some legislators and voters are unwilling to fund expensive intervention programs that do not pay off until decades later.

That may be changing. In some nations, preschool education is now considered a right, not a privilege: Young children from families of all incomes are educated without cost to the parents. Beyond those nations already mentioned, many others offer everyone some free preschool or give parents a child-care subsidy. For example, England provides 15 free hours per week, New Zealand 20, and Canada pays $100 a month for each child under age 6.

Among developed nations, the United States is an outlier, least likely to support new mothers or young children. However in the past decade, some states (e.g., Oklahoma, Georgia, Florida, New Jersey, and Illinois) and some cities (e.g., New York, Boston, Cleveland, San Antonio, Los Angeles) have offered preschool to every 4-year-old. Although this investment generally results in fewer children needing special education later on, implementation and results are controversial—a topic for further research.

As of 2012, 40 states sponsored some public education for young children—usually only for 4-year-olds. In 2012–2013, more than a million children (1,338,737) attended state-sponsored preschools, including Head Start. That is 28 percent of all 4-year-olds, twice as many as a decade earlier (Barnett et al., 2013).

Most state programs pay only for children living in poverty, but many wealthy families pay tuition for preschool education. Private schools may be very expensive—as much as $30,000 a year. Not surprisingly, in the United States, families in the highest income quartile are more likely to have their 3- and 4-year-olds in an educational program (see Visualizing Development, p. 306).

The increases in preschool for 4-year-olds is good news, but developmentalists wish more younger children were in good preschools. In contrast to years past, much more is known about what young children can learn; 2- and 3-year-olds are capable of learning languages, concepts, and much else. What a child learns before age 6 is pivotal for later schooling and adult life. The amazing potential of young children is also a theme of the next chapter, where we discuss other kinds of learning—in emotional regulation, social skills, and more.

Early-Childhood Schooling

Preschool can be an academic and social benefit to children. Around the world, increasing numbers of children are enrolled in early-childhood-education programs.

Early-childhood-education programs are described as "teacher-directed" or "child-centered," but in reality, most teachers' styles reflect a combination of both approaches. Some students benefit more from the order and structure of a teacher-directed classroom, while others work better in a more collaborative and creative environment.

TEACHER-DIRECTED APPROACH

Focused on Getting Preschoolers Ready to Learn

Direct instruction

Teacher as formal authority

Students learn by listening

Classroom is orderly and quiet

Teacher fully manages lesssons

Fosters autonomy of each individual

Encourages academics

Students learn from teacher

CHILD-CENTERED APPROACH

Focused on Individual Development and Growth

Teacher as facilitator

Teacher as delegator

Students learn actively

Classroom is designed for collaborative work

Students influence content

Fosters collaboration among students

Encourages artistic expression

Students learn from each other

PHOTO: ©2016 MACMILLAN

DIFFERENT STUDENTS, DIFFERENT TEACHERS

There is clearly no "one right way" to teach children. Each approach has potential benefits and pitfalls. A classroom full of creative, self-motivated students can thrive when a gifted teacher acts as a competent facilitator. But students who are distracted or annoyed by noise, or who are shy or intimidated by other children, can blossom under an engaging and encouraging teacher in a more traditional environment.

Well Done

- engaging teacher
- clear, consistent assessment
- reading and math skills emphasized
- quiet, orderly classroom
- all students treated equally

- emphasizes social skills and emotion regulation
- encourages critical thinking
- builds communication skills
- fosters individual achievement
- encourages creativity and curiosity

Teacher-Directed ⟵   ⟶ **Child-Centered**

- bored students
- passive learning
- less independent, critical thinking
- teacher may dominate

- chaotic/noisy classrooms
- students may miss avoid important knowledge and skills
- inconclusive assessment of student progress
- some students may dominate classroom

Done Poorly

SUMMING UP   Young children can learn a great deal before kindergarten, in either a child-centered or teacher-directed preschool, or in an excellent home setting. Montessori and Reggio Emilia schools advance children's learning. Both emphasize individual accomplishments and child development, with emphasis on creativity and exploration.

Teacher-directed programs stress readiness for school and teach letters and numbers that all children should know, as well as proper student behavior. Head Start and other programs are designed to advance learning for low-income children. Longitudinal research finds that some of the benefits of preschool programs are evident in adulthood. However, quality and accessibility are variable. The best programs are expensive; the benefits are apparent only decades later.

WHAT HAVE YOU LEARNED?

1. What do most preschools provide that most homes do not?
2. In child-centered programs, what do the teachers do?
3. What makes the Reggio Emilia program different from most other preschool programs?
4. Why are Montessori schools still functioning, 100 years after the first such schools opened?
5. What are the advantages and disadvantages of teacher-directed preschools?
6. What are the goals of Head Start?
7. What are the long-term results of intervention preschools?

SUMMARY

Thinking During Early Childhood

1. Piaget stressed the egocentric and illogical aspects of thought during early childhood. He called this stage of thinking pre-operational intelligence because young children do not yet use logical operations to think about their observations and experiences.

2. Young children, according to Piaget, sometimes focus on only one thing (centration) and see things only from their own viewpoint (egocentrism), remaining stuck on appearances and current reality. They may believe that living spirits reside in inanimate objects and that nonhuman animals have the same characteristics they themselves have, a belief called animism.

3. Vygotsky stressed the social aspects of childhood cognition, noting that children learn by participating in various experiences, guided by more knowledgeable adults or peers. Such guidance assists learning within the zone of proximal development, which encompasses the knowledge children are close to understanding and the skills they can almost master.

4. According to Vygotsky, the best teachers use various hints, guidelines, and other tools to provide a child with a scaffold for new learning. Language is a bridge that provides social mediation between the knowledge that the child already has and the learning that society hopes to impart. For Vygotsky, words are tools for learning.

5. Children develop theories, especially to explain the purpose of life and their role in it. One theory about children's thinking is called "theory-theory"—the hypothesis that children develop theories because all humans innately seek explanations for everything they observe.

6. An example of the developing cognition of young children is theory of mind—an understanding of what others may be thinking. Theory of mind begins at around age 4, partly the result of maturation of the brain. Culture and experiences also influence its development.

Language Learning

7. Language develops rapidly during early childhood, a sensitive period but not a critical one for language learning. Vocabulary increases dramatically, with thousands of words added between ages 2 and 6. In addition, basic grammar is mastered.

8. Many children learn to speak more than one language, gaining cognitive as well as social advantages. Early childhood is the best time to learn two languages. The benefits of bilingualism are lifelong.

Early-Childhood Schooling

9. Organized educational programs during early childhood advance cognitive and social skills, although specifics vary a great deal. Quality of a program cannot be judged by the name or by appearance.

10. Montessori and Reggio Emilia are two child-centered programs that began in Italy and are now offered in many nations. They stress individual interests of each child, including creative play, inspired by Piaget and Vygotsky.

11. Behaviorist principles led to many specific practices of teacher-directed programs. Children learn to listen to teachers and become ready for kindergarten.

12. Head Start is a U.S. federal government program primarily for low-income children. Longitudinal research finds that early-childhood education reduces the risk of later problems, such as needing special education. High-quality programs increase the likelihood that a child will become a law-abiding, gainfully employed adult.

13. Many types of preschool programs are successful. It is the quality of early education that matters. Children learn best if teachers follow a defined curriculum and if the child/adult ratio is low. The training, warmth, and continuity of early-childhood teachers benefit the children in many ways.

KEY TERMS

preoperational intelligence
  (p. 277)
symbolic thought (p. 278)
animism (p. 278)
centration (p. 278)
egocentrism (p. 278)

focus on appearance (p. 278)
static reasoning (p. 278)
irreversibility (p. 279)
conservation (p. 279)
scaffolding (p. 282)
overimitation (p. 283)

private speech (p. 284)
social mediation (p. 284)
theory-theory (p. 286)
theory of mind (p. 287)
fast-mapping (p. 292)
overregularization (p. 294)

pragmatics (p. 294)
Montessori schools (p. 300)
Reggio Emilia (p. 300)
Head Start (p. 303)

APPLICATIONS

The best way to understand thinking in early childhood is to listen to a child, as applications 1 and 2 require. If some students have no access to children, they should do application 3 or 4.

1. Replicate one of Piaget's conservation experiments. The easiest one is conservation of liquids (Figure 9.1). Work with a child under age 5 who tells you that two identically shaped glasses contain the same amount of liquid. Then carefully pour one glass of liquid into a narrower, taller glass. Ask the child if one glass now contains more or if the glasses contain the same amount.

2. To demonstrate how rapidly language is learned, show a preschool child several objects and label one with a nonsense word the child has never heard. (*Toma* is often used; so is *wug.*) Or choose a word the child does not know, such as *wrench, spatula,* or the name of a coin from another nation. Test the child's fast-mapping.

3. Theory of mind emerges at about age 4, but many adults still have trouble understanding other people's thoughts and motives. Ask several people why someone in the news did whatever he or she did (e.g., a scandal, a crime, a heroic act). Then ask your informants how sure they are of their explanation. Compare and analyze the reasons as well as the degrees of certainty. (One person may be sure of an explanation that someone else thinks is impossible.)

4. Think about an experience in which you learned something that was initially difficult. To what extent do Vygotsky's concepts (guided participation, zone of proximal development) explain the experience? Write a detailed, step-by-step account of your learning process as Vygotsky would have described it.

CHAPTER 10

Early Childhood:
Psychosocial Development

What Will You Know?

1. Why do 2-year-olds have more sudden tempers, tears, and terrors than 6-year-olds?
2. If a child never plays, is that a problem?
3. Should girls play with trucks and boys with dolls?
4. What happens if you never punish a child?

It was a hot summer afternoon. Rachel, almost 3, and Bethany, age 4, were with me in the kitchen, which was in one corner of our living/dining area. Rachel opened the refrigerator and grabbed a glass bottle of orange juice. The sticky bottle slipped, shattering on the tile floor. My stunned daughters looked at me, at the shards, at the spreading juice with extra pulp. I picked my girls up and plopped them on the couch.

"Stay there," I yelled.

They did, quiet, wide-eyed, and puzzled at my loud fury. Rachel had not deliberately dropped the juice, and Bethany had done nothing wrong, but they both knew that sometimes I demanded unquestioning obedience and they saw the signs that this was one of those times.

As they watched me pick, sweep, and mop, I understood how parents could hit their kids. By the end of this chapter, I hope you also realize that a moment like this—in the summer heat, with two small children causing unexpected work—can turn a loving, patient parent into something else. It is not easy, day after day, being the guide and model that parents should be.

Fortunately, many safeguards prevented me from serious maltreatment: The girls had learned when to obey, I knew not to punish in anger—our shared morality kept discipline within bounds. I hugged them when I took them off the couch. As children learn to manage their emotions, as parents learn to guide their children, as the macrosystem and microsystem (beliefs and income) influence adult–child interaction, many aspects of psychosocial development affect how children develop from ages 2 to 6. This chapter describes all that.

Emotional Development

Children gradually learn when and how to express emotions, becoming more capable in every aspect of their lives. Controlling the expression of emotions, called **emotional regulation,** is the preeminent psychosocial task between ages 2 and 6. Emotional regulation is a lifelong endeavor, affected by temperament and time, but early childhood is a

emotional regulation The ability to control when and how emotions are expressed.

A Poet and We Know It She is the proud winner of a national poetry contest. Is she as surprised, humbled, and thankful as an adult winner would be?

effortful control The ability to regulate one's emotions and actions through effort, not simply through natural inclination.

initiative versus guilt Erikson's third psychosocial crisis, in which children undertake new skills and activities and feel guilty when they do not succeed at them.

self-concept A person's understanding of who he or she is, in relation to self-esteem, appearance, personality, and various traits.

OBSERVATION QUIZ Does this mother deserve praise? (see answer, page 315)

crucial period for its development (Gross, 2014; Lewis, 2013). Difficulty with emotional regulation predicts many psychosocial problems later on.

Such regulation is virtually impossible in infancy, but when the emotional hot spots of the limbic system connect to the prefrontal cortex, children become better able to control their reactions. This is not easy; it requires practice, maturation, and work, called **effortful control** (Eisenberg et al., 2014).

By age 6, children can usually be angry but not explosive, frightened but not terrified, sad but not inconsolable, anxious but not withdrawn, proud but not boastful. Depending on each child's temperament, some emotions are easier to control than others, but even temperamentally angry or fearful children can learn to modify the expression of their emotions (Moran et al., 2013, Tan et al., 2013).

Emotional regulation is a lifelong necessity; no one does it perfectly all the time. When Rachel dropped the orange juice, I should not have yelled. Fortunately, my unregulated expression of anger stopped there. Learning to regulate emotion is a long process.

Initiative Versus Guilt

During Erikson's third developmental stage, **initiative versus guilt,** children acquire many skills and competencies in addition to emotional regulation. *Initiative* can mean several things—saying something new, expanding an ability, beginning a project. Depending on the outcome (especially reactions from other people), children feel proud or guilty.

Usually, North American parents encourage enthusiasm, effort, and pride in their 2- to 6-year-olds, and also prevent guilt from becoming self-hatred. If, instead, parents ignore rather than guide emotions, a child may not learn emotional regulation (Morris et al., 2007).

Protective Optimism

Adults may think that children should have an accurate view of their abilities. But that is not typical of preschool children, nor should it be. Children are proud of themselves, optimistically overestimating their prowess. That helps them try new things, which advances skills of all kinds. As Erikson predicted, their optimistic self-concept protects them from guilt and shame.

Children's beliefs about their worth require first a sense that they are a person (self-awareness, usually attained at 18 months), accompanied by lack of self-criticism. This flourishes with parental confirmation, especially when parents remind their children of their positive accomplishments ("You helped Daddy sweep the sidewalk. You made it very clean.").

Remember that Erikson described autonomy at ages 1 and 2, a stage often characterized by stubbornness and nicknamed "the terrible twos." By age 3, autonomy is transformed to become initiative, as children act on their eagerness to learn new skills (Rubin et al., 2009). This chapter's opening anecdote is an example: Rachel was learning to get juice when she was thirsty. Both autonomy and initiative are more prized in Western cultures than in Eastern ones, where children learn to be socially attuned and interdependent (Keller & Otto, 2011).

Children in North America and Europe develop a strong **self-concept,** an understanding of themselves. For example, young children are given choices: "Apple or banana?" "Blue pajamas or red ones?" Choosing makes people believe they are

Genuinely Helpful Children of all ages can be helpful to their families, but their actions depend on family and cohort. Thirty years ago more children gathered freshly laid eggs than recycled plastic milk bottles. Indeed, no blue recycling bins existed until tens of thousands of environmentalists advocated reducing our carbon footprint.

independent agents (Kim & Chu, 2011). Preschool children do not usually realize the limits of their choices, as my friend did when his 4-year-old daughter wanted him to make a valentine. He did not want to do it, but she gave him only two choices: a valentine for his mother or his wife.

In the United States, self-concept quickly includes gender and size. Girls are usually happy to be girls; boys to be boys; both are glad they aren't babies. "Cry-baby" is an insult; praise for being "a big kid" is welcomed; pride in being able to do something better than a younger child is boasted out loud.

Erikson recognized that young children are not realistic. They believe that they are strong, smart, and good-looking—and thus that any goal is achievable. Whatever they are (self-concept) is thought to be good.

For instance, young children not only believe that their nation and religion are best; they feel sorry for children who do not belong to their country or church. At this age, a protective optimism encourages children to try unfamiliar activities, make friends, begin school, and so on (Boseovski, 2010). The same is true for mastering skills: They learn to pour juice, zip pants, and climb trees, undeterred by overflowing juice, stuck zippers, or a perch too high. Faith in themselves helps them persist.

Moreover, children are cognitively ready to understand group categories, not only of ethnicity, gender, and nationality, but even categories that are irrelevant, such as children whose names begin with the same letter. Such categories seem to be part of human thinking lifelong, so group identity appears spontaneously once the child is old enough. One amusing example occurred when preschoolers were asked to explain why one fictional creature would steal from another. They immediately suggested a reason, as you would expect from theory-theory.

> "Why did a Zaz steal a toy from a Flurp?"
> "Because he's a Zaz, but he's a Flurp. They're not the same kind. . . ."
> "Why did a Zaz steal a toy from a Zaz?
> "Because he's a very mean boy."

[Rhodes, 2013, p. 259]

Brain Maturation

The new initiative that Erikson describes results from myelination of the limbic system, growth of the prefrontal cortex, and a longer attention span—all the result of neurological maturation. (**Developmental Link:** Brain maturation is described in detail in Chapter 5 and Chapter 8.) Emotional regulation and cognitive maturation develop together, each enabling the other to advance (Bell & Calkins, 2011; Lewis, 2013).

Normally, neurological advances in the pre-frontal cortex at about age 4 or 5 make children less likely to throw tantrums, pick fights, or giggle during prayer. Throughout early childhood, violent outbursts, uncontrolled crying, and terrifying *phobias* (irrational, crippling fears) diminish. The capacity for self-control, such as not opening a present immediately if asked to wait and not expressing disappointment at an undesirable gift, becomes more evident.

For example in one study, researchers asked children to wait 8 minutes while their mothers did some paperwork before opening a wrapped present in front of

Proud Peruvian In rural Peru, a program of early education (Pronoei) encourages community involvement and traditional culture. Preschoolers, like this girl in a holiday parade, are proud to be themselves, and that helps them become healthy and strong.

© MIKE THEISS/NATIONAL GEOGRAPHIC SOCIETY/CORBIS

FADEDINK.NET/SHUTTERSTOCK

Video Activity: Can Young Children Delay Gratification illustrates how most young children are unable to overcome temptation even when promised a reward for doing so.

them (Cole et al., 2011). The children used strategies to help them wait, including distractions and private speech.

Keisha was one of the study participants:

> "Are you done, Mom?" . . . "I wonder what's in it" . . . "Can I open it now?"
>
> Each time her mother reminds Keisha to wait, eventually adding, "If you keep interrupting me, I can't finish and if I don't finish . . ." Keisha plops in her chair, frustrated. "I really want it," she laments, aloud but to herself. "I want to talk to mommy so I won't open it. If I talk, Mommy won't finish. If she doesn't finish, I can't have it." She sighs deeply, folds her arms, and scans the room. . . . The research assistant returns. Keisha looks at her mother with excited anticipation. Her mother says, "OK, now." Keisha tears open the gift.
>
> [Cole et al., 2011, p. 59]

According to a longitudinal study of preschoolers who managed to wait before eating a marshmallow in order to get two marshmallows, the ability to delay gratification correlates with success in adulthood (Mischel, 2014).

Motivation

Motivation (the impulse that propels someone to act) comes either from a person's own desires or from the social context.

Intrinsic motivation comes from within, when people do something for the joy of doing it: A musician might enjoy making music even when no one else hears it. Intrinsic motivation is thought to advance creativity, innovation, and emotional well-being (Weinstein & DeHaan, 2014).

Extrinsic motivation comes from outside, when people do something to gain praise or another reinforcement. A musician might play for applause or money. Humans seek such external rewards, but if the reward stops, the behavior stops.

Intrinsic motivation is crucial for young children, with almost all of them playing, questioning, and exploring for the sheer joy of it. That serves them well. A study found that 3-year-olds who were strong in intrinsic motivation were, two years later, especially strong in early math and reading skills (Mokrova et al., 2013).

Child-centered preschools, as described in Chapter 9, depend on the reality that children love to talk, play, and move. Praise and prizes might be appreciated, but that's not why children work at what they do. When playing a game, they might not keep score; the fun is in the activity (intrinsic), not the winning.

Intrinsic motivation is apparent when children invent dialogues for their toys, concentrate on creating a work of art or architecture, and converse with **imaginary friends.** Such conversations with invisible companions are rarely encouraged by adults (i.e., no extrinsic motivation), but from about age 2 to 7, imaginary friends are increasingly common. Children know their imaginary friends are pretend, but conjuring them up meets intrinsic needs (M. Taylor et al., 2009).

In a classic experiment designed to understand more about why children do what they do, preschool children were given markers and paper for drawing and assigned to one of three groups who received, respectively: (1) no award, (2) an expected award (they were told *before* they had drawn anything that they would get a certificate), and (3) an unexpected award (*after* they had drawn something, they heard, "You were a big help," and got a certificate) (Lepper et al., 1973).

Later, observers noted how often children in each group chose to draw on their own. Those who received the expected award were less likely to draw than those who were unexpectedly rewarded. The interpretation was that extrinsic motivation (condition #2) undercut intrinsic motivation.

This research triggered a flood of studies seeking to understand whether, when, and how positive reinforcement should be given. The consensus is that praising

intrinsic motivation A drive, or reason to pursue a goal, that comes from inside a person, such as the desire to feel smart or competent.

extrinsic motivation A drive, or reason to pursue a goal, that arises from the need to have one's achievements rewarded from outside, perhaps by receiving material possessions or another person's esteem.

Especially for College Students Is extrinsic or intrinsic motivation more influential in your study efforts? (see response, page 316)

imaginary friends Make-believe friends who exist only in a child's imagination; increasingly common from ages 3 through 7. They combat loneliness and aid emotional regulation.

Especially for Teachers One of your students tells you about a child who plays, sleeps, and talks with an imaginary friend. Does this mean that that child is emotionally disturbed? (see response, page 316) or paying a person *after* an accomplishment sometimes encourages that behavior. However, if payment is promised in advance, that extrinsic reinforcement may backfire (Deci et al., 1999; Cameron & Pierce, 2002; Gottfried et al., 2009).

Praise is effective when it is connected to the particular production, not to a general trait. For example, the adult might say, "You did a good drawing," not "You are a great artist." The goal is to help the child realize that effort paid off, which motivates a repeat performance (Zentall & Morris, 2010).

In another set of experiments that suggest that specific praise for effort is better than generalized statements, some 4- to 7-year-old children were told that boys (or girls) are good at a particular game. Knowing that made their scores on the game lower than those of other children. They apparently feared that they would not be as good as most children of their age and sex. They "felt less happy and less competent, liked the game less, and were less persistent" (Cimpian, 2013, p. 272). By contrast, children who were told that one particular child was good at the game believed that personal effort mattered. That belief was motivating; their scores were higher than those told the general statement.

Culture and Emotional Control

As you know, cultural differences are apparent in every aspect of development. This is quite obvious in emotional expression. Children may be encouraged to laugh/cry/yell or the opposite, to hide those emotions. Some adults guffaw, slap their knees, and stomp their feet for joy; others cover their mouths with their hands if a smile spontaneously appears. Children learn to do the same.

Control strategies vary culturally as well. Peers, parents, and strangers sometimes ignore emotional outbursts, sometimes deflect them, sometimes punish them. Shame is used when social reputation is a priority. In some cultures, "pride goeth before a fall" and people who "have no shame" are considered mentally ill (Stein, 2006).

Finally, families, cultures, and nations differ as to which emotions most need to be regulated. Cohort changes and social stereotypes distort any attempt to link specific nations with the emotions each attempts to regulate, but the following illustrates the idea of cultural variations:

- Fear (United States)
- Anger (Iran)
- Pride (China)
- Selfishness (Japan)
- Impatience (many Native American communities)
- Defiance (Mexico)
- Moodiness (the Netherlands)

(Chen, 2011; Harkness et al., 2011; J. G. Miller, 2004; Stubben, 2001; Tahmouresi et al., 2014).

Temperaments vary, which makes people within the same culture unlike one another. "Cultures are inevitably more complicated than the framework that is supposed to explain them" (Harkness et al., 2011, p. 92). Nonetheless, parents everywhere teach emotional regulation, hoping their children will adapt to the norms of their culture, and cultures differ in which emotions are particularly unwelcome (Kim & Sasaki, 2014).

Especially for Teachers of Young Children Should you put gold stars on children's work? (see response, page 317)

// ANSWER TO OBSERVATION QUIZ (from page 312) Yes—even if you don't consider recycling important. Notice her face and body: She is smiling and kneeling, and her hands are on her legs, all suggesting that she knows how to encourage without interfering. Even more commendable is her boys' behavior: Many brothers would be grabbing, shoving, and throwing, but, at least at this moment, shared cooperation is evident. Kudos to Mom.

Learning Emotional Regulation Like this girl in Hong Kong, all 2-year-olds burst into tears when something upsets them—a toy breaks, a pet refuses to play, or it's time to go home. A mother who comforts them and helps them calm down is teaching them to regulate their emotions.

Seeking Emotional Balance

Universally, at every age, in all cultures and cohorts, caregivers try to prevent **psychopathology,** an illness or disorder (*-pathology*) of the mind (*psycho-*). Although symptoms and diagnoses are influenced by culture (rebellion is expected in some cultures and pathological in others), impaired emotional regulation signals mental imbalance everywhere. Parents guide young children toward "an optimal balance" between emotional expression and emotional control (Blair & Dennis, 2010; Trommsdorff & Cole, 2011).

Without adequate regulation, emotions are overwhelming. Intense reactions can occur in opposite ways, as you might expect from the activate/inhibit nature of neurons, as explained in Chapter 8.

Some people have **externalizing problems:** Their powerful feelings burst out uncontrollably. They externalize rage, for example, by lashing out or breaking things. Without emotional regulation, an angry child might pummel another person or lie down screaming and kicking. By age 5, children usually have learned more self-control, perhaps pouting or cursing, not hitting and screaming.

Other people have **internalizing problems:** They are fearful and withdrawn, turning distress inward. Emotions may be internalized via headaches or stomach aches. Although the cause is psychological, the ache is real. Girls tend to internalize and boys to externalize, although children of both sexes do both.

With maturity, the extreme fears of some 2-year-olds (e.g., terror of the bathtub drain, of an imagined tidal wave, of a stranger on crutches) diminish. The fear isn't gone, but expression is regulated. A frightened 2-year-old might hide in the closet; a 5-year-old might be afraid of kindergarten but will bravely let go of Mother's hand and enter the classroom.

Both undercontrol, which produces externalizing behavior, and overcontrol, which leads to internalizing behavior, are much more common in 3-year-olds than in 5-year-olds. Experiences during those years interact with brain maturation, ideally strengthening emotional regulation (Lewis, 2013).

Sex differences in internalizing and externalizing behavior are traditionally assumed to be biological, perhaps hormonal, but a cultural explanation is also possible. Do parents and cultures teach young girls to restrain externalizing actions ("not ladylike"), while teaching boys to avoid crying ("be a man")? Trying to understand the causes of sex or gender differences is a concern of thousands of researchers (Eagly & Wood, 2013). Conflicting theories and evidence are presented

psychopathology Literally, an illness of the mind, or psyche. Various cultures and groups within cultures have different concepts of specific psychopathologies. A recent compendium of symptoms and disorders in the United States is in the DSM-5. Many other nations use an international set of categories, the ICD-10.

externalizing problems Difficulty with emotional regulation that involves expressing powerful feelings through uncontrolled physical or verbal outbursts, as by lashing out at other people or breaking things.

internalizing problems Difficulty with emotional regulation that involves turning one's emotional distress inward, as by feeling excessively guilty, ashamed, or worthless.

Age or Gender? Probably both. Brother and sister are reacting typically for their age and sex, as the 4-year-old boy moves his book away from his sister, who cries instead of grabbing it. Culture may be a factor, too, as these siblings are in Korea, where physical fighting between siblings is not allowed.

// Response for College Students (from page 314): Both are important. Extrinsic motivation includes parental pressure and the need to get a good job after graduation. Intrinsic motivation includes the joy of learning, especially if you can express that learning in ways others recognize. Have you ever taken a course that was not required and was said to be difficult? That was intrinsic motivation.

// Response for Teachers (from page 314): No, unless the child is over age 10. In fact, imaginary friends are quite common, especially among creative children. The child may be somewhat lonely, though; you could help him or her find a friend.

later in this chapter. In any case, unless they master emotional regulation during early childhood, boys tend to throw and hit and girls tend to sob or hide.

Cute or Too Shy? Cute, of course. Universally, girls and women are expected to be reticent. They cling more to their mothers in kindergarten, they wait to be asked to dance or date, they talk less in co-ed groups. If she were a he, would he be considered too shy?

SUMMING UP   Achieving emotional regulation is the crucial psychosocial task in early childhood. Erikson thought young children are naturally motivated to take initiative, with joy at new tasks. He also thought that during early childhood, guilt feelings may come to the fore, as parents criticize unrestrained emotional expression. As children develop their self-concept, motivation to do well increases as does the belief that one's own group (e.g., gender, nationality, ethnicity) is better than others. Brain maturation and family guidance help children regulate their emotions, avoiding either extreme externalizing or internalizing reactions. Universally, 2- to 6-year-olds become better able to control and express their emotions, but cultures differ in which emotions should be controlled and how emotions should be expressed.

WHAT HAVE YOU LEARNED?

1. How might protective optimism lead to a child's acquisition of new skills and competencies?
2. How would a child's self-concept affect his or her motivation?
3. What is an example of an intrinsic motivation for reading?
4. What is an example of an extrinsic motivation for reading?
5. What seem to be sex differences in externalizing and internalizing behavior?
6. What is the connection between psychopathology and emotional regulation?
7. What is universal and what is culture-specific in emotional expression?

Play

Play is timeless and universal—apparent in every part of the world for thousands of years. Many developmentalists believe that play is the most productive as well as the most enjoyable activity that children undertake (Elkind, 2007; Bateson & Martin, 2013; P. K. Smith, 2010). Whether play is essential for normal growth or is merely fun is "a controversial topic of study" (Pellegrini, 2011, p. 3).

This controversy underlies many of the disputes regarding preschool education, which increasingly stresses academic skills. One consequence is that "play in school has become an endangered species" (Trawick-Smith, 2012, p. 259). Among the leading theorists of human development, Vygotsky is well known for his respect for child's play, which makes a playing child "a head taller" than their actual height (Vygotsky, 1980).

Some educators want children to play less in order to focus on reading and math; others predict emotional and academic problems for children who rarely play. It does seem that children who are deprived of activity for a long period tend to play more vigorously when they finally have the chance (Pellegrini et al., 2013), and that for children of all ages, taking a break from concentrated intellectual work enhances learning.

There are two general kinds of play, *pretend play* that often occurs by a child alone, and *social play,* that occurs when children are together. The idea that "pretend play is a crucial engine of child development" has been explored in hundreds of studies, carefully reviewed (Lillard et al., 2013, p. 24).

The reviewers do not confuse correlation with causation. They report that evidence is weak regarding pretend play, but they suggest that preventing social play will not only make children less happy, it may impair learning (Lillard et al., 2013). They conclude that play—especially social play—is one way that children develop their minds and social skills, although not the only way.

// **Response for Teachers of Young Children** (from page 315): Perhaps, but only after the work is completed and if the child has put genuine effort into it. You do not want to undercut intrinsic motivation, as happens with older students who know a particular course will be an "easy A."

Less Play, Less Safe?

Play is universal—all young children do it when they are with each other, if they can. For children, play takes up more time than anything else, whether their family is rich or poor.

WHAT 3-YEAR-OLDS DO WITH THEIR TIME

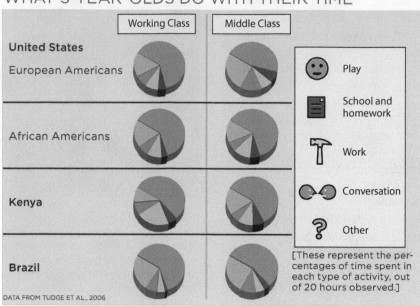

	Working Class	Middle Class
United States European Americans		
African Americans		
Kenya		
Brazil		

😐 Play

📄 School and homework

🔨 Work

Conversation

❓ Other

[These represent the percentages of time spent in each type of activity, out of 20 hours observed.]

DATA FROM TUDGE ET AL., 2006

However, many developmentalists worry that active play has decreased as screen time has increased, especially in the United States (on average, 2.1 hours per day for 2- to 4-year-olds).

Parents worry that children will be injured if they play outside, but the data suggest the opposite. Only 166 out of every thousand children need to go to the emergency room per year, and almost all of those were injured in the home, or in a car.

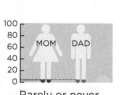

PERCENT OF KIDS WHOSE PARENTS PLAY OUTDOORS WITH THEM

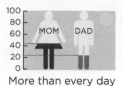

More than every day

A few times a week

A few times a month

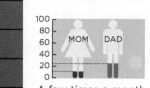

Rarely or never

From what kind of injuries do young children suffer?

Compare 1- to 4-year-olds and 5- to 14-year-olds

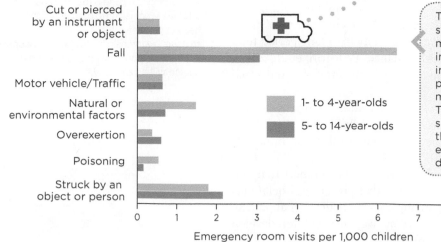

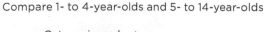

- Cut or pierced by an instrument or object
- Fall
- Motor vehicle/Traffic
- Natural or environmental factors
- Overexertion
- Poisoning
- Struck by an object or person

■ 1- to 4-year-olds
■ 5- to 14-year-olds

Emergency room visits per 1,000 children

The injuries most likely to occur outside are lumped together as environmental or natural—usually animal or insect bites. And the most common injury, falls—which may result from poor balance and motor control—is more problematic for inactive children. The next most common injury is being struck by a person—almost always that person is an adult at home. At every age, physical fitness is the best defense against accidental injury.

DATA FROM EMERGENCY ROOM VISITS, 2009–2010, CHILDSTATS.GOV.

Playmates

How, then, should children play? Young children play best with *peers,* that is, people of about the same age and social status. Although even infants are intrigued by other small children, most infant play is either solitary or with a parent. Some maturation is required for social play, which may advance brain development and creativity (Bateson & Martin, 2013).

Such an advance can be seen over the years of early childhood. Toddlers are too self-absorbed to be good playmates, but they learn quickly. By age 6, most children are quite skilled: Some know how to join a peer group, manage conflict, take turns, find friends, and keep playmates (Şendil & Erden, 2014; Göncü & Gaskins, 2011). As they become better playmates, they learn emotional regulation, empathy, and cultural understanding.

Parents have an obvious task: Find peers and arrange play dates. Of course, some parents play with their children, which benefits both of them. But even the most playful parent is outmatched by another child at negotiating the rules of tag, at play-fighting, at pretending to be sick, at killing dragons. Specifics vary, but "play with peers is one of the most important areas in which children develop positive social skills" (Xu, 2010, p. 496).

Culture and Cohort

All young children play; "everywhere, a child playing is a sign of healthy development" (Gosso, 2010, p. 95). Play is the favorite activity of young children, as illustrated in Visualizing Development, page 318. Basic play is similar in every culture: throwing and catching; chasing and exploring; pretending to be adults; drawing with chalk, felt pens, sticks, or anything that can make a mark. Accordingly, developmentalists think play is *experience-expectant.*

Some specifics are *experience-dependent,* however, reflecting culture and SES. (**Developmental Link:** Experience-expectant and experience-dependent brain development are explained in Chapter 5.) Chinese children fly kites, Alaskan Natives tell dreams and stories, Sami children of Scandinavia pretend to be reindeer, Cameroonian children hunt mice, and so on. Parents in some cultures consider play important and willingly engage in games and dramas. In other places, sheer survival takes time and energy, and children must help by doing chores. In those places, if children have any time for play, it is with each other, not with adults who spend all their energy on basic tasks (Kalliala, 2006; Roopnarine, 2011).

As children grow older, play becomes more social, influenced by brain maturation, playmate availability, and the physical setting. One developmentalist bemoans the twenty-first century's "swift and pervasive rise of electronic media" and adults who lean "more toward control than freedom" (Chudacoff, 2011, p. 108). He praises children who find places to play independently and "conspire ways to elude adult management."

This opinion may be extreme, but it is echoed in more common concerns. As you remember, one dispute in preschool education is the proper balance between unstructured, creative play and teacher-directed learning. Before the electronic age, and in places where technology was rare, most families had several children and few mothers worked outside the home. Then all children played outside with others, and groups often included children of several ages.

Play Ball! In every nation, young children play with balls, but the specific games they play vary with the culture. Soccer is the favorite game in many countries, including Brazil, where these children are practicing their dribbling on Copacabana Beach in Rio de Janeiro.

OBSERVATION QUIZ Does kicking a soccer ball, as shown above, require fine or gross motor skills? (see answer, page 322)

That was true in the United States a century ago. In 1932, the American sociologist Mildred Parten described the development of five kinds of social play, each more advanced than the previous one:

1. *Solitary play*: A child plays alone, unaware of any other children playing nearby.
2. *Onlooker play*: A child watches other children play.
3. *Parallel play*: Children play with similar objects in similar ways but not together.
4. *Associative play*: Children interact, sharing material, but their play is not reciprocal.
5. *Cooperative play*: Children play together, creating dramas or taking turns.

Parten thought that progress in social play was age-related, with 1-year-olds usually playing alone and 6-year-olds usually cooperatively.

Research on contemporary children finds much more age variation, perhaps because family size is smaller and parents invest heavily in each child. Many Asian parents teach 3-year-olds to take turns, share, and otherwise cooperate (stage 5). Many North American children, encouraged to be individuals, still engage in parallel play at age 6 (stage 3). Given all the social, political, and economic changes over the past century, many forms of social play (not necessarily in Parten's five-step sequence) are normal (Xu, 2010).

No Grabbing Maybe the child on the left or the right will soon try to grab. If sharing continues, is it because these children have been raised within Asian families?

Active Play

Children need physical activity to develop muscle strength and control. Peers provide an audience, role models, and sometimes competition. For instance, running skills develop best when children chase or race each other, not when a child runs alone. Gross motor play is favored among young children, who enjoy climbing, kicking, and tumbling (Case-Smith & Kuhaneck, 2008).

Active social play—not solitary play—correlates with peer acceptance and a healthy self-concept and may help regulate emotions (Becker et al., 2014; Sutton-Smith, 2011). Adults need to remember this when they want children to sit still and be quiet. Among nonhuman primates, deprivation of social play warps later life, rendering some monkeys unable to mate, to make friends, or even to survive alongside other monkeys (Herman et al., 2011; Palagi, 2011). Is the same true for human primates?

Active play advances planning and self-control. Two-year-olds merely chase and catch each other, but older children keep the interaction fair, long lasting, and fun. In the game of tag, for instance, children set rules (adjusted to local terrains and dangers), and each child decides how far to venture from base. If one child is "it" for too long, another child (often a friend) makes it easy to be caught. In that way, all the children can enjoy the game.

Rough-and-Tumble Play

rough-and-tumble play Play that mimics aggression through wrestling, chasing, or hitting, but in which there is no intent to harm.

The most common form of active play is called **rough-and-tumble play** because it looks quite rough and because the children seem to tumble over one another. The term was coined by British scientists who studied primates in East Africa (Blurton-Jones, 1976). They noticed that monkeys often chased, attacked, rolled over in the dirt, and wrestled quite roughly, but without injuring one another.

If a young male monkey wanted to play, he would simply catch the eye of a peer and then run a few feet away. This invitation to rough-and-tumble play was almost always accepted with a *play face* (smiling, not angry). Puppies, kittens, and young baboons behave similarly.

When these scientists returned to London, they saw that their own children, like baby monkeys, engage in rough-and-tumble play, signified by the play face. Children chase, wrestle, and grab each other, developing games like tag and cops-and-robbers, with various conventions, expressions, and gestures that children use to signify "just pretend."

Rough-and-tumble play happens everywhere (although cops-and-robbers can be "robots-and-humans" or many other iterations) and has probably been common among children for thousands of years (Fry, 2014). It is much more common among boys than girls and flourishes best in ample space with minimal supervision (Pellegrini, 2013).

Many scientists think that rough-and-tumble play helps the prefrontal cortex develop, as children learn to regulate emotions, practice social skills, and strengthen their bodies (Pellis & Pellis, 2011). Indeed, some believe that play in childhood, especially rough-and-tumble play between father and son, may prevent antisocial behavior (even murder) later on (Fry, 2014; Wenner, 2009).

Drama and Pretending

Another major type of active play is **sociodramatic play,** in which children act out various roles and plots. Through such acting, children:

- Explore and rehearse social roles
- Learn to explain their ideas and persuade playmates
- Practice emotional regulation by pretending to be afraid, angry, brave, and so on
- Develop self-concept in a nonthreatening context

Sociodramatic play builds on pretending, which emerges in toddlerhood. But preschoolers do more than pretend; they combine their imagination with that of their friends, advancing in theory of mind (Kavanaugh, 2011). The beginnings of sociodramatic play are illustrated by the following pair, a 3-year-old girl and a 2-year-old boy. The girl wanted to act out the role of a baby, and she persuaded a boy in her nursery school to be the parent.

> **Boy:** Not good. You bad.
> **Girl:** Why?
> **Boy:** 'Cause you spill your milk.
> **Girl:** No. 'Cause I bit somebody.
> **Boy:** Yes, you did.
> **Girl:** Say, "Go to sleep. Put your head down."
> **Boy:** Put your head down.
> **Girl:** No.
> **Boy:** Yes.
> **Girl:** No.
> **Boy:** Yes. Okay, I will spank you. Bad boy. [*Spanks her, not hard*]
> **Girl:** No. My head is up. [*Giggles*] I want my teddy bear.
> **Boy:** No. Your teddy bear go away.
> [*At this point she asked if he was really going to take the teddy bear away.*]
>
> [*from Garvey, reported in Cohen, 2006, p. 72*]

Note the social interaction in this form of play, with the 3-year-old clearly more mature than the 2-year-old. She created, directed, and

Joy Supreme Pretend play in early childhood is thrilling and powerful. For this 7-year-old from the Park Slope neighborhood of Brooklyn, New York, pretend play overwhelms mundane realities, such as an odd scarf or awkward arm.

sociodramatic play Pretend play in which children act out various roles and themes in stories that they create.

Machine Guns Ready Good versus evil is a universal theme, but children need parents, community, or television to tell them who is evil and what must be done to them. During the civil war in Liberia, these boys practiced killing the enemy. That war ended. Hopefully these boys, now older, also developed more constructive play. Sadly, elsewhere— Syria? Ukraine? Palestine?—children take up the fight.

played her part, sometimes accepting what the boy said and sometimes not. The boy took direction, yet also made up his own dialogue and actions ("Bad boy"). It is noteworthy that the 2-year-old boy was willing to cooperate. When children are a few years older than these two, play is almost exclusively with peers of the same sex, if they are available (Leaper, 2013).

A slightly older girl might want to play with the boys, but the older boys usually do not allow her (Pellegrini, 2013). Boy-versus-girl play emerges later, at puberty, but toward the end of early childhood both sexes usually stick to their own unless a particular neighborhood group is quite small, and then the girls and boys play with each other.

Older preschoolers are not only more gender-conscious, their sociodramatic play is much more elaborate. This was evident in four boys, about age 5, in a day-care center in Finland. Joni plays the role of the evil one who menaces the other boys; Tuomas directs the drama and acts in it as well.

Tuomas: And now he [Joni] would take me and would hang me. . . . This would be the end of all of me.

Joni: Hands behind.

Tuomas: I can't help it. I have to. *[The two other boys follow his example.]*

Joni: I would put fire all around them.
[All three brave boys lie on the floor with hands tied behind their backs. Joni piles mattresses on them, and pretends to light a fire, which crackles closer and closer.]

Tuomas: Everything is lost.
[One boy starts to laugh.]

Petterl: Better not to laugh, soon we will all be dead. . . . I am saying my last words.

Tuomas: Now you can say your last wish. . . . And now I say I wish we can be terribly strong.
[At that point, the three boys suddenly gain extraordinary strength, pushing off the mattresses and extinguishing the fire. Good triumphs over evil, but not until the last moment, because, as one boy explains, "Otherwise this playing is not exciting at all."]

[adapted from Kalliala, 2006, p. 83]

Good versus evil is a favorite theme of boys' sociodramatic play, with danger part of the plot but victory in the end. By contrast, girls often act out domestic scenes, with themselves as the adults. In the same day-care center where Joni piled mattresses on his playmates, the girls say their play is "more beautiful and peaceful . . . [but] boys play all kinds of violent games" (Kalliala, 2006, p. 110).

The prevalence of sociodramatic play varies by culture, with parents often following cultural norms. Some cultures find make-believe frivolous and discourage it; In other cultures, parents teach toddlers to be lions, or robots, or ladies drinking tea. Then children elaborate on those themes (Kavanaugh, 2011). Many children are avid television watchers, and they act out superhero themes. Some parents never let their children watch videos of any kind, especially ones with violent themes.

That children act out superheroes and villains from video screens

Stopped In Her Tracks The birthday balloon or the tiny horse on the floor are no match for the bright images on the screen, designed to capture every child's attention. Are you critical of the parents who bought, placed, and turned on that large television for their 2-year-old, or the culture that allows such programming? Would you report this as child neglect?

ART DIRECTORS & TRIP/ALAMY

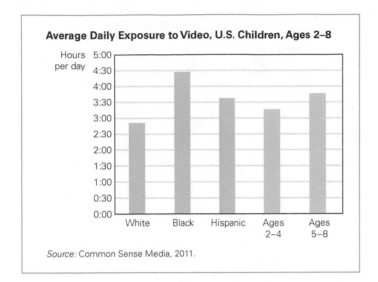

Average Daily Exposure to Video, U.S. Children, Ages 2–8

Source: Common Sense Media, 2011.

FIGURE 10.1

Learning by Playing Fifty years ago, the average child spent three hours a day in outdoor play. Video games and television have largely replaced that play time, especially in cities. Children seem safer if parents can keep an eye on them, but what are the long-term effects on brain and body?

is troubling to many developmentalists. They prefer prefer that children's dramas come from their own imagination, not from the media. Of course, some children learn from videos, especially if adults watch with them and reinforce the lessons. However, children on their own rarely select educational programs over fast-paced cartoons, in which characters hit, shoot, and kick. And then they act out what they have seen.

Canadian as well as U.S. organizations of professionals in child welfare (e.g., pediatricians) suggest children under age 2 have no screen time, and those over age 2 have less than an hour a day. However about half of all North American children exceed those limits, with screen time increasing as income falls (Carson et al., 2013; Fletcher et al., 2014). Professionals are concerned for many reasons: (1) violent media teaches aggression; (2) gender and ethnic stereotypes are pervasive; and (3) passive watching reduces time for family interaction and active play (see Figure 10.1).

SUMMING UP   As they have done in every era, all children everywhere play during early childhood, which makes many developmentalists think play is essential for healthy development. Some parents and other adults are not convinced; they would rather children help at home or learn academic skills.

Social play teaches social skills. In that way, at least, there is no doubt that children benefit from play with peers even more than from solitary play or play with adults. Specific games and dramas vary by culture and gender. Rough-and-tumble play is active play that boys particularly enjoy; sociodramatic play is common in children of both sexes. Boys tend to prefer good-versus-evil dramas, with themselves as heroes who defeat the bad guys; girls may prefer domestic scenes, with themselves as the adults. Imaginary play is considered healthy for preschoolers; "screen time" is discouraged by most experts in child development.

WHAT HAVE YOU LEARNED?

1. What are children thought to gain from play?
2. Why might playing with peers help children build muscles and develop self-control?
3. What do children learn from rough-and-tumble play?
4. What do children learn from sociodramatic play?
5. Why do many experts want to limit children's screen time?

Video: The Impact of Media in Early Childhood
http://qrs.ly/on4ep0n

Challenges for Caregivers

We have seen that young children's emotions and actions are affected by many factors, including brain maturation, culture, and peers. Now we focus on another primary influence on young children: their caregivers. Parents are crucial, and alternate caregivers become pivotal as well.

Caregiving Styles

Many researchers have studied the effects of parenting strategies and emotions. Of course, genes and cultures differ, and that shapes children. Beyond that, however, some parental practices lead to psychopathology while others encourage children to become outgoing, caring adults (Deater-Deckard, 2013).

Baumrind's Three Styles of Caregiving

Although thousands of researchers have traced the effects of parenting on child development, the work of one person, 50 years ago, continues to be influential. In her original research, Diana Baumrind (1967, 1971) studied 100 preschool children, all from California, almost all middle-class European Americans. (The cohort and cultural limitations of this sample were not obvious at the time.)

Baumrind found that parents differed on four important dimensions:

1. *Expressions of warmth.* Some parents are warm and affectionate; others, cold and critical.
2. *Strategies for discipline.* Parents vary in how they explain, criticize, persuade, and punish.
3. *Communication.* Some parents listen patiently; others demand silence.
4. *Expectations for maturity.* Parents vary in expectations for responsibility and self-control.

On the basis of these dimensions, Baumrind identified three parenting styles (summarized in Table 10.1).

Authoritarian parenting. The authoritarian parent's word is law, not to be questioned. Misconduct brings strict punishment, usually physical. Authoritarian parents set down clear rules and hold high standards. They do not expect children to offer opinions; discussion about emotions is especially rare. (One adult from such a family said that "How do you feel?" had only two possible answers: "Fine" and "Tired.") Authoritarian parents seem cold, rarely showing affection.

Permissive parenting. Permissive parents (also called *indulgent*) make few demands, hiding any impatience they feel. Discipline is lax, partly because they have low expectations for maturity. Permissive parents are nurturing and accepting, listening to whatever their offspring say, even if it is profanity or criticism of the parent.

Authoritative parenting. Authoritative parents set limits, but they are flexible. They encourage maturity, but they usually listen and forgive (not punish) if the child falls short. They consider themselves guides, not authorities (unlike authoritarian parents) and not friends (unlike permissive parents).

Other researchers describe a fourth style, called **neglectful/uninvolved parenting,** which may be confused with permissive but is quite different. The similarity is that neither permissive nor neglectful parents use physical punishment. However, neglectful parents are oblivious to their children's behavior; they seem

---

authoritarian parenting An approach to child rearing that is characterized by high behavioral standards, strict punishment for misconduct, and little communication from child to parent.

permissive parenting An approach to child rearing that is characterized by high nurturance and communication but little discipline, guidance, or control. (Also called *indulgent parenting.*)

authoritative parenting An approach to child rearing in which the parents set limits but listen to the child and are flexible.

neglectful/uninvolved parenting An approach to child rearing in which the parents are indifferent toward their children and unaware of what is going on in their children's lives.

Especially for Political Scientists Many observers contend that children learn their political attitudes at home, from the way their parents teach them. Is this true? (see response, page 326)

OBSERVATION QUIZ Is the father below authoritarian, authoritative, or permissive? (see answer, page 326)

Protect Me From the Water Buffalo These two are at the Carabao Kneeling Festival. In rural Philippines, hundreds of these large but docile animals kneel on the steps of the church, part of a day of gratitude for the harvest.

TABLE 10.1 | Characteristics of Parenting Styles Identified by Baumrind

Style	Warmth	Discipline	Expectations of Maturity	Communication Parent to Child	Communication Child to Parent
Authoritarian	Low	Strict, often physical	High	High	Low
Permissive	High	Rare	Low	Low	High
Authoritative	High	Moderate, with much discussion	Moderate	High	High

not to care. By contrast, permissive parents care very much: They defend their children, arrange play dates, and sacrifice to buy coveted toys.

The following long-term effects of parenting styles have been reported, not only in the United States but in many other nations as well (Baumrind, 2005; Baumrind et al., 2010; Chan & Koo, 2011; Huver et al., 2010; Rothrauff et al., 2009; Deater-Deckard, 2013).

- *Authoritarian* parents raise children who become conscientious, obedient, and quiet but not especially happy. Such children tend to feel guilty or depressed, internalizing their frustrations and blaming themselves when things don't go well. As adolescents, they sometimes rebel, leaving home before age 20.
- *Permissive* parents raise children who lack self-control, especially in the give-and-take of peer relationships. Inadequate emotional regulation makes them immature and impedes friendships, so they are unhappy. They tend to continue to live at home, still dependent on their parents, in early adulthood.
- *Authoritative* parents raise children who are successful, articulate, happy with themselves, and generous with others. These children are usually liked by teachers and peers, especially in cultures that value individual initiative (e.g., the United States).
- *Neglectful/uninvolved* parents raise children who are immature, sad, lonely, and at risk of injury and abuse, not only in early childhood but also lifelong.

Problems with Baumrind's Styles

Baumrind's classification schema is often criticized. Problems include the following:

- Her participants were not diverse in SES, ethnicity, or culture.
- She focused more on adult attitudes than on adult actions.
- She overlooked children's temperamental differences.
- She did not recognize that some "authoritarian" parents are also affectionate.
- She did not realize that some "permissive" parents provide extensive verbal guidance.

We now know that a child's temperament powerfully affects caregivers. Caring for a child is an interactive process, and good caregivers treat each child as an individual who needs personalized care. That may make outsiders misinterpret the parental practices they see.

For example, fearful children require reassurance while impulsive ones need strong guidelines. Parents of such children may, to outsiders, seem permissive or authoritarian. Of course, some parents *are* too lax or too rigid, but every child needs some protection and guidance; some more than others. Overprotection and hypervigilance are both a cause and consequence of childhood anxiety (McShane & Hastings, 2009; Deater-Deckard, 2013), but the right balance depends on the particular child, as differential susceptibility makes clear.

"He's just doing that to get attention."

Pay Attention Children develop best with lots of love and attention. They shouldn't have to ask for it!

// **ANSWER TO OBSERVATION QUIZ** (from page 324): It is impossible to be certain based on one moment, but the best guess is authoritative. He seems patient and protective, providing comfort and guidance, neither forcing (authoritarian) nor letting the child do whatever he wants (permissive).

// **Response for Political Scientists** (from page 324): There are many parenting styles, and it is difficult to determine each one's impact on children's personalities. At this point, attempts to connect early child rearing with later political outlook are speculative.

Cultural Variations

The significance of context is obvious when children of various ethnic groups are compared because parents in various cultures have heartfelt, and sometimes opposite, child-rearing strategies. One explanation is genetic: Certain alleles may be more common in some ethnic groups, which may affect child temperament and thus make a certain style of parenting more effective. However, a much more plausible reason for cultural differences is that caregivers anticipate the social context in which the child must function.

U.S. parents of Chinese, Caribbean, or African heritage are often stricter than those of European backgrounds, yet their children seem to develop better than if their parents were easygoing (Parke & Buriel, 2006; Ng et al., 2014). Latino parents are sometimes thought to be too intrusive, other times too permissive—but their children seem to be happier than the children of European American parents who behave the same way (García & Garcia, 2009; Ispa et al., 2004).

Does culture erase the effects of each of the four styles of parenting? No. However, the outcome of any parenting style is affected by the child's temperament, the parent's personality, and the social context. This later factor may be particularly important for minority children growing up in a majority culture (Henry, 2011).

In a detailed study of 1,477 instances in which Mexican American mothers of 4-year-olds tried to get their children to do something they were not doing, most of the time the mothers simply uttered a command and the children complied (Livas-Dlott et al., 2010). This simple strategy, with the mother asserting authority and the children obeying without question, might be considered authoritarian.

Almost never, however, did the mothers use physical punishment or even harsh threats when the children did not immediately do as they were told—which happened 14 percent of the time. For example,

> Hailey [the 4-year-old] decided to look for another doll and started digging through her toys, throwing them behind her as she dug. Maricruz [the mother] told Hailey she should not throw her toys. Hailey continued to throw toys, and Maricruz said her name to remind her to stop. Hailey continued her misbehavior, and her mother repeated "Hailey" once more. When Hailey continued, Maricruz raised her voice but calmly directed, "Hailey, look at me." Hailey continued but then looked at Maricruz as she explained, "You don't throw toys; you could hurt someone." Finally, Hailey complied and stopped.
>
> [Livas-Dlott et al., 2010, p. 572]

Note that the mother's first three efforts failed, and then a look accompanied by an explanation (albeit inaccurate in that setting, as no one could be hurt) succeeded. The researchers explain that these Mexican American families did not fit any of Baumrind's categories; respect for adult authority did not mean a cold mother–child relationship. Instead, the relationship shows evident *carino* (caring) (Livas-Dlott et al., 2010).

Warmth and caring may be the crucial aspect of parenting style in every ethnic group. Other research also finds that parental affection and warmth allow children to develop self-respect and to become compassionate adults, and this can occur in any of the three common parenting styles within any culture (Deater-Deckard, 2013; Eisenberg et al., 2013).

Given a multicultural and multicontextual perspective, developmentalists hesitate to be too specific in recommending any particular parenting style. That does not mean that all families function equally well—far from it. Signs of emotional distress, including a child's anxiety, aggression, and inability to play with others, indicate that the family may not be the safe haven of support and guidance that it should be. Ineffective, abusive, and neglectful parents are one cause of child distress, but not the only one. It is a mistake to assume that the parents are to blame whenever the child is troubled.

Becoming Boys or Girls: Sex and Gender

Biology determines whether a baby is male or female except in very rare cases when genes do not function normally. As you remember from Chapter 4, at about 8 weeks after conception, the SRY gene directs growth of external reproductive organs, and then male hormones exert subtle control over the brain, body, and later behavior. Without that gene, the fetus develops female organs, which produce female hormones that also affect the brain and behavior.

Sometimes the sex hormones are inactive prenatally and the child does not develop like the typical boy or girl (Hines, 2013). That is rare; most children are male or female in all three ways: chromosomes, genitals, and hormones. That is their nature, but obviously nurture affects sexual development lifelong.

During early childhood, patterns of behavior and preferences related to gender become important to children and apparent to adults. Before age 2, children apply gender labels (*Mrs., Mr., lady, man*) consistently. By age 4, children are convinced that certain toys (such as dolls or trucks) and roles (not just Daddy or Mommy, but also nurse, teacher, police officer, soldier) are "best suited" for one sex or the other.

Sexual stereotypes often become obvious and rigid between ages 3 and 6. Dynamic-systems theory suggests that concepts of male and female behavior are affected by many developmental aspects of biology and culture, changing as humans grow older (Martin & Ruble, 2010).

Many scientists distinguish **sex differences,** which are biological differences between males and females, from **gender differences,** which are culturally prescribed roles and behaviors. In theory, this distinction seems straightforward, but, as with every nature–nurture distinction, the interaction between sex and gender makes it hard to separate the two. Scientists need to "treat culture and biology not as separate influences but as interacting components of nature and nurture" (Eagly & Wood, 2013, p. 349).

Young children are often confused about the origin of male-female differences. One little girl said she would grow a penis when she got older, and one little boy offered to buy his mother one. Ignorance about biology was demonstrated by a 3-year-old who went with his father to see a neighbor's newborn kittens. Returning home, the child told his mother that there were three girl kittens and two boy kittens. "How do you know?" she asked. "Daddy picked them up and read what was written on their tummies," he replied.

Many preschool children do not realize that their own biological sex is permanent. In one preschool, the children themselves decided that one wash-up basin was for boys and the other for girls, a decision that reflects young children's insistence on gender distinctions. One girl started to use the boys' basin.

> **Boy:** This is for the boys.
> **Girl:** Stop it. I'm not a girl and a boy, so I'm here.
> **Boy:** What?
> **Girl:** I'm a boy and also a girl.
> **Boy:** You, now, are you today a boy?
> **Girl:** Yes.
> **Boy:** And tomorrow what will you be?
> **Girl:** A girl. Tomorrow I'll be a girl. Today I'll be a boy.
> **Boy:** And after tomorrow?
> **Girl:** I'll be a girl.
>
> [*Ehrlich & Blum-Kulka, 2014, p.31*]

sex differences Biological differences between males and females, in organs, hormones, and body type.

gender differences Differences in the roles and behaviors of males and females that are prescribed by the culture.

Same Situation, Far Apart: Culture Clash? He wears the orange robes of a Buddhist monk and she wears the hijab of a Muslim girl. Although he is at a week-long spiritual retreat led by the Dalai Lama and she is in an alley in Pakistan, both carry universal toys—a pop gun and a bride doll, identical to those found almost everywhere.

Test Your Imagination Preschool children have impressive imaginations and strong social impulses. When two friends are together, they launch into amazing fun, drinking tea, crossing swords, wearing special masks or bracelets, or whatever. Adults may be more limited—can you picture these two scenes with genders switched, the boys in the tea party and the girls in the sword fight?

phallic stage Freud's third stage of development, when the penis becomes the focus of concern and pleasure.

Oedipus complex The unconscious desire of young boys to replace their father and win their mother's romantic love.

superego In psychoanalytic theory, the judgmental part of the personality that internalizes the moral standards of the parents.

Electra complex The unconscious desire of girls to replace their mother and win their father's romantic love.

identification An attempt to defend one's self-concept by taking on the behaviors and attitudes of someone else.

As already mentioned, girls tend to play with other girls and boys with other boys. Despite their parents' and teachers' wishes, children say, "No girls [or boys] allowed." Most older children consider ethnic discrimination immoral, but they accept some sex discrimination (Møller & Tenenbaum, 2011). Why?

Theories of Gender Development

A dynamic-systems approach reminds us that attitudes, roles, and even the biology of gender differences change from one developmental period to the next. Theories about how and why this occurs suggest explanations (Martin & Ruble, 2010; Leaper, 2013). Consider the five broad theories first described in Chapter 2.

Psychoanalytic Theory

Freud (1938/1995) called the period from about ages 3 to 6 the **phallic stage,** named after the *phallus,* the Greek word for penis. At about 3 or 4 years of age, said Freud, boys become aware of their male sexual organ. They masturbate, fear castration, and develop sexual feelings toward their mother.

These feelings make every young boy jealous of his father—so jealous, according to Freud, that he wants to replace his dad. Freud called this the **Oedipus complex,** after Oedipus, son of a king in Greek mythology. Abandoned as an infant and raised in a distant kingdom, Oedipus returned to his birthplace and, without realizing it, killed his father and married his mother. When he discovered the horror, he blinded himself.

Freud believed that this ancient story dramatizes the overwhelming emotions that all boys feel about their parents—both love and hate. Every male feels guilty about his unconscious incestuous and murderous impulses. In self-defense, he develops a powerful conscience called the **superego,** which is quick to judge and punish.

That marks the beginning of morality, according to psychoanalytic theory. This theory contends that a boy's fascination with superheroes, guns, kung fu, and the like arises from his unconscious impulse to kill his father. Further, an adult man's homosexuality, homophobia, or obsession with guns, prostitutes, and hell arise from problems at the phallic stage.

Freud offered several descriptions of the moral development of girls. One centers on the **Electra complex** (also named after a figure in classical mythology). The Electra complex is similar to the Oedipus complex in that the little girl wants to eliminate the same-sex parent (her mother) and become intimate with the other-sex parent (her father). That may also lead girls to develop a superego.

According to psychoanalytic theory, at the phallic stage, children cope with guilt and fear through **identification;** that is, they try to become like the same-sex parent. Consequently, young boys copy their fathers' mannerisms, opinions, and actions, and girls copy their mothers'. Both sexes exaggerate the male or female role, which is why 5-year-olds have such sexist ideas.

Most psychologists have rejected Freud's theory regarding sex and gender. They favor one or another of many other theories to explain the young child's sex and gender awareness.

a case to study

My Daughters

Since the superego arises from the phallic stage, and since Freud believed that sexual identity and expression are crucial for mental health, his theory suggests that parents should encourage children to accept and follow gender roles. Many social scientists disagree. They contend that the psychoanalytic explanation of sexual and moral development "flies in the face of sociological and historical evidence" (David et al., 2004, p. 139).

Accordingly, I learned in graduate school that Freud was unscientific, and I deliberately dressed my baby girls in blue, not pink. However, as explained in Chapter 2, developmental scientists seek to connect research, theory, and experience. My own experience has made me rethink my rejection of Freud, as episodes with my four daughters illustrate.

My rethinking began with a conversation with my eldest daughter, Bethany, when she was about 4 years old:

Bethany: When I grow up, I'm going to marry Daddy.
    Me: But Daddy's married to me.
Bethany: That's all right. When I grow up, you'll probably be dead.
    Me: *[Determined to stick up for myself]* Daddy's older than me, so when I'm dead, he'll probably be dead, too.
Bethany: That's OK. I'll marry him when he gets born again.

I was dumbfounded, without a good reply. I had no idea where she had gotten the concept of reincarnation. Bethany saw my face fall, and she took pity on me:

Bethany: Don't worry, Mommy. After you get born again, you can be our baby.

The second episode was a conversation I had with my daughter Rachel when she was about 5:

Rachel: When I get married, I'm going to marry Daddy.
    Me: Daddy's already married to me.
Rachel: *[With the joy of having discovered a wonderful solution]* Then we can have a double wedding!

The third episode was considerably more graphic. It took the form of a "valentine" left on my husband's pillow on February 14th by my daughter Elissa (see Figure 10.2).

Finally, when Sarah turned 5, she also said she would marry her father. I told her she couldn't, because he was married to me. Her response revealed one more hazard of watching TV: "Oh, yes, a man can have two wives. I saw it on television."

As you remember from Chapter 1, a single example (or four daughters from one family) does not prove that Freud was correct. I still think Freud was wrong on many counts. But his description of the phallic stage seems less bizarre than I once thought.

COURTESY KATHLEEN BERGER

FIGURE 10.2
Pillow Talk Elissa placed this artwork on my husband's pillow. My pillow, beside it, had a less colorful, less elaborate note— an afterthought. It read, "Dear Mom, I love you too."

Behaviorism

Behaviorists believe that virtually all roles, values, and morals are learned. To behaviorists, gender distinctions are the product of ongoing reinforcement and punishment, as well as social learning. Parents, peers, and teachers all reward behavior that is "gender appropriate" more than behavior that is "gender inappropriate" (Berenbaum et al., 2008).

For example, "adults compliment a girl when she wears a dress but not when she wears pants" (Ruble et al., 2006, p. 897), and a boy who asks for both a train and a doll for his birthday is likely to get the train. Boys are rewarded for boyish requests, not for girlish ones. Indeed, the parental push toward traditional gender behavior in play and chores is among the most robust findings of decades of research on this topic (Eagly & Wood, 2013).

Social learning is considered an extension of behaviorism. According to that theory, people model themselves after people they perceive to be nurturing, powerful, and yet similar to themselves. For young children, those people are usually their parents.

As it happens, adults are the most sex-typed of their entire lives when they are raising young children. If an employed woman ever leaves her job to become a housewife, it is when she has a baby. Fathers behave differently than mothers with young children, who learn sex roles from their parents. No wonder they are quite sexist (Hallers-Haalboom et al., 2014).

Furthermore, although national policies (e.g., subsidizing preschool) impact gender roles and many fathers are involved caregivers, women in every nation do much more child care, house cleaning, and meal preparation than do men (Hook, 2010). Children follow those examples, unaware that the behavior they see is caused partly by their very existence: Before children are born, many couples share domestic work, but baby care often changes that.

Cognitive Theory

Cognitive theory offers an alternative explanation for the strong gender identity that becomes apparent at about age 5 (Kohlberg et al., 1983). Remember that cognitive theorists focus on how children understand various ideas. A **gender schema** is the child's understanding of male–female differences (Martin et al., 2011).

gender schema A cognitive concept or general belief based on one's experiences—in this case, a child's understanding of sex differences.

Cognitive theorists point out that young children have many gender-related experiences but not much cognitive depth. They see the world in simple, egocentric terms, as explained in Chapter 9. For this reason, their gender schemas categorize male and female as opposites. Nuances, complexities, exceptions, and gradations about gender (as well as just about everything else) are beyond them.

As Piaget noted, during the preoperational stage, appearance trumps logic. One group of researchers who advocate the cognitive interpretation noted that "[m]any young children pass through a stage of gender appearance rigidity; girls insist on wearing dresses, often pink and frilly, whereas boys refuse to wear anything with a hint of femininity" (Halim et al., 2014, p. 1091). In the research reported by this group, parents sometimes were quite unisex, in attitude or action, but that did not necessarily sway a preschool girl who wanted a bright pink tutu and a sparkly tiara. The child's gender schema overcame the child's experience.

Sociocultural Theory

Sociocultural theory stresses the importance of cultural values and customs. Some aspects of a culture are transmitted through the parents, as explained in the discussion of behaviorism, but many more arise from the larger community. This varies from place to place and time to time, as would be expected for any cultural value.

Consider a meta-analysis of international research. In many cultures, men prefer younger, more attractive women as mates, and women seek older, more established men. But this preference changes as cultures change, when nations become more equitable in treatment of men and women (Zentner & Mitura, 2012).

Thus, national culture affects even personal adult choices such as marriage partners. Children are influenced by norms. That is why boys want to be soldiers, or engineers, or football players—ambitions more apparent in some cultures than others.

My 4-year-old daughter said she wanted to be a nurse when she grew up. I replied, "Nurses are wonderful, but why don't you become a doctor?" She looked at me as if I were stupid: "Oh Mommy, the girls are nurses and the boys are doctors." She was right: I knew possibilities, but I forgot her personal experience.

Universal Theories

Humanism stresses the hierarchy of needs, beginning with survival, then safety, then love and belonging. The final two needs—respect and self-actualization—are not considered priorities for people until the earlier three have been satisfied.

Ideally, babies have all their basic needs met, and toddlers learn to feel safe, which makes love and belonging crucial during early childhood. Children increasingly strive for admiration from their peers. Therefore, the girls seek to be one of the girls and the boys to be one of the boys.

In a study of slightly older children, participants wanted to be part of same-sex groups, not because they disliked the other sex, but because that satisfied their need to belong (Zosuls et al., 2011). As we have already seen, children increasingly prefer to play with children of their own sex because humans are social beings who want to be validated for who they are. By age 6, they are astute "gender detectives" who scan their environment for differences between boys and girls, not always accurately, as in this example:

> On her first day of school, Mia sits at the lunch table eating a peanut butter and jelly sandwich. She notices that a few boys are eating peanut butter and jelly, but not one girl is. When her father picks her up from school, Mia runs up to him and exclaims, "Peanut butter and jelly is for boys! I want a turkey sandwich tomorrow."
>
> *[Quoted in Miller et al., 2013, p. 307]*

Humanism would interpret this as evidence that Mia's need to belong to the girls in her class overruled her earlier basic need, which was satisfied with peanut butter and jelly.

Evolutionary theory holds that male–female sexual passion is one of humankind's basic drives, because all creatures have two essential urges—to survive and to reproduce. For this reason, males and females try to look attractive to the other sex—walking, talking, and laughing in gendered ways. If girls see their mothers wearing make-up and high heels, they want to do likewise.

According to evolutionary theory, the species' need to reproduce is part of everyone's genetic heritage, which makes young boys and girls copy adult behavior that is sexually alluring. For example, one 6-year-old girl, when she was taking a bath and her father came into the bathroom, put her hands on her chest to cover her nipples. Children begin to model themselves after adult men and women, so that they will be ready after puberty to mate and a new generation will be born, as evolution requires.

Thus, according to this theory, over millennia of human history, genes, chromosomes, and hormones have evolved to allow the species to survive. Genes dictate that boys are more active (rough-and-tumble play) and girls more domestic (playing house) because that prepares them for adulthood, when fathers defend against predators and mothers care for the home and children: To deny that is to deny nature.

What Is Best?

Each of the major developmental theories strives to explain the ideas that young children express and the roles they follow. No consensus has been reached. Regarding sex or gender, those who contend that nature is more important than nurture, or that nurture is more important than nature, tend to design, cite, and believe studies that endorse their perspective. Only recently has a true interactionist

perspective (that is a perspective that emphasizes that nature affects nurture and vice versa) on gender been endorsed (Eagly & Wood, 2013).

These theories raise important questions: What roles *should* parents and other caregivers teach? Should every child learn to combine the best of both sexes (called *androgyny*), thereby causing gender stereotypes to crumble as children become more mature, much as a belief in Santa and the Tooth Fairy disappears? Or should male–female distinctions be encouraged as essential for human reproduction and family life?

Answers vary among developmentalists as well as among parents and cultures. Generally, children become more stereotyped in the gender behaviors they endorse, a tendency some adults encourage and others do not. A few children rebel. They are called transgender, or gender dysphoric, or non-conforming, with each label controversial because of the implications for the child and the family (Drescher, 2014). During most of childhood, such children often hide their feelings to prevent being rejected by peers. This is particularly true during the preschool years, when peers and parents usually expect every child to follow gender norms (Cotton, 2014).

Determining how to raise children who are happy to be themselves but not prejudiced against those of the other sex or against those who are gender non-conforming is one challenge that all caregivers face.

SUMMING UP   Caregiving styles vary, ranging from very strict, cold, and demanding to very lax, warm, and permissive. Baumrind's classic research categorized parenting as authoritarian, authoritative, and permissive; these categories still seem relevant, even though the original research was limited in many ways. A fourth type, neglectful/uninvolved, has also been described. Cross-cultural research questions Baumrind's categories but finds, in general, that a middle ground—neither strict nor lax—seems best. Parental warmth seems more crucial than other aspects of style. Neglectful and uninvolved parenting is, in every culture, harmful.

The young child's ideas and stereotypes about males and females are quite rigid during early childhood. Norms are changing. Theorists differ in their explanations and interpretations of gender differences, some emphasizing biological and brain differences, others stressing the impact of culture. That is true for caregivers as well: All are affected by their culture and assumptions, but some believe that the primary impetus for boy–girl behavior is biological, others that culture is far more influential.

WHAT HAVE YOU LEARNED?

1. Which parenting style seems to promote the happiest, most successful children?
2. Why do U.S. childhood professionals advise limitations on electronic media for young children?
3. What did Freud believe about the attitudes young children have regarding their mothers and fathers?
4. What do behaviorists say about the origins of gender roles?
5. How is the idea of the sexes as opposites related to cognitive theory?
6. How does evolutionary theory explain why children follow gender norms?
7. Why is the nature–nurture debate likely to arise when gender roles are considered?●

Moral Development

Children develop increasingly complex moral values, judgments, and behaviors as they mature. Emotional regulation, sexual differences, and parenting practices are all moral issues, as "morality is multifaceted and includes affective, cognitive, and behavioral components" (Smetana, 2013). Thus, moral development is evident in every topic already discussed.

Rough-and-tumble play, for instance, teaches children not to hurt their playmates. Concern for helping other people is also apparent in sociodramatic play, especially the rescue fantasies and caregiving routines that are commonly acted out. Children learn to take turns and to share, and they believe it unfair when another child does not do so (Utendale & Hastings, 2011).

Piaget thought that moral development began when children learned games with rules, which he connected with concrete operational thought at about age 7 (Piaget, 1932/2013). We now know that Piaget was mistaken: Both games with rules and moral development are evident much earlier.

Some precursors of morality appear in infancy (Narvaez & Lapsley, 2009). By age 3 or even earlier, children evidence many moral emotions and behaviors. For example, when given rewards to distribute, 3-year-olds try to be fair, giving each person an equal amount unless someone has been helpful or mean, and then they are rewarded by getting more or punished by getting less (Baumard et al., 2012).

With maturation and adult guidance over the preschool years, children develop guilt (as Erikson explained) and self-control. That helps them behave in ethical ways and feel pride when they do so (Kochanska et al., 2009; Konner, 2010; R. Thompson, 2014).

Video: Interview with Lawrence Walker discusses what parents can do to encourage their children's moral development.

Nature and Nurture

Many parents, teachers, and other adults consider children's "good" behavior more important than any other advancement already described, including health, motor skills, intelligence, language, and social play. Perhaps for this reason, debate rages over how children internalize standards, develop virtues, and avoid vices. Scholars in many social sciences hold conflicting perspectives—nature versus nurture again.

The *nature* perspective suggests that morality is genetic, an outgrowth of natural bonding, attachment, and cognitive maturation. That would explain why young children help and defend their parents, no matter what the parents do, and punish other children who violate moral rules. Even infants have a sense of what is fair and not, expecting adults to reward effort. An experiment with 6-month-old babies found that they preferred a puppet who helped another puppet, rather than one who did not (Hamlin, 2014).

Morality, if defined as behavior that helps others without immediate reward to oneself, may be in human DNA. According to evolutionary theory, humans protect, cooperate, and even sacrifice for one another because each individual is defenseless and vulnerable to weather, strangers, and wild animals. To survive, people need to rely on other people, and from that need springs a moral sense (Dunning, 2011). The body produces hormones, specifically oxytocin, that naturally push people toward trusting and loving each other (Zak, 2012).

The *nurture* perspective contends that culture is crucial to moral development. That would explain why young children emulate people who follow the rules of their community, even if the actual behavior is not innately good or bad. Although children understand the intellectual difference between morality and custom, some children believe that people who eat raw fish, or hamburgers, or bacon, or dogs are immoral (Turiel, 2002).

Developmentalists distinguish between ethical behavior (seeking not to harm others) and conventional behavior (seeking to follow norms), but that distinction is not always apparent, and may itself be cultural (Haidt, 2013). Consider gun use, abortion, the death penalty, disobeying an elder, stealing food—all considered immoral in some cultures, conventional in others, and morally right (not wrong) in some communities under particular circumstances.

Both nature and nurture are influential in standards of conduct, and the interaction between the two is essential—and well worth discussion and debate. Beyond that truism, specifics cannot be settled here.

However, it is apparent that morality appears during early childhood and that parental practices are crucial as they teach children—explicitly and by example—how to behave (R. Thompson, 2014). Accordingly, we explore two moral issues that arise from age 2 to age 6: children's aggression and adults' disciplinary practices. Nature and nurture are crucial in both.

Empathy and Antipathy

Moral emotions are evident as children play with one another. With increasing social experiences and decreasing egocentrism, children develop **empathy,** an understanding of other people's feelings and concerns, and **antipathy,** a feeling of dislike or even hatred. Experience is crucial at every age; people with more friends of various backgrounds are more empathetic to those of another race or immigration status.

Prosocial Behavior

Scientists studying young humans and other primates report spontaneous efforts to help others who are hurt, crying, or in need of help: Those efforts are evidence of empathy and compassion, which then lead to **prosocial behavior**—extending helpfulness and kindness without any obvious benefit to oneself.

Expressing concern, offering to share, and including a shy child in a game or conversation are examples of prosocial behavior among young children. Jack, age 3, showed empathy when he "refused to bring snacks with peanuts to school because another boy had to sit alone during snack because he was allergic to nuts. Jack wanted to sit with him" (Lovecky, 2009, p. 161).

Prosocial behavior seems to result more from emotion than from intellect, more from empathy than from theory of mind (Eggum et al., 2011). The origins of prosocial behavior may arise from parents helping their children become aware of their own emotions, not from telling children what emotions others might have (Brownell et al., 2013).

The link between empathy and later prosocial behavior in early childhood was traced longitudinally in children from 18 months to 6 years of age. A preschooler's empathy at ages 2 to 4 predicted prosocial behavior in first grade: Those empathetic preschoolers were more likely to share help, and include other children. Neither parents' education nor income predicted prosocial behavior (Taylor et al., 2013).

Prosocial reactions are not automatic. Some children limit empathy by "avoiding contact with the person in need [which illustrates] . . . the importance of emotion development and regulation in the development of prosocial behavior" and the critical influence of cultural norms (Trommsdorff & Cole, 2011, p. 136). Feeling distress may be a part of nature; whether a child expresses that emotion, and how a child responds to his or her feelings of distress, may be nurture.

Antisocial Actions

Antipathy can lead to **antisocial behavior**—deliberately hurting another person, including people who have done nothing wrong. Antisocial actions include verbal insults, social exclusion, and physical assaults (Calkins & Keane, 2009). An antisocial 4-year-old might look another child in the eye, scowl, and then kick him hard without provocation. In general, children become more prosocial and less antisocial as they mature (Ramani et al., 2010).

empathy The ability to understand the emotions and concerns of another person, especially when those emotions and concerns differ from one's own.

antipathy Feelings of dislike or even hatred for another person.

prosocial behavior Actions that are helpful and kind but are of no obvious benefit to oneself.

antisocial behavior Actions that are deliberately hurtful or destructive to another person.

Pinch, Poke, or Pat Antisocial and prosocial responses are actually a sign of maturation: Babies do not recognize the impact of their actions. These children have much more to learn, but they already are quite social.

In some ways, antisocial behavior comes naturally (Seguin & Tremblay, 2013). For 2-year-olds, it is hard to let another child use a crayon that they have already used. Preschool children have a definite sense of ownership: If a crayon belongs to the teacher, it should be shared, but a child who owns it is allowed to be selfish (Neary & Friedman, 2014). The rules of ownership are understood by children as young as 3, who apply them more rigidly than adults from the same community.

At every age, antisocial behavior may indicate a failure of empathy. That may be brain-based; sometimes something is missing in the neuroanatomy of the person (Portnoy et al., 2013). But it also may result directly from parents who do not talk about emotions or respond to the emotions of the child (Taylor et al., 2013; Richards et al., 2014).

Aggression

Not surprisingly, given the moral sensibilities of young children, 5-year-olds already judge whether another child's aggression is justified or not. Children are particularly focused on effects, not motives: A child who accidentally spilled water on another's painting may be the target of that child's justified anger.

As with adults, impulsive self-defense is more readily forgiven than is a deliberate, unprovoked attack. As young children gain in social understanding, particularly theory of mind, they gradually become better at understanding someone else's intentions, and that makes them less likely to judge an accidental action as a hostile one (Choe et al., 2013a).

Researchers recognize four general types of aggression, all of which are evident in early childhood (see Table 10.2). **Instrumental aggression** is common among 2-year-olds, who often want something they do not have and simply try to take it. An aggressive reaction from the other child—crying, hitting, and resisting the grab of the instrumentally aggressive child—is also more typical at age 2 than earlier or later.

Reactive aggression is therefore common among young children; almost every child reacts when hurt, whether or not the hurt was deliberate. Children are less likely to respond with physical aggression as they develop emotional control and theory of mind (Olson et al., 2011).

instrumental aggression Behavior that hurts someone else because the aggressor wants to get or keep a possession or a privilege.

reactive aggression An impulsive verbal or physical retaliation for another person's intentional or accidental action.

relational aggression Nonphysical acts, such as insults or social rejection, aimed at harming the social connection between the victim and other people.

bullying aggression Unprovoked, repeated physical or verbal attacks, especially on victims who are unlikely to defend themselves.

Relational aggression (usually verbal) destroys another child's self-esteem and disrupts the victim's social networks, becoming more hurtful as children mature. A young child might tell another, "You can't be my friend" or "You are fat," hurting another's feelings. These are examples of relational aggression.

The fourth and most ominous type is **bullying aggression,** done to dominate someone else. It is not rare among young children but should be stopped before school age, when it becomes particularly destructive. Not only does it destroy the self-esteem of victims, it impairs the later development of the bullies, who learn behavior patterns that will harm them in adulthood. (**Developmental Link:** An in-depth discussion of bullying appears in Chapter 13.)

TABLE 10.2	The Four Forms of Aggression	
Type of Aggression	**Definition**	**Comments**
Instrumental aggression	Hurtful behavior that is aimed at gaining something (such as a toy, a place in line, or a turn on the swing) that someone else has	Often increases from age 2 to 6; involves objects more than people; quite normal; more egocentric than antisocial.
Reactive aggression	An impulsive retaliation for a hurt (intentional or accidental) that can be verbal or physical	Indicates a lack of emotional regulation, characteristic of 2-year-olds. A 5-year-old can usually stop and think before reacting.
Relational aggression	Nonphysical acts, such as insults or social rejection, aimed at harming the social connections between the victim and others	Involves a personal attack and thus is directly antisocial; can be very hurtful; more common as children become socially aware.
Bullying aggression	Unprovoked, repeated physical or verbal attack, especially on victims who are unlikely to defend themselves	In both bullies and victims, a sign of poor emotional regulation; adults should intervene before the school years. (Bullying is discussed in Chapter 13.)

All forms of aggression become less common from ages 2 to 6, as the brain matures and empathy increases. In addition, children learn to use aggression selectively, and that decreases both victimization and aggression later on (Ostrov et al., 2014). Parents, peers, and preschool teachers are pivotal mentors in this process.

It is a mistake to expect children to regulate their emotions on their own. If they are not guided, they may develop destructive patterns. It is also a mistake to punish aggressors too harshly because that may remove them from their zone of proximal development, where they can learn to regulate their anger.

In other words, although there is evidence that preschool children spontaneously judge others who harm people, with the emphasis on the actual hurt more than the intention, there also is evidence that prosocial and antisocial behavior is learned (Smetana, 2013). Preschool teachers are often instrumental in this education because they have many opportunities to teach: Aggression often arises in a social setting with other children.

A longitudinal study found that close teacher–student relationships in preschool predicted less aggression and less victimization in elementary school, presumably because close relationships led teachers to guide the children to control their own reactive aggression (Runions & Shaw, 2013).

Good Behavior

For people everywhere, part of human development is learning the moral standards of their culture. Each culture has particular moral principles; parents form

personal standards based on these principle and then guide their children in developing good behavior.

However, no child always does exactly what parents want. Indeed, if a child is too quiet and proper, that may be a sign that the child is fearful of a parent's rage. Some disagreements, some protests, some untoward impulses and unexpected rebellion are part of the normal process of growing up.

Lest anyone imagine that children will always be good if they have benevolent parents, consider a study of mothers and 3-year-olds during late afternoon (a stressful time). Conflicts (including verbal disagreements) arose about every two minutes (Laible et al., 2008). Here is one example that began with an activity recommended for every parent; the mother was about to take her daughter for a walk:

> **Child:** I want my other shoes.
> **Mother:** You don't need your other shoes. You wear your Pooh sandals when we go for a walk.
> **Child:** Noooooo.
> **Mother:** [Child's name]! You don't need your other shoes.
> **Child:** [Cries loudly]
> **Mother:** No, you don't need your other shoes. You wear your Pooh sandals when we go for a walk.
> **Child:** Ahhhh. Want pretty dress. [Crying]
> **Mother:** Your pretty dress!
> **Child:** Yeah.
> **Mother:** You can wear them some other day.
> **Child:** Noooooo. [Crying]
>
> [from Laible et al., 2008, pp. 442–443]

In this study, those 3-year-olds who had been securely attached at age 1 (an indication of responsive parenting) had as many conflicts as those who had been insecurely attached. Obviously, responsive parents do not always have children who are peaceful and obedient.

However, unlike the situation in the snippet above, the mothers of securely attached children more often compromised and explained (Laible et al., 2008). Is that the best response? Should this mother have offered reasons why the other shoes were not appropriate, or should she have let her daughter wear them? Alternatively, should she have slapped the child for crying, or said, "I won't walk with you if you fuss"?

Discipline

Since misbehavior is part of growing up, parents must respond. How to respond is a major moral issue for the parents, with each type of response teaching the child something about moral behavior.

Physical Punishment

In the United States, young children are slapped, spanked, or beaten more often than are infants or older children. They are physically disciplined more often than children in Canada or Western Europe but less often than children in Africa or South America. Not only in the United States but also in many developing nations, adults remember being physically punished and think it works. In some ways, they are correct: Physical punishment (called **corporal punishment** because it hurts the body) succeeds at the moment—it is impossible to misbehave while being spanked, and afterwards children are usually quiet.

Longitudinal research finds, however, that children who are physically punished are more likely to become bullies, delinquents, and then abusive adults.

Especially for Parents of 3-Year-Olds How could a parent compromise with a child who wants to wear "other shoes"? (see response, page 339)

corporal punishment Punishment that physically hurts the body, such as slapping, spanking, etc.

Especially for Parents Suppose you agree that spanking is destructive, but you sometimes get so angry at your child's behavior that you hit him or her. Is your reaction appropriate? (see response, page 340)

They are also less likely to learn quickly in school or attend college (Straus & Paschall, 2009). In fact, although children who misbehave in externalizing ways (hitting, yelling, throwing things) are more likely to be spanked, longitudinal research finds that children who are not spanked are more likely to learn self-control. As spanking increases, so does misbehavior (Gershoff, 2013).

In 33 nations (mostly in Europe), corporal punishment is illegal; in many nations on other continents, it is the norm. In the United States, parents use it often. Even in U.S. schools, paddling is legal (but rarely used) in 19 of the 50 states. Most of those states are in the Southeast, and most of the children who are paddled are African American boys, which raises questions about the justice of the punishment (Morones, 2013).

Although some adults believe that physical punishment will "teach a lesson" of obedience, the lesson that children learn may be that "might makes right." When they become bigger and stronger, children who have been physically disciplined then tend to use corporal punishment on others—their classmates, their wives or husbands, their children. Most developmentalists advise against corporal punishment, but this issue is controversial. Many parents believe that spanking is sometimes necessary.

Smack Will the doll learn never to disobey her mother again?

💬 opposing perspectives

Is Spanking Okay?

Opinions about spanking are influenced by past experiences and cultural norms, making it hard for opposing perspectives to be understood by people on the other side (Ferguson, 2013).

What might be right with spanking? One argument is that over the centuries many parents have done it, so it has stood the test of time. Indeed, spanking is probably the most common punishment in the United States: One study found that 85% of United States teenagers remember being slapped or spanked by their mothers (Bender et al., 2007).

Another argument is that the correlations often reported between spanking and later depression, crime, low achievement, and so on may reflect SES differences, not spanking. As you remember from Chapter 1, sometimes a correlation is the result of a third variable, which is the cause of both of the two variables that correlate. Since people who do not spank their children tend to have more education than people who do, SES may be the real reason children who are not spanked tend to do better in school. A study that attempted to parcel out all the possible third variables between punishment style and later development found a much smaller correlation between spanking and future problems than most other studies report (Ferguson, 2013).

What might be wrong with spanking? One problem is the emotions of the adult, as angry spankers sometimes become abusive. Another problem is the child's cognition. Many children do not understand the reason behind the spanking. Parents assume the transgression is obvious, but many children think the parents' emotions, not the child's actions, triggered the spanking (Harkness et al., 2011).

Almost all the research finds that children who are spanked continue to suffer in many ways. They are more depressed, more antisocial, more likely to hate school, and less likely to have close friends. While critical thinking demands that we consider all sides until the evidence is clear, one developmentalist says, "We know enough now to stop hitting our children" (Gershof, 2013, p. 133). Most other child advocates agree.

Yet the evidence is not clear enough to satisfy everyone. For example, one study of parents who attend religiously conservative Protestant churches found that, as expected, they spanked their children more often than other parents did. However, unexpectedly, children spanked during early (but not middle) childhood did not develop the lower self-esteem and increased aggression that has been found with other spanked children (Ellison et al., 2011). Indeed, the opposite was more likely.

Many studies of children from all family constellations find that physical punishment of young children correlates with delayed theory of mind and increased aggression (Olson et al., 2011). To prove cause without a doubt would require parents of monozygotic twins to raise them identically, except that one twin would be spanked often and the other never. Of course, that is unethical as well as impossible.

Nonetheless, most developmentalists wonder why parents would take the chance. The best argument in favor of spanking is that alternative punishments may be worse (Larzelere et al., 2010). Let us consider other options.

Psychological Control

A common method of discipline is called **psychological control,** in which children's shame, guilt, and gratitude are used to control their behavior (Barber, 2002). Psychological control may reduce academic achievement and emotional understanding, just as spanking is thought to do (Alegre, 2011).

Consider the results of a several studies in Finland, in which parents were asked about psychological control (Aunola et al., 2013). If parents strongly agreed with the following questions, they were considered to use psychological control:

1. "My child should be aware of how much I have done for him/her."
2. "I let my child see how disappointed and shamed I am if he/she misbehaves."
3. "My child should be aware of how much I sacrifice for him/her."
4. "I expect my child to be grateful and appreciate all the advantages he/she has."

// **Response for Parents of 3-Year-Olds** (from page 337): Remember, authoritative parents listen but do not usually give in. A parent could ask why the child did not want the Pooh sandals (ugly? too tight? old?) and explain why the "other shoes" were not appropriate (raining? save for special occasions? hard to walk in?). A promise for the future (e.g., "Let's save your other shoes and pretty dress for the birthday party tomorrow") might stop the "Noooo."

psychological control A disciplinary technique that involves threatening to withdraw love and support and that relies on a child's feelings of guilt and gratitude to the parents.

The authors of the study suggest that, since spanking was the norm, conservative Protestant children do not perceive being spanked as stigmatizing or demeaning. Moreover, spanking may be accompanied by induction: Religious leaders also tell parents to explain transgressions, to assure children that they are loved, and never to spank in anger. As a result, their children may view mild-to-moderate corporal punishment as legitimate, appropriate, and even a sign of parental involvement, commitment, and concern (Ellison et al., 2011, p. 957).

As I write these words, I realize that the opposing perspective is mine. As you saw in the opening of this chapter, I believe that children should never be hit. I am one of many developmentalists convinced that alternatives to spanking are better for the child as well as a safeguard against abuse.

But a dynamic-systems view considers discipline as one aspect of a complex web. A multi-cultural understanding makes it apparent that, whenever cultures differ radically about any aspect of child development, it is wise to reflect before judging.

I do not think children should be spanked. Yet I know that I am influenced by my background and context; I also know that I am not always right. Whatever your opinion, consider the alternatives.

She understands? Children who are spanked remember the pain and anger, but not the reason for the punishment. It is better for parents to explain what the misbehavior was. However, sometimes explanations are not understood.

The higher the parents scored on these four measures of psychological control, the lower the children's math scores were—and this connection grew stronger over time. Moreover, the children tended to have negative emotions (depression, anger, and so on).

Time-Out and Induction

A disciplinary technique often used with young children in North America is the **time-out,** in which an adult requires a misbehaving child to sit quietly, without toys or playmates, for a short time. Time-out is favored by many experts. For example, in the large, longitudinal evaluation of the Head Start program highlighted in Chapter 9, an increase in time-outs and a decrease in spankings were considered signs of improved parental discipline (U.S. Department of Health and Human Services, 2010).

time-out A disciplinary technique in which a child is separated from other people for a specified time.

The crucial idea behind time-out is that it not be done in anger, or for too long; it is recommended that parents use a calm voice and that the time-out last only one to five minutes (Morawska & Sanders, 2011). It works as a punishment if the child really enjoys "time-in," when the child is happily engaged with the parents or with peers. Time-outs must not be done with hostility.

Often combined with the time-out is another alternative to physical punishment and psychological control—**induction,** in which the parents talk extensively with the offender, helping the child understand why his or her behavior was wrong. Ideally, time-out allows the child to calm down, and a strong and affectionate parent–child relationship allows the child to explain his or her emotions and the parent to listen carefully. The parent then encourages the child to imagine what he or she *might have* done instead of what *was* done.

induction A disciplinary technique in which the parent tries to get the child to understand why a certain behavior was wrong. Listening, not lecturing, is crucial."

Such conversation helps children internalize standards, but induction takes time and patience. Since 3-year-olds confuse causes with consequences, they cannot answer an angry "Why did you do that?" or appreciate a lengthy explanation of why the behavior was wrong. Simple induction ("You made him sad") may be more appropriate, but even that is hard before a child develops theory of mind.

Nonetheless, induction seems to pay off over time. Children whose parents used induction when they were 3 years old became children with fewer externalizing problems in elementary school (Choe et al., 2013b).

// **Response for Parents** (from page 338): No. The worst time to spank a child is when you are angry. You might seriously hurt the child, and the child will associate anger with violence. You would do better to learn to control your anger and develop other strategies for discipline and for prevention of misbehavior.

Bad Boy or Bad Parent? For some children and in some cultures, sitting alone is an effective form of punishment. Sometimes, however, it produces an angry child without changing the child's behavior.

SUMMING UP   Children's moral development often advances during early childhood, as they develop empathy while their theory of mind advances and their emotions become better regulated. New empathy usually helps a child act prosocially, making the child able to share, take turns, and so on. Children can also increasingly develop antipathy, another emotion that indicates cognitive advances. All young children are sometimes aggressive, engaging in instrumental (to get something) or reactive aggression. Those who hurt other children without a self-protective reason are bullies and need to learn more prosocial ways to act.

Parents, guided by their culture, teach morality in many ways. One way is that children learn from parents' strategies for discipline, sometimes learning the wrong lesson, such as that people who are stronger can hurt other people. Every means of punishment may have long-term effects, with physical punishment especially criticized for encouraging aggression. Psychological control seems better, in that it discourages externalizing problems, but it may increase internalizing difficulties. Time-out and induction are generally thought to be best, but individual and cultural differences affect the efficacy of every mode of discipline.

WHAT HAVE YOU LEARNED?

1. What did Piaget believe about the moral development of children?
2. How might evolutionary theory explain moral development?
3. What is the nature perspective on how people develop morals?
4. What is the nurture perspective on how people develop morals?
5. How might children develop empathy and antipathy as they play with one another?
6. What is the connection between empathy and prosocial behavior?
7. What are the four kinds of aggression?
8. How does moral development relate to discipline?
9. Why have some nations made corporal punishment illegal?
10. How could psychological control be harmful?
11. When and how would time-out and induction be most effective?

SUMMARY

Emotional Development

1. Learning to regulate and control emotions is crucial during early childhood. Emotional regulation is made possible by maturation of the brain, as well as by experience.

2. In Erikson's psychosocial theory, the crisis of *initiative versus guilt* occurs during early childhood. Children normally feel pride, sometimes mixed with feelings of guilt. Self-concept develops; preschoolers think they are quite wonderful.

3. Both externalizing and internalizing problems signify impaired self-control. Some emotional problems that indicate psychopathology are first evident during early childhood.

Play

4. All young children enjoy playing—preferably with other children of the same sex, who teach lessons in social interaction that their parents do not.

5. Active play takes many forms, with rough-and-tumble play fostering social skills and sociodramatic play fostering emotional regulation.

Challenges for Caregivers

6. Three classic styles of parenting have been identified: authoritarian, permissive, and authoritative. Generally, children are more successful and happier when their parents are authoritative, expressing warmth and setting guidelines.

7. A fourth style of parenting, neglectful/uninvolved, is always harmful. The particulars of parenting reflect the culture as well as the temperament of the child.

8. Awareness of gender differences begins early, particularly in clothes, toys, playmates, and future careers.

9. Freud emphasized that children are attracted to the opposite-sex parent and eventually seek to identify, or align themselves, with the same-sex parent. Behaviorists hold that gender-related behaviors are learned through reinforcement, punishment (especially for males), and social modeling.

10. Cognitive theorists note that preoperational thinking leads to gender schemas and therefore stereotypes. Sociocultural theorists stress that cultures vary a great deal in the specific of gender norms, and children learn from what they observe.

11. Universal theories note that in all cultures, humans have the powerful need to belong to their group; evolutionary theory contends that gender differences aid the reproduction of the species.

Moral Development

12. Both nature and nurture affect moral development, which is intertwined with emotional regulation and the emergence of empathy. Throughout early childhood, children develop standards of right and wrong.

13. Prosocial emotions lead to caring for others; antisocial emotions lead to harming others. Patterns of behavior, learned in early childhood, continue later in childhood and beyond.

14. Punishments can have long-term consequences. Both corporal punishment and psychological control may have adverse effects. Time-out and induction may be more effective.

KEY TERMS

emotional regulation (p. 311)
effortful control (p. 312)
initiative versus guilt (p. 312)
self-concept (p. 312)
intrinsic motivation (p. 314)
extrinsic motivation (p. 314)
imaginary friends (p. 314)
psychopathology (p. 316)
externalizing problems (p. 316)
internalizing problems (p. 316)

rough-and-tumble play (p. 320)
sociodramatic play (p. 321)
authoritarian parenting (p. 324)
permissive parenting (p. 324)
authoritative parenting (p. 324)
neglectful/uninvolved parenting (p. 324)
sex differences (p. 327)
gender differences (p. 327)

phallic stage (p. 328)
Oedipus complex (p. 328)
superego (p. 328)
Electra complex (p. 328)
identification (p. 328)
gender schema (p. 330)
empathy (p. 334)
antipathy (p. 334)
prosocial behavior (p. 334)

antisocial behavior (p. 334)
instrumental aggression (p. 335)
reactive aggression (p. 335)
relational aggression (p. 336)
bullying aggression (p. 336)
corporal punishment (p. 337)
psychological control (p. 339)
time-out (p. 340)
induction (p. 340)

APPLICATIONS

In all three cases, record data and then draw conclusions.

1. Children's television programming is rife with stereotypes. Watch an hour of children's TV and describe the content of both the programs and the commercials.

2. Gender indicators often go unnoticed. Go to a public place and quantify gender differences, such as articles of clothing, mannerisms, interaction patterns, and activities.

3. Ask three parents about punishment, both how they were punished and how they punish, at what age, and for what.

PART 3

The Developing Person So Far:
Early Childhood

BIOSOCIAL

Body Changes Children continue to grow from ages 2 to 6, but at a slower rate. Normally, the BMI (body mass index) is lower at about ages 5 and 6 than at any other time of life. Children often eat too much unhealthy food and refuse to eat certain other foods altogether. Parents do not realize that appetites are small.

Brain Development and Motor Skills The proliferation of neural pathways continues and myelination is ongoing. Parts of the brain (e.g., the corpus callosum, prefrontal cortex, amygdala, hippocampus, and hypothalamus) connect. This not only also leads to a decline in impulsivity and perseveration but also allows lateralization of the brain's left and right hemispheres and better coordination of the left and right sides of the body, facilitating motor skill development.

Injuries and Maltreatment Far more children worldwide die of avoidable accidents than of diseases. All forms of child maltreatment—including abuse and neglect—require primary, secondary, and tertiary prevention. Neighborhood stability, parental education, income support, and fewer unwanted children reduce maltreatment. Parents are the most common abusers, but everyone in the community can help with prevention.

COGNITIVE

Thinking During Early Childhood Piaget stressed the young child's egocentric, illogical perspective, which prevents the child from grasping concepts such as conservation. Vygotsky stressed the cultural context, noting that children learn from mentors—which include parents, teachers, peers—and from the social context. Children develop their own theories, including a theory of mind, as they realize that not everyone thinks as they do.

Language Learning Language develops rapidly. By age 6, the average child knows 10,000 words and demonstrates extensive grammatical knowledge. Young children can learn two (or more) languages equally well during these years if their social context is encouraging. Mistakes, in overregularization, in pronunciation, and in precise use of vocabulary are common.

Early-Childhood Schooling Young children are avid learners. Child-centered, teacher-directed, and intervention programs, such as Head Start, can all nurture learning; the outcome depends on the warmth and skill of teachers and on the specifics of the curriculum.

PSYCHOSOCIAL

Emotional Development Self-esteem is usually high during early childhood. Self-concept emerges in Erikson's stage of *initiative versus guilt*, as does the ability to regulate emotions. Externalizing problems may be the result of too little emotional regulation; internalizing problems may result from too much control.

Play All young children play, and they play best with peers. Rough and tumble and dramatic play are particularly likely to foster emotional regulation, empathy, and cultural understanding.

Challenges for Caregivers The authoritative caregiving style—which is warm and encouraging, with good communication as well as high expectations—is most effective in promoting the child's self-esteem, autonomy, and self-control. The authoritarian and permissive styles are less beneficial, although cultural variations are apparent. Children develop stereotypic concepts of sex (biological) and gender (cultural); current developmental theories give contradictory explanations. Morals develop in response to cultural norms and practices.

middle childhood

Every age has joys and sorrows, gains and losses. But if you were pushed to choose one best time, you might select ages 6 to 11. In middle childhood, many people experience good health and steady growth as they master new athletic skills, learn thousands of words, and enter a wider social world than that of younger children. Life is safe and happy: the dangers of adolescence (drugs, early sex, violence) are still distant.

But that is not always true. For some, these years are the worst, not the best. They hate school or fear home; they may suffer with asthma or learning disabilities, or they may be the victim of bullies. Adults argue over what occurs during these years: Should children with special needs take medication? What do international tests signify? How are children affected by single parenthood, divorce, or cohabitation? The next three chapters describe these joys and problems.

CHAPTER 11

Middle Childhood:
Biosocial Development

My daughter seemed lonely in the early weeks of first grade. Her teacher told me that she was admired, not rejected, and that she might become friends with Alison, who was also shy and bright. I spoke to Alison's mother, a friendly, big-boned woman named Sharon, and we arranged a play date. Soon Bethany and Alison became best friends, as the teacher had predicted, and their friendship has lasted for years.

Unpredicted, however, is that Sharon became my friend. She and her husband, Rick (an editor of a fashion magazine), had one other child, a pudgy boy two years older.

When my daughter and Alison were in fifth grade, I mentioned to Rick my interest in longitudinal research. He recalled a friend, a professional photographer, who took pictures of Alison and her brother every year. The friend wanted them for his portfolio; Rick was happy to oblige. He then retrieved an old album with stunning depictions of sibling relationships and personality development from infancy on. Alison was smiling and coy, even as an infant, and her brother was gaunt and serious until Alison was born, when he seemed to relax.

Rick was happy with my interest; Sharon was not.

"I hate that album," she said, slamming it shut. She explained that she told the pediatrician that she thought her baby boy was hungry, but the doctor insisted she stick to a four-hour breast-feeding schedule and told her to never give him formula. That's why she hated that album; it was evidence of an inexperienced mother heeding a doctor while starving her son.

Decades later, my daughter and I are still friends with Alison and Sharon, whose adult son is obese. His photo as a thin, serious infant haunts me now as well.

Did Sharon cause his obesity by underfeeding him when he was little, or by over-feeding him later on? Or did his genes and culture interact in a destructive way? Or was he rebelling against his father, whose profession glorifies appearance?

This chapter begins our description of middle childhood, which is usually a happy time. This chapter also describes some problems of this period, and the interaction of genes and environment that cause them. Consequences and solutions are complex:

Sharon and Rick are not the only aging parents who still wonder what they could have done differently and how they can help their adult children now. I wonder, too.

A Healthy Time

middle childhood The period between early childhood and early adolescence, approximately from ages 6 to 11.

Genes and environment safeguard **middle childhood,** as the years from about 6 to 11 are called (Konner, 2010). Fatal diseases and accidents are rare; both nature and nurture make these years the healthiest of the entire life span. In the United States in 2012, the death rate for 5- to 14-year-olds was half the rate for 1- to 4-year-olds and one-fifth the rate for 15- to 24-year-olds.

The reasons are (1) genetic diseases are more threatening in early infancy or old age than in middle childhood, (2) infectious diseases are kept away via immunization, and (3) fatal accidents—although the most common cause of death in early childhood—are rare until adolescence.

The already low death rate has been further reduced recently. For example, in the United States in 1950, the death rate per 100,000 children aged 5 to 14 was 60; in 2010, it was 13. Even the incidence of minor illnesses, such as ear infections, infected tonsils, and flu, has been reduced, in part because of better medicine and immunization (National Center for Health Statistics, 2013).

Slower Growth, Greater Strength

Unlike infants or adolescents, school-age children grow slowly and steadily. Self-care is easy—from dressing to bathing, from making lunch to getting to school. Brain maturation allows children to sit and learn in class without breaking their pencils, tearing their papers, or elbowing their classmates. In these middle years, children are much more self-sufficient than younger children and not yet troubled by adolescent body changes.

Teeth

Important to the individual child is the loss of baby teeth, with the entire set replaced by permanent teeth beginning at about age 6 (with girls a few months ahead of boys) and complete by puberty.

Important to society is oral health overall. Worldwide sixty years ago, many children neither brushed their teeth nor saw a dentist, and fluoride was almost never added to water. That's why many of the oldest-old have missing teeth, as do some younger adults because of disease (especially diabetes) or trauma. In developed nations, teeth are replaced with implants or dentures; in poor nations, many of the elderly have gaps in their mouths or visible gold teeth—a sign of wealth in nations where good dentists were scarce.

Currently, most school-age children brush their teeth, and many communities—including all the larger U.S. cities—add fluoride to drinking water. According to a national survey, about 75 percent of U.S. children saw a dentist for preventive care in the past year, and for 70 percent of them, the condition of their teeth was very good (Iida & Rozier, 2013).

Children's Health Habits

Good childhood habits protect later adult health. The health that most school-age children naturally enjoy may either continue or be disrupted, depending on daily actions, including eating a balanced diet, getting enough exercise and sleep, and breathing clean air. Unfortunately, children who have poor health for economic or social reasons (such as no regular medical care) are vulnerable lifelong, even if their socioeconomic status improves later on, because of epigenetic factors in childhood (Miller & Chen, 2010; Blair & Raver, 2012).

Children's habits during these years are strongly affected by peers and parents. When children see others routinely care for their health, social learning pushes them to do the same. Camps for children with asthma, cancer, diabetes, sickle cell anemia, and other chronic illnesses are particularly beneficial because the example of other children and the guidance of knowledgeable adults help children learn self-care. Such care needs to become routine—not a matter of parental insistence—in childhood, lest teenage rebellion leads to ignoring special diets, pills, warning signs, and doctors (Dean et al., 2010; Naughton et al., 2014).

Physical Activity

Beyond the sheer fun of playing, the benefits of physical activity—especially games with rules, which school-age children are now able to follow—can last a lifetime. Exercise not only improves physical health and reduces depression, it may also improve academic achievement (Efrat, 2011; Carlson et al., 2008).

How could body movement improve brain functioning? A review of the research suggests several possible mechanisms, including direct benefits of better cerebral blood flow and increased neurotransmitters, as well as the indirect results of better mood (Singh et al., 2012).

A new concept in psychology is *embodied cognition,* that human thoughts are affected by body health, comfort, position and so on. If this is true, then a well-functioning body helps thinking. In addition, playing games with other children teaches cooperation, problem-solving, and respect for teammates and opponents, who may be of many backgrounds. Where can children reap these benefits?

Expert Eye–Hand Coordination The specifics of motor skill development in middle childhood depend on the culture. These flute players are carrying on the European Baroque musical tradition that thrives among the poor, remote Guarayo people of Bolivia.

Neighborhood Games

Neighborhood play is flexible. Rules and boundaries are adapted to the context (out of bounds is "past the tree" or "behind the parked truck"). Stickball, touch football, tag, hide-and-seek, and dozens of other running and catching games go on forever—or at least until dark. The play is active, interactive, and inclusive—ideal for children. It also teaches ethics. As one scholar notes:

> Children play tag, hide and seek, or pickup basketball. They compete with one another but always according to rules, and rules that they enforce themselves without recourse to an impartial judge. The penalty for not playing by the rules is not playing, that is, social exclusion.
>
> [Gillespie, 2010, p. 298]

For school-age children, "social exclusion" is a steep price to pay for insisting on their own way. Instead, most cooperate.

Unfortunately, modern life has undercut informal neighborhood games. Vacant lots and empty fields have largely disappeared, and parents fear "stranger danger"—thinking that a stranger will somehow hurt their child (which is exceedingly rare) and ignoring the many benefits of outside play, which are universal. As one advocate of more unsupervised, creative childhood play sadly notes:

> Actions that would have been considered paranoid in the '70s—walking third-graders to school, forbidding your kid to play ball in the street, going down the slide with your child in your lap—are now routine.
>
> [Rosin, 2014]

Idyllic Two 8-year-olds, each with a 6-year-old sister, all four daydreaming or exploring in a very old tree beside a lake in Denmark—what could be better? Ideally, all the world's children would be so fortunate, but most are not.

Indoor activities such as homework, television, and video games crowd out outdoor play, partly because parents always want to see where their children are and what they are doing.

Many parents enroll their children in organizations that offer—depending on the culture—tennis, karate, cricket, rugby, baseball, or soccer. Unfortunately, in every nation, childhood sports leagues are less likely to include children of low SES or children with disabilities. As a result, the children most likely to benefit are least likely to participate, even when enrollment is free. The reasons are many, the consequences sad (Dearing et al., 2009). Another group unlikely to participate are older girls, again a group particularly likely to benefit from athletic activity (Kremer et al., 2014).

Exercise in School

When opportunities for neighborhood play are scarce, physical education in school is a logical alternative. However, because schools are pressured to focus on test scores in academic subjects, time for physical education and recess has declined. A study of Texas elementary schools found that 24 percent had no recess at all and only 1 percent had recess several times a day (W. Zhu et al., 2010).

Texas, unfortunately, is no exception. A survey asking teachers of more than 10,000 third-graders nationwide found that about one-third of the children had less than 15 minutes of recess each day. Children deprived of recess were more often lower SES, in classes that were "hard to manage," in public schools, and in cities. They also had fewer scheduled gym periods (Barros et al., 2009).

These researchers write that "many children from disadvantaged backgrounds are not free to roam their neighborhoods or even their own yards unless they are accompanied by adults. For many of these children, recess periods may be the only opportunity for them to practice their social skills with other children" (Barros et al., 2009, p. 434). Thus, school exercise is least likely for children who most need it—city-dwellers who live in crowded urban neighborhoods, with fearful parents who don't let them go out to play.

Even when gym is required, classes may be too crowded to allow extensive active play, or the school may implement gym on paper but not in practice. For instance, although Alabama requires elementary schools to have daily physical education for at least 30 minutes, a study of all primary schools in one district found that only 22 minutes a day was actually devoted to gym. None of the schools had recess or after-school sports (Robinson et al., 2014). One reason for the lack of after-school sports is that schools fear liability if children are hurt.

Several organizations have developed guidelines to prevent concussions among 7- and 8-year-olds in football practice, as well as to halt full-body impact among children under age 12 playing ice hockey. The fact that regulations need to protect

"Just remember, son, it doesn't matter whether you win or lose—unless you want Daddy's love."

children from brain damage is sobering (Toporek, 2012). Of course, games for young children could be designed to prevent injury, but the usual reaction from adults is to provide protective equipment, such as better helmets for young players.

Ironically, schools in Japan, where many children score well on international tests, usually have several recess breaks totaling more than an hour each day. Japanese public schools typically have good equipment for physical activity, including an indoor gym and a pool.

Why Helmets? Sports organized by adults, such as this football team of 7- to 8-year-old boys sponsored by the Lyons and Police Athletic League of Detroit, may be harmful to children. The best games are those that require lots of running and teamwork—but no pushing or shoving.

JIM WEST/AGE FOTOSTOCK

SUMMING UP School-age children are usually healthy, strong, and capable. Genes as well as immunization protect them against contagious diseases, and medical awareness and care have improved over the past decades. This is particularly evident in oral health. Moreover, children's maturation adds strength, understanding, and coordination, and enables them to undertake self-care and learn health habits to sustain them lifelong. Although neighborhood play, school physical education, and community sports leagues all provide needed activity, energetic play is much more likely for some children than for others. Unfortunately, those who need it most are the least likely to have it.

WHAT HAVE YOU LEARNED?

1. What physical abilities emerge from age 6 to age 11?
2. How do childhood health habits affect adult health?
3. What are the main advantages and disadvantages of physical play during middle childhood?
4. How do children benefit from physical education in school?

Especially for Physical Education Teachers A group of parents of fourth- and fifth-graders have asked for your help in persuading the school administration to sponsor a competitive sports team. How should you advise the group to proceed? (see response, page 355)

Health Problems in Middle Childhood

Some chronic health conditions, including Tourette syndrome, stuttering, and allergies, often worsen during the school years. Even minor problems—wearing glasses, repeatedly coughing or blowing one's nose, or having a visible birthmark—can make children self-conscious, interfering with friendship formation.

Researchers increasingly recognize "that the expression and outcome for any problem will depend on the configuration and timing of a host of surrounding circumstances" (Hayden & Mash, 2014, p. 49). Parents and children are not merely reactive: In a dynamic-systems manner, individuals and contexts influence each other. Consider two examples: obesity and asthma.

Childhood Obesity

Body mass index (BMI) is a measure of body fat that depends on how heavy a person is at their height. **Childhood overweight** is usually defined as a BMI above the 85th percentile, and **childhood obesity** is defined as a BMI above the 95th percentile for children at a particular age. In 2012, 18 percent of 6- to 11-year-olds in the United States were obese (Ogden et al., 2014).

childhood overweight In a child, having a BMI above the 85th percentile, according to the U.S. Centers for Disease Control's 1980 standards for children of a given age.

childhood obesity In a child, having a BMI above the 95th percentile, according to the U.S. Centers for Disease Control's 1980 standards for children of a given age.

VISUALIZING DEVELOPMENT

Childhood Obesity Around the Globe

Obesity now causes more deaths worldwide than malnutrition. Reductions are possible. A multi-faceted prevention effort—including mothers, preschools, pediatricians, grocery stores, and even the White House—has reduced obesity in the United States for 2- to 5-year-olds. It was 13.9 percent in 2002 and was 8.4 percent in 2012. However, obesity rates from age 6 to 60 remain high everywhere.

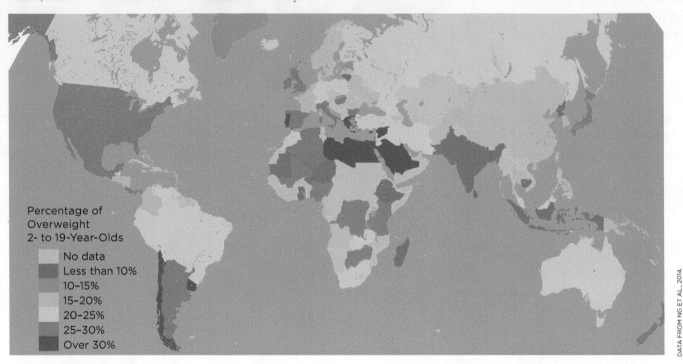

Percentage of Overweight 2- to 19-Year-Olds

- No data
- Less than 10%
- 10–15%
- 15–20%
- 20–25%
- 25–30%
- Over 30%

DATA FROM NG ET AL., 2014.

ADS AND OBESITY

Nations differ in children's exposure to televised ads for unhealthy food. The amount of this advertising continues to correlate with childhood obesity (e.g., Hewer, 2014). Parents can reduce overweight by limiting screen time and playing outside with their children. The community matters as well: When neighborhoods have no safe places to play, rates of obesity soar.

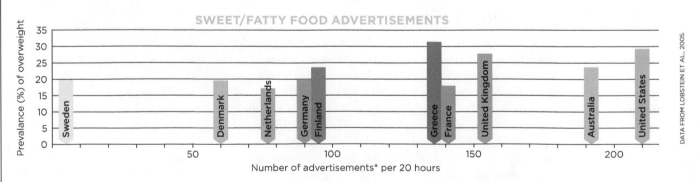

SWEET/FATTY FOOD ADVERTISEMENTS

Prevalance (%) of overweight — Number of advertisements* per 20 hours

Sweden, Denmark, Netherlands, Germany, Finland, Greece, France, United Kingdom, Australia, United States

DATA FROM LOBSTEIN ET AL., 2005.

WORLD HEALTH ORGANIZATION (WHO) RECOMMENDATIONS FOR PHYSICAL ACTIVITY FOR CHILDREN

 1 Children ages 5 to 17 should be active for at least an hour a day.

 2 More than an hour of exercise each day brings additional benefits.

 3 Most physical activity should be aerobic. Vigorous activities should occur 3 times per week or more.

WHO also recommends daily exercise for adults of every age—including centenarians.

ADAPTED FROM WORLD HEALTH ORGANIZATION, 2011.

Childhood obesity is increasing worldwide, having more than doubled since 1980 in all three nations of North America (Mexico, the United States, and Canada) (Ogden et al., 2011). Since 2000, rates seem to have leveled off in the United States and have actually declined in preschool children, but for older children, they continue to increase in most nations, including the most populous two, China and India (Gupta et al., 2012; Ji et al., 2013) (see Visualizing Development, p. 352).

Childhood overweight correlates with asthma, high blood pressure, and elevated cholesterol (especially LDL, the "lousy" cholesterol). As excessive weight builds, average school achievement decreases, self-esteem falls, and loneliness rises (Harrist et al., 2012).

Especially for Teachers A child in your class is overweight, but you are hesitant to say anything to the parents, who are also overweight, because you do not want to offend them. What should you do? (see response, page 356)

Especially for Parents Suppose that you always serve dinner with the television on, tuned to a news broadcast. Your hope is that your children will learn about the world as they eat. Can this practice be harmful? (see response, page 356)

a view from science

What Causes Childhood Obesity?

There are "hundreds if not thousands of contributing factors" for childhood obesity, from the cells of the body to the norms of the society (Harrison et al., 2011, p. 51). Dozens of genes affect weight by influencing activity level, hunger, food preferences, body type, and metabolism. New genes and alleles that affect obesity—and that never act alone—are discovered virtually every month (Dunmore, 2013).

Knowing that genes are involved may slow down the impulse to blame people for being overweight. However, genes cannot explain why obesity rates have increased dramatically, since genes change little from one generation to the next (Harrison et al., 2011). Instead, cohort changes must be responsible.

Look at the figure on obesity among 6- to 11-year-olds in the United States (see Figure 11.1).

At first glance, one might think that the large ethnic gaps (such as 9 percent of Asian Americans and 26 percent of Hispanic Americans) might be genetic. But consider gender: Non-Hispanic white *girls* are twice as likely to be obese as boys, but in the other groups *boys* are more often obese than girls. Something cultural, not biological, must be the reason. Further evidence that social context, not genes, affects obesity was found in a study that controlled for family income and early parenting: Ethnic differences in childhood obesity almost disappeared (Taveras et al., 2013).

What parenting practices make children too heavy? Obesity rates rise if: infants are not breast-fed and begin eating solid foods before 4 months; preschoolers have televisions in their bedrooms and drink high quantities of soda; school-age children sleep too little but have several hours each day of "screen time" (TV, videos, games), rarely playing outside (Hart et al., 2011; Taveras et al., 2013).

Although family habits in infancy and early childhood can set a child on the path to obesity, during middle childhood, children themselves have *pester power*—the ability to get adults to do what they want (Powell et al., 2011). Often they pester their parents to buy calorie-dense foods that are advertised on television.

On average, family contexts changed for the worse toward the end of the twentieth century in North America and are spreading worldwide. For instance, family size has decreased, and as a result, pester power has increased, and

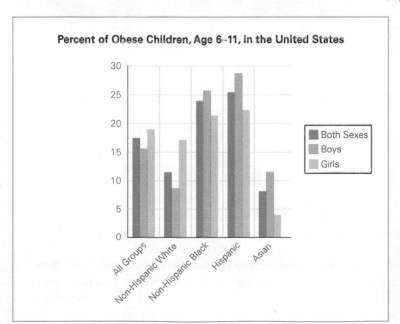

Percent of Obese Children, Age 6–11, in the United States

Both Sexes
Boys
Girls

FIGURE 11.1

Fatter and Fatter The incidence of obesity (defined here as a BMI above the 95th percentile, according to the Centers for Disease Control and Prevention 2000 growth charts) increases with age. Infants and preschoolers have lower rates than schoolchildren, which suggests that nurture is more influential than nature.

more food is available for each child. That makes childhood obesity collateral damage from reduction of birth rate—a worldwide trend in the early twenty-first century.

Attempts to limit sugar and fat clash with the goals of many corporations, since snacks and processed foods are very profitable. On the plus side, many schools have policies that foster good nutrition. A national survey in the United States found that schools are reducing all types of commercial food advertising. However, vending machines are still prevalent in high schools, and free food coupons are often used as incentives in elementary schools (Terry-McElrath et al., 2014).

Overall, simply offering healthy food is not enough to convince children to change their diet; context and culture are crucial (Hanks et al., 2013). Communities can build parks, bike paths, and sidewalks, and nations can decrease subsidies for sugar and corn oil and syrup. As educators try to improve children's eating habits, cultural sensitivity is crucial, since each ethnic group has preferred foods and family patterns. To work against culture is foolish, but working within cultures can protect the children.

For example, African American parents may consider fried fish and potatos part of their culture, but so are baked fish and a variety of greens; Mexican American parents may enjoy rice and beans, but those can be cooked without added fat. Immigrants who want to "eat American" may not be aware of the correlation between fast food and childhood obesity (Alviola et al., 2013).

Home cooking is usually better. In the United States, older adults who immigrated after childhood have lower rates of obesity than do the native born, yet their children are more often obese than other children, a statistic that should give everyone pause.

Rather than trying to zero in on any single factor, a dynamic-systems approach is needed: Many factors, over time, make a child overweight (Harrison et al., 2011). Changing just one factor is not enough. The answer to the second "What Will You Know?" question at the start of this chapter: Everyone is to blame.

Same Situation, Far Apart Children have high energy but small stomachs, so they enjoy frequent snacks more than big meals. Yet snacks are typically poor sources of nutrition. Who is healthier: the Hispanic children eating lollypops at a theme park in Florida or the Japanese children eating *takoyaki* (an octopus dumpling) as part of a traditional celebration near Tokyo?

Asthma

asthma A chronic disease of the respiratory system in which inflammation narrows the airways from the nose and mouth to the lungs, causing difficulty in breathing. Signs and symptoms include wheezing, shortness of breath, chest tightness, and coughing.

Asthma is a chronic inflammatory disorder of the airways that makes breathing difficult. Sufferers have periodic attacks, sometimes requiring a rush to the hospital emergency room, a frightening experience for children who know that asthma might kill them (although it almost never does in childhood).

In the United States, childhood asthma rates have tripled since 1980. (See Figure 11.2 for current rates for those younger than 18 years old.) Parents report that 14 percent of U.S. 5- to 11-year-olds have been diagnosed with asthma at some time, and about 9 percent still suffer from it (National Center for Health Statistics, 2013).

Researchers have long sought the causes of asthma. A few alleles have been identified as contributing factors, but none acts in isolation. Several aspects of modern life—carpets, pollution, house pets, airtight windows, parental smoking, cockroaches, dust mites, less outdoor play—correlate with asthma attacks, but no single factor is the sole trigger. Some children are more susceptible to certain allergens, and a combination of sensitivity to allergies, early respiratory infections, and compromised lung functioning increases wheezing and shortness of breath (Mackenzie et al., 2014).

Some experts suggest a *hygiene hypothesis*: that "the immune system needs to tangle with microbes when we are young" (Leslie, 2012, p. 1428). Children may be overprotected from viruses and bacteria. In their concern about hygiene, parents prevent exposure to minor infections, diseases, and family pets that would strengthen their child's immunity. This hypothesis is supported by data showing that (1) first-born children develop asthma more often than later-born ones; (2) asthma and allergies are less common among farm children; and (3) children born by cesarean delivery (very sterile) have a greater incidence of asthma. Overall, it may be "that despite what our mothers told us, cleanliness sometimes leads to sickness" (Leslie, 2012, p. 1428).

None of these factors, however, *proves* the hygiene hypothesis. Perhaps farm children are protected by drinking unpasteurized milk, by outdoor chores, or by alleles that are more common in farm families, rather than by exposure to a range of bacteria (von Mutius & Vercelli, 2010). In fact, there are "many paths to asthma," with no one cause identified as the crucial one (H. Kim et al., 2010). One review of the hygiene hypothesis notes "the picture can be dishearteningly complex" (Couzin-Frankel, 2010, p. 1168).

However, there is hope. Consider a study of 133 Latino adult smokers, all caregivers of children with asthma. They agreed to allow a Spanish-speaking counselor to come repeatedly to their homes (Borrelli et al., 2010). The counselor placed a smoke monitor in the child's bedroom. A week later she told the caregiver how much smoke exposure the child had experienced. Then, in three sessions, she provided specific suggestions for how to quit smoking, based on research on addiction, with particular sensitivity to Latino values.

Three months later, one-fourth of the caregivers had quit smoking completely, and many of the rest had cut down. The average child's exposure to smoke was cut in half, and asthma attacks diminished (Borrelli et al., 2010). Having data on their child and getting personal encouragement was crucial.

Pride and Prejudice In some city schools, asthma is so common that using an inhaler is a sign of pride, as may be true here. The "prejudice" is beyond the walls of this school nurse's room, in a society that allows high rates of childhood asthma.

// Response for Physical Education Teachers (from page 351): Discuss with the parents their reasons for wanting the team. Children need physical activity, but some aspects of competitive sports are better suited to adults than to children.

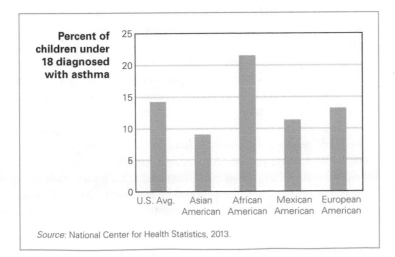

Source: National Center for Health Statistics, 2013.

FIGURE 11.2

Not Breathing Easy Of all U.S. children younger than 18, 14 percent have been diagnosed at least once with asthma. Why are Puerto Rican and African American children more likely to have asthma? Does the answer have to do with nature or nurture, genetics, or pollution?

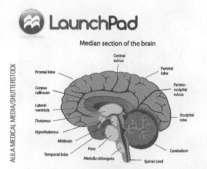

Video Activity: Brain Development: Middle Childhood depicts the changes that occur in a child's brain from age 6 to age 11.

SUMMING UP Some children have chronic health problems that interfere with school and friendship. Among these are obesity and asthma, both of which are increasing in every nation and have genetic and environmental causes. Childhood obesity may seem harmless, but it leads to social problems among classmates and severe health problems later on. Asthma's harm is more immediate: Children with asthma often miss school and may be rushed to emergency rooms, gasping for air. Although genes predispose some children to each particular health problem, family practices and neighborhood context can increase rates of obesity and asthma, and many society-wide policies and cultural customs make the problems worse.

WHAT HAVE YOU LEARNED?

1. What are the national and cohort differences in childhood obesity?
2. Why does a thin 6-year-old not need to "fatten up"?
3. What roles do nature and nurture play in childhood asthma?
4. Why is childhood asthma a concern for developmentalists?

Brain Development

Recall that emotional regulation, theory of mind, and left–right coordination emerge in early childhood. The maturing corpus callosum connects the hemispheres of the brain, enabling balance and two-handed coordination, while myelination adds speed. Maturation of the prefrontal cortex—the executive part of the brain—allows the child to begin to plan, monitor, and evaluate. All of these neurological developments continue. We now look at additional advances in middle childhood.

Coordinating Connections

Increasing maturation results in connections between the various lobes and regions of the brain. Such connections are crucial for the complex tasks that children must master, which require "smooth coordination of large numbers of neurons" (Stern, 2013, p. 577). Certain areas of the brain, called *hubs,* are locations where massive numbers of axons meet. Hubs tend to be near the corpus callosum, and damage to them correlates with brain dysfunction (as in dementia and schizophrenia) (Crossley et al., 2014).

The importance of hubs means that the brain connections formed in middle childhood are crucial for healthy brain functioning. Particularly important are links between the hypothalamus and the amygdala, because emotions need to be regulated so learning can occur. Stress impairs these connections: Slow academic mastery in middle childhood is one more consequence of early maltreatment (Hanson et al., 2014).

One example of the need for brain connections is learning to read, perhaps the most important intellectual accomplishment of middle childhood. Reading is not instinctual: Our ancestors never did it, and until recent centuries, only a few scribes and scholars could make sense of marks on paper. Consequently, the brain has no areas dedicated to reading, the way it does for talking or gesturing (Sousa, 2014).

Instead, reading uses many parts of the brain—one for sounds, another for recognizing letters, another for sequencing, another for comprehension and more. By working together, those parts first foster listening, talking, and thinking, and then put it all together (Lewandowski & Lovett, 2014). Indeed, every skill mastered in middle childhood requires connections between many neurons in several brain regions.

// **Response for Teachers** (from page 353): Speak to the parents, not accusingly (because you know that genes and culture have a major influence on body weight) but helpfully. Alert them to the potential social and health problems their child's weight poses. Most parents are very concerned about their child's well-being and will work with you to improve the child's snacks and exercise levels.

// **Response for Parents** (from page 353): Habitual TV watching correlates with obesity, so you may be damaging your children's health rather than improving their intellect. Your children would probably profit more if you were to make dinner a time for family conversation about world events.

Think Quick; Too Slow

Advance planning and impulse control are aided by faster **reaction time,** which is how long it takes to respond to a stimulus. Increasing myelination reduces reaction time every year from birth until about age 16. Skill at games is an obvious example, from scoring on a video game, to swinging at a pitch, to kicking a speeding soccer ball toward a teammate.

Many more complex examples involve social and academic skills. For instance, being able to discern when to utter a witty remark and when to stay quiet is something few 6-year-olds can do. By age 10, some children have quick reactions, allowing them to (1) realize that a comment could be made and (2) decide what it could be, (3) think about the other person's possible response, and in the same split second (4) know when something should NOT be said.

Both quick replies and quick inhibition develop. Children become less likely to blurt out wrong answers but more likely to enjoy games that require speed. Interestingly, children with reading problems are slower as well as more variable in reaction time, and that itself slows down every aspect of reading (Tamm et al., 2014).

reaction time The time it takes to respond to a stimulus, either physically (with a reflexive movement such as an eyeblink) or cognitively (with a thought).

selective attention The ability to concentrate on some stimuli while ignoring others.

Pay Attention

Neurological advances allow children not only to process information quickly but also to pay special heed to the most important elements of their environment. **Selective attention,** the ability to concentrate on some stimuli while ignoring others, improves markedly at about age 7.

School-age children not only notice various stimuli (which is one form of attention) but also select appropriate responses when several possibilities conflict (Wendelken et al., 2011). Selective attention improves as neurological maturity continues (Stevens & Bavelier, 2012).

For example in school, children listen, take notes, and ignore distractions (all difficult at age 6, easier by age 10). Unfazed by the din of the cafeteria, children react quickly to gestures and facial expressions. On the baseball diamond, older batters ignore the other team's attempts to distract them, and fielders start moving into position as soon as the bat hits the ball.

Pay Attention Some adults think that computers can make children lazy, because they can look up whatever they don't know. But imagine the facial expressions of these children if they were sitting at their desks with 30 classmates, listening to a lecture.

Automatization

One final advance in brain function in middle childhood is **automatization,** the process by which a sequence of thoughts and actions is repeated until it becomes automatic. At first, almost all behaviors that are deliberate require careful thought. After many repetitions, neurons fire in sequence, and less thinking is needed because the firing of one neuron sets off a chain reaction: That is automatization.

Consider again learning to read. At first, eyes (sometimes aided by a guiding finger) focus intensely, painstakingly making out letters and sounding out each one. This leads to the perception of syllables and then words. Eventually, the process becomes so routine that as people drive along on a highway, they read billboards that they have no interest in reading. Children do the same, gradually learning to read without conscious control.

Automatic reading aids other academic skills. One longitudinal study of second-graders—from the beginning to the end of the school year—found a reciprocal process from one type of academic proficiency to another, with automatic processing advancing as learning continues (Lai et al., 2014).

automatization A process in which repetition of a sequence of thoughts and actions makes the sequence routine, so that it no longer requires conscious thought.

Learning to speak a second language, to recite the multiplication tables, and to write one's name also is slow at first but gradually becomes automatic. Habits and routines learned in childhood are useful lifelong—and when they are not, they are hard to break. That's automatization.

Measuring the Mind

In ancient times, if adults were strong and fertile, that was usually enough to be considered a solid member of the community. A few wise men were admired, but most people were not expected to think quickly and profoundly. Over the centuries, though, we humans have placed higher and higher values on intelligence, and have developed ways to measure it.

Aptitude, Achievement, and IQ

In theory, **aptitude** is the potential to master a specific skill or to learn a certain body of knowledge. The brain functions which have just been described—reaction time, selective attention, and automatization—may be the foundation of aptitude, whether the specific aptitude is the ability to become a proficient soccer player, seamstress, chef, student, or whatever.

Measuring the brain directly is complicated, however. Therefore, intellectual aptitude is usually measured by answers to a series of questions. The underlying assumption is that there is one general thing called *intelligence* (often referred to as *g,* for general intelligence) and that correct answers measure *g.*

Originally, IQ tests produced a score that was literally an Intelligence Quotient: Mental age (the average chronological age of children who answer a certain number of questions correctly) was divided by the chronological age of the child who took the test. The result of that division (the quotient) was multiplied by 100.

Thus if the average 10-year-old answered say, exactly 60 questions correctly, then people who got 60 questions right would have a mental age of 10—no matter how old they were. Anyone whose mental age was the same as their chronological age (in this example, a 10-year-old who got 60 questions right) the quotient would be 10 ÷ 10 = 1. The IQ would be 100 (1 × 100), exactly average.

If a 10-year-old answered the questions as well as a typical 12-year-old, the score would be 12 ÷ 10 × 100, or 120. The current method of calculating IQ is more complex, but an IQ within one standard deviation of 100 (between 85 and 115) is still considered average (see Figure 11.3).

> **aptitude** The potential to master a specific skill or to learn a certain body of knowledge.

OBSERVATION QUIZ If a person's IQ is 110, what category is he or she in? (see answer, page 360)

FIGURE 11.3

In Theory, Most People Are Average
Almost 70 percent of IQ scores fall within the normal range. Note, however, that this is a norm-referenced test. In fact, actual IQ scores have risen in many nations; 100 is no longer exactly the midpoint. Furthermore, in practice, scores below 50 are slightly more frequent than indicated by the normal curve shown here because severe disability is not the result of normal distribution, but of genetic and prenatal factors.

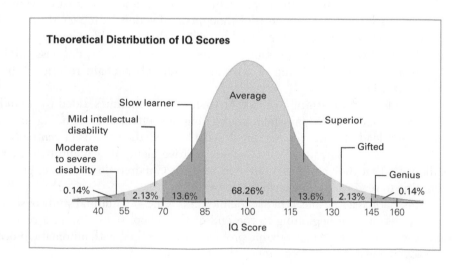

Theoretical Distribution of IQ Scores

- Slow learner
- Average
- Mild intellectual disability
- Superior
- Moderate to severe disability
- Gifted
- Genius

0.14%   2.13%   13.6%   68.26%   13.6%   2.13%   0.14%

40   55   70   85   100   115   130   145   160

IQ Score

In theory, achievement is what has actually been learned, not learning potential (aptitude). School **achievement tests** compare scores to norms established for each grade. For example, children of any age who read as well as the average third-grader would be at the third-grade level in reading achievement.

The words *in theory* precede the definitions of *aptitude* and *achievement* above because, although potential and accomplishment are supposed to be distinct, the data find substantial overlap. IQ and achievement scores are strongly correlated.

It was once assumed that aptitude was a fixed characteristic, present at birth. Longitudinal data show otherwise. Young children with a low IQ can become above average or even gifted adults, like my nephew David (discussed in Chapter 1). Indeed, the average IQ scores of entire nations have risen substantially every decade for the past century—a phenomenon called the **Flynn effect,** named after the researcher who first described it (Flynn, 1999, 2012).

Most psychologists now agree that the brain is like a muscle, affected by mental exercise—which often is encouraged or discouraged by the social setting. Brain structures grow or shrink depending on past learning. This is proven in language and music and probably is true in other areas as well (Zatorre, 2013). During middle childhood, speed of thought is crucial for high IQ, with working memory also influential (Demetriou et al., 2013). Both speed and memory are affected by experience, evident in the Flynn effect.

Criticisms of Testing

Since scores change over time, IQ tests are much less definitive than they were once thought to be. Some scientists doubt whether any single test can measure the complexities of the human brain, especially if the test is designed to measure *g*, one general aptitude. According to some experts, children inherit many abilities, some high and some low, rather than any *g* (e.g., Q. Zhu et al., 2010).

Two leading developmentalists (Sternberg and Gardner) are among those who believe that humans have **multiple intelligences,** not just one. Gardner originally described seven intelligences: linguistic, logical-mathematical, musical, spatial, bodily-kinesthetic (movement), interpersonal (social understanding), and intrapersonal (self-understanding), each associated with a particular brain region (Gardner, 1983). He subsequently added an eighth (naturalistic: understanding nature, as in biology, zoology, or farming) and a ninth (spiritual/existential: thinking about life and death) (Gardner, 1999, 2006; Gardner & Moran, 2006).

Although every normal person has some of all nine intelligences, Gardner believes each individual excels in particular ones. For example, someone might be gifted spatially but not linguistically (a visual artist who cannot describe her work) or might have interpersonal but not naturalistic intelligence (an astute clinical psychologist whose houseplants die). Gardner's concepts regarding multiple intelligences influence the curriculum in many primary schools. For instance, children might be allowed to demonstrate their understanding of a historical event via a poster with drawings instead of writing a paper with a bibliography.

Sternberg described three kinds of intelligence: analytic, creative, and practical (1985, 2011). He contends that schools emphasize analysis (academics), but that creative and practical intelligence should also be valued. He added a fourth type of intelligence —called wisdom—as crucial in adulthood. He writes:

achievement test A measure of mastery or proficiency in reading, mathematics, writing, science, or some other subject.

Flynn effect The rise in average IQ scores that has occurred over the decades in many nations.

©2016 MACMILLAN

Typical 7-Year-Old? In many ways this boy is typical. He likes video games and school, he usually appreciates his parents, he gets himself dressed every morning. This photo shows him using blocks to construct a design to match a picture, one of the ten kinds of challenges that comprise the WISC, a widely used IQ test. His attention to the task is not unusual for children his age, but his actual performance is more like that of an older child. That makes his IQ score significantly above 100.

multiple intelligences The idea that human intelligence is composed of a varied set of abilities rather than a single, all-encompassing one.

Especially for Teachers What are the advantages and disadvantages of using Gardner's nine intelligences to guide your classroom curriculum? (see response, page 361)

One needs creativity to generate novel ideas, analytical intelligence to ascertain whether they are good ideas, practical intelligence to implement the ideas and persuade others of their value, and wisdom to ensure that the ideas help reach a common good.

[Sternberg, 2012, p. 21]

Gardner, Sternberg, and many other scholars find that cultures and families dampen or encourage particular intelligences. For instance, if two children are born with creative, musical intelligence, the child whose parents are musicians is more likely to develop musical intelligence than a child whose parents are tone-deaf.

Every test reflects the culture of the people who create, administer, and take it. This is obvious for achievement tests: A child may score low because of home, school, or culture, not because of ability. Indeed, IQ tests are still used partly because achievement tests do not necessarily reflect aptitude.

Scores on aptitude tests are also influenced by culture. Some experts have tried to develop tests that are culture-free, asking children to identify pictures, draw shapes, repeat stories, hop on one foot, name their classmates, sort objects, and so on.

An obvious precaution, required by most IQ tests, is that a friendly, trained adult ask questions of an individual student, in order to avoid cultural test-taking skills. Yet experience still matters. For example, some children are told to never talk to strangers, and so they do not answer the examiner's questions.

Brain Scans

One way to indicate aptitude is to measure the brain directly, avoiding the cultural biases of written exams or individual questions. Brain scans do not correlate with scores on IQ tests in childhood, but they do in adolescence (Brouwer et al., 2014). That suggests that one or the other of these tests is flawed when measuring the intelligence of children. The brain seems to have several localized hubs and lobes, which suggests multiple intelligence, but overall speed of reaction seems a characteristic of the entire brain, which may underlie g. Variation is vast in children's brains, which makes experts hesitant to argue for any one interpretation of IQ tests and brain scans (e.g., Goddings & Giedd, 2014).

For example, although it seems logical that less brain activity means less intelligence, that is not always the case. In fact, automatization reduces the need for brain activity, so the smartest children might have less active brains. Another puzzle is that a thicker cortex sometimes correlates with high IQ, but cortex thinness predicts greater vocabulary in 9- to 11-year-olds (Menary et al., 2013; Karama et al., 2009; G. Miller, 2006). Brain patterns in creative children differ from those who score high on IQ tests (Jung & Ryman, 2013). These results are puzzling—but so is much brain research.

Neuroscientists agree, however, on three conclusions:

1. Brain development depends on specific experiences. Thus, a brain scan is accurate only for the moment at which is done.
2. Brain development continues throughout life: Middle childhood is a crucial time, but developments before and after these years are also significant for brain functioning.
3. Children with disorders often have unusual brain patterns, and training their brains may help. However, brain complexity and normal variation mean that diagnosis and remediation are far from perfect.

This leads to the final topics of this chapter, children with special needs and how they should be taught.

// **Response for Teachers** (from page 359): The advantages are that all the children learn more aspects of human knowledge and that many children can develop their talents. Art, music, and sports should be an integral part of education, not just a break from academics. The disadvantage is that they take time and attention away from reading and math, which might lead to less proficiency in those subjects on standard tests and thus to criticism from parents and supervisors.

SUMMING UP During middle childhood, neurological maturation allows faster, more automatic reactions. Selective attention enables focused concentration in school and in play. IQ tests, which measure aptitude for learning, compare mental age to chronological age. Actual learning is measured by achievement tests.

As children and cultures adapt to changing contexts, IQ scores change much more than was originally imagined. Some scientists believe that certain abilities, perhaps speed of thought and working memory, undergird general intelligence, known as *g*. However, the concept that intelligence arises from one underlying aptitude is challenged by several scientists who believe that people have not just one type of intelligence but multiple intelligences. Further challenges to traditional IQ tests come from social scientists, who find marked cultural differences in what children are taught to do, and from neuroscientists, who see that brain activity does not reliably correlate with IQ scores.

WHAT HAVE YOU LEARNED?

1. Why does quicker reaction time improve the ability to learn?
2. How does selective attention make it easier for a child to sit in a classroom?
3. When would a teacher give an aptitude test instead of an achievement test?
4. If the theory of multiple intelligences is correct, should IQ tests be discarded? Why or why not?
5. Which intellectual abilities are more valued than others in the United States? Give examples.
6. Should brain scans replace traditional intelligence tests? Why or why not? •

Developmental Psychopathology

Some children have special needs because of their brain and behavior patterns. **Developmental psychopathology** links the study of usual development with the study of special needs (Cicchetti, 2013b; Hayden & Mash, 2014). Every topic already described, including "genetics, neuroscience, developmental psychology, . . . must be combined to understand how psychopathology develops and can be prevented" (Dodge, 2009, p. 413).

At the outset, four general principles should be emphasized.

1. *Abnormality is normal.* Most children sometimes act oddly. At the same time, children with serious disorders are, in many respects, like everyone else.
2. *Disability changes year by year.* Most disorders are **comorbid,** which means that more than one problem is evident in the same person. Which particular disorder is most disabling at a particular time changes, as does the degree of impairment.
3. *Life may be better or worse in adulthood.* Prognosis is difficult. Many children with severe disabilities (e.g., blindness) become productive adults. Conversely, some conditions (e.g., conduct disorder) may become more disabling.
4. *Diagnosis and treatment reflect the social context.* Each individual interacts with the surrounding setting—including family, school, community, and culture—to modify, worsen, or even create psychopathology.

> **developmental psychopathology** The field that uses insights into typical development to understand and remediate developmental disorders.

> **comorbid** Refers to the presence of two or more unrelated disease conditions at the same time in the same person.

Special Needs in Middle Childhood

Developmental psychopathology is relevant lifelong because "[e]ach period of life, from the prenatal period through senescence, ushers in new biological and psychological challenges, strengths, and vulnerabilities" (Cicchetti, 2013b, p. 458). Turning points, opportunities, and past influences are always apparent.

However in middle childhood, children are grouped by age. For some parents and teachers it suddenly becomes obvious that a particular child differs markedly from others the same age. Fortunately, the effects of most disorders can be mitigated if treatment is early and properly targeted.

Therein lies a problem: Although early treatment is more successful, early and accurate diagnosis is difficult, not only because many disorders are comorbid but also because symptoms differ by age. As you learned in Chapter 7, infants have temperamental differences that might or might not become problems, and Chapter 10 explained that some aggression is normal. Difference is not necessarily deficit, but that does not mean that all differences are benign.

Two basic principles of developmental psychopathology lead to caution in diagnosis and treatment (Hayden & Mash, 2014; Cicchetti, 2013b). First is **multifinality,** which means that one cause can have many (multiple) final manifestations. For example, an infant who has been flooded with stress hormones may become a hypervigilant or an unusually calm kindergartener, may be easily angered or quick to cry, or may not be affected at all.

The second principle is **equifinality** (equal in final form), which means that one symptom can have many causes. For instance, a nonverbal child may be autistic, hard of hearing, not fluent in the dominant language, or pathologically shy.

The complexity of diagnosis is evident in the *Diagnostic and Statistical Manual of Mental Disorders,* 5th edition (American Psychiatric Association, 2013), often referred to as DSM-5. A major problem is recognizing the cutoff between normal childish behavior and pathology. Some suggest that childhood psychopathology was underdiagnosed in early editions of the DSM and now is overdiagnosed (Hayden & Mash, 2014). As examples of the many complexities regarding children with special needs, we discuss three particularly common and troubling disorders. Appendix A lists the DSM-5 criteria for these three.

multifinality A basic principle of developmental psychopathology that holds that one cause can have many (multiple) final manifestations.

equifinality A basic principle of developmental psychopathology that holds that one symptom can have many causes.

attention-deficit/hyperactivity disorder (ADHD) A condition characterized by a persistent pattern of inattention and/or by hyperactive or impulsive behaviors; ADHD interferes with a person's functioning or development.

Attention-Deficit/Hyperactivity Disorder

Someone with **attention-deficit/hyperactivity disorder (ADHD)** is often inattentive and unusually active and impulsive, so much so that his or her ability to function is affected. The diagnosis in DSM-5 says symptoms must start before age 12 (in DSM-IV it was age 7) and must impact daily life. (DSM-IV said *impaired,* not just *impacted.*) Thus more children are considered to have ADHD than was the case 10 years ago.

Some impulsive, active, and creative actions are normal for children. However, children with ADHD

> are so active and impulsive that they cannot sit still, are constantly fidgeting, talk when they should be listening, interrupt people all the time, can't stay on task, . . . accidentally injure themselves." All this makes them "difficult to parent or teach."
>
> [Nigg & Barkley, 2014, p. 75]

They tend to have academic difficulties; they are less likely to graduate from high school and college; they become unhappy with themselves and with everyone else.

A River Is Better Than a School People must be quick and active to avoid capsizing in white-water rafting, but these children are up to the task. They have been diagnosed with ADHD; they are quite able to respond to fast-changing currents.

Problems with Diagnosis

There is no biological marker for ADHD. Current research, nonetheless, suggests the origin of the disorder is neurological, with problems in brain regulation either because of genes, complications of pregnancy, or toxins (such as lead) (Nigg & Barkely, 2014).

ADHD is comorbid with other conditions, including biological problems such as sleep deprivation or allergic reactions. Explosive rages, later followed by deep regret, are typical for children with many disorders, including ADHD. One surprising comorbidity is deafness: Children with severe hearing loss often are affected in balance and activity, and that seems to make them prone to developing ADHD (Antoine et al., 2013). In this way, ADHD is an example of equifinality; many causes produce one disorder.

Although the U.S. rates of children with ADHD were about 5 percent in 1980, recent data find that 7 percent of all 4- to 9-year-olds, 13 percent of all 10- to 13-year-olds, and 15 percent of all 14- to 17-year-olds have been diagnosed with ADHD (Schwarz & Cohen, 2013). These numbers are called "astronomical" by one pediatric neurologist (Graf, quoted in Schwarz & Cohen, 2013).

Rates of ADHD in most other nations are lower than in the United States, but they are rising everywhere (e.g., Al-Yagon et al., 2013; Hsia & Maclennan, 2009, van den Ban et al., 2010). Most research finds the highest rates in North America and lowest rates in East Asia (Erskine et al., 2014), but since diagnosis depends on someone's judgment, it is probably not helpful to compare nations. Increases everywhere are worrisome for at least three reasons:

- *Misdiagnosis.* If ADHD is diagnosed when another disorder is the problem, treatment might make the problem worse, not better (Miklowitz & Cicchetti, 2010). Many psychoactive drugs alter moods, so a child with disruptive mood dysregulation disorder (formerly called childhood-onset bipolar disorder) might be harmed by drugs that help children with ADHD.
- *Drug abuse.* Although drugs that reduce the symptoms of ADHD reduce one cause of later drug abuse, some adolescents may use a diagnosis of ADHD in order to obtain amphetamines with a doctor's prescription.
- *Normal behavior considered pathological.* In young children, high activity, impulsiveness, and curiosity are normal. If a normal child is diagnosed as abnormal, that may affect the child's self-concept and adult expectations. Could normal male activity be one reason ADHD is much more common in boys than girls?

Many adults (71 percent in one study) who were diagnosed with ADHD as children say they no longer have the condition (Barbaresi et al., 2013). Do people overcome or outgrow ADHD, or do adults minimize their symptoms, or do parents and teachers over-report?

Treatment for ADHD involves: (1) training for the family and the child, (2) special education for teachers, and (3) medication. But, as equifinality suggests, most disorders vary in causes, so treatment that helps one child does not necessarily work for another (Mulligan et al., 2013).

Drug Treatment for ADHD and Other Disorders

Because many adults are upset by what young children normally do and because any physician can write a prescription to quiet a child, thousands of children may be overmedicated. But because many parents do not recognize that their child

Almost Impossible The concentration needed to do homework is almost beyond this boy, age 11, who takes medication for ADHD. Note his furrowed brow, resting head, and sad face.

OBSERVATION QUIZ Is he able to write? (see answer, page 364)

Especially for Health Workers Parents ask that some medication be prescribed for their kindergarten child, who they say is much too active for them to handle. How do you respond? (see response, page 365)

// ANSWER TO OBSERVATION QUIZ
(from page 363) Yes, ADHD does not
preclude reading and writing. However,
ADHD makes it hard to think and write at the
same time. That's why his teacher writes for
him. She also tries to keep him focused on
his work—very difficult for this boy.

needs help, or they are suspicious of drugs and psychologists (Moldavsky & Sayal, 2013; Rose, 2008), thousands of children may suffer needlessly.

In the United States, more than 2 million people younger than 18 take prescription drugs to regulate their emotions and behavior (see Figure 11.4). The rates are about 14 percent for teenagers (Merikangas et al., 2013), about 10 percent for 6- to 11-year-olds, and less than 1 percent for 2- to 5-year-olds (Olfson et al., 2010). In China, parents rarely use psychoactive medication for children: A Chinese child with ADHD symptoms is thought to need correction rather than medication (Yang et al., 2013). Wise or cruel?

The most commonly prescribed drug for ADHD is Ritalin, but at least 20 other psychoactive drugs treat depression, anxiety, intellectual disability, autism spectrum disorder, disruptive mood dysregulation disorder, and many other conditions in middle childhood. Many child psychologists believe that drugs can be helpful, and they worry that the public discounts the devastation and lost learning that occur when a child's serious disorder is not recognized or treated.

But all agree that finding the best drug at the right strength is difficult, in part because each child's genes and personality are unique, and in part because children's weight and metabolism change every year. Given all that, it is troubling that only half of all children who take psychoactive drugs are evaluated and monitored by a mental health professional (Olfson et al., 2010). Most experts also believe that contextual interventions (instructing parents and teachers on child management) should be tried first (Daley et al., 2009; Leventhal, 2013; Pelham & Fabiano, 2008) and provide the best long-term solution.

Drugs may help, but they are not a cure. In one careful study, when children with ADHD were given appropriate medication, carefully calibrated, they were more able to concentrate. However, eight years later, many had stopped taking their medicine. At this follow-up, both those on medication and those who had stopped taking it often had learning difficulties (Molina et al., 2009).

Ethnic differences are found in parent responses, teacher responses, and treatment for children with ADHD symptoms. In the U.S., it seems that, when African American and Hispanic children are diagnosed with ADHD, their parents are less likely to give them medication compared to European American parents (Morgan et al., 2013). However, genes, culture, health care, education, religion, and stereo-

FIGURE 11.4

One Child In Every Classroom Or maybe two, if the class has more than 20 students or is in Alabama. This figure shows the percent of 6- to 17-year-olds prescribed psychoactive drugs in the previous six months. About half of these children have been diagnosed with ADHD, and the rest have anxiety, mood, and other disorders. These data are averages, gathered from many communities. In fact, some schools, even in the South, have very few medicated children, and others, even in the West, have many in every class. The regional variations evident here are notable, but much more dramatic are rates by school, community, and doctor—some of whom are much quicker to medicate children than others.

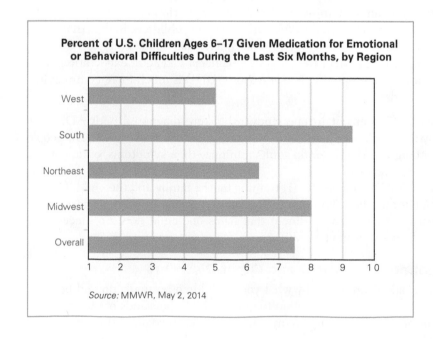

Percent of U.S. Children Ages 6–17 Given Medication for Emotional or Behavioral Difficulties During the Last Six Months, by Region

Source: MMWR, May 2, 2014

types could all affect ethnic differences. As two experts explain, "disentangling these will be extremely valuable to improving culturally competent assessment in an increasingly diverse society" (Nigg & Barkely, 2014, p. 98).

When appropriately used, drugs for ADHD may help children make friends, learn in school, feel happier, and behave better. These drugs also seem to help adolescents and adults with ADHD (Surman et al., 2013). However, as the just-cited longitudinal study found, problems do not disappear: Adolescents and adults who were diagnosed with ADHD as children are less successful academically and personally, whether or not they were medicated (Molina et al., 2013). Drugs do not erase special needs. Consider the following case.

// Response for Health Workers (from page 363): Medication helps some hyperactive children but not all. It might be useful for this child, but other forms of intervention should be tried first. Compliment the parents on their concern about their child, but refer them to an expert in early childhood for an evaluation and recommendations. Behavior-management techniques geared to the particular situation, not medication, are the first strategy.

a case to study

Lynda Is Getting Worse

Even experts differ in diagnosis of problems and recommended treatments. For instance, one study asked 158 child psychologists—half of them from England and half from the United States—to diagnose an 11-year-old girl with the following symptoms.

> Parents say Lynda has been hyperactive, with poor boundaries and disinhibited behavior since she was a toddler. . . . Lynda has taken several stimulants since age 8. She is behind in her school work, but IQ normal. . . .
>
> At school she is oppositional and "lazy" but not disruptive in class. Psychological testing, age 8, described frequent impulsivity, tendencies to discuss topics unrelated to tasks she was completing, intermittent expression of anger and anxiety, significantly elevated levels of physical activity, difficulties sitting still, and touching everything. Over the past year Lynda has become very angry, irritable, destructive and capricious. She is provocative and can be cruel to pets and small children. She has been sexually inappropriate with peers and families, including expressing interest in lewd material on the Internet, *Playgirl* magazine, hugging and kissing peers. She appears to be grandiose, telling her family that she will be attending medical school, or will become a record producer, a professional wrestler, or an acrobat. Throughout this period there have been substantial marital difficulties between the parents.
>
> *[Dubicka et al., 2008, appendix p. 3]*

Most (81 percent) of the clinicians diagnosing Lynda thought she had ADHD, and most thought she had another disorder as well. The Americans were likely to suggest a second and third disorder, with 75 percent of them specifying bipolar disorder. Only 33 percent of the British psychologists said bipolar (Dubicka et al., 2008).

Clinicians did not finger the family context or teacher's attitudes. This is a serious omission, since, for both nature and nurture reasons, parents who have ADHD or mood disorders are more likely to have children with disorders. It would have made sense for the parents to be tested and treated as well as 8-year-old Lynda. The family context matters. Many studies find that school and home environment can be crucial for a young child with ADHD (Nigg & Barkely 2014).

In this case, her parents thought Lynda had ADHD since toddlerhood; a pediatrician agreed, and at age 8 put her on drugs. Now, at age 11, she seems to be getting worse, not better, while her parents are increasingly hostile to each other. Family interaction, especially a close parental alliance, might have forestalled the problem.

Of course, it is impossible to know what would have happened if intensive intervention had taken place for the entire family when Lynda was a toddler. Might marital problems have been avoided? In any case, the four principles of developmental psychopathology suggest that developmental patterns and social contexts needed to be considered. That might have led to improvement, as apparently three years of medication did not.

Specific Learning Disorders

The DSM-5 diagnosis of **specific learning disorder** now includes disabilities in both perception and processing of information, with lower achievement than expected in reading, math, or writing (including spelling) (Lewandowski & Lovett, 2014). Learning disorders make it difficult for children to master a particular skill that most children acquire easily.

specific learning disorder (learning disability) A marked deficit in a particular area of learning that is not caused by an apparent physical disability, by an intellectual disability, or by an unusually stressful home environment.

Video: Dyslexia: Expert and Children
http://qrs.ly/cg4ep0v

dyslexia Unusual difficulty with reading; thought to be the result of some neurological underdevelopment.

Happy Reading Those large prism glasses keep the letters from jumping around on the page, a boon for this 8-year-old French boy. Unfortunately, each child with dyslexia needs individualized treatment: These glasses help some, but not most, children who find reading difficult.

dyscalculia Unusual difficulty with math, probably originating from a distinct part of the brain.

Some learning disabilities are not debilitating (e.g., the off-key singer learns to be quiet in chorus), but as DSM-5 notes, every schoolchild is expected to read, calculate, and write. Disabilities in these areas undercut academic achievement, destroy self-esteem, and qualify a child for special education (according to U.S. law) or formal diagnosis (according to DSM-5). Hopefully, such children find (or are taught) ways to compensate, and other abilities shine. Winston Churchill, Albert Einstein, and Hans Christian Andersen are all said to have had learning disabilities.

Dyslexia

The most commonly diagnosed learning disorder is **dyslexia**—unusual difficulty with reading. No single test accurately diagnoses dyslexia (or any learning disability) because every academic achievement involves many distinct factors (Riccio & Rodriguez, 2007). One child with a reading disability might have trouble sounding out words but might excel in comprehension and memory of printed text; another child might have the opposite problem. Dozens of types and causes of dyslexia have been identified, so no single strategy will help every child with dyslexia (O'Brien et al., 2012).

Early theories hypothesized that visual difficulties—for example, reversals of letters (reading *god* instead of *dog*) and mirror writing (*b* instead of *d*)—were the cause of dyslexia, but we now know that dyslexia more often originates with speech and hearing difficulties (Gabrieli, 2009; Swanson, 2013). An early warning occurs if a 3-year-old does not talk clearly or has not had a naming explosion. (**Developmental Link:** Both explained in Chapter 6.) Early therapy improves speech and might also reduce or prevent later dyslexia.

Traditionally, dyslexia was diagnosed only if a child had difficulty reading despite normal IQ, normal hearing and sight, and normal behavior. This approach usually meant waiting until the third grade or so, when the reading difficulty became apparent. Now difficulty with the basic skills for beginning reading (naming letters and sounds, hearing rhymes) is recognized in kindergarten, and children receive earlier remediation.

Dyscalculia and Dysgraphia

Another common learning disorder is **dyscalculia,** unusual difficulty with math. For example, when asked to estimate the height of a normal room, second-graders with dyscalculia might answer "200 feet," or, when asked which card is higher, the 5 or the 8 of hearts, the child might correctly answer 8—but only after using their fingers to count the number of hearts on each card (Butterworth et al., 2011).

Dyslexia and dyscalculia are often comorbid, although each originates from several distinct parts of the brain. Early encouragement with counting and calculating (long before first grade) can teach a child math basics, limiting dyscalculia and avoiding the emotional stress children feel if other children grasp math more easily (Butterworth et al., 2011).

Similar concerns regard very poor spelling and writing, known as dysgraphia, and again early remediation is useful, because the origin is probably in the brain as well as the social context. Remediation is best done early, at age 6 not age 10, not only because the brain is more flexible but also because the young child's eagerness to learn has not yet been crushed by failure. Every person, learning disabled or not, has strengths and interests, and almost everyone can learn basic skills if they are given extensive and targeted teaching, encouragement, and practice.

Autism Spectrum Disorder

Of all the children with special needs, those with **autism spectrum disorder (ASD)** are probably the most troubling. Their problems are severe, but both causes and treatments are hotly disputed. Thomas Insel, director of the National Institute of Mental Health, describes the parents and other advocates of children with autism as "the most polarized, fragmented community I know" (quoted in Solomon, 2012, p. 280).

Many children with ASD show symptoms in the first year of life, but some seem normal and then suddenly regress at about age 2 or 3, perhaps because a certain level of brain development, or a particular medical insult, occurs (Klinger et al., 2014). Most are diagnosed at age 4 or later (MMWR, March 28, 2014).

Symptoms

Autism spectrum disorder is characterized by woefully inadequate social understanding, coupled with repetitive or restrictive patterns of behavior, such as lining up toys by color rather than playing with them, or fascination with trains, lights, or spinning objects. More than a century ago, autism was considered rare, affecting fewer than 1 in 1,000 children with "an extreme aloneness that, whenever possible, disregards, ignores, shuts out anything . . . from the outside" (Kanner, 1943).

Years ago, children who developed slowly, and who would now be likely to be diagnosed with ASD, were usually diagnosed as being "mentally retarded" or as having a "pervasive developmental disorder." (The term "mental retardation," which was used in DSM-IV, has been replaced with "intellectual disability" in DSM-5.)

Much has changed. Far more children are diagnosed with autism spectrum disorder, and far fewer with intellectual disability. In the United States, among 8-year-olds, one child in every 68 is said to have an autism spectrum disorder (MMWR, March 28, 2014). Almost five times as many boys as girls, and about one-third more European Americans than Hispanic, Asian, or African Americans, are diagnosed with autism.

The DSM-5 autism diagnosis, formerly reserved for children who were mute or violent, now includes mild, moderate, or severe categories. Children who once were said to have Asperger syndrome are now said to have "autism spectrum disorder without language or intellectual impairment" (American Psychiatric Association, 2013, p. 32).

Children with any form of ASD find it difficult to understand the emotions of others, which makes them feel alien, like "an anthropologist on Mars," as Temple Grandin, an educator and writer with ASD, expressed it (quoted in Sacks, 1995). Consequently, they are less likely to talk or play with anyone, and they are delayed in developing theory of mind. *Severely impaired* children never speak, rarely smile, and play for hours with one object (such as a spinning top or a toy train). *Mildly impaired* children appear normal at first, and may be talented in some specialized area, such as drawing or geometry. Many (46 percent) score in the 'normal' or 'above normal' range on IQ tests (MMWR, March 28, 2014).

Most children with autism spectrum disorder show signs in early infancy (no social smile, for example, or less gazing at faces and eyes than most toddlers). Some improve by age 3; others deteriorate. Late onset occurs with several brain disorders, including *Rett syndrome*, in which a

autism spectrum disorder (ASD) A developmental disorder marked by difficulty with social communication and interaction—including difficulty seeing things from another person's point of view—and restricted, repetitive patterns of behavior, interests, or activities.

LaunchPad

Video: Current Research into Autism Spectrum Disorder explores why the causes of ASD are still largely unknown.

Precious Gifts Many children with autism spectrum disorder are gifted artists. This boy attends a school in Montmoreau, France, that features workshops in which children with ASD develop social, play, and learning skills.

newborn girl (boys with the Rett gene never survive) has "normal psychomotor development through the first 5 months after birth," but then her brain develops very slowly, severely limiting movement and language (Bienvenu, 2005).

Many children with ASD have an opposite problem—too much neurological activity, not too little. Their head grows too fast, and by age 2 it is larger than average. Their sensory cortex may be hypersensitive, making them unusually upset by noise, light, and other sensations. That suggests that the core problem in ASD is neurological. Literally hundreds of genes and dozens of brain abnormalities are more common in people diagnosed with autism than in the general population.

As mentioned above, in the United States far more children are found to have ASD now than in 1990. The incidence of this disorder may have actually increased, or the definition has expanded, or more children receive that diagnosis because educational services are more available (Klinger et al., 2014).

Underlying the estimate of frequency is the problem that no definitive measure diagnoses autism spectrum disorder: Many adults are socially inept, insensitive to other people's emotions, and poor at communication—are they all on the spectrum? One expert believes that the reason so many more boys than girls are designated with autism is that females are naturally more empathetic and males more likely to systematize, so biological sex differences protect girls who are genetically vulnerable (Baron-Cohen, 2010).

A related issue is whether autism is a disorder needing a cure, or whether the real problem is in parents and society that expect everyone to be fluent talkers, gregarious, and flexible—the opposite of people with autism. Advocates of **neurodiversity,** suggests that the neurological diversity of human beings is to be accepted, appreciated, even celebrated (Kapp et al., 2013). Do typical humans foolishly want no one to be atypical?

neurodiversity The idea that people have diverse brain structures, with each person having neurological strengths and weaknesses that should be appreciated, in much the same way diverse cultures and ethnicities are welcomed. A person who is adept at numbers and systems but inept in social skills and metaphors might be recognized as having unusual gifts, rather than pitied for having an autism spectrum disorder.

Treatment

The neurodiversity perspective is one reaction to the many treatments that converge on autism. When a child is diagnosed with ASD, parental responses vary from irrational hope to deep despair, from blaming doctors and chemical additives to feeling guilty for what they did wrong. Many parents sue schools, or doctors, or the government; many spend all their money and change their lives; many subject their children to treatments that are, at best, harmless, and at worst, painful and even fatal.

Andrew Solomon (2012) writes about one child, who was medicated with

> Abilify, Topamax, Seroquel, Prozac, Ativan, Depakote, trazodone, Risperdal, Anafranil, Lamictal, Benadryl, melatonin, and the homeopathic remedy, Calms Forté. Every time I saw her, the meds were being adjusted again . . . .[He also describes] physical interventions—putting children in hyperbaric oxygen chambers, putting them in tanks with dolphins, giving them blue-green algae, or megadosing them on vitamins . . . usually neither helpful nor harmful, though they can have dangers, are certainly disorienting, and cost a lot
>
> [p. 229, 270]

Equifinality certainly applies to ASD: A child can have autistic symptoms for many reasons; no single gene causes the disorder. That makes treatment difficult; an intervention that seems to help one child proves worthless for another. It is known, however, that biology is crucial (genes, copy number abnormalities, birth complications, prenatal injury, perhaps chemicals during fetal or infant development) and that family nurture is not the cause of ASD but may modify it. Social and language engagement of the child early in life seems the most promising treatment.

SUMMING UP Many children have special learning needs that originate with problems in the development of their brains. Developmental psychopathologists emphasize that no child is typical in every way; the passage of time sometimes brings improvement and sometimes not. Children with attention-deficit/hyperactivity disorder, learning disorders, and autism spectrum disorders may function adequately as adults or may have lifelong problems, depending on many variables, including: (1) the severity of the problem, (2) family support, (3) school strategies, and (4) comorbid conditions. In general, the earlier diagnosis and treatment occurs, the better, but it is during middle childhood that many problems become apparent.

WHAT HAVE YOU LEARNED?
1. How does normal childhood behavior differ between the United States and Asia?
2. What is the difference between multifinality and equifinality?
3. Why is medication recommended for children with ADHD?
4. Why might parents ask a doctor to prescribe Ritalin for their child?
5. What are dyslexia, dyscalculia, and dysgraphia?
6. How might an adult have a learning disability that has never been diagnosed?
7. What are the three primary signs of autism spectrum disorder?
8. What are the implications of neurodiversity?

All Together Now Kiemel Lamb (*top center*) leads children with autism in song, a major accomplishment. For many of these children, music is soothing, words are difficult, and handholding in a group is almost impossible.

Special Education

The overlap of the biosocial, cognitive, and psychosocial domains is evident to developmentalists, as is the need for parents, teachers, therapists, and researchers to work together to help each child. However, deciding whether or not a child should be designated as needing special education is not straightforward, nor is it closely related to specific special needs.

Labels, Laws, and Learning

In the United States, recognition that the distinction between normal and abnormal is not clear-cut (the first principle of developmental psychopathology) led to a series of reforms. Dramatic changes occurred in the treatment and education of children with special needs.

According to the 1975 Education of All Handicapped Children Act, children with special needs must be educated in the **least restrictive environment (LRE).** That law has been revised several times, but the goal remains that children should not be segregated from other children unless it is not possible to remediate problems within the regular classroom.

Consequently, LRE usually means educating children with special needs in a regular class, a practice once called *mainstreaming,* rather than in a special classroom or school. Sometimes a child is sent for a few hours a week to a *resource room,* with a teacher who provides targeted tutoring. Sometimes a class is an *inclusion class,* which means that children with special needs are "included" in the general classroom, with "appropriate aids and services" (ideally from a trained teacher who works with the regular teacher).

A more recent educational strategy is called **response to intervention (RTI)** (Fletcher & Vaughn, 2009; Shapiro et al., 2011; Ikeda, 2012). All children are

least restrictive environment (LRE) A legal requirement that children with special needs be assigned to the most general educational context in which they can be expected to learn.

response to intervention (RTI) An educational strategy intended to help children who demonstrate below-average achievement in early grades, using special intervention.

taught specific skills; for instance, learning the sounds that various letters make. Then the children are each tested, and those who did not master the skill receive special "intervention"—practice and individualized teaching, usually within the regular class. Then they are tested again, and, if need be, intervention occurs again. Only when a child does not respond adequately to repeated, focused intervention is the child referred for testing and observation to diagnose the problem.

RTI is used in some nations with success (e.g., Sahlberg, 2011) and is now implemented in many U.S. schools. Most children respond to intervention, but those who do not are then tested to determine if they have special needs. In that case, the school proposes an **individual education plan (IEP)** with the parents.

The basic assumption of the IEP is that schools need to "design learning pathways for each individual sufferer." The label, or specific diagnosis, is supposed to help target effective remediation. Yet this rarely occurs in practice (Butterworth & Kovas, 2013, p. 304). Instead, the special needs that attract most research on remediation are not the more common ones. One example: In the United States, "research funding in 2008–2009 for autistic spectrum disorder was 31 times greater than for dyslexia and 540 times greater than for dyscalculia" (Butterworth & Kovas, 2013, p. 304).

In the United States, historical shifts are notable in which children are recognized by educators as having special needs, and what their needs are labeled. As Figure 11.5 shows, the proportion of children designated with special needs rose in the United States from 10 percent in 1980 to 13 percent in 2011, primarily because more children are called learning disabled or autistic (National Center for Education Statistics, 2013b).

There is no separate category for ADHD. To receive special services, children with ADHD are often designated as having a specific learning disorder. Since most disorders are comorbid, the particular special needs category in the school

individual education plan (IEP) A document that specifies educational goals and plans for a child with special needs.

FIGURE 11.5

Nature or Nurture Communities have always had some children with special needs, with physical, emotional, and neurological disorders. In some eras, and today in some nations, the education of such children was neglected. Indeed, many children were excluded from normal life even before they quit trying. Now in the United States, every child is entitled to school. Categories have changed, probably because of nurture, not nature. Thus, teratogens and changing parental and community practice probably caused the rise in autism spectrum disorder and developmental delay, the decrease in intellectual disability, and the fluctuation in learning disorders apparent here.

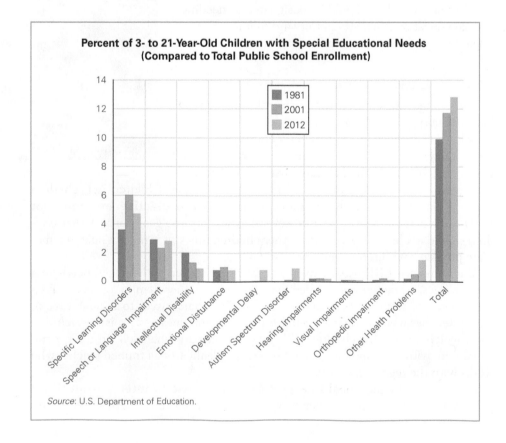

Percent of 3- to 21-Year-Old Children with Special Educational Needs (Compared to Total Public School Enrollment)

Legend: 1981, 2001, 2012

Categories: Specific Learning Disorders, Speech or Language Impairment, Intellectual Disability, Emotional Disturbance, Developmental Delay, Autism Spectrum Disorder, Hearing Impairments, Visual Impairments, Orthopedic Impairment, Other Health Problems, Total

Source: U.S. Department of Education.

system may not be the diagnosis given by a psychologist. One result is that teachers, therapists, and parents may work at cross-purposes to educate a child.

Internationally, the connection between special needs and education varies, again for cultural and historical reasons more than child-related ones (Rotatori et al., 2014). In many African and Latin American nations, almost no child receives special education in public schools; in many Asian nations, diagnosis refers primarily to physical disability. The U.S. school system designates more children as having special needs than does any other nation: Whether this is a reason for national pride or shame depends on one's perspective.

Gifted and Talented

Children who are unusually gifted are often thought to have special needs as well, but they are not covered by federal laws in the United States. Instead, each U.S. state selects and educates gifted and talented children in a particular way, a variation that leads to controversy.

A scholar writes: "The term *gifted* . . . has never been more problematic than it is today" (Dai, 2010, p. 8). Educators, political leaders, scientists, and everyone else argue about who is gifted and what should be done about them. Are gifted children unusually intelligent, or talented, or creative? Should they be skipped, segregated, enriched, or left alone?

A hundred years ago, the definition of gifted was simple: high IQ. A famous longitudinal study followed a thousand "genius" children, all of whom scored above 140 on the Stanford-Binet IQ test (Terman, 1925). Even today, some school systems define gifted as having an IQ of 130 or above (attained by 1 child in 50). Other children are unusually talented, recognized by their parents at a young age, by the general public after they die—but not usually by their teachers when they are in elementary school. Mozart composed music at age 3; Pablo Picasso created works of art at age 4.

A hundred years ago, school placement was simple for high IQ children. They were taught with children who were their mental age, not their chronological age. This practice was called **acceleration.** Today that is rarely done because many accelerated children never learned how to get along with others. As one woman remembers:

> Nine-year-old little girls are so cruel to younger girls. I was much smaller than them, of course, and would have done anything to have a friend. Although I could cope with the academic work very easily, emotionally I wasn't up to it. Maybe it was my fault and I was asking to be picked on. I was a weed at the edge of the playground.
>
> *[Rachel, quoted in Freeman, 2010, p. 27]*

Calling herself a weed suggests that she never overcame her conviction that she was less cherished than the other children. Her intellectual needs may have been met by her skipping two grades, but her emotional and social needs were severely neglected.

Historically, many famous musicians, artists, and scientists were child prodigies whose fathers recognized their talent (often because the father was talented) and taught them. Often they did not attend regular school, because laws requiring attendance did not exist. Mozart's father transcribed his earliest pieces and toured Europe with his gifted son. Picasso's father removed him from school in second grade so he could create all day.

That solution also had pitfalls. Although intense early education at home nourishes talent, neither Mozart nor Picasso had happy adult lives. Moreover, Picasso said he never learned to read or write, and Mozart had a poor understanding of

acceleration Educating gifted children alongside other children of the same mental, not chronological, age.

Gifted. Then What? Mercan Türkoğlu was awarded a Bambi, the German equivalent of an Oscar, for her star performance in the film *Three Quarter Moon*. She is German of Turkish ancestry, Muslim, and a talented actress. What education will best prepare her for adulthood?

math and money. Similar patterns are still apparent, as exemplified by gifted athletes (e.g., Tiger Woods and Steffi Graf) as well as those in less public specialties. Here is one example:

> Sufiah Yusof started her maths degree at Oxford [the leading University in England] in 2000, at the age of 13. She too had been dominated and taught by her father. But she ran away the day after her final exam. She was found by police but refused to go home, demanding of her father in an email: "Has it ever crossed your mind that the reason I left home was because I've finally had enough of 15 years of physical and emotional abuse?" Her father claimed she'd been abducted and brainwashed. She refuses to communicate with him. She is now a very happy, high-class, high-earning prostitute.
>
> [Freeman, 2010, p. 286]

Some children who might need special education are unusually creative (Sternberg et al., 2011). They are *divergent thinkers,* finding many solutions and even more questions for every problem. Such students joke in class, resist drudgery, ignore homework, and bedevil their teachers. They may become innovators, inventors, and creative forces of the future.

Creative children do not conform to social standards. They are not *convergent thinkers,* who choose the correct answer on school exams. One such person was Charles Darwin, whose "school reports complained unendingly that he wasn't interested in studying, only shooting, riding, and beetle-collecting" (Freeman, 2010, p. 283). Other creative geniuses who were poor students are Einstein, Freud, Newton, Steve Jobs. Again, such people are not usually recognized until late in adulthood, or after death.

Neuroscience has recently discovered that children who develop their musical talents with extensive practice in early childhood grow specialized brain structures, as do child athletes and mathematicians. Since plasticity means that children learn whatever their context teaches, special talents may be enhanced with special education, an argument for elementary school teaching to accommodate creative children.

Since both acceleration and intense parental tutoring have led to later problems, a third education strategy has become popular, at least in the United States. Children who are bright, talented, and/or creative—all the same age but each with special abilities—are taught together in their own classroom. Ideally, such children are neither bored nor lonely; each is challenged and appreciated by their classmates.

Classes for gifted students require unusual teachers, smart and creative, able to appreciate divergent thinking and challenge the very bright. They must be flexible: providing a 7-year-old artist freedom, guidance, and inspiration for magnificent art and simultaneously providing patient, step-by-step reading instruction if that same child is a typical new reader. Similarly, a 7-year-old who reads at the twelfth-grade level might have immature social skills, needing a teacher who finds another child to befriend him or her and who then helps both of them share, compromise, and take turns.

Should such teachers be available only for the gifted? Every child may need talented teachers and individualized instruction, no matter what the child's abilities or disabilities may be. Many educators complain that the system of education in the United States, where each school district and sometimes each school hires and assigns teachers, results in the best teachers having the most able students, when it should be the opposite. This trend is furthered by tracking, putting children with special needs together, and allowing private or charter schools to select certain students and leave the rest behind.

Some nations educate all children together, assuming that the best learners are not naturally gifted but are able to work harder at learning. Thus, the teacher's job is to motivate and challenge every child. U.S. law says all children can learn, and it is the job of schools to teach them. Every special and ordinary form of education can benefit by applying what we know about children's minds (De Corte, 2013). That is the topic of the next chapter.

SUMMING UP   No child learns or behaves exactly like another, and no educational strategy always succeeds. Various strategies are apparent not only for children with disabilities but also for those who are unusually gifted and talented. Mainstreaming and inclusion of children with special needs occur because educators believe that children benefit from learning with other children. It is not straightforward to balance that belief with the need for some children to have an individual education plan, or a gifted and talented class.

WHAT HAVE YOU LEARNED?
1. What do mainstreaming and inclusion have in common?
2. Why is response to intervention considered an alternative to special education?
3. Why are children who are smarter than their peers no longer allowed to skip grades?
4. What are the arguments for and against special classes for gifted children?   ●

SUMMARY

A Healthy Time

1. Middle childhood is a time of steady growth and few serious illnesses. Increasing independence and self-care allow most school-age children to be relatively happy and competent.

2. Advances in medical care have reduced childhood sickness and death. During these years, health habits, including daily oral care, protect children from later health problems.

3. Physical activity aids health and joy in many ways. However, current social and environmental conditions make informal neighborhood play rare. School physical education is less prevalent than it was formerly. Children who most need physical activity may be least likely to have it.

Health Problems in Middle Childhood

4. Childhood obesity is a worldwide epidemic. Although genes are part of the problem, too little exercise and the greater availability of unhealthy foods are the main reasons today's youth are heavier than their counterparts of 50 years ago. Parents and policies share the blame.

5. The incidence of asthma is increasing overall, with notable ethnic differences. The origins of asthma are genetic; the main triggers are specific environmental allergens, although research on asthma finds marked variation in causes, triggers, and consequences. Preventive measures include longer breast-feeding, increased outdoor play, and less air pollution, particularly from motor vehicles.

Brain Development

6. Brain development continues during middle childhood, enhancing every aspect of development. Notable are advances in reaction time and automatization, allowing faster and better coordination of many parts of the brain and body. Experience enhances coordination of brain impulses.

7. IQ tests quantify intellectual aptitude, which increases in middle childhood. Most such tests emphasize language and logic ability and predict school achievement. IQ scores may change over time, as culture and experience enhance particular abilities.

8. Achievement tests measure accomplishment, often in specific academic areas. Aptitude and achievement are correlated, both for individuals and for nations, and have risen in the past decades.

9. Critics of IQ testing contend that intelligence is manifested in multiple ways, which makes conventional IQ tests that assume *g*, too narrow and limited. Multiple intelligences include creative and practical abilities as well as many skills not usually valued in typical North American schools.

Developmental Psychopathology

10. Developmental psychopathology uses an understanding of normal development to inform the study of unusual development. Four general lessons have emerged: Abnormality is normal; disability changes over time; a condition may get better or worse in adolescence and adulthood; diagnosis depends on context.

11. Children with attention-deficit/hyperactivity disorder (ADHD) have potential problems in three areas: inattention, impulsiveness, and activity. Stimulant medication often helps children with ADHD to learn, but any drug use by children must be carefully monitored.

12. People with a specific learning disorder have unusual difficulty in mastering a specific skill or skills that other people learn easily. The most common learning disorders that impair achievement in middle childhood are dyslexia (unusual difficulty with reading), dyscalculia (unusual difficulty with math), and dysgraphia (unusual difficulty with writing and spelling).

13. Children with autism spectrum disorder typically have problems with social interactions and language. They often exhibit restricted, repetitive patterns of behavior, interests, and activities. Many causes are hypothesized. ASD is partly genetic; no one now views ASD as primarily the result of inadequate parenting. Treatments are diverse and controversial.

Special Education

14. About 13 percent of all school-age children in the United States receive special education services. These services begin with an IEP (individual education plan) and assignment to the least restrictive environment (LRE), usually the regular classroom.

15. A strategy to reduce the number of children with special needs is to notice when children are having difficulty and then providing special help. This strategy, called response to intervention, allows most children to learn.

16. Some children are unusually intelligent, talented, or creative. Many states and nations provide special education for them. The traditional strategy—skipping a grade—no longer seems beneficial. Instead, in the United States, gifted and talented children are usually educated as a special group.

KEY TERMS

middle childhood (p. 348)
childhood overweight (p. 351)
childhood obesity (p. 351)
asthma (p. 354)
reaction time (p. 357)
selective attention (p. 357)
automatization (p. 357)
aptitude (p. 358)

achievement test (p. 359)
Flynn effect (p. 359)
multiple intelligences (p. 359)
developmental psychopathology
  (p. 361)
comorbid (p. 361)
multifinality (p. 362)
equifinality (p. 362)

attention-deficit/hyperactivity
  disorder (ADHD) (p. 362)
specific learning disorder
  (learning disability) (p. 365)
dyslexia (p. 366)
dyscalculia (p. 366)
autism spectrum disorder (ASD)
  (p. 367)

neurodiversity (p. 368)
least restrictive environment
  (LRE) (p. 369)
response to intervention (RTI)
  (p. 369)
individual education plan (IEP)
  (p. 370)
acceleration (p. 371)

APPLICATIONS

1. Compare outdoor play spaces for children in different neighborhoods—ideally, urban, suburban, and rural areas. Note size, safety, and use. How might children's weight and motor skills be affected by the differences you observe?

2. Developmental psychologists believe that every teacher should be skilled at teaching children with a wide variety of needs. Does the teacher-training curriculum at your college or university reflect this goal? Should all teachers take the same courses, or should some teachers be specialized? Give reasons for your opinions.

3. Internet sources on any topic vary in quality. This is particularly true of websites designed for parents of children with special needs. Pick one childhood disability or disease and find several Web sources devoted to that condition. How might parents evaluate the information provided?

4. Special education teachers are in great demand. In your local public school, what is the ratio of regular to special education teachers? How many of those special education teachers are in self-contained classrooms, resource rooms, and inclusion classrooms? What do your data reveal about the education of children with special needs in your community?

12

Middle Childhood:
Cognitive Development

What Will You Know?

1. Does cognition improve naturally with age, or is teaching crucial to its development?
2. Why do children use slang, curse words, and bad grammar?
3. What type of school is best during middle childhood?

At age 9, I wanted a puppy. My parents said no; we already had Dusty, our family dog. I dashed off a poem, promising "to brush his hair as smooth as silk" and "to feed him milk." Twice wrong. Not only poor cadence, but also, puppies get sick on cow's milk. But my father praised my poem; I got Taffy, a blonde cocker spaniel.

At age 10, my daughter Sarah wanted her ears pierced. I said no, it would be unfair to her three older sisters, who had had to wait for ear piercing until they were teenagers. Sarah wrote an affidavit and persuaded all three to sign "No objection." She got gold posts.

Our wishes differed by cohort and our strategies by family. Sarah knew I wouldn't budge for doggerel but that signed documents might work. In the end, we were both typical school-age children, mastering whatever circumstances offer, wanting something that we did not need. Depending on the context, children learn to divide fractions, text friends, memorize baseball stats, load rifles, and persuade parents.

This chapter describes the cognitive accomplishments that make all that possible. We begin with Piaget, Vygotsky, and information processing. Then we discuss applications of those theories to language and formal education, nationally and internationally. Everyone agrees that extensive learning occurs; adults disagree sharply about how best to teach.

Building on Theory

Learning is rapid. By age 11, some children beat their elders at chess, play music that adults pay to hear, publish poems, or win trophies for spelling or sports or some other learned skill. Others survive on the streets or kill in wars, mastering lessons that no child should have to study. How do they learn so quickly?

Piaget and School-Age Children

Piaget called the cognition of middle childhood **concrete operational thought,** characterized by new concepts that enable children to use logic. *Operational* comes

concrete operational thought Piaget's term for the ability to reason logically about direct experiences and perceptions.

Product of Cognition Concrete thinking is specific, such as caring for a lamb until it becomes an award-winning sheep, as this New Jersey 4-H member did.

from the Latin word *operare,* meaning "to work; to produce." By calling this period operational, Piaget emphasized productive thinking.

The school-age child, no longer limited by egocentrism, performs logical operations. Children apply their new reasoning skills to *concrete* situations, which are situations grounded in actual experience, like the concrete of a cement sidewalk. Concrete thinking arises from what is visible, tangible, and real, not abstract and theoretical (as at the next stage, formal operational thought). A shift from preoperational to concrete operational thinking occurs between ages 5 and 7: Children become more systematic, objective, scientific—and educable.

A Hierarchy of Categories

classification The logical principle that things can be organized into groups (or categories or classes) according to some characteristic they have in common.

One logical operation is **classification,** the organization of things into groups (or *categories* or *classes*) according to some characteristic that they share. For example, *family* includes parents, siblings, and cousins. Other common classes are animals, toys, and food. Each class includes some elements and excludes others; each is part of a hierarchy.

Food, for instance, is an overarching category, with the next-lower level of the hierarchy being meat, grains, fruits, and so on. Most subclasses can be further divided: Meat includes poultry, beef, and pork, each of which can be divided again. Adults realize that items at the bottom of a classification hierarchy belong to every higher level: Bacon is always pork, meat, and food, but most food, meat, and pork are not bacon. However, the mental operation of moving up and down the hierarchy is beyond preoperational children.

seriation The concept that things can be arranged in a logical series, such as the number sequence or the alphabet.

Piaget devised many classification experiments. For example, a child is shown a bunch of nine flowers—seven yellow daisies and two white roses. Then the child is asked, "Are there more daisies or more flowers?"

Until about age 7, most children answer, "More daisies." The youngest children offer no justification, but some 6-year-olds explain that "there are more yellow ones than white ones" or "because daisies are daisies, they aren't flowers" (Piaget et al., 2001). By age 8, most children can classify: "More flowers than daisies," they say.

Other Logical Concepts

Several logical concepts were already discussed in Chapter 9—in the explanation of ideas that are beyond preoperational children, such as conservation and reversibility.

Math and Money Third-grader Perry Akootchook understands basic math, so he might beat his mother at "spinning for money," shown here. Compare his concrete operational skills with that of a typical preoperational child, who would not be able to play this game and might give a dime for a nickel.

Another example of concrete logic is **seriation,** the knowledge that things can be arranged in a logical *series.* Seriation is crucial for using (not merely memorizing) the alphabet or the number sequence. By age 5, most children can count up to 100, but because they do not yet grasp seriation, they cannot correctly estimate where any particular two-digit number would be placed on a line that starts at zero and ends at 100 (Meadows, 2006).

Concrete operational thought correlates with primary school math achievement, although many other factors contribute (Desoete et al., 2009). For example, logic helps with arithmetic: Children at the stage of concrete operational thought eventually understand that 12 + 3 = 3 + 12 and that 15 is always 15 (conservation), that all the numbers from 20 to 29 are in the 20s (classification), that 134 is less than 143 (seriation), and that if $5 \times 3 = 15$, then $15 \div 5$ is 3 (reversibility). (**Developmental Link:** These concepts are explained in Chapter 9 and detailed in a recently reissued classic, Inhelder & Piaget, 1964/2013a.)

The Significance of Piaget's Findings

Logic connects to math ability, as just shown. However, researchers find more continuity than discontinuity as children master number skills. Thus, Piaget's stage idea was mistaken: There is no sudden shift in logic between preoperational and concrete operational intelligence.

Nonetheless, Piaget's experiments revealed something important. School-age children can use mental categories and subcategories more flexibly, inductively, and simultaneously than younger children can. They are cognitively advanced, capable of thinking in ways that younger children are not.

Vygotsky and School-Age Children

Like Piaget, Vygotsky felt that educators should consider children's thought processes, not just the outcomes. He appreciated the fact that children are curious, creative learners. For that reason, Vygotsky believed that an educational system based on rote memorization rendered the child "helpless in the face of any sensible attempt to apply any of this acquired knowledge" (Vygotsky, 1994a, pp. 356–357).

The Role of Instruction

Unlike Piaget, Vygotsky stressed the centrality of instruction. Vygotsky believed school could be crucial for cognitive growth. He thought that peers and teachers provide the bridge between developmental potential and needed skills via guided participation and scaffolding, in the zone of proximal development. (**Developmental Link:** Vygotsky's theory is discussed in Chapters 2 and 9.)

Confirmation of the role of social interaction and instruction comes from a U.S. study of children who, because of their school's entry-date cutoff, are either relatively old kindergartners or quite young first-graders. At the end of the school year, achievement scores of the 6-year-old first-graders far exceeded those of kindergarten 6-year-olds who were only one month younger (Lincove & Painter, 2006). Obviously, they had learned a great deal from their year of first grade instruction.

Internationally as well, children who begin first grade earlier tend to be ahead in academic achievement compared to those who enter later, an effect noted even at age 15. The author of this study noted that Vygotsky's theory is not the only one that explains this finding and that these results were not found in every nation (Sprietsma, 2010). However, no matter what explanation is correct, children's academic achievement seems influenced by social context.

Vygotsky would certainly agree with that, and he would explain those national differences by noting that education before first grade in some nations is far better than in others. Remember that Vygotsky believed education occurs everywhere, not only in school. Children learn as they play with peers, watch television, eat with their families, walk down the street. Every experience, from birth on, teaches them something, with some contexts much more educational than others.

For instance, a study of the reading and math achievement of more than one thousand third- and fifth-grade children from ten U.S. cities found that high-scoring primary school children were likely to have had extensive cognitive stimulation. There were three main sources of intellectual activity:

1. Families (e.g., parents read to them daily when they were toddlers)
2. Preschool programs (e.g., a variety of learning activities)
3. First-grade curriculum (e.g., emphasis on literacy, with individualized evaluation and instruction)

Video Activity: The Balance Scale Task shows children of various ages completing the task and gives you an opportunity to try it, too.

Especially for Teachers How might Piaget's and Vygotsky's ideas help in teaching geography to a class of third-graders? (see response, page 381)

Girls Can't Do It As Vygotsky recognized, children learn whatever their culture teaches. Fifty years ago girls were in cooking and sewing classes. No longer. This 2012 photo shows 10-year-olds Kamrin and Caitlin in a Kentucky school, preparing for a future quite different from that of their grandmothers.

MIRANDA PEDERSON/DAILY NEWS/ASSOCIATED PRESS

In this study, most children from families of low socioeconomic status did not experience all three sources of stimulation, but those who did showed more cognitive advances by fifth grade than the average high-SES child (Crosnoe et al., 2010).

Generally, poverty reduces children's achievement because they are less likely to have these three sources of stimulation. However, for low-SES children especially, maternal education makes a notable difference in academic achievement—presumably because educated mothers read, listen, and talk to their children more. Also, an educated mother is more likely to place her child in a preschool with a curriculum that encourages learning.

International Contexts

Vygotsky's emphasis on sociocultural contexts contrasts with Piaget's maturational, self-discovery approach. Vygotsky believed that cultures (tools, customs, and mentors) are powerful educators. For example, if a child is surrounded by reading adults, by full bookcases, by daily newspapers, and by street signs, that child will read better than a child who has had little exposure to print, even if both are in the same classroom.

The same applies to math. If children learn math in school, they are proficient at school math; if they learn math out of school, they are adept at solving mathematical problems in situations similar to the context in which they learned (Abreu, 2008). Ideally, though, children learn math both in and out of school.

Context affects more than academic learning. A stunning example of knowledge acquired from the social context comes from Varanasi, a city in northeast India. Many Varanasi children have an extraordinary sense of spatial orientation: They know whether they are facing north or south, even when they are inside a room with no windows. In one experiment, children were blindfolded, spun around, and led to a second room, yet many still knew which way they were now facing (Mishra et al., 2009). How did they know? Perhaps social context.

In Varanasi, everyone refers to the spatial orientation to locate objects. (The English equivalent might be, not that the dog is sleeping by the door, but that the dog is sleeping southeast.) From their early days, children learn north/south/east/west in order to communicate. By middle childhood, they have an internal sense of direction.

Culture affects how children learn, not just what they learn. This was evident in a two-session study in California of 80 Mexican American children, each with a sibling (Silva et al., 2010). Half of the sibling pairs were from indigenous Mexican families, in which children learn by watching, guided by other children. The other half were from families acculturated to U.S. learning, via direct instruction, not observation. Those acculturated children had learned to work independently, sitting at desks, not collaboratively, crowding around a teacher.

In the first session of this study, a Spanish-speaking "toy lady" showed each child how to make a toy while his or her sibling sat nearby. First, the younger sibling waited while the older sibling made a toy mouse, and then the older sibling waited while the younger sibling made a toy frog. Each waiting child's behavior was videotaped and coded every 5 seconds as *sustained attention* (alert and focused on the activity), *glancing* (sporadic interest, but primary focus elsewhere), or *not attending* (looking away).

A week later, each child individually was told there was some extra material to make the toy that his or her sibling had made the week before, and was encouraged to make

Never Lost These children of Varanasi sleep beside the Ganges in the daytime. At night they use their excellent sense of direction to guide devotees from elsewhere.

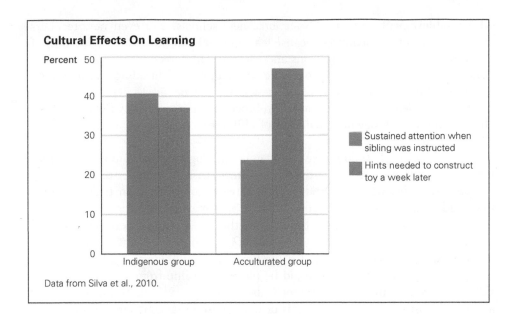

Cultural Effects On Learning

Data from Silva et al., 2010.

FIGURE 12.1
Two Ways to Learn Even when children currently live in the same settings and attend the same schools, they follow family cultural traditions in the way they learn.

the mouse or the frog (whichever one that child had not already made). In this second session, the toy lady did not give the children step-by-step instructions as she had for the sibling a week earlier, but she had a long list of hints she could give *if* the child needed them.

The purpose of this experiment was to see how much the children had learned by observation the week before. The children from indigenous backgrounds scored higher, needing fewer hints, because they had been more attentive when their siblings made the toy (Silva et al., 2010) (see Figure 12.1).

The same conclusions have been found in other research. For example, in another study, children born and raised in the United States who are accustomed to learning by observation (as in some Native American cultures) were more proficient at remembering an overheard folktale (Tsethlikai & Rogoff, 2013).

Information Processing

Today's educators and psychologists regard both Piaget and Vygotsky as insightful. International research confirms the merits of their theories. Piaget described universal changes; Vygotsky noted cultural impact.

A third approach to understanding cognition adds crucial insight. The *information-processing perspective* benefits from technology that allows much more detailed data and analysis than was possible for Piaget or Vygotsky. (**Developmental Link:** Information processing is introduced in Chapter 2.)

Thousands of researchers who study cognition can be said to use the information-processing approach. Not all of them would describe themselves as doing so because "information processing is not a single theory but, rather, a framework characterizing a large number of research programs" (Miller, 2011, p. 266).

The basic assumption of all such research programs is that, like computers, people can access large amounts of information. They then: (1) seek relevant units of information (as a search engine does), (2) analyze (as software programs do), and (3) express their conclusions so that another person can understand (as a networked computer or a printout might do). By tracing the paths and links of each of these functions, scientists better understand the learning process.

The brain's gradual growth, now seen in neurological scans, confirms the usefulness of the information-processing perspective. So does data on children's

// Response for Teachers (from page 379): Here are two of the most obvious ways. (1) Use logic. Once children can grasp classification and class inclusion, they can understand cities within states, states within nations, and nations within continents. Organize your instruction to make logical categorization easier. (2) Make use of children's need for concrete and personal involvement. You might have the children learn first about their own location, then about the places where relatives and friends live, and finally about places beyond their personal experience (via books, photographs, videos, and guest speakers).

Skills of the Street Children In many nations, children sell to visitors, using math and business skills that few North American children know. This boy was offering necklaces to visitors at the Blue Mosque in Afghanistan.

Arithmetic Strategies: The Research of Robert Siegler http://qrs.ly/o84ep10

sensory memory The component of the information-processing system in which incoming stimulus information is stored for a split second to allow it to be processed. (Also called the *sensory register*.)

working memory The component of the information-processing system in which current conscious mental activity occurs. (Formerly called *short-term memory*.)

school achievement: Absences, vacations, new schools, and even new teachers may set back a child's learning because learning each day builds on the learning of the previous day. Brain connections and pathways are forged from repeated experiences, allowing advances in processing. Without careful building and repetition of various skills, fragile connections between neurons break.

One of the leaders of the information-processing perspective is Robert Siegler. He has studied the day-by-day details of children's cognition in math (Siegler & Chen, 2008).

Apparently, children do not suddenly grasp the logic of the number system, as Piaget expected at the concrete operational stage. Instead, number understanding accrues gradually, with new and better strategies for calculation tried, ignored, half-used, abandoned, and finally adopted. Siegler compared the acquisition of knowledge to waves on an ocean beach when the tide is rising. There is substantial ebb and flow, although eventually a new level is reached.

One example is the ability to estimate where a number might fall on a line, such as where the number 53 would be placed on a line from zero to 100. This skill predicts later math achievement (Libertus et al., 2013). U.S. kindergartners are usually lost when asked to do this task; Chinese kindergartners are somewhat better (Siegler & Mu, 2008).

Everywhere, proficiency gradually builds from the first grade on, predicting later math skills (Feigenson et al., 2013). This has led many information-processing experts to advocate giving children practice with number lines in order to develop math ability, such as the ability to do multiplication and division.

Curiously, knowing how to count to high numbers seems less important for math mastery than being able to estimate magnitude (Thompson & Siegler, 2010). For example, understanding the size of fractions (e.g., that 3/16 is smaller than 1/4) is connected to a thorough grasp of the relationship between one number and another, a skill that predicts later math achievement internationally, according to a study of school children in China, Belgium, and the United States (Torbeyns et al., 2014). Overall, information processing guides teachers who want to know exactly which concepts and skills are crucial foundations for mastery, not only for math but for reading and writing as well.

Memory

Many scientists who study memory take an information-processing approach. They have learned that various methods of input, storage, and retrieval affect the increasing cognitive ability of the schoolchild. Each of the three major steps in the memory process—sensory memory, working memory, and long-term memory—is affected by both maturation and experience.

Sensory memory (also called the *sensory register*) is the first component of the human information-processing system. It stores incoming stimuli for a split second, with sounds retained slightly longer than sights. To use terms explained in Chapter 5, *sensations* are retained for a moment, and then some become *perceptions*. This first step of sensory awareness is already quite good in early childhood. Sensory memory improves slightly until about age 10 and remains adequate until late adulthood.

Once some sensations become perceptions, the brain selects the meaningful ones and transfers them to working memory for further analysis. It is in **working memory** (formerly called *short-term memory*) that current, conscious mental activity occurs. Processing, not mere exposure, is essential for getting information into working memory; for this reason, working memory improves markedly in middle childhood (Cowan & Alloway, 2009) (see Table 12.1).

TABLE 12.1	Advances in Memory from Infancy to Age 11
Child's Age	**Memory Capabilities**
Under 2 years	Infants remember actions and routines that involve them. Memory is implicit, triggered by sights and sounds (an interactive toy, a caregiver's voice).
2–5 years	Words are now used to encode and retrieve memories. Explicit memory begins, although children do not yet use memory strategies. Children remember things by rote (their phone number, nursery rhymes).
5–7 years	Children realize they need to remember some things, and they try to do so, usually via rehearsal (repeating an item again and again). This is not the most efficient strategy, but repetition can lead to automatization.
7–9 years	Children can learn new strategies, including visual clues (remembering how a particular spelling word looks) and auditory hints (rhymes, letters), evidence of brain functions called the visual-spatial sketchpad and phonological loop. Children benefit from organizing things to be remembered.
9–11 years	Memory becomes more adaptive and strategic as children become able to learn various memory techniques from teachers and other children. They can organize material themselves, developing their own memory aids.

Source: Based on Meadows, 2006.

As Siegler's waves metaphor suggests, memory strategies for processing information do not appear suddenly. Gradual improvement occurs from toddlerhood through adolescence (Schneider & Lockl, 2008). Children develop strategies to increase working memory (Camos & Barrouillet, 2011), and they use these strategies occasionally at first, then consistently.

Cultural differences are evident. For example, many Muslim children are taught to memorize all 80,000 words of the Quran, so they learn strategies to remember long passages. These strategies are unknown to non-Muslim children, and they help with other cognitive tasks (Hein et al., 2014). A very different example is the ability to draw a face, an ability admired by U.S. children. They learn strategies to improve their drawing, such as knowing where to put the eyes, mouth, and chin when drawing a face. (Few spontaneously draw the eyes mid-face, rather than at the top, but most learn to do so.)

Finally, information from working memory may be transferred to **long-term memory,** to be stored for minutes, hours, days, months, or years. The capacity of long-term memory—how much can be crammed into one brain—is huge by the end of middle childhood. Together with sensory memory and working memory, long-term memory organizes ideas and reactions, fostering more effective learning over the years (Wendelken et al., 2011).

Crucial to long-term memory is not merely *storage* (how much material has been deposited) but also *retrieval* (how readily past learning can be brought into working memory). For everyone at every age, retrieval is easier for some memories (especially of vivid, emotional experiences) than for others. And for everyone, long-term memory is imperfect: We all forget and distort memories, with strategies needed for accurate recall.

Knowledge

Research on information processing finds that the more people already know, the more information they can learn. Having an extensive **knowledge base,** or a broad body of knowledge in a particular subject, makes it easier to remember and understand related new information. As children gain knowledge during the

long-term memory The component of the information-processing system in which virtually limitless amounts of information can be stored indefinitely.

Especially for Teachers How might your understanding of memory help you teach a 2,000-word vocabulary list to a class of fourth-graders? (see response, page 385)

knowledge base A body of knowledge in a particular area that makes it easier to master new information in that area.

school years, they become better able to judge what is true or false, what is worth remembering, and what is insignificant (Woolley & Ghossainy, 2013).

Three factors facilitate increases in the knowledge base: past experience, current opportunity, and personal motivation. The last item in this list explains why children's knowledge base is not what their parents or teachers might prefer. Some schoolchildren memorize words and rhythms of hit songs, know plots and characters of television programs, or can recite the names and histories of basketball players, and yet they do not know whether World War I was in the nineteenth or twentieth century or whether Pakistan is in Asia or Africa.

Motivation provides a clue for teachers: New concepts are learned best if they are connected to personal and emotional experiences. Children who themselves are from South Asia, or who have classmates who are, learn the boundaries of Pakistan more readily.

Control Processes

The mechanisms that put memory, processing speed, and the knowledge base together are **control processes;** they regulate the analysis and flow of information within the system. Control processes include *emotional regulation* and *selective attention* (explained in Chapters 10 and 11, respectively).

Equally important is **metacognition,** sometimes defined as "thinking about thinking," understanding how to learn. Metacognition is the ultimate control process because it allows a person to evaluate a cognitive task, determine how to accomplish it, monitor performance, and then make adjustments. According to scholars of cognition, "Middle childhood may be crucial for the development of metacognitive monitoring and study of control processes" (Metcalfe & Finn, 2013, p. 19).

Control processes require the brain to organize, prioritize, and direct mental operations, much as the CEO (chief executive officer) of a business organizes, prioritizes, and directs business operations. For that reason, control processes are also called *executive processes,* and the ability to use them is called **executive function** (already mentioned in Chapter 9), which allows a person to step back from the specifics of learning and thinking and consider more general goals and strategies. Executive function is evident whenever people concentrate on the relevant parts of a task, using the knowledge base to comprehend new information and apply memory strategies.

Executive function ability is a foundation for learning in early and middle childhood, measurable already by age 5, and more evident among 10-year-olds than among 4- or 6-year-olds (Masten, 2014; Bjorklund et al., 2009). For example, fourth-grade students can listen to the teacher talk about the river Nile, ignoring classmates who are chewing gum or passing notes.

Deliberate selectivity is a control process at work. A child can decide to do homework before watching television or to review spelling words before breakfast, creating mnemonics to remember the tricky parts. All these signify executive function.

Both metacognition and control processes improve with age and experience. For instance, in one study, children took a fill-in-the-blanks test and indicated how confident they were of each answer. Then they were allowed to delete some questions, with the remaining ones counting more. Already by age 9, they were able to estimate correctness; by age 11, they were skilled at knowing what to delete (Roebers et al., 2009).

Sometimes, experience that is not directly related has an impact. This seems to be true for fluently bilingual children, who must learn to inhibit one language while using another. They are advanced in control processes, obviously in language but also in more abstract measures of control (Bialystok, 2010).

What Does She See? It depends on her knowledge base and personal experiences. Perhaps this trip to an aquarium in North Carolina is no more than a break from the school routine, with the teachers merely shepherding the children to keep them safe. Or, perhaps she has learned about sharks and dorsal fins, about scales and gills, about warm-blooded mammals and cold-blooded fish, so she is fascinated by the swimming creatures she watches. Or, if her personal emotions shape her perceptions, she feels sad about the fish in their watery cage or finds joy in their serenity and beauty.

control processes Mechanisms (including selective attention, metacognition, and emotional regulation) that combine memory, processing speed, and knowledge to regulate the analysis flow of information within the information-processing system. (Also called *executive processes.*)

metacognition "Thinking about thinking," or the ability to evaluate a cognitive task in order to determine how best to accomplish it, and then to monitor and adjust one's performance on that task.

executive function The cognitive ability to organize and prioritize the many thoughts that arise from the various parts of the brain, allowing the person to anticipate, strategize, and plan behavior.

Control processes develop spontaneously as the prefrontal cortex matures, but they can also be taught. Sometimes teaching is explicit, more so in some nations (e.g., Germany) than in others (e.g., the United States) (Bjorklund et al., 2009). Examples that may be familiar include spelling rules ("*i* before *e* except after *c*") and ways to remember how to turn a light bulb (lefty-loosey, righty-tighty). Preschoolers ignore such rules or use them only on command; 7-year-olds begin to use them; 9-year-olds can create and master more complicated rules.

Many factors beyond specific instruction affect learning. For example, if children do not master emotional control in early childhood, their school achievement is likely to suffer for years (Bornstein et al., 2013).

Given the complexity of factors and goals, educators disagree as to what should be deliberately taught versus what is best discovered by the child. However, understanding the early steps that lead to later knowledge, as information processing seeks to do, may guide instruction and hence improve learning. Exactly how to do that is an important topic of current research, as you will see in A View from Science on page 391. But first, consider one specific domain of learning that advances during middle childhood, language.

SUMMING UP   Every theory of cognitive development recognizes that school-age children are avid learners who actively build on the knowledge they already have. Piaget emphasized that children's own grasp of logic, via maturation and experience, allows them to reach the cognitive stage he called concrete operational thought. Then they can apply that logic to learning math and many other academic tasks. Research inspired by Vygotsky and the sociocultural perspective reveals that cultural differences can be powerful: Both what is learned and how it is learned are influenced by the context of instruction and everyday experience. Because cultures vary, children also vary in what they learn and how they learn it.

An information-processing analysis highlights the many components of thinking that advance, step-by-step, during middle childhood. Although sensory and long-term memory do not change much during these years, the speed and efficiency of working memory improve dramatically, making school-age children better thinkers as well as more strategic learners as they grow older. With every passing year children expand their knowledge base, which makes new material easier to connect with past learning and thus easier to learn. As control processes and metacognition advance, children are better able to direct their minds toward whatever they want to learn. Executive function is crucial, as children who are more capable with executive processes are also better able to learn.

WHAT HAVE YOU LEARNED?

1. Why did Piaget call cognition in middle childhood *concrete operational thought?*
2. How would one express classification in a category other than those listed in the text, such as transportation or plants?
3. How do Vygotsky and Piaget differ in their explanation of cognitive advances in middle childhood?
4. How are the children of Varanasi an example of Vygotsky's theory?
5. How does information-processing theory differ from traditional theories of cognitive development?
6. According to Siegler, what is the pattern of learning math concepts?
7. What aspects of memory improve markedly during middle childhood?
8. How and why does the knowledge base increase in middle childhood?
9. How might executive function help a student learn?

// Response for Teachers (from page 383): Children this age can be taught strategies for remembering by forming links between working memory and long-term memory. You might break down the vocabulary list into word clusters, grouped according to root words, connections to the children's existing knowledge, applications, or (as a last resort) first letters or rhymes. Active, social learning is useful; perhaps in groups, the students could write a story each day that incorporates 15 new words. Each group could read its story aloud to the class.

Language

As you will remember, many aspects of language advance during early childhood. By age 6, children have mastered the basic vocabulary and grammar of their first language. Many also speak a second language fluently. Those linguistic abilities allow the formation of a strong knowledge base, enabling some school-age children to learn up to 20 new words a day and to apply complex grammar rules. Here are some specifics.

Vocabulary

By age 6, children know the names of thousands of objects, and they use many parts of speech—adjectives and adverbs as well as nouns and verbs. As Piaget stressed, their thinking soon becomes more flexible and logical; they can understand prefixes, suffixes, compound words, phrases, and metaphors. For example, 2-year-olds know *egg*, but 10-year-olds also know *egg salad, egg-drop soup, egghead,* and *last one in is a rotten egg.* They know that each of these expressions is distinct from the uncooked eggs in the refrigerator.

Understanding Metaphors

Metaphors, jokes, and puns are finally comprehended. Some jokes ("What is black and white and read all over?" "Why did the chicken cross the road?") are funny only during middle childhood. Younger children don't understand why they provoke laughter, and teenagers find them lame and stale, but the new cognitive flexibility of 6- to 11-year-olds allows them to enjoy puns, unexpected answers to normal questions, as well as metaphors and similes.

Indeed, a lack of metaphorical understanding, even if a child has a large vocabulary, signifies cognitive problems (Thomas et al., 2010). Humor, or lack of it, is a diagnostic tool.

Many adults do not realize how difficult it is for young children or adults who are learning a new language to grasp figures of speech. The humorist James Thurber remembered what he called "the enchanted private world" of his early boyhood:

> In this world, businessmen who phoned their wives to say they were tied up at the office sat roped to their swivel chairs, and probably gagged, unable to move or speak except somehow, miraculously, to telephone. . . . Then there was the man who left town under a cloud. Sometimes I saw him all wrapped up in the cloud and invisible. . . . At other times it floated, about the size of a sofa, above him wherever he went. . . . [I remember] the old lady who was always up in the air, the husband who did not seem able to put his foot down, the man who lost his head during a fire but was still able to run out of the house yelling.
>
> *[Thurber, 1999, p. 40]*

Metaphors are context-specific, building on the knowledge base. An American who lives in China notes phrases that U.S. children learn but that children in cultures without baseball do not, including "dropped the ball," "on the ball," "play ball," "throw a curve," "strike out" (Davis, 1999). If a teacher says "keep your eyes on the ball," some immigrant children might not pay attention because they are looking for that ball.

Because school-age children can create metaphors and similes, asking them to do so reveals emotions that they do not express in other ways. For instance, in a study of how children felt about their asthma, one 11-year-old said that his asthma

> is like a jellyfish, which has a deadly sting and vicious bite and tentacles which could squeeze your throat and make your bronchioles get smaller and make breathing harder. Or like a boa constrictor squeezing life out of you.
>
> *[quoted in Peterson & Sterling, 2009, p. 97]*

Especially for Parents You've had an exhausting day but are setting out to buy groceries. Your 7-year-old son wants to go with you. Should you explain that you are so tired that you want to make a quick solo trip to the supermarket this time? (see response, page 388)

That boy was terrified of his disease, which he considered evil and dangerous —and beyond his parents' help. Other children in the same study responded differently. One girl thought asthma would attack her only if she was not good and that her "guardian angel" would keep it away as long as she behaved herself. Adults who want to know how a child feels about something might ask for a metaphor.

Adjusting Vocabulary to the Context

One aspect of language that advances markedly in middle childhood is pragmatics, already defined in Chapter 9. Pragmatics is evident in the contrast between talking formally to teachers (never calling them a *rotten egg*) and informally with friends (who can be rotten eggs or worse). As children master pragmatics, they become more adept at making friends. Shy 6-year-olds cope far better with the social pressures of school if they use pragmatics well (Coplan & Weeks, 2009). By contrast, children with autism who have learned to talk are usually very poor at pragmatics (Klinger et al., 2014).

Mastery of pragmatics allows children to change styles of speech, or "linguistic codes," depending on their audience. Each code includes many aspects of language—tone, pronunciation, gestures, sentence length, idioms, vocabulary, and grammar. Sometimes the switch is between *formal code* (used in academic contexts) and *informal code* (used with friends); sometimes it is between standard (or proper) speech and dialect or vernacular (used on the street). Code used in texting—numbers (411), abbreviations (LOL), emoticons (:-D), and spelling (r u ok?)—shows exemplary pragmatics.

Some children may not realize that informal expressions are wrong in formal language. All children need instruction to become fluent in the formal code because the logic of grammar (whether *who* or *whom* is correct or how to spell *you*) is almost impossible to deduce. The peer group teaches the informal code, and each local community transmits dialect, metaphors, and pronunciation.

Educators must teach the formal code. However, they should not make children feel that their neighborhood or family grammar or pronunciation is shameful.

Bilingual Education

Code changes are obvious when children speak one language at home and another at school. Every nation includes many such children; most of the world's 6,000 languages are not school languages. For instance, English is the language of instruction in Australia, but 17 percent of the children speak one of 246 other languages at home (Centre for Community Child Health & Telethon Institute for Child Health Research, 2009).

In the United States, almost 1 school-age child in 4 speaks a language other than English at home. Most of them also speak English well, according to their parents (see Figure 12.2).

In addition, many other children speak a dialect of English that differs from the pronunciation and grammar taught at school. All these alternate codes have distinct patterns of timing, grammar, and emphasis, as well as vocabulary, so all require much more than literal translation.

Typical Yet Unusual It's not unusual that these children are texting in French; they live in Bordeaux, and children everywhere text their friends. The oddity is that a girl and a boy are lying head to head, which rarely occurs in middle childhood. The explanation? They are siblings. Like dogs and cats that grow up together, familiarity overtakes hostility.

FIGURE 12.2

Hurray for Teachers More children in the United States are now bilingual and more of them speak English well, from about 60 percent in 1980 to 75 percent in 2011.

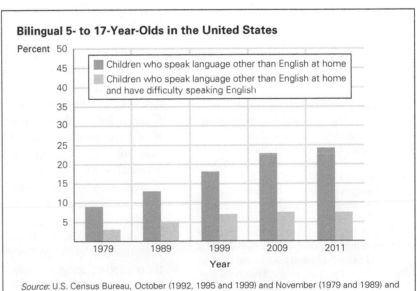

Bilingual 5- to 17-Year-Olds in the United States

Percent

- Children who speak language other than English at home
- Children who speak language other than English at home and have difficulty speaking English

Source: U.S. Census Bureau, October (1992, 1995 and 1999) and November (1979 and 1989) and Current Population Surveys and 2000–2011 American Community Survey.

If a child learns only one language in the early years, but then masters a second language during middle childhood, the brain must adjust. A study found no brain differences between monolingual and bilingual children if they spoke both languages from infancy. However, from about age 4 through adolescence, the older children are when they learn a second language, the more likely their brains will reveal differences that result from the need to accommodate their dual languages.

Specifically, children who learn a second language later have greater cortical thickness on the left side (the language side) and thinness on the right (Klein et al., 2014). This reflects what we know about language learning: School-age children can master a second language they did not know before, but they must work at it.

In the United States, some children of every ethnicity are called **ELLs,** or **English Language Learners,** based on their proficiency in speaking, writing, and reading English. Among U.S. children with Latin American heritage, those who speak English well are much better at reading than those who do not. Age, schooling, and SES all have an effect, but even some of higher SES may be less adept at reading than the average European American child (Howard et al., 2014). Culture may be the reason, as their learning style may not be the same as their teachers' teaching style, even though they speak and understand English well.

Teaching approaches range from **immersion,** in which instruction occurs entirely in the new language, to the opposite, in which children are taught in their first language until the second language can be taught as a "foreign" tongue (a strategy rare in the United States but common elsewhere). Between these extremes lies **bilingual schooling,** with instruction in two languages, and **ESL (English as a Second Language),** with all non-English speakers taught English in one multilingual group. ESL is intended to be a short and intense program to prepare students for regular classes.

Methods for teaching a second language sometimes succeed and sometimes fail, with the research not yet clear as to which approach is best (Gandara & Rumberger, 2009). The success of any method seems to depend on the literacy of the home environment (frequent reading, writing, and listening in any language helps); the warmth, training, and skill of the teacher; and the national context.

Specifics differ for each state and grade level, but the general trends are dismal. ELLs fall more behind their peers with each passing grade, becoming high school dropouts at higher rates than other students their age. For instance, in Pennsylvania in 2009, the percent of fourth graders proficient in reading was 74 percent for the non-ELLs but only 30 percent for the ELLs. The gap in math scores was not quite as wide, but in every subject and every grade, the gap widened as children grew older (O'Conner et al., 2012).

Using an information-processing perspective, scholars have discovered that each aspect of language learning follows a distinct developmental path, and this can help teachers target exactly the learning that each child needs. Between ages 5 and 8, for children who speak Spanish at home and English in school, the length of each sentence in English (average number of words) dips during summer vacation but fluency improves steadily (words per minute). Especially for them, the 3-month-long summer break is destructive of education (Rojas & Iglesias, 2013).

For these bilingual children, knowledge of Spanish follows another trajectory. It does not improve much during kindergarten and first grade (presumably because children focus on English), and then advances markedly at the end of second grade (Rojas & Iglesias, 2013). Schools can affect this by having Spanish classes for all the youngest children, so those whose home language is Spanish will appreciate their mother tongue. These are averages; specifics of learning and effective educational strategies depend on the particular experiences of the child at home and school, just as information-processing theory would predict.

ELLs (English Language Learners) Children in the United States whose proficiency in English is low—usually below a cutoff score on an oral or written test. Many children who speak a non-English language at home are also capable in English; they are *not* ELLs.

immersion A strategy in which instruction in all school subjects occurs in the second (usually the majority) language that a child is learning.

bilingual schooling A strategy in which school subjects are taught in both the learner's original language and the second (majority) language.

ESL (English as a Second Language) A U.S. approach to teaching English that gathers all the non-English speakers together and provides intense instruction in English. Their first language is never used; the goal is to prepare them for regular classes in English.

// Response for Parents (from page 386): Your son would understand your explanation, but you should take him along if you can do so without losing patience. You wouldn't ignore his need for food or medicine, so don't ignore his need for learning. While shopping, you can teach vocabulary (does he know pimientos, pepperoni, polenta?), categories (root vegetables, freshwater fish), and math (which size box of cereal is cheaper?). Explain in advance that you need him to help you find items and carry them and that he can choose only one item that you wouldn't normally buy. Seven-year-olds can understand rules, and they enjoy being helpful.

Differences in Language Learning

Learning to speak, read, and write the school language is pivotal for primary school education. Some differences in ability may be innate: A child with a language disability will have trouble with both the school and home languages.

It is a mistake to assume that a child who does not speak English well is learning disabled (difference is not deficit), but it is also is a mistake to assume that such a child's only problem is lack of English knowledge (deficits do occur among all children, no matter what their background). To discover whether a child has difficulty learning language, it is best to test in the home language—even when the child has been speaking the second language from kindergarten on (Erdos et al., 2014).

Although some children from every language background have disabilities, most of the language gap between one child and another is the result of the social context, not brain abnormality. Two crucial factors are SES and expectations.

Socioeconomic Status

Decades of research throughout the world have found a strong correlation between academic achievement and socioeconomic status. Language is a major reason. Not only do children from low-SES families usually have smaller vocabularies than those from higher-SES families, but their grammar is also simpler (fewer compound sentences, dependent clauses, and conditional verbs), and their sentences are shorter (Hart & Risley, 1995; Hoff, 2013). That slows down school learning in every subject.

With regard to language learning, the information-processing perspective focuses on specifics that might affect the brain and thus the ability to learn. Brain scans confirm that development of the hippocampus is particularly affected by SES, as is language learning (Jednoróg et al., 2012). That is correlation; many researchers have sought the cause of the connection between SES and language. Possibilities abound—inadequate prenatal care, exposure to lead, no breakfast, overcrowded households, few books at home, teenage parents, authoritarian child rearing, inexperienced teachers, few neighborhood role models . . . the list could go on and on. All of these conditions correlate with low SES and less learning, but it is difficult to isolate the impact of any specific one.

However, one factor seems clearly a cause, not just a correlate, of language proficiency: language heard during the first five years of life. If it is extensive and elaborate, the child is likely to speak and then read well.

The mothers' education seems crucial. Many less-educated parents talk and listen much less to their infants and young children than college-educated parents do. For instance, among mothers of 2-year-olds, 24 percent of those with less than a high school education read books daily to their children, but 70 percent of the mothers with at least a BA do so (National Center for Education Statistics, 2009) (see Figure 12.3).

Even independent of income, research has shown that children who grow up in homes with many books accumulate, on average, three years more schooling than children who

FIGURE 12.3

Red Fish, Blue Fish As you can see, most mothers sing to their little children, but the college-educated mothers are much more likely to know that book reading is important. Simply knowing how to turn a page or hearing new word combinations (hop on pop?) correlates with reading ability later on.

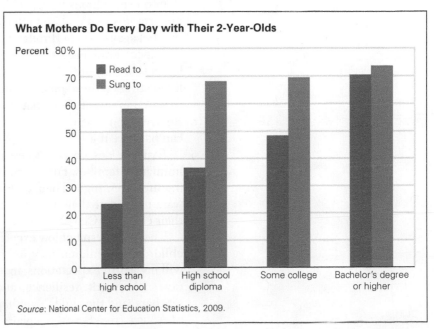

What Mothers Do Every Day with Their 2-Year-Olds

Percent

Source: National Center for Education Statistics, 2009.

Priorities This family in London is low-income, evident in the stained walls, peeling paint, and old toilet, but that does not necessarily limit the girl's future. More important is what she learns about values and behavior. If this scene is typical, this mother is teaching her daughter about appearance and obedience. What would happen if the child had to care for her own grooming? Tangles? Short hair? Independence? Linguistic advances?

OBSERVATION QUIZ What in the daughter's behavior suggests that maternal grooming is a common event in her life? (see answer, page 392)

grow up in homes with no books (Evans et al., 2010), presumably because the parents of the latter group rarely read. Language exposure is the direct cause here, not household income. Indeed, children from high-SES families who rarely hear language also do poorly in school, and some low-SES families encourage language and their children do well.

Book-reading is not the only way to increase language learning in children (some families rarely read to their children but engage them in conversation about the interesting sights around them), but book-reading often indicates how much verbal input a child receives. Another way to surround children with language is to sing to a child, not just a few simple songs, but dozens of songs, with varied vocabulary in many stanzas.

Ideally, parents read to, sing to, and converse with each child daily, and also provide extensive vocabulary about various activities. For example, as parent and child are walking down the street: "The sidewalk is narrow (or wide, or cracked, or cement) here." "See the wilted rose. Is it red or magenta or maroon?" "That truck has six huge tires. Why does it have so many?" Children offer comments of their own, and adults can respond with "Yes," "That's interesting," "I never thought of that"—never ignoring the child or commanding, "Be quiet!"

Expectations

Beyond direct language encouragement, a second cause of low achievement in middle childhood is teachers' and parents' expectations. Although substantial research has found that children are influenced by adults' positive expectations, the relationship between expectation and achievement becomes complicated as children grow older. One crucial factor seems to be whether parents and teachers have shared expectations for the children, rather than working at cross-purposes. Also important is that children internalize those expectations rather than feel the need to rebel against them (Froiland & Davison, 2014).

Expectations need to be explicit, not idealistic. For instance, children should know that they are expected to read for pleasure rather than watch television, to learn advanced academic vocabulary (e.g., *negotiate, evolve, allegation, deficit*), and to have important ideas that the parent will listen to attentively and with respect. Remember, though, that authoritarian parenting, which includes high standards, can backfire if it is not accompanied by warmth.

Expectations do not necessarily follow along income lines, especially among immigrant families. For low-SES Latinos especially, family expectations for learning are often high. Their children try to meet those expectations because they want to validate their parents' decision to leave their native land to improve life for their children (Ceballo et al., 2014; Fuller & García Coll, 2010).

The worst result of low expectations by adults is that they are transmitted to the child. Schoolchildren may internalize their parents' or teachers' belief that they will not learn. Expectations, motivation, and achievement go hand in hand. Qualities such as grit, resilience, and emotional regulation—all affected by parents, teachers, and the child's own hopes—are crucial for learning at every stage of life, as A View from Science explains.

a view from science

True Grit

Thousands of social scientists—psychologists, educators, sociologists, economists—have realized that, for cognitive development from middle childhood through late adulthood, characteristics beyond IQ scores, test grades, and family SES are sometimes pivotal. One leading proponent of this idea is Paul Tough, who wrote: "We have been focusing on the wrong skills and abilities in our children, and we have been using the wrong strategies to help nurture and teach those skills" (Tough, 2012, p. xv). Instead of focusing on test scores, we should focus on character, Tough believes.

Many scientists agree that executive control processes with many names (grit, emotional regulation, conscientiousness, resilience, executive function, effortful control) develop over the years of middle childhood and are crucial for cognitive growth. Over the long term, these aspects of character predict achievement in high school, college, and adulthood. Developmentalists disagree about exactly which qualities are crucial for achievement, with grit considered crucial by some and not others (Ivcevic & Brackett, 2014; Duckworth & Kern, 2011), but no one denies that success depends on personality traits, not just on intellect.

This concept appears in almost every chapter of this textbook, from the discussion of plasticity in Chapter 1 to the evidence in Chapter 11 regarding children who overcome notable learning disabilities. One of the best longitudinal studies we have (the Dunedin study of an entire cohort of children from New Zealand) found that measures of self-control before age 10 predicted health, happiness, education, and accomplishment many years later, even when IQ and SES were already taken into account (Moffitt et al., 2011).

Among the many influences on children, a pivotal one is having at least one adult who encourages accomplishment. For many children, that adult is their mother, although, especially when parents are neglectful or abusive, a teacher, a religious leader, a coach, or someone else can be the mentor and advocate who helps a child overcome adversity (Masten, 2014).

Remember that school-age children are ready for intellectual growth (Piaget) and are responsive to mentors (Vygotsky). These universals were evident in one study that occurred in two places, 12,000 miles apart: the Northeastern United States and Taiwan. More than 200 mothers were asked to recall and then discuss with their 6- to 10-year-olds two learning-related incidents that they knew their child experienced. In one incident, the child had a "good attitude or behavior in learning"; in the other, "not perfect" (Li et al., 2014).

All the mothers were married and middle-class, and all tried to encourage their children, stressing the value of education and the importance of doing well in school. All the children reflected their mothers' attitudes.

Although the researchers noted these universal aspects of the mother–child dialogues, they also found that the Chinese mothers were about 50 percent more likely to mention what the researchers called "learning virtues," such as practice, persistence, and concentration—all of which are part of grit. The American mothers were 25 percent more likely to mention "positive affect," such as happiness and pride.

This distinction is evident in the following two excepts:

First, Tim and his American mother discussed a "not perfect" incident.

Mother: I wanted to talk to you about . . . that time when you had that one math paper that . . . mostly everything was wrong and you never bring home papers like that. . . .

Tim: I just had a clumsy day.

Mother: You had a clumsy day. You sure did, but there was, when we finally figured out what it was that you were doing wrong, you were pretty happy about it . . . and then you were happy to practice it, right? . . . Why do you think that was?

Tim: I don't know, because I was frustrated, and then you sat down and went over it with me, and I figured it out right with no distraction and then I got it right.

Mother: So it made you feel good to do well?

Tim: Uh-huh.

Mother: And it's okay to get some wrong sometimes.

Tim: And I, I never got that again, didn't I?

The next excerpt occurred when Ren and his Chinese mother discuss a "good attitude or behavior."

Mother: Oh, why does your teacher think that you behave well?

Ren: It's that I concentrate well in class.

Mother: Is your good concentration the concentration to talk to your peer at the next desk?

Ren: I listen to teachers.

Mother: Oh, is it so only for Mr. Chang's class or is it for all classes?

Ren: Almost all classes like that. . . .

Mother: So you want to behave well because you want to get an . . . honor award. Is that so?

Ren: Yes.

Mother: Or is it also that you yourself want to behave better?

Ren: Yes. I also want to behave better myself.

[Li et al., 2014, p. 1218]

Both Tim and Ren are likely to be good students in their respective schools. When parents support and encourage their child's learning, almost always the child masters the basic skills required of elementary school students, and almost never does the child become crushed by life experiences. Instead, the child has sufficient strengths to overcome most challenges (Masten, 2014).

However, the specifics of parental encouragement affect the child's achievement. Some research has found that parents in Asia emphasize that education requires hard work, whereas parents in North America stress the joy of learning. It may be that some parents push their children to excel because they believe that their children's accomplishments reflect on them. The result, according to one group of researchers, is that U.S. children are happier but less accomplished than Asian ones (Ng et al., 2014).

SUMMING UP Children continue to learn language rapidly during the school years. They become more flexible, logical, and knowledgeable, figuring out the meanings of new words and grasping metaphors, jokes, and compound words. Many converse with friends using informal speech and master formal code in school. They learn whatever grammar and vocabulary they are taught, and they succeed at pragmatics —the practical task of adjusting their language to friends, teachers, or family. Millions become proficient in a second language, a process facilitated by teachers and peers, as well as by the overall culture and the parents' use of language. For academic achievement during middle childhood, both past exposure to language—ideally extensive, with varied vocabulary—and adults' expectations are influential.

WHAT HAVE YOU LEARNED?

1. How does learning language progress between the ages of 6 and 10?
2. How does a child's age affect the understanding of metaphors and jokes?
3. Why would a child's linguistic code be criticized by teachers but admired by friends?
4. What factors in a child's home and school affect language-learning ability?
5. What are three research conclusions regarding U.S. children whose home language is not English?
6. How and why does low SES affect language learning?

Teaching and Learning

As we have just described, school-age children are great learners, using logic, developing strategies, accumulating knowledge, and expanding language proficiency. In every nation, new responsibilities and formal instruction begin at about age 6, because that is when the human body and brain are ready for them.

Traditionally, learning occurred at home, but now United Nations data find that more than 95 percent of the world's 7-year-olds are in school; that is where their parents and political leaders want them to be. (See Visualizing Development, p. 404, for U.S. and international statistics on education in middle childhood.)

Indeed, in many developing nations the number of students in elementary school exceeds the number of school-age children, because many older children who missed some early learning are enrolled in primary education. In 2012, Ghana, El Salvador, and China were among the nations with significantly more students enrolled in primary school than the total population of children who were primary school age (UNESCO, 2012). That is not a good sign: Many of them eventually drop out without having learned to read, write, and calculate.

International Schooling

Everywhere children are taught to read, write, and do arithmetic. Because of brain maturation and sequenced learning, 6-year-olds are not expected to multiply three-digit numbers or read paragraphs fluently out loud, but every nation teaches 10-year-olds to do so. Some of the sequences recognized universally are listed in the At About This Time tables.

Nations also want their children to be good citizens. However, citizenship is not easy to teach. There is no consensus as to what good citizenship means or what developmental paths should be followed for children to learn it (Cohen & Malin, 2010). Accordingly, many children simply follow their parents example regarding everything from picking up trash to supporting a candidate for president.

Differences by Nation

Although literacy and numeracy (reading and math, respectively) are valued everywhere, many curriculum specifics vary by nation, by community, and by school. These variations are evident in the results of international tests, in the mix of school subjects, and in the relative power of parents, educators, and political leaders.

For example, daily physical activity is mandated in some schools but not in others. Many schools in Japan have swimming pools, virtually no schools in Africa or Latin America do. As you read in Chapter 11, some U.S. schools have no recess at all.

Geography, music, and art are essential in some places, not in others. Half of all U.S. 18- to 24-year-olds say they had no arts education in childhood, either in school or anywhere else (Rabkin & Hedberg, 2011) (see Figure 12.4). By contrast, schools in Finland consider arts education essential, with a positive impact on learning (Nevanen et al., 2014).

Educational practices may differ even between nations that are geographically and culturally close. For example, the average child in a primary school in Spain spends twice as much school time studying science as does the average child in Italy (145 versus 78 hours per year, respectively). Similar disparities occur in nations in which each region or district

at about this time

Math

Age	Norms and Expectations
4–5 years	• Count to 20. • Understand one-to-one correspondence of objects and numbers. • Understand *more* and *less*. • Recognize and name shapes.
6 years	• Count to 100. • Understand *bigger* and *smaller*. • Add and subtract one-digit numbers.
8 years	• Add and subtract two-digit numbers. • Understand simple multiplication and division. • Understand word problems with two variables.
10 years	• Add, subtract, multiply, and divide multidigit numbers. • Understand simple fractions, percentages, area, and perimeter of shapes. • Understand word problems with three variables.
12 years	• Begin to use abstract concepts, such as formulas, algebra.

Math learning depends heavily on direct instruction and repeated practice, which means that some children advance more quickly than others. This list is only a rough guide, meant to illustrate the importance of sequence.

at about this time

Reading

Age	Norms and Expectations
4–5 years	• Understand basic book organization, such as, for children learning English, that books are written front to back and that letters make words from left to right. • Recognize letters—name the letters on sight. • Recognize and spell own name.
6–7 years	• Know the sounds of the consonants and vowels, including those that have two sounds (e.g., *c, g, o*) and combinations (*th, br*). • Use sounds to figure out words. • Read simple words, such as *cat, sit, ball, jump.*
8 years	• Read simple sentences out loud, 50 words per minute, including words of two syllables. • Understand basic punctuation, consonant–vowel blends. • Comprehend what is read.
9–10 years	• Read and understand paragraphs and chapters, including advanced punctuation (e.g., the colon). • Answer comprehension questions about concepts as well as facts. • Read polysyllabic words (e.g., *vegetarian, population, multiplication*).
11–12 years	• Demonstrate rapid and fluent oral reading (more than 100 words per minute). • Vocabulary includes words that have specialized meaning in various fields. For example, in civics, *liberties, federal, parliament,* and *environment.* • Comprehend paragraphs about unfamiliar topics. • Sound out new words, figuring out meaning using cognates and context. • Read for pleasure.
13+ years	• Continue to build vocabulary, with greater emphasis on comprehension than on speech. Understand textbooks.

Reading is a complex mix of skills, dependent on brain maturation, education, and culture. The sequence given here is approximate; it should not be taken as a standard to measure any particular child.

FIGURE 12.4

Focus on Facts As achievement test scores become the measure of learning, education in art, music, and movement has been squeezed out. Artists worry that creativity and imagination may be lost as well.

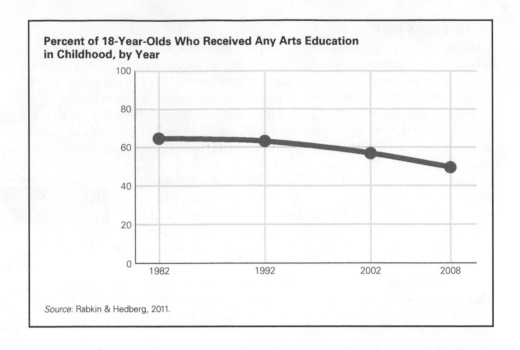

Percent of 18-Year-Olds Who Received Any Arts Education in Childhood, by Year

Source: Rabkin & Hedberg, 2011.

hidden curriculum The unofficial, unstated, or implicit rules and priorities that influence the academic curriculum and every other aspect of learning in a school.

Same Situation, Far Apart: Spot the Hidden Curriculum Literacy is central to the curriculum for schoolchildren everywhere, no matter how far apart they live. However, in the U.S. classroom at the left, boys and girls learn together, clothes are casual, history books are paperback and illustrated, and children of every background read the same stories with the same patriotic—but not religious—themes. The hidden curriculum is quite different for the boy memorizing his holy book on the right.

is allowed to set local standards. For example in Canada, children in the province of Quebec study science about half as much as those in Ontario (50 compared to 92 hours per year) (Snyder & Dillow, 2013).

Differences between one nation and another, and, in the United States, between one school and another, may be dramatic in the **hidden curriculum**, which includes all the implicit values and assumptions of the school. The hidden curriculum is evident in course offerings, schedules, tracking, teacher characteristics, discipline, teaching methods, sports competition, student government, extracurricular activities, and so on.

Whether students should be quiet or talkative in the classroom is part of the hidden curriculum, taught from kindergarten on. I realized this when I taught at the United Nations high school. One student, newly arrived from India, never spoke in class so I called on him. He immediately stood up to answer—to the surprise of his classmates. Soon he learned to stay seated, but he never spoke spontaneously. Students are taught to express opinions or not, and that correlates with their later political responses in their nation, as passive or active citizens (Lin, 2014).

Having Fun? Not necessarily.

The hidden curriculum is also thought to be the underlying reason for a disheartening difference in whether elementary school students respond to their teachers' offer of special assistance. In one study, middle-class children were likely to ask for help but lower-SES students were not: They wanted to avoid special attention, fearing it would lead to criticism (Calarco, 2014). This researcher concluded that the hidden curriculum of the social context, as well as the teachers' expectations, affected learning, unintentionally benefitting the middle-class students.

More generally, if teachers' gender, ethnicity, or economic background is unlike that of the students, children may conclude that education is irrelevant for them. If the school has gifted classes, the hidden message may be that all the rest of the students are not very capable.

The physical setting of the school also sends a message. Some schools have spacious classrooms, wide hallways, and large, grassy playgrounds; others have cramped, poorly equipped classrooms and cement play yards. In some nations, school is held outdoors, with no chairs, desks, or books. Sessions are canceled when it rains. What does that tell the students?

International Testing

Over the past two decades, more than 50 nations have participated in at least one massive international test of educational achievement. Longitudinal data reveal that when achievement rises, the national economy advances with it; this sequence seems causal, not merely correlational (Hanushek & Woessmann, 2009). Apparently, better-educated adults become more productive workers.

Science and math achievement are tested in the **Trends in Math and Science Study (TIMSS).** The main test of reading is the **Progress in International Reading Literacy Study (PIRLS).** These tests are given every few years, with East Asian nations usually ranking at the top. The rank of the United States has risen over the past two decades, but it is still below several nations in Eastern and Western Europe, as well as in Asia (see Tables 12.2 and 12.3). Most developing nations in Africa or South America do not give these tests, but when they do, their scores are low.

After a wholesale reform of the educational system, Finland's scores increased dramatically from about 1990 to 2011. Changes occurred over several years, including the abolishment of ability grouping in 1985 and curriculum reform in 1994 to encourage collaboration and active learning. Strict requirements for becoming a teacher are in place. Only the top 3 percent of Finland's high school graduates are

OBSERVATION QUIZ What three differences do you see between recess in New York City (left) and Santa Rosa, California (right)? (see answer, page 397)

Trends in Math and Science Study (TIMSS) An international assessment of the math and science skills of fourth- and eighth-graders. Although the TIMSS is very useful, different countries' scores are not always comparable because sample selection, test administration, and content validity are hard to keep uniform.

Progress in International Reading Literacy Study (PIRLS) Inaugurated in 2001, a planned five-year cycle of international trend studies in the reading ability of fourth-graders.

TABLE 12.2	TIMSS Ranking and Average Scores of Math Achievement for Fourth-Graders, 2011	
Rank*	**Country**	**Score**
1.	Singapore	606
2.	Korea	605
3.	Hong Kong	602
4.	Chinese Taipei	591
5.	Japan	585
6.	N. Ireland	562
7.	Belgium	549
8.	Finland	545
9.	England	542
10.	Russia	542
11.	United States	541
12.	Netherlands	540
	Canada (Quebec)	533
	Germany	528
	Canada (Ontario)	518
	Australia	516
	Italy	508
	Sweden	504
	New Zealand	486
	Iran	431
	Yemen	248

*The top 12 groups are listed in order, but after that, not all the jurisdictions that took the test are listed. Some nations have improved over the past 15 years (notably, Hong Kong, England) and some have declined (Austria, Netherlands), but most continue about where they have always been.

Source: Provasnik et al., 2012; Mullis et al., 2012a.

TABLE 12.3	PIRLS Distribution of Reading Achievement
Country	**Score**
Hong Kong	571
Russia	568
Finland	568
Singapore	567
N. Ireland	558
United States	556
Denmark	554
Chinese Taipei	553
Ireland	552
England	552
Canada	548
Italy	541
Germany	541
Israel	541
New Zealand	531
Australia	527
Poland	526
France	520
Spain	513
Iran	457
Colombia	448
Indonesia	428
Morocco	310

Source: Adapted from Mullis et al., 2012b.

admitted to teachers' colleges. They study five years at the university at no charge, earning a master's degree in the theory and practice of education.

Finnish teachers are also granted more autonomy within their classrooms than is typical in other systems, and since the 1990s, they have had more time and encouragement to work with colleagues (Sahlberg, 2011). Buildings are designed to foster collaboration, with comfortable teacher's lounges (Sparks, 2012) that reflect a hidden curriculum regarding teacher professionalism. The teachers also belong to a union—again, a sign of respect.

Respect for teaching might be the reason for Finland's success, or perhaps the reasons are more basic, such as Finland's size, population, culture, or history.

The crucial difference may be expectations: Every child is assumed to have strengths and weaknesses that the teacher uses to find the right combination of approaches that will foster learning. Almost no child is designated for special education because *all* are given individualized attention.

International test results reflect educational approaches in various nations, as well as cultural values. TIMSS experts videotaped 231 math classes in Japan, Germany, and the United States (Stigler & Hiebert, 2009). The U.S. teachers taught math at a lower level than did their German and Japanese counterparts, presenting more definitions disconnected to prior learning. Few U.S. students seemed engaged in math because they felt the "teachers seem to believe that learning terms and practicing skills is not very exciting" (p. 89).

By contrast, the Japanese teachers were excited about math instruction, working collaboratively and structuring lessons so that the children developed proofs and alternative solutions, both alone and in groups. Teachers used social interaction and followed an orderly sequence (building lessons on previous knowledge). Japanese teaching reflected all three theories of cognition: children's creative problem solving from Piaget, collaborative learning from Vygotsky,

Sharing Answers After individually subtracting 269 from 573, these two third-graders check their answers two ways—first by adding and then by showing their work to each other. As you can see, he is not embarrassed at his mistake because students in this class enjoy learning from each other.

© DEBBIE NODA/MODESTO BEE/ZUMAPRESS.COM/ALAMY LIMITED

and sequencing from information processing. Since Japanese students excel on the TIMSS, the teachers' use of strategies from all three theories may lead to student success.

Problems with International Benchmarks

Elaborate and extensive measures are in place to make the PIRLS and the TIMSS valid. For instance, test items are designed to be fair and culture-free, and participating children represent the diversity (economic, ethnic, etc.) of the child population. Consequently, most social scientists respect the data gathered from these tests.

The tests are far from perfect, however. Designing test items that are equally challenging to every student in every nation is impossible. Should fourth-graders be expected to understand fractions, graphs, and simple geometry, or should the test examine only basic operations with whole numbers? Once such general issues are decided so that every child has an equal chance, then specific items need to be written, again with an effort to be equally fair to every culture. The following item was used to test fourth-grade math:

> Al wanted to find out how much his cat weighed. He weighed himself and noted that the scale read 57 kg. He then stepped on the scale holding his cat and found that it read 62 kg. What was the weight of the cat in kilograms?

This problem involves simple subtraction, yet 40 percent of U.S. fourth-graders got it wrong. Were they unable to subtract 57 from 62? Did they not understand the example? Did the abbreviation for kilograms confuse them because—unlike children in most nations—they are more familiar with pounds? On this item, children from Yemen were at the bottom, with 95 percent of them failing. Is that because few of them have cats for pets or weigh themselves on a scale? As you see, national and cultural contexts may affect test scores.

Gender Differences in School Performance

In addition to marked national, ethnic, and economic differences, gender differences in achievement scores are reported. The PIRLS finds girls ahead of boys in verbal skills in every nation by an average of 16 points. The female advantage is not that high in the United States, with the 2011 PIRLS finding girls 10 points ahead. This meant that they were about 2 percent ahead of the average boy, an advantage—similar to Canada, Germany, and the Netherlands—suggesting that those nations are closer in gender equality than the average PIRLS nation.

Traditionally, boys were ahead of girls in math and science. However, the 2011 TIMSS reported that gender differences among fourth-graders in math have narrowed or disappeared. In most nations, boys are still slightly ahead, with the United States showing the greatest male advantage (9 points). However in many nations, girls are ahead, sometimes by a great deal, such as 14 points in Thailand and 35 points in Kuwait. Such results lead to a *gender-similarities hypothesis* that males and females are similar on most test measures, with "trivial" exceptions (Hyde et al., 2008, p. 494).

Unlike test results, classroom performance during elementary school shows gender differences in almost every nation. Girls have higher report card grades overall, including in math and science. Then, at puberty, girls' grades dip, especially in science, and in college, fewer women choose STEM (Science, Technology, Engineering, Math) majors, and even fewer pursue STEM careers. For instance, in the United States as in most nations, although women earn more college degrees than men, in 2011 only 22 percent of the doctorates in engineering were awarded to women (Snyder & Dillow, 2013).

// ANSWER TO OBSERVATION QUIZ
(from page 395): The most obvious is the play equipment, but there are two others that make some New York children eager for recess to end. Did you notice the concrete play surface and the winter jackets?

Video Activity: Educating the Girls of the World examines the situation of girls' education around the world while stressing the importance of education for all children.

Many reasons for gender differences in educational attainment have been suggested, with the social context of the elementary school classroom being crucial (Legewie & DiPrete, 2012). Perhaps school itself is more connected with feminism than masculinity. Indeed, children are all expected to sit still and concentrate, which may be easier for girls than boys. If sexual attractiveness becomes crucial at puberty, girls may underachieve because they think boys will not be attracted to them if they are too smart. As adults they believe that a career in science will clash with becoming good mothers and wives.

An alternate explanation is that social prejudice and the hidden curriculum favors young girls but not young women. Since most elementary school teachers are women, girls in the early grades may feel (or be) more encouraged than boys. Then, when adolescents begin to prepare for adulthood, most seek the roles that have typically been held by their sex—nurse, not doctor; secretary, not CEO; and definitely not mathematician, physicist, or engineer. Explanations for the gender gap in STEM fields have shifted over the past 40 years: Analysts once blamed the female brain or body; currently blame more often falls on culture or society (Kanny et al., 2014).

The following A Case to Study is an example: Do you think Paul became a low achiever because he was male, or because he was Mexican, or because his school failed him?

a case to study

Two Immigrants

Two children, both Mexican American, describe their experiences in their local public school in California.

Yolanda:

When I got here [from Mexico at age 7], I didn't want to stay here, 'cause I didn't like the school. And after a little while, in third grade, I started getting the hint of it and everything and I tried real hard in it. I really got along with the teachers. . . . They would start talking to me, or they kinda like pulled me up some grades, or moved me to other classes, or took me somewhere. And they were always congratulating me.

Paul:

I grew up . . . ditching school, just getting in trouble, trying to make a dollar, that's it, you know? Just go to school, steal from the store, and go sell candies at school. And that's what I was doing in the third or fourth grade. . . . I was always getting in the principal's office, suspended, kicked out, everything, starting from the third grade.

[quoted in Nieto, 2000, pp. 220, 249]

Note that initially Yolanda didn't like the United States because of school, but her teachers "kind of pulled me up." By third grade, she was beginning to get "the hint of it."

For Paul, school was where he sold stolen candy and where his third-grade teacher sent him to the principal, who suspended him. Ms. Nelson's fifth grade was "a good year," but it was too late; he had already learned he was "just a mess-up," and his expectations for himself were low.

Paul was later sent to a special school, and the text implies that he was in jail by age 18. Yolanda became a successful young woman, fluently bilingual.

It would be easy to conclude that the difference was gender, since girls generally do better in school than boys, but that is too simple. Some Mexican-born boys do well in California schools, which raises the question of how teachers impact children: What could the third-grade teacher have done for Paul?

Schooling in the United States

Although most national tests indicate improvements in U.S. children's academic performance over the past decade, when U.S. children are compared with children in other nations, they are still far from the top. A particular concern is that a child's achievement seems to be more influenced by income and ethnicity in the

United States than in other nations. Some high-scoring nations have more ethnic groups and immigrants than the United States, so diversity itself is not the reason.

Each state and each school district in the United States determines school policy and funding, with one result being notable disparities. For example, Massachusetts and Minnesota are consistently at the top of state achievement, and West Virginia, Mississippi, and New Mexico are at the bottom—in part because of the investment in education within those states as well as the proportion of students of high or low SES (which itself affects state spending) (Pryor, 2014).

Also in the United States, although many educators and political leaders have attempted to eradicate performance disparities linked to a child's background, the gap between fourth-grade European Americans and their Latino and African American peers is as wide as it was 15 years ago (Snyder & Dillow, 2013). Furthermore, the gap between low- and high-income U.S. students is widening, as is the gap between Native Americans and other groups (Maxwell, 2012).

National Standards

International comparisons as well as disparities within the United States led to passage of the **No Child Left Behind Act (NCLB)** of 2001, a federal law promoting high national standards for public schools. One controversial aspect of the law is that it requires frequent testing to measure whether standards are being met. Low-scoring schools lose funding and may be closed. An unfortunate result is that children of average achievement are pushed to meet the benchmark, while children far above or far below may be ignored.

Most people agree with the NCLB goals (accountability and higher achievement) but not with the strategies that must be used (Frey et al., 2012). NCLB troubles those who value the arts, social studies, or physical education because those subjects are often squeezed out when reading and math achievement are the ultimate priorities (Dee et al., 2013). States have been granted substantial power of implementation. Teacher evaluation and preparation has increased, but class size has not decreased, and the tests, and testing, remain controversial (Frey et al., 2012; Dee et al., 2013).

For decades, federally sponsored tests called the **National Assessment of Educational Progress (NAEP)** have measured achievement in reading, mathematics, and other subjects. Many critics believe that the NAEP is more realistic than state tests because the NAEP labels fewer children proficient. For example in the state of New York, state tests found 62 percent proficient in math, but the NAEP found only 32 percent; 51 percent were found proficient in reading on the state tests but only 35 percent according to NAEP (Martin, 2014).

Disagreement about state tests and standards led the governors of all 50 states to designate a group of experts who developed a *Common Core* of standards, finalized in 2010, for use nationwide. The standards, more rigorous than most state standards, are quite explicit, with half a dozen or more specific expectations for achievement in each subject for each grade. (Table 12.4 provides a sample of the specific standards.) As of 2013, forty-four states adopted this Common Core for both reading and math. Minnesota is a partial adopter, in reading but not in math, and five states—Texas, Virginia, Alaska, Indiana, and Nebraska—opted out of the Common Core.

Most teachers were initially in favor of the Common Core, but implementation has turned many against it. In 2013, a poll by Education Next found only 12 percent of teachers were opposed to the Common Core; a year later, 40 percent were (Gewertz, 2014). Likewise, many state legislators as well as the general public have doubts about the Common Core. This is another example of a general finding: Issues regarding how best to teach children, and what they need to learn, are controversial among teachers, parents, and political leaders.

"Big deal, an A in math. That would be a D in any other country."

MIKE TWOHY/THE NEW YORKER COLLECTION/WWW.CARTOONBANK.COM

No Child Left Behind Act A U.S. law enacted in 2001 that was intended to increase accountability in education by requiring states to qualify for federal educational funding by administering standardized tests to measure school achievement.

National Assessment of Educational Progress (NAEP) An ongoing and nationally representative measure of U.S. children's achievement in reading, mathematics, and other subjects over time; nicknamed "the Nation's Report Card."

TABLE 12.4	The Common Core: Sample Items for Each Grade	
Grade	Reading and Writing	Math
Kindergarten	Pronounce the primary sound for each consonant.	Know number names and the count sequence.
First	Decode regularly spelled one-syllable words.	Relate counting to addition and subtraction (e.g., by counting 2 more to add 2).
Second	Decode words with common prefixes and suffixes.	Measure the length of an object twice, using different units of length for the two measurements; describe how the two measurements relate to the size of the unit chosen.
Third	Decode multisyllabic words.	Understand division as an unknown-factor problem; for example, find 32 ÷ 8 by finding the number that makes 32 when multiplied by 8.
Fourth	Use combined knowledge of all letter–sound correspondences, syllable patterns, and morphology (e.g., roots and affixes) to read accurately unfamiliar multisyllabic words in context and out of context.	Apply and extend previous understandings of multiplication to multiply a fraction by a whole number.
Fifth	With guidance and support from peers and adults, develop and strengthen writing as needed by planning, revising, editing, and rewriting, or trying a new approach.	Graph points on the coordinate plane to solve real-world and mathematical problems.

Source: National Governors Association, 2010.

Learning a Second Language

One example of such a controversy involves determining when, how, to whom, and whether schools should provide second-language instruction. These questions are answered in opposite ways from one nation to another. Some nations teach two or more languages throughout elementary school, and others punish children who utter any word in any language other than the majority one.

In the United States, less than 5 percent of children under age 11 study a language other than English in school (Robelen, 2011). (In secondary school, most U.S. students take a year or two of a language other than English, but studies of brain maturation suggest that this is too late for efficient language learning.)

Some U.S. educators note that almost every child studies two languages by age 10 in Canada as well as in most nations of Europe. African children who are talented and fortunate enough to reach high school often speak three languages. The implications of this for U.S. language instruction are often ignored because of debates about immigration and globalization. Instead of trying to teach English-speaking children a second language during the years when they are best able to learn it, educators in the United States debate how best to teach English to children who do not speak it, a topic discussed above.

Choices and Complications

An underlying issue for almost any national or international school is the proper role of parents. In most nations, matters regarding public education—curriculum, funding, teacher training, and so on—are set by the central government. Almost all children attend the local school, whose resources and standards are similar to those of the other schools in that nation. In those nations, the parents' job is to support the child's learning, by checking homework and so on.

All the Same These five children all speak a language other than English at home and are now learning English as a new language at school. Although such classes should ideally be taught to true English language learners (ELLs), children who already speak English are sometimes mistakenly included in them (like 8-year-old Elena, from Mexico).

AP PHOTO/DANIEL SHANKEN

In contrast to that model, local districts in the United States provide most of the funds and guidelines, and parents, as voters and volunteers, are often active in their child's school. As part of the trend toward fewer children per family, parents are increasingly ready to move their children from one public school to another. Parents befriend their child's teacher, join parent–teacher associations (PTAs), move to another school zone, vote for local officials who have particular policies in education, and so on.

Although most U.S. parents send their children to the nearest public school, almost one-third do not. Other choices include a more distant public school, a public charter school, a private school, or home schooling (see Figure 12.5).

The existence of all of these options creates a problem: It is difficult for parents to decide the best school for their child, partly because neither the test scores of students in any of these schools, nor the moral values a particular school may espouse, correlate with the cognitive skills that developmentalists seek to foster (Finn et al., 2014). Thus, parents may choose a school that may not actually be the best educational experience for their child. Schools that enroll only children from selected families may publish high scores, but not because of the school.

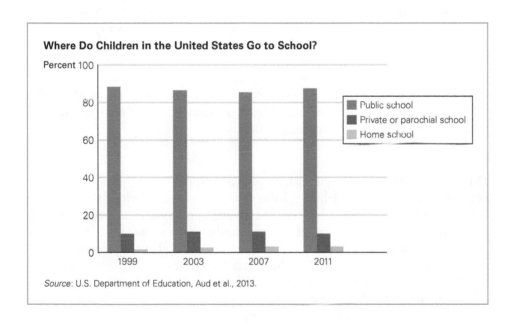

Source: U.S. Department of Education, Aud et al., 2013.

FIGURE 12.5

Where'd You Go to School? You can see that home schooling is still the least-chosen option, but the number of home-schooled children is increasing, while the number of children attending private is slightly decreasing. Although any child can be home-schooled in the United States (not in some other nations), detailed data indicate that home schooling is more common in the early grades, especially when public schools are not nearby (as in Alaska and Texas), and less common in high school.

Charter Schools

Charter schools are public schools funded and licensed by states or local districts. Typically, they also have private money and sponsors. They are exempt from some regulations, especially those negotiated by teacher unions (hours, class size, etc.), and they control admissions and expulsions. They are more ethnically segregated and enroll fewer children with special needs (Stern et al., 2014).

On average, teachers at charter schools are younger and work longer hours than regular public school teachers, and school size is smaller than in traditional schools. Perhaps 4 percent of U.S. children are in charter schools.

Some charter schools are remarkably successful; others are not (Clark et al., 2014). A major criticism is that not every child who enters a charter school stays to graduate; one scholar reports that "the dropout rate for African American males is shocking" (Miron, quoted in Zehr, 2011b, p. 1). Children and teachers leave charter schools more often than they leave regular public schools, a disturbing statistic.

charter school A public school with its own set of standards that is funded and licensed by the state or local district in which it is located.

Loved and Rewarded Marissa Ochoa, a third-grade public school teacher near San Diego, California, is shown moments after she learned that she won $5,000 as a star educator. Which do you think is more rewarding to her, the money or the joy of her students?

OBSERVATION QUIZ The photo above shows Marissa's students congratulating their teacher. What do you see in the hidden curriculum? (see answer, page 405)

private school A school funded by tuition charges, endowments, and often religious or other nonprofit sponsors.

voucher A public subsidy for tuition payment at a nonpublic school. Vouchers vary a great deal from place to place, not only in amount and availability but also in restrictions as to who gets them and what schools accept them.

home schooling Education in which children are taught at home, usually by their parents.

Overall, the charter school question is complex, with so much variation from state to state, and school to school (some schools sought by many parents, some avoided for good reasons) that it is difficult to judge charters as a group.

Private Schools

Private schools are funded by tuition, endowments, and church sponsors. Traditionally in the United States, most private schools were parochial (church related), organized by the Catholic Church to teach religion and to resist the anti-Catholic rhetoric of many public schools. Tuition was low since teachers were nuns who earned little pay.

Recently, many Catholic schools have closed, and other church-related schools have opened as have more independent private schools. All told, about 10 percent of students in the United States attend private schools. Economic factors are a major concern: High tuition means that few private-school children are poor or even middle class.

To solve that problem, some U.S. jurisdictions issue **vouchers,** money that parents can use to pay some or all of the tuition at a private school, including a church-sponsored one. This practice is controversial, not only because it decreases public school support but also because public funds go to religious institutions, contrary to the U.S. principle of separation of church and state. Advocates say that vouchers increase competition and improve all schools; critics counter that they weaken public schools and are costly to taxpayers.

Home Schools

Home schooling occurs when parents avoid both public and private schools by educating their children at home. In most U.S. states, authorities set standards for what a child must learn, but home-schooling families decide specifics of curriculum, schedules, and discipline. This choice has become more common: About 2 percent of all children were home schooled in 2003, about 3 percent in 2007, and perhaps slightly more in 2012 (Snyder & Dillow, 2013; Ray, 2013). Numbers are not expected to continue to increase, because home schooling requires an adult at home, typically the mother in a two-parent family, who is willing to teach the children. Such mothers are increasingly scarce.

The major problem with home schooling is not academic (some mothers are conscientious teachers and some home-schooled children score high on achievement tests) but social: Children have no interaction with classmates. To compensate, many home-schooling parents plan activities with other home-schooling families. This practice reflects local culture: Home schooling is more common in some parts of the United States (in the South and the Northwest more than in the Northeast or Midwest), which affects how readily parents can find other home-schooled children.

How to Decide?

The underlying problem with all these options is that people disagree about the best education for a 6- to 11-year-old and about how to measure learning. For example, many parents consider class size to be a major issue: They may choose private school, if they can afford it, because fewer students are in each class. They also insist that children have homework, beginning in the first grade. Yet few developmentalists are convinced that either small classes or daily homework are essential for cognitive development during middle childhood.

Mixed evidence comes from nations where children score high on international tests. Sometimes they have large student–teacher ratios (Korea's average is 28 to 1) and sometimes small (Finland's is 14 to 1). Fourth-graders with no homework sometimes have higher achievement scores than those with homework (Snyder & Dillow, 2010). This does not prove that small classes and extensive homework are worthless. Perhaps weaker students are assigned to smaller classes with more homework? If so, the data on homework or class size may be the results of low-scoring children, not vice versa. Nevertheless, these correlations raise doubts.

Who should decide what children should learn and how? Every developmental theory can lead to suggestions about education, but implementation is difficult. Statistical analysis raises questions about homeschooling and about charter schools (Lubienski et al., 2013; Finn et al., 2014), but as our discussion of NAEP, Common Core, TIMSS, and so on makes clear, the evidence allows many interpretations. As one review notes, "the modern day, home-based, parent-led education movement . . . stirs up many a curious query, negative critique, and firm praise" (Ray, 2013, p. 378). Parents, politicians, and developmental experts all agree that school is vital for development and that some children learn much more than others, but disagreement about teachers and curriculum—hidden or overt—abound.

A Word on Ethnic Diversity

As of 2014 in the United States, the nation's public schools are said to have become "majority minority," which means that most students are from groups that once were called minorities—such as African American, Latino, or Asian American (Krogstad & Fry, 2014) (see Figure 12.6). From a developmental perspective, the terms *majority* and *minority* are misleading, since the majority category includes many children whose ancestors came from distinct parts of Europe, and the minority category likewise includes many groups. Regarding cognitive development, though,

Especially for School Administrators Children who wear uniforms in school tend to score higher on reading tests. Why? (see response, page 405)

OBSERVATION QUIZ Why is the earlier data reported every few years, and the later years every year? (see answer, page 405)

FIGURE 12.6

Opportunity Increasing As you know, each ethnic group measured by U.S. statistics is much more diverse than the broad categories shown here. On this chart, the "white" category may be particularly misleading, since children with heritage from Siberia, Baghdad, Dublin, and Oslo are all in that category, despite many religious and cultural differences among them. The two most numerous white categories are children of German or English heritage, but some of their ancestors arrived on the Mayflower and some by jet, with the largest wave coming by steerage between 1870 to 1930. Arrival date and circumstances affect each family. Nonetheless, crude as it is, this chart shows increasing intellectual opportunity: Cognitive growth occurs when people from diverse backgrounds listen to each other.

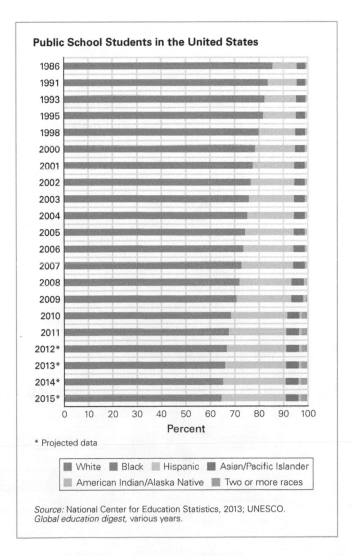

Public School Students in the United States

Source: National Center for Education Statistics, 2013; UNESCO. *Global education digest,* various years.

As you remember from Chapter 1, "race" is a questionable category. In the United States, Hispanic people are of any race, but all are Latino with heritage from Mexico or farther south. Some of them speak only English and have lived in the United States for generations. The category "two or more races" was not offered until recently. Therefore it has not increased as much as it seems to have, since biracial students were considered to be of one race before 2008. This chart shows public school students only, but since 90 percent of U.S. students are in public schools, and since overt racial discrimination is illegal, the addition of private school students would not change the totals significantly.

VISUALIZING DEVELOPMENT

Education in Middle Childhood Around the World

Only a decade ago, gender differences in education around the world were stark, with far fewer girls in school than boys. Now girls have almost caught up. However, many of today's children suffer from past educational inequality: Recent data find that the best predictor of childhood health and learning is an educated mother.

WORLDWIDE PRIMARY SCHOOL ENROLLMENT, 2011

Enrollments in elementary school are increasing around the world, but poor countries still lag behind more wealthy ones, and in all countries, more boys attend school than girls. These data are for almost all 6- to 11-year-olds. About 10 percent leave school by age 10.

BARBARA DELGADO/SHUTTERSTOCK

BOYS — Countries: All, Poor
GIRLS — All, Poor

SOURCE: THE WORLD BANK, 2014

WORLDWIDE, BASIC ELEMENTARY EDUCATION LEADS TO:

LESS −
- Child and maternal mortality
- Transmission of HIV
- Early marriage and childbirth
- War

MORE +
- Better-paying jobs
- Agricultural productivity
- Use of medical care
- Voting

SOURCE: HANUSHEK & WÖSSMANN, 2007

HOW ARE U.S. FOURTH-GRADERS DOING?

Primary school enrollment is high in the United States, but not every student is learning. While numbers are improving, less than half of fourth-graders are proficient in math and reading.

PROFICIENCY LEVELS FOR U.S. FOURTH-GRADERS

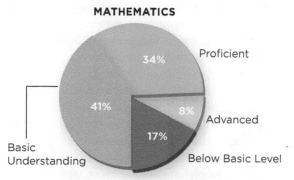

MATHEMATICS
- Proficient: 34%
- Advanced: 8%
- Below Basic Level: 17%
- Basic Understanding: 41%

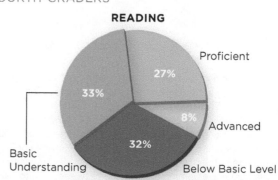

READING
- Proficient: 27%
- Advanced: 8%
- Below Basic Level: 32%
- Basic Understanding: 33%

SOURCE: ADAPTED FROM NATIONAL CENTER FOR EDUCATION STATISTICS, 2013A, FIGURES 4 AND 5

CHANGE IN AVERAGE SCORES FOR U.S. FOURTH-GRADERS — NAEP (NATIONAL ASSESSMENT OF ACADEMIC PROGRESS)

29 pts — MATH: 1990, 2011, 2013

5 pts — READING: 1990, 2011, 2013

SOURCE: NATIONAL CENTER FOR EDUCATION STATISTICS, 2013A, FIGURE 1

in middle childhood, every child advances, with specifics dependent far more on each individual's particular experiences than on his or her ethnic background.

Cognitive research leaves no doubt that, barring severe impairment, all school-age children *can* learn a second language and become skilled in math, reading, writing, and so on if they are taught logically, step-by-step. Whether they do so, however, is affected by SES, expectations, school practices, and national policies.

Children also learn best from personal contact, as might be expected during the period of concrete operational thinking. If well taught during middle childhood, children can learn about various groups, becoming sensitive to prejudice against any of their peers—whether based on gender, ethnicity, religion, or national origin (Bigler & Wright, 2014).

School children's ability to be logical and teachable, now that they are no longer preoperational and egocentric, makes this a good time to teach them to be proud of who they are, as well as to learn about their classmates. Ideally, they are fortunate enough to have a diverse classroom and a teacher who appreciates differences and similarities. Schools and homes both have a marked impact on what a child learns, and, as this chapter details again and again, children are ready to learn whatever their social context teaches them.

SUMMING UP   Societies throughout the world recognize that school-age children are avid learners and that educated citizens are essential to economic development. This has led to increased school enrollment: Almost all 6- to 11-year-olds are in school. Schools differ in what and how children are taught. International tests find that some nations are far more successful than others in educating their young. Among the top-scoring nations on the TIMSS and the PIRLS are Finland and the nations of East Asia. Since the United States is far from the best, internationally, many parents and politicians have implemented reforms, including No Child Left Behind, the Common Core, charter schools, and vouchers. It is not clear which, if any, of these, improves learning for school-age children. Test scores, as well as the nature and content of education, raise ideological and political passions. Teachers are crucial, and so are parents, who foster children's basic skills and motivation.

WHAT HAVE YOU LEARNED?

1. What do all nations have in common regarding education in middle childhood?
2. How does the hidden curriculum differ from the stated school curriculum?
3. What are three different ways in which ELLs are taught English in school?
4. What are the TIMSS and the PIRLS?
5. What are the national and international differences in school achievement of girls and boys?
6. What problems do the Common Core standards attempt to solve?
7. How do charter schools, private schools, and home schools differ?

// **ANSWER TO OBSERVATION QUIZ**
(from page 402): All the closest students are girls. What have the boys learned that is not part of the official curriculum?

// **Response for School Administrators**
(from page 403): The relationship reflects correlation, not causation. Wearing uniforms is more common when the culture of the school emphasizes achievement and study, with strict discipline in class and a policy of expelling disruptive students.

// **ANSWER TO OBSERVATION QUIZ**
(from page 403): Every year is needed to show recent trends. As you see, there was less yearly change before 2000. Note also that these numbers are *percentages* of children of various backgrounds. The absolute numbers have increased in every group.

SUMMARY

Building on Theory

1. According to Piaget, middle childhood is the time of concrete operational thought, when egocentrism diminishes and logical thinking begins. School-age children can understand classification, conservation, and seriation.

2. Vygotsky stressed the social context of learning, including the specific lessons of school and learning from peers and adults. Culture affects not only what children learn but also how they learn.

3. An information-processing approach examines each step of the thinking process, from input to output, using the computer as a model. This approach is useful for understanding memory, perception, and expression.

4. Memory begins with information that reaches the brain from the sense organs. Then, selection processes, benefiting from past experience, allow some information to reach working memory. Finally, long-term memory indefinitely stores images and ideas that can be retrieved when needed.

5. A broader knowledge base, logical strategies for retrieval, and faster processing advance every aspect of memory and cognition. Control processes are crucial. Children become better at controlling and directing their thinking as the prefrontal cortex matures. Metacognition and executive processing improve over the years of middle childhood and beyond.

Language

6. Language learning advances in many practical ways, including expanded vocabulary. Words are logically linked together and an understanding of metaphors begins.

7. Children excel at pragmatics during middle childhood, often using one code with their friends and another in school. Many children become fluent in the school language while speaking their first language at home.

8. Children of low SES are usually lower in linguistic skills, primarily because they hear less language at home and because adult expectations for their learning are low. This is not inevitable for low-SES families, however.

Teaching and Learning

9. Nations and experts agree that education is critical during middle childhood. Almost all the world's children now attend primary school. Schools differ in what and how they teach, especially with regard to religion, languages, and the arts.

10. International assessments are useful as comparisons, partly because few objective measures of learning are available. Reading is assessed with the PIRLS, math and science with the TIMSS. On both measures, children in East Asia excel and children in the United States are in the middle ranks.

11. In the United States, the No Child Left Behind Act and the National Assessment of Educational Progress (NAEP) attempt to raise the standard of education, with mixed success. The Common Core, developed with the sponsorship of the governors of the 50 states, is an effort to raise national standards and improve accountability.

12. Nations differ in how much overall control the central government has on education and how much choice and influence parents have. Unlike almost all other countries, in the United States, each state, each district, and sometimes each school retains significant control. Education is a political issue as much or more than a developmental one.

13. Disagreements about the best type of school are frequent; some parents choose charter schools, others prefer private schools, and still others opt for home schooling. However, some parents value particular aspects of schooling (class size, homework) more than do many educators. More research is needed to discover what is best.

KEY TERMS

concrete operational thought (p. 377)
classification (p. 378)
seriation (p. 378)
sensory memory (p. 382)
working memory (p. 382)
long-term memory (p. 383)
knowledge base (p. 383)
control processes (p. 384)

metacognition (p. 384)
executive function (p. 384)
ELLs (English Language Learners) (p. 388)
immersion (p. 388)
bilingual schooling (p. 388)
ESL (English as a Second Language) (p. 388)
hidden curriculum (p. 394)

Trends in Math and Science Study (TIMSS) (p. 395)
Progress in International Reading Literacy Study (PIRLS) (p. 395)
No Child Left Behind Act (p. 399)

National Assessment of Educational Progress (NAEP) (p. 399)
charter school (p. 401)
private school (p. 402)
voucher (p. 402)
home schooling (p. 402)

APPLICATIONS

1. Visit a local elementary school and look for the hidden curriculum. For example, do the children line up? Why or why not, when and how? Does gender, age, ability, or talent affect the grouping of children or the selection of staff? What is on the walls? Are parents involved? If so, how? For everything you observe, speculate about the underlying assumptions.

2. Interview a 6- to 11-year-old child to find out what he or she knows *and understands* about mathematics. Relate both correct and incorrect responses to the logic of concrete operational thought.

3. What do you remember about how you learned to read? Compare your memories with those of two other people, one at least 10 years older and the other at least 5 years younger than you are. Can you draw any conclusions about effective reading instruction? If so, what are they? If not, why not?

4. Talk to two parents of primary school children. What do they think are the best and worst parts of their children's education? Ask specific questions and analyze the results.

13

Middle Childhood:
Psychosocial Development

What Will You Know?

1. What helps some children thrive in a difficult family, school, or neighborhood?
2. Should parents marry, risking divorce, or not marry, and thus avoid divorce?
3. What can be done to stop a bully?
4. When would children lie to adults to protect a friend?

"But Dad, that's not fair! Why does Keaton get to kill zombies and I can't?"

"Well, because you are too young to kill zombies. Your cousin Keaton is older than you, so that's why he can do it. You'll get nightmares."

"That's soooo not fair."

"Next year, after your birthday, I'll let you kill zombies."

[adapted from Asma, 2013]

This conversation between a professor and his 8-year-old illustrates psychosocial development in middle childhood, explained in this chapter. All children want to do what the bigger children do, and all parents seek to protect their children, sometimes ineffectively. Throughout middle childhood, issues of parents and peers, fairness and justice, inclusion and exclusion are pervasive. Age takes on new importance, as concrete operational thinking makes chronology more salient, and age-based cutoffs are the usual mode that schools, camps, and athletic leagues decide if a given child is "ready."

I still remember who was the youngest, and the oldest, child in my fourth grade class—even though we all were born within the same 12 months. In the excerpt above, the professor hoped his son would no longer want to kill zombies when he was 9, but as you will see, a child's sense of fairness often differs from an adult's. Morality is the final topic of this chapter, but even the first topic, the nature of the child, raises ethical as well as psychosocial questions.

The Nature of the Child

As explained in the previous two chapters, steady growth, brain maturation, and intellectual advances make middle childhood a time for more independence (see At About This Time). One practical result is that between ages 6 and 11, children learn to care for themselves. They not only hold their own spoon but also make their own lunch, not

Adults Stay Out In middle childhood, children want to do things themselves. What if parents grabbed each child's hand and wanted to jump in, too? That would spoil the fun.

industry versus inferiority The fourth of Erikson's eight psychosocial crises, during which children attempt to master many skills, developing a sense of themselves as either industrious or inferior, competent or incompetent.

latency Freud's term for middle childhood, during which children's emotional drives and psychosexual needs are quiet (latent). Freud thought that sexual conflicts from earlier stages are only temporarily submerged, bursting forth again at puberty.

only zip their own pants but also pack their own suitcases, not only walk to school but also organize games with friends.

They venture outdoors alone, if their parents let them, and some experts think that parents should do just that (Rosin, 2014). Over the same years, parent–child interactions shift from primarily physical care (bathing, dressing, and so on) to include more conversation. Parents talk to their children about values, a trend particularly apparent with boys and their fathers (Keown & Palmer, 2014). The child's budding independence fosters growth. Parental guidance is still important even though the specifics may change.

Industry and Inferiority

Throughout the centuries and in every culture, school-age children are industrious. They busily master whatever skills their culture values. Physical and cognitive maturation, described in the previous chapters, makes such activity possible.

Erikson's Insights

With regard to his fourth psychosocial crisis, **industry versus inferiority,** Erikson noted that the child "must forget past hopes and wishes, while his exuberant imagination is tamed and harnessed to the laws of impersonal things," becoming "ready to apply himself to given skills and tasks" (Erikson, 1963, pp. 258, 259).

Think of learning to read and add, both of which are painstaking and boring. For instance, slowly sounding out "Jane has a dog" or writing "3 + 4 = 7" for the hundredth time is not exciting. Yet school-age children busily practice reading and math: They are intrinsically motivated to read a page, finish a worksheet, memorize a spelling word, color a map, and so on.

This was apparent in Chapter 12, in the comparison of mothers from Taiwan and New England. When Tim's mother helped him figure out how to do a particular kind of math problem that had him "clumsy" in class, she wrote out a page of problems for him, and then he did "the whole thing likety-split . . . [which made him] very happy" (Li et al., 2014, p. 1218). Similarly, children enjoy collecting, categorizing, and counting whatever they gather—perhaps stamps, stickers, stones, or seashells. That is industry.

Overall, children judge themselves as either *industrious* or *inferior*—deciding whether they are competent or incompetent, productive or useless, winners or losers. Self-pride depends not necessarily on actual accomplishments, but on how others, especially peers, view one's accomplishments. Social rejection is both a cause and a consequence of feeling inferior (Rubin et al., 2013).

Freud on Latency

Sigmund Freud described this period as **latency,** a time when emotional

---

🗓 at about this time

Signs of Psychosocial Maturation over the Years of Middle Childhood*

Children responsibly perform specific chores.

Children make decisions about a weekly allowance.

Children can tell time, and they have set times for various activities.

Children have homework, including some assignments over several days.

Children are less often punished than when they were younger.

Children try to conform to peers in clothes, language, and so on.

Children voice preferences about their after-school care, lessons, and activities.

Children are responsible for younger children, pets, and, in some places, work.

Children strive for independence from parents.

*Of course, culture is crucial. For example, giving a child an allowance has been typical for middle-class families in developed nations since about 1960. It was rare, or completely absent, in earlier times and other places.

drives are quiet (latent) and unconscious sexual conflicts are submerged. Some experts complain that "middle childhood has been neglected at least since Freud relegated these years to the status of an uninteresting 'latency period'" (Huston & Ripke, 2006, p. 7).

But in one sense, Freud was correct: Sexual impulses are absent, or at least hidden. Even when children were betrothed before age 12 (rare today but common earlier in some nations), the young husband and wife had little interaction.

Everywhere, boys and girls typically choose to be with others of their own sex. Indeed, boys who write "Girls stay out!" and girls who complain that "Boys stink!" are typical. From a developmental perspective, latency is a dynamic stage, not a gradual progression, as children shift away from sexual interests—only to reverse themselves when the hormones of puberty push them to do so (Knight, 2014).

Self-Concept

As children mature, they develop their *self-concept,* which is their idea about themselves, including their intelligence, personality, abilities, gender, and ethnic background. Self-concept begins earlier. As you remember, the very notion that they are individuals is a discovery in toddlerhood, and a positive, global self-concept is typical in early childhood. Complexity appears in middle childhood.

The self-concept gradually becomes more specific and logical, as cognitive development and social awareness increase. Children realize they are not the fastest, smartest, prettiest person. At some point between ages 6 and 11 when they win a race with their mother, they realize that she could have run faster if she had tried.

Crucial during middle childhood is **social comparison**—comparing one's self to others (Davis-Kean et al., 2009; Dweck, 2013). Ideally, social comparison helps school-age children value themselves and abandon the imaginary, rosy self-evaluation of preschoolers. The self-concept becomes more realistic, incorporating comparison to peers and judgments from the overall society (Davis-Kean et al., 2009).

social comparison The tendency to assess one's abilities, achievements, social status, and other attributes by measuring them against those of other people, especially one's peers.

This means that some children—especially those from minority ethnic or religious groups—become newly aware of social prejudices they need to overcome. Children also become aware of gender discrimination, with girls complaining that they are not allowed to play tougher sports and boys complaining that teachers favor the girls (Brown et al., 2011). Over the years of middle childhood, children most likely to develop healthy self-esteem are those who recognize prejudice and react by affirming pride in their backgrounds (Corenblum, 2014).

Affirming pride is an important counterbalance, because, for all children, their increasing self-understanding and social awareness come at a price. Self-criticism and self-consciousness rise from ages 6 to 11, and "by middle childhood this [earlier] overestimate of their ability or judgments decreases" (Davis-Kean et al., 2009, p. 184) while global self-esteem falls. Children's self-concept becomes influenced by the opinions of others, even by other children whom they do not know (Thomaes et al., 2010).

In addition, because children think concretely during middle childhood, materialism increases, and attributes that adults might find superficial (hair texture, sock patterns) become important, making self-esteem fragile (Chaplin & John, 2007). Insecure 10-year-olds might desperately want the latest jackets, cell phones, and so on.

Culture and Self-Esteem

Academic and social competence are aided by realistic self-perception. Unrealistically high self-esteem reduces effortful control (deliberately modifying one's impulses and emotions), and less effortful control leads to lower achievement and increased aggression.

The same consequences occur if self-esteem is unrealistically low. Obviously then, the goal is to find a middle ground. This is not easy: Children may be too self-critical or not self-critical enough. Cultures differ in defining what that the middle ground is.

Same Situation, Far Apart: Helping at Home Sichuan, in China, and Virginia, in the United States, provide vastly different contexts for child development. For instance in some American suburbs, laws require recycling and forbid hanging laundry outside—but not in rural China. Nonetheless, everywhere children help their families with household chores, as these two do.

High self-esteem is not universally valued. Many cultures expect children to be modest, not prideful. For example, Australians say that "tall poppies are cut down," the Chinese say "the nail that sticks up is hammered," and the Japanese discourage social comparison aimed at making oneself feel superior. This makes self-esteem a moral issue: *Should* people believe that they are better than other people, as is typical in the United States? Answers vary (Robins et al., 2012; Buhrmester et al., 2011).

Often in the United States, children's successes are praised and teachers are wary of being critical, especially in middle childhood. For example, some schools issue report cards with grades ranging from "Excellent" to "Needs improvement" instead of from A to F. An opposite trend is found in the national reforms of education, explained in Chapter 12. Because of the No Child Left Behind Act, some schools are rated as failing. Obviously culture, cohort, and age all influence attitudes about high self-esteem: The effects are debatable.

One component of self-concept has received considerable research attention (Dweck, 2013). As children become more self-aware, they benefit from praise for their process, not for their person: for *how* they learn, *how* they relate to others, and so on, not for static qualities such as intelligence and popularity. This encourages growth.

For example, children who fail a test are devastated if failure means they are not smart. However, process-oriented children consider failure a "learning opportunity," a time to figure out how to study the next time. The self-conscious emotions (pride, shame, guilt) develop during middle childhood, and serve to guide social interaction. However, those same emotions can overcome a child's self-concept, leading to psychopathology (Muris & Meesters, 2014).

Watch **Video: Interview with Carol Dweck** to learn about how children's mindsets affect their intellectual development.

Thus, as with most developmental advances, the potential for psychological growth is evident in the advance a child makes in self-concept in middle childhood. However, improvement is not automatic—family, culture, and social context affect whether this advance will be a burden or a blessing.

Resilience and Stress

In infancy and early childhood, children depend on their immediate families for food, learning, and life itself. Then "experiences in middle childhood can sustain, magnify, or reverse the advantages or disadvantages that children acquire in the preschool years" (Huston & Ripke, 2006, p. 2). Some children continue to benefit from supportive families, and others escape destructive family influences by finding their own niche in the larger world.

Surprisingly, some children seem unscathed by early experiences. They have been called "resilient" or even "invincible." Current thinking about resilience (see Table 13.1), with insights from dynamic-systems theory, emphasizes that no one is impervious to past history or current context, and many suffer lifelong harm from early maltreatment, but some weather early storms and a few not only survive but come out stronger (Masten, 2014).

Differential susceptibility is apparent, not only because of genes but also because of early child rearing, preschool education, and sociocultural values. As Chapter 1 explains, some children are hardy, more like dandelions than orchids, but all are influenced by their situation (Ellis & Boyce, 2008).

Resilience has been defined as "a dynamic process encompassing positive adaptation within the context of significant adversity" (Luthar et al., 2000, p. 543) and "the capacity of a dynamic system to adapt successfully to disturbances that

resilience The capacity to adapt well to significant adversity and to overcome serious stress.

TABLE 13.1	Dominant Ideas About Resilience, 1965–Present
1965	All children have the same needs for healthy development.
1970	Some conditions or circumstances—such as "absent father," "teenage mother," "working mom," and "day care"—are harmful for every child.
1975	All children are *not* the same. Some children are resilient, coping easily with stressors that cause harm in other children.
1980	Nothing inevitably causes harm. All the factors thought to be risks in 1970 (e.g., day care) are sometimes beneficial.
1985	Factors beyond the family, both in the child (low birthweight, prenatal alcohol exposure, aggressive temperament) and in the community (poverty, violence), can harm children.
1990	Risk–benefit analysis finds that some children are "invulnerable" to, or even benefit from, circumstances that destroy others.
1995	No child is invincibly resilient. Risks are always harmful—if not in education, then in emotions; if not immediately, then long term.
2000	Risk–benefit analysis involves the interplay among many biological, cognitive, and social factors, some within the child (genes, disability, temperament), the family (function as well as structure), and the community (including neighborhood, school, church, and culture).
2005	Focus on strengths, not risks. Assets in child (intelligence, personality), family (secure attachment, warmth), community (schools, after-school programs), and nation (income support, health care) are crucial.
2010	Strengths vary by culture and national values. Both universal needs and local variations must be recognized and respected.
2012	Genes, family structures, and cultural practices can be either strengths or weaknesses. Differential sensitivity means identical stressors can benefit one child and harm another.
2014	All children have the capacity to grow despite many impediments, a phenomenon called "ordinary magic." However multiple, accumulated stresses, such as usually occur when a child is poor and homeless, make resilience difficult.

threaten system function, viability, or development" (Masten, 2014, p. 10). Note that both leading researchers emphasize three factors in their definitions:

- Resilience is *dynamic,* not a stable trait. That means a given person may be resilient at some periods but not at others, and the effects from one period reverberate as time goes on.
- Resilience is a *positive adaptation* to stress. For example, if parental rejection leads a child to a closer relationship with another adult, that is positive adaptation, not mere passive endurance. That child is resilient.
- Adversity must be *significant,* a threat to the processes of development or even to life itself (viability).

Cumulative Stress

One important discovery is that stress accumulates over time, including stressful minor disturbances (called "daily hassles"). A long string of hassles, day after day, is more devastating than an isolated major stress. Almost every child can withstand one trauma, but repeated stresses make resilience difficult; "the likelihood of problems increased as the number of risk factors increased" (Masten, 2014, p. 14; Jaffee et al., 2007).

One international example comes from Sri Lanka, where many children in the first decade of the twenty-first century were exposed to war, a tsunami, poverty, deaths of relatives, and relocation. A study of the Sri Lankan children found that accumulated stresses, more than any single problem, increased pathology and decreased academic achievement. The authors point to "the importance of multiple contextual, past, and current factors in influencing children's adaptation" (Catani et al., 2010, p. 1188).

The social context—especially supportive adults who do not blame the child—is crucial. A chilling example comes from the "child soldiers" in the 1991–2002 civil war in Sierra Leone (Betancourt et al., 2013). Children witnessed and often participated in murder, rape, and other traumas. When the war was over, 529 war-affected youth, then aged 10 to 17, were interviewed. Many were pathologically depressed or anxious, as one might expect.

These war-damaged children were interviewed again two and six years later. Surprisingly, many had overcome their trauma and were functioning normally. Recovery was more likely if they were in middle childhood, not adolescence, when the war occurred. If at least one caregiver survived, if their communities did not reject them, and if their daily routines were restored, the children usually regained emotional normality.

An example from the United States comes from children temporarily living in a shelter for homeless families. (Cutuli et al., 2013; Obradović, 2012). Compared to other children from the same kinds of families (typically high poverty, often single parent), they are "significantly behind their low-income, but residentially more stable peers" in every measure of development (Obradović et al., 2009, p. 513). Presumably the residential disruption, when added to their other stresses, was too much. They suffered physiologically, as measured by cortisol levels, blood pressure, and weight; they also suffered psychologically, as measured by learning in school and number of good friends.

Again, protective factors buffered the impact: Having a parent with them who was supportive and who provided affection, hope, and stable routines enabled some homeless children to be resilient.

This echoes research from England during World War II, when many children were sent to loving families in rural areas to escape

Death and Disruption Children are astonishingly resilient. This girl is in a refugee camp in Northern Syria in 2013, having fled the civil war that killed thousands in her community. Nonetheless, she is with her family and is adequately fed and clothed, and that is enough for a smile.

AAMIR QURESHI/AFP/GETTY IMAGES

the daily bombing of London. To the surprise of the researchers, those children who stayed in London, hearing bombs and frequently fleeing to air raid shelters, were more resilient than those who were physically safe but had no parent nearby (Freud & Burlingham, 1943).

Similar results were found in a longitudinal study of children exposed to a sudden, wide-ranging, terrifying wild fire in Australia. Almost all the children suffered stress reactions at the time, but 20 years later, the crucial factor in their reactions was not how close they had been to the blaze but whether or not they were separated from their mothers (McFarlane & Van Hooff, 2009).

Cognitive Coping

Obviously, these examples are extreme, but the general finding appears in other research as well. Disasters take a toll, but resilience is possible. Factors in the child (especially problem-solving ability), in the family (consistency and care), and in the community (good schools and welcoming religious institutions) all help children recover (Masten, 2014).

One pivotal factor is the child's own interpretation of events (Lagattuta, 2014). Cortisol increases in low-income children *if* they interpret events connected to their family's poverty as a personal threat and *if* the family lacks order and routines (thus increasing daily hassles) (E. Chen et al., 2010). When low-SES children do not take things personally and their family is not chaotic, they may be resilient.

Think of people you know: Many adults whose childhood family income was low did not consider themselves poor. They may have had to share a bed with a sibling, and they may have eaten macaroni day after day, but that did not bother them because their parents seemed strong and happy, or at least not erratic and angry. They did not realize how poor they were. Therefore, poverty did not harm them lifelong.

In general, a child's interpretation of a family situation (poverty, divorce, and so on) determines how it affects him or her. Some children consider the family they were born into a temporary hardship; they look forward to the day when they can leave childhood behind. If they also have personal strengths, such as problem-solving abilities and intellectual openness, they may shine in adulthood—evident in the United States in thousands of success stories, from Abraham Lincoln to Oprah Winfrey.

The opposite reaction is called *parentification,* when children feel responsible for the entire family, acting as parents who take care of everyone, including their actual parents. Here again, the child's interpretation is crucial.

If children feel burdened and wish they could have a carefree childhood, they are likely to suffer, but if they think they are helpful and their parents and community respect their contribution, they are likely to be resilient. This may explain a curious finding: European American children are more likely to suffer from parentification than African Americans are (Khafi et al., 2014).

In another example, children who endured hurricane Katrina were affected by their thoughts, positive and negative, more than by other expected factors, including their caregivers' distress (Kilmer & Gil-Rivas, 2010). Especially in disasters, getting school routines started again quickly is sometimes especially helpful because children benefit from their cognitive accomplishments and the expectations for their future. Spiritual convictions and restoring religious routines (prayer, attending services) also help children cope if they provide hope and meaning (Masten, 2014).

Prayer may also foster resilience, because it changes a person's thinking. In one study, adults were required to pray for a specific person for several weeks. Their attitude about that person changed (Lambert et al., 2010). Ethics precludes such an

Video Activity: Child Soldiers and Child Peacemakers examines the state of child soldiers in the world, and then explores how developmental components of adolescent cognition relate to the decisions of five teenage peace activists.

Same Situation, Far Apart: Praying Hands
Differences are obvious between the Northern Indian girls entering their Hindu school and the West African boy in a Christian church, even in their clothes and hand positions. But underlying similarities are more important. In every culture, many 8-year-olds are more devout than their elders.

experiment with children, but it is known that children often pray, expecting that prayer will make them feel better, especially when they are sad or angry (Bamford & Lagattuta, 2010). As already explained, expectations and interpretations can be powerful.

SUMMING UP Children advance in maturity and responsibility during the school years. According to Erikson, the crisis of industry versus inferiority generates feelings of confidence or self-doubt as children try to accomplish whatever their family, school, and culture expect them to do. Freud thought latency enables children to master new skills because sexual impulses are quiet.

Often children develop more realistic self-concepts, with the help of their families and their own attitudes, as social comparison becomes more possible. Some children are resilient, coping with major adversity including war and natural disasters. Resilience is more likely if the stress is temporary and coping measures and social support are available. School achievement, helpful adults, stable routines, and religious beliefs help many children overcome whatever problems they face.

WHAT HAVE YOU LEARNED?

1. How do Erikson's stages for preschool and school-age children differ?
2. Why is social comparison particularly powerful during middle childhood?
3. Why do cultures differ in how they value pride or modesty?
4. Why and when might minor stresses be more harmful than major stresses?
5. What factors in the social context help children cope with major disasters?
6. How might a child's interpretation affect the ability to cope with repeated stress? ●

Families and Children

No one doubts that genes affect personality as well as ability, that peers are vital, and that schools and cultures influence what, and how much, children learn. Some have gone farther, suggesting that genes, peers, and communities have so much influence that parenting has little impact—unless it is grossly abusive (Harris, 1998, 2002; McLeod et al., 2007). This suggestion arose from studies about the impact of the environment on child development.

Shared and Nonshared Environments

Many studies have found that children are much less affected by *shared environment* (influences that arise from being in the same environment, such as two siblings living in one home, raised by their parents) than by *nonshared environment* (e.g., the experiences in the school or neighborhood that differ between one child and another).

Most personality traits and intellectual characteristics can be traced to genes and nonshared environments, with little left over for the shared influence of being raised together. Even psychopathology, happiness, and sexual orientation (Burt, 2009; Långström et al., 2010; Bartels et al., 2013) arise primarily from genes and nonshared environment.

Since many research studies find that shared environment has little impact, could it be that parents are merely caretakers, necessary for providing basics (food, shelter), harmful when abusive, but inconsequential in their daily restrictions, routines, and responses? Could it be that it doesn't matter much if parents enforce a set bath and bedtime, or if the parents let the child wash and sleep when he wishes? If a child becomes a murderer or a hero, maybe that is genetic and non-shared, so we should not blame or credit the parents!

Recent findings, however, reassert parent power. The analysis of shared and nonshared influences was correct, but the conclusion was based on a false assumption. Siblings raised together do *not* share the same environment.

For example, if relocation, divorce, unemployment, or a new job occurs in a family, the impact on each child depends on the child's age, genes, resilience, and gender. Moving to another town upsets a school-age child more than an infant, divorce harms boys more than girls, poverty may hurt preschoolers the most, and so on.

The variations above do not apply for all siblings: Differential susceptibility means that one child is more affected, for better or worse, than another (Pluess & Belsky, 2010). When siblings are raised together, all experiencing the same dysfunctional family, each children's genes, age, and gender may lead one child to become antisocial, another to be pathologically anxious, and a third to be resilient, capable, and strong (Beauchaine et al., 2009). Further, parents do not treat each child the same, even when the children look identical, as the following makes clear.

Family Unity Thinking about any family—even a happy, wealthy family like this one—makes it apparent that each child's family experiences differ. For instance, would you expect this 5-year-old boy to be treated the same way as his two older sisters? And how about each child's feelings toward the parents? Even though the 12-year-olds are twins, one may favor her mother while the other favors her father.

Especially for Scientists How would you determine whether or not parents treat all their children the same? (see response, page 418)

 # a view from science

"I Always Dressed One in Blue Stuff . . ."

To separate the effects of genes and environment, many researchers have studied twins. As you remember from Chapter 3, some twins are dizygotic, with only half of their genes in common, and some are monozygotic, identical in all their genes. It was assumed that children growing up with the same parents would have the same nurture, so that if dizygotic twins were less alike than monozygotic twins (and they often are), their differences must be genetic. However, if one monozygotic twin was unlike the other, that must be the result of nonshared environment (i.e., non-family influences).

That logical idea was the basis for research that found that genes and nonshared environment had a greater effect on twins than shared family environment, and, by extension, on everyone. Comparing monozygotic and dizygotic twins continues to be a useful research strategy. Recently it led to interesting conclusions

about the interplay of nature and nurture in topics from food preferences of 3-year-olds (parents are influential in a child's taste in junk food, less so for fruits and vegetables) to 25-year-olds' relationships with their parents (genes are more influential in adulthood than in adolescence, when peers are more important) (Fildes et al., 2014; Samek et al., 2014).

However, those research conclusions are now tempered by another finding: Siblings raised in the same households do not necessarily share the same home environment. A seminal study in this regard occurred with twins in England.

An expert team of scientists compared 1,000 sets of monozygotic twins reared by their biological parents (Caspi et al., 2004). Obviously, the pairs were identical in genes, sex, and age. The researchers asked the mothers to describe each twin. Descriptions ranged from very positive ("my ray of sunshine") to very negative

("I wish I never had her. . . . She's a cow, I hate her") (quoted in Caspi et al., 2004, p. 153). Many mothers noted personality differences between their twins. For example, one mother said:

> Susan can be very sweet. She loves babies . . . she can be insecure . . . she flutters and dances around. . . . There's not much between her ears. . . . She's exceptionally vain, more so than Ann. Ann loves any game involving a ball, very sporty, climbs trees, very much a tomboy. One is a serious tomboy and one's a serious girlie girl. Even when they were babies I always dressed one in blue stuff and one in pink stuff.
>
> [quoted in Caspi et al., 2004, p. 156]

Some mothers rejected one twin but not the other:

> He was in the hospital and everyone was all "poor Jeff, poor Jeff" and I started thinking, "Well, what about me? I'm the one's just had twins. I'm the one's going through this, he's a seven-week-old baby and doesn't know a thing about it . . ." I sort of detached and plowed my emotions into Mike. [Jeff's twin brother.]
>
> [quoted in Caspi et al., 2004, p. 156]

This mother later blamed Jeff for favoring his father: "Jeff would do anything for Don but he wouldn't for me, and no matter what I did for either of them [Don or Jeff] it wouldn't be right" (p. 157). She said Mike was much more lovable.

The researchers measured personality at age 5 (assessing, among other things, antisocial behavior as reported by kindergarten teachers) and then measured each twin's personality two years later. They found that if a mother was more negative toward one of her twins, that twin *became* more antisocial, more likely to fight, steal, and hurt others at age 7 than at age 5, unlike the favored twin.

These researchers acknowledge that many other nonshared factors—peers, teachers, and so on—are significant. But this personality difference in monozygotic twins confirms that parents matter. This will surprise no one who has a brother or a sister. Children from the same family do not always share the same family experience.

Family Structure and Family Function

family structure The legal and genetic relationships among relatives; includes nuclear family, extended family, stepfamily, and so on.

family function The way a family works to meet the needs of its members. Children need families to provide basic material necessities, to encourage learning, to help them develop self-respect, to nurture friendships, and to foster harmony and stability.

Family structure refers to the legal and genetic connections among related people. Legal connections may be marriage or adoption; genetic connections may be from parent to child, or more broadly as between cousins, or grandparents and grandchildren, or even between great aunts and second cousins.

Family function refers to how the people in a family care for each other: Some families function well, others are dysfunctional.

Function is more important than structure; everyone needs family love and encouragement, which can come from parents, grandparents, siblings, or any other relative. Beyond that, people's needs differ depending on how old they are: Infants need responsive caregiving, teenagers need guidance, young adults need freedom, the aged need respect.

The Needs of Children in Middle Childhood

What do school-age children need? Ideally, their families provide five things:

1. *Physical necessities.* Although 6- to 11-year-olds eat, dress, and go to sleep without help, families provide food, clothing, and shelter. Ideally, children live in a household where adults meet their basic needs.
2. *Learning.* These are prime learning years: Families support, encourage, and guide education.
3. *Self-respect.* Because children at about age 6 become much more self-critical and socially aware, families provide opportunities for success (in academic pursuits, in sports, in the arts, or whatever).
4. *Peer relationships.* Families choose schools and neighborhoods with friendly children and then arrange play dates, group activities, overnights, and so on.
5. *Harmony and stability.* Families provide protective, predictable routines in a home that is a safe, peaceful haven.

// **Response for Scientists** (from page 417): Proof is very difficult when human interaction is the subject of investigation, since random assignment is impossible. Ideally, researchers would find identical twins being raised together and would then observe the parents' behavior over the years.

The final item on the list above is especially crucial in middle childhood: Children cherish safety and stability, they do not like change (Turner et al., 2012). Ironically, many parents move from one neighborhood or school to another during these years. Children who move frequently are significantly harmed, academically and psychologically, but resilience is possible (Cutuli et al., 2013).

The problems arising from instability are evident for U.S. children in military families. Enlisted parents tend to have higher incomes, better health care, and more education than do civilians from the same backgrounds. But they have one major disadvantage: They move.

Military children have more emotional problems and lower school achievement than do their peers from civilian families. In reviewing earlier research, a scientist reports "[m]ilitary parents are continually leaving, returning, leaving again. . . school work suffers, more for boys than for girls, . . .and that reports of depression and behavioral problems go up when a parent is deployed" (Hall, 2008, p. 52).

About half the military personnel on active duty have children, and many of their children learn to cope with the stresses they experience (Russo & Fallon, 2014). To help them, the U.S. military has instituted special programs to help children whose parents are deployed. Caregivers of such children are encouraged to avoid changes in the child's life: no new homes, new rules, or new schools (Lester et al., 2011). Similar concerns arise when a deployed parent comes home: He or she is welcomed, of course, but sometimes return signifies changes in the child's life, and that is difficult.

On a broader level, children who are repeatedly displaced because of storms, fire, war, and the like are particularly likely to suffer in middle childhood. At this age, many children try to protect their parents by not telling them how distressed they are, but the data reveal that moving from place to place impairs a child's health and school learning (Masten, 2014).

Diverse Structures

Worldwide today, there are more single-parent households, more divorces and re-marriages, and fewer children per family than in the past (see Visualizing Development, p. 423). The specifics vary from decade to decade and nation to nation (see Figure 13.1). Nevertheless, although the proportions differ, the problems are similar worldwide.

Such diversity should be acknowledged but not exaggerated. Almost two-thirds of all U.S. school-age children live with two married parents (see Table 13.2), most often their biological parents. A **nuclear family** is a family composed only of children and their biological parents (married or not). Other two-parent structures include adoptive, foster, grandparents without parents, stepfamilies, and same-sex couples.

Rates of single-parenthood vary greatly worldwide. U.S. rates are among the highest, with about 31 percent of all U.S. 6- to 11-year olds living in a **single-parent family.** Rates change depending on the age of the child: More than half of all contemporary U.S. children will live in a single-parent family at least for a year before they reach age 18. However, as far as we can deduce, at any given moment most 6- to 11-year-olds live with two parents.

An **extended family** includes relatives in addition to parents and children. Usually the additional persons are grandparents, sometimes uncles, aunts, or cousins of the child.

The crucial distinction between types of families is based on who lives together in the same household. Many so-called single-parent families actually have two parents involved in the child's life. However, the two parents do not live together. Likewise, some children see their grandparents every day, even though they do not

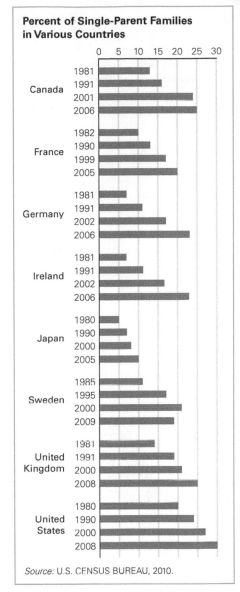

Percent of Single-Parent Families in Various Countries

Source: U.S. CENSUS BUREAU, 2010.

FIGURE 13.1

Single Parents A rising percentage of all households with children are headed by a single parent. In some countries, many households are headed by two unmarried parents, a structure not shown here. With the exception of Ireland, whose data are from family-based statistics, these data are from household-based statistics.

nuclear family A family that consists of a father, a mother, and their biological children under age 18.

single-parent family A family that consists of only one parent and his or her biological children under age 18.

extended family A family of three or more generations living in one household.

polygamous family A family consisting of one man, several wives, and their children.

live with them. In that case, the family functions like an extended family, but it is not categorized as such.

In many nations, the **polygamous family** (one husband with two or more wives) is an acceptable family structure. Generally in polygamous families, income per child is reduced, and education, especially for the girls, is limited (Omariba & Boyle, 2007). Polygamy is rare—and illegal—in the United States. Even in nations where it is allowed, polygamy is less common than it was 30 years ago. In Ghana, for example, men with several wives and a dozen children are now unusual (Heaton & Darkwah, 2011).

TABLE 13.2 | Family Structures (percent of U.S. 6- to 11-year-olds in each type)*

Two-Parent Families (69%)

1. **Nuclear family** (46%) Named after the nucleus (the tightly connected core particles of an atom), the nuclear family consists of a man and a woman and their biological offspring under 18 years of age. In middle childhood, almost half of all children live in nuclear families.

2. **Extended family** (10%) If both biological parents are present and other relatives live with them (usually a grandparent, sometimes an aunt or uncle), that is an extended family. About 10 percent of school-age children live in such families.

3. **Stepparent family** (9%) Divorced fathers usually remarry; divorced mothers remarry about half the time. When children from a former relationship live with the new couple, it makes a stepparent family. If the stepparent family includes children born to two or more couples (such as children from the spouses' previous marriages and/or children of the new couple), that is called a *blended family*.

4. **Adoptive family** (2%) Although as many as one-third of infertile couples adopt children, few adoptable children are available, so most adoptive couples have only one or two children. Thus, only 2 percent of children are adopted, although the overall percentage of adoptive families is higher than that.

5. **Both grandparents, no parents** (1%) Grandparents take on parenting for some children when biological parents are absent (dead, imprisoned, sick, addicted, etc.).

6. **Two same-sex parents** (1%) Some two-parent families are headed by a same-sex couple, with the biological child of one of them. (When same-sex couples adopt a child, that is listed as an adoptive family, above.)

Single-Parent Families (31%)

One-parent families are increasing, but they average fewer children than two-parent families. So in middle childhood, only 31 percent of children have a lone parent.

1. **Single mother—never married** (14%) More than half of all U. S. women under age 30 who gave birth in 2010 or later were unmarried. However, by the time their children reach middle childhood, often the mothers have married or the children are cared for by someone else. At any given moment, about 13 percent of 6- to 11-year-olds are with their never-married mothers.

2. **Single mother—divorced, separated, or widowed** (12%) Although many marriages end in divorce (almost half in the United States, fewer in other nations), many divorcing couples have no children. Others remarry. Thus, only 12 percent of school-age children currently live with single, formerly married mothers.

3. **Single father** (4%) About 1 father in 25 has physical custody of his children and raises them without their mother or a new wife. This category increased at the start of the twenty-first century but has decreased since 2005.

4. **Grandparent alone** (1%) Sometimes a single grandparent (usually the grandmother) becomes the sole caregiving adult for a child.

*Less than 1 percent of U.S. children live without any caregiving adult; they are not included in this table.

Source: The percentages in this table are estimates, based on data in U.S. Census Bureau, *Statistical Abstract* and Current Population Reports, *America's Families and Living Arrangements,* and Pew Research Center reports. The category "extended family" in this table is higher than in most published statistics, since some families do not tell official authorities about relatives living with them.

⚗️ a view from science

Divorce

Scientists try to provide analysis and insight based on empirical data (of course), but the task goes far beyond reporting facts. Regarding divorce, thousands of studies and several opposing opinions need to be considered, analyzed, and combined—no easy task. One scholar who has attempted this analysis is Andrew Cherlin, who has written 13 books and over 200 articles since 1988.

Among the facts that need analysis are these:

1. The United States leads the world in the rates of marriage, divorce, and remarriage, with almost half of all marriages ending in divorce.
2. Single parents, cohabiting parents, and stepparents sometimes provide good care, but children tend to do best in nuclear families with married parents.
3. Divorce often impairs children's academic achievement and psychosocial development for years, even decades.

Each of these is troubling. Why does this occur? The problem, Cherlin (2009) contends, is that U.S. culture is conflicted: Marriage is idolized, but so is personal freedom. As a result, many people assert their independence by marrying without consulting their parents or community. Then, child care often becomes overwhelming and family support is lacking.

Because the United States does not provide paid parental leave or public child care, marriages become strained. Divorce seems to be the solution. However, because marriage remains the ideal, divorced adults blame their former mate or their own poor decisions, not the institution or the society.

Consequently, they seek another marriage, which may lead to another divorce. (Divorced people are more likely to remarry than single people their age are to marry, but second marriages fail more often than first marriages.) Repeated transitions allow personal freedom for the adults but harm the children.

This leads to a related insight. Cherlin suggests that the main reason children are harmed by divorce—as well as by cohabitation, single parenthood, and stepparenthood—is not the legal status of their parents but the lack of stability. For example, divorces typically include numerous disruptions: in residence, in school, in family members, and—this may be crucial—in the relationship between child and parent. Divorced parents may become too strict or too lenient, impose premature responsibility or independence, or trouble the child by sharing confidences that relieve the adult's anger or loneliness.

Scholars now describe divorce as a process, with transitions and conflicts before and after the formal event (H. S. Kim, 2011; Putnam, 2011). As you remember, resilience is difficult when the child must contend with repeated changes and ongoing hassles—yet that is what divorce brings. Coping is particularly hard when children are at an age that involves their own developmental transition, such as entering first grade or beginning puberty.

Didn't Want to Marry This couple were happily cohabiting and strongly committed to each other but didn't wed until they learned that her health insurance would not cover him unless they were legally married.

Beyond analysis and insight, the other task of developmental science is to provide practical suggestions. Most scholars would agree with the following:

1. Marriage commitments need to be made slowly and carefully, to minimize the risk of divorce. It takes time to develop intimacy and commitment.
2. Once married, couples must work to keep the relationship strong. Often happiness dips after the birth of the first child. New parents need to do together what they love—dancing, traveling, praying, whatever.
3. Divorcing parents need to minimize transitions and maintain a child's relationships with both parents. A mediator—who advocates for the child, not for either parent—may help.
4. In middle childhood, schools can provide vital support. Routines, friendships, and academic success may be especially crucial when a child's family is chaotic.

This may sound idealistic. However, another scientist, who has also studied divorced families for decades, writes:

> Although divorce leads to an increase in stressful life events, such as poverty, psychological and health problems in parents, and inept parenting, it also may be associated with escape from conflict, the building of new more harmonious fulfilling relationships, and the opportunity for personal growth and individuation.
>
> [Hetherington, 2006, p. 204]

Not every parent should marry, not every marriage should continue, and divorce does not harm every child. However, every child benefits if families fulfill all five needs of school-age children. Scientists hope they will.

Connecting Family Structure and Function

How a family functions is more important for the children than the structure of their family. That does not make structure irrelevant. The two are related; structure influences—but does not determine—function. The crucial question is whether the structure makes it more or less likely that the five family functions mentioned earlier (physical necessities, learning, self-respect, friendship, and harmony/stability) will be fulfilled.

Two-Parent Families

On average, nuclear families function best; children in the nuclear structure tend to achieve better in school with fewer psychological problems. A scholar who summarized dozens of studies concludes: "Children living with two biological married parents experience better educational, social, cognitive, and behavioral outcomes than do other children" (Brown, 2010, p. 1062). Why? Does this mean that everyone should marry before they have a child, and then stay married? Not necessarily. The case for nuclear families is not as strong as it appears. Some benefits are correlates, not causes.

Same Situation, Far Apart: Happy Families
The boys in both photos are about 4 years old. Roberto (*left*) lives with his single mother in Chicago. She pays $360 a month for her two children to attend a day-care center. The youngest child in the Balmedina family (*right*) lives with his nuclear family—no day care needed—in the Philippines. Which boy has the better life? The answer is not known; family function is more crucial than family structure.

Education, earning potential, and emotional maturity all make it more likely that people will marry, have children, stay married, and establish a nuclear family. For example, first-time mothers in the United States are usually married when they conceive their first child if they are highly educated (78 percent), but usually not married if they are low in SES (89 percent unmarried at conception) (Gibson-Davis & Rackin, 2014).

Thus, brides and grooms may have personal assets *before* they marry and become parents. That means that the correlation between child success and married parents occurs partly because of who marries, not because of the wedding. For some unmarried mothers, making a legal, binding commitment would actually render them less able to devote the attention and love that their child needs.

Income also correlates with family structure. Usually, if everyone can afford it, relatives live independently, apart from the married couple. That means that, at least in the United States, an extended family suggests that someone is financially dependent.

SOURCE: SOCIAL TRENDS INSTITUTE, 2012.

SOURCE: U.S. CENSUS BUREAU, 2012; COPEN ET AL., 2012.

VISUALIZING DEVELOPMENT

A Wedding, or Not? Family Structures Around the World

Children fare best when both parents actively care for them every day. This is most likely to occur if the parents are married, although there are many exceptions. Many developmentalists now focus on the rate of single parenthood, shown on this map. Some single parents raise children well, but the risk of neglect, poverty, and instability in single-parent households increases the chances of child problems.

RATES OF SINGLE PARENTHOOD

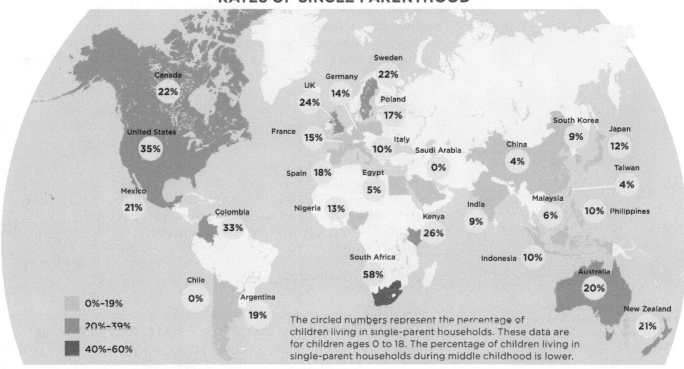

Canada **22%**

Sweden **22%**

Germany **14%**

UK **24%**

Poland **17%**

United States **35%**

France **15%**

Italy **10%**

Saudi Arabia **0%**

China **4%**

South Korea **9%**

Japan **12%**

Taiwan **4%**

Spain **18%**

Egypt **5%**

Mexico **21%**

Colombia **33%**

Nigeria **13%**

Kenya **26%**

India **9%**

Malaysia **6%**

10% Philippines

Chile **0%**

Argentina **19%**

South Africa **58%**

Indonesia **10%**

Australia **20%**

New Zealand **21%**

0%–19%

20%–39%

40%–60%

The circled numbers represent the percentage of children living in single-parent households. These data are for children ages 0 to 18. The percentage of children living in single-parent households during middle childhood is lower.

A young couple in love and committed to each other—what next?

IN THE UNITED STATES:

Influence of family and religion:
relatively weak

Likelihood of cohabitation:
70%

Likelihood of woman's marriage before age 25:
40%

IN NIGERIA:

influence of family and religion:
relatively strong

(Islam in northern Nigeria, evangelical Christianity in eastern Nigeria)

Likelihood of cohabitation:
1%

Likelihood of woman's marriage before age 25:
80%

Cohabitation and marriage rates change from year to year and from culture to culture. These two examples are illustrative and approximate. Family-structure statistics like these often focus on marital status and may make it seem as if Nigerian children are more fortunate than American children. However, actual household functioning is more complex than that, and involves many other factors.

These two factors—mate selection and income—explain some of the correlation between nuclear families and child well-being, but not all of it (Brown, 2010). The fact that the nuclear family is "not as strong as it appears" does not mean that marriage does not matter. For many couples, marriage leads to mutual affection and support, and then both partners become wealthier and healthier than either would alone. Further, when both parents live with their children day and night, a *parental alliance* is likely to form and benefit the child.

The parental alliance is important in every nation, but its influence is particularly apparent in Russia, where recent economic upheaval has reduced the male average life span from age 64 in 1985 to 59 in 2000. Those most at risk for a premature death are single men, who have higher rates of depression and alcoholism. The husband/father role leads men to take better care of themselves, so they can care for their children (Ashwin & Isupova, 2014). (**Developmental Link:** The parental alliance was first discussed in Chapter 4.)

Shared parenting also decreases the risk of child maltreatment and makes it more likely that children will have someone to read to them, check their homework, invite their friends over, buy them new clothes, and save for their education. Of course, having two married parents does not guarantee an alliance. One of my students wrote:

> My mother externalized her feelings with outbursts of rage, lashing out and breaking things, while my father internalized his feelings by withdrawing, being silent and looking the other way. One could say I was being raised by bipolar parents. Growing up, I would describe my mom as the Tasmanian devil and my father as the ostrich, with his head in the sand. . . . My mother disciplined with corporal punishment as well as with psychological control, while my father was permissive. What a pair.
>
> [C., 2013]

This student never experienced a well-functioning parental alliance. That may help explain why she is now a single parent, having twice married, given birth, and divorced. More generally, childhood family experiences echo in adulthood. Fathers who live apart from the mothers of their children tend to be most involved when the children are young. Later, their former partners and the children themselves make meaningful relationships difficult, so divorced fathers increasingly distance themselves from their children as time goes on.

One consequence: When children reach "the age of majority" (usually 18) and fathers are no longer legally responsible for their children, many divorced or unmarried fathers stop child support. Unfortunately, most emerging adults need substantial funds if they want to attend college or live independently, so a long-ago divorce still hinders their development (Goldfarb, 2014).

The lack of financial support for older adolescents is not simply because two-parent families are wealthier than one-parent families. Even remarried adults, whose household income is comparable to that of nuclear parents, contribute less, on average, to children from their first marriage (Turley & Desmond, 2011).

Stepfathers tend to spend very little time caring for their stepchildren, even when they live together (Kalil et al., 2014). When they grow up, their children are more likely to live farther from either father than children from nuclear families are (Seltzer et al., 2013). The parental alliance is weaker in such families in childhood, and that becomes a weaker family alliance lifelong.

Middle American Family This photo seems to show a typical breakfast in Brunswick, Ohio—Cheerios for 1-year-old Carson, pancakes that 7-year-old Carter does not finish eating, and family photos crowded on the far table. The one apparent difference—that both parents are women—does not necessarily create or avoid children's problems.

DAVID MAXWELL/THE NEW YORK TIMES/REDUX

Adoptive and same-sex parents usually function well for children, not only in middle childhood but lifelong. Stepfamilies can also function well, if the biological parent has chosen a new partner who will be a good parent. Especially when children are under age 2 and the stepparent and the biological parent develop a strong, healthy relationship, the children who live with them may thrive (Ganong et al., 2011). Of course, no structure always functions well, but particular circumstances for all three family types can nudge in the right direction.

All three family types (step-, adoptive, and same-sex) risk instability, so children may not have the fifth family function that they need (harmony and stability). Instability is particularly likely in stepfamilies. Compared with other two-parent families, stepfamilies often change residence and community. In addition, family constellations shift: Older stepchildren leave home more often than older biological children, new babies capture parental attention and affection, additional relatives may join the household, and divorce is more common.

Further, harmony is more difficult in stepfamilies (Martin-Uzzi, & Duval-Tsioles, 2013). Often the child's loyalty to both biological parents is challenged by ongoing disputes between them. A solid parental alliance is elusive when it includes three adults—two of whom had such profound differences that they divorced, plus another adult who is a newcomer to the child.

Children who gain a stepparent may be angry or sad; for both reasons, they often act out (for example, fight with friends, fail in school, refuse to follow household rules). That causes disagreements for their newly married parents, who often have opposite strategies for child-rearing.

Further, disputes between half-siblings in blended families are common. Remember, however, that structure affects function but does not determine it. Many stepparent families are difficult for children, but others function well for everyone (van Eeden-Moorefield & Pasley, 2013).

Finally, the grandparent family is often idealized, but reality is much more complex. If a household has grandparents and parents, often conflicts arise, and sometimes the grandparents are care-receivers more than caregivers. When grandparents provide full-time care with no parents present (called a *skipped-generation family*, a common form of foster care), the hope is that their experience and maturity will benefit the grandchildren.

But the grandparents usually do not benefit. On average, grandparents in skipped-generation families are poorer, sicker, and less stable than other grandparents. Rates of single parenthood are also higher, as many skipped-generation families are headed by the grandmother alone. To make matters worse, grandchildren who have been removed from their parents often have health or behavioral problems themselves (Hayslip et al., 2014). They are less likely to succeed in school or have supportive, enduring friendships.

Despite all these problems, skipped-generation families receive fewer services for children. Judges, schools, and social workers are sometimes ignorant of the special needs of such families, and where child care is concerned, neighbors and friends are less likely to help a grandmother than a mother (Baker & Mutchler, 2010; Hayslip & Smith, 2013).

Single-Parent Families

On average, the single-adult structure functions less well for children because one adult has less income, time, and stability than two adults who share responsibility. Most single parents fill many roles—including wage earner, daughter or son (single parents often depend on their own parents), and lover (many seek a new partner), which diminishes their ability to provide steady emotional and academic support for their children.

Don't Judge We know this is a mother and her child, but structure and function could be wonderful or terrible. These two could be half of a nuclear family, or a single mother with one adoptive child, or part of four other family structures. That does not matter as much as family function: If this scene is typical, with both enjoying physical closeness in the great outdoors, this family functions well.

Especially for Single Parents You have heard that children raised in one-parent families will have difficulty in establishing intimate relationships as adolescents and adults. What can you do about this possibility? (see response, page 427)

Rates of single parenthood and single grandparenthood are far higher among African Americans than other ethnic groups. This increases the neighborhood acceptance but does not lighten the burden. If a single parent is depressed (and many are), that compounds the problem. The following case is an example.

a case to study

How Hard Is It to Be a Kid?

Neesha's fourth-grade teacher referred her to the school guidance team because Neesha often fell asleep in class, was late 51 days, and was absent 15 days. Although she was only 10 years old and had missed much of the fourth grade, testing found Neesha scoring at the seventh-grade level in reading and writing, and at the fifth-grade level in math. Since achievement was not Neesha's problem, something psychosocial must be amiss.

The counselor spoke to Neesha's mother, Tanya, a depressed single parent who was worried about paying rent on the tiny apartment where she had moved when Neesha's father left three years earlier. He lived with his girlfriend, now with a new baby. Tanya said she had no problems with Neesha, who was "more like a little mother than a kid," unlike her 15-year-old son, Tyrone, who suffered from fetal alcohol effects and whose behavior worsened when his father left.

Tyrone was recently beaten up badly as part of a gang initiation, a group he considered "like a family." He was currently in juvenile detention, after being arrested for stealing bicycle parts. Note the nonshared environment here: Although the siblings grew up together, when their father left, 12-year-old Tyrone became rebellious whereas 7-year-old Neesha became parentified, "a little mother."

The school counselor spoke with Neesha.

> Neesha volunteered that she worried a lot about things and that sometimes when she worries she has a hard time falling asleep. . . . she got in trouble for being late so many times, but it was hard to wake up. Her mom was sleeping late because she was working more nights cleaning offices. . . . Neesha said she got so far behind that she just gave up. She was also having problems with the other girls in

the class, who were starting to tease her about sleeping in class and not doing her work. She said they called her names like "Sleepy" and "Dummy." She said that at first it made her very sad, and then it made her very mad. That's when she started to hit them to make them stop.
>
> [Wilmshurst, 2011, pp. 152–153]

Neesha was coping with poverty, a depressed mother, an absent father, a delinquent brother, and classmate bullying. She seemed to have been resilient—her achievement scores were impressive—but shortly after the counselor spoke with her,

> The school principal received a call from Neesha's mother, who asked that her daughter not be sent home from school because she was going to kill herself. She was holding a loaded gun in her hand and she had to do it, because she was not going to make this month's rent. She could not take it any longer, but she did not want Neesha to come home and find her dead. . . . While the guidance counselor continued to keep the mother talking, the school contacted the police, who apprehended [the] mom while she was talking on her cell phone. . . . The loaded gun was on her lap. . . . The mother was taken to the local psychiatric facility.
>
> [Wilmshurst, 2011, pp. 154–155]

Whether Neesha will be able to cope with her problems depends on whether she can find support beyond her family. Perhaps the school counselor will help:

> When asked if she would like to meet with the school psychologist once in a while, just to talk about her worries, Neesha said she would like that very much. After she left the office, she turned and thanked the psychologist for working with her, and added, "You know, sometimes it's hard being a kid."
>
> [Wilmshurst, 2011, p. 154]

Family structure encourages or undercuts healthy function, but many parents and communities overcome structural problems to support their children. Contrary to the averages, thousands of nuclear families are destructive, thousands of stepparents provide excellent care, and thousands of single-parent families are wonderful. In some European nations, single parents are given many public resources; in other nations, they are shamed as well as unsupported. Children benefit or suffer accordingly (Abela & Walker, 2014).

Culture is always influential. In contrast to data from the United States, a study in the slums of Mumbai, India, found rates of psychological disorders among school-age children *higher* in nuclear families than in extended families, presumably because grandparents, aunts, and uncles provided more care and stability in that city than two parents alone (Patil et al., 2013). On the other hand, another student found that college students in India who injured themselves (e.g., cutting) were more often from extended families than nuclear ones (Kharsati & Bhola, 2014). One explanation is that these two studies had different populations: College students tend to be from wealthier families, unlike the children in Mumbai.

Overall, single parents are much less common in many nations than in the United States, but in both these studies in India as in research throughout the world, children in single-parent families are more likely to have emotional or academic problems than children living with two parents.

Family Trouble

All the generalities just explained are averages, with many exceptions. However, two factors interfere with family function in every structure, ethnic group, and nation: low income and high conflict. Many families experience both, because financial stress increases conflict and vice versa.

Wealth and Poverty

Family income correlates with both function and structure. Marriage rates fall in times of recession, and divorce correlates with unemployment. The effects of poverty are cumulative; low socioeconomic status (SES) is especially damaging for children if it begins in infancy and continues through middle childhood (G. Duncan et al., 2010). Low SES correlates with many other problems, and "risk factors pile up in the lives of some children, particularly among the most disadvantaged" (Masten, 2014, p. 95).

Several scholars have developed the *family-stress model,* which holds that any risk factor (such as low income, divorce, single parenthood, or unemployment) damages a family if, and only if, it increases stress on the parents, who then become less patient and responsive to their children. This is true among families of many structures, ethnic groups, and cultures (Emmen et al., 2013).

If economic hardship is ongoing, if uncertainty about the future is high, if parents have little education—all these factors reduce the parents' ability to be the mentors and advocates that children need. Instead, adults become tense and hostile toward their partners and children. Thus, as many studies have found, although low SES makes many stresses more likely, and adults certainly should not be blamed if worries about food and housing make them less patient with their children, nonetheless the parents' *reaction* to their situation is more important than income alone (Valdez et al., 2013; Evans & Kim, 2013; D. Lee et al., 2013).

Adults whose upbringing included less education and impaired emotional control often find it difficult to find employment and care for their children, and then low income adds to their difficulties (Schofield et al., 2011). Health problems in infancy may lead to "biologically embedded" stresses that impair adult well-being, which affects the next generation (Masten, 2013).

If all this is so, more income means better family functioning, especially if the income is stable, not a windfall. For example, children in single-mother households do much better if their father reliably pays child support, even if he is not actively involved in the child's daily life (Huang, 2009). Nations that subsidize single parents (e.g., Austria and Iceland) also have smaller achievement gaps between low- and middle-SES children on the TIMSS. This finding is suggestive,

// Response for Single Parents (from page 425): Do not get married mainly to provide a second parent for your child. If you were to do so, things would probably get worse rather than better. Do make an effort to have friends of both sexes with whom your child can interact.

You Idiot! Ideally, parents never argue in front the children, as these two do here. However, *how* they argue is crucial. Every couple disagrees about specifics of family life; dysfunctional families call each other names. Hopefully, he said "I know how to fit this bike into the car" and she answered "I was just trying to help," rather than either one escalating the fight by saying "It was your stupid idea to take this trip!"

but controversial and value-laden. Some developmentalists report that raising income does *not,* by itself, improve parenting (L. Berger et al., 2009).

In fact, reaction to wealth may also cause difficulty. Children in high-income families develop more than their share of developmental problems. Wealthy parents may be stressed by needing to maintain their achievements. In addition, they may pressure their children to excel, or they may become too lax in reacting to early use of alcohol and other drugs. That may create externalizing and internalizing problems in middle childhood that lead to drug use, delinquency, and poor academic performance (Luthar & Barkin, 2012).

Conflict

There is no disagreement about conflict: Every researcher agrees that family conflict harms children, especially when adults fight about child rearing. Such fights are more common in stepfamilies, divorced families, and extended families, but nuclear families are not immune. In every family, children suffer not only if they are abused, physically or emotionally, but also if they merely witness their parents' abuse. Fights between siblings can be harmful, too (Turner et al., 2012).

Researchers have hypothesized that children are emotionally troubled in families with feuding parents because of their genes, not because of witnessing the parents fighting. The idea is that the parents' genes lead to marital problems and that children who inherit those same genes will have similar temperaments. If that is the case, then it doesn't matter if children are exposed to their parents' conflicts.

This idea was tested in a longitudinal study of 867 twin pairs (388 monozygotic pairs and 479 dizygotic pairs), all married with an adolescent child. Each adolescent was compared to his or her cousin, the child of one parent's twin (Schermerhorn et al., 2011). Thus, this study had data on family conflict from 5,202 individuals—one-third of them adult twins, one-third of them spouses of twins, and one-third of them adolescents who were genetically linked to another adolescent.

The researchers found that, although genes had some influence, witnessing conflict had a more powerful effect, causing externalizing problems in boys and internalizing problems in girls. In this study, quiet disagreements did little harm, but open conflict (such as yelling when children could hear) or divorce did (Schermerhorn et al., 2011). That leads to an obvious conclusion: Parents should not fight in front of their children.

SUMMING UP Families serve five crucial functions for school-age children: to supply basic necessities, to encourage learning, to develop self-respect, to nurture friendships, and to provide harmony and stability.

Nuclear families (headed by two biological parents) are the most common family structure and tend to provide more income, stability, and parental attention, all of which benefit children. Many other families are headed by a single parent, usually the mother—half because she never married and half because she divorced. Many other family types are possible.

Children sometimes do well in every structure, but each structure has vulnerabilities. Although structures affect function, no structure inevitably harms children, and no structure (including nuclear) guarantees optimal function. Poverty and wealth can both cause stress, which interferes with family function: When parents worry about income, they are less likely to be patient and responsive with their children. Conflict between the parents affects the children, no matter what the family structure.

1. How is it that siblings raised together do not share the exact same environment?
2. What is the difference between family structure and family function?
3. Why is a harmonious, stable home particularly important during middle childhood?
4. Describe the characteristics of four different family structures.
5. What are the advantages for children in a nuclear family structure?
6. List three reasons why the single-parent structure might function less well for children.
7. In what ways are family structure and family function affected by culture?
8. Using the family-stress model, explain how low family income might affect family function.

The Peer Group

Peers become increasingly important in middle childhood. With their new awareness of reality (concrete operations), children are painfully aware of their classmates' opinions, judgments, and accomplishments.

The Culture of Children

Peer relationships, unlike adult–child relationships, involve partners who negotiate, compromise, share, and defend themselves as equals. Consequently, children learn social lessons from one another that grown-ups cannot teach (Rubin et al., 2013). Adults sometimes command obedience, sometimes are subservient, but they are always much older and bigger, with their own values and experiences.

Child culture includes the customs, rules, and rituals that are passed down to younger children from slightly older ones. Jump-rope rhymes, insults, and superstitions are often part of peer society. Even nursery games echo child culture. For instance, "Ring around the rosy/Pocketful of posy/Ashes, ashes/We all fall down," may have originated as children coped with the Black Death, which killed half the population of Europe in the fourteenth century (Kastenbaum, 2012). (*Rosy* may be short for *rosary,* the circle of prayer beads of Roman Catholics; posy may be the dried flowers of the herbs thought to deflect sickness—but no one knows for sure.)

Throughout the world, child culture encourages independence from adults. Many children reject clothes that parents buy as too loose, too tight, too long, too short, or wrong in color, style, brand, decoration, or some other aspect that adults might not notice.

Appearance is important in child culture, but more important is a measure of independence from adults. Classmates pity those (especially boys) whose parents kiss them ("mama's boy"), tease children who please the teachers ("teacher's pet," "suck-up"), and despise those who betray children to adults ("tattletale," "grasser," "snitch," "rat"). Keeping secrets from parents and teachers is a moral mandate (Gillis, 2008).

The culture of children is not always benign. For example, because communication with peers is vital, children learn the necessary languages. Parents proudly note how well their children speak a second language, but may be distressed when their children spout their peers' curses, accents, and slang. Because they value independence, children find friends who defy authority, sometimes harmlessly (passing a note in class), sometimes not (shoplifting, smoking). If a bully teases or isolates a child, it is hard for the other children to defend the one who is shunned.

child culture The particular habits, styles, and values that reflect the set of rules and rituals that characterize children as distinct from adult society.

No Toys Boys in middle childhood are happiest playing outside with equipment designed for work. This wheelbarrow is perfect, especially because at any moment the pusher might tip it.

Friendships

Teachers may try to separate friends, but developmentalists find that friends teach each other academic and social skills (Bagwell & Schmidt, 2011). It is a mistake to assume that friends are the source of trouble, although obviously each relationship is distinct. Aggressive children seek other aggressive children, and then they both exclude outsiders, but at least they learn loyalty via the friendship (Rubin et al., 2013).

Remember Yolanda and Paul from Chapter 12? Their friends guided them:

Yolanda:

There's one friend . . . she's always been with me, in bad or good . . . She's always telling me, "Keep on going and your dreams are gonna come true."

Paul:

I think right now about going Christian, right? Just going Christian, trying to do good, you know? Stay away from drugs, everything. And every time it seems like I think about that, I think about the homeboys. And it's a trip because a lot of the homeboys are my family, too, you know?

[quoted in Nieto, 2000, pp. 220, 249]

Yolanda later went to college; Paul went to jail.

Children want to be liked; consequently they learn faster and feel happier when they have friends. If they had to choose between being friendless but popular (looked up to by many peers) or having close friends but being unpopular (ignored by peers), most would choose to have friends (Bagwell & Schmidt, 2011). A wise choice.

Friendships become more intense and intimate over the years of middle childhood, as social cognition and effortful control advance. Six-year-olds may like anyone of the same sex and age who is willing to play with them. By age 10, children demand more of their friends. They share secrets and expect loyalty. Compared to younger children, older children change friends less often, become more upset when a friendship breaks up, and find it harder to make new friends.

Older children tend to choose friends whose interests, values, and backgrounds are similar to their own. By the end of middle childhood, close friendships are almost always between children of the same sex, age, ethnicity, and socioeconomic status (Rubin et al., 2013). This occurs not because children naturally become more prejudiced over the course of middle childhood (they do not) but because they seek friends who understand and agree with them.

Gender differences persist in activities (girls converse more whereas boys play more active games), but both boys and girls want best friends and usually find them. Having no close friends at age 11 predicts depression at age 13 (Brendgen et al., 2010).

Popular and Unpopular Children

In North American culture, shy children are not popular, but a 1990 survey in Shanghai found that shy children were liked and respected (X. Chen et al., 1992). Twelve years later, assertiveness became more valued in China: A survey from the same schools found shy children less popular than their shy predecessors had been (X. Chen et al., 2005). A few years later, a third study in rural China found shyness still valued; it predicted adult adjustment (X. Chen et al., 2009).

Finally, a fourth study from a Chinese city found that shyness in middle childhood predicted unhappiness later on—unless the shy child was also academically superior, in which case shyness was not a disability (X. Chen et al., 2013). Obviously, cohort and context matter.

In the United States, two types of popular children and three types of unpopular children are apparent in middle childhood (Cillessen & Marks, 2011). First, at every age, children who are friendly and cooperative are well liked. By the end of middle childhood, status becomes as important as likeability. Consequently, a second type of popularity begins: Children who are dominant and somewhat aggressive are also popular (Shi & Xie, 2012).

As for the three types of unpopular children, some are *neglected*, not rejected, ignored but not shunned. The other two types are actively rejected. Some are **aggressive-rejected,** disliked because they are antagonistic and confrontational. Others are **withdrawn-rejected,** disliked because they are timid and anxious.

Both aggressive-rejected and withdrawn-rejected children often misinterpret social situations, lack emotional regulation, and experience mistreatment at home. Each of these problems causes rejection, and then rejection makes home and school worse for the child (Stenseng et al., 2014). If they are not guided toward friendship with at least one other child, they may become bullies and victims.

Bullies and Victims

Bullying is defined as repeated, systematic attacks intended to harm those who are unable or unlikely to defend themselves. It occurs in every nation, in every community, and in every kind of school (religious or secular, public or private, progressive or traditional, large or small) and perhaps in every child. As one girl said, "There's a little bit of bully in everyone" (Guerra et al., 2011, p. 303).

As one boy explained:

> You can get bullied because you are weak or annoying or because you are different. Kids with big ears get bullied. Dorks get bullied. You can also get bullied because you think too much of yourself and try to show off. Teacher's pet gets bullied. If you say the right answer too many times in class you can get bullied. There are lots of popular groups who bully each other and other groups, but you can get bullied within your group too. If you do not want to get bullied, you have to stay under the radar, but then you might feel sad because no one pays attention to you.
>
> *[quoted in Guerra et al., 2011, p. 306]*

Bullying may be of four types:

- *Physical* (hitting, pinching, shoving, or kicking)
- *Verbal* (teasing, taunting, or name-calling)
- *Relational* (destroying peer acceptance)
- *Cyberbullying* (using electronic means to harm another)

The first three types are common in primary school and begin even earlier, in preschool. Cyberbullying is more common later on. (**Developmental Link:** Cyberbullying is discussed in Chapter 15.)

A key word in the definition of bullying is *repeated*. Almost every child experiences an isolated attack or is called a derogatory name at some point. Victims of bullying, however, endure shameful experiences again and again—being forced to hand over lunch money, laugh at insults, drink milk mixed with detergent, and so on—with no one defending them. Victims tend to be "cautious, sensitive, quiet . . . lonely and abandoned at school. As a rule, they do not have a single good friend in their class" (Olweus et al., 1999, p. 15).

Victims are chosen not because of their perceived appearance or behavior but because of their emotional vulnerability and social isolation. Children new to a school, or whose background and home culture are unlike that of their peers, are especially vulnerable.

aggressive-rejected Rejected by peers because of antagonistic, confrontational behavior.

withdrawn-rejected Rejected by peers because of timid, withdrawn, and anxious behavior.

bullying Repeated, systematic efforts to inflict harm through physical, verbal, or social attack on a weaker person.

PHOTOS ARE BEING USED FOR ILLUSTRATIVE PURPOSES ONLY, PERSONS DEPICTED IN THE PHOTOS ARE MODELS.

Who Suffers More? Physical bullying is typically the target of anti-bullying laws and policies, because it is easier to spot than relational bullying. Moreover, it is easier to stop—a boy can learn to never put his hands on another boy. But being rejected from the group, especially with gossip and lies, is more devastating to the victim and harder to control. How would the girls respond if the teacher said "She has to be your friend"?

bully-victims People who attack others and who are attacked as well. (Also called *provocative victims* because they do things that elicit bullying.)

Bullying: Interview with Nicki Crick explains the characteristics of bullies.

http://qrs.ly/nq4ep13

©2016 MACMILLAN

Remember the three types of unpopular children? Neglected children are not victimized; they are ignored, "under the radar." If their family relationships are good, they suffer less even if they are bullied (which they usually are not) (Bowes et al., 2010).

Withdrawn-rejected children are often victims; they are isolated, feel depressed, and are friendless. Aggressive-rejected children are called **bully-victims** (or *provocative victims*), with neither friends nor sympathizers. They suffer the most because they strike back ineffectively, which increases the bullying (Dukes et al., 2009).

Unlike bully-victims, most bullies are *not* rejected. Although some have low self-esteem, others are proud; they are pleased with themselves, they have friends who admire them and classmates who fear them (Guerra et al., 2011). As already mentioned, some are quite popular, with bullying a form of social dominance and authority (Pellegrini et al., 2012). Over the years of middle childhood, bullies become skilled at avoiding adult awareness, picking victims who are rejected by most classmates and who will not resist or tell.

Boys bully more than girls, usually physically attacking smaller, weaker boys. Girl bullies usually use words to attack shyer, more soft-spoken girls. Young boys can sometimes bully girls, but by puberty (about age 11), boys who bully girls are not admired (Veenstra et al., 2010), although sexual teasing is. Especially in the final years of middle childhood, boys who are thought to be gay become targets, with suicide attempts one consequence (Hong & Garbarino, 2012).

Causes and Consequences of Bullying

Bullying may originate with a genetic predisposition or a brain abnormality, but when a toddler is aggressive, parents, teachers, and peers usually teach emotional regulation and effortful control. If home life is stressful, if discipline is ineffectual, if siblings are hostile, or if attachment is insecure, those lessons may not be learned or even taught. Instead, vulnerable young children develop externalizing and internalizing problems, becoming bullies or victims in middle childhood (Turner et al., 2012).

Peers are crucial. Some peer groups approve of relational bullying, and then children entertain their classmates by mocking and insulting each other (Werner & Hill, 2010). On the other hand, when students themselves disapprove of bullying, its incidence is reduced (Guerra & Williams, 2010). Age is also an important factor. For most of childhood, bullies are disliked, but a switch occurs at about age 11, when bullying becomes a way to gain social status (Caravita & Cillessen, 2012).

The consequences of bullying can echo for years, worsening with age. Many victims become depressed; many bullies become increasingly cruel. The worst bullies seem unmoved by their victims' distress: Such bullies tend to become more aggressive with age (Willoughby et al., 2014).

Unless bullies are deterred, they and their victims risk impaired social understanding, lower school achievement, and relationship difficulties. Decades later they have higher rates of mental illness (Copeland et al., 2013; Ttofi et al., 2014). Compared to other adults the same age, former bullies are more likely to die young, be jailed, or have destructive marriages. Bystanders suffer, too: They learn less when bullying is common, and they are often distressed but afraid to help the victim (Juvonen & Graham, 2014; Monks & Coyne, 2011).

Can Bullying Be Stopped?

Most victimized children find ways to halt ongoing bullying—by ignoring, retaliating, defusing, or avoiding. Friends defend each other and restore self-esteem (Bagwell & Schmidt, 2011). Friendships help individual victims, but what can be done to halt a culture of bullying?

We know what does *not* work: simply increasing students' awareness of bullying, instituting zero tolerance for fighting, or putting bullies together in a therapy group or a classroom (Baldry & Farrington, 2007; Monks & Coyne, 2011). This last measure tends to make daily life easier for some teachers, but it increases aggression. Another strategy is to talk to the parents of the bully, but this may backfire. Since one cause of bullying is poor parent–child interaction, talking to the bully's or victim's parents may "create even more problems for the child, for the parents, and for their relationship" (Rubin et al., 2013, p. 267).

The school community as a whole—teachers and bystanders, parents and aides, bullies and victims and bystanders—needs to change. In fact, the entire school can either increase the rate of bullying or decrease it (Juvonen & Graham, 2014). For example, a Colorado study found that, when the overall school climate encouraged learning and cooperation, children with high self-esteem were unlikely to be bullies; when the school climate was hostile, those with high self-esteem were often bullies (Gendron et al., 2011).

Again, peers are crucial: They must do more than simply notice bullying, becoming aware without doing anything to counter it. In fact, some bystanders feel morally disengaged from the victims, which increases bullying. Others are sympathetic but feel powerless (Thornberg & Jungert, 2013). However, if they empathize with victims, feel effective (high in effortful control), and refuse to admire bullies, classroom aggression is reduced (Salmivalli, 2010).

Efforts to change the entire school are credited with recent successful efforts to decrease bullying in 29 schools in England (Cross et al., 2011), throughout Norway, in Finland (Kärnä et al., 2011), and often in the United States (Allen, 2010; Limber, 2011).

A review of ways to halt bullying (Berger, 2007) finds that:

- Everyone in the school must change, not just the identified bullies.
- Intervention is more effective in the earlier grades.
- Evaluation is critical: Programs that seem good might be harmful.

This final point merits emphasis. Longitudinal research finds that some programs make a difference and some do not. Variations depend on the age of the children and the indicators (peer report of bullying or victimization, teacher report of incidents reported, and so on). Objective follow-up efforts suggest that bullying can be reduced but not eliminated.

It is foolhardy to blame only the bully and, of course, wrong to blame the victim: The entire school community—including the culture of the school—needs to change. That leads to the final topic of this chapter, moral development.

> **Especially for Parents of an Accused Bully**
> Another parent has told you that your child is a bully. Your child denies it and explains that the other child doesn't mind being teased. (see response, page 435)

SUMMING UP   School-age children develop their own culture, with customs that encourage them to be loyal to one another. All 6- to 11-year-olds want and need social acceptance and close, mutual friendships to protect against loneliness and depression. Children of all ages value peers who are kind and outgoing. By the end of middle childhood, peers who are self-assured and aggressive may be admired as well. Friendship is more valued than popularity; being rejected is painful.

Most children experience occasional peer rejection. However, some children are victims—repeatedly rejected and friendless—and experience physical, verbal, or relational bullying. Bullies may have friends and social power in middle childhood and early adolescence, but as time goes on, they may become increasingly cruel and less admired. Some efforts to reduce bullying succeed and some do not. A whole-school approach seems best, with the bystanders crucial to establishing an anti-bullying culture.

Children's Moral Values

The origins of morality are debatable (see Chapter 10), but there is no doubt that middle childhood is prime time for moral development. These are:

> years of eager, lively searching on the part of children . . . as they try to understand things, to figure them out, but also to weigh the rights and wrongs. . . . This is the time for growth of the moral imagination, fueled constantly by the willingness, the eagerness of children to put themselves in the shoes of others.
>
> [Coles, 1997, p. 99]

Many forces drive children's growing interest in moral issues. Three of them are (1) child culture, (2) personal experience, and (3) empathy. As already explained, the culture of children includes moral values, such as loyalty to friends and keeping secrets. Personal experiences also matter.

For all children, empathy increases in middle childhood as children become more socially perceptive. This increasing perception can backfire, however. One example was just described: Bullies become adept at picking victims (Veenstra et al., 2010). An increase in social understanding makes noticing and defending rejected children possible, but in a social context that allows bullying, bystanders may decide to be self-protective rather than to intervene (Pozzoli & Gini, 2013).

Children who are slow to develop theory of mind—which, as discussed in Chapter 9, is affected by family and culture—are also slow to develop empathy (Caravita et al., 2010). The authors of a study of 7-year-olds "conclude that moral *competence* may be a universal human characteristic, but that it takes a situation with specific demand characteristics to translate this competence into actual prosocial performance" (van Ijzendoorn et al., 2010, p. 1). In other words, school-age children can think and act morally, but they do not always do so.

Moral Reasoning

Piaget wrote extensively about the moral development of children, as they developed and enforced their own rules for playing games together (Piaget, 1932/1997). His emphasis on how children think about moral issues led to a famous description of cognitive stages of morality (Kohlberg, 1963).

Kohlberg's Levels of Moral Thought

Lawrence Kohlberg described three levels of moral reasoning and two stages at each level (see Table 13.3), with parallels to Piaget's stages of cognition.

- **Preconventional moral reasoning** is similar to preoperational thought in that it is egocentric, with children most interested in their personal pleasure or avoiding punishment.
- **Conventional moral reasoning** parallels concrete operational thought in that it relates to current, observable practices: Children watch what their parents, teachers, and friends do, and try to follow suit.
- **Postconventional moral reasoning** is similar to formal operational thought because it uses abstractions, going beyond what is concretely observed, willing to question "what is" in order to decide "what should be."

Wonderfully Conventional Krysta Caltabiano displays her poster, "Ways to Be a Good Citizen," which won the Good Citizenship Contest sponsored by the Connecticut Secretary of State.

preconventional moral reasoning Kohlberg's first level of moral reasoning, emphasizing rewards and punishments.

conventional moral reasoning Kohlberg's second level of moral reasoning, emphasizing social rules.

postconventional moral reasoning Kohlberg's third level of moral reasoning, emphasizing moral principles.

According to Kohlberg, intellectual maturation advances moral thinking. During middle childhood, children's answers shift from being primarily preconventional to being more conventional: Concrete thought and peer experiences help children move past the first two stages (level I) to the next two (level II). Postconventional reasoning is not usually present until adolescence or adulthood, if then.

Kohlberg posed moral dilemmas to school-age boys (and eventually girls, teenagers, and adults). The most famous example of these dilemmas involves a poor man named Heinz, whose wife was dying. He could not pay for the only drug that could cure his wife, a drug that a local druggist sold for 10 times what it cost to make.

> Heinz went to everyone he knew to borrow the money, but he could only get together about half of what it cost. He told the druggist that his wife was dying and asked him to sell it cheaper or let him pay later. But the druggist said "no." The husband got desperate and broke into the man's store to steal the drug for his wife. Should the husband have done that? Why?
>
> *[Kohlberg, 1963, p. 19]*

The crucial element in Kohlberg's assessment of moral stages is not what a person answers but the reasons given. For instance, suppose a child says that Heinz should steal the drug. That itself does not indicate the child's level of moral reasoning. The reason could be that Heinz needs his wife to care for him (preconventional), or that people will blame him if he lets his wife die (conventional), or that a human life is more important than obeying a law (postconventional).

Or suppose another child says Heinz should not steal. The reason could be that he will go to jail (preconventional), or that the child has been taught that stealing is wrong (conventional), or that for a community to function, no one should take another person's livelihood (postconventional).

Criticisms of Kohlberg

Kohlberg has been criticized for not appreciating cultural or gender differences. For example, loyalty to family overrides any other value in some cultures, so some people might avoid postconventional actions that hurt their family. Also, Kohlberg's original participants were all boys, which may have led him to discount nurturance and relationships, thought to be more valued by females than males (Gilligan, 1982). Overall, Kohlberg seemed to value abstract principles more than individual needs and to evaluate people on how rational they are.

However, emotional thinking may be more influential than logic in moral development (Haidt, 2013). Thus, according to critics of Kohlberg, emotional regulation, empathy, and social understanding, all of which develop throughout childhood, may be more crucial for morality than intellectual development is.

Furthermore, Kohlberg did not seem to recognize that although children's morality differs from that of adults, they may be quite moral. School-age children tend to

// **Response for Parents of an Accused Bully** (from page 433): The future is ominous if the charges are true. Your child's denial is a sign that there is a problem. (An innocent child would be worried about the misperception instead of categorically denying that any problem exists.) You might ask the teacher what the school is doing about bullying. Family counseling might help. Because bullies often have friends who egg them on, you may need to monitor your child's friendships and perhaps befriend the victim. Talk matters over with your child. Ignoring the situation might lead to heartache later on.

TABLE 13.3	Kohlberg's Three Levels and Six Stages of Moral Reasoning

Level I: Preconventional Moral Reasoning

The goal is to get rewards and avoid punishments; this is a self-centered level.

- *Stage one: Might makes right* (a punishment-and-obedience orientation). The most important value is to maintain the appearance of obedience to authority, avoiding punishment while still advancing self-interest. Don't get caught!

- *Stage two: Look out for number one* (an instrumental and relativist orientation). Each person tries to take care of his or her own needs. Be nice to other people so that they will be nice to you.

Level II: Conventional Moral Reasoning

Emphasis on social rules; this is a family, community, and cultural level.

- *Stage three: Good girl and nice boy.* Proper behavior pleases other people. Social approval is more important than any specific reward.

- *Stage four: Law and order.* Proper behavior means being a dutiful citizen and obeying the laws set down by society, even when no police are nearby.

Level III: Postconventional Moral Reasoning

Emphasis is placed on moral principles; this level is centered on ideals.

- *Stage five: Social contract.* Social rules are obeyed when they benefit everyone and are established by mutual agreement. If the rules become destructive or if one party doesn't live up to the agreement, the contract is no longer binding. Under those circumstances, disobeying the law may be moral.

- *Stage six: Universal ethical principles.* Universal principles, not individual situations (level I) or community practices (level II), determine right and wrong. Ethical values (such as "life is sacred") are established by thought and prayer. They may contradict egocentric (level I) or social and community (level II) values.

question or ignore adult rules that seem unfair (Turiel, 2006, 2008), and that may indicate postconventional thinking.

In one respect, however, Kohlberg was undeniably correct. He was right in noting that children use their intellectual abilities to justify their moral actions. In one experiment, children aged 8 to 18 were grouped with two others about the same age and were allotted some money. They were then asked to decide how much to share with another trio of children.

No age trends were found in sharing: Some groups chose to share equally; other groups were more selfish. However, there were age differences in the reasons. Older children suggested more complex rationalizations for their choices, both selfish and altruistic (Gummerum et al., 2008).

What Children Value

Many lines of research have shown that children develop their own morality, guided by peers, parents, and culture (Killen & Smetana, 2014). Some prosocial values are evident in early childhood including caring for close family members, cooperating with other children, and not hurting anyone intentionally.

Even very young children think stealing is wrong, and even infants seem to appreciate social support and punish mean behavior in experiments with a good and a mean puppet (Hamlin, 2014). If a puppet is seen hitting another puppet for no good reason, and then a child is asked to allocate candy to the two puppets, the child might give candy to the victim, not the bully.

As children become more aware of themselves and others in middle childhood, they realize that one person's values may conflict with another's. Concrete operational cognition, which gives children the ability to understand and use logic, propels them to think about morality. In the opening anecdote of this chapter, when the boy argued that it was "so unfair" that he could not kill zombies in the video game, a sense of morality was evident.

Adults Versus Peers

When child culture conflicts with adult morality, children often align themselves with peers. A child might lie to protect a friend, for instance. Friendship itself has a hostile side: Many close friends reject other children who want to join a game, or conversation, with friends (Rubin et al., 2013). They may also protect a bully if he or she is a friend.

The conflict between the morality of children and that of adults is evident in the value that children place on education. Adults usually prize school and respect teachers, but children may encourage one another to play hooky, cheat on tests, harass a substitute teacher, and so on.

Three common moral imperatives among 6- to 11-year-olds are the following:

- Protect your friends.
- Don't tell adults what is happening.
- Conform to peer standards of dress, talk, behavior.

These three can explain both apparent boredom and overt defiance, as well as standards of dress that mystify adults (such as jeans so loose that they fall off or so tight that they impede digestion—both styles worn by my children, who grew up in different cohorts). This may seem like mere social conformity, but children may elevate it to a standard of right and wrong, as adults might do for whether or not a woman wears a head covering, a revealing dress, or even high

Not Victims An outsider might worry that these two boys would be bullied, one because he is African American and the other because he appears to be disabled. But both are well liked for the characteristics shown here: friendliness and willingness to help and be helped.

KIDSTOCK/GETTY IMAGES

heels. Given what is known about middle childhood, it is no surprise that children do not echo adult morality.

Fortunately, peers during adulthood as well as childhood help one another develop morals. Research finds that children are better at stopping bullying than adults are, because bystanders are pivotal. Since bullies tend to be low on empathy, they need peers to teach them that their actions are not admired (many bullies believe people admire their aggression). During middle childhood, morality can be scaffolded just as cognitive skills are, with mentors—peers or adults—using moral dilemmas to advance moral understanding, while they also advance the underlying moral skills of empathy and emotional regulation (Hinnant et al., 2013).

Developing Moral Values

Throughout middle childhood, moral judgment becomes more comprehensive, considering psychological as well as physical harm, intentions as well as consequences. In one study 5- to 11-year-olds saw pictures depicting situations when a child hurt another to prevent further harm (stopping a friend from a dangerous climb to retrieve a ball) or when one child was simply mean (such as pushing a friend off the swings so the child can swing). The younger children were more likely to judge based on results, but the older children considered intention.

When harm was psychological, not physical (hurting the child's feelings, not hitting) more than half of the older children considered intentions, but only about 5 percent of the younger children did. Compared to the younger children, the older children more often said justifiable harm was okay but unjustifiable harm should be punished (Jambon & Smetana, 2014).

A detailed examination of the effect of peers on morality began with an update on one of Piaget's moral issues: whether punishment should seek *retribution* (hurting the transgressor) or *restitution* (restoring what was lost). Piaget found that children advance from retribution to restitution between ages 8 and 10 (Piaget, 1932/1997).

To learn how this occurs, researchers asked 133 9-year-olds to consider this scenario:

> Late one afternoon there was a boy who was playing with a ball on his own in the garden. His dad saw him playing with it and asked him not to play with it so near the house because it might break a window. The boy didn't really listen to his dad, and carried on playing near the house. Then suddenly, the ball bounced up high and broke the window in the boy's room. His dad heard the noise and came to see what had happened. The father wonders what would be the fairest way to punish the boy. He thinks of two punishments. The first is to say: "Now, you didn't do as I asked. You will have to pay for the window to be mended, and I am going to take the money from your pocket money." The second is to say: "Now, you didn't do as I asked. As a punishment you have to go to your room and stay there for the rest of the evening." Which of these punishments do you think is the fairest?
>
> [Leman & Björnberg, 2010, p. 962]

The children were split almost equally in their initial responses. Then 24 pairs were formed of children who had opposite views. Each pair was asked to discuss the issue, trying to reach agreement. (The other children did not discuss it.) Six pairs were boy–boy, six were boy–girl with the boy favoring restitution, six were boy–girl with the girl favoring restitution, and six were girl–girl.

The conversations typically took only five minutes, and the retribution side was more often chosen—which Piaget would consider a moral backslide, since more restitution than retribution advocates switched. However, two weeks and eight weeks later all the children were queried again. Many responses changed toward the more advanced, restitution response (see Figure 13.2). This advance occurred even for the children who merely thought about the dilemma again (no discussion)

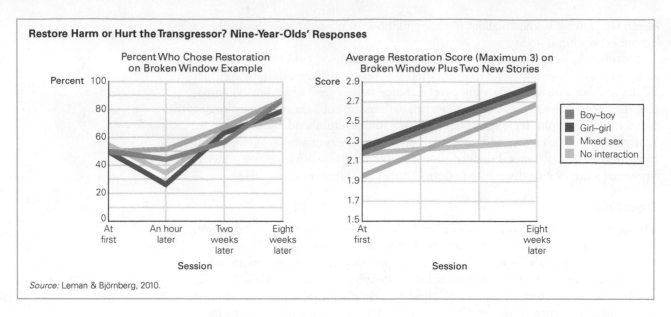

Restore Harm or Hurt the Transgressor? Nine-Year-Olds' Responses

Source: Leman & Björnberg, 2010.

FIGURE 13.2

Benefits of Time and Talking The graph on the left shows that most children, immediately after their initial punitive response, became even more likely to seek punishment rather than to repair damage. However, after some time and reflection, they chose the response Piaget considered more mature. The graph on the right indicates that children who had talked about the broken window example moved toward restorative justice even in examples they had not heard before. That was not true for those who had not talked about the first story.

but children who had discussed it with another child were particularly likely to decide that restitution was best.

The main conclusion from this study was that "conversation on a topic may stimulate a process of individual reflection that triggers developmental advances" (Leman & Björnberg, 2010, p. 969). Parents and teachers take note: Raising moral issues, and letting children discuss them, advances morality—not immediately, but soon.

Think again about the opening anecdote for this chapter (killing zombies) or the previous chapter (piercing ears). In both cases, the parent used age as a criterion, and in both cases the child rejected that argument. A better argument might raise a higher standard—in the first example, for instance, that killing is never justified. The child might disagree, but such conversations might help the child think more deeply about moral values, as happened in this experiment. That deeper thought might protect the child during adolescence, when life-changing moral issues arise, which is described in the next three chapters.

SUMMING UP Moral issues are of great interest to children in middle childhood, when children become more aware of the values of their cultures, their parents, and particularly of their peers. Kohlberg's stages of moral thought are based on advancing rationalism, in parallel to Piaget's stages of development. He believed the progression is universal, from the young child's egocentrism to the adults' highest level of morality, which transcends the norms of any particular nation. Kohlberg has been criticized for not having a multicultural understanding, but he seems correct in his conclusion that moral judgment advances from ages 6 to 11. Children develop moral standards that they try to follow. These may differ from adult morals, in part because children's morality includes loyalty to peers. Maturation, reflection, and discussion all foster moral development.

WHAT HAVE YOU LEARNED?

1. Using your own example, illustrate Kohlberg's three levels of moral reasoning.
2. What are the main criticisms of Kohlberg's theory?
3. What three values are common among school-age children?
4. What seems to advance moral thought from the beginning to the end of middle childhood?

SUMMARY

The Nature of the Child

1. All theories of development acknowledge that school-age children become more independent and capable in many ways.

2. Erikson emphasized industry, when children busily strive to master various tasks. If they are unable to do so, they feel inferior. Freud described latency, when psychosexual needs are quiet.

3. Children develop their self-concept during middle childhood, basing it on a more realistic assessment of their competence than they had in earlier years.

4. Self-respect is always helpful, but high self-esteem may reduce effort and is not valued in every culture. Low self-esteem is also harmful.

5. Both daily hassles and major stresses take a toll on children, with accumulated stresses more likely to impair development than any single event on its own. Resilience is aided by the child's interpretation of the situation and the availability of supportive adults, peers, and institutions.

Families and Children

6. Families influence children in many ways, as do genes and peers. Although most siblings share a childhood home and parents, each sibling experiences different (nonshared) circumstances within the family.

7. The five functions of a supportive family are to satisfy children's physical needs, to encourage learning, to support friendships, to protect self-respect, and to provide a safe, stable, and harmonious home.

8. The most common family structure worldwide is the nuclear family, usually with other relatives nearby. Other two-parent families include adoptive, same-sex, grandparent, and step-families, each of which is capable of functioning well for children. However, each also has vulnerabilities.

9. On average, children have fewer emotional problems and learn more in school if they live with two parents rather than one, especially if the two have a good parental alliance, so that both adults are caregivers.

10. Single-parent families have higher rates of change—for example, in where they live and who belongs to the family. On average, such families have less income, which may cause stress. Nonetheless, some single parents are better parents than they would be if the child's other parent were in the household.

11. Income affects family function, for two-parent as well as single-parent households. Poor children are at greater risk for emotional and behavioral problems because the stresses that often accompany poverty hinder effective parenting.

12. No matter what the family SES, instability and conflict are harmful. Children suffer even when the conflict does not involve them directly, but their parents or siblings fight.

The Peer Group

13. Peers teach crucial social skills during middle childhood. Each cohort of children has a culture, passed down from slightly older children. Close friends are wanted and needed.

14. Popular children may be cooperative and easy to get along with or may be competitive and aggressive. Children's judgment of popularity is affected by culture as well as the age of the children.

15. Rejected children may be neglected, aggressive, or withdrawn. Aggressive and withdrawn children have difficulty with social cognition; their interpretation of the normal give-and-take of childhood is impaired.

16. Bullying is common among school-age children and has long-term consequences for both bullies and victims. Bullies themselves may be admired, which makes their behavior more difficult to stop.

17. Overall, a multifaceted, long-term, whole-school approach—with parents, teachers, and bystanders working together—seems the best way to halt bullying.

Children's Moral Values

18. School-age children seek to differentiate right from wrong. Peer values, cultural standards, and family practices are all part of their personal morality.

19. Children advance in moral thinking as they mature. Kohlberg described three levels of moral reasoning, each related to cognitive maturity. His description has been criticized for ignoring cultural and gender differences and for stressing rationality at the expense of emotions.

20. When values conflict, children often choose loyalty to peers over adult standards of behavior. As children grow older, especially when they discuss moral issues, they develop more thoughtful answers to moral questions, considering intentions as well as consequences.

KEY TERMS

industry versus inferiority (p. 410)

latency (p. 410)

social comparison (p. 411)

resilience (p. 413)

family structure (p. 418)

family function (p. 418)

nuclear family (p. 419)

single-parent family (p. 419)

extended family (p. 419)

polygamous family (p. 420)

child culture (p. 429)

aggressive-rejected (p. 431)

withdrawn-rejected (p. 431)

bullying (p. 431)

bully-victim (p. 432)

preconventional moral reasoning (p. 434)

conventional moral reasoning (p. 434)

postconventional moral reasoning (p. 434)

APPLICATIONS

1. Go someplace where school-age children congregate (such as a schoolyard, a park, or a community center) and use naturalistic observation for at least half an hour. Describe what popular, average, withdrawn, and rejected children do. Note at least one potential conflict (bullying, rough-and-tumble play, etc.). Describe the sequence and the outcome.

2. Focusing on verbal bullying, describe at least two times when someone said something hurtful to you and two times when you said something that might have been hurtful to someone else. What are the differences between the two types of situations?

3. How would your childhood have been different if your family structure had been different, such as if you had (or had not) lived with your grandparents, if your parents had (or had not) gotten divorced, if you had (or had not) been adopted?

4. Interview two parents, one in a nuclear family and one in a single-parent family. Ask them about the advantages and disadvantages of that family structure. If they do not know, ask about specifics (homework, rules, punishments, meals). Analyze the results, illustrating them with quotations.

PART 4

The Developing Person So Far:
Middle Childhood

BIOSOCIAL

A Healthy Time During middle childhood, children grow more slowly than they did earlier or than they will during adolescence. Physical play is crucial for health and happiness. Prevalent physical problems, including obesity and asthma, have genetic roots and are influenced by environmental factors; both have psychosocial consequences.

Brain Development Brain maturation continues, leading to faster reactions and better self-control. The specific skills a child masters depend largely on culture, gender, and inherited ability. Children have multiple intellectual abilities, most of which are not reflected in standard IQ tests.

Children with Special Needs Many children have special learning needs, ranging from severe (e.g., autism spectrum disorder) to wonderful (e.g., gifted). Early recognition, targeted education, and psychological support are needed.

COGNITIVE

Building on Theory Piaget noted that beginning at about age 7, children attain the logic of concrete operational thought, including the concepts of classification and seriation. Vygotsky emphasized that children become more open to learning from mentors. Information-processing abilities increase, resulting in greater memory, a broader knowledge base, control processes, and metacognition.

Language Children's increasing ability to understand the structures and possibilities of language enables them to extend their cognitive powers. Children have the cognitive capacity to become bilingual and bicultural, although much depends on the teacher.

Teaching and Learning International comparisons reveal marked variations in the overt and hidden curriculums, as well as in learning, between one nation and another. In the United States, most children attend regular public schools in their neighborhood, but some attend charter schools, private schools, or are home-schooled.

PSYCHOSOCIAL

The Nature of the Child Theorists agree that many school-age children develop competencies, emotional control, and attitudes to defend against stress. Some children are resilient, coping with problems and finding support in friends, family, school, religion, and community.

Families and Children Parents influence children, especially as they exacerbate or buffer problems in school and the community. Families need to meet basic needs, encourage learning, foster self-respect, nurture friendship, and—most important—provide harmony and stability. Nuclear families often provide this, and one-parent, foster, same-sex, or grandparent families can also function well for children. Sufficient household income, minimal conflict, and family stability benefit children of all ages and in every family structure.

The Peer Group Children depend less on their parents and more on friends for help, loyalty, and sharing of mutual interests. Rejection and bullying become serious problems.

Children's Moral Values Moral development, influenced by peers, advances during these years. Children develop moral standards that they try to follow, although these may differ from the moral standards of adults. Loyality to peers is a prime value for school-age children.

adolescence

A century ago, puberty began at age 15 or so. Soon after that age, most girls married and most boys found work. It is said that *adolescence begins with biology and ends with culture.* If so, then a hundred years ago, adolescence lasted a few months. Now adolescence lasts many years. Puberty starts before the teen years, and adult responsibilities are often postponed until emerging adulthood or later.

In the next three chapters (covering ages 11 to 18), we begin with biology (this chapter), consider cognition (Chapter 15), and then discuss culture (Chapter 16). Adolescence attracts extremes, arousing the highest hopes and the worst fears of parents, teachers, police officers, social workers, and children themselves. Patterns and events can catapult a teenager to destruction or celebration. Understanding this phase of development is the first step toward ensuring that the teenagers you know, and the millions you never met, experience a fulfilling, not devastating, adolescence.

Adolescence:
Biosocial Development

What Will You Know?

1. How can you predict when puberty will begin for a particular child?
2. Why do some teenagers avoid eating for days, even months?
3. What makes teenage sex a problem instead of a joy?

I overheard a conversation among three teenagers, including my daughter Rachel, all of them past their awkward years and now becoming beautiful. They were discussing the imperfections of their bodies. One spoke of her fat stomach (what stomach? I could not see it), another of her long neck (hidden by her silky, shoulder-length hair). Rachel complained not only about a bent pinky finger but also about her feet!

The reality that children grow into men and women is no shock to any adult. But for teenagers, heightened self-awareness often triggers surprise or even horror, joy, and despair at the specifics of their development. Like these three, adolescents pay attention to details of their growth. Gender differences also become prominent. Girls tend to bond as they discuss their flaws; boys are more likely to boast than to complain, yet almost all teenagers become simultaneously self-conscious and social, needing each other for validation.

This chapter describes the biosocial specifics of growing bodies and emerging sexuality. It all begins with hormones, but other invisible changes may be even more potent—such as the timing of neurological maturation that does not yet allow adolescents like these three to realize that minor imperfections are insignificant.

Puberty Begins

Puberty refers to the years of rapid physical growth and sexual maturation that end childhood, producing a person of adult size, shape, and sexuality. The forces of puberty are unleashed by a cascade of hormones that produce external growth and internal changes, including heightened emotions and sexual desires.

The process of puberty normally starts sometime between ages 8 and 14. Most physical growth and maturation ends about four years after the first signs appear, although some individuals (especially boys) add height, weight, and muscle until age 20 or so. Over the past decades the age of puberty has decreased, perhaps for both sexes, although the evidence is more solid for girls (Biro et al., 2013; Herman-Giddens, 2013).

For girls, the observable changes of puberty usually begin with nipple growth. Soon a few pubic hairs are visible, followed by a peak growth spurt, widening of the hips, the first menstrual period (**menarche**), a full pubic-hair pattern, and breast maturation

puberty The time between the first onrush of hormones and full adult physical development. Puberty usually lasts three to five years. Many more years are required to achieve psychosocial maturity.

menarche A girl's first menstrual period, signaling that she has begun ovulation. Pregnancy is biologically possible, but ovulation and menstruation are often irregular for years after menarche.

Video: The Timing of Puberty
http://qrs.ly/m34ep16

(Susman et al., 2010). The average age of menarche among normal-weight girls is about 12 years, 4 months (Biro et al., 2013) although variation in timing is quite normal.

For boys, the usual sequence is growth of the testes, initial pubic-hair growth, growth of the penis, first ejaculation of seminal fluid (**spermarche**), appearance of facial hair, a peak growth spurt, deepening of the voice, and final pubic-hair growth (Biro et al., 2001; Herman-Giddens et al., 2012; Susman et al., 2010). The typical age of spermarche is just under 13 years, almost a year later than menarche. Averages as well as age vary markedly, as soon discussed: The averages above are for well-nourished adolescents in the United States.

Unseen Beginnings

Just described are the visible changes of puberty, but the entire process begins with an invisible event—a marked increase in hormones. **Hormones** are body chemicals that regulate hunger, sleep, moods, stress, sexual desire, immunity, reproduction, and many other bodily functions and processes, including puberty. Throughout adolescence, hormone levels correlate with physiological changes and self-reported developments (Shirtcliff et al., 2009).

You learned in Chapter 8 that the production of many hormones is regulated deep within the brain, where biochemical signals from the hypothalamus signal another brain structure, the **pituitary,** to go into action. The pituitary produces hormones that stimulate the **adrenal glands,** located above the kidneys at either side of the lower back. The adrenal glands produce more hormones.

Many hormones that regulate puberty follow this route, known as the **HPA (hypothalamus–pituitary–adrenal) axis** (see Figure 14.1). Abnormalities of the HPA axis in adolescence are associated with eating disorders, anxiety, and depression. These conditions and many other types of psychopathology, appearing for the first time or worsening at puberty, are connected to hormones and genes (Dahl & Gunnar, 2009).

spermarche A boy's first ejaculation of sperm. Erections can occur as early as infancy, but ejaculation signals sperm production. Spermarche may occur during sleep (in a "wet dream") or via direct stimulation.

hormone An organic chemical substance that is produced by one body tissue and conveyed via the bloodstream to another to affect some physiological function.

pituitary A gland in the brain that responds to a signal from the hypothalamus by producing many hormones, including those that regulate growth and that control other glands, among them the adrenal and sex glands.

adrenal glands Two glands, located above the kidneys, that produce hormones (including the "stress hormones" epinephrine [adrenaline] and norepinephrine).

HPA (hypothalamus–pituitary–adrenal) axis A sequence of hormone production originating in the hypothalamus and moving to the pituitary and then to the adrenal glands.

Same Situation, Far Apart: Eye Openers Nature often grows eyelashes straight or slightly curly, but adolescent girls want them curlier. The main difference between these two settings is not the goal but the equipment. Girls in Pinellas Park, Florida, have large mirrors and metal tools designed for lash curling—both are rare in Beijing, China.

Especially for Parents of Teenagers Why would parents blame adolescent moods on hormones? (see response, page 448)

Indeed, abnormalities of the HPA axis probably cause the sudden increases in clinical depression among young adolescent girls (Guerry & Hastings, 2011). Further, HPA disruptions are one result of childhood sexual abuse (discussed soon) (Trickett et al., 2011).

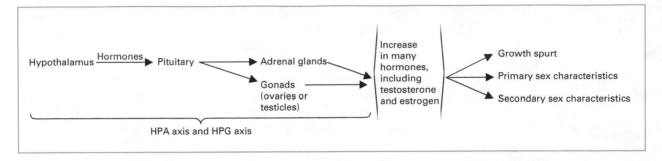

Hypothalamus → Hormones → Pituitary → Adrenal glands / Gonads (ovaries or testicles) → Increase in many hormones, including testosterone and estrogen → Growth spurt / Primary sex characteristics / Secondary sex characteristics

HPA axis and HPG axis

Sex Hormones

Late in childhood, the pituitary activates not only the adrenal glands but also the **gonads,** or sex glands (ovaries in females; testes, or testicles, in males), following another sequence called the **HPG (hypothalamus–pituitary–gonad) axis.** One hormone in particular, GnRH (gonadotropin-releasing hormone), causes the gonads to enlarge and dramatically increase their production of sex hormones, chiefly **estradiol** in girls and **testosterone** in boys. These hormones affect the body's shape and function and produce additional hormones that regulate stress and immunity (Young et al., 2008).

Estrogens (including estradiol) are female hormones and *androgens* (including testosterone) are male hormones, although both sexes have some of both. The biochemical messages from the HPG axis activate the ovaries to produce high levels of estrogens and the testes to produce dramatic increases in androgens. This "surge of hormones" affects bodies, brains, and behavior before any visible signs of puberty appear, "well before the teens" (Peper & Dahl, 2013, p. 134).

The activated gonads produce mature sperm or ova, released in menarche or spermarche. Conception is possible, although fertility peaks several years later.

Hormonal increases and differences may also underlie sex differences in psychopathology. Compared to the other sex, adolescent males are almost twice as likely to develop schizophrenia and adolescent females more than twice as likely to develop depression. Of course, hormones are not the sole cause of psychopathology in anyone (Tackett et al., 2014; Rudolph, 2014).

One psychological effect of hormones at puberty has been proven: Hormones awaken interest in sex. The first sexual objects are usually unattainable—a film star, a teacher—but by mid-adolescence, fantasies typically settle on another teenager.

Emotional surges and lustful impulses may begin with hormones, but remember that body, brain, and behavior always interact. Sexual thoughts themselves can *cause* physiological and neurological processes, not just result from them.

Cortisol levels rise at puberty, and that makes adolescents quicker to become angry or upset (Goddings et al., 2012; Klein & Romeo, 2013). Then those emotions, in turn, increase levels of various other hormones. Bodies, brains, and behavior each affect the other two.

For example, when other people react to emerging breasts or beards, that evokes thoughts and frustrations in the adolescent, which then raise hormone levels, propel physiological development, and trigger emotions, which then affect people's reactions. Thus the internal and external changes of puberty each impact the other.

Body Rhythms

The brain of every living creature responds to the environment with natural rhythms that rise and fall by the hours, days, and seasons. For example, body weight and height are affected by time of year: Children's growth rate increases

FIGURE 14.1

Biological Sequence of Puberty Puberty begins with a hormonal signal from the hypothalamus to the pituitary gland, both deep within the brain. The pituitary, in turn, sends a hormonal message through the bloodstream to the adrenal glands and the gonads to produce more hormones.

gonads The paired sex glands (ovaries in females, testicles in males). The gonads produce hormones and gametes.

HPG (hypothalamus–pituitary–gonad) axis A sequence of hormone production originating in the hypothalamus and moving to the pituitary and then to the gonads.

estradiol A sex hormone, considered the chief estrogen. Females produce much more estradiol than males do.

testosterone A sex hormone, the best known of the androgens (male hormones); secreted in far greater amounts by males than by females.

Especially for Teenagers Some 14-year-olds have unprotected sex and then are relieved to realize that conception did not occur. Does this mean they do not need to worry about contraception? (see response, page 450)

I Covered That Teachers everywhere complain that students don't remember what they were taught. Maybe schedules, not daydreaming, are to blame.

....

circadian rhythm A day–night cycle of biological activity that occurs approximately every 24 hours. (*Circadian* means "about a day.")

OBSERVATION QUIZ As you see, girls get even less sleep than boys. Why is that? (see answer, page 452)

// Response for Parents of Teenagers (from page 446): If something causes adolescents to shout "I hate you," to slam doors, or to cry inconsolably, parents may decide that hormones are the problem. This makes it easy to dismiss the teenager's anger. However, research on stress and hormones suggests that this comforting attribution is too simplistic.

for height in summer and for weight in winter. Some *biorhythms* are on a day–night cycle that occurs approximately every 24 hours, called the **circadian rhythm.** (*Circadian* means "about a day.") Puberty affects both seasonal and daily biorhythms.

The hypothalamus and the pituitary regulate the hormones that affect patterns of stress, appetite, sleep, and so on. At puberty, these hormones cause a *phase delay* in the circadian sleep–wake cycles. The delay is in the body's reaction to daylight and dark.

For most people, daylight awakens the brain. That's why people experiencing jet lag are urged to take an early morning walk. The phase delay at puberty makes many teens wide awake and hungry at midnight but half asleep, with no appetite or energy, all morning.

In addition to circadian changes in adolescent bodies, some individuals (especially males) are naturally more alert in the evening than in the morning, a genetic trait called *eveningness*. Exacerbated by pubertal phase delay, eveningness puts adolescents at risk for antisocial activities because they are awake when adults are asleep. Another result, if school is scheduled for adults, not teenagers, is that students are sleep deprived (Carskadon, 2011). In many nations, sleep deprivation increases during adolescence (see Figure 14.2) (Roenneberg et al., 2012).

To make it worse, "the blue spectrum light from TV, computer, and personal-device screens may have particularly strong effects on the human circadian system" (Peper & Dahl, 2013, p. 137). Watching late-night TV, working on the computer, or texting friends at 10 P.M. interferes with normal nighttime sleepiness. Sleeping late on weekend mornings is a sign of deprivation, not compensation.

Sleep deprivation and irregular sleep schedules lead to several specific dangers, including insomnia, nightmares, mood disorders (depression, conduct disorder, anxiety), and falling asleep while driving. In addition, sleepy people do not learn as well as they might when rested. Many adults ignore these facts, as the following Opposing Perspectives explains.

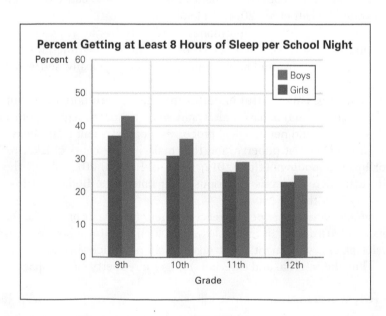

FIGURE 14.2

Sleepyheads Three of every four high school seniors are sleep deprived. Even if they go to sleep at midnight, as many do, they must get up before 8, as almost all do. Then all day they are tired.

opposing perspectives

Algebra at 7 A.M.? Get Real!

Parents sometimes fight biology. This is evident with sexual curiosity ("you're too young to think about boys") and circadian rhythm ("go to sleep, you need to get up at dawn"). Adults set early curfews. For example in 2014, Baltimore implemented a law that requires everyone under age 14 to be home by 9 P.M., and 14- to 16-year-olds to be off the streets by 10 P.M. on school nights and 11 P.M. on weekends. Baltimore may be an extreme case, but some parents everywhere stay awake until their teenager comes home from a party, or drag their teenager out of bed for school—the same child who, a decade earlier, was commanded to stay in bed until 7 A.M.

For many adolescents, however, early sleep and early rising are almost impossible. Sleep-deprived teenagers nod off in class (see Figure 14.3) and sometimes use drugs to stay awake or go to sleep (Mueller et al., 2011; Patrick & Schulenberg, 2011).

Data on circadian rhythm and the teenage brain convinced social scientists at the University of Minnesota to ask 17 school districts to start high school at 8:30 A.M. or later. Parents disagreed. Many (42 percent) thought high school should begin before 8:00 A.M. Some (20 percent) wanted their teenagers out of the house by 7:15 A.M., but only 1 percent of parents with younger children wanted them out by that hour (Wahlstrom, 2002).

Other adults had their own reasons for wanting high school to begin early. Teachers thought that learning was more efficient in the morning; bus drivers hated rush hour; cafeteria workers liked to be done by mid-afternoon; police wanted teenagers off the streets by 4:00 P.M.; coaches needed after-school sports events to end before dark; business owners hired teens for the early evening shift; community groups wanted the school gyms available in the late afternoon.

Initially only one Minnesota school district (Edina) changed the schedule, from 7:25 A.M.–2:05 P.M. to 8:30 A.M.–3:10 P.M. After a trial year, most parents (93 percent) and virtually all students approved. One student said, "I have only fallen asleep in school once this whole year, and last year I fell asleep about three times a week" (quoted in Wahlstrom, 2002, p. 190). Fewer students were absent, late, disruptive, or sick (the school nurse became an advocate). Grades rose.

Other school districts noticed. Minneapolis high schools changed their start time from 7:15 A.M. to 8:40 A.M. Again, attendance and graduation rates improved.

School boards in South Burlington (Vermont), West Des Moines (Iowa), Tulsa (Oklahoma), Arlington (Virginia), Palo Alto (California), and Milwaukee (Wisconsin) voted to start high school later, from an average of 7:45 A.M. to an average of 8:30 A.M. (Tonn, 2006; Snider, 2012). Unexpected advantages appeared: more efficient energy use, less adolescent depression, and in Tulsa, unprecedented athletic championships.

Many school districts remain stuck to their traditional schedules (set before the hazards of sleep deprivation were known)—scheduling school buses to drop off teenagers at school and then go back to pick up the younger children. Although "the science is there, the will to change is not" (Snider, 2012).

One example comes from Fairfax (Virginia) where two opposing groups: SLEEP (Start Later for Excellence in Education Proposal) versus WAKE (Worried About Keeping Extra-Curriculars) argued. One sports reporter wrote:

> The later start would hinder teams without lighted practice fields. Hinder kids who work after-school jobs to save for college or to help support their families. Hinder teachers who work second jobs or take late-afternoon college classes. Hinder commuters who would get stopped behind more buses during peak traffic times. Hinder kids who might otherwise seek after-school academic help, or club or team affiliation. Hinder families that depend on high school children to watch younger siblings after school. Hinder community groups that use school and park facilities in the late afternoons and evenings.
>
> *[Williams, 2009]*

Note that he never argued that learning in high school would be hindered, because the evidence is that it would not. He wrote that science was on the side of change but reality was not. To

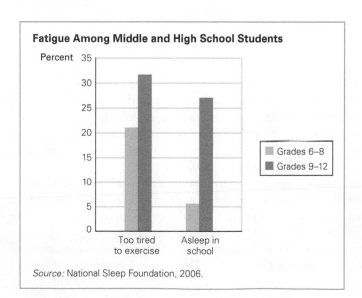

Fatigue Among Middle and High School Students

Legend:
- Grades 6–8
- Grades 9–12

Source: National Sleep Foundation, 2006.

FIGURE 14.3

Dreaming and Learning? This graph shows the percentage of U.S. students who, once a week or more, fall asleep in class or are too tired to exercise. Not shown are those who are too tired overall (59 percent of high school students) or who doze in class "almost every day" (8 percent).

developmentalists, of course, science *is* reality. In 2009, the Fairfax school board voted to keep high school start at 7:20 A.M.

The SLEEP advocates kept trying. On the eighth try, the Fairfax school board in 2012 finally set a goal: High schools should not start before 8 A.M. They hired a team to figure out how to implement that goal. As of 2014, the Fairfax school board had not yet decided on the new start time.

They now have a new reason to change. In August 2014, the American Academy of Pediatrics concluded that high school should not begin until 8:30 or 9 A.M., because adolescent sleep deprivation causes a cascade of intellectual and behavioral problems. They noted that 43 percent of high schools in the United States start *before* 8 A.M. The clash between tradition and science, or between adult expectations and adolescent bodies, continues.

RADIUS IMAGES/CORBIS

Ancient Rivals or New Friends One of the best qualities of adolescents is that they identify more with their generation than their ethnic group, here Turk and German. Do the expressions of these 13-year-olds convey respect or hostility? Impossible to be sure, but given that they are both about mid-puberty (face shape, height, shoulder size), and both in the same school, they may become friends.

// **Response for Teenagers** (from page 447): No. Early sex has many hazards. Pregnancy is less likely (although quite possible) before age 15. This may lead to a false sense of security, which may disappear with a crash; fertility is higher in the late teens than at any other time. In addition, STIs are especially common with adolescent sex, another reason to use a condom.

secular trend The long-term upward or downward direction of various measurements, as a result of modern conditions. For example, improved nutrition and medical care over the past 200 years has led to earlier puberty and greater average height.

Age and Puberty

Normally, pubertal hormones begin to increase between ages 8 and 14, and visible signs of puberty appear a year later. That six-year range is too great for many parents, teachers, and children, who want to know when a given child will begin puberty. Fortunately, if a child's genes, gender, body fat, and stress level are known, some prediction is possible (see Visualizing Development, p. 451).

Genes and Gender

About two-thirds of the variation in age of puberty is genetic, evident not only in families but also in ethnic groups (Dvornyk & Waqar-ul-Haq, 2012; Biro et al., 2013). African Americans reach puberty about seven months earlier than European or Hispanic Americans, while Chinese Americans average several months later. Ethnic differences are apparent on other continents as well. For instance, northern European girls reach menarche at 13 years, 4 months, on average; southern European girls do so at 12 years, 5 months (Alsaker & Flammer, 2006).

The sex chromosomes have a marked effect. In height, the average girl is about two years ahead of the average boy: The female height spurt occurs *before* menarche, whereas for boys the increase in height is relatively late, *after* spermarche.

When it comes to hormonal and sexual changes themselves, though, girls may be less than a year ahead of boys. A sixth-grade boy with sexual fantasies about the taller girls in his class is neither perverted nor precocious; his hormones are simply ahead of his height.

Body Fat

Another major influence on the onset of puberty is body fat. Heavy girls reach menarche years earlier than malnourished ones do. Most girls must weigh at least 100 pounds (45 kilograms) before they experience their first period (Berkey et al., 2000). Although malnutrition always delays puberty, body fat may not be as necessary for well-fed boys. Indeed, in developed nations obese boys are more often delayed in puberty, unlike girls (Crocker et al., 2014).

Body fat also explains why youths reach puberty at age 15 or later in some parts of Africa, although their genetic relatives in North America mature much earlier. Similarly, malnutrition may explain why puberty began at about age 17 in sixteenth-century Europe.

Since then, puberty has occurred at younger and younger ages (an example of what is called the **secular trend,** the trend of changes in human growth as nutrition improved). Increased food availability has led to weight gain in childhood,

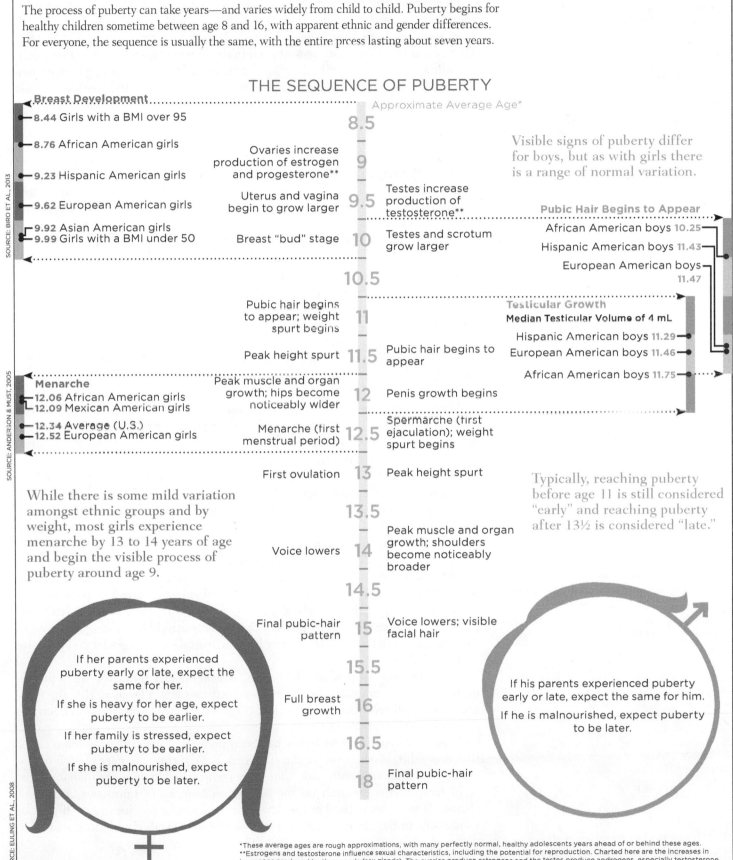

VISUALIZING DEVELOPMENT

The Timing of Puberty

The process of puberty can take years—and varies widely from child to child. Puberty begins for healthy children sometime between age 8 and 16, with apparent ethnic and gender differences. For everyone, the sequence is usually the same, with the entire process lasting about seven years.

THE SEQUENCE OF PUBERTY

Approximate Average Age*

Breast Development

- **8.44** Girls with a BMI over 95
- **8.76** African American girls
- **9.23** Hispanic American girls
- **9.62** European American girls
- **9.92** Asian American girls
- **9.99** Girls with a BMI under 50

SOURCE: BIRO ET AL, 2013

Menarche
- **12.06** African American girls
- **12.09** Mexican American girls
- **12.34** Average (U.S.)
- **12.52** European American girls

SOURCE: ANDERSON & MUST, 2005

Ovaries increase production of estrogen and progesterone**

Uterus and vagina begin to grow larger

Breast "bud" stage

Pubic hair begins to appear; weight spurt begins

Peak height spurt

Peak muscle and organ growth; hips become noticeably wider

Menarche (first menstrual period)

First ovulation

Voice lowers

Final pubic-hair pattern

Full breast growth

8.5
9
9.5
10
10.5
11
11.5
12
12.5
13
13.5
14
14.5
15
15.5
16
16.5
18

Testes increase production of testosterone**

Testes and scrotum grow larger

Penis growth begins

Spermarche (first ejaculation); weight spurt begins

Peak height spurt

Peak muscle and organ growth; shoulders become noticeably broader

Voice lowers; visible facial hair

Final pubic-hair pattern

Visible signs of puberty differ for boys, but as with girls there is a range of normal variation.

Pubic Hair Begins to Appear

African American boys **10.25**

Hispanic American boys **11.43**

European American boys **11.47**

Testicular Growth
Median Testicular Volume of 4 mL

Hispanic American boys **11.29**

European American boys **11.46**

African American boys **11.75**

SOURCE FOR BOY DATA HERMAN-GIDDENS, ET AL, 2012

While there is some mild variation amongst ethnic groups and by weight, most girls experience menarche by 13 to 14 years of age and begin the visible process of puberty around age 9.

Typically, reaching puberty before age 11 is still considered "early" and reaching puberty after 13½ is considered "late."

If her parents experienced puberty early or late, expect the same for her.

If she is heavy for her age, expect puberty to be earlier.

If her family is stressed, expect puberty to be earlier.

If she is malnourished, expect puberty to be later.

SOURCE: EULING ET AL, 2008

If his parents experienced puberty early or late, expect the same for him.

If he is malnourished, expect puberty to be later.

*These average ages are rough approximations, with many perfectly normal, healthy adolescents years ahead of or behind these ages.
**Estrogens and testosterone influence sexual characteristics, including the potential for reproduction. Charted here are the increases in hormones produced by the gonads (sex glands). The ovaries produce estrogens and the testes produce androgens, especially testosterone. Adrenal glands produce some of both kinds of hormones (not shown) in both sexes.

Especially for Parents Worried About Early Puberty Suppose your cousin's 9-year-old daughter has just had her first period, and your cousin blames hormones in the food supply for this "precocious" puberty. Should you change your young daughter's diet? (see response, page 454)

// ANSWER TO OBSERVATION QUIZ
(from page 448): Girls tend to spend more time studying, talking to friends, and getting ready in the morning. Other data show that many girls get less than 7 hours of sleep per night.

leptin A hormone that affects appetite and is believed to affect the onset of puberty. Leptin levels increase during childhood and peak at around age 12.

and that has led to earlier puberty for girls and taller average height for both sexes. Because of the secular trend, for centuries every generation has reached puberty before the previous one (Floud et al., 2011; Fogel & Grotte, 2011).

One curious bit of evidence of the secular trend is that U.S. presidents have been taller in recent decades than they were earlier (James Madison, the fourth president, was shortest at 5 feet, 4 inches; Barack Obama is 6 feet, 1 inch tall). The secular trend seems to have stopped in developed nations, because now nutrition allows everyone to attain their genetic potential. Currently, young men no longer usually look down at their short fathers, or girls at their little mothers, unless the parents were born in Asia or Africa, where the secular trend continues.

Exceptions and Hormones

There is an exception in developed nations to the statement "the secular trend has stopped." Puberty that begins before age 8, called *precocious puberty,* seems more common now, although still rare (perhaps 2 percent). The increase may be caused by childhood obesity or by exposure to new chemicals and may be more common in girls than boys.

Some research finds, however, that puberty is delayed, not accelerated, in boys who were exposed to phthalates and bisphenol A when they were in the womb (Ferguson et al., 2014) or who experience heavy doses of pesticides in boyhood (Lam et al., 2014). Another study found that phthalates delay puberty in girls of normal weight, but the authors note that other research has found earlier puberty (Wolff et al., 2014).

Caution, not panic, is needed here. No doubt, heavy doses of many chemicals and pesticides affect fish, frogs, insects, and birds, causing reproductive problems. However, as noted in Chapter 4, experts disagree about the impact on humans of specific environmental toxins, as well as about what dose is safe.

Many researchers focus on sex hormones as factors that accelerate puberty. Of course, estrogens and androgens affect body shape, reproduction, height, and weight, but these sex hormones may also work directly to trigger the onset of puberty, even before visible changes occur.

Many scientists suspect that precocious or delayed puberty is caused by hormones in the food supply, especially in milk. Cattle are fed steroids to increase bulk and milk production, and hundreds of chemicals and hormones are used to produce most of the meat and milk that children consume. All these *might* affect appetite, body fat, and sex hormones, with effects suspected at puberty (Clayton et al., 2014; Wiley, 2011; Synovitz & Chopak-Foss, 2013).

Leptin, a hormone naturally produced by the human body, definitely affects the onset of puberty. Leptin affects appetite and energy; without it, puberty does not occur. However, high levels of leptin correlate with obesity. A girl with this problem may experience early puberty that ends relatively soon, stopping growth. Thus the heaviest third-grade girl may become the tallest fifth grader and then the shortest high school graduate.

Normally, body fat produces leptin (one reason puberty is delayed is if a person overexercises or undereats), and starvation increases leptin levels so that the hungry person will seek food. Once weight is gained, higher levels of leptin decrease the appetite (Elias & Purohit, 2013).

Most of the research on leptin has been done with mice; they become fat or thin depending on the levels of this hormone, but the consequences of high or low leptin, especially artificially added, are more complicated for humans than for mice.

In fact, all the research on the effects on humans of hormones and other chemicals, whether natural or artificial, is complex. The precise impact of all the substances in the air, water, or diet on the human sexual-reproductive system is unknown. It seems that the female system is especially sensitive not only to leptin but also to other factors in the environment. Leptin is one factor in puberty onset, but many other hormones, chemicals, genes, and psychosocial forces are involved (Elias, 2012).

Stress

Stress hastens the hormonal onset of puberty, especially if a child's parents are sick, drug-addicted, or divorced, or if the neighborhood is violent and impoverished. One study of sexually abused girls found that they began puberty seven months earlier, on average, than did a matched comparison group (Trickett et al., 2011). Particularly for girls who are genetically sensitive, puberty comes early if their family interaction is stressful but late if their family is supportive (Ellis et al., 2011; James et al., 2012).

This is one explanation for the fact that many internationally adopted children experience early puberty, especially if their first few years of life were in an institution or a chaotic home. An alternate explanation is that their age at adoption was underestimated, so puberty appears to occur early but actually occurs at the expected time (Hayes, 2013).

Most developmentalists agree that age of menarche is influenced by genes and experience, as differential susceptibility would predict. Minor stresses—first day of a new school, summer camp away from home, a fight with a best friend—also trigger menarche in a girl whose body is ready.

Twenty years ago many scientists were skeptical about a direct link between stress and puberty. Perhaps early puberty caused stress rather than the other way around? Now, however, the link seems clear. (See A View from Science.)

⚗️ a view from science

Stress and Puberty

Hypothetically, the connection between stress and early puberty could be indirect. For example, perhaps children in dysfunctional families eat worse and watch TV more, and that makes them overweight. Or perhaps they inherit genes for early puberty from their distressed mothers, and those genes led the mothers to become pregnant too young, creating a stressful family environment.

Either poor nutrition or genetic risk could cause early puberty. Then stress would be an indirect byproduct, not a cause.

However, several longitudinal studies show a *direct* link between stress and puberty. For example, one longitudinal study of 756 children found parents who demanded respect, often spanked, and rarely hugged their babies were, a decade later, likely to have daughters who reached puberty earlier than other girls in the same study (Belsky et al., 2007). The likely reason: Harsh parenting increases cortisol levels, and cortisol affects puberty.

A follow-up of the same girls at age 15, controlling for genetic differences, found that harsh treatment in childhood increased sexual risk (more sex partners, pregnancies, sexually transmitted infections) but *not* other risks (drugs, crime) (Belsky et al., 2010). This suggests that stress triggers earlier increases of sex hormones but not increases in generalized rebellion. The direct impact of stress on puberty seems proven.

Why would higher cortisol trigger puberty? The opposite effect—delayed puberty—makes more sense. Then stressed teens would still look and act childlike, which might evoke adult protection rather than lust or anger. Protection is especially needed in conflict-ridden or stressed single-parent homes, yet such homes produce earlier puberty and less parental nurturance. Is this a biological mistake? Not according to evolutionary theory:

> Maturing quickly and breeding promiscuously would enhance reproductive fitness more than would delaying development, mating cautiously, and investing heavily in parenting. The latter strategy, in contrast, would make biological sense, for virtually the same reproductive-fitness-enhancing reasons, under conditions of contextual support and nurturance.
>
> [Belsky et al., 2010, p. 121]

In other words, thousands of years ago, when harsh conditions threatened survival of the species, adolescents needed to reproduce early and often. Natural selection would hasten puberty to increase the birth rate.

By contrast, in peaceful times with plentiful food, puberty could occur later, allowing children to postpone maturity and instead enjoy extra years of nurturance from parents and grandparents. Genes evolved to respond differently to war and peace.

Of course, this evolutionary rationale no longer applies. Today, early sexual activity and reproduction are more likely to destruct than protect communities.

However, the genome has been shaped over millennia; if there is a puberty-starting allele that responds to social conditions, it will respond today as it did thousands of years ago. This idea complements behavioral genetic understanding of differential susceptibility (Harkness, 2014). Because of genetic protections, not every distressed girl experiences early puberty, but also for genetic reasons, family stress may speed up age of menarche.

// Response for Parents Worried About Early Puberty (from page 452): Probably not. If she is overweight, her diet should change, but the hormone hypothesis is speculative. Genes are the main factor; she shares only one-eighth of her genes with her cousin.

Too Early, Too Late

For most adolescents, these links between puberty, genes, fat, stress, and hormones are irrelevant. Only one aspect of timing matters: their friends' schedules. No one wants to be too early or too late.

Girls

Think about the early-maturing girl. If she has visible breasts at age 10, the boys her age tease her; they are unnerved by the sexual creature in their midst. She must fit her developing body into a school chair designed for smaller children; she might hide her breasts in large T-shirts and bulky sweaters; she might refuse to undress for gym. Early-maturing girls tend to have lower self-esteem, more depression, and poorer body image than do other girls (Galvao et al., 2014; Compian et al., 2009).

All the Same? All four girls are 13, all from the same community in England. But as you see, each is on her own timetable, and that affects the clothes and expressions. Why is one in a tank top and shorts while another is in a heavy shirt and pants?

OBSERVATION QUIZ Who is least developed and who is most? (see answer, page 456)

© REDSNAPPER/ALAMY

Sometimes early-maturing girls have older boyfriends, who are attracted to their womanly shape and girlish innocence. Having an older boyfriend gives these girls status, but it also increases their risk of problems (including drug and alcohol abuse) that arise from an older peer group (Mrug et al., 2014). Early-maturing girls enter abusive relationships more often than other girls do. Is that because they are lonely and their social judgment is immature?

Boys

Research over the past 100 years has always found that early female maturation is more often harmful than helpful, but cohort seems crucial for males. Early-maturing boys who were born around 1930 often became leaders in high school and earned more money as adults (Jones, 1965; Taga et al., 2006). Since about 1960, however, the risks associated with early male maturation have outweighed the benefits.

In the twenty-first century, early-maturing boys are more aggressive, lawbreaking, and alcohol-abusing than the average boy (Biehl et al., 2007; Lynne et al., 2007; Mendle et al., 2012). This is not surprising: A boy who is experiencing rapid increases in testosterone, and whose body looks more like a man than a child, is likely to cause trouble with parents, peers, schools, and the police.

Early puberty is particularly stressful if it happens suddenly: The boys most likely to become depressed are those for whom puberty was both early and quick (Mendle et al., 2010). In adolescence, depression is often masked as anger. That fuming, flailing 12-year-old boy may be more sad than mad.

Late puberty may also be difficult, especially for boys (Benoit et al., 2013). Slow-developing boys tend to be more anxious, depressed, and afraid of sex. Girls are less attracted to them, coaches less often want them on their teams, peers bully or tease them. If a boy still looks childish, unlike the other boys and girls, he is likely to react in ways that are not healthy for him.

Every adolescent wants to hit puberty "on time." They often overestimate or underestimate their maturation, or become depressed, if they are not average (Conley & Rudolph, 2009; Shirtcliff et al., 2009; Benoit et al., 2013). These effects are not caused by biology alone; family contexts and especially peer pressure can make early and late puberty worse (Mendle et al., 2012; Benoit et al., 2013).

Ethnic Differences

Puberty that is late by world norms, at age 14 or so, is not troubling if one's friends are late as well. Well-nourished Africans tend to experience puberty a few months earlier and Asians a few months later than Europeans, but they all function well if their peers are on the same schedule (Al-Sahab et al., 2010). This is true within those continents, as well as within nations such as the United States and Canada that are home to many teenagers with roots elsewhere.

For adolescents of all ethnic backgrounds, peer approval is more important than adult approval or historic understanding. The effects of early puberty vary not only by sex but also by ethnicity and culture. For instance, one study found that, in contrast to European Americans, early-maturing African American girls were not depressed, but early-maturing African American boys were (Hamlat et al., 2014a, 2014b).

European research finds that Swedish early-maturing girls were likely to encounter problems with boys and early drug abuse, but similar Slovak girls were not (Skoog & Stattin, 2014). Finally, among Mexican American boys, early maturers were likely to experience trouble with the police and with other boys if they lived in neighborhoods with relatively few Mexican Americans but not if they lived in ethnic enclaves (White et al., 2013).

None of these trends is true for all children, of course, as ethnicity is only one influence on development. However, all three studies confirm that contextual factors interact with biological ones, and both have significant implications for individuals. Always, relationships with peers and parents make off-time puberty better or worse (Benoit et al., 2013).

SUMMING UP   Puberty usually begins between ages 8 and 14 (typically around age 11) in response to a chain reaction of hormones from the hypothalamus, to the pituitary, to the adrenal and sex glands.

Hormones interact with emotions: Adolescent outbursts of sudden anger, sadness, and lust are affected both by hormones and by reactions from other people to the young person's changing body. The dynamic interaction among hormones, genes, adolescent behavior, and social regulations is evident in the clash between circadian rhythm and high school schedules. Many teenagers are sleep deprived, which affects their learning and emotions.

Genes, body fat, hormones, and stress affect the onset of puberty, especially among girls. For both sexes, early or late puberty is less desirable than puberty at the same age as one's peers; off-time maturation may lead to depression, drug abuse, and other problems.

WHAT HAVE YOU LEARNED?

1. What are the first visible signs of puberty?
2. What body parts of a teenage boy or girl are the last to reach full growth?
3. How do hormones affect the physical and psychological aspects of puberty?
4. Why do adolescents experience sudden, intense emotions?
5. How does the circadian rhythm affect adolescents?
6. What are the consequences of sleep deprivation?
7. What are the gender differences in the growth spurt?
8. What are the ethnic and cultural differences in the timing of puberty?
9. How does off-time puberty affect girls?
10. How does off-time puberty affect boys?

Growth and Nutrition

Puberty entails transformation of every part of the body, each change affecting the others. Here we discuss biological growth, the nutrition that fuels that growth, and the eating disorders that disrupt it. Next we will focus on the two other aspects of pubertal transformation, brain reorganization and sexual maturation.

Growing Bigger and Stronger

growth spurt The relatively sudden and rapid physical growth that occurs during puberty. Each body part increases in size on a schedule: Weight usually precedes height, and growth of the limbs precedes growth of the torso.

The first set of changes is called the **growth spurt**—a sudden, uneven jump in the size of almost every body part, turning children into adults. Growth proceeds from the extremities to the core (the opposite of the earlier proximodistal growth). Thus, fingers and toes lengthen before hands and feet, hands and feet before arms and legs, arms and legs before the torso. This growth is not always symmetrical: One foot, one breast, or even one ear may grow later than the other.

Because the torso is the last body part to grow, many pubescent children are temporarily big-footed, long-legged, and short-wasted. If young teenagers complain that their jeans don't fit, they are probably correct—even if those same jeans fit when their parents bought them a month earlier. (Advance warning about rapid body growth occurs when parents buy their children's shoes in the adult section).

Sequence: Weight, Height, Muscles

As the growth spurt begins, children eat more and gain weight. Exactly when, where, and how much weight they gain depends on heredity, hormones, diet, exercise, and gender. By age 17, the average girl has twice the percentage of body fat as her male classmate, whose increased weight is mostly muscle.

A height spurt follows the weight spurt; then a year or two later a muscle spurt occurs. Thus, the pudginess and clumsiness of early puberty are usually gone by late adolescence. Keep in mind, however, that puberty may dislodge the usual relationship between height and overweight or underweight. A child may be eating too much or too little for their height, but that may not be apparent in conventional measures of BMI (Golden et al., 2012).

At puberty, all the muscles increase in power. Arm muscles develop particularly in boys, doubling in strength from age 8 to 18. Other muscles are gender neutral. Both sexes run faster with each year of adolescence, with boys not much faster than girls (unless the girls choose to slow down) until the end of high school (see Figure 14.4).

Organ Growth

In both sexes, organs mature in much the same way. Lungs triple in weight; consequently, adolescents breathe more deeply and slowly. The heart (another muscle) doubles in size as the heartbeat slows, decreasing the pulse rate while increasing blood pressure (Malina et al., 2004). Consequently, endurance improves: Some teenagers can run for miles or dance for hours. Red blood cells increase in both sexes, but dramatically more so in boys, which aids oxygen transport during intense exercise.

Both weight and height increase *before* muscles and internal organs: To protect immature muscles and organs, athletic training and weight lifting should be tailored to an adolescent's size the previous year. Sports injuries are the most common school accidents, and they increase at puberty. One reason is that the height spurt precedes increases in bone mass, making young adolescents particularly vulnerable to fractures (Mathison & Agrawal, 2010).

One organ system, the lymphoid system (which includes the tonsils and adenoids), *decreases* in size, so teenagers are less susceptible to respiratory ailments. Mild asthma, for example, often switches off at puberty—half as many teenagers as children are asthmatic (MMWR, June 8, 2012). In addition, teenagers have fewer colds and allergies than younger children. This reduction in susceptibility is aided by growth of the larynx, which also deepens the voice, dramatically noticeable in boys but also evident in girls.

Another organ system, the skin, becomes oilier, sweatier, and more prone to acne. Hair also changes, becoming coarser and darker. New hair grows under arms, on faces, and over sex organs (pubic hair, from the same Latin root as *puberty*). Visible facial and chest hair is sometimes considered a sign of manliness, although hairiness in either sex depends on genes as well as on hormones.

Girls pluck or wax any facial hair they see and shave their legs, while boys proudly grow sideburns, soul patches, chinstraps, moustaches, and so on—with specifics dependent on culture and cohort. Sexual attraction is the goal.

Often teenagers cut, style, or grow their hair in ways their parents do not like, as a sign of independence. To become more attractive, many adolescents spend considerable time, money, and thought on their visible hair—growing, gelling, shaving, curling, straightening, highlighting, brushing, combing, styling, dyeing, wetting, and/or drying. . . . In many ways, hair is far more than a growth characteristic; it is a display of sexuality.

Diet Deficiencies

All the changes of puberty depend on adequate nourishment, yet many adolescents do not eat well. Teenagers often skip breakfast, binge at midnight, guzzle

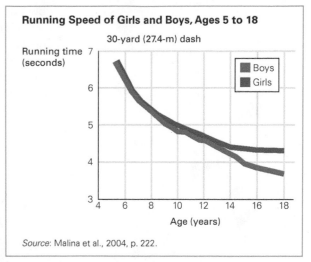

Running Speed of Girls and Boys, Ages 5 to 18

30-yard (27.4-m) dash

Source: Malina et al., 2004, p. 222.

FIGURE 14.4

Little Difference Both sexes develop longer and stronger legs during puberty, but eventually, females are somewhat slower than males.

down unhealthy energy drinks, and munch on salty, processed snacks. One reason for their eating patterns is that their hormones affect the circadian rhythm of their appetites; another reason is that their drive for independence makes them avoid family dinners, refusing to eat what their mothers say they should. Family dinners in supportive families correlate with healthy adolescent eating and well-being, but that is less true when family relationships are poor (Meier & Musick, 2014).

Cohort and age are crucial. In the United States, each new generation eats less well than the previous one, and each 18-year-old tends to eat a less balanced diet than he or she did at age 10 (Larson et al., 2007). Most adolescents consume enough calories, but in 2013 only 16 percent of high school seniors ate the recommended three or more servings of vegetables a day (MMWR, June 13, 2014).

Deficiencies of iron, calcium, zinc, and other minerals are especially common during adolescence. Because menstruation depletes iron, anemia is more likely among adolescent girls than among any other age group. This is true everywhere, especially in South Asia and sub-Saharan Africa, where teenage girls rarely eat iron-rich meat and green vegetables.

Reliable laboratory analysis of blood iron on a large sample of young girls in developing nations is not available, but all indications suggest that many are anemic.

For the Audience Teenage eating behavior is influenced by other adolescents. Note the evident approval from the slightly older teenager, not from the younger boys. Would the eater have put his head back and mouth wide open if the only onlookers were his parents?

Data is available for 18- to 23-year-old college women in Saudi Arabia (not among the poorest nations). About a fourth (24 percent) were clinically anemic and another fourth (28 percent) were iron-deficient (Al-Sayes et al., 2011). These numbers are especially troubling since almost all college women in Saudi Arabia are in good health, from wealthy families, and have never been pregnant. Those factors put them among the better-nourished young women in that nation.

Boys everywhere may also be iron-deficient if they engage in physical labor or intensive sports: Muscles need iron for growth and strength. The cutoff for iron-deficiency anemia is higher for boys than girls because boys require more iron to be healthy (Morón & Viteri, 2009). Yet in developed as well as developing nations, many adolescents of both sexes spurn iron-rich foods (green vegetables, eggs, and meat) in favor of iron-poor chips, sweets, and fries.

Similarly, although the daily recommended intake of calcium for teenagers is 1,300 milligrams, the average U.S. teen consumes less than 500 milligrams a day. About half of adult bone mass is acquired from ages 10 to 20, which means many contemporary teenagers will develop osteoporosis (fragile bones), a major cause of disability, injury, and death in late adulthood, especially for women.

One reason for calcium deficiency is that milk drinking has declined. In 1961, most North American children drank at least 24 ounces (about three-fourths of a liter) of milk each day, providing almost all (about 900 milligrams) of their daily calcium requirement. Fifty years later, only 12.5 percent of high school students drank that much milk and 19 percent (more girls than boys) drank no milk at all (MMWR, June 13, 2014).

Choices Made

Many economists advocate a "nudge" to encourage people to make better choices, not only in nutrition but also in all other aspects of their lives (Thaler & Sunstein, 2008). Teenagers are often nudged in the wrong direction. Nutritional deficiencies result from the food choices that young adolescents are enticed to make.

Fast-food establishments cluster around high schools, often with extra seating that encourages teenagers to eat and socialize. This is especially true for high schools with large Hispanic populations, who are most at risk for obesity (Taber et al., 2011). Forty percent of Hispanic girls in U.S. high schools describe themselves as overweight, as do 27 percent of Hispanic boys (MMWR, June 13, 2014).

Price influences food choices, especially for adolescents, and healthy fast foods cost more than unhealthy ones. For example, compare the prices of a McDonald's salad and a hamburger.

Nutritional deficiencies increase when schools have vending machines that offer soda and snacks, especially for middle school students (Rovner et al., 2011). An increasing number of laws require schools to encourage healthy eating, but effects are more apparent in elementary schools than high schools (Mâsse et al., 2013; Terry-McElrath et al., 2014).

Many adolescents spurn school lunches in favor of unhealthy snacks sold by in-school vending machines (who pay the school for prime placement) and nearby businesses. No wonder rates of obesity increase at about age 12.

Rates of obesity are falling in childhood but not in adolescence. Only three U.S. states (Kentucky, Mississippi, Tennessee) had high-school obesity rates at 15 percent or more in 2003; 22 states were that high in 2013 (MMWR, June 13, 2014). In Latin America, the nutritional focus is still on preventing underweight not preventing overweight, yet overall, about 1 teenager in 4 is overweight or obese (Rivera et al., 2014).

Body Image

One reason for poor nutrition among teenagers is anxiety about **body image**—that is, a person's idea of how his or her body looks. Few teenagers welcome every change in their bodies. Instead, they tend to focus on and exaggerate imperfections

Diet Worldwide, adolescent obesity is increasing. Parental responses differ, from indifference to major focus. For some U.S. parents the response is to spend thousands of dollars trying to change their children, as is the case for the parents of these girls eating breakfast at Wellspring, a California boarding school for overweight teenagers which costs $6,250 a month. Every day, these girls exercise more than 10,000 steps (tracked with a pedometer) and eat less than 20 grams of fat (normal is more than 60 grams).

body image A person's idea of how his or her body looks.

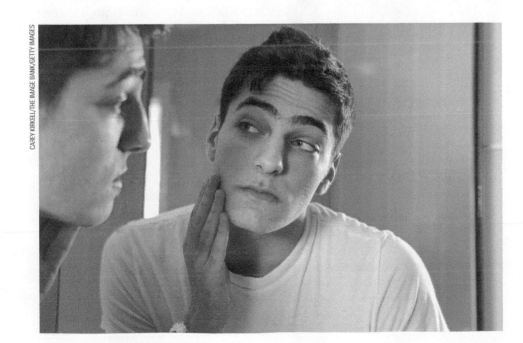

If Your Mirror Showed This You might be happy. He has thick hair, distinctive eyebrows, blue-green eyes—a handsome young man. Yet he worries about his smooth skin, probably because his facial hair is not yet full grown, or perhaps he fears he hasn't shaved close enough. Adolescents almost always find something amiss in how they look.

(as did the three girls in the anecdote that opens this chapter). Two-thirds of U.S. high-school girls are trying to lose weight, even though only one-fourth are actually overweight or obese (MMWR, June 8, 2012).

Few adolescents are happy with their bodies, partly because almost none look like the bodies portrayed online and in magazines, movies, and television programs that are marketed to teenagers (Bell & Dittmar, 2011). Unhappiness with appearance—especially with weight for girls—is documented worldwide: including in South Korea, China, and Greece (Kim & Kim, 2009; Chen & Jackson, 2009; Argyrides & Kkeli, 2014).

Eating Disorders

Dissatisfaction with body image can be dangerous, even deadly. Many teenagers, mostly girls, eat erratically or ingest drugs (especially diet pills) to lose weight; others, mostly boys, take steroids to increase muscle mass. (**Developmental Link:** Teenage drug abuse is discussed in Chapter 16.) Eating disorders are rare in childhood but increase dramatically at puberty, accompanied by distorted body image, food obsession, and depression (Le Grange & Lock, 2011). Such disorders are often unrecognized until they get worse in emerging adulthood.

Adolescents sometimes switch from obsessive dieting, to overeating, to overexercising, and back again. Obesity is an eating disorder at every age. (**Developmental Link:** Obesity is discussed in Chapter 8 and in the epilogue.) Here we describe three other eating disorders likely to begin in adolescence.

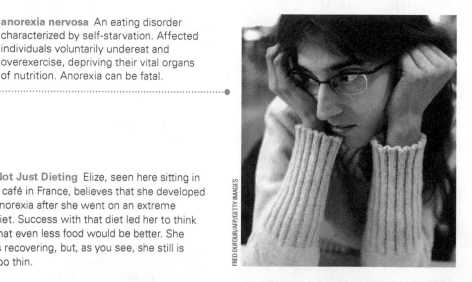

FRED DUFOUR/AFP/GETTY IMAGES

> **anorexia nervosa** An eating disorder characterized by self-starvation. Affected individuals voluntarily undereat and overexercise, depriving their vital organs of nutrition. Anorexia can be fatal.

Not Just Dieting Elize, seen here sitting in a café in France, believes that she developed anorexia after she went on an extreme diet. Success with that diet led her to think that even less food would be better. She is recovering, but, as you see, she still is too thin.

> **bulimia nervosa** An eating disorder characterized by binge eating and subsequent purging, usually by induced vomiting and/or use of laxatives.

Anorexia Nervosa

A body mass index (BMI) of 17 or lower, or loss of more than 10 percent of body weight within a month or two, indicates **anorexia nervosa,** a disorder characterized by voluntary starvation and a destructive and distorted attitude about one's own body fat. The affected person becomes very thin, risking death by organ failure. Staying too thin becomes an obsession.

Although anorexia existed earlier, it was not identified until about 1950, when some high-achieving, upper-class young women became so emaciated that they died. Soon anorexia was evident among teenagers and young adults of every income, nation, and ethnicity; the rate spikes at puberty and again in emerging adulthood.

Certain alleles increase the risk of developing anorexia (Young, 2010), with higher risk among girls with close relatives who suffer from eating disorders or severe depression. Although far more common in girls, boys are also at risk.

Bulimia Nervosa and Binge Eating Disorder

About three times as common as anorexia is **bulimia nervosa** (also called *binge–purge syndrome*). This disorder is clinically present in 1 to 3 percent of female teenagers and young adults in the United States. They overeat compulsively, consuming thousands of calories within an hour or two, and then purge through vomiting or laxatives. Most are close to normal in weight and therefore unlikely to starve. However, they risk serious health problems, including damage to their gastrointestinal systems and cardiac arrest from electrolyte imbalance.

Binging and purging are common among adolescents. For instance, a survey found that in the last 30 days of 2013, 6.6 percent of U.S. high-school girls and 2.2 percent of the boys vomited or took laxatives to lose weight, with marked variation by state—from 3.6 percent in Nebraska to 9 percent in Arizona (MMWR, June 13, 2014).

A disorder newly recognized in DSM-5 is *binge eating disorder*. Some adolescents periodically and compulsively overeat, quickly consuming large amounts of ice cream, cake, or any snack food until their stomachs hurt. When bingeing becomes a disorder, overeating is typically done in private, at least once weekly for three months. The sufferer does not purge (hence this is not bulimia) but feels out of control, distressed, and depressed.

All adolescents are vulnerable to unhealthy eating. Autonomy and body image can lead to disorders. Teenagers try new diets, go without food for 24 hours (as did 19 percent of U.S. high-school girls in one typical month), or take diet drugs (6.6 percent) (MMWR, June 13, 2014). Many eat oddly (e.g., only rice or only carrots), begin unusual diets, or exercise intensely.

Parents are slow to recognize eating disorders, and delay getting help that their children need (Thomson et al., 2014). Yet the research on all the eating disorders finds that family function (not structure) is crucial (Tetzlaff & Hilbert, 2014).

A combination of causes leads to obesity, anorexia, bulimia, or bingeing. At least five general elements—cultural images, stress, puberty, hormones, and childhood experiences—make disordered eating more likely.

A developmental perspective notes that healthy eating begins with childhood habits and family routines. Most overweight or underweight newborns never develop nutritional problems, but children who are overweight or underweight are at risk. Particularly in adolescence, family-based therapy for eating disorders is more successful than therapy that focuses only on the individual (Couturier et al., 2013; Murray et al., 2014).

SUMMING UP   The transformations of puberty are dramatic. Boys and girls become men or women, both physically and neurologically, although full maturity takes a decade or so. Growth proceeds from the extremities to the center, so the limbs grow before the internal organs do. Increase in weight precedes that in height, which precedes growth of the muscles and of the internal organs.

All adolescents are vulnerable to poor nutrition; few are well nourished day after day, year after year. Insufficient iron and calcium is particularly common as fast food and nutrient-poor snacks often replace family meals. Both boys and girls often choose junk food instead of a balanced diet, in part because they and their peers are concerned about physical appearance and social acceptance. The combination of nutritional deficiencies, peer culture, and anxiety about body image sometimes causes obesity, anorexia, or bulimia, influenced by heredity and childhood patterns. All adolescent nutrition problems have lifelong, life-threatening consequences.

WHAT HAVE YOU LEARNED?
1. What is the pattern of growth in adolescent bodies?
2. What complications result from the sequence of growth (weight/height/muscles)?
3. Why are many adolescents unhappy with their appearance?
4. What interferes with the ability of adolescents to get enough iron and calcium?
5. Why would anyone voluntarily starve to death?
6. Why would anyone make herself or himself throw up?

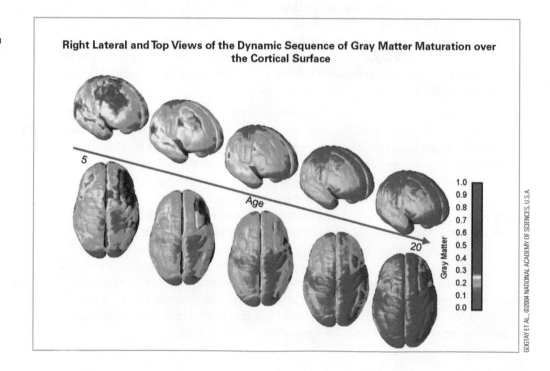

LaunchPad

Median section of the brain

Video Activity: Brain Development: Adolescence features animations and illustrations of the changes that occur in the teenage brain.

Brain Development

Like the other parts of the body, different parts of the brain grow at different rates. Myelination and maturation occur in sequence, proceeding from the lower and inner parts of the brain to the cortex and from the back to the prefrontal cortex (Sowell et al., 2007). That means that the limbic system (site of fear, anxiety, and other intense emotions) matures before regions where planning, emotional regulation, and impulse control occur.

Furthermore, pubertal hormones target the amygdala and other crucial parts of the HPA axis directly (Romeo, 2013), but full functioning of the cortex requires maturation and experience beyond the teen years. Thus, the instinctual and emotional areas of the adolescent brain develop ahead of the reflective, analytic areas. Puberty means emotional rushes, unchecked by caution. Immediate impulses thwart long-term planning.

Brain scans confirm that emotional control, revealed by fMRI studies, is not fully developed until adulthood. During adolescence, the prefrontal cortex is limited in connections and engagement (Luna et al., 2013).

When compared with the brains of emerging adults, adolescent brains show heightened arousal in the brain's reward centers. Teens seek excitement and pleasure, especially the social pleasure of a peer's admiration (Galván, 2013). In fact, when others are watching, teens find it thrilling to take dramatic risks that produce social acclaim, risks they would not dare take alone (Albert et al., 2013).

FIGURE 14.5

Same People, But Not the Same Brain These brain scans are part of a longitudinal study that repeatedly compared the proportion of gray matter from childhood through adolescence. (Gray matter refers to the cell bodies of neurons, which are less prominent with age as some neurons are unused.) Gray matter is reduced as white matter increases, in part because pruning during the teen years (the last two pairs of images here) allows intellectual connections to build. As the authors of one study that included this chart explained, teenagers may "look like an adult, but cognitively they are not there yet" (K. Powell, 2006, p. 865).

Especially for Health Practitioners How might you encourage adolescents to seek treatment for STIs? (see response, page 464)

The fact that the frontal lobes are the last to mature may explain something that has long bewildered adults: Especially when they are with their friends, many adolescents seek the thrill of new experiences and sensations, forgetting the caution that their parents have tried to instill. The following is one example.

a case to study

"What Were You Thinking?"

Laurence Steinberg is a noted expert on adolescence (e.g., Steinberg, 2014). He is also a father.

> When my son, Benjamin, was 14, he and three of his friends decided to sneak out of the house where they were spending the night and visit one of their girlfriends at around two in the morning. When they arrived at the girl's house, they positioned themselves under her bedroom window, threw pebbles against her windowpanes, and tried to scale the side of the house. Modern technology, unfortunately, has made it harder to play Romeo these days. The boys set off the house's burglar alarm, which activated a siren and simultaneously sent a direct notification to the local police station, which dispatched a patrol car. When the siren went off, the boys ran down the street and right smack into the police car, which was heading to the girl's home. Instead of stopping and explaining their activity, Ben and his friends scattered and ran off in different directions through the neighborhood. One of the boys was caught by the police and taken back to his home, where his parents were awakened and the boy questioned.
>
> I found out about this affair the following morning, when the girl's mother called our home to tell us what Ben had done. . . . After his near brush with the local police, Ben had returned to the house out of which he had snuck, where he slept soundly until I awakened him with an angry telephone call, telling him to gather his clothes and wait for me in front of his friend's house. On our drive home, after delivering a long lecture about what he had done and about the dangers of running from armed police in the dark when they believe they may have interrupted a burglary, I paused.
>
> "What were you thinking?" I asked.
>
> "That's the problem, Dad," Ben replied, "I wasn't."
>
> [Steinberg, 2004, pp. 51, 52]

Steinberg realized that his son was right: When emotions are intense, especially when friends are nearby, the logical part of the brain shuts down. This shutdown is not reflected in questionnaires that require teenagers to respond to paper-and-pencil questions regarding hypothetical dilemmas. On those tests, most teenagers think carefully and answer correctly. In fact, when strong emotions are not activated, teenagers may be more logical than adults (Casey & Caudle, 2013). They remember facts they have learned in biology or health class about sex and drugs. However,

> the prospect of visiting a hypothetical girl from class cannot possibly carry the excitement about the possibility of surprising someone you have a crush on with a visit in the middle of the night. It is easier to put on a hypothetical condom during an act of hypothetical sex than it is to put on a real one when one is in the throes of passion. It is easier to just say no to a hypothetical beer than it is to a cold frosty one on a summer night.
>
> [Steinberg, 2004, p. 53]

Ben reached adulthood safely. Some other teenagers, with less cautious police or less diligent parents, do not. Brain immaturity makes teenagers vulnerable to social pressures and stresses, which typically bombard young people today (Casey & Caudle, 2013).

Indeed, brain immaturity coupled with the stresses of adolescence may help explain why many types of psychopathology increase at puberty, especially when puberty is early. Two experts write that "higher rates of psychopathology among early maturers are expected because their slow-developing neurocognitive systems are mismatched with the fast-approaching social and affective challenges at the onset of puberty" (Ge & Natsuaki, 2009, p. 329).

Of course, as with all the changes of adolescence, social context is crucial. It is as irrational for adults to blame teenage problems solely on their brains as it is for teenagers to follow every impulse.

The normal sequence of brain maturation (limbic system at puberty, then prefrontal cortex sometime in the early 20s) combined with the earlier onset of puberty means that, for contemporary teenagers, emotions rule behavior for a decade. The limbic system makes powerful sensations—loud music, speeding cars, strong drugs—compelling.

It is not that the prefrontal cortex shuts down. Actually, it continues to mature throughout childhood and adolescence, and, when they think about it, adolescents are able to assess risks better than children are (Pfeifer et al., 2011). The balance and coordination between the various parts of the brain is awry, even as the brain continues to develop (Casey et al., 2011).

When stress, arousal, passion, sensory bombardment, drug intoxication, or deprivation is extreme, the adolescent brain is flooded with impulses that might shame adults. Teenagers brag about being so drunk that they were "wasted," "bombed," "smashed"—a state most adults try to avoid and would not admit.

// **Response for Health Practitioners** (from page 462): Many adolescents are intensely concerned about privacy and fearful of adult interference. This means your first task is to convince the teenagers that you are nonjudgmental and that everything is confidential.

Also, unlike most adults, many teenagers *choose* to spend a night without sleep, to eat nothing all day, to exercise in pain, or to risk parenthood or an STI by not using a condom. The parts of the brain dedicated to analysis are immature until long after the first hormonal rushes and sexual urges begin.

Sadly, teenagers have access to fast cars, lethal weapons, and dangerous drugs before their brains are ready. My friend said to his neighbor, who gave his son a red convertible for high school graduation, "Why didn't you just give him a loaded gun?" The mother of the 20-year-old who killed 20 children and 7 adults (including the mother) in Newtown, Connecticut, did just that.

A more common example of the cautious part of the brain being overwhelmed by emotions comes from teens sending text messages while they are driving. In one survey, among U.S. high school seniors who have driven a car in the past month, 60 percent texted while driving, even though that is illegal almost everywhere (MMWR, June 13, 2014).

More generally, despite quicker reflexes and better vision than adults, far more teenagers die in motor-vehicle accidents than older drivers do. Thoughtless impulses and poor decisions are almost always to blame, not skill.

Any decision, from whether to eat a peach to where to go to college, requires balancing risk and reward, caution and attraction. Experiences, memories, emotions, and the prefrontal cortex help people choose to avoid some actions and perform others. Since the reward parts of adolescents' brains are stronger than the inhibition parts (Luna et al., 2013), many adolescents act in ways that seem foolhardy to adults.

Benefits of Adolescent Brain Development

It is easy to criticize adolescent behavior and blame it on hormones, peers, culture, or the latest chosen culprit, brains. Yet remember that difference is not always deficit. Gains as well as losses are part of every developmental period. There are benefits as well as hazards in the adolescent brain.

For instance, with increased myelination and slower inhibition, reactions become lightning fast. Such speed is valuable, making adolescent athletes potential superstars, quick and fearless as they steal a base, tackle a fullback, or sprint when their lungs feel about to burst. Ideally, coaches have the wisdom to channel such bravery.

Furthermore, as the brain's reward areas activate positive neurotransmitters, teenagers become happier. A new love, a first job, a college acceptance, or even an A on a term paper can produce a rush of joy, to be remembered and cherished lifelong.

Societies need some people who question assumptions, and adolescents are primed to question everything, often raising issues that need to be raised. As social and ecological circumstances change, someone needs to think critically about having lots of children, or eating bacon every breakfast, or burning fossil fuels. If tradition were never questioned, customs would ossify, and societies die.

Further, teenagers need to take risks and learn new things, because "the fundamental task of adolescence—to achieve adult levels of social competence—requires a great deal of learning about the social complexities of human social interactions" (Peper & Dahl, 2013, p. 135). That is exactly what their brains enable adolescents to do.

Synaptic growth enhances moral development as well. Adolescents question their elders and forge their own standards. Values embraced during adolescence are more likely to endure than those acquired later, after brain connections are

Yes, Not No Diving into cold water with your friends is thrilling if you are a teenage boy and a girl is watching. Adult prohibition increases the joy.

firmly established. This is an asset if adolescent values are less self-centered than those of children or are more culturally attuned than those of older generations.

Thus the developing prefrontal cortex "confers benefits as well as risks. It helps explain the creativity of adolescence and early adulthood, before the brain becomes set in its ways" (Monastersky, 2007, p. A17). The emotional intensity of adolescents "intertwines with the highest levels of human endeavor: passion for ideas and ideals, passion for beauty, passion to create music and art" (Dahl, 2004, p. 21). One application: Since adolescents are learning lessons about life, adults who care about the next generation need to ensure those lessons are good ones.

SUMMING UP   The brain develops unevenly during adolescence, with the limbic system ahead of the prefrontal cortex. That makes the brain's reward centers more active than the cautionary areas, especially when adolescents are with each other. As a result, adolescents are quick to react, before having second thoughts or considering consequences. Without impulse control, anger can lead to hurtful words or even serious injury, lust can lead to disease or pregnancy, self-hatred can lead to self-destruction. These same brain qualities can be positive, as adolescents fall in love, throw themselves into work or study, question social traditions that are no longer relevant. Adolescent brain development allows joy and despair; teenagers are vulnerable to some of the best as well as some of the worst experiences life has to offer.

WHAT HAVE YOU LEARNED?
1. Why does laboratory research generally show advanced thinking in adolescence?
2. Why do adolescents often make decisions that adults consider foolish?
3. Since adolescents have quicker reflexes and better vision than adults, why are they more likely to die in a motor-vehicle accident than from any other cause?
4. How might the timing of brain maturation during adolescence create problems?
5. In what ways is adolescent brain functioning better than adult brain functioning? ●

Sexual Maturation

Sexuality is a complex aspect of human development. Here we consider biological changes at puberty and some of the cultural variations and implications. Variations are discussed again in later chapters, as is sex education.

Sexual Characteristics

The body characteristics that are directly involved in conception and pregnancy are called **primary sex characteristics.** During puberty, every primary sex organ (the ovaries, the uterus, the penis, and the testes) increases dramatically in size and matures in function. By the end of the process, reproduction is possible.

At the same time that maturation of the primary sex characteristics occurs, secondary sex characteristics develop. **Secondary sex characteristics** are bodily features that do not directly affect reproduction (hence they are secondary) but that signify masculinity or femininity.

One secondary characteristic is shape. Young boys and girls have similar shapes, but at puberty males widen at the shoulders and grow about 5 inches taller than females, while girls widen at the hips and develop breasts. Those female curves are often considered signs of womanhood, but neither breasts nor wide hips are required for conception; thus, they are secondary, not primary, sex characteristics.

primary sex characteristics The parts of the body that are directly involved in reproduction, including the uterus, ovaries, testicles, and penis.

secondary sex characteristics Physical traits that are not directly involved in reproduction but that indicate sexual maturity, such as a man's beard and a woman's breasts.

The pattern of hair growth at the scalp line (widow's peak), the prominence of the larynx (Adam's apple), and several other anatomical features differ for men and women; all are secondary sex characteristics that few people notice. As previously explained, facial hair increases in both sexes, affected by sex hormones as well as genes.

Secondary sex characteristics are important psychologically, if not biologically. Breasts are an obvious example. Many adolescent girls buy "minimizer," "maximizer," "training," or "shaping" bras in the hope that their breasts will conform to an idealized body image. During the same years, many overweight boys are horrified to notice a swelling around their nipples—a temporary result of the erratic hormones of early puberty. If a boy's breast growth is very disturbing, tamoxifen or plastic surgery can reduce the swelling, although many doctors prefer to let time deal with the problem (Morcos & Kizy, 2012).

Sexual Activity

The primary and secondary sex characteristics just described are not the only evidence of sex hormones. Fantasizing, flirting, hand-holding, staring, standing, sitting, walking, displaying, and touching are all done in particular ways to reflect sexuality. As already explained, hormones trigger thoughts, but the culture shapes thoughts into enjoyable fantasies, shameful preoccupations, frightening impulses, or actual contact (see Figure 14.6).

A recent study on sexual behaviors such as hand-holding and cuddling among young adolescents found that biological maturation was only one factor in whether or not such activities occurred: Especially among young European Americans, those girls with lower self-esteem were more likely to engage in sexual intimacy (Hipwell et al., 2010).

Regarding sex-related impulses, some experts believe that boys are more influenced by hormones and girls by culture (Baumeister & Blackhart, 2007). Perhaps.

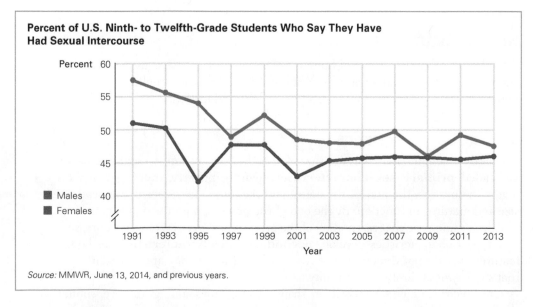

Percent of U.S. Ninth- to Twelfth-Grade Students Who Say They Have Had Sexual Intercourse

Source: MMWR, June 13, 2014, and previous years.

FIGURE 14.6

Boys and Girls Together Boys tend to be somewhat more sexually experienced than girls during the high school years, but since the Youth Risk Behavior Survey began in 1991, the overall trend has been toward equality in rates of sexual activity.

If a relationship includes sexual intimacy, girls seem more concerned than boys about the depth of the romance, and women are more concerned with commitment to a long-term relationship than men are, a difference less marked among college students than among others (Del Giudice, 2011). Girls hope their partners say, "I'll love you forever"; boys like to hear, "I want you now."

Everyone, however, is influenced by hormones and society, biology and culture. All adolescents have sexual interests they did not previously have (biology), which produce behaviors engaged in by teenagers in some nations that teenagers of other nations would not engage in (culture). Since only girls can become pregnant, their wish for long-term commitment may be a consequence of biology, not culture.

For whatever reason, the gender gap in experience is narrowing. It has already been reversed in some European nations, such as Norway, where sex education begins in childhood. By adolescence, today's Norwegian teenagers know how to prevent the unwanted consequences of intercourse. In 1987, Norwegian boys had their first sexual intercourse almost a year younger than girls did; by 2002, the sexes flipped, with girls averaging half a year younger than boys (Stigum et al., 2010).

In the United States, rates of sexual activity are almost even, with minor gender differences. For example, among high school students, 46 percent of the girls and 47.5 percent of the boys say they have had sexual intercourse, 35 percent of the girls and 33 percent of the boys say they have had intercourse in the past 3 months, and 13 percent of the girls and 17 percent of the boys say they have had 4 or more sexual partners (MMWR, June 13, 2014).

Within nations, ethnic differences are narrowing as well, with every group less sexually active than the previous cohort. Between 1991 and 2013, according to an anonymous questionnaire, intercourse experience among African American high school students decreased 25 percent (to 61 percent); among European Americans, down 12 percent (45 percent); and among Latinos, down 9 percent (47 percent) (MMWR, June 13, 2014).

One statistic illustrates this new trend. In 1991, 62 percent of U.S. eleventh-graders said they had had intercourse, but in 2013 only 47 percent said so. Rates vary by state as well, from a low of 35 percent of Nebraska high school students (ninth to twelfth grade) to a high of 54 percent in Mississippi (MMWR, June 13, 2014); both represent a decrease from earlier.

The trend toward later sexual activity is international, although as marriages occur later, rates of premarital sex are rising. More teenagers worldwide are virgins than was true a decade ago, a trend documented in China, where, unlike earlier, first intercourse does not occur until age 20, on average (Yu et al., 2013).

All these examples demonstrate that a universal experience (rising hormones) that produces another universal experience (growth of primary and secondary sex characteristics) is influenced by cohort, gender, and culture. Other research finds that the most powerful influence on adolescents' sexual activity is their close friends, not national or local norms for their gender or their ethnic group.

Sexual Problems in Adolescence

Sexual interest and interaction are part of adolescence; healthy adult relationships are more likely to develop when adolescent impulses are not haunted by shame and fear (Tolman & McClelland, 2011). Although guidance is needed, teenagers are healthy and normal, not depraved or evil, in experiencing sexual urges. Before focusing on the hazards of adolescent sex, we should note that several "problems" are less troubling now than in earlier decades. Here are three specifics:

Prom and Proper This prom picture shows a happy young couple from Michigan who reflect the standards of their community. Note the matching clothes and flowers, and consider that in many cultures of the world, a 17-year-old girl would never publicly cling so tightly to a classmate.

Don't Worry Contemporary teenagers, like this couple, are more likely to be seen in public hugging and kissing but are less likely to be sexually active than similar couples were 20 years ago.

- *Teen births have decreased in every nation.* Teen births have been declining (World Health Organization, December 1, 2012). In the United States, births to teenage mothers (aged 15 to 19) decreased 25 percent between 2007 and 2011 across race and ethnicity, with the biggest drop among Hispanic teens (Martin et al., 2010; Centers for Disease Control and Prevention, June 16, 2014). Similar declines are evident in other nations. In China, the teen pregnancy rate was cut in half from 1960 to 2010 (reducing the United Nations' projections of the world's population in 2050 by about 1 billion).
- *The use of "protection" has risen.* Contraception, particularly condom use among adolescent boys, has increased markedly in most nations since 1990 (Santelli & Melnikas, 2010). The U.S. Youth Risk Behavior Survey found that 63 percent of sexually active ninth-grade boys used a condom during their most recent intercourse (MMWR, June 13, 2014).
- *The teen abortion rate is down.* In general, the teen abortion rate in the United States has declined every year since abortion became legal. The rate today is about half that of 20 years earlier (Kost & Henshaw, 2013), even as the rate among older women has increased. The reason is primarily that contraception is more prevalent, so unwanted teen pregnancies are less common. Internationally, however, abortion rates among teenagers are very difficult to track. An estimated three million girls aged 15 to 19 undergo unsafe abortions each year, mostly in low- and middle-income countries (World Health Organization, December 1, 2012).

These are positive trends, but many aspects of adolescent sexual activity remain problematic.

Sex Too Soon

Sex can, of course, be thrilling and affirming, providing a bonding experience. However, compared to a century ago, adolescent sexual activity—especially if it results in birth—is more hazardous because four circumstances have changed:

1. Earlier puberty and weaker social taboos mean some very young teens have sexual experiences. Early sex correlates with depression and drug abuse.
2. Most teenage mothers have no husbands to help them. A century ago, teenage mothers were married; now, in the United States, 85 percent are unwed.
3. Raising a child has become more complex and expensive, and most young grandmothers are employed, so fewer of them provide full-time care.
4. Sexually transmitted infections are more common and dangerous.

See the Joy Some young mothers are wonderful, as seems the case here. This mother–infant pair have many advantages, not only their mutual love but also a supportive community. (Note the floor of the play room—colorful, non-toxic and soft—perfect for toddlers.)

As you just read, teen births are declining, as are teen abortions. However, the U.S. rate of adolescent pregnancy is the highest of any developed nation (true among every ethnic group). Such pregnancies are risky. If a pregnant girl is under 16 (most are not), she is more likely than pregnant teenagers who are a year or two older to experience complications—including spontaneous or induced abortion, high blood pressure, stillbirth, preterm birth, and an underweight newborn.

There are many reasons in addition to age for these hazards. Poverty and lack of education correlate with teen pregnancy and with every problem just listed (Santelli & Melnikas, 2010). Beyond that, younger pregnant teenagers are often malnourished and postpone prenatal care (Borkowski et al., 2007).

After birth, adolescents are often less responsive, so insecure attachment is more common. For children as well as adults, the decline in teen pregnancy is good news. (**Developmental Link:** Attachment types and the importance of early attachment were discussed in Chapter 7.)

Even without pregnancy, teenagers who have sex risk psychosocial problems. A study of 3,923 adult women in the United States found that those who *voluntarily* had sex before age 16 were more likely to divorce later on, whether or not they became pregnant or later married their first sexual partner. The same study found that adolescents whose first sexual experience was *unwanted* (either "really didn't want it" or "had mixed feelings") were also more likely to divorce (Paik, 2011).

Forced sex is much worse, of course, as now explained.

Sexual Abuse

Teenage births are risky, but sexual abuse is devastating: It harms development lifelong. **Child sexual abuse** is defined as any sexual activity (including fondling and photographing) between a juvenile and an adult, with age 18 the usual demarcation (although legal age varies by state). Girls are particularly vulnerable, although boys are also at risk.

The rate of sexual abuse increases at puberty, a sensitive time because many young adolescents are confused about their own sexual urges and identity (Graber et al., 2010). Virtually every adolescent problem, including pregnancy, drug abuse, eating disorders, and suicide, is more frequent in adolescents who are sexually abused.

This is true worldwide. The United Nations reports that millions of girls in their early teens are forced into marriage or prostitution (often across national borders) each year (Pinheiro, 2006). Adolescent girls are common victims of sex trafficking, not only because their youth makes them more alluring but also because their immaturity makes them more vulnerable (McClain & Garrity, 2011). Some believe they are helping their families by earning money to support them, others are literally sold by their families (Kara, 2009).

That is less likely in developed nations, where sexual abuse of children usually occurs within homes. In the United States, the person most likely to sexually abuse a child or young adolescent is a family member, who typically isolates the victim, depriving him or her of the friendships and romances that aid in developing a healthy and satisfying life. Sometimes that family member is a biological parent, but more often it is a stepfather or uncle, trusted by the mother and therefore with access to the child. Young people who are sexually exploited tend to fear sex and to devalue themselves lifelong.

A longitudinal study in Washington, D.C. of 84 reported victims of child sexual abuse (all girls) included interviews with each of them six times over 23 years (Trickett et al., 2011). In order to isolate the effects of abuse, the researchers also followed the development of individuals from the same backgrounds (SES, ethnicity, and so on) who were not sexually abused.

child sexual abuse Any erotic activity that arouses an adult and excites, shames, or confuses a child, whether or not the victim protests and whether or not genital contact is involved.

Especially for Parents Worried About Their Teenager's Risk Taking You remember the risky things you did at the same age, and you are alarmed by the possibility that your child will follow in your footsteps. What should you do? (see response, page 471)

Every possible problem that was studied was far more common in the victims than in their nonvictimized peers. Problems included attitudes directly related to abuse (e.g., most of those abused by their biological fathers thought of sex as dirty, shameful, and dangerous) and behaviors seemingly unconnected (e.g., although their body weight was normal in childhood, 42 percent were obese in their 20s).

Cognitive development—school achievement as well as language use—was also impaired. Among the most troubling results were much higher rates of self-harm, aggression, and repeated victimization—both sexual and physical in nature (Trickett et al., 2011). The reason—low self-esteem.

Almost half of the girls who were abused became mothers. They had a total of 78 children, three of whom died in infancy and nine of whom were permanently removed from their mothers, who had severely maltreated them. These rates are much higher than rates among the nonvictimized mothers from the same income and ethnic groups.

Early in this chapter, we noted that the HPA system regulates puberty and many other physiological responses. Many of the formerly abused women had abnormal HPA regulation, with alteration of their cortisol responses. That condition produced heightened stress reactions in early adolescence but then abnormally low-stress responses in adulthood.

Smirking or Non-Smirking?

Fortunately, now that sexual abuse is reported more often, it has become less common, with "large declines in sexual abuse from 1992 to 2010" in the United States (Finkelhor & Jones, 2012, p. 3). Worldwide, about 13 percent of women say they were sexually abused as children (Stoltenborgh et al., 2011). Of course, even one instance is too many.

Our discussion of sex abuse focuses on girls, because they are the most common victims. However, teenage boys may be sexually abused as well, a direct attack on their fledgling identity as men (Dorais, 2009).

Remember that perpetrators of all kinds of abuse are often people known to the child. After puberty, although sometimes abusers are parents, coaches, or other authorities, often they are other teenagers. In the Youth Risk Behavior Survey of U.S. high school students, 14 percent of the girls and 6 percent of the boys said they had been kissed, touched, or forced to have sex within a dating relationship when they did not want to (MMWR June 13, 2014). Sex education is discussed in Chapter 16; obviously teenagers have much to learn.

Sexually Transmitted Infections

Unlike teen pregnancy and sexual abuse, the other major problem of teenage sex shows no signs of abating. A **sexually transmitted infection (STI)** (sometimes called a sexually transmitted disease [STD]) is any infection transmitted through sexual contact. Worldwide, sexually active teenagers have higher rates of the most common STIs—gonorrhea, genital herpes, and chlamydia—than do sexually active people of any other age group.

sexually transmitted infection (STI) A disease spread by sexual contact, including syphilis, gonorrhea, genital herpes, chlamydia, and HIV.

In the United States, half of all new STIs occur in people ages 15 to 25, even though this age group has less than one-fourth of the sexually active people (Satterwhite et al., 2013). Rates are particularly high among sexually active adolescents, ages 15–19 (MMWR, September 26, 2014). Biology provides one reason: Pubescent girls are particularly likely to catch an STI compared to fully developed women, probably because adult women have more vaginal secretions that reduce infections. Further, if symptoms appear, teens are less likely to alert their partners or seek treatment unless pain requires it.

There are hundreds of STIs. *Chlamydia* is the most frequently reported one; it often begins without symptoms, yet it can cause permanent infertility. Worse is *human papillomavirus (HPV)*, which has no immediate consequences but increases the risk of "serious, life-threatening cancer" in both sexes (MMWR, July 25, 2014, p. 622). Immunization before the first intercourse has reduced the rate of HPV, but in 2013 among 13- to 17-year-olds, only 38 percent of the girls and 14 percent of the boys had all three recommended doses (MMWR, July 25, 2014).

National variations in laws and rates of STIs are large. Rates among U.S. teenagers are higher than those in any other medically advanced nation, but lower than rates in some developing nations. HIV rates are not declining, despite increased awareness.

Internationally, a comparison of 30 developed nations found that French teenagers were among the most likely to use condoms, while those in the United States were least likely to do so (MMWR, June 13, 2014; Nic Gabhainn et al., 2009) (see Table 14.1). One reason French teenagers use condoms may be that, by law, every French high school (including Catholic ones) must offer free, confidential medical care and condoms. By contrast, providing either is illegal at many U.S. schools.

Once again, it is apparent that a universal experience (the biology of puberty) varies remarkably depending on culture. As we stated earlier, adolescence begins with biology and ends with culture. You will see more examples in the next chapter, as you learn that schools for adolescents vary a great deal in how and what they teach.

TABLE 14.1	Condom Use Among 15-Year-Olds (Tenth Grade)	
Country	Sexually Active (% of total)	Used Condom at Last Intercourse (% of those sexually active)
France	20	84
England	29	83
Canada	23	78
Russia	33	75
Israel	14	72
United States	40	62

Sources: MMWR, June 13, 2014, Nic Gabhainn et al., 2009.

SUMMING UP Sexual differentiation is another example of the dramatic transformations of puberty. Primary sex characteristics, which are directly connected to reproduction, develop; so do secondary sex characteristics, which signify masculinity or femininity but are not necessary for pregnancy. Sexual interest increases as bodies mature and hormone levels rise, with differences between males and females in sexual activity more apparent in some nations than others. Early parenthood, sexual abuse, and sexually transmitted infections are increasingly hazardous. The first two of these are becoming less frequent, but STIs are alarmingly common among teenagers, especially in the United States. Untreated, some of these lead to lifelong infertility, while others lead to death in adulthood. Some nations have policies in place to help protect adolescents from such hazards, but many others do not.

// Response for Parents Worried About Their Teenager's Risk Taking (from page 469): You are right to be concerned, but you cannot keep your child locked up for the next decade or so. Since you know that some rebellion and irrationality are likely, try to minimize them by not boasting about your own youthful exploits, by reacting sternly to the inevitable minor infractions so your child can rebel without disastrous consequences, and by making allies of your child's teachers.

WHAT HAVE YOU LEARNED?

1. What are examples of the difference between primary and secondary sex characteristics?
2. Why are there fewer problems caused by adolescent sexuality now than a few decades ago?
3. What are the problems with adolescent pregnancy?
4. Among sexually active people, why do adolescents have more STIs than adults?
5. What are the effects of child sexual abuse?

SUMMARY

Puberty Begins

1. Puberty refers to the various changes that transform a child's body into an adult one. Even before the teenage years, biochemical signals from the hypothalamus to the pituitary gland to the adrenal glands (the HPA axis) increase production of testosterone, estrogen, and various other hormones, which causes the body to grow rapidly and become capable of reproduction.

2. Some emotional reactions, such as quick mood shifts, are directly caused by hormones, as are thoughts about sex. The reactions of others to adolescents and their own reactions to the physical changes they are undergoing also trigger emotional responses, which, in turn, affect hormones.

3. Hormones regulate all the body rhythms of life, by day, by season, and by year. Changes in these rhythms in adolescence often result in sleep deprivation, partly because the natural circadian rhythm makes teenagers wide awake at night. Sleep deprivation causes numerous health and learning problems.

4. Puberty normally begins anytime from about age 8 to about age 14—most often between ages 10 and 13. The young person's sex, genetic background, body fat, and level of stress all contribute to this variation in timing.

5. Girls generally begin and end puberty before boys do, although the time gap in sexual maturity is much shorter than the two-year gender gap in reaching peak height.

6. Adolescents who reach puberty earlier or later than their friends experience additional stresses. Generally (depending on culture, community, and cohort), early-maturing girls and early- or late-maturing boys have a particularly difficult time.

Growth and Nutrition

7. The growth spurt is an acceleration of growth in every part of the body. Peak weight usually precedes peak height, which is then followed by peak muscle growth. This sequence makes adolescents particularly vulnerable to sports injuries. The lungs and the heart also increase in size and capacity.

8. All the changes of puberty depend on adequate nourishment, yet adolescents do not always make healthy food choices. One reason for poor nutrition is the desire to lose (or, less often, gain) weight because of anxiety about body image. This is a worldwide problem, involving cultural as well as biological factors.

9. Although serious eating disorders such as anorexia and bulimia are not usually diagnosed until emerging adulthood, their precursors are evident during puberty. Many adolescents eat too much of the wrong foods or too little food overall, with bingeing and obesity common.

Brain Development

10. Because of the sequence of brain development, many adolescents seek intense emotional experiences, unchecked by rational thought. For the same reason, adolescents are quick to react, explore, and learn. As a result, adolescents take risks, bravely or foolishly, with potential for harm as well as for good.

11. Various parts of the brain mature during puberty and in the following decade. The regions dedicated to emotional arousal (including the amygdala) mature before those that regulate and rationalize emotional expression (the prefrontal cortex).

Sexual Maturation

12. Male–female differences in bodies and behavior become apparent at puberty. The maturation of primary sex characteristics means that by age 13 or so, after experiencing menarche or spermarche, teenagers are capable of reproducing, although peak fertility is several years later.

13. Secondary sex characteristics are not directly involved in reproduction but signify that the child is becoming a man or a woman. Body shape, breasts, voice, body hair, and numerous other features differentiate males from females. Sexual activity is influenced more by culture than by physiology.

14. Among the problems that adolescents face is the tendency to become sexually active before their bodies and minds are ready. Pregnancy before age 16 takes a physical toll on a growing girl; it also puts her baby at risk of physical and psychological problems. Teen births are much less common today than earlier.

15. Sexual abuse, which includes any sexually provocative activity that involves a juvenile and an adult, is more likely to occur in early adolescence than at other ages. Girls are more often victims than boys are; perpetrators are often family members or close family friends. Rates are declining in the United States, but international sex trafficking is a global problem.

16. Untreated STIs at any age can lead to infertility and even death. Rates among sexually active teenagers are rising for many reasons.

KEY TERMS

puberty (p. 445)
menarche (p. 445)
spermarche (p. 446)
hormone (p. 446)
pituitary (p. 446)
adrenal glands (p. 446)

HPA (hypothalamus–pituitary–adrenal) axis (p. 446)
gonads (p. 447)
HPG (hypothalamus–pituitary–gonad) axis (p. 447)
estradiol (p. 447)
testosterone (p. 447)

circadian rhythm (p. 448)
secular trend (p. 450)
leptin (p. 452)
growth spurt (p. 456)
body image (p. 459)
anorexia nervosa (p. 460)
bulimia nervosa (p. 460)

primary sex characteristics (p. 465)
secondary sex characteristics (p. 465)
child sexual abuse (p. 469)
sexually transmitted infection (STI) (p. 470)

APPLICATIONS

1. Visit a fifth-, sixth-, or seventh-grade class. Note variations in the size and maturity of the students. Do you see any patterns related to gender, ethnicity, body fat, or self-confidence?

2. Interview two to four of your friends who are in their late teens or early 20s about their memories of menarche or spermarche, including their memories of others' reactions. Do their comments indicate that these events are, or are not, emotionally troubling for young people?

3. Talk with someone who became a teenage parent. Were there any problems with the pregnancy, the birth, or the first years of parenthood? Would the person recommend teen parenthood? What would have been different had the baby been born three years earlier or three years later?

4. Find two or three adults who, as adolescents, acted impulsively and did something that could have potentially caused great harm to themselves and/or other people. What do they recall about their thinking at the time of the incident? How would their actions differ now? What do their answers reveal about the adolescent mind?

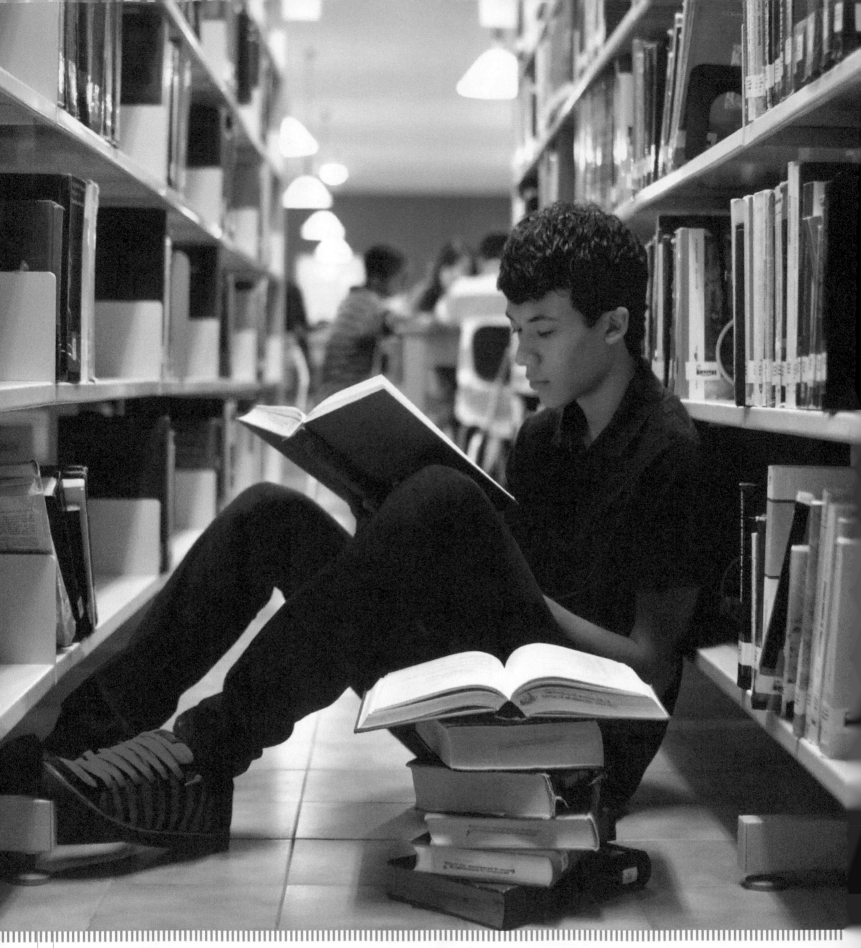

Adolescence:
Cognitive Development

What Will You Know?

1. Why are young adolescents often egocentric?

2. Why does emotion sometimes overwhelm reason?

3. Is cyberbullying worse than bullying directly?

4. What kind of school is best for teenagers?

I have taught at four universities, educating thousands of college students. Most of the content of my courses is standard. That allows me to focus on updating, adding current examples, and adjusting to the particular students. I change methods depending on the particular topic and class (lecture, discussion, polls, groups, video clip, pair/share, role play, written responses, quizzes, and more).

No class is exactly like any other. Group dynamics change, in part because of the individuals in the class. Ideally I know who needs encouragement ("Good question"), who needs prompts ("Do you agree with —"), who should think before they speak ("What is your evidence?"), whose background needs to be understood by others ("Is that what it was like when you were a child in . . . ?"). Deciding who should learn what, when, and how is my challenge and my joy.

A few years ago, I taught a course for college credit to advanced high school students. They grasped concepts quickly, they studied diligently, they completed papers on time—in all those ways they were good students. But they also presented new pedagogical challenges. For example, one day I was explaining Freud and the following exchange occurred.

> **Student:** I don't agree with Freud.
>   **Me:** You don't have to agree, just learn the terms and concepts.
> **Student:** Why should I do that?
>   **Me:** You need to understand Freud, so you can then disagree.
> **Student:** But I have my own ideas, and I like them better than Freud's.

I was taken aback. None of my college students had ever been so egocentric as to claim that their own ideas were so good that they didn't need to bother with Freud. That does not mean they agreed with psychoanalytic theory: Some expressed insightful critiques. But none resisted learning about Freud, especially by deciding in advance that they liked their ideas better.

Then I remembered: Bright as they were, these students were adolescents. I adjusted my teaching accordingly.

This chapter describes adolescent cognition, sometimes impressively brilliant, sometimes surprisingly abstract, and sometimes amazingly egocentric. Then we describe how adolescents are taught—in middle school, in high school, and around the world—and how that aligns or clashes with adolescent cognition.

Logic and Self

Brain maturation, additional years of schooling, moral challenges, increased independence, and intense conversations all occur between the ages of 11 and 18. These aspects of adolescents' development propel impressive cognitive growth, as teenagers move from egocentrism to abstract logic.

Egocentrism

During puberty, young people center on themselves, in part because maturation of the brain heightens self-consciousness (Sebastian et al., 2008). Young adolescents grapple with conflicting feelings about their parents and friends, thinking deeply (but not always realistically) about their future. Adolescents ruminate (going over problems via phone, text, conversation, and self-talk, as when they lie in bed, unable to sleep) about each nuance of everything they have done, are doing, and might do.

Adolescent egocentrism—that is, adolescents thinking intensely about themselves and about what others think of them—was first described by David Elkind (1967). In egocentrism, adolescents regard themselves as much more unique, special, and admired or disliked than anyone else considers them to be. Consequently, they have difficulty understanding other points of view. For example, few adolescent girls are attracted to boys with pimples and braces, but Edgar's eagerness to be recognized as growing up kept him from realizing this, according to his older sister:

> Now in the 8th grade, Edgar has this idea that all the girls are looking at him in school. He got his first pimple about three months ago. I told him to wash it with my face soap but he refused, saying, "Not until I go to school to show it off." He called the dentist, begging him to approve his braces now instead of waiting for a year. The perfect gifts for him have changed from action figures to a bottle of cologne, a chain, and a fitted baseball hat like the rappers wear.
>
> *[adapted from Eva, personal communication]*

Egocentrism leads adolescents to interpret everyone else's behavior as if it were a judgment on them. A stranger's frown or a teacher's critique can make a teenager conclude that "No one likes me" and then deduce that "I am unlovable" or even "I can't leave the house." More positive casual reactions—a smile from a sales clerk or an extra-big hug from a younger brother—could lead to "I am great" or "Everyone loves me," with similarly distorted self-perception.

Acute self-consciousness about physical appearance may be more prevalent between the ages of 10 and 14 than at any other time, in part because every adolescent notices that the changes in his or her particular body during puberty do not exactly conform to norms, ideals, and fantasies (Guzman & Nishina, 2014). Most young adolescents would rather not stand out from their peers, hoping instead to blend in, although they may want to flaunt adult standards. Conformity rules, and body changes do not always follow the rules.

All Eyes on Me Egocentrism and obsession with appearance are hallmarks of adolescence, as shown by these high school cheerleaders. Given teenage thinking, it is not surprising that many boys and girls seek stardom, sometimes making competition within teams and between schools fierce. Cooperation and moderation are more difficult.

adolescent egocentrism A characteristic of adolescent thinking that leads young people (ages 10 to 13) to focus on themselves to the exclusion of others.

Because adolescents focus on their own perspectives, oblivious to other viewpoints, their emotions may not be grounded in reality. For example, a study of 1,310 Dutch and Belgian adolescents found that egocentrism was strong, and self-esteem and loneliness were more closely tied to their *perception* of how others saw them, not to their actual popularity. Gradually, after about age 15, some gained more perspective and became less depressed (Vanhalst et al., 2013).

Fables

The **personal fable** is the belief that one is unique, destined to have a heroic, fabled, even legendary life. Some 12-year-olds plan to star in the NBA, or to become billionaires, or to cure cancer. Some believe they are destined to die an early, tragic death; for them, the fact that smoking, eating junk food, or other habits could lead to midlife cancer or heart disease are irrelevant.

Adolescents markedly overestimate the chance that they will die soon. One study found that teens estimate 1 chance in 5 that they will die before age 20, when in fact the odds are less than 1 in 1,000. Even those most at risk of early death (urban African American males) survive at least to age 20 more than 99 times in 100. But if the peer group thinks that some of them will die young, they are more likely to do self-destructive things, such as risking jail, HIV, or drug addiction (Haynie et al., 2014).

The personal fable may coexist with the **invincibility fable,** the idea that death will not occur unless it is destined, which is another reason that some adolescents believe that fast driving, unprotected sex, or addictive drugs will do them no harm unless "their number is up."

In every nation, most army volunteers—hoping for combat—are under age 20. Young recruits take more risks than older, more experienced soldiers (Killgore et al., 2006). Another example of the invincibility fable comes from online chat rooms: Despite adult warnings, teenagers reveal personal information that they should keep private (McCarty et al., 2011).

The Imaginary Audience

Egocentrism creates an **imaginary audience** in the minds of many adolescents. They believe they are at center stage, with all eyes on them, and they imagine how others might react to their appearance and behavior.

One woman remembers:

> When I was 14 and in the 8th grade, I received an award at the end-of-year school assembly. Walking across the stage, I lost my footing and stumbled in front of the entire student body. To be clear, this was not falling flat on one's face, spraining an ankle, or knocking over the school principal—it was a small misstep noticeable only to those in the audience who were paying close attention. As I rushed off the stage, my heart pounded with embarrassment and self-consciousness, and weeks of speculation about the consequence of this missed step were set into motion. There were tears and loss of sleep. Did my friends notice? Would they stop wanting to hang out with me? Would a reputation for clumsiness follow me to high school?
>
> [Somerville, 2013, p. 121]

This woman went on to become an expert on the adolescent brain. She remembered from personal experience that "adolescents are hyperaware of other's evaluations and feel they are under constant scrutiny by an imaginary audience" (Somerville, 2013, p. 124).

personal fable An aspect of adolescent egocentrism characterized by an adolescent's belief that his or her thoughts, feelings, and experiences are unique, more wonderful, or more awful, than anyone else's.

invincibility fable An adolescent's egocentric conviction that he or she cannot be overcome or even harmed by anything that might defeat a normal mortal, such as unprotected sex, drug abuse, or high-speed driving.

imaginary audience The other people who, in an adolescent's egocentric belief, are watching and taking note of his or her appearance, ideas, and behavior. This belief makes many teenagers very self-conscious.

Duck, Duck, Goose Far more teens are injured in bicycle accidents than hunting ones, because almost all young people ride bicycles and relatively few are hunters. However, especially when no adult is present, young hunters are less likely is to wear blaze orange, to attend safety classes, and be licensed to hunt. Most likely these boys will return home safe, without the duck they seek. However, guns and off-road vehicles are leading causes of male death under age 18, so this scene is not a comforting one.

A Proud Teacher "Is it possible to train a cockroach?" This hypothetical question, an example of formal operational thought, was posed by 15-year-old Tristan Williams of New Mexico. In his award-winning science project, he succeeded in conditioning Madagascar cockroaches to hiss at the sight of a permanent marker. (His parents' logic about sharing their home with 600 cockroaches is unknown.)

formal operational thought In Piaget's theory, the fourth and final stage of cognitive development, characterized by more systematic logical thinking and by the ability to understand and systematically manipulate abstract concepts.

A librarian acknowledges that libraries are rule-driven places that are supposed to be quiet and that this conflicts with the cognition of teenagers. He explains that the imaginary audience is the "reason why teens are so loud—they simply want to be sure that no one needs to strain to hear what their life is like today. [B]ecause of personal fable, a teenager will believe himself to be the exception to any rule" (Sexton, 2002). The librarian explains how research on adolescent thinking and brain development can help those in his field react to teenagers.

Another venue where the imaginary audience dominates is online. Teens post comments on Twitter, Instagram, Facebook, and so on, and they expect others to understand, laugh, or sympathize. Their imaginary audience is their friends and other teenagers, not parents, teachers, college admission officers, or future employers who might have another interpretation (boyd, 2014).

Too much can be made of adolescent egocentrism. Indeed, one team of researchers considers adolescent egocentrism a "largely discredited notion" (Laursen & Hartl, 2013, p. 1266). Nonetheless, they and many others find some truth in it. Adults must not exaggerate the idea or blame every adolescent behavior on it, but understanding egocentrism may help understanding adolescence.

Formal Operational Thought

Piaget described a shift to **formal operational thought** as adolescents move past concrete operational thinking and consider abstractions, including "assumptions that have no necessary relation to reality" (Piaget, 1972, p. 148).

Is Piaget correct? Many educators think so. They adjust the curriculum between primary and secondary school, reflecting a shift from concrete to formal, logical thought. Here are three examples:

- *Math.* Younger children multiply real numbers, such as $4 \times 3 \times 8$; adolescents can multiply unreal numbers, such as $(2x)(3y)$ or even $(25xy^2)(-3zy^3)$.
- *Social studies.* Younger children study other cultures by considering daily life—drinking goat's milk or building an igloo, for instance. Adolescents consider the effect of GNP (gross national product) and TFR (total fertility rate) on global politics. They ponder the relationship between the Egyptian Spring and the size of the young adult cohort, for instance.
- *Science.* Younger students water plants; adolescents test H_2O in the lab and learn about invisible molecules and distant galaxies.

Piaget's Experiments

Piaget and his colleagues devised a number of tasks to assess formal operational thought (Inhelder & Piaget, 1958). In these tasks, "in contrast to concrete operational children, formal operational adolescents imagine all possible determinants . . . [and] systematically vary the factors one by one, observe the results correctly, keep track of the results, and draw the appropriate conclusions" (P. H. Miller, 2011, p. 57).

One of their experiments (diagrammed in Figure 15.1) required balancing a scale by hooking weights onto the scale's arms. To master this task, a person must realize the reciprocal interaction between distance from the center and heaviness of the weight. Therefore, a heavy weight close to the center can be counterbalanced with a light weight far from the center on the other side.

Balancing was not understood by the 3- to 5-year-olds. By age 7, children balanced the scale by putting the same amount of weight on each arm, but they didn't realize how the distance from the center mattered. By age 10, children experimented with the weights, using trial and error, not logic. Finally, by about age 13 or 14, some children hypothesized about reciprocity, developing the correct formula (Piaget & Inhelder, 1969).

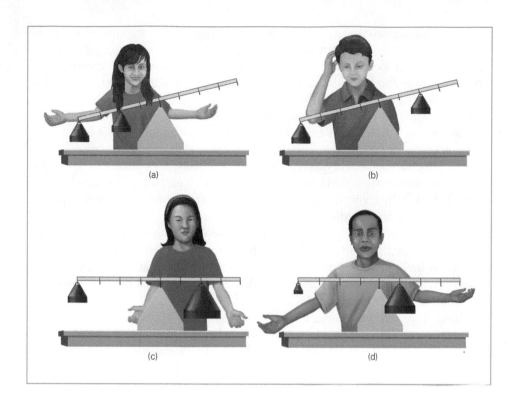

FIGURE 15.1
How to Balance a Scale Piaget's balance-scale test of formal reasoning, as it is attempted by (*a*) a 4-year-old, (*b*) a 7-year-old, (*c*) a 10-year-old, and (*d*) a 14-year-old. The key to balancing the scale is to make weight times distance from the center equal on both sides of the center; the realization of that principle requires formal operational thought.

Hypothetical-Deductive Reasoning

One hallmark of formal operational thought is the capacity to think of possibility, not just reality. "Here and now" is only one of many possibilities, including "there and then," "long, long ago," "not yet," and "never." As Piaget said:

> The adolescent . . . thinks beyond the present and forms theories about everything, delighting especially in considerations of that which is not. . . .
>
> *[Piaget, 1972, p. 148]*

Adolescents are therefore primed to engage in **hypothetical thought,** reasoning about *if–then* propositions that do not reflect reality. For example, consider this question (adapted from De Neys & Van Gelder, 2009):

> If all mammals can walk,
> And whales are mammals,
> Can whales walk?

Children answer "No!" They know that whales swim, not walk; the logic escapes them. Some adolescents answer "Yes." They understand the conditional *if,* and therefore the counterfactual phrase "if all mammals."

> *Possibility* no longer appears merely as an extension of an empirical situation or of action actually performed. Instead, it is *reality* that is now secondary to *possibility.*
>
> *[Inhelder & Piaget, 1958, p. 251; emphasis in original]*

Hypothetical thought transforms perceptions, not necessarily for the better. Zombies and robots become fascinating, sometimes frightening.

Adolescents criticize everything from their mother's spaghetti (it's not *al dente*) to the Gregorian calendar (it's not the Chinese or Jewish one). They criticize what *is* because of their hypothetical thinking and their awareness of other families and cultures. That complicates immediate, practical decisions (Moshman, 2011).

hypothetical thought Reasoning that includes propositions and possibilities that may not reflect reality.

Triple Winners Sharing the scholarship check of $100,000, these high school students are not only high achievers, but they also have learned to collaborate within a comprehensive public school (Hewlett). They were taught much more than formal operational logic.

deductive reasoning Reasoning from a general statement, premise, or principle, through logical steps, to figure out (deduce) specifics. (Also called *top-down reasoning*.)

inductive reasoning Reasoning from one or more specific experiences or facts to reach (induce) a general conclusion. (Also called *bottom-up reasoning*.)

Especially for Natural Scientists Some ideas that were once universally accepted, such as the belief that the sun moved around the Earth, have been disproved. Is it a failure of inductive or deductive reasoning that leads to false conclusions? (see response, page 482)

In developing the capacity to think hypothetically, by age 14 or so adolescents become more capable of **deductive reasoning,** or *top-down reasoning,* which begins with an abstract idea or premise and then uses logic to draw specific conclusions. In the example above, "if all mammals can walk" is a premise. By contrast, **inductive reasoning,** or *bottom-up reasoning,* predominates during the school years, as children accumulate facts and experiences (the knowledge base) to aid their thinking. Since they know whales cannot walk, that knowledge trumps the logic.

In essence, a child's reasoning goes like this: "This creature waddles and quacks. Ducks waddle and quack. Therefore, this must be a duck." This is inductive: It progresses from particulars ("waddles" and "quacks") to a general conclusion ("a duck"). By contrast, deduction progresses from the general to the specific: "If it's a duck, it will waddle and quack" (see Figure 15.2).

An example of the progress toward deductive reasoning comes from how children, adolescents, and adults change in their understanding of the causes of racism. Even before adolescence, almost everyone is aware that racism exists—and almost everyone opposes it. However, children tend to believe the core problem is that some people are prejudiced.

Using inductive reasoning, children conclude that the remedy is education. They argue against racism when they hear other people express it. By contrast, older adolescents think, deductively, that racism is a society-wide problem that requires policy solutions.

This example arises from a study of adolescent opinions regarding policies to remedy racial discrimination (Hughes & Bigler, 2011). Not surprisingly, most students of all ages in an interracial U.S. high school recognized disparities between African and European Americans and believed that racism was a major cause.

However, the age of the students made a difference. Among those who recognized marked inequalities, older adolescents (ages 16 to 17) more often supported systemic solutions (e.g., affirmative action and desegregation) than did younger adolescents (ages 14 to 15). Hughes and Bigler wrote: "[D]uring adolescence, cognitive development facilitates the understanding that discrimination exists at the social-systemic level . . . [and] racial awareness begins to inform views of race-conscious policies" (2011, p. 489).

FIGURE 15.2

Bottom Up or Top Down? Children, as concrete operational thinkers, are likely to draw conclusions on the basis of their own experiences and what they have been told. This is called inductive, or bottom-up, reasoning. Adolescents can think deductively, from the top down.

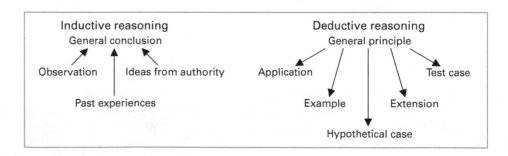

sunk cost fallacy The mistaken belief that if money, time, or effort that cannot be recovered (a "sunk cost," in economic terms) has already been invested in some endeavor, then more should be invested in an effort to reach the goal. Because of this fallacy, people spend money trying to fix a "lemon" of a car or send more troops to fight a losing battle.

Logical Fallacies

Many cognitive scientists study how people of all ages sometimes think illogically. Such failures are apparent throughout adolescence (Albert & Steinberg, 2011), but there is one age-related difference: Younger adolescents are more confident of their illogical ideas than older adolescents are (De Neys & Feremans, 2013).

One example is the **sunk cost fallacy:** When people have spent money, time, or effort that cannot be recovered (a cost already "sunk"), they hold the fallacy that they must continue to pursue their goal because otherwise all previous effort will have been wasted (Cunha & Caldieraro, 2009). This fallacy leads people to pour money into repairing a "lemon" of a car, to remain in a class they are failing, to stay in an abusive relationship, and so on.

Another common fallacy is **base rate neglect,** in which people ignore information about the frequency of a phenomenon. For example (cited by Kahneman, 2011, p. 151), if a stranger on the subway is reading the *New York Times,* which is more likely?

> She does not have a college degree.
> She has a PhD.

The answer is no college degree. Far more subway riders have no degree than have a PhD (perhaps 50:1). But people tend to ignore that base rate, and instead conclude that a PhD recipient is more likely to read the *New York Times* than someone without a degree. That is base rate neglect.

Egocentrism makes base rate neglect more likely and more personal. For instance, a teen might not wear a bicycle helmet, feeling invincible despite statistics, until a friend is brain-damaged in a biking accident. "When adolescents take unjustified risks, it is often because of the weakness of their analytic systems, which provide an inadequate check on impulsive or ill-considered decisions" (Sunstein, 2008, p. 145).

Many have criticized Piaget's stage theory, as you know from previous chapters. That is apparent regarding formal operational thinking as well. For instance, research has found that adults long past adolescence sometimes reason like concrete operational or even preoperational children. Logical fallacies occur at every age, and "No contemporary scholarly reviewer of research evidence endorses the emergence of a discrete new cognitive structure at adolescence that closely resembles . . . formal operations" (Kuhn & Franklin, 2006, p. 954).

Nonetheless, something shifts in cognition after puberty: Piaget was correct when he concluded that most older adolescents possess the ability to think more logically and hypothetically than most children do.

> **base rate neglect** A common fallacy in which a person ignores the overall frequency of some behavior or characteristic (called the *base rate*) in making a decision. For example, a person might bet on a "lucky" lottery number without considering the odds that that number will be selected.

SUMMING UP Thinking reaches heightened self-consciousness at puberty. Some adolescents are egocentric, with unrealistic notions about their place in the social world, as evidenced by the personal fable and the imaginary audience. They often imagine themselves to be invincible, unique, and the center of attention. Adolescent egocentrism is an exaggerated focus on oneself, which is typical of adolescents, and can lead to a fatalistic attitude about death and risk taking that does not consider the future.

Piaget's *formal operational thought,* which includes his fourth and final stages of intelligence, begins in adolescence. He found that adolescents' deductive logic and hypothetical reasoning improve. That is reflected in the curricula of high schools as well as the adolescent's readiness to argue with adults. Other scholars note logical lapses at every age and much more variability in adolescent thought than Piaget's description implies.

WHAT HAVE YOU LEARNED?

1. How does adolescent egocentrism differ from early-childhood egocentrism?
2. What perceptions arise from belief in the imaginary audience?
3. Why are the personal fable and the invincibility fable called "fables"?
4. What are the practical implications of adolescent cognition?
5. What are the advantages and disadvantages of using inductive rather than deductive reasoning?
6. What objections are raised by contemporary scholars to Piaget's description of adolescent cognition?

Two Modes of Thinking

Advanced logic in adolescence is counterbalanced by the increasing power of intuitive thinking. A **dual-process model** of cognition has been formulated (Albert & Steinberg, 2011) (see Visualizing Development, p. 483).

Intuition Versus Analysis

Most cognitive psychologists recognize two modes of thought, using various terms and descriptions to describe them. The terms include: intuitive/analytic, implicit/explicit, creative/factual, contextualized/decontextualized, unconscious/conscious, gist/quantitative, emotional/intellectual, experiential/rational, hot/cold, systems 1 and 2. Here we refer to them as *intuitive* and *analytical*. Although they interact and can overlap, each mode is independent (Kuhn, 2013).

The thinking described by the first half of each pair is easier and quicker, preferred in everyday life. Sometimes, however, circumstances necessitate the second mode, when more careful thought is demanded. The discrepancy between the maturation of the limbic system and the prefrontal cortex reflects this duality. (**Developmental Link:** Timing differences in maturation of various parts of the brain is discussed in Chapter 14.)

The Irrational Adolescent

In describing adolescent cognition, intuitive and analytic thought are defined as follows:

- **Intuitive thought** begins with a belief, assumption, or general rule (called a *heuristic*) rather than logic. Intuition is quick and powerful; it feels "right."
- **Analytic thought** is the formal, logical, hypothetical-deductive thinking described by Piaget. It involves rational analysis of many factors whose interactions must be calculated, as in the scale-balancing problem.

When the two modes of thinking conflict, people of all ages sometimes use one and sometimes the other: We are all "predictably irrational" at times (Ariely, 2009). Adolescents tend to think quickly, because their reaction time is shorter than at any other time of life. That typically makes them "fast and furious" intuitive thinkers, unlike their teachers and parents, who prefer slower, more analytic thinking.

At every age, experiences and role models influence choices, not only in deciding what to do but also in choosing which intellectual process to use in making the decision. Conversations, observations, and debate all advance cognition and lead to conclusions that come from a deeper consideration of the facts (Kuhn, 2013).

Paul Klaczynski conducted dozens of studies comparing the thinking of children, young adolescents, and older adolescents (usually 9-, 12-, and 15-year-olds) (Holland & Klaczynski, 2009; Klaczynski, 2001, 2011; Klaczynski et al., 2009). Variation in thinking is evident at every age. Klaczynski reports that almost every adolescent is analytical and logical on some problems but not on others, with some passing the same questions that others fail. As they grow older, adolescents sometimes gain

dual-process model The notion that two networks exist within the human brain, one for emotional processing of stimuli and one for analytical.

// Response for Natural Scientists (from page 480): Probably both. Our false assumptions are not logically tested because we do not realize that they might need testing.

intuitive thought Thought that arises from an emotion or a hunch, beyond rational explanation, and is influenced by past experiences and cultural assumptions.

analytic thought Thought that results from analysis, such as a systematic ranking of pros and cons, risks and consequences, possibilities and facts. Analytic thought depends on logic and rationality.

Impressive Connections This robot is about to compete in the Robotics Competition in Atlanta, Georgia, but much more impressive are the brains of the Oregon high school team (including Melissa, shown here) who designed the robot.

Thinking in Adolescence

We are able to think both intuitively and analytically, but adolescents tend to rely more on intuitive thinking than do adults.

INDUCTIVE vs. DEDUCTIVE REASONING

INDUCTIVE: Conclusion reached after many of the following. Note that the problem is that the adolescent's nimble mind can rationalize many specifics. Only when the evidence is overwhelming is the conclusion reached.

DEDUCTIVE: The principle is the starting point, not the end point.

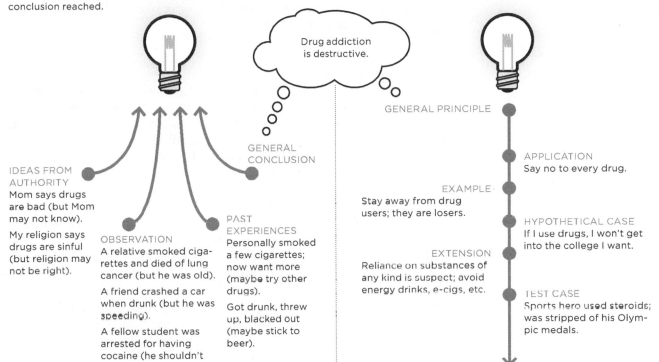

Drug addiction is destructive.

GENERAL CONCLUSION

IDEAS FROM AUTHORITY
Mom says drugs are bad (but Mom may not know).

My religion says drugs are sinful (but religion may not be right).

OBSERVATION
A relative smoked cigarettes and died of lung cancer (but he was old).

A friend crashed a car when drunk (but he was speeding).

A fellow student was arrested for having cocaine (he shouldn't have carried it).

PAST EXPERIENCES
Personally smoked a few cigarettes; now want more (maybe try other drugs).

Got drunk, threw up, blacked out (maybe stick to beer).

GENERAL PRINCIPLE

APPLICATION
Say no to every drug.

EXAMPLE
Stay away from drug users; they are losers.

HYPOTHETICAL CASE
If I use drugs, I won't get into the college I want.

EXTENSION
Reliance on substances of any kind is suspect; avoid energy drinks, e-cigs, etc.

TEST CASE
Sports hero used steroids; was stripped of his Olympic medals.

CHANGES IN AGE

INTUITIVE THINKING

ANALYTICAL THINKING

age

YOUNGER

OLDER

This singer is cute and fun ═ I'll listen to her

This singer is very popular

➕ She sometimes writes her own songs

➕ She makes creative videos

➕ I agree with her morals ═ I'll listen to her music

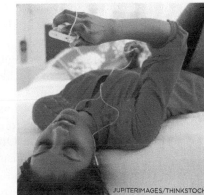

JUPITERIMAGES/THINKSTOCK

As people age, their thinking tends to move from intuitive processing to more analytic processing. Virtually all cognitive psychologists note these two alternative processes and describe a developmental progression toward more dispassionate logic with maturity. However, the terms used and the boundaries between the two vary. They are roughly analogous to Kahneman's System 1 (which "operates automatically and quickly") and System 2 ("the conscious, reasoning self") (Kahneman, 2011, pp. 20–21), as well as to the traditional distinction between inductive and deductive reasoning, and to Piaget's concrete operational versus formal operational thought. Although experts vary in their descriptions, and individuals vary in when and how they use these two processes, overall adolescents tend to favor intuitive rather than analytic thinking.

in logic and sometimes regress, with the social context and training in statistics becoming major influences on cognition (Klaczynski & Felmban, 2014).

To test yourself on intuitive and analytic thinking, answer the following three problems:

1. A bat and a ball cost $1.10 in total. The bat costs $1 more than the ball. How much does the ball cost?
2. If it takes 5 minutes for 5 machines to make 5 widgets, how long would it take 100 machines to make 100 widgets?
3. In a lake, there is a patch of lily pads. Every day the patch doubles in size. If it takes 48 days for the patch to cover the entire lake, how long would it take for the patch to cover half the lake?

[From Gervais & Norenzayan, 2012]

Answers are on page 485.

Although many researchers find that logic gradually overcomes biased reasoning during adolescence, whether such analysis is used depends on specifics. For instance, older adolescents who idealized thinness were *less* likely to use logic to judge the weight of Jennifer, a hypothetical girl described as lazy and not well liked. Compared to younger adolescents, older adolescents *more* often jumped to the conclusion that Jennifer was obese (Klaczynski & Felmban, 2014).

In dozens of studies, being smarter as measured by an intelligence test does not advance logic as much as having more experience, in school and in life. Students can learn to use statistics and to respect expert opinion, and that helps them think more rationally—but not always (Kail, 2013).

Even though teenagers *can* use logic, sometimes they increasingly reason intuitively with age, especially when that intuitive reasoning activates stereotypes. Thus, "in certain domains, social variables are better predictors of age differences in heuristics and biases than cognitive abilities" (Klaczynski & Felmban, 2014, p. 103–104). Competence does not always predict performance.

Preferring Emotions

Why not use formal operational thinking? Klaczynski's participants had all learned the scientific method in school, and they knew that scientists use empirical evidence and deductive reasoning. But they did not always think like scientists. Why not?

Dozens of experiments and extensive theorizing have found some answers (Albert & Steinberg, 2011). Essentially, logic is more difficult than intuition, and it requires questioning ideas that are comforting and familiar. Once people of any age reach an emotional conclusion (sometimes called a "gut feeling"), they resist changing their minds. Prejudice does not quickly disappear because it is not seen as prejudice.

As people gain experience in making decisions and thinking things through, they may become better at knowing when analysis is needed (Milkman et al., 2009). For example, in contrast to younger students, when judging whether a rule is legitimate, older adolescents are more suspicious of authority and more likely to consider mitigating circumstances (Klaczynski, 2011). That may be wise—sometimes.

Both suspicion of authority and awareness of context advance reasoning, but both also complicate simple issues or lead to impulsive but destructive actions. Indeed, suspicion of authority may propel adolescents to respond illogically. One of my students argued with a police officer who was about to charge her cousin, falsely, with playing hooky: When he moved to grab the cousin, she bit his hand— and spent months in jail. [Then I appeared in court on her behalf; the judge released her because he listened to me but not to her, an example of the "social variables" that Klacynzinki describes.]

Rational judgment is difficult when egocentrism dominates, and when the social demands outweigh the intellectual ones. Another psychologist discovered this personally when her teenage son phoned to be picked up from a party that had "gotten out of hand." The boy heard

> his frustrated father lament "drinking and trouble—haven't you figured out the connection?" Despite the late hour and his shaky state, the teenager advanced a lengthy argument to the effect that his father had the causality all wrong and the trouble should be attributed to other covariates, among them bad luck.
>
> *[Kuhn & Franklin, 2006, p. 966]*

Answers	Intuitive (Incorrect)	Analytic (Correct)
1.	10 cents	5 cents
2.	100 minutes	5 minutes
3.	24 days	47 days

Better Thinking

Sometimes adults conclude that more mature thought processes are wiser, since they lead to caution (as in the father's connection between "drinking and trouble"). Adults are particularly critical when egocentrism makes an impulsive teenager risk future addiction by experimenting with drugs or risk pregnancy and AIDS by not using a condom.

But adults may themselves be egocentric in making such judgments if they assume that adolescents share their values. Parents want healthy, long-lived children, so they blame faulty reasoning when adolescents risk their lives. Adolescents, however, value social warmth and friendship, and their hormones and brains are more attuned to those values than to long-term consequences (Crone & Dahl, 2012).

A 15-year-old who is offered a cigarette, for example, might rationally choose peer acceptance and the possibility of romance over the distant risk of cancer. Think of a teenager who wants to be "cool" or "bad," and then decide how likely he or she is to say, "No thank you, my mother wouldn't approve."

Furthermore, weighing alternatives and thinking of possibilities can be paralyzing. The systematic, analytic thought that Piaget described is slow and costly, not fast and frugal, wasting precious time when a young person wants to act. Some risks are taken impulsively and foolishly.

Other risks are calculated in advance. The calculation may not be what the parents would do, but that does not mean the choice is not thought out (Maslowsky et al., 2011). Thus when parents discover that their child has done something contrary to the parents' wishes, it is not necessarily because the heat of the moment overwhelmed cool rationality; it could be that the child rejected the parents' directives after careful thought.

As the knowledge base increases and the brain matures, as impulses become less insistent and past experiences accumulate, both modes of thought become more forceful. With maturity, education, and conversation with those who disagree, adolescents are neither paralyzed by too much analysis nor plummeted into danger via intuition.

On average, logic increases from adolescence to adulthood (and then decreases somewhat in old age) (De Neys & Van Gelder, 2009; Kuhn, 2013). Always, however, the specific context, including superstitions and assumptions, makes a difference: We cannot assume that adolescent decisions are better than, or worse than, those of either children or adults (Furlan et al., 2013).

Thinking About Religion

As you remember from Chapter 1, scientists build on previous research or theories, replicating, extending, or refuting the work of others. Assumptions are questioned, empirical evidence is gathered to verify or criticize new theories and old cultural myths. This is a formal operational approach.

Some impressionistic descriptions of teenagers and religion (e.g., Flory & Miller, 2000) emphasize cults and sects. One observer reports that young congregants gather "dressed as they are, piercings and all, and express their commitment by means of hip-hop and rap music, multimedia presentations, body modification, and anything else that can be infused with religious meaning" (Ream & Savin-Williams, 2003, p. 51). Likewise, some television programs and movies depict innocent girls attracted to destructive, freakish, mesmerizing cults (Neal, 2011).

These stereotypes evoke emotions—the quick, intuitive responses that judge piercings and rap to be the antithesis of religious tradition. When another team of researchers began by "reading many published overview reports on adolescence . . . [they got] the distinct impression that American youth simply do not have religious or spiritual lives" (Smith, 2005, p. 4).

Seeking evidence, not impressions, they surveyed 3,360 13- to 17-year-olds and their parents and tallied quantitative results. Then they added qualitative depth by interviewing 287 teenagers privately, in long, structured conversations.

They found that most adolescents (71 percent) felt close to God. They believed in heaven, hell, and angels and affirmed the same religion as their parents. Some were agnostic (2 percent), and 16 percent said they were not religious—although many of those prayed and attended services and said their parents were not particularly religious, either. Less than 1 percent were "unconventional" (e.g., Wiccan), contrary to the accounts the researchers had read.

They also found that adolescents' religious beliefs were often egocentric: Faith was a personal tool to be used in times of difficulty (e.g., while taking an exam). Many (82 percent) claimed their beliefs were important in daily life. One boy explained that religion kept him from doing "bad things, like murder or something," and one girl said:

> [Religion] influences me a lot with the people I choose not to be around. I would not hang with people that are, you know, devil worshipers because that's just not my thing. I could not deal with that negativity.
>
> *[quoted in Smith, 2005, p. 139]*

The researchers doubt that "socializing with Satanists is a real issue in this girl's life" or that this boy "struggles with murderous tendencies" (Smith, 2005, p. 139). However, they also noted that few adolescents (less than 1 percent) used theology to guide them in the actual issues of daily life, such as seeking justice or loving one's neighbor. For most, religious beliefs were intuitive, not analytic.

As good developmentalists, the researchers surveyed the same individuals three years later. They found a "shifting away from conventional religious beliefs" (Denton et al., 2008, p. 3). This trend was confirmed by another study of Canadian undergraduates about the same age as the U.S. participants at follow-up. For them, religiosity decreased as analytic thinking increased (Gervais & Norenzayan, 2012).

But, despite less certainty about God, angels, or an afterlife, the older adolescents in the U.S. study tended to feel they had become more, not less, religious over the three-year period. One possible reason is that "as adolescents develop and mature, they take more ownership over their own beliefs and practices so that their religiosity feels stronger and more authentic" (Denton et al., 2008, p. 32). In other words, maturation, independence, and years of questioning may advance thinking about religion as well as about everything else.

Seeking a Higher Power Amidst the Depths Religious faith is very powerful for young Mormons, who are expected to spend a mission year at the end of adolescence. Rodney Mills and Robert Keach pray after preaching in Kensington, Philadelphia, a neighborhood of heroin addicts, male and female sex workers, prescription drug sellers, and, in 2010, a serial killer who specialized in strangling prostitutes. All emerging adults seek the meaning of life; obviously some answers are more powerful than others.

JONATHAN WILSON/MCT/LANDOV

What does this imply for adults who hope to instill values in the next generation? In many ways, these data are encouraging: Most adolescents adhere to the faith of their parents. However, the authors wish that adults would encourage teenagers to discuss complex spiritual issues (e.g., stewardship of the environment, poverty, implications of scriptures). This would require parents and church leaders themselves to engage their analytic processes.

Dual Processing and the Brain

The brain maturation described in Chapter 14 seems directly related to the dual processes just explained. Because the limbic system is activated by puberty but the prefrontal cortex matures more gradually, it is easy to understand why adolescents are swayed by their intuition instead of by analysis.

Since adolescent brains respond quickly and deeply to social rejection, teens readily follow impulses that promise social approval. In experiments in which adults and adolescents, alone or with peers, play video games in which taking risks might lead to crashes or gaining points, adolescents are much more likely than adults are to risk crashing, especially when they are with peers (Albert et al., 2013) (see Figure 15.3).

This explains why motor-vehicle accidents in adolescence result in more deaths per vehicle than crashes in adulthood: Teenage drivers often have many friends in the car whose admiration they seek by speeding, passing trucks, beating the train at the railroad crossing, and so on.

Per mile driven, drivers under 20 have fatal crashes about ten times more often than adults do. Don't blame this only on inexperience; blame it on the need for acclaim. Some states now prohibit teen drivers from transporting other teenagers, a law that reduces deaths even as it bans one activity that adolescents enjoy.

Risk-taking experiments show notable differences in brain activity (specifically in the *ventral striatum*) between adolescents and adults. When they are with other adults, the adults' brains give more signals of caution (inhibition)—opposite to adolescents' brains when they are with peers (Albert et al., 2013).

Because experiments that include brain scans are expensive, they rarely include many participants. However, less-costly research methods confirm these results.

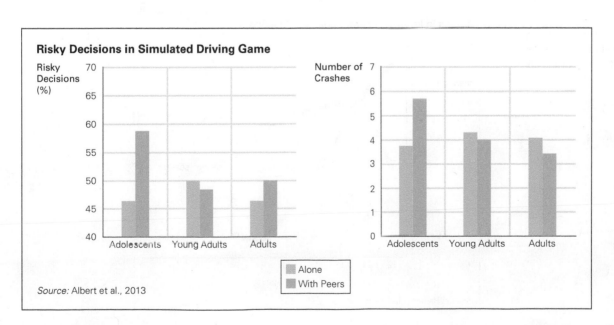

Risky Decisions in Simulated Driving Game

Source: Albert et al., 2013

Alone
With Peers

FIGURE 15.3

Losing Is Winning In this game, risk-taking led to more crashes and fewer points. As you see, adolescents were strongly influenced by the presence of peers, so much so that they lost points they would have kept if they had played alone. In fact, sometimes they laughed when they crashed, instead of bemoaning their loss. Note the contrast with emerging adults, who were more likely to take risks when alone.

One longitudinal survey repeatedly queried more than 7,000 adolescents, beginning at age 12 and ending at age 24, about their ideas, activities, and plans.

The results of that survey were "consistent with neurobiological research indicating that cortical regions involved in impulse control and planning continue to mature through early adulthood [and that] subcortical regions that respond to emotional novelty and reward are more responsive in middle adolescence than in either children or adults" (Harden & Tucker-Drob, 2011, p. 743).

Specifically, this longitudinal survey traced sensation seeking (e.g., "I enjoy new and exciting experiences") from early adolescence to the mid-20s. Increases were notable from ages 12 to 14 (see Figure 15.4). Sensation seeking leads to intuitive thinking, direct from the gut to the brain.

The researchers also studied impulsivity, as indicated by agreement with statements such as "I often get in a jam because I do things without thinking." A decline in impulsive action occurs as analytic thinking increases.

On average, sensation seeking accelerated rapidly at puberty, and both sensation seeking and impulsivity slowly decline with maturation. However, trajectories varied individually: Sensation seeking did not necessarily correlate with impulsivity. Thus, biology (the HPA system) is not necessarily linked to experience (the prefrontal cortex) (Harden & Tucker-Drob, 2011). Both affect behavior: Risky sex correlates with both sensation seeking and with impulsivity (Charnigo et al., 2013), but each has an independent impact.

For example, hormone rushes in two adolescents might produce intense and identical drives for sex, but one teenager might have learned (directly or indirectly) to curb desire, while the other has had the opposite experiences. For the first, impulsivity would decline rapidly, as practice at saying no increases. This would not be true for the second adolescent, who would seek sexual pleasure as seen on a video, heard from a friend, or experienced before. Thus, both might experience equal sensation-seeking impulses, but their impulses would diverge.

A practical application of this research comes from a program that teaches middle school students to avoid dating violence, both physical (e.g., hitting, kicking, pushing) and emotional (e.g., name-calling, put-downs, spreading rumors) (Peskin et al., 2014). Five middle schools in Texas were assigned a special curriculum that stressed healthy sexual relationships. Homework required discussions with parents.

FIGURE 15.4

Look Before You Leap As you can see, adolescents become less impulsive as they mature, but they still enjoy the thrill of a new sensation.

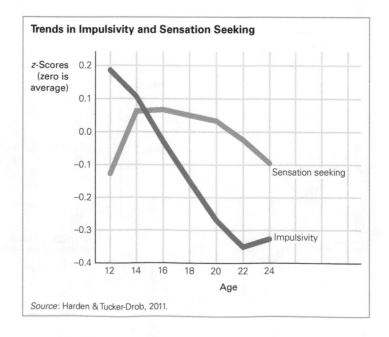

Trends in Impulsivity and Sensation Seeking

Source: Harden & Tucker-Drob, 2011.

A similar group of five other Texas schools had health classes as usual. The intervention reduced dating violence three years later, from 32 percent in the control group to 24 percent in the intervention group (Peskin et al., 2014). In other words, the classroom and parent discussions ("cold processing") allowed the more reflective part of the students' brains to grow—and lessened impulsive, "hot" cognition in intimate settings.

SUMMING UP Current research recognizes that there are at least two modes of cognition, here called intuitive reasoning and analytical thought, although many other terms indicate two similar pairs. Intuitive thinking is experiential, quick, and impulsive, unlike formal operational thought. Both forms develop during adolescence. Sometimes intuitive processes crowd out analytic ones because emotions overwhelm logic, especially when adolescents are together. Each form of thinking is appropriate in some contexts. The capacity for logical, reflective thinking increases with neurological maturation, as the prefrontal cortex matures.

WHAT HAVE YOU LEARNED?

1. When might intuition and analysis lead to contrasting conclusions?
2. What mode of thinking—intuitive or analytic—do most people prefer, and why?
3. How does personal experience increase the probability of base rate neglect?
4. How does egocentrism account for the clashing priorities of parents and adolescents?
5. When is intuitive thinking better than analytic thinking?
6. How can it be that adolescents attend services less often but claim to be more spiritual as they age?
7. What is the relationship between adolescent brain development and the two modes of thought?

Digital Natives

Adults over age 40 grew up without the Internet, instant messaging, Twitter, Snapchat, blogs, cell phones, smartphones, MP3 players, tablets, or digital cameras. At first, the Internet was only for the military, then primarily for businesses and the educated elite. Until 2006, only students at elite colleges could join Facebook.

In contrast, today's teenagers have been called *digital natives,* although if that term implies that they know everything about digital communication, it is a misnomer (boyd, 2014). There is no doubt, however, that today's adolescents have been networking, texting, and clicking for definitions, directions, and data all their lives. Their cell phones are within reach, day and night.

A huge gap between those with and without computers was bemoaned a decade ago; it divided boys from girls and rich from poor (Dijk, 2005; Norris, 2001). Now that *digital divide* is shrinking.

In developed nations, virtually every school and library is connected to the Internet, as are many in developing nations. This opens up new ideas and allows access to like-minded people, both especially important for teens who feel isolated within their communities, such as those with Down syndrome, or who are gay, or deaf, or simply at odds with their neighbors in beliefs or priorities.

As costs tumble, the device that has been particularly important at creating digital natives among low-SES adolescents of every ethnic group is the smartphone, used primarily to connect with friends (Madden et al., 2013). Connection to peers has always been important to teenagers, and has always been feared by adults—who in earlier generations feared that the automobile, or the shopping mall, or rock and roll, would lead their children astray.

Although discrepancies in number and quality of devices still follow SES lines, the most notable digital divide is now age: Each older generation is less likely to use the Internet than the next younger one. That may explain why people bemoaning the effects of technology on adolescent minds tend to be over age 50.

Not Isolating Adults sometimes think that technology encourages social isolation. Not true: Adolescents use cell phones to connect with each other. Who are these girls texting? The answer might be "each other."

OBSERVATION QUIZ Beyond the smartphones, what two signs of adolescent conformity are apparent? (see answer, page 492)

Technology and Cognition

In general, educators accept, even welcome, students' facility with technology. In many high schools, teachers use laptops, smartphones, and so on as tools for learning. In some districts, students are required to take at least one class completely online. There are "virtual" schools, in which students earn all their credits online, never entering a school building, and in Maine all high school students have laptops (Silvernail et al., 2011).

Some programs and games have been designed for high school classes. For example, ten teachers were taught how to use a game (*Mission Biotech*) to teach genetics and molecular biology. Their students—even in advanced classes but especially in general education—scored higher on tests of the standard biology curriculum than students who did not use the game (Sadler et al., 2013). This suggests that, when carefully used, computer games can enhance learning.

Remember that research before the technology explosion found that instruction, practice, conversation, and experience advance adolescent thought. Social networking via technology may speed up this process, as teens communicate daily with dozens—perhaps even hundreds or thousands—of "friends" via e-mail, texting, and cell phone.

Most secondary students check facts, read explanations, view videos, and thus grasp concepts they would not have understood without technology. For some adolescents, the Internet is their only source of information about health and sex. Almost every high school student in the United States uses the Internet for research, finding it quicker and its range of information more extensive than books on library shelves.

A major concern is that adolescents do not evaluate what they see on the screen as carefully as they should, nor understand the implications of sending a message on impulse. Messages endure, and can be seen by hundreds, sometimes thousands, of unintended recipients, sometimes with unanticipated harm to others or oneself (boyd, 2014).

Teachers use the Internet not only for research and assignments but also to judge whether or not a student's paper is plagiarized. Educators claim that the most difficult aspect of technology is teaching students how to evaluate sources, some reputable, some nonsensical. To this end, teachers explain the significance of .com, .org, .edu, and .gov (O'Hanlon, 2013).

In Maine, giving each student a laptop to use in school seems a cost-effective way to advance learning; however, even when students have laptops, some teachers are better at online instruction than others (Silvernail et al., 2011).

A New Addiction?

Parents worry about sexual abuse via the Internet. Research is reassuring: Although sexual predators lurk online, most teens never encounter them. Sexual abuse is a serious problem, but if sexual abuse is defined as a perverted older stranger taking advantage of an innocent teenager, it is "extremely rare" (Mitchell et al., 2013, p. 1226).

Between 2000 and 2010, percent of teenagers who say that someone online tried to get them to talk about sex declined from 10 percent to 1 percent. Those 1 percent were almost always solicited by another young person whom the teenager knew in person—a Facebook friend, for instance (Mitchell et al., 2013).

Teenagers are actually more suspicious of strangers than they were before the Internet, partly because parents and the police have alerted them to the danger. A Web-based program to teach children how to recognize and avoid sex abuse seems to have had some benefit (Müller et al., 2014). However, such programs may reassure adults more than help teenagers. As one review asserts:

> Our data suggest that it would be beneficial for policy-makers and youth-serving professionals, including educators, law enforcement, and mental health personnel, to help youth in general improve healthy sexual and relationship decision-making, improving efforts to communicate with friends, being more assertive, and becoming more skilled at refusing solicitations instead of focusing on specific Internet behaviors.
>
> *[Mitchell et al., 2013, p. 1233]*

As the next chapter explains, teenagers have much to learn about sex and self-protection.

These myth-busting facts do not mean that unwanted harassment is no problem. Ten years after high school, former bullies and victims—online or offline, sexual or otherwise—are less likely to have graduated from college and less likely to have good jobs or any job at all (Sigurdson et al., 2014). Parents and teachers need to worry less about protecting teenagers against older online predators and worry more about the teenagers who victimize each other.

Even when no social harm occurs, technology may present some dangers, however. It encourages rapid shifts of attention, multitasking without reflection, and visual learning instead of invisible analysis (Greenfield, 2009). Video games with violent content promote aggression (Gentile, 2011).

For some adolescents, chat rooms, video games, and Internet gambling are considered addictive, taking time from active play, schoolwork, and friendship. For teenagers with a troubled family life, Internet addiction is considered a problem worldwide, particularly in China (Tang et al., 2014).

This is not mere speculation. A study of almost two thousand older children and adolescents in the United States found that the *average* person played video games two hours a day. Some played much more, and only 3 percent of the boys

FIGURE 15.5

More Than Eating The average adolescent boy spends more time playing video games than reading, eating, doing homework, talking with friends, playing sports, or almost anything else except sleeping or sitting in class. Indeed, some skip school or postpone sleep to finish a game.

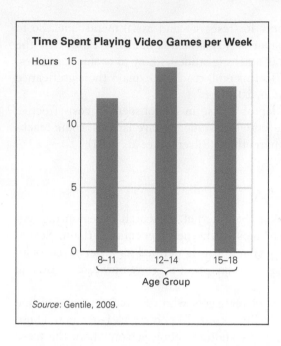

Time Spent Playing Video Games per Week

Source: Gentile, 2009.

and 21 percent of the girls never played (Gentile, 2011) (see Figure 15.5). Another survey found that almost one-third of all high school students use technology more than three hours a day (this does not include using computers at school), with use higher among boys and non-whites (MMWR, June 8, 2012). The rate has been increasing steadily since 1990.

At what point and for whom does this become truly addictive instead of normal teen behavior? Many adolescents in the first survey admit that video-game playing takes time away from household chores and homework. Worse, one-fourth used video games to escape from problems, and one-fifth had "done poorly on a school assignment or test" because of spending too much time on video games. The heaviest users got lower school grades and had more physical fights than did the average users (Gentile, 2011).

Using criteria for addiction developed by psychiatrists for other addictions (gambling, drugs, and so on), one study found that 12 percent of the boys and 3 percent of the girls were addicted to playing video games. However, correlation is not causation: Perhaps low school achievement led to video game playing rather than vice versa. Some scholars worry that adults tend to pathologize normal teen behavior, once again particularly in China, where rehabilitation centers are strict—some would say abusive—in keeping teenagers from Internet use (Bax, 2014).

Studies in many nations judge a sizable minority of high school students (e.g., 15 percent in Turkey, 12 percent in India) as "addicted" to computer use (Şaşmaz et al., 2014; Yadav et al., 2013). Reviewing research from many nations, one team of researchers report addiction rates from 0 to 26 percent. The variation was caused more by differing definitions and procedures among researchers than by differences among students in any particular place (Y. Lee et al., 2014).

The fear that the Internet may undercut school achievement seems justified, however. A study began with younger boys whose parents intended to buy them a video game system. (Such a study could not have been done with adolescents, because almost all adolescents who want to play games online already have the equipment to do so.) Randomly, half of them were given the system, and the other half had to wait four months. Those who immediately received the video game system had lower reading and writing achievement after four months than did their peers who waited (Weis & Cerankosky, 2010).

Most screen time occurs in the child's own bedroom. About half of all parents place no restrictions on technology use, as long as their adolescent is safe at home. Other parents place many restrictions on their children—not only regarding technology, but on contact with peers, either at home or in a public place (such as a movie theater or store). To socialize, some teens have no choice but to text or log in when their parents are not watching (boyd, 2014).

Some suggest that technology should be banned from schools and bedrooms, but, as one critic writes, "we don't ban pencils and paper because students pass

// ANSWER TO OBSERVATION QUIZ
(from page 490) Hair and jeans. A few decades ago, if girls wore jeans, they might be black or green, and hair was curly. But now, at least for these three at a Texas high school, jeans must be blue and tight, and hair straight and long—with a visible part. Texas girls may have once slept with curlers in their hair; now some iron their hair every morning to straighten it.

notes" (Shuler, 2009, p. 35). Some teachers confiscate computers and cell phones used in class, others ignore them, and still others include them in the curriculum.

Whether extensive use of the Internet qualifies as an addiction is controversial. The psychiatrists who wrote the new DSM-5, after careful consideration of the evidence, did *not* include it as an addiction. They decided that further study was needed.

Cyber Danger

Now let us focus on the danger from Internet use that seems most valid. When a person is bullied via electronic devices, usually via social media, text messages, or cell phone videos, that is **cyberbullying** (Tokunaga, 2010). The adolescents most involved in cyberbullying are usually already bullies or victims or both, with bully-victims especially likely to engage in, and suffer from, cyberbullying. (**Developmental Link:** Bullying is discussed in Chapter 13.) Technology does not create bullies; it gives them another means to act and a larger audience, which multiplies the harm (Kowalski et al., 2014).

> **cyberbullying** Bullying that occurs when one person spreads insults or rumors about another by means of social media posts, e-mails, text messages, or cell phone videos.

Fake Face in Georgia Alex stands behind a phony Facebook page that portrays her as a racist, sexually active drug user. She is 14, a late developer, which may be why she became a cyberbullying target. Also shown are her parents, Amy and Chris Boston, who are suing her classmates for libel. No matter what happens in court, the worst has already happened: Alex thought those girls were her friends.

Worst in Adolescence

Texted and posted rumors and insults can "go viral," reaching thousands, transmitted day and night. The imaginary audience magnifies the shame. Not only words but also photos and videos can be easily sent: Some adolescents take video of others drunk, naked, or crying and send that to dozens of others, who may send it to yet others, who may post it on YouTube or Vine. Since young adolescents are impulsive and low on judgment, cyberbullying is particularly prevalent and sometimes thoughtlessly cruel between ages 11 and 14.

While the causes of all forms of bullying are similar, each form has its own sting: Cyberbullying may be worst when the victim believes in the imaginary audience, when the identity is forming, when sexual impulses are new, and when impulsive thoughts precede analytic ones—all of which are characteristic of many young adolescents.

Adolescent victims are likely to suffer from depression, because cyberbullying adds to the typical rise in depression that occurs at puberty. In extreme cases, cyberbullying may be the final straw that triggers suicide (Bonanno & Hymel, 2013).

The school climate affects all forms of bullying. When students consider school a good place to be—with supportive teachers, friendly students, opportunities for growth (clubs, sports, theater, music), and the like—those with high self-esteem are less likely to engage in cyberbullying and more likely to disapprove of it. That reduces incidence. However, when the school climate is negative, those with high self-esteem are often bullies (Gendron et al., 2011).

Some people believe that cyberbullying is unstoppable. Nonetheless, teens themselves use successful strategies, such as deleting messages from bullies (Parris et al., 2012). As with other forms of bullying, cyberbullies and victims are influenced by the context, which can make it more or less harmful (Kowalski et al., 2014).

One complication is that most adolescents trust technology while many adults ignore it. Parents often are unaware of cyberbullying, and few laws and policies successfully prevent it. Some school administrators insist they cannot stop cyberbullying because it does not emanate from school computers. However, cyberbullying usually occurs among classmates and can poison the school climate, and thus educators must be concerned. Adolescents are vulnerable; they need more protection than most adults realize (boyd, 2014).

Sexting

The vulnerability of adolescence was tragically evident in the suicide of a California 15-year-old, Audrie Pott (Sulek, 2013). At a sleepover, Audrie and her friends found alcohol. She got so drunk that she blacked out, or passed out. When she came to, she realized she had been raped. On the next school day, three boys in her school were bragging that they had had sex with her, showing pictures to classmates. The next weekend, Audrie hanged herself. Only then did her parents learn what had happened.

One aspect of this tragedy will come as no surprise to adolescents: "sexting," as sending sexual photographs is called. As many as 30 percent of adolescents re-

Something Worth Sharing
But what is it? Is it the same as boys everywhere, or is it something specific to their culture? The four are in England: We do not know if they see a football (soccer) score, a prime minister's proclamation, or a sexy female.

port having received sexting photos, with marked variation by school, gender, and ethnicity and often in attitude: Many teens send their own sexy "selfies" and are happy to receive sext messages (Temple et al., 2014). As with Internet addiction, researchers have yet to agree on how to measure sexting or how harmful it is.

There are evidently two dangers: (1) pictures may be forwarded without the naked person's knowledge, and (2) senders who deliberately send erotic self-images risk serious depression if the reaction is not what they wished (Temple et al., 2014). Remember that body image formation is crucial during early adolescence, and that many teens have distorted self-concepts—no wonder sexting is fraught with trouble.

Other Hazards

Internet connections allow troubled adolescents to connect with others who share their prejudices and self-destructive obsessions, such as anorexia or cutting. The people they connect with are those who confirm and inform their twisted cognition. This is another reason parents and teachers need to continue their close relationships with their adolescents. Note the absence of parents at Audrie's alcoholic sleepover, rape, cyberbullying, and suicide. (Parent–child relationships are a central theme of the next chapter.)

The danger of all forms of technology lies not in the equipment but in the cognition of the user. As is true of many aspects of adolescence (puberty, brain development, egocentric thought, use of contraception, and so on), context, adults, peers, and the adolescent's own personality and temperament "shape, mediate, and/or modify effects" of technology (Oakes, 2009, p. 1142).

One careful observer claims that instead of being *native* users of technology, many teenager are *naïve* users. They believe they have privacy settings that they do not have, trust sites that are markedly biased, misunderstand how to search for and verify information (boyd, 2014).

Educators can help with all this—but only if they themselves understand technology and teens. Teens are intuitive, impulsive, and egocentric, often unaware of the impact of what they send or overestimating the validity of what they read. Adults should know better, but everyone is sometimes illogical and emotional: We all need time and experience to use technology wisely.

SUMMING UP   In fostering adolescent cognition, technology has many positive aspects: A computer is a tool for learning and providing information far more specific and wide-ranging than any teacher could. Further, online connections promote social outreach and reduce isolation, especially for those who feel marginalized. Friends often connect via texting and e-mail, and social-networking sites expand the social circle. However, technology also has a dark side, especially evident in cyberbullying, sexting, and video game addiction. This negative aspect of technology can interfere with education and friendship rather than enhance them.

WHAT HAVE YOU LEARNED?
1.   What benefits come from adolescents' use of technology?
2.   Why is adult fear of online adult predators exaggerated?
3.   How do video games affect student learning?
4.   Who is most and least involved in cyberbullying?
5.   Why might sexting be a problem?
6.   In what way is the term "digital native" valid and how is it misleading?

Teaching and Learning

What does our knowledge of adolescent thought imply about school? Educators, developmentalists, political leaders, and parents wonder exactly which curricula and school structures are best for 11- to 18-year-olds. There are dozens of options: academic knowledge/vocational skills, single sex/co-ed, competitive/cooperative, large/small, public/private, religious/secular, charter/voucher, and more.

To complicate matters, adolescents are far from a homogeneous group. As a result,

> some youth thrive at school—enjoying and benefiting from most of their experiences there; others muddle along and cope as best they can with the stress and demands of the moment; and still others find school an alienating and unpleasant place to be.
>
> [Eccles & Roeser, 2011, p. 225]

Given all these variations, no single school structure or style of pedagogy seems best for everyone. Various scientists, nations, schools, and teachers try many strategies, some based on opposite but logical hypotheses. To begin to analyze this complexity, we present definitions, facts, issues, and possibilities.

Definitions and Facts

Each year of schooling advances human potential, a fact recognized by leaders and scholars in every nation and discipline. As you have read, adolescents are capable of deep and wide-ranging thought, no longer limited by concrete experience, yet they are often egocentric and impulsive, and their thinking intuitive. The quality of education matters: A year can propel thinking forward or can have little impact (Hanushek & Woessmann, 2010).

secondary education Literally, the period after primary education (elementary or grade school) and before tertiary education (college). It usually occurs from about ages 12 to 18, although there is some variation by school and by nation.

Secondary education—traditionally grades 7 through 12—denotes the school years after elementary or grade school (known as *primary education*) and before college or university (known as *tertiary education*). Adults are healthier and wealthier if they complete primary education, learning to read and write, and then continue on through secondary and tertiary education. This is true within nations and between them.

Even cigarette-smoking by European American adults—seemingly unrelated to education—is almost three times as common among those with no high school diploma than it is among those with BA degrees (40 percent versus 15 percent, respectively) (National Center for Health Statistics, 2013).

These cigarette data are typical: Data on almost every condition, from every nation and ethnic group, confirm that high school and college graduation correlates with better health, wealth, and family life. Some reasons are indirectly related to education (e.g., income and place of residence), but even when poverty and toxic neighborhoods are equalized, education confers benefits.

Partly because political leaders recognize that educated adults advance national wealth and health, every nation is increasing the number of students in secondary schools. Education is compulsory until at least age 12 almost everywhere, and new high schools and colleges open daily in developing nations.

The two most populous countries, China and India, are characterized by massive growth in education. In India, for example, less than 1 percent of the population graduated from high school in 1950; the 2002 rate was 37 percent; the 2010 rate was 50 percent; now it is even higher (Bagla & Stone, 2013).

In many nations, two levels of secondary education are provided. Traditionally, secondary education was divided into junior high (usually grades 7 and 8) and senior high (usually grades 9 through 12). As the average age of puberty declined, **middle schools** were created for grades 6 to 8, and sometimes for grades 5 to 8.

Middle School

Adjusting to middle school is bound to be stressful, as teachers, classmates, and expectations all change. Regarding learning, "researchers and theorists commonly view early adolescence as an especially sensitive developmental period" (McGill et al., 2012, p. 1003). Yet many developmentalists find middle schools to be "developmentally regressive" (Eccles & Roeser, 2010, p. 13), which means learning goes backward.

> **middle school** A school for children in the grades between elementary and high school. Middle school usually begins with grade 6 and ends with grade 8.

Same Situation, Far Apart: No Romance Here Young adolescents around the globe, such as these in California (*left*) and Pakistan (*right*), attend middle school, but what they learn differs. Many North American schools encourage collaboration and hands-on learning (these girls are dissecting a squid), whereas many South Asian schools stress individual writing. Both classrooms are single-sex—unusual in the United States but standard in many developing nations. What do students learn from that?

Increasing Behavioral Problems

For many middle school students, academic achievement slows down and behavioral problems increase. Puberty itself is part of the problem. At least for other animals studied, especially when they are under stress, learning is reduced at puberty (McCormick et al., 2010).

For people, the biological and psychological stresses of puberty are not the only reason learning suffers in early adolescence. Cognition matters, too: How much new middle school students like their school affects how much they learn (Riglin et al., 2013).

A longitudinal study found a decline in school interests and grades from age 7 to 16, with a notable dip in the transition to middle school (Dotterer et al., 2009). African American and Latino middle school students particularly seem less engaged in school (McGill et al., 2012; Hayes et al., 2014). Students become aware of expectations for them in the larger community. This makes the decline in academics particularly steep for young adolescents of ethnic minorities.

Unfortunately, many students of every group have reasons to dislike middle school compared to elementary school. Bullying is common in middle school, particularly in the first year (Baly et al., 2014). Middle schools undercut student–teacher relationships (Meece & Eccles, 2010), and parents are less involved, partly because students want to seem independent.

> **Especially for Teachers** You are stumped by a question your student asks. What do you do? (see response, page 499)

Unlike primary school, when each classroom has one teacher all year, middle school teachers may have hundreds of students. They become impersonal and distant, opposite to the direct, personal engagement that young adolescents need.

a case to study

James, the High-Achieving Dropout

A longitudinal study in Massachusetts followed children from preschool through high school. James was one of the most promising. In his early school years, he was an excellent reader whose mother took great pride in him, her only child. Once James entered middle school, however, something changed:

> Although still performing well academically, James began acting out. At first his actions could be described as merely mischievous, but later he engaged in much more serious acts, such as drinking and fighting, which resulted in his being suspended from school.
>
> *[Snow et al., 2007, p. 59]*

Family problems increased. James and his father blamed each other for their poor relationship, and his mother bragged "about how independent James was for being able to be left alone to fend for himself," while James "described himself as isolated and closed off" (Snow et al., 2007, p. 59).

James said, "The kids were definitely afraid of me but that didn't stop them" from associating with him (Snow et al., 2007, p. 59). James's experience is not unusual. Generally, aggressive and drug-using students are admired in middle school more than those who are conscientious and studious—a marked difference from elementary school (Rubin et al., 2013). Students dislike those who are unlike them, which may mean general antipathy toward those who excel (Laursen et al., 2010). Some adolescents sacrifice academics to avoid social exclusion.

This is not true only for African American boys like James. There is "an abundance of evidence of middle school declines on a number of academic outcomes" (McGill et al., 2012). There is also evidence that middle school achievement predicts which students will graduate from high school and then who will go to college (Center for Education Policy, 2012).

Although girls' achievement also declines in middle school, they are less likely to quit than boys. For the past four decades (since 1977) in the United States and in many other nations, fewer boys have graduated from high school than girls. As a result, according to U.S. data for 2011, males ages 16 to 24 were 18 percent more likely than females to leave high school before graduation (National Center for Education Statistics, 2013c).

At the end of primary school, James planned to go to college; in middle school, he said he had "a complete lack of motivation"; in tenth grade, he dropped out.

As was true for James, the early signs of a future high school dropout are found in middle school. Those students most at risk of leaving before graduation are low-SES boys from minority ethnic groups, yet almost no middle school has male guidance counselors or teachers who are African American or Latino. Given the egocentric and intuitive thinking of many young adolescents, they may stop trying to achieve if they do not see role models of successful, educated men (Morris & Morris, 2013).

Finding Acclaim

To pinpoint the developmental mismatch between students' needs and the middle school context, note that just when egocentrism leads young people to feelings of shame or fantasies of stardom (the imaginary audience), schools typically require them to change rooms, teachers, and classmates every 40 minutes or so. That makes both public acclaim and supportive new friendships difficult to achieve.

Recognition for academic excellence is especially elusive because middle school teachers mark more harshly than their primary school counterparts. Effort without accomplishment is not recognized, and achievement that was earlier "outstanding" is now only average. Acclaim for after-school activities is also elusive, because many art, drama, dance, and other programs put adolescents of all ages together, and 11- to 13-year-olds are not as skilled as older adolescents. Finally, athletic teams become competitive; those with fragile egos avoid them.

Many middle school students seek acceptance from their peers. Bullying increases, physical appearance becomes more important, status symbols are displayed (from gang colors to trendy sunglasses), expensive clothes are coveted, and sexual conquests are flaunted. Of course, much depends on the cultural context, but almost every middle school student seeks peer approval in ways that adults disapprove (Véronneau & Dishion, 2010), a topic further discussed in the next chapter.

Coping with Middle School

One way to cope with stress is directly cognitive, that is, to blame classmates, teachers, parents, or governments for any problems. This may explain the surprising results of a Los Angeles study: Students in schools that were *more* ethnically mixed felt safer and *less* lonely. They did not necessarily have friends from other groups, but students who felt rejected could "attribute their plight to the prejudice of other people" rather than blame themselves (Juvonen et al., 2006, p. 398). Furthermore, since each group was a minority, the students tended to support and defend other members of their group, giving each individual some ethnic allies.

Another way middle school students avoid failure is to quit trying. Then they can blame a low grade on their choice ("I didn't study") rather than on their ability. Pivotal is how they think of their potential.

If they hold to the **entity theory of intelligence** (i.e., that ability is innate, a fixed quantity present at birth), then they conclude that nothing they do can improve their academic skill. If they think they are innately incompetent at math, or reading, or whatever, they mask that self-assessment by claiming not to study, try, or care. Thus, entity belief reduces stress, but it also reduces learning.

By contrast, if adolescents adopt the **incremental theory of intelligence** (i.e., that intelligence can increase if they work to master whatever they seek to understand), they will pay attention, participate in class, study, complete their homework, and learn. That is also called *mastery motivation,* an example of intrinsic motivation. (**Developmental Link:** Intrinsic and extrinsic motivation are discussed in Chapter 10; stereotype threat in the epilogue.)

This is not hypothetical. In the first year of middle school, students with entity beliefs do not achieve much, whereas those with mastery motivation improve academically, as found in many nations including Norway (Diseth et al., 2014), China (Zhao & Wang, 2014), and the United States (Burnette et al., 2013).

The implicit belief that skills can be mastered is crucial for learning social skills as well as academic ones (Dweck, 2013). Students are highly motivated to improve their peer relationships. Adults need to convince them that improvement is possible, and then guide them. That advances academic as well as social skills.

The contrast between the entity and incremental theories is apparent not only for individual adolescents but also for teachers, parents, schools, and cultures. If the hidden curriculum endorses competition among students and tells some students they are not "college material," then everyone believes the entity theory, and students are unlikely to help each other (Eccles & Roeser, 2011). If a teacher believes that some children cannot learn much, then they won't.

International comparisons reveal that educational systems that track students into higher or lower classes, that expel low-achieving students, and that allow competition between schools for the brightest students (all reflecting entity, not incremental, theory) also show lower average achievement and a larger gap between the scores of students at the highest and lowest score quartiles (OECD, 2011).

// **Response for Teachers** (from page 497): Praise a student by saying, "What a great question!" Egos are fragile, so it's best to always validate the question. Seek student engagement, perhaps asking whether any classmates know the answer or telling the student to discover the answer online or saying you will find out. Whatever you do, don't fake it; if students lose faith in your credibility, you may lose them completely.

entity theory of intelligence An approach to understanding intelligence that sees ability as innate, a fixed quantity present at birth; those who hold this view do not believe that effort enhances achievement.

incremental theory of intelligence An approach to understanding intelligence that holds that intelligence can be directly increased by effort; those who subscribe to this view believe they can master whatever they seek to learn if they pay attention, participate in class, study, complete their homework, and so on.

Especially for Middle School Teachers You think your lectures are interesting and you know you care about your students, yet many of them cut class, come late, or seem to sleep through it. What do you do? (see response, page 503)

Same Situation, Far Apart: How to Learn Although developmental psychologists find that adolescents learn best when they are actively engaged with ideas, most teenagers are easier to control when they are taking tests (*top,* Winston-Salem, North Carolina, United States) or reciting scripture (*bottom,* Kabul, Afghanistan).

Especially for High School Teachers You are much more interested in the nuances and controversies than in the basic facts of your subject, but you know that your students will take high-stakes tests on the basics and that their scores will have a major impact on their futures. What should you do? (see response, page 504)

> **high-stakes test** An evaluation that is critical in determining success or failure. If a single test determines whether a student will graduate or be promoted, it is a high-stakes test.

High School

Many of the patterns and problems of middle school continue in high school, although with puberty over, adolescents are better able to cope. As we have seen, adolescents become increasingly able to think abstractly, analytically, hypothetically, and logically (all formal operational thought) as well as subjectively, emotionally, intuitively, and experientially. High school curricula and teaching methods often require the former mode.

The College-Bound

From a developmental perspective, the fact that high schools emphasize formal thinking makes sense, since many older adolescents are capable of abstract logic.

In several nations, attempts are underway to raise standards so that all high school graduates will be ready for college. For that reason, U.S. schools are increasing the number of students who take classes that are assessed by externally scored exams, either the IB (International Baccalaureate) or the AP (Advanced Placement).

Such classes satisfy some college requirements if the student scores well. More and more students are taking AP and IB classes: 33 percent of high school graduates did so in 2013, compared to 19 percent in 2003 (Adams, 2014).

Some students are discouraged from taking the AP exams, and those who avoid taking AP classes are often African or Latino American. Some students who might pass do not enroll—because the class is not offered, the student is not motivated or encouraged, or the cost of the test ($91) is prohibitive.

Another problem is that taking an AP class does not necessarily lead to college readiness (Sadler et al., 2010). One study showed that overall, almost a third of those who took the exam failed. Failure rates were higher among African Americans, lower among Latino and Asian Americans (Adams, 2014). The IB is less common, but again, few receive the highest scores.

Students who score well on AP or IB tests tend to do well in college. Since students who are capable and motivated, and who have college-educated parents, are most likely to take advanced high school courses, later success in college may be the result of who they are, not what they have learned (Challenge Success, 2013).

Of course, AP and IB exams are not the only measure of high school rigor. Another indicator is an increase in the requirements to receive an academic diploma. (In many U.S. schools, no one is allowed to earn a vocational or general diploma unless parents request it.) Graduation requirements usually include two years of math beyond algebra, two years of laboratory science, three years of history, and four years of English. Learning a language other than English is often required as well. Standards within those classes have often been raised by the Common Core, accepted by some, not all, high schools.

In addition to mandated courses, 24 U.S. states now also require students to pass a **high-stakes test** in order to graduate. (Any exam for which the consequences of failing are severe is called a high-stakes test.) A decade ago no state had such a test as a graduation requirement. Because the more populous states more often have high-stakes tests, 74 percent of U.S. high school students must take exit exams before graduation. This requirement is controversial, as the following explains.

opposing perspectives

Testing

Secondary students in the United States take many more tests than they did even a decade ago. This includes many high-stakes tests—not only tests to earn a high school diploma, but also tests to get into college (the SAT and ACT, achievement and aptitude) and tests to earn college credits while in high school.

Testing begins long before high school: Many students take high-stakes tests to pass third, fifth, and eighth grades, and some take tests to enter special kindergarten classes. Further, the Common Core, explained in Chapter 12, requires testing in reading and math, and will do so soon in science, history, and geography.

All tests may be high stakes for teachers, who can earn extra pay or lose their job based on how their students score, and for schools, which may gain resources or be closed because of test scores. Even entire school systems are rated on test scores, and this is said to be one reason widespread cheating occurred in Atlanta beginning in 2009 (Severson & Blinder, 2014).

Opposing perspectives on testing are voiced within many schools, parent groups, and state legislatures. In 2013, Alabama dropped its high-stakes test for graduation while Pennsylvania instituted such a test. In the same year Texas reduced the number of tests required for graduation from 15 (the result of a 2007 law) to 5 (Robelen, 2013). At the same time, Texas instituted rigorous standards for entering high school, to be assessed in tests of eighth graders beginning in 2021.

Overall, high school graduation rates in the United States have increased every year for the past decade, reaching 80 percent in 2012 (see Figure 15.6). Some say that tests and standards are part of the reason, but the data suggest that the high-stakes tests may actually discourage some students while making graduation too easy for others who have not done well in their classes (Hyslop, 2014).

Students who fail exams are often those with designated learning disabilities, one-third of whom do not graduate (Samuels, 2013), and those from low-income households who attend less rigorous schools. Some argue that the tests punish students, when the real culprit is the school, the community, or the entire nation. Passing graduation exit exams does not correlate with excellence in college, but failing them increases the risk of harm—including prison later on (Baker & Lang, 2013).

A panel of experts found that too much testing reduces learning rather than advances it (Hout & Elliot, 2011). But how much is "too much"?

One expert recommends "using tests to motivate students and teachers" (Walberg, 2011, p. 7). He believes that well-constructed tests benefit everyone—teachers, students, and the taxpayers. Other experts contend that the most important learning is deeper and more enduring than any machine-scored test can measure (Au & Tempel, 2012; David, 2011).

Ironically, just when U.S. schools are raising requirements, many East Asian nations, including China, Singapore, and Japan (all with high scores on international tests), are moving in the opposite direction. Particularly in Singapore, national high-stakes tests are being phased out, and local autonomy is increasing (Hargreaves, 2012).

By contrast, other nations, including Australia, the United States, and the United Kingdom, have instituted high-stakes tests since 2000, amid the same opposing views. Obviously, no consensus yet.

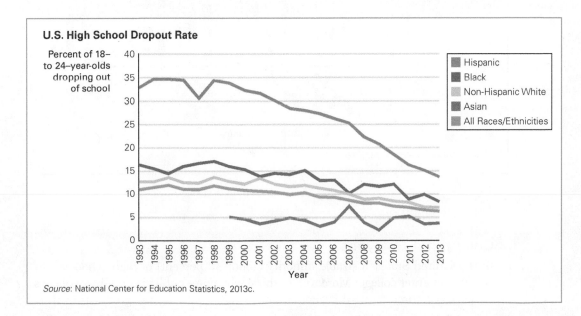

U.S. High School Dropout Rate

Percent of 18- to 24-year-olds dropping out of school

Legend: Hispanic, Black, Non-Hispanic White, Asian, All Races/Ethnicities

Year

Source: National Center for Education Statistics, 2013c.

FIGURE 15.6

Mostly Good News

This depicts wonderful improvements in high school graduation rates, especially among Hispanic youth, who drop out only half as often as they did twenty years ago. However, since high school graduation is increasingly necessary for lifetime success, even the rates shown here may not have kept pace with the changing needs of the economy. Future health, income, and happiness for anyone who drops out may be in jeopardy.

A team of Australian educators reviewed all the evidence and concluded:

> What emerges consistently across this range of studies are serious concerns regarding the impact of high stakes testing on student health and well-being, learning, teaching and curriculum.
>
> [Polesel et al., 2012, p. 5]

International data support both sides of this controversy. One nation whose children generally score well is South Korea, where high-stakes tests have resulted in extensive studying. Many South Korean parents hire tutors to teach their children after school and on weekends to improve their test scores (Lee & Shouse, 2011).

On the opposite side of the globe, students in Finland also score very well on international tests, and yet they have no national tests until the end of high school. Nor do they spend much time on homework or after-school education. A Finnish expert proudly states that "schoolteachers teach in order to help their students learn, not to pass tests" (Sahlberg, 2011, p. 26). He believes that teachers do their best with each child because there is no external standard that makes them "teach to the test."

The most recent international data suggest that U.S. high school students are not doing well, despite more high-stakes tests. As reviewed in Chapter 12, two international tests, the TIMSS (Trends in International Mathematics and Science Study) and the PIRLS (Progress in International Reading Literacy Study), find that the United States is far from the top on student learning.

A third set of international tests, the PISA (Programme for International Student Assessment, to be explained soon), places U.S. students even lower. The 2012 results from the 65 nations that took the tests puts the U.S. 36th in math, 28th in science, and 24th in reading—all lower than in 2009, when the United States scores were 31st, 23rd, and 17th among 75 nations.

Again in 2012 as in former years, China, Japan, Singapore, and Korea were at the top. Tellingly, the results for the United States lagged behind the nation most similar in ethnicity and location—Canada. Some results were surprising—Finland was the best-performing European nation, and Poland and Estonia also scored very well. Not surprising were the nations with the lowest results: Peru, Indonesia, and Qatar.

In many nations, scores on those three international tests as well as other metrics compel reexamination of school policies and practices. That certainly is true in the United States, which trails other developed nations in high school graduation rate (see Figure 15.7). Whether tests will change that is controversial: Many legislators believe so; many educators disagree.

FIGURE 15.7

Children Left Behind High school graduation rates in almost every nation and ethnic group are improving. However, the United States still lags behind other nations, and ethnic differences persist, with the rate among Native Americans lowest and among Asian Americans highest. High school diplomas are only one sign of educational accomplishment: Nations at the top of this chart tend also to rank highest in preschool attendance, in middle school achievement, and in college graduation. Raising the graduation rate involves the entire educational system, not simply more rigorous or more lenient graduation standards.

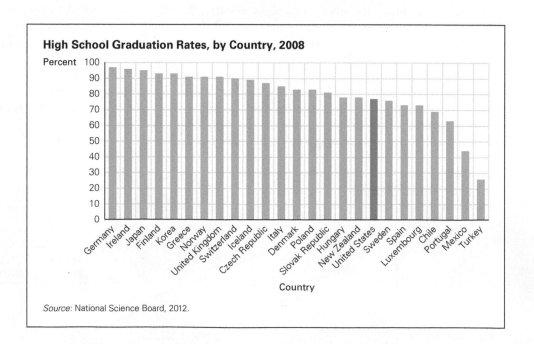

High School Graduation Rates, by Country, 2008

Source: National Science Board, 2012.

College for Everyone?

In the United States, a sizable minority (about 30 percent) of high school graduates do not enter college. Moreover, of those who enter public community colleges, most (about three-fourths) do not complete their associate's degree within three years, and almost half of those entering public or private four-year schools do not graduate. Some simply take longer, or enter the job market first, but even 10 years after the usual age for high school graduation, only 34 percent of U.S. young adults have earned a bachelor's degree (National Center for Education Statistics, 2013c).

Rates are even lower in many of the largest cities. For example, only 18 percent of the approximately 60,000 students entering ninth grade public schools in the district of Philadelphia managed to graduate on time from high school and then complete at least two years of college (Center for Education Policy, 2013).

The 82 percent who fell off track are often a disappointment to their parents: In Philadelphia and nationwide, almost all parents hope their children will graduate from college. The students may be a disappointment to themselves as well. Many quit high school before their senior year, but among the Philadelphia seniors, 84 percent plan to go to college but only 47 percent enroll the following September. Some will begin college later, but their chance of college completion is low.

These sobering statistics underlie another debate among educators. Should students be encouraged to "dream big" early in high school, aspiring for tertiary learning? This suggestion originates from studies that find a correlation between dreaming big in early adolescence and going to college years later (Domina et al., 2011a, 2011b). Others suggest that college is a "fairy tale dream" that may lead to low self-esteem (Rosenbaum, 2011). If adolescents fail academic classes, will they feel bored, stupid, and disengaged?

Business leaders have another concern: that high school graduates are not ready for the demands of work because their education has been too abstract. They have not learned enough through discussion, emotional maturation, and real-world experience.

Internationally, vocational education that explicitly prepares students for jobs via a combination of academic classes and practical experience seems to succeed better than a general curriculum (Eichhorst et al., 2012). On the other hand, in the United States, many students whose test scores suggest they could succeed at a four-year college do not enroll. Some high schools do better than others.

For example, students who entered high school with high scores in two major cities in neighboring states (Albuquerque, New Mexico and Fort Worth, Texas) had markedly different college enrollment rates (Albuquerque was 83 percent, compared to 58 percent in Fort Worth) (Center for Education Policy, 2012).

Overall, the data present a dilemma for educators. Suggesting that a student should not go to college may be racist, classist, sexist, or worse. On the other hand, many students who begin college do not graduate, so they lose time and gain debt when they could have advanced in a vocation. Everyone agrees that adolescents need to be educated for life as well as employment, but it is difficult to decide what that means.

Measuring Practical Cognition

Employers usually provide on-the-job training, which is much more specific and current than what high schools provide. They hope their future employees will have learned in secondary school how to think, explain, write, concentrate, and get along with other people.

As one executive of Boeing (which hired 33,000 new employees in two years) wrote:

> We believe that professional success today and in the future is more likely for those who have practical experience, work well with others, build strong relationships, and are able to think and do, not just look things up on the Internet.
>
> [Stephens & Richey, 2013]

// Response for Middle School Teachers (from page 499): Students need both challenge and involvement; avoid lessons that are too easy or too passive. Create small groups; assign oral reports, debates, and role-plays; and so on. Remember that adolescents like to hear one another's thoughts and their own voices.

PISA (Programme for International Student Assessment) An international test taken by 15-year-olds in 50 nations that is designed to measure problem solving and cognition in daily life.

Those skills are hard to measure, especially on national high-stakes tests or on the two international tests explained in Chapter 12, the PIRLS and the TIMSS.

The third set of international tests mentioned above, the **PISA (Programme for International Student Assessment),** was designed to measure students' ability to apply what they have learned. The PISA is taken by 15-year-olds, an age chosen because some 15-year-olds are close to the end of their formal school career. The questions are written to be practical, measuring knowledge that might apply at home or on the job. As a PISA report described it:

> The tests are designed to generate measures of the extent to which students can make effective use of what they have learned in school to deal with various problems and challenges they are likely to experience in everyday life.
>
> [PISA, 2009, p. 12]

For example, among the 2012 math questions is this one:

> Chris has just received her car driving license and wants to buy her first car. The table below shows the details of four cars she finds at a local car dealer.

Model	Alpha	Bolte	Castel	Dezal
Year	2003	2000	2001	1999
Advertised price (zeds)	4800	4450	4250	3990
Distance travelled (kilometers)	105 000	115 000	128 000	109 000
Engine capacity (liters)	1.79	1.796	1.82	1.783

What car's engine capacity is the smallest?

A. Alpha   B. Bolte   C. Castel   D. Dezal

For that and the other questions on the PISA, the calculations are quite simple—most 10-year-olds can do them; no calculus, calculators, or complex formulas required. However, almost half of the 15-year-olds worldwide got that question wrong. (The answer is D.) One problem is decimals: Some students do not remember how to interpret them when a practical question, not an academic one, is asked. Even in Singapore and Hong Kong, one out of five 15-year-olds got this question wrong. Another problem is that distance traveled is irrelevant, yet many students are distracted by it.

As noted in Opposing Perspectives, overall the U.S. students perform lower on the PISA compared to many other nations. International analysis finds that the following items correlate with high achievement (OECD, 2010, p. 6):

// Response for High School Teachers
(from page 500): It would be nice to follow your instincts, but the appropriate response depends partly on pressures within the school and on the expectations of the parents and administration. A comforting fact is that adolescents can think about and learn almost anything if they feel a personal connection to it. Look for ways to teach the facts your students need for the tests as the foundation for the exciting and innovative topics you want to teach. Everyone will learn more, and the tests will be less intimidating to your students.

1. Leaders, parents, and citizens value education overall, with individualized approaches to learning so that all students learn what they need.
2. Standards are high and clear, so every student knows what he or she must do, with a "focus on the acquisition of complex, higher-order thinking skills."
3. Teachers and administrators are valued, and they are given "considerable discretion . . . in determining content" and sufficient salary as well as time for collaboration.
4. Learning is prioritized "across the entire system," with high-quality teachers working in the most challenging environments.

The PISA and international comparisons of high school dropout rates suggest that U.S. secondary education can be improved, especially for those who do not go to college. Surprisingly, students who are capable of passing their classes, at least as measured on IQ tests, drop out almost as often as those who are less capable. Persistence, engagement, and motivation seem more crucial than intellectual ability alone (Archambault et al., 2009; Tough, 2012).

An added complication is that adolescents themselves vary: Some are thoughtful, some are impulsive, some are ready for analytic challenges, some are egocentric. All of them, however, need personal encouragement.

A study of student emotional and academic engagement from the fifth to the eighth grade found that, as expected, the overall average was a slow and steady decline of engagement. However, about 18 percent were highly engaged throughout while about 5 percent dramatically reduced engagement year by year (Li & Lerner, 2011). The 18 percent do well in high school. The 5 percent usually drop out, but some of them are late bloomers who could succeed in college if given time and encouragement. Thus, schools and teachers need many strategies if they hope to reach every adolescent.

Now let us seek practical, general conclusions for this chapter. The cognitive skills that boost national economic development and personal happiness are creativity, flexibility, relationship building, and analytic ability. Whether or not an adolescent is college-bound, those skills are exactly what the adolescent mind can develop—with proper education and guidance. Every cognitive theorist and researcher believes that adolescents' logical, social, and creative potential is not always realized, but that it can be. Does that belief end this chapter on a hopeful note?

SUMMING UP Worldwide, nations realize that high school education adds to national health and wealth, and thus many nations have increased the number of students in high schools. The United States is no longer the leader in the rate of high school graduation.

Middle schools tend to be less personal, less flexible, and more tightly regulated than elementary schools, which may contribute to a general finding: declining student achievement. Teachers grade more harshly, students are more rebellious, and because teachers specialize in a particular subject, every teacher has far more students overall than the typical primary school teacher. All of this works against what young adolescents need most, an adult who cares about their personal education.

Ideally, secondary education advances formal operational thinking, but this is not always the case. Variations in the structure of testing in high schools are vast, nationally and internationally. On international tests and measures, the United States is far from the top. Most high school graduates try college, but many do not graduate. The idea that high schools should prepare students to enter the workforce is controversial, with college attendance and then graduation the goal for many, but not the reality.

WHAT HAVE YOU LEARNED?

1. Why have most junior high schools disappeared?
2. What characteristics of middle schools make them more difficult for students than elementary schools?
3. Why does puberty affect a person's ability to learn?
4. How do beliefs about intelligence affect motivation and learning?
5. What are the advantages and disadvantages of high-stakes testing?
6. What are the problems with Advanced Placement classes and tests?
7. Should high schools prepare everyone for college? Why or why not?
8. How does the PISA differ from other international tests?

SUMMARY

Logic and Self

1. Cognition in early adolescence may be egocentric, a kind of self-centered thinking. Adolescent egocentrism gives rise to the personal fable, the invincibility fable, and the imaginary audience.

2. *Formal operational thought* is Piaget's term for the last of his four periods of cognitive development. He tested and demonstrated formal operational thought with various problems that students in a high school science or math class might encounter.

3. Piaget realized that adolescents are no longer earthbound and concrete in their thinking; they imagine the possible, the probable, and even the impossible, instead of focusing only on what is real. They develop hypotheses and explore, using deductive reasoning. However, few developmentalists find that adolescents move suddenly from concrete to formal thinking.

Two Modes of Thinking

4. Many cognitive theories describe two types of thinking during adolescence. One set of names for these two types is intuitive and analytic. Both become more forceful during adolescence, but brain development means that intuitive emotional thinking matures before analytic, logical thought.

5. Few teenagers always use logic, although they are capable of doing so. Emotional, intuitive thinking is quicker and more satisfying, and sometimes better, than analytic thought.

6. Neurological as well as survey research find that adolescent thinking is characterized by more rapid development of the limbic system and slower development of the prefrontal cortex. Peers further increase emotional impulses, so adolescents may make choices their parents believe to be foolish.

Digital Natives

7. Adolescents use technology, particularly the Internet, more than people of any other age. They reap many educational benefits, and many teachers welcome the accessibility of information and the research advances made possible by the Internet. Social connections are encouraged as well.

8. However, technology can be destructive. Some adolescents may be addicted to video games, some use cell phones and instant messages for cyberbullying, some find like-minded peers to support eating disorders and other pathologies, some engage in sexting. Overall, adults may mistakenly attribute normal teen behavior to technology use.

Teaching and Learning

9. Achievement in secondary education—after primary education (grade school) and before tertiary education (college)—correlates with the health and wealth of individuals and nations.

10. In middle school, many students struggle both socially and academically. One reason may be that middle schools are not structured to accommodate egocentrism or intuitive thinking. Students' beliefs about the nature of intelligence may also affect their learning.

11. Education in high school emphasizes formal operational thinking. In the United States, the demand for more accountability has led to an increase in the requirements for graduation and to more Advanced Placement (AP) classes and high-stakes testing.

12. A sizable number of high school students do not graduate or go on to college. Many more leave college without a degree. Current high school education does not seem to meet their needs.

13. The PISA test, taken by 15-year-olds in 50 nations, measures how well students can apply the knowledge they have been taught. Students in the United States seem to have particular difficulty with such tests.

KEY TERMS

adolescent egocentrism (p. 476)
personal fable (p. 477)
invincibility fable (p. 477)
imaginary audience (p. 477)
formal operational thought
 (p. 478)

hypothetical thought (p. 479)
deductive reasoning (p. 480)
inductive reasoning (p. 480)
sunk cost fallacy (p. 480)
base rate neglect (p. 481)
dual-process model (p. 482)

intuitive thought (p. 482)
analytic thought (p. 482)
cyberbullying (p. 493)
secondary education (p. 496)
middle school (p. 497)
entity theory of intelligence
 (p. 499)

incremental theory of
 intelligence (p. 499)
high-stakes test (p. 500)
PISA (Programme for
 International Student
 Assessment) (p. 504)

APPLICATIONS

1. Describe a time when you overestimated how much other people were thinking about you. How was your mistake similar to and different from adolescent egocentrism?

2. Talk to a teenager about politics, families, school, religion, or any other topic that might reveal the way he or she thinks. Do you hear any adolescent egocentrism? Intuitive thinking? Systematic thought? Flexibility? Cite examples.

3. Think of a life-changing decision you have made. How did logic and emotion interact? What would have changed if you had given the matter more thought—or less?

4. Describe what happened and what you thought in the first year you attended a middle school or high school. What made it better or worse than later years in that school?

Adolescence:
Psychosocial Development

What Will You Know?

1. Why might a teenager be a jock one year and a nerd the next?
2. Should parents back off when their teenager disputes every rule, wish, or suggestion they make?
3. Who are the best, and worst, sources of information about sex?
4. Should we worry more about teen suicide or juvenile delinquency?
5. Why are adolescents forbidden to drink and smoke, when adults are allowed to do so?

It's not easy being a teenager, as the previous chapters make clear, but neither is it easy being the parent of one. Sometimes I was too lenient. For example, once my daughter came home late; I was worried, angry, and upset, but I did not think about punishing her until she asked, "How long am I grounded?" And sometimes I was too strict. For years I insisted that my daughters and their friends wash the dinner dishes until all my children told me that none of their friends had such mean mothers.

At times, parents like me ricochet. When our children were infants, my husband and I had discussed how we would react when they became teenagers: We were ready to be firm, united, and consistent regarding illicit drugs, unsafe sex, and serious law-breaking. More than a decade later, when our children actually reached that stage, none of those issues appeared. Instead, unanticipated challenges caused us to react, sometimes in ways that surprised us. My husband said, "I knew they would become adolescents. I didn't expect us to become parents of adolescents."

This chapter is about adolescents' behavior and their relationships with friends, parents, and the larger society. It begins with identity and ends with drugs, both of which might appear to be the result of personal choice but actually are strongly affected by other people. I realize now that my children's actions and my reactions were influenced by personal history (I washed family dishes as a teenager) and by current norms (their friends did not).

Identity

Psychosocial development during adolescence is often understood as a search for a consistent understanding of oneself. Self-expression and self-concept become increasingly important at puberty. Each young person wants to know, "Who am I?"

According to Erik Erikson, life's fifth psychosocial crisis is **identity versus role confusion:** Working through the complexities of finding one's own identity is the

identity versus role confusion
Erikson's term for the fifth stage of development, in which the person tries to figure out "Who am I?" but is confused as to which of many possible roles to adopt.

identity achievement Erikson's term for the attainment of identity, or the point at which a person understands who he or she is as a unique individual, in accord with past experiences and future plans.

role confusion A situation in which an adolescent does not seem to know or care what his or her identity is. (Sometimes called *identity* or *role diffusion*.)

foreclosure Erikson's term for premature identity formation, which occurs when an adolescent adopts parents' or society's roles and values wholesale, without questioning or analysis.

moratorium An adolescent's choice of a socially acceptable way to postpone making identity-achievement decisions. Going to college is a common example.

primary task of adolescence (Erikson, 1968/1994). He said this crisis is resolved with **identity achievement,** when adolescents have reconsidered the goals and values of their parents and culture, accepting some and discarding others, forging their own identity.

The result is neither wholesale rejection nor unquestioning acceptance of social norms (Côté, 2009). With their new autonomy, teenagers maintain continuity with the past so that they can move to the future. Each person must achieve his or her own identity. Simply adopting parental norms does not work, because the social context of each generation differs.

Not Yet Achieved

Erikson's insights have inspired thousands of researchers. Notable among those was James Marcia, who described and measured four specific ways young people cope with the identity crisis: (1) role confusion, (2) foreclosure, (3) moratorium, and finally (4) identity achievement (Marcia, 1966).

Over the past half-century, major psychosocial shifts have lengthened the duration of adolescence and made identity achievement more complex (Côté, 2006; Kroger et al., 2010; Meeus, 2011). However, the above three way stations on the road to identity achievement still seem evident (Kroger & Marcia, 2011).

Role confusion is the opposite of identity achievement. It is characterized by lack of commitment to any goals or values. Erikson originally called this *identity diffusion* to emphasize that some adolescents seem diffuse, unfocused, and unconcerned about their future. Perhaps worse, adolescents in role confusion see no goals or purpose in their life, and thus they flounder, unable to move forward (Hill et al., 2013).

Identity **foreclosure** occurs when, in order to avoid the confusion of not knowing who they are, young people accept traditional roles and values (Marcia, 1966; Marcia et al., 1993). They might follow customs transmitted from their parents or culture, never exploring alternatives. Or they might foreclose on an oppositional, *negative identity*—the direct opposite of whatever their parents want—again without thoughtful questioning. Foreclosure is comfortable. For many, it is a temporary shelter, to be followed by more exploration (Meeus, 2011).

A more mature shelter is **moratorium,** a time-out that includes some exploration, either in breadth (trying many things) or in depth (following one path but with a tentative, temporary commitment) (Meeus, 2011). In high school, a student might become focused on playing in a band, not expecting this to be a lifelong career. A few years later, during emerging adulthood, someone might choose a moratorium by signing up for two years in the army. Moratoria are more common after age 18, because some maturity is required to reject some paths while choosing others (Kroger et al., 2010).

Several aspects of the search for identity, especially sexual and vocational identity, have become more arduous than they were when Erikson described them, and establishing a personal identity is more difficult. Fifty years ago, the drive to become independent and autonomous was thought to be the "key normative psychosocial task of adolescence" (Zimmer-Gembeck & Collins, 2003, p. 177). Adolescents still search for identity, but a review of "studies among adults revealed that identity progression is a life-long process" (Meeus, 2011).

No Role Confusion These are high school students in Junior ROTC training camp. For many youths who cannot afford college, the military offers a temporary identity, complete with haircut, uniform, and comrades.

LaunchPad

Video Activity: Adolescence Around the World: Rites of Passage presents a comparison of adolescent initiation customs in industrialized and developing societies.

Four Arenas of Identity Formation

Erikson (1968/1994) highlighted four aspects of identity: religious, political, vocational, and sexual. Terminology and emphasis have changed for all four, as has timing. In fact, if an 18-year-old is no longer open to new possibilities in any of these four areas, that may indicate foreclosure, not achievement—and identity might shift again.

None of these four identity statuses occurs in social isolation: Parents and peers are influential, as detailed later in this chapter, and the ever-changing chronosystem (historical context) makes identity dynamic. Nonetheless, each of these four arenas remains integral to adolescence. (**Developmental Link:** The chronosystem is explained in Chapter 1.) A crucial question is whether the adolescent ponders the possibilities and actively chooses an identity, or whether identity comes from external pressures (Lillevoll et al., 2013), either to conform or to rebel.

Religious Identity

For most adolescents, their *religious identity* is similar to that of their parents and community. Few adolescents totally reject religion if they've grown up following a particular faith, especially if they have a good relationship with their parents (Kim-Spoon et al., 2012).

Past parental practices influence adolescent religious identity, although some adolescents express that identity in ways that their parents did not anticipate: A Muslim girl might start to wear a headscarf, a Catholic boy might study for the priesthood, or a Baptist teenager might join a Pentecostal youth group, each surprising their less devout parents.

Such new practices are relatively minor, not a new religious identity. Thus, almost no young Muslims convert to Judaism, and almost no teenage Baptists become Hindu—although such conversions can occur in adulthood. Most adolescents question beliefs because their cognitive processes allow more analytic thinking, but few teenagers have a crisis of faith unless unusual circumstances propel it (King & Roeser, 2009).

Same Situation, Far Apart: Chosen, Saved, or Just Another Teenager? An Orthodox Jewish boy lighting Hanukkah candles in Israel and an evangelical Christian girl at a religious rally in Michigan are much alike, despite distance and appearance. Many teenagers express such evident religious devotion that outsiders consider them fanatics.

Rebels Not Prophets Teenagers are often on the forefront of political activism, especially if their parents have instilled values that make them want to do something dramatic to help earthquake victims, or reverse abortion laws, or, as with these Egyptians in Tahrir Square, topple a repressive regime. However, their political sentiments are not yet the product of their own identity achievement: Given the cognition of adolescence as described in Chapter 15, joining a group protest may be based more on emotion than analysis.

Political Identity

Parents also influence their children's *political identity*. In the twenty-first century in the United States, party identification is weakening, with more adults saying they are independent rather than Republican, Democrat, or any other party. Their teenage children reflect their lack of party affiliation; some proudly say they do not care about politics, echoing their parents without realizing it.

For everyone, adolescent political leanings are likely to continue in adulthood, although there is also a trend among current young adults toward more liberal leanings than their parents (Taylor, 2014). That doesn't usually happen during adolescence: Hillary Clinton's parents were Republican and she was a Young Republican at age 17, becoming a Democrat at age 21.

Related to political identity is *ethnic identity,* not a topic discussed by Erikson. Historical changes over the past few decades have made ethnic identity crucial for adolescents in the United States. High school senior Natasha Scott "just realized that my race is something I have to think about." Her mother is Asian and her father is African American, which had not been a concern of hers as she was growing up. However, college applications (and the 2010 Census) required choices regarding ethnic identity (Saulny & Steinberg, 2011).

Natasha is not the only one. In the United States and Canada, almost half of all adolescents are of African, Asian, Latino, or Native American (First Nations, in Canada) heritage, and many of them also have ancestors of another ethnic group. Although the census lumps all people of each of these groups together, teenagers forging their personal identity must become more specific.

Hispanic youth, for instance, must figure out their personal identity in relation to, for example, having grandparents from Mexico, Peru, or Spain, and/or California, Texas, or New York. Many also have ancestors from both Europe and Africa. Similarly, those who are European American must decide the significance of having grandparents from, say, Italy, Ireland, or Sweden. No teenager adopts, wholesale, the identity of their ancestors, but each one must incorporate, somehow, their family's history. Often ethnic identity blends into political identity.

Vocational Identity

Vocational identity originally meant envisioning oneself as a worker in a particular occupation. Choosing a future career made sense for teenagers a century ago, when most girls became housewives and most boys became farmers, small businessmen, or factory workers. Those few in professions were mostly generalists (doctors did family medicine, lawyers handled all kinds of cases, teachers taught all subjects).

Obviously, early vocational identity is no longer appropriate. No teenager can realistically choose among the tens of thousands of careers available today; most adults change vocations (not just employers) many times.

Vocational identity takes years to establish, and most jobs demand specific skills and knowledge that are best learned at the workplace. Currently, vocational identity is best seen as a dynamic, flexible path: People find a career, or even better, a calling, that can lead to a variety of specific jobs (Skorikov & Vondracek, 2011).

Although some adults hope that having a job will keep teenagers out of trouble as they identify as workers, the opposite may occur (Staff & Schulenberg, 2010). Research that controlled for SES found that adolescents who are employed more than 20 hours a week during the school year tend to quit school, fight with parents, smoke cigarettes, and hate their jobs—not only when they are teenagers but also later on.

Typically, teenagers with a paycheck spend their wages on clothes, cars, drugs, fast food, and music, not on supporting their families or saving for college (Mortimer, 2013). Grades fall: Employment interferes with homework and school attendance (see Figure 16.1).

Sexual Identity

As you remember from Chapter 10, for social scientists *sex* and *sexual* refer to biological characteristics, whereas *gender* refers to cultural and social attributes that differentiate males and females. A half-century ago, Erikson and other theorists thought of the two sexes as opposites (P. Y. Miller & Simon, 1980). They assumed that adolescents who were confused about their *sexual identity* would soon adopt "proper" male or female roles (Erikson, 1968/1994; A. Freud, 2000).

Adolescence was once a time for "gender intensification," when people increasingly identified as male or female. No longer (Priess et al., 2009). Erikson's term *sexual identity* has been replaced by **gender identity** (Denny & Pittman, 2007), which refers primarily to a person's self-definition as male, female, or transgender.

Gender identity often (not always) began with the person's biological sex and led to a gender role that society considered appropriate. Gender roles once meant that only men were employed; they were *breadwinners* (good providers) and women were *housewives* (married to their houses). As women entered the labor market, gender roles expanded but were still strong (nurse/doctor, secretary/businessman, pink collar/blue collar).

Now, gender roles are changing everywhere. The speed and specifics of the change vary dramatically by culture and cohort, and gender theorists note that specifics are complex (Doucet & Lee, 2014). Some gender roles seem resistant to change, but almost everywhere, women do less housework than they did when Erikson wrote, while men do more.

Gender roles have changed particularly in parenting. According to data from many European nations, when fertility is low and education is high, fathers often provide direct child care (Sullivan et al., 2014). In the United States, single mothers still far outnumber single fathers (fathers were 13 percent of all single parents in 1980; 17 percent in 2013). However, since the total number of single-parent households is increasing, far more children (especially teenagers) are in single-father families than even two decades ago, and most adolescent boys expect to become active fathers.

Achieving gender identity is a lifelong task, because possibilities and roles keep changing. Gender identity is particularly complex for adolescents who feel their sex at birth is not their true gender identity. In former decades, people with "a strong and persistent cross-gender identification" were thought to have a *gender identity disorder,* a serious diagnosis in DSM-IV.

The DSM-5 instead describes *gender dysphoria,* when people are distressed at their biological gender. A "disorder" means something is wrong, no matter

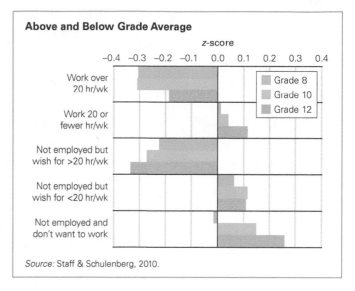

Above and Below Grade Average

Source: Staff & Schulenberg, 2010.

FIGURE 16.1

Don't Think About It There was a time when high-school employment correlated with lifetime success. This is no longer true. The surprise is that even wanting a full-time job (and the extra income it would bring) reduces achievement—or is it the other way around? The scores in the chart above are z-scores, or standard scores, which show the difference from the group average. A z-score of 2 is a dramatic difference; a z-score of 3 is extreme.

gender identity A person's acceptance of the roles and behaviors that society associates with the biological categories of male and female.

Who and Where? As Erikson explained in 1968, the pride of self-discovery is universal for adolescents: These could be teenagers anywhere. But a closer look reveals gay teenagers in Atlanta, Georgia, where this march would not have occurred 50 years ago.

how the person feels, whereas dysphoria implies that the psychological problem is emotional distress, not necessarily gender identity (Zucker et al., 2013). Social conditions and self-perception can relieve dysphoria, allowing someone to take on a new gender identity and be psychologically healthy. Fifty years ago, psychiatrists never contemplated that possibility.

SUMMING UP Erikson's fifth psychosocial crisis—identity versus role confusion—was first described more than half a century ago. Adolescence was characterized as a time to search for a personal identity in order to reach identity achievement by adulthood. Whereas the identity crisis still occurs and role confusion, foreclosure, and moratorium are apparent, timing has changed. The identity crisis lasts much longer; fewer young people develop a firm sense of who they are and what path they will follow by age 18.

Specific aspects of identity—religious, political, vocational, and sexual—have taken new forms, with complexities that Erikson did not anticipate. This is especially true for vocational identity: The vast array of possible jobs, and the training required for each one, means that adolescents need years of exploration and education. Likewise, adolescents are aware of many more religious, political, and gender identities than adults once recognized. All these forms of identity may begin during adolescence, but many emerging adults still are experimenting. Identity begins to be established during adolescence, as teenagers reject some aspects of the identities prescribed by their elders, but the identity crisis continues past adolescence.

WHAT HAVE YOU LEARNED?

1. What is Erikson's fifth psychosocial crisis, and how is it resolved?
2. How does identity foreclosure differ from identity moratorium?
3. What has changed over the past decades regarding political identity?
4. What role do parents play as adolescents form religious and political identity?
5. Why is it premature for today's adolescents to achieve vocational identity?
6. What assumptions about sexual identity did most adults hold 50 years ago?
7. What variations in sexual identity are apparent worldwide?

Relationships with Adults

Adolescence is often characterized as a period of waning adult influence, when children distance themselves from their elders. This picture is only half true. Adult influence is less immediate but no less important.

Parents

The fact that parent–adolescent relationships are pivotal does not mean that they are peaceful (Laursen & Collins, 2009). Disputes are common because the adolescent's drive for independence, arising from biological as well as psychological impulses and social expectations, clashes with the parents' desire for control.

Normally, conflict peaks in early adolescence, especially between mothers and daughters. The most common conflict is not fighting but instead *bickering*—repeated, petty arguments (more nagging than fighting) about routine, day-to-day concerns such as cleanliness, clothes, chores, and schedules (Eisenberg et al., 2008).

Each generation tends to misjudge the other, and that adds to the conflict. Parents think their offspring resent them more than they actually do, and adolescents imagine their parents want to dominate them more than they actually do (Sillars et al., 2010).

Unspoken concerns need to be aired so both generations better understand each other. Imagine a parent seeing filthy socks on the living room floor. The parent might interpret that as a deliberate mark of disrespect and react angrily, yelling "Pick up those socks right now." But perhaps the adolescent was merely distracted, oblivious to the parent's desire for a neat house. If so, then the parent could merely sigh and put the socks in the hamper, or in the child's bedroom.

Some bickering may indicate a healthy family, since close relationships almost always include conflict. A study of mothers and their adolescents suggested that "although too much anger may be harmful . . . , some expression of anger may be adaptive" (Hofer et al., 2013). In this study, as well as generally, the parent–child relationship usually improved with time.

Over the years, teenagers learn to regulate their moods and parents to grant autonomy. By age 18, many teenagers appreciate their parents (and put socks in the hamper), and many parents adjust to their child's independence (suggesting socks belong in the child's room) (Masche, 2010).

You already know that authoritative parenting is usually best for children and that uninvolved parenting is worst. (**Developmental Link:** Parenting styles are discussed in Chapter 10.) This continues in adolescence. Although teenagers may claim that their parents are irrelevant, that is not true. Neglect is always destructive and authoritarian parenting can backfire, resulting in children who lie or leave.

"So I blame you for everything—whose fault is that?"

a view from science

Parents, Genes, and Risks

Research on human development has many practical applications. This was evident in a longitudinal study of African American families in rural Georgia that involved 611 parents and their 11-year-olds (Brody et al., 2009).

Half of them were assigned to the comparison group, with no special intervention. The other half were invited to seven two-hour training sessions. Groups were small, and leaders were well prepared and selected to be likely role models. Parents and their 11-year-olds were taught in two separate groups for an hour and then brought together.

The parents learned the following:

- The importance of being nurturing and involved
- The importance of conveying pride in being African American (called racial socialization)
- How monitoring and control benefit adolescents
- Why clear norms and expectations reduce substance use
- Strategies for communication about sex

The 11-year-olds learned the following:

- The importance of having household rules
- Adaptive behaviors when encountering racism
- The need for making plans for the future
- The differences between them and peers who use alcohol

After that first hour, the parents and 11-year-olds were led in games, structured interactions, and modeling designed to improve family communication and cohesion. Three years after the intervention, both the experimental and comparison groups were reassessed regarding sex and alcohol/drug activity. The results were disappointing: The intervention helped but not very much.

Then, four years after the study began, the researchers read new research that found heightened risks of depression, delinquency, and other problems for people with the short allele of the 5-HTTLPR gene. To see whether this applied to their African American teenagers, they collected and analyzed the DNA of 16-year-olds who had been, at age 11, in either the special training group or the comparison group. As Figure 16.2 shows, the training had virtually no impact on those with the long allele, but it had a major impact on those with the short one.

The fact that 14 hours or fewer of training (some families skipped sessions) had an impact on genetically sensitive boys is amazing, given all the other influences surrounding these boys over the years. Apparently, since the parent–child relationship is crucial throughout adolescence, those seven sessions provided in-sights and connections that affected each vulnerable dyad from then on.

Genetic sensitivity was crucial. In a follow up study when the boys were 19, those boys with the short 5-HTTLPR gene had in-creased levels of many indicators of poor health—physical and psychological—if their family environment was not supportive (Brody et al., 2013). Again, nature and nurture work together.

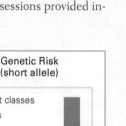

Source: Brody et al., 2009.

FIGURE 16.2

Not Yet The risk score was simply one point for each of the following: had drunk alcohol, had smoked marijuana, had had sex. As shown, most of the 11-year-olds had done none of these. By age 14, most had done one (usually had drunk beer or wine)—except for those at genetic risk who did not have the seven-session training. Some of them had done all three, and many had done at least two. As you see, for those youths without genetic risk, the usual parenting was no better or worse than the parenting that benefited from the special classes: The average 14-year-old in either group had tried only one risky behavior. But for those at genetic risk, the special program made a decided difference.

Cultural Differences

Expectations vary by culture, as do justifications (Brown & Bakken, 2011). For example, in Chile, adolescents usually obey their parents, but if they do something their parents might not like, they keep it secret (Darling et al., 2008). By contrast, many U.S. adolescents deliberately provoke an argument by boldly proclaiming what should be allowed, even if it is something they themselves never do (Cumsille et al., 2010).

Several researchers have compared parent–child relationships in various cultures: Everywhere, parent–child communication and encouragement reduce teenage depression, suicide, and low self-esteem, and increase aspirations and achievements (e.g., Kwok & Shek, 2010; Leung et al., 2010; Qin et al., 2009). Culture shapes specifics, but the overall pattern shows that parents remain role models and guides.

Closeness Within the Family

More important than family conflict or individual autonomy may be family close-ness, which has four aspects:

1. Communication (Do family members talk openly with one another?)
2. Support (Do they rely on one another?)
3. Connectedness (How emotionally close are they?)
4. Control (Do parents encourage or limit adolescent autonomy?)

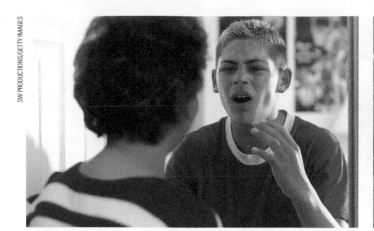 

A Study in Contrasts? These two teenagers appear to be opposites: one yelling at his mother and the other conscientiously helping his father. However, adolescent moods can change in a flash, especially with parents. Later in the day, these two might switch roles.

No social scientist doubts that the first two, communication and support, are helpful, perhaps essential, for healthy development. Patterns set in place during childhood continue, ideally buffering some of the turbulence of adolescence (Cleveland et al., 2005; Laursen & Collins, 2009). Regarding the next two, connectedness and control, consequences vary and observers differ in what they see. How do you react to this example, written by one of my students?

> I got pregnant when I was sixteen years old, and if it weren't for the support of my parents, I would probably not have my son. And if they hadn't taken care of him, I wouldn't have been able to finish high school or attend college. My parents also helped me overcome the shame that I felt when . . . my aunts, uncles, and especially my grandparents found out that I was pregnant.
>
> *[I., personal communication]*

My student is grateful to her parents, but did teenage motherhood give her parents too much control, requiring her to depend on them instead of seeking her identity? Indeed, had they unconsciously encouraged pregnancy by permitting her to be with a boy but not explaining contraception?

An added complexity is that this young woman's parents had emigrated from South America. Cultural expectations affect everyone's responses, so her dependence may have been normative in her culture but not elsewhere. A longitudinal study of nonimmigrant adolescent mothers in the United States found that most (not all) fared best if their parents were supportive but did not take over child care (Borkowski et al., 2007). Whether this is true in other nations has not been reported.

A related issue is **parental monitoring**—that is, parental knowledge about each child's whereabouts, activities, and companions. Many studies have shown that, when parental knowledge is the result of a warm, supportive relationship, adolescents are likely to become confident, well-educated adults, avoiding drugs and risky sex. However, if the parents are cold, strict, and punitive, monitoring may lead to rebellion.

Adolescents play an active role in their own monitoring: Some happily tell parents about their activities, whereas others are secretive (Vieno et al., 2009). A "dynamic interplay between parents and children" (Abar et al., 2014. p. 2177) is particularly apparent in adolescence. Most teenagers disclose only part of the truth to their parents, selectively omitting whatever their parents would not approve (Brown & Bakken, 2011).

Thus, monitoring may signify a mutual, close interaction (Kerr et al., 2010). However, monitoring may be harmful when it derives from suspicion. Especially

parental monitoring Parents' ongoing awareness of what their children are doing, where, and with whom.

Video: Parenting in Adolescence examines how family structure and communication styles and can help or hinder parent–teen relationships.

in early adolescence, if adolescents resist telling their parents much of anything, they are more likely to develop problems such as aggression against peers, law-breaking, and drug abuse (Laird et al., 2013). But lack of communication may be the symptom, not the cause.

Control is another aspect of parenting that can backfire. Adolescents expect parents to exert some control, especially over moral issues. However, overly restrictive and controlling parenting correlates with many adolescent problems, including severe depression (Brown & Bakken, 2011). Further, parents sometimes restrict the wrong activity. One researcher laments that parents sometimes refuse to let their children use social media, inadvertently limiting their ability to sustain supportive friendships (boyd, 2014).

Other Adults

Parents are important but so are many other adults. One of the admirable characteristics of most adolescents is that they know many people, sometimes seeking advice and help from neighbors, teachers, relatives, and so on. This is characteristic of resilient teenagers, who find the support they need (Masten, 2014).

The impact is notable when adults take time to listen. For many youths, the most patient advisors are family members—older siblings, cousins, aunts and uncles, grandparents. Sometimes parents delegate a sibling (the adolescent's aunt or uncle) to discuss taboo topics, such as sex or delinquency (Milardo, 2010). Links between teenagers and relatives are especially common in developing nations and among immigrant groups for two reasons: Relatives often live together or nearby, and cultural values make family central.

Adults with no biological relationship to the young person can also be significant (Chang et al., 2010; Scales et al., 2006). For instance, regarding the four arenas of identity development (religion, politics, vocation, sex), clergy affect a young person's faith, political leaders mold values, school counselors influence vocational aspirations, and adults in satisfying partnerships are role models (Lerner & Steinberg, 2009). In addition, many adolescents admire celebrities—in sports, music, and film—and try to be like them, for good or ill.

SUMMING UP   Relationships with adults are essential during adolescence. Parents and adolescents often bicker over small things, especially common with mothers and daughters in early puberty, but squabbling between parents and teenagers does not mean that the relationship is destructive. In fact, parental guidance and ongoing communication promote adolescents' psychosocial health. Among the signs of a healthy parent–adolescent relationship are that parents know what their child is doing (parental monitoring) and that adolescents talk with their parents about their concerns. The adolescent's relationships with parents and other adults are powerfully affected by culture, by past relationships, and by the adolescent's maturity. Either extreme neglect or excessive control can lead to adolescent rebellion. The firm but flexible guidance of authoritative parenting continues to be effective. Other relatives and non-relatives also sometimes become guides and mentors, especially when parental advice is limited or resisted.

WHAT HAVE YOU LEARNED?

1.   Why do parents and adolescents often bicker?
2.   How do parent–adolescent relationships change over time?
3.   When is parental monitoring a sign of a healthy parent–adolescent relationship?
4.   When can a parent–child relationship be considered too close?
5.   How and when do adults other than parents affect adolescents?

Peer Power

Adolescents rely on peers to help them navigate the physical changes of puberty, the intellectual challenges of high school, and the social changes of leaving childhood. Friendships are important at every stage, but during early adolescence, popularity (not just friendship) is most coveted (LaFontana & Cillessen, 2010).

Peers and Parents

Adults are sometimes unaware of adolescents' desire for respect from their contemporaries. I did not recognize this at the time with my own children:

- Our oldest daughter wore the same pair of jeans in tenth grade, day after day. She washed them each night by hand and asked me to put them in the dryer early each morning. My husband was bewildered. "Is this some weird female ritual?" he asked. Years later, she explained that she was afraid that if she wore different pants each day, her classmates would think she cared about her clothes and then criticize her choices.
- Our second daughter, at 16, pierced her ears for the third time. When I asked if this meant she would do drugs, she laughed at my naiveté. I later saw that many of her friends had multiple holes in their ear lobes.
- At age 15, our third daughter was diagnosed with cancer. My husband and I weighed opinions from four physicians, each explaining treatment that would minimize the risk of death. She had other priorities: "I don't care what you choose, as long as I keep my hair." (Now her health is good, and her hair grew back.)
- In sixth grade, our youngest refused to wear her jacket (it was new; she had chosen it), even in midwinter. Not until high school did she tell me she did it so that her classmates would think she was tough.

In retrospect, I am amazed that I was unaware of the power of peers.

Sometimes adults conceptualize adolescence as a tug of war between peers and parents, with the peers winning. This is not true. Relationships with parents are the prototype for peer relationships: Healthy communication and support from parents make constructive peer relationships likely. Both usually pull on the same side.

Parents and peers are often mutually reinforcing, although many adolescents downplay the influence of their parents and many parents are unaware of the influence of peers, as I was. Only when parents are harsh or neglectful does peer influence reign alone (Brown & Bakken, 2011).

Closeness to parents protects adolescent self-esteem. However, if adolescents have a poor relationship with parents, then it is particularly beneficial for the adolescent to have some good friends (Birkeland et al., 2014).

Helpful friends can be of either sex. Although same-sex friends are often preferred, many adolescents have members of the other sex as close friends. Opposite-sex friends increase the likelihood of drug use and early romance, but much depends on the social context: Parents should not assume that a good friend of the other sex means trouble (Lam et al., 2014).

Same Situation, Far Apart: Friends Together Teenagers in the middle of the United States (Illinois) and in the middle of Sudan (Khartoum) prefer to spend their free time with peers (these are all 15- to 17-year-olds), not with adults. Generational loyalty is stronger during these years than during any other stage of life.

OBSERVATION QUIZ There are dramatic differences among teenagers in these two nations as well. What three differences you see? (See answer, page 521)

Peer Pressure

peer pressure Encouragement to conform to one's friends or contemporaries in behavior, dress, and attitude; usually considered a negative force, as when adolescent peers encourage one another to defy adult authority.

Parents worry about **peer pressure;** that is, they fear that peers will push their child to use drugs, break laws, and so on. If biological and social stresses are overwhelming, however, peers can be more helpful than harmful, especially in early adolescence. In later adolescence, teenagers are less susceptible to peer pressure, either positive or negative (Monahan et al., 2009). Some adolescents are more influenced by peers than others, because genes and early experiences differ (Prinstein et al., 2011; Choukas-Bradly et al., 2014).

Everyday Danger After cousins Alex and Arthur, ages 16 and 20, followed family wishes to shovel snow around their Denver home, they followed their inner risk impulses and jumped from the roof. Not every young man can afford the expense of motocross or hang-gliding, but almost every one leaps into risks that few 40-year-olds would dare.

MATTHEW STAVER/BLOOMBERG VIA GETTY IMAGES

Peers are particularly needed by adolescents of minority and immigrant groups as they strive to achieve ethnic identity, attaining their own firm identity (not confused or foreclosed), understanding what it means to be Asian, African, Latino, and so on. The larger society provides stereotypes and prejudice, parents ideally describe ethnic heroes and reasons to be proud (Umana-Taylor et al., 2010).

Then peers from the same background help with self-esteem. For example, a study of Hispanic adolescents found that those who experienced ethnic prejudice were more likely to abuse drugs, but not if their parents and peers made them proud to identify as Latino (Grigsby et al., 2014).

The particular peers who are influential are those with the adolescent at the moment. This was found in a study in which all the eleventh graders in several public schools in Los Angeles were offered a free, online SAT prep course (worth $200) that they could take if they signed up on a paper the organizers distributed (Bursztyn & Jensen, 2014). Students were *not* allowed to talk before deciding whether or not to accept the offer, so they did not know that, although all the papers had identical, detailed descriptions of the SAT program, one word differed in who would learn of their decision—either no other students or only the students in that particular class.

The two versions were either:

> *Your decision to sign up for the course will be kept completely private from everyone, except the other students in the room.*

or:

> *Your decision to sign up for the course will be kept completely private from everyone, including the other students in the room.*

A marked difference was found if they thought their classmates would learn of their decision. The honors students were more likely to sign up, and the non-honors students less likely, if they thought their classmates would know.

To make sure this was a peer effect, not just divergent motivation and ability, the researchers compared 107 students who took exactly two honors classes and several non-honors ones. Some happened to be sitting in an honors classroom when they filled out their sign-up sheets; others were not.

When the decisions of this subgroup were kept totally private, acceptance rates were similar (72 and 79 percent) no matter which class they were in at the moment. But if they thought their classmates might know their decision, *imagined* peer pressure affected them. When in an honors class, 97 percent signed up for the SAT program, but if similar students were in a non-honors class, only 54 percent did—a 43 percent difference (Bursztyn & Jensen, 2014).

Social Networking

You read in Chapter 15 about the dangers of technology. Remember, however, that technology is a tool that might exacerbate depression or self-destruction but does not cause it (Yom-Tov et al., 2012). "Stranger danger" is more a problem in the adult mind than in the adolescent reality (boyd, 2014).

Despite adult fears to the contrary, technology usually brings friends together in adolescence (Mesch & Talmud, 2010). This is obvious with texting, e-mail, and social media, but it also occurs with video games. Many games now pit one player against another or require cooperation among several players (Collins & Freeman, 2013). Technology users, including video game players, are usually at least as extroverted and socially connected as other adolescents.

Although most social networking is between friends who know each other well, the Internet may be a lifeline for teenagers who are isolated because of their sexual orientation, culture, religion, or home language.

Networking may be vital if adolescents have special health needs. During these years, many refuse to follow special diets, take medication, see doctors, do exercises, or whatever. Technology combats that rebellion, as shown with teenagers who have diabetes: They monitor their insulin via cell phone, talk to the doctor via Skype, and talk to other young people with diabetes via Internet chat (Harris et al., 2012).

The adolescent need for social connections has always been strong, as have parental fears about it. What has changed is the particular target of the parental fears. Once it was novels or comic books, the schoolyard or the mall; now it is the computer and the cell phone (boyd, 2014).

Selecting Friends

Of course, peers *can* lead one another into trouble. Collectively, they may provide **deviancy training,** whereby one person shows another how to resist social norms (Dishion et al., 2001). However, innocent teens are not corrupted by deviants. Adolescents choose their friends and models—not always wisely, but never randomly.

A developmental progression can be traced: The combination of "problem behavior, school marginalization, and low academic performance" at age 11 leads to gang involvement two years later, deviancy training two years after that, and violent behavior at age 18 or 19 (Dishion et al., 2010, p. 603). This cascade is not inevitable; adults need to engage marginalized 11-year-olds instead of blaming their friends years later.

To further understand the impact of peers, examination of two concepts is helpful: *selection* and *facilitation*. Teenagers *select* friends whose values and interests

Social or Solitary? Adults have criticized the Internet for allowing teenagers to keep friends at a distance. By contrast, sitting around an outdoor fire is romanticized as a bonding experience. Which is more accurate here? Are these two girls about to talk about what they are reading?

Especially for Parents of a Teenager Your 13-year-old comes home after a sleepover at a friend's house with a new, weird hairstyle—perhaps cut or colored in a bizarre manner. What do you say and do? (see response, page 525)

deviancy training Destructive peer support in which one person shows another how to rebel against authority or social norms.

they share, abandoning former friends who follow other paths. Then friends *facilitate* destructive or constructive behaviors. It is easier to do wrong ("Let's all skip school on Friday") or right ("Let's study together for the chem exam") with friends. Peer facilitation helps adolescents do things they are unlikely to do alone.

Thus, adolescents select and facilitate, choose and are chosen. Happy, energetic, and successful teens have close friends who themselves are high achievers, with no major emotional problems. The opposite also holds: Those who are drug users, sexually active, and alienated from school choose compatible friends.

A study of identical twins from ages 14 to 17 found that selection typically precedes facilitation, rather than the other way around. Those who *later* rebelled chose law-breaking friends at age 14 more often than did their more conventional twin (Burt et al., 2009).

Research on teenage cigarette smoking also found that selection preceded peer pressure (Kiuru et al., 2010); yet another study found that young adolescents tend to select peers who drink alcohol, and then start drinking themselves (Osgood et al., 2013). Finally, a third study of teenage sexual activity again found that selection was the crucial peer influence on behavior (van de Bongardt et al., 2014). In general, peers provide opportunity, companionship, and encouragement for what adolescents already are inclined to do.

Romance

Half a century ago, Dexter Dunphy (1963) described the sequence of male–female relationships during childhood and adolescence:

1. Groups of friends, exclusively one sex or the other
2. A loose association of girls and boys, with public interactions within a crowd
3. Small mixed-sex groups of the advanced members of the crowd
4. Formation of couples, with private intimacies

Culture affects the timing and manifestation of each step on Dunphy's list, but subsequent research in many nations validates the sequence. Heterosexual youths worldwide (and even the young of other primates) avoid the other sex in childhood and are attracted to them by adulthood. Biology underlies this universal sequence.

The peer group is part of the process. Romantic partners, especially in early adolescence, are selected not for their individual traits as much as for the traits that peers admire. If the leader of a girls' group of close friends pairs with the leader of a boys' group, the unattached members of the two cliques tend to pair off as well.

A classic example is football players and cheerleaders: They often socialize together, and then pair off with someone from the other group. Which particular football player or cheerleader is chosen depends more on availability than compatibility, which helps explain why adolescent romantic partners tend to have less in common, in personality and attitudes, than adult couples do (Zimmer-Gembeck & Ducat, 2010).

First Love

Teens' first romances typically occur in high school, with girls having a steady partner more often than boys do. Exclusive commitment is the ideal, but hard to maintain: "Cheating," flirting, switching, and disloyalty are rife. Breakups are common, as are unreciprocated crushes. All of this can be devastating, and emotions sometimes go to opposite extremes, from exhilaration to despair, leading to revenge or depression. In such cases, peer support can be a lifesaver; friends help adolescents cope with romantic ups and downs (Mehta & Strough, 2009).

Contrary to adult fears, many teenage romances do not include coitus. In the United States in 2013, even though more than one-third of all tenth grade students had experienced vaginal intercourse, about another one-third were virgins at high school graduation (see Figure 16.3). Norms vary markedly from group to group, school to school, city to city, and nation to nation.

For instance, more than twice as many ninth- to twelfth-graders in Memphis as in San Francisco say they have had intercourse (60 percent versus 26 percent) (MMWR, June 13, 2014). Within every city are many subgroups, each with their own norms.

Parents have an impact. Thus, when parent–child relationships are good, girls from religious families tend to be romantically involved with boys from religious families, and their shared values typically slow down sexual activity (Kim-Spoon et al., 2012).

Same-Sex Romances

Some adolescents are attracted to peers of the same sex. **Sexual orientation** refers to the direction of a person's erotic desires. One meaning of *orient* is to "turn toward"; thus, sexual orientation refers to whether a person is romantically attracted to (turned on by) people of the other sex, the same sex, or both sexes.

Sexual orientation can be strong, weak, overt, secret, or unconscious, and it is surprisingly fluid during the teen years. Girls often recognize their orientation only after their first sexual experiences; many adult lesbians had other-sex relationships in adolescence (Saewyc, 2011). In one detailed study, 10 percent of sexually active teenagers had had same-sex partners, but more than one-third of that 10 percent nonetheless identified themselves as heterosexual (Pathela & Schillinger, 2010). In that study, those most at risk of sexual violence and sexually transmitted infections (STIs) were those who had partners of both sexes. This specific finding in confirmed by more general studies (e.g., Russell et al., 2014).

Obviously, culture and cohort are powerful. Some cultures accept youth who are gay, lesbian, bisexual, or transgender (the census in India asks people to identify as male, female, or Hijra [transgender]) and others criminalize them (as do 38 of the 53 African nations), some even killing them (Uganda). Worldwide, many gay youths date members of the other sex to hide their orientation; deception puts them at risk for binge-drinking, suicidal thoughts, and drug use. Those hazards are less common in cultures where same-sex partnerships are accepted (see Figure 16.4), especially when parents affirm their offspring's sexuality.

At least in the United States, adolescents have similar difficulties and strengths whether they are gay or straight (Saewyc, 2011). However, lesbian, gay, transgender, and bisexual youth have a higher risk of depression and anxiety,

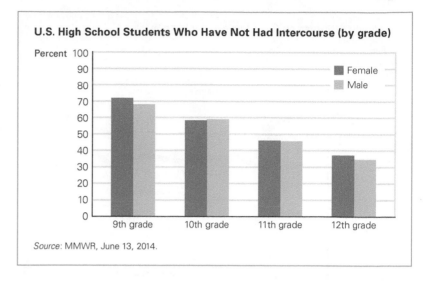

U.S. High School Students Who Have Not Had Intercourse (by grade)

Source: MMWR, June 13, 2014.

FIGURE 16.3

Many Virgins For 30 years, the Youth Risk Behavior Survey has asked high school students from all over the United States dozens of confidential questions about their behavior. As you can see, about one-third of all students have already had sex by the ninth grade, and about one-third have not yet had sex by their senior year—a group whose ranks have been increasing in recent years. Other research finds that sexual behaviors are influenced by peers, with members of some groups all sexually experienced by age 14 and members of others not until age 18 or older.

sexual orientation A term that refers to whether a person is sexually and romantically attracted to others of the same sex, the opposite sex, or both sexes.

Girls Together These two girls from Sweden seem comfortable lying close to one another. Many boys of this age wouldn't want their photograph taken if they were this close together. Around the world, there are cultural and gender norms about what are acceptable expressions of physical affection among friends during adolescence.

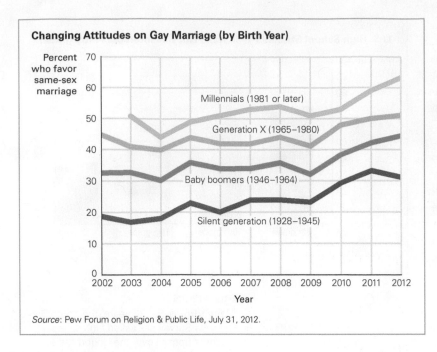

Changing Attitudes on Gay Marriage (by Birth Year)

Millennials (1981 or later)

Generation X (1965–1980)

Baby boomers (1946–1964)

Silent generation (1928–1945)

Source: Pew Forum on Religion & Public Life, July 31, 2012.

FIGURE 16.4

Young and Old Everyone knows that attitudes about same-sex relationships are changing. Less well known is that cohort differences are greater than the historical shifts.

Video: Romantic Relationships in Adolescence explores teens' attitudes and assumptions about romance and sexuality.

Especially for Sex Educators Suppose adults in your community never talk to their children about sex or puberty. Is that a mistake? (see response, page 526)

for reasons from every level of Bronfenbrenner's ecological approach (Mustanski et al., 2014). (**Developmental Link:** Ecological systems are described in Chapter 1.)

Sex Education

Many adolescents have strong sexual urges but minimal logic about pregnancy and disease, as might be expected from the 10-year interval between maturation of the body and of the brain. Millions of teenagers worry that they are over-sexed, undersexed, or deviant—unaware that thousands, maybe millions, of people are just like them.

As a result, "students seem to waffle their way through sexually relevant encounters driven both by the allure of reward and the fear of negative consequences" (Wagner, 2011, p. 193). They have much to learn. Where do they learn it?

From the Media

Many adolescents learn about sex from the media. The Internet is a common source. Unfortunately, Web sites are often frightening (featuring pictures of diseased sexual organs) or mesmerizing (containing pornography), and young adolescents are particularly naive.

Media consumption peaks at puberty. The TV shows most watched by teenagers include sexual content almost seven times per hour (Steinberg & Monahan, 2011). That content is alluring: Almost never does a television character develop an STI, deal with an unwanted pregnancy, or mention (much less use) a condom. Magazines may be worse. One study found that men's magazines convince teenage boys that maleness means sexual conquests (Ward et al., 2011).

Adolescents with intense exposure to sexual content on the screen and in music are more often sexually active, but the direction of this correlation is controversial (Collins et al., 2011; Steinberg & Monahan, 2011). Are teenagers drawn to sexy images because they are sexually active, or does their exposure to sexual content in the media cause them to be sexually involved? One analysis concludes that "the most important influences on adolescents' sexual behavior may be closer to home than Hollywood" (Steinberg & Monahan, 2011, p. 575).

From Parents and Peers

As that quote implies, sex education begins at home. Every study finds that parental communication influences adolescents' behavior, and many programs of sex education explicitly require parental participation (Silk & Romero, 2014).

However, some parents wait too long and are uninformed about current STIs and contraception. Parents tend to express clichés and generalities, unaware of their adolescents' sexuality, and adolescents tend to believe their parents know nothing about sex. Embarrassment and ignorance are common on both sides.

It is not unusual for parents to think their own child is not sexually active, while fearing that the child's social connections are far too sexual (Elliott, 2012). One study makes the point: Parents of 12-year-old girls were asked whether their daughters had hugged or kissed a boy "for a long time" or hung out with older boys (signs that sex information is urgently needed). Only 5 percent of the parents, but 38 percent of the girls, said yes (O'Donnell et al., 2008).

What should parents say? That is the wrong question, according to a longitudinal study of thousands of adolescents. Teens who were most likely to risk an STI had parents who warned them to stay away from all sex. In contrast, adolescents were more likely to remain virgins if they had a warm relationship with their parents—specific information was less important than open communication (Deptula et al., 2010). Parents should not shy away from discussions about sex, but honest conversation between parent and child provides better protection than specific sex-related discussions (Hicks et al., 2013).

Especially when parents are silent, forbidding, or vague, adolescent sexual behavior is strongly influenced by peers. Boys learn about sex from other boys (Henry et al., 2012), girls from other girls, with the strongest influence being what peers say they have done, not something abstract (Choukas-Bradley et al., 2014).

Partners also teach each other. However, their lessons are more about pleasure than consequences: Most U.S. adolescent couples do not decide together *before* they have sex how they will prevent pregnancy and disease, and what they will do if their prevention efforts fail. Adolescents were asked whom they discussed sexual issues with. Friends were the most common confidants, then parents, and last of all dating partners. Indeed, only half of them had *ever* discussed anything about sex with their sexual partner (Widman et al., 2014).

From Educators

Sex education from teachers varies dramatically by nation. The curriculum for middle schools in most European nations includes information about masturbation, same-sex romance, oral and anal sex, and specific uses and failures of various methods of contraception. These subjects almost never are covered in U.S. classes.

Rates of teenage pregnancy in most European nations are less than half those in the United States. Perhaps early and extensive education is the reason, although obviously, curriculum is part of the larger culture. Cultural differences regarding sex are vast.

Within the United States, the timing and content of sex education vary by state and community. Some high schools provide comprehensive education, free condoms, and medical treatment; others provide nothing. Some school systems begin sex education in the sixth grade; others wait until senior year of high school. Some middle school sex-education programs successfully increase condom use and delay the age when adolescents become sexually active, but other programs have no impact (Hamilton et al., 2013; Kirby & Laris, 2009).

One controversy has been whether sexual abstinence should be taught as the only acceptable strategy. It is true, of course, that abstaining from sex (including oral and anal sex) prevents STIs, and that abstinence precludes pregnancy. But longitudinal data on abstinence-only education four to six years after adolescents were taught are disappointing. In careful comparison studies, about half the students in the abstinence-only group and the comprehensive sex education group had had sex by age 16 (Trenholm et al., 2007). Students in the abstinence group knew slightly less about preventing disease and pregnancy, but sexual activity was similar in both groups.

A developmental concern is that for the past thirty years, adolescents in the United States have more STIs and unwanted pregnancies than adolescents in other developed nations. In some European nations, sex education is part of the curriculum even before puberty, although politics sometimes clashes with comprehensive, early sex education everywhere (Parker et al., 2009).

// **Response for Parents of a Teenager** (from page 521): Remember: Communicate, do not control. Let your child talk about the meaning of the hairstyle. Remind yourself that a hairstyle in itself is harmless. Don't say "What will people think?" or "Are you on drugs?" or anything that might give your child reason to stop communicating.

// **Response for Sex Educators** (from page 524): Yes, but forgive them. Ideally, parents should talk to their children about sex, presenting honest information and listening to the children's concerns. However, many parents find it very difficult to do so because they feel embarrassed and ignorant. You might schedule separate sessions for adults over 30, for emerging adults, and for adolescents.

Some social scientists contend that the problem is that U.S. educators and parents present morals and facts to adolescents, but teen behavior is driven by social values and emotions. Sexual behavior does not spring from the prefrontal cortex: Knowing how and why to use a condom does not guarantee a careful, wise choice when passions run high. Consequently, effective sex education must engage emotions more than logic. Role-playing with other teens and frank discussions with parents are both crucial (Suleiman & Brindis, 2014).

SUMMING UP Contrary to what some adults may think, peer pressure can be positive. Many adolescents rely on friends of both sexes to help them with the concerns and troubles of the teen years. Romances are typical in high school, but early, exclusive, long-lasting romances are more often a sign of emotional trouble than of maturity. Some adolescents are romantically attracted to others of their own sex; the psychological impact of same-sex orientation depends on the adolescent's family and community.

The media and peers are the most common sources for sex information, but not the most accurate. Parents are influential role models, but few provide detailed and current information before adolescents begin experimenting with sex. School instruction may be helpful, but not every curriculum is equally effective. Schools vary in what they teach about sex, and when. International research suggests that sex education should begin early in adolescence and be more informative than prohibitive.

WHAT HAVE YOU LEARNED?

1. How does the influence of peers and parents differ for adolescents?
2. Why do many adults misunderstand the role of peer pressure?
3. What is the role of parents, peers, and society in helping an adolescent develop an ethnic identity?
4. How do adolescents choose romantic partners, and what do they do together?
5. How does culture affect sexual orientation?
6. From whom do adolescents usually learn about sex?
7. What does the research say about sex education in schools?

Sadness and Anger

Adolescence is usually a wonderful time, perhaps better for current generations than for any earlier cohort. Nonetheless, troubles plague about 20 percent of youths. For instance, one specific survey of over ten thousand 13- to 17-year-olds in the United States using the categories of the DSM-IV found that 23 percent had a disorder in the past month (Kessler et al., 2012). Most disorders are *comorbid,* with several problems occurring at once. Distinguishing between pathology and normal moodiness, between behavior that is seriously troubled versus merely unsettling, is complex.

It is typical for an adolescent to be momentarily less happy and more angry than younger children, but teen emotions often change quickly (Neumann et al., 2011). For a few, however, negative emotions cloud every moment, becoming intense, chronic, even deadly.

Depression

The general emotional trend from childhood to early adolescence is toward less confidence and higher rates of depression, and then, gradually, self-esteem increases. A dip in self-esteem at puberty is found for children of every ethnicity and gender (Fredricks & Eccles, 2002; Greene & Way, 2005; Kutob et al., 2010; Zeiders et al., 2013). Often, self-esteem rises in high school (especially for African American girls and European American boys), but reports vary, and every study finds notable individual differences.

Universal trends, as well as family effects, are apparent. A report from China also finds a dip in self-esteem at seventh grade (when many Chinese experience puberty) and then a gradual rise. Recent cohorts of Chinese teenagers have lower self-esteem than earlier cohorts. The authors ascribe this to reduced social connections: Many youth have no siblings or cousins, many parents are employed far from their children, and divorce has become more common (Liu & Xin, 2014).

On average, self-esteem in adolescence is higher in boys than girls, higher in African Americans than European Americans, who themselves have higher self-esteem than Asian Americans. It is also higher in older adolescents than younger ones (Bachman et al., 2011).

These generalities regarding depression apply to most disorders (Kessler et al., 2012). All studies find notable variability among people the same age, yet continuity within each person. Severe depression may lift but rarely disappears (Huang, 2010).

Context matters. One cultural norm is **familism**—the belief that family members should sacrifice personal freedom and success to care for one another. For immigrant Latino youth, self-esteem and ethnic pride are higher than for most other groups, and a rise over the years of adolescence is common. When compared to the high rates of depression among European American girls, the Latina rise in self-esteem is particularly notable (Zeiders et al., 2013). Perhaps familism is the reason: Latinas become increasingly helpful at home, which makes their parents appreciative and them proud, unlike other U.S. teenage girls.

Clinical Depression

Some adolescents sink into **clinical depression,** a deep sadness and hopelessness that disrupts all normal activities. The causes, including genes and early care, predate adolescence. Then the onset of puberty—with its myriad physical and emotional ups and downs—pushes some vulnerable children, especially girls, into despair. The rate of clinical depression more than doubles during this time, to an estimated 15 percent, affecting about 1 in 5 girls and 1 in 10 boys.

Hormones are probably part of the reason for these gender differences, but girls also experience social pressures from their families, peers, and cultures that boys do not (Naninck et al., 2011). Perhaps the combination of biological and psychosocial stresses causes some to slide into depression.

Differential susceptibility is apparent. One study found that the short allele of the serotonin transporter promoter gene (5-HTTLPR) increased the rate of depression among girls everywhere but increased depression among boys only if they lived in low-SES communities (Uddin et al., 2010). It is not surprising that vulnerability to depression is partly genetic, but why does neighborhood affect boys more than girls? Perhaps cultural factors depress females everywhere, but boys may be protected unless jobs, successful adult men, and encouragement within their community are scarce.

A cognitive explanation for gender differences in depression focuses on **rumination**—talking about, brooding over, and mentally replaying past experiences. Girls ruminate much more than boys, and rumination often

familism The belief that family members should support one another, sacrificing individual freedom and success, if necessary, in order to preserve family unity and protect the family from outside sources.

clinical depression Feelings of hopelessness, lethargy, and worthlessness that last two weeks or more.

rumination Repeatedly thinking and talking about past experiences; can contribute to depression.

Hanging Out These three adolescents live on the Rosebud Sioux Reservation in South Dakota. Adolescence can be challenging for all teenagers, but the suicide rate among Native American teenagers is more than three times the rate for U.S. adolescents overall. Tribal officials in South Dakota are trying to improve the lives of young people so they feel more hope for the future.

KEVIN MOLONEY/THE NEW YORK TIMES/REDUX

leads to depression (Michl et al., 2013). For that reason, close mother–daughter relationships may be depressing if the pair ruminate about the mother's problems (Waller & Rose, 2010). On the other hand, when rumination occurs with a close friend after a stressful event, the friend's support may be helpful (Rose et al., 2014). Differential susceptibility again.

Suicide

Serious, distressing thoughts about killing oneself (called **suicidal ideation**) are most common at about age 15. The 2013 Youth Risk Behavior Survey revealed that more than one-third (35 percent) of U.S. high school girls felt so hopeless that they stopped doing some usual activities for two weeks or more in the previous year (an indication of depression), and more than one-fifth (22.4 percent) seriously thought about suicide. The corresponding rates for boys were 20 percent and 11.6 percent (MMWR, June 13, 2014).

Suicidal ideation can lead to **parasuicide,** also called *attempted suicide* or *failed suicide.* Parasuicide includes any deliberate self-harm that could have been lethal. *Parasuicide* is the best word to use because "failed" suicide implies that to die is to succeed (!); suicide "attempt" is likewise misleading because, especially in adolescence, the difference between attempt and actual suicide may be luck and prompt treatment, not intent.

As you see in Figure 16.5, parasuicide can be divided according to instances that require medical attention (surgery, pumped stomachs, etc.) and those who do not, but any parasuicide is a warning. If there is a next time, the person may die. Thus parasuicide must be taken very seriously.

One form of psychotherapy that seems to reduce the risk of completed suicide is *dialectical behavior therapy,* designed to help the adolescent accept their moods, but not act on them (Miller et al., 2007). This seems a promising, although replicated experimental research regarding this therapy is needed (Berk et al., 2014).

Internationally, rates of teenage parasuicide range between 6 and 20 percent. Among U.S. high school students in 2013, 10.6 percent of the girls and 5.4 percent of the boys tried to kill themselves in the previous year (MMWR, June 13, 2014; see Figure 16.5).

suicidal ideation Thinking about suicide, usually with some serious emotional and intellectual or cognitive overtones.

parasuicide Any potentially lethal action against the self that does not result in death. (Also called *attempted suicide* or *failed suicide.*)

FIGURE 16.5
Sad Thoughts Completed suicide is rare in adolescence, but serious thoughts about killing oneself are frequent. Depression and parasuicide are more common in girls than in boys, but rates are high even in boys. There are three reasons to suspect the rates for boys are underestimates: Boys tend to be less willing to divulge their emotions, boys consider it unmanly to try but fail to kill themselves, and completed suicide is higher in males than in females.

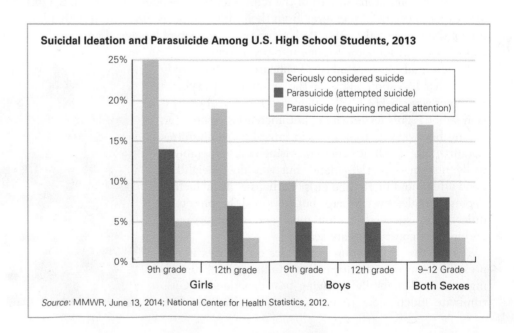

Although suicidal ideation during adolescence is common, completed suicides are rare. The U.S. annual rate of completed suicide for people aged 15 to 19 (in school or not) is less than 8 per 100,000, or 0.008 percent, which is only half the rate for adults aged 20 and older (Parks et al., 2014). This is an important statistic to keep in mind whenever someone claims that adolescent suicide is "epidemic." It is not. Of course, even one teenage suicide is one too many.

Because they are not logical and analytical, adolescents are particularly affected when they hear about someone's suicide, either through the media or from peers (Niedzwiedz et al., 2014). That makes them susceptible to **cluster suicides,** which are several suicides within a group over a brief span of time. For that reason, media portrayal of a tragic suicide may inadvertently trigger more deaths.

In every large nation except China, girls are more likely to *attempt* suicide, but boys are more likely to *complete* it. In the United States, adolescent boys kill themselves four times more often than girls (Parks et al., 2014). The reason may be method: Males typically jump from high places or shoot themselves (immediately lethal), whereas females often swallow pills or cut their wrists, which allows time for conversation, intervention, and second thoughts. Given adolescent volatility, second thoughts are protective.

European American youth are three times more likely to commit suicide than African, Hispanic, or Asian Americans. Suicide is one of very few causes of death that increase with SES.

Delinquency and Defiance

Like low self-esteem and suicidal ideation, bouts of anger are common in adolescence. In fact, a moody adolescent could be both depressed and delinquent because externalizing and internalizing behavior are closely connected during these years (Loeber & Burke, 2011). This may explain suicide in jail: Teenagers jailed for assault (externalizing) are higher suicide risks (internalizing) than adult prisoners.

Especially for Journalists You just heard that a teenage cheerleader jumped off a tall building and died. How should you report the story? (see response, page 531)

cluster suicides Several suicides committed by members of a group within a brief period of time.

Hope and Anger Adolescents and young adults everywhere demonstrate against adult authority, with varied strategies and results. In Cairo's Tahrir Square (*left*), this young man flashes the peace sign hours before President Mubarak's resignation. French students (*right*) protested cuts in high school staff, but their demands were resisted by the government. Worldwide, social change is fueled by youthful aspirations—sometimes leading to victory, sometimes to despair, and often (as in Egypt) with high emotions that seem unrealistic later on. The French students (*right*) seem to have lost all hope—a sign of political despair.

Externalizing actions are obvious. Many adolescents slam doors, curse parents, and tell friends exactly how badly other teenagers (or siblings or teachers) have behaved. Some teenagers—particularly boys—"act out" by breaking laws. They steal, damage property, or injure others.

One issue is whether teenage anger is not only common but also necessary for normal development. That is what Anna Freud (Sigmund's daughter, herself a

AARON ST. CLAIR/SPLASH NEWS/NEWSCOM

What Next? Jenelle Evans, famous as *Teen Mom 2*, has photographers following her even to court. Here she returns to court with her then boyfriend, Kieffer Delp, both accused of breaking and entering and drug possession. Those charges were dropped, but the judge sentenced her to two days in jail because she tested positive for marijuana. Limited or persistent?

adolescence-limited offender A person whose criminal activity stops by age 21.

life-course-persistent offender A person whose criminal activity typically begins in early adolescence and continues throughout life; a career criminal.

prominent psychoanalyst) thought. She wrote that adolescent resistance to parental authority was "welcome . . . beneficial . . . inevitable." She explained:

> We all know individual children who as late as the ages of fourteen, fifteen or sixteen, show no such outer evidence of inner unrest. They remain, as they have been during the latency period, "good" children, wrapped up in their family relationships, considerate sons of their mothers, submissive to their fathers, in accord with the atmosphere, ideas and ideals of their childhood background. Convenient as this may be, it signifies a delay of their normal development and is, as such, a sign to be taken seriously.
>
> [A. Freud, 2000, p. 263]

However, most contemporary psychologists, teachers, and parents are quite happy with well-behaved, considerate teenagers, who often grow up to be happy adults. The 30-year Dunedin, New Zealand study first mentioned in Chapter 1 found that adults who had never been arrested usually earned degrees, "held high-status jobs, and expressed optimism about their own futures" (Moffitt, 2003, p. 61).

Some psychologists suggest that adolescent rebellion is a social construction. It might be an idea created and endorsed by many Western adults but not expected or usual in Asian nations (Russell et al., 2010).

Breaking the Law

Both the prevalence (how widespread) and the incidence (how frequent) of criminal actions are higher during adolescence than earlier or later. Arrest statistics in every nation reflect this fact, with 30 percent of African American males and 22 percent of European American males being arrested at least once before age 18 (Brame et al., 2014).

It would be good to know how many young people have broken the law but not been caught, or caught but not arrested. Confidential self-reports suggest that most adolescents (male or female) break the law at least once before age 20.

However, the actual percentage is unknown, as some adolescents refuse to answer and some might brag (falsely) about skipping school, drinking underage, shoplifting, hurting another person, vandalism, and so on. Others might deny (again falsely) ever having done such a thing. Researchers in the Netherlands found that one-third of those interrogated by the police said that they had no police contact (van Batenburg-Eddes et al., 2012).

Research on confessions to a crime is interesting in this regard. In the United States, about 20 percent of confessions are false: That is, people confess to a crime they did not commit. False confessions are more likely in adolescence, partly because of brain immaturity and partly because young people want to help their family members and please adults—including the police (Feld, 2013; Steinberg, 2009).

Many researchers in delinquency suggest that we need to distinguish two kinds of teenage lawbreakers (Monahan et al., 2013), as first proposed by Terri Moffitt (2001, 2003). Most juvenile delinquents are **adolescence-limited offenders,** whose criminal activity stops by age 21. They break the law with their friends, facilitated by their chosen antisocial peers. More boys than girls are in this group, but some gangs include both sexes (the gender gap in law-breaking is narrower in late adolescence than earlier or later).

The other delinquents are **life-course-persistent offenders,** who break the law before and after adolescence as well as during it. Their law-breaking is more often done alone than as part of a gang, and the cause is neurological impairment (either inborn or caused by early experiences). Symptoms include not only childhood defiance but also early problems with language and learning.

Although suicidal ideation during adolescence is common, completed suicides are rare. The U.S. annual rate of completed suicide for people aged 15 to 19 (in school or not) is less than 8 per 100,000, or 0.008 percent, which is only half the rate for adults aged 20 and older (Parks et al., 2014). This is an important statistic to keep in mind whenever someone claims that adolescent suicide is "epidemic." It is not. Of course, even one teenage suicide is one too many.

Because they are not logical and analytical, adolescents are particularly affected when they hear about someone's suicide, either through the media or from peers (Niedzwiedz et al., 2014). That makes them susceptible to **cluster suicides,** which are several suicides within a group over a brief span of time. For that reason, media portrayal of a tragic suicide may inadvertently trigger more deaths.

In every large nation except China, girls are more likely to *attempt* suicide, but boys are more likely to *complete* it. In the United States, adolescent boys kill themselves four times more often than girls (Parks et al., 2014). The reason may be method: Males typically jump from high places or shoot themselves (immediately lethal), whereas females often swallow pills or cut their wrists, which allows time for conversation, intervention, and second thoughts. Given adolescent volatility, second thoughts are protective.

European American youth are three times more likely to commit suicide than African, Hispanic, or Asian Americans. Suicide is one of very few causes of death that increase with SES.

Delinquency and Defiance

Like low self-esteem and suicidal ideation, bouts of anger are common in adolescence. In fact, a moody adolescent could be both depressed and delinquent because externalizing and internalizing behavior are closely connected during these years (Loeber & Burke, 2011). This may explain suicide in jail: Teenagers jailed for assault (externalizing) are higher suicide risks (internalizing) than adult prisoners.

Especially for Journalists You just heard that a teenage cheerleader jumped off a tall building and died. How should you report the story? (see response, page 531)

cluster suicides Several suicides committed by members of a group within a brief period of time.

Hope and Anger Adolescents and young adults everywhere demonstrate against adult authority, with varied strategies and results. In Cairo's Tahrir Square (*left*), this young man flashes the peace sign hours before President Mubarak's resignation. French students (*right*) protested cuts in high school staff, but their demands were resisted by the government. Worldwide, social change is fueled by youthful aspirations—sometimes leading to victory, sometimes to despair, and often (as in Egypt) with high emotions that seem unrealistic later on. The French students (*right*) seem to have lost all hope—a sign of political despair.

Externalizing actions are obvious. Many adolescents slam doors, curse parents, and tell friends exactly how badly other teenagers (or siblings or teachers) have behaved. Some teenagers—particularly boys—"act out" by breaking laws. They steal, damage property, or injure others.

One issue is whether teenage anger is not only common but also necessary for normal development. That is what Anna Freud (Sigmund's daughter, herself a

AARON ST. CLAIR/SPLASH NEWS/NEWSCOM

What Next? Jenelle Evans, famous as *Teen Mom 2*, has photographers following her even to court. Here she returns to court with her then boyfriend, Kieffer Delp, both accused of breaking and entering and drug possession. Those charges were dropped, but the judge sentenced her to two days in jail because she tested positive for marijuana. Limited or persistent?

adolescence-limited offender A person whose criminal activity stops by age 21.

life-course-persistent offender A person whose criminal activity typically begins in early adolescence and continues throughout life; a career criminal.

prominent psychoanalyst) thought. She wrote that adolescent resistance to parental authority was "welcome . . . beneficial . . . inevitable." She explained:

> We all know individual children who as late as the ages of fourteen, fifteen or sixteen, show no such outer evidence of inner unrest. They remain, as they have been during the latency period, "good" children, wrapped up in their family relationships, considerate sons of their mothers, submissive to their fathers, in accord with the atmosphere, ideas and ideals of their childhood background. Convenient as this may be, it signifies a delay of their normal development and is, as such, a sign to be taken seriously.
>
> [A. Freud, 2000, p. 263]

However, most contemporary psychologists, teachers, and parents are quite happy with well-behaved, considerate teenagers, who often grow up to be happy adults. The 30-year Dunedin, New Zealand study first mentioned in Chapter 1 found that adults who had never been arrested usually earned degrees, "held high-status jobs, and expressed optimism about their own futures" (Moffitt, 2003, p. 61).

Some psychologists suggest that adolescent rebellion is a social construction. It might be an idea created and endorsed by many Western adults but not expected or usual in Asian nations (Russell et al., 2010).

Breaking the Law

Both the prevalence (how widespread) and the incidence (how frequent) of criminal actions are higher during adolescence than earlier or later. Arrest statistics in every nation reflect this fact, with 30 percent of African American males and 22 percent of European American males being arrested at least once before age 18 (Brame et al., 2014).

It would be good to know how many young people have broken the law but not been caught, or caught but not arrested. Confidential self-reports suggest that most adolescents (male or female) break the law at least once before age 20.

However, the actual percentage is unknown, as some adolescents refuse to answer and some might brag (falsely) about skipping school, drinking underage, shoplifting, hurting another person, vandalism, and so on. Others might deny (again falsely) ever having done such a thing. Researchers in the Netherlands found that one-third of those interrogated by the police said that they had no police contact (van Batenburg-Eddes et al., 2012).

Research on confessions to a crime is interesting in this regard. In the United States, about 20 percent of confessions are false: That is, people confess to a crime they did not commit. False confessions are more likely in adolescence, partly because of brain immaturity and partly because young people want to help their family members and please adults—including the police (Feld, 2013; Steinberg, 2009).

Many researchers in delinquency suggest that we need to distinguish two kinds of teenage lawbreakers (Monahan et al., 2013), as first proposed by Terri Moffitt (2001, 2003). Most juvenile delinquents are **adolescence-limited offenders,** whose criminal activity stops by age 21. They break the law with their friends, facilitated by their chosen antisocial peers. More boys than girls are in this group, but some gangs include both sexes (the gender gap in law-breaking is narrower in late adolescence than earlier or later).

The other delinquents are **life-course-persistent offenders,** who break the law before and after adolescence as well as during it. Their law-breaking is more often done alone than as part of a gang, and the cause is neurological impairment (either inborn or caused by early experiences). Symptoms include not only childhood defiance but also early problems with language and learning.

Although suicidal ideation during adolescence is common, completed suicides are rare. The U.S. annual rate of completed suicide for people aged 15 to 19 (in school or not) is less than 8 per 100,000, or 0.008 percent, which is only half the rate for adults aged 20 and older (Parks et al., 2014). This is an important statistic to keep in mind whenever someone claims that adolescent suicide is "epidemic." It is not. Of course, even one teenage suicide is one too many.

Because they are not logical and analytical, adolescents are particularly affected when they hear about someone's suicide, either through the media or from peers (Niedzwiedz et al., 2014). That makes them susceptible to **cluster suicides,** which are several suicides within a group over a brief span of time. For that reason, media portrayal of a tragic suicide may inadvertently trigger more deaths.

In every large nation except China, girls are more likely to *attempt* suicide, but boys are more likely to *complete* it. In the United States, adolescent boys kill themselves four times more often than girls (Parks et al., 2014). The reason may be method: Males typically jump from high places or shoot themselves (immediately lethal), whereas females often swallow pills or cut their wrists, which allows time for conversation, intervention, and second thoughts. Given adolescent volatility, second thoughts are protective.

European American youth are three times more likely to commit suicide than African, Hispanic, or Asian Americans. Suicide is one of very few causes of death that increase with SES.

Delinquency and Defiance

Like low self-esteem and suicidal ideation, bouts of anger are common in adolescence. In fact, a moody adolescent could be both depressed and delinquent because externalizing and internalizing behavior are closely connected during these years (Loeber & Burke, 2011). This may explain suicide in jail: Teenagers jailed for assault (externalizing) are higher suicide risks (internalizing) than adult prisoners.

Especially for Journalists You just heard that a teenage cheerleader jumped off a tall building and died. How should you report the story? (see response, page 531)

cluster suicides Several suicides committed by members of a group within a brief period of time.

Hope and Anger Adolescents and young adults everywhere demonstrate against adult authority, with varied strategies and results. In Cairo's Tahrir Square (*left*), this young man flashes the peace sign hours before President Mubarak's resignation. French students (*right*) protested cuts in high school staff, but their demands were resisted by the government. Worldwide, social change is fueled by youthful aspirations—sometimes leading to victory, sometimes to despair, and often (as in Egypt) with high emotions that seem unrealistic later on. The French students (*right*) seem to have lost all hope—a sign of political despair.

Externalizing actions are obvious. Many adolescents slam doors, curse parents, and tell friends exactly how badly other teenagers (or siblings or teachers) have behaved. Some teenagers—particularly boys—"act out" by breaking laws. They steal, damage property, or injure others.

One issue is whether teenage anger is not only common but also necessary for normal development. That is what Anna Freud (Sigmund's daughter, herself a

prominent psychoanalyst) thought. She wrote that adolescent resistance to parental authority was "welcome . . . beneficial . . . inevitable." She explained:

> We all know individual children who as late as the ages of fourteen, fifteen or sixteen, show no such outer evidence of inner unrest. They remain, as they have been during the latency period, "good" children, wrapped up in their family relationships, considerate sons of their mothers, submissive to their fathers, in accord with the atmosphere, ideas and ideals of their childhood background. Convenient as this may be, it signifies a delay of their normal development and is, as such, a sign to be taken seriously.
>
> [A. Freud, 2000, p. 263]

However, most contemporary psychologists, teachers, and parents are quite happy with well-behaved, considerate teenagers, who often grow up to be happy adults. The 30-year Dunedin, New Zealand study first mentioned in Chapter 1 found that adults who had never been arrested usually earned degrees, "held high-status jobs, and expressed optimism about their own futures" (Moffitt, 2003, p. 61).

Some psychologists suggest that adolescent rebellion is a social construction. It might be an idea created and endorsed by many Western adults but not expected or usual in Asian nations (Russell et al., 2010).

Breaking the Law

Both the prevalence (how widespread) and the incidence (how frequent) of criminal actions are higher during adolescence than earlier or later. Arrest statistics in every nation reflect this fact, with 30 percent of African American males and 22 percent of European American males being arrested at least once before age 18 (Brame et al., 2014).

It would be good to know how many young people have broken the law but not been caught, or caught but not arrested. Confidential self-reports suggest that most adolescents (male or female) break the law at least once before age 20.

However, the actual percentage is unknown, as some adolescents refuse to answer and some might brag (falsely) about skipping school, drinking underage, shoplifting, hurting another person, vandalism, and so on. Others might deny (again falsely) ever having done such a thing. Researchers in the Netherlands found that one-third of those interrogated by the police said that they had no police contact (van Batenburg-Eddes et al., 2012).

Research on confessions to a crime is interesting in this regard. In the United States, about 20 percent of confessions are false: That is, people confess to a crime they did not commit. False confessions are more likely in adolescence, partly because of brain immaturity and partly because young people want to help their family members and please adults—including the police (Feld, 2013; Steinberg, 2009).

Many researchers in delinquency suggest that we need to distinguish two kinds of teenage lawbreakers (Monahan et al., 2013), as first proposed by Terri Moffitt (2001, 2003). Most juvenile delinquents are **adolescence-limited offenders,** whose criminal activity stops by age 21. They break the law with their friends, facilitated by their chosen antisocial peers. More boys than girls are in this group, but some gangs include both sexes (the gender gap in law-breaking is narrower in late adolescence than earlier or later).

The other delinquents are **life-course-persistent offenders,** who break the law before and after adolescence as well as during it. Their law-breaking is more often done alone than as part of a gang, and the cause is neurological impairment (either inborn or caused by early experiences). Symptoms include not only childhood defiance but also early problems with language and learning.

What Next? Jenelle Evans, famous as *Teen Mom 2*, has photographers following her even to court. Here she returns to court with her then boyfriend, Kieffer Delp, both accused of breaking and entering and drug possession. Those charges were dropped, but the judge sentenced her to two days in jail because she tested positive for marijuana. Limited or persistent?

adolescence-limited offender A person whose criminal activity stops by age 21.

life-course-persistent offender A person whose criminal activity typically begins in early adolescence and continues throughout life; a career criminal.

Although suicidal ideation during adolescence is common, completed suicides are rare. The U.S. annual rate of completed suicide for people aged 15 to 19 (in school or not) is less than 8 per 100,000, or 0.008 percent, which is only half the rate for adults aged 20 and older (Parks et al., 2014). This is an important statistic to keep in mind whenever someone claims that adolescent suicide is "epidemic." It is not. Of course, even one teenage suicide is one too many.

Because they are not logical and analytical, adolescents are particularly affected when they hear about someone's suicide, either through the media or from peers (Niedzwiedz et al., 2014). That makes them susceptible to **cluster suicides,** which are several suicides within a group over a brief span of time. For that reason, media portrayal of a tragic suicide may inadvertently trigger more deaths.

In every large nation except China, girls are more likely to *attempt* suicide, but boys are more likely to *complete* it. In the United States, adolescent boys kill themselves four times more often than girls (Parks et al., 2014). The reason may be method: Males typically jump from high places or shoot themselves (immediately lethal), whereas females often swallow pills or cut their wrists, which allows time for conversation, intervention, and second thoughts. Given adolescent volatility, second thoughts are protective.

European American youth are three times more likely to commit suicide than African, Hispanic, or Asian Americans. Suicide is one of very few causes of death that increase with SES.

Delinquency and Defiance

Like low self-esteem and suicidal ideation, bouts of anger are common in adolescence. In fact, a moody adolescent could be both depressed and delinquent because externalizing and internalizing behavior are closely connected during these years (Loeber & Burke, 2011). This may explain suicide in jail: Teenagers jailed for assault (externalizing) are higher suicide risks (internalizing) than adult prisoners.

Hope and Anger Adolescents and young adults everywhere demonstrate against adult authority, with varied strategies and results. In Cairo's Tahrir Square (*left*), this young man flashes the peace sign hours before President Mubarak's resignation. French students (*right*) protested cuts in high school staff, but their demands were resisted by the government. Worldwide, social change is fueled by youthful aspirations—sometimes leading to victory, sometimes to despair, and often (as in Egypt) with high emotions that seem unrealistic later on. The French students (*right*) seem to have lost all hope—a sign of political despair.

© JAMES MAY/ALAMY

REUTERS/PHILIPPE WOJAZER/LANDOV

Externalizing actions are obvious. Many adolescents slam doors, curse parents, and tell friends exactly how badly other teenagers (or siblings or teachers) have behaved. Some teenagers—particularly boys—"act out" by breaking laws. They steal, damage property, or injure others.

One issue is whether teenage anger is not only common but also necessary for normal development. That is what Anna Freud (Sigmund's daughter) herself a

Especially for Journalists You just heard that a teenage cheerleader jumped off a tall building and died. How should you report the story? (see response, page 531)

cluster suicides Several suicides committed by members of a group within a brief period of time.

What Next? Jenelle Evans, famous as *Teen Mom 2*, has photographers following her even to court. Here she returns to court with her then boyfriend, Kieffer Delp, both accused of breaking and entering and drug possession. Those charges were dropped, but the judge sentenced her to two days in jail because she tested positive for marijuana. Limited or persistent?

adolescence-limited offender A person whose criminal activity stops by age 21.

life-course-persistent offender A person whose criminal activity typically begins in early adolescence and continues throughout life; a career criminal.

prominent psychoanalyst) thought. She wrote that adolescent resistance to parental authority was "welcome . . . beneficial . . . inevitable." She explained:

> We all know individual children who as late as the ages of fourteen, fifteen or sixteen, show no such outer evidence of inner unrest. They remain, as they have been during the latency period, "good" children, wrapped up in their family relationships, considerate sons of their mothers, submissive to their fathers, in accord with the atmosphere, ideas and ideals of their childhood background. Convenient as this may be, it signifies a delay of their normal development and is, as such, a sign to be taken seriously.
>
> [*A. Freud, 2000, p. 263*]

However, most contemporary psychologists, teachers, and parents are quite happy with well-behaved, considerate teenagers, who often grow up to be happy adults. The 30-year Dunedin, New Zealand study first mentioned in Chapter 1 found that adults who had never been arrested usually earned degrees, "held high-status jobs, and expressed optimism about their own futures" (Moffitt, 2003, p. 61).

Some psychologists suggest that adolescent rebellion is a social construction. It might be an idea created and endorsed by many Western adults but not expected or usual in Asian nations (Russell et al., 2010).

Breaking the Law

Both the prevalence (how widespread) and the incidence (how frequent) of criminal actions are higher during adolescence than earlier or later. Arrest statistics in every nation reflect this fact, with 30 percent of African American males and 22 percent of European American males being arrested at least once before age 18 (Brame et al., 2014).

It would be good to know how many young people have broken the law but not been caught, or caught but not arrested. Confidential self-reports suggest that most adolescents (male or female) break the law at least once before age 20.

However, the actual percentage is unknown, as some adolescents refuse to answer and some might brag (falsely) about skipping school, drinking underage, shoplifting, hurting another person, vandalism, and so on. Others might deny (again falsely) ever having done such a thing. Researchers in the Netherlands found that one-third of those interrogated by the police said that they had no police contact (van Batenburg-Eddes et al., 2012).

Research on confessions to a crime is interesting in this regard. In the United States, about 20 percent of confessions are false: That is, people confess to a crime they did not commit. False confessions are more likely in adolescence, partly because of brain immaturity and partly because young people want to help their family members and please adults—including the police (Feld, 2013; Steinberg, 2009).

Many researchers in delinquency suggest that we need to distinguish two kinds of teenage lawbreakers (Monahan et al., 2013), as first proposed by Terri Moffitt (2001, 2003). Most juvenile delinquents are **adolescence-limited offenders,** whose criminal activity stops by age 21. They break the law with their friends, facilitated by their chosen antisocial peers. More boys than girls are in this group, but some gangs include both sexes (the gender gap in law-breaking is narrower in late adolescence than earlier or later).

The other delinquents are **life-course-persistent offenders,** who break the law before and after adolescence as well as during it. Their law-breaking is more often done alone than as part of a gang, and the cause is neurological impairment (either inborn or caused by early experiences). Symptoms include not only childhood defiance but also early problems with language and learning.

During adolescence, the criminal records of both types may be similar. However, if adolescence-limited delinquents can be protected from various snares (such as quitting school, entering prison, drug addiction, early parenthood), they outgrow their criminal behavior. This is confirmed by other research: Few delinquent youths who are not imprisoned continue to be criminals in early adulthood (Monahan et al., 2009).

Causes of Delinquency

One way to reduce adolescent crime is to consider earlier behavior patterns and then stop delinquency before the police become involved. Parents and schools need to develop strong and protective relationships with children, teaching them emotional regulation and prosocial behavior, as explained in earlier chapters. In early adolescence, three pathways to dire consequences can be seen:

1. *Stubbornness* can lead to defiance, which can lead to running away. Runaways are often victims as well as criminals (e.g., falling in with prostitutes and petty thieves).

2. *Shoplifting* can lead to arson and burglary. Things become more important than people.

3. *Bullying* can lead to assault, rape, and murder.

Each of these pathways demands a different response. The rebelliousness of the first can be channeled or limited until less impulsive anger prevails with maturation. Those on the second pathway require stronger human relationships and moral education. Those on the third present the most serious problem; their bullying should have been stopped in childhood, as Chapters 10 and 13 explained. In all cases, early warning signs are present, and intervention is more effective earlier than later (Loeber & Burke, 2011).

Adolescent crime in the United States and many other nations has decreased in the past 20 years. Only half as many juveniles under age 18 are currently arrested for murder than were in 1990. For almost every crime, boys are arrested at least twice as often as girls are.

No explanation for declining rates or gender differences is accepted by all scholars. Regarding gender, it is true that boys are more overtly aggressive and rebellious at every age, but this may be nurture, not nature (Loeber et al., 2013). Some studies find that female aggression is typically limited to family and friends and therefore less likely to lead to an arrest.

Regarding the drop in adolescent crime, many possibilities have been suggested: fewer high school dropouts (more education means less crime); wiser judges (who now have community service as an option); better policing (arrests for misdemeanors are up, which may warn parents); smaller families (parents are more attentive to each of two children than of twelve); better contraception and legal abortion (wanted children are less likely to become criminals); stricter drug laws (binge drinking and crack use increase crime); more immigrants (who are more law-abiding); less lead in the blood (early lead poisoning reduces brain functioning); and more.

Nonetheless, adolescents remain more likely to break the law than adults. To be specific, the arrest rate for 15- to 17-year-olds is twice that for those over 18. The disproportion is true for almost every crime (fraud, forgery, and embezzlement are exceptions) (FBI, 2013). Jail increases the chance that a temporary rebellion will be a lifetime pattern, but that does not mean that delinquency should be ignored. As with depression, angry adolescents cannot be ignored: They harm as well as others.

// **Response for Journalists** (from page 529): Since teenagers seek admiration from their peers, be careful not to glorify the victim's life or death. Facts are needed, as is, perhaps, inclusion of warning signs that were missed or cautions about alcohol abuse. Avoid prominent headlines or anything that might encourage another teenager to do the same thing.

SUMMING UP   Compared with people of other ages, many adolescents experience sudden and extreme emotions that lead to powerful sadness and explosive anger. Supportive families, friends, neighborhoods, and cultures usually contain and channel such feelings. For some teenagers, however, emotions are unchecked or intensified by their social contexts. This situation can lead to parasuicide (especially for girls), to minor lawbreaking (for both sexes), and less often, to completed suicide or jail (especially for boys). Incidence statistics sometimes counter public impressions: Teenage suicide is much less common than adult suicide (even though many teenagers contemplate suicide), and almost all teenagers break the law (although arrest and imprisonment rates are much higher for boys). Developmentalists distinguish between adolescent-limited and life-course-persistent criminals. Pathways to crime can be seen in childhood and early adolescence: Intervention is most effective then as well.

WHAT HAVE YOU LEARNED?

1. What is the difference between adolescent sadness and clinical depression?
2. Why do many adults think adolescent suicide is more common than it is?
3. How can rumination contribute to gender differences in depression?
4. Why are cluster suicides more common in adolescence than in later life?
5. What are the similarities between life-course-persistent and adolescence-limited offenders?
6. What factors increase or decrease deliquency?

Drug Use and Abuse

Hormonal surges, the brain's reward centers, and cognitive immaturity make adolescents particularly attracted to the sensations produced by psychoactive drugs. But their immature bodies and brains make drug use especially hazardous.

Variations in Drug Use

Most teenagers try *psychoactive drugs,* that is, drugs that activate the brain. Cigarettes, alcohol, and many prescription medicines are as addictive and damaging as illegal drugs such as cocaine and heroin.

Age Trends

For many developmental reasons, adolescence is a sensitive time for experimentation, daily use, and eventual addiction to psychoactive drugs (Schulenberg et al., 2014). Both prevalence and incidence of drug use increase from about ages 10 to 25 and then decreases, as adult responsibilities and experiences make drugs less attractive.

Most worrisome is drinking alcohol and smoking cigarettes before age 15, because early use escalates. That makes depression, sexual abuse, bullying, and later addiction more likely (Merikangas & McClaire, 2012; Mennis & Mason, 2012).

Although drug use increases as adolescents mature, we need to mention one exception: inhalants (fumes from aerosol containers, glue, cleaning fluid, etc.). Sadly, the youngest adolescents are most likely to try inhalants, because they find it easy to get and they are least able, cognitively, to understand the risk of one time use—brain damage and even death. For all drugs, close family relationships are protective (Baltazar et al., 2013).

Variations by Place, Generation, and Gender

Nations vary markedly. Consider the most common drugs: alcohol and to[...]

In most European nations, alcohol is part of every dinner, and child[...] as adults partake. The opposite is true in much of the Middle East, [...]

Video: Risk-Taking in Adolescence: Substance Use
http://qrs.ly/xf4ep1k

Especially for Police Officers You see some 15-year-olds drinking beer in a local park when they belong in school. What do you do? (see response, page 535)

is illegal and teenagers almost never drink. The only alcohol available is concocted illegally; it is dangerous—in one recent incident, 7 young Iranian men died from drinking it (Erdbrink, 2013).

Cigarettes are available everywhere, but national differences are dramatic. In many Asian nations, anyone anywhere may smoke cigarettes; in the United States, adolescents are forbidden to buy or smoke, and smoking by anyone of any age is prohibited in many places. Nonetheless, 48 percent of U.S. high school seniors have tried smoking (MMWR, June 13, 2014).

In Canada, cigarette advertising is outlawed. Cigarette packs have graphic pictures of diseased lungs, rotting teeth, and so on; fewer Canadian 15- to 19-year-olds smoke.

Variations within nations are also marked. In the United States, three-fourths of high school seniors have tried alcohol and almost half are current drinkers; about a third have tried marijuana (MMWR, June 13, 2014), but a significant minority (about 25 percent) have never used any drugs,

How to Escape Imagine living where these boys do, or on the streets in Tegucigalpa, the capital city of Honduras—the nation with the world's highest murder rate. These homeless teenagers are sniffing paint thinner for a dangerous moment of joy.

including alcohol and cigarettes.

Cohort differences are evident, even over a few years. Use of most drugs has decreased in the United States since 1976 (see Figure 16.6), with the most notable decreases in marijuana and the most recent decreases in synthetic narcotics and prescription drugs (Johnston et al., 2014). As mentioned in Chapter 1, vaping (using e-cigarettes) is increasing rapidly during adolescence, but neither lawmakers, nor doctors, nor parents yet know if this bodes ill or well for their future.

Longitudinal data show that the availability of drugs does not have much impact on use: Most high school students say they could easily get alcohol, cigarettes, and marijuana if they wish. However, perception of risks varies from cohort to cohort, and that has a large effect on use.

With some exceptions, adolescent boys use more drugs and use them more often than girls do (Mennis & Mason, 2012). In Asia and South America, about four times as many boys as girls smoke. Although the exact proportion varies by nation, in Asia adolescent girls never smoke nearly as much as boys (Giovino et al., 2012).

FIGURE 16.6
Rise and Fall By asking the same questions year after year, the Monitoring the Future study shows notable historical effects. It is encouraging that something in society, not in the adolescent, makes drug use increase and decrease and that the most recent data show a decline in use. However, as Chapter 1 emphasized, survey research cannot prove what causes change.

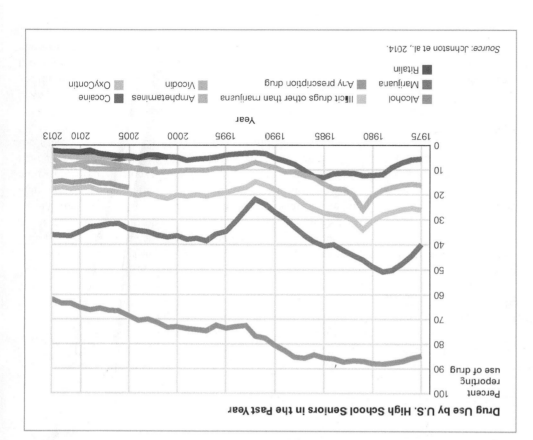

Drug Use by U.S. High School Seniors in the Past Year

Percent reporting use of drug

Year

Legend: Alcohol, Illicit drugs other than marijuana, Marijuana, Any prescription drug, Ritalin, Cocaine, Amphetamines, Vicodin, OxyContin

Source: Johnston et al., 2014.

JASON LEE/REUTERS/LANDOV

A Man Now This boy in Tibet is proud to be a smoker—in many Asian nations, smoking is considered manly.

These gender differences are reinforced by social constructions about proper male and female behavior. In Indonesia, for instance, 38 percent of the boys smoke cigarettes, but only 5 percent of the girls do. One Indonesian boy explained, "If I don't smoke, I'm not a real man" (quoted in Ng et al., 2007).

In the United States, females smoke cigarettes about as often as males (for high school seniors the rates of smoking in the past month are 19 and 20 percent, respectively), but they drink alcohol at younger ages (MMWR, June 13, 2014). Body image is important for both sexes, which is why boys use more steroids and girls use more diet drugs. (**Developmental Link:** Body image is discussed in Chapter 14.)

Harm from Drugs

Many researchers find that drug use before maturity is particularly likely to harm body and brain growth, as well as predict addiction. However, adolescents typically deny that they ever could become addicted. Few adolescents notice when they move past *use* (experimenting) to *abuse* (experiencing harm) and then to *addiction* (needing the drug to avoid feeling nervous, anxious, sick, or in pain).

Each drug is harmful in a particular way. An obvious negative effect of *tobacco* is that it impairs digestion and nutrition, slowing down growth. This is true not only for cigarettes but also for bidis, cigars, pipes, and chewing tobacco, and probably e-cigarettes. Since internal organs continue to mature after the height spurt, drug-using teenagers who appear to be fully grown may damage their developing hearts, lungs, brains, and reproductive systems.

---

opposing perspectives

E-Cigarettes: Path to Addiction or Healthy Choice?

Controversial is the use of *e-cigarettes,* which are increasingly available and often tried by adolescents. If using e-cigs, or vaping, helps smokers quit, then e-cigarettes literally save lives. Smokers with asthma, heart disease, or lung cancer who find it impossible to stop smoking cigarettes are often able to switch to vaping with notable health benefits (Burstyn, 2014; Franck et al., 2014; Hajek et al., 2014).

However, the fear is that adolescents who try e-cigarettes will become addicted to nicotine and be harmed by some other ingredients. Part of the problem is that e-cigarettes are marketed with flavors and an appearance that make them attractive to teenagers. It is known that menthol cigarettes and hookah bars increase the rate of cigarette-smoking among young people (Giovino et al., 2013; Sterling & Mermelstein, 2011); e-cigs may do the same (Hajek et al., 2014; Bhatnagar et al., 2014; Dutra & Glantz, 2014).

A victory of North American public health campaigns has been a marked reduction in smoking regular cigarettes. Not only are there only half as many adult smokers as there were in 1950, there are numerous public places where smoking is forbidden, and many people now forbid anyone to smoke in their homes.

In the United States, such homes were the majority (83 percent) in 2010, an increase from almost zero in 1970 and 43 percent in 1992. Many of those homes have no smoking residents, but cigarettes are banned at 46 percent of the homes where a smoker lives (MMWR, September 5, 2014). Adolescent smoking has markedly declined.

That is clearly a victory for public health, one to celebrate. Therein lies the danger. If e-cigarettes make smoking more acceptable, will adolescents pick up the habits that their elders gave up? E-cigs are illegal for people under age 18, but they are sold in flavors like bubble gum, can be placed for a fee in Hollywood movies, and are permitted in public places. If the image of smoking changes from a "cancer stick" to a "glamour accessory," will public health progress stop?

The argument from distributers of e-cigarettes is that they are a healthier alternative to cigarettes, that people should be able to make their own choices, and that the fear of adolescent vaping is exaggerated—part of the irrational fear that everything teenagers do is trouble. As with all opposing perspectives, attitudes depend on who is judging, not yet on a consensus among scientists.

Alcohol is the most frequently abused drug in the United States. Heavy drinking impairs memory and self-control, damaging the hippocampus and the prefrontal cortex, distorting the reward circuits of the brain lifelong (Guerri & Pascual, 2010).

Adolescence is a particularly sensitive period, because the regions of the brain that are connected to pleasure are more strongly affected by alcohol during adolescence than at later ages. That makes teenagers less conscious of the "intoxicating, aversive, and sedative effects" of alcohol (Spear, 2013, p. 155). Brain damage by alcohol during adolescence has been proven with controlled research on mice, with the results seeming to extend to humans as well.

Marijuana seems harmless to many people (especially teenagers), partly because users seem more relaxed than inebriated. Yet adolescents who regularly smoke marijuana are more likely to drop out of school, become teenage parents, be depressed, and later be unemployed. Marijuana affects memory, language proficiency, and motivation—all of which are especially crucial during adolescence (Chassin et al., 2014). Many developmentalists fear that more acceptance of marijuana among adults will lead to less learning and poorer health among teenagers.

Marijuana is often the drug of choice among wealthier adolescents, who then become less motivated to achieve in school and more likely to develop other problems (Ansary & Luthar, 2009). It seems as if, rather than lack of ambition leading to marijuana use, marijuana destroys ambition.

Twenty-three U.S. states have legalized marijuana for medical use, with many more states about to do so. In Colorado, Washington, Alaska, and Oregon, it is legal for recreational use as well. The law everywhere forbids marijuana, as well as cigarettes and alcohol, for teenagers, because of the aforementioned harm to adolescent bodies and brains. It remains to be seen whether adolescents will access marijuana as readily as they do alcohol, and whether this is as harmful as some fear.

Some researchers wonder whether these are correlations, not causes. It is true that depressed and abused adolescents are more likely to use drugs, and that later these same people are likely to be more depressed and further abused. Maybe the stresses of adolescence lead to drug use, not vice versa.

However, longitudinal research suggests that drug use *causes* more problems than it solves, often *preceding* anxiety disorders, depression, and rebellion (Maslowsky et al., 2014). Further, adolescents who use alcohol, cigarettes, and marijuana recreationally as teenagers are more likely to abuse these and other drugs after age 20 (Moss et al., 2014). Longitudinal studies of twins (which allow control for genetics and family influences) find that, although many problems predate drug use, drugs themselves add to the problems (Lynskey et al., 2012; Korhonen et al., 2012).

Most adolescents covet the drugs that slightly older youth use. Many 18-year-olds will buy drugs for younger siblings and classmates, supposedly being kind but actually doing harm.

New Zealand lowered the age for legal purchase of alcohol from 20 to 18 in 1999, and experienced more hospital admissions for intoxication, car crashes, and injuries from assault in both 18- to 19-year-olds and 16- to 17-year-olds (Kypri et al., 2006; 2014). Developmentalists fear adolescent drug use but wonder what will reduce it.

Preventing Drug Abuse: What Works?

Drug abuse is progressive, beginning with a social occasion and ending alone. The first use usually occurs with friends; occasional use seems to be a common expression of friendship or generational solidarity. An early sign of trouble is lower school achievement, but few notice that as early as they should (see Visualizing Development, p. 536, for school dropout rates).

Especially for Parents Who Drink Socially You have heard that parents should allow their children to drink at home, to teach them to drink responsibly and not get crunk elsewhere. Is that wise? (see response, page 537)

// **Response for Police Officers** (from page 532): Avoid both extremes: Don't let them think this situation is either harmless or serious. You might take them to the police station and call their parents. These adolescents are probably not life-course-persistent offenders; jailing them or grouping them with other lawbreakers might encourage more crime.

VISUALIZING DEVELOPMENT

How Many Adolescents Are in School?

Attendance in secondary school is a psychosocial topic as much as a cognitive one. Whether or not an adolescent is in school reflects every aspect of the social context, including national policies, family support, peer pressures, employment prospects, and other economic concerns. Rates of violence, delinquency, poverty, and births to girls younger than 17 increase as school attendance decreases.

PERCENTAGE OF SECONDARY SCHOOL-AGED CHILDREN NOT IN SCHOOL

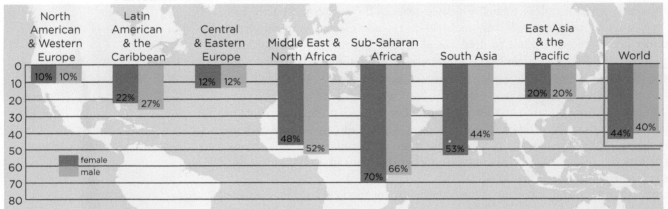

DATA FROM UNESCO, 2011; UNICEF, JULY, 2014.

SELECTED SECONDARY SCHOOL GRADUATION RATES

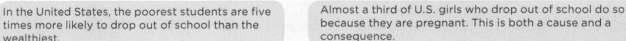

DATA FROM OECD, 2013.

Finland	Japan	Germany	Israel	Poland	United States	China	Greece	Turkey
96	95.58	92.45	84.7	83.7	74.4	73.13	67.52	56.2

U.S. HIGH SCHOOL GRADUATION RATE, CLASS OF 2012

In the United States, the poorest students are five times more likely to drop out of school than the wealthiest.

(RUMBERGER, 2012)

Almost a third of U.S. girls who drop out of school do so because they are pregnant. This is both a cause and a consequence.

(SHUGER, 2012)

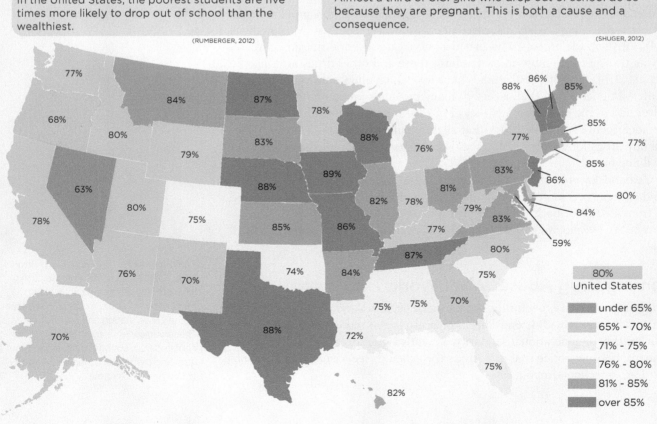

80%
United States

under 65%
65% – 70%
71% – 75%
76% – 80%
81% – 85%
over 85%

DATA FROM EDUCATION WEEK, 2013; U.S. DEPARTMENT OF EDUCATION, NATIONAL CENTER FOR EDUCATION STATISTICS, COMMON CORE OF DATA (CCD), "NCES COMMON CORE OF DATA STATE DROPOUT AND GRADUATION RATE DATA FILE," SCHOOL YEAR 2011–12, PRELIMINARY VERSION 1A.

However, the Monitoring the Future study found that in 2013:

- 22 percent of high school seniors reported having had five drinks in a row in the past two weeks.
- 9 percent smoked cigarettes every day for the past month.
- 6.5 percent smoked marijuana every day.

[Johnston et al., 2014]

These figures are ominous, suggesting that addiction is the next step. Another problem is synthetic marijuana ("spice"), which was not widely available until 2009 and was used by 11 percent of high school seniors in 2012 (Johnston et al., 2014). And although prescription drug use may seem harmless since the source originally was a physician, many adolescents are addicted to prescription drugs.

Remember that most adolescents think they are exceptions, sometimes feeling invincible, sometimes extremely fearful of social disapproval, but almost never worried that they themselves will become addicts. They rarely realize that every psychoactive drug excites the limbic system and interferes with the prefrontal cortex.

Because of these neurological reactions, drug users are more emotional (varying from euphoria to terror, from paranoia to rage) than they would otherwise be. They are also less reflective. Moodiness and impulsivity are characteristic of adolescents, and drugs make them worse. Every hazard—including car crashes, unsafe sex, and suicide—is more common among teens who have taken a psychoactive drug.

With harmful drugs, as with many other aspects of life, each generation prefers to learn things for themselves. A common phenomenon is **generational forgetting,** the idea that each new generation forgets what the previous generation learned (Chassin et al., 2014; Johnston et al., 2012). Mistrust of the older generation, added to loyalty to one's peers, leads not only to generational forgetting but also to a backlash. When adults forbid something, that is a reason to try it, especially if the adolescent realizes that some adults exaggerated the dangers. If a friend passes out from drug use, adolescents may hesitate to get medical help.

Some antidrug curricula and advertisements actually make drugs seem exciting. Antismoking announcements produced by cigarette companies (such as a clean-cut young person advising viewers to think before they smoke) actually increase use (Strasburger et al., 2009).

This does not mean that trying to halt early drug use is hopeless. Massive ad campaigns by public health advocates in Florida and California cut adolescent smoking almost in half, in part because the publicity appealed to the young. Public health advocates have learned that teenagers respond to graphic images. In one example:

> A young man walks up to a convenience store counter and asks for a pack of cigarettes. He throws some money on the counter, but the cashier says "that's not enough." So the young man pulls out a pair of pliers, wrenches out one of his teeth, and hands it over. . . . A voiceover asks: "What's a pack of smokes cost? Your teeth."
>
> *[Krisberg, 2014]*

Parental example and social changes also make a difference. Throughout the United States, higher prices, targeted warnings, and better law enforcement have led to a marked decline in cigarette smoking among younger adolescents. In 2012, only 5 percent of eighth-graders had smoked cigarettes in the past month, compared with 21 percent in 1996 (Johnston et al., 2012). (Use of other drugs has not declined as much.)

// Response for Parents Who Drink Socially (from page 535): No. Alcohol is particularly harmful for young brains. It is best to drink only when your children are not around. Children who are encouraged to drink with their parents are more likely to drink when no adults are present. Adolescents are rebellious, and they may drink even if you forbid it. But if you allow alcohol, they might rebel with other drugs.

generational forgetting The idea that each new generation forgets what the previous generation learned. As used here, the term refers to knowledge about the harm drugs can do.

Serious Treatment A nurse checks Steve Duffer's blood pressure after a dose of Naltrexone, a drug with many side effects that combats severe addiction, in this case addiction to heroin. Steve is now 24.

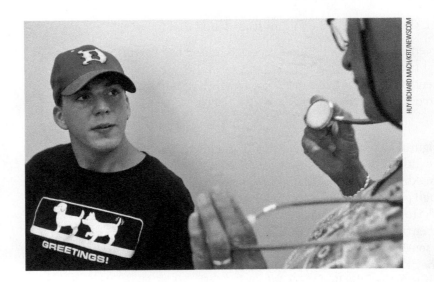

Looking broadly at the past three chapters and the past 40 years in the United States, we see that universal biological processes do not lead to universal psychosocial problems. Sharply declining rates of teenage births and abortions (Chapter 14), increasing numbers graduating from high school (Chapter 15), and less misuse of legal and illegal drugs are apparent in many nations. Adolescence starts with puberty; that much is universal. But what happens next depends on parents, peers, schools, communities, and cultures.

SUMMING UP   Most adolescents worldwide try drugs, most commonly cigarettes and alcohol. Drug use and abuse vary depending on age, culture, cohort, laws, and gender, with most adolescents in some nations using drugs that are never tried in other nations. Drug use early in adolescence is especially risky, since many drugs reduce learning and growth, harm the developing brain, and make later addiction more likely. Every cohort is offered new drugs, with e-cigarettes the most recent in a long line of drugs that are flavored and packaged to appeal to the young. Generational forgetting is one reason each cohort has distinctive drug-use patterns, and many efforts to stop drug use have failed. Other efforts have succeeded, such as well-designed ads, targeted public education, and graphic package design. The overall trend is positive: Drug use is lower in the United States and in many other nations (though not for all drugs) than it was a few decades ago.

WHAT HAVE YOU LEARNED?

1.   Why are psychoactive drugs particularly attractive in adolescence?
2.   Why are psychoactive drugs particularly destructive in adolescence?
3.   What specific harm occurs with tobacco products?
4.   Why are developmentalists particularly worried about e-cigarettes?
5.   What methods to reduce adolescent drug use are successful?

SUMMARY

Identity

1. Adolescence is a time for self-discovery. According to Erikson, adolescents seek their own identity, sorting through the traditions and values of their families and cultures.

2. Many young adolescents foreclose on their options without exploring possibilities, and many experience role confusion. Older adolescents might seek a moratorium. Identity achievement takes longer for contemporary adolescents than it did half a century ago, when Erikson first described it.

3. Identity achievement occurs in many domains, including religion, politics, vocation, and sex. Each of these remains important over the life span, but timing, contexts, and, often, terminology have changed since Erikson and Marcia first described them. Achieving vocational and sexual (gender) identity is particularly difficult in adolescence.

Relationships with Adults

4. Parents continue to influence their growing children, despite bickering between them over minor issues. Ideally, communication and warmth remain high within the family, while parental control decreases and adolescents develop autonomy.

5. There are cultural differences in the timing of conflicts and in the particulars of parental monitoring. Too much parental control is harmful, as is neglect. Parents need to find a balance between granting freedom and providing guidance.

6. Adults other than parents sometimes provide important mentoring and modeling for adolescents, making resilience possible. Adult relatives, teachers, religious and community leaders, and even public figures can be influential.

Peer Power

7. Peers and peer pressure can be beneficial or harmful, depending on the particular friends. Adolescents select their friends, including friends of the other sex, who then facilitate constructive and/or destructive behavior. Adolescents seek the approval of their peers, sometimes engaging in risky behavior to gain such approval.

8. Like adults, adolescents experience diverse sexual needs and may be involved in short-term or long-term romances, depending in part on their peer group. Finding a life partner is a long process, typically involving emotional ups and downs. Early, exclusive sexual relationships are often a sign of emotional immaturity.

9. Some youths are sexually attracted to people of the same sex. Depending on the culture and cohort, they may have a more difficult adolescence than others, including being bullied or worse.

10. Many adolescents learn about sex from peers and the media—sources that do not provide a balanced picture. Ideally, parents are the best teachers about sex, but many are silent and naive.

11. Most parents want schools to teach adolescents about sex. Education varies from nation to nation, with some nations providing comprehensive education beginning in the early grades. In the United States, no curriculum (including abstinence-only programs) markedly changes the age at which adolescents become sexually active, although some help reduce rates of pregnancy and STIs.

Sadness and Anger

12. Almost all adolescents become self-conscious and self-critical. A few become chronically sad and depressed. Many adolescents (especially girls) think about suicide, and some attempt it. Few adolescents actually kill themselves; most who do so are boys.

13. At least in Western societies, almost all adolescents become more independent and angry as part of growing up, although most still respect their parents. Breaking the law as well as bursts of anger are common; boys are more likely to be arrested for violent offenses than are girls.

14. Adolescence-limited delinquents should be prevented from hurting themselves or others; their criminal behavior will disappear with maturation. Life-course-persistent offenders are aggressive in childhood and may continue to be so in adulthood.

Drug Use and Abuse

15. Most adolescents experiment with drugs, especially alcohol and tobacco, although such substances impair growth of the body and the brain. National culture has a powerful influence on which specific drugs are used as well as on frequency of use. Age, gender, community, and parents are also influential.

16. Alcohol and marijuana are particularly harmful in adolescence, as they affect the developing brain and threaten the already shaky impulse control. However, adults who exaggerate harm, or who abuse drugs themselves, are unlikely to prevent teen drug use.

17. Prevention and moderation of adolescent drug use and abuse are possible. Antidrug programs and messages need to be carefully designed to avoid a backlash or generational forgetting.

KEY TERMS

identity versus role confusion (p. 509)

identity achievement (p. 510)

role confusion (p. 510)

foreclosure (p. 510)

moratorium (p. 510)

gender identity (p. 513)

parental monitoring (p. 517)

peer pressure (p. 520)

deviancy training (p. 521)

sexual orientation (p. 523)

familism (p. 527)

clinical depression (p. 527)

rumination (p. 527)

suicidal ideation (p. 528)

parasuicide (p. 528)

cluster suicides (p. 529)

adolescence-limited offender (p. 530)

life-course-persistent offender (p. 530)

generational forgetting (p. 537)

APPLICATIONS

1. Interview people who spent their teenage years in U.S. schools of various sizes, or in another nation, about the peer relationships in their high schools. Describe and discuss any differences you find.

2. Locate a news article about a teenager who committed suicide. Can you find evidence in the article that there were warning signs that were ignored? Does the report inadvertently encourage cluster suicides?

3. Research suggests that most adolescents have broken the law but that few have been arrested or incarcerated. Ask 10 of your fellow students whether they broke the law when they were under 18 and if so, how often, in what ways, and with what consequences. (Assure them of confidentiality.) What hypothesis arises about lawbreaking in your cohort?

4. Cultures have different standards for drug use among children, adolescents, and adults. Interview three people from different cultures (not necessarily from different nations; each occupation, generation, or religion can be said to have a culture) about their culture's drug-use standards. Ask your respondents to explain the reasons for any differences.

PART 5

The Developing Person So Far:
Adolescence

BIOSOCIAL

Puberty Begins Puberty begins adolescence, as the child's body becomes much bigger (the growth spurt) and more sexual. Hormones of the HPA and HPG axes influence growth and sexual maturation as well as body rhythms, which change so that adolescents are more wakeful at night. The normal range for the beginning of puberty is age 8 to age 14.

Growth and Nutrition Many teens do not get enough iron or calcium because they often consume fast food and soda instead of family meals and milk. Some suffer from serious eating disorders such as anorexia and bulimia. The limbic system typically matures faster than the prefrontal cortex. As a result, adolescents are more likely to act impulsively.

Sexual Maturation Both sexes experience increased hormones, new reproductive potential, and primary as well as secondary sexual characteristics. Every adolescent is more interested in sexual activities, with possible hazards of early pregnancy and sexual abuse.

COGNITIVE

Logic and Self Adolescents think differently than younger children do. Piaget stressed the adolescent's new analytical ability—using abstract logic (part of formal operational thought). Adolescents use two modes of cognition, intuitive reasoning and analytic thought. Intuitive thinking is experiential, quick, and impulsive, unlike formal operational thought; intuitive processes sometimes crowd out analytical ones. Technology has both positive and negative aspects. Positives include enhancement of learning and promotion of social outreach and reduced isolation through online connections. Negatives are evident in cyberbullying and video game addiction.

Teaching and Learning Secondary education promotes individual and national success. International tests find marked differences in achievement. In the United States, high-stakes tests and more rigorous course requirements before high school graduation are intended to improve standards.

PSYCHOSOCIAL

Identity Adolescent development includes a search for identity, as Erikson described. Adolescents combine childhood experiences, cultural values, and their unique aspirations in forming an identity. The contexts of identity are religion, politics/ethnicity, vocation, and sex/gender.

Relationships Families continue to be influential, despite rebellion and bickering. Adolescents seek autonomy but also rely on parental support. Parental guidance and ongoing communication promote adolescents' psychosocial health. Friends and peers of both sexes are increasingly important.

Sadness and Anger Depression and rebellion become serious problems for a minority of adolescents. Many adolescents break the law, but their delinquency is limited to their adolescent years; the great majority eventually become law-abiding adults. Some, however, are life-course-persistent offenders. Adolescents are attracted to psychoactive drugs yet such drugs are particularly harmful during the teen years.

EPILOGUE

Emerging Adulthood

What Will You Know?

1. Why are young adults having so few children?
2. Does college change the way people think?
3. Do emerging adults still need and want their parents in their lives?

- **Biosocial Development**
  Strong and Active Bodies
  Taking Risks
  A CASE TO STUDY: An Adrenaline Junkie

- **Cognitive Development**
  Postformal Thought and Brain Development
  Countering Stereotypes
  A VIEW FROM SCIENCE: Stereotype Threat
  The Effects of College

- **Psychosocial Development**
  Identity Achieved
  Personality in Emerging Adulthood
  Intimacy
  Emerging Adults and Their Parents

C onsider this brief chapter both a review and a preview. It follows the same sequence as at earlier stages—body, mind, and social context—always noting the impact of genetic, prenatal, and early experiences and consequences for later development. You will see many familiar themes—echoes of early relationships, cultural differences, contextual and cohort effects. **Emerging adulthood** is a time when people continue learning and exploring, postponing marriage, parenthood, and career (see At About This Time), and preparing for the rest of life.

emerging adulthood The period of life between the ages of 18 and 25. Emerging adulthood is now widely thought of as a separate developmental stage.

at about this time

Following Certain Patterns, by Average Age

Age 17–18—Graduate from high school (about 20 percent do not)

Age 18–19—Enroll in college (between 20 and 30 percent of high school graduates do not)

Age 22—Earn college degree (about half of those who enter college)

Age 25—Steady employment in chosen field (rate fluctuates, depends on economy)

Age 25—Women's first birth* (for those who will have children; about 20 percent will not)

Age 26—Women's first marriage (about 18 percent never marry)

Age 28—Men's first marriage (about 25 percent never marry)

*By ethnicity: Age 23—African American or Hispanic; age 26—European American; age 29—Asian American

Source: U.S. Census Bureau, 2011 and previous years.

These are norms, which convey the median age for these events, each traditionally considered signs of adulthood. Note that most people do *not* achieve college graduation and that the median age for family commitment is at the end of emerging adulthood. Furthermore, many people do not follow this normative path.

I followed this path myself. Between ages 18 and 25, I attended four colleges or universities, changed majors five times, rejected marriage offers from four young men, lived in ten different places, and started several jobs—none lasting more than 18 months.

Peak Performance Because this is a soccer match, of course we see skilled feet and strong legs—but also notice the arms, torsos, and feats of balance. Deniz Naki and Luis Gustavo, professional soccer players in their 20s, are in better shape than most emerging adults, but imagine these two a decade earlier or later and you will realize why, physiologically, the early 20s are considered the prime of life.

organ reserve The capacity of organs to allow the body to cope with stress, via extra, unused functioning ability.

homeostasis The balanced adjustment of all the body's systems to keep physiological functions in a state of equilibrium.

allostasis A dynamic body adjustment, related to homeostasis, that affects overall physiology over time. Homeostasis requires an immediate response, whereas allostasis requires longer-term adjustment.

allostatic load The stresses of basic body systems that combine to limit overall functioning. Higher allostatic load makes a person more vulnerable to illness.

Following that period of rapid change, I stayed put—decades later I still have had one husband, one neighborhood, one career, and since age 30, one main employer. The restlessness of my early 20s once seemed odd, but now such restlessness is apparent worldwide. As with all adult developments, the chronological ages at which they happen vary: In some nations, people "settle down" by age 20, in others by age 30. Nonetheless, emerging adulthood is evident everywhere.

Biosocial Development

Biologically, the years from ages 18 to 25 are prime time for hard physical work and safe reproduction. However, the reality that young adults can carry rocks, plow fields, or haul water is no longer admired, nor is their fertility. If a contemporary young couple had a baby every year, their neighbors would be more appalled than approving. Now, societies, families, and young adults themselves expect more education, later marriage, and fewer children than was the norm a few decades ago.

Strong and Active Bodies

Health has not changed, except maybe to improve. As always, every body system—including the digestive, respiratory, circulatory, and sexual-reproductive systems—functions optimally at the end of adolescence. Serious diseases are not yet apparent, and some childhood ailments are outgrown.

To understand this, it is helpful to understand three aspects of body functioning that keep emerging adults healthy: organ reserve, homeostasis, and allostatic load.

Organ reserve refers to the extra power that every organ can call upon when needed. That reserve power decreases each year, but in emerging adulthood, it usually allows speedy recovery from excess demands on the body, such as exercising for hours, staying awake all night, or drinking too much alcohol.

Closely related to organ reserve is **homeostasis**—a balance between various body functions that keeps every physical function in sync with every other. For example, if the air temperature rises, people sweat, move slowly, and thirst for cold drinks—three aspects of body functioning that cool them. Homeostasis is quickest in early adulthood.

The next time you read about heat-wave deaths (as in England in 2013 or Australia in 2014), note the age of the victims. Because homeostasis slows down, the body dissipates heat less well with age. Even middle-aged adults are less protected from temperature changes—or any other stress on the body—than emerging adults (Larose et al., 2013).

Related to homeostasis is **allostasis,** a dynamic body adjustment that gradually changes overall physiology. The main difference between homeostasis and allostasis is time: Homeostasis requires an immediate response from body systems, whereas allostasis refers to long-term adjustment.

The effects of early life are apparent. Organ reserve usually protects emerging adults, because some reserve is used to maintain health. In a measure called **allostatic load,** daily, weekly, monthly, and yearly adjustments accumulate, gradually affecting the burden, or load, that weighs down

A Moment or a Lifetime? These three in New Delhi enjoy free pizza at the opening of the 600th Domino's in India, just one of more than 5,000 outside the United States. Cheese and pepperoni may satisfy homeostatic drive, but they now increase the allostatic load in every nation.

health. Few emerging adults reach the threshold that results in serious illness, but health habits early in life are already evident by age 25 in metabolism, weight, lung capacity, cholesterol or so on. Even the nutrition of the mother when she was pregnant affects the fetus, the child, and then the young adult.

For example, how much a person eats is affected by many factors. An empty stomach immediately triggers hormones, stomach pains, low blood sugar, and so on, all of which lead a person to eat again. That is homeostasis. But if a person begins a serious diet, ignoring hunger messages for days and weeks, rapid weight loss soon triggers new homeostatic reactions, allowing the person to function with a reduced calorie intake, which makes it harder to lose more weight (Tremblay & Chaput, 2012).

Over the years, allostasis becomes crucial. If a person overeats or starves day after day, the body adjusts: Appetite increases or decreases accordingly. But continued homeostasis may take a toll on health, increasing the allostatic load. Obesity is one cause of diabetes, heart disease, high blood pressure, and so on—all the result of physiological adjustment (allostasis) to day-after-day overeating (Sterling, 2012).

TABLE EP.1	U.S. Deaths from the Top Three Causes (Heart Disease, Stroke, Cancer)
Age Group	Annual Rate per 100,000
15–24	7
25–34	17
35–44	55
45–54	207
55–64	560
65–74	1,280
75–84	2,974
85+	7,730

Source: National Center for Health Statistics, 2013

Keep Moving

Another example comes from exercise. After a few minutes of exercise, the heart beats faster and breathing becomes heavier—these are homeostatic responses. Because of organ reserve, the temporary stresses on the body in early adulthood are no problem. Over time, homeostasis adjusts and allows the person to exercise longer and harder. That decreases allostatic load by reducing the health risks evident in the blood and weight.

The opposite is also true. One study (CARDIA—Coronary Artery Risk Development in Adulthood) began with healthy 18- to 30-year-olds, most of them (3,154) reexamined 7 and 20 years later. Those who were the least fit at the first assessment (more than 400 of them, with higher metabolic risk) were four times more likely to have diabetes and high blood pressure in middle age.

In CARDIA, problems began but were unnoticed (except in blood work) when participants were in their 20s. Organ reserve allowed them to function. Nonetheless, each year their allostatic load increased, unless their daily habits changed (Camhi et al., 2013). By late adulthood, the load is deadly (see Table EP.1).

Fertility, Then and Now

As already mentioned, the sexual-reproductive system is at its strongest during emerging adulthood: Orgasms are frequent, the sex drive is powerful, erotic responses are joyful, fertility is optimal, miscarriage is less common, serious birth complications are rare. Historically, most people married by age 20, had their first child within two years, and often a second and third before age 25.

That has changed dramatically. The bodies of emerging adults still crave sex, but their minds know they are not ready for parenthood. For many, the solution is sex without pregnancy, made possible by modern contraception. The world's 2010 birth rate for 15- to 25-year-olds is half of what it was in 1960 (United Nations, 2013).

Taking Risks

Remember that each age group has its own gains and losses, characteristics that can be a blessing or a burden. This is apparent with risk-taking. Some emerging adults bravely, or foolishly, take risks—a behavior that is gender- and age-related,

Anywhere In some ways, life in China is radically different from life elsewhere, but universals are also apparent. This emerging-adult couple poses in front of a Beijing stadium.

OBSERVATION QUIZ One detail in the young man's hands suggests that the setting is Asia, not North America. What is it? (see answer, page 547)

as well as genetic and hormonal. Those who are genetically impulsive *and* male *and* emerging adults are most likely to be brave and foolish.

Societies as well as individuals benefit because emerging adults take chances. Enrolling in college, moving to a new state or nation, getting married, having a baby—all are risky. So is starting a business, filming a documentary, entering an athletic contest, enlisting in the military, or joining the Peace Corps.

Yet risk-taking is often destructive. Although their bodies are strong and their reactions quick, emerging adults nonetheless have more serious accidents than do people of any other age. The low rate of disease between ages 18 and 25 is counterbalanced by a high rate of violent death (see Table EP.1).

Destructive risks that are common in emerging adulthood include unprotected sex with a new partner, driving fast without a seat belt, carrying a loaded gun, abusing drugs, and addictive gambling—all done partly for a rush of adrenaline (Cosgrave, 2010). Accidents, homicides, and suicides are the leading causes of death among young adults—killing more adults under age 30 than all diseases combined, even in nations where infectious diseases and malnutrition are rampant.

Risky Sex

Premarital sex, while avoiding parenthood, seems a good solution to the conflict between physical and psychological maturation, but it has serious consequences. Sexually transmitted infections (STIs) are increasing, which may cause lifetime infertility and disease, including some that seem unrelated, such as cancer and tuberculosis.

In earlier times, prostitution was local, which kept STIs local as well. Now, with globalization, an STI caught in one place quickly spreads. Sex-trafficking adds to the problem: Women and girls from one nation sent to another sometimes bring infections and sometimes catch diseases they never would have contracted at home.

This proliferation is particularly tragic with HIV/AIDS. Within 30 years, primarily because of the sexual activities of young adults, HIV has become a worldwide epidemic, with more female than male victims (Fan et al., 2014).

Young adults remain the prime STI vectors (those who spread disease) as well as the new victims. Genetic research on DNA and on STIs have proven that the subtypes and recombinations of HIV—once quite localized—are now present in many regions (Tatem et al., 2012).

Indeed, tracing HIV in Africa shows that it originally was only in the capital of what now is the Democratic Republic of the Congo. Then it spread following the route of the railroads built as part of modernization: carriers of HIV took the disease to nations where it had not been (Faria et al., 2014). Travel benefits emerging adults in many ways, expanding the mind and fostering cultural understanding, but newcomers introduce diseases, and catch diseases, that were once controlled by local conditions.

Risky Sports

Many young adults enjoy risks in recreation: They climb mountains, swim in oceans, run in pain, play past exhaustion, and so on. Skydiving, bungee jumping, pond swooping, parkour, potholing (in caves), waterfall kayaking, ziplining, and many more activities have been invented to increase excitement. Serious injury is not the goal, but risk adds to the thrill.

extreme sports Forms of recreation that include apparent risk of injury or death and that are attractive and thrilling as a result.

Competitive **extreme sports** (such as *motocross*—motorcycle jumping off a ramp into "big air," doing tricks during the fall, and hoping to land upright) are new sports for some emerging adults, who find golf, bowling, and so on too tame (Breivik, 2010).

a case to study

An Adrenaline Junkie

The fact that extreme sports are age-related is evident in Travis Pastrana, "an extreme sports renaissance man—a pro adrenaline junkie/daredevil/speed demon—whatever you want to call him" (Giblin, 2014). After several accidents that almost killed him, he won the 2006 X Games motocross competition at age 22 with a double backflip because, he explained, "The two main things are that I've been healthy and able to train at my fullest, and a lot of guys have had major crashes this year" (quoted in Higgins, 2006, p. D-7).

Four years later, Pastrana set a new record for leaping through big air in an automobile, as he drove over the ocean from a ramp on the California shoreline to a barge more than 250 feet out. He crashed into a barrier on the boat but emerged, seemingly ecstatic and unhurt, to the thunderous cheers of thousands of other young adults on the shore (Roberts, 2010).

In 2011, a broken foot and ankle made him temporarily halt extreme sports—but soon he was back risking his life to the acclaim of his cohort, winning races rife with flips and other hazards. In 2013, after some more serious injuries, he said he was "still a couple of surgeries away" from being able to race on a motorcycle, so he turned to NASCAR auto racing.

In 2014, after becoming a husband and a father (twice), he quit NASCAR. He says his most hazardous race days are over. He is an icon for the next generation of daredevil young men.

JOHN HARRELSON/GETTY IMAGES

Dangerous Pleasure Here Travis Pastrana prepares to defy death once again as a NASCAR driver. Two days later, his first child was born, and two months later, he declared his race record disappointing. At age 30 he quit, declaring on Facebook that he would devote himself to his wife and family. Is that maturation, fatherhood, or failure?

Drug Abuse

The same impulse that is admired in extreme sports leads to behaviors that are destructive, not only for individuals but for the community. The most studied of these is drug abuse (Reith, 2005).

By definition, **drug abuse** occurs whenever a drug (legal or illegal, prescribed or not) is used in a harmful way, damaging a person's physical, cognitive, or psychosocial well-being. From an emerging-adult perspective, the potential for abuse and arrest is part of the allure in buying, carrying, and using an illegal drug. Illegal drug use peaks at about age 20 and declines sharply with age (see Figure EP.1). The thrill is gone. Addiction to legal drugs (not immediately dangerous) may continue in adulthood, but after age 25, most adults want to quit cigarettes and avoid alcohol abuse. That is difficult for many, but unlike emerging adults, they no longer enjoy it.

Drug abuse is more common among college students than among their peers who are not in college, partly because groups of emerging adults urge each other on. For instance, college students are most likely to engage in extreme drinking, with 25 percent of young college men reporting that they consumed 10 or more drinks in a row at least once in the previous two weeks (Johnston et al., 2009). Such extreme behavior arises from the same drive as extreme sports or other risks—with the same possible consequence: death.

drug abuse The ingestion of a drug to the extent that it impairs the user's biological or psychological well-being.

// **ANSWER TO OBSERVATION QUIZ**
(from page 545) It is the cigarette, not the camera. Most young men in Canada and the United States do not smoke, especially publicly and casually, as this man does.

FIGURE EP.1

Too Old for That As you can see, emerging adults are the biggest substance abusers, but illegal drug use drops much faster than does cigarette use or binge drinking.

Especially for Substance Abuse Counselors
Can you think of three possible explanations for the more precipitous drop in the use of illegal drug compared to legal ones? (see response, page 550)

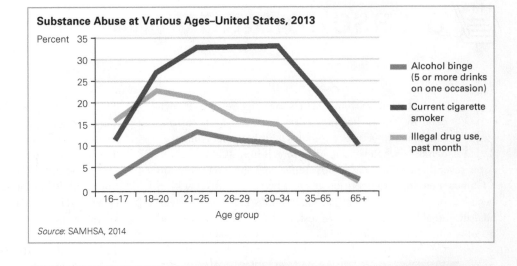

Substance Abuse at Various Ages–United States, 2013

Legend:
- Alcohol binge (5 or more drinks on one occasion)
- Current cigarette smoker
- Illegal drug use, past month

Source: SAMHSA, 2014

DANNY SMYTHE/SHUTTERSTOCK

Video: College Binge Drinking shows college students engaging in (and rationalizing) this risky behavior.

postformal thought A proposed adult stage of cognitive development, following Piaget's four stages. Postformal thought goes beyond adolescent thinking by being more practical, more flexible, and more dialectical (i.e., more capable of combining contradictory elements into a comprehensive whole).

SUMMING UP Emerging adults are physiologically at their prime, with strong and healthy bodies. One strength is the sexual-reproductive system, which pushes many contemporary young adults to engage in premarital sex. The thrill of risk-taking can become a problem, since it leads emerging adults to extreme sports, unprotected sex, drug abuse, and serious injuries. Accidents, homicide, and suicide are leading causes of death among young adults worldwide.

WHAT HAVE YOU LEARNED?

1. Why is maximum physical strength usually attained in emerging adulthood?
2. What has changed, and what has not changed, in the past decades regarding sexual and reproductive development?
3. Why are STIs more common currently than 50 years ago?
4. What are the social benefits of risk taking?
5. Why are some sports more attractive at some ages than others?
6. Why are serious accidents more common in emerging adulthood than later?
7. Why are college students more likely to abuse drugs than those not in college?

Cognitive Development

You remember that each of Piaget's four periods of child and adolescent development is characterized by major advances in cognition, with each advance representing a new stage. Adult thinking similarly differs from earlier thinking: It is more practical, more flexible, and better able to coordinate objective and subjective perspectives.

Postformal Thought and Brain Development

Many developmentalists believe that Piaget's fourth stage, formal operational thought, is inadequate to describe adult thinking. Some propose a fifth stage, called **postformal thought,** a "type of logical, adaptive problem solving that is a step more complex than scientific formal-level Piagetian tasks" (Sinnott, 2014, p. 3). As one group of scholars explained, in postformal thought "one can conceive of multiple logics, choices, or perceptions . . . in order to better understand the complexities and inherent biases in 'truth'" (Griffin et al., 2009, p. 173).

As you remember from Chapter 15, adolescents use two modes of thought (dual processing) but they have difficulty combining them. They use formal analysis to

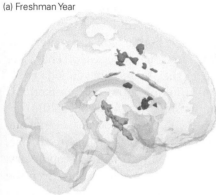

(a) Freshman Year

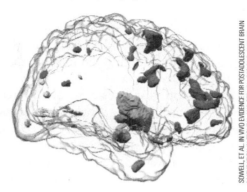

(b) Adolescence and Emerging Adulthood

Thinking Away from Home (*a*) Entering a residential college means experiencing new foods, new friends, and new neurons. A longitudinal study of 18-year-old students at the beginning and end of their first year in college (Dartmouth) found increases in the brain areas that integrate emotion and cognition—namely, the cingulate (blue and yellow), caudate (red), and insula (orange). Researchers also studied one-year changes in the brains of students over age 25 at the same college and found no dramatic growth. (*b*) Shown here are the areas of change in one person's brain from age 14 to 25. The frontal cortex (purple) demonstrated many changes in particular parts, as did the areas for processing speech (green and blue)—a crucial aspect of young adult learning. Areas for visual processing (yellow) showed less change.

Neuroscience reveals that brains mature in many ways between adolescence and adulthood; scientists are not yet sure of the cognitive implications.

learn science, distill principles, develop arguments, and resolve the world's problems; alternatively, they think spontaneously and emotionally about personal issues. They prefer quick reactions, only later realizing the consequences.

Postformal thinkers are less impulsive and reactive. They take a more flexible and comprehensive approach, with forethought, noting difficulties and anticipating problems, not denying, avoiding, or procrastinating. As a result, postformal thinking is more practical, creative, and imaginative than thinking in previous cognitive stages (Wu & Chiou, 2008). It is particularly useful in human relationships (Sinnott, 2014).

As you have read, Piaget's stage theory of childhood cognition is not accepted by all developmentalists. Many more question this fifth stage. As two scholars writing about emerging adulthood wrote, "Who needs stages anyway?" (Hendry & Kloep, 2011).

Piaget himself never labeled or described postformal cognition. Certainly, if cognitive *stage* means attaining a new set of intellectual abilities (such as the symbolic use of language that distinguishes sensorimotor from preoperational thought), then adulthood has no stages.

However, as described in Chapter 14, the prefrontal cortex is not fully mature until the early 20s, and new dendrites connect throughout life. As more is understood about brain development after adolescence, it seems that thinking may change as the brain matures (Lemieux 2012). Several studies find that adult cognition benefits from a wider understanding and greater experience of the social world (Sinnott, 2014).

Countering Stereotypes

Cognitive flexibility, particularly the ability to change childhood assumptions, helps counter stereotypes. Young adults show many signs of such flexibility. The very fact that emerging adults marry later than previous generations did suggests that, couple by couple, their thinking processes are not determined by their childhood culture or by traditional norms. Early experiences are influential, but postformal thinkers are not stuck in them.

The Threat of Bias If students fear that others expect them to do poorly in school because of their ethnicity or gender, they might not identify with academic achievement and therefore do worse on exams than they otherwise would have. Any, or all, of these three could be self-handicapping at this very moment.

Especially for Someone Who Has to Make an Important Decision Which is better: to go with your gut feelings or to consider pros and cons as objectively as you can? (see response, page 551)

 LaunchPod

Median section of the brain

For a quick look at the changes that occur in a person's brain between ages 18 and 25, try **Video Activity: Brain Development: Emerging Adulthood.**

// **Response for Substance Abuse Counselors** (from page 548) Legal drugs could be more addictive, the thrill of illegality may diminish with age, or the fear of arrest may increase. In any case, treatment for young-adult substance abusers may differ from that for older ones.

stereotype threat The possibility that one's appearance or behavior will be misread to confirm another person's oversimplified, prejudiced attitudes.

Research on racial prejudice is another example. Many people are less prejudiced than their parents, and they believe they are not biased. However, tests may reveal implicit discrimination. Thus, many adults have both unconscious prejudice and rational tolerance—a combination that illustrates dual processing. The wider the gap between explicit and implicit, the stronger their stereotypes (Shoda et al., 2014). Postformal reasoning may allow rational thinking to overcome emotional reactions, with responses dependent on reality, not stereotypes (Sinnott, 2014).

Unfortunately, many people do not recognize their own stereotypes, even when false beliefs harm them. One of the most pernicious results is **stereotype threat,** arising in people who worry that other people might judge them as stupid, lazy, oversexed, or worse because of their ethnicity, sex, age, or appearance. Even the *possibility* of being stereotyped arouses emotions and hijacks memory, disrupting cognition (Schmader, 2010). That is stereotype threat.

a view from science

Stereotype Threat

One statistic has troubled social scientists for decades: African American men have lower grades in high school and earn only half as many college degrees as African American women. This cannot be genetic, since the women have the same genes (except one chromosome) as the men. Most scientists have blamed the context and historical discrimination that fell particularly hard on men (Arnett & Brody, 2008).

One African American scholar thought of another possibility, one that originated in the mind, not the social context. He labeled it *stereotype threat,* a "threat in the air," not in reality (Steele, 1997). The mere *possibility* of being negatively stereotyped may arouse emotions that disrupt cognition as well as emotional regulation.

The hypothesis is that if African American males are aware of the stereotype that they are poor scholars, they become anxious in educational settings. That anxiety may increase stress hormones that reduce their ability to focus on intellectual challenges.

Then, if they score low, they might protect their pride by denigrating academics. That leads to disengagement from studying and still lower achievement. The more threatening the context, the worse they will do (Taylor & Walton, 2011).

Stereotype threat is more than a hypothesis. Hundreds of studies show that it harms almost all humans, not just African American men. Women underperform in math, older people are more forgetful, bilingual students stumble with English.

Every member of a stigmatized minority in every nation seems to handicap themselves because of what they imagine others might think (Inzlicht & Schmader, 2012). Not only academics but athletic prowess and health habits may be impaired if stereotype threat makes people anxious (Aronson et al., 2013).

The worst part of stereotype threat is that it is self-imposed. People alert to the possibility of prejudice are not only hypersensitive when it occurs, but it hijacks their minds, undercutting ability. Eventually they disengage, but their initial reaction may be to try harder to prove the stereotype wrong, and that extra effort may backfire (Mangels et al., 2012; Aronson et al., 2013).

The harm from anxiety is familiar to those who study sports psychology. When star athletes unexpectedly underperform because of stress (called "choking"), stereotype threat arising from past team losses may be the cause (Jordet et al., 2012). Many female players imagine they are not expected to play as well as men (e.g., someone told them "you throw like a girl"), and that itself impairs performance (Hively & El-Alayli, 2014).

The researchers who first recognized stereotype threat wondered if it could be eliminated, or at least reduced. They hypothesized that if African American college men *internalize* (believe wholeheartedly, not just intellectually) that intelligence is plastic (incremental theory) rather than the inalterable product of genes and gender (entity theory), that belief might protect them from stereotype threat.

Using a clever combination of written material, mentoring, and videotaping, these scientists convinced African American students at Stanford University that their ability and hence their achievement depended on their personal efforts. That reduced stereotype threat and led to higher grades (Aronson et al., 2002).

This experiment intrigued the scientific community, but it involved only 79 exceptional students—not enough to validate the concept. Might other stereotyped groups respond differently?

Soon thousands of scientists replicated and varied this study with many other populations. The results confirm that stereotype threat is pervasive but that it can be alleviated (Inzlicht & Schmader 2012; Sherman et al., 2013; Dennehy et al., 2014).

Does this finding from science apply to the general public? The answer depends on whether anxiety about what other people think ever affected your performance.

The Effects of College

A major reason why emerging adulthood has become a new period of development, when people postpone the usual markers of adult life (marriage, a steady job), is that many older adolescents seek further education instead of taking on adult responsibilities. However, some aspects of higher education are controversial.

Massification

There is no dispute that tertiary education improves health and wealth. Because of that, every nation has increased the number of college students—a phenomenon called *massification,* based on the idea that college could benefit almost everyone (the masses) (Altbach et al., 2010). The United States was the first major nation to endorse massification. That is why, among the over-age-60 population, the United States leads in the percentage of college graduates. However, other nations have increased public funding for college education while the United States has decreased it. Now, many other nations have higher rates of BA degree holders (see Figure EP.2).

U.S. Census data and surveys of individuals find that college education pays off even more than it did thirty years ago, with the average college man earning $17,558 more per year than a high school graduate. Women also benefit from college, but not as much: Graduates earn $10,393 more per year (Autor, 2014).

The typical person with a master's degree earns twice as much over a lifetime as the typical one with only a high school diploma (Doubleday, 2013) (see Figure EP.3). Parents almost universally want their children to go to college, and new college students expect to earn a degree. Only about half of them do so.

College and Cognition

For developmentalists interested in cognition, the crucial question about college education is not about wealth, health, rates, or even graduation. Does college advance critical thinking and postformal thought?

According to one classic study (Perry, 1981, 1970/1998), thinking progresses through nine levels of complexity over the four years that lead to a bachelor's degree, moving from a simplistic dualism (right or wrong, yes or no, success or failure) to a relativism that recognizes a multiplicity of perspectives (see Table EP.2).

FIGURE EP.2

Send Your Children to College In many nations, the younger generations more often earn bachelor's degrees (BA or BS) than their parents and grandparents. This table shows OECD nations and rates for 2011, the most recent year for which an international comparison is available. In many nations, the 2013 rates are somewhat higher, as the economic recession sent more young people to college, but the United States still lags behind.

Especially for Those Considering Studying Abroad Given the effects of college, would it be better for a student to study abroad in the first year or last year of a college education? (see response, page 555)

// Response for Someone Who Has to Make an Important Decision (from page 549) Both are necessary. Mature thinking requires a combination of emotions and logic. To make sure you use both, take your time (don't act on your first impulse) and talk with people you trust. Ultimately, you will live with your decision, so do not ignore either intuitive or logical thought.

Video: The Effects of Mentoring on Intellectual Development: The University-Community Links Project shows how an after-school study enhancement program has proven beneficial for both its mentors and the at-risk students who attend it.

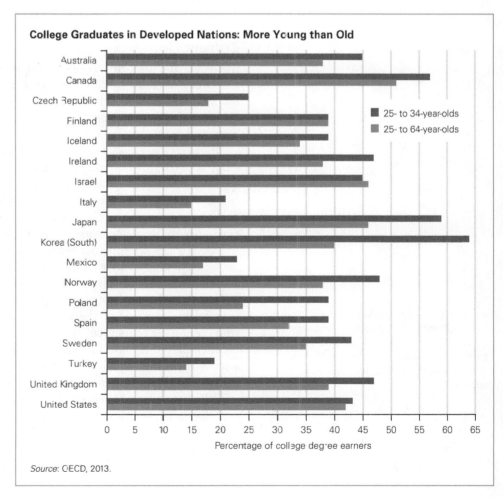

College Graduates in Developed Nations: More Young than Old

- 25- to 34-year-olds
- 25- to 64-year-olds

Percentage of college degree earners

Source: OECD, 2013.

FIGURE EP.3

Older, Wiser, and Richer
Adolescents find it easier to think about their immediate experiences (a boring math class) rather than their middle-age income, so some drop out of high school to take a job that will someday pay $500 a week. But over an average of 40 years of employment, someone who completes a master's degree earns half a million dollars more than someone who leaves school in eleventh grade. That translates into about $90,000 for each year of education from twelfth grade to a master's. The earnings gap is even wider than those numbers indicate because this chart compares adults who have jobs, yet finding work is more difficult for those with less education.

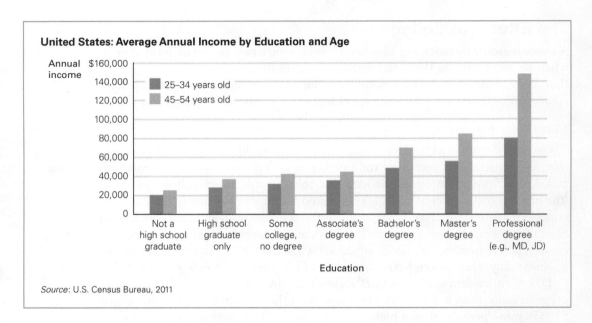

United States: Average Annual Income by Education and Age

Source: U.S. Census Bureau, 2011

Especially for High School Teachers One of your brightest students doesn't want to go to college. She would rather keep waitressing in a restaurant, where she makes good money in tips. What do you say? (see response, page 554)

Perry found that the college experience itself causes this progression: Peers, professors, books, and class discussion all stimulate new questions and thoughts. Other research confirmed Perry's conclusions. In general, the more years of higher education a person has, the deeper and more postformal that person's reasoning becomes (Pascarella & Terenzini, 1991).

Current Contexts

But wait. You probably noticed that Perry's study was first published in 1981. Hundreds of other studies also found that college education deepens cognition, but most of that research occurred in the twentieth century. Since you know that cohort and culture are crucial influences, you may wonder whether those conclusions still hold.

Many recent books criticize college education on exactly those grounds. Notably, a twenty-first-century longitudinal study of a cross-section of U.S. college students found that students' growth in critical thinking, analysis, and communication over the four years of college was only half as much as among college students two decades ago. This analysis of the first two years of college found that 45 percent of the students made no significant advances at all (Arum & Roksa, 2011).

The reasons were many: Students study less, professors expect less, and students avoid classes in which they must read at least 40 pages a week or write 20 pages a semester. Administrators and faculty still hope for intellectual growth, but rigorous classes are canceled or not required.

A follow-up study of the same individuals after graduation found that those who spent most of their college time socializing rather than studying were likely to be unemployed or have low-income jobs. What they had gained from college was a sense that things would get better, but not the critical-thinking skills or the self-discipline that is needed for adult success (Arum & Roksa, 2014).

Other observers blame the faculty, or the wider culture, for forcing colleges to follow a corporate model, with students as customers who need to be satisfied rather than intellectual youth who need to be challenged (Deresiewicz, 2014). Customers, apparently, demand dormitories and sports facilities that are costly, and students take out loans to pay for them. The fact that the United States has slipped in massification is not surprising, given the political, economic, and cultural contexts of contemporary college.

Two new pedagogical techniques may foster greater learning, or may be evidence of the decline of standards. One is called the *flipped class*, in which students are required to watch videos of a lecture on their computers before class, using class time for discussion, with the professor prodding and encouraging but not lecturing. The other technique is classes that are totally online, including **massive open online courses (MOOCs).** Thousands of students enroll in MOOCs and do all of the work hundreds or thousands of miles away.

MOOCs are most effective for students who are highly motivated and adept at computers. They learn best if they

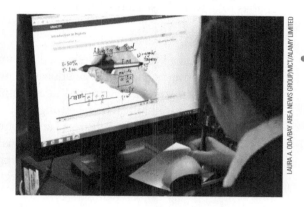

massive open online course (MOOC) A course that is offered solely online for college credit. Typically, tuition is very low, and thousands of students enroll.

Writing on the Wall In Oakland, California, Selina Wong is learning physics online from a MOOC offered by San Jose University. The most common criticism of online courses is that they are not interactive, but as you see, this is not always true.

TABLE EP.2	Perry's Scheme of Cognitive and Ethical Development During College	
Freshmen	Position 1	Authorities know, and if we work hard, read every word, and learn Right Answers, all will be well.
Dualism modified	Transition	But what about other opinions, uncertainties, disagreements? Some people disagree with each other or don't seem to know, and some authorities give us problems instead of Answers.
	Position 2	Authorities must be Right; the others are frauds. Others must be different and Wrong. Good Authorities give us problems so we can learn to find the Right Answer by our own independent thought.
	Transition	But even Good Authorities admit they don't know all the answers yet!
	Position 3	Then some uncertainties and different opinions are real and legitimate temporarily, even for Authorities. They're working on them to get to the Truth.
	Transition	But there are so many things they don't know the Answers to! And they won't for a long time.
Relativism discovered	Position 4a	Where Authorities don't know the Right Answers, everyone has a right to his own opinion; no one is wrong!
	Transition	Then what right have They to grade us?
	Position 4b	In certain courses, Authorities are not asking for the Right Answer. They want us to think about things in a certain way, supporting opinion with data. That's what they grade us on.
	Position 5	Then all thinking must be relative, even for Them. You have to understand each context. Theories are not Truth but metaphors. You have to think about your thinking.
	Transition	But if everything is relative, am I relative, too? How can I know I'm making the Right Choice?
	Position 6	I see I'm going to have to make my own decisions in an uncertain world with no one to tell me I'm Right.
	Transition	I'm lost if I don't. When I decide on my career (or marriage or values), everything will straighten out.
Commitments in relativism developed	Position 7	Well, I've made my first Commitment!
	Transition	Why didn't that settle everything?
	Position 8	I've made several commitments. I've got to balance them—how many, how deep? How certain, how tentative?
	Transition	Things are getting contradictory. I can't make logical sense out of life's dilemmas.
Seniors	Position 9	This is how life will be. I must be wholehearted while tentative, fight for my values yet respect others, believe my deepest values are right yet be ready to learn. I shall be retracing this whole journey over and over, but, I hope, more wisely.

Source: Perry, 1981, 1970/1998. The Modern American college by CHICKERING, ARTHUR W. Reproduced with permission of JOHN WILEY & SONS, INCORPORATED in the format Educational/Instructional Program via Copyright Clearance Center

// **Response for High School Teachers** (from page 552) Even more than ability, motivation is crucial for college success, so don't insist that she attend college. Since your student has money and a steady job (prime goals for today's college-bound youth), she may not realize what she would be missing. Ask her what she hopes for herself, in work and lifestyle, over the many decades ahead.

have another classmate, or an expert, as a personal guide: Face-to-face interaction seems to help motivation and learning (Breslow et al., 2013). Most MOOC students drop out; sometimes only about 10 percent of enrollees complete all the work and pass the class. The MOOC saves money and commuting; educators disagree as to how much students learn.

Motivation to Attend College

Motivation is crucial for every intellectual accomplishment. An underlying problem in the controversy about college education may be that people disagree about its purpose. Thus, students motivated to accomplish one thing clash with professors who are motivated to teach something else.

Developmentalists, most professors, and many college graduates believe that the main purpose of higher education is "personal and intellectual growth," which means that professors should focus on fostering critical thinking and analysis. However, adults who have never attended college believe that "acquiring specific skills and knowledge" is more important.

In the Arum and Roksa report (2011), students majoring in business and other career fields were less likely to gain in critical thinking compared to those in the liberal arts (courses that demand more reading and writing). These researchers suggest that colleges, professors, and students themselves who seek easier, more popular courses are short-changing themselves for future maturity and success (Arum & Roksa, 2014).

However, many students attend college primarily for career reasons (see Figure EP.4). They want jobs with good pay; they select majors and institutions accordingly, not for intellectual challenge and advanced communication skills. Professors are often critical when college success is measured via the salaries of graduates, but that metric may be what the public expects college to provide.

In 1955, most U.S. colleges were four-year institutions, and most students majored in the liberal arts. There were only 275 junior colleges; in 2014, there were almost 1,920 such colleges, now called community colleges. (Some also offer four-year degrees, but their primary focus is on two-year associate's degrees.)

Similarly, for-profit colleges were scarce until about 1980; now the United States has more than 752, a number reduced from over a thousand four years ago (Chronicle of Higher Education, 2014). Everywhere, fewer students major in liberal arts.

No nation has reached consensus on the purpose of college. For example in China, where the number of college students now exceeds the United States (but remember that the Chinese population is much larger), the central government has fostered thousands of new institutions of higher learning, primarily to advance the economy, not to deepen intellectual understanding. However, even in that centralized government, disagreement about the goals and practices of college is evident (Ross & Wang, 2013).

In 2009, a new Chinese university (called South University of Science and Technology of China, SUSTC) was founded to encourage analysis and critical thinking. SUSTC does not require

FIGURE EP.4

Cohort Shift Students in 1980 thought new ideas and a philosophy of life were prime reasons to go to college—they were less interested in jobs, careers, and money than are students in 2010. If this thinking causes a conflict between student motivation and professor's goals, who should adjust?

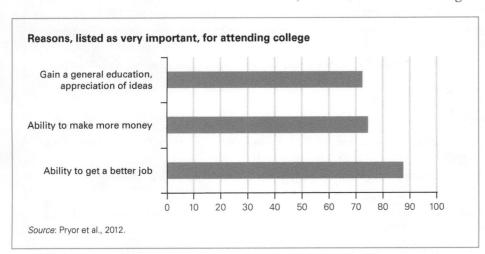

Reasons, listed as very important, for attending college

Source: Pryor et al., 2012.

prospective students to take the national college entry exam (*Gao Kao*); instead, "creativity and a passion for learning" are the admission criteria (Stone, 2011, p. 161). It is not clear whether SUSTC is successful, in part because people disagree about how to measure success. The Chinese government praises SUSTC's accomplishments but has not replicated it (Shenzhen Daily, 2014).

The Effects of Diversity

At least one characteristic of the twenty-first-century college scene in every nation bodes well for cognition—the diversity of the student body. The most obvious change is gender: In 1970, at least two-thirds of college students were male; now in every developed nation (except Germany), more than half are female. Most formerly single-sex colleges are now co-ed.

In addition, students' ethnic, economic, religious, and cultural backgrounds are more varied. Compared to 1970, more students are parents, are older than age 24, are of non-European heritage, attend part time, and live and work off-campus, although most students are still 18 to 22 years old and attend college full time. This is true not only in North America but also worldwide.

// **Response for Those Considering Studying Abroad** (from page 551) Since one result of college is that students become more open to other perspectives while developing their commitment to their own values, foreign study might be most beneficial after several years of college. If they study abroad too early, some students might be either too narrowly patriotic (they are not yet open) or too quick to reject everything about their national heritage (they have not yet developed their own commitments).

Unlike Their Parents Both photos show large urban colleges in the United States, with advantages the older college generations did not have: wireless technology (in use by all three on the left) and classmates from 50 nations (evident on the right).

OBSERVATION QUIZ Which is a community college? (see answer, page 557)

Discussion among people of different backgrounds and perspectives leads to intellectual challenge and deeper thought. The benefits of a diverse student body last for years after graduation (Pascarella et al., 2014). Colleges that make use of their new diversity—via curriculum, assignments, discussions, cooperative education, learning communities, and so on—stretch student understanding, not only of other people but also of themselves (Harper & Yeung, 2013).

When 18-year-old high school graduates of similar backgrounds and abilities are compared, those who enter the labor market rather than pursuing higher education achieve less and are less satisfied by middle age than those who earned a college degree (Hout, 2012). The lifelong financial benefits of college seem particularly strong for ethnic minorities and low-income families, who actually are less likely to attend college. Of course there are always exceptions, but as Chapter 1 explains, scientific conclusions should not be based on one person.

SUMMING UP   Emerging adults often become more flexible, creative, and coordinated thinkers than they were as adolescents, an advancement sometimes described as postformal thought. College education brings health and wealth to graduates, and nations worldwide have increased the number of students in college. Research in earlier decades in the United States finds that college also advances cognition, helping students become more critical thinkers as well as more flexible. However, some find that those cognitive effects are less evident than they were previously, especially since many current students seek skills and knowledge for career purposes, not for intellectual challenge. Nonetheless, college typically broadens a person's perspective, as the diversity of students and the opportunity to understand and debate new ideas lead to deeper, more flexible, thought.

WHAT HAVE YOU LEARNED?

1. Why did scholars choose the term *postformal* to describe the fifth stage of cognition?
2. How does postformal thinking differ from typical adolescent thought?
3. Why might the threat of a stereotype affect cognition?
4. Who is vulnerable to stereotype threat and why?
5. How do current college enrollment patterns differ from those of 50 years ago?
6. Why do people disagree about the goals of a college education?

Psychosocial Development

A theme of human development is that continuity and change are evident throughout life. In emerging adulthood, the legacy of early development is apparent amidst new achievements. Erikson recognized this ongoing process in his description of the fifth of his eight stages, identity versus role confusion. Remember that the crisis of identity versus role confusion begins in adolescence, but it is not usually resolved then.

Identity Achieved

As already mentioned, Erikson believed that the outcome of earlier crises provides the foundation for each new stage. The identity crisis is an example (see Table EP.3); adults of all ages continue to reflect on their identities.

TABLE EP.3	Erikson's Eight Stages of Development	
Stage	**Virtue / Pathology**	**Possible in Emerging Adulthood if Not Successfully Resolved**
Trust vs. Mistrust	Hope / Withdrawal	Suspicious of others, making close relationships difficult
Autonomy vs. Shame and Doubt	Will / Compulsion	Obsessively driven, single-minded, not socially responsive
Initiative vs. Guilt	Purpose / Inhibition	Fearful, regretful (e.g., very homesick in college)
Industry vs. Inferiority	Competence / Inertia	Self-critical of any endeavor, procrastinating, perfectionistic
Identity vs. Role Confusion	Fidelity / Repudiation	Uncertain and negative about values, lifestyle, friendships
Intimacy vs. Isolation	Love / Exclusivity	Anxious about close relationships, jealous, lonely
Generativity vs. Stagnation	Care / Rejection	[In the future] Fear of failure
Integrity vs. Despair	Wisdom / Disdain	[In the future] No "mindfulness," no life plan

Source: Erikson, 1982/1998.

Developmental psychologists, influenced by Erikson and emerging adults themselves, consider establishing a vocational identity to be part of growing up (Arnett, 2004). Emerging adulthood is a "critical stage for the acquisition of resources"—including the education, skills, and experience needed for vocational success (Tanner et al., 2009, p. 34).

Current emerging adults often quit one job and seek another. Between ages 18 and 25, the average U.S. worker changes jobs every year, with the college-educated changing jobs more than those who are less educated (U.S. Bureau of Labor Statistics, July 25, 2012). They want work that interests them, with co-workers who share their values, which makes them likely to seek a new job more often.

Young workers are not ready to climb a particular vocational ladder, rung by rung. That is a problem for employers, who must interview, choose, and train new employees (Meister, 2012). It is less problematic for the young adults themselves, since exploration is part of the identity search.

Emerging adulthood is a crucial time for developing values regarding work. Are job security and salary (extrinsic rewards) more important than the joy of doing the work one loves (intrinsic rewards)?

The economic recession, apparent worldwide beginning roughly in 2008, is likely to affect how those entering the job market develop their vocational identity (Johnson et al., 2012; Chow et al., 2014). For all emerging adults, the development of personal identity and a sense of purpose are likely to further vocational identity and result in a happier work life (Porfeli et al., 2013).

// **ANSWER TO OBSERVATION QUIZ**
(from page 555) The one with the flags is Kingsborough Community College, in Brooklyn, New York; the one with a colonnade is UCLA (University of California in Los Angeles). If you guessed right, what clues did you use?

Same Situation, Far Apart: Connecting with Their Generation Neither of these young women considers her job a vocation, but both use skills and knowledge that few older adults have. The DJ (*left*) mixes music for emerging adults who crowd thousands of clubs in China to drink, dance, and socialize despite regulations that attempt to close down such establishments. More than 10,000 Apple Store "geniuses" (*right*) work at low pay to meet the booming young-adult demand for the latest social networking tools.

Personality in Emerging Adulthood

Continuity and change are evident in personality. Of course, temperament, childhood trauma, and emotional habits endure lifelong: If self-doubt, anxiety, depression, and so on are present in childhood and adolescence, they are often still evident years later. Traits strongly present at age 5 or 15 do not disappear by age 25.

Yet personality is not static. After adolescence, new characteristics appear and negative traits diminish. Emerging adults make choices that break with the past. This age period is now characterized by years of freedom from a settled lifestyle, which allows shifts in attitude and personality. Overall, a study with almost a million adolescents and adults from 62 nations found that "[d]uring early adulthood, individuals from different cultures across the world tend to become more agreeable, more conscientious, and less neurotic" (Bleidorn et al., 2013, p. 2530).

Rising Self-Esteem

Psychological research finds both continuity and improvement. For example, one longitudinal study found that 17-year-olds who saw life in positive terms maintained their outlook as time went on, while those who were negative often changed for the better (Blonigen et al., 2008). A study of college students found a dip in self-confidence over their freshman year, and then gradual improvement, with a significant—but not large—rise in self-esteem from the beginning to the end of college (Chung et al., 2014).

This positive trend of increasing happiness has become more evident over recent decades, perhaps because young adults are more likely than adolescents to make their own life decisions and move past the role confusion at the beginning of the identity search (Schwartz et al., 2011).

Plasticity

Emerging adults are open to new experiences (a reflection of their adventuresome spirit), and this allows personality shifts as well as eagerness for more education (McAdams & Olson, 2010). Going to college, leaving home, paying one's way, stopping drug abuse, moving to a new city, finding satisfying work and performing it well, making new friends, committing to a partner—each of these might alter a person's life course. The feeling of self-efficacy builds with each successful accomplishment.

Total transformation does not occur since genes, childhood experiences, and family circumstances always affect people. Nor do new experiences always lead to improvement. Cohort effects are always possible: Perhaps the rising self-esteem now documented in longitudinal research will no longer be found if unemployment and financial distress cause lower self-esteem in today's young adults. But there is no doubt that personality *can* shift after adolescence.

Intimacy

In Erikson's theory, after achieving identity, people experience the sixth crisis of development, **intimacy versus isolation.** This crisis arises from the powerful desire to share one's personal life with someone else. Without intimacy, adults suffer from loneliness and isolation. Erikson (1963) explains:

> The young adult, emerging from the search for and the insistence on identity, is eager and willing to fuse his identity with others. He is ready for intimacy, that is, the capacity to commit himself to concrete affiliations and partnerships and to develop the ethical strength to abide by such commitments, even though they call for significant sacrifices and compromises.
>
> *[p. 263]*

The urge for social connection is a powerful human impulse, one reason our species has thrived. Other theorists use different words (*affiliation, affection, interdependence, communion, belonging, love*) for the same human need. Attachment experienced in infancy may well be a precursor to adult intimacy, especially if the person has developed a working model of attachment (Chow & Ruhl, 2014; Phillips et al., 2013). Adults seek to become friends, lovers, companions, and partners.

All intimate relationships (friendship, family ties, and romance) have much in common—in both the psychic needs they satisfy and in the behaviors they require. Intimacy progresses from attraction to close connection to ongoing commitment. Each relationship demands some personal sacrifice, including vulnerability that brings deeper self-understanding and shatters the isolation caused by too much self-protection.

intimacy versus isolation The sixth of Erikson's eight stages of development. Adults seek someone with whom to share their lives in an enduring and self-sacrificing commitment. Without such commitment they risk profound loneliness and isolation.

As Erikson (1963) explains, to establish intimacy, the emerging adult must

> face the fear of ego loss in situations which call for self-abandon: in the solidarity of close affiliations [and] sexual unions, in close friendship and in physical combat, in experiences of inspiration by teachers and of intuition from the recesses of the self. The avoidance of such experiences . . . may lead to a deep sense of isolation and consequent self-absorption.
>
> *[pp. 163–164]*

According to a more recent theory, an important aspect of close human connections is "self-expansion," the idea that each of us enlarges our understanding, our experiences, and our resources through our intimate friends and lovers (Aron et al., 2013). Casual sex, as in "hook-ups" and fleeting acquaintances, are contrary to the intimacy that Erikson thought was crucial for psychosocial health.

Romantic Partners

Love, romance, and commitment are still important for emerging adults, although specifics have changed. Most emerging adults are thought to be postponing, not abandoning, marriage. As one U.S. sociologist explains, "despite the culture of divorce, Americans remain optimistic about and even eager to enter marriages" (Hill, 2007, p. 295). One of the hottest political issues in 2014 in the United States was whether gay and lesbian couples can marry legally. The fact that people care deeply about this issue indicates that marriage is still considered desirable.

The relationship between love and marriage depends on era and culture. Three distinct patterns are evident.

In about one-third of the world's families, love does not precede marriage because parents arrange marriages to join two families together.

In another one-third, adolescents meet only a select group. (Single-sex schools keep them from meeting unsuitable mates.) Parents supervise all male–female interactions. When young people decide to marry someone of that preselected group, the young man asks the young woman's father for "her hand in marriage." Historically, if parental approval was not forthcoming, the teens parted sorrowfully or eloped—neither of which occurs as often today.

The third pattern is relatively new, although familiar to most readers of this book. Young people socialize with hundreds of others and pair off but do not marry until they are able, financially and emotionally, to be independent. Their choices tilt toward personal qualities observable at the moment, such as physical appearance, personal hygiene, personality, sexuality, a sense of humor, not qualities more important to parents, such as religion, ethnicity, or long-term stability.

Suggesting "one-third" for each of these is a rough approximation. In former times, most marriages were of the first type; young people almost never met and married people unknown to their parents. Currently, in developing nations, a pattern called *modern traditionalism* often blends the first two types. For example, in Qatar, couples believe they have a choice, but more than half the marriages are between cousins, often anticipated by relatives from the time they were children (Harkness & Khaled, 2014).

For Western emerging adults, the third type is idealized. Love is considered a prerequisite for marriage and then sexual exclusiveness is expected, as found in a survey of 14,121 people of many ethnic groups and orientations (Meier et al., 2009). They were asked to rate from 1 to 10 the importance of money, same racial background, long-term commitment, love, and faithfulness for a successful marriage or a serious, committed relationship.

Faithfulness to one's partner was considered most important of all (rated 10 by 89 percent) and love was almost as high (rated 10 by 86 percent). By contrast, most thought being of the same race did not matter much (57 percent rated it 1, 2, or 3). Money, while important to many, was not nearly as crucial as love and fidelity.

This survey was conducted in North America, but emerging adults worldwide share many of the same values. Six thousand miles away, emerging adults in Kenya also reported that love was the primary reason for couples to connect and stay together; money was less important (S. Clark et al., 2010).

Finding Each Other

One major innovation of the current cohort of emerging adults is the use of social networks. Web sites such as Facebook and Instagram allow individuals to post their photos and personal information on the Internet, sharing the details of their daily lives with thousands of others. College students almost all (93 percent) use social media sites, particularly to connect with each other (Chronicle of Higher Education, 2014). Many also use Internet matching sites to find potential partners.

Modern Match-ups These couples stare into each other's eyes as part of a singles meeting in Manhattan. Maybe some of them will end up like Alex and Sarah (*right*) who met online and are now among the 2 million U.S. residents who met online and married in 2011.

One problem is that social networking may produce dozens of potential partners, increasing *choice overload* when too many options are available. Choice overload increases second thoughts after a choice is made. (People wonder whether they would have been happier with another choice.) Some people, overloaded with possibilities, refuse to make any selection (Iyengar & Lepper, 2000; Reutskaja & Hogarth, 2009).

Choice overload has been demonstrated with consumer goods—jams, chocolates, pens, restaurants—and now it seems true also for choosing a date, a hook-up, or a mate (Sprecher & Metts, 2013). Contrary to the assumptions of most emerging adults, some research finds that love flourishes better when choice is limited.

Living Together

A second major innovation among emerging adults is **cohabitation,** the term for living together in a romantic partnership without being married. Cohabitation varies widely from one generation and one nation to another.

Two-thirds of all newly married couples in the United States have lived with their partner before marriage (Manning et al., 2014), as have most couples in Canada, northern Europe, England, and Australia. Many couples in Sweden, France, Jamaica, and Puerto Rico live with a partner and plan to stay together, never mar-

cohabitation An arrangement in which a couple live together in a committed romantic relationship but are not formally married.

rying. In other nations—including Japan, Ireland, and Italy—fewer people cohabit, although the rate is rising everywhere.

Research from 30 nations finds that acceptance of cohabitation within their nation affects the happiness of those who cohabit. Demographic differences within those 30 nations (such as education, income, age, and religion among both the married and cohabiting couples) affect happiness as well (Soons & Kalmijn, 2009).

In the United States, cohabiting couples have higher rates of breakups than married couples. Furthermore, children born to cohabiting couples are more likely to have academic, health, or emotional difficulties (Schmeer, 2011). Although there are practical reasons for cohabitation—it saves money and postpones commitment—no longitudinal research has found that it improves psychosocial development.

On the other hand, it is not proven that, for contemporary couples, cohabitation is harmful. Some factors—such as a couple being already engaged to marry before moving in together and being financially secure (rare for most cohabiting couples)—mitigate such problems. Further, the likelihood of divorce when marriage follows cohabitation is closely related to the age of those who cohabit. If a pair of 20-year-olds live together and then marry, their divorce risk is much higher than for a pair of 30-year-olds who do the same (Kuperberg, 2014).

Emerging Adults and Their Parents

It is hard to overestimate the importance of the family during any period of the life span. Although a family is made up of individuals, it is much more than the persons who belong to it. In the dynamic synergy of a well-functioning family, children grow, adults find support, and everyone is part of a unit that gives meaning to, and provides models for, daily life.

If anything, parents today are more important to emerging adults than ever. Two experts in human development write: "[W]ith delays in marriage, more Americans choosing to remain single, and high divorce rates, a tie to a parent may be the most important bond in a young adult's life" (Fingerman & Furstenberg, 2012).

All members of each family have **linked lives;** that is, the experiences and needs of each family member at one stage of life are affected by every other family member (Elder, 1998; Macmillan & Copher, 2005). We have seen this in earlier chapters: Children are affected by their parents' relationship, even if the children are not directly involved in their parents' domestic disputes, financial stresses, parental alliances, and so on. Brothers and sisters can be abusers or protectors, role models for good or for ill.

Many emerging adults still live at home, though the percentage varies from nation to nation. Almost all unmarried

Cohabitation in the United States

Unmarried partner (male/female) households (in millions)

Source: U.S. Census Bureau, 2011 and earlier years.

FIGURE EP.5

More Together, Fewer Married As you see, the number of cohabitating male–female households in the United States has increased dramatically over the past decades. These numbers are an underestimate: Couples do not always tell the U.S. Census that they are living together, nor are cohabitants counted within their parents' households. Same-sex couples (not tallied until 2000) are also not included here.

linked lives Lives in which the success, health, and well-being of each family member are connected to those of other members, including members of another generation, as in the relationship between parents and children.

Love, Not Marriage Andrew and Jessica decided to raise their daughter together but not to marry. They live in White Bear, Minnesota, a relatively conservative area, but cohabiting couples are increasingly common everywhere.

Brilliant, Unemployed, and Laughing
This is not an unusual combination for contemporary college graduates. Melissa, in Missoula, Montana, graduated summa cum laude from George Washington University and is now one of the many college graduates who live with their parents. The arrangement provides financial and family benefits, but it is not known who cooked dinner and who will wash the dishes.

helicopter parents The label used for parents who hover (like a helicopter) over their emerging adult children. The term is pejorative, but parental involvement is sometimes helpful.

young adults in Italy and Japan live with their parents. Fewer do so in the United States, but many parents underwrite their young-adult children's independent living if they can afford to do so (Furstenberg, 2010). When they do not live at home, emerging adults see their parents, on average, several times a week and phone them even more often (Fingerman et al., 2012b).

There is a downside to parental support: It may impede independence. The most dramatic example is the so-called **helicopter parent,** hovering over an emerging adult child, ready to swoop down if any problem arises (Fingerman et al., 2012a).

All Together Now

When we look at actual lives, not the cultural ideal of independence or interdependence, emerging adults worldwide have much in common, including close family connections and a new freedom from parental limits. Family members continue to feel obligated to one another no matter where they live or how old they are.

On the first page of Chapter 1, you learned that the science of human development is about how people change over time and that change is ongoing, with variations by culture, family, SES, and history. Every chapter describes potential problems as well as strategies that help most individuals survive and thrive.

This chapter began by explaining that emerging adulthood provides a review and a preview. Both are now apparent: Most 18- to 25-year-olds survive risks (e.g., overcome substance abuse, combat loneliness, and deal with other problems through further education, friends, family, and maturation). Ideally, surviving risks and thriving is what every developing person does at every age.

SUMMING UP Patterns of psychosocial development in emerging adulthood evidence continuity and change. Personality traits endure, but improvement is often apparent as young adults experience rising self-esteem and self-confidence. The need for social support is lifelong. Among young adults, marriage is often postponed and, at least in contemporary North America, it is more often a personal choice, rather than a family arrangement. Parental support is ongoing, with different particulars in various nations and cultures.

WHAT HAVE YOU LEARNED?

1. Why is vocational identity particularly elusive in current times?
2. How does personality change from adolescence to adulthood?
3. What do emerging adults seek in a close relationship?
4. How has the process of mate selection changed over the past decades?
5. Why do many emerging adults cohabit instead of marrying?
6. What kinds of support do parents provide their young-adult children?

SUMMARY

Biosocial Development

1. Emerging adults usually have strong and healthy bodies. Death from disease is rare, although violent deaths are not uncommon.

2. The sexual-reproductive system reaches a peak during these years. The sex drive is strong and orgasms frequent. Problem-free conception, pregnancy, and birth are more likely between ages 18 and 25 than earlier or later, although most current emerging adults postpone childbearing until age 25 or later.

3. Willingness to take risks is characteristic of emerging adults. This allows positive behaviors, such as entering college, meeting new people, volunteering for difficult tasks, or finding new jobs. It also leads to destructive actions, such as unprotected sex and drug use.

4. Extreme sports are attractive to some emerging adults. Attempting to understand this, developmentalists posit that the risk of injury and even of death can be thrilling at this age and that boredom is to be avoided.

Cognitive Development

5. Adult thinking is more advanced than adolescent thought in that it is more flexible, better able to coordinate the objective and the subjective. Some scholars consider adult thinking a fifth stage of cognition called postformal thought.

6. The flexibility of young-adult thought allows people to reexamine stereotypes from their childhood. This is particularly important in decreasing stereotype threat, which may impair adult cognition if left unchecked.

7. Worldwide, there are far more college students than there were a few decades ago. Everywhere the students' backgrounds and current situations are more diverse than formerly.

8. Although a college education has been shown to have health and income benefits, observers disagree as to how, or even whether, college improves cognition. Evidence suggests that it does, but perhaps not as much as in earlier generations.

Psychosocial Development

9. Identity continues to be worked out in emerging adulthood. Vocational identity is particularly difficult in today's job market, with emerging adults likely to change jobs often.

10. Personality traits from childhood do not disappear in emerging adulthood, but many people learn to modify or compensate for whatever negative traits they have. Personality is much more plastic than people once thought or experienced.

11. The need for social connections and relationships is lifelong. In earlier times and in some cultures currently, emerging adults followed their parents' wishes in seeking marriage partners. Today's youth are more likely to choose their own partners and postpone marriage.

12. Cohabitation is the current norm for emerging adults in many nations, although not in others. Some research finds that this increases marital and childrearing problems later on, but that may vary by culture and cohort.

13. Family members continue to be important to emerging adults: Parental support—financial as well as emotional—may be more crucial than in earlier times.

KEY TERMS

emerging adulthood (p. 543)
organ reserve (p. 544)
homeostasis (p. 544)
allostasis (p. 544)

allostatic load (p. 544)
extreme sports (p. 546)
drug abuse (p. 547)
postformal thought (p. 548)

stereotype threat (p. 550)
massive open online courses (MOOCs) (p. 553)
intimacy versus isolation (p. 558)

cohabitation (p. 560)
linked lives (p. 561)
helicopter parent (p. 562)

APPLICATIONS

1. Describe an incident during your emerging adulthood when taking a risk could have led to disaster. What were your feelings at the time? What would you do if you knew that a child of yours was about to do the same thing?

2. Read a biography or autobiography that includes information about the person's thinking from adolescence through adulthood. How did personal experiences, education, and maturation affect the person's thinking?

3. Statistics on cohort and culture in students and colleges are fascinating, but only a few are reported here. Compare your nation, state, or province with another. Analyze the data and discuss causes and implications of differences.

4. Talk to three people with whom you would expect to have contrasting views on love and marriage (differences in age, gender, upbringing, experience, and religion might affect attitudes). Ask each the same questions and then compare their answers.

Appendix
More About Research
Methods

This appendix explains how to learn about any topic. It is crucial that you distinguish valid conclusions from wishful thinking. Such learning begins with your personal experience.

Make It Personal

Think about your life, observe your behavior, and watch the people around you. Pay careful attention to details of expression, emotion, and behavior. The more you see, the more fascinated, curious, and reflective you will become. Ask questions and listen carefully and respectfully to what other people say regarding development.

Whenever you ask specific questions as part of an assignment, **remember that observing ethical standards (see Chapter 1) comes first.** *Before* you interview anyone, inform the person of your purpose and assure him or her of confidentiality. Promise not to identify the person in your report (use a pseudonym) and do not repeat any personal details that emerge in the interview to anyone (friends or strangers). Your instructor will provide further ethical guidance. If you might publish what you've learned, get in touch with your college's Institutional Review Board (IRB).

Read the Research

No matter how deeply you think about your own experiences, and no matter how intently you listen to others whose background is unlike yours, you also need to read scholarly published work in order to fully understand any topic that interests you. Be skeptical about magazine or newspaper reports; some are bound to be simplified, exaggerated, or biased.

Professional Journals and Books

Part of the process of science is that conclusions are not considered solid until they are corroborated in many studies, which means that you should consult several sources on any topic. **Four journals in human development** are:

- *Developmental Psychology* (published by the American Psychological Association)
- *Child Development* (Society for Research in Child Development)
- *Developmental Review* (Elsevier)
- *Human Development* (Karger)

These journals differ in the types of articles and studies they publish, but all are well respected and peer-reviewed, which means that other scholars review each article submitted and recommend that it be accepted, rejected, or revised. Every article includes references to other recent work.

Also look at journals that specialize in longer reviews from the perspective of a researcher.

- *Child Development Perspectives* (from Society for Research in Child Development)
- *Perspectives on Psychological Science* (This is published by the Association for Psychological Science. APS publishes several excellent journals, none specifically on development but every issue has at least one article that is directly relevant.)

Beyond these six are literally thousands of other professional journals, each with a particular perspective or topic, including many in sociology, family studies, economics, and so on. To judge them, look for journals that are peer-reviewed. Also consider the following details: the background of the author (research funded by corporations tends to favor their products); the nature of the publisher (professional organizations, as in the first two journals above, protect their reputations); how long the journal has been published (the volume number tells you that). Some interesting work does not meet these criteria, but these are guides to quality.

Many **books** cover some aspect of development. Single-author books are likely to present only one viewpoint. That view may be insightful, but it is limited. You might consult a *handbook,* which is a book that includes many authors and many topics. One good handbook in development, now in its seventh edition (a sign that past scholars have found it useful) is:

- *Handbook of Child Psychology and Developmental Science. Edited by Richard M. Lerner (7th ed.), 2015, Wiley.*

Again, dozens of good handbooks are available, many of which focus on a particular age, perspective, or topic.

The Internet

The **Internet** is a mixed blessing, useful to every novice and experienced researcher but dangerous as well. Every library worldwide and most homes in North America, Western Europe, and East Asia have computers that provide access to journals and other information. If you're doing research in a library, ask for help from the librarians; many of them can guide you in the most effective ways to conduct online searches. In addition, other students, friends, and even strangers can be helpful.

Virtually everything is on the Internet, not only massive national and international statistics but also accounts of very personal experiences. Photos, charts, quizzes, ongoing experiments, newspapers from around the world, videos, and much more are available at a click. Every journal has a Web site, with tables of contents, abstracts, and sometimes full texts. (An abstract gives the key findings; for the full text, you may need to consult the library's copy of the print version.)

Unfortunately, you can spend many frustrating hours sifting through information that is useless, trash, or tangential. *Directories* (which list general topics or areas and then move you step by step in the direction you choose) and *search engines* (which give you all the sites that use a particular word or words) can help you select appropriate information. Each directory or search engine provides somewhat different lists; none provides only the most comprehensive and accurate sites. Sometimes organizations figure out ways to make their links appear first, even though they are biased. With experience and help, you will find the best sites for you, but you will also encounter some junk no matter how experienced you are.

Anybody can put anything online, regardless of its truth or fairness, so you need a very critical eye. Make sure you have several divergent sources for every "fact" you find; consider who provided the information and why. Every controversial issue has sites that forcefully advocate opposite viewpoints, sometimes with biased statistics and narrow perspectives.

Here are five Internet sites that are quite reliable:

- *embryo.soad.umich.edu* The Multidimensional Human Embryo. Presents MRI images of a human embryo at various stages of development, accompanied by brief explanations.
- *childdevelopmentinfo.com* Child Development Institute. A useful site, with links and articles on child development and information on common childhood psychological disorders.
- *eric.ed.gov* Education Resources Information Center (ERIC). Provides links to many education-related sites and includes brief descriptions of each.
- *www.nia.nih.gov* National Institute on Aging. Includes information about current research on aging (in case you want to expand your search beyond child development).
- *www.cdc.gov/nchs/hus.htm* The National Center for Health Statistics issues an annual report on health trends, called *Health, United States.*

Every source—you, your interviewees, journals, books, and the Internet—is helpful. Do not depend on any particular one. Avoid plagiarism and prejudice by citing every source and noting objectivity, validity, and credibility. Your own analysis, opinions, words, and conclusions are crucial, backed up by science, as explained in Chapter 1.

Additional Terms and Concepts

As emphasized throughout this text, the study of development is a science. Social scientists spend years in graduate school, studying methods and statistics. Chapter 1 touches on some of these matters (observation and experiments; correlation and statistical significance; independent and dependent variables; experimental and control groups; cross-sectional, longitudinal, and cross-sequential research), but there is much more. A few additional aspects of research are presented here to help you evaluate research wherever you find it.

Who Participates?

The entire group of people about whom a scientist wants to learn is called a **population.** Generally, a research population is quite large—not usually the world's entire population of more than 7 billion, but perhaps all the 4 million babies born in the United States last year, or all the 31 million Japanese currently over age 65.

The particular individuals who are studied in a specific research project are called the **participants.** They are used as a **sample** of the larger group. Ideally, the participants are a **representative sample,** that is, a sample that reflects the entire population. Every peer-reviewed, published study reports details on the sample.

Selection of the sample is crucial. People who volunteer, or people who have telephones, or people who have some particular condition are not a *random sample;*

population The entire group of individuals who are of particular concern in a scientific study, such as all the children of the world or all newborns who weigh less than 3 pounds.

participants The people who are studied in a research project. Participants is the term now used in psychology; other disciplines still call these people "subjects."

sample A group of individuals drawn from a specified population. A sample might be the low-birthweight babies born in four particular hospitals that are representative of all hospitals.

representative sample A group of research participants who reflect the relevant characteristics of the larger population whose attributes are under study.

in a random sample, everyone in a particular population is equally likely to be selected. To avoid *selection bias,* some studies are *prospective,* beginning with an entire cluster of people (for instance, every baby born on a particular day) and then tracing the development of some particular characteristic.

For example, prospective studies find the antecedents of heart disease, or child abuse, or high school dropout rates—all of which are much harder to find if the study is *retrospective,* beginning with those who had heart attacks, experienced abuse, or left school. Thus, although retrospective research finds that most high school dropouts say they disliked school, prospective research finds that some who like school still decide to drop out and then later say they hated school, while others dislike school but stay to graduate. Prospective research discovers how many students are in these last two categories; retrospective research on people who have already dropped out does not.

Research Design

Every researcher begins not only by formulating a hypothesis but also by learning what other scientists have discovered about the topic in question and what methods might be useful and ethical in designing research. Often they include measures to guard against inadvertently finding only the results they expect. For example, the people who actually gather the data may not know the purpose of the research. Scientists say that these data gatherers are **blind** to the hypothesized outcome. Participants are sometimes "blind" as well, because otherwise they might, for instance, respond the way they think they should.

Another crucial aspect of research design is to define exactly what is to be studied. Researchers establish an **operational definition** of whatever phenomenon they will be examining, defining each variable by describing specific, observable behavior. This is essential in quantitative research, but it is also useful in qualitative research. For example, if a researcher wants to know when babies begin to walk, does walking include steps taken while holding on? Is one unsteady step enough? Some parents say yes, but the usual operational definition of *walking* is "takes at least three steps without holding on." This operational definition allows comparisons worldwide, making it possible to discover, for example, that well-fed African babies tend to walk earlier than well-fed European babies.

Operational definitions are difficult to formulate, but they are essential when personality traits are studied. How should *aggression* or *sharing* or *shyness* be defined? Lack of an operational definition leads to contradictory results. For instance, critics report that infant day care makes children more aggressive, but advocates report that it makes them less passive. In this case, both may be seeing the same behavior but defining it differently. For any scientist, operational definitions are crucial, and studies usually include descriptions of how they measured attitudes or behavior.

Reporting Results

You already know that results should be reported in sufficient detail so that another scientist can analyze the conclusions and replicate the research. Various methods, populations, and research designs may produce divergent conclusions. For that reason, handbooks, some journals, and some articles are called *reviews:* They summarize past research. Often, when studies are similar in operational definitions and methods, the review is a **meta-analysis,** which combines the findings of many studies to present an overall conclusion.

blind The condition of data gatherers (and sometimes participants, as well) who are deliberately kept ignorant of the purpose of the research so that they cannot unintentionally bias the results.

operational definition A description of the specific, observable behavior that will constitute the variable that is to be studied, so that any reader will know whether that behavior occurred or not. Operational definitions may be arbitrary (e.g., an IQ score at or above 130 is operationally defined as "gifted"), but they must be precise.

meta-analysis A technique of combining results of many studies to come to an overall conclusion. Meta-analysis is powerful, in that small samples can be added together to lead to significant conclusions, although variations from study to study sometimes make combining them impossible.

Table 1.2 (p. 22) describes some statistical measures. One of them is *statistical significance,* which indicates whether or not a particular result could have occurred by chance.

A crucial statistic is **effect size,** a way of measuring how much impact one variable has on another. Effect size ranges from 0 (no effect) to 1 (total transformation, never found in actual studies). Effect size may be particularly important when the sample size is large, because a large sample often leads to highly "significant" results (results that are unlikely to have occurred by chance) that have only a tiny effect on the variable of interest.

Hundreds of statistical measures are used by developmentalists. Often the same data can be presented in many ways. Some scientists examine statistical analysis intently before they accept conclusions as valid. A specific example involved methods to improve students' writing ability between grades 4 and 12. A meta-analysis found that many methods of writing instruction have a significant impact, but effect size is much larger for some methods (teaching strategies and summarizing) than for others (prewriting exercises and studying models). For teachers, this statistic is crucial, for they want to know what has a big effect, not merely what is better than chance (significant).

Numerous articles published in the past decade are meta-analyses that combine similar studies to search for general trends. Often effect sizes are also reported, which is especially helpful for meta-analyses since standard calculations almost always find some significance if the number of participants is in the thousands.

effect size A way of indicating statistically how much of an impact the independent variable in an experiment had on the dependent variable.

Glossary

23rd pair The chromosome pair that, in humans, determines sex. The other 22 pairs are autosomes, inherited equally by males and females.

A

acceleration Educating gifted children alongside other children of the same mental, not chronological, age.

accommodation The restructuring of old ideas to include new experiences.

achievement test A measure of mastery or proficiency in reading, mathematics, writing, science, or some other subject.

adolescence-limited offender A person whose criminal activity stops by age 21.

adolescent egocentrism A characteristic of adolescent thinking that leads young people (ages 10 to 13) to focus on themselves to the exclusion of others.

adoption A legal proceeding in which an adult or couple is granted the joys and obligations of being a child's parent(s).

adrenal glands Two glands, located above the kidneys, that produce hormones (including the "stress hormones" epinephrine [adrenaline] and norepinephrine).

affordance An opportunity for perception and interaction that is offered by a person, place, or object in the environment.

age of viability The age (about 22 weeks after conception) at which a fetus might survive outside the mother's uterus if specialized medical care is available.

aggressive-rejected Rejected by peers because of antagonistic, confrontational behavior.

allele A variation that makes a gene different in some way from other genes for the same characteristics. Many genes never vary; others have several possible alleles.

allocare Literally, "other-care"; the care of children by people other than the biological parents.

allostasis A dynamic body adjustment, related to homeostasis, that affects overall physiology over time. Homeostasis requires an immediate response, whereas allostasis requires longer-term adjustment.

allostatic load The stresses of basic body systems that combine to limit overall functioning. Higher allostatic load makes a person more vulnerable to illness.

amygdala A tiny brain structure that registers emotions, particularly fear and anxiety.

analytic thought Thought that results from analysis, such as a systematic ranking of pros and cons, risks and consequences, possibilities and facts. Analytic thought depends on logic and rationality.

animism The belief that natural objects and phenomena are alive.

anorexia nervosa An eating disorder characterized by self-starvation. Affected individuals voluntarily undereat and overexercise, depriving their vital organs of nutrition. Anorexia can be fatal.

anoxia A lack of oxygen that, if prolonged, can cause brain damage or death.

antipathy Feelings of dislike or even hatred for another person.

antisocial behavior Actions that are deliberately hurtful or destructive to another person.

Apgar scale A quick assessment of a newborn's health. The baby's color, heart rate, reflexes, muscle tone, and respiratory effort are given a score of 0, 1, or 2 twice—at one minute and five minutes after birth—and each time the total of all five scores is compared with the maximum score of 10 (rarely attained).

apprenticeship in thinking Vygotsky's term for how cognition is stimulated and developed in people by more skilled members of their community.

aptitude The potential to master a specific skill or to learn a certain body of knowledge.

assimilation The reinterpretation of new experiences to fit into old ideas.

assisted reproductive technology (ART) A general term for the techniques designed to help infertile couples conceive and then sustain a pregnancy.

asthma A chronic disease of the respiratory system in which inflammation narrows the airways from the nose and mouth to the lungs, causing difficulty in breathing. Signs and symptoms include wheezing, shortness of breath, chest tightness, and coughing.

attachment According to Ainsworth, "an affectional tie" that an infant forms with a caregiver—a tie that binds them together in space and endures over time.

attention-deficit/hyperactivity disorder (ADHD) A condition characterized by a persistent pattern of inattention and/or by hyperactive or impulsive behaviors; ADHD interferes with a person's functioning or development.

authoritarian parenting An approach to child rearing that is characterized by high behavioral standards, strict punishment for misconduct, and little communication from child to parent.

authoritative parenting An approach to child rearing in which the parents set limits but listen to the child and are flexible.

autism spectrum disorder (ASD) A developmental disorder marked by difficulty with social communication and interaction—including difficulty seeing things from another person's point of view—and restricted, repetitive patterns of behavior, interests, or activities.

automatization A process in which repetition of a sequence of thoughts and actions makes the sequence routine, so that it no longer requires conscious thought.

autonomy versus shame and doubt Erikson's second crisis of psychosocial development. Toddlers either succeed or fail in gaining a sense of self-rule over their actions and their bodies.

axon A fiber that extends from a neuron and transmits electrochemical impulses from that neuron to the dendrites of other neurons.

B

babbling An infant's repetition of certain syllables, such as *ba-ba-ba*, that begins when babies are between 6 and 9 months old.

base rate neglect A common fallacy in which a person ignores the overall frequency of some behavior or characteristic (called the *base rate*) in making a decision. For example, a person might bet on a "lucky" lottery number without considering the odds that that number will be selected.

bed-sharing When two or more people sleep in the same bed. If one of those people is an infant, some researchers worry that the adult will roll over on the infant.

behavioral teratogens Agents and conditions that can harm the prenatal brain, impairing the future child's intellectual and emotional functioning.

behaviorism A grand theory of human development that studies observable behavior. Behaviorism is also called *learning theory* because it describes the laws and processes by which behavior is learned.

Big Five The five basic clusters of personality traits that remain quite stable throughout life: openness, conscientiousness, extroversion, agreeableness, and neuroticism.

bilingual schooling A strategy in which school subjects are taught in both the learner's original language and the second (majority) language.

binocular vision The ability to focus the two eyes in a coordinated manner in order to see one image.

body image A person's idea of how his or her body looks.

Brazelton Neonatal Behavioral Assessment Scale (NBAS) A test often administered to newborns that measures responsiveness and records 46 behaviors, including 20 reflexes.

bulimia nervosa An eating disorder characterized by binge eating and subsequent purging, usually by induced vomiting and/or use of laxatives.

bully-victims People who attack others and who are attacked as well. (Also called *provocative victims* because they do things that elicit bullying.)

bullying aggression Unprovoked, repeated physical or verbal attacks, especially on victims who are unlikely to defend themselves.

bullying Repeated, systematic efforts to inflict harm through physical, verbal, or social attack on a weaker person.

C

carrier A person whose genotype includes a gene that is not expressed in the phenotype. The carried gene occurs in half of the carrier's gametes and thus is passed on to half of the carrier's children. If such a gene is inherited from both parents, the characteristic appears in the phenotype.

case study An in-depth study of one person, usually requiring personal interviews to collect background information and various follow-up discussions, tests, questionnaires, and so on.

centration A characteristic of preoperational thought in which a young child focuses (centers) on one idea, excluding all others.

cerebral palsy A disorder that results from damage to the brain's motor centers. People with cerebral palsy have difficulty with muscle control, so their speech and/or body movements are impaired.

cesarean section (c-section) A surgical birth, in which incisions through the mother's abdomen and uterus allow the fetus to be removed quickly, instead of being delivered through the vagina. (Also called simply *section*.)

charter school A public school with its own set of standards that is funded and licensed by the state or local district in which it is located.

child abuse Deliberate action that impairs a child's physical, emotional, or sexual well-being.

child culture The particular habits, styles, and values that reflect the set of rules and rituals that characterize children as distinct from adult society.

child maltreatment Intentional harm to, or avoidable endangerment of, anyone under 18 years of age.

child neglect Failure to meet a child's basic physical, educational, or emotional needs.

child sexual abuse Any erotic activity that arouses an adult and excites, shames, or confuses a child, whether or not the victim protests and whether or not genital contact is involved.

child-directed speech The high-pitched, simplified, and repetitive way adults speak to infants and children. (Also called *baby talk* or *motherese*.)

childhood obesity In a child, having a BMI above the 95th percentile, according to the U.S. Centers for Disease Control's 1980 standards for children of a given age.

childhood overweight In a child, having a BMI above the 85th percentile, according to the U.S. Centers for Disease Control's 1980 standards for children of a given age.

chromosome One of the 46 structures made of DNA (in 23 pairs) that almost every cell of the human body contains and that, together, contain all the genes. Other species have more or fewer chromosomes.

circadian rhythm A day–night cycle of biological activity that occurs approximately every 24 hours. (*Circadian* means "about a day.")

classical conditioning The learning process in which a meaningful stimulus (such as the smell of food to a hungry animal) is connected with a neutral stimulus (such as the sound of a tone) that had no special meaning before conditioning. (Also called *respondent conditioning*.)

classification The logical principle that things can be organized into groups (or categories or classes) according to some characteristic they have in common.

clinical depression Feelings of hopelessness, lethargy, and worthlessness that last two weeks or more.

cluster suicides Several suicides committed by members of a group within a brief period of time.

co-sleeping A custom in which parents and their children (usually infants) sleep together in the same room.

code of ethics A set of moral principles or guidelines that members of a profession or group are expected to follow.

cognitive equilibrium In cognitive theory, a state of mental balance in which people are not confused because they can use their existing thought processes to understand current experiences and ideas.

cognitive theory A grand theory of human development that focuses on changes in how people think over time. According to this theory, our thoughts shape our attitudes, beliefs, and behaviors.

cohabitation An arrangement in which a couple live together in a committed romantic relationship but are not formally married.

cohort People born within the same historical period who therefore move through life together, experiencing the same events, new technologies, and cultural shifts at the same ages. For example, the effect of the Internet varies depending on what cohort a person belongs to.

comorbid Refers to the presence of two or more unrelated disease conditions at the same time in the same person.

concrete operational thought Piaget's term for the ability to reason logically about direct experiences and perceptions.

conditioning According to behaviorism, the processes by which responses become linked to particular stimuli and learning takes place. The word *conditioning* is used to emphasize the importance of repeated practice, as when an athlete *conditions* his or her body.

conservation The principle that the amount of a substance remains the same (i.e., is conserved) even when its appearance changes.

control processes Mechanisms (including selective attention, metacognition, and emotional regulation) that combine memory, processing speed, and knowledge to regulate the analysis flow of information within the information-processing system. (Also called *executive processes.*)

conventional moral reasoning Kohlberg's second level of moral reasoning, emphasizing social rules.

copy number variations Genes with various repeats or deletions of base pairs.

corporal punishment Punishment that physically hurts the body, such as slapping, spanking, etc.

corpus callosum A long, thick band of nerve fibers that connects the left and right hemispheres of the brain and allows communication between them.

correlation A number between +1.0 and −1.0 that indicates the degree of relationship between two variables, expressed in terms of the likelihood that one variable will (or will not) occur when the other variable does (or does not). A correlation indicates only that two variables are somehow related, not that one variable causes the other to occur.

cortex The outer layers of the brain in humans and other mammals. Most thinking, feeling, and sensing involves the cortex.

cortisol The primary stress hormone; fluctuations in the body's cortisol level affect human emotions.

couvade Symptoms of pregnancy and birth experienced by fathers.

critical period A time when a particular type of developmental growth (in body or behavior) must happen for normal development to occur.

cross-sectional research A research design that compares groups of people who differ in age but are similar in other important characteristics.

cross-sequential research A research design in which researchers first study several groups of people of different ages (a cross-sectional approach) and then follow those groups over the years (a longitudinal approach). (Also called *cohort-sequential research* or *time-sequential research.*)

culture A system of shared beliefs, norms, behaviors, and expectations that persist over time and prescribe social behavior and assumptions.

cyberbullying Bullying that occurs when one person spreads insults or rumors about another by means of social media posts, e-mails, text messages, or cell phone videos.

D

deductive reasoning Reasoning from a general statement, premise, or principle, through logical steps, to figure out (deduce) specifics. (Also called *top-down reasoning.*)

deferred imitation A sequence in which an infant first perceives something done by someone else and then performs the same action hours or even days later.

dendrite A fiber that extends from a neuron and receives electrochemical impulses transmitted from other neurons via their axons.

deoxyribonucleic acid (DNA) The chemical composition of the molecules that contain the genes, which are the chemical instructions for cells to manufacture various proteins.

dependent variable In an experiment, the variable that may change as a result of whatever new condition or situation the experimenter adds. In other words, the dependent variable *depends* on the independent variable.

developmental psychopathology The field that uses insights into typical development to understand and remediate developmental disorders.

developmental theory A group of ideas, assumptions, and generalizations that interpret and illuminate the thousands of observations that have been made about human growth. A developmental theory provides a framework for explaining the patterns and problems of development.

deviancy training Destructive peer support in which one person shows another how to rebel against authority or social norms.

difference-equals-deficit error The mistaken belief that a deviation from some norm is necessarily inferior to behavior or characteristics that meet the standard. Often the "norm" is the standard for the observer, and difference is anyone unlike oneself.

differential susceptibility The idea that people vary in how sensitive they are to particular experiences. Often such differences are genetic, which makes some people affected "for better *and* for worse" by life events. (Also called *differential sensitivity.*)

disorganized attachment A type of attachment that is marked by an infant's inconsistent reactions to the caregiver's departure and return.

distal parenting Caregiving practices that involve remaining distant from the baby, providing toys, food, and face-to-face communication with minimal holding and touching.

dizygotic (DZ) twins Twins who are formed when two separate ova are fertilized by two separate sperm at roughly the same time. (Also called *fraternal* twins.)

dominant–recessive pattern The interaction of a heterozygous pair of alleles in such a way that the phenotype reflects one allele (the dominant gene) more than the other (the recessive gene).

doula Someone who helps with the birth process. Traditionally in Latin America, a doula was the only professional who attended childbirth. Now doulas are likely to arrive at the woman's home during early labor and later work alongside a hospital's staff.

Down syndrome A condition in which a person has 47 chromosomes instead of the usual 46, with 3 rather than 2 chromosomes at the 21st site. People with Down syndrome typically have distinctive characteristics, including unusual facial features, heart abnormalities, and language difficulties. (Also called *trisomy-21.*)

drug abuse The ingestion of a drug to the extent that it impairs the user's biological or psychological well-being.

dual-process model The notion that two networks exist within the human brain, one for emotional processing of stimuli and one for analytical.

dynamic perception Perception that is primed to focus on movement and change.

dynamic-systems approach A view of human development as an ongoing, ever-changing interaction between the physical, cognitive, and psychosocial influences. The crucial understanding is that development is never static but is always affected by, and affects, many systems of development.

dyscalculia Unusual difficulty with math, probably originating from a distinct part of the brain.

dyslexia Unusual difficulty with reading; thought to be the result of some neurological underdevelopment.

E

eclectic perspective The approach taken by most developmentalists, in which they apply aspects of each of the various theories of development rather than adhering exclusively to one theory.

ecological-systems approach A perspective on human development that considers all the influences from the various contexts of development. (Later renamed *bioecological theory*.)

effortful control The ability to regulate one's emotions and actions through effort, not simply through natural inclination.

egocentrism Piaget's term for children's tendency to think about the world entirely from their own personal perspective.

Electra complex The unconscious desire of girls to replace their mother and win their father's romantic love.

ELLs (English Language Learners) Children in the United States whose proficiency in English is low—usually below a cutoff score on an oral or written test. Many children who speak a non- English language at home are also capable in English; they are *not* ELLs.

embryo The name for a developing human organism from about the third through the eighth week after conception.

embryonic period The stage of prenatal development from approximately the third through the eighth week after conception, during which the basic forms of all body structures, including internal organs, develop.

emerging adulthood The period of life between the ages of 18 and 25. Emerging adulthood is now widely thought of as a separate developmental stage.

emotional regulation The ability to control when and how emotions are expressed.

empathy The ability to understand the emotions and concerns of another person, especially when those emotions and concerns differ from one's own.

empirical Based on observation, experience, or experiment; not theoretical.

entity theory of intelligence An approach to understanding intelligence that sees ability as innate, a fixed quantity present at birth; those who hold this view do not believe that effort enhances achievement.

epigenetics The study of how environmental factors affect genes and genetic expression—enhancing, halting, shaping, or altering the expression of genes and resulting in a phenotype that may differ markedly from the genotype.

equifinality A basic principle of developmental psychopathology that holds that one symptom can have many causes.

ESL (English as a Second Language) A U.S. approach to teaching English that gathers all the non-English speakers together and provides intense instruction in English. Their first language is never used; the goal is to prepare them for regular classes in English.

estradiol A sex hormone, considered the chief estrogen. Females produce much more estradiol than males do.

ethnic group People whose ancestors were born in the same region and who often share a language, culture, and religion.

executive function The cognitive ability to organize and prioritize the many thoughts that arise from the various parts of the brain, allowing the person to anticipate, strategize, and plan behavior.

experience-dependent brain functions Brain functions that depend on particular, variable experiences and that therefore may or may not develop in a particular infant.

experience-expectant brain functions Brain functions that require certain basic common experiences (which an infant can be expected to have) in order to develop normally.

experiment A method to determine cause and effect. Researchers control the participants and the interventions, which makes it easier to understand what causes what, for whom.

extended family A family of three or more generations living in one household.

externalizing problems Difficulty with emotional regulation that involves expressing powerful feelings through uncontrolled physical or verbal outbursts, as by lashing out at other people or breaking things.

extreme sports Forms of recreation that include apparent risk of injury or death and that are attractive and thrilling as a result.

extremely low birthweight (ELBW) A body weight at birth of less than 2 pounds, 3 ounces (1,000 grams).

extrinsic motivation A drive, or reason to pursue a goal, that arises from the need to have one's achievements rewarded from outside, perhaps by receiving material possessions or another person's esteem.

F

failure to thrive A serious medical condition in early infancy, when the baby does not gain weight as rapidly as he or she is expected to.

false positive The result of a laboratory test that reports something as true when in fact it is not true. This can occur for pregnancy tests, when a woman might not be pregnant even though the test says she is, or during pregnancy when a problem is reported that actually does not exist.

familism The belief that family members should support one another, sacrificing individual freedom and success, if necessary, in order to preserve family unity and protect the family from outside sources.

family function The way a family works to meet the needs of its members. Children need families to provide basic material necessities, to encourage learning, to help them develop self-respect, to nurture friendships, and to foster harmony and stability.

family structure The legal and genetic relationships among relatives; includes nuclear family, extended family, stepfamily, and so on.

fast-mapping The speedy and sometimes imprecise way in which children learn new words by tentatively placing them in mental categories according to their perceived meaning.

fetal alcohol syndrome (FAS) A cluster of birth defects, including abnormal facial characteristics, slow physical growth, and reduced intellectual ability, that may occur in the fetus of a woman who drinks alcohol while pregnant.

fetal period The stage of prenatal development from the ninth week after conception until birth, during which the fetus gains about 7 pounds (more than 3,000 grams) and organs become more mature, gradually able to function on their own.

fetus The name for a developing human organism from the start of the ninth week after conception until birth.

fine motor skills Physical abilities involving small body movements, especially of the hands and fingers, such as drawing and picking up a coin. (The word *fine* here means "small.")

Flynn effect The rise in average IQ scores that has occurred over the decades in many nations.

fMRI Functional magnetic resonance imaging, a measuring technique in which the brain's electrical excitement indicates activation anywhere in the brain; fMRI helps researchers locate neurological responses to stimuli.

focus on appearance A characteristic of preoperational thought in which a young child ignores all attributes that are not apparent.

foreclosure Erikson's term for premature identity formation, which occurs when an adolescent adopts parents' or society's roles and values wholesale, without questioning or analysis.

formal operational thought In Piaget's theory, the fourth and final stage of cognitive development, characterized by more systematic logical thinking and by the ability to understand and systematically manipulate abstract concepts.

foster care A legal, publicly supported system in which a maltreated child is removed from the parents' custody and entrusted to another adult or family. Foster care providers are reimbursed for expenses incurred in meeting the child's needs.

fragile X syndrome A genetic disorder in which part of the X chromosome seems to be attached to the rest of it by a very thin string of molecules. The cause is a single gene that has more than 200 repetitions of one triplet.

G

gamete A reproductive cell; that is, a sperm or ovum that can produce a new individual if it combines with a gamete from the other sex to make a zygote.

gender differences Differences in the roles and behaviors of males and females that are prescribed by the culture.

gender identity A person's acceptance of the roles and behaviors that society associates with the biological categories of male and female.

gender schema A cognitive concept or general belief based on one's experiences—in this case, a child's understanding of sex differences.

gene A small section of a chromosome; the basic unit for the transmission of heredity. A gene consists of a string of chemicals that provide instructions for the cell to manufacture certain proteins.

generational forgetting The idea that each new generation forgets what the previous generation learned. As used here, the term refers to knowledge about the harm drugs can do.

genetic counseling Consultation and testing by trained experts that enables individuals to learn about their genetic heritage, including harmful conditions that they might pass along to any children they may conceive.

genome The full set of genes that are the instructions to make an individual member of a certain species.

genotype An organism's entire genetic inheritance, or genetic potential.

germinal period The first two weeks of prenatal development after conception, characterized by rapid cell division and the beginning of cell differentiation.

gonads The paired sex glands (ovaries in females, testicles in males). The gonads produce hormones and gametes.

goodness of fit A similarity of temperament and values that produces a smooth interaction between an individual and his or her social context, including family, school, and community.

grammar All the methods—word order, verb forms, and so on—that languages use to communicate meaning, apart from the words themselves.

gross motor skills Physical abilities involving large body movements, such as walking and jumping. (The word *gross* here means "big.")

growth spurt The relatively sudden and rapid physical growth that occurs during puberty. Each body part increases in size on a schedule: Weight usually precedes height, and growth of the limbs precedes growth of the torso.

guided participation The process by which people learn from others who guide their experiences and explorations. This learning is direct and interactive.

H

habituation The process of becoming accustomed to an object or event through repeated exposure to it, and thus becoming less interested in it.

Head Start A federally funded early-childhood intervention program for low-income children of preschool age.

head-sparing A biological mechanism that protects the brain when malnutrition disrupts body growth. The brain is the last part of the body to be damaged by malnutrition.

helicopter parents The label used for parents who hover (like a helicopter) over their emerging adult children. The term is pejorative, but parental involvement is sometimes helpful.

heritability A statistic that indicates what percentage of the variation in a particular trait within a particular population, in a particular context and era, can be traced to genes.

heterozygous Referring to two genes of one pair that differ in some way. Typically one allele has only a few base pairs that differ from the other member of the pair.

hidden curriculum The unofficial, unstated, or implicit rules and priorities that influence the academic curriculum and every other aspect of learning in a school.

high-stakes test An evaluation that is critical in determining success or failure. If a single test determines whether a student will graduate or be promoted, it is a high-stakes test.

hippocampus A brain structure that is a central processor of memory, especially memory for locations.

holophrase A single word that is used to express a complete, meaningful thought.

home schooling Education in which children are taught at home, usually by their parents.

homeostasis The balanced adjustment of all the body's systems to keep physiological functions in a state of equilibrium.

homozygous Referring to two genes of one pair that are exactly the same in every letter of their code. Most gene pairs are homozygous.

hormone An organic chemical substance that is produced by one body tissue and conveyed via the bloodstream to another to affect some physiological function.

HPA (hypothalamus–pituitary–adrenal) axis A sequence of hormone production originating in the hypothalamus and moving to the pituitary and then to the adrenal glands.

HPG (hypothalamus–pituitary–gonad) axis A sequence of hormone production originating in the hypothalamus and moving to the pituitary and then to the gonads.

Human Genome Project An international effort to map the complete human genetic code. This effort was essentially completed in 2001, though analysis is ongoing.

humanism A theory that stresses the potential of all humans for good and the belief that all people have the same basic needs, regardless of culture, gender, or background.

hypothalamus A brain area that responds to the amygdala and the hippocampus to produce hormones that activate other parts of the brain and body.

hypothesis A specific prediction that can be tested.

hypothetical thought Reasoning that includes propositions and possibilities that may not reflect reality.

I

identification An attempt to defend one's self-concept by taking on the behaviors and attitudes of someone else.

identity achievement Erikson's term for the attainment of identity, or the point at which a person understands who he or she is as a unique individual, in accord with past experiences and future plans.

identity versus role confusion Erikson's term for the fifth stage of development, in which the person tries to figure out "Who am I?" but is confused as to which of many possible roles to adopt.

imaginary audience The other people who, in an adolescent's egocentric belief, are watching and taking note of his or her appearance, ideas, and behavior. This belief makes many teenagers very self-conscious.

imaginary friends Make-believe friends who exist only in a child's imagination; increasingly common from ages 3 through 7. They combat loneliness and aid emotional regulation.

immersion A strategy in which instruction in all school subjects occurs in the second (usually the majority) language that a child is learning.

immigrant paradox The surprising, paradoxical fact that low SES immigrant women tend to have fewer birth complications than native-born peers with higher incomes.

immunization A process that stimulates the body's immune system by causing production of antibodies to defend against attack by a particular contagious disease. Creation of antibodies may be accomplished either naturally (by having the disease), by injection, by drops that are swallowed, or by a nasal spray. (These imposed methods are also called *vaccination*.)

implantation The process, beginning about 10 days after conception, in which the developing organism burrows into the placenta that lines the uterus, where it can be nourished and protected as it continues to develop.

impulse control The ability to postpone or deny the immediate response to an idea or behavior.

in vitro fertilization (IVF) Fertilization that takes place outside a woman's body (as in a glass laboratory dish). The procedure involves mixing sperm with ova that have been surgically removed from the woman's ovary. If a zygote is produced, it is inserted into a woman's uterus, where it may implant and develop into a baby.

incremental theory of intelligence An approach to understanding intelligence that holds that intelligence can be directly increased by effort; those who subscribe to this view believe they can master whatever they seek to learn if they pay attention, participate in class, study, complete their homework, and so on.

independent variable In an experiment, the variable that is introduced to see what effect it has on the dependent variable. (Also called *experimental variable*.)

individual education plan (IEP) A document that specifies educational goals and plans for a child with special needs.

induction A disciplinary technique in which the parent tries to get the child to understand why a certain behavior was wrong. Listening, not lecturing, is crucial."

inductive reasoning Reasoning from one or more specific experiences or facts to reach (induce) a general conclusion. (Also called *bottom-up reasoning*.)

industry versus inferiority The fourth of Erikson's eight psychosocial crises, during which children attempt to master many skills, developing a sense of themselves as either industrious or inferior, competent or incompetent.

information-processing theory A perspective that compares human thinking processes, by analogy, to computer analysis of data, including sensory input, connections, stored memories, and output.

information-processing theory A perspective that compares human thinking processes, by analogy, to computer analysis of data, including sensory input connections, stored memories, and output.

initiative versus guilt Erikson's third psychosocial crisis, in which children undertake new skills and activities and feel guilty when they do not succeed at them.

injury control/harm reduction Practices that are aimed at anticipating, controlling, and preventing dangerous activities. These practices reflect the beliefs that accidents are not random and that injuries can be made less harmful if proper controls are in place.

insecure-avoidant attachment A pattern of attachment in which an infant avoids connection with the caregiver. The infant seems not to care about the caregiver's presence, departure, or return.

insecure-resistant/ambivalent attachment A pattern of attachment in which an infant's anxiety and uncertainty are evident, as when the infant becomes very upset at separation from the caregiver and both resists and seeks contact on reunion.

instrumental aggression Behavior that hurts someone else because the aggressor wants to get or keep a possession or a privilege.

internalizing problems Difficulty with emotional regulation that involves turning one's emotional distress inward, as by feeling excessively guilty, ashamed, or worthless.

intimacy versus isolation The sixth of Erikson's eight stages of development. Adults seek someone with whom to share their lives in an enduring and self-sacrificing commitment. Without such commitment they risk profound loneliness and isolation.

intra-cytoplasmic sperm injection (ICSI) An in vitro fertilization technique in which a single sperm cell is injected directly into an ovum.

intrinsic motivation A drive, or reason to pursue a goal, that comes from inside a person, such as the desire to feel smart or competent.

intuitive thought Thought that arises from an emotion or a hunch, beyond rational explanation, and is influenced by past experiences and cultural assumptions.

invincibility fable An adolescent's egocentric conviction that he or she cannot be overcome or even harmed by anything that might defeat a normal mortal, such as unprotected sex, drug abuse, or high-speed driving.

irreversibility A characteristic of preoperational thought in which a young child thinks that nothing can be undone. A thing cannot be restored to the way it was before a change occurred.

K

kangaroo care A form of newborn care in which mothers (and sometimes fathers) rest their babies on their naked chests, like kangaroo mothers that carry their immature newborns in a pouch on their abdomen.

kinship care A form of foster care in which a relative of a maltreated child, usually a grandparent, becomes the approved caregiver.

knowledge base A body of knowledge in a particular area that makes it easier to master new information in that area.

kwashiorkor A disease of chronic malnutrition during childhood, in which a protein deficiency makes the child more vulnerable to other diseases, such as measles, diarrhea, and influenza.

L

language acquisition device (LAD) Chomsky's term for a hypothesized mental structure that enables humans to learn language, including the basic aspects of grammar, vocabulary, and intonation.

latency Freud's term for middle childhood, during which children's emotional drives and psychosexual needs are quiet (latent). Freud thought that sexual conflicts from earlier stages are only temporarily submerged, bursting forth again at puberty.

lateralization Literally, "sidedness," referring to the specialization in certain functions by each side of the brain, with one side dominant for each activity. The left side of the brain controls the right side of the body, and vice versa.

least restrictive environment (LRE) A legal requirement that children with special needs be assigned to the most general educational context in which they can be expected to learn.

leptin A hormone that affects appetite and is believed to affect the onset of puberty. Leptin levels increase during childhood and peak at around age 12.

life-course-persistent offender A person whose criminal activity typically begins in early adolescence and continues throughout life; a career criminal.

linked lives Lives in which the success, health, and well-being of each family member are connected to those of other members, including members of another generation, as in the relationship between parents and children.

"little scientist" The stage-five toddler (age 12 to 18 months) who experiments without anticipating the results, using trial and error in active and creative exploration.

long-term memory The component of the information-processing system in which virtually limitless amounts of information can be stored indefinitely.

longitudinal research A research design in which the same individuals are followed over time, as their development is repeatedly assessed.

low birthweight (LBW) A body weight at birth of less than 5. pounds (2,500 grams).

M

marasmus A disease of severe protein-calorie malnutrition during early infancy, in which growth stops, body tissues waste away, and the infant eventually dies.

massive open online course (MOOC) A course that is offered solely online for college credit. Typically, tuition is very low, and thousands of students enroll.

mean length of utterance (MLU) The average number of words and meaningful sounds (such as -ing and huh?) in a typical sentence (called utterance, because children may not talk in complete sentences). MLU is often used to indicate how advanced a child's language development is.

menarche A girl's first menstrual period, signaling that she has begun ovulation. Pregnancy is biologically possible, but ovulation and menstruation are often irregular for years after menarche.

metacognition "Thinking about thinking," or the ability to evaluate a cognitive task in order to determine how best to accomplish it, and then to monitor and adjust one's performance on that task.

middle childhood The period between early childhood and early adolescence, approximately from ages 6 to 11.

middle school A school for children in the grades between elementary and high school. Middle school usually begins with grade 6 and ends with grade 8.

modeling The central process of social learning, by which a person observes the actions of others and then copies them.

monozygotic (MZ) twins Twins who originate from one zygote that splits apart very early in development. (Also called *identical twins*.) Other monozygotic multiple births (such as triplets and quadruplets) can occur as well.

Montessori schools Schools that offer early-childhood education based on the philosophy of Maria Montessori, which emphasizes careful work and tasks that each young child can do.

moratorium An adolescent's choice of a socially acceptable way to postpone making identity-achievement decisions. Going to college is a common example.

motor skills The learned abilities to move some part of the body, in actions ranging from a large leap to a flicker of the eyelid. (The word *motor* here refers to movement of muscles.)

multifactorial Referring to a trait that is affected by many factors, both genetic and environmental, that enhance, halt, shape, or alter the expression of genes, resulting in a phenotype that may differ markedly from the genotype.

multifinality A basic principle of developmental psychopathology that holds that one cause can have many (multiple) final manifestations.

multiple intelligences The idea that human intelligence is composed of a varied set of abilities rather than a single, all-encompassing one.

myelination The process by which axons become coated with myelin, a fatty substance that speeds the transmission of nerve impulses from neuron to neuron.

N

naming explosion A sudden increase in an infant's vocabulary, especially in the number of nouns, that begins at about 18 months of age.

National Assessment of Educational Progress (NAEP) An ongoing and nationally representative measure of U.S. children's achievement in reading, mathematics, and other subjects over time; nicknamed "the Nation's Report Card."

nature In development, nature refers to the traits, capacities, and limitations that each individual inherits genetically from his or her parents at the moment of conception.

neglectful/uninvolved parenting An approach to child rearing in which the parents are indifferent toward their children and unaware of what is going on in their children's lives.

neurodiversity The idea that people have diverse brain structures, with each person having neurological strengths and weaknesses that should be appreciated, in much the same way diverse cultures and ethnicities are welcomed. A person who is adept at numbers and systems but inept in social skills and metaphors might be recognized as having unusual gifts, rather than pitied for having an autism spectrum disorder.

neuron One of billions of nerve cells in the central nervous system, especially in the brain.

neurotransmitter A brain chemical that carries information from the axon of a sending neuron to the dendrites of a receiving neuron.

No Child Left Behind Act A U.S. law enacted in 2001 that was intended to increase accountability in education by requiring states to qualify for federal educational funding by administering standardized tests to measure school achievement.

norm An average, or typical, standard of behavior or accomplishment, such as the norm for age of walking or the norm for greeting a stranger.

nuclear family A family that consists of a father, a mother, and their biological children under age 18.

nurture In development, nurture includes all the environmental influences that affect the individual after conception. This includes everything from the mother's nutrition while pregnant to the implicit values of the nation.

O

object permanence The realization that objects (including people) still exist when they can no longer be seen, touched, or heard.

Oedipus complex The unconscious desire of young boys to replace their father and win their mother's romantic love.

operant conditioning The learning process by which a particular action is followed by something desired (which makes the person or animal more likely to repeat the action) or by something unwanted (which makes the action less likely to be repeated). (Also called *instrumental conditioning*.)

organ reserve The capacity of organs to allow the body to cope with stress, via extra, unused functioning ability.

overimitation When a person imitates an action that is not a relevant part of the behavior to be learned. Overimitation is common among 2- to 6-year-olds when they imitate adult actions that are unnecessary.

overregularization The application of rules of grammar even when exceptions occur, making the language seem more "regular" than it actually is.

P

parasuicide Any potentially lethal action against the self that does not result in death. (Also called *attempted suicide* or *failed suicide*.)

parent–infant bond The strong, loving connection that forms as parents hold, examine, and feed their newborn.

parental alliance Cooperation between a mother and a father based on their mutual commitment to their children. In a parental alliance, the parents support each other in their shared parental roles.

parental monitoring Parents' ongoing awareness of what their children are doing, where, and with whom.

peer pressure Encouragement to conform to one's friends or contemporaries in behavior, dress, and attitude; usually considered a negative force, as when adolescent peers encourage one another to defy adult authority.

people preference A universal principle of infant perception, specifically an innate attraction to other humans, evident in visual, auditory, and other preferences.

percentile A point on a ranking scale of 0 to 100. The 50th percentile is the midpoint; half the people in the population being studied rank higher and half rank lower.

perception The mental processing of sensory information when the brain interprets a sensation.

permanency planning An effort by child-welfare authorities to find a long-term living situation that will provide stability and support for a maltreated child. A goal is to avoid repeated changes of caregiver or school, which can be harmful to the child.

permissive parenting An approach to child rearing that is characterized by high nurturance and communication but little discipline, guidance, or control. (Also called *indulgent parenting*.)

perseveration The tendency to persevere in, or stick to, one thought or action for a long time.

personal fable An aspect of adolescent egocentrism characterized by an adolescent's belief that his or her thoughts, feelings, and experiences are unique, more wonderful, or more awful, than anyone else's.

phallic stage Freud's third stage of development, when the penis becomes the focus of concern and pleasure.

phenotype The observable characteristics of a person, including appearance, personality, intelligence, and all other traits.

PISA (Programme for International Student Assessment) An international test taken by 15-year-olds in 50 nations that is designed to measure problem solving and cognition in daily life.

pituitary A gland in the brain that responds to a signal from the hypothalamus by producing many hormones, including those that regulate growth and that control other glands, among them the adrenal and sex glands.

plasticity The idea that abilities, personality, and other human characteristics can change over time. Plasticity is particularly evident during childhood, but even older adults are not always "set in their ways."

polygamous family A family consisting of one man, several wives, and their children.

polygenic Referring to a trait that is influenced by many genes.

post-traumatic stress disorder (PTSD) An anxiety disorder that develops after a profoundly shocking or frightening event, such as rape, severe beating, war, or natural disaster. Symptoms may include flashbacks to the event, hyperactivity and hypervigilance, displaced anger, sleeplessness, nightmares, sudden terror or anxiety, and confusion between fantasy and reality.

postconventional moral reasoning Kohlberg's third level of moral reasoning, emphasizing moral principles.

postformal thought A proposed adult stage of cognitive development, following Piaget's four stages. Postformal thought goes beyond adolescent thinking by being more practical, more flexible, and more dialectical (i.e., more capable of combining contradictory elements into a comprehensive whole).

postpartum depression A new mother's feelings of inadequacy and sadness in the days and weeks after giving birth.

pragmatics The practical use of language that includes the ability to adjust language communication according to audience and context.

preconventional moral reasoning Kohlberg's first level of moral reasoning, emphasizing rewards and punishments.

prefrontal cortex The area of the cortex at the very front of the brain that specializes in anticipation, planning, and impulse control.

preoperational intelligence Piaget's term for cognitive development between the ages of about 2 and 6; it includes language and imagination (which involve symbolic thought), but logical, operational thinking is not yet possible at this stage.

preterm A birth that occurs 3 or more weeks before the full 38 weeks of the typical pregnancy—that is, at 35 or fewer weeks after conception.

primary circular reactions The first of three types of feedback loops in sensorimotor intelligence, this one involving the infant's own body. The infant senses motion, sucking, noise, and other stimuli and tries to understand them.

primary prevention Actions that change overall background conditions to prevent harm

primary sex characteristics The parts of the body that are directly involved in reproduction, including the uterus, ovaries, testicles, and penis.

private school A school funded by tuition charges, endowments, and often religious or other nonprofit sponsors.

private speech The internal dialogue that occurs when people talk to themselves (either silently or out loud).

Progress in International Reading Literacy Study (PIRLS) Inaugurated in 2001, a planned five-year cycle of international trend studies in the reading ability of fourth-graders.

prosocial behavior Actions that are helpful and kind but are of no obvious benefit to oneself.

protein-calorie malnutrition A condition in which a person does not consume sufficient food of any kind. This deprivation can result in several illnesses, severe weight loss, and even death.

proximal parenting Caregiving practices that involve being physically close to the baby, with frequent holding and touching.

pruning When applied to brain development, the process by which unused connections in the brain atrophy and die.

psychoanalytic theory A grand theory of human development that holds that irrational, unconscious drives and motives, often originating in childhood, underlie human behavior.

psychological control A disciplinary technique that involves threatening to withdraw love and support and that relies on a child's feelings of guilt and gratitude to the parents.

psychopathology Literally, an illness of the mind, or psyche. Various cultures and groups within cultures have different concepts of specific psychopathologies. A recent compendium of symptoms and disorders in the United States is in the DSM-5. Many other nations use an international set of categories, the ICD-10.

puberty The time between the first onrush of hormones and full adult physical development. Puberty usually lasts three to five years. Many more years are required to achieve psychosocial maturity.

R

race A group of people who are regarded by themselves or by others as distinct from other groups on the basis of physical appearance, typically skin color. Social scientists think race is a misleading concept, as biological differences are not signified by outward appearance.

reaction time The time it takes to respond to a stimulus, either physically (with a reflexive movement such as an eyeblink) or cognitively (with a thought).

reactive aggression An impulsive verbal or physical retaliation for another person's intentional or accidental action.

reflex An unlearned, involuntary action or movement in response to a stimulus. A reflex occurs without conscious thought.

Reggio Emilia A program of early-childhood education that originated in the town of Reggio Emilia, Italy, and that encourages each child's creativity in a carefully designed setting.

reinforcement When a behavior is followed by something desired, such as food for a hungry animal or a welcoming smile for a lonely person.

relational aggression Nonphysical acts, such as insults or social rejection, aimed at harming the social connection between the victim and other people.

REM (rapid eye movement) sleep A stage of sleep characterized by flickering eyes behind closed lids, dreaming, and rapid brain waves.

reminder session A perceptual experience that helps a person recollect an idea, a thing, or an experience.

replication Repeating a study, usually using different participants.

reported maltreatment Harm or endangerment about which someone has notified the authorities.

resilience The capacity to adapt well to significant adversity and to overcome serious stress.

response to intervention (RTI) An educational strategy intended to help children who demonstrate below-average achievement in early grades, using special intervention.

role confusion A situation in which an adolescent does not seem to know or care what his or her identity is. (Sometimes called *identity* or *role diffusion*.)

rough-and-tumble play Play that mimics aggression through wrestling, chasing, or hitting, but in which there is no intent to harm.

rumination Repeatedly thinking and talking about past experiences; can contribute to depression.

S

scaffolding Temporary support that is tailored to a learner's needs and abilities and aimed at helping the learner master the next task in a given learning process.

science of human development The science that seeks to understand how and why people of all ages and circumstances change or remain the same over time.

scientific method A way to answer questions using empirical research and data-based conclusions.

scientific observation A method of testing a hypothesis by unobtrusively watching and recording participants' behavior in a systematic and objective manner—in a natural setting, in a laboratory, or in searches of archival data.

secondary circular reactions The second of three types of feedback loops in sensorimotor intelligence, this one involving people and objects. Infants respond to other people, to toys, and to any other object they can touch or move.

secondary education Literally, the period after primary education (elementary or grade school) and before tertiary education (college). It usually occurs from about ages 12 to 18, although there is some variation by school and by nation.

secondary prevention Actions that avert harm in a high-risk situation, such as holding a child's hand while crossing the street.

secondary sex characteristics Physical traits that are not directly involved in reproduction but that indicate sexual maturity, such as a man's beard and a woman's breasts.

secular trend The long-term upward or downward direction of various measurements, as a result of modern conditions. For example, improved nutrition and medical care over the past 200 years has led to earlier puberty and greater average height.

secure attachment A relationship in which an infant obtains both comfort and confidence from the presence of his or her caregiver.

selective adaptation The process by which living creatures (including people) adjust to their environment. Genes that enhance survival and reproductive ability are selected, over the generations, to become more prevalent.

selective attention The ability to concentrate on some stimuli while ignoring others.

self-awareness A person's realization that he or she is a distinct individual whose body, mind, and actions are separate from those of other people.

self-concept A person's understanding of who he or she is, in relation to self-esteem, appearance, personality, and various traits.

self-righting The inborn drive to remedy a developmental deficit; literally, to return to sitting or standing upright after being tipped over. People of all ages have self-righting impulses, seeking emotional as well as physical balance.

sensation The response of a sensory system (eyes, ears, skin, tongue, nose) when it detects a stimulus.

sensitive period A time when a certain type of development is most likely, although it may still happen later with more difficulty. For example, early childhood is considered a sensitive period for language learning.

sensorimotor intelligence Piaget's term for the way infants think—by using their senses and motor skills—during the first period of cognitive development.

sensory memory The component of the information-processing system in which incoming stimulus information is stored for a split second to allow it to be processed. (Also called the *sensory register*.)

separation anxiety An infant's distress when a familiar caregiver leaves; most obvious between 9 and 14 months.

seriation The concept that things can be arranged in a logical series, such as the number sequence or the alphabet.

sex differences Biological differences between males and females, in organs, hormones, and body type.

sexual orientation A term that refers to whether a person is sexually and romantically attracted to others of the same sex, the opposite sex, or both sexes.

sexually transmitted infection (STI) A disease spread by sexual contact, including syphilis, gonorrhea, genital herpes, chlamydia, and HIV.

shaken baby syndrome A life-threatening injury that occurs when an infant is forcefully shaken back and forth, a motion that ruptures blood vessels in the brain and breaks neural connections.

single-parent family A family that consists of only one parent and his or her biological children under age 18.

small for gestational age (SGA) (Also called *small-for-dates*.) A term for a baby whose birthweight is significantly lower than expected, given the time since conception. For example, a 5-pound (2,265-gram) newborn is considered SGA if born on time but not SGA if born two months early.

social comparison The tendency to assess one's abilities, achievements, social status, and other attributes by measuring them against those of other people, especially one's peers.

social construction An idea that is built on shared perceptions, not on objective reality. Many age-related terms (such as *childhood, adolescence, yuppie,* and *senior citizen*) are social constructions, strongly influenced by social assumptions.

social learning The acquisition of behavior patterns by observing the behavior of others.

social learning theory An extension of behaviorism that emphasizes the influence that other people have over a person's behavior. Even without specific reinforcement, every individual learns through observation and imitation of other people. (Also called *observational learning*.)

social mediation Human interaction that expands and advances understanding, often through words that one person uses to explain something to another.

social referencing Seeking information about how to react to an unfamiliar or ambiguous object or event by observing someone else's expressions and reactions. That other person becomes a social reference.

social smile A smile evoked by a human face normally first evident in infants about 6 weeks after birth.

sociocultural theory A newer theory that holds that development results from the dynamic interaction of each person with the surrounding social and cultural forces.

sociodramatic play Pretend play in which children act out various roles and themes in stories that they create.

socioeconomic status (SES) A person's position in society as determined by income, occupation, education, and place of residence. (Sometimes called *social class*.)

specific learning disorder (learning disability) A marked deficit in a particular area of learning that is not caused by an apparent physical disability, by an intellectual disability, or by an unusually stressful home environment.

spermarche A boy's first ejaculation of sperm. Erections can occur as early as infancy, but ejaculation signals sperm production. Spermarche may occur during sleep (in a "wet dream") or via direct stimulation.

static reasoning A characteristic of pre-operational thought in which a young child thinks that nothing changes. Whatever is now has always been and always will be.

stem cells Cells from which any other specialized type of cell can form.

stereotype threat The possibility that one's appearance or behavior will be misread to confirm another person's oversimplified, prejudiced attitudes.

still-face technique An experimental practice in which an adult keeps his or her face unmoving and expressionless in face-to-face interaction with an infant.

Strange Situation A laboratory procedure for measuring attachment by evoking infants' reactions to the stress of various adults' comings and goings in an unfamiliar playroom.

stranger wariness An infant's expression of concern—a quiet stare while clinging to a familiar person, or a look of fear—when a stranger appears.

stunting The failure of children to grow to a normal height for their age due to severe and chronic malnutrition.

substantiated maltreatment Harm or endangerment that has been reported, investigated, and verified.

sudden infant death syndrome (SIDS) A situation in which a seemingly healthy infant, usually between 2 and 6 months old, suddenly stops breathing and dies unexpectedly while asleep.

suicidal ideation Thinking about suicide, usually with some serious emotional and intellectual or cognitive overtones.

sunk cost fallacy The mistaken belief that if money, time, or effort that cannot be recovered (a "sunk cost," in economic terms) has already been invested in some endeavor, then more should be invested in an effort to reach the goal. Because of this fallacy, people spend money trying to fix a "lemon" of a car or send more troops to fight a losing battle.

superego In psychoanalytic theory, the judgmental part of the personality that internalizes the moral standards of the parents.

survey A research method in which information is collected from a large number of people by interviews, written questionnaires, or some other means.

symbolic thought A major accomplishment of preoperational intelligence that allows a child to think symbolically, including understanding that words can refer to things not seen and that an item, such as a flag, can symbolize something else (in this case, a country).

synapse The intersection between the axon of one neuron and the dendrites of other neurons.

synaptic gap The pathway across which neurotransmitters carry information from the axon of the sending neuron to the dendrites of the receiving neuron.

synchrony A coordinated, rapid, and smooth exchange of responses between a caregiver and an infant.

T

temperament Inborn differences between one person and another in emotions, activity, and self-regulation. It is measured by the person's typical responses to the environment.

teratogen An agent or condition, including viruses, drugs, and chemicals, that can impair prenatal development and result in birth defects or even death.

tertiary circular reactions The third of three types of feedback loops in sensorimotor intelligence, this one involving active exploration and experimentation. Infants explore a range of new activities, varying their responses as a way of learning about the world.

tertiary prevention Actions, such as immediate and effective medical treatment, that reduce harm or prevent disability after injury.

testosterone A sex hormone, the best known of the androgens (male hormones); secreted in far greater amounts by males than by females.

theory A comprehensive set of ideas.

theory of mind A person's theory of what other people might be thinking. In order to have a theory of mind, children must realize that other people are not necessarily thinking the same thoughts that they themselves are. That realization seldom occurs before age 4.

theory-theory The idea that children attempt to explain everything they see and hear by constructing theories.

threshold effect In prenatal development, when a teratogen is relatively harmless in small doses but becomes harmful once exposure reaches a certain level (the threshold).

time-out A disciplinary technique in which a child is separated from other people for a specified time.

transient exuberance The great but temporary increase in the number of dendrites that develop in an infant's brain during the first two years of life.

Trends in Math and Science Study (TIMSS) An international assessment of the math and science skills of fourth- and eighth-graders. Although the TIMSS is very useful, different countries' scores are not always comparable because sample selection, test administration, and content validity are hard to keep uniform.

trust versus mistrust Erikson's first crisis of psychosocial development. Infants learn basic trust if the world is a secure place where their basic needs (for food, comfort, attention, and so on) are met.

U

ultrasound An image of a fetus (or an internal organ) produced by using high-frequency sound waves. (Also called *sonogram*.)

V

very low birthweight (VLBW) A body weight at birth of less than 3 pounds, 5 ounces (1,500 grams).

visual cliff An experimental apparatus that gives the illusion of a sudden drop-off between one horizontal surface and another.

voucher A public subsidy for tuition payment at a nonpublic school. Vouchers vary a great deal from place to place, not only in amount and availability but also in restrictions as to who gets them and what schools accept them.

W

wasting The tendency for children to be severely underweight for their age as a result of malnutrition.

withdrawn-rejected Rejected by peers because of timid, withdrawn, and anxious behavior.

working memory The component of the information-processing system in which current conscious mental activity occurs. (Formerly called *short-term memory.*)

working model In cognitive theory, a set of assumptions that the individual uses to organize perceptions and experiences. For example, a person might assume that other people are trustworthy and be surprised by an incident in which this working model of human behavior is erroneous.

X

X-linked A gene carried on the X chromosome. If a male inherits an X-linked recessive trait from his mother, he expresses that trait because the Y from his father has no counteracting gene. Females are more likely to be carriers of X-linked traits but are less likely to express them.

XX A 23rd chromosome pair that consists of two X-shaped chromosomes, one each from the mother and the father. XX zygotes become females.

XY A 23rd chromosome pair that consists of an X-shaped chromosome from the mother and a Y-shaped chromosome from the father. XY zygotes become males.

Z

zone of proximal development In sociocultural theory, a metaphorical area, or "zone," surrounding a learner that includes all the skills, knowledge, and concepts that the person is close ("proximal") to acquiring but cannot yet master without help.

zygote The single cell formed from the union of two gametes, a sperm and an ovum.

References

Aarnoudse-Moens, Cornelieke S. H.; Smidts, Diana P.; Oosterlaan, Jaap; Duivenvoorden, Hugo J. & Weisglas-Kuperus, Nynke. (2009). Executive function in very preterm children at early school age. *Journal of Abnormal Child Psychology*, 37(7), 981–993. doi: 10.1007/s10802-009-9327-z

Abar, Caitlin C.; Jackson, Kristina M. & Wood, Mark. (2014). Reciprocal relations between perceived parental knowledge and adolescent substance use and delinquency: The moderating role of parent–teen relationship quality. *Developmental Psychology*, 50(9), 2176–2187. doi: 10.1037/a0037463

Abela, Angela & Walker, Janet (Eds.). (2014). *Contemporary issues in family studies: Global perspectives on partnerships, parenting and support in a changing world*. Malden, MA: Wiley.

Abreu, Guida de. (2008). From mathematics learning out-of-school to multicultural classrooms: A cultural psychology perspective. In Lyn D. English (Ed.), *Handbook of international research in mathematics education* (2nd ed., pp. 323–353). New York, NY: Routledge.

Accardo, Pasquale. (2006). Who's training whom? *The Journal of Pediatrics*, 149(2), 151–152. doi: 10.1016/j.jpeds.2006.04.026

Adams, Caralee. (2014). High school students' participation in advanced placement continues to grow. Education Week. Retrieved from http://blogs.edweek.org/edweek/college_bound/2014/02/high_school_students_participating_in_advanced_placement_continues_to_grow.html

Adamson, Lauren B. & Bakeman, Roger. (2006). Development of displaced speech in early mother-child conversations. *Child Development*, 77(1), 186–200. doi: 10.1111/j.1467-8624.2006.00864.x

Adamson, Lauren B.; Bakeman, Roger; Deckner, Deborah F. & Nelson, P. Brooke. (2014). From interactions to conversations: The development of joint engagement during early childhood. *Child Development*, 85(3), 941–955. doi: 10.1111/cdev.12189

Adolph, Karen E. & Berger, Sarah E. (2005). Physical and motor development. In Marc H. Bornstein & Michael E. Lamb (Eds.), *Developmental science: An advanced textbook* (5th ed., pp. 223–281). Mahwah, NJ: Lawrence Erlbaum Associates.

Adolph, Karen E.; Cole, Whitney G.; Komati, Meghana; Garciaguirre, Jessie S.; Badaly, Daryaneh; Lingeman, Jesse M., . . . Sotsky, Rachel B. (2012). How do you learn to walk? Thousands of steps and dozens of falls per day. *Psychological Science*, 23(11), 1387–1394. doi: 10.1177/0956797612446346

Adolph, Karen E. & Kretch, Kari S. (2012). Infants on the edge: Beyond the visual cliff. In Alan M. Slater & Paul C. Quinn (Eds.), *Developmental psychology: Revisiting the classic studies*. Thousand Oaks, CA: Sage.

Adolph, Karen E. & Robinson, Scott. (2013). The road to walking: What learning to walk tells us about development. In Philip D. Zelazo (Ed.), *The Oxford handbook of developmental psychology* (Vol. 1, pp. 402–447). New York, NY: Oxford University Press.

Adolph, Karen E.; Vereijken, Beatrix & Shrout, Patrick E. (2003). What changes in infant walking and why. *Child Development*, 74(2), 475–497. doi: 10.1111/1467-8624.7402011

Ahmed, Parvez & Jaakkola, Jouni J. K. (2007). Maternal occupation and adverse pregnancy outcomes: A Finnish population-based study. *Occupational Medicine*, 57(6), 417–423. doi: 10.1093/occmed/kqm038

Ainsworth, Mary D. Salter. (1967). *Infancy in Uganda: Infant care and the growth of love*. Baltimore, MD: Johns Hopkins Press.

Ainsworth, Mary D. Salter. (1973). The development of infant-mother attachment. In Bettye M. Caldwell & Henry N. Ricciuti (Eds.), *Child development and social policy* (pp. 1–94). Chicago, IL: University of Chicago Press.

Akhtar, Nameera & Jaswal, Vikram K. (2013). Deficit or difference? Interpreting diverse developmental paths: An introduction to the special section. *Developmental Psychology*, 49(1), 1–3. doi: 10.1037/a0029851

Aksglaede, Lise; Link, Katarina; Giwercman, Aleksander; Jørgensen, Niels; Skakkebæk, Niels E. & Juul, Anders. (2013). 47,XXY Klinefelter syndrome: Clinical characteristics and age-specific recommendations for medical management. *American Journal of Medical Genetics Part C: Seminars in Medical Genetics*, 163(1), 55–63. doi: 10.1002/ajmg.c.31349

Al-Namlah, Abdulrahman S.; Meins, Elizabeth & Fernyhough, Charles. (2012). Self-regulatory private speech relates to children's recall and organization of autobiographical memories. *Early Childhood Research Quarterly*, 27(3), 441–446. doi: 10.1016/j.ecresq.2012.02.005

Al-Sahab, Ban; Ardern, Chris I.; Hamadeh, Mazen J. & Tamim, Hala. (2010). Age at menarche in Canada: Results from the National Longitudinal Survey of Children & Youth. *BMC Public Health*, 10(1), 736–743. doi: 10.1186/1471-2458-10-736

Al-Sayes, Fatin; Gari, Mamdooh; Qusti, Safaa; Bagatian, Nadiah & Abuzenadah, Adel. (2011). Prevalence of iron deficiency and iron deficiency anemia among females at university stage. *Journal of Medical Laboratory and Diagnosis*, 2(1), 5–11.

Al-Yagon, Michal; Cavendish, Wendy; Cornoldi, Cesare; Fawcett, Angela J.; Grünke, Matthias; Hung, Li-Yu, . . . Vio, Claudio. (2013). The proposed changes for DSM-5 for SLD and ADHD: International perspectives—Australia, Germany, Greece, India, Israel, Italy, Spain, Taiwan, United Kingdom, and United States. *Journal of Learning Disabilities*, 46(1), 58–72. doi: 10.1177/0022219412464353

Albert, Dustin; Chein, Jason & Steinberg, Laurence. (2013). The teenage brain: Peer influences on adolescent decision making. *Current Directions in Psychological Science*, 22(2), 114–120. doi: 10.1177/0963721412471347

Albert, Dustin & Steinberg, Laurence. (2011). Judgment and decision making in adolescence. *Journal of Research on Adolescence*, 21(1), 211–224. doi: 10.1111/j.1532-7795.2010.00724.x

Alegre, Alberto. (2011). Parenting styles and children's emotional intelligence: What do we know? *The Family Journal*, 19(1), 56–62. doi: 10.1177/1066480710387486

Alkire, Blake C.; Vincent, Jeffrey R.; Burns, Christy T.; Metzler, Ian S.; Farmer, Paul E. & Meara, John G. (2012). Obstructed labor and caesarean delivery: The cost and benefit of surgical intervention. *PLoS ONE*, 7(4), e34595. doi: 10.1371/journal.pone.0034595

Allen, Kathleen P. (2010). A bullying intervention system in high school: A two-year school-wide follow-up. *Studies In Educational Evaluation*, 36(3), 83–92. doi: 10.1016/j.stueduc.2011.01.002

Almomani, Basima; Hawwa, Ahmed F.; Millership, Jeffrey S.; Heaney, Liam; Douglas, Isabella; McElnay, James C. & Shields, Michael D. (2013). Can certain genotypes predispose to poor asthma control in children? A pharmacogenetic study of 9 candidate genes in children with difficult asthma. *PLoS ONE*, 8(4), e60592. doi: 10.1371/journal.pone.0060592

Almond, Douglas. (2006). Is the 1918 influenza pandemic over? Long-term effects of in utero influenza exposure in the post-1940 U.S. population.

Journal of Political Economy, 114(4), 672–712. doi: 10.1086/507154

Alper, Meryl. (2013). Developmentally appropriate New Media Literacies: Supporting cultural competencies and social skills in early childhood education. *Journal of Early Childhood Literacy, 13*(2), 175–196. doi: 10.1177/1468798411430101

Alsaker, Françoise D. & Flammer, August. (2006). Pubertal development. In Sandy Jackson & Luc Goossens (Eds.), *Handbook of adolescent development* (pp. 30–50). New York, NY: Psychology Press.

Altbach, Philip G.; Reisberg, Liz & Rumbley, Laura E. (2010). Tracking a global academic revolution. *Change: The Magazine of Higher Learning, 42*(2), 30–39. doi: 10.1080/00091381003590845

Alviola, Pedro A.; Nayga, Rodolfo M. & Thomsen, Michael. (2013). Food deserts and childhood obesity. *Applied Economic Perspectives and Policy, 35*(1), 106–124. doi: 10.1093/aepp/pps035

Amato, Michael S.; Magzamen, Sheryl; Imm, Pamela; Havlena, Jeffrey A.; Anderson, Henry A.; Kanarek, Marty S. & Moore, Colleen F. (2013). Early lead exposure (<3 years old) prospectively predicts fourth grade school suspension in Milwaukee, Wisconsin (USA). *Environmental Research, 126*, 60–65. doi: 10.1016/j.envres.2013.07.008

Ambady, Nalini & Bharucha, Jamshed. (2009). Culture and the brain. *Current Directions in Psychological Science, 18*(6), 342–345. doi: 10.1111/j.1467-8721.2009.01664.x

American Academy of Pediatrics. (2014). School start times for adolescents. *Pediatrics, 134*(3), 642–649. doi: 10.1542/peds.2014-1697

American College of Obstetricians and Gynecologists Committee on Obstetric Practice. (2011). Committee opinion no. 476: Planned home birth. *Obstetrics & Gynecology, 117*(2), 425–428. doi: 10.1097/AOG.0b013e31820eee20

American Psychiatric Association. (2013). *Diagnostic and statistical manual of mental disorders: DSM-5* (5th ed.). Washington, DC: American Psychiatric Association.

American Psychological Association. (2010). Ethical principles of psychologists and code of conduct: Including 2010 amendments. http://www.apa.org/ethics/code/index.aspx

Anderson, Robert N.; Kochanek, Kenneth D. & Murphy, Sherry L. (1997). *Report of final mortality statistics, 1995.* Hyattsville, MD: Centers for Disease Control and Prevention, National Center for Health Statistics, 45(11, Suppl. 2).

Anderson, Sarah E. & Must, Aviva. (2005). Interpreting the continued decline in the average age at menarche: Results from two nationally representative surveys of U.S. girls studied 10 years apart. *The Journal of Pediatrics, 147*(6), 753–760. doi: 10.1016/j.jpeds.2005.07.016

Andrews, Nick; Miller, Elizabeth; Grant, Andrew; Stowe, Julia; Osborne, Velda & Taylor, Brent. (2004). Thimerosal exposure in infants and developmental disorders: A retrospec-

tive cohort study in the United Kingdom does not support a causal association. *Pediatrics, 114*(3), 584–591. doi: 10.1542/peds.2003-1177-L

Ansary, Nadia S. & Luthar, Suniya S. (2009). Distress and academic achievement among adolescents of affluence: A study of externalizing and internalizing problem behaviors and school performance. *Development and Psychopathology, 21*(1), 319–341. doi: 10.1017/S0954579409000182

Antenucci, Antonio. (2013, November 26). Cop who bought homeless man boots promoted. *New York Post.*

Antoine, Michelle W.; Hübner, Christian A; Arezzo, Joseph C. & Hébert, Jean M. (2013). A causative link between inner ear defects and long-term striatal dysfunction. *Science, 341*(6150), 1120–1123. doi: 10.1126/science.1240405

Apgar, Virginia. (1953). A proposal for a new method of evaluation of the newborn infant. *Current Researches in Anesthesia and Analgesia, 32,* 260–267.

Archambault, Isabelle; Janosz, Michel; Fallu, Jean-Sébastien & Paganim, Linda S. (2009). Student engagement and its relationship with early high school dropout. *Journal of Adolescence, 32*(3), 651–670. doi: 10.1016/j.adolescence.2008.06.007

Argyrides, Marios & Kkeli, Natalie. (2014). Predictive factors of disordered eating and body image satisfaction in Cyprus. *International Journal of Eating Disorders.* doi: 10.1002/eat.22310

Ariely, Dan. (2009). *Predictably irrational: The hidden forces that shape our decisions.* New York, NY: Harper.

Arnett, Jeffrey J. (2004). *Emerging adulthood: The winding road from the late teens through the twenties.* New York, NY: Oxford University Press.

Arnett, Jeffrey J. & Brody, Gene H. (2008). A fraught passage: The identity challenges of African American emerging adults. *Human Development, 51*(5–6), 291–293. doi: 10.1159/000170891

Aron, Arthur; Lewandowski, Gary W.; Mashek, Debra & Aron, Elaine N. (2013). The self-expansion model of motivation and cognition in close relationships. In Jeffry A. Simpson & Lorne Campbell (Eds.), *The Oxford handbook of close relationships* (pp. 90–115). New York, NY: Oxford University Press.

Aronson, Joshua; Burgess, Diana; Phelan, Sean M. & Juarez, Lindsay. (2013). Unhealthy interactions: The role of stereotype threat in health disparities. *American Journal of Public Health, 103*(1), 50–56. doi: 10.2105/AJPH.2012.300828

Aronson, Joshua; Fried, Carrie B. & Good, Catherine. (2002). Reducing the effects of stereotype threat on African American college students by shaping theories of intelligence. *Journal of Experimental Social Psychology, 38*(2), 113–125. doi: 10.1006/jesp.2001.1491

Arum, Richard & Roksa, Josipa. (2011). *Academically adrift: Limited learning on college campuses.* Chicago, IL: University of Chicago Press.

Arum, Richard & Roksa, Josipa. (2014). *Aspiring adults adrift: Tentative transitions of col-*

lege graduates. Chicago, IL: University of Chicago Press.

Arum, Richard; Roksa, Josipa & Cho, Esther. (2011). *Improving undergraduate learning: Findings and policy recommendations from the SSRC-CLA Longitudinal Project.* New York, NY: Social Science Research Council.

Ash, Caroline; Jasny, Barbara R.; Roberts, Leslie; Stone, Richard & Sugden, Andrew M. (2008). Reimagining cities. *Science, 319*(5864), 739. doi: 10.1126/science.319.5864.739

Ashraf, Quamrul & Galor, Oded. (2013). The 'Out of Africa' hypothesis, human genetic diversity, and comparative economic development. *American Economic Review, 103*(1), 1–46. doi: 10.1257/aer.103.1.1

Ashwin, Sarah & Isupova, Olga. (2014). "Behind every great man…": The male marriage wage premium examined qualitatively. *Journal of Marriage and Family, 76*(1), 37–55. doi: 10.1111/jomf.12082

Aslin, Richard N. (2012). Language development: Revisiting Eimas et al.'s /ba/ and /pa/ study. In Alan M. Slater & Paul C. Quinn (Eds.), *Developmental psychology: Revisiting the classic studies.* Thousand Oaks, CA: Sage.

Asma, Stephen T. (2013). *Against fairness.* Chicago, IL: University of Chicago Press.

Atzil, Shir; Hendler, Talma & Feldman, Ruth. (2014). The brain basis of social synchrony. *Social Cognitive & Affective Neuroscience, 9*(8), 1193–1202. doi: 10.1093/scan/nst105

Au, Wayne & Tempel, Melissa B. (Eds.). (2012). *Pencils down: Rethinking high-stakes testing and accountability in public schools.* Milwaukee, WI: Rethinking Schools.

Aud, Susan; Wilkinson-Flicker, Sidney; Kristapovich, Paul; Rathbun, Amy; Wang, Xiaolei & Zhang, Jijun. (2013). *The condition of education 2013.* Washington, DC: U.S. Department of Education, National Center for Education Statistics.

Audrey, Suzanne; Holliday, Jo & Campbell, Rona. (2006). It's good to talk: Adolescent perspectives of an informal, peer-led intervention to reduce smoking. *Social Science & Medicine, 63*(2), 320–334. doi: 10.1016/j.socscimed.2005.12.010

Aunola, Kaisa; Tolvanen, Asko; Viljaranta, Jaana & Nurmi, Jari-Erik. (2013). Psychological control in daily parent–child interactions increases children's negative emotions. *Journal of Family Psychology, 27*(3), 453–462. doi: 10.1037/a0032891

Autor, David H. (2014). Skills, education, and the rise of earnings inequality among the "other 99 percent". *Science, 344*(6186), 843–851. doi: 10.1126/science.1251868

Aven, Terje. (2011). On some recent definitions and analysis frameworks for risk, vulnerability, and resilience. *Risk Analysis, 31*(4), 515–522. doi: 10.1111/j.1539-6924.2010.01528.x

Ayyanathan, Kasirajan (Ed.). (2014). *Specific gene expression and epigenetics: The interplay*

between the genome and its environment. Oakville, Canada: Apple Academic Press.

Azrin, Nathan H. & Foxx, Richard M. (1974). *Toilet training in less than a day.* New York, NY: Simon & Schuster.

Babchishin, Lyzon K.; Weegar, Kelly & Romano, Elisa. (2013). Early child care effects on later behavioral outcomes using a Canadian nation-wide sample. *Journal of Educational and Developmental Psychology*, 3(2), 15–29. doi: 10.5539/jedp.v3n2p15

Babineau, Vanessa; Green, Cathryn Gordon; Jolicoeur-Martineau, Alexis; Minde, Klaus; Sassi, Roberto; St-André, Martin, . . . Wazana, Ashley. (2014). Prenatal depression and 5-HTTLPR interact to predict dysregulation from 3 to 36 months—A differential susceptibility model. *Journal of Child Psychology and Psychiatry.* doi: 10.1111/jcpp.12246

Bachman, Jerald G.; O'Malley, Patrick M.; Freedman-Doan, Peter; Trzesniewski, Kali H. & Donnellan, M. Brent. (2011). Adolescent self-esteem: Differences by race/ethnicity, gender, and age. *Self Identity*, 10(4), 445–473. doi: 10.1080/15298861003794538

Bagla, Pallava & Stone, Richard. (2013). Science for all. *Science*, 340(6136), 1032–1036. doi: 10.1126/science.340.6136.1032

Bagwell, Catherine L. & Schmidt, Michelle E. (2011). *Friendships in childhood & adolescence.* New York, NY: Guilford Press.

Baillargeon, Renée. (2000). How do infants learn about the physical world? In Darwin Muir & Alan Slater (Eds.), *Infant development: The essential readings* (pp. 195–212). Malden, MA: Blackwell.

Baillargeon, Renée & DeVos, Julie. (1991). Object permanence in young infants: Further evidence. *Child Development*, 62(6), 1227–1246. doi: 10.1111/j.1467-8624.1991.tb01602.x

Baillargeon, Renée; Stavans, Maayan; Wua, Di; Gertner, Yael; Setoh, Peipei; Kittredge, Audrey K. & Bernard, Amélie. (2012). Object individuation and physical reasoning in infancy: An integrative account. *Language Learning and Development*, 8(1), 4–46. doi: 10.1080/15475441.2012.630610

Baker, Jeffrey P. (2000). Immunization and the American way: 4 childhood vaccines. *American Journal of Public Health*, 90(2), 199–207. doi: 10.2105/AJPH.90.2.199

Baker, J. R. & Hudson, J. L. (2013). Friendship quality and social information processing in clinically anxious children. *Child Psychiatry & Human Development*, 45(1), 12–23. doi: 10.1007/s10578-013-0374-x

Baker, Lindsey A. & Mutchler, Jan E. (2010). Poverty and material hardship in grandparent-headed households. *Journal of Marriage and Family*, 72(4), 947–962. doi: 10.1111/j.1741-3737.2010.00741.x

Baker, Olesya & Lang, Kevin. (2013). *The effect of high school exit exams on graduation, employment, wages and incarceration.* Cambridge, MA: National Bureau Of Economic Research. doi: 10.3386/w19182

Baldry, Anna C. & Farrington, David P. (2007). Effectiveness of programs to prevent school bullying. *Victims & Offenders*, 2(2), 183–204. doi: 10.1080/15564880701263155

Baldwin, Dare A. (1993). Infants' ability to consult the speaker for clues to word reference. *Journal of Child Language*, 20(2), 395–418. doi: 10.1017/S0305000900008345

Ball, Helen L. & Volpe, Lane E. (2013) Sudden Infant Death Syndrome (SIDS) risk reduction and infant sleep location – Moving the discussion forward. *Social Science & Medicine*, 79(1), 84–91. doi: 10.1016/j.socscimed.2012.03.025

Baltazar, Alina; Hopkins, Gary; McBride, Duane; Vanderwaal, Curt; Pepper, Sara & Mackey, Sarah. (2013). Parental influence on inhalant use. *Journal of Child & Adolescent Substance Abuse*, 22(1), 25–37. doi: 10.1080/1067828X.2012.729904

Baly, Michael W.; Cornell, Dewey G. & Lovegrove, Peter. (2014). A longitudinal investigation of self- and peer reports of bullying victimization across middle school. *Psychology in the Schools*, 51(3), 217–240. doi: 10.1002/pits.21747

Bamford, Christi & Lagattuta, Kristin H. (2010). A new look at children's understanding of mind and emotion: The case of prayer. *Developmental Psychology*, 46(1), 78–92. doi: 10.1037/a0016694

Bandura, Albert. (1986). *Social foundations of thought and action: A social cognitive theory.* Englewood Cliffs, NJ: Prentice-Hall.

Bandura, Albert. (1997). The anatomy of stages of change. *American Journal of Health Promotion*, 12(1), 8–10.

Bandura, Albert. (2006). Toward a psychology of human agency. *Perspectives on Psychological Science*, 1(2), 164–180. doi: 10.1111/j.1745-6916.2006.00011.x

Banks, Jane W. (2003). Ka'nisténhsera Teiakotíhsnie's: A native community rekindles the tradition of breastfeeding. *AWHONN Lifelines*, 7(4), 340–347. doi: 10.1177/1091592303257828

Bannon, Michael J.; Johnson, Magen M.; Michelhaugh, Sharon K.; Hartley, Zachary J.; Halter, Steven D.; David, James A., . . . Schmidt, Carl J. (2014). A molecular profile of cocaine abuse includes the differential expression of genes that regulate transcription, chromatin, and dopamine cell phenotype. *Neuropsychopharmacology*, 39(9), 2191–2199. doi: 10.1038/npp.2014.70

Barbaresi, William J.; Colligan, Robert C.; Weaver, Amy L.; Voigt, Robert G.; Killian, Jill M. & Katusic, Slavica K. (2013). Mortality, ADHD, and psychosocial adversity in adults with childhood ADHD: A prospective study. *Pediatrics*, 131(4), 637–644. doi: 10.1542/peds.2012-2354

Barber, Brian K. (Ed.). (2002). *Intrusive parenting: How psychological control affects children and adolescents.* Washington, DC: American Psychological Association.

Barboza, Carolyn F.; Monteiro, Sarojini M. D. R.; Barradas, Susana C.; Sarmiento, Olga L.; Rios, Paola; Ramirez, Andrea, . . . Pratt, Michael. (2013). Physical activity, nutrition and behavior change in Latin America: A systematic review. *Global Health Promotion*, 20(4 Suppl.), 65–81. doi: 10.1177/1757975913502240

Barinaga, Marcia. (2003). Newborn neurons search for meaning. *Science*, 299(5603), 32–34. doi: 10.1126/science.299.5603.32

Barnett, Kylie J.; Finucane, Ciara; Asher, Julian E.; Bargary, Gary; Corvin, Aiden P.; Newell, Fiona N. & Mitchell, Kevin J. (2008). Familial patterns and the origins of individual differences in synaesthesia. *Cognition*, 106(2), 871–893. doi: 10.1016/j.cognition.2007.05.003

Barnett, Mark; Watson, Ruth & Kind, Peter. (2006). Pathways to barrel development. In Reha Erzurumlu, et al. (Eds.), *Development and plasticity in sensory thalamus and cortex* (pp. 138–157). New York, NY: Springer. doi: 10.1007/978-0-387-38607-2_9

Barnett, W. Steven; Carolan, Megan E.; Squires, James H. & Brown, Kirsty C. (2013). *The state of preschool, 2013: State preschool yearbook.* New Brunswick, NJ: The National Institute for Early Education Research.

Baron-Cohen, Simon. (2010). Empathizing, systemizing, and the extreme male brain theory of autism. In Ivanka Savic (Ed.), *Progress in brain research: Sex differences in the human brain, their underpinnings and implications* (pp. 167–175). New York, NY: Elsevier. doi: 10.1016/B978-0-444-53630-3.00011-7

Baron-Cohen, Simon; Tager-Flusberg, Helen & Lombardo, Michael (Eds.). (2013). *Understanding other minds: Perspectives from developmental social neuroscience* (3rd ed.). New York, NY: Oxford University Press.

Barr, Rachel. (2013). Memory constraints on infant learning from picture books, television, and touchscreens. *Child Development Perspectives*, 7(4), 205–210. doi: 10.1111/cdep.12041

Barros, Romina M.; Silver, Ellen J. & Stein, Ruth E. K. (2009). School recess and group classroom behavior. *Pediatrics*, 123(2), 431–436. doi: 10.1542/peds.2007-2825

Bartels, Meike; Cacioppo, John T.; van Beijsterveldt, Toos C. E. M. & Boomsma, Dorret I. (2013). Exploring the association between well-being and psychopathology in adolescents. *Behavior Genetics*, 43(3), 177–190. doi: 10.1007/s10519-013-9589-7

Bateson, Patrick & Martin, Paul. (2013). *Play, playfulness, creativity and innovation.* New York, NY: Cambridge University Press.

Bauer, Patricia J.; San Souci, Priscilla & Pathman, Thanujeni. (2010). Infant memory. *Wiley Interdisciplinary Reviews: Cognitive Science*, 1(2), 267–277. doi: 10.1002/wcs.38

Baumard, Nicolas; Mascaro, Olivier & Chevallier, Coralie. (2012). Preschoolers are able to take merit into account when distributing goods. *Developmental Psychology*, 48(2), 492–498. doi: 10.1037/a0026598

Baumeister, Roy F. & Blackhart, Ginnette C. (2007). Three perspectives on gender differences in adolescent sexual development. In Rutger C. M. E. Engels, et al. (Eds.), *Friends, lovers, and groups: Key relationships in adolescence* (pp. 93–104). Hoboken, NJ: Wiley.

Baumrind, Diana. (1967). Child care practices anteceding three patterns of preschool behavior. *Genetic Psychology Monographs, 75*(1), 43–88.

Baumrind, Diana. (1971). Current patterns of parental authority. *Developmental Psychology, 4*(1, Pt. 2), 1–103. doi: 10.1037/h0030372

Baumrind, Diana. (2005). Patterns of parental authority and adolescent autonomy. *New Directions for Child and Adolescent Development, 2005*(108), 61–69. doi: 10.1002/cd.128

Baumrind, Diana; Larzelere, Robert E. & Owens, Elizabeth B. (2010). Effects of preschool parents' power assertive patterns and practices on adolescent development. *Parenting, 10*(3), 157–201. doi: 10.1080/15295190903290790

Bax, Trent. (2014). *Youth and internet addiction in China.* New York, NY: Routledge.

Bazinger, Claudia & Kühberger, Anton. (2012). Theory use in social predictions. *New Ideas in Psychology, 30*(3), 319–321. doi: 10.1016/j.newideapsych.2012.02.003

Beal, Susan. (1988). Sleeping position and sudden infant death syndrome. *The Medical Journal of Australia, 149*(10), 562.

Beauchaine, Theodore P.; Klein, Daniel N.; Crowell, Sheila E.; Derbidge, Christina & Gatzke-Kopp, Lisa. (2009). Multifinality in the development of personality disorders: A Biology × Sex × Environment interaction model of antisocial and borderline traits. *Development and Psychopathology, 21*(3), 735–770. doi: 10.1017/S0954579409000418

Beck, Melinda. (2009, May 26). How's your baby? Recalling the Apgar score's namesake. *The Wall Street Journal,* p. D–1.

Beck, Martha N. (1999). *Expecting Adam: A true story of birth, rebirth, and everyday magic.* New York, NY: Times Books.

Becker, Derek R.; McClelland, Megan M.; Loprinzi, Paul & Trost, Stewart G. (2014). Physical activity, self-regulation, and early academic achievement in preschool children. *Early Education and Development, 25*(1), 56–70. doi: 10.1080/10409289.2013.780505

Begos, Kevin. (2010). A wounded hero. *CR: Collaborations, Results, 5*(1), 30–35, 62–63.

Beilin, Lawrence & Huang, Rae-Chi. (2008). Childhood obesity, hypertension, the metabolic syndrome and adult cardiovascular disease. *Clinical and Experimental Pharmacology and Physiology, 35*(4), 409–411. doi: 10.1111/j.1440-1681.2008.04887.x

Beise, Jan & Voland, Eckart. (2002). A multilevel event history analysis of the effects of grandmothers on child mortality in a historical German population: Krummhörn, Ostfriesland, 1720–1874. *Demographic Research, 7*(13), 469–498. doi: 10.4054/DemRes.2002.7.13

Bell, Beth T. & Dittmar, Helga. (2011). Does media type matter? The role of identification in adolescent girls' media consumption and the impact of different thin-ideal media on body image. *Sex Roles, 65*(7/8), 478–490. doi: 10.1007/s11199-011-9964-x

Bell, Martha Ann & Calkins, Susan D. (2011). Attentional control and emotion regulation in early development. In Michael I. Posner (Ed.), *Cognitive neuroscience of attention* (2nd ed., pp. 322–330). New York, NY: Guilford Press.

Belsky, Jay; Bakermans-Kranenburg, Marian J. & van IJzendoorn, Marinus H. (2007). For better and for worse: Differential susceptibility to environmental influences. *Current Directions in Psychological Science, 16*(6), 300–304. doi: 10.1111/j.1467-8721.2007.00525.x

Belsky, Jay & Pluess, Michael. (2009). The nature (and nurture?) of plasticity in early human development. *Perspectives on Psychological Science, 4*(4), 345–351. doi: 10.1111/j.1745-6924.2009.01136.x

Belsky, Jay & Pluess, Michael. (2012). Differential susceptibility to long-term effects of quality of child care on externalizing behavior in adolescence? *International Journal of Behavioral Development, 36*(1), 2–10. doi: 10.1177/0165025411406855

Belsky, Jay; Steinberg, Laurence; Houts, Renate M. & Halpern-Felsher, Bonnie L. (2010). The development of reproductive strategy in females: Early maternal harshness → earlier menarche → increased sexual risk taking. *Developmental Psychology, 46*(1), 120–128. doi: 10.1037/a0015549

Benacerraf, Beryl R. (2007). *Ultrasound of fetal syndromes* (2nd ed.). Philadelphia, PA: Churchill Livingstone.

Bender, Heather L.; Allen, Joseph P.; Mcelhaney, Kathleen Boykin; Antonishak, Jill; Moore, Cynthia M.; Kelly, Heather O'beirne & Davis, Steven M. (2007). Use of harsh physical discipline and developmental outcomes in adolescence. *Development and Psychopathology, 19*(1), 227–242. doi: 10.1017/S0954579407070125

Benigno, Joann P.; Byrd, Dana L.; McNamara, Joseph P. H.; Berg, W. Keith & Farrar, M. Jeffrey. (2011). Talking through transitions: Microgenetic changes in preschoolers' private speech and executive functioning. *Child Language Teaching and Therapy, 27*(3), 269–285. doi: 10.1177/0265659010394385

Benjamin, Georges C. (2004). The solution is injury prevention. *American Journal of Public Health, 94*(4), 521. doi: 10.2105/AJPH.94.4.521

Bennett, Craig M. & Baird, Abigail A. (2006). Anatomical changes in the emerging adult brain: A voxel-based morphometry study. *Human Brain Mapping, 27*(9), 766–777. doi: 10.1002/hbm.20218

Benoit, Amelie; Lacourse, Eric & Claes, Michel. (2013). Pubertal timing and depressive symptoms in late adolescence: The moderating role of individual, peer, and parental factors. *Development and Psychopathology, 25*(2), 455–471. doi: 10.1017/S0954579412001174

Bentley, Gillian R. & Mascie-Taylor, C. G. Nicholas. (2000). Introduction. In Gillian R. Bentley & C. G. Nicholas Mascie-Taylor (Eds.), *Infertility in the modern world: Present and future prospects* (pp. 1–13). New York, NY: Cambridge University Press.

Berenbaum, Sheri A.; Martin, Carol Lynn; Hanish, Laura D.; Briggs, Phillip T. & Fabes, Richard A. (2008). Sex differences in children's play. In Jill B. Becker, et al. (Eds.), *Sex differences in the brain: From genes to behavior* (pp. 275–290). New York, NY: Oxford University Press.

Berg, Sandra J. & Wynne-Edwards, Katherine E. (2002). Salivary hormone concentrations in mothers and fathers becoming parents are not correlated. *Hormones & Behavior, 42*(4), 424–436. doi: 10.1006/hbeh.2002.1841

Berger, Kathleen S. (1980). *The developing person* (1st ed.). New York, NY: Worth.

Berger, Kathleen S. (2007). Update on bullying at school: Science forgotten? *Developmental Review, 27*(1), 90–126. doi: 10.1016/j.dr.2006.08.002

Berger, Lawrence M.; Paxson, Christina & Waldfogel, Jane. (2009). Income and child development. *Children and Youth Services Review, 31*(9), 978–989. doi: 10.1016/j.childyouth.2009.04.013

Berk, Michele; Adrian, Molly; McCauley, Elizabeth; Asarnow, Joan; Avina, Claudia & Linehan, Marsha. (2014). Conducting research on adolescent suicide attempters: Dilemmas and decisions. *Behavior Therapist, 37*(3), 65–69.

Berkey, Catherine S.; Gardner, Jane D.; Frazier, A. Lindsay & Colditz, Graham A. (2000). Relation of childhood diet and body size to menarche and adolescent growth in girls. *American Journal of Epidemiology, 152*(5), 446–452. doi: 10.1093/aje/152.5.446

Bernard, Kristin & Dozier, Mary. (2010). Examining infants' cortisol responses to laboratory tasks among children varying in attachment disorganization: Stress reactivity or return to baseline? *Developmental Psychology, 46*(6), 1771–1778. doi: 10.1037/a0020660

Bernard, Kristin; Lind, Teresa & Dozier, Mary. (2014). Neurobiological consequences of neglect and abuse. In Jill E. Korbin & Richard D. Krugman (Eds.), *Handbook of child maltreatment* (pp. 205–223). New York, NY: Springer. doi: 10.1007/978-94-007-7208-3_11

Bers, Marina; Seddighin, Safoura & Sullivan, Amanda. (2013). Ready for robotics: Bringing together the T and E of STEM in early childhood teacher education. *Journal of Technology and Teacher Education, 21*(3), 355–377.

Betancourt, Theresa S.; McBain, Ryan; Newnham, Elizabeth A. & Brennan, Robert T. (2013). Trajectories of internalizing problems in war-affected Sierra Leonean youth: Examining conflict and postconflict factors. *Child Development, 84*(2), 455–470. doi: 10.1111/j.1467-8624.2012.01861.x

Bhatia, Tej K. & Ritchie, William C. (Eds.). (2013). *The handbook of bilingualism and multilingualism* (2nd ed.). Malden, MA: Wiley-Blackwell.

Bhatnagar, Aruni; Whitsel, Laurie P.; Ribisl, Kurt M.; Bullen, Chris; Chaloupka, Frank; Piano, Mariann R., . . . Benowitz, Neal. (2014). Electronic cigarettes: A policy statement from the American Heart Association. *Circulation, 130*(16), 1418–1436. doi: 10.1161/CIR.0000000000000107

Bhutta, Zulfiqar A.; Ali, Samana; Cousens, Simon; Ali, Talaha M.; Haider, Batool A.; Rizvi, Arjumand, . . . Black, Robert E. (2008). Interventions to address maternal, newborn, and child survival: What difference can integrated primary health care strategies make? *The Lancet, 372*(9642), 972–989. doi: 10.1016/S0140-6736(08)61407-5

Bialystok, Ellen. (2010). Global-local and trail-making tasks by monolingual and bilingual children: Beyond inhibition. *Developmental Psychology, 46*(1), 93–105. doi: 10.1037/a0015466

Bianconi, Eva; Piovesan, Allison; Facchin, Federica; Beraudi, Alina; Casadei, Raffaella; Frabetti, Flavia, . . . Canaider, Silvia. (2013). An estimation of the number of cells in the human body. *Annals of Human Biology, 40*(6), 463–471. doi: 10.3109/03014460.2013.807878

Biehl, Michael C.; Natsuaki, Misaki N. & Ge, Xiaojia. (2007). The influence of pubertal timing on alcohol use and heavy drinking trajectories. *Journal of Youth and Adolescence, 36*(2), 153–167. doi: 10.1007/s10964-006-9120-z

Bienvenu, Thierry. (2005). Rett syndrome. In Merlin G. Butler & F. John Meaney (Eds.), *Genetics of developmental disabilities* (pp. 477–519). Boca Raton, FL: Taylor & Francis.

Bigler, Rebecca S. & Wright, Yamanda F. (2014). Reading, writing, arithmetic, and racism? Risks and benefits to teaching children about intergroup biases. *Child Development Perspectives, 8*(1), 18–23. doi: 10.1111/cdep.12057

Birdsong, David. (2006). Age and second language acquisition and processing: A selective overview. *Language Learning, 56*(Suppl. 1), 9–49. doi: 10.1111/j.1467-9922.2006.00353.x

Birkeland, Marianne S.; Breivik, Kyrre & Wold, Bente. (2014). Peer acceptance protects global self-esteem from negative effects of low closeness to parents during adolescence and early adulthood. *Journal of Youth and Adolescence, 43*(1), 70–80. doi: 10.1007/s10964-013-9929-1

Biro, Frank M.; Greenspan, Louise C.; Galvez, Maida P.; Pinney, Susan M.; Teitelbaum, Susan; Windham, Gayle C., . . . Wolff, Mary S. (2013). Onset of breast development in a longitudinal cohort. *Pediatrics, 132*(6), 1019–1027. doi: 10.1542/peds.2012-3773

Biro, Frank M.; McMahon, Robert P.; Striegel-Moore, Ruth; Crawford, Patricia B.; Obarzanek, Eva; Morrison, John A., . . . Falkner, Frank. (2001). Impact of timing of pubertal maturation on growth in black and white female adolescents: The National Heart, Lung, and Blood Institute Growth and Health Study. *Journal*

of Pediatrics, 138(5), 636–643. doi: 10.1067/mpd.2001.114476

Bisiacchi, Patrizia Silvia; Mento, Giovanni & Suppiej, Agnese. (2009). Cortical auditory processing in preterm newborns: An ERP study. *Biological Psychology, 82*(2), 176–185. doi: 10.1016/j.biopsycho.2009.07.005

Bjorklund, David F.; Dukes, Charles & Brown, Rhonda D. (2009). The development of memory strategies. In Mary L. Courage & Nelson Cowan (Eds.), *The development of memory in infancy and childhood* (2nd ed., pp. 145–175). New York, NY: Psychology Press.

Bjorklund, David F. & Sellers, Patrick D. (2014). Memory development in evolutionary perspective. In Patricia Bauer & Robyn Fivush (Eds.), *The Wiley handbook on the development of children's memory* (Vol. 1, pp. 126–150). Malden, MA: Wiley.

Blad, Evie. (2014). Some states overhauling vaccine laws. *Education Week, 33*(31).

Blair, Clancy & Dennis, Tracy. (2010). An optimal balance: The integration of emotion and cognition in context. In Susan D. Calkins & Martha Ann Bell (Eds.), *Child development at the intersection of emotion and cognition* (pp. 17–35). Washington, DC: American Psychological Association.

Blair, Clancy & Raver, C. Cybele. (2012). Child development in the context of adversity: Experiential canalization of brain and behavior. *American Psychologist, 67*(4), 309–318. doi: 10.1037/a0027493

Blandon, Alysia Y.; Calkins, Susan D. & Keane, Susan P. (2010). Predicting emotional and social competence during early childhood from toddler risk and maternal behavior. *Development and Psychopathology, 22*(1), 119–132. doi: 10.1017/S0954579409990307

Bleidorn, Wiebke; Klimstra, Theo A.; Denissen, Jaap J. A.; Rentfrow, Peter J.; Potter, Jeff & Gosling, Samuel D. (2013). Personality maturation around the world: A cross-cultural examination of social-investment theory. *Psychological Science, 24*(12), 2530–2540. doi: 10.1177/0956797613498396

Bliss, Catherine. (2012). *Race decoded: The genomic fight for social justice.* Stanford, CA: Stanford University Press.

Blonigen, Daniel M.; Carlson, Marie D.; Hicks, Brian M.; Krueger, Robert F. & Iacono, William G. (2008). Stability and change in personality traits from late adolescence to early adulthood: A longitudinal twin study. *Journal of Personality, 76*(2), 229–266. doi: 10.1111/j.1467-6494.2007.00485.x

Blum, Deborah. (2002). *Love at Goon Park: Harry Harlow and the science of affection.* Cambridge, MA: Perseus.

Blurton-Jones, Nicholas G. (1976). Rough-and-tumble play among nursery school children. In Jerome S. Bruner, et al. (Eds.), *Play: Its role in development and evolution* (pp. 352–363). New York, NY: Basic Books.

Bögels, Susan M.; Knappe, Susanne & Clark, Lee Anna. (2013). Adult separation anxiety disorder in DSM-5. *Clinical Psychology Review, 33*(5), 663–674. doi: 10.1016/j.cpr.2013.03.006

Bombard, Jennifer M.; Robbins, Cheryl L.; Dietz, Patricia M. & Valderrama, Amy L. (2013). Preconception care: The perfect opportunity for health care providers to advise lifestyle changes for hypertensive women. *American Journal of Health Promotion, 27*(3), S43–S49. doi: 10.4278/ajhp.120109-QUAN-6

Bonanno, Rina A. & Hymel, Shelley. (2013). Cyber bullying and internalizing difficulties: Above and beyond the impact of traditional forms of bullying. *Journal of Youth and Adolescence, 42*(5), 685–697. doi: 10.1007/s10964-013-9937-1

Booth, Alan & Dunn, Judy (Eds.). (2014). *Stepfamilies: Who benefits? Who does not?* New York, NY: Routledge.

Borke, Jörn; Lamm, Bettina; Eickhorst, Andreas & Keller, Heidi. (2007). Father-infant interaction, paternal ideas about early child care, and their consequences for the development of children's self-recognition. *Journal of Genetic Psychology, 168*(4), 365–379. doi: 10.3200/GNTP.168.4.365-380

Borkowski, John G.; Farris, Jaelyn Renee; Whitman, Thomas L.; Carothers, Shannon S.; Weed, Keri & Keogh, Deborah A. (Eds.). (2007). *Risk and resilience: Adolescent mothers and their children grow up.* Mahwah, NJ: Lawrence Erlbaum Associates.

Bornstein, Marc H. (2014). Human infancy... and the rest of the lifespan. *Annual Review of Psychology, 65,* 121–158. doi: 10.1146/annurev-psych-120710-100359

Bornstein, Marc H.; Arterberry, Martha E. & Mash, Clay. (2005). Perceptual development. In Marc H. Bornstein & Michael E. Lamb (Eds.), *Developmental science: An advanced textbook* (5th ed., pp. 283–325). Mahwah, NJ: Lawrence Erlbaum Associates.

Bornstein, Marc H. & Colombo, John. (2012). Infant cognitive functioning and mental development. In Sabina Pauen (Ed.), *Early childhood development and later outcome.* New York, NY: Cambridge University Press.

Bornstein, Marc H.; Hahn, Chun-Shin & Wolke, Dieter. (2013). System and cascades in cognitive development and academic achievement. *Child Development, 84*(1), 154–162. doi: 10.1111/j.1467-8624.2012.01849.x

Bornstein, Marc H.; Mortimer, Jeylan T.; Lutfey, Karen & Bradley, Robert. (2011). Theories and processes in life-span socialization. In Karen L. Fingerman, et al. (Eds.), *Handbook of life-span development* (pp. 27–56). New York, NY: Springer.

Borrelli, Belinda; McQuaid, Elizabeth L.; Novak, Scott P.; Hammond, S. Katharine & Becker, Bruce. (2010). Motivating Latino caregivers of children with asthma to quit smoking: A randomized trial. *Journal of Consulting and Clinical Psychology, 78*(1), 34–43. doi: 10.1037/a0016932

Boseovski, Janet J. (2010). Evidence for "rose-colored glasses": An examination of the positivity bias in young children's personality judgments. *Child Development Perspectives, 4*(3), 212–218. doi: 10.1111/j.1750-8606.2010.00149.x

Bosworth, Hayden B. & Hertzog, Christopher. (2009). *Aging and cognition: Research methodologies and empirical advances.* Washington, DC: American Psychological Association. doi: 10.1037/11882-000

Bower, Bruce. (2007). Net heads: Huge numbers of brain cells may navigate small worlds. *Science News, 171*(7), 104–106. doi: 10.1002/scin.2007.5591710709

Bowes, Lucy; Maughan, Barbara; Caspi, Avshalom; Moffitt, Terrie E. & Arseneault, Louise. (2010). Families promote emotional and behavioural resilience to bullying: Evidence of an environmental effect. *Journal of Child Psychology and Psychiatry, 51*(7), 809–817. doi: 10.1111/j.1469-7610.2010.02216.x

boyd, danah. (2014). *It's complicated: The social lives of networked teens.* New Haven, CT: Yale University Press.

Boyd, Wendy; Walker, Susan & Thorpe, Karen. (2013). Choosing Work and Care: Four Australian women negotiating return to paid work in the first year of motherhood. *Contemporary Issues in Early Childhood, 14*(2), 168–178. doi: 10.2304/ciec.2013.14.2.168

Bracken, Bruce A. & Crawford, Elizabeth. (2010). Basic concepts in early childhood educational standards: A 50-state review. *Early Childhood Education Journal, 37*(5), 421–430. doi: 10.1007/s10643-009-0363-7

Bradley, Rachel & Slade, Pauline. (2011). A review of mental health problems in fathers following the birth of a child. *Journal of Reproductive and Infant Psychology, 29*(1), 19–42. doi: 10.1080/02646838.2010.513047

Brainerd, Charles J.; Reyna, Valerie F. & Ceci, Stephen J. (2008). Developmental reversals in false memory: A review of data and theory. *Psychological Bulletin, 134*(3), 343–382. doi: 10.1037/0033-2909.134.3.343

Brakefield, Tiffany A.; Mednick, Sara C.; Wilson, Helen W.; De Neve, Jan-Emmanuel; Christakis, Nicholas A. & Fowler, James H. (2014). Same-sex sexual attraction does not spread in adolescent social networks. *Archives of Sexual Behavior, 43*(2), 335–344. doi: 10.1007/s10508-013-0142-9

Brame, Robert; Bushway, Shawn D.; Paternoster, Ray & Turner, Michael G. (2014). Demographic patterns of cumulative arrest prevalence by ages 18 and 23. *Crime & Delinquency, 60*(3), 471–486. doi: 10.1177/0011128713514801

Brandone, Amanda C.; Horwitz, Suzanne R.; Aslin, Richard N. & Wellman, Henry M. (2014). Infants' goal anticipation during failed and successful reaching actions. *Developmental Science, 17*(1), 23–34. doi: 10.1111/desc.12095

Brazelton, T. Berry & Sparrow, Joshua D. (2006). *Touchpoints, birth to 3: Your child's emotional and behavioral development* (2nd ed.). Cambridge, MA: Da Capo Press.

Breivik, Gunnar. (2010). Trends in adventure sports in a post-modern society. *Sport in Society: Cultures, Commerce, Media, Politics, 13*(2), 260–273. doi: 10.1080/17430430903522970

Bremner, J. Gavin & Wachs, Theodore D. (Eds.). (2010). *The Wiley-Blackwell handbook of infant development* (2nd ed.). Malden, MA: Wiley-Blackwell.

Brendgen, Mara; Lamarche, Véronique; Wanner, Brigitte & Vitaro, Frank. (2010). Links between friendship relations and early adolescents' trajectories of depressed mood. *Developmental Psychology, 46*(2), 491–501. doi: 10.1037/a0017413

Brennan, Arthur; Ayers, Susan; Ahmed, Hafez & Marshall-Lucette, Sylvie. (2007). A critical review of the Couvade syndrome: The pregnant male. *Journal of Reproductive and Infant Psychology, 25*(3), 173–189. doi: 10.1080/02646830701467207

Breslow, Lori; Pritchard, David E.; Deboer, Jennifer; Stump, Glenda S.; Ho, Andrew D. & Seaton, Daniel T. (2013). Studying learning in the worldwide classroom research into edX's first MOOC. *Research and Practice in Assessment, 8*(1), 13–25.

Bretherton, Inge. (2010). Fathers in attachment theory and research: A review. *Early Child Development and Care, 180*(1/2), 9–23. doi: 10.1080/03004430903414661

Brickhouse, Tegwyn H.; Rozier, R. Gary & Slade, Gary D. (2008). Effects of enrollment in Medicaid versus the State Children's Health Insurance Program on kindergarten children's untreated dental caries. *American Journal of Public Health, 98*(5), 876–881. doi: 10.2105/ajph.2007.111468

Brody, Gene H.; Beach, Steven R. H.; Philibert, Robert A.; Chen, Yi-fu & Murry, Velma McBride. (2009). Prevention effects moderate the association of 5-HTTLPR and youth risk behavior initiation: Gene × environment hypotheses tested via a randomized prevention design. *Child Development, 80*(3), 645–661. doi: 10.1111/j.1467-8624.2009.01288.x

Brody, Gene H.; Yu, Tianyi; Chen, Yi-fu; Kogan, Steven M.; Evans, Gary W.; Windle, Michael, . . . Philibert, Robert A. (2013). Supportive family environments, genes that confer sensitivity, and allostatic load among rural African American emerging adults: A prospective analysis. *Journal of Family Psychology, 27*(1), 22–29. doi: 10.1037/a0027829

Brody, Jane E. (2012, July 24). The ideal and the real of breast-feeding. *The New York Times.*

Brody, Jane E. (2013, February 26). Too many pills in pregnancy. *The New York Times,* p. D5.

Bronfenbrenner, Urie. (1977). Toward an experimental ecology of human development. *American Psychologist, 32*(7), 513–531. doi: 10.1037//0003-066X.32.7.513

Bronfenbrenner, Urie. (1986). Recent advances in research on the ecology of human development. In Rainer Silbereisen, et al. (Eds.), *Development as action in context problem behavior and normal youth development* (pp. 287–309). New York, NY: Springer.

Bronfenbrenner, Urie & Morris, Pamela A. (2006). The bioecological model of human development. In William Damon & Richard M. Lerner (Eds.), *Handbook of child psychology* (6th ed., Vol. 1, pp. 793–828). Hoboken, NJ: Wiley.

Brooker, Robert J. (2009). *Genetics: Analysis & principles* (3rd ed.). New York, NY: McGraw-Hill.

Brooker, Rebecca J.; Buss, Kristin A.; Lemery-Chalfant, Kathryn; Aksan, Nazan; Davidson, Richard J. & Goldsmith, H. Hill. (2013). The development of stranger fear in infancy and toddlerhood: Normative development, individual differences, antecedents, and outcomes. *Developmental Science, 16*(6), 864–878. doi: 10.1111/desc.12058

Brouwer, Rachel M.; van Soelen, Inge L. C.; Swagerman, Suzanne C.; Schnack, Hugo G.; Ehli, Erik A.; Kahn, René S., . . . Boomsma, Dorret I. (2014). Genetic associations between intelligence and cortical thickness emerge at the start of puberty. *Human Brain Mapping, 35*(8), 3760–3773. doi: 10.1002/hbm.22435

Brown, B. Bradford & Bakken, Jeremy P. (2011). Parenting and peer relationships: Reinvigorating research on family–peer linkages in adolescence. *Journal of Research on Adolescence, 21*(1), 153–165. doi: 10.1111/j.1532-7795.2010.00720.x

Brown, Christia Spears; Alabi, Basirat O.; Huynh, Virginia W. & Masten, Carrie L. (2011). Ethnicity and gender in late childhood and early adolescence: Group identity and awareness of bias. *Developmental Psychology, 47*(2), 463–471. doi: 10.1037/a0021819

Brown, Susan L. (2010). Marriage and child well-being: Research and policy perspectives. *Journal of Marriage and Family, 72*(5), 1059–1077. doi: 10.1111/j.1741-3737.2010.00750.x

Brownell, Celia A.; Svetlova, Margarita; Anderson, Ranita; Nichols, Sara R. & Drummond, Jesse. (2013). Socialization of early prosocial behavior: Parents' talk about emotions is associated with sharing and helping in toddlers. *Infancy, 18*(1), 91–119. doi: 10.1111/j.1532-7078.2012.00125.x

Bruck, Maggie; Ceci, Stephen J. & Principe, Gabrielle F. (2006). The child and the law. In William Damon & Richard M. Lerner (Eds.), *Handbook of child psychology* (6th ed., Vol. 4, pp. 776–816). Hoboken, NJ: Wiley.

Bryant, Gregory A. & Barrett, H. Clark. (2007). Recognizing intentions in infant-directed speech: Evidence for universals. *Psychological Science, 18*(8), 746–751. doi: 10.1111/j.1467-9280.2007.01970.x

Brymer, Eric. (2010). Risk and extreme sports: A phenomenological perspective. *Annals of Leisure Research, 13*(1/2), 218–239. doi: 10.1080/11745398.2010.9686845

Buhrmester, Michael D.; Blanton, Hart & Swann, William B. (2011). Implicit self-esteem:

Nature, measurement, and a new way forward. *Journal of Personality and Social Psychology, 100*(2), 365–385. doi: 10.1037/a0021341

Bulpitt, Christopher J.; Beckett, Nigel; Peters, Ruth; Staessen, Jan A.; Wang, Ji-Guang; Comsa, Marius, . . . Rajkumar, Chakravarthi. (2013). Does white coat hypertension require treatment over age 80? Results of the hypertension in the very elderly trial ambulatory blood pressure side project. *Hypertension, 61*(1), 89–94. doi: 10.1161/HYPERTENSIONAHA.112.191791

Burnette, Jeni L.; O'Boyle, Ernest H.; VanEpps, Eric M.; Pollack, Jeffrey M. & Finkel, Eli J. (2013). Mind-sets matter: A meta-analytic review of implicit theories and self-regulation. *Psychological Bulletin, 139*(3), 655–701. doi: 10.1037/a0029531

Burstyn, Igor. (2014). Peering through the mist: Systematic review of what the chemistry of contaminants in electronic cigarettes tells us about health risks. *BMC Public Health, 14*(1), 18. doi: 10.1186/1471-2458-14-18

Bursztyn, Leonardo & Jensen, Robert. (2014). How does peer pressure affect educational investments? *NBER working paper series*, (Working Paper 20714).

Burt, S. Alexandra. (2009). Rethinking environmental contributions to child and adolescent psychopathology: A meta-analysis of shared environmental influences. *Psychological Bulletin, 135*(4), 608–637. doi: 10.1037/a0015702

Burt, S. Alexandra; McGue, Matt & Iacono, William G. (2009). Nonshared environmental mediation of the association between deviant peer affiliation and adolescent externalizing behaviors over time: Results from a cross-lagged monozygotic twin differences design. *Developmental Psychology, 45*(6), 1752–1760. doi: 10.1037/a0016687

Buss, David M.; Shackelford, Todd K.; Kirkpatrick, Lee A. & Larsen, Randy J. (2001). A half century of mate preferences: The cultural evolution of values. *Journal of Marriage and Family, 63*(2), 491–503. doi: 10.1111/j.1741-3737.2001.00491.x

Butler, Merlin G. & Meaney, F. John (Eds.). (2005). *Genetics of developmental disabilities*. Boca Raton, FL: Taylor & Francis.

Buttelmann, David; Zmyj, Norbert; Daum, Moritz & Carpenter, Malinda. (2013). Selective imitation of in-group over out-group members in 14-month-old infants. *Child Development, 84*(2), 22–428. doi: 10.1111/j.1467-8624.2012.01860.x

Butterworth, Brian & Kovas, Yulia. (2013). Understanding neurocognitive developmental disorders can improve education for all. *Science, 340*(6130), 300–305. doi: 10.1126/science.1231022

Butterworth, Brian; Varma, Sashank & Laurillard, Diana. (2011). Dyscalculia: From brain to education. *Science, 332*(6033), 1049–1053. doi: 10.1126/science.1201536

Byard, Roger W. (2014). "Shaken baby syndrome" and forensic pathology: An uneasy interface. *Forensic Science, Medicine, and Pathology, 10*(2), 239–241. doi: 10.1007/s12024-013-9514-7

Byers-Heinlein, Krista; Burns, Tracey C. & Werker, Janet F. (2010). The roots of bilingualism in newborns. *Psychological Science, 21*(3), 343–348. doi: 10.1177/0956797609360758

Calarco, Jessica McCrory. (2014). The inconsistent curriculum: Cultural tool kits and student interpretations of ambiguous expectations. *Social Psychology Quarterly, 77*(2), 185–209. doi: 10.1177/0190272514521438

Calkins, Susan D. & Keane, Susan P. (2009). Developmental origins of early antisocial behavior. *Development and Psychopathology, 21*(4), 1095–1109. doi: 10.1017/S095457940999006X

Callaghan, Tara. (2013). Symbols and symbolic thought. In Philip D. Zelazo (Ed.), *The Oxford handbook of developmental psychology* (Vol. 1). New York, NY: Oxford University Press. doi: 10.1093/oxfordhb/9780199958450.013.0034

Calvert, Karin. (2003). Patterns of childrearing in America. In Willem Koops & Michael Zuckerman (Eds.), *Beyond the century of the child: Cultural history and developmental psychology* (pp. 62–81). Philadelphia, PA: University of Pennsylvania Press.

Cameron, Judy & Pierce, W. David. (2002). *Rewards and intrinsic motivation: Resolving the controversy.* Westport, CT: Bergin & Garvey.

Camhi, Sarah M.; Katzmarzyk, Peter T.; Broyles, Stephanie; Church, Timothy S.; Hankinson, Arlene L.; Carnethon, Mercedes R., . . . Lewis, Cora E. (2013). Association of metabolic risk with longitudinal physical activity and fitness: Coronary artery risk development in young adults (CARDIA). *Metabolic Syndrome and Related Disorders, 11*(3), 195–204. doi: 10.1089/met.2012.0120

Camos, Valérie & Barrouillet, Pierre. (2011). Developmental change in working memory strategies: From passive maintenance to active refreshing. *Developmental Psychology, 47*(3), 898–904. doi: 10.1037/a0023193

Campbell, Frances; Conti, Gabriella; Heckman, James J.; Moon, Seong H.; Pinto, Rodrigo; Pungello, Elizabeth & Pan, Yi. (2014). Early childhood investments substantially boost adult health. *Science, 343*(6178), 1478–1485. doi: 10.1126/science.1248429

Campbell, Frances A.; Pungello, Elizabeth P.; Miller-Johnson, Shari; Burchinal, Margaret & Ramey, Craig T. (2001). The development of cognitive and academic abilities: Growth curves from an early childhood educational experiment. *Developmental Psychology, 37*(2), 231–242. doi: 10.1037/0012-1649.37.2.231

Camras, Linda A. & Shutter, Jennifer M. (2010). Emotional facial expressions in infancy. *Emotion Review, 2*(2), 120–129. doi: 10.1177/1754073909352529

Canadian Paediatric Society. (2008). Adolescent sexual orientation. *Paediatrics & Child Health, 13*(7), 619–623.

Canagarajah, A. Suresh & Wurr, Adrian J. (2011). Multilingual communication and language acquisition: New research directions. *The Reading Matrix, 11*(1), 1–15.

Caravita, Simona C. S. & Cillessen, Antonius H. N. (2012). Agentic or communal? Associations between interpersonal goals, popularity, and bullying in middle childhood and early adolescence. *Social Development, 21*(2), 376–395. doi: 10.1111/j.1467-9507.2011.00632.x

Caravita, Simona C. S.; Di Blasio, Paola & Salmivalli, Christina. (2010). Early adolescents' participation in bullying: Is ToM involved? *The Journal of Early Adolescence, 30*(1), 138–170. doi: 10.1177/0272431609342983

Cardoso-Leite, Pedro & Bavelier, Daphne. (2014). Video game play, attention, and learning: How to shape the development of attention and influence learning? *Current Opinion in Neurology, 27*(2), 185–191. doi: 10.1097/WCO.0000000000000077

Carey, Susan. (2009). *The origin of concepts.* New York, NY: Oxford University Press.

Carey, Susan. (2010). Beyond fast mapping. *Language Learning and Development, 6*(3), 184–205. doi: 10.1080/15475441.2010.484379

Carlson, Susan A.; Fulton, Janet E.; Lee, Sarah M.; Maynard, L. Michele; Brown, David R.; Kohl, Harold W. & Dietz, William H. (2008). Physical education and academic achievement in elementary school: Data from the early childhood longitudinal study. *American Journal of Public Health, 98*(4), 721–727. doi: 10.2105/ajph.2007.117176

Carlson, Stephanie M.; Koenig, Melissa A. & Harms, Madeline B. (2013). Theory of mind. *Wiley Interdisciplinary Reviews: Cognitive Science, 4*(4), 391–402. doi: 10.1002/wcs.1232

Carpenter, Siri. (2012). Psychology's bold initiative. *Science, 335*(6076), 1558–1561. doi: 10.1126/science.335.6076.1558

Carskadon, Mary A. (2011). Sleep in adolescents: The perfect storm. *Pediatric Clinics of North America, 58*(3), 637–647. doi: 10.1016/j.pcl.2011.03.003

Carson, Valerie; Tremblay, Mark S.; Spence, John C.; Timmons, Brian W. & Janssen, Ian. (2013). The Canadian Sedentary Behaviour Guidelines for the Early Years (zero to four years of age) and screen time among children from Kingston, Ontario. *Paediatrics & Child Health, 18*(1), 25–28.

Caruso, Federica. (2013). Embedding early childhood education and care in the socio-cultural context: The case of Italy. In Jan Georgeson & Jane Payler (Eds.), *International perspectives on early childhood education and care.* New York, NY: Open University Press.

Case-Smith, Jane & Kuhaneck, Heather Miller. (2008). Play preferences of typically developing children and children with developmental delays between ages 3 and 7 years. *OTJR: Occupation, Participation and Health, 28*(1), 19–29. doi: 10.3928/15394492-20080101-01

Casey, B. J. & Caudle, Kristina. (2013). The teenage brain: Self control. *Current Directions*

in *Psychological Science, 22*(2), 82–87. doi: 10.1177/0963721413480170

Casey, B. J.; Jones, Rebecca M. & Somerville, Leah H. (2011). Braking and accelerating of the adolescent brain. *Journal of Research on Adolescence, 21*(1), 21–33. doi: 10.1111/j.1532-7795.2010.00712.x

Caspi, Avshalom; Moffitt, Terrie E.; Morgan, Julia; Rutter, Michael; Taylor, Alan; Arseneault, Louise, . . . Polo-Tomas, Monica. (2004). Maternal expressed emotion predicts children's antisocial behavior problems: Using monozygotic-twin differences to identify environmental effects on behavioral development. *Developmental Psychology, 40*(2), 149–161. doi: 10.1037/0012-1649.40.2.149

Cassia, Viola Macchi; Kuefner, Dana; Picozzi, Marta & Vescovo, Elena. (2009). Early experience predicts later plasticity for face processing: Evidence for the reactivation of dormant effects. *Psychological Science, 20*(7), 853–859. doi: 10.1111/j.1467-9280.2009.02376.x

Castellani, Valeria; Pastorelli, Concetta; Eisenberg, Nancy; Gerbino, Maria; Giunta, Laura Di; Ceravolo, Rosalba & Milioni, Michela. (2014). Hostile, aggressive family conflict trajectories during the transition to adulthood: Associations with adolescent Big Five and emerging adulthood adjustment problems. *Journal of Adolescence, 37*(5), 647–658. doi: 10.1016/j.adolescence.2013.12.002

Catani, Claudia; Gewirtz, Abigail H.; Wieling, Elizabeth; Schauer, Elizabeth; Elbert, Thomas & Neuner, Frank. (2010). Tsunami, war, and cumulative risk in the lives of Sri Lankan schoolchildren. *Child Development, 81*(4), 1176–1191. doi: 10.1111/j.1467-8624.2010.01461.x

Cavalari, Rachel N. S. & Donovick, Peter J. (2014). Agenesis of the corpus callosum: Symptoms consistent with developmental disability in two siblings. *Neurocase: The Neural Basis of Cognition.* doi: 10.1080/13554794.2013.873059

Ceballo, Rosario; Maurizi, Laura K.; Suarez, Gloria A. & Aretakis, Maria T. (2014). Gift and sacrifice: Parental involvement in Latino adolescents' education. *Cultural Diversity and Ethnic Minority Psychology, 20*(1), 116–127. doi: 10.1037/a0033472

Ceci, Stephen J. & Bruck, Maggie. (1995). *Jeopardy in the courtroom: A scientific analysis of children's testimony.* Washington, DC: American Psychological Association.

Cecil, Kim M.; Brubaker, Christopher J.; Adler, Caleb M.; Dietrich, Kim N.; Altaye, Mekibib; Egelhoff, John C., . . . Lanphear, Bruce P. (2008). Decreased brain volume in adults with childhood lead exposure. *PloS Medicine, 5*(5), 741–750. doi: 10.1371/journal.pmed.0050112

Center for Education Policy. (2012). *SDP strategic performance indicator: The high school effect on college-going.* Cambridge, MA: Harvard University, Center for Education Policy Research.

Center for Education Policy. (2013). *SDP college-going diagnostic: The school district of Philadelphia.* Cambridge, MA: Harvard University, Center for Education Policy Research.

Centers for Disease Control and Prevention. (2012). HIV diagnoses (2012). from NCHHSTP Atlas http://gis.cdc.gov/GRASP/NCHHSTPAtlas/main.html

Centers for Disease Control and Prevention. (2012, August). *Breastfeeding report card—United States, 2012.* Atlanta, GA: National Center for Chronic Disease Prevention and Health Promotion, Centers for Disease Control and Prevention.

Centers for Disease Control and Prevention. (2012, May). *Epidemiology and prevention of vaccine-preventable diseases* (William Atkinson, et al. Eds. Revised 12th ed.). Washington DC: Public Health Foundation.

Centers for Disease Control and Prevention. (2013, February). *Incidence, prevalence, and cost of sexually transmitted infections in the United States: CDC Fact Sheet.* Atlanta, GA: Centers for Disease Control and Prevention, Division of STD Prevention.

Centers for Disease Control and Prevention. (2013, July). *Breastfeeding report card—United States, 2013.* Atlanta, GA: National Center for Chronic Disease Prevention and Health Promotion, Centers for Disease Control and Prevention.

Centers for Disease Control and Prevention. (2014). *Breastfeeding among U.S. children born 2001–2011, CDC National Immunization Survey.* Atlanta, GA: National Center for Chronic Disease Prevention and Health Promotion, Centers for Disease Control and Prevention.

Centers for Disease Control and Prevention. (2014). Underlying cause of death 1999–2012. Retrieved January 21, 2015, from CDC WONDER Online Database http://wonder.cdc.gov/ucd-icd10.html

Centers for Disease Control and Prevention. (2014, December 16). *2013 Sexually transmitted diseases surveillance: Table 45. Selected STDs and complications—Initial visits to physicians' offices, national disease and therapeutic index, United States, 1966–2013.* Atlanta, GA: Centers for Disease Control and Prevention.

Centers for Disease Control and Prevention. (2014, January). *2014 Recommended immunizations for children from birth through 6 years old.* Atlanta, GA: U.S. Department of Health and Human Services, Centers For Disease Control and Prevention.

Centers for Disease Control and Prevention. (2014, July). *Breastfeeding report card—United States, 2014.* Atlanta, GA: National Center for Chronic Disease Prevention and Health Promotion, Centers for Disease Control and Prevention.

Centers for Disease Control and Prevention. (2014, June 16). Teen birth rates drop, but disparities persist. http://www.cdc.gov/features/ds-teenpregnancy/

Centers for Disease Control and Prevention. (2014, October 17). *Updates on CDC's Polio eradication efforts.* Atlanta, GA: Centers for Disease Control and Prevention.

Centre for Community Child Health & Telethon Institute for Child Health Research. (2009). *A snapshot of early childhood development in Australia: Australian Early Development Index (AEDI) national report 2009.* Canberra, Australia: Australian Government Department of Education.

Cespedes, Elizabeth M.; McDonald, Julia; Haines, Jess; Bottino, Clement J.; Schmidt, Marie Evans & Taveras, Elsie M. (2013). Obesity-related behaviors of US- and non-US-born parents and children in low-income households. *Journal of Developmental & Behavioral Pediatrics, 34*(8), 541–548. doi: 10.1097/DBP.0b013e3182a509fb

Chafen, Jennifer J. S.; Newberry, Sydne J.; Riedl, Marc A.; Bravata, Dena M.; Maglione, Margaret; Suttorp, Marika J., . . . Shekelle, Paul G. (2010). Diagnosing and managing common food allergies. *JAMA, 303*(18), 1848–1856. doi: 10.1001/jama.2010.582

Challenge Success. (2013). *The advanced placement program: Living up to its promise?* Stanford, CA: Challenge Success.

Chambers, John R.; Swan, Lawton K. & Heesacker, Martin. (2014). Better off than we know: Distorted perceptions of incomes and income inequality in America. *Psychological Science, 25*(2), 613–618. doi: 10.1177/0956797613504965

Champagne, Frances A. & Curley, James P. (2010). Maternal care as a modulating influence on infant development. In Mark S. Blumberg, et al. (Eds.), *Oxford handbook of developmental behavioral neuroscience* (pp. 323–341). New York, NY: Oxford University Press. doi: 10.1093/oxfordhb/9780195314731.013.0017

Chan, Cheri C. Y.; Tardif, Twila; Chen, Jie; Pulverman, Rachel B.; Zhu, Liqi & Meng, Xiangzhi. (2011). English- and Chinese-learning infants map novel labels to objects and actions differently. *Developmental Psychology, 47*(5), 1459–1471. doi: 10.1037/a0024049

Chan, David W. & Zhao, Yongjun. (2010). The relationship between drawing skill and artistic creativity: Do age and artistic involvement make a difference? *Creativity Research Journal, 22*(1), 27–36. doi: 10.1080/10400410903579528

Chan, Tak Wing & Koo, Anita. (2011). Parenting style and youth outcomes in the UK. *European Sociological Review, 27*(3), 385–399. doi: 10.1093/esr/jcq013

Chang, Esther S.; Greenberger, Ellen; Chen, Chuansheng; Heckhausen, Jutta & Farruggia, Susan P. (2010). Nonparental adults as social resources in the transition to adulthood. *Journal of Research on Adolescence, 20*(4), 1065–1082. doi: 10.1111/j.1532-7795.2010.00662.x

Chaplin, Lan Nguyen & John, Deborah Roedder. (2007). Growing up in a material world: Age differences in materialism in children and adolescents. *Journal of Consumer Research, 34*(4), 480–493. doi: 10.1086/518546

Charnigo, Richard; Noar, Seth M.; Garnett, Christopher; Crosby, Richard; Palmgreen, Philip & Zimmerman, Rick S. (2013). Sensation seeking and impulsivity: Combined associations with risky sexual behavior in a large sample of young adults. *The Journal of Sex Research, 50*(5), 480–488. doi: 10.1080/00224499.2011.652264

Chartier, Karen G.; Scott, Denise M.; Wall, Tamara L.; Covault, Jonathan; Karriker-Jaffe, Katherine J.; Mills, Britain A., . . . Arroyo, Judith A. (2014). Framing ethnic variations in alcohol outcomes from biological pathways to neighborhood context. *Alcoholism: Clinical and Experimental Research, 38*(3), 611–618. doi: 10.1111/acer.12304

Chassin, Laurie; Bountress, Kaitlin; Haller, Moira & Wang, Frances. (2014). Adolescent substance use disorders. In Eric J. Mash & Russell A. Barkley (Eds.), *Child psychopathology* (3rd ed., pp. 180–124). New York, NY: Guilford Press.

Chassin, Laurie; Hussong, Andrea & Beltran, Iris. (2009). Adolescent substance use. In Richard M. Lerner & Laurence Steinberg (Eds.), *Handbook of adolescent psychology* (3rd ed., Vol. 1, pp. 723–763). Hoboken, NJ: Wiley.

Chen, Edith; Cohen, Sheldon & Miller, Gregory E. (2010). How low socioeconomic status affects 2-year hormonal trajectories in children. *Psychological Science, 21*(1), 31–37. doi: 10.1177/0956797609355566

Chen, Gong & Gao, Yuan. (2013). Changes in social participation of older adults in Beijing. *Ageing International, 38*(1), 15–27. doi: 10.1007/s12126-012-9167-y

Chen, Hong & Jackson, Todd. (2009). Predictors of changes in weight esteem among mainland Chinese adolescents: A longitudinal analysis. *Developmental Psychology, 45*(6), 1618–1629. doi: 10.1037/a0016820

Chen, Xinyin. (2011). Culture and children's socioemotional functioning: A contextual-developmental perspective. In Xinyin Chen & Kenneth H. Rubin (Eds.), *Socioemotional development in cultural context* (pp. 29–52). New York, NY: Guilford Press.

Chen, Xinyin; Cen, Guozhen; Li, Dan & He, Yunfeng. (2005). Social functioning and adjustment in Chinese children: The imprint of historical time. *Child Development, 76*(1), 182–195. doi: 10.1111/j.1467-8624.2005.00838.x

Chen, Xinyin; Rubin, Kenneth H. & Sun, Yuerong. (1992). Social reputation and peer relationships in Chinese and Canadian children: A cross-cultural study. *Child Development, 63*(6), 1336–1343. doi: 10.1111/j.1467-8624.1992.tb01698.x

Chen, Xinyin; Wang, Li & Wang, Zhengyan. (2009). Shyness-sensitivity and social, school, and psychological adjustment in rural migrant and urban children in China. *Child Development, 80*(5), 1499–1513. doi: 10.1111/j.1467-8624.2009.01347.x

Chen, Xinyin; Yang, Fan & Wang, Li. (2013). Relations between shyness-sensitivity and internalizing problems in Chinese children: Moderating effects of academic achievement. *Journal of Abnormal Child Psychology, 41*(5), 825–836. doi: 10.1007/s10802-012-9708-6

Chen, Yi; Li, Guanghui; Ruan, Yan; Zou, Liying; Wang, Xin & Zhang, Weiyuan. (2013). An epidemiological survey on low birth weight infants in China and analysis of outcomes of full-term low birth weight infants. *BMC Pregnancy and Childbirth, 13*, 242. doi: 10.1186/1471-2393-13-242

Cheng, Diana; Kettinger, Laurie; Uduhiri, Kelechi & Hurt, Lee. (2011). Alcohol consumption during pregnancy: Prevalence and provider assessment. *Obstetrics & Gynecology, 117*(2), 212–217. doi: 10.1097/AOG.0b013e3182078569

Cheng, Yvonne W.; Shaffer, Brian; Nicholson, James & Caughey, Aaron B. (2014). Second stage of labor and epidural use: A larger effect than previously suggested. *Obstetrics & Gynecology, 123*(3), 527–535. doi: 10.1097/AOG.0000000000000134

Cherlin, Andrew J. (2009). *The marriage-go-round: The state of marriage and the family in America today.* New York, NY: Knopf.

Cheslack-Postava, Keely; Liu, Kayuet & Bearman, Peter S. (2011). Closely spaced pregnancies are associated with increased odds of autism in California sibling births. *Pediatrics, 127*(2), 246–253. doi: 10.1542/peds.2010-2371

Child Care Aware® of America. (2014). *Child care in America: 2014 State fact sheets.* Arlington, VA: Child Care Aware® of America.

Child Trends. (2013). *World family map 2013. Mapping family change and child well-being outcomes.* Bethesda, MD: Child Trends.

Choe, Daniel E.; Lane, Jonathan D.; Grabell, Adam S. & Olson, Sheryl L. (2013a). Developmental precursors of young school-age children's hostile attribution bias. *Developmental Psychology, 49*(12), 2245–2256. doi: 10.1037/a0032293

Choe, Daniel E.; Olson, Sheryl L. & Sameroff, Arnold J. (2013b). The interplay of externalizing problems and physical and inductive discipline during childhood. *Developmental Psychology, 49*(11), 2029–2039. doi: 10.1037/a0032054

Chomsky, Noam. (1968). *Language and mind.* New York, NY: Harcourt Brace & World.

Chomsky, Noam. (1980). *Rules and representations.* New York, NY: Columbia University Press.

Choukas-Bradley, Sophia; Giletta, Matteo; Widman, Laura; Cohen, Geoffrey L. & Prinstein, Mitchell J. (2014). Experimentally measured susceptibility to peer influence and adolescent sexual behavior trajectories: A preliminary study. *Developmental Psychology, 50*(9), 2221–2227. doi: 10.1037/a0037300

Chow, Angela; Krahn, Harvey J. & Galambos, Nancy L. (2014). Developmental trajectories of work values and job entitlement beliefs in the transition to adulthood. *Developmental Psychology, 50*(4), 1102–1115. doi: 10.1037/a0035185

Chow, Chong Man & Ruhl, Holly. (2014). Friendship and romantic stressors and depression in emerging adulthood: Mediating and moderating roles of attachment representations. *Journal of Adult Development, 21*(2), 106–115. doi: 10.1007/s10804-014-9184-z

Christian, Cindy W. & Block, Robert. (2009). Abusive head trauma in infants and children. *Pediatrics, 123*(5), 1409–1411. doi: 10.1542/peds.2009-0408

Christiansen, Sofie; Axelstad, Marta; Boberg, Julie; Vinggaard, Anne M.; Pedersen, Gitte A. & Hass, Ulla. (2014). Low-dose effects of bisphenol A on early sexual development in male and female rats. *Reproduction, 147*(4), 477–487. doi: 10.1530/REP-13-0377

Chronicle of Higher Education. (2010). *Almanac of higher education 2010–2011.* Washington, DC.

Chronicle of Higher Education. (2014). *Almanac of higher education 2014.* Washington, DC.

Chudacoff, Howard P. (2011). The history of children's play in the United States. In Anthony D. Pellegrini (Ed.), *The Oxford handbook of the development of play* (pp. 101–109). New York, NY: Oxford University Press. doi: 10.1093/oxfordhb/9780195393002.013.0009

Chung, Joanne M.; Robins, Richard W.; Trzesniewski, Kali H.; Noftle, Erik E.; Roberts, Brent W. & Widaman, Keith F. (2014). Continuity and change in self-esteem during emerging adulthood. *Journal of Personality and Social Psychology, 106*(3), 469–483. doi: 10.1037/a0035135

Cicchetti, Dante. (2013a). Annual Research Review: Resilient functioning in maltreated children – past, present, and future perspectives. *Journal of Child Psychology and Psychiatry, 54*(4), 402–422. doi: 10.1111/j.1469-7610.2012.02608.x

Cicchetti, Dante. (2013b). An overview of developmental psychopathology. In Philip D. Zelazo (Ed.), *The Oxford handbook of developmental psychology* (Vol. 2, pp. 455–480). New York, NY: Oxford University Press. doi: 10.1093/oxfordhb/9780199958474.013.0018

Cicconi, Megan. (2014). Vygotsky meets technology: A reinvention of collaboration in the early childhood mathematics classroom. *Early Childhood Education Journal, 42*(1), 57–65. doi: 10.1007/s10643-013-0582-9

Cillessen, Antonius H. N. & Marks, Peter E. L. (2011). Conceptualizing and measuring popularity. In Antonius H. N. Cillessen, et al. (Eds.), *Popularity in the peer system* (pp. 25–56). New York, NY: Guilford Press.

Cimpian, Andrei. (2013). Generic statements, causal attributions, and children's naive theories. In Mahzarin R. Banaji & Susan A. Gelman (Eds.), *Navigating the social world: What infants, children, and other species can teach us* (pp. 269–274). New York, NY: Oxford University Press.

Clark, Caron A. C.; Fang, Hua; Espy, Kimberly A.; Filipek, Pauline A.; Juranek, Jenifer; Bangert, Barbara, . . . Taylor, H. Gerry. (2013). Relation of neural structure to persistently low academic achievement: A longitudinal study of children with differing birth weights. *Neuropsychology, 27*(3), 364–377. doi: 10.1037/a0032273

Clark, Nina A.; Demers, Paul A.; Karr, Catherine J.; Koehoorn, Mieke; Lencar, Cornel; Tamburic, Lillian & Brauer, Michael. (2010). Effect of early life exposure to air pollution on development of childhood asthma. *Environmental Health Perspectives, 118*(2), 284–290. doi: 10.1289/ehp.0900916

Clark, Shelley; Kabiru, Caroline & Mathur, Rohini. (2010). Relationship transitions among youth in urban Kenya. *Journal of Marriage and Family, 72*(1); 73–88. doi: 10.1111/j.1741-3737.2009.00684.x

Clayton, P. E.; Gill, M. S.; Tillmann, V. & Westwood, M. (2014). Translational neuroendocrinology: Control of human growth. *Journal of Neuroendocrinology, 26*(6), 349–355. doi: 10.1111/jne.12156

Cleveland, Michael J.; Gibbons, Frederick X.; Gerrard, Meg; Pomery, Elizabeth A. & Brody, Gene H. (2005). The impact of parenting on risk cognitions and risk behavior: A study of mediation and moderation in a panel of African American adolescents. *Child Development, 76*(4), 900–916. doi: 10.1111/j.1467-8624.2005.00885.x

Cohen, David. (2006). *The development of play* (3rd ed.). New York, NY: Routledge.

Cohen, Jon. (2007). Hope on new AIDS drugs, but breast-feeding strategy backfires. *Science, 315*(5817), 1357. doi: 10.1126/science.315.5817.1357

Cohen, Joel E. & Malin, Martin B. (Eds.). (2010). *International perspectives on the goals of universal basic and secondary education*. New York, NY: Routledge.

Cohen, Larry; Chávez, Vivian & Chehimi, Sana (Eds.). (2010). *Prevention is primary: Strategies for community well-being* (2nd ed.). San Francisco, CA: Jossey-Bass.

Cohen, Leslie B. & Cashon, Cara H. (2006). Infant cognition. In William Damon & Richard M. Lerner (Eds.), *Handbook of child psychology* (6th ed., Vol. 2, pp. 214–251). Hoboken, NJ: Wiley.

Colaco, Marc; Johnson, Kelly; Schneider, Dona & Barone, Joseph. (2013). Toilet training method is not related to dysfunctional voiding. *Clinical Pediatrics, 52*(1), 49–53. doi: 10.1177/0009922812464042

Cole, Pamela M.; Tan, Patricia Z.; Hall, Sarah E.; Zhang, Yiyun; Crnic, Keith A.; Blair, Clancy B. & Li, Runze. (2011). Developmental changes in anger expression and attention focus: Learning to wait. *Developmental Psychology, 47*(4), 1078–1089. doi: 10.1037/a0023813

Coles, Robert. (1997). *The moral intelligence of children: How to raise a moral child*. New York, NY: Random House.

Collins, Emily & Freeman, Jonathan. (2013). Do problematic and non-problematic video game players differ in extraversion, trait empathy, social capital and prosocial tendencies? *Computers in Human Behavior, 29*(5), 1933–1940. doi: 10.1016/j.chb.2013.03.002

Collins, Rebecca L.; Martino, Steven C.; Elliott, Marc N. & Miu, Angela. (2011). Relationships between adolescent sexual outcomes and exposure to sex in media: Robustness to propensity-based analysis. *Developmental Psychology, 47*(2), 585–591. doi: 10.1037/a0022563

Colson, Eve R.; Willinger, Marian; Rybin, Denis; Heeren, Timothy; Smith, Lauren A.; Lister, George & Corwin, Michael J. (2013). Trends and factors associated with infant bed sharing, 1993–2010: The National Infant Sleep Position study. *JAMA Pediatrics, 167*(11), 1032–1037. doi: 10.1001/jamapediatrics.2013.2560

Common Sense Media. (2011). *Zero to eight: Children's media use in America*. San Francisco, CA: Common Sense.

Compian, Laura J.; Gowen, L. Kris & Hayward, Chris. (2009). The interactive effects of puberty and peer victimization on weight concerns and depression symptoms among early adolescent girls. *The Journal of Early Adolescence, 29*(3), 357–375. doi: 10.1177/0272431608323656

Complaints.com. (2011, April 3).

Confer, Jaime C.; Easton, Judith A.; Fleischman, Diana S.; Goetz, Cari D.; Lewis, David M. G.; Perilloux, Carin & Buss, David M. (2010). Evolutionary psychology: Controversies, questions, prospects, and limitations. *American Psychologist, 65*(2), 110–126. doi: 10.1037/a0018413

Conger, John J. (1975). Proceedings of the American Psychological Association, Incorporated, for the year 1974: Minutes of the annual meeting of the Council of Representatives. *American Psychologist, 30*(6), 620–651. doi: 10.1037/h0078455

Conley, Colleen S. & Rudolph, Karen D. (2009). The emerging sex difference in adolescent depression: Interacting contributions of puberty and peer stress. *Development and Psychopathology, 21*(2), 593–620. doi: 10.1017/S0954579409000327

Conwell, Erin & Morgan, James L. (2012). Is it a noun or is it a verb? Resolving the ambicategoricality problem. *Language Learning and Development, 8*(2), 87–112. doi: 10.1080/15475441.2011.580236

Coon, Carleton S. (1962). *The origin of races*. New York, NY: Knopf.

Coovadia, Hoosen M. & Wittenberg, Dankwart F. (Eds.). (2004). *Paediatrics and child health: A manual for health professionals in developing countries* (5th ed.). New York, NY: Oxford University Press.

Copeland, William E.; Wolke, Dieter; Angold, Adrian & Costell, E. Jane. (2013). Adult psychiatric outcomes of bullying and being bullied by peers in childhood and adolescence. *JAMA Psychiatry, 70*(4), 419–426. doi: 10.1001/jamapsychiatry.2013.504

Copen, Casey E.; Daniels, Kimberly & Mosher, William D. (2013). *First premarital cohabitation in the United States: 2006–2010 national survey of family growth*. Hyattsville, MD: U.S. Department of Health and Human Services, Centers for Disease Control and Prevention, National Center for Health Statistics.

Coplan, Robert J. & Weeks, Murray. (2009). Shy and soft-spoken: Shyness, pragmatic language, and socio-emotional adjustment in early childhood. *Infant and Child Development, 18*(3), 238–254. doi: 10.1002/icd.622

Corballis, Michael C. (2011). *The recursive mind: The origins of human language, thought, and civilization*. Princeton, NJ: Princeton University Press.

Corda, Larisa; Khanapure, Amita & Karoshi, Mahantesh. (2012). Biopanic, advanced maternal age and fertility outcomes. In Mahantesh Karoshi, et al. (Eds.), *A Textbook of Preconceptional Medicine and Management*. London, UK: Sapiens.

Corenblum, Barry. (2014). Relationships between racial–ethnic identity, self-esteem and in-group attitudes among first nation children. *Journal of Youth and Adolescence, 43*(3), 387–404. doi: 10.1007/s10964-013-0081-8

Cosgrave, James F. (2010). Embedded addiction: The social production of gambling knowledge and the development of gambling markets. *Canadian Journal of Sociology, 35*(1), 113–134.

Costa, Albert & Sebastián-Gallés, Núria. (2014). How does the bilingual experience sculpt the brain? *Nature Reviews Neuroscience, 15*(5), 336–345. doi: 10.1038/nrn3709

Côté, James E. (2006). Emerging adulthood as an institutionalized moratorium: Risks and benefits to identity formation. In Jeffrey Jensen Arnett & Jennifer Lynn Tanner (Eds.), *Emerging adults in America: Coming of age in the 21st century* (pp. 85–116). Washington, DC: American Psychological Association. doi: 10.1037/11381-004

Côté, James E. (2009). Identity formation and self-development in adolescence. In Richard M. Lerner & Laurence Steinberg (Eds.), *Handbook of adolescent psychology* (3rd ed., Vol. 1, pp. 266–304). Hoboken, NJ: Wiley.

Côté, Sylvana M.; Borge, Anne I.; Geoffroy, Marie-Claude; Rutter, Michael & Tremblay, Richard E. (2008). Nonmaternal care in infancy and emotional/behavioral difficulties at 4 years old: Moderation by family risk characteristics. *Developmental Psychology, 44*(1), 155–168. doi: 10.1037/0012-1649.44.1.155

Cotton, Richard. (2014). Supporting transgender students in schools. *British Journal of School Nursing, 9*(3), 141–143. doi: 10.12968/bjsn.2014.9.3.141

Couturier, Jennifer; Kimber, Melissa & Szatmari, Peter. (2013). Efficacy of family-based treatment for adolescents with eating disorders: A systematic review and meta-analysis. *International Journal of Eating Disorders, 46*(1), 3–11. doi: 10.1002/eat.22042

Couzin-Frankel, Jennifer. (2010). Bacteria and asthma: Untangling the links. *Science, 330*(6008), 1168–1169. doi: 10.1126/science.330.6008.1168

Couzin-Frankel, Jennifer. (2011). A pitched battle over life span. *Science*, 333(6042), 549–550. doi: 10.1126/science.333.6042.549

Couzin-Frankel, Jennifer. (2013). Return of unexpected DNA results urged. *Science*, 339(6127), 1507–1508. doi: 10.1126/science.339.6127.1507

Cowan, Nelson (Ed.). (1997). *The development of memory in childhood*. Hove, East Sussex, UK: Psychology Press.

Cowan, Nelson & Alloway, Tracy. (2009). Development of working memory in childhood. In Mary L. Courage & Nelson Cowan (Eds.), *The development of memory in infancy and childhood* (2nd ed., pp. 303–342). New York, NY: Psychology Press.

Crain, William C. (2005). *Theories of development: Concepts and applications* (5th ed.). Upper Saddle River, NJ: Prentice Hall.

Cramer, Robert; Lipinski, Ryan; Bowman, Ashley & Carollo, Tanner. (2009). Subjective distress to violations of trust in Mexican American close relationships conforms to evolutionary principles. *Current Psychology*, 28(1), 1–11. doi: 10.1007/s12144-009-9049-y

Cristia, Alejandrina; Seidl, Amanda; Junge, Caroline; Soderstrom, Melanie & Hagoort, Peter. (2014). Predicting individual variation in language from infant speech perception measures. *Child Development*, 85(4), 1330–1345. doi: 10.1111/cdev.12193

Crocker, Melissa K.; Stern, Elizabeth A.; Sedaka, Nicole M.; Shomaker, Lauren B.; Brady, Sheila M.; Ali, Asem H., . . . Yanovski, Jack A. (2014). Sexual dimorphisms in the associations of BMI and body fat with indices of pubertal development in girls and boys. *The Journal of Clinical Endocrinology & Metabolism*, 99(8), E1519–E1529. doi: 10.1210/jc.2014-1384

Crone, Eveline A. & Dahl, Ronald E. (2012). Understanding adolescence as a period of social–affective engagement and goal flexibility. *Nature Reviews Neuroscience*, 13(9), 636–650. doi: 10.1038/nrn3313

Crone, Eveline A. & Ridderinkhof, K. Richard. (2011). The developing brain: From theory to neuroimaging and back. *Developmental Cognitive Neuroscience*, 1(2), 101–109. doi: 10.1016/j.dcn.2010.12.001

Crone, Eveline A. & Westenberg, P. Michiel. (2009). A brain-based account of developmental changes in social decision making. In Michelle de Haan & Megan R. Gunnar (Eds.), *Handbook of developmental social neuroscience* (pp. 378–396). New York, NY: Guilford Press.

Crosnoe, Robert & Johnson, Monica Kirkpatrick. (2011). Research on adolescence in the twenty-first century. *Annual Review of Sociology*, 37(1), 439–460. doi: 10.1146/annurev-soc-081309-150008

Crosnoe, Robert; Leventhal, Tama; Wirth, Robert John; Pierce, Kim M. & Pianta, Robert C. (2010). Family socioeconomic status and consistent environmental stimulation in early childhood. *Child Development*, 81(3), 972–987. doi: 10.1111/j.1467-8624.2010.01446.x

Cross, Donna; Monks, Helen; Hall, Marg; Shaw, Thérèse; Pintabona, Yolanda; Erceg, Erin, . . . Lester, Leanne. (2011). Three-year results of the Friendly Schools whole-of-school intervention on children's bullying behaviour. *British Educational Research Journal*, 37(1), 105–129. doi: 10.1080/01411920903420024

Crossley, Nicolas A.; Mechelli, Andrea; Scott, Jessica; Carletti, Francesco; Fox, Peter T.; McGuire, Philip & Bullmore, Edward T. (2014). The hubs of the human connectome are generally implicated in the anatomy of brain disorders. *Brain*, 137(8), 2382–2395. doi: 10.1093/brain/awu132

Cruz, Alvaro A.; Bateman, Eric D. & Bousquet, Jean. (2010). The social determinants of asthma. *European Respiratory Journal*, 35(2), 239–242. doi: 10.1183/09031936.00070309

Cruz-Inigo, Andres E.; Ladizinski, Barry & Sethi, Aisha. (2011). Albinism in Africa: Stigma, slaughter and awareness campaigns. *Dermatologic Clinics*, 29(1), 79–87. doi: 10.1016/j.det.2010.08.015

Cubillo, Ana; Halari, Rozmin; Smith, Anna; Taylor, Eric & Rubia, Katya. (2012). A review of fronto-striatal and fronto-cortical brain abnormalities in children and adults with Attention deficit hyperactivity disorder (ADHD) and new evidence for dysfunction in adults with ADHD during motivation and attention. *Cortex*, 48(2), 194–215. doi: 10.1016/j.cortex.2011.04.007

Cuijpers, P.; van Straten, A.; van Oppen, P. & Andersson, G. (2010). Welke psychologische behandeling, uitgevoerd door wie, is het meest effectief bij depressie? *Gedragstherapie*, 43, 79–113.

Cumsille, Patricio; Darling, Nancy & Martínez, M. Loreto. (2010). Shading the truth: The patterning of adolescents' decisions to avoid issues, disclose, or lie to parents. *Journal of Adolescence*, 33(2), 285–296. doi: 10.1016/j.adolescence.2009.10.008

Cunha, Marcus & Caldieraro, Fabio. (2009). Sunk-cost effects on purely behavioral investments. *Cognitive Science*, 33(1), 105–113. doi: 10.1111/j.1551-6709.2008.01005.x

Currie, Janet & Widom, Cathy S. (2010). Long-term consequences of child abuse and neglect on adult economic well-being. *Child Maltreatment*, 15(2), 111–120. doi: 10.1177/1077559509355316

Cutuli, J. J.; Desjardins, Christopher David; Herbers, Janette E.; Long, Jeffrey D.; Heistad, David; Chan, Chi-Keung, . . . Masten, Ann S. (2013). Academic achievement trajectories of homeless and highly mobile students: Resilience in the context of chronic and acute risk. *Child Development*, 84(3), 841–857. doi: 10.1111/cdev.12013

Daddis, Christopher. (2010). Adolescent peer crowds and patterns of belief in the boundaries of personal authority. *Journal of Adolescence*, 33(5), 699–708. doi: 10.1016/j.adolescence.2009.11.001

Dahl, Ronald E. (2004). Adolescent brain development: A period of vulnerabilities and opportunities, keynote address. *Annals of the New York Academy of Sciences*, 1021, 1–22. doi: 10.1196/annals.1308.001

Dahl, Ronald E. & Gunnar, Megan R. (2009). Heightened stress responsiveness and emotional reactivity during pubertal maturation: Implications for psychopathology. *Development and Psychopathology*, 21(1), 1–6. doi: 10.1017/S0954579409000017

Dai, David Yun. (2010). *The nature and nurture of giftedness: A new framework for understanding gifted education*. New York, NY: Teachers College Press.

Daley, Dave; Jones, Karen; Hutchings, Judy & Thompson, Margaret. (2009). Attention deficit hyperactivity disorder in pre-school children: Current findings, recommended interventions and future directions. *Child: Care, Health and Development*, 35(6), 754–766. doi: 10.1111/j.1365-2214.2009.00938.x

Dalman, Christina; Allebeck, Peter; Gunnell, David; Harrison, Glyn; Kristensson, Krister; Lewis, Glyn, . . . Karlsson, Håkan. (2008). Infections in the CNS during childhood and the risk of subsequent psychotic illness: A cohort study of more than one million Swedish subjects. *American Journal of Psychiatry*, 165(1), 59–65. doi: 10.1176/appi.ajp.2007.07050740

Damashek, Amy & Kuhn, Jennifer. (2014). Promise and challenges: Interventions for the prevention of unintentional injuries among young children. *Clinical Practice in Pediatric Psychology*, 2(3), 250–262. doi: 10.1037/cpp0000064

Damasio, Antonio R. (2012). *Self comes to mind: Constructing the conscious brain*. New York, NY: Vintage.

Danel, Isabella; Berg, Cynthia; Johnson, Christopher H. & Atrash, Hani. (2003). Magnitude of maternal morbidity during labor and delivery: United States, 1993–1997. *American Journal of Public Health*, 93(4), 631–634. doi: 10.2105/AJPH.93.4.631

Darling, Nancy; Cumsille, Patricio & Martinez, M. Loreto. (2008). Individual differences in adolescents' beliefs about the legitimacy of parental authority and their own obligation to obey: A longitudinal investigation. *Child Development*, 79(4), 1103–1118. doi: 10.1111/j.1467-8624.2008.01178.x

Darwin, Charles. (1859). *On the origin of species by means of natural selection*. London, UK: J. Murray.

Daum, Moritz M.; Ulber, Julia & Gredebäck, Gustaf. (2013). The development of pointing perception in infancy: Effects of communicative signals on covert shifts of attention. *Developmental Psychology*, 49(10), 1898–1908. doi: 10.1037/a0031111

David, Barbara; Grace, Diane & Ryan, Michelle K. (2004). The gender wars: A self-categorization perspective on the development of gender identity. In Mark Bennett & Fabio Sani (Eds.), *The development of the social self* (pp. 135–157). New York, NY: Psychology Press.

David, Jane L. (2011). High-stakes testing narrows the curriculum. *Educational Leadership*, 68(6), 78–80.

Davidson, Julia O'Connell. (2005). *Children in the global sex trade*. Malden, MA: Polity.

Davis, Elysia Poggi; Parker, Susan W.; Tottenham, Nim & Gunnar, Megan R. (2003). Emotion, cognition, and the hypothalamic-pituitary-adrenocortical axis: A developmental perspective. In Michelle de Haan & Mark H. Johnson (Eds.), *The cognitive neuroscience of development* (pp. 181–206). New York, NY: Psychology Press.

Davis, Linell. (1999). *Doing culture: Cross-cultural communication in action*. Beijing, China: Foreign Language Teaching & Research Press.

Davis, R. Neal; Davis, Matthew M.; Freed, Gary L. & Clark, Sarah J. (2011). Fathers' depression related to positive and negative parenting behaviors with 1-year-old children. *Pediatrics*, 127(4), 612–618. doi: 10.1542/peds.2010-1779

Davis-Kean, Pamela E.; Jager, Justin & Collins, W. Andrew. (2009). The self in action: An emerging link between self-beliefs and behaviors in middle childhood. *Child Development Perspectives*, 3(3), 184–188. doi: 10.1111/j.1750-8606.2009.00104.x

Dawson, Geraldine; Jones, Emily J. H.; Merkle, Kristen; Venema, Kaitlin; Lowy, Rachel; Faja, Susan, . . . Webb, Sara J. (2012). Early behavioral intervention is associated with normalized brain activity in young children with autism. *Journal of the American Academy of Child & Adolescent Psychiatry*, 51(11), 1150–1159. doi: 10.1016/j.jaac.2012.08.018

Dawson, Lorne L. (2010). The study of new religious movements and the radicalization of home-grown terrorists: Opening a dialogue. *Terrorism and Political Violence*, 22(1), 1–21. doi: 10.1080/09546550903409163

De Cock, Kevin M. (2011). *Trends in global health and CDC's international role, 1961–2011*. Atlanta, GA: Centers for Disease Control and Prevention, 60(Suppl. 4), 104–111.

De Corte, Erik. (2013). Giftedness considered from the perspective of research on learning and instruction. *High Ability Studies*, 24(1), 3–19. doi: 10.1080/13598139.2013.780967

de Haan, Amaranta D.; Prinzie, Peter & Dekovic, Maja. (2009). Mothers' and fathers' personality and parenting: The mediating role of sense of competence. *Developmental Psychology*, 45(6), 1695–1707. doi: 10.1037/a0016121

de Heering, Adelaide; de Liedekerke, Claire; Deboni, Malorie & Rossion, Bruno. (2010). The role of experience during childhood in shaping the other-race effect. *Developmental Science*, 13(1), 181–187. doi: 10.1111/j.1467-7687.2009.00876.x

de Hoog, Marieke L. A.; Kleinman, Ken P.; Gillman, Matthew W.; Vrijkotte, Tanja G. M.; van Eijsden, Manon & Taveras, Elsie M. (2014). Racial/ethnic and immigrant differences in early childhood diet quality. *Public Health Nutrition*, 17(6), 1308–1317. doi: 10.1017/S1368980013001183

de Jonge, Ank; Mesman, Jeanette A. J. M.; Manniën, Judith; Zwart, Joost J.; van Dillen, Jeroen & van Roosmalen, Jos. (2013). Severe adverse maternal outcomes among low risk women with planned home versus hospital births in the Netherlands: Nationwide cohort study. *BMJ*, 346, f3263. doi: 10.1136/bmj.f3263

de la Croix, David. (2013). *Fertility, education, growth, and sustainability*. New York, NY: Cambridge University Press.

De Lee, Joseph Bolivar. (1938). *The principles and practice of obstetrics* (7th ed.). Philadelphia, PA: W. B. Saunders Co.

De Neys, Wim & Feremans, Vicky. (2013). Development of heuristic bias detection in elementary school. *Developmental Psychology*, 49(2), 258–269. doi: 10.1037/a0028320

De Neys, Wim & Van Gelder, Elke. (2009). Logic and belief across the lifespan: The rise and fall of belief inhibition during syllogistic reasoning. *Developmental Science*, 12(1), 123–130. doi: 10.1111/j.1467-7687.2008.00746.x

de Weerth, Carolina; Zijlmans, Maartje; Mack, Simon & Beijers, Roseriet. (2013). Cortisol reactions to a social evaluative paradigm in 5- and 6-year-old children. *Stress*, 16(1), 65–72. doi: 10.3109/10253890.2012.684112

Dean, Angela J.; Walters, Julie & Hall, Anthony. (2010). A systematic review of interventions to enhance medication adherence in children and adolescents with chronic illness. *Archives of Disease in Childhood*, 95(9), 717–723. doi: 10.1136/adc.2009.175125

Dearing, Eric; Wimer, Christopher; Simpkins, Sandra D.; Lund, Terese; Bouffard, Suzanne M.; Caronongan, Pia, . . . Weiss, Heather. (2009). Do neighborhood and home contexts help explain why low-income children miss opportunities to participate in activities outside of school? *Developmental Psychology*, 45(6), 1545–1562. doi: 10.1037/a0017359

Deater-Deckard, Kirby. (2013). The social environment and the development of psychopathology. In Philip D. Zelazo (Ed.), *The Oxford handbook of developmental psychology* (Vol. 2, pp. 527–548). New York, NY: Oxford University Press. doi: 10.1093/oxfordhb/9780199958474.013.0021

Deci, Edward L.; Koestner, Richard & Ryan, Richard M. (1999). A meta-analytic review of experiments examining the effects of extrinsic rewards on intrinsic motivation. *Psychological Bulletin*, 125(6), 627–668. doi: 10.1037//0033-2909.125.6.627

Dee, Thomas; Jacob, Brian A. & Schwartz, Nathaniel. (2013). The effects of NCLB on school resources and practices. *Educational Evaluation and Policy Analysis*, 35(2), 252–279. doi: 10.3102/0162373712467080

Degenhardt, Louisa; Coffey, Carolyn; Carlin, John B.; Swift, Wendy; Moore, Elya & Patton, George C. (2010). Outcomes of occasional cannabis use in adolescence: 10-year follow-up study in Victoria, Australia. *The British Journal of Psychiatry*, 196(4), 290–295. doi: 10.1192/bjp.bp.108.056952

Degnan, Kathryn A.; Hane, Amie Ashley; Henderson, Heather A.; Moas, Olga Lydia; Reeb-Sutherland, Bethany C. & Fox, Nathan A. (2011). Longitudinal stability of temperamental exuberance and social–emotional outcomes in early childhood. *Developmental Psychology*, 47(3), 765–780. doi: 10.1037/a0021316

DeKeyser, Robert M. (2013). Age effects in second language learning: Stepping stones toward better understanding. 63(Suppl. 1), 52–67. doi: 10.1111/j.1467-9922.2012.00737.x

Del Giudice, Marco. (2011). Sex differences in romantic attachment: A meta-analysis. *Personality and Social Psychology Bulletin*, 37(2), 193–214. doi: 10.1177/0146167210392789

Delaunay-El Allam, Maryse; Soussignan, Robert; Patris, Bruno; Marlier, Luc & Schaal, Benoist. (2010). Long-lasting memory for an odor acquired at the mother's breast. *Developmental Science*, 13(6), 849–863. doi: 10.1111/j.1467-7687.2009.00941.x

DeLisi, Matt. (2014). Low self-control is a brain-based disorder. In Kevin M. Beaver, et al. (Eds.), *The nurture versus biosocial debate in criminology: On the origins of criminal behavior and criminality* (pp. 172–183). Thousand Oaks, CA: Sage.

DeLoache, Judy S.; Chiong, Cynthia; Sherman, Kathleen; Islam, Nadia; Vanderborght, Mieke; Troseth, Georgene L., . . . O'Doherty, Katherine. (2010). Do babies learn from baby media? *Psychological Science*, 21(11), 1570–1574. doi: 10.1177/0956797610384145

Demetriou, Andreas; Spanoudis, George; Shayer, Michael; Mouyi, Antigoni; Kazi, Smaragda & Platsidou, Maria. (2013). Cycles in speed-working memory-G relations: Towards a developmental–differential theory of the mind. *Intelligence*, 41(1), 34–50. doi: 10.1016/j.intell.2012.10.010

Demorest, Amy P. (2004). *Psychology's grand theorists: How personal experiences shaped professional ideas*. New York: Psychology Press.

Dennehy, Tara C.; Ben-Zeev, Avi & Tanigawa, Noriko. (2014). 'Be prepared': An implemental mindset for alleviating social-identity threat. *British Journal of Social Psychology*, 53(3), 585–594. doi: 10.1111/bjso.12071

Denny, Dallas & Pittman, Cathy. (2007). Gender identity: From dualism to diversity. In Mitchell Tepper & Annette Fuglsang Owens (Eds.), *Sexual Health* (Vol. 1, pp. 205–229). Westport, CT: Praeger.

Denton, Melinda L.; Pearce, Lisa D. & Smith, Christian. (2008). *Religion and spirituality on the path through adolescence*. Chapel Hill, NC: National Study of Youth and Religion, University of North Carolina at Chapel Hill.

Deptula, Daneen P.; Henry, David B. & Schoeny, Michael E. (2010). How can parents make a difference? Longitudinal associations with adolescent sexual behavior. *Journal of Family Psychology*, 24(6), 731–739. doi: 10.1037/a0021760

Deresiewicz, William. (2014). *Excellent sheep: The miseducation of the American elite and the way to a meaningful life*. New York, NY: Free Press.

Desai, Rishi J.; Hernandez-Diaz, Sonia; Bateman, Brian T. & Huybrechts, Krista F.

(2014). Increase in prescription opioid use during pregnancy among medicaid-enrolled women. *Obstetrics & Gynecology, 123*(5), 997–1002. doi: 10.1097/AOG.0000000000000208

Desoete, Annemie; Stock, Pieter; Schepens, Annemie; Baeyens, Dieter & Roeyers, Herbert. (2009). Classification, seriation, and counting in grades 1, 2, and 3 as two-year longitudinal predictors for low achieving in numerical facility and arithmetical achievement? *Journal of Psychoeducational Assessment, 27*(3), 252–264. doi: 10.1177/0734282908330588

Dewey, Lauren; Allwood, Maureen; Fava, Joanna; Arias, Elizabeth; Pinizzotto, Anthony & Schlesinger, Louis. (2013). Suicide by cop: Clinical risks and subtypes. *Archives of Suicide Research, 17*(4), 448–461. doi: 10.1080/13811118.2013.801810

Dezutter, Jessie; Waterman, Alan S.; Schwartz, Seth J.; Luyckx, Koen; Beyers, Wim; Meca, Alan, . . . Caraway, S. Jean. (2014). Meaning in life in emerging adulthood: A person-oriented approach. *Journal of Personality, 82*(1), 57–68. doi: 10.1111/jopy.12033

Diamond, Lisa M. & Fagundes, Christopher P. (2010). Psychobiological research on attachment. *Journal of Social and Personal Relationships, 27*(2), 218–225. doi: 10.1177/0265407509360906

Diamond, Marian C. (1988). *Enriching heredity: The impact of the environment on the anatomy of the brain.* New York, NY: Free Press.

Diamond, Mathew E. (2007). Neuronal basis of perceptual intelligence. In Flavia Santoianni & Claudia Sabatano (Eds.), *Brain development in learning environments: Embodied and perceptual advancements* (pp. 98–108). Newcastle, UK: Cambridge Scholars Publishing.

Diener, Marissa. (2000). Gift from the gods: A Balinese guide to early child rearing. In Judy S. DeLoache & Alma Gottlieb (Eds.), *A world of babies: Imagined childcare guides for seven societies* (pp. 96–116). New York, NY: Cambridge University Press.

Dijk, Jan A. G. M. van. (2005). *The deepening divide: Inequality in the information society.* Thousand Oaks, CA: Sage.

Dinh, Michael M.; Bein, Kendall; Roncal, Susan; Byrne, Christopher M.; Petchell, Jeffrey & Brennan, Jeffrey. (2013). Redefining the golden hour for severe head injury in an urban setting: The effect of prehospital arrival times on patient outcomes. *Injury, 44*(5), 606–610. doi: 10.1016/j.injury.2012.01.011

Diseth, Åge; Meland, Eivind & Breidablik, Hans J. (2014). Self-beliefs among students: Grade level and gender differences in self-esteem, self-efficacy and implicit theories of intelligence. *Learning and Individual Differences, 35,* 1–8. doi: 10.1016/j.lindif.2014.06.003

Dishion, Thomas J.; Poulin, François & Burraston, Bert. (2001). Peer group dynamics associated with iatrogenic effects in group interventions with high-risk young adolescents. In Douglas W. Nangle & Cynthia A. Erdley (Eds.), *The role of friendship in psychological adjustment* (pp. 79–92). San Francisco, CA: Jossey-Bass.

Dishion, Thomas J.; Véronneau, Marie-Hélène & Myers, Michael W. (2010). Cascading peer dynamics underlying the progression from problem behavior to violence in early to late adolescence. *Development and Psychopathology, 22*(3), 603–619. doi: 10.1017/S0954579410000313

Dix, Theodore & Yan, Ni. (2014). Mothers' depressive symptoms and infant negative emotionality in the prediction of child adjustment at age 3: Testing the maternal reactivity and child vulnerability hypotheses. *Development and Psychopathology, 26*(1), 111–124. doi: 10.1017/S0954579413000898

Dobson, Velma; Candy, T. Rowan; Hartmann, E. Eugenie; Mayer, D. Luisa; Miller, Joseph M. & Quinn, Graham E. (2009). Infant and child vision research: Present status and future directions. *Optometry & Vision Science, 86*(6), 559–560. doi: 10.1097/OPX.0b013e3181aa06d5

Dodge, Kenneth A. (2009). Mechanisms of gene-environment interaction effects in the development of conduct disorder. *Perspectives on Psychological Science, 4*(4), 408–414. doi: 10.1111/j.1745-6924.2009.01147.x

Domina, Thurston; Conley, AnneMarie & Farkas, George. (2011a). The case for dreaming big. *Sociology of Education, 84*(2), 118–121. doi: 10.1177/0038040711401810

Domina, Thurston; Conley, AnneMarie & Farkas, George. (2011b). The link between educational expectations and effort in the college-for-all era. *Sociology of Education, 84*(2), 93–112. doi: 10.1177/1941406411401808

Dorais, Michel. (2009). *Don't tell: The sexual abuse of boys* (2nd ed.). Montreal, Canada: McGill-Queen's University Press.

dosReis, Susan; Mychailyszyn, Matthew P.; Evans-Lacko, Sara E.; Beltran, Alicia; Riley, Anne W. & Myers, Mary Anne. (2009). The meaning of Attention-deficit/hyperactivity disorder medication and parents' initiation and continuity of treatment for their child. *Journal of Child and Adolescent Psychopharmacology, 19*(4), 377–383. doi: 10.1089/cap.2008.0118

Dotterer, Aryn M.; McHale, Susan M. & Crouter, Ann C. (2009). The development and correlates of academic interests from childhood through adolescence. *Journal of Educational Psychology, 101*(2), 509–519. doi: 10.1037/a0013987

Doubleday, Justin. (2013). Earnings gap narrows, but college education still pays, report says. *The Chronicle Of Higher Education,* A14.

Doucet, Andrea & Lee, Robyn. (2014). Fathering, feminism(s), gender, and sexualities: Connections, tensions, and new pathways. *Journal of Family Theory & Review, 6*(4), 355–373. doi: 10.1111/jftr.12051

Drabant, Emily M.; Ramel, Wiveka; Edge, Michael D.; Hyde, Luke W.; Kuo, Janice R.; Goldin, Philippe R., . . . Gross, James J. (2012). Neural mechanisms underlying 5-HTTLPR-related sensitivity to acute stress. *PsychiatryOnline, 169*(4), 397–405. doi: 10.1176/appi.ajp.2011.10111699

Drake, Kim; Belsky, Jay & Fearon, R. M. Pasco. (2014). From early attachment to engagement with learning in school: The role of self-regulation and persistence. *Developmental Psychology, 50*(5), 1350–1361. doi: 10.1037/a0032779

Drescher, Jack. (2014). Controversies in gender diagnoses. *LGBT Health, 1*(1), 10–14. doi: 10.1089/lgbt.2013.1500

Drover, James; Hoffman, Dennis R.; Castañeda, Yolanda S.; Morale, Sarah E. & Birch, Eileen E. (2009). Three randomized controlled trials of early long-chain polyunsaturated fatty acid supplementation on means-end problem solving in 9-month-olds. *Child Development, 80*(5), 1376–1384. doi: 10.1111/j.1467-8624.2009.01339.x

Dubicka, Bernadka; Carlson, Gabrielle A.; Vail, Andy & Harrington, Richard. (2008). Prepubertal mania: Diagnostic differences between US and UK clinicians. *European Child & Adolescent Psychiatry, 17*(3), 153–161. doi: 10.1007/s00787-007-0649-5

Duckworth, Angela Lee & Kern, Margaret L. (2011). A meta-analysis of the convergent validity of self-control measures. *Journal of Research in Personality, 45*(3), 259–268. doi: 10.1016/j.jrp.2011.02.004

Dukes, Richard L.; Stein, Judith A. & Zane, Jazmin I. (2009). Effect of relational bullying on attitudes, behavior and injury among adolescent bullies, victims and bully-victims. *The Social Science Journal, 46*(4), 671–688. doi: 10.1016/j.soscij.2009.05.006

Dumas, A.; Simmat-Durand, L. & Lejeune, C. (2014). Pregnancy and substance use in France: A literature review. *Journal de Gynécologie Obstétrique et Biologie de la Reproduction.* doi: 10.1016/j.jgyn.2014.05.008

Duncan, Greg J. & Magnuson, Katherine. (2013). Investing in preschool programs. *Journal of Economic Perspectives, 27*(2), 109–132. doi: 10.1257/jep.27.2.109

Duncan, Greg J.; Ziol-Guest, Kathleen M. & Kalil, Ariel. (2010). Early-childhood poverty and adult attainment, behavior, and health. *Child Development, 81*(1), 306–325. doi: 10.1111/j.1467-8624.2009.01396.x

Dunmore, Simon J. (2013). Of fat mice and men: The rise of the adipokines. *Journal of Endocrinology, 216*(1), E1–E2. doi: 10.1530/JOE-12-0513

Dunning, David. (2011). *Social motivation.* New York, NY: Psychology Press.

Dunphy, Dexter C. (1963). The social structure of urban adolescent peer groups. *Sociometry, 26*(2), 230–246. doi: 10.2307/2785909

DuPaul, George J.; Gormley, Matthew J. & Laracy, Seth D. (2013). Comorbidity of LD and ADHD: Implications of DSM-5 for assessment and treatment. *Journal of Learning Disabilities, 46*(1), 43–51. doi: 10.1177/0022219412464351

DuPont, Robert L. & Lieberman, Jeffrey A. (2014). Young brains on drugs. *Science, 344*(6184), 557. doi: 10.1126/science.1254989

Dutra, Lauren M. & Glantz, Stanton A. (2014). Electronic cigarettes and conventional cigarette use among US adolescents: A cross-sectional study. *JAMA Pediatrics, 168*(7), 610–617. doi: 10.1001/jamapediatrics.2013.5488

Dvornyk, Volodymyr & Waqar-ul-Haq. (2012). Genetics of age at menarche: A systematic review. *Human Reproduction Update, 18*(2), 198–210. doi: 10.1093/humupd/dmr050

Dweck, Carol S. (2013). Social Development. In Philip D. Zelazo (Ed.), *The Oxford handbook of developmental psychology* (Vol. 2, pp. 167–190). New York, NY: Oxford University Press. doi: 10.1093/oxfordhb/9780199958474.013.0008

Eagly, Alice H. & Wood, Wendy. (2013). The nature–nurture debates: 25 years of challenges in understanding the psychology of gender. *Perspectives on Psychological Science, 8*(3), 340–357. doi: 10.1177/1745691613484767

Earth Policy Institute. (2011). *Two stories of disease: Smallpox and polio.* Washington, DC: Earth Policy Institute.

Eccles, Jacquelynne S. & Roeser, Robert W. (2010). An ecological view of schools and development. In Judith L. Meece & Jacquelynne S. Eccles (Eds.), *Handbook of research on schools, schooling, and human development* (pp. 6–22). New York, NY: Routledge.

Eccles, Jacquelynne S. & Roeser, Robert W. (2011). Schools as developmental contexts during adolescence. *Journal of Research on Adolescence, 21*(1), 225–241. doi: 10.1111/j.1532-7795.2010.00725.x

Eckholm, Erik. (2013, October 24). Case explores rights of fetus versus mother. *The New York Times,* pp. A1, A16.

Edwards, Judge Leonard P. (2007). Achieving timely permanency in child protection courts: The importance of frontloading the court process. *Juvenile and Family Court Journal, 58*(2), 1–37. doi: 10.1111/j.1755-6988.2007.tb00136.x

Efrat, Merav. (2011). The relationship between low-income and minority children's physical activity and academic-related outcomes: A review of the literature. *Health Education & Behavior, 38*(5), 441–451. doi: 10.1177/1090198110375025

Eggum, Natalie D.; Eisenberg, Nancy; Kao, Karen; Spinrad, Tracy L.; Bolnick, Rebecca; Hofer, Claire, . . . Fabricius, William V. (2011). Emotion understanding, theory of mind, and prosocial orientation: Relations over time in early childhood. *The Journal of Positive Psychology, 6*(1), 4–16. doi: 10.1080/17439760.2010.536776

Ehrlich, Sara Z. & Blum-Kulka, Shoshana. (2014). 'Now I said that Danny becomes Danny again': A multifaceted view of kindergarten children's peer argumentative discourse. In Asta Cekaite, et al. (Eds.), *Children's peer talk: Learning from each other* (pp. 23–41). New York, NY: Cambridge University Press.

Eichhorst, Werner; Rodríguez-Planas, Núria; Schmidl, Ricarda & Zimmermann, Klaus F. (2012). *A roadmap to vocational education and training systems around the world.* Bonn, Germany: Institute for the Study of Labor.

Eisenberg, Nancy; Hofer, Claire; Spinrad, Tracy L.; Gershoff, Elizabeth T.; Valiente, Carlos; Losoya, Sandra, . . . Maxon, Elizabeth. (2008). Understanding mother-adolescent conflict discussions: Concurrent and across-time prediction from youths' dispositions and parenting. *Monographs of the Society for Research in Child Development, 73*(2), vii–viii. doi: 10.1111/j.1540-5834.2008.00470.x

Eisenberg, Nancy; Hofer, Claire; Sulik, Michael J. & Liew, Jeffrey. (2013). The development of prosocial moral reasoning and a prosocial orientation in young adulthood: Concurrent and longitudinal correlates. *Developmental Psychology, 50*(1), 58–70. doi: 10.1037/a0032990

Eisenberg, Nancy; Hofer, Claire; Sulik, Michael J. & Spinrad, Tracy L. (2014). Self-regulation, effortful control, and their socioemotional correlates. In James J. Gross (Ed.), *Handbook of emotion regulation* (2nd ed., pp. 157–172). New York, NY: Guilford Press.

Elder, Glen H. (1998). The life course as developmental theory. *Child Development, 69*(1), 1–12. doi: 10.1111/j.1467-8624.1998.tb06128.x

Elias, Carol F. (2012). Leptin action in pubertal development: Recent advances and unanswered questions. *Trends in Endocrinology & Metabolism, 23*(1), 9–15. doi: 10.1016/j.tem.2011.09.002

Elias, Carol F. & Purohit, Darshana. (2013). Leptin signaling and circuits in puberty and fertility. *Cellular and Molecular Life Sciences, 70*(5), 841–862. doi: 10.1007/s00018-012-1095-1

Elicker, James; Ruprecht, Karen M. & Anderson, Treshawn. (2014). Observing infants' and toddlers' relationships and interactions in group care. In Linda J. Harrison & Jennifer Sumsion (Eds.), *Lived spaces of infant-toddler education and care: Exploring diverse perspectives on theory, research and practice* (pp. 131–145). Dordrecht, Netherlands: Springer. doi: 10.1007/978-94-017-8838-0_10

Elkind, David. (1967). Egocentrism in adolescence. *Child Development, 38*(4), 1025–1034.

Elkind, David. (2007). *The power of play: How spontaneous, imaginative activities lead to happier, healthier children.* Cambridge, MA: Da Capo Press.

Ellingsaeter, Anne L. (2014). Towards universal quality early childhood education and care: The Norwegian model. In Ludovica Gambaro, et al. (Eds.), *An equal start?: Providing quality early education and care for disadvantaged children* (pp. 53–76). Chicago, IL: Policy Press.

Elliott, Sinikka. (2012). *Not my kid: What parents believe about the sex lives of their teenagers.* New York, NY: New York University Press.

Ellis, Bruce J. & Boyce, W. Thomas. (2008). Biological sensitivity to context. *Current Directions in Psychological Science, 17*(3), 183–187. doi: 10.1111/j.1467-8721.2008.00571.x

Ellis, Bruce J.; Del Giudice, Marco; Dishion, Thomas J.; Figueredo, Aurelio José; Gray, Peter; Griskevicius, Vladas, . . . Wilson, David Sloan. (2012). The evolutionary basis of risky adolescent behavior: Implications for science, policy, and practice. *Developmental Psychology, 48*(3), 598–623. doi: 10.1037/a0026220

Ellis, Bruce J.; Shirtcliff, Elizabeth A.; Boyce, W. Thomas; Deardorff, Julianna & Essex, Marilyn J. (2011). Quality of early family relationships and the timing and tempo of puberty: Effects depend on biological sensitivity to context. *Development and Psychopathology, 23*(1), 85–99. doi: 10.1017/S0954579410000660

Ellison, Christopher G.; Musick, Marc A. & Holden, George W. (2011). Does conservative Protestantism moderate the association between corporal punishment and child outcomes? *Journal of Marriage and Family, 73*(5), 946–961. doi: 10.1111/j.1741-3737.2011.00854.x

Elmadfa, I; Meyer, A; Nowak, V; Hasenegger, V; Putz, P; Verstraeten, R, . . . Margetts, B. (2009). *European nutrition and health report 2009: Forum of nutrition.* European Commission, Health and Consumer Protection, 62.

Emmen, Rosanneke A. G.; Malda, Maike; Mesman, Judi; van IJzendoorn, Marinus H.; Prevoo, Mariëlle J. L. & Yeniad, Nihal. (2013). Socioeconomic status and parenting in ethnic minority families: Testing a minority family stress model. *Journal of Family Psychology, 27*(6), 896–904. doi: 10.1037/a0034693

Engelberts, Adèle C. & de Jonge, Guustaaf Adolf. (1990). Choice of sleeping position for infants: Possible association with cot death. *Archives of Disease in Childhood, 65*(4), 462–467. doi: 10.1136/adc.65.4.462

Enserink, Martin. (2011). Can this DNA sleuth help catch criminals? *Science, 331*(6019), 838–840. doi: 10.1126/science.331.6019.838

Epps, Chad & Holt, Lynn. (2011). The genetic basis of addiction and relevant cellular mechanisms. *International Anesthesiology Clinics, 49*(1), 3–14. doi: 10.1097/AIA.0b013e3181f2bb66

Epstein, Jeffery N.; Langberg, Joshua M.; Lichtenstein, Philip K.; Altaye, Mekibib; Brinkman, William B.; House, Katherine & Stark, Lori J. (2010). Attention-deficit/hyperactivity disorder outcomes for children treated in community-based pediatric settings. *Archives of Pediatrics & Adolescent Medicine, 164*(2), 160–165. doi: 10.1001/archpediatrics.2009.263

Erdbrink, Thomas. (2013, June 3). Seven die in Iran after drinking homemade alcohol. *The New York Times,* p. A3.

Erdman, Phyllis & Ng, Kok-Mun (Eds.). (2010). *Attachment: Expanding the cultural connections.* New York, NY: Routledge.

Erdos, Caroline; Genesee, Fred; Savage, Robert & Haigh, Corinne. (2014). Predicting risk for oral and written language learning difficulties in students educated in a second language. *Applied Psycholinguistics, 35*(2), 371–398. doi: 10.1017/S0142716412000422

Erikson, Erik H. (1963). *Childhood and society* (2nd ed.). New York, NY: Norton.

Erikson, Erik H. (1968). *Identity: Youth and crisis.* New York, NY: Norton.

Erikson, Erik H. (1982). *The life cycle completed: A review*. New York, NY: Norton.

Erikson, Erik H. (1994). *Identity: Youth and crisis*. New York, NY: Norton.

Erikson, Erik H. (1998). *The life cycle completed*. New York, NY: Norton.

Erskine, Holly E.; Ferrari, Alize J.; Nelson, Paul; Polanczyk, Guilherme V.; Flaxman, Abraham D.; Vos, Theo, . . . Scott, James G. (2013). Research Review: Epidemiological modelling of Attention-deficit/hyperactivity disorder and conduct disorder for the Global Burden of Disease Study 2010. *Journal of Child Psychology and Psychiatry*, 54(12), 1263–1274. doi: 10.1111/jcpp.12144

Euling, Susan Y.; Herman-Giddens, Marcia E.; Lee, Peter A.; Selevan, Sherry G.; Juul, Anders; Sørensen, Thorkild I. A., . . . Swan, Shanna H. (2008). Examination of US puberty-timing data from 1940 to 1994 for secular trends: Panel findings. *Pediatrics*, 121(Suppl. 3), S172–S191. doi: 10.1542/peds.2007-1813D

Evans, Angela D.; Xu, Fen & Lee, Kang. (2011). When all signs point to you: Lies told in the face of evidence. *Developmental Psychology*, 47(1), 39–49. doi: 10.1037/a0020787

Evans, Gary W. & Kim, Pilyoung. (2013). Childhood poverty, chronic stress, self-regulation, and coping. *Child Development Perspectives*, 7(1), 43–48. doi: 10.1111/cdep.12013

Evans, M. D. R.; Kelley, Jonathan; Sikora, Joanna & Treiman, Donald J. (2010). Family scholarly culture and educational success: Books and schooling in 27 nations. *Research in Social Stratification and Mobility*, 28(2), 171–197. doi: 10.1016/j.rssm.2010.01.002

Eyer, Diane E. (1992). *Mother-infant bonding: A scientific fiction*. New Haven, CT: Yale University Press.

Fairhurst, Merle T.; Löken, Line & Grossmann, Tobias. (2014). Physiological and behavioral responses reveal 9-month-old infants' sensitivity to pleasant touch. *Psychological Science*, 25(5), 1124–1131. doi: 10.1177/0956797614527114

Falconi, A.; Gemmill, A.; Dahl, R. E. & Catalano, R. (2014). Adolescent experience predicts longevity: evidence from historical epidemiology. *Journal of Developmental Origins of Health and Disease*, 5(3), 171–177. doi: 10.1017/S2040174414000105

Fan, Hung; Conner, Ross F. & Villarreal, Luis P. (2014). *AIDS: Science and society* (7th ed.). Burlington, MA: Jones & Bartlett Learning.

Farahani, Mansour; Subramanian, S. V. & Canning, David. (2009). The effect of changes in health sector resources on infant mortality in the short-run and the long-run: A longitudinal econometric analysis. *Social Science & Medicine*, 68(11), 1918–1925. doi: 10.1016/j.socscimed.2009.03.023

Faria, Nuno R.; Rambaut, Andrew; Suchard, Marc A.; Baele, Guy; Bedford, Trevor; Ward, Melissa J., . . . Lemey, Philippe. (2014). The early spread and epidemic ignition of HIV-1 in human populations. *Science*, 346(6205), 56–61. doi: 10.1126/science.1256739

Fauser, B. C. J. M.; Devroey, P.; Diedrich, K.; Balaban, B.; Bonduelle, M.; Delemarre-van de Waal, H. A., . . . Wells, D. (2014). Health outcomes of children born after IVF/ICSI: A review of current expert opinion and literature. *Reproductive BioMedicine Online*, 28(2), 162–182. doi: 10.1016/j.rbmo.2013.10.013

Fazzi, Elisa; Signorini, Sabrina G.; Bomba, Monica; Luparia, Antonella; Lanners, Josée & Balottin, Umberto. (2011). Reach on sound: A key to object permanence in visually impaired children. *Early Human Development*, 87(4), 289–296. doi: 10.1016/j.earlhumdev.2011.01.032

FBI. (2013). *Crime in the United States, 2012*. Clarksburg, WV: U.S. Department of Justice. Federal Bureau of Investigation, Criminal Justice Information Services Division.

Feeley, Nancy; Sherrard, Kathryn; Waitzer, Elana & Boisvert, Linda. (2013). The father at the bedside: Patterns of involvement in the NICU. *Journal of Perinatal & Neonatal Nursing*, 27(1), 72–80. doi: 10.1097/JPN.0b013e31827fb415

Feigenson, Lisa; Libertus, Melissa E. & Halberda, Justin. (2013). Links between the intuitive sense of number and formal mathematics ability. *Child Development Perspectives*, 7(2), 74–79. doi: 10.1111/cdep.12019

Feld, Barry C. (2013). *Kids, cops, and confessions: Inside the interrogation room*. New York, NY: New York University Press.

Feldman, Ruth. (2007). Parent-infant synchrony and the construction of shared timing; Physiological precursors, developmental outcomes, and risk conditions. *Journal of Child Psychology and Psychiatry*, 48(3/4), 329–354. doi: 10.1111/j.1469-7610.2006.01701.x

Feldman, Ruth; Gordon, Ilanit & Zagoory-Sharon, Orna. (2011). Maternal and paternal plasma, salivary, and urinary oxytocin and parent–infant synchrony: Considering stress and affiliation components of human bonding. *Developmental Science*, 14(4), 752–761. doi: 10.1111/j.1467-7687.2010.01021.x

Feldman, Ruth; Weller, Aron; Sirota, Lea & Eidelman, Arthur I. (2002). Skin-to-skin contact (kangaroo care) promotes self-regulation in premature infants: Sleep-wake cyclicity, arousal modulation, and sustained exploration. *Developmental Psychology*, 38(2), 194–207. doi: 10.1037//0012-1649.38.2.194

Feltis, Brooke B.; Powell, Martine B.; Snow, Pamela C. & Hughes-Scholes, Carolyn H. (2010). An examination of the association between interviewer question type and story-grammar detail in child witness interviews about abuse. *Child Abuse & Neglect*, 34(6), 407–413. doi: 10.1016/j.chiabu.2009.09.019

Feng, Xing Lin; Wang, Ying; An, Lin & Ronsmans, Carine. (2014). Cesarean section in the People's Republic of China: Current perspectives. *International Journal of Women's Health*, 6(1), 59–74. doi: 10.2147/IJWH.S41410

Fentiman, Linda C. (2009). Pursuing the perfect mother: Why America's criminalization of maternal substance abuse is not the answer—A comparative legal analysis. *Michigan Journal of Gender & Law*, 15(2).

Ferber, Sari G. & Makhoul, Imad R. (2004). The effect of skin-to-skin contact (kangaroo care) shortly after birth on the neurobehavioral responses of the term newborn: A randomized, controlled trial. *Pediatrics*, 113(4), 858–865. doi: 10.1542/peds.113.4.858

Ferguson, Christopher J. (2013). Spanking, corporal punishment and negative long-term outcomes: A meta-analytic review of longitudinal studies. *Clinical Psychology Review*, 33(1), 196–208. doi: 10.1016/j.cpr.2012.11.002

Ferguson, Christopher J. & Donnellan, M. Brent. (2014). Is the association between children's baby video viewing and poor language development robust? A reanalysis of Zimmerman, Christakis, and Meltzoff (2007). *Developmental Psychology*, 50(1), 129–137. doi: 10.1037/a0033628

Ferguson, Gail M.; Iturbide, Maria I. & Gordon, Beverly P. (2014). Tridimensional (3d) acculturation: Ethnic identity and psychological functioning of tricultural Jamaican immigrants. *International Perspectives in Psychology: Research, Practice, Consultation*, 3(4), 238–251. doi: 10.1037/ipp0000019

Ferguson, Kelly K.; Peterson, Karen E.; Lee, Joyce M.; Mercado-García, Adriana; Blank-Goldenberg, Clara; Téllez-Rojo, Martha M. & Meeker, John D. (2014). Prenatal and peripubertal phthalates and bisphenol A in relation to sex hormones and puberty in boys. *Reproductive Toxicology*, 47, 70–76. doi: 10.1016/j.reprotox.2014.06.002

Fewtrell, Mary; Wilson, David C.; Booth, Ian & Lucas, Alan. (2011). Six months of exclusive breast feeding: How good is the evidence? *BMJ*, 342, c5955. doi: 10.1136/bmj.c5955

Figueiredo, B.; Canário, C. & Field, T. (2014). Breastfeeding is negatively affected by prenatal depression and reduces postpartum depression. *Psychological Medicine*, 44(5), 927–936. doi: 10.1017/S0033291713001530

Fildes, Alison; van Jaarsveld, Cornelia H. M.; Llewellyn, Clare H.; Fisher, Abigail; Cooke, Lucy & Wardle, Jane. (2014). Nature and nurture in children's food preferences. *The American Journal of Clinical Nutrition*, 99(4), 911–917. doi: 10.3945/ajcn.113.077867

Filová, Barbora; Ostatníková, Daniela; Celec, Peter & Hodosy, Július. (2013). The effect of testosterone on the formation of brain structures. *Cells Tissues Organs*, 197(3), 169–177. doi: 10.1159/000345567

Fine, J. S.; Calello, D. P.; Marcus, S. M. & Lowry, J. A. (2012). 2011 Pediatric fatality review of the National Poison Center Database. *Clinical Toxicology*, 50(10), 872–874. doi: 10.3109/15563650.2012.752494

Finer, Lawrence B. & Zolna, Mia R. (2014). Shifts in intended and unintended pregnancies in the United States, 2001–2008. *American Journal of Public Health, 104*(S1), S43–S48. doi: 10.2105/AJPH.2013.301416

Fingerman, Karen L.; Cheng, Yen-Pi; Birditt, Kira & Zarit, Steven. (2012a). Only as happy as the least happy child: Multiple grown children's problems and successes and middle-aged parents' well-being. *The Journals of Gerontology Series B: Psychological Sciences and Social Sciences, 67B*(2), 184–193. doi: 10.1093/geronb/gbr086

Fingerman, Karen L.; Cheng, Yen-Pi; Tighe, Lauren; Birditt, Kira S. & Zarit, Steve. (2012b). Relationships between young adults and their parents. In Alan Booth, et al. (Eds.), *Early adulthood in family context* (pp. 59–85). New York, NY: Springer. doi: 10.1007/978-1-4614-1436-0_5

Fingerman, Karen L. & Furstenberg, Frank F. (2012, May 30). You can go home again. *The New York Times*, p. A29.

Finkelhor, David & Jones, Lisa. (2012). *Have sexual abuse and physical abuse declined since the 1990s?* Durham, NH: Crimes Against Children Research Center, University of New Hampshire.

Finn, Amy S.; Kraft, Matthew A.; West, Martin R.; Leonard, Julia A.; Bish, Crystal E.; Martin, Rebecca E., . . . Gabrieli, John D. E. (2014). Cognitive skills, student achievement tests, and schools. *Psychological Science, 25*(3), 736–744. doi: 10.1177/0956797613516008

Fiset, Sylvain & Plourde, Vickie. (2013). Object permanence in domestic dogs (Canis lupus familiaris) and gray wolves (Canis lupus). *Journal of Comparative Psychology, 127*(2), 115–127. doi: 10.1037/a0030595

Fletcher, Erica N.; Whitaker, Robert C.; Marino, Alexis J. & Anderson, Sarah E. (2014). Screen time at home and school among low-income children attending Head Start. *Child Indicators Research, 7*(2), 421–436. doi: 10.1007/s12187-013-9212-8

Fletcher, Jack M. & Vaughn, Sharon. (2009). Response to intervention: Preventing and remediating academic difficulties. *Child Development Perspectives, 3*(1), 30–37. doi: 10.1111/j.1750-8606.2008.00072.x

Fletcher, Richard; St. George, Jennifer & Freeman, Emily. (2013). Rough and tumble play quality: Theoretical foundations for a new measure of father–child interaction. *Early Child Development and Care, 183*(6), 746–759. doi: 10.1080/03004430.2012.723439

Floris, Dorothea L.; Chura, Lindsay R.; Holt, Rosemary J.; Suckling, John; Bullmore, Edward T.; Baron-Cohen, Simon & Spencer, Michael D. (2013). Psychological correlates of handedness and corpus callosum asymmetry in autism: The left hemisphere dysfunction theory revisited. *Journal of Autism and Developmental Disorders, 4*(8), 1758–1772. doi: 10.1007/s10803-012-1720-8

Flory, Richard W. & Miller, Donald E. (Eds.). (2000). *GenX religion*. New York, NY: Routledge.

Floud, Roderick; Fogel, Robert W.; Harris, Bernard & Hong, Sok Chul. (2011). *The changing body: Health, nutrition, and human development in the western world since 1700.* New York, NY: Cambridge University Press.

Flynn, James R. (1999). Searching for justice: The discovery of IQ gains over time. *American Psychologist, 54*(1), 5–20. doi: 10.1037/0003-066X.54.1.5

Flynn, James R. (2012). *Are we getting smarter?: Rising IQ in the twenty-first century.* New York, NY: Cambridge University Press.

Fogel, Robert W. & Grotte, Nathaniel. (2011). *An overview of the changing body: Health, nutrition, and human development in the western world since 1700.* Cambridge, MA: National Bureau Of Economic Research.

Forbes, Deborah. (2012). The global influence of the Reggio Emilia Inspiration. In Robert Kelly (Ed.), *Educating for creativity: A global conversation* (pp. 161–172). Calgary, Canada: Brush Education.

Forget-Dubois, Nadine; Dionne, Ginette; Lemelin, Jean-Pascal; Pérusse, Daniel; Tremblay, Richard E. & Boivin, Michel. (2009). Early child language mediates the relation between home environment and school readiness. *Child Development, 80*(3), 736–749. doi: 10.1111/j.1467-8624.2009.01294.x

Fortuna, Keren & Roisman, Glenn I. (2008). Insecurity, stress, and symptoms of psychopathology: Contrasting results from self-reports versus interviews of adult attachment. *Attachment & Human Development, 10*(1), 11–28. doi: 10.1080/14616730701868571

Foster, Eugene A.; Jobling, Mark A.; Taylor, P. G.; Donnelly, Peter; de Knijff, Peter; Mieremet, Rene, . . . Tyler-Smith, C. (1998). Jefferson fathered slave's last child. *Nature, 396*(6706), 27–28. doi: 10.1038/23835

Fox, Nathan A.; Henderson, Heather A.; Marshall, Peter J.; Nichols, Kate E. & Ghera, Melissa M. (2005). Behavioral inhibition: Linking biology and behavior within a developmental framework. *Annual Review of Psychology, 56*, 235–262. doi: 10.1146/annurev.psych.55.090902.141532

Fox, Nathan A.; Henderson, Heather A.; Rubin, Kenneth H.; Calkins, Susan D. & Schmidt, Louis A. (2001). Continuity and discontinuity of behavioral inhibition and exuberance: Psychophysiological and behavioral influences across the first four years of life. *Child Development, 72*(1), 1–21. doi: 10.1111/1467-8624.00262

Fox, Nathan A.; Reeb-Sutherland, Bethany C. & Degnan, Kathryn A. (2013). Personality and emotional development. In Philip D. Zelazo (Ed.), *The Oxford handbook of developmental psychology* (Vol. 2, pp. 15–44). New York, NY: Oxford University Press. doi: 10.1093/oxfordhb/9780199958474.013.0002

Fragouli, Elpida & Wells, Dagan. (2011). Aneuploidy in the human blastocyst. *Cytogenetic and Genome Research, 133*(2–4), 149–159. doi: 10.1159/000323500

Franck, Caroline; Budlovsky, Talia; Windle, Sarah B.; Filion, Kristian B. & Eisenberg, Mark J. (2014). Electronic cigarettes in North America: History, use, and implications for smoking cessation. *Circulation, 129*(19), 1945–1952. doi: 10.1161/CIRCULATIONAHA.113.006416

Frankenburg, William K.; Dodds, Josiah; Archer, Philip; Shapiro, Howard & Bresnick, Beverly. (1992). The Denver II: A major revision and restandardization of the Denver Developmental Screening Test. *Pediatrics, 89*(1), 91–97.

Franklin, Sarah. (2013). *Biological relatives: IVF, stem cells, and the future of kinship.* Durham, NC: Duke University Press.

Frayling, Timothy M.; Timpson, Nicholas J.; Weedon, Michael N.; Zeggini, Eleftheria; Freathy, Rachel M.; Lindgren, Cecilia M., . . . McCarthy, Mark I. (2007). A common variant in the FTO gene is associated with body mass index and predisposes to childhood and adult obesity. *Science, 316*(5826), 889–894. doi: 10.1126/science.1141634

Frazier, A. Lindsay; Camargo, Carlos A.; Malspeis, Susan; Willett, Walter C. & Young, Michael C. (2014). Prospective study of peripregnancy consumption of peanuts or tree nuts by mothers and the risk of peanut or tree nut allergy in their offspring. *JAMA Pediatrics, 168*(2), 156–162. doi: 10.1001/jamapediatrics.2013.4139

Frazier, Thomas W.; Keshavan, Matcheri S.; Minshew, Nancy J. & Hardan, Antonio Y. (2012). A two-year longitudinal MRI study of the corpus callosum in autism. *Journal of Autism and Developmental Disorders, 42*(11), 2312–2322. doi: 10.1007/s10803-012-1478-z

Fredricks, Jennifer A. & Eccles, Jacquelynne S. (2002). Children's competence and value beliefs from childhood through adolescence: Growth trajectories in two male-sex-typed domains. *Developmental Psychology, 38*(4), 519–533. doi: 10.1037/0012-1649.38.4.519

Freeman, Joan. (2010). *Gifted lives: What happens when gifted children grow up?* New York, NY: Routledge.

Frenda, Steven J.; Nichols, Rebecca M. & Loftus, Elizabeth F. (2011). Current issues and advances in misinformation research. *Current Directions in Psychological Science, 20*(1), 20–23. doi: 10.1177/0963721410396620

Freud, Anna. (2000). Adolescence. In James B. McCarthy (Ed.), *Adolescent development and psychopathology* (pp. 29–52). Lanham, MD: University Press of America.

Freud, Anna & Burlingham, Dorothy T. (1943). *War and children.* New York, NY: Medical War Books.

Freud, Sigmund. (1935). *A general introduction to psychoanalysis.* New York, NY: Liveright.

Freud, Sigmund. (1938). *The basic writings of Sigmund Freud.* New York, NY: Modern Library.

Freud, Sigmund. (1989). *Introductory lectures on psycho-analysis.* New York, NY: Liveright.

Freud, Sigmund. (1995). *The basic writings of Sigmund Freud.* New York, NY: Modern Library.

Freud, Sigmund. (2001). An outline of psychoanalysis. *The standard edition of the complete*

psychological works of Sigmund Freud (Vol. 23). London, UK: Vintage.

Frey, Andy J.; Mandlawitz, Myrna & Alvarez, Michelle. (2012). Leaving NCLB behind. *Children and Schools, 34*(2), 67–69. doi: 10.1093/cs/cds021

Friend, Stephen H. & Schadt, Eric E. (2014). Clues from the resilient. *Science, 344*(6187), 970–972. doi: 10.1126/science.1255648

Fries, Alison B. Wismer & Pollak, Seth D. (2007). Emotion processing and the developing brain. In Donna Coch, et al. (Eds.), *Human behavior, learning, and the developing brain: Atypical development* (pp. 329–361). New York, NY: Guilford Press.

Froiland, John M. & Davison, Mark L. (2014). Parental expectations and school relationships as contributors to adolescents' positive outcomes. *Social Psychology of Education, 17*(1), 1–17. doi: 10.1007/s11218-013-9237-3

Fry, Douglas P. (2014). Environment of evolutionary adaptedness, rough-and-tumble play, and the selection of restraint in human aggression. In Darcia Narvaez, et al. (Eds.), *Ancestral landscapes in human evolution: Culture, childrearing and social wellbeing* (pp. 169–188). New York, NY: Oxford University Press.

Fuligni, Allison Sidle; Howes, Carollee; Huang, Yiching; Hong, Sandra Soliday & Lara-Cinisomo, Sandraluz. (2012). Activity settings and daily routines in preschool classrooms: Diverse experiences in early learning settings for low-income children. *Early Childhood Research Quarterly, 27*(2), 198–209. doi: 10.1016/j.ecresq.2011.10.001

Fuller, Bruce & García Coll, Cynthia. (2010). Learning from Latinos: Contexts, families, and child development in motion. *Developmental Psychology, 46*(3), 559–565. doi: 10.1037/a0019412

Furey, Terrence S. & Sethupathy, Praveen. (2013). Genetics driving epigenetics. *Science, 342*(6159), 705–706. doi: 10.1126/science.1246755

Furlan, Sarah; Agnoli, Franca & Reyna, Valerie F. (2013). Children's competence or adults' incompetence: Different developmental trajectories in different tasks. *Developmental Psychology, 49*(8), 1466–1480. doi: 10.1037/a0030509

Furstenberg, Frank F. (2010). On a new schedule: Transitions to adulthood and family change. *Future of Children, 20*(1), 67–87. doi: 10.1353/foc.0.0038

Furukawa, Emi; Tangney, June & Higashibara, Fumiko. (2012). Cross-cultural continuities and discontinuities in shame, guilt, and pride: A study of children residing in Japan, Korea and the USA. *Self and Identity, 11*(1), 90–113. doi: 10.1080/15298868.2010.512748

Fusaro, Maria & Harris, Paul L. (2013). Dax gets the nod: Toddlers detect and use social cues to evaluate testimony. *Developmental Psychology, 49*(3), 514–522. doi: 10.1037/a0030580

Gabrieli, John D. E. (2009). Dyslexia: A new synergy between education and cognitive neuroscience. *Science, 325*(5938), 280–283. doi: 10.1126/science.1171999

Galván, Adriana. (2013). The teenage brain: Sensitivity to rewards. *Current Directions in Psychological Science, 22*(2), 88–93. doi: 10.1177/0963721413480859

Galvao, Tais F.; Silva, Marcus T.; Zimmermann, Ivan R.; Souza, Kathiaja M.; Martins, Silvia S. & Pereira, Mauricio G. (2014). Pubertal timing in girls and depression: A systematic review. *Journal of Affective Disorders, 155*, 13–19. doi: 10.1016/j.jad.2013.10.034

Gambaro, Ludovica; Stewart, Kitty & Waldfogel, Jane (Eds.). (2014). *An equal start?: Providing quality early education and care for disadvantaged children.* Chicago, IL: Policy Press.

Ganapathy, Thilagavathy. (2014). Couvade syndrome among 1st time expectant fathers. *Muller Journal of Medical Science Research, 5*(1), 43–47. doi: 10.4103/0975-9727.128944

Gandara, Patricia & Rumberger, Russell W. (2009). Immigration, language, and education: How does language policy structure opportunity? *Teachers College Record, 111*(3), 750–782.

Gandini, Leila; Hill, Lynn; Cadwell, Louise & Schwall, Charles (Eds.). (2005). *In the spirit of the studio: Learning from the atelier of Reggio Emilia.* New York, NY: Teachers College Press.

Gangestad, Steven W. & Simpson, Jeffry A. (Eds.). (2007). *The evolution of mind: Fundamental questions and controversies.* New York, NY: Guilford Press.

Ganong, Lawrence H.; Coleman, Marilyn & Jamison, Tyler. (2011). Patterns of stepchild–stepparent relationship development. *Journal of Marriage and Family, 73*(2), 396–413. doi: 10.1111/j.1741-3737.2010.00814.x

García Coll, Cynthia T. & Marks, Amy K. (2012). *The immigrant paradox in children and adolescents: Is becoming American a developmental risk?* Washington, DC: American Psychological Association.

García, Fernando & Gracia, Enrique. (2009). Is always authoritative the optimum parenting style? Evidence from Spanish families. *Adolescence, 44*(173), 101–131.

Gardner, Howard. (1983). *Frames of mind: The theory of multiple intelligences.* New York, NY: Basic Books.

Gardner, Howard. (1999). Are there additional intelligences? The case for naturalist, spiritual, and existential intelligences. In Jeffrey Kane (Ed.), *Education, information and transformation: Essays on learning and thinking* (pp. 111–131). Upper Saddle River, NJ: Merrill.

Gardner, Howard. (2006). *Multiple intelligences: New horizons in theory and practice.* New York, NY: Basic Books.

Gardner, Howard & Moran, Seana. (2006). The science of multiple intelligences theory: A response to Lynn Waterhouse. *Educational Psychologist, 41*(4), 227–232. doi: 10.1207/s15326985ep4104_2

Gardner, Paula & Hudson, Bettie L. (1996). *Advance report of final mortality statistics, 1993.* Hyattsville, MD: National Center for Health Statistics, 44(7, Suppl.).

Gathwala, Geeta; Singh, Bir & Singh, Jagjit. (2010). Effect of Kangaroo Mother Care on physical growth, breastfeeding and its acceptability. *Tropical Doctor, 40*(4), 199–202. doi: 10.1258/td.2010.090513

Gauvain, Mary; Beebe, Heidi & Zhao, Shuheng. (2011). Applying the cultural approach to cognitive development. *Journal of Cognition and Development, 12*(2), 121–133. doi: 10.1080/15248372.2011.563481

Ge, Xiaojia & Natsuaki, Misaki N. (2009). In search of explanations for early pubertal timing effects on developmental psychopathology. *Current Directions in Psychological Science, 18*(6), 327–331. doi: 10.1111/j.1467-8721.2009.01661.x

Gendron, Brian P.; Williams, Kirk R. & Guerra, Nancy G. (2011). An analysis of bullying among students within schools: Estimating the effects of individual normative beliefs, self-esteem, and school climate. *Journal of School Violence, 10*(2), 150–164. doi: 10.1080/15388220.2010.539166

Genesee, Fred. (2008). Early dual language learning. *Zero to Three, 29*(1), 17–23.

Gentile, Douglas A. (2009). Pathological video-game use among youth ages 8 to 18: A national study. *Psychological Science, 20*(5), 594–602. doi: 10.1111/j.1467-9280.2009.02340.x

Gentile, Douglas A. (2011). The multiple dimensions of video game effects. *Child Development Perspectives, 5*(2), 75–81. doi: 10.1111/j.1750-8606.2011.00159.x

Georgas, James; Berry, John W.; van de Vijver, Fons J. R.; Kagitçibasi, Çigdem & Poortinga, Ype H. (Eds.). (2006). *Families across cultures: A 30-nation psychological study.* New York, NY: Cambridge University Press.

Georgeson, Jan & Payler, Jane (Eds.). (2013). *International perspectives on early childhood education and care.* New York, NY: Open University Press.

Geraerts, Elke; Lindsay, D. Stephen; Merckelbach, Harald; Jelicic, Marko; Raymaekers, Linsey; Arnold, Michelle M. & Schooler, Jonathan W. (2009). Cognitive mechanisms underlying recovered-memory experiences of childhood sexual abuse. *Psychological Science, 20*(1), 92–98. doi: 10.1111/j.1467-9280.2008.02247.x

Gershoff, Elizabeth T. (2013). Spanking and child development: We know enough now to stop hitting our children. *Child Development Perspectives, 7*(3), 133–137. doi: 10.1111/cdep.12038

Gervais, Will M. & Norenzayan, Ara. (2012). Analytic thinking promotes religious disbelief. *Science, 336*(6080), 493–496. doi: 10.1126/science.1215647

Gettler, Lee T. & McKenna, James J. (2010). Never sleep with baby? Or keep me close but keep me safe: Eliminating inappropriate safe infant sleep rhetoric in the United States. *Current Pediatric Reviews*, 6(1), 71–77. doi: 10.2174/157339610791317250

Gewertz, Catherine. (2014, August 19). Support slipping for common core, especially among teachers, poll finds [Web log post]. Education week: Curriculum matters. Retrieved from http://blogs.edweek.org/edweek/curriculum/2014/08/education_next_poll_shows_comm.html

Giardino, Angelo P. & Alexander, Randell. (2005). *Child maltreatment: A clinical guide and reference* (3rd ed.). St. Louis, MO: G. W. Medical.

Giblin, Chris. (2014). Travis Pastrana makes comeback for Red Bull's inaugural straight rhythm competition. *Men's Fitness*.

Gibson, Eleanor J. (1969). *Principles of perceptual learning and development*. New York, NY: Appleton-Century-Crofts.

Gibson, Eleanor J. (1988). Exploratory behavior in the development of perceiving, acting, and the acquiring of knowledge. *Annual Review of Psychology*, 39, 1–42. doi: 10.1146/annurev.ps.39.020188.000245

Gibson, Eleanor J. (1997). An ecological psychologist's prolegomena for perceptual development: A functional approach. In Cathy Dent-Read & Patricia Zukow-Goldring (Eds.), *Evolving explanations of development: Ecological approaches to organism-environment systems* (1st ed., pp. 23–54). Washington, DC: American Psychological Association.

Gibson, Eleanor J. & Walk, Richard D. (1960). The "visual cliff". *Scientific American*, 202(4), 64–71. doi: 10.1038/scientificamerican0460-64

Gibson, James J. (1979). *The ecological approach to visual perception*. Boston, MA: Houghton Mifflin.

Gibson-Davis, Christina & Rackin, Heather. (2014). Marriage or carriage? Trends in union context and birth type by education. *Journal of Marriage and Family*, 76(3), 506–519. doi: 10.1111/jomf.12109

Giles, Amy & Rovee-Collier, Carolyn. (2011). Infant long-term memory for associations formed during mere exposure. *Infant Behavior and Development*, 34(2), 327–338. doi: 10.1016/j.infbeh.2011.02.004

Gilles, Floyd H. & Nelson, Marvin D. (2012). *The developing human brain: Growth and adversities*. London, UK: Mac Keith Press.

Gillespie, Michael A. (2010). Players and spectators: Sports and ethical training in the American university. In Elizabeth Kiss & J. Peter Euben (Eds.), *Debating moral education: Rethinking the role of the modern university* (pp. 293–316). Durham, NC: Duke University Press.

Gilliam, Mary; Stockman, Michael; Malek, Meaghan; Sharp, Wendy; Greenstein, Deanna; Lalonde, Francois, . . . Shaw, Philip. (2011). Developmental trajectories of the corpus callosum in Attention-deficit/hyperactivity

disorder. *Biological Psychiatry*, 69(9), 839–846. doi: 10.1016/j.biopsych.2010.11.024

Gilligan, Carol. (1982). *In a different voice: Psychological theory and women's development*. Cambridge, MA: Harvard University Press.

Gillis, John R. (2008). The islanding of children: Reshaping the mythical landscapes of childhood. In Marta Gutman & Ning de Coninck-Smith (Eds.), *Designing modern childhoods: History, space, and the material culture of children* (pp. 316–329). New Brunswick, NJ: Rutgers University Press.

Gilroy, Paul. (2000). *Against race: Imagining political culture beyond the color line*. Cambridge, MA: Belknap Press of Harvard University Press.

Giovino, Gary A.; Mirza, Sara A.; Samet, Jonathan M.; Gupta, Prakash C.; Jarvis, Martin J.; Bhala, Neeraj, . . . Asma, Samira. (2012). Tobacco use in 3 billion individuals from 16 countries: An analysis of nationally representative cross-sectional household surveys. *The Lancet*, 380(9842), 668–679. doi: 10.1016/S0140-6736(12)61085-X

Giuffrè, Mario; Piro, Ettore & Corsello, Giovanni. (2012). Prematurity and twinning. *Journal of Maternal-Fetal and Neonatal Medicine*, 25(3), 6–10. doi: 10.3109/14767058.2012.712350

Gjerdingen, Dwenda; McGovern, Patricia; Attanasio, Laura; Johnson, Pamela Jo & Kozhimannil, Katy B. (2014). Maternal depressive symptoms, employment, and social support. *Journal of the American Board of Family Medicine*, 27(1), 87–96. doi: 10.3122/jabfm.2014.01.130126

Glenberg, Arthur M.; Witt, Jessica K. & Metcalfe, Janet. (2013). From the revolution to embodiment: 25 years of cognitive psychology. *Perspectives on Psychological Science*, 8(5), 573–585. doi: 10.1177/1745691613498098

Gluckman, Peter D. & Hanson, Mark A. (2006). *Developmental origins of health and disease*. New York, NY: Cambridge University Press.

Göbel, Silke M.; Shaki, Samuel & Fischer, Martin H. (2011). The cultural number line: A review of cultural and linguistic influences on the development of number processing. *Journal of Cross-Cultural Psychology*, 42(4), 543–565. doi: 10.1177/0022022111406251

Goddings, Anne-Lise & Giedd, Jay N. (2014). Structural brain development during childhood and adolescence. In Michael S. Gazzaniga & George R. Mangun (Eds.), *The cognitive neurosciences* (5th ed., pp. 15–22). Cambridge, MA: The MIT Press.

Goddings, Anne-Lise; Heyes, Stephanie Burnett; Bird, Geoffrey; Viner, Russell M. & Blakemore, Sarah-Jayne. (2012). The relationship between puberty and social emotion processing. *Developmental Science*, 15(6), 801–811. doi: 10.1111/j.1467-7687.2012.01174.x

Godinet, Meripa T.; Li, Fenfang & Berg, Teresa. (2014). Early childhood maltreatment and trajectories of behavioral problems: Exploring gender and racial differences. *Child Abuse & Neglect*, 38(3), 544–556. doi: 10.1016/j.chiabu.2013.07.018

Godlike Productions. (2012). Lawns: Wasteful, unquestioned totems of conformity [Web log post]. Retrieved from http://www.godlikeproductions.com/forum1/message1925689/pg1

Gogtay, Nitin; Giedd, Jay N.; Lusk, Leslie; Hayashi, Kiralee M.; Greenstein, Deanna; Vaituzis, A. Catherine, . . . Ungerleider, Leslie G. (2004). Dynamic mapping of human cortical development during childhood through early adulthood. *Proceedings of the National Academy of Sciences of the United States of America*, 10(21), 8174–8179. doi: 10.1073/pnas.0402680101

Golden, Neville H.; Yang, Wei; Jacobson, Marc S.; Robinson, Thomas N. & Shaw, Gary M. (2012). Expected body weight in adolescents: Comparison between weight-for-stature and BMI methods. *Pediatrics*, 130(6), e1607–e1613. doi: 10.1542/peds.2012-0897

Goldfarb, Sally F. (2014). Who pays for the 'boomerang generation'?: A legal perspective on financial support for young adults. *Harvard Journal of Law and Gender*, 37, 46–106.

Goldin-Meadow, Susan & Alibali, Martha W. (2013). Gesture's role in speaking, learning, and creating language. *Annual Review of Psychology*, 64, 257–283. doi: 10.1146/annurev-psych-113011-143802

Goldstein, Michael H.; Schwade, Jennifer A. & Bornstein, Marc H. (2009). The value of vocalizing: Five-month-old infants associate their own noncry vocalizations with responses from caregivers. *Child Development*, 80(3), 636–644. doi: 10.1111/j.1467-8624.2009.01287.x

Golinkoff, Roberta M. & Hirsh-Pasek, Kathy. (2008). How toddlers begin to learn verbs. *Trends in Cognitive Sciences*, 12(10), 397–403. doi: 10.1016/j.tics.2008.07.003

Göncü, Artin & Gaskins, Suzanne. (2011). Comparing and extending Piaget's and Vygotsky's understandings of play: Symbolic play as individual, sociocultural, and educational interpretation. In Anthony D. Pellegrini (Ed.), *The Oxford handbook of the development of play* (pp. 48–57). New York, NY: Oxford University Press.

Gonzalez-Gomez, Nayeli; Hayashi, Akiko; Tsuji, Sho; Mazuka, Reiko & Nazzi, Thierry. (2014). The role of the input on the development of the LC bias: A crosslinguistic comparison. *Cognition*, 132(3), 301–311. doi: 10.1016/j.cognition.2014.04.004

Goodlad, James K.; Marcus, David K. & Fulton, Jessica J. (2013). Lead and Attention-deficit/hyperactivity disorder (ADHD) symptoms: A meta-analysis. *Clinical Psychology Review*, 33(3), 417–425. doi: 10.1016/j.cpr.2013.01.009

Goodman, Judith C.; Dale, Philip S. & Li, Ping. (2008). Does frequency count? Parental input and the acquisition of vocabulary. *Journal of Child Language*, 35(3), 515–531. doi: 10.1017/S0305000907008641

Goodman, J. David. (2012, November 29). Photo of officer giving boots to barefoot man warms hearts online. *The New York Times*, p. A22.

Goodman, Sherryl H. & Gotlib, Ian H. (Eds.). (2002). *Children of depressed parents: Mechanisms of risk and implications for treatment*. Washington, DC: American Psychological Association.

Gopnik, Alison. (2001). Theories, language, and culture: Whorf without wincing. In Melissa Bowerman & Stephen C. Levinson (Eds.), *Language acquisition and conceptual development* (pp. 45–69). New York, NY: Cambridge University Press.

Gopnik, Alison. (2012). Scientific thinking in young children: Theoretical advances, empirical research, and policy implications. *Science, 337*(6102), 1623–1627. doi: 10.1126/science.1223416

Gosso, Yumi. (2010). Play in different cultures. In Peter K. Smith (Ed.), *Children and play: Understanding children's worlds* (pp. 80–98). Malden, MA: Wiley-Blackwell.

Gottesman, Irving I.; Laursen, Thomas Munk; Bertelsen, Aksel & Mortensen, Preben Bo. (2010). Severe mental disorders in offspring with 2 psychiatrically ill parents. *Archives of General Psychiatry, 67*(3), 252–257. doi: 10.1001/archgenpsychiatry.2010.1

Gottfried, Adele E.; Marcoulides, George A.; Gottfried, Allen W. & Oliver, Pamella H. (2009). A latent curve model of parental motivational practices and developmental decline in math and science academic intrinsic motivation. *Journal of Educational Psychology, 101*(3), 729–739. doi: 10.1037/a0015084

Gottlieb, Alma. (2000). Luring your child into this life: A Beng path for infant care. In Judy S. DeLoache & Alma Gottlieb (Eds.), *A world of babies: Imagined childcare guides for seven societies* (pp. 55–90). New York, NY: Cambridge University Press.

Gough, Ethan K.; Moodie, Erica E. M.; Prendergast, Andrew J.; Johnson, Sarasa M. A.; Humphrey, Jean H.; Stoltzfus, Rebecca J., . . . Manges, Amee R. (2014). The impact of antibiotics on growth in children in low and middle income countries: Systematic review and meta-analysis of randomised controlled trials. *BMJ, 348*, g2267. doi: 10.1136/bmj.g2267

Graber, Julia A.; Nichols, Tracy R. & Brooks-Gunn, Jeanne. (2010). Putting pubertal timing in developmental context: Implications for prevention. *Developmental Psychobiology, 52*(3), 254–262. doi: 10.1002/dev.20438

Grady, Jessica S.; Ale, Chelsea M. & Morris, Tracy L. (2012). A naturalistic observation of social behaviours during preschool drop-off. *Early Child Development and Care, 182*(12), 1683–1694. doi: 10.1080/03004430.2011.649266

Grady, Rosheen; Alavi, Nika; Vale, Rachel; Khandwala, Mohammad & McDonald, Sarah D. (2012). Elective single embryo transfer and perinatal outcomes: A systematic review and meta-analysis. *Fertility and Sterility, 97*(2), 324–331. doi: 10.1016/j.fertnstert.2011.11.033

Graignic-Philippe, R.; Dayan, J.; Chokron, S.; Jacquet, A-Y. & Tordjman, S. (2014). Effects of prenatal stress on fetal and child development: A critical literature review. *Neuroscience & Biobehavioral Reviews, 43*(5), 137–162. doi: 10.1016/j.neubiorev.2014.03.022

Grant, Kristen; Goldizen, Fiona C.; Sly, Peter D.; Brune, Marie-Noel; Neira, Maria; van den Berg, Martin & Norman, Rosana E. (2013). Health consequences of exposure to e-waste: A systematic review. *The Lancet Global Health, 1*(6), e350–e361. doi: 10.1016/S2214-109X(13)70101-3

Grayson, David S.; Ray, Siddharth; Carpenter, Samuel; Iyer, Swathi; Dias, Taciana G. Costa; Stevens, Corinne, . . . Fair, Damien A. (2014). Structural and functional rich club organization of the brain in children and adults. *PLoS ONE, 9*(2), e88297. doi: 10.1371/journal.pone.0088297

Green, James A.; Whitney, Pamela G. & Potegal, Michael. (2011). Screaming, yelling, whining, and crying: Categorical and intensity differences in vocal expressions of anger and sadness in children's tantrums. *Emotion, 11*(5), 1124–1133. doi: 10.1037/a0024173

Greene, Melissa L. & Way, Niobe. (2005). Self-esteem trajectories among ethnic minority adolescents: A growth curve analysis of the patterns and predictors of change. *Journal of Research on Adolescence, 15*(2), 151–178. doi: 10.1111/j.1532-7795.2005.00090.x

Greenfield, Patricia M. (2009). Technology and informal education: What is taught, what is learned. *Science, 323*(5910), 69–71. doi: 10.1126/science.1167190

Greenough, William T.; Black, James E. & Wallace, Christopher S. (1987). Experience and brain development. *Child Development, 58*(3), 539–559. doi: 10.1111/j.1467-8624.1987.tb01400.x

Greenough, William T. & Volkmar, Fred R. (1973). Pattern of dendritic branching in occipital cortex of rats reared in complex environments. *Experimental Neurology, 40*(2), 491–504. doi: 10.1016/0014-4886(73)90090-3

Gregg, Christopher. (2010). Parental control over the brain. *Science, 330*(6005), 770–771. doi: 10.1126/science.1199054

Gregg, Norman McAlister. (1941). Congenital cataract following German measles in the mother. *Transactions of the Ophthalmological Society of Australia, 3*, 35–46.

Griffin, James; Gooding, Sarah; Semesky, Michael; Farmer, Brittany; Mannchen, Garrett & Sinnott, Jan D. (2009). Four brief studies of relations between postformal thought and non-cognitive factors: Personality, concepts of god, political opinions, and social attitudes. *Journal of Adult Development, 16*(3), 173–182. doi: 10.1007/s10804-009-9056-0

Grigsby, Timothy J. H.; Forster, Myriam; Soto, Daniel W.; Baezconde-Garbanati, Lourdes & Unger, Jennifer B. (2014). Problematic substance use among Hispanic adolescents and young adults: Implications for prevention efforts. *Substance Use & Misuse, 49*(8), 1025–1038. doi: 10.3109/10826084.2013.852585

Grobman, Kevin H. (2008). Learning & teaching developmental psychology: Attachment theory, infancy, & infant memory development. http://www.devpsy.org/questions/attachment_theory_memory.html

Gross, James J. (Ed.). (2014). *Handbook of emotion regulation* (2nd ed.). New York, NY: Guilford Press.

Grossmann, Klaus E.; Bretherton, Inge; Waters, Everett & Grossmann, Karin (Eds.). (2014). *Mary Ainsworth's enduring influence on attachment theory, research, and clinical applications*. New York, NY: Routledge.

Grossmann, Tobias. (2013). Mapping prefrontal cortex functions in human infancy. *Infancy, 18*(3), 303–324. doi: 10.1111/infa.12016

Grotevant, Harold D. & McDermott, Jennifer M. (2014). Adoption: Biological and social processes linked to adaptation. *Annual Review of Psychology, 65*, 235–265. doi: 10.1146/annurev-psych-010213-115020

Guerra, Nancy G. & Williams, Kirk R. (2010). Implementing bullying prevention in diverse settings: Geographic, economic, and cultural influences. In Eric M. Vernberg & Bridget K. Biggs (Eds.), *Preventing and treating bullying and victimization* (pp. 319–336). New York, NY: Oxford University Press.

Guerra, Nancy G.; Williams, Kirk R. & Sadek, Shelly. (2011). Understanding bullying and victimization during childhood and adolescence: A mixed methods study. *Child Development, 82*(1), 295–310. doi: 10.1111/j.1467-8624.2010.01556.x

Guerri, Consuelo & Pascual, María. (2010). Mechanisms involved in the neurotoxic, cognitive, and neurobehavioral effects of alcohol consumption during adolescence. *Alcohol, 44*(1), 15–26. doi: 10.1016/j.alcohol.2009.10.003

Guerry, John & Hastings, Paul. (2011). In search of HPA axis dysregulation in child and adolescent depression. *Clinical Child and Family Psychology Review, 14*(2), 135–160. doi: 10.1007/s10567-011-0084-5

Gummerum, Michaela; Keller, Monika; Takezawa, Masanori & Mata, Jutta. (2008). To give or not to give: Children's and adolescents' sharing and moral negotiations in economic decision situations. *Child Development, 79*(3), 562–576. doi: 10.1111/j.1467-8624.2008.01143.x

Guo, Sufang; Padmadas, Sabu S.; Zhao, Fengmin; Brown, James J. & Stones, R. William. (2007). Delivery settings and caesarean section rates in China. *Bulletin of the World Health Organization, 85*(10), 755–762. doi: 10.2471/BLT.06.035808

Gupta, Nidhi; Goel, Kashish; Shah, Priyali & Misra, Anoop. (2012). Childhood obesity in developing countries: Epidemiology, determinants, and prevention. *Endocrine Reviews, 33*(1), 48–70. doi: 10.1210/er.2010-0028

Guzman, Natalie S. de & Nishina, Adrienne. (2014). A longitudinal study of body dissatisfaction and pubertal timing in an ethnically diverse adolescent sample. *Body Image, 11*(1), 68–71. doi: 10.1016/j.bodyim.2013.11.001

Haden, Catherine A. (2010). Talking about science in museums. *Child Development Perspectives*, 4(1), 62–67. doi: 10.1111/j.1750-8606.2009.00119.x

Haidt, Jonathan. (2013). *The righteous mind: Why good people are divided by politics and religion.* New York, NY: Vintage Books.

Hajek, Peter; Etter, Jean-François; Benowitz, Neal; Eissenberg, Thomas & McRobbie, Hayden. (2014). Electronic cigarettes: Review of use, content, safety, effects on smokers and potential for harm and benefit. *Addiction*, 109(11), 1801–1810. doi: 10.1111/add.12659

Halim, May Ling; Ruble, Diane N.; Tamis-LeMonda, Catherine S.; Zosuls, Kristina M.; Lurye, Leah E. & Greulich, Faith K. (2014). Pink frilly dresses and the avoidance of all things "girly": Children's appearance rigidity and cognitive theories of gender development. *Developmental Psychology*, 50(4), 1091–1101. doi: 10.1037/a0034906

Hall, Lynn K. (2008). *Counseling military families: What mental health professionals need to know.* New York, NY: Taylor & Francis.

Hallers-Haalboom, Elizabeth T.; Mesman, Judi; Groeneveld, Marleen G.; Endendijk, Joyce J.; van Berkel, Sheila R.; van der Pol, Lotte D. & Bakermans-Kranenburg, Marian J. (2014). Mothers, fathers, sons and daughters: Parental sensitivity in families with two children. *Journal of Family Psychology*, 28(2), 138–147. doi: 10.1037/a0036004

Hamerton, John L. & Evans, Jane A. (2005). Sex chromosome anomalies. In Merlin G. Butler & F. John Meaney (Eds.), *Genetics of developmental disabilities* (pp. 585–650). Boca Raton, FL: Taylor & Francis.

Hamilton, Alice. (1914). Lead poisoning in the United States. *American Journal of Public Health*, 4(6), 477–480. doi: 10.2105/AJPH.4.6.477-a

Hamilton, Rashea; Sanders, Megan & Anderman, Eric M. (2013). The multiple choices of sex education. *Phi Delta Kappan*, 94(5), 34–39.

Hamlat, Elissa J.; Shapero, Benjamin G.; Hamilton, Jessica L.; Stange, Jonathan P.; Abramson, Lyn Y. & Alloy, Lauren B. (2014a). Pubertal timing, peer victimization, and body esteem differentially predict depressive symptoms in African American and Caucasian girls. *The Journal of Early Adolescence*. doi: 10.1177/0272431614534071

Hamlat, Elissa J.; Stange, Jonathan P.; Abramson, Lyn Y. & Alloy, Lauren B. (2014b). Early pubertal timing as a vulnerability to depression symptoms: Differential effects of race and sex. *Journal of Abnormal Child Psychology*, 42(4), 527–538. doi: 10.1007/s10802-013-9798-9

Hamlin, J. Kiley. (2014). The origins of human morality: Complex socio-moral evaluations by preverbal infants. In Jean Decety & Yves Christen (Eds.), *New frontiers in social neuroscience* (pp. 165–188). New York, NY: Springer. doi: 10.1007/978-3-319-02904-7_10

Hammond, Christopher J.; Andrew, Toby; Mak, Ying Tat & Spector, Tim D. (2004).

A susceptibility locus for myopia in the normal population is linked to the PAX6 gene region on chromosome 11: A genomewide scan of dizygotic twins. *American Journal of Human Genetics*, 75(2), 294–304. doi: 10.1086/423148

Han, Euna; Norton, Edward C. & Powell, Lisa M. (2011). Direct and indirect effects of body weight on adult wages. *Economics & Human Biology*, 9(4), 381–392. doi: 10.1016/j.ehb.2011.07.002

Hanania, Rima. (2010). Two types of perseveration in the dimension change card sort task. *Journal of Experimental Child Psychology*, 107(3), 325–336. doi: 10.1016/j.jecp.2010.05.002

Hane, Amie Ashley; Cheah, Charissa; Rubin, Kenneth H. & Fox, Nathan A. (2008). The role of maternal behavior in the relation between shyness and social reticence in early childhood and social withdrawal in middle childhood. *Social Development*, 17(4), 795–811. doi: 10.1111/j.1467-9507.2008.00481.x

Hanks, Andrew S.; Just, David R. & Wansink, Brian. (2013). Smarter lunchrooms can address new school lunchroom guidelines and childhood obesity. *The Journal of Pediatrics*, 162(4), 867–869. doi: 10.1016/j.jpeds.2012.12.031

Hanson, Jamie L.; Nacewicz, Brendon M.; Sutterer, Matthew J.; Cayo, Amelia A.; Schaefer, Stacey M.; Rudolph, Karen D., . . . Davidson, Richard J. (2014). Behavioral problems after early life stress: Contributions of the hippocampus and amygdala. *Biological Psychiatry*, (In Press). doi: 10.1016/j.biopsych.2014.04.020

Hanushek, Eric A. & Woessmann, Ludger. (2009). Do better schools lead to more growth? Cognitive skills, economic outcomes, and causation. *Journal of Economic Growth*, 17(4), 267–321. doi: 10.1007/s10887-012-9081-x

Hanushek, Eric A. & Woessmann, Ludger. (2010). *The high cost of low educational performance: The long-run economic impact of improving PISA outcomes.* Paris: OECD Publishing. doi: 10.1787/9789264077485-en

Hanushek, Eric A. & Wößmann, Ludger. (2007). *The role of education quality in economic growth.* Washington, DC: World Bank, *World Bank Policy Research Working Paper No. 4122.*

Harden, K. Paige & Tucker-Drob, Elliot M. (2011). Individual differences in the development of sensation seeking and impulsivity during adolescence: Further evidence for a dual systems model. *Developmental Psychology*, 47(3), 739–746. doi: 10.1037/a0023279

Hare, Kelly M. & Cree, Alison. (2010). Incidence, causes and consequences of pregnancy failure in viviparous lizards: Implications for research and conservation settings. *Reproduction, Fertility and Development*, 22(5), 761–770. doi: 10.1071/RD09195

Hargreaves, Andy. (2012). Singapore: The Fourth Way in action? *Educational Research for Policy and Practice*, 11(1), 7–17. doi: 10.1007/s10671-011-9125-6

Harjes, Carlos E.; Rocheford, Torbert R.; Bai, Ling; Brutnell, Thomas P.; Kandianis,

Catherine Bermudez; Sowinski, Stephen G., . . . Buckler, Edward S. (2008). Natural genetic variation in lycopene epsilon cyclase tapped for maize biofortification. *Science*, 319(5861), 330–333. doi: 10.1126/science.1150255

Harkness, Geoff & Khaled, Rana. (2014). Modern traditionalism: Consanguineous marriage in Qatar. *Journal of Marriage & Family*, 76(3), 587–603. doi: 10.1111/jomf.12106

Harkness, Sara. (2014). Is biology destiny for the whole family? Contributions of evolutionary life history and behavior genetics to family theories. *Journal of Family Theory & Review*, 6(1), 31–34. doi: 10.1111/jftr.12032

Harkness, Sara; Super, Charles M. & Mavridis, Caroline J. (2011). Parental ethnotheories about children's socioemotional development. In Xinyin Chen & Kenneth H. Rubin (Eds.), *Socioemotional development in cultural context* (pp. 73–98). New York, NY: Guilford Press.

Harlor, Allen D. Buz & Bower, Charles. (2009). Hearing assessment in infants and children: Recommendations beyond neonatal screening. *Pediatrics*, 124(4), 1252–1263. doi: 10.1542/peds.2009-1997

Harper, Casandra E. & Yeung, Fanny. (2013). Perceptions of institutional commitment to diversity as a predictor of college students' openness to diverse perspectives. *The Review of Higher Education*, 37(1), 25–44. doi: 10.1353/rhe.2013.0065

Harris, Judith R. (1998). *The nurture assumption: Why children turn out the way they do.* New York, NY: Free Press.

Harris, Judith R. (2002). Beyond the nurture assumption: Testing hypotheses about the child's environment. In John G. Borkowski, et al. (Eds.), *Parenting and the child's world: Influences on academic, intellectual, and social-emotional development* (pp. 3–20). Mahwah, NJ: Erlbaum.

Harris, M. A.; Hood, K. K. & Mulvaney, S. A. (2012). Pumpers, skypers, surfers and texters: Technology to improve the management of diabetes in teenagers. *Diabetes, Obesity and Metabolism*, 14(11), 967–972. doi: 10.1111/j.1463-1326.2012.01599.x

Harrison, Denise; Bueno, Mariana; Yamada, Janet; Adams-Webber, Thomasin & Stevens, Bonnie. (2010). Analgesic effects of sweet-tasting solutions for infants: Current state of equipoise. *Pediatrics*, 126(5), 894–902. doi: 10.1542/peds.2010-1593

Harrison, Kristen; Bost, Kelly K.; McBride, Brent A.; Donovan, Sharon M.; Grigsby-Toussaint, Diana S.; Kim, Juhee, . . . Jacobsohn, Gwen Costa. (2011). Toward a developmental conceptualization of contributors to overweight and obesity in childhood: The Six-Cs model. *Child Development Perspectives*, 5(1), 50–58. doi: 10.1111/j.1750-8606.2010.00150.x

Harrison, Linda J.; Elwick, Sheena; Vallotton, Claire D. & Kappler, Gregor. (2014). Spending time with others: A time-use diary for infant-toddler child care. In Linda J. Harrison & Jennifer Sumsion (Eds.), *Lived spaces*

of infant-toddler education and care: Exploring diverse perspectives on theory, research and practice (pp. 59–74). Dordrecht, Netherlands: Springer. doi: 10.1007/978-94-017-8838-0_5

Harrist, Amanda W.; Topham, Glade L.; Hubbs-Tait, Laura; Page, Melanie C.; Kennedy, Tay S. & Shriver, Lenka H. (2012). What developmental science can contribute to a transdisciplinary understanding of childhood obesity: An interpersonal and intrapersonal risk model. *Child Development Perspectives*, 6(4), 445–455. doi: 10.1111/cdep.12004

Hart, Betty & Risley, Todd R. (1995). *Meaningful differences in the everyday experience of young American children.* Baltimore, MD: P.H. Brookes.

Hart, Chantelle N.; Cairns, Alyssa & Jelalian, Elissa. (2011). Sleep and obesity in children and adolescents. *Pediatric Clinics of North America*, 58(3), 715–733. doi: 10.1016/j.pcl.2011.03.007

Harter, Susan. (2012). *The construction of the self: Developmental and sociocultural foundations* (2nd ed.). New York, NY: Guilford Press.

Hatch, J. Amos. (2012). From theory to curriculum: Developmental theory and its relationship to curriculum and instruction in early childhood education. In Nancy File, et al. (Eds.), *Curriculum in early childhood education: Re-examined, rediscovered, renewed.* New York, NY: Routledge.

Hatzenbuehler, Mark L. (2014). Structural stigma and the health of lesbian, gay, and bisexual populations. *Current Directions in Psychological Science*, 23(2), 127–132. doi: 10.1177/0963721414523775

Hawthorne, Joanna. (2009). Promoting development of the early parent-infant relationship using the Neonatal Behavioural Assessment Scale. In Jane Barlow & P. O. Svanberg (Eds.), *Keeping the baby in mind: Infant mental health in practice* (pp. 39–51). New York, NY: Routledge.

Hayden, Ceara; Bowler, Jennifer O.; Chambers, Stephanie; Freeman, Ruth; Humphris, Gerald; Richards, Derek & Cecil, Joanne E. (2013). Obesity and dental caries in children: A systematic review and meta-analysis. *Community Dentistry and Oral Epidemiology*, 41(4), 289–308. doi: 10.1111/cdoe.12014

Hayden, Elizabeth P. & Mash, Eric J. (2014). Child psychopathology: A developmental-systems perspective. In Eric J. Mash & Russell A. Barkley (Eds.), *Child psychopathology* (3rd ed., pp. 3–72). New York, NY: Guilford Press.

Haydon, Jo. (2007). *Genetics in practice: A clinical approach for healthcare practitioners.* Hoboken, NJ: Wiley.

Hayes, DeMarquis; Blake, Jamilia J.; Darensbourg, Alicia & Castillo, Linda G. (2014). Examining the academic achievement of Latino adolescents: The role of parent and peer beliefs and behaviors. *The Journal of Early Adolescence.* doi: 10.1177/0272431614530806

Hayes, Peter. (2013). International adoption, "early" puberty, and underrecorded age. *Pediatrics*, 131(6), 1029–1031. doi: 10.1542/peds.2013-0232

Hayes, Rachel A. & Slater, Alan. (2008). Three-month-olds' detection of alliteration in syllables. *Infant Behavior and Development*, 31(1), 153–156. doi: 10.1016/j.infbeh.2007.07.009

Hayne, Harlene & Simcock, Gabrielle. (2009). Memory development in toddlers. In Mary L. Courage & Nelson Cowan (Eds.), *The development of memory in infancy and childhood* (2nd ed., pp. 43–68). New York, NY: Psychology Press.

Haynie, Dana L.; Soller, Brian & Williams, Kristi. (2014). Anticipating early fatality: Friends', schoolmates' and individual perceptions of fatality on adolescent risk behaviors. *Journal of Youth and Adolescence*, 43(2), 175–192. doi: 10.1007/s10964-013-9968-7

Hayslip, Bert; Blumenthal, Heidemarie & Garner, Ashley. (2014). Health and grandparent–grandchild well-being: One-year longitudinal findings for custodial grandfamilies. *Journal of Aging and Health*, 26(4), 559–582. doi: 10.1177/0898264314525664

Hayslip, Bert & Smith, Gregory C. (Eds.). (2013). *Resilient grandparent caregivers: A strengths-based perspective.* New York, NY: Routledge.

Heaton, Tim B. & Darkwah, Akosua. (2011) Religious differences in modernization of the family: Family demographics trends in Ghana. *Journal of Family Issues*, 32(12), 1576–1596. doi: 10.1177/0192513x1398951

Hein, Sascha; Tan, Mei; Aljughaiman, Abdullah & Grigorenko, Elena L. (2014). Characteristics of the home context for the nurturing of gifted children in Saudi Arabia. *High Ability Studies*, 25(1), 23–33. doi: 10.1080/13598139.2014.906970

Hemminki, Kari; Sundquist, Jan & Bermejo, Justo L. (2008). Familial risks for cancer as the basis for evidence-based clinical referral and counseling. *The Oncologist*, 13(3), 239–247. doi: 10.1634/theoncologist.2007-0242

Hendry, Leo B. & Kloep, Marion. (2011). Lifestyles in emerging adulthood: Who Needs stages anyway? In Jeffrey Jensen Arnett, et al. (Eds.), *Debating emerging adulthood: Stage or process?* (pp. 77–104). New York, NY: Oxford University Press. doi: 10.1093/acprof:oso/9780199757176.003.0005

Henry, David B.; Deptula, Daneen P. & Schoeny, Michael E. (2012). Sexually transmitted infections and unintended pregnancy: A longitudinal analysis of risk transmission through friends and attitudes. *Social Development*, 21(1), 195–214. doi: 10.1111/j.1467-9507.2011.00626.x

Henry, P. J. (2011). The role of stigma in understanding ethnicity differences in authoritarianism. *Political Psychology*, 32(3), 419–438. doi: 10.1111/j.1467-9221.2010.00816.x

Herek, Gregory M. (2010). Sexual orientation differences as deficits: Science and stigma in the history of American psychology. *Perspectives on Psychological Science*, 5(6), 693–699. doi: 10.1177/1745691610388770

Herman, Khalisa N.; Paukner, Annika & Suomi, Stephen J. (2011). Gene × environment interactions and social play: Contributions from rhesus macaques. In Anthony D. Pellegrini (Ed.), *The Oxford handbook of the development of play* (pp. 58–69). New York, NY: Oxford University Press. doi: 10.1093/oxfordhb/9780195393002.013.0006

Herman-Giddens, Marcia E. (2013). The enigmatic pursuit of puberty in girls. *Pediatrics*, 132(6), 1125–1126. doi: 10.1542/peds.2013-3058

Herman-Giddens, Marcia E.; Steffes, Jennifer; Harris, Donna; Slora, Eric; Hussey, Michael; Dowshen, Steven A., . . . Reiter, Edward O. (2012). Secondary sexual characteristics in boys: Data from the pediatric research in office settings network. *Pediatrics*, 130(5), e1058–e1068. doi: 10.1542/peds.2011-3291

Herrmann, Esther; Call, Josep; Hernàndez-Lloreda, María Victoria; Hare, Brian & Tomasello, Michael. (2007). Humans have evolved specialized skills of social cognition: The cultural intelligence hypothesis. *Science*, 317(5843), 1360–1366. doi: 10.1126/science.1146282

Herschensohn, Julia R. (2007). *Language development and age.* New York, NY: Cambridge University Press.

Hetherington, E. Mavis. (2006). The influence of conflict, marital problem solving and parenting on children's adjustment in nondivorced, divorced and remarried families. In Alison Clarke-Stewart & Judy Dunn (Eds.), *Families count: Effects on child and adolescent development* (pp. 203–237). New York, NY: Cambridge University Press.

Hewer, Mariko. (2014). Selling sweet nothings: Science shows food marketing's effects on children's minds—and appetites. *Observer*, 27(10).

Hicks, Meredith S.; McRee, Annie-Laurie & Eisenberg, Marla E. (2013). Teens talking with their partners about sex: The role of parent communication. *American Journal of Sexuality Education*, 8(1–2), 1–17. doi: 10.1080/15546128.2013.790219

Higgins, Matt. (2006, August 7). A series of flips creates some serious buzz. *The New York Times*, p. D7.

Hill, Patrick L.; Burrow, Anthony L. & Sumner, Rachel. (2013). Addressing important questions in the field of adolescent purpose. *Child Development Perspectives*, 7(4), 232–236. doi: 10.1111/cdep.12048

Hill, Shirley A. (2007). Transformative processes: Some sociological questions. *Journal of Marriage and Family*, 69(2), 293–298. doi: 10.1111/j.1741-3737.2007.00363.x

Hines, Melissa. (2013). Sex and sex differences. In Philip D. Zelazo (Ed.), *The Oxford handbook of developmental psychology* (Vol. 1, pp. 162–201). New York, NY: Oxford University Press. doi: 10.1093/oxfordhb/9780199958450.013.0007

Hinnant, J. Benjamin; Nelson, Jackie A.; O'Brien, Marion; Keane, Susan P. & Calkins, Susan D. (2013). The interactive roles of parenting, emotion regulation and executive functioning in moral reasoning during middle childhood. *Cognition and Emotion*, 27(8), 1460–1468. doi: 10.1080/02699931.2013.789792

Hipwell, Alison E.; Keenan, Kate; Loeber, Rolf & Battista, Deena. (2010). Early predictors of sexually intimate behaviors in an urban sample of young girls. *Developmental Psychology, 46*(2), 366–378. doi: 10.1037/a0018409

Hirvonen, Riikka; Aunola, Kaisa; Alatupa, Saija; Viljaranta, Jaana & Nurmi, Jari-Erik. (2013). The role of temperament in children's affective and behavioral responses in achievement situations. *Learning and Instruction, 27*, 21–30. doi: 10.1016/j.learninstruc.2013.02.005

Hively, Kimberly & El-Alayli, Amani. (2014). "You throw like a girl:" The effect of stereotype threat on women's athletic performance and gender stereotypes. *Psychology of Sport and Exercise, 15*(1), 48–55. doi: 10.1016/j.psychsport.2013.09.001

Ho, Emily S. (2010). Measuring hand function in the young child. *Journal of Hand Therapy, 23*(3), 323–328. doi: 10.1016/j.jht.2009.11.002

Hoeve, Machteld; Dubas, Judith S.; Gerris, Jan R. M.; van der Laan, Peter H. & Smeenk, Wilma. (2011). Maternal and paternal parenting styles: Unique and combined links to adolescent and early adult delinquency. *Journal of Adolescence, 34*(5), 813–827. doi: 10.1016/j.adolescence.2011.02.004

Hofer, Claire; Eisenberg, Nancy; Spinrad, Tracy L.; Morris, Amanda S.; Gershoff, Elizabeth; Valiente, Carlos, . . . Eggum, Natalie D. (2013). Mother-adolescent conflict: Stability, change, and relations with externalizing and internalizing behavior problems. *Social Development, 22*(2), 259–279. doi: 10.1111/sode.12012

Hoff, Erika. (2013). Interpreting the early language trajectories of children from low-SES and language minority homes: Implications for closing achievement gaps. *Developmental Psychology, 49*(1), 4–14. doi: 10.1037/a0027238

Hoff, Erika; Core, Cynthia; Place, Silvia; Rumiche, Rosario; Señor, Melissa & Parra, Marisol. (2012). Dual language exposure and early bilingual development. *Journal of Child Language, 39*(1), 1–27. doi: 10.1017/S0305000910000759

Hoff, Erika; Rumiche, Rosario; Burridge, Andrea; Ribota, Krystal M. & Welsh, Stephanie N. (2014). Expressive vocabulary development in children from bilingual and monolingual homes: A longitudinal study from two to four years. *Early Childhood Research Quarterly, 29*(4), 433–444. doi: 10.1016/j.ecresq.2014.04.012

Hoffman, Jessica L.; Teale, William H. & Paciga, Kathleen A. (2013). Assessing vocabulary learning in early childhood. *Journal of Early Childhood Literacy.* doi: 10.1177/1468798413501184

Holden, Constance. (2009). Fetal cells again? *Science, 326*(5951), 358–359. doi: 10.1126/science.326_358

Holden, Constance. (2010). Myopia out of control. *Science, 327*(5961), 17. doi: 10.1126/science.327.5961.17-c

Holland, James D. & Klaczynski, Paul A. (2009). Intuitive risk taking during adolescence. *Prevention Researcher, 16*(2), 8–11.

Hollich, George J.; Hirsh-Pasek, Kathy; Golinkoff, Roberta M.; Brand, Rebecca J.; Brown, Ellie; Chung, He Len, . . . Rocroi, Camille. (2000). *Breaking the language barrier: An emergentist coalition model for the origins of word learning.* Malden, MA: Blackwell.

Holmboe, K.; Nemoda, Z.; Fearon, R. M. P.; Sasvari-Szekely, M. & Johnson, M. H. (2011). Dopamine D4 receptor and serotonin transporter gene effects on the longitudinal development of infant temperament. *Genes, Brain and Behavior, 10*(5), 513–522. doi: 10.1111/j.1601-183X.2010.00669.x

Holsti, Liisa; Grunau, Ruth E. & Shany, Eilon. (2011). Assessing pain in preterm infants in the neonatal intensive care unit: Moving to a brain-oriented approach. *Pain Management, 1*(2), 171–179. doi: 10.2217/pmt.10.19

Holtzman, Jennifer. (2009). Simple, effective—and inexpensive—strategies to reduce tooth decay in children. *ICAN: Infant, Child, & Adolescent Nutrition, 1*(4), 225–231. doi: 10.1177/1941406409338861

Hong, David S. & Reiss, Allan L. (2014). Cognitive and neurological aspects of sex chromosome aneuploidies. *The Lancet Neurology, 13*(3), 306–318. doi: 10.1016/S1474-4422(13)70302-8

Hong, Jun Sung; Algood, Carl L.; Chiu, Yu-Ling & Lee, Stephanie Ai-Ping. (2011). An ecological understanding of kinship foster care in the United States. *Journal of Child and Family Studies, 20*(6), 863–872. doi: 10.1007/s10826-011-9454-3

Hong, Jun Sung & Garbarino, James. (2012). Risk and protective factors for homophobic bullying in schools: An application of the social–ecological framework. *Educational Psychology Review, 24*(2), 271–285. doi: 10.1007/s10648-012-9194-y

Hong, Soo-Young; Torquati, Julia & Molfese, Victoria J. (2013). Theory guided professional development in early childhood science education. In Lynn E. Cohen & Sandra Waite-Stupiansky (Eds.), *Learning across the early childhood curriculum* (pp. 1–32). Bingley, UK: Emerald.

Hook, Jennifer L. (2010). Gender inequality in the welfare state: Sex segregation in housework, 1965–2003. *American Journal of Sociology, 115*(5), 1480–1523. doi: 10.1086/651384

Hopkins, J. Roy. (2011). The enduring influence of Jean Piaget. *Observer, 24*(10).

Horowitz, Alice M.; Kleinman, Dushanka V. & Wang, Min Qi. (2013). What Maryland adults with young children know and do about preventing dental caries. *American Journal of Public Health, 103*(6), e69–e76. doi: 10.2105/AJPH.2012.301038

Horton, Megan K.; Kahn, Linda G.; Perera, Frederica; Barr, Dana B. & Rauh, Virginia. (2012). Does the home environment and the sex of the child modify the adverse effects of prenatal exposure to chlorpyrifos on child working memory? *Neurotoxicology and Teratology, 34*(5), 534–541. doi: 10.1016/j.ntt.2012.07.004

Horwitz, Ralph I.; Cullen, Mark R.; Abell, Jill & Christian, Jennifer B. (2013). (De)Personalized medicine. *Science, 339*(6124), 1155–1156. doi: 10.1126/science.1234106

Hougaard, Karin S. & Hansen, Åse M. (2007). Enhancement of developmental toxicity effects of chemicals by gestational stress: A review. *Neurotoxicology and Teratology, 29*(4), 425–445. doi: 10.1016/j.ntt.2007.02.003

Hout, Michael. (2012). Social and economic returns to college education in the United States. *Annual Review of Sociology, 39*, 379–400. doi: 10.1146/annurev.soc.012809.102503

Hout, Michael & Elliott, Stuart W. (Eds.). (2011). *Incentives and test-based accountability in education.* Washington, DC: National Academies Press.

Howard, Elizabeth R.; Páez, Mariela M.; August, Diane L.; Barr, Christopher D.; Kenyon, Dorry & Malabonga, Valerie. (2014). The importance of SES, home and school language and literacy practices, and oral vocabulary in bilingual children's English reading development. *Bilingual Research Journal, 37*(2), 120–141. doi: 10.1080/15235882.2014.934485

Howell, Diane M.; Wysocki, Karen & Steiner, Michael J. (2010). Toilet training. *Pediatrics in Review, 31*(6), 262–263. doi: 10.1542/pir.31-6-262

Hoyert, Donna L.; Kochanek, Kenneth D. & Murphy, Sherry L. (1999). *Deaths: Final data for 1997.* Hyattsville, MD: National Center for Health Statistics, 47(19).

Hoyert, Donna L.; Kung, Hsiang-Ching & Smith, Betty L. (2005). *Deaths: Preliminary data for 2003.* Hyattsville, MD: National Center for Health Statistics, 53(15).

Hoyert, Donna L. & Xu, Jiaquan. (2012). *Deaths: Preliminary data for 2011.* Hyattsville, MD: National Center for Health Statistics, 61(6).

Hrdy, Sarah B. (2009). *Mothers and others: The evolutionary origins of mutual understanding.* Cambridge, MA: Harvard University Press.

Hsia, Yingfen & Maclennan, Karyn. (2009). Rise in psychotropic drug prescribing in children and adolescents during 1992–2001: A population-based study in the UK. *European Journal of Epidemiology, 24*(4), 211–216. doi: 10.1007/s10654-009-9321-3

Huang, Chiungjung. (2010). Mean-level change in self-esteem from childhood through adulthood: Meta-analysis of longitudinal studies. *Review of General Psychology, 14*(3), 251–260. doi: 10.1037/a0020543

Huang, Chien-Chung. (2009). Mothers' reports of nonresident fathers' involvement with their children: Revisiting the relationship between child support payment and visitation. *Family Relations, 58*(1), 54–64. doi: 10.1111/j.1741-3729.2008.00534.x

Hugdahl, Kenneth & Westerhausen, René (Eds.). (2010). *The two halves of the brain:*

Information processing in the cerebral hemispheres. Cambridge, MA: The MIT Press.

Hughes, Julie M. & Bigler, Rebecca S. (2011). Predictors of African American and European American adolescents' endorsement of race-conscious social policies. *Developmental Psychology*, 47(2), 479–492. doi: 10.1037/a0021309

Hughey, Matthew W. & Parks, Gregory. (2014). *The wrongs of the right: Language, race, and the Republican Party in the age of Obama.* New York, NY: New York University Press.

Huh, Susanna Y.; Rifas-Shiman, Sheryl L.; Taveras, Elsie M.; Oken, Emily & Gillman, Matthew W. (2011). Timing of solid food introduction and risk of obesity in preschool-aged children. *Pediatrics*, 127(3), e544–e551. doi: 10.1542/peds.2010-0740

Huh, Susanna Y.; Rifas-Shiman, Sheryl L.; Zera, Chloe A.; Edwards, Janet W. Rich; Oken, Emily; Weiss, Scott T. & Gillman, Matthew W. (2012). Delivery by caesarean section and risk of obesity in preschool age children: A prospective cohort study. *Archives of the Diseases of Childhood*, 97(7), 610–616. doi: 10.1136/archdischild-2011-301141

Hultman, C. M.; Sandin, S.; Levine, S. Z.; Lichtenstein, P. & Reichenberg, A. (2011). Advancing paternal age and risk of autism: New evidence from a population-based study and a meta-analysis of epidemiological studies. *Molecular Psychiatry*, 16(12), 1203–1212. doi: 10.1038/mp.2010.121

Huntsinger, Carol S.; Jose, Paul E.; Krieg, Dana B. & Luo, Zupei. (2011). Cultural differences in Chinese American and European American children's drawing skills over time. *Early Childhood Research Quarterly*, 26(1), 134–145. doi: 10.1016/j.ecresq.2010.04.002

Huston, Aletha C. & Ripke, Marika N. (2006). Middle childhood: Contexts of development. In Aletha C. Huston & Marika N. Ripke (Eds.), *Developmental contexts in middle childhood: Bridges to adolescence and adulthood* (pp. 1–22). New York, NY: Cambridge University Press.

Hutchinson, Esther A.; De Luca, Cinzia R.; Doyle, Lex W.; Roberts, Gehan & Anderson, Peter J. (2013). School-age outcomes of extremely preterm or extremely low birth weight children. *Pediatrics*, 131(4), e1053–e1061. doi: 10.1542/peds.2012-2311

Huver, Rose M. E.; Otten, Roy; de Vries, Hein & Engels, Rutger C. M. E. (2010). Personality and parenting style in parents of adolescents. *Journal of Adolescence*, 33(3), 395–402. doi: 10.1016/j.adolescence.2009.07.012

Huynh, Jimmy L. & Casaccia, Patrizia. (2013). Epigenetic mechanisms in multiple sclerosis: Implications for pathogenesis and treatment. *The Lancet Neurology*, 12(2), 195–206. doi: 10.1016/S1474-4422(12)70309-5

Hyde, Janet S. (2014). Gender similarities and differences. *Annual Review of Psychology*, 65, 373–398. doi: 10.1146/annurev-psych-010213-115057

Hyde, Janet S.; Lindberg, Sara M.; Linn, Marcia C.; Ellis, Amy B. & Williams, Caroline C. (2008). Gender similarities characterize math performance. *Science*, 321(5888), 494–495. doi: 10.1126/science.1160364

Hyslop, Anne. (2014). *The case against exit exams.* Washington DC: New America Education Policy Program.

Iacovidou, Nicoletta; Varsami, Marianna & Syggellou, Angeliki. (2010). Neonatal outcome of preterm delivery. *Annals of the New York Academy of Sciences*, 1205, 130–134. doi: 10.1111/j.1749-6632.2010.05657 x

Iida, Hiroko & Rozier, R. Gary. (2013). Mother-Perceived social capital and children's oral health and use of dental care in the United States. *American Journal of Public Health*, 103(3), 480–487. doi: 10.2105/AJPH.2012.300845

Ikeda, Martin J. (2012). Policy and practice considerations for response to intervention: Reflections and commentary. *Journal of Learning Disabilities*, 45(3), 274–277. doi: 10.1177/0022219412442170

ILO. (2011). Database of conditions of work and employment laws. from International Labour Organization http://www.ilo.org/dyn/travail/travmain.home

Imai, Mutsumi; Kita, Sotaro; Nagumo, Miho & Okada, Hiroyuki. (2008). Sound symbolism facilitates early verb learning. *Cognition*, 109(1), 54–65. doi: 10.1016/j.cognition.2008.07.015

Inan, Hatice Z.; Trundle, Kathy C. & Kantor, Rebecca. (2010). Understanding natural sciences education in a Reggio Emilia-inspired preschool. *Journal of Research in Science Teaching*, 47(10), 1186–1208. doi: 10.1002/tea.20375

Inhelder, Bärbel & Piaget, Jean. (1958). *The growth of logical thinking from childhood to adolescence: An essay on the construction of formal operational structures.* New York, NY: Basic Books.

Inhelder, Bärbel & Piaget, Jean. (1964). *The early growth of logic in the child: Classification and seriation.* New York, NY: Harper & Row.

Inhelder, Bärbel & Piaget, Jean. (2013a). *The early growth of logic in the child: Classification and seriation.* New York, NY: Routledge.

Inhelder, Bärbel & Piaget, Jean. (2013b). *The growth of logical thinking from childhood to adolescence: An essay on the construction of formal operational structures.* New York, NY: Routledge.

Insel, Thomas R. (2014). Mental disorders in childhood: Shifting the focus from behavioral symptoms to neurodevelopmental trajectories. *JAMA*, 311(17), 1727–1728. doi: 10.1001/jama.2014.1193

Institute of Medicine (U.S.). Immunization Safety Review Committee. (2004). *Immunization safety review: Vaccines and autism.* Washington, DC: National Academies Press.

Inzlicht, Michael & Schmader, Toni. (2012). *Stereotype threat: Theory, process, and application.* New York, NY: Oxford University Press.

Irwin, Scott; Galvez, Roberto; Weiler, Ivan Jeanne; Beckel-Mitchener, Andrea & Greenough, William. (2002). Brain structure and the functions of FMR1 protein. In Randi Jenssen Hagerman & Paul J. Hagerman (Eds.), *Fragile X syndrome: Diagnosis, treatment, and research* (3rd ed., pp. 191–205). Baltimore, MD: Johns Hopkins University Press.

Ishii, Nozomi; Kono, Yumi; Yonemoto, Naohiro; Kusuda, Satoshi & Fujimura, Masanori. (2013). Outcomes of infants born at 22 and 23 weeks' gestation. *Pediatrics*, 132(1), 62–71. doi: 10.1542/peds.2012-2857

Ispa, Jean M.; Fine, Mark A.; Halgunseth, Linda C.; Harper, Scott; Robinson, JoAnn; Boyce, Lisa, . . . Brady-Smith, Christy. (2004). Maternal intrusiveness, maternal warmth, and mother-toddler relationship outcomes: Variations across low-income ethnic and acculturation groups. *Child Development*, 75(6), 1613–1631. doi: 10.1111/j.1467-8624.2004.00806.x

Ivcevic, Zorana & Brackett, Marc. (2014). Predicting school success: Comparing conscientiousness, grit, and emotion regulation ability. *Journal of Research in Personality*, 52, 29–36. doi: 10.1016/j.jrp.2014.06.005

Iyengar, Sheena S. & Lepper, Mark R. (2000). When choice is demotivating: Can one desire too much of a good thing? *Journal of Personality and Social Psychology*, 79(6), 995–1006. doi: 10.1037//0022-3514.79.6.995

Izard, Carroll E. (2009). Emotion theory and research: Highlights, unanswered questions, and emerging issues. *Annual Review of Psychology*, 60, 1–25. doi: 10.1146/annurev.psych.60.110707.163539

Jaffe, Arthur C. (2011). Failure to thrive: Current clinical concepts. *Pediatrics in Review*, 32(3), 100–108. doi: 10.1542/pir.32-3-100

Jaffe, Eric. (2004). Mickey Mantle's greatest error: Yankee star's false belief may have cost him years. *Observer*, 17(9), 37.

Jaffee, Sara R.; Caspi, Avshalom; Moffitt, Terrie E.; Polo-Tomás, Monica & Taylor, Alan. (2007). Individual, family, and neighborhood factors distinguish resilient from non-resilient maltreated children: A cumulative stressors model. *Child Abuse & Neglect*, 31(3), 231–253. doi: 10.1016/j.chiabu.2006.03.011

Jambon, Marc & Smetana, Judith G. (2014). Moral complexity in middle childhood: Children's evaluations of necessary harm. *Developmental Psychology*, 50(1), 22–33. doi: 10.1037/a0032992

James, Jenée; Ellis, Bruce J.; Schlomer, Gabriel L. & Garber, Judy. (2012). Sex-specific pathways to early puberty, sexual debut, and sexual risk taking: Tests of an integrated evolutionary–developmental model. *Developmental Psychology*, 48(3), 687–702. doi: 10.1037/a0026427

Jansen, Jarno; Beijers, Roseriet; Riksen-Walraven, Marianne & de Weerth, Carolina. (2010). Cortisol reactivity in young infants. *Psychoneuroendocrinology*, 35(3), 329–338. doi: 10.1016/j.psyneuen.2009.07.008

Jarcho, Johanna M.; Fox, Nathan A.; Pine, Daniel S.; Etkin, Amit; Leibenluft, Ellen; Shechner, Tomer & Ernst, Monique. (2013). The neural correlates of emotion-based cognitive control in adults with early childhood behavioral inhibition. *Biological Psychology*, 92(2), 306–314. doi: 10.1016/j.biopsycho.2012.09.008

Jasny, Barbara R.; Chin, Gilbert; Chong, Lisa & Vignieri, Sacha. (2011). Again, and again, and again... *Science*, 334(6060), 1225. doi: 10.1126/science.334.6060.1225

Jednoróg, Katarzyna; Altarelli, Irene; Monzalvo, Karla; Fluss, Joel; Dubois, Jessica; Billard, Catherine, . . . Ramus, Franck. (2012). The influence of socioeconomic status on children's brain structure. *PLoS ONE*, 7(8), e42486. doi: 10.1371/journal.pone.0042486

Ji, Cheng Ye; Chen, Tian Jiao & Working Group on Obesity in China (WGOC). (2013). Empirical changes in the prevalence of overweight and obesity among Chinese students from 1985 to 2010 and corresponding preventive strategies. *Biomedical and Environmental Sciences*, 26(1), 1–12. doi: 10.3967/0895-3988.2013.01.001

Johnson, Elizabeth K. & Tyler, Michael D. (2010). Testing the limits of statistical learning for word segmentation. *Developmental Science*, 13(2), 339–345. doi: 10.1111/j.1467-7687.2009.00886.x

Johnson, Mark H. (2011). *Developmental cognitive neuroscience: An introduction* (3rd ed.). Malden, MA: Wiley-Blackwell.

Johnson, Mark H. & Fearon, R. M. Pasco. (2011). Commentary: Disengaging the infant mind: Genetic dissociation of attention and cognitive skills in infants—Reflections on Leppänen et al. (2011). *Journal of Child Psychology and Psychiatry*, 52(11), 1153–1154. doi: 10.1111/j.1469-7610.2011.02433.x

Johnson, Monica K.; Sage, Rayna A. & Mortimer, Jeylan T. (2012). Work values, early career difficulties, and the U.S. economic recession. *Social Psychology Quarterly*, 75(3), 242–267. doi: 10.1177/0190272512451754

Johnson, Susan C.; Dweck, Carol S.; Chen, Frances S.; Stern, Hilarie L.; Ok, Su-Jeong & Barth, Maria. (2010). At the intersection of social and cognitive development: Internal working models of attachment in infancy. *Cognitive Science*, 34(5), 807–825. doi: 10.1111/j.1551-6709.2010.01112.x

Johnson, Teddi D. (2011). Report calls for examination of chemical safety: National coalition notes difficulty determining exposures. *The Nation's Health*, 41(6), 9.

Johnston, Lloyd D.; O'Malley, Patrick M.; Bachman, Jerald G. & Schulenberg, John E. (2009). *Monitoring the future, national survey results on drug use, 1975–2008: College students and adults ages 19–50.* Bethesda, MD: National Institute on Drug Abuse.

Johnston, Lloyd D.; O'Malley, Patrick M.; Bachman, Jerald G. & Schulenberg, John E. (2012). *Monitoring the future, national survey results on drug use, 1975–2011, Volume I: Secondary school students.* Ann Arbor, MI: Institute for Social Research, The University of Michigan.

Johnston, Lloyd D.; O'Malley, Patrick M.; Bachman, Jerald G.; Schulenberg, John E. & Miech, Richard A. (2014). *Monitoring the future, national survey results on drug use, 1975–*

2013: Volume 1, Secondary school students. Ann Arbor, MI: Institute for Social Research, The University of Michigan.

Jones, Andrea M. & Morris, Tracy L. (2012). Psychological adjustment of children in foster care: Review and implications for best practice. *Journal of Public Child Welfare*, 6(2), 129–148. doi: 10.1080/15548732.2011.617272

Jones, Mary C. (1965). Psychological correlates of somatic development. *Child Development*, 36(4), 899–911.

Jong, Jyh-Tsorng; Kao, Tsair; Lee, Liang-Yi; Huang, Hung-Hsuan; Lo, Po-Tsung & Wang, Hui-Chung. (2010). Can temperament be understood at birth? The relationship between neonatal pain cry and their temperament: A preliminary study. *Infant Behavior and Development*, 33(3), 266–272. doi: 10.1016/j.infbeh.2010.02.001

Jonsson, Maria; Cnattingius, Sven & Wikström, Anna-Karin. (2013). Elective induction of labor and the risk of cesarean section in low-risk parous women: A cohort study. *Acta Obstetricia et Gynecologica Scandinavica*, 92(2), 198–203. doi: 10.1111/aogs.12043

Jordet, Geir; Hartman, Esther & Vuijk, Pieter J. (2012). Team history and choking under pressure in major soccer penalty shootouts. *British Journal of Psychology*, 103(2), 268–283. doi: 10.1111/j.2044-8295.2011.02071.x

Juan, Shan. (2010, January 14). C-section epidemic hits China: WHO. *China Daily*.

Juang, Linda P.; Syed, Moin & Cookston, Jeffrey T. (2012). Acculturation-based and everyday parent–adolescent conflict among Chinese American adolescents: Longitudinal trajectories and implications for mental health. *Journal of Family Psychology*, 26(6), 916–926. doi: 10.1037/a0030057

Julian, Megan M. (2013). Age at adoption from institutional care as a window into the lasting effects of early experiences. *Clinical Child and Family Psychology Review*, 16(2), 101–145. doi: 10.1007/s10567-013-0130-6

Jung, Rex E. & Ryman, Sephira G. (2013). Imaging creativity. In Kyung Hee Kim, et al. (Eds.), *Creatively gifted students are not like other gifted students: Research, theory, and practice* (pp. 69–87). Rotterdam, The Netherlands: SensePublishers. doi: 10.1007/978-94-6209-149-8_6

Juvonen, Jaana & Graham, Sandra. (2014). Bullying in schools: The power of bullies and the plight of victims. *Annual Review of Psychology*, 65, 159–185. doi: 10.1146/annurev-psych-010213-115030

Juvonen, Jaana; Nishina, Adrienne & Graham, Sandra. (2006). Ethnic diversity and perceptions of safety in urban middle schools. *Psychological Science*, 17(5), 393–400. doi: 10.1111/j.1467-9280.2006.01718.x

Kachel, A. Friederike; Premo, Luke S. & Hublin, Jean-Jacques. (2011). Modeling the effects of weaning age on length of female reproductive period: Implications for the evolution of human life history. *American Journal of Human Biology*, 23(4), 479–487. doi: 10.1002/ajhb.21157

Kagan, Jerome. (2011). Three lessons learned. *Perspectives on Psychological Science*, 6(2), 107–113. doi: 10.1177/1745691611400205

Kahana-Kalman, Ronit & Walker-Andrews, Arlene S. (2001). The role of person familiarity in young infants' perception of emotional expressions. *Child Development*, 72(2), 352–369. doi: 10.1111/1467-8624.00283

Kahneman, Daniel. (2011). *Thinking, fast and slow.* New York, NY: Farrar, Straus and Giroux.

Kail, Robert V. (2013). Influences of credibility of testimony and strength of statistical evidence on children's and adolescents' reasoning. *Journal of Experimental Child Psychology*, 116(3), 747–754. doi: 10.1016/j.jecp.2013.04.004

Kaiser, Jocelyn. (2013). Researchers to explore promise, risks of sequencing newborns' DNA. *Science*, 341(6151), 1163. doi: 10.1126/science.341.6151.1163

Kaiser, Jocelyn. (2014). Gearing up for a closer look at the human placenta. *Science*, 344(6188), 1073. doi: 10.1126/science.344.6188.1073

Kalil, Ariel; Ryan, Rebecca & Chor, Elise. (2014). Time investments in children across family structures. *The ANNALS of the American Academy of Political and Social Science*, 654(1), 50–168. doi: 10.1177/0002716214528276

Kalliala, Marjatta. (2006). *Play culture in a changing world.* Maidenhead, UK: Open University Press.

Kandel, Denise B. (Ed.). (2002). *Stages and pathways of drug involvement: Examining the gateway hypothesis.* New York, NY: Cambridge University Press.

Kang, Hye-Kyung. (2014). Influence of culture and community perceptions on birth and perinatal care of immigrant women: Doulas' perspective. *The Journal of Perinatal Education*, 23(1), 25–32. doi: 10.1891/1058-1243.23.1.25

Kanner, Leo. (1943). Autistic disturbances of affective contact. *Nervous Child*, 2, 217–250.

Kanny, Mary A.; Sax, Linda J. & Riggers-Piehl, Tiffani A. (2014). Investigating forty years of STEM research: How explanations for the gender gap have evolved over time. *Journal of Women and Minorities in Science and Engineering*, 20(2), 127–148. doi: 10.1615/JWomenMinorScienEng.2014007246

Kapp, Steven K.; Gillespie-Lynch, Kristen; Sherman, Lauren E. & Hutman, Ted. (2013). Deficit, difference, or both? Autism and neurodiversity. *Developmental Psychology*, 49(1), 59–71. doi: 10.1037/a0028353

Kara, Siddharth. (2009). *Sex trafficking: Inside the business of modern slavery.* New York, NY: Columbia University Press.

Karama, Sherif; Ad-Dab'bagh, Yasser; Haier, Richard J.; Deary, Ian J.; Lyttelton, Oliver C.; Lepage, Claude & Evans, Alan C. (2009). Positive association between cognitive ability and cortical thickness in a representative US sample of healthy 6 to 18-year-olds. *Intelligence*, 37(2), 145–155. doi: 10.1016/j.intell.2008.09.006

Kärnä, Antti; Voeten, Marinus; Little, Todd D.; Poskiparta, Elisa; Kaljonen, Anne & Salmivalli, Christina. (2011). A large-scale evaluation of the KiVa antibullying program: Grades 4–6. *Child Development, 82*(1), 311–330. doi: 10.1111/j.1467-8624.2010.01557.x

Kärtner, Joscha; Borke, Jörn; Maasmeier, Kathrin; Keller, Heidi & Kleis, Astrid. (2011). Sociocultural influences on the development of self-recognition and self-regulation in Costa Rican and Mexican toddlers. *Journal of Cognitive Education and Psychology, 10*(1), 96–112. doi: 10.1891/1945-8959.10.1.96

Kärtner, Joscha; Keller, Heidi & Yovsi, Relindis D. (2010). Mother–infant interaction during the first 3 months: The emergence of culture-specific contingency patterns. *Child Development, 81*(2), 540–554. doi: 10.1111/j.1467-8624.2009.01414.x

Kastenbaum, Robert J. (2012). *Death, society, and human experience* (11th ed.). Boston, MA: Pearson.

Kavanaugh, Robert D. (2011). Origins and consequences of social pretend play. In Anthony D. Pellegrini (Ed.), *The Oxford handbook of the development of play* (pp. 296–307). New York, NY: Oxford University Press. doi: 10.1093/oxfordhb/9780195393002.013.0022

Keil, Frank C. (2011). Science starts early. *Science, 331*(6020), 1022–1023. doi: 10.1126/science.1195221

Keller, Heidi. (2014). Introduction: Understanding relationships. In Hiltrud Otto & Heidi Keller (Eds.), *Different faces of attachment: Cultural variations on a universal human need* (pp. 3–25). New York, NY: Cambridge University Press.

Keller, Heidi; Borke, Jörn; Chaudhary, Nandita; Lamm, Bettina & Kleis, Astrid. (2010). Continuity in parenting strategies: A cross-cultural comparison. *Journal of Cross-Cultural Psychology, 41*(3), 391–409. doi: 10.1177/0022022109359690

Keller, Heidi & Otto, Hiltrud. (2011). Different faces of autonomy. In Xinyin Chen & Kenneth H. Rubin (Eds.), *Socioemotional development in cultural context* (pp. 164–185). New York, NY: Guilford Press.

Keller, Heidi; Yovsi, Relindis; Borke, Joern; Kärtner, Joscha; Jensen, Henning & Papaligoura, Zaira. (2004). Developmental consequences of early parenting experiences: Self-recognition and self-regulation in three cultural communities. *Child Development, 75*(6), 1745–1760. doi: 10.1111/j.1467-8624.2004.00814.x

Kellman, Philip J. & Arterberry, Martha E. (2006). Infant visual perception. In William Damon & Richard M. Lerner (Eds.), *Handbook of child psychology* (6th ed., Vol. 2, pp. 109–160). Hoboken, NJ: Wiley.

Kelly, Daniel; Faucher, Luc & Machery, Edouard. (2010). Getting rid of racism: Assessing three proposals in light of psychological evidence. *Journal of Social Philosophy, 41*(3), 293–322. doi: 10.1111/j.1467-9833.2010.01495.x

Kempe, Ruth S. & Kempe, C. Henry. (1978). *Child abuse.* Cambridge, MA: Harvard University Press.

Kendall-Taylor, Nathaniel; Lindland, Eric; O'Neil, Moira & Stanley, Kate. (2014). Beyond prevalence: An explanatory approach to reframing child maltreatment in the United Kingdom. *Child Abuse & Neglect, 38*(5), 810–821. doi: 10.1016/j.chiabu.2014.04.019

Kenrick, Douglas T.; Griskevicius, Vladas; Neuberg, Steven L. & Schaller, Mark. (2010). Renovating the pyramid of needs: Contemporary extensions built upon ancient foundations. *Perspectives on Psychological Science, 5*(3), 292–314. doi: 10.1177/1745691610369469

Keown, Louise J. & Palmer, Melanie. (2014). Comparisons between paternal and maternal involvement with sons: Early to middle childhood. *Early Child Development and Care, 184*(1), 99–117. doi: 10.1080/03004430.2013.773510

Kerr, Margaret; Stattin, Håkan & Burk, William J. (2010). A reinterpretation of parental monitoring in longitudinal perspective. *Journal of Research on Adolescence, 20*(1), 39–64. doi: 10.1111/j.1532-7795.2009.00623.x

Kesselring, Thomas & Müller, Ulrich. (2011). The concept of egocentrism in the context of Piaget's theory. *New Ideas in Psychology, 29*(3), 327–345. doi: 10.1016/j.newideapsych.2010.03.008

Kessler, Ronald C.; Avenevoli, Shelli; Costello, E. Jane; Georgiades, Katholiki; Green, Jennifer G.; Gruber, Michael J., . . . Merikangas, Kathleen R. (2012). Prevalence, persistence, and sociodemographic correlates of DSM-IV disorders in the National Comorbidity Survey Replication Adolescent Supplement. *Archives of General Psychiatry, 69*(4), 372–380. doi: 10.1001/archgenpsychiatry.2011.160

Khafi, Tamar Y.; Yates, Tuppett M. & Luthar, Suniya S. (2014). Ethnic differences in the developmental significance of parentification. *Family Process, 53*(2), 267–287. doi: 10.1111/famp.12072

Khanna, Sunil K. (2010). *Fetal/fatal knowledge: New reproductive technologies and family-building strategies in India.* Belmont, CA: Wadsworth/Cengage Learning.

Kharsati, Naphisabet & Bhola, Poornima. (2014). Patterns of non-suicidal self-injurious behaviours among college students in India. *International Journal of Social Psychiatry.* doi: 10.1177/0020764014535755

Killen, Melanie & Smetana, Judith G. (Eds.). (2014). *Handbook of moral development* (2nd ed.). New York, NY: Psychology Press.

Killgore, William D. S.; Vo, Alexander H.; Castro, Carl A. & Hoge, Charles W. (2006). Assessing risk propensity in American soldiers: Preliminary reliability and validity of the Evaluation of Risks (EVAR) scale–English version. *Military Medicine, 171*(3), 233–239.

Kilmer, Ryan P. & Gil-Rivas, Virginia. (2010). Exploring posttraumatic growth in children impacted by Hurricane Katrina: Correlates of the phenomenon and developmental considerations.

Child Development, 81(4), 1211–1227. doi: 10.1111/j.1467-8624.2010.01463.x

Kim, Dong-Sik & Kim, Hyun-Sun. (2009). Body-image dissatisfaction as a predictor of suicidal ideation among Korean boys and girls in different stages of adolescence: A two-year longitudinal study. *The Journal of Adolescent Health, 45*(1), 47–54. doi: 10.1016/j.jadohealth.2008.11.017

Kim, Geunyoung; Walden, Tedra A. & Knieps, Linda J. (2010). Impact and characteristics of positive and fearful emotional messages during infant social referencing. *Infant Behavior and Development, 33*(2), 189–195. doi: 10.1016/j.infbeh.2009.12.009

Kim, Hojin I. & Johnson, Scott P. (2013). Do young infants prefer an infant-directed face or a happy face? *International Journal of Behavioral Development, 37*(2), 125–130. doi: 10.1177/0165025413475972

Kim, Hyun Sik. (2011). Consequences of parental divorce for child development. *American Sociological Review, 76*(3), 487–511. doi: 10.1177/0003122411407748

Kim, Heejung S. & Chu, Thai Q. (2011). Cultural variation in the motivation of self-expression. In David Dunning (Ed.), *Social motivation* (pp. 57–78). New York, NY: Psychology Press.

Kim, Heejung S. & Sasaki, Joni Y. (2014). Cultural neuroscience: Biology of the mind in cultural contexts. *Annual Review of Psychology, 65*, 487–514. doi: 10.1146/annurev-psych-010213-115040

Kim, Hye Young; DeKruyff, Rosemarie H. & Umetsu, Dale T. (2010). The many paths to asthma: Phenotype shaped by innate and adaptive immunity. *Nature Immunology, 11*(7), 577–584. doi: 10.1038/ni.1892

Kim, Joon Sik. (2011). Excessive crying: Behavioral and emotional regulation disorder in infancy. *Korean Journal of Pediatrics, 54*(6), 229–233. doi: 10.3345/kjp.2011.54.6.229

Kim-Spoon, Jungmeen; Longo, Gregory S. & McCullough, Michael E. (2012). Parent-adolescent relationship quality as a moderator for the influences of parents' religiousness on adolescents' religiousness and adjustment. *Journal of Youth and Adolescence, 41*(12), 1576–1587. doi: 10.1007/s10964-012-9796-1

King, Bruce M. (2013). The modern obesity epidemic, ancestral hunter-gatherers, and the sensory/reward control of food intake. *American Psychologist, 68*(2), 88–96. doi: 10.1037/a0030684

King, Pamela E. & Roeser, Robert W. (2009). Religion and spirituality in adolescent development. In Richard M. Lerner & Laurence Steinberg (Eds.), *Handbook of adolescent psychology* (3rd ed., Vol. 1, pp. 435–478). Hoboken, NJ: Wiley.

Kinney, Hannah C. & Thach, Bradley T. (2009). The sudden infant death syndrome. *New England Journal of Medicine, 361*, 795–805. doi: 10.1056/NEJMra0803836

Kirby, Douglas & Laris, B. A. (2009). Effective curriculum-based sex and STD/HIV education programs for adolescents. *Child Development*

Perspectives, 3(1), 21–29. doi: 10.1111/j.1750-8606.2008.00071.x

Kirk, Elizabeth; Howlett, Neil; Pine, Karen J. & Fletcher, Ben. (2013). To sign or not to sign? The impact of encouraging infants to gesture on infant language and maternal mind-mindedness. *Child Development, 84*(2), 574–590. doi: 10.1111/j.1467-8624.2012.01874.x

Kiuru, Noona; Burk, William J.; Laursen, Brett; Salmela-Aro, Katariina & Nurmi, Jari-Erik. (2010). Pressure to drink but not to smoke: Disentangling selection and socialization in adolescent peer networks and peer groups. *Journal of Adolescence, 33*(6), 801–812. doi: 10.1016/j.adolescence.2010.07.006

Klaczynski, Paul A. (2001). Analytic and heuristic processing influences on adolescent reasoning and decision-making. *Child Development, 72*(3), 844–861. doi: 10.1111/1467-8624.00319

Klaczynski, Paul A. (2011). Age differences in understanding precedent-setting decisions and authorities' responses to violations of deontic rules. *Journal of Experimental Child Psychology, 109*(1), 1–24. doi: 10.1016/j.jecp.2010.10.010

Klaczynski, Paul A.; Daniel, David B. & Keller, Peggy S. (2009). Appearance idealization, body esteem, causal attributions, and ethnic variations in the development of obesity stereotypes. *Journal of Applied Developmental Psychology, 30*(4), 537–551. doi: 10.1016/j.appdev.2008.12.031

Klaczynski, Paul A. & Felmban, Wejdan S. (2014). Heuristics and biases during adolescence: Developmental reversals and individual differences. In Henry Markovits (Ed.), *The developmental psychology of reasoning and decision-making* (pp. 84–111). New York, NY: Psychology Press.

Klassen, Terry P.; Kiddoo, Darcie; Lang, Mia E.; Friesen, Carol; Russell, Kelly; Spooner, Carol & Vandermeer, Ben. (2006). *The effectiveness of different methods of toilet training for bowel and bladder control.* Rockville, MD: Agency for Healthcare Research and Quality, U.S. Department of Health and Human Services.

Klaus, Marshall H. & Kennell, John H. (1976). *Maternal-infant bonding: The impact of early separation or loss on family development.* St. Louis, MO: Mosby.

Klein, Denise; Mok, Kelvin; Chen, Jen-Kai & Watkins, Kate E. (2014). Age of language learning shapes brain structure: A cortical thickness study of bilingual and monolingual individuals. *Brain and Language, 131,* 20–24. doi: 10.1016/j.bandl.2013.05.014

Klein, Hilary. (1991). Couvade syndrome: Male counterpart to pregnancy. *International Journal of Psychiatry in Medicine, 21*(1), 57–69. doi: 10.2190/FLE0-92JM-C4CN-J83T

Klein, Zoe A. & Romeo, Russell D. (2013). Changes in hypothalamic–pituitary–adrenal stress responsiveness before and after puberty in rats. *Hormones and Behavior, 64*(2), 357–363. doi: 10.1016/j.yhbeh.2013.01.012

Klinger, Laura G.; Dawson, Geraldine; Burner, Karen & Crisler, Megan. (2014).

Autism spectrum disorder. In Eric J. Mash & Russell A. Barkley (Eds.), *Child psychopathology* (3rd ed., pp. 531–572). New York, NY: Guilford Press.

Klug, William S.; Cummings, Michael R.; Spencer, Charlotte A. & Palladino, Michael A. (2008). *Concepts of genetics* (9th ed.). San Francisco, CA: Benjamin Cummings.

Knight, Rona. (2014). A hundred years of latency: From Freudian psychosexual theory to dynamic systems nonlinear development in middle childhood. *Journal of the American Psychoanalytic Association, 62*(2), 203–235. doi: 10.1177/0003065114531044

Kochanek, Kenneth D.; Xu, Jiaquan; Murphy, Sherry L.; Miniño, Arialdi M. & Kung, Hsiang-Ching. (2011). *Deaths: Preliminary data for 2009.* Hyattsville, MD: National Center for Health Statistics, 59(4).

Kochanska, Grazyna; Barry, Robin A.; Jimenez, Natasha B.; Hollatz, Amanda L. & Woodard, Jarilyn. (2009). Guilt and effortful control: Two mechanisms that prevent disruptive developmental trajectories. *Journal of Personality and Social Psychology, 97*(2), 322–333. doi: 10.1037/a0015471

Kohlberg, Lawrence. (1963). The development of children's orientations toward a moral order: I. Sequence in the development of moral thought. *Vita Humana, 6*(1/2), 11–33. doi: 10.1159/000269667

Kohlberg, Lawrence; Levine, Charles & Hewer, Alexandra. (1983). *Moral stages: A current formulation and a response to critics.* New York, NY: Karger.

Kolb, Bryan & Whishaw, Ian Q. (2013). *An introduction to brain and behavior* (4th ed.). New York, NY: Worth.

Konner, Melvin. (2007). Evolutionary foundations of cultural psychology. In Shinobu Kitayama & Dov Cohen (Eds.), *Handbook of cultural psychology* (pp. 77–105). New York, NY: Guilford Press.

Konner, Melvin. (2010). *The evolution of childhood: Relationships, emotion, mind.* Cambridge, MA: Harvard University Press.

Kopp, Claire B. (2011). Development in the early years: Socialization, motor development, and consciousness. *Annual Review of Psychology, 62,* 165–187. doi: 10.1146/annurev.psych.121208.131625

Korhonen, Tellervo; Latvala, Antti; Dick, Danielle M.; Pulkkinen, Lea; Rose, Richard J.; Kaprio, Jaakko & Huizink, Anja C. (2012). Genetic and environmental influences underlying externalizing behaviors, cigarette smoking and illicit drug use across adolescence. *Behavior Genetics, 42*(4), 614–625. doi: 10.1007/s10519-012-9528-z

Kost, Kathryn & Henshaw, Stanley. (2013). *U.S. teenage pregnancies, births and abortions, 2008: State trends by age, race and ethnicity.* New York, NY: Guttmacher Institute.

Koster-Hale, Jorie & Saxe, Rebecca. (2013). Functional neuroimaging of theory of mind. In Simon Baron-Cohen, et al. (Eds.), *Understanding other minds: Perspectives from developmental social*

neuroscience (3rd ed., pp. 132–163). New York, NY: Oxford University Press.

Kouider, Sid; Stahlhut, Carsten; Gelskov, Sofie V.; Barbosa, Leonardo S.; Dutat, Michel; de Gardelle, Vincent, . . . Dehaene-Lambertz, Ghislaine. (2013). A neural marker of perceptual consciousness in infants. *Science, 340*(6130), 376–380. doi: 10.1126/science.1232509

Kowalski, Robin M.; Giumetti, Gary W.; Schroeder, Amber N. & Lattanner, Micah R. (2014). Bullying in the digital age: A critical review and meta-analysis of cyberbullying research among youth. *Psychological Bulletin, 140*(4), 1073–1137. doi: 10.1037/a0035618

Kozhimannil, Katy B.; Law, Michael R. & Virnig, Beth A. (2013). Cesarean delivery rates vary tenfold among US hospitals; Reducing variation may address quality and cost issues. *Health Affairs, 32*(3), 527–535. doi: 10.1377/hlthaff.2012.1030

Krebs, John R. (2009). The gourmet ape: Evolution and human food preferences. *American Journal of Clinical Nutrition, 90*(3), 707S–711S. doi: 10.3945/ajcn.2009.27462B

Kremer, Peter; Elshaug, Christine; Leslie, Eva; Toumbourou, John W.; Patton, George C. & Williams, Joanne. (2014). Physical activity, leisure-time screen use and depression among children and young adolescents. *Journal of Science and Medicine in Sport, 17*(2), 183–187. doi: 10.1016/j.jsams.2013.03.012

Krentz, Ursula C. & Corina, David P. (2008). Preference for language in early infancy: The human language bias is not speech specific. *Developmental Science, 11*(1), 1–9. doi: 10.1111/j.1467-7687.2007.00652.x

Kretch, Kari S. & Adolph, Karen E. (2013). No bridge too high: Infants decide whether to cross based on the probability of falling not the severity of the potential fall. *Developmental Science, 16*(3), 336–351. doi: 10.1111/desc.12045

Krisberg, Kim. (2014). Public health messaging: How it is said can influence behaviors: Beyond the facts. *The Nation's Health, 44*(6), 1–20.

Kroger, Jane & Marcia, James E. (2011). The identity statuses: Origins, meanings, and interpretations. In Seth J. Schwartz, et al. (Eds.), *Handbook of identity theory and research* (pp. 31–53). New York, NY: Springer. doi: 10.1007/978-1-4419-7988-9_2

Kroger, Jane; Martinussen, Monica & Marcia, James E. (2010). Identity status change during adolescence and young adulthood: A meta-analysis. *Journal of Adolescence, 33*(5), 683–698. doi: 10.1016/j.adolescence.2009.11.002

Krogstad, Jens M. & Fry, Richard. (2014, August 18). *Dept. of Ed. projects public schools will be 'majority-minority' this fall.* Washington, DC: Pew Research Center.

Kuehn, Bridget M. (2011). Scientists find promising therapies for fragile X and Down syndromes. *JAMA, 305*(4), 344–346. doi: 10.1001/jama.2010.1960

Kuhn, Deanna. (2013). Reasoning. In Philip D. Zelazo (Ed.), *The Oxford handbook of developmental psychology* (Vol. 1, pp. 744–764). New York, NY: Oxford University Press. doi: 10.1093/oxfordhb/9780199958450.013.0026

Kuhn, Deanna & Franklin, Sam. (2006). The second decade: What develops (and how). In William Damon & Richard M. Lerner (Eds.), *Handbook of child psychology* (6th ed., Vol. 2, pp. 953–993). Hoboken, NJ: Wiley.

Kuhn, Louise; Reitz, Cordula & Abrams, Elaine J. (2009). Breastfeeding and AIDS in the developing world. *Current Opinion in Pediatrics, 21*(1), 83–93. doi: 10.1097/MOP.0b013e328320d894

Kulkofsky, Sarah & Klemfuss, J. Zoe. (2008). What the stories children tell can tell about their memory: Narrative skill and young children's suggestibility. *Developmental Psychology, 44*(5), 1442–1456. doi: 10.1037/a0012849

Kundu, Tapas K. (Ed.). (2013). *Epigenetics: Development and disease.* New York, NY: Springer. doi: 10.1007/978-94-007-4525-4

Kuperberg, Arielle. (2014). Age at coresidence, premarital cohabitation, and marriage dissolution: 1985–2009. *Journal of Marriage and Family, 76*(2), 352–369. doi: 10.1111/jomf.12092

Kushnerenko, Elena; Tomalski, Przemyslaw; Ballieux, Haiko; Ribeiro, Helena; Potton, Anita; Axelsson, Emma L., . . . Moore, Derek G. (2013). Brain responses to audiovisual speech mismatch in infants are associated with individual differences in looking behaviour. *European Journal of Neuroscience, 38*(9), 3363–3369. doi: 10.1111/ejn.12317

Kutob, Randa M.; Senf, Janet H.; Crago, Marjorie & Shisslak, Catherine M. (2010). Concurrent and longitudinal predictors of self-esteem in elementary and middle school girls. *Journal of School Health, 80*(5), 240–248. doi: 10.1111/j.1746-1561.2010.00496.x

Kuwahara, Keisuke; Kochi, Takeshi; Nanri, Akiko; Tsuruoka, Hiroko; Kurotani, Kayo; Pham, Ngoc Minh, . . . Mizoue, Tetsuya. (2014). Flushing response modifies the association of alcohol consumption with markers of glucose metabolism in Japanese men and women. *Alcoholism: Clinical and Experimental Research, 38*(4), 1042–1048. doi: 10.1111/acer.12323

Kwok, Sylvia Y. C. Lai & Shek, Daniel T. L. (2010). Hopelessness, parent-adolescent communication, and suicidal ideation among Chinese adolescents in Hong Kong. *Suicide and Life-Threatening Behavior, 40*(3), 224–233. doi: 10.1521/suli.2010.40.3.224

Kypri, Kypros; Davie, Gabrielle; McElduff, Patrick; Connor, Jennie & Langley, John. (2014). Effects of lowering the minimum alcohol purchasing age on weekend assaults resulting in hospitalization in New Zealand. *American Journal of Public Health, 104*(8), 1396–1401. doi: 10.2105/AJPH.2014.301889

Kypri, Kypros; Voas, Robert B.; Langley, John D.; Stephenson, Shaun C. R.; Begg, Dorothy J.; Tippetts, A. Scott & Davie, Gabrielle S.

(2006). Minimum purchasing age for alcohol and traffic crash injuries among 15- to 19-year-olds in New Zealand. *American Journal of Public Health, 96*(1), 126–131. doi: 10.2105/AJPH.2005.073122

Kyriakidou, Marilena; Blades, Mark & Carroll, Dan. (2014). Inconsistent findings for the eyes closed effect in children: The implications for interviewing child witnesses. *Frontiers in Psychology, 5,* 488. doi: 10.3389/fpsyg.2014.00448

LaBar, Kevin S. (2007). Beyond fear: Emotional memory mechanisms in the human brain. *Current Directions in Psychological Science, 16*(4), 173–177. doi: 10.1111/j.1467-8721.2007.00498.x

LaFontana, Kathryn M. & Cillessen, Antonius H. N. (2010). Developmental changes in the priority of perceived status in childhood and adolescence. *Social Development, 19*(1), 130–147 doi: 10.1111/j.1467-9507.2008.00522.x

Lagattuta, Kristin H. (2014). Linking past, present, and future: Children's ability to connect mental states and emotions across time. *Child Development Perspectives, 8*(2), 90–95. doi: 10.1111/cdep.12065

Lai, Stephanie A.; Benjamin, Rebekah G.; Schwanenflugel, Paula J. & Kuhn, Melanie R. (2014). The longitudinal relationship between reading fluency and reading comprehension skills in second-grade children. *Reading & Writing Quarterly: Overcoming Learning Difficulties, 30*(2), 116–138. doi: 10.1080/10573569.2013.789785

Laible, Deborah; Panfile, Tia & Makariev, Drika. (2008). The quality and frequency of mother-toddler conflict: Links with attachment and temperament. *Child Development, 79*(2), 426–443. doi: 10.1111/j.1467-8624.2007.01134.x

Laird, Robert D.; Marrero, Matthew D.; Melching, Jessica A. & Kuhn, Emily S. (2013). Information management strategies in early adolescence: Developmental change in use and transactional associations with psychological adjustment. *Developmental Psychology, 49*(5), 928–937. doi: 10.1037/a0028845

Lake, Neil. (2012). Labor, interrupted: Cesareans, "cascading interventions," and finding a sense of balance. *Harvard Magazine, 115*(2), 21–26.

Lam, Chun Bun; McHale, Susan M. & Crouter, Ann C. (2014). Time with peers from middle childhood to late adolescence: Developmental course and adjustment correlates. *Child Development, 85*(4), 1677–1693. doi: 10.1111/cdev.12235

Lam, Thuy; Williams, Paige L.; Lee, Mary M.; Korrick, Susan A.; Birnbaum, Linda S.; Burns, Jane S., . . . Hauser, Russ. (2014). Prepubertal organochlorine pesticide concentrations and age of pubertal onset among Russian boys. *Environment International, 73,* 135–142. doi: 10.1016/j.envint.2014.06.020

Lamb, Michael E. (1982). Maternal employment and child development: A review. In Michael E. Lamb (Ed.), *Nontraditional families: Parenting and child development* (pp. 45–69). Hillsdale, NJ: Erlbaum.

Lamb, Michael E. (Ed.). (2010). *The role of the father in child development* (5th ed.). Hoboken, NJ: Wiley.

Lamb, Michael E. (Ed.). (2013). *The father's role: Cross cultural perspectives.* New York, NY: Routledge.

Lamb, Michael E. (2014). How I got started: Drawn into the life of crime: Learning from, by, and for child victims and witnesses. *Applied Cognitive Psychology, 28*(4), 607–611. doi: 10.1002/acp.3031

Lambert, Nathaniel M.; Fincham, Frank D.; Stillman, Tyler F.; Graham, Steven M. & Beach, Steven R. H. (2010). Motivating change in relationships. *Psychological Science, 21*(1), 126–132. doi: 10.1177/0956797609355634

Landgren, Kajsa; Lundqvist, Anita & Hallström, Inger. (2012). Remembering the chaos—But life went on and the wound healed: A four year follow up with parents having had a baby with infantile colic. *The Open Nursing Journal, 6,* 53–69. doi: 10.2174/1874434601206010053

Lando, Amy M. & Lo, Serena C. (2014). Consumer understanding of the benefits and risks of fish consumption during pregnancy. *American Journal Of Lifestyle Medicine, 8*(2), 88–92. doi: 10.1177/1559827613514704

Lane, Jonathan D. & Harris, Paul L. (2014). Confronting, representing, and believing counterintuitive concepts: Navigating the natural and the supernatural. *Perspectives on Psychological Science, 9*(2), 144–160. doi: 10.1177/1745691613518078

Långström, Niklas; Rahman, Qazi; Carlström, Eva & Lichtenstein, Paul. (2010). Genetic and environmental effects on same-sex sexual behavior: A population study of twins in Sweden. *Archives of Sexual Behavior, 39*(1), 75–80. doi: 10.1007/s10508-008-9386-1

Lara-Cinisomo, Sandraluz; Fuligni, Allison Sidle & Karoly, Lynn A. (2011). Preparing preschoolers for kindergarten. In DeAnna M. Laverick & Mary Renck Jalongo (Eds.), *Transitions to early care and education* (Vol. 4, pp. 93–105). New York, NY: Springer. doi: 10.1007/978-94-007-0573-9_9

Larose, Joanie; Boulay, Pierre; Sigal, Ronald J.; Wright, Heather E. & Kenny, Glen P. (2013). Age-related decrements in heat dissipation during physical activity occur as early as the age of 40. *PLoS ONE, 8*(12), e83148. doi: 10.1371/journal.pone.0083148

Larson, Nicole I.; Neumark-Sztainer, Dianne; Hannan, Peter J. & Story, Mary. (2007). Trends in adolescent fruit and vegetable consumption, 1999–2004: Project EAT. *American Journal of Preventive Medicine, 32*(2), 147–150. doi: 10.1016/j.amepre.2006.10.011

Larzelere, Robert; Cox, Ronald & Smith, Gail. (2010). Do nonphysical punishments reduce antisocial behavior more than spanking? A comparison using the strongest previous causal evidence against spanking. *BMC Pediatrics, 10*(10). doi: 10.1186/1471-2431-10-10

Lau, Carissa; Ambalavanan, Namasivayam; Chakraborty, Hrishikesh; Wingate, Martha S. & Carlo, Waldemar A. (2013). Extremely low birth weight and infant mortality rates in the United States. *Pediatrics, 131*(5), 855–860. doi: 10.1542/peds.2012-2471

Laurent, Heidemarie K. (2014). Clarifying the contours of emotion regulation: Insights from parent–child stress research. *Child Development Perspectives, 8*(1), 30–35. doi: 10.1111/cdep.12058

Laurino, Mercy Y.; Bennett, Robin L.; Saraiya, Devki S.; Baumeister, Lisa; Doyle, Debra L.; Leppig, Kathleen, . . . Raskind, Wendy H. (2005). Genetic evaluation and counseling of couples with recurrent miscarriage: Recommendations of the National Society of Genetic Counselors. *Journal of Genetic Counseling, 14*(3), 165–181. doi: 10.1007/s10897-005-3241-5

Laursen, Brett; Bukowski, William M.; Nurmi, Jari-Eri; Marion, Donna; Salmela-Aro, Katariina & Kiuru, Noona. (2010). Opposites detract: Middle school peer group antipathies. *Journal of Experimental Child Psychology, 106*(4), 240–256. doi: 10.1016/j.jecp.2010.03.001

Laursen, Brett & Collins, W. Andrew. (2009). Parent-child relationships during adolescence. In Richard M. Lerner & Laurence Steinberg (Eds.), *Handbook of adolescent psychology* (3rd ed., Vol. 2, pp. 3–42). Hoboken, NJ: Wiley.

Laursen, Brett & Hartl, Amy C. (2013). Understanding loneliness during adolescence: Developmental changes that increase the risk of perceived social isolation. *Journal of Adolescence, 36*(6), 1261–1268. doi: 10.1016/j.adolescence.2013.06.003

Lavelli, Manuela & Fogel, Alan. (2005). Developmental changes in the relationship between the infant's attention and emotion during early face-to-face communication: The 2-month transition. *Developmental Psychology, 41*(1), 265–280. doi: 10.1037/0012-1649.41.1.265

Le Grange, Daniel & Lock, James (Eds.). (2011). *Eating disorders in children and adolescents: A clinical handbook.* New York, NY: Guilford Press.

Leach, Penelope. (2011). The EYFS and the real foundations of children's early years. In Richard House (Ed.), *Too much, too soon?: Early learning and the erosion of childhood.* Stroud, UK: Hawthorn.

Leaper, Campbell. (2013). Gender development during childhood. In Philip D. Zelazo (Ed.), *The Oxford handbook of developmental psychology* (Vol. 2, pp. 326–377). New York, NY: Oxford University Press. doi: 10.1093/oxfordhb/9780199958474.013.0014

Leavitt, Judith W. (2009). *Make room for daddy: The journey from waiting room to birthing room.* Chapel Hill, NC: University of North Carolina Press.

Lee, Dohoon; Brooks-Gunn, Jeanne; McLanahan, Sara S.; Notterman, Daniel & Garfinkel, Irwin. (2013). The Great Recession, genetic sensitivity, and maternal harsh parenting. *Proceedings of the National Academy of Sciences, 110*(34), 13780–13784. doi: 10.1073/pnas.1312398110

Lee, Jihyun & Porretta, David L. (2013). Enhancing the motor skills of children with autism spectrum disorders: A pool-based approach. *JOPERD: The Journal Of Physical Education, Recreation & Dance, 84*(1), 41–45. doi: 10.1080/07303084.2013.746154

Lee, RaeHyuck; Zhai, Fuhua; Brooks-Gunn, Jeanne; Han, Wen-Jui & Waldfogel, Jane. (2014). Head start participation and school readiness: Evidence from the early childhood longitudinal study–birth cohort. *Developmental Psychology, 50*(1), 202–215. doi: 10.1037/a0032280

Lee, Soojeong & Shouse, Roger C. (2011). The impact of prestige orientation on shadow education in South Korea. *Sociology of Education, 84*(3), 212–224. doi: 10.1177/0038040711411278

Lee, Yuan-Hsuan; Ko, Chih-Hung & Chou, Chien. (2014). Re-visiting internet addiction among Taiwanese students: A cross-sectional comparison of students' expectations, online gaming, and online social interaction. *Journal of Abnormal Child Psychology.* doi: 10.1007/s10802-014-9915-4

Legewie, Joscha & DiPrete, Thomas A. (2012). School context and the gender gap in educational achievement. *American Sociological Review, 77*(3), 463–485. doi: 10.1177/0003122412440802

Lehner, Ben. (2013). Genotype to phenotype: Lessons from model organisms for human genetics. *Nature Reviews Genetics, 14*(3), 168–178. doi: 10.1038/nrg3404

Leman, Patrick J. & Björnberg, Marina. (2010). Conversation, development, and gender: A study of changes in children's concepts of punishment. *Child Development, 81*(3), 958–971. doi: 10.1111/j.1467-8624.2010.01445.x

Lemieux, André. (2012). Post-formal thought in gerontagogy or beyond Piage. *Journal of Behavioral and Brain Science, 2,* 399–406. doi: 10.4236/jbbs.2012.23046

Lemish, Daphna & Kolucki, Barbara. (2013). Media and early childhood development. In Pia Rebello Britto, et al. (Eds.), *Handbook of early childhood development research and its impact on global policy.* New York, NY: Oxford University Press.

Leonard, Hayley C. & Hill, Elisabeth L. (2014). Review: The impact of motor development on typical and atypical social cognition and language: A systematic review. *Child and Adolescent Mental Health, 19*(3), 163–170. doi: 10.1111/camh.12055

Lepper, Mark R.; Greene, David & Nisbett, Richard E. (1973). Undermining children's intrinsic interest with extrinsic reward: A test of the "overjustification" hypothesis. *Journal of Personality and Social Psychology, 28*(1), 129–137. doi: 10.1037/h0035519

Lerner, Claire & Dombro, Amy Laura. (2004). Finding your fit: Some temperament tips for parents. *Zero to Three, 24*(4), 42–45.

Lerner, Richard M. (Ed.). (2015). *Handbook of child psychology and developmental science* (7th ed.). Hoboken, NJ: Wiley.

Lerner, Richard M. & Steinberg, Laurence D. (Eds.). (2009). *Handbook of adolescent psychology* (3rd ed.). Hoboken, NJ: Wiley.

Leslie, Mitch. (2012). Gut microbes keep rare immune cells in line. *Science, 335*(6075), 1428. doi: 10.1126/science.335.6075.1428

Lester, Patricia; Leskin, Gregory; Woodward, Kirsten; Saltzman, William; Nash, William; Mogil, Catherine, . . . Beardslee, William. (2011). Wartime deployment and military children: Applying prevention science to enhance family resilience. In Shelley MacDermid Wadsworth & David Riggs (Eds.), *Risk and resilience in U.S. military families* (pp. 149–173). New York, NY: Springer. doi: 10.1007/978-1-4419-7064-0_8

Leung, Angel Nga-Man; Wong, Stephanie Siu-fong; Wong, Iris Wai-yin & McBride-Chang, Catherine. (2010). Filial piety and psychosocial adjustment in Hong Kong Chinese early adolescents. *The Journal of Early Adolescence, 30*(5), 651–667. doi: 10.1177/0272431609341046

Leventhal, Bennett L. (2013). Complementary and alternative medicine: Not many compliments but lots of alternatives. *Journal of Child and Adolescent Psychopharmacology, 23*(1), 54–56. doi: 10.1089/cap.2013.2312

Lewallen, Lynne P. (2011). The importance of culture in childbearing. *Journal of Obstetric, Gynecologic, & Neonatal Nursing, 40*(1), 4–8. doi: 10.1111/j.1552-6909.2010.01209.x

Lewandowski, Lawrence J. & Lovett, Benjamin J. (2014). Learning disabilities. In Eric J. Mash & Russell A. Barkley (Eds.), *Child psychopathology* (3rd ed., pp. 625–669). New York, NY: Guilford Press.

Lewin, Kurt. (1943). Psychology and the process of group living. *Journal of Social Psychology, 17*(1), 113–131. doi: 10.1080/00224545.1943.9712269

Lewis, Charlotte W.; Linsenmayer, Kristi A. & Williams, Alexis. (2010). Wanting better: A qualitative study of low-income parents about their children's oral health. *Pediatric Dentistry, 32*(7), 518–524.

Lewis, John D.; Theilmann, Rebecca J.; Townsend, Jeanne & Evans, Alan C. (2013). Network efficiency in autism spectrum disorder and its relation to brain overgrowth. *Frontiers in Human Neuroscience, 7,* 845. doi: 10.3389/fnhum.2013.00845

Lewis, Lawrence B.; Antone, Carol & Johnson, Jacqueline S. (1999). Effects of prosodic stress and serial position on syllable omission in first words. *Developmental Psychology, 35*(1), 45–59. doi: 10.1037//0012-1649.35.1.45

Lewis, Michael. (2010). The emergence of human emotions. In Michael Lewis, et al. (Eds.), *Handbook of emotions* (3rd ed.). New York, NY: Guilford Press.

Lewis, Michael & Brooks, Jeanne. (1978). Self-knowledge and emotional development. In Michael Lewis & L. A. Rosenblum (Eds.), *Genesis of behavior* (Vol. 1, pp. 205–226). New York, NY: Plenum Press.

Lewis, Michael & Kestler, Lisa (Eds.). (2012). *Gender differences in prenatal substance exposure.* Washington, DC: American Psychological Association.

Lewis, Michael & Ramsay, Douglas. (2005). Infant emotional and cortisol responses to goal blockage. *Child Development*, 76(2), 518–530. doi: 10.1111/j.1467-8624.2005.00860.x

Lewis, Marc D. (2013). The development of emotional regulation: Integrating normative and individual differences through developmental neuroscience. In Philip D. Zelazo (Ed.), *The Oxford handbook of developmental psychology* (Vol. 2, pp. 81–97). New York, NY: Oxford University Press. doi: 10.1093/oxfordhb/9780199958474.013.0004

Lewkowicz, David J. (2010). Infant perception of audio-visual speech synchrony. *Developmental Psychology*, 46(1), 66–77. doi: 10.1037/a0015579

Li, Jin; Fung, Heidi; Bakeman, Roger; Rae, Katharine & Wei, Wanchun. (2014). How European American and Taiwanese mothers talk to their children about learning. *Child Development*, 85(3), 1206–1221. doi: 10.1111/cdev.12172

Li, Weilin; Farkas, George; Duncan, Greg J.; Burchinal, Margaret R. & Vandell, Deborah Lowe. (2013). Timing of high-quality child care and cognitive, language, and preacademic development. *Developmental Psychology*, 49(8), 1440–1451. doi: 10.1037/a0030613

Li, Yibing & Lerner, Richard M. (2011). Trajectories of school engagement during adolescence: Implications for grades, depression, delinquency, and substance use. *Developmental Psychology*, 47(1), 233–247. doi: 10.1037/a0021307

Libertus, Klaus & Needham, Amy. (2010). Teach to reach: The effects of active vs. passive reaching experiences on action and perception. *Vision Research*, 50(24), 2750–2757. doi: 10.1016/j.visres.2010.09.001

Libertus, Melissa E.; Feigenson, Lisa & Halberda, Justin. (2013). Is approximate number precision a stable predictor of math ability? *Learning and Individual Differences*, 25, 126–133. doi: 10.1016/j.lindif.2013.02.001

Lillard, Angeline S. (2013). Playful learning and Montessori education. *American Journal of Play*, 5(2), 157–186.

Lillard, Angeline S. & Else-Quest, Nicole. (2006). Evaluating Montessori education. *Science*, 313(5795), 1893–1894. doi: 10.1126/science.1132362

Lillard, Angeline S.; Lerner, Matthew D.; Hopkins, Emily J.; Dore, Rebecca A.; Smith, Eric D. & Palmquist, Carolyn M. (2013). The impact of pretend play on children's development: A review of the evidence. *Psychological Bulletin*, 139(1), 1–34. doi: 10.1037/a0029321

Lillevoll, Kjersti R.; Kroger, Jane & Martinussen, Monica. (2013). Identity status and locus of control: A meta-analysis. *Identity: An International Journal of Theory and Research*, 13(3), 253–265. doi: 10.1080/15283488.2013.799471

Limber, Susan P. (2011). Development, evaluation, and future directions of the Olweus Bullying Prevention Program. *Journal of School Violence*, 10(1), 71–87. doi: 10.1080/15388220.2010.519375

Lin, Alex R. (2014). Examining students' perception of classroom openness as a predictor of civic knowledge: A cross-national analysis of 38 countries. *Applied Developmental Science*, 18(1), 17–30. doi: 10.1080/10888691.2014.864204

Lincove, Jane A. & Painter, Gary. (2006). Does the age that children start kindergarten matter? Evidence of long-term educational and social outcomes. *Educational Evaluation and Policy Analysis*, 28(2), 153–179 doi: 10.3102/01623737028002153

Liszkowski, Ulf; Schäfer, Marie; Carpenter, Malinda & Tomasello, Michael. (2009). Prelinguistic infants, but not chimpanzees, communicate about absent entities. *Psychological Science*, 20(5), 654–660. doi: 10.1111/j.1467-9280.2009.02346.x

Liszkowski, Ulf & Tomasello, Michael. (2011). Individual differences in social, cognitive, and morphological aspects of infant pointing. *Cognitive Development*, 26(1), 16–29. doi: 10.1016/j.cogdev.2010.10.001

Liu, Dong & Xin, Ziqiang. (2014). Birth cohort and age changes in the self-esteem of Chinese adolescents: A cross-temporal meta-analysis, 1996–2009. *Journal of Research on Adolescence*. doi: 10.1111/jora.12134

Livas-Dlott, Alejandra; Fuller, Bruce; Stein, Gabriela L.; Bridges, Margaret; Mangual Figueroa, Ariana & Mireles, Laurie. (2010). Commands, competence, and *cariño*: Maternal socialization practices in Mexican American families. *Developmental Psychology*, 46(3), 566–578. doi: 10.1037/a0018016

Lloyd-Fox, Sarah; Blasi, Anna; Volein, Agnes; Everdell, Nick; Elwell, Claire E. & Johnson, Mark H. (2009). Social perception in infancy: A near infrared spectroscopy study. *Child Development*, 80(4), 986–999. doi: 10.1111/j.1467-8624.2009.01312.x

Lobstein, Tim & Dibb, Sue. (2005). Evidence of a possible link between obesogenic food advertising and child overweight. *Obesity Reviews*, 6(3), 203–208. doi: 10.1111/j.1467-789X.2005.00191.x

LoBue, Vanessa. (2013). What are we so afraid of? How early attention shapes our most common fears. *Child Development Perspectives*, 7(1), 38–42. doi: 10.1111/cdep.12012

Lock, Margaret. (2013). The lure of the epigenome. *The Lancet*, 381(9881), 1896–1897. doi: 10.1016/S0140-6736(13)61149-6

Loeber, Rolf & Burke, Jeffrey D. (2011). Developmental pathways in juvenile externalizing and internalizing problems. *Journal of Research on Adolescence*, 21(1), 34–46. doi: 10.1111/j.1532-7795.2010.00713.x

Loeber, Rolf; Capaldi, Deborah M. & Costello, Elizabeth. (2013). Gender and the development of aggression, disruptive behavior, and delinquency from childhood to early adulthood. In Patrick H. Tolan & Bennett L. Leventh (Eds.), *Disruptive behavior disorders* (pp. 137–160). New York, NY: Springer. doi: 10.1007/978-1-4614-7557-6_6

Longo, Lawrence D. (2013). *The rise of fetal and neonatal physiology: Basic science to clinical care*. New York, NY: Springer.

Lorber, Michael F. & Egeland, Byron. (2011). Parenting and infant difficulty: Testing a mutual exacerbation hypothesis to predict early onset conduct problems. *Child Development*, 82(6), 2006–2020. doi: 10.1111/j.1467-8624.2011.01652.x

Lovecky, Deirdre V. (2009). Moral sensitivity in young gifted children. In Tracy Cross & Don Ambrose (Eds.), *Morality, ethics, and gifted minds* (pp. 161–176). New York, NY: Springer. doi: 10.1007/978-0-387-89368-6_13

Lowell, Darcy I.; Carter, Alice S.; Godoy, Leandra; Paulicin, Belinda & Briggs-Gowan, Margaret J. (2011). A randomized controlled trial of Child FIRST: A comprehensive home-based intervention translating research into early childhood practice. *Child Development*, 82(1), 193–208. doi: 10.1111/j.1467-8624.2010.01550.x

Lowrey, Annie. (2014, March 16). Income gap, meet the longevity gap. *The New York Times*, p. BU1.

Lubienski, Christopher; Puckett, Tiffany & Brewer, T. Jameson. (2013). Does home-schooling "work"? A critique of the empirical claims and agenda of advocacy organizations. *Peabody Journal of Education*, 88(3), 378–392. doi: 10.1080/0161956X.2013.798516

Luecken, Linda J.; Lin, Betty; Coburn, Shayna S.; MacKinnon, David P.; Gonzales, Nancy A. & Crnic, Keith A. (2013). Prenatal stress, partner support, and infant cortisol reactivity in low-income Mexican American families. *Psychoneuroendocrinology*, 38(12), 3092–3101. doi: 10.1016/j.psyneuen.2013.09.006

Lukas, D. & Clutton-Brock, T. H. (2013). The evolution of social monogamy in mammals. *Science*, 341(6145), 526–530. doi: 10.1126/science.1238677

Luna, Beatriz; Paulsen, David J.; Padmanabhan, Aarthi & Geier, Charles. (2013). The teenage brain: Cognitive control and motivation. *Current Directions in Psychological Science*, 22(2), 94–100. doi: 10.1177/0963721413478416

Luo, Rufan; Tamis-LeMonda, Catherine S.; Kuchirko, Yana; Ng, Florrie F. & Liang, Eva. (2014). Mother–child book-sharing and children's storytelling skills in ethnically diverse, low-income families. *Infant and Child Development*, 23(4), 402–425. doi: 10.1002/icd.1841

Lupski, James R. (2013). Genome mosaicism: One human, multiple genomes. *Science*, 341(6144), 358–359. doi: 10.1126/science.1239503

Luthar, Suniya S. & Barkin, Samuel H. (2012). Are affluent youth truly "at risk"? Vulnerability and resilience across three diverse samples. *Development and Psychopathology*, 24(2), 429–449. doi: 10.1017/S0954579412000089

Luthar, Suniya S.; Cicchetti, Dante & Becker, Bronwyn. (2000). The construct of resilience: A critical evaluation and guidelines for future work. *Child Development*, 71(3), 543–562. doi: 10.1111/1467-8624.00164

Lynne, Sarah D.; Graber, Julia A.; Nichols, Tracy R.; Brooks-Gunn, Jeanne & Botvin,

Gilbert J. (2007). Links between pubertal timing, peer influences, and externalizing behaviors among urban students followed through middle school. *Journal of Adolescent Health*, 40(2), 181.e187—181.e113. doi: 10.1016/j.jadohealth.2006.09.008

Lynskey, Michael T.; Agrawal, Arpana; Henders, Anjali; Nelson, Elliot C.; Madden, Pamela A. F. & Martin, Nicholas G. (2012). An Australian twin study of cannabis and other illicit drug use and misuse, and other psychopathology. *Twin Research and Human Genetics*, 15(5), 631–641. doi: 10.1017/thg.2012.41

Lyon, Thomas D.; Malloy, Lindsay C.; Quas, Jodi A. & Talwar, Victoria A. (2008). Coaching, truth induction, and young maltreated children's false allegations and false denials. *Child Development*, 79(4), 914–929. doi: 10.1111/j.1467-8624.2008.01167.x

Lyons, Kristen E.; Ghetti, Simona & Cornoldi, Cesare. (2010). Age differences in the contribution of recollection and familiarity to false-memory formation: A new paradigm to examine developmental reversals. *Developmental Science*, 13(2), 355–362. doi: 10.1111/j.1467-7687.2009.00889.x

Lyons-Ruth, Karlen; Bronfman, Elisa & Parsons, Elizabeth. (1999). Maternal frightened, frightening, or atypical behavior and disorganized infant attachment patterns. *Monographs of the Society for Research in Child Development*, 64(3), 67–96. doi: 10.1111/1540-5834.00034

MacDorman, Marian F. & Rosenberg, Harry M. (1993). *Trends in infant mortality by cause of death and other characteristics, 1960–88.* Hyattsville, MD: National Center for Health Statistics, 20(20).

Macgregor, Stuart; Lind, Penelope A.; Bucholz, Kathleen K.; Hansell, Narelle K.; Madden, Pamela A. F.; Richter, Melinda M., . . . Whitfield, John B. (2009). Associations of ADH and ALDH2 gene variation with self report alcohol reactions, consumption and dependence: An integrated analysis. *Human Molecular Genetics*, 18(3), 580–593. doi: 10.1093/hmg/ddn372

Mackenzie, K. J.; Anderton, S. M. & Schwarze, J. (2014). Viral respiratory tract infections and asthma in early life: Cause and effect? *Clinical & Experimental Allergy*, 44(1), 9–19. doi: 10.1111/cea.12139

MacLeod, Andrea; Fabiano-Smith, Leah; Boegner-Pagé, Sarah & Fontolliet, Salomé. (2013). Simultaneous bilingual language acquisition: The role of parental input on receptive vocabulary development. *Child Language Teaching and Therapy*, 29(1), 131–142. doi: 10.1177/0265659012466862

Macmillan, Ross & Copher, Ronda. (2005). Families in the life course: Interdependency of roles, role configurations, and pathways. *Journal of Marriage and Family*, 67(4), 858–879. doi: 10.1111/j.1741-3737.2005.00180.x

Macosko, Evan Z. & McCarroll, Steven A. (2013). Our fallen genomes. *Science*, 342(6158), 564–565. doi: 10.1126/science.1246942

Madden, Mary; Lenhart, Amanda; Duggan, Maeve; Cortesi, Sandra & Gasser, Urs. (2013). *Teens and technology 2013.* Washington, DC: Pew Research Center, Pew Internet & American Life Project.

Madsen, Kreesten M.; Lauritsen, Marlene B.; Pedersen, Carsten B.; Thorsen, Poul; Plesner, Anne-Marie; Andersen, Peter H. & Mortensen, Preben B. (2003). Thimerosal and the occurrence of autism: Negative ecological evidence from Danish population-based data. *Pediatrics*, 112(3), 604–606.

Magnuson, Katherine & Waldfogel, Jane. (2014). Delivering high-quality early childhood education and care to low-income children: How well is the US doing? In Ludovica Gambaro, et al. (Eds.), *An equal start?: Providing quality early education and care for disadvantaged children* (pp. 193–218). Chicago, IL: Policy Press.

Majdandžić, Mirjana; Möller, Eline L.; de Vente, Wieke; Bögels, Susan M. & van den Boom, Dymphna C. (2013). Fathers' challenging parenting behavior prevents social anxiety development in their 4-year-old children: A longitudinal observational study. *Journal of Abnormal Child Psychology*, 42(2), 301–310. doi: 10.1007/s10802-013-9774-4

Majercsik, Eszter. (2005). Hierachy of needs of geriatric patients. *Gerontology*, 51(3), 170–173. doi: 10.1159/000083989

Makimoto, Kiyoko. (1998). Drinking patterns and drinking problems among Asian-Americans and Pacific Islanders. *Alcohol Health and Research World*, 22(4), 270–275.

Malina, Robert M.; Bouchard, Claude & Bar-Or, Oded. (2004). *Growth, maturation, and physical activity* (2nd ed.). Champaign, IL: Human Kinetics.

Malloy, Michael H. (2009). Impact of cesarean section on intermediate and late preterm births: United States, 2000–2003. *Birth*, 36(1), 26–33. doi: 10.1111/j.1523-536X.2008.00292.x

Mandler, Jean M. (2004). *The foundations of mind: Origins of conceptual thought.* New York, NY: Oxford University Press.

Mandler, Jean M. & DeLoache, Judy. (2012). The beginnings of conceptual development. In Sabina M. Pauen (Ed.), *Early childhood development and later outcome.* New York, NY: Cambridge University Press.

Mangels, Jennifer A.; Good, Catherine; Whiteman, Ronald C.; Maniscalco, Brian & Dweck, Carol S. (2012). Emotion blocks the path to learning under stereotype threat. *Social Cognitive Affective Neuroscience*, 7(2), 230–241. doi: 10.1093/scan/nsq100

Mann, Joshua R.; McDermott, Suzanne; Bao, Haikun & Bersabe, Adrian. (2009). Maternal genitourinary infection and risk of cerebral palsy. *Developmental Medicine & Child Neurology*, 51(4), 282–288. doi: 10.1111/j.1469-8749.2008.03226.x

Manning, Wendy D.; Brown, Susan L. & Payne, Krista K. (2014). Two decades of stability and change in age at first union formation. *Journal of Marriage and Family*, 76(2), 247–260. doi: 10.1111/jomf.12090

Månsson, Johanna & Stjernqvist, Karin. (2014). Children born extremely preterm show significant lower cognitive, language and motor function levels compared with children born at term, as measured by the Bayley-III at 2.5 years. *Acta Paediatrica*, 103(5), 504–511. doi: 10.1111/apa.12585

Manuck, Stephen B. & McCaffery, Jeanne M. (2014). Gene-environment interaction. *Annual Review of Psychology*, 65, 41–70. doi: 10.1146/annurev-psych-010213-115100

Mar, Raymond A. (2011). The neural bases of social cognition and story comprehension. *Annual Review of Psychology*, 62, 103–134. doi: 10.1146/annurev-psych-120709-145406

Marazita, John M. & Merriman, William E. (2010). Verifying one's knowledge of a name without retrieving it: A U-shaped relation to vocabulary size in early childhood. *Language Learning and Development*, 7(1), 40–54. doi: 10.1080/15475441.2010.496099

March, John S.; Franklin, Martin E.; Leonard, Henrietta L. & Foa, Edna B. (2004). Obsessive-compulsive disorder. In Tracy L. Morris & John S. March (Eds.), *Anxiety disorders in children and adolescents* (2nd ed., pp. 212–240). New York, NY: Guilford Press.

Marcia, James E. (1966). Development and validation of ego-identity status. *Journal of Personality and Social Psychology*, 3(5), 551–558. doi: 10.1037/h0023281

Marcia, James E.; Waterman, Alan S.; Matteson, David R.; Archer, Sally L. & Orlofsky, Jacob L. (1993). *Ego identity: A handbook for psychosocial research.* New York, NY: Springer-Verlag.

Marcovitch, Stuart; Boseovski, Janet J.; Knapp, Robin J. & Kane, Michael J. (2010). Goal neglect and working memory capacity in 4- to 6-year-old children. *Child Development*, 81(6), 1687–1695. doi: 10.1111/j.1467-8624.2010.01503.x

Marcus, Gary F. & Rabagliati, Hugh. (2009). Language acquisition, domain specificity, and descent with modification. In John Colombo, et al. (Eds.), *Infant pathways to language: Methods, models, and research disorders* (pp. 267–285). New York, NY: Psychology Press.

Mareschal, Denis & Kaufman, Jordy. (2012). Object permanence in infancy: Revisiting Baillargeon's drawbridge study. In Alan M. Slater & Paul C. Quinn (Eds.), *Developmental psychology: Revisiting the classic studies.* Thousand Oaks, CA: Sage.

Marette, André & Picard-Deland, Eliane. (2014). Yogurt consumption and impact on health: Focus on children and cardiometabolic risk. *American Journal Clinical Nutrition*, 99(5), 1243S–1247S. doi: 10.3945/ajcn.113.073379

Marshall, Eliot. (2011). Waiting for the revolution. *Science*, 331(6017), 526–529. doi: 10.1126/science.331.6017.526

Marshall, Eliot. (2014). An experiment in zero parenting. *Science, 345*(6198), 752–754. doi: 10.1126/science.345.6198.752

Martin, Carmel. (2014). *Common core implementation best practices.* Washington, DC: Center for American Progress.

Martin, Carol L.; Fabes, Richard; Hanish, Laura; Leonard, Stacie & Dinella, Lisa. (2011). Experienced and expected similarity to same-gender peers: Moving toward a comprehensive model of gender segregation. *Sex Roles, 65*(5/6), 421–434. doi: 10.1007/s11199-011-0029-y

Martin, Carol L. & Ruble, Diane N. (2010). Patterns of gender development. *Annual Review of Psychology, 61*, 353–381. doi: 10.1146/annurev.psych.093008.100511

Martin, Joyce A.; Hamilton, Brady E.; Sutton, Paul D.; Ventura, Stephanie J.; Mathews, T. J. & Osterman, Michelle J. K. (2010). *Births: Final data for 2008.* Hyattsville, MD: U.S. Department of Health and Human Services, Centers for Disease Control and Prevention, National Center for Health Statistics, National Vital Statistics System.

Martin-Uzzi, Michele & Duval-Tsioles, Denise. (2013). The experience of remarried couples in blended families. *Journal of Divorce & Remarriage, 54*(1), 43–57. doi: 10.1080/10502556.2012.743828

Martinez, Gilbert A.; Dodd, David, A. & Samartgedes, Jo Ann. (1981). Milk feeding patterns in the United States during the first 12 months of life. *Pediatrics, 68*(6), 863–868.

Martorell, Reynaldo & Young, Melissa F. (2012). Patterns of stunting and wasting: Potential explanatory factors. *Advances in Nutrition, 3*(2), 227–233. doi: 10.3945/an.111.001107

Marvasti, Amir B. & McKinney, Karyn D. (2011). Does diversity mean assimilation? *Critical Sociology, 37*(5), 631–650. doi: 10.1177/0896920510380071

Mascarelli, Amanda. (2013). Growing up with pesticides. *Science, 341*(6147), 740–741. doi: 10.1126/science.341.6147.740

Masche, J. Gowert. (2010). Explanation of normative declines in parents' knowledge about their adolescent children. *Journal of Adolescence, 33*(2), 271–284. doi: 10.1016/j.adolescence.2009.08.002

Maski, Kiran P. & Kothare, Sanjeev V. (2013). Sleep deprivation and neurobehavioral functioning in children. *International Journal of Psychophysiology, 89*(2), 259–264. doi: 10.1016/j.ijpsycho.2013.06.019

Maslow, Abraham H. (1997). *Motivation and personality* (3rd ed.). New York, NY: Pearson.

Maslow, Abraham H. (1999). *Toward a psychology of being* (3rd ed.). New York, NY: Wiley.

Maslowsky, Julie; Keating, Daniel P.; Monk, Christopher S. & Schulenberg, John. (2011). Planned versus unplanned risks: Neurocognitive predictors of subtypes of adolescents' risk behavior. *International Journal of Behavioral Development, 35*(2), 152–160. doi: 10.1177/0165025410378069

Maslowsky, Julie; Schulenberg, John E. & Zucker, Robert A. (2014). Influence of conduct problems and depressive symptomatology on adolescent substance use: Developmentally proximal versus distal effects. *Developmental Psychology, 50*(4), 1179–1189. doi: 10.1037/a0035085

Mâsse, Louise C.; Perna, Frank; Agurs-Collins, Tanya & Chriqui, Jamie F. (2013). Change in school nutrition-related laws from 2003 to 2008: Evidence from the School Nutrition-Environment State Policy Classification System. *American Journal of Public Health, 103*(9), 1597–1603. doi: 10.2105/AJPH.2012.300896

Masten, Ann S. (2013). Risk and resilience in development. In Philip D. Zelazo (Ed.), *The Oxford handbook of developmental psychology* (Vol. 2, pp. 579–607). New York, NY: Oxford University Press. doi: 10.1093/oxfordhb/9780199958474.013.0023

Masten, Ann S. (2014). *Ordinary magic: Resilience in development.* New York, NY: Guilford Press.

Mathews, T. J.; Menacker, Fay & MacDorman, Marian F. (2003). *Infant mortality statistics from the 2001 period linked birth/infant death data set.* Hyattsville, MD: National Center for Health Statistics, 52(2).

Mathison, David J. & Agrawal, Dewesh. (2010). An update on the epidemiology of pediatric fractures. *Pediatric Emergency Care, 26*(8), 594–603. doi: 10.1097/PEC.0b013e3181eb838d

Mattar, Rejane; de Campos Mazo, Daniel Ferraz & Carrilho, Flair José. (2012). Lactose intolerance: Diagnosis, genetic, and clinical factors. *Clinical and Experimental Gastroenterology, 5*, 113–121. doi: 10.2147/CEG.S32368

Maxwell, Lesli A. (2012). Achievement gaps tied to income found widening. *Education Week, 31*(23), 1, 22–23.

Mayes, Rick; Bagwell, Catherine & Erkulwater, Jennifer L. (2009). *Medicating children: ADHD and pediatric mental health.* Cambridge, MA: Harvard University Press.

McAdams, Dan P. & Olson, Bradley D. (2010). Personality development: Continuity and change over the life course. *Annual Review of Psychology, 61*, 517–542. doi: 10.1146/annurev.psych.093008.100507

McAdams, Dan P. & Pals, Jennifer L. (2006). A new Big Five: Fundamental principles for an integrative science of personality. *American Psychologist, 61*(3), 204–217. doi: 10.1037/0003-066X.61.3.204

McAlister, Anna R. & Peterson, Candida C. (2013). Siblings, theory of mind, and executive functioning in children aged 3–6 years: New longitudinal evidence. *Child Development, 84*(4), 1442–1458. doi: 10.1111/cdev.12043

McCabe, Janice. (2011). Doing multiculturalism: An interactionist analysis of the practices of a multicultural sorority. *Journal of Contemporary Ethnography, 40*(5), 521–549. doi: 10.1177/0891241611403588

McCall, Robert B. (2013). The consequences of early institutionalization: Can institutions be improved?—Should they? *Child and Adolescent Mental Health, 18*(4), 193–201. doi: 10.1111/camh.12025

McCarthy, Neil & Eberhart, Johann K. (2014). Gene–ethanol interactions underlying fetal alcohol spectrum disorders. *Cellular and Molecular Life Sciences, 71*(14), 2699–2706. doi: 10.1007/s00018-014-1578-3

McCartney, Kathleen; Burchinal, Margaret; Clarke-Stewart, Alison; Bub, Kristen L.; Owen, Margaret T. & Belsky, Jay. (2010). Testing a series of causal propositions relating time in child care to children's externalizing behavior. *Developmental Psychology, 46*(1), 1–17. doi: 10.1037/a0017886

McCarty, Cheryl; Prawitz, Aimee D.; Derscheid, Linda E. & Montgomery, Bette. (2011). Perceived safety and teen risk taking in online chat sites. *Cyberpsychology, Behavior, and Social Networking, 14*(3), 169–174. doi: 10.1089/cyber.2010.0050

McClain, Natalie M. & Garrity, Stacy E. (2011). Sex trafficking and the exploitation of adolescents. *Journal of Obstetric, Gynecologic, & Neonatal Nursing, 40*(2), 243–252. doi: 10.1111/j.1552-6909.2011.01221.x

McCormick, Cheryl M.; Mathews, Iva Z.; Thomas, Catherine & Waters, Patti. (2010). Investigations of HPA function and the enduring consequences of stressors in adolescence in animal models. *Brain and Cognition, 72*(1), 73–85. doi: 10.1016/j.bandc.2009.06.003

McCowan, Lesley M. E.; Dekker, Gustaaf A.; Chan, Eliza; Stewart, Alistair; Chappell, Lucy C.; Hunter, Misty, . . . North, Robyn A. (2009). Spontaneous preterm birth and small for gestational age infants in women who stop smoking early in pregnancy: Prospective cohort study. *BMJ, 338*, b1081. doi: 10.1136/bmj.b1081

McCright, Aaron M. & Dunlap, Riley E. (2011). The politicization of climate change and polarization in the American public's views of global warming, 2001–2010. *Sociological Quarterly, 52*(2), 155–194. doi: 10.1111/j.1533-8525.2011.01198.x

McFarlane, Alexander C. & Van Hooff, Miranda. (2009). Impact of childhood exposure to a natural disaster on adult mental health: 20-year longitudinal follow-up study. *The British Journal of Psychiatry, 195*(2), 142–148. doi: 10.1192/bjp.bp.108.054270

McGill, Rebecca K.; Hughes, Diane; Alicea, Stacey & Way, Niobe. (2012). Academic adjustment across middle school: The role of public regard and parenting. *Developmental Psychology, 48*(4), 1003–1018. doi: 10.1037/a0026006

McIntyre, Donald A. (2002). *Colour blindness: Causes and effects.* Chester, UK: Dalton Publishing.

McKusick, Victor A. (2007). Mendelian inheritance in man and its online version, OMIM. *The American Journal of Human Genetics, 80*(4), 588–604. doi: 10.1086/514346

McLaren, Paul J.; Fellay, Jacques & Telenti, Amalio. (2013). European genetic diversity and susceptibility to pathogens. *Human Heredity*, 76(3–4), 187–193. doi: 10.1159/000357758

McLaurin, Jennie A. (2014). Migrant farm worker health. In Jacob C. Warren & K. Bryant Smalley (Eds.), *Rural public health: Best practices and preventive models* (pp. 227–240). New York, NY: Springer.

McLeod, Bryce D.; Wood, Jeffrey J. & Weisz, John R. (2007). Examining the association between parenting and childhood anxiety: A meta-analysis. *Clinical Psychology Review*, 27(2), 155–172. doi: 10.1016/j.cpr.2006.09.002

McManus, I. Chris; Moore, James; Freegard, Matthew & Rawles, Richard. (2010). Science in the making: Right Hand, Left Hand. III: Estimating historical rates of left-handedness. *Laterality: Asymmetries of Body, Brain and Cognition*, 15(1/2), 186–208. doi: 10.1080/13576500802565313

McShane, Kelly E. & Hastings, Paul D. (2009). The New Friends Vignettes: Measuring parental psychological control that confers risk for anxious adjustment in preschoolers. *International Journal of Behavioral Development*, 33(6), 481–495. doi: 10.1177/0165025409103874

Meadows, Sara. (2006). *The child as thinker: The development and acquisition of cognition in childhood* (2nd ed.). New York, NY: Routledge.

Meece, Judith L. & Eccles, Jacquelynne S. (Eds.). (2010). *Handbook of research on schools, schooling, and human development*. New York, NY: Routledge.

Meeus, Wim. (2011). The study of adolescent identity formation 2000–2010: A review of longitudinal research. *Journal of Research on Adolescence*, 21(1), 75–94. doi: 10.1111/j.1532-7795.2010.00716.x

Mehta, Clare M. & Strough, JoNell. (2009). Sex segregation in friendships and normative contexts across the life span. *Developmental Review*, 29(3), 201–220. doi: 10.1016/j.dr.2009.06.001

Meier, Ann; Hull, Kathleen E. & Ortyl, Timothy A. (2009). Young adult relationship values at the intersection of gender and sexuality. *Journal of Marriage and Family*, 71(3), 510–525. doi: 10.1111/j.1741-3737.2009.00616.x

Meier, Ann & Musick, Kelly. (2014). Variation in associations between family dinners and adolescent well-being. *Journal of Marriage and Family*, 76(1), 13–23. doi: 10.1111/jomf.12079

Meister, Jeanne. (2012). Job hopping is the 'new normal' for millennials: Three ways to prevent a human resource nightmare. *Forbes*.

Meltzoff, Andrew N. & Gopnik, Alison. (2013). Learning about the mind from evidence: Children's development of intuitive theories of perception and personality. In Simon Baron-Cohen, et al. (Eds.), *Understanding other minds: Perspectives from developmental social neuroscience* (3rd ed., pp. 19–34). New York, NY: Oxford University Press. doi: 10.1093/acprof:oso/9780199692972.001.0001

Meltzoff, Andrew N. & Moore, M. Keith. (1999). A new foundation for cognitive development in infancy: The birth of the representa-

tional infant. In Ellin K. Scholnick, et al. (Eds.), *Conceptual development: Piaget's legacy* (pp. 53–78). Mahwah, NJ: Lawrence Erlbaum Associates.

Menary, Kyle; Collins, Paul F.; Porter, James N.; Muetzel, Ryan; Olson, Elizabeth A.; Kumar, Vipin, . . . Luciana, Monica. (2013). Associations between cortical thickness and general intelligence in children, adolescents and young adults. *Intelligence*, 41(5), 597–606. doi: 10.1016/j.intell.2013.07.010

Mendle, Jane; Harden, K. Paige; Brooks-Gunn, Jeanne & Graber, Julia A. (2010). Development's tortoise and hare: Pubertal timing, pubertal tempo, and depressive symptoms in boys and girls. *Developmental Psychology*, 46(5), 1341–1353. doi: 10.1037/a0020205

Mendle, Jane; Harden, K. Paige; Brooks-Gunn, Jeanne & Graber, Julia A. (2012). Peer relationships and depressive symptomatology in boys at puberty. *Developmental Psychology*, 48(2), 429–435. doi: 10.1037/a0026425

Mennis, Jeremy & Mason, Michael J. (2012). Social and geographic contexts of adolescent substance use: The moderating effects of age and gender. *Social Networks*, 34(1), 150–157. doi: 10.1016/j.socnet.2010.10.003

Merikangas, Kathleen R.; He, Jian-ping; Rapoport, Judith; Vitiello, Benedetto & Olfson, Mark. (2013). Medication use in US youth with mental disorders. *JAMA Pediatrics*, 167(2), 141–148. doi: 10.1001/jamapediatrics.2013.431

Merikangas, Kathleen R. & McClair, Vetisha L. (2012). Epidemiology of substance use disorders. *Human Genetics*, 131(6), 779–789. doi: 10.1007/s00439-012-1168-0

Meririnne, Esa; Kiviruusu, Olli; Karlsson, Linnea; Pelkonen, Mirjami; Ruuttu, Titta; Tuisku, Virpi & Marttunen, Mauri. (2010). Brief report: Excessive alcohol use negatively affects the course of adolescent depression: One year naturalistic follow-up study. *Journal of Adolescence*, 33(1), 221–226. doi: 10.1016/j.adolescence.2009.07.010

Mersky, J. P.; Topitzes, J. & Reynolds, A. J. (2013). Impacts of adverse childhood experiences on health, mental health, and substance use in early adulthood: A cohort study of an urban, minority sample in the U.S. *Child Abuse & Neglect*, 37(11), 917–925. doi: 10.1016/j.chiabu.2013.07.011

Merz, Emily C. & McCall, Robert B. (2011). Parent ratings of executive functioning in children adopted from psychosocially depriving institutions. *Journal of Child Psychology and Psychiatry*, 52(5), 537–546. doi: 10.1111/j.1469-7610.2010.02335.x

Mesch, Gustavo S. & Talmud, Ilan. (2010). *Wired youth: The social world of adolescence in the information age*. New York, NY: Routledge.

Messinger, Daniel M.; Ruvolo, Paul; Ekas, Naomi V. & Fogel, Alan. (2010). Applying machine learning to infant interaction: The development is in the details. *Neural Networks*, 23(8/9), 1004–1016. doi: 10.1016/j.neunet.2010.08.008

Metcalfe, Janet & Finn, Bridgid. (2013). Metacognition and control of study choice in children. *Metacognition and Learning*, 8(1), 19–46. doi: 10.1007/s11409-013-9094-7

Metcalfe, Lindsay A.; Harvey, Elizabeth A. & Laws, Holly B. (2013). The longitudinal relation between academic/cognitive skills and externalizing behavior problems in preschool children. *Journal of Educational Psychology*, 105(3), 881–894. doi: 10.1037/a0032624

Michl, Louisa C.; McLaughlin, Katie A.; Shepherd, Kathrine & Nolen-Hoeksema, Susan. (2013). Rumination as a mechanism linking stressful life events to symptoms of depression and anxiety: Longitudinal evidence in early adolescents and adults. *Journal of Abnormal Psychology*, 122(2), 339–352. doi: 10.1037/a0031994

Miklowitz, David J. & Cicchetti, Dante (Eds.). (2010). *Understanding bipolar disorder: A developmental psychopathology perspective*. New York, NY: Guilford Press.

Milardo, Robert M. (2010). *The forgotten kin: Aunts and uncles*. New York, NY: Cambridge University Press.

Miles, Lynden K. (2009). Who is approachable? *Journal of Experimental Social Psychology*, 45(1), 262–266. doi: 10.1016/j.jesp.2008.08.010

Milkman, Katherine L.; Chugh, Dolly & Bazerman, Max H. (2009). How can decision making be improved? *Perspectives on Psychological Science*, 4(4), 379–383. doi: 10.1111/j.1745-6924.2009.01142.x

Miller, Alec L.; Rathus, Jill H. & Linehan, Marsha M. (2007). *Dialectical behavior therapy with suicidal adolescents*. New York, NY: Guilford Press.

Miller, Cindy F.; Martin, Carol Lynn; Fabes, Richard A. & Hanish, Laura D. (2013). Bringing the cognitive and the social together: How gender detectives and gender enforcers shape children's gender development. In Mahzarin R. Banaji & Susan A. Gelman (Eds.), *Navigating the social world: What infants, children, and other species can teach us* (pp. 306–313). New York, NY: Oxford University Press.

Miller, Greg. (2006). The thick and thin of brainpower: Developmental timing linked to IQ. *Science*, 311(5769), 1851. doi: 10.1126/science.311.5769.1851

Miller, Greg. (2010). New clues about what makes the human brain special. *Science*, 330(6008), 1167. doi: 10.1126/science.330.6008.1167

Miller, Gregory E. & Chen, Edith. (2010). Harsh family climate in early life: Presages the emergence of a proinflammatory phenotype in adolescence. *Psychological Science*, 21(6), 848–856. doi: 10.1177/0956797610370161

Miller, Joan G. (2004). The cultural deep structure of psychological theories of social development. In Robert J. Sternberg & Elena L. Grigorenko (Eds.), *Culture and competence: Contexts of life success* (pp. 111–138). Washington, DC: American Psychological Association.

Miller, Orlando J. & Therman, Eeva. (2001). *Human chromosomes* (4th ed.). New York, NY: Springer.

Miller, Portia; Votruba-Drzal, Elizabeth; Coley, Rebekah Levine & Koury, Amanda S. (2014). Immigrant families' use of early childcare: Predictors of care type. *Early Childhood Research Quarterly*, 29(4), 484–498. doi: 10.1016/j.ecresq.2014.05.011

Miller, Patricia H. (2011). *Theories of developmental psychology* (5th ed.). New York, NY: Worth Publishers.

Miller, Patricia Y. & Simon, William. (1980). The development of sexuality in adolescence. In Joseph Adelson (Ed.), *Handbook of adolescent psychology* (pp. 383–407). New York, NY: Wiley.

Mills, Jon (Ed.). (2004). *Psychoanalysis at the limit: Epistemology, mind, and the question of science*. Albany, NY: State University of New York Press.

Mills, James L.; McPartlin, Joseph M.; Kirke, Peadar N.; Lee, Young J.; Conley, Mary R.; Weir, Donald G. & Scott, John M. (1995). Homocysteine metabolism in pregnancies complicated by neural-tube defects. *The Lancet*, 345(8943), 149–151. doi: 10.1016/S0140-6736(95)90165-5

Mills-Koonce, W. Roger; Garrett-Peters, Patricia; Barnett, Melissa; Granger, Douglas A.; Blair, Clancy & Cox, Martha J. (2011). Father contributions to cortisol responses in infancy and toddlerhood. *Developmental Psychology*, 47(2), 388–395. doi: 10.1037/a0021066

Milunsky, Aubrey. (2011). *Your genes, your health: A critical family guide that could save your life*. New York, NY: Oxford University Press.

Minagawa-Kawai, Yasuyo; van der Lely, Heather; Ramus, Franck; Sato, Yutaka; Mazuka, Reiko & Dupoux, Emmanuel. (2011). Optical brain imaging reveals general auditory and language-specific processing in early infant development. *Cerebral Cortex*, 21(2), 254–261. doi: 10.1093/cercor/bhq082

Mindell, Jodi A.; Sadeh, Avi; Wiegand, Benjamin; How, Ti Hwei & Goh, Daniel Y. T. (2010). Cross-cultural differences in infant and toddler sleep. *Sleep Medicine*, 11(3), 274–280. doi: 10.1016/j.sleep.2009.04.012

Miniño, Arialdi M.; Heron, Melonie P.; Murphy, Sherry L. & Kochanek, Kenneth D. (2007). *Deaths: Final data for 2004*. Hyattsville, MD: National Center for Health Statistics, 55(19).

Minogue, Kristen. (2010). China's brain mappers zoom in on neural connections. *Science*, 330(6005), 747. doi: 10.1126/science.330.6005.747

Mischel, Walter. (2014). *The marshmallow test: Mastering self-control*. New York, NY: Little, Brown and Company.

Mishra, Ramesh C.; Singh, Sunita & Dasen, Pierre R. (2009). Geocentric dead reckoning in Sanskrit- and Hindi-medium school children. *Culture & Psychology*, 15(3), 386–408. doi: 10.1177/1354067x09343330

Misra, Dawn P.; Caldwell, Cleopatra; Young, Alford A. & Abelson, Sara. (2010). Do fathers matter? Paternal contributions to birth outcomes and racial disparities. *American Journal of Obstetrics and Gynecology*, 202(2), 99–100. doi: 10.1016/j.ajog.2009.11.031

Missana, Manuela; Rajhans, Purva; Atkinson, Anthony P. & Grossmann, Tobias. (2014). Discrimination of fearful and happy body postures in 8-month-old infants: An event-related potential study. *Frontiers in Human Neuroscience*, 8, 531. doi: 10.3389/fnhum.2014.00531

Mitchell, Edwin A. (2009). SIDS: Past, present and future. *Acta Paediatrica*, 98(11), 1712–1719. doi: 10.1111/j.1651-2227.2009.01503.x

Mitchell, Kimberly J.; Finkelhor, David; Jones, Lisa M. & Wolak, Janis. (2012). Prevalence and characteristics of youth sexting: A national study. *Pediatrics*, 129(1), 13–20. doi: 10.1542/peds.2011-1730

Mitchell, Kimberly J.; Jones, Lisa M.; Finkelhor, David & Wolak, Janis. (2013). Understanding the decline in unwanted online sexual solicitations for U.S. youth 2000–2010: Findings from three Youth Internet Safety Surveys. *Child Abuse & Neglect*, 37(12), 1225–1236. doi: 10.1016/j.chiabu.2013.07.002

Mitchell, Philip B.; Meiser, Bettina; Wilde, Alex; Fullerton, Janice; Donald, Jennifer; Wilhelm, Kay & Schofield, Peter R. (2010). Predictive and diagnostic genetic testing in psychiatry. *Psychiatric Clinics of North America*, 33(1), 225–243. doi: 10.1016/j.psc.2009.10.001

Miyata, Susanne; MacWhinney, Brian; Otomo, Kiyoshi; Sirai, Hidetosi; Oshima-Takane, Yuriko; Hirakawa, Makiko, . . . Itoh, Keiko. (2013). Developmental sentence scoring for Japanese. *First Language*, 33(2), 200–216. doi: 10.1177/0142723713479436

Mize, Krystal D.; Pineda, Melannie; Blau, Alexis K.; Marsh, Kathryn & Jones, Nancy A. (2014). Infant physiological and behavioral responses to a jealousy provoking condition. *Infancy*, 19(3), 338–348. doi: 10.1111/infa.12046

MMWR. (2002, September 13). *Folic acid and prevention of spina bifida and anencephaly: 10 years after the U.S. public health service recommendation*. Atlanta, GA: U.S. Department of Health and Human Services, Centers for Disease Control and Prevention, 51(RR13), 1–3.

MMWR. (2008, January 18). *School-associated student homicides—United States, 1992–2006*. Atlanta, GA: U.S. Department of Health and Human Services, Centers for Disease Control and Prevention, 57(2), 33–36.

MMWR. (2010, June 4). *Youth risk behavior surveillance—United States, 2009*. Atlanta, GA: U.S. Department of Health and Human Services, Centers for Disease Control and Prevention, 59(SS05).

MMWR. (2011, January 7). *Notifiable diseases and mortality tables*. Atlanta, GA: U.S. Department of Health and Human Services, Centers for Disease Control and Prevention, 59(52), 1704–1717.

MMWR. (2012, July 20). *Alcohol Use and Binge Drinking Among Women of Childbearing Age—United States, 2006–2010*. Atlanta, GA: U.S. Department of Health and Human Services, Centers for Disease Control and Prevention, 61(28), 534–538.

MMWR. (2012, June 8). *Youth risk behavior surveillance—United States, 2011*. Atlanta, GA: U.S. Department of Health and Human Services, Centers for Disease Control and Prevention, 61(4).

MMWR. (2013, April 5). *Blood lead levels in children aged 1–5 Years—United States, 1999–2010*. Atlanta, GA: U.S. Department of Health and Human Services, Centers for Disease Control and Prevention, 62(13), 245–248.

MMWR. (2013, August 9). *Vital signs: Obesity among low-income, preschool-aged children—United States, 2008–2011*. Atlanta, GA: U.S. Department of Health and Human Services, Centers for Disease Control and Prevention, 62(31), 629–634.

MMWR. (2013, January 18). *Obesity prevalence among low-income, preschool-aged children—New York City and Los Angeles County, 2003–2011*. Atlanta, GA: U.S. Department of Health and Human Services, Centers for Disease Control and Prevention, 62(2), 17–22.

MMWR. (2014, August 29). *National, state, and selected local area vaccination coverage among children aged 19–35 months—United States, 2013*. Atlanta, GA: U.S. Department of Health and Human Services, Centers for Disease Control and Prevention, 63(34), 741–748.

MMWR. (2014, July 25). *Human papillomavirus vaccination coverage among adolescents, 2007–2013, and postlicensure vaccine safety monitoring, 2006–2014—United States*. Atlanta, GA: U.S. Department of Health and Human Services, Centers for Disease Control and Prevention, 63(29).

MMWR. (2014, June 6). *Measles—United States, January 1–May 23, 2014*. Atlanta, GA: U.S. Department of Health and Human Services, Centers for Disease Control and Prevention, 63(22), 496–499.

MMWR. (2014, June 13). *Youth risk behavior surveillance—United States, 2013*. Atlanta, GA: U.S. Department of Health and Human Services, Centers for Disease Control and Prevention, 63(4).

MMWR. (2014, March 7). *Impact of requiring influenza vaccination for children in licensed child care or preschool programs—Connecticut, 2012–13 influenza season*. Atlanta, GA: U.S. Department of Health and Human Services, Centers for Disease Control and Prevention, 63(9), 181–185.

MMWR. (2014, March 28). *Prevalence of autism spectrum disorder among children aged 8 years—Autism and Developmental Disabilities Monitoring Network, 11 sites, United States, 2010*. Atlanta, GA: U.S. Department of Health and Human Services, Centers for Disease Control and Prevention, 63(2).

MMWR. (2014, May 2). *QuickStats: Percentage of children aged 6–17 years prescribed medication during the preceding 6 months for emotional or behavioral difficulties, by census region—National*

Health Interview Survey, United States, 2011–2012. Atlanta, GA: Centers for Disease Control and Prevention, 63(17), 389–389.

MMWR. (2014, May 16). *Racial/ethnic disparities in fatal unintentional drowning among persons aged ≤29 years—United States, 1999–2010.* Atlanta, GA: U.S. Department of Health and Human Services, Centers for Disease Control and Prevention, 63(19), 421–426.

MMWR. (2014, September 5). *Prevalence of smokefree home rules—United States, 1992–1993 and 2010–2011.* Atlanta, GA: Department of Health and Human Services, Centers for Disease Control and Prevention, 63(35), 765–769.

MMWR. (2014, September 26). *Prevalence of Chlamydia trachomatis genital infection among persons aged 14–39 Years—United States, 2007–2012.* Atlanta, GA: Department of Health and Human Services, Centers for Disease Control and Prevention, 63(38), 834–838.

Moffitt, Terrie E. (2003). Life-course-persistent and adolescence-limited antisocial behavior: A 10-year research review and a research agenda. In Benjamin B. Lahey, et al. (Eds.), *Causes of conduct disorder and juvenile delinquency* (pp. 49–75). New York, NY: Guilford Press.

Moffitt, Terrie E.; Arseneault, Louise; Belsky, Daniel; Dickson, Nigel; Hancox, Robert J.; Harrington, HonaLee, . . . Casp, Avshalom. (2011). A gradient of childhood self-control predicts health, wealth, and public safety. *Proceedings of the National Academy of Sciences of the United States of America, 108*(7), 2693–2698. doi: 10.1073/pnas.1010076108

Moffitt, Terrie E.; Caspi, Avshalom; Rutter, Michael & Silva, Phil A. (2001). *Sex differences in antisocial behaviour: Conduct disorder, delinquency, and violence in the Dunedin Longitudinal Study.* New York, NY: Cambridge University Press.

Mokrova, Irina L.; O'Brien, Marion; Calkins, Susan D.; Leerkes, Esther M. & Marcovitch, Stuart. (2013). The role of persistence at preschool age in academic skills at kindergarten. *European Journal of Psychology of Education, 28*(4), 1495–1503. doi: 10.1007/s10212-013-0177-2

Moldavsky, Maria & Sayal, Kapil. (2013). Knowledge and attitudes about Attention-deficit/hyperactivity disorder (ADHD) and its treatment: The views of children, adolescents, parents, teachers and healthcare professionals. *Current Psychiatry Reports, 15,* 377. doi: 10.1007/s11920-013-0377-0

Molina, Brooke S. G.; Hinshaw, Stephen P.; Arnold, L. Eugene; Swanson, James M.; Pelham, William E.; Hechtman, Lily, . . . Marcus, Sue. (2013). Adolescent substance use in the Multimodal Treatment Study of Attention-deficit/hyperactivity disorder (ADHD) (MTA) as a function of childhood ADHD, random assignment to childhood treatments, and subsequent medication. *Journal of the American Academy of Child & Adolescent Psychiatry, 52*(3), 250–263. doi: 10.1016/j.jaac.2012.12.014

Molina, Brooke S. G.; Hinshaw, Stephen P.; Swanson, James W.; Arnold, L. Eugene; Vitiello, Benedetto; Jensen, Peter S., . . . Houck, Patricia R. (2009). The MTA at 8 years:

Prospective follow-up of children treated for combined-type ADHD in a multisite study. *Journal of the American Academy of Child and Adolescent Psychiatry, 48*(5), 484–500. doi: 10.1097/CHI.0b013e31819c23d0

Møller, Signe J. & Tenenbaum, Harriet R. (2011). Danish majority children's reasoning about exclusion based on gender and ethnicity. *Child Development, 82*(2), 520–532. doi: 10.1111/j.1467-8624.2010.01568.x

Monahan, Kathryn C.; Steinberg, Laurence & Cauffman, Elizabeth. (2009). Affiliation with antisocial peers, susceptibility to peer influence, and antisocial behavior during the transition to adulthood. *Developmental Psychology, 45*(6), 1520–1530. doi: 10.1037/a0017417

Monahan, Kathryn C.; Steinberg, Laurence; Cauffman, Elizabeth & Mulvey, Edward P. (2013). Psychosocial (im)maturity from adolescence to early adulthood: Distinguishing between adolescence-limited and persisting antisocial behavior. *Development and Psychopathology, 25*(4), 1093–1105. doi: 10.1017/S0954579413000394

Monastersky, Richard. (2007). Who's minding the teenage brain? *Chronicle of Higher Education,* 53(19), A14–A18.

Monks, Claire P. & Coyne, Iain (Eds.). (2011). *Bullying in different contexts.* New York, NY: Cambridge University Press.

Monte, Lindsay M. & Ellis, Renee R. (2014). *Fertility of women in the United States, 2012: Population characteristics.* Washington, DC: U.S. Department of Commerce, Economics and Statistics Administration, U.S. Census Bureau.

Monteiro, Carlos A.; Conde, Wolney L. & Popkin, Barry M. (2004). The burden of disease from undernutrition and overnutrition in countries undergoing rapid nutrition transition: A view from Brazil. *American Journal of Public Health, 94*(3), 433–434. doi: 10.2105/AJPH.94.3.433

Monteiro, Carlos A.; Levy, Renata B.; Claro, Rafael M.; Ribeiro de Castro, Inês Rugani & Cannon, Geoffrey. (2011). Increasing consumption of ultra-processed foods and likely impact on human health: Evidence from Brazil. *Public Health Nutrition, 14*(1), 5–13. doi: 10.1017/S1368980010003241

Monthly Vital Statistics Report. (1980). *Final mortality statistics, 1978: Advance report.* Hyattsville, MD: National Center for Health Statistics, 29(6, Suppl. 2).

Moore, Keith L. & Persaud, T. V. N. (2007). *The developing human: Clinically oriented embryology* (8th ed.). Philadelphia, PA: Saunders/Elsevier.

Moore, Keith L. & Persaud, T. V. N. (2008). *The developing human: Clinically oriented embryology* (8th ed.). Philadelphia, PA: Saunders.

Moran, Lyndsey R.; Lengua, Liliana J. & Zalewski, Maureen. (2013). The interaction between negative emotionality and effortful control in early social-emotional development. *Social Development, 22*(2), 340–362. doi: 10.1111/sode.12025

Morawska, Alina & Sanders, Matthew. (2011). Parental use of time out revisited: A useful

or harmful parenting strategy? *Journal of Child and Family Studies, 20*(1), 1–8. doi: 10.1007/s10826-010-9371-x

Morcos, Roy N. & Kizy, Thomas. (2012). Gynecomastia: When is treatment indicated? *Journal of Family Practice, 61*(12), 719–725.

Morelli, Gilda A. & Rothbaum, Fred. (2007). Situating the child in context: Attachment relationships and self-regulation in different cultures. In Shinobu Kitayama & Dov Cohen (Eds.), *Handbook of cultural psychology* (pp. 500–527). New York, NY: Guilford Press.

Morgan, Ian G.; Ohno-Matsui, Kyoko & Saw, Seang-Mei. (2012). Myopia. *The Lancet,* 379(9827), 1739–1748. doi: 10.1016/S0140-6736(12)60272-4

Morgan, Paul L.; Staff, Jeremy; Hillemeier, Marianne M.; Farkas, George & Maczuga, Steven. (2013). Racial and ethnic disparities in ADHD diagnosis from kindergarten to eighth grade. *Pediatrics, 132*(1), 85–93. doi: 10.1542/peds.2012-2390

Morning, Ann. (2008). Ethnic classification in global perspective: A cross-national survey of the 2000 census round. *Population Research and Policy Review, 27*(2), 239–272. doi: 10.1007/s11113-007-9062-5

Morón, Cecilio & Viteri, Fernando E. (2009). Update on common indicators of nutritional status: Food access, food consumption, and biochemical measures of iron and anemia. *Nutrition Reviews, 67*(Suppl. 1), S31–S35. doi: 10.1111/j.1753-4887.2009.00156.x

Morones, Alyssa. (2013). Paddling persists in U.S. schools. *Education Week, 33*(9), 1, 10–11.

Morris, Amanda S.; Silk, Jennifer S.; Steinberg, Laurence; Myers, Sonya S. & Robinson, Lara R. (2007). The role of the family context in the development of emotion regulation. *Social Development, 16*(2), 361–388. doi: 10.1111/j.1467-9507.2007.00389.x

Morris, Vivian G. & Morris, Curtis L. (2013). A call for African American male teachers: The supermen expected to solve the problems of low-performing schools. In Chance W. Lewis & Ivory A. Toldson (Eds.), *Black male teachers: Diversifying the United States' teacher workforce* (pp. 151–165). Bingley, UK: Emerald Group.

Morrissey, Taryn. (2009). Multiple child-care arrangements and young children's behavioral outcomes. *Child Development, 80*(1), 59–76. doi: 10.1111/j.1467-8624.2008.01246.x

Mortimer, Jeylan. (2013). Work and its positive and negative effects on youth's psychosocial development. In Carol W. Runyan, et al. (Eds.), *Health and safety of young workers: Proceedings of a U.S. and Canadian series of symposia* (pp. 66–79). Washington, DC: U.S. Department of Health and Human Services, Centers for Disease Control and Prevention, National Institute for Occupational Safety and Health.

Mosher, William D.; Jones, Jo & Abma, Joyce C. (2012). *Intended and unintended births in the United States: 1982–2010.* Hyattsville, MD: U.S. Department of Health and Human Services,

Centers for Disease Control and Prevention, National Center for Health Statistics, 55, 1–27.

Moshman, David. (2011). *Adolescent rationality and development: Cognition, morality, and identity* (3rd ed.). New York, NY: Psychology Press.

Moshman, David. (2014). *Epistemic cognition and development: The psychology of truth and justification.* New York, NY: Psychology Press.

Moss, Howard B.; Chen, Chiung M. & Yi, Hsiao-ye. (2014). Early adolescent patterns of alcohol, cigarettes, and marijuana polysubstance use and young adult substance use outcomes in a nationally representative sample. *Drug & Alcohol Dependence, 136*(Suppl. 1), 51–62. doi: 10.1016/j.drugalcdep.2013.12.011

Motel, Seth. (2014). *6 facts about marijuana.* Washington, DC: Pew Research Center.

Moulson, Margaret C.; Westerlund, Alissa; Fox, Nathan A.; Zeanah, Charles H. & Nelson, Charles A. (2009). The effects of early experience on face recognition: An event-related potential study of institutionalized children in Romania. *Child Development, 80*(4), 1039–1056. doi: 10.1111/j.1467-8624.2009.01315.x

Moyer, Virginia A. (2014). Prevention of dental caries in children from birth through age 5 years: US Preventive Services Task Force Recommendation Statement. *Pediatrics, 133*(6), 1102–1111. doi: 10.1542/peds.2014-0483

Mrug, Sylvie; Elliott, Marc N.; Davies, Susan; Tortolero, Susan R.; Cuccaro, Paula & Schuster, Mark A. (2014). Early puberty, negative peer influence, and problem behaviors in adolescent girls. *Pediatrics, 133*(1), 7–14. doi: 10.1542/peds.2013-0628

Mueller, Christian E.; Bridges, Sara K. & Goddard, Michelle S. (2011). Sleep and parent-family connectedness: Links, relationships and implications for adolescent depression. *Journal of Family Studies, 17*(1), 9–23.

Mulder, Pamela J. & Johnson, Teresa S. (2010). The Beginning Breastfeeding Survey: Measuring mothers' perceptions of breastfeeding effectiveness during the postpartum hospitalization. *Research in Nursing & Health, 33*(4), 329–344. doi: 10.1002/nur.20384

Mullally, Sinéad L. & Maguire, Eleanor A. (2014). Learning to remember: The early ontogeny of episodic memory. *Developmental Cognitive Neuroscience, 9*(13), 12–29. doi: 10.1016/j.dcn.2013.12.006

Müller, Anna R.; Röder, Mandy & Fingerle, Michael. (2014). Child sexual abuse prevention goes online: Introducing "Cool and Safe" and its effects. *Computers & Education, 78*, 60–65. doi: 10.1016/j.compedu.2014.04.023

Müller, Ulrich; Dick, Anthony S.; Gela, Katherine; Overton, Willis F. & Zelazo, Philip D. (2006). The role of negative priming in preschoolers' flexible rule use on the dimensional change card sort task. *Child Development, 77*(2), 395–412. doi: 10.1111/j.1467-8624.2006.00878.x

Mulligan, A.; Anney, R.; Butler, L.; O'Regan, M.; Richardson, T.; Tulewicz, E. M., . . . Gill, M. (2013). Home environment: Association with hyperactivity/impulsivity in children with ADHD and their non-ADHD siblings. *Child: Care, Health & Development, 39*(2), 202–212. doi: 10.1111/j.1365-2214.2011.01345.x

Mullis, Ina V. S.; Martin, Michael O.; Foy, Pierre & Arora, A. (2012a). *TIMSS 2011 International Results in Mathematics.* Chestnut Hill, MA: TIMSS & PIRLS International Study Center, Boston College.

Mullis, Ina V. S.; Martin, Michael O.; Foy, Pierre & Drucker, Kathleen T. (2012b). *PIRLS 2011 international results in reading.* Chestnut Hill, MA: TIMSS & PIRLS International Study Center, Boston College.

Muñoz, Carmen & Singleton, David. (2011). A critical review of age-related research on L2 ultimate attainment. *Language Teaching, 44*(1), 1–35. doi: 10.1017/S0261444810000327

Muraskas, Jonathan K.; Rau, Brian J.; Castillo, Patricia Rae; Gianopoulos, John & Boyd, Lauren A. C. (2012). Long-term follow-up of 2 newborns with a combined birth weight of 540 grams. *Pediatrics, 129*(1), e174–e178. doi: 10.1542/peds.2010-0039

Muris, Peter & Meesters, Cor. (2014). Small or big in the eyes of the other: On the developmental psychopathology of self-conscious emotions as shame, guilt, and pride. *Clinical Child and Family Psychology Review, 17*(1), 19–40. doi: 10.1007/s10567-013-0137-z

Murphy, Sherry L.; Xu, Jiaquan & Kochanek, Kenneth D. (2012). *Deaths: Preliminary data for 2010.* Hyattsville, MD: National Center for Health Statistics, 60(4).

Murray, Stuart B.; Loeb, Katharine L. & Le Grange, Daniel. (2014). Indexing psychopathology throughout family-based treatment for adolescent anorexia nervosa: Are we on track? *Advances in Eating Disorders: Theory, Research and Practice, 2*(1), 93–96. doi: 10.1080/21662630.2013.831522

Murray, Thomas H. (2014). Stirring the simmering "designer baby" pot. *Science, 343*(6176), 1208–1210. doi: 10.1126/science.1248080

Mustanski, Brian; Birkett, Michelle; Greene, George J.; Hatzenbuehler, Mark L. & Newcomb, Michael E. (2014). Envisioning an America without sexual orientation inequities in adolescent health. *American Journal of Public Health, 104*(2), 218–225. doi: 10.2105/AJPH.2013.301625

Naci, Huseyin; Chisholm, Dan & Baker, T. D. (2009). Distribution of road traffic deaths by road user group: A global comparison. *Injury Prevention, 15*(1), 55–59. doi: 10.1136/ip.2008.018721

Nadeau, Joseph H. & Dudley, Aimée M. (2011). Systems genetics. *Science, 331*(6020), 1015–1016. doi: 10.1126/science.1203869

NAEYC. The 10 NAEYC program standards. http://families.naeyc.org/accredited-article/10-naeyc-program-standards#1

NAEYC. (2014). *NAEYC Early Childhood Program Standards and Accreditation Criteria & Guidance for Assessment.* Washington, DC: National Association for the Education of Young Children.

Naninck, Eva F. G.; Lucassen, Paul J. & Bakker, Julie. (2011). Sex differences in adolescent depression: Do sex hormones determine vulnerability? *Journal of Neuroendocrinology, 23*(5), 383–392. doi: 10.1111/j.1365-2826.2011.02125.x

Narayan, Chandan R.; Werker, Janet F. & Beddor, Patrice Speeter. (2010). The interaction between acoustic salience and language experience in developmental speech perception: Evidence from nasal place discrimination. *Developmental Science, 13*(3), 407–420. doi: 10.1111/j.1467-7687.2009.00898.x

Narvaez, Darcia & Lapsley, Daniel K. (2009). Moral identity, moral functioning, and the development of moral character. *Psychology of Learning and Motivation, 50*, 237–274. doi: 10.1016/S0079-7421(08)00408-8

National Center for Education Statistics. (2009). *The condition of education 2009.* Washington, DC: Institute of Education Sciences, U.S. Department of Education.

National Center for Education Statistics. (2013, May). *Table 202.10: Enrollment of 3-, 4-, and 5-year-old children in preprimary programs, by level of program, control of program, and attendance status: Selected years, 1965 through 2012.* Washington, DC: Institute of Education Sciences, U.S. Department of Education.

National Center for Education Statistics. (2013a). *The Nation's report card: A first look: 2013 mathematics and reading.* Washington, DC: Institute of Education Sciences, U.S. Department of Education.

National Center for Education Statistics. (2013b). *Table 204.30: Children 3 to 21 years old served under Individuals with Disabilities Education Act (IDEA), Part B, by type of disability: Selected years, 1976–77 through 2011–12.* Washington, DC: Institute of Education Sciences, U.S. Department of Education.

National Center for Education Statistics. (2013c). *Annual diploma counts and the Averaged Freshmen Graduation Rate (AFGR) in the United States by race/ethnicity: School years 2007–08 through 2011–12.* Washington, DC: U.S. Department of Education, Institute of Education Sciences, National Center for Education Statistics.

National Center for Education Statistics. (2014). *Fast facts: Back to school statistics.* Washington, DC: U.S. Department of Education, Institute of Education Sciences, National Center for Education Statistics.

National Center for Environmental Health. (2012). *Tested and confirmed elevated blood lead levels by state, year and blood lead level group for children <72 months.* Atlanta, GA: Centers for Disease Control and Prevention.

National Center for Health Statistics. (2012). *Health, United States, 2011: With special feature on socioeconomic status and health.* Hyattsville, MD: U.S. Department of Health and Human Services, Centers for Disease Control and Prevention.

National Center for Health Statistics. (2013). *Health, United States, 2012: With special feature on emergency care.* Hyattsville, MD: U.S. Department of Health and Human Services, Centers for Disease Control and Prevention.

National Governors Association Center for Best Practices (NGA Center) and the Council of Chief State School Officers (CCSSO). (2010, October 25). *Common core state standards initiative.* Washington, DC: National Governors Association.

National Science Board. (2012). *Science and Engineering Indicators 2012.* Arlington, VA: National Science Foundation.

National Sleep Foundation. (2006). *Summary findings of the 2006 Sleep in America poll.* Washington, DC: National Sleep Foundation & WBA Market Research.

National Vital Statistics Reports. (2013). *Table 3. Number of deaths and death rates, by age, race, and sex: United States, 2012.* Atlanta, GA: U.S. Department of Health and Human Services, Centers for Disease Control and Prevention.

National Vital Statistics Reports. (Forthcoming). *Deaths: Final data for 2012.* Hyattsville, MD: National Center for Health Statistics, 63(9).

Natsuaki, Misaki N.; Leve, Leslie D.; Neiderhiser, Jenae M.; Shaw, Daniel S.; Scaramella, Laura V.; Ge, Xiaojia & Reiss, David. (2013). Intergenerational transmission of risk for social inhibition: The interplay between parental responsiveness and genetic influences. *Development and Psychopathology, 25*(1), 261–274. doi: 10.1017/S0954579412001010

Naudé, H.; Marx, J.; Pretorius, E. & Hislop-Esterhuyzen, N. (2007). Evidence of early childhood defects due to prenatal overexposure to vitamin A: A case study. *Early Child Development and Care, 177*(3), 235–253. doi: 10.1080/03004430500456149

Naughton, Michelle J.; Yi-Frazier, Joyce P.; Morgan, Timothy M.; Seid, Michael; Lawrence, Jean M.; Klingensmith, Georgeanna J., . . . Loots, Beth. (2014). Longitudinal associations between sex, diabetes self-care, and health-related quality of life among youth with type 1 or type 2 diabetes mellitus. *The Journal of Pediatrics, 164*(6), 1376–1383.e1371. doi: 10.1016/j.jpeds.2014.01.027

Neal, Lynn S. (2011). "They're freaks!": The cult stereotype in fictional television shows, 1958–2008. *Nova Religio: The Journal of Alternative and Emergent Religions, 14*(3), 81–107. doi: 10.1525/nr.2011.14.3.81

Neary, Karen R. & Friedman, Ori. (2014). Young children give priority to ownership when judging who should use an object. *Child Development, 85*(1), 326–337. doi: 10.1111/cdev.12120

Neary, Marianne T. & Breckenridge, Ross A. (2013). Hypoxia at the heart of sudden infant death syndrome? *Pediatric Research, 74*(4), 375–379. doi: 10.1038/pr.2013.122

Needleman, Herbert L. & Gatsonis, Constantine A. (1990). Low-level lead exposure and the IQ of children: A meta-analysis of modern studies. *JAMA, 263*(5), 673–678. doi: 10.1001/jama.1990.03440050067035

Needleman, Herbert L.; Schell, Alan; Bellinger, David; Leviton, Alan & Allred, Elizabeth N. (1990). The long-term effects of exposure to low doses of lead in childhood. *New England Journal of Medicine, 322*(2), 83–88. doi: 10.1056/NEJM199001113220203

Neggers, Yasmin & Crowe, Kristi. (2013). Low birth weight outcomes: Why better in Cuba than Alabama? *Journal of the American Board of Family Medicine, 26*(2), 187–195. doi: 10.3122/jabfm.2013.02.120227

Neigh, Gretchen N.; Gillespie, Charles F. & Nemeroff, Charles B. (2009). The neurobiological toll of child abuse and neglect. *Trauma, Violence, & Abuse, 10*(4), 389–410. doi: 10.1177/1524838009339758

Nelson, Charles A.; Fox, Nathan A. & Zeanah, Charles H. (2014). *Romania's abandoned children: Deprivation, brain development, and the struggle for recovery.* Cambridge, MA: Harvard University Press.

Nelson, Charles A.; Zeanah, Charles H.; Fox, Nathan A.; Marshall, Peter J.; Smyke, Anna T. & Guthrie, Donald. (2007). Cognitive recovery in socially deprived young children: The Bucharest Early Intervention Project. *Science, 318*(5858), 1937–1940. doi: 10.1126/science.1143921

Nelson, Eric E.; Lau, Jennifer Y. F. & Jarcho, Johanna M. (2014). Growing pains and pleasures: How emotional learning guides development. *Trends in Cognitive Sciences, 18*(2), 99–108. doi: 10.1016/j.tics.2013.11.003

Nelson, Geoffrey & Caplan, Rachel. (2014). The prevention of child physical abuse and neglect: An update. *Journal of Applied Research on Children: Informing Policy for Children at Risk, 5*(1).

Nelson, R. Michael & DeBacker, Teresa K. (2008). Achievement motivation in adolescents: The role of peer climate and best friends. *Journal of Experimental Education, 76*(2), 170–189. doi: 10.3200/JEXE.76.2.170-190

Nesdale, Drew; Zimmer-Gembeck, Melanie J. & Roxburgh, Natalie. (2014). Peer group rejection in childhood: Effects of rejection ambiguity, rejection sensitivity, and social acumen. *Journal of Social Issues, 70*(1), 12–28. doi: 10.1111/josi.12044

Neuman, Susan B.; Kaefer, Tanya; Pinkham, Ashley & Strouse, Gabrielle. (2014). Can babies learn to read? A randomized trial of baby media. *Journal of Educational Psychology, 106*(3), 815–830. doi: 10.1037/a0035937

Neumann, Anna; van Lier, Pol; Frijns, Tom; Meeus, Wim & Koot, Hans. (2011). Emotional dynamics in the development of early adolescent psychopathology: A one-year longitudinal study. *Journal of Abnormal Child Psychology, 39*(5), 657–669. doi: 10.1007/s10802-011-9509-3

Nevanen, Saila; Juvonen, Antti & Ruismäki, Heikki. (2014). Does arts education develop school readiness? Teachers' and artists' points of view on an art education project. *Arts Education Policy Review, 115*(3), 72–81. doi: 10.1080/10632913.2014.913970

Nevin, Rick. (2007). Understanding international crime trends: The legacy of preschool lead exposure. *Environmental Research, 104*(3), 315–336. doi: 10.1016/j.envres.2007.02.008

Newnham, Carol A.; Milgrom, Jeannette & Skouteris, Helen. (2009). Effectiveness of a modified mother-infant transaction program on outcomes for preterm infants from 3 to 24 months of age. *Infant Behavior and Development, 32*(1), 17–26. doi: 10.1016/j.infbeh.2008.09.004

Ng, Florrie Fei-Yin; Pomerantz, Eva M. & Deng, Ciping. (2014). Why are Chinese mothers more controlling than American mothers? "My child is my report card". *Child Development, 85*(1), 355–369. doi: 10.1111/cdev.12102

Ng, Marie; Fleming, Tom; Robinson, Margaret; Thomson, Blake; Graetz, Nicholas; Margono, Christopher, . . . Gakidou, Emmanuela. (2014). Global, regional, and national prevalence of overweight and obesity in children and adults during 1980–2013: A systematic analysis for the Global Burden of Disease Study 2013. *The Lancet, 384*(9945), 766–781. doi: 10.1016/S0140-6736(14)60460-8

Ng, Nawi; Weinehall, Lars & Öhman, Ann. (2007). 'If I don't smoke, I'm not a real man'– Indonesian teenage boys' views about smoking. *Health Education Research, 22*(6), 794–804. doi: 10.1093/her/cyl104

Ngui, Emmanuel; Cortright, Alicia & Blair, Kathleen. (2009). An investigation of paternity status and other factors associated with racial and ethnic disparities in birth outcomes in Milwaukee, Wisconsin. *Maternal and Child Health Journal, 13*(4), 467–478. doi: 10.1007/s10995-008-0383-8

Nguyen, H.T.; Geens, Mieke & Spits, C. (2013). Genetic and epigenetic instability in human pluripotent stem cells. *Human Reproduction Update, 19*(2), 187–205. doi: 10.1093/humupd/dms048

Nic Gabhainn, Saoirse; Baban, Adriana; Boyce, William & Godeau, Emmanuelle. (2009). How well protected are sexually active 15-year olds? Cross-national patterns in condom and contraceptive pill use 2002–2006. *International Journal of Public Health, 54*(Suppl. 2), 209–215. doi: 10.1007/s00038-009-5412-x

Niclasen, Janni; Andersen, Anne-Marie N.; Strandberg-Larsen, Katrine & Teasdale, Thomas W. (2014). Is alcohol binge drinking in early and late pregnancy associated with behavioural and emotional development at age 7 years? *European Child & Adolescent Psychiatry.* doi: 10.1007/s00787-013-0511-x

Niedzwiedz, Claire; Haw, Camilla; Hawton, Keith & Platt, Stephen. (2014). The definition and epidemiology of clusters of suicidal behavior: A systematic review. *Suicide and Life-Threatening Behavior, 44*(5), 569–581. doi: 10.1111/sltb.12091

Nielsen, Mark & Tomaselli, Keyan. (2010). Overimitation in Kalahari Bushman children and the origins of human cultural cognition. *Psychological Science, 21*(5), 729–736. doi: 10.1177/0956797610368808

Nielsen, Mark; Tomaselli, Keyan; Mushin, Ilana & Whiten, Andrew. (2014). Exploring tool innovation: A comparison of Western and Bushman children. *Journal of Experimental Child Psychology, 126*, 384–394. doi: 10.1016/j.jecp.2014.05.008

Nieto, Sonia. (2000). *Affirming diversity: The sociopolitical context of multicultural education* (3rd ed.). New York, NY: Longman.

Nigg, Joel T. & Barkley, Russell A. (2014). Attention-deficit/hyperactivity disorder. In Eric J. Mash & Russell A. Barkley (Eds.), *Child psychopathology* (3rd ed., pp. 75–144). New York, NY: Guilford Press.

Norris, Pippa. (2001). *Digital divide: Civic engagement, information poverty, and the internet worldwide.* New York, NY: Cambridge University Press.

Nugent, J. Kevin; Petrauskas, Bonnie J. & Brazelton, T. Berry (Eds.). (2009). *The newborn as a person: Enabling healthy infant development worldwide.* Hoboken, NJ: Wiley.

O'Brien, Beth A.; Wolf, Maryanne & Lovett, Maureen W. (2012). A taxometric investigation of developmental dyslexia subtypes. *Dyslexia, 18*(1), 16–39. doi: 10.1002/dys.1431

O'Doherty, Kieran. (2006). Risk communication in genetic counselling: A discursive approach to probability. *Theory & Psychology, 16*(2), 225–256. doi: 10.1177/0959354306062537

O'Donnell, Lydia; Stueve, Ann; Duran, Richard; Myint-U, Athi; Agronick, Gail; Doval, Alexi San & Wilson-Simmons, Renée. (2008). Parenting practices, parents' underestimation of daughters' risks, and alcohol and sexual behaviors of urban girls. *Journal of Adolescent Health, 42*(5), 496–502. doi: 10.1016/j.jadohealth.2007.10.008

O'Hanlon, Leslie H. (2013). Teaching students the skills to be savvy researchers. *Education Week, 32*(32), s12, s15, s16.

O'Leary, Colleen M.; Nassar, Natasha; Zubrick, Stephen R.; Kurinczuk, Jennifer J.; Stanley, Fiona & Bower, Carol. (2010). Evidence of a complex association between dose, pattern and timing of prenatal alcohol exposure and child behaviour problems. *Addiction, 105*(1), 74–86. doi: 10.1111/j.1360-0443.2009.02756.x

O'Conner, Rosemarie; Abedi, Jamal & Tung, Stephanie. (2012). *A descriptive analysis of enrollment and achievement among English language learner students in Pennsylvania.* Washington, DC: U.S. Department of Education, Institute of Education Sciences, National Center for Education Evaluation and Regional Assistance, Regional Educational Laboratory Mid-Atlantic.

Oakes, J. Michael. (2009). The effect of media on children: A methodological assessment from a social epidemiologist. *American Behavioral Scientist, 52*(8), 1136–1151. doi: 10.1177/0002764209331538

Oakes, Lisa M.; Cashon, Cara; Casasola, Marianella & Rakison, David (Eds.). (2011). *Infant perception and cognition: Recent advances, emerging theories, and future directions.* New York,

NY: Oxford University Press. doi: 10.1093/acprof:oso/9780195366709.001.0001

Obradović, Jelena. (2012). How can the study of physiological reactivity contribute to our understanding of adversity and resilience processes in development? *Development and Psychopathology, 24*(2), 371–387. doi: 10.1017/S0954579412000053

Obradović, Jelena; Long, Jeffrey D.; Cutuli, J. J.; Chan, Chi-Keung; Hinz, Elizabeth; Heistad, David & Masten, Ann S. (2009). Academic achievement of homeless and highly mobile children in an urban school district: Longitudinal evidence on risk, growth, and resilience. *Development and Psychopathology, 21*(2), 493–518. doi: 10.1017/S0954579409000273

OECD. (2010). *PISA 2009 results: Learning to learn: Student engagement, strategies and practices* (Vol. 3): PISA, OECD Publishing. doi: 10.1787/9789264083943-en

OECD. (2011). *Education at a glance 2011: OECD indicators.* Paris, France: Organisation for Economic Cooperation and Development. doi: 10.1787/eag-2011-en

OECD. (2013). *Education at a glance 2013: OECD indicators.* Paris, France: Organisation for Economic Cooperation and Development. doi: 10.1787/19991487

Offit, Paul A. (2011). *Deadly choices: How the anti-vaccine movement threatens us all.* New York, NY: Basic Books.

Ogden, Cynthia L.; Carroll, Margaret D.; Kit, Brian K. & Flegal, Katherine M. (2014). Prevalence of childhood and adult obesity in the United States, 2011–2012. *JAMA, 311*(8), 806–814. doi: 10.1001/jama.2014.732

Ogden, Cynthia L.; Gorber, Sarah C.; Dommarco, Juan A. Rivera; Carroll, Margaret; Shields, Margot & Flegal, Katherine. (2011). The epidemiology of childhood obesity in Canada, Mexico and the United States. In Luis A. Moreno, et al. (Eds.), *Epidemiology of obesity in children and adolescents* (Vol. 2, pp. 69–93). New York, NY: Springer. doi: 10.1007/978-1-4419-6039-9_5

Oh, Seungmi & Lewis, Charlie. (2008). Korean preschoolers' advanced inhibitory control and its relation to other executive skills and mental state understanding. *Child Development, 79*(1), 80–99. doi: 10.1111/j.1467-8624.2007.01112.x

Olds, David L. (2006). The nurse–family partnership: An evidence-based preventive intervention. *Infant Mental Health Journal, 27*(1), 5–25. doi: 10.1002/imhj.20077

Olfson, Mark; Crystal, Stephen; Huang, Cecilia & Gerhard, Tobias. (2010). Trends in antipsychotic drug use by very young, privately insured children. *Journal of the American Academy of Child and Adolescent Psychiatry, 49*(1), 13–23. doi: 10.1016/j.jaac.2009.09.003

Olson, Kristina R. & Dweck, Carol S. (2009). Social cognitive development: A new look. *Child Development Perspectives, 3*(1), 60–65. doi: 10.1111/j.1750-8606.2008.00078.x

Olson, Sheryl L.; Lopez-Duran, Nestor; Lunkenheimer, Erika S.; Chang, Hyein &

Sameroff, Arnold J. (2011). Individual differences in the development of early peer aggression: Integrating contributions of self-regulation, theory of mind, and parenting. *Development and Psychopathology, 23*(1), 253–266. doi: 10.1017/S0954579410000775

Olweus, Dan; Limber, Sue & Mahalic, Sharon F. (1999). *Bullying prevention program.* Boulder, CO: Center for the Study and Prevention of Violence, Institute of Behavioral Science, University of Colorado at Boulder.

Omariba, D. Walter Rasugu & Boyle, Michael H. (2007). Family structure and child mortality in sub-Saharan Africa: Cross-national effects of polygyny. *Journal of Marriage and Family, 69*(2), 528–543. doi: 10.1111/j.1741-3737.2007.00381.x

Oosterman, Mirjam; Schuengel, Carlo; Slot, N. Wim; Bullens, Ruud A. R. & Doreleijers, Theo A. H. (2007). Disruptions in foster care: A review and meta-analysis. *Children and Youth Services Review, 29*(1), 53–76. doi: 10.1016/j.childyouth.2006.07.003

Osgood, D. Wayne; Ragan, Daniel T.; Wallace, Lacey; Gest, Scott D.; Feinberg, Mark E. & Moody, James. (2013). Peers and the emergence of alcohol use: Influence and selection processes in adolescent friendship networks. *Journal of Research on Adolescence, 23*(3), 500–512. doi: 10.1111/jora.12059

Osher, David; Bear, George G.; Sprague, Jeffrey R. & Doyle, Walter. (2010). How can we improve school discipline? *Educational Researcher, 39*(1), 48–58. doi: 10.3102/0013189X09357618

Osorio, Snezana N. (2011). Reconsidering kwashiorkor. *Topics in Clinical Nutrition, 26*(1), 10–13. doi: 10.1097/TIN.0b013e318209e3b6

Ostfeld, Barbara M.; Esposito, Linda; Perl, Harold & Hegyi, Thomas. (2010). Concurrent risks in sudden infant death syndrome. *Pediatrics, 125*(3), 447–453. doi: 10.1542/peds.2009-0038

Ostrov, Jamie M.; Kamper, Kimberly E.; Hart, Emily J.; Godleski, Stephanie A. & Blakely-McClure, Sarah J. (2014). A gender-balanced approach to the study of peer victimization and aggression subtypes in early childhood. *Development and Psychopathology, 26*(3), 575–587. doi: 10.1017/S0954579414000248

Otheguy, Ricardo & Stern, Nancy. (2011). On so-called Spanglish. *International Journal of Bilingualism, 15*(1), 85–100. doi: 10.1177/1367006910379298

Otto, Bailey. (2014, July 11). Missouri death by snake bite uncommon. *St. Louis Post-Dispatch.*

Otto, Hiltrud & Keller, Heidi (Eds.). (2014). *Different faces of attachment: Cultural variations on a universal human need.* New York, NY: Cambridge University Press.

Over, Harriet & Gattis, Merideth. (2010). Verbal imitation is based on intention understanding. *Cognitive Development, 25*(1), 46–55. doi: 10.1016/j.cogdev.2009.06.004

Oyekale, Abayomi S. & Oyekale, Tolulope O. (2009). Do mothers' educational levels matter in child malnutrition and health outcomes in Gambia and Niger? *The Social Sciences, 4*(1), 118–127.

Ozturk, Ozge; Krehm, Madelaine & Vouloumanos, Athena. (2013). Sound symbolism in infancy: Evidence for sound–shape cross-modal correspondences in 4-month-olds. *Journal of Experimental Child Psychology, 114*(2), 173–186. doi: 10.1016/j.jecp.2012.05.004

Paik, Anthony. (2011). Adolescent sexuality and the risk of marital dissolution. *Journal of Marriage and Family, 73*(2), 472–485. doi: 10.1111/j.1741-3737.2010.00819.x

Palagi, Elisabetta. (2011). Playing at every age: Modalities and potential functions in non-human primates. In Anthony D. Pellegrini (Ed.), *The Oxford handbook of the development of play* (pp. 70–82). New York, NY: Oxford University Press. doi: 10.1093/oxfordhb/9780195393002.013.0007

Panksepp, Jaak & Watt, Douglas. (2011). What is basic about basic emotions? Lasting lessons from affective neuroscience. *Emotion Review, 3*(4), 387–396. doi: 10.1177/1754073911410741

Papandreou, Maria. (2014). Communicating and thinking through drawing activity in early childhood. *Journal of Research in Childhood Education, 28*(1), 85–100. doi: 10.1080/02568543.2013.851131

Park, D. J. J. & Congdon, Nathan G. (2004). Evidence for an "epidemic" of myopia. *Annals Academy of Medicine Singapore, 33*(1), 21–26.

Park, Hyun; Bothe, Denise; Holsinger, Eva; Kirchner, H. Lester; Olness, Karen & Mandalakas, Anna. (2011). The impact of nutritional status and longitudinal recovery of motor and cognitive milestones in internationally adopted children. *International Journal of Environmental Research and Public Health, 8*(1), 105–116. doi: 10.3390/ijerph8010105

Parke, Ross D. (2013). Gender differences and similarities in parental behavior. In Bradford Wilcox & Kathleen K. Kline (Eds.), *Gender and parenthood: Biological and social scientific perspectives* (pp. 120–163). New York, NY: Columbia University Press.

Parke, Ross D. & Buriel, Raymond. (2006). Socialization in the family: Ethnic and ecological perspectives. In William Damon & Richard M. Lerner (Eds.), *Handbook of child psychology* (6th ed., Vol. 3, pp. 429–504). Hoboken, NJ: Wiley.

Parker, Andrew. (2012). *Ethical problems and genetics practice.* New York, NY: Cambridge University Press.

Parker, Rachael; Wellings, Kaye & Lazarus, Jeffrey V. (2009). Sexuality education in Europe: An overview of current policies. *Sex Education: Sexuality, Society and Learning, 9*(3), 227–242. doi: 10.1080/14681810903059060

Parks, Sharyn E.; Johnson, Linda L.; McDaniel, Dawn D. & Gladden, Matthew. (2014, January 17). *Surveillance for violent deaths—National Violent Death Reporting System, 16 states, 2010.* Atlanta, GA: U.S. Department of Health and Human Services, Centers for Disease Control and Prevention, Morbidity and Mortality Weekly Report, 63(SS01), 1–33.

Parladé, Meaghan V. & Iverson, Jana M. (2011). The interplay between language, gesture, and affect during communicative transition: A dynamic systems approach. *Developmental Psychology, 47*(3), 820–833. doi: 10.1037/a0021811

Parris, Leandra; Varjas, Kris; Meyers, Joel & Cutts, Hayley. (2012). High school students' perceptions of coping with cyberbullying. *Youth & Society, 44*(2), 284–306. doi: 10.1177/0044118x11398881

Pascarella, Ernest T.; Martin, Georgianna L.; Hanson, Jana M.; Trolian, Teniell L.; Gillig, Benjamin & Blaich, Charles. (2014). Effects of diversity experiences on critical thinking skills over 4 years of college. *Journal of College Student Development, 55*(1), 86–92. doi: 10.1353/csd.2014.0009

Pascarella, Ernest T. & Terenzini, Patrick T. (1991). *How college affects students: Findings and insights from twenty years of research.* San Francisco, CA: Jossey-Bass.

Pathela, Preeti & Schillinger, Julia A. (2010). Sexual behaviors and sexual violence: Adolescents with opposite-, same-, or both-sex partners. *Pediatrics, 126*(5), 879–886. doi: 10.1542/peds.2010-0396

Patil, Rakesh N.; Nagaonkar, Shashikant N.; Shah, Nilesh B. & Bhat, Tushar S. (2013). A cross-sectional study of common psychiatric morbidity in children aged 5 to 14 years in an urban slum. *Journal of Family Medicine and Primary Care, 2*(2), 164–168. doi: 10.4103/2249-4863.117413

Patrick, Megan E. & Schulenberg, John E. (2011). How trajectories of reasons for alcohol use relate to trajectories of binge drinking: National panel data spanning late adolescence to early adulthood. *Developmental Psychology, 47*(2), 311–317. doi: 10.1037/a0021939

Patton, George C.; Hemphill, Sheryl A.; Beyers, Jennifer M.; Bond, Lyndal; Toumbourou, John W.; McMorris, Barbara J. & Catalano, Richard F. (2007). Pubertal stage and deliberate self-harm in adolescents. *Journal of the American Academy of Child and Adolescent Psychiatry, 46*(4), 508–514. doi: 10.1097/chi.0b013e31803065c7

Pauler, Florian M.; Barlow, Denise P. & Hudson, Quanah J. (2012). Mechanisms of long range silencing by imprinted macro noncoding RNAs. *Current Opinion in Genetics & Development, 22*(3), 283–289. doi: 10.1016/j.gde.2012.02.005

Paulsell, Diane; Del Grosso, Patricia & Supplee, Lauren. (2014). Supporting replication and scale-up of evidence-based home visiting programs: Assessing the implementation knowledge base. *American Journal of Public Health, 104*(9), 1624–1632. doi: 10.2105/AJPH.2014.301962

Paulus, Frank W.; Backes, Aline; Sander, Charlotte S.; Weber, Monika & von Gontard, Alexander. (2014). Anxiety disorders and behavioral inhibition in preschool children: A population-based study. *Child Psychiatry & Human Development.* doi: 10.1007/s10578-014-0460-8

Pawlik, Amy J. & Kress, John P. (2013). Issues affecting the delivery of physical therapy services for individuals with critical illness. *Physical Therapy, 93*(2), 256–265. doi: 10.2522/ptj.20110445

Pearce, Matt. (2012, November 29). Photo of N.Y. cop aiding homeless man draws bittersweet reaction. *Los Angeles Times.*

Pedersen, Daphne E. & Kilzer, Gabe. (2014). Work-to-family conflict and the maternal gatekeeping of dual-earner mothers with young children. *Journal of Family and Economic Issues, 35*(2), 251–262. doi: 10.1007/s10834-013-9370-3

Peffley, Mark & Hurwitz, Jon. (2010). *Justice in America: The separate realities of blacks and whites.* New York, NY: Cambridge University Press.

Pelham, William E. & Fabiano, Gregory A. (2008). Evidence-based psychosocial treatments for Attention-deficit/hyperactivity disorder. *Journal of Clinical Child & Adolescent Psychology, 37*(1), 184–214. doi: 10.1080/15374410701818681

Pellegrini, Anthony D. (2011). Introduction. In Anthony D. Pellegrini (Ed.), *The Oxford handbook of the development of play* (pp. 3–6). New York, NY: Oxford University Press. doi: 10.1093/oxfordhb/9780195393002.013.0001

Pellegrini, Anthony D. (2013). Play. In Philip D. Zelazo (Ed.), *The Oxford handbook of developmental psychology* (Vol. 2, pp. 276–299). New York, NY: Oxford University Press. doi: 10.1093/oxfordhb/9780199958474.013.0012

Pellegrini, Anthony D.; Roseth, Cary J.; Van Ryzin, Mark J. & Solberg, David W. (2011). Popularity as a form of social dominance: An evolutionary perspective. In Antonius H. N. Cillessen, et al. (Eds.), *Popularity in the peer system* (pp. 123–139). New York, NY: Guilford Press.

Pellis, Sergio M. & Pellis, Vivien C. (2011). Rough-and-tumble play: Training and using the social brain. In Anthony D. Pellegrini (Ed.), *The Oxford handbook of the development of play* (pp. 245–259). New York, NY: Oxford University Press. doi: 10.1093/oxfordhb/9780195393002.013.0019

Peng, Duan & Robins, Philip K. (2010). Who should care for our kids? The effects of infant child care on early child development. *Journal of Children and Poverty, 16*(1), 1–45. doi: 10.1080/10796120903575085

Peper, Jiska S. & Dahl, Ronald E. (2013). The teenage brain: Surging hormones—brain-behavior interactions during puberty. *Current Directions in Psychological Science, 22*(2), 134–139. doi: 10.1177/0963721412473755

Perfetti, Jennifer; Clark, Roseanne & Fillmore, Capri-Mara. (2004). Postpartum depression: Identification, screening, and treatment. *Wisconsin Medical Journal, 103*(6), 56–63.

Perner, Josef. (2000). Communication and representation: Why mentalistic reasoning is a lifelong endeavour. In Peter Mitchell & Kevin John Riggs (Eds.), *Children's reasoning and the mind* (pp. 367–401). Hove, UK: Psychology Press.

Perry, William G. (1970). *Forms of intellectual and ethical development in the college years: A scheme.* New York, NY: Holt, Rinehart and Winston.

Perry, William G. (1981). Cognitive and ethical growth: The making of meaning. In Arthur Chickering (Ed.), *The modern American college: Responding to the new realities of diverse students and a changing society* (pp. 76–116). San Francisco, CA: Jossey-Bass.

Perry, William G. (1998). *Forms of intellectual and ethical development in the college years: A scheme.* San Francisco, CA: Jossey-Bass.

Persaud, Trivedi V. N.; Chudley, Albert E. & Skalko, Richard G. (1985). *Basic concepts in teratology.* New York, NY: Liss.

Persico, Antonio M. & Merelli, Sara. (2014). Environmental factors in the onset of autism spectrum disorder. *Current Developmental Disorders Reports, 1*(1), 8–19. doi: 10.1007/s40474-013-0002-2

Peskin, Melissa F.; Markham, Christine M.; Shegog, Ross; Baumler, Elizabeth R.; Addy, Robert C. & Tortolero, Susan R. (2014). Effects of the It's Your Game . . . Keep It Real program on dating violence in ethnic-minority middle school youths: A group randomized trial. *American Journal of Public Health, 104*(8), 1471–1477. doi: 10.2105/AJPH.2014.301902

Peters, Stacey L.; Lind, Jennifer N.; Humphrey, Jasmine R.; Friedman, Jan M.; Honein, Margaret A.; Tassinari, Melissa S., . . . Broussard, Cheryl S. (2013). Safe lists for medications in pregnancy: Inadequate evidence base and inconsistent guidance from Web-based information, 2011. *Pharmacoepidemiology and Drug Safety, 22*(3), 324–328. doi: 10.1002/pds.3410

Peterson, Jane W. & Sterling, Yvonne M. (2009). Children's perceptions of asthma: African American children use metaphors to make sense of asthma. *Journal of Pediatric Health Care, 23*(2), 93–100. doi: 10.1016/j.pedhc.2007.10.002

Petrenko, Christie L. M.; Friend, Angela; Garrido, Edward F.; Taussig, Heather N. & Culhane, Sara E. (2012). Does subtype matter? Assessing the effects of maltreatment on functioning in preadolescent youth in out-of-home care. *Child Abuse & Neglect, 36*(9), 633–644. doi: 10.1016/j.chiabu.2012.07.001

Pew Forum on Religion & Public Life. (2012, July 31). *Two-thirds of democrats now support gay marriage.* Washington, DC: Pew Research Center.

Pew Research Center. (2010). *Millennials, a portrait of Generation Next: Confident. Connected. Open to change.* Washington, DC: Pew Research Center.

Pew Research Center. (2014, April 2). *America's new drug policy landscape: Two-thirds favor treatment, not jail, for use of heroin, cocaine.* Washington, DC: Pew Research Center.

Pew Research Center. (2014, March 7). *Millennials in adulthood: Detached from institutions, networked with friends.* Washington, DC: Pew Research Center.

Pew Research Center, U.S. Politics & Policy. (2014, April 2). *America's new drug policy landscape: Two-thirds favor treatment, not jail, for use of heroin, cocaine.* Washington, DC: Pew Research Center.

Pew Social & Demographic Trends. (2011, May 16). *Is college worth it? College presidents, public assess value, quality and mission of higher education.* Washington. DC: Pew Research Center.

Peyser, James A. (2011). Unlocking the secrets of high-performing charters. *Education Next, 11*(4). 36–43.

Pfeifer, Jennifer H.; Masten, Carrie L.; Moore, William E.; Oswald, Tasha M.; Mazziotta, John C.; Iacoboni, Marco & Dapretto, Mirella. (2011). Entering adolescence: Resistance to peer influence, risky behavior, and neural changes in emotion reactivity. *Neuron, 69*(5), 1029–1036. doi: 10.1016/j.neuron.2011.02.019

Phillips, Deborah A.; Fox, Nathan A. & Gunnar, Megan R. (2011). Same place, different experiences: Bringing individual differences to research in child care. *Child Development Perspectives, 5*(1), 44–49. doi: 10.1111/j.1750-8606.2010.00155.x

Phillips, Tommy M.; Wilmoth, Joe D.; Wall, Sterling K.; Peterson, Donna J.; Buckley, Rhonda & Phillips, Laura E. (2013). Recollected parental care and fear of intimacy in emerging adults. *The Family Journal, 21*(3), 335–341. doi: 10.1177/1066480713476848

Piaget, Jean. (1932). *The moral judgment of the child.* London, UK: K. Paul, Trench, Trubner & Co

Piaget, Jean. (1952). *The origins of intelligence in children.* Oxford, UK: International Universities Press.

Piaget, Jean. (1954). *The construction of reality in the child.* New York, NY: Basic Books.

Piaget, Jean. (1962). *Play, dreams and imitation in childhood.* New York, NY: Norton.

Piaget, Jean. (1972). *The psychology of intelligence.* Totowa, NJ: Littlefield.

Piaget, Jean. (1997). *The moral judgment of the child.* New York, NY: Simon & Schuster.

Piaget, Jean. (2011). *The origins of intelligence in children.* New York, NY: Routledge.

Piaget, Jean. (2013). *The moral judgment of the child.* New York, NY: Routledge.

Piaget, Jean & Inhelder, Bärbel. (1969). *The psychology of the child.* New York, NY: Basic Books.

Piaget, Jean; Voelin-Liambey, Daphne & Berthoud-Papandropoulou, Ioanna. (2001). Problems of class inclusion and logical implication. In Robert L. Campbell (Ed.), *Studies in reflecting abstraction* (pp. 105–137). Hove, UK: Psychology Press.

Pickles, Andrew; Hill, Jonathan; Breen, Gerome; Quinn, John; Abbott, Kate; Jones, Helen & Sharp, Helen. (2013). Evidence for interplay between genes and parenting on infant temperament in the first year of life: Monoamine oxidase A polymorphism moderates effects of maternal sensitivity on infant anger proneness. *Journal of Child Psychology and Psychiatry, 54*(12), 1308–1317. doi: 10.1111/jcpp.12081

Pietrantonio, Anna Marie; Wright, Elise; Gibson, Kathleen N.; Alldred, Tracy; Jacobson, Dustin & Niec, Anne. (2013). Mandatory reporting of child abuse and neglect: Crafting a positive process for health professionals and caregivers. *Child Abuse & Neglect, 37*(2/3), 102–109. doi: 10.1016/j.chiabu.2012.12.007

Pilarz, Alejandra Ros & Hill, Heather D. (2014). Unstable and multiple child care arrangements and young children's behavior. *Early Childhood Research Quarterly, 29*(4), 471–483. doi: 10.1016/j.ecresq.2014.05.007

Pin, Tamis; Eldridge, Beverley & Galea, Mary P. (2007). A review of the effects of sleep position, play position, and equipment use on motor development in infants. *Developmental Medicine & Child Neurology, 49*(11), 858–867. doi: 10.1111/j.1469-8749.2007.00858.x

Pinheiro, Paulo Sérgio. (2006). *World report on violence against children.* Geneva, Switzerland: United Nations.

Pinker, Steven. (2007). *The stuff of thought: Language as a window into human nature.* New York, NY: Viking.

Pinker, Steven. (2011). *The better angels of our nature: Why violence has declined.* New York, NY: Viking.

PISA. (2009). *Learning mathematics for life: A perspective from PISA.* Paris, France: OECD. doi: 10.1787/9789264075009-en

PISA. (2014a). *Pisa 2012 results: What students know and can do, student performance in mathematics, reading and science.* Paris, France: OECD, 1.

PISA. (2014b). *PISA 2012 results in focus: What 15-year-olds know and what they can do with what they know.* Paris, France: OECD.

Piteo, A. M.; Roberts, R. M.; Nettelbeck, T.; Burns, N.; Lushington, K.; Martin, A. J. & Kennedy, J. D. (2013). Postnatal depression mediates the relationship between infant and maternal sleep disruption and family dysfunction. *Early Human Development, 89*(2), 69–74. doi: 10.1016/j.earlhumdev.2012.07.017

Plomin, Robert; DeFries, John C.; Knopik, Valerie S. & Neiderhiser, Jenae M. (2013). *Behavioral genetics.* New York, NY: Worth Publishers.

Plows, Alexandra. (2011). *Debating human genetics: Contemporary issues in public policy and ethics.* New York, NY: Routledge.

Pluess, Michael & Belsky, Jay. (2010). Differential susceptibility to parenting and quality child care. *Developmental Psychology, 46*(2), 379–390. doi: 10.1037/a0015203

Pogrebin, Abigail. (2010). *One and the same: My life as an identical twin and what I've learned about everyone's struggle to be singular.* New York, NY: Anchor.

Polesel, John; Dulfer, Nicky & Turnbull, Malcolm. (2012). *The experience of education: The impacts of high stakes testing on school students and their families. Literature review.* Rydalmere NSW, Australia: The Whitlam Institute within the University of Western Sydney.

Porfeli, Erik J.; Lee, Bora & Vondracek, Fred W. (2013). Identity development and careers in adolescents and emerging adults. In W.

Bruce Walsh, et al. (Eds.), *Handbook of vocational psychology: Theory, research, and practice* (pp. 133–154). New York, NY: Routledge.

Portnoy, Jill; Gao, Yu; Glenn, Andrea L.; Niv, Sharon; Peskin, Melissa; Rudo-Hutt, Anna, . . . Raine, Adrian. (2013). The biology of childhood crime and antisocial behavior. In Chris L. Gibson & Marvin D. Krohn (Eds.), *Handbook of life-course criminology: Emerging trends and directions for future research* (pp. 21–42). New York, NY: Springer. doi: 10.1007/978-1-4614-5113-6_2

Posner, Michael I.; Rothbart, Mary K.; Sheese, Brad E. & Tang, Yiyuan. (2007). The anterior cingulate gyrus and the mechanism of self-regulation. *Cognitive, Affective & Behavioral Neuroscience, 7*(4), 391–395. doi: 10.3758/CABN.7.4.391

Powell, Cynthia M. (2013). Sex chromosomes, sex chromosome disorders, and disorders of sex development. In Steven L. Gersen & Martha B. Keagle (Eds.), *The principles of clinical cytogenetics* (pp. 175–211). New York, NY: Springer. doi: 10.1007/978-1-4419-1688-4_10

Powell, Kendall. (2006). Neurodevelopment: How does the teenage brain work? *Nature, 442*(7105), 865–867. doi: 10.1038/442865a

Powell, Shaun; Langlands, Stephanie & Dodd, Chris. (2011). Feeding children's desires? Child and parental perceptions of food promotion to the "under 8s". *Young Consumers: Insight and Ideas for Responsible Marketers, 12*(2), 96–109. doi: 10.1108/17473611111141560

Pozzoli, Tiziana & Gini, Gianluca. (2013). Why do bystanders of bullying help or not? A multidimensional model. *The Journal of Early Adolescence, 33*(3), 315–340. doi: 10.1177/0272431612440172

Priess, Heather A.; Lindberg, Sara M. & Hyde, Janet Shibley. (2009). Adolescent gender-role identity and mental health: Gender intensification revisited. *Child Development, 80*(5), 1531–1544. doi: 10.1111/j.1467-8624.2009.01349.x

Prinstein, Mitchell J.; Brechwald, Whitney A. & Cohen, Geoffrey L. (2011). Susceptibility to peer influence: Using a performance-based measure to identify adolescent males at heightened risk for deviant peer socialization. *Developmental Psychology, 47*(4), 1167–1172. doi: 10.1037/a0023274

Proctor, Laura J. & Dubowitz, Howard. (2014). Child neglect: Challenges and controversies. In Jill E. Korbin & Richard D. Krugman (Eds.), *Handbook of child maltreatment* (pp. 27–61). New York, NY: Springer. doi: 10.1007/978-94-007-7208-3_2

Propper, Cathi B. & Holochwost, Steven J. (2013). The influence of proximal risk on the early development of the autonomic nervous system. *Developmental Review, 33*(3), 151–167. doi: 10.1016/j.dr.2013.05.001

Provasnik, Stephen; Kastberg, David; Ferraro, David; Lemanski, Nita; Roey, Stephen & Jenkins, Frank. (2012). *Highlights from TIMSS 2011: Mathematics and science achievement of U.S. fourth- and eighth-grade students in an international context.* Washington, DC: National Center for Education Statistics, Institute of Education Sciences, U.S. Department of Education.

Pruden, Shannon M.; Hirsh-Pasek, Kathy; Golinkoff, Roberta M. & Hennon, Elizabeth A. (2006). The birth of words: Ten-month-olds learn words through perceptual salience. *Child Development, 77*(2), 266–280. doi: 10.1111/j.1467-8624.2006.00869.x

Pryor, Frederic L. (2014). A note on the determinants of recent pupil achievement. *Scientific Research, 5,* 1265–1268. doi: 10.4236/ce.2014.514143

Pryor, John H.; Eagan, Kevin; Palucki Blake, Laura; Hurtado, Sylvia; Berdan, Jennifer & Case, Matthew H. (2012). *The American freshman: National norms fall 2012.* Los Angeles, CA: Higher Education Research Institute, UCLA.

Pulvermüller, Friedemann & Fadiga, Luciano. (2010). Active perception: Sensorimotor circuits as a cortical basis for language. *Nature Reviews Neuroscience, 11*(5), 351–360. doi: 10.1038/nrn2811

Puri, Sunita; Adams, Vincanne; Ivey, Susan & Nachtigall, Robert D. (2011). "There is such a thing as too many daughters, but not too many sons": A qualitative study of son preference and fetal sex selection among Indian immigrants in the United States. *Social Science & Medicine, 72*(7), 1169–1176. doi: 10.1016/j.socscimed.2011.01.027

Purves, Dale; Augustine, George J.; Fitzpatrick, David; Hall, William C.; LaMantia, Anthony-Samuel; McNamara, James O. & Williams, S. Mark (Eds.). (2004). *Neuroscience* (3rd ed.). Sunderland, MA: Sinauer Associates.

Putnam, Richard R. (2011). First comes marriage, then comes divorce: A perspective on the process. *Journal of Divorce & Remarriage, 52*(7), 557–564. doi: 10.1080/10502556.2011.615661

Qin, Desiree B. & Chang, Tzu-Fen. (2013). Asian fathers. In Natasha J. Cabrera & Catherine S. Tamis-LeMonda (Eds.), *Handbook of father involvement: Multidisciplinary perspectives* (2nd ed., pp. 261–281). New York, NY: Routledge.

Qin, Lili; Pomerantz, Eva M. & Wang, Qian. (2009). Are gains in decision-making autonomy during early adolescence beneficial for emotional functioning? The case of the United States and China. *Child Development, 80*(6), 1705–1721. doi: 10.1111/j.1467-8624.2009.01363.x

Rabin, Roni C. (2011, October 25). Drugs to treat A.D.H.D. reach the preschool set. *The New York Times,* p. D5.

Rabipour, Sheida & Raz, Amir. (2012). Training the brain: Fact and fad in cognitive and behavioral remediation. *Brain and Cognition, 79*(2), 159–179. doi: 10.1016/j.bandc.2012.02.006

Rabkin, Nick & Hedberg, Eric C. (2011). *Arts education in America: What the declines mean for arts participation.* Washington, DC: National Endowment for the Arts.

Race Ethnicity and Genetics Working Group. (2005). The use of racial, ethnic, and ancestral categories in human genetics research. *American Journal of Human Genetics, 77*(4), 519–532. doi: 10.1086/491747

Raeburn, Paul. (2014). *Do fathers matter?: What science is telling us about the parent we've overlooked.* New York, NY: Farrar, Straus and Giroux.

Rajaratnam, Julie Knoll; Marcus, Jake R.; Flaxman, Abraham D.; Wang, Haidong; Levin-Rector, Alison; Dwyer, Laura, . . . Murray, Christopher J. L. (2010). Neonatal, postneonatal, childhood, and under-5 mortality for 187 countries, 1970–2010: A systematic analysis of progress towards Millennium Development Goal 4. *The Lancet, 375*(9730), 1988–2008. doi: 10.1016/S0140-6736(10)60703-9

Ramakrishnan, Usha; Goldenberg, Tamar & Allen, Lindsay H. (2011). Do multiple micronutrient interventions improve child health, growth, and development? *Journal of Nutrition, 141*(11), 2066–2075. doi: 10.3945/jn.111.146845

Ramani, Geetha B.; Brownell, Celia A. & Campbell, Susan B. (2010). Positive and negative peer interaction in 3- and 4-year-olds in relation to regulation and dysregulation. *Journal of Genetic Psychology, 171*(3), 218–250. doi: 10.1080/00221320903300353

Ramscar, Michael & Dye, Melody. (2011). Learning language from the input: Why innate constraints can't explain noun compounding. *Cognitive Psychology, 62*(1), 1–40. doi: 10.1016/j.cogpsych.2010.10.001

Ramscar, Michael; Dye, Melody; Gustafson, Jessica W. & Klein, Joseph. (2013). Dual routes to cognitive flexibility: Learning and response-conflict resolution in the dimensional change card sort task. *Child Development, 84*(4), 1308–1323. doi: 10.1111/cdev.12044

Rasinger, Sebastian M. (2013). Language shift and vitality perceptions amongst London's second-generation Bangladeshis. *Journal of Multilingual and Multicultural Development, 34*(1), 46–60. doi: 10.1080/01434632.2012.707202

Raspberry, Kelly A. & Skinner, Debra. (2011). Negotiating desires and options: How mothers who carry the fragile X gene experience reproductive decisions. *Social Science & Medicine, 72*(6), 992–998. doi: 10.1016/j.socscimed.2011.01.010

Ratnarajah, Nagulan; Rifkin-Graboi, Anne; Fortier, Marielle V.; Chong, Yap Seng; Kwek, Kenneth; Saw, Seang-Mei, . . . Qiu, Anqi. (2013). Structural connectivity asymmetry in the neonatal brain. *NeuroImage, 75,* 187–194. doi: 10.1016/j.neuroimage.2013.02.052

Ravizza, Kenneth. (2007). Peak experiences in sport. In Daniel Smith & Michael Bar-Eli (Eds.), *Essential readings in sport and exercise psychology* (pp. 122–125). Champaign, IL: Human Kinetics.

Ray, Brian D. (2013). Homeschooling rising into the twenty-first century: Editor's introduction. *Peabody Journal of Education, 88*(3), 261–264. doi: 10.1080/0161956X.2013.796822

Raymond, Neil; Beer, Charlotte; Glazebrook, Cristine & Sayal, Kapil. (2009). Pregnant women's attitudes towards alcohol consumption. *BMC*

Public Health, 9(1), 175–183. doi: 10.1186/1471-2458-9-175

Ream, Geoffrey L. & Savin-Williams, Ritch C. (2003). Religious development in adolescence. In Gerald R. Adams & Michael D. Berzonsky (Eds.), *Blackwell handbook of adolescence* (pp. 51–59). Malden, MA: Blackwell.

Reavey, Daphne; Haney, Barbara M.; Atchison, Linda; Anderson, Betsi; Sandritter, Tracy & Pallotto, Eugenia K. (2014). Improving pain assessment in the NICU: A quality improvement project. *Advances in Neonatal Care, 14*(3), 144–153. doi: 10.1097/ANC.0000000000000034

Reche, Marta; Valbuena, Teresa; Fiandor, Ana; Padial, Antonia; Quirce, Santiago & Pascual, Cristina. (2011). Induction of tolerance in children with food allergy. *Current Nutrition & Food Science, 7*(1), 33–39. doi: 10.2174/157340111794941085

Reddy, Marpadga A. & Natarajan, Rama. (2013). Role of epigenetic mechanisms in the vascular complications of diabetes. In Tapas K. Kundu (Ed.), *Epigenetics: Development and disease* (pp. 435–454). New York, NY: Springer. doi: 10.1007/978-94-007-4525-4_19

Reith, Gerda. (2005). On the edge: Drugs and the consumption of risk in late modernity. In Stephen Lyng (Ed.), *Edgework: The sociology of risk taking* (pp. 227–246). New York, NY: Routledge.

Rendell, Luke; Fogarty, Laurel; Hoppitt, William J. E.; Morgan, Thomas J. H.; Webster, Mike M. & Laland, Kevin N. (2011). Cognitive culture: Theoretical and empirical insights into social learning strategies. *Trends in Cognitive Sciences, 15*(2), 68–76. doi: 10.1016/j.tics.2010.12.002

Reutskaja, Elena & Hogarth, Robin M. (2009). Satisfaction in choice as a function of the number of alternatives: When "goods satiate". *Psychology and Marketing, 26*(3), 197–203. doi: 10.1002/mar.20268

Reynolds, Arthur J. (2000). *Success in early intervention: The Chicago child-parent centers.* Lincoln, NE: University of Nebraska Press.

Reynolds, Arthur J. & Ou, Suh-Ruu. (2011). Paths of effects from preschool to adult well-being: A confirmatory analysis of the child-parent center program. *Child Development, 82*(2), 555–582. doi: 10.1111/j.1467-8624.2010.01562.x

Reynolds, Arthur J.; Temple, Judy A.; White, Barry A. B.; Ou, Suh-Ruu & Robertson, Dylan L. (2011). Age 26 cost–benefit analysis of the child-parent center early education program. *Child Development, 82*(1), 379–404. doi: 10.1111/j.1467-8624.2010.01563.x

Rhodes, Marjorie. (2013). The conceptual structure of social categories: The social allegiance hypothesis. In Mahzarin R. Banaji & Susan A. Gelman (Eds.), *Navigating the social world: What infants, children, and other species can teach us* (pp. 258–262). New York, NY: Oxford University Press.

Riccio, Cynthia A. & Rodriguez, Olga L. (2007). Integration of psychological assessment approaches in school psychology. *Psychology in the Schools, 44*(3), 243–255. doi: 10.1002/pits.20220

Richards, Jennifer S.; Hartman, Catharina A.; Franke, Barbara; Hoekstra, Pieter J.; Heslenfeld, Dirk J.; Oosterlaan, Jaap, . . . Buitelaar, Jan K. (2014). Differential susceptibility to maternal expressed emotion in children with ADHD and their siblings? Investigating plasticity genes, prosocial and antisocial behaviour. *European Child & Adolescent Psychiatry.* doi: 10.1007/s00787-014-0567-2

Richardson, Rick & Hayne, Harlene. (2007). You can't take it with you: The translation of memory across development. *Current Directions in Psychological Science, 16*(4), 223–227. doi: 10.1111/j.1467-8721.2007.00508.x

Richert, Rebekah A.; Robb, Michael B. & Smith, Erin I. (2011). Media as social partners: The social nature of young children's learning from screen media. *Child Development, 82*(1), 82–95. doi: 10.1111/j.1467-8624.2010.01542.x

Riglin, Lucy; Frederickson, Norah; Shelton, Katherine H. & Rice, Frances. (2013). A longitudinal study of psychological functioning and academic attainment at the transition to secondary school. *Journal of Adolescence, 36*(3), 507–517. doi: 10.1016/j.adolescence.2013.03.002

Riordan, Jan & Wambach, Karen (Eds.). (2009). *Breastfeeding and human lactation* (4th ed.). Sudbury, MA: Jones and Bartlett Publishers.

Rivera, Juan Ángel; de Cossío, Teresita González; Pedraza, Lilia S.; Aburto, Tania C.; Sánchez, Tania G. & Martorell, Reynaldo. (2014). Childhood and adolescent overweight and obesity in Latin America: A systematic review. *The Lancet Diabetes & Endocrinology, 2*(4), 321–332. doi: 10.1016/S2213-8587(13)70173-6

Robelen, Erik W. (2011). More students enrolling in Mandarin Chinese. *Education Week, 30*(27), 5.

Robelen, Erik W. (2013). Texas trying to scale back graduation requirements. *Education Week, 32*(27), 7.

Roberts, Leslie. (2013). The art of eradicating polio. *Science, 342*(6154), 28–35. doi: 10.1126/science.342.6154.28

Roberts, Soraya. (2010, January 1). Travis Pastrana breaks world record for longest rally car jump on New Year's Eve. *New York Daily News.*

Robins, Richard W.; Trzesniewski, Kali H. & Donnellan, M. Brent. (2012). A brief primer on self-esteem. *Prevention Researcher, 19*(2), 3–7.

Robinson, Leah E.; Wadsworth, Danielle D.; Webster, E. Kipling & Bassett, David R. (2014). School reform: The role of physical education policy in physical activity of elementary school children in Alabama's Black Belt region. *American Journal of Health Promotion, 38*(sp3), S72–S76. doi: 10.4278/ajhp.130430-ARB-207

Rochat, Philippe. (2013). Self-conceptualizing in development. In Philip D. Zelazo (Ed.), *The Oxford handbook of developmental psychology* (Vol. 2, pp. 378–397). New York, NY: Oxford University Press. doi: 10.1093/oxfordhb/9780199958474.013.0015

Roebers, Claudia M.; Schmid, Corinne & Roderer, Thomas. (2009). Metacognitive monitoring and control processes involved in primary school children's test performance. *British Journal of Educational Psychology, 79*(4), 749–767. doi: 10.1348/978185409X429842

Roenneberg, Till; Allebrandt, Karla; Merrow, Martha & Vetter, Céline. (2012). Social jetlag and obesity. *Current Biology, 22*(10), 939–943. doi: 10.1016/j.cub.2012.03.038

Rogers, Carl R. (2004). *On becoming a person: A therapist's view of psychotherapy.* London, UK: Constable.

Rogers-Chapman, M. Felicity. (2013). Accessing STEM-focused education: Factors that contribute to the opportunity to attend STEM high schools across the United States. *Education and Urban Society, 46*(6), 716–737. doi: 10.1177/0013124512469815

Rogoff, Barbara. (2003). *The cultural nature of human development.* New York, NY: Oxford University Press.

Rogoff, Barbara. (2011). *Developing destinies: A Mayan midwife and town.* New York, NY: Oxford University Press.

Rojas, Raúl & Iglesias, Aquiles. (2013). The language growth of Spanish-speaking English Language Learners. *Child Development, 84*(2), 2630–2646. doi: 10.1111/j.1467-8624.2012.01871.x

Romeo, Russell D. (2013). The teenage brain: The stress response and the adolescent brain. *Current Directions in Psychological Science, 22*(2), 140–145. doi: 10.1177/0963721413475445

Rondal, Jean A. (2010). Language in Down syndrome: A life-span perspective. In Marcia A. Barnes (Ed.), *Genes, brain, and development: The neurocognition of genetic disorders* (pp. 122–142). New York, NY: Cambridge University Press.

Rook, Graham A. W.; Lowry, Christopher A. & Raison, Charles L. (2014). Hygiene and other early childhood influences on the subsequent function of the immune system. *Brain Research* (Corrected Proof). doi: 10.1016/j.brainres.2014.04.004

Roopnarine, Jaipaul L. (2011). Cultural variations in beliefs about play, parent-child play, and children's play: Meaning for childhood development. In Anthony D. Pellegrini (Ed.), *The Oxford handbook of the development of play* (pp. 19–39). New York, NY: Oxford University Press. doi: 10.1093/oxfordhb/9780195393002.013.0003

Roopnarine, Jaipaul L. & Hossain, Ziarat. (2013). African American and African Caribbean fathers. In Natasha J. Cabrera & Catherine S. Tamis-LeMonda (Eds.), *Handbook of father involvement: Multidisciplinary perspectives* (2nd ed., pp. 223–243). New York, NY: Routledge.

Rose, Amanda J.; Schwartz-Mette, Rebecca A.; Glick, Gary C.; Smith, Rhiannon L. & Luebbe, Aaron M. (2014). An observational study of co-rumination in adolescent friendships. *Developmental Psychology, 50*(9), 2199–2209. doi: 10.1037/a0037465

Rose, Steven. (2008). Drugging unruly children is a method of social control. *Nature*, 451(7178), 521. doi: 10.1038/451521a

Roseberry, Sarah; Hirsh-Pasek, Kathy; Parish-Morris, Julia & Golinkoff, Roberta M. (2009). Live action: Can young children learn verbs from video? *Child Development*, 80(5), 1360–1375. doi: 10.1111/j.1467-8624.2009.01338.x

Rosenbaum, James E. (2011). The complexities of college for all. *Sociology of Education*, 84(2), 113–117. doi: 10.1177/0038040711401809

Rosin, Hanna. (2014, March 19). The overprotected kid. *The Atlantic*.

Ross, Heidi & Wang, Yimin. (2013). Reforms to the college entrance examination in China: Key issues, developments, and dilemmas. *Chinese Education & Society*, 46(1), 3–9. doi: 10.2753/CED1061-1932460100

Rossignol, Michel; Chaillet, Nils; Boughrassa, Faiza & Moutquin, Jean-Marie. (2014). Interrelations between four antepartum obstetric interventions and cesarean delivery in women at low risk: A systematic review and modeling of the cascade of interventions. *Birth*, 41(1), 70–78. doi: 10.1111/birt.12088

Rotatori, Anthony; Bakken, Jeffrey P.; Burkhardt, Sandra A.; Obiakor, Festus E. & Sharma, Umesh. (2014). *Special education international perspectives: Practices across the globe*. Bingley, UK: Emerald.

Roth, Guy & Assor, Avi. (2012). The costs of parental pressure to express emotions: Conditional regard and autonomy support as predictors of emotion regulation and intimacy. *Journal of Adolescence*, 35(4), 799–808. doi: 10.1016/j.adolescence.2011.11.005

Rothrauff, Tanja C.; Cooney, Teresa M. & An, Jeong Shin. (2009). Remembered parenting styles and adjustment in middle and late adulthood. *The Journals of Gerontology Series B: Psychological Sciences and Social Sciences*, 64B(1), 137–146. doi: 10.1093/geronb/gbn008

Rottenberg, Jonathan. (2014). *The depths: The evolutionary origins of the depression epidemic*. New York, NY: Basic Books.

Rouchka, Eric C. & Cha, I. Elizabeth. (2009). Current trends in pseudogene detection and characterization. *Current Bioinformatics*, 4(2), 112–119. doi: 10.2174/157489309788184792

Rovee-Collier, Carolyn. (1987). Learning and memory in infancy. In Joy Doniger Osofsky (Ed.), *Handbook of infant development* (2nd ed., pp. 98–148). New York, NY: Wiley.

Rovee-Collier, Carolyn. (1990). The "memory system" of prelinguistic infants. *Annals of the New York Academy of Sciences*, 608, 517–542. doi: 10.1111/j.1749-6632.1990.tb48908.x

Rovee-Collier, Carolyn & Cuevas, Kimberly. (2009). The development of infant memory. In Mary L. Courage & Nelson Cowan (Eds.), *The development of memory in infancy and childhood* (2nd ed., pp. 11–41). New York, NY: Psychology Press.

Rovee-Collier, Carolyn & Hayne, Harlene. (1987). Reactivation of infant memory: Implications for cognitive development. In Hayne W. Reese (Ed.), *Advances in child development and behavior* (Vol. 20, pp. 185–238). London, UK: Academic Press.

Rovner, Alisha J.; Nansel, Tonja R.; Wang, Jing & Iannotti, Ronald J. (2011). Food sold in school vending machines is associated with overall student dietary intake. *Journal of Adolescent Health*, 48(1), 13–19. doi: 10.1016/j.jadohealth.2010.08.021

Rubertsson, C.; Hellström, J.; Cross, M. & Sydsjö, G. (2014). Anxiety in early pregnancy: Prevalence and contributing factors. *Archives of Women's Mental Health*, 17(3), 221–228. doi: 10.1007/s00737-013-0409-0

Rubin, Kenneth H.; Bowker, Julie C.; McDonald, Kristina L. & Menzer, Melissa. (2013). Peer relationships in childhood. In Philip D. Zelazo (Ed.), *The Oxford handbook of developmental psychology* (Vol. 2, pp. 242–275). New York, NY: Oxford University Press. doi: 10.1093/oxfordhb/9780199958474.013.0011

Rubin, Kenneth H.; Coplan, Robert J. & Bowker, Julie C. (2009). Social withdrawal in childhood. *Annual Review of Psychology*, 60, 141–171. doi: 10.1146/annurev.psych.60.110707.163642

Ruble, Diane N.; Martin, Carol Lynn & Berenbaum, Sheri. (2006). Gender development. In William Damon & Richard M. Lerner (Eds.), *Handbook of child psychology* (6th ed., Vol. 3, pp. 858–932). Hoboken, NJ: Wiley.

Rudolph, Karen D. (2014). Puberty as a developmental context of risk for psychopathology. In Michael Lewis & Karen D. Rudolph (Eds.), *Handbook of developmental psychopathology* (pp. 331–354). New York, NY: Springer. doi: 10.1007/978-1-4614-9608-3_17

Rumberger, Russell W. (2012). *Dropping out: Why students drop out of high school and what can be done about it*. Cambridge, MA: Harvard University Press.

Runions, Kevin C. & Shaw, Thérèse. (2013). Teacher–child relationship, child withdrawal and aggression in the development of peer victimization. *Journal of Applied Developmental Psychology*, 34(6), 319–327. doi: 10.1016/j.appdev.2013.09.002

Russell, Charlotte K.; Robinson, Lyn & Ball, Helen L. (2013). Infant sleep development: Location, feeding and expectations in the postnatal period. *The Open Sleep Journal*, 6(1), 68–76. doi: 10.2174/1874620901306010068

Russell, Stephen T.; Chu, June Y.; Crockett, Lisa J. & Lee, Sun-A. (2010). Interdependent independence: The meanings of autonomy among Chinese American and Filipino American adolescents. In Stephen Thomas Russell, et al. (Eds.), *Asian American parenting and parent-adolescent relationships* (pp. 101–116). New York, NY: Springer. doi: 10.1007/978-1-4419-5728-3_6

Russell, Stephen T.; Everett, Bethany G.; Rosario, Margaret & Birkett, Michelle. (2014). Indicators of victimization and sexual orientation among adolescents: Analyses from youth risk behavior surveys. *American Journal of Public Health*, 104(2), 255–261. doi: 10.2105/AJPH.2013.301493

Russo, Theresa J. & Fallon, Moira A. (2014). Coping with stress: Supporting the needs of military families and their children. *Early Childhood Education Journal*. doi: 10.1007/s10643-014-0665-2

Rutter, Michael; Sonuga-Barke, Edmund J.; Beckett, Celia; Castle, Jennifer; Kreppner, Jana; Kumsta, Robert, . . . Gunnar, Megan R. (2010). Deprivation-specific psychological patterns: Effects of institutional deprivation. *Monographs of the Society for Research in Child Development*, 75(1). doi: 10.1111/j.1540-5834.2010.00547.x

Ryan, Alan S. (1997). The resurgence of breast-feeding in the United States. *Pediatrics*, 99(4), E12.

Ryan, Alan S.; Rush, David; Krieger, Fritz W. & Lewandowski, Gregory E. (1991). Recent declines in breast-feeding in the United States, 1984 through 1989. *Pediatrics*, 88(4), 719–727.

Ryan, Alan S.; Zhou, Wenjun & Acosta, Andrew. (2002). Breastfeeding continues to increase into the new millennium. *Pediatrics*, 110(6), 1103–1109. doi: 10.1542/peds.110.6.1103

Ryan, Erin L. (2012). "They are kind of like magic": Why U.S. mothers use baby videos with 12- to 24-month-olds. *Journalism and Mass Communication*, 2(7), 771–785.

Rymer, Russ. (1994). *Genie: A scientific tragedy*. New York: Harper Perennial.

Saarni, Carolyn; Campos, Joseph J.; Camras, Linda A. & Witherington, David. (2006). Emotional development: Action, communication, and understanding. In William Damon & Richard M. Lerner (Eds.), *Handbook of child psychology* (6th ed., Vol. 3, pp. 226–299). Hoboken, NJ: Wiley.

Sabol, T. J.; Soliday Hong, S. L.; Pianta, R. C. & Burchinal, M. R. (2013). Can rating Pre-K programs predict children's learning? *Science*, 341(6148), 845–846. doi: 10.1126/science.1233517

Sacks, Oliver W. (1995). *An anthropologist on Mars: Seven paradoxical tales*. New York, NY: Knopf.

Sadeh, Avi; Mindell, Jodi A.; Luedtke, Kathryn & Wiegand, Benjamin. (2009). Sleep and sleep ecology in the first 3 years: A web-based study. *Journal of Sleep Research*, 18(1), 60–73. doi: 10.1111/j.1365-2869.2008.00699.x

Sadeh, Avi; Tikotzky, Liat & Scher, Anat. (2010). Parenting and infant sleep. *Sleep Medicine Reviews*, 14(2), 89–96. doi: 10.1016/j.smrv.2009.05.003

Sadler, Philip Michael; Sonnert, Gerhard; Tai, Robert H. & Klopfenstein, Kristin (Eds.). (2010). *AP: A critical examination of the advanced placement program*. Cambridge, MA: Harvard Education Press.

Sadler, Troy D.; Romine, William L.; Stuart, Parker E. & Merle-Johnson, Dominike. (2013). Game-based curricula in biology classes: Differential effects among varying academic levels. *Journal of Research in Science Teaching, 50*(4), 479–499. doi: 10.1002/tea.21085

Sadler, Thomas W. (2012). *Langman's medical embryology* (12th ed.). Philadelphia, PA: Lippincott Williams & Wilkins.

Saewyc, Elizabeth M. (2011). Research on adolescent sexual orientation: Development, health disparities, stigma, and resilience. *Journal of Research on Adolescence, 21*(1), 256–272. doi: 10.1111/j.1532-7795.2010.00727.x

Saffran, Jenny R.; Werker, Janet F. & Werner, Lynne A. (2006). The infant's auditory world: Hearing, speech, and the beginnings of language. In William Damon & Richard M. Lerner (Eds.), *Handbook of child psychology* (6th ed., Vol. 2, pp. 58–108). Hoboken, NJ: Wiley.

Sagarin, Brad J.; Martin, Amy L.; Coutinho, Savia A.; Edlund, John E.; Patel, Lily; Skowronski, John J. & Zengel, Bettina. (2012). Sex differences in jealousy: A meta-analytic examination. *Evolution and Human Behavior, 33*(6), 595–614. doi: 10.1016/j.evolhumbehav.2012.02.006

Sahlberg, Pasi. (2011). *Finnish lessons: What can the world learn from educational change in Finland?* New York, NY: Teachers College Press.

Salkind, Neil J. (2004). *An introduction to theories of human development.* Thousand Oaks, CA: Sage.

Salmivalli, Christina. (2010). Bullying and the peer group: A review. *Aggression and Violent Behavior, 15*(2), 112–120. doi: 10.1016/j.avb.2009.08.007

Samek, D. R.; Hicks, B. M.; Keyes, M. A.; Bailey, J.; McGue, M. & Iacono, W. G. (2014). Gene–environment interplay between parent–child relationship problems and externalizing disorders in adolescence and young adulthood. *Psychological Medicine.* doi: 10.1017/S0033291714001445

SAMHSA. (2014). *Results from the 2013 National Survey on Drug Use and Health: Summary of national findings.* Rockville, MD: U.S. Department Of Health And Human Services, Substance Abuse and Mental Health, Services Administration Center for Behavioral Health Statistics and Quality.

Samuels, Christina A. (2013). Study reveals gaps in graduation rates: Diplomas at risk. *Education Week, 32*(32), 5.

Samuels, Christina A. & Klein, Alyson. (2013). States faulted on preschool spending levels. *Education Week, 32*(30), 21, 24.

Sanson, Ann; Smart, Diana & Misson, Sebastian. (2011). Children's socio-emotional, physical, and cognitive outcomes: Do they share the same drivers? *Australian Journal of Psychology, 63*(1), 56–74. doi: 10.1111/j.1742-9536.2011.00007.x

Santelli, John S. & Melnikas, Andrea J. (2010). Teen fertility in transition: Recent and historic trends in the United States. *Annual Review of Public Health, 31,* 371–383. doi: 10.1146/annurev.publhealth.29.020907.090830

Saraiva, Linda; Rodrigues, Luís P.; Cordovil, Rita & Barreiros, João. (2013).

Influence of age, sex and somatic variables on the motor performance of pre-school children. *Annals of Human Biology, 40*(5), 444–450. doi: 10.3109/03014460.2013.802012

Şaşmaz, Tayyar; Öner, Seva; Kurt, A. Öner; Yapıcı, Gülçin; Yazıcı, Aylin Ertekin; Buğdaycı, Resul & Şiş, Mustafa. (2014). Prevalence and risk factors of Internet addiction in high school students. *European Journal of Public Health, 24*(1), 15–20. doi: 10.1093/eurpub/ckt051

Satterwhite, Catherine Lindsey; Torrone, Elizabeth; Meites, Elissa; Dunne, Eileen F.; Mahajan, Reena; Ocfemia, M. Cheryl Bañez, . . . Weinstock, Hillard. (2013). Sexually transmitted infections among US women and men: Prevalence and incidence estimates, 2008. *Sexually Transmitted Diseases, 40*(3), 187–193. doi: 10.1097/OLQ.0b013e318286bb53

Saulny, Susan & Steinberg, Jacques. (2011, June 13). On college forms, a question of race, or races, can perplex. *The New York Times,* p. A1.

Saw, Seang-Mei; Cheng, Angela; Fong, Allan; Gazzard, Gus; Tan, Donald T. H. & Morgan, Ian. (2007). School grades and myopia. *Ophthalmic and Physiological Optics, 27*(2), 126–129. doi: 10.1111/j.1475-1313.2006.00455.x

Saxton, Matthew. (2010). *Child language: Acquisition and development.* Thousand Oaks, CA: Sage.

Scales, Peter C.; Benson, Peter L. & Mannes, Marc. (2006). The contribution to adolescent well-being made by nonfamily adults: An examination of developmental assets as contexts and processes. *Journal of Community Psychology, 34*(4), 401–413. doi: 10.1002/jcop.20106

Scarr, Sandra. (1985). Constructing psychology: Making facts and fables for our times. *American Psychologist, 40*(5), 499–512. doi: 10.1037/0003-066x.40.5.499

Schachner, Adena & Hannon, Erin E. (2011). Infant-directed speech drives social preferences in 5-month-old infants. *Developmental Psychology, 47*(1), 19–25. doi: 10.1037/a0020740

Schafer, Markus H.; Morton, Patricia M. & Ferraro, Kenneth F. (2014). Child maltreatment and adult health in a national sample: Heterogeneous relational contexts, divergent effects? *Child Abuse & Neglect, 38*(3), 395–406. doi: 10.1016/j.chiabu.2013.08.003

Schanler, Richard. J. (2011). Outcomes of human milk-fed premature infants. *Seminars in Perinatology, 35*(1), 29–33. doi: 10.1053/j.semperi.2010.10.005

Schardein, James L. (1976). *Drugs as teratogens.* Cleveland, OH: CRC Press.

Scheffler, Richard M.; Brown, Timothy T.; Fulton, Brent D.; Hinshaw, Stephen P.; Levine, Peter & Stone, Susan. (2009). Positive association between Attention-deficit/hyperactivity disorder medication use and academic achievement during elementary school. *Pediatrics, 123*(5), 1273–1279. doi: 10.1542/peds.2008-1597

Schermerhorn, Alice C.; D'Onofrio, Brian M.; Turkheimer, Eric; Ganiban, Jody M.; Spotts, Erica L.; Lichtenstein, Paul, . . .

Neiderhiser, Jenae M. (2011). A genetically informed study of associations between family functioning and child psychosocial adjustment. *Developmental Psychology, 47*(3), 707–725. doi: 10.1037/a0021362

Schifrin, Barry S. & Cohen, Wayne R. (2013). The effect of malpractice claims on the use of caesarean section. *Best Practice & Research Clinical Obstetrics & Gynaecology, 27*(2), 269–283. doi: 10.1016/j.bpobgyn.2012.10.004

Schmader, Toni. (2010). Stereotype threat deconstructed. *Current Directions in Psychological Science, 19*(1), 14–18. doi: 10.1177/0963721409359292

Schmeer, Kammi K. (2011). The child health disadvantage of parental cohabitation. *Journal of Marriage and Family, 73*(1), 181–193. doi: 10.1111/j.1741-3737.2010.00797.x

Schmid, Monika S.; Gilbers, Steven & Nota, Amber. (2014). Ultimate attainment in late second language acquisition: Phonetic and grammatical challenges in advanced Dutch–English bilingualism. *Second Language Research, 30*(2), 129–157. doi: 10.1177/0267658313505314

Schneider, Wolfgang & Lockl, Kathrin. (2008). Procedural metacognition in children: Evidence for developmental trends. In John Dunlosky & Robert A. Bjork (Eds.), *Handbook of metamemory and memory* (pp. 391–409). New York, NY: Psychology Press.

Schofield, Thomas J.; Martin, Monica J.; Conger, Katherine J.; Neppl, Tricia M.; Donnellan, M. Brent & Conger, Rand D. (2011). Intergenerational transmission of adaptive functioning: A test of the interactionist model of SES and human development. *Child Development, 82*(1), 33–47. doi: 10.1111/j.1467-8624.2010.01539.x

Schön, Daniele; Boyer, Maud; Moreno, Sylvain; Besson, Mireille; Peretz, Isabelle & Kolinsky, Régine. (2008). Songs as an aid for language acquisition. *Cognition, 106*(2), 975–983. doi: 10.1016/j.cognition.2007.03.005

Schore, Allan & McIntosh, Jennifer. (2011). Family law and the neuroscience of attachment, part I. *Family Court Review, 49*(3), 501–512. doi: 10.1111/j.1744-1617.2011.01387.x

Schulenberg, John; Patrick, Megan E.; Maslowsky, Julie & Maggs, Jennifer L. (2014). The epidemiology and etiology of adolescent substance use in developmental perspective. In Michael Lewis & Karen D. Rudolph (Eds.), *Handbook of Developmental Psychopathology* (pp. 601–620). New York, NY: Springer. doi: 10.1007/978-1-4614-9608-3_30

Schwartz, Carl E.; Kunwar, Pratap S.; Greve, Douglas N.; Moran, Lyndsey R.; Viner, Jane C.; Covino, Jennifer M., . . . Wallace, Stuart R. (2010). Structural differences in adult orbital and ventromedial prefrontal cortex predicted by infant temperament at 4 months of age. *Archives of General Psychiatry, 67*(1), 78–84. doi: 10.1001/archgenpsychiatry.2009.171

Schwartz, Seth J.; Beyers, Wim; Luyckx, Koen; Soenens, Bart; Zamboanga, Byron

L.; Forthun, Larry F., . . . Waterman, Alan S. (2011). Examining the light and dark sides of emerging adults' identity: A study of identity status differences in positive and negative psychosocial functioning. *Journal of Youth and Adolescence*, 40(7), 839–859. doi: 10.1007/s10964-010-9606-6

Schwarz, Alan & Cohen, Sarah. (2013, March 31). A.D.H.D. seen in 11% of U.S. children as diagnoses rise. *The New York Times*.

Schweinhart, Lawrence J.; Montie, Jeanne; Xiang, Zongping; Barnett, W. Steven; Belfield, Clive R. & Nores, Milagros. (2005). *Lifetime effects: The High/Scope Perry Preschool Study through age 40.* Ypsilanti, MI: High/Scope Press.

Schweinhart, Lawrence J. & Weikart, David P. (1997). *Lasting differences: The High/Scope Preschool curriculum comparison study through age 23.* Ypsilanti, MI: High/Scope Educational Research Foundation.

Schytt, Erica & Waldenström, Ulla. (2010). Epidural analgesia for labor pain: Whose choice? *Acta Obstetricia et Gynecologica Scandinavica*, 89(2), 238–242. doi: 10.3109/00016340903280974

Scott, Diane L.; Lee, Chang-Bae; Harrell, Susan W. & Smith-West, Mary B. (2013). Permanency for children in foster care: Issues and barriers for adoption. *Child & Youth Services*, 34(3), 290–307. doi: 10.1080/0145935X.2013.826045

Scott, Lisa S. & Monesson, Alexandra. (2010). Experience-dependent neural specialization during infancy. *Neuropsychologia*, 48(6), 1857–1861. doi: 10.1016/j.neuropsychologia.2010.02.008

Scott, Lisa S.; Pascalis, Olivier & Nelson, Charles A. (2007). A domain-general theory of the development of perceptual discrimination. *Current Directions in Psychological Science*, 16(4), 197–201. doi: 10.1111/j.1467-8721.2007.00503.x

Sear, Rebecca & Mace, Ruth. (2008). Who keeps children alive? A review of the effects of kin on child survival. *Evolution and Human Behavior*, 29(1), 1–18. doi: 10.1016/j.evolhumbehav.2007.10.001

Sebastian, Catherine; Burnett, Stephanie & Blakemore, Sarah-Jayne. (2008). Development of the self-concept during adolescence. *Trends in Cognitive Sciences*, 12(11), 441–446. doi: 10.1016/j.tics.2008.07.008

Sebastián-Gallés, Núria. (2007). Biased to learn language. *Developmental Science*, 10(6), 713–718. doi: 10.1111/j.1467-7687.2007.00649.x

Sedlak, Andrea J. & Ellis, Raquel T. (2014). Trends in child abuse reporting. In Jill E. Korbin & Richard D. Krugman (Eds.), *Handbook of child maltreatment* (pp. 3–26). New York, NY: Springer. doi: 10.1007/978-94-007-7208-3_1

Séguin, Jean R. & Tremblay, Richard E. (2013). Aggression and antisocial behavior: A developmental perspective. In Philip D. Zelazo (Ed.), *The Oxford handbook of developmental psychology* (Vol. 2, pp. 507–526). New York, NY: Oxford University Press. doi: 10.1093/oxfordhb/9780199958474.013.0020

Seifer, Ronald; Dickstein, Susan; Parade, Stephanie; Hayden, Lisa C.; Magee, Karin D. & Schiller, Masha. (2014). Mothers' appraisal of goodness of fit and children's social development. *International Journal of Behavioral Development*, 38(1), 86–97. doi: 10.1177/0165025413507172

Seiver, Elizabeth; Gopnik, Alison & Goodman, Noah D. (2013). Did she jump because she was the big sister or because the trampoline was safe? Causal inference and the development of social attribution. *Child Development*, 84(2), 443–454. doi: 10.1111/j.1467-8624.2012.01865.x

Seligman, Hilary K. & Schillinger, Dean. (2010). Hunger and socioeconomic disparities in chronic disease. *New England Journal of Medicine*, 363(1), 6–9. doi: 10.1056/NEJMp1000072

Seligman, Martin E. P.; Railton, Peter; Baumeister, Roy F. & Sripada, Chandra. (2013). Navigating into the future or driven by the past. *Perspectives on Psychological Science*, 8(2), 119–141. doi: 10.1177/1745691612474317

Seltzer, Judith A.; Yahirun, Jenjira J. & Bianchi, Suzanne M. (2013). Coresidence and geographic proximity of mothers and adult children in stepfamilies. *Journal of Marriage and Family*, 75(5), 1164–1180. doi: 10.1111/jomf.12058

Şendil, Çağla Öneren & Erden, Feyza Tantekin. (2014). Peer preference: A way of evaluating social competence and behavioural well-being in early childhood. *Early Child Development and Care*, 184(2), 230–246. doi: 10.1080/03004430.2013.778254

Senior, Jennifer. (2014). *All joy and no fun: The paradox of modern parenthood.* New York, NY: Ecco.

Seppa, Nathan. (2013). Urban eyes: Too much time spent indoors may be behind a surge in nearsightedness. *Science News*, 183(3), 22–25. doi: 10.1002/scin.5591830323

Seppa, Nathan. (2014). Whooping cough bounces back: Replacement vaccine is not so great at protecting kids. *Science News*, 185(8), 22–26. doi: 10.1002/scin.5591850817

Settle, Jaime E.; Dawes, Christopher T.; Christakis, Nicholas A. & Fowler, James H. (2010). Friendships moderate an association between a dopamine gene variant and political ideology. *The Journal of Politics*, 72(4), 1189–1198. doi: 10.1017/S0022381610000617

Severson, Kim & Blinder, Alan. (2014, January 7). Test scandal in Atlanta brings more guilty pleas. *The New York Times*, p. A9.

Sexton, John. (2002). From hanging out to homework: Teens in the library. *OLA Quarterly*, 8(3), 10–12, 19. doi: 10.7710/1093-7374.1620

Shah, Nirvi. (2011). Policy fight brews over discipline. *Education Week*, 31(7), 1, 12.

Shah, Prakesh; Balkhair, Taiba; Ohlsson, Arne; Beyene, Joseph; Scott, Fran & Frick, Corine. (2011). Intention to become pregnant and low birth weight and preterm birth: A systematic review. *Maternal and Child Health Journal*, 15(2), 205–216. doi: 10.1007/s10995-009-0546-2

Shahin, Hashem; Walsh, Tom; Sobe, Tama; Lynch, Eric; King, Mary-Claire; Avraham,

Karen B. & Kanaan, Moien. (2002). Genetics of congenital deafness in the Palestinian population: Multiple connexin 26 alleles with shared origins in the Middle East. *Human Genetics*, 110(3), 284–289. doi: 10.1007/s00439-001-0674-2

Shanahan, Timothy & Lonigan, Christopher J. (2010). The National Early Literacy Panel: A summary of the process and the report. *Educational Researcher*, 39(4), 279–285. doi: 10.3102/0013189x10369172

Shanks, Laurie. (2011). Child sexual abuse: How to move to a balanced and rational approach to the cases everyone abhors. *American Journal of Trial Advocacy*, 34(3).

Shapiro, Edward S.; Zigmond, Naomi; Wallace, Teri & Marston, Doug (Eds.). (2011). *Models for implementing response to intervention: Tools, outcomes, and implications.* New York, NY: Guilford Press.

Shapiro, Melanie F. (2011). *Mothers' feelings about physical and emotional intimacy twelve to fifteen months after the birth of a first child.* (Thesis). School for Social Work. Northampton, MA: Smith College. https://dspace.smith.edu/handle/11020/23004

Sheeran, Paschal; Harris, Peter R. & Epton, Tracy. (2014). Does heightening risk appraisals change people's intentions and behavior? A meta-analysis of experimental studies. *Psychological Bulletin*, 140(2), 511–543. doi: 10.1037/a0033065

Shenzhen Daily. (2014, April 8). The pros and cons of SUSTC's development. *Shenzhen Daily*.

Sherman, David K.; Hartson, Kimberly A.; Binning, Kevin R.; Purdie-Vaughns, Valerie; Garcia, Julio; Taborsky-Barba, Suzanne, . . . Cohen, Geoffrey L. (2013). Deflecting the trajectory and changing the narrative: How self-affirmation affects academic performance and motivation under identity threat. *Journal of Personality and Social Psychology*, 104(4), 591–618. doi: 10.1037/a0031495

Shi, Bing & Xie, Hongling. (2012). Popular and nonpopular subtypes of physically aggressive preadolescents: Continuity of aggression and peer mechanisms during the transition to middle school. *Merrill-Palmer Quarterly*, 58(4), 530–553. doi: 10.1353/mpq.2012.0025

Shi, Rushen. (2014). Functional morphemes and early language acquisition. *Child Development Perspectives*, 8(1), 6–11. doi: 10.1111/cdep.12052

Shields, Margot & Tremblay, Mark S. (2010). Canadian childhood obesity estimates based on WHO, IOTF and CDC cut-points. *International Journal of Pediatric Obesity*, 5(3), 265–273. doi: 10.3109/17477160903268282

Shirtcliff, Elizabeth A.; Dahl, Ronald E. & Pollak, Seth D. (2009). Pubertal development: Correspondence between hormonal and physical development. *Child Development*, 80(2), 327–337. doi: 10.1111/j.1467-8624.2009.01263.x

Shoda, Tonya M.; McConnell, Allen R. & Rydell, Robert J. (2014). Having explicit-implicit evaluation discrepancies triggers race-based motivated reasoning. *Social Cognition*, 32(2), 190–202. doi: 10.1521/soco.2014.32.2.190

Shonkoff, Jack P.; Siegel, Benjamin S.; Dobbins, Mary I.; Earls, Marian F.; Garner, Andrew S.; McGuinn, Laura, . . . Wood, David L. (2012). The lifelong effects of early childhood adversity and toxic stress. *Pediatrics*, *129*(1), e232–e246. doi: 10.1542/peds.2011-2663

Shuger, Lisa. (2012). *Teen pregnancy and high school dropout: What communities can do to address these issues.* Washington, DC: The National Campaign to Prevent Teen and Unplanned Pregnancy and America's Promise Alliance.

Shuler, Carly. (2009). *Pockets of potential: Using mobile technologies to promote children's learning.* New York, NY: The Joan Ganz Cooney Center at Sesame Workshop.

Shutts, Kristin; Kinzler, Katherine D. & DeJesus, Jasmine M. (2013). Understanding infants' and children's social learning about foods: Previous research and new prospects. *Developmental Psychology*, *49*(3), 419–425. doi: 10.1037/a0027551

Siegal, Michael & Surian, Luca (Eds.). (2012). *Access to language and cognitive development.* New York, NY: Oxford University Press.

Siegler, Robert S. (2009). Improving the numerical understanding of children from low-income families. *Child Development Perspectives*, *3*(2), 118–124. doi: 10.1111/j.1750-8606.2009.00090.x

Siegler, Robert S. & Chen, Zhe. (2008). Differentiation and integration: Guiding principles for analyzing cognitive change. *Developmental Science*, *11*(4), 433–448. doi: 10.1111/j.1467-7687.2008.00689.x

Siegler, Robert S. & Mu, Yan. (2008). Chinese children excel on novel mathematics problems even before elementary school. *Psychological Science*, *19*(8), 759–763. doi: 10.1111/j.1467-9280.2008.02153.x

Sigurdson, J. F.; Wallander, J. & Sund, A. M. (2014). Is involvement in school bullying associated with general health and psychosocial adjustment outcomes in adulthood? *Child Abuse & Neglect*, *38*(10), 1607–1617. doi: 10.1016/j.chiabu.2014.06.001

Silk, Jessica & Romero, Diana. (2014). The role of parents and families in teen pregnancy prevention: An analysis of programs and policies. *Journal of Family Issues*, *35*(10), 1339–1362. doi: 10.1177/0192513X13481330

Silk, Timothy J. & Wood, Amanda G. (2011). Lessons about neurodevelopment from anatomical magnetic resonance imaging. *Journal of Developmental & Behavioral Pediatrics*, *32*(2), 158–168. doi: 10.1097/DBP.0b013e318206d58f

Sillars, Alan; Smith, Traci & Koerner, Ascan. (2010). Misattributions contributing to empathic (in)accuracy during parent-adolescent conflict discussions. *Journal of Social and Personal Relationships*, *27*(6), 727–747. doi: 10.1177/0265407510373261

Silton, Nava R.; Flannelly, Laura T.; Flannelly, Kevin J. & Galek, Kathleen. (2011). Toward a theory of holistic needs and the brain. *Holistic Nursing Practice*, *25*(5), 258–265. doi: 10.1097/HNP.0b013e31822a0301

Silva, Katie G.; Correa-Chávez, Maricela & Rogoff, Barbara. (2010). Mexican-heritage children's attention and learning from interactions directed to others. *Child Development*, *81*(3), 898–912. doi: 10.1111/j.1467-8624.2010.01441.x

Silvernail, David L.; Pinkham, Caroline A.; Wintle, Sarah E.; Walker, Leanne C. & Bartlett, Courtney L. (2011). *A middle school one-to-one laptop program: The Maine experience.* Gorham, ME: Maine Education Policy Research Institute, University of Southern Maine.

Simmons, Joseph P.; Nelson, Leif D. & Simonsohn, Uri. (2011). False-positive psychology: Undisclosed flexibility in data collection and analysis allows presenting anything as significant. *Psychological Science*, *22*(11), 1359–1366. doi: 10.1177/0956797611417632

Simpson, Jeffry A. & Kenrick, Douglas. (2013). *Evolutionary social psychology.* Hoboken, NJ: Taylor & Francis.

Simpson, Jeffry A. & Rholes, W. Steven (Eds.). (2015). *Attachment theory and research: New directions and emerging themes.* New York, NY: Guilford.

Sinclair, Samantha & Carlsson, Rickard. (2013). What will I be when I grow up? The impact of gender identity threat on adolescents' occupational preferences. *Journal of Adolescence*, *36*(3), 465–474. doi: 10.1016/j.adolescence.2013.02.001

Singh, Amika; Uijtdewilligen, Léonie; Twisk, Jos W. R.; van Mechelen, Willem & Chinapaw, Mai J. M. (2012). Physical activity and performance at school: A systematic review of the literature including a methodological quality assessment. *Archives of Pediatrics & Adolescent Medicine*, *166*(1), 49–55. doi: 10.1001/archpediatrics.2011.716

Singh, Leher. (2008). Influences of high and low variability on infant word recognition. *Cognition*, *106*(2), 833–870. doi: 10.1016/j.cognition.2007.05.002

Sinnott, Jan D. (2014). *Adult development: Cognitive aspects of thriving close relationships.* New York, NY: Oxford University Press.

Sjöström, Lars; Peltonen, Markku; Jacobson, Peter; Ahlin, Sofie; Andersson-Assarsson, Johanna; Anveden, Åsa, . . . Carlsson, Lena M. S. (2014). Association of bariatric surgery with long-term remission of type 2 diabetes and with microvascular and macrovascular complications. *JAMA*, *311*(22), 2297–2304. doi: 10.1001/jama.2014.5988

Skinner, B. F. (1953). *Science and human behavior.* New York, NY: Macmillan.

Skinner, B. F. (1957). *Verbal behavior.* New York, NY: Appleton-Century-Crofts.

Skoog, Thérèse & Stattin, Håkan. (2014). Why and under what contextual conditions do early-maturing girls develop problem behaviors? *Child Development Perspectives*, *8*(3), 158–162. doi: 10.1111/cdep.12076

Skorikov, Vladimir B. & Vondracek, Fred W. (2011). Occupational identity. In Seth J. Schwartz, et al. (Eds.), *Handbook of identity theory and research* (pp. 693–714). New York, NY: Springer. doi: 10.1007/978-1-4419-7988-9_29

Slack, Jonathan. (2012). *Stem cells: A very short introduction.* New York, NY: Oxford University Press.

Slater, Alan M. (2012). Imitation in infancy: Revisiting Meltzoff and Moore's (1977) study. In Alan M. Slater & Paul C. Quinn (Eds.), *Developmental psychology: Revisiting the classic studies.* Thousand Oaks, CA: Sage.

Slavich, George M. & Cole, Steven W. (2013). The emerging field of human social genomics. *Clinical Psychological Science*, *1*(3), 331–348. doi: 10.1177/2167702613478594

Slining, Meghan; Adair, Linda S.; Goldman, Barbara D.; Borja, Judith B. & Bentley, Margaret. (2010). Infant overweight is associated with delayed motor development. *The Journal of Pediatrics*, *157*(1), 20–25.e21. doi: 10.1016/j.jpeds.2009.12.054

Sloan, Mark. (2009). *Birth day: A pediatrician explores the science, the history, and the wonder of childbirth.* New York, NY: Ballantine Books.

Sloane, Stephanie; Baillargeon, Renée & Premack, David. (2012). Do infants have a sense of fairness? *Psychological Science*, *23*(2), 196–204. doi: 10.1177/0956797611422072

Smetana, Judith G. (2013). Moral development: The Social Domain Theory view. In Philip D. Zelazo (Ed.), *The Oxford handbook of developmental psychology* (Vol. 1, pp. 832–866). New York, NY: Oxford University Press. doi: 10.1093/oxfordhb/9780199958450.013.0029

Smith, Christian. (2005). *Soul searching: The religious and spiritual lives of American teenagers.* New York, NY: Oxford University Press.

Smith, Michelle I.; Yatsunenko, Tanya; Manary, Mark J.; Trehan, Indi; Mkakosya, Rajhab; Cheng, Jiye, . . . Gordon, Jeffrey I. (2013). Gut microbiomes of Malawian twin pairs discordant for kwashiorkor. *Science*, *339*(6119), 548–554. doi: 10.1126/science.1229000

Smith, Peter K. (2010). *Children and play: Understanding children's worlds.* Malden, MA: Wiley-Blackwell.

Smithells, R. W.; Sheppard, S.; Schorah, C. J.; Seller, M. J.; Nevin, N. C.; Harris, R., . . . Fielding, D. W. (2011). Apparent prevention of neural tube defects by periconceptional vitamin supplementation. *International Journal of Epidemiology*, *40*(5), 1146–1154. doi: 10.1093/ije/dyr143

Smokowski, Paul R.; Rose, Roderick & Bacallao, Martica. (2010). Influence of risk factors and cultural assets on Latino adolescents' trajectories of self-esteem and internalizing symptoms. *Child Psychiatry & Human Development*, *41*(2), 133–155. doi: 10.1007/s10578-009-0157-6

Snider, Terra Ziporyn. (2012). Later school start times are a public-health issue. *Education Week*, *31*(31), 25, 27.

Snow, Catherine E.; Porche, Michelle V.; Tabors, Patton O. & Harris, Stephanie R. (2007). *Is literacy enough? Pathways to academic success for adolescents*. Baltimore, MD: Brookes Publishing Company.

Snyder, Thomas D. & Dillow, Sally A. (2010). *Digest of education statistics, 2009*. Washington, DC: National Center for Education Statistics, Institute of Education Sciences, U.S. Department of Education.

Snyder, Thomas D. & Dillow, Sally A. (2013). *Digest of education statistics, 2012*. National Center for Education Statistics, Institute of Education Science, U.S. Department of Education.

Sobal, Jeffery & Hanson, Karla L. (2011). Marital status, marital history, body weight, and obesity. *Marriage & Family Review, 47*(7), 474–504. doi: 10.1080/01494929.2011.620934

Soderstrom, Melanie; Ko, Eon-Suk & Nevzorova, Uliana. (2011). It's a question? Infants attend differently to yes/no questions and declaratives. *Infant Behavior and Development, 34*(1), 107–110. doi: 10.1016/j.infbeh.2010.10.003

Soley, Gaye & Hannon, Erin E. (2010). Infants prefer the musical meter of their own culture: A cross-cultural comparison. *Developmental Psychology, 46*(1), 286–292. doi: 10.1037/a0017555

Solomon, Andrew. (2012). *Far from the tree: Parents, children and the search for identity*. New York, NY: Scribner.

Somerville, Leah H. (2013). The teenage brain: Sensitivity to social evaluation. *Current Directions in Psychological Science, 22*(2), 121–127. doi: 10.1177/0963721413476512

Soons, Judith P. M. & Kalmijn, Matthijs. (2009). Is marriage more than cohabitation? Well-being differences in 30 European countries. *Journal of Marriage and Family, 71*(5), 1141–1157. doi: 10.1111/j.1741-3737.2009.00660.x

Sophian, Catherine. (2013). Vicissitudes of children's mathematical knowledge: Implications of developmental research for early childhood mathematics education. *Early Education and Development, 24*(4), 436–442. doi: 10.1080/10409289.2013.773255

Soska, Kasey C.; Adolph, Karen E. & Johnson, Scott P. (2010). Systems in development: Motor skill acquisition facilitates three-dimensional object completion. *Developmental Psychology, 46*(1), 129–138. doi: 10.1037/a0014618

Sousa, David A. (2014). *How the brain learns to read* (2nd ed.). Thousand Oaks, CA: SAGE.

Sowell, Elizabeth R.; Thompson, Paul M.; Holmes, Colin J.; Jernigan, Terry L. & Toga, Arthur W. (1999). In vivo evidence for post-adolescent brain maturation in frontal and striatal regions. *Nature Neuroscience, 2*(10), 859–862.

Sowell, Elizabeth R.; Thompson, Paul M. & Toga, Arthur W. (2007). Mapping adolescent brain maturation using structural magnetic resonance imaging. In Daniel Romer & Elaine F. Walker (Eds.), *Adolescent psychopathology and the developing brain: Integrating brain and prevention science* (pp. 55–84). New York, NY: Oxford University Press.

Sparks, Sarah D. (2012). Form + function = Finnish schools. *Education Week, 31*(36), 9.

Spear, Linda. (2013). The teenage brain: Adolescents and alcohol. *Current Directions in Psychological Science, 22*(2), 152–157. doi: 10.1177/0963721412472192

Spelke, Elizabeth S. (1993). Object perception. In Alvin I. Goldman (Ed.), *Readings in philosophy and cognitive science* (pp. 447–460). Cambridge, MA: The MIT Press.

Spencer, John P.; Blumberg, Mark S.; McMurray, Bob; Robinson, Scott R.; Samuelson, Larissa K. & Tomblin, J. Bruce. (2009). Short arms and talking eggs: Why we should no longer abide the nativist–empiricist debate. *Child Development Perspectives, 3*(2), 79–87. doi: 10.1111/j.1750-8606.2009.00081.x

Sperry, Debbie M. & Widom, Cathy S. (2013). Child abuse and neglect, social support, and psychopathology in adulthood: A prospective investigation. *Child Abuse & Neglect, 37*(6), 415–425. doi: 10.1016/j.chiabu.2013.02.006

Sprecher, Susan & Metts, Sandra. (2013). Logging on, hooking up: The changing nature of romantic relationship initiation and romantic relating. In Cindy Hazan & Mary I. Campa (Eds.), *Human bonding: The science of affectional ties* (pp. 197–225). New York, NY: The Guilford Press.

Sprietsma, Maresa. (2010). Effect of relative age in the first grade of primary school on long-term scholastic results: International comparative evidence using PISA 2003. *Education Economics, 18*(1), 1–32. doi: 10.1080/09645290802201961

Staff, Jeremy & Schulenberg, John. (2010). Millennials and the world of work: Experiences in paid work during adolescence. *Journal of Business and Psychology, 25*(2), 247–255. doi: 10.1007/s10869-010-9167-4

Standing, E. M. (1998). *Maria Montessori: Her life and work*. New York, NY: Plume.

Statistics Canada. (2013). *Table 2: Distribution (number and percentage) and percentage change of census families by family structure, Canada, provinces and territories, 2011*. Government of Canada.

Steele, Claude M. (1997). A threat in the air: How stereotypes shape intellectual identity and performance. *American Psychologist, 52*(6), 613–629. doi: 10.1037//0003-066X.52.6.613

Stein, Arlene. (2006). *Shameless: Sexual dissidence in American culture*. New York, NY: New York University Press.

Steinberg, Laurence. (2004). Risk taking in adolescence: What changes, and why? *Annals of the New York Academy of Sciences, 1021*, 51–58. doi: 10.1196/annals.1308.005

Steinberg, Laurence. (2009). Should the science of adolescent brain development inform public policy? *American Psychologist, 64*(8), 739–750. doi: 10.1037/0003-066x.64.8.739

Steinberg, Laurence. (2014). *Age of opportunity: Lessons from the new science of adolescence*. Boston, MA: Houghton Mifflin Harcourt.

Steinberg, Laurence & Monahan, Kathryn C. (2011). Adolescents' exposure to sexy media does not hasten the initiation of sexual intercourse. *Developmental Psychology, 47*(2), 562–576. doi: 10.1037/a0020613

Steiner, Meir & Young, Elizabeth A. (2008). Hormones and mood. In Jill B. Becker, et al. (Eds.), *Sex differences in the brain: From genes to behavior* (pp. 405–426). New York, NY: Oxford University Press.

Stenseng, Frode; Belsky, Jay; Skalicka, Vera & Wichstrøm, Lars. (2014). Social exclusion predicts impaired self-regulation: A 2-year longitudinal panel study including the transition from preschool to school. *Journal of Personality*. doi: 10.1111/jopy.12096

Stephens, Nicole M.; Markus, Hazel Rose & Fryberg, Stephanie A. (2012). Social class disparities in health and education: Reducing inequality by applying a sociocultural self model of behavior. *Psychological Review, 119*(4), 723–744. doi: 10.1037/a0029028

Stephens, Rick & Richey, Mike. (2013). A business view on U.S. education. *Science, 340*(6130), 313–314. doi: 10.1126/science.1230728

Sterling, Kymberle L. & Mermelstein, Robin. (2011). Examining hookah smoking among a cohort of adolescent ever smokers. *Nicotine & Tobacco Research, 13*(12), 1202–1209. doi: 10.1093/ntr/ntr146

Sterling, Peter. (2012). Allostasis: A model of predictive regulation. *Physiology & Behavior, 106*(1), 5–15. doi: 10.1016/j.physbeh.2011.06.004

Stern, Mark; Clonan, Sheila; Jaffee, Laura & Lee, Anna. (2014). The normative limits of choice: Charter schools, disability studies, and questions of inclusion. *Educational Policy*. doi: 10.1177/0895904813510779

Stern, Peter. (2013). Connection, connection, connection.... *Science, 342*(6158), 577. doi: 10.1126/science.342.6158.577

Sternberg, Robert J. (1985). *Beyond IQ: A triarchic theory of human intelligence*. New York, NY: Cambridge University Press.

Sternberg, Robert J. (2008). Schools should nurture wisdom. In Barbara Z. Presseisen (Ed.), *Teaching for intelligence* (2nd ed., pp. 61–88). Thousand Oaks, CA: Corwin Press.

Sternberg, Robert J. (2011). The theory of successful intelligence. In Robert J. Sternberg & Scott Barry Kaufman (Eds.), *The Cambridge handbook of intelligence* (pp. 504–526). New York, NY: Cambridge University Press.

Sternberg, Robert J. (2012). Why I became an administrator . . . and why you might become one too: Applying the science of psychology to the life of a university. *Observer, 25*(2), 21–22.

Sternberg, Robert J.; Jarvin, Linda & Grigorenko, Elena L. (2011). *Explorations in giftedness*. New York, NY: Cambridge University Press.

Stetser, Marie C. & Stillwell, Robert. (2014). *Public high school four-year on-time graduation rates and event dropout rates: School years 2010–11 and 2011–12*. Washington, DC: Department of Education, National Center for Education Statistics.

Stevens, Courtney & Bavelier, Daphne. (2012). The role of selective attention on academic foundations: A cognitive neuroscience perspective. *Developmental Cognitive Neuroscience, 2*(Suppl. 1), S30–S48. doi: 10.1016/j.dcn.2011.11.001

Stevenson, Richard J.; Oaten, Megan J.; Case, Trevor I.; Repacholi, Betty M. & Wagland, Paul. (2010). Children's response to adult disgust elicitors: Development and acquisition. *Developmental Psychology, 46*(1), 165–177. doi: 10.1037/a0016692

Stieb, David M.; Chen, Li; Eshoul, Maysoon & Judek, Stan. (2012). Ambient air pollution, birth weight and preterm birth: A systematic review and meta-analysis. *Environmental Research, 117,* 100–111. doi: 10.1016/j.envres.2012.05.007

Stigler, James W. & Hiebert, James. (2009). *The teaching gap: Best ideas from the world's teachers for improving education in the classroom.* New York, NY: Free Press.

Stigum, Hein; Samuelsen, Sven-Ove & Traeen, Bente. (2010). Analysis of first coitus. *Archives of Sexual Behavior, 39*(4), 907–914. doi: 10.1007/s10508-009-9494-6

Stiles, Joan & Jernigan, Terry. (2010). The basics of brain development. *Neuropsychology Review, 20*(4), 327–348. doi: 10.1007/s11065-010-9148-4

Stipek, Deborah. (2013). Mathematics in early childhood education: Revolution or evolution? *Early Education & Development, 24*(4), 431–435. doi: 10.1080/10409289.2013.777285

Stolt, Suvi; Matomäki, Jaakko; Lind, Annika; Lapinleimu, Helena; Haataja, Leena & Lehtonen, Liisa. (2014). The prevalence and predictive value of weak language skills in children with very low birth weight—a longitudinal study. *Acta Paediatrica, 103*(6), 651–658. doi: 10.1111/apa.12607

Stoltenborgh, Marije; van IJzendoorn, Marinus H.; Euser, Eveline M. & Bakermans-Kranenburg, Marian J. (2011). A global perspective on child sexual abuse: Meta-analysis of prevalence around the world. *Child Maltreatment, 16*(2), 79–101. doi: 10.1177/1077559511403920

Stone, Richard. (2011). Daring experiment in higher education opens its doors. *Science, 332*(6026), 161. doi: 10.1126/science.332.6026.161

Stoneking, Mark & Delfin, Frederick. (2010). The human genetic history of East Asia: Weaving a complex tapestry. *Current Biology, 20*(4), R188–R193. doi: 10.1016/j.cub.2009.11.052

Strait, Dana L.; Parbery-Clark, Alexandra; O'Connell, Samantha & Kraus, Nina. (2013). Biological impact of preschool music classes on processing speech in noise. *Developmental Cognitive Neuroscience, 6,* 51–60. doi: 10.1016/j.dcn.2013.06.003

Strasburger, Victor C.; Wilson, Barbara J. & Jordan, Amy B. (2009). *Children, adolescents, and the media* (2nd ed.). Los Angeles, CA: Sage.

Straus, Murray A. & Paschall, Mallie J. (2009). Corporal punishment by mothers and development of children's cognitive ability: A longitudinal study of two nationally representative age cohorts. *Journal of Aggression, Maltreatment & Trauma, 18*(5), 459–483. doi: 10.1080/10926770903035168

Stremmel, Andrew J. (2012). A situated framework: The Reggio experience. In Nancy File, et al. (Eds.), *Curriculum in early childhood education: Re-examined, rediscovered, renewed* (pp. 133–145). New York, NY: Routledge.

Stroebe, Wolfgang; Postmes, Tom & Spears, Russell. (2012). Scientific misconduct and the myth of self-correction in science. *Perspectives on Psychological Science, 7*(6), 670–688. doi: 10.1177/1745691612460687

Stubben, Jerry D. (2001). Working with and conducting research among American Indian families. *American Behavioral Scientist, 44*(9), 1466–1481. doi: 10.1177/00027642010440090004

Stupica, Brandi; Sherman, Laura J. & Cassidy, Jude. (2011). Newborn irritability moderates the association between infant attachment security and toddler exploration and sociability. *Child Development, 82*(5), 1381–1389. doi: 10.1111/j.1467-8624.2011.01638.x

Suchy, Frederick J.; Brannon, Patsy M.; Carpenter, Thomas O.; Fernandez, Jose R.; Gilsanz, Vicente; Gould, Jeffrey B., . . . Wolf, Marshall A. (2010). National Institutes of Health Consensus Development Conference: Lactose intolerance and health. *Annals of Internal Medicine, 152*(12), 792–796. doi: 10.7326/0003-4819-152-12-201006150-00248

Suleiman, Ahna B. & Brindis, Claire D. (2014). Adolescent school-based sex education: Using developmental neuroscience to guide new directions for policy and practice. *Sexuality Research and Social Policy, 11*(2), 137–152. doi: 10.1007/s13178-014-0147-8

Sulek, Julia P. (2013, April 30). Audrie Pott suicide: Parents share grief, quest for justice in exclusive interview. *San Jose Mercury News.*

Sullivan, Oriel; Billari, Francesco C. & Altintas, Evrim. (2014). Fathers' changing contributions to child care and domestic work in very low–fertility countries: The effect of education. *Journal of Family Issues, 35*(8), 1048–1065. doi: 10.1177/0192513X14522241

Sullivan, Shannon. (2014). *Good white people: The problem with middle-class white anti-racism.* Albany, NY: State University of New York Press.

Sun, Min & Rugolotto, Simone. (2004). Assisted infant toilet training in a Western family setting. *Journal of Developmental & Behavioral Pediatrics, 25*(2), 99–101. doi: 10.1097/00004703-200404000-00004

Sunstein, Cass R. (2008). Adolescent risk-taking and social meaning: A commentary. *Developmental Review, 28*(1), 145–152. doi: 10.1016/j.dr.2007.11.003

Suomi, Steven J. (2002). Parents, peers, and the process of socialization in primates. In John G. Borkowski, et al. (Eds.), *Parenting and the child's world: Influences on academic, intellectual, and social-emotional development* (pp. 265–279). Mahwah, NJ: Erlbaum.

Surman, Craig B. H.; Hammerness, Paul G.; Pion, Katie & Faraone, Stephen V. (2013). Do stimulants improve functioning in adults with ADHD?: A review of the literature. *European Neuropsychopharmacology, 23*(6), 528–533. doi: 10.1016/j.euroneuro.2012.02.010

Susman, Elizabeth J.; Houts, Renate M.; Steinberg, Laurence; Belsky, Jay; Cauffman, Elizabeth; DeHart, Ganie, . . . Halpern-Felsher, Bonnie L. (2010). Longitudinal development of secondary sexual characteristics in girls and boys between ages 9-1/2 and 15-1/2 years. *Archives of Pediatrics & Adolescent Medicine, 164*(2), 166–173. doi: 10.1001/archpediatrics.2009.261

Sutton-Smith, Brian. (2011). The antipathies of play. In Anthony D. Pellegrini (Ed.), *The Oxford handbook of the development of play* (pp. 110–115). New York, NY: Oxford University Press. doi: 10.1093/oxfordhb/9780195393002.013.0010

Swanson, Christopher B. (2014). Graduation rate breaks 80 percent. *Education Week, 33*(33 Suppl. 1), 24–26.

Swanson, H. Lee. (2013). Meta-analysis of research on children with learning disabilities. In H. Lee Swanson, et al. (Eds.), *Handbook of learning disabilities* (2nd ed., pp. 627–642). New York, NY: Guilford Press.

Synovitz, Linda & Chopak-Foss, Joanne. (2013). Precocious puberty: Pathology, related risks, and support strategies. *Open Journal of Preventive Medicine, 3*(9), 504–509. doi: 10.4236/ojpm.2013.39068

Taber, Daniel R.; Stevens, June; Evenson, Kelly R.; Ward, Dianne S.; Poole, Charles; Maciejewski, Matthew L., . . . Brownson, Ross C. (2011). State policies targeting junk food in schools: Racial/ethnic differences in the effect of policy change on soda consumption. *American Journal of Public Health, 101*(9), 1769–1775. doi: 10.2105/ajph.2011.300221

Tackett, Jennifer L.; Herzhoff, Kathrin; Harden, K. Paige; Page-Gould, Elizabeth & Josephs, Robert A. (2014). Personality × hormone interactions in adolescent externalizing psychopathology. *Personality Disorders: Theory, Research, and Treatment, 5*(3), 235–246. doi: 10.1037/per0000075

Taga, Keiko A.; Markey, Charlotte N. & Friedman, Howard S. (2006). A longitudinal investigation of associations between boys' pubertal timing and adult behavioral health and well-being. *Journal of Youth and Adolescence, 35*(3), 380–390. doi: 10.1007/s10964-006-9039-4

Tahmouresi, Niloufar; Bender, Caroline; Schmitz, Julian; Baleshzar, Alireza & Tuschen-Caffier, Brunna. (2014). Similarities and differences in emotion regulation and psychopathology in Iranian and German school-children: A cross-cultural study. *International Journal of Preventive Medicine, 5*(1), 52–60.

Tajalli, Hassan & Garba, Houmma A. (2014). Discipline or prejudice? Overrepresentation of minority students in disciplinary alternative education programs. *The Urban Review*. doi: 10.1007/s11256-014-0274-9

Tamis-LeMonda, Catherine S.; Bornstein, Marc H. & Baumwell, Lisa. (2001). Maternal responsiveness and children's achievement of language milestones. *Child Development*, 72(3), 748–767. doi: 10.1111/1467-8624.00313

Tamis-LeMonda, Catherine S.; Kuchirko, Yana & Song, Lulu. (2014). Why is infant language learning facilitated by parental responsiveness? *Current Directions in Psychological Science*, 23(2), 121–126. doi: 10.1177/0963721414522813

Tamm, Leanne; Epstein, Jeffery N.; Denton, Carolyn A.; Vaughn, Aaron J.; Peugh, James & Willcutt, Erik G. (2014). Reaction time variability associated with reading skills in poor readers with ADHD. *Journal of the International Neuropsychological Society*, 20(3), 292–301. doi: 10.1017/S1355617713001495

Tan, Patricia Z.; Armstrong, Laura M. & Cole, Pamela M. (2013). Relations between temperament and anger regulation over early childhood. *Social Development*, 22(4), 755–772. doi: 10.1111/j.1467-9507.2012.00674.x

Tang, Jie; Yu, Yizhen; Du, Yukai; Ma, Ying; Zhang, Dongying & Wang, Jiaji. (2014). Prevalence of internet addiction and its association with stressful life events and psychological symptoms among adolescent internet users. *Addictive Behaviors*, 39(3), 744–747. doi: 10.1016/j.addbeh.2013.12.010

Tanner, Jennifer L.; Arnett, Jeffrey J. & Leis, Julie A. (2009). Emerging adulthood: Learning and development during the first stage of adulthood. In M. Cecil Smith & Nancy DeFrates-Densch (Eds.), *Handbook of research on adult learning and development* (pp. 34–67). New York, NY: Routledge.

Tarullo, Amanda R.; Garvin, Melissa C. & Gunnar, Megan R. (2011). Atypical EEG power correlates with indiscriminately friendly behavior in internationally adopted children. *Developmental Psychology*, 47(2), 417–431. doi: 10.1037/a0021363

Tatem, Andrew J.; Hemelaar, Joris; Gray, Rebecca & Salemi, Marco. (2012). Spatial accessibility and the spread of HIV-1 subtypes and recombinants. *AIDS*, 26(18), 2351–2360. doi: 10.1097/QAD.0b013e328359a904

Taveras, Elsie M.; Gillman, Matthew W.; Kleinman, Ken P.; Rich-Edwards, Janet W. & Rifas-Shiman, Sheryl L. (2013). Reducing racial/ethnic disparities in childhood obesity: The role of early life risk factors. *JAMA Pediatrics*, 167(8), 731–738. doi: 10.1001/jamapediatrics.2013.85

Tay, Marc Tze-Hsin; Au Eong, Kah Guan; Ng, C. Y. & Lim, M. K. (1992). Myopia and educational attainment in 421,116 young Singaporean males. *Annals Academy of Medicine Singapore*, 21(6), 785–791.

Taylor, Marjorie; Shawber, Alison B. & Mannering, Anne M. (2009). Children's imaginary companions: What is it like to have an invisible friend? In Keith D. Markman, et al. (Eds.), *Handbook of imagination and mental simulation* (pp. 211–224). New York, NY: Psychology Press.

Taylor, Paul. (2014). *The next America: Boomers, millennials, and the looming generational showdown.* New York, NY: PublicAffairs.

Taylor, Rachael W.; Murdoch, Linda; Carter, Philippa; Gerrard, David F.; Williams, Sheila M. & Taylor, Barry J. (2009). Longitudinal study of physical activity and inactivity in preschoolers: The FLAME study. *Medicine & Science in Sports & Exercise*, 41(1), 96–102. doi: 10.1249/MSS.0b013e3181849d81

Taylor, Valerie J. & Walton, Gregory M. (2011). Stereotype threat undermines academic learning. *Personality and Social Psychology Bulletin*, 37(8), 1055–1067. doi: 10.1177/0146167211406506

Taylor, Zoe E.; Eisenberg, Nancy; Spinrad, Tracy L.; Eggum, Natalie D. & Sulik, Michael J. (2013). The relations of ego-resiliency and emotion socialization to the development of empathy and prosocial behavior across early childhood. *Emotion*, 13(5), 822–831. doi: 10.1037/a0032894

Teiser, Johanna; Lamm, Bettina; Böning, Mirjam; Graf, Frauke; Gudi, Helene; Goertz, Claudia, . . . Keller, Heidi. (2014). Deferred imitation in 9-month-olds: How do model and task characteristics matter across cultures? *International Journal of Behavioral Development*, 38(3), 247–254. doi: 10.1177/0165025413513706

Telzer, Eva H.; Flannery, Jessica; Shapiro, Mor; Humphreys, Kathryn L.; Goff, Bonnie; Gabard-Durman, Laurel, . . . Gee, Nim. (2013). Early experience shapes amygdala sensitivity to race: An international adoption design. *The Journal of Neuroscience*, 33(33), 13484–13488. doi: 10.1523/JNEUROSCI.1272-13.2013

Temple, Jeff R.; Le, Vi Donna; van den Berg, Patricia; Ling, Yan; Paul, Jonathan A. & Temple, Brian W. (2014). Brief report: Teen sexting and psychosocial health. *Journal of Adolescence*, 37(1), 33–36. doi: 10.1016/j.adolescence.2013.10.008

Teoh, Yee San & Lamb, Michael E. (2013). Interviewer demeanor in forensic interviews of children. *Psychology, Crime & Law*, 19(2), 145–159. doi: 10.1080/1068316X.2011.614610

Terman, Lewis M. (1925). *Genetic studies of genius.* Stanford, CA: Stanford University Press.

Terry-McElrath, Yvonne M.; Turner, Lindsey; Sandoval, Anna; Johnston, Lloyd D. & Chaloupka, Frank J. (2014). Commercialism in US elementary and secondary school nutrition environments: Trends from 2007 to 2012. *JAMA Pediatrics*, 168(3), 234–242. doi: 10.1001/jamapediatrics.2013.4521

Tessier, Karen. (2010). Effectiveness of hands-on education for correct child restraint use by parents. *Accident Analysis & Prevention*, 42(4), 1041–1047. doi: 10.1016/j.aap.2009.12.011

Tetzlaff, A. & Hilbert, A. (2014). The role of the family in childhood and adolescent binge eating. A systematic review. *Appetite*, 76(1), 208. doi: 10.1016/j.appet.2014.01.050

Thaler, Richard H. & Sunstein, Cass R. (2008). *Nudge: Improving decisions about health, wealth, and happiness.* New Haven, CT: Yale University Press.

The Chronicle of Higher Education. (2014). Almanac of higher education 2014–15. *The Chronicle Of Higher Education*, 60(45).

Thelen, Esther & Corbetta, Daniela. (2002). Microdevelopment and dynamic systems: Applications to infant motor development. In Nira Granott & Jim Parziale (Eds.), *Microdevelopment: Transition processes in development and learning* (pp. 59–79). New York, NY: Cambridge University Press.

Thelen, Esther & Smith, Linda B. (2006). Dynamic systems theories. In Richard M. Lerner & William Damon (Eds.), *Handbook of child psychology* (6th ed., Vol. 1, pp. 258–312). Hoboken, NJ: Wiley.

Thomaes, Sander; Reijntjes, Albert; Orobio de Castro, Bram; Bushman, Brad J.; Poorthuis, Astrid & Telch, Michael J. (2010). I like me if you like me: On the interpersonal modulation and regulation of preadolescents' state self-esteem. *Child Development*, 81(3), 811–825. doi: 10.1111/j.1467-8624.2010.01435.x

Thomas, Alexander & Chess, Stella. (1977). *Temperament and development.* New York, NY: Brunner/Mazel.

Thomas, Michael S. C.; Van Duuren, Mike; Purser, Harry R. M.; Mareschal, Denis; Ansari, Daniel & Karmiloff-Smith, Annette. (2010). The development of metaphorical language comprehension in typical development and in Williams syndrome. *Journal of Experimental Child Psychology*, 106(2/3), 99–114. doi: 10.1016/j.jecp.2009.12.007

Thompson, Charis. (2014). Reproductions through technology. *Science*, 344(6182), 361–362. doi: 10.1126/science.1252641

Thompson, Clarissa A. & Siegler, Robert S. (2010). Linear numerical-magnitude representations aid children's memory for numbers. *Psychological Science*, 21(9), 1274–1281. doi: 10.1177/0956797610378309

Thompson, Ross A. (2006). The development of the person: Social understanding, relationships, conscience, self. In William Damon & Richard M. Lerner (Eds.), *Handbook of child psychology* (6th ed., Vol. 3, pp. 24–98). Hoboken, NJ: Wiley.

Thompson, Ross A. (2014). Conscience development in early childhood. In Melanie Killen & Judith G. Smetana (Eds.), *Handbook of moral development* (2nd ed., pp. 73–92). New York, NY: Psychology Press.

Thompson, Ross A. & Nelson, Charles A. (2001). Developmental science and the media: Early brain development. *American Psychologist*, 56(1), 5–15. doi: 10.1037//0003-066X.56.1.5

Thompson, Ross A. & Raikes, H. Abigail. (2003). Toward the next quarter-century:

Conceptual and methodological challenges for attachment theory. *Development and Psychopathology, 15*(3), 691–718. doi: 10.1017/S0954579403000348

Thomson, Samuel; Marriott, Michael; Telford, Katherine; Law, Hou; McLaughlin, Jo & Sayal, Kapil. (2014). Adolescents with a diagnosis of anorexia nervosa: Parents' experience of recognition and deciding to seek help. *Clinical Child Psychology Psychiatry, 19*(1), 43–57. doi: 10.1177/1359104512465741

Thornberg, Robert & Jungert, Tomas. (2013). Bystander behavior in bullying situations: Basic moral sensitivity, moral disengagement and defender self-efficacy. *Journal of Adolescence, 36*(3), 475–483. doi: 10.1016/j.adolescence.2013.02.003

Thurber, James. (1999). The secret life of James Thurber. *The Thurber carnival* (pp. 35–41). New York, NY: Harper Perennial.

Tikotzky, Liat; Sharabany, Ruth; Hirsch, Idit & Sadeh, Avi. (2010). "Ghosts in the nursery:" Infant sleep and sleep-related cognitions of parents raised under communal sleeping arrangements. *Infant Mental Health Journal, 31*(3), 312–334. doi: 10.1002/imhj.20258

Tishkoff, Sarah A.; Reed, Floyd A.; Friedlaender, Françoise R.; Ehret, Christopher; Ranciaro, Alessia; Froment, Alain, . . . Williams, Scott M. (2009). The genetic structure and history of Africans and African Americans. *Science, 324*(5930), 1035–1044. doi: 10.1126/science.1172257

Titzmann, Peter F. & Silbereisen, Rainer K. (2009). Friendship homophily among ethnic German immigrants: A longitudinal comparison between recent and more experienced immigrant adolescents. *Journal of Family Psychology, 23*(3), 301–310. doi: 10.1037/a0015493

Tobey, Emily A.; Thal, Donna; Niparko, John K.; Eisenberg, Laurie S.; Quittner, Alexandra L. & Wang, Nae-Yuh. (2013). Influence of implantation age on school-age language performance in pediatric cochlear implant users. *International Journal of Audiology, 52*(4), 219–229. doi: 10.3109/14992027.2012.759666

Tokunaga, Robert S. (2010). Following you home from school: A critical review and synthesis of research on cyberbullying victimization. *Computers in Human Behavior, 26*(3), 277–287. doi: 10.1016/j.chb.2009.11.014

Tolman, Deborah L. & McClelland, Sara I. (2011). Normative sexuality development in adolescence: A decade in review, 2000–2009. *Journal of Research on Adolescence, 21*(1), 242–255. doi: 10.1111/j.1532-7795.2010.00726.x

Tomalski, Przemyslaw & Johnson, Mark H. (2010). The effects of early adversity on the adult and developing brain. *Current Opinion in Psychiatry, 23*(3), 233–238. doi: 10.1097/YCO.0b013e3283387a8c

Tomasello, Michael. (2006). Acquiring linguistic constructions. In William Damon & Richard M. Lerner (Eds.), *Handbook of child psychology* (6th ed., Vol. 2, pp. 255–298). Hoboken, NJ: Wiley.

Tomasello, Michael. (2009). Cultural transmission: A view from chimpanzees and human infants. In Ute Schönpflug (Ed.), *Cultural transmission: Psychological, developmental, social, and methodological aspects* (pp. 33–47). New York, NY: Cambridge University Press.

Tomasello, Michael & Herrmann, Esther. (2010). Ape and human cognition. *Current Directions in Psychological Science, 19*(1), 3–8. doi: 10.1177/0963721409359300

Tonn, Jessica L. (2006). Later high school start times a reaction to research. *Education Week, 25*(28), 5, 17.

Tonyan, Holli A.; Mamikonian-Zarpas, Ani & Chien, Dorothy. (2013). Do they practice what they preach? An ecocultural, multidimensional, group-based examination of the relationship between beliefs and behaviours among child care providers. *Early Child Development and Care, 183*(12), 1853–1877. doi: 10.1080/03004430.2012.759949

Toporek, Bryan. (2012). Sports rules revised as research mounts on head injuries. *Education Week, 31*(22), 8.

Torbeyns, Joke; Schneider, Michael; Xin, Ziqiang & Siegler, Robert S. (2014). Bridging the gap: Fraction understanding is central to mathematics achievement in students from three different continents. *Learning and Instruction*, (In Press). doi: 10.1016/j.learninstruc.2014.03.002

Tough, Paul. (2012). *How children succeed: Grit, curiosity, and the hidden power of character.* Boston, MA: Houghton Mifflin Harcourt.

Trawick-Smith, Jeffrey. (2012). Teacher–child play interactions to achieve learning outcomes: Risks and opportunities. In Robert C. Pianta (Ed.), *Handbook of early childhood education* (pp. 259–277). New York, NY: Guilford Press.

Tremblay, Angelo & Chaput, Jean-Philippe. (2012). Obesity: The allostatic load of weight loss dieting. *Physiology & Behavior, 106*(1), 16–21. doi: 10.1016/j.physbeh.2011.05.020

Trenholm, Christopher; Devaney, Barbara; Fortson, Ken; Quay, Lisa; Wheeler, Justin & Clark, Melissa. (2007). *Impacts of four Title V, Section 510 abstinence education programs final report.* Washington, DC: U.S. Department of Health and Human Services, Mathematica Policy Research, Inc.

Trickett, Penelope K.; Noll, Jennie G. & Putnam, Frank W. (2011). The impact of sexual abuse on female development: Lessons from a multigenerational, longitudinal research study. *Development and Psychopathology, 23*(2), 453–476. doi: 10.1017/S0954579411000174

Trommsdorff, Gisela & Cole, Pamela M. (2011). Emotion, self-regulation, and social behavior in cultural contexts. In Xinyin Chen & Kenneth H. Rubin (Eds.), *Socioemotional development in cultural context* (pp. 131–163). New York, NY: Guilford Press.

Tronick, Edward. (1989). Emotions and emotional communication in infants. *American Psychologist, 44*(2), 112–119. doi: 10.1037//0003-066X.44.2.112

Tronick, Edward & Beeghly, Marjorie. (2011). Infants' meaning-making and the development of mental health problems. *American Psychologist, 66*(2), 107–119. doi: 10.1037/a0021631

Tronick, Edward & Weinberg, M. Katherine. (1997). Depressed mothers and infants: Failure to form dyadic states of consciousness. In Lynne Murray & Peter J. Cooper (Eds.), *Postpartum depression and child development* (pp. 54–81). New York, NY: Guilford Press.

Tsao, Feng-Ming; Liu, Huei-Mei & Kuhl, Patricia K. (2004). Speech perception in infancy predicts language development in the second year of life: A longitudinal study. *Child Development, 75*(4), 1067–1084. doi: 10.1111/j.1467-8624.2004.00726.x

Tsethlikai, Monica & Rogoff, Barbara. (2013). Involvement in traditional cultural practices and American Indian children's incidental recall of a folktale. *Developmental Psychology, 49*(3), 568–578. doi: 10.1037/a0031308

Ttofi, Maria M.; Bowes, Lucy; Farrington, David P. & Lösel, Friedrich. (2014). Protective factors interrupting the continuity from school bullying to later internalizing and externalizing problems: A systematic review of prospective longitudinal studies. *Journal of School Violence, 13*(1), 5–38. doi: 10.1080/15388220.2013.857345

Tucker-Drob, Elliot M.; Rhemtulla, Mijke; Harden, K. Paige; Turkheimer, Eric & Fask, David. (2011). Emergence of a gene × socioeconomic status interaction on infant mental ability between 10 months and 2 years. *Psychological Science, 22*(1), 125–133. doi: 10.1177/0956797610392926

Tudge, Jonathan. (2008). *The everyday lives of young children: Culture, class, and child rearing in diverse societies.* New York, NY: Cambridge University Press.

Tudge, Jonathan R. H.; Doucet, Fabienne; Odero, Dolphine; Sperb, Tania M.; Piccinini, Cesar A. & Lopes, Rita S. (2006). A window into different cultural worlds: Young children's everyday activities in the United States, Brazil, and Kenya. *Child Development, 77*(5), 1446–1469. doi: 10.1111/j.1467-8624.2006.00947.x

Tummeltshammer, Kristen S.; Wu, Rachel; Sobel, David M. & Kirkham, Natasha Z. (2014). Infants track the reliability of potential informants. *Psychological Science, 25*(9), 1730–1738. doi: 10.1177/0956797614540178

Turiel, Elliot. (2002). *The culture of morality: Social development, context, and conflict.* New York, NY: Cambridge University Press.

Turiel, Elliot. (2006). The development of morality. In William Damon & Richard M. Lerner (Eds.), *Handbook of child psychology* (6th ed., Vol. 3, pp. 789–857). Hoboken, NJ: Wiley.

Turiel, Elliot. (2008). Thought about actions in social domains: Morality, social conventions, and social interactions. *Cognitive Development, 23*(1), 136–154. doi: 10.1016/j.cogdev.2007.04.001

Turley, Ruth N. López & Desmond, Matthew. (2011). Contributions to college costs by married, divorced, and remarried parents.

Journal of Family Issues, 32(6), 767–790. doi: 10.1177/0192513x10388013

Turner, Heather A.; Finkelhor, David; Ormrod, Richard; Hamby, Sherry; Leeb, Rebecca T.; Mercy, James A. & Holt, Melissa. (2012). Family context, victimization, and child trauma symptoms: Variations in safe, stable, and nurturing relationships during early and middle childhood. *American Journal of Orthopsychiatry, 82*(2), 209–219. doi: 10.1111/j.1939-0025.2012.01147.x

U.S. Bureau of Labor Statistics. (2011). *The employment situation – November 2011.* Washington, DC: U.S. Department of Labor.

U.S. Bureau of Labor Statistics. (2012, July 25). *Number of jobs held, labor market activity, and earnings growth among the youngest baby boomers: Results from a longitudinal survey summary.* Washington, DC: U.S. Department of Labor.

U.S. Bureau of Labor Statistics. (2013, April 30). *Employment characteristics of families, 2012.* Washington, DC: U.S. Department of Labor.

U.S. Census Bureau. (1981). *Current population survey: November, 1979.* Ann Arbor, MI: U.S. Department of Commerce, Bureau of the Census.

U.S. Census Bureau. (1989). *Current population survey: November, 1989.* Ann Arbor, MI: U.S. Department of Commerce, Bureau of the Census.

U.S. Census Bureau. (1992). *Current population survey: October, 1992.* Washington, DC: U.S. Department of Commerce, Economic and Statistics Administration, U.S. Census Bureau.

U.S. Census Bureau. (1995). *Current population survey: October, 1995.* Washington, DC: U.S. Department of Commerce, Economic and Statistics Administration, U.S. Census Bureau.

U.S. Census Bureau. (1999). *Current population survey: October, 1999.* Washington, DC: U.S. Department of Commerce, Economic and Statistics Administration, U.S. Census Bureau.

U.S. Census Bureau. (2010). *Annual estimates of the resident population by sex, race, and Hispanic origin for the United States: April 1, 2000 to July 1, 2009.* Washington, DC: U.S. Census Bureau.

U.S. Census Bureau. (2011). *America's families and living arrangements: 2011.* U.S. Department of Commerce, Economics and Statistics Administration, U.S. Census Bureau.

U.S. Census Bureau. (2013, April). *Who's minding the kids? Child care arrangements: 2011—Detailed tables.* Retrieved from: https://www.census.gov/programs-surveys/sipp/data/tables/2008-panel/2011-tables.html

U.S. Census Bureau. (2013a). *America's families and living arrangements: 2012.* Washington, DC: U.S. Department of Commerce, Economics and Statistics Administration, U.S. Census Bureau.

U.S. Census Bureau. (2013b). *2009–2013 American Community Survey 5-year estimates: Poverty.* Washington, DC: U.S. Department of Commerce, United States Census Bureau.

U.S. Department of Agriculture & U.S. Department of Health and Human Services. (2010). *Dietary Guidelines for Americans, 2010.*

Washington, DC: U.S. Government Printing Office.

U.S. Department of Health and Human Services. (2003). *Child maltreatment 2001.* Washington, DC: Administration for Children and Families, Administration on Children Youth and Families, Children's Bureau.

U.S. Department of Health and Human Services. (2008). *Child maltreatment 2006.* Washington, DC: Administration for Children and Families, Administration on Children Youth and Families, Children's Bureau.

U.S. Department of Health and Human Services. (2010). *Head Start impact study: Final report.* Washington, DC: Administration for Children and Families.

U.S. Department of Health and Human Services. (2011). *The Surgeon General's call to action to support breastfeeding.* Washington, DC: U.S. Department of Health and Human Services, Office of the Surgeon General.

U.S. Department of Health and Human Services. (2011). *Child maltreatment 2010.* Washington, DC: Administration for Children and Families, Administration on Children Youth and Families, Children's Bureau.

U.S. Department of Health and Human Services. (2012). *Child maltreatment 2011.* Washington, DC: Administration for Children and Families, Administration on Children Youth and Families, Children's Bureau.

U.S. Department of Health and Human Services. (2012, November). *National surveillance of asthma: United States, 2001–2010.* Hyattsville, MD: U.S. Department of Health and Human Services, Centers for Disease Control and Prevention, National Center for Health Statistics, 3(35), 31, Table 32.

U.S. Department of Health and Human Services. (2013, December). *Child maltreatment 2012.* Washington, DC: Administration for Children and Families, Administration on Children Youth and Families, Children's Bureau.

U.S. Department of Transportation. (2013a). *Traffic safety facts, pedestrians: 2011 data.* Washington, DC: National Center for Statistics and Analysis.

U.S. Department of Transportation. (2013b). *Traffic safety facts, children: 2011 data.* Washington, DC: National Center for Statistics and Analysis.

Uddin, Monica; Koenen, Karestan C.; de los Santos, Regina; Bakshis, Erin; Aiello, Allison E. & Galea, Sandro. (2010). Gender differences in the genetic and environmental determinants of adolescent depression. *Depression and Anxiety, 27*(7), 658–666. doi: 10.1002/da.20692

Uekermann, J.; Kraemer, M.; Abdel-Hamid, M.; Schimmelmann, B. G.; Hebebrand, J.; Daum, I., . . . Kis, B. (2010). Social cognition in Attention-deficit hyperactivity disorder (ADHD). *Neuroscience & Biobehavioral Reviews, 34*(5), 734–743. doi: 10.1016/j.neubiorev.2009.10.009

Umana-Taylor, Adriana J. & Guimond, Amy B. (2010). A longitudinal examination of parenting behaviors and perceived discrimination

predicting Latino adolescents' ethnic identity. *Developmental Psychology, 46*(3), 636–650. doi: 10.1037/a0019376

UNESCO. (2011). Institute for statistics database. Retrieved from: http://www.uis.unesco.org/Pages/default.aspx

UNESCO. (2012). *Global education digest, 2012: Opportunities lost: The impact of grade repetition and early school leaving.* Montreal, Canada: United Nations Educational, Scientific and Cultural Organization Institute for Statistics.

UNICEF. (2012). *The state of the world's children 2012: Children in an urban world.* New York, NY: United Nations.

UNICEF. (2014, July). Education: Secondary net attendance ration—Percentage. UNICEF Global Databases. Retrieved from: http://data.unicef.org/education/secondary

UNICEF. (2014a, October). Low birthweight: Percentage of infants weighing less than 2,500 grams at birth. UNICEF global databases, based on DHS, MICS, other national household surveys, data from routine reporting systems, UNICEF and WHO. Retrieved from: http://data.unicef.org/nutrition/low-birthweight

UNICEF. (2014b, October). Infant and young child feeding. UNICEF Global Databases. Retrieved from: http://www.unicef.org/nutrition/index_breastfeeding.html

United Nations. (2011). *The millennium development goals report 2011.* New York, NY: United Nations.

United Nations. (2013). *World population prospects: The 2012 revision, Volume 1: Comprehensive tables.* New York, NY: Population Division of the United Nations Department of Economic and Social Affairs of the United Nations Secretariat, Department of Economic and Social Affairs.

United Nations Children's Fund; World Health Organization & The World Bank. (2012). *Levels and trends in child malnutrition: UNICEF–WHO–World Bank joint child malnutrition estimates.* UNICEF, New York; WHO, Geneva; The World Bank, Washington, DC.

Ursache, Alexandra; Blair, Clancy; Stifter, Cynthia & Voegtline, Kristin. (2013). Emotional reactivity and regulation in infancy interact to predict executive functioning in early childhood. *Developmental Psychology, 49*(1), 127–137. doi: 10.1037/a0027728

Utendale, William T. & Hastings, Paul D. (2011). Developmental changes in the relations between inhibitory control and externalizing problems during early childhood. *Infant and Child Development, 20*(2), 181–193. doi: 10.1002/icd.691

Vaala, Sarah E.; Linebarger, Deborah L.; Fenstermacher, Susan K.; Tedone, Ashley; Brey, Elizabeth; Barr, Rachel, . . . Calvert, Sandra L. (2010). Content analysis of language-promoting teaching strategies used in infant-directed media. *Infant and Child Development, 19*(6), 628–648. doi: 10.1002/icd.715

Valdez, Carmen R.; Chavez, Tom & Woulfe, Julie. (2013). Emerging adults' lived experience of formative family stress: The family's lasting influence. *Qualitative Health Research, 23*(8), 1089–1102. doi: 10.1177/1049732313494271

Valsiner, Jaan. (2006). Developmental epistemology and implications for methodology. In Richard M. Lerner & William Damon (Eds.), *Handbook of child psychology* (6th ed., Vol. 1, pp. 166–209). Hoboken, NJ: Wiley.

van Batenburg-Eddes, Tamara; Butte, Dick & van de Looij-Jansen, Petra. (2012). Measuring juvenile delinquency: How do self-reports compare with official police statistics? *European Journal of Criminology, 9*(1), 23–37. doi: 10.1177/1477370811421644

van de Bongardt, Daphne; Reitz, Ellen; Sandfort, Theo & Deković, Maja. (2014). A meta-analysis of the relations between three types of peer norms and adolescent sexual behavior. *Personality and Social Psychology Review.* doi: 10.1177/1088868314544223

van den Akker, Alithe; Deković, Maja; Prinzie, Peter & Asscher, Jessica. (2010). Toddlers' temperament profiles: Stability and relations to negative and positive parenting. *Journal of Abnormal Child Psychology, 38*(4), 485–495. doi: 10.1007/s10802-009-9379-0

van den Ban, Els; Souverein, Patrick; Swaab, Hanna; van Engeland, Herman; Heerdink, Rob & Egberts, Toine. (2010). Trends in incidence and characteristics of children, adolescents, and adults initiating immediate- or extended-release methylphenidate or atomoxetine in the Netherlands during 2001–2006. *Journal of Child and Adolescent Psychopharmacology, 20*(1), 55–61. doi: 10.1089/cap.2008.0153

van Eeden-Moorefield, Brad & Pasley, Kay. (2013). Remarriage and stepfamily life. In Gary W. Peterson & Kevin R. Bush (Eds.), *Handbook of marriage and the family* (pp. 517–546). New York, NY: Springer. doi: 10.1007/978-1-4614-3987-5_22

van Hof, Paulion; van der Kamp, John & Savelsbergh, Geert J. P. (2008). The relation between infants' perception of catchableness and the control of catching. *Developmental Psychology, 44*(1), 182–194. doi: 10.1037/0012-1649.44.1.182

van IJzendoorn, Marinus H.; Bakermans-Kranenburg, Marian J.; Pannebakker, Fieke & Out, Dorothée. (2010). In defence of situational morality: Genetic, dispositional and situational determinants of children's donating to charity. *Journal of Moral Education, 39*(1), 1–20. doi: 10.1080/03057240903528535

Van Puyvelde, Martine; Vanfleteren, Pol; Loots, Gerrit; Deschuyffeleer, Sara; Vinck, Bart; Jacquet, Wolfgang & Verhelst, Werner. (2010). Tonal synchrony in mother-infant interaction based on harmonic and pentatonic series. *Infant Behavior and Development, 33*(4), 387–400. doi: 10.1016/j.infbeh.2010.04.003

van Soelen, Inge L. C.; Brouwer, Rachel M.; Peper, Jiska S.; van Beijsterveldt, Toos C. E. M.; van Leeuwen, Marieke; de Vries, Linda S., . . . Boomsma, Dorret I. (2010). Effects of gestational age and birth weight on brain volumes in healthy 9 year-old children. *The Journal of Pediatrics, 156*(6), 896–901. doi: 10.1016/j.jpeds.2009.12.052

Vandermassen, Griet. (2005). *Who's afraid of Charles Darwin? Debating feminism and evolutionary theory.* Lanham, MD: Rowman & Littlefield.

Vanhalst, Janne; Luyckx, Koen; Scholte, Ron H. J.; Engels, Rutger C. M. E. & Goossens, Luc. (2013). Low self-esteem as a risk factor for loneliness in adolescence: Perceived—but not actual—social acceptance as an underlying mechanism. *Journal of Abnormal Child Psychology, 41*(7), 1067–1081. doi: 10.1007/s10802-013-9751-y

Varga, Colleen M.; Gee, Christina B. & Munro, Geoffrey. (2011). The effects of sample characteristics and experience with infidelity on romantic jealous. *Sex Roles, 65*(11/12), 854–866. doi: 10.1007/s11199-011-0048-8

Varga, M. E.; Pavlova, O. G. & Nosova, S. V. (2010). The counting function and its representation in the parietal cortex in humans and animals. *Neuroscience and Behavioral Physiology, 40*(2), 185–196. doi: 10.1007/s11055-009-9238-z

Veenstra, René; Lindenberg, Siegwart; Munniksma, Anke & Dijkstra, Jan Kornelis. (2010). The complex relation between bullying, victimization, acceptance, and rejection: Giving special attention to status, affection, and sex differences. *Child Development, 81*(2), 480–486. doi: 10.1111/j.1467-8624.2009.01411.x

Vennemann, Mechtild M.; Hense, Hans-Werner; Bajanowski, Thomas; Blair, Peter S.; Complojer, Christina; Moon, Rachel Y. & Kiechl-Kohlendorfer, Ursula. (2012). Bed sharing and the risk of sudden infant death syndrome: Can we resolve the debate? *The Journal of Pediatrics, 160*(1), 44–48 doi: 10.1016/j.jpeds.2011.06.052

Vered, Karen O. (2008). *Children and media outside the home: Playing and learning in after-school care.* New York, NY: Palgrave Macmillan.

Verona, Sergiu. (2003). Romanian policy regarding adoptions. In Victor Littel (Ed.), *Adoption update* (pp. 5–10). New York, NY: Nova Science.

Véronneau, Marie-Hélène & Dishion, Thomas. (2010). Predicting change in early adolescent problem behavior in the middle school years: A mesosystemic perspective on parenting and peer experiences. *Journal of Abnormal Child Psychology, 38*(8), 1125–1137. doi: 10.1007/s10802-010-9431-0

Vieno, Alessio; Nation, Maury; Pastore, Massimiliano & Santinello, Massimo. (2009). Parenting and antisocial behavior: A model of the relationship between adolescent self-disclosure, parental closeness, parental control, and adolescent antisocial behavior. *Developmental Psychology, 45*(6), 1509–1519. doi: 10.1037/a0016929

Vignoles, Vivian L.; Schwartz, Seth J. & Luyckx, Koen. (2011). Introduction: Toward an integrative view of identity. In Seth J. Schwartz, et al. (Eds.), *Handbook of identity theory and research* (pp. 1–27). New York, NY: Springer. doi: 10.1007/978-1-4419-7988-9_1

Vitale, Susan; Sperduto, Robert D. & Ferris, Frederick L. (2009). Increased prevalence of myopia in the United States between 1971–1972 and 1999–2004. *Archives of Ophthalmology, 127*(12), 1632–1639. doi: 10.1001/archophthalmol.2009 303

Vogel, Gretchen. (2010). Diseases in a dish take off. *Science, 330*(6008), 1172–1173. doi: 10.1126/science.330.6008.1172

von Mutius, Erika & Vercelli, Donata. (2010). Farm living: Effects on childhood asthma and allergy. *Nature Reviews Immunology, 10*(12), 861–868. doi: 10.1038/nri2871

Vonderheid, Susan C.; Kishi, Rieko; Norr, Kathleen F. & Klima, Carrie. (2011). Group prenatal care and doula care for pregnant women. In Arden Handler, et al. (Eds.), *Reducing racial/ethnic disparities in reproductive and perinatal outcomes: The evidence from population-based interventions* (pp. 369–400). New York, NY: Springer. doi: 10.1007/978-1-4419-1499-6_15

Vong, Keang-Ieng. (2013). China: Pedagogy today and the move towards creativity. In Jan Georgeson & Jane Payler (Eds.), *International perspectives on early childhood education and care.* New York, NY: Open University Press.

Vouloumanos, Athena & Werker, Janet F. (2007). Listening to language at birth: Evidence for a bias for speech in neonates. *Developmental Science, 10*(2), 159–164. doi: 10.1111/j.1467-7687.2007.00549.x

Vuolo, Mike; Mortimer, Jeylan T. & Staff, Jeremy. (2014). Adolescent precursors of pathways from school to work. *Journal of Research on Adolescence, 24*(1), 145–162. doi: 10.1111/jora.12038

Vygotsky, Lev S. (1980). *Mind in society: The development of higher psychological processes.* Cambridge, MA: Harvard University Press.

Vygotsky, Lev S. (1987). Thinking and speech. In Robert W. Rieber & Aaron S. Carton (Eds.), *The collected works of L. S. Vygotsky* (Vol. 1, pp. 39–285). New York, NY: Springer.

Vygotsky, Lev S. (1994a). The development of academic concepts in school aged children. In René van der Veer & Jaan Valsiner (Eds.), *The Vygotsky reader* (pp. 355–370). Cambridge, MA: Blackwell.

Vygotsky, Lev S. (1994b). Principles of social education for deaf and dumb children in Russia. In Rene van der Veer & Jaan Valsiner (Eds.), *The Vygotsky reader* (pp. 19–26). Cambridge, MA: Blackwell.

Vygotsky, Lev S. (2012). *Thought and language.* Cambridge, MA: The MIT Press.

Wagner, Katie; Dobkins, Karen & Barner, David. (2013). Slow mapping: Color word learning as a gradual inductive process. *Cognition, 127*(3), 307–317. doi: 10.1016/j.cognition.2013.01.010

Wagner, Laura & Lakusta, Laura. (2009). Using language to navigate the infant mind. *Perspectives on Psychological Science, 4*(2), 177–184. doi: 10.1111/j.1745-6924.2009.01117.x

Wagner, Paul A. (2011). Socio-sexual education: A practical study in formal thinking and teachable moments. *Sex Education: Sexuality,*

Society and Learning, 11(2), 193–211. doi: 10.1080/14681811.2011.558427

Wahlstrom, Dustin; Collins, Paul; White, Tonya & Luciana, Monica. (2010). Developmental changes in dopamine neurotransmission in adolescence: Behavioral implications and issues in assessment. *Brain and Cognition*, 72(1), 146–159. doi: 10.1016/j.bandc.2009.10.013

Wahlstrom, Kyla L. (2002). Accommodating the sleep patterns of adolescents within current educational structures: An uncharted path. In Mary A. Carskadon (Ed.), *Adolescent sleep patterns: Biological, social, and psychological influences* (pp. 172–197). New York, NY: Cambridge University Press.

Wakefield, A. J.; Murch, S. H.; Anthony, A.; Linnell, J.; Casson, D. M.; Malik, M., . . . Walker-Smith, J. A. (1998). Ileal-lymphoid-nodular hyperplasia, non-specific colitis, and pervasive developmental disorder in children. *The Lancet*, 351(9103), 637–641.

Walberg, Herbert J. (2011). *Tests, testing, and genuine school reform*. Stanford, CA: Education Next Books.

Walker, Peter; Bremner, J. Gavin; Mason, Uschi; Spring, Jo; Mattock, Karen; Slater, Alan & Johnson, Scott P. (2010). Preverbal infants' sensitivity to synaesthetic cross-modality correspondences. *Psychological Science*, 21(1), 21–25. doi: 10.1177/0956797609354734

Walle, Eric A. & Campos, Joseph J. (2014). Infant language development is related to the acquisition of walking. *Developmental Psychology*, 50(2), 336–348. doi: 10.1037/a0033238

Waller, Erika M. & Rose, Amanda J. (2010). Adjustment trade-offs of co-rumination in mother-adolescent relationships. *Journal of Adolescence*, 33(3), 487–497. doi: 10.1016/j.adolescence.2009.06.002

Wallis, Claudia. (2014). Gut reactions: Intestinal bacteria may help determine whether we are lean or obese. *Scientific American*, 310(6), 30–33. doi: 10.1038/scientificamerican0614-30

Wambach, Karen & Riordan, Jan. (2014). *Breastfeeding and human lactation* (5th ed.). Burlington, MA: Jones & Bartlett Publishers.

Wang, Chao; Xue, Haifeng; Wang, Qianqian; Hao, Yongchen; Li, Dianjiang; Gu, Dongfeng & Huang, Jianfeng. (2014). Effect of drinking on all-cause mortality in women compared with men: A meta-analysis. *Journal of Women's Health*, 23(5). doi: 10.1089/jwh.2013.4414

Wang, Jingyun & Candy, T. Rowan. (2010). The sensitivity of the 2- to 4-month-old human infant accommodation system. *Investigative Ophthalmology and Visual Science*, 51(6), 3309–3317. doi: 10.1167/iovs.09-4667

Wang, Qi; Shao, Yi & Li, Yexin Jessica. (2010). "My way or mom's way?" The bilingual and bicultural self in Hong Kong Chinese children and adolescents. *Child Development*, 81(2), 555–567. doi: 10.1111/j.1467-8624.2009.01415.x

Wang, Xueli. (2013). Modeling entrance into STEM fields of study among students beginning at community colleges and four-year institutions.

Research in Higher Education, 54(6), 664–692. doi: 10.1007/s11162-013-9291-x

Ward, L. Monique; Epstein, Marina; Caruthers, Allison & Merriwether, Ann. (2011). Men's media use, sexual cognitions, and sexual risk behavior: Testing a mediational model. *Developmental Psychology*, 47(2), 592–602. doi: 10.1037/a0022669

Warren, Charles W.; Jones, Nathan R.; Eriksen, Michael P. & Asma, Samira. (2006). Patterns of global tobacco use in young people and implications for future chronic disease burden in adults. *The Lancet*, 367(9512), 749–753. doi: 10.1016/S0140-6736(06)68192-0

Washington, Harriet A. (2006). *Medical apartheid: The dark history of medical experimentation on Black Americans from colonial times to the present*. New York, NY: Doubleday.

Watkins-Lewis, Karen M. & Hamre, Bridget K. (2012). African-American parenting characteristics and their association with children's cognitive and academic school readiness. *Journal of African American Studies*, 16(3), 390–405. doi: 10.1007/s12111-011-9195-9

Watrin, João P. & Darwich, Rosângela. (2012). On behaviorism in the cognitive revolution: Myth and reactions. *Review of General Psychology*, 16(3), 269–282. doi: 10.1037/a0026766

Watson, John B. (1928). *Psychological care of infant and child*. New York, NY: Norton.

Watson, John B. (1998). *Behaviorism*. New Brunswick, NJ: Transaction.

Waxman, Sandra; Fu, Xiaolan; Arunachalam, Sudha; Leddon, Erin; Geraghty, Kathleen & Song, Hyun-joo. (2013). Are nouns learned before verbs? Infants provide insight into a long-standing debate. *Child Development Perspectives*, 7(3), 155–159. doi: 10.1111/cdep.12032

Waxman, Sandra R. & Lidz, Jeffrey L. (2006). Early word learning. In William Damon & Richard M. Lerner (Eds.), *Handbook of child psychology* (6th ed., Vol. 2, pp. 299–335). Hoboken, NJ: Wiley.

Weikum, Whitney M.; Vouloumanos, Athena; Navarra, Jordi; Soto-Faraco, Salvador; Sebastian-Galles, Nuria & Werker, Janet F. (2007). Visual language discrimination in infancy. *Science*, 316(5828), 1159. doi: 10.1126/science.1137686

Weinstein, Netta & DeHaan, Cody. (2014). On the mutuality of human motivation and relationships. In Netta Weinstein (Ed.), *Human motivation and interpersonal relationships: Theory, research, and applications* (pp. 3–25). New York, NY: Springer. doi: 10.1007/978-94-017-8542-6_1

Weis, Robert & Cerankosky, Brittany C. (2010). Effects of video-game ownership on young boys' academic and behavioral functioning: A randomized, controlled study. *Psychological Science*, 21(4), 463–470. doi: 10.1177/0956797610362670

Weisman, Omri; Zagoory-Sharon, Orna & Feldman, Ruth. (2014). Oxytocin administration, salivary testosterone, and father–infant social behavior. *Progress in Neuro-Psychopharmacology and Biological Psychiatry*, 49(3), 47–52. doi: 10.1016/j.pnpbp.2013.11.006

Weismer, Susan E.; Venker, Courtney E.; Evans, Julia L. & Moyle, Maura J. (2013). Fast mapping in late-talking toddlers. *Applied Psycholinguistics*, 34(1), 69–89. doi: 10.1017/S0142716411000610

Weiss, Nicole H.; Tull, Matthew T.; Lavender, Jason & Gratz, Kim L. (2013). Role of emotion dysregulation in the relationship between childhood abuse and probable PTSD in a sample of substance abusers. *Child Abuse & Neglect*, 37(11), 944–954. doi: 10.1016/j.chiabu.2013.03.014

Weiss, Noel S. & Koepsell, Thomas D. (2014). *Epidemiologic methods: Studying the occurrence of illness* (2nd ed.). New York, NY: Oxford University Press.

Wellman, Henry M.; Fang, Fuxi & Peterson, Candida C. (2011). Sequential progressions in a theory-of-mind scale: Longitudinal perspectives. *Child Development*, 82(3), 780–792. doi: 10.1111/j.1467-8624.2011.01583.x

Wen, Xiaoli; Elicker, James G. & McMullen, Mary B. (2011). Early childhood teachers' curriculum beliefs: Are they consistent with observed classroom practices? *Early Education & Development*, 22(6), 945–969. doi: 10.1080/10409289.2010.507495

Wendelken, Carter; Baym, Carol L.; Gazzaley, Adam & Bunge, Silvia A. (2011). Neural indices of improved attentional modulation over middle childhood. *Developmental Cognitive Neuroscience*, 1(2), 175–186. doi: 10.1016/j.dcn.2010.11.001

Wenner, Melinda. (2009). The serious need for play. *Scientific American Mind*, 20(1), 22–29. doi: 10.1038/scientificamericanmind0209-22

Werner, Nicole E. & Hill, Laura G. (2010). Individual and peer group normative beliefs about relational aggression. *Child Development*, 81(3), 826–836. doi: 10.1111/j.1467-8624.2010.01436.x

White, Rebecca M. B.; Deardorff, Julianna; Liu, Yu & Gonzales, Nancy A. (2013). Contextual amplification or attenuation of the impact of pubertal timing on Mexican-origin boys' mental health symptoms. *Journal of Adolescent Health*, 53(6), 692–698. doi: 10.1016/j.jadohealth.2013.07.007

Whiteside-Mansell, Leanne; Bradley, Robert H.; Casey, Patrick H.; Fussell, Jill J. & Conners-Burrow, Nicola A. (2009). Triple risk: Do difficult temperament and family conflict increase the likelihood of behavioral maladjustment in children born low birth weight and preterm? *Journal of Pediatric Psychology*, 34(4), 396–405. doi: 10.1093/jpepsy/jsn089

Whitfield, Keith E. & McClearn, Gerald. (2005). Genes, environment, and race: Quantitative genetic approaches. *American Psychologist*, 60(1), 104–114. doi: 10.1037/0003-066X.60.1.104

Whittle, Sarah; Yap, Marie B. H.; Sheeber, Lisa; Dudgeon, Paul; Yücel, Murat; Pantelis, Christos, . . . Allen, Nicholas B. (2011). Hippocampal volume and sensitivity to maternal aggressive behavior: A prospective study of adolescent depressive symptoms. *Development and Psychopathology*, 23(1), 115–129. doi: 10.1017/S0954579410000684

Wicherts, Jelte M.; Dolan, Conor V. & van der Maas, Han L. J. (2010). The dangers of unsystematic selection methods and the representativeness of 46 samples of African test-takers. *Intelligence*, 38(1), 30–37. doi: 10.1016/j.intell.2009.11.003

Widman, Laura; Choukas-Bradley, Sophia; Helms, Sarah W.; Golin, Carol E. & Prinstein, Mitchell J. (2014). Sexual communication between early adolescents and their dating partners, parents, and best friends. *The Journal of Sex Research*, 51(7), 731–741. doi: 10.1080/00224499.2013.843148

Wiley, Andrea S. (2011). Milk intake and total dairy consumption: Associations with early menarche in NHANES 1999–2004. *PLoS ONE*, 6(2), e14685. doi: 10.1371/journal.pone.0014685

Wilhelm, Miriam; Dahl, Edgar; Alexander, Henry; Brähler, Elmar & Stöbel-Richter, Yve. (2013). Ethical attitudes of German specialists in reproductive medicine and legal regulation of preimplantation sex selection in Germany. *PloS*, 8(2), e56390. doi: 10.1371/journal.pone.0056390

Williams, Lela Rankin; Fox, Nathan A.; Lejuez, C. W.; Reynolds, Elizabeth K.; Henderson, Heather A.; Perez-Edgar, Koraly E., . . . Pine, Daniel S. (2010). Early temperament, propensity for risk-taking and adolescent substance-related problems: A prospective multimethod investigation. *Addictive Behaviors*, 35(2), 1148–1151. doi: 10.1016/j.addbeh.2010.07.005

Williams, Preston. (2009, March 5). Teens might need to sleep more, but schools have to work efficiently. *The Washington Post*, p. LZ10.

Willoughby, Michael T.; Mills-Koonce, W. Roger; Gottfredson, Nisha C. & Wagner, Nicholas J. (2014). Measuring callous unemotional behaviors in early childhood: Factor structure and the prediction of stable aggression in middle childhood. *Journal of Psychopathology and Behavioral Assessment*, 36(1), 30–42. doi: 10.1007/s10862-013-9379-9

Wilmshurst, Linda. (2011). *Child and adolescent psychopathology: A casebook* (2nd ed.). Thousand Oaks, CA: Sage.

Wilson, Kathryn R.; Hansen, David J. & Li, Ming. (2011). The traumatic stress response in child maltreatment and resultant neuropsychological effects. *Aggression and Violent Behavior*, 16(2), 87–97. doi: 10.1016/j.avb.2010.12.007

Winsler, Adam; Fernyhough, Charles & Montero, Ignacio (Eds.). (2009). *Private speech, executive functioning, and the development of verbal self-regulation*. New York, NY: Cambridge University Press.

Winter, Suzanne M. (2011). Culture, health, and school readiness. In DeAnna M. Laverick & Mary Renck Jalongo (Eds.), *Transitions to early care and education* (Vol. 4, pp. 117–133). New York, NY: Springer. doi: 10.1007/978-94-007-0573-9_11

Wittassek, Matthias; Koch, Holger Martin; Angerer, Jürgen & Brüning, Thomas. (2011).

Assessing exposure to phthalates—The human biomonitoring approach. *Molecular Nutrition & Food Research*, 55(1), 7–31. doi: 10.1002/mnfr.201000121

Wolak, Janis; Finkelhor, David; Mitchell, Kimberly J. & Ybarra, Michele L. (2008). Online "predators" and their victims: Myths, realities, and implications for prevention and treatment. *American Psychologist*, 63(2), 111–128. doi: 10.1037/0003-066X.63.2.111

Wolfe, Christy D.; Zhang, Jing; Kim-Spoon, Jungmeen & Bell, Martha Ann. (2014). A longitudinal perspective on the association between cognition and temperamental shyness. *International Journal of Behavioral Development*, 38(3), 266–276. doi: 10.1177/0165025413516257

Wolff, Mary S.; Teitelbaum, Susan; McGovern, K.; Windham, Gayle C.; Pinney, Susan M.; Galvez, Maida P., . . . Biro, Frank M. (2014). Phthalate exposure and pubertal development in a longitudinal study of US girls. *Human Reproduction*, 29(7), 1558–1566. doi: 10.1093/humrep/deu081

Woodrow, Christine. (2014). Refocusing our attention to children's learning and the complex interplay of context and culture. *International Journal of Early Years Education*, 22(1), 1–3. doi: 10.1080/09669760.2014.902639

Woodward, Amanda L. & Markman, Ellen M. (1998). Early word learning. In Deanna Kuhn & Robert S. Siegler (Eds.), *Handbook of child psychology* (5th ed., Vol. 2, pp. 371–420). Hoboken, NJ: Wiley.

Woodward, B. J.; Papile, L.-A.; Lowe, J. R.; Laadt, V. L.; Shaffer, M. L.; Montman, R. & Watterberg, K. L. (2011). Use of the Ages and Stages Questionnaire and Bayley Scales of Infant Development-II in neurodevelopmental follow-up of extremely low birth weight infants. *Journal of Perinatology*, 31(10), 641–646. doi: 10.1038/jp.2011.1

Woolley, Jacqueline D. & Ghossainy, Maliki E. (2013). Revisiting the fantasy–reality distinction: Children as naïve skeptics. *Child Development*, 84(5), 1496–1510. doi: 10.1111/cdev.12081

World Bank. (1994) *World development report 1994: Infrastructure for development*. New York, NY: Oxford University Press.

World Bank. (2014). *Table 2.11: World Development indicators, participation in education*. Washington, DC: World Bank.

World Bank. (2015). Population estimates and projections: Fertility and mortality by country. Retrieved from: http://datatopics.worldbank.org/hnp/popestimates#

World Health Organization. (2006). WHO Motor Development Study: Windows of achievement for six gross motor development milestones. *Acta Paediatrica*, 95(Suppl. 450), 86–95. doi: 10.1111/j.1651-2227.2006.tb02379.x

World Health Organization. (2010). WHO global infobase: NCD indicators https://apps.who.int/infobase/Indicators.aspx

World Health Organization. (2011). WHO global infobase: NCD indicators. https://apps.who.int/infobase/Indicators.aspx

World Health Organization. (2012, December 1). *Early marriages, adolescent and young pregnancies: Report by the Secretariat*. Geneva, Switzerland: World Health Organization.

World Health Organization. (2012, May 18). Progress toward interruption of wild poliovirus transmission—Worldwide, January 2011–March 2012 weekly. *Morbidity and Mortality Weekly Report*, 61(19), 353–357.

World Health Organization. (2014). Malnutrition prevalence, height for age (% of children under 5). from The World Bank

World Health Organization. (2014). Infant and young child feeding data by country. Retrieved from: http://www.who.int/nutrition/databases/infantfeeding/countries/en/

Wosje, Karen S.; Khoury, Philip R.; Claytor, Randal P.; Copeland, Kristen A.; Hornung, Richard W.; Daniels, Stephen R. & Kalkwarf, Heidi J. (2010). Dietary patterns associated with fat and bone mass in young children. *American Journal of Clinical Nutrition*, 92(2), 294–303. doi: 10.3945/ajcn.2009.28925

Wu, Pai-Lu & Chiou, Wen-Bin. (2008). Postformal thinking and creativity among late adolescents: A post-Piagetian approach. *Adolescence*, 43(170), 237–251.

Xu, Fei. (2013). The object concept in human infants: Commentary on fields. *Human Development*, 56(3), 167–170. doi: 10.1159/000351279

Xu, Fei & Kushnir, Tamar. (2013). Infants are rational constructivist learners. *Current Directions in Psychological Science*, 22(1), 28–32. doi: 10.1177/0963721412469396

Xu, Yaoying. (2010). Children's social play sequence: Parten's classic theory revisited. *Early Child Development and Care*, 180(4), 489–498. doi: 10.1080/03004430802090430

Yadav, Priyanka; Banwari, Girish; Parmar, Chirag & Maniar, Rajesh. (2013). Internet addiction and its correlates among high school students: A preliminary study from Ahmedabad, India. *Asian Journal of Psychiatry*, 6(6), 500–505. doi: 10.1016/j.ajp.2013.06.004

Yamaguchi, Susumu; Greenwald, Anthony G.; Banaji, Mahzarin R.; Murakami, Fumio; Chen, Daniel; Shiomura, Kimihiro, . . . Krendl, Anne. (2007). Apparent universality of positive implicit self-esteem. *Psychological Science*, 18(6), 498–500. doi: 10.1111/j.1467-9280.2007.01928.x

Yang, Rongwang; Zhang, Suhan; Li, Rong & Zhao, Zhengyan. (2013). Parents' attitudes toward stimulants use in China. *Journal of Developmental & Behavioral Pediatrics*, 34(3), 225. doi: 10.1097/DBP.0b013e318287cc27

Yom-Tov, Elad; Fernandez-Luque, Luis; Weber, Ingmar & Crain, Steven P. (2012). Pro-anorexia and pro-recovery photo sharing: A tale of two warring tribes. *Journal of Medical Internet Research*, 14(6), e151. doi: 10.2196/jmir.2239

Young, Elizabeth A.; Korszun, Ania; Figueiredo, Helmer F.; Banks-Solomon, Matia & Herman, James P. (2008). Sex differences in HPA axis regulation. In Jill B. Becker, et al. (Eds.), *Sex differences in the brain: From genes to behavior* (pp. 95–105). New York, NY: Oxford University Press.

Young, John K. (2010). Anorexia nervosa and estrogen: Current status of the hypothesis. *Neuroscience & Biobehavioral Reviews, 34*(8), 1195–1200. doi: 10.1016/j.neubiorev.2010.01.015

Yu, Xiao-ming; Guo, Shuai-jun & Sun, Yu-ying. (2013). Sexual behaviours and associated risks in Chinese young people: A meta-analysis. *Sexual Health, 10*(5), 424–433. doi: 10.1071/SH12140

Yurovsky, Daniel; Fricker, Damian C.; Yu, Chen & Smith, Linda B. (2014). The role of partial knowledge in statistical word learning. *Psychonomic Bulletin & Review, 21*(1), 1–22. doi: 10.3758/s13423-013-0443-y

Zachry, Anne H. & Kitzmann, Katherine M. (2011). Caregiver awareness of prone play recommendations. *American Journal of Occupational Therapy, 65*(1), 101–105. doi: 10.5014/ajot.2011.09100

Zahn-Waxler, Carolyn; Park, Jong-Hyo; Usher, Barbara; Belouad, Francesca; Cole, Pamela & Gruber, Reut. (2008). Young children's representations of conflict and distress: A longitudinal study of boys and girls with disruptive behavior problems. *Development and Psychopathology, 20*(1), 99–119. doi: 10.1017/S0954579408000059

Zak, Paul J. (2012). *The moral molecule: The source of love and prosperity.* New York, NY: Dutton.

Zalenski, Robert J. & Raspa, Richard. (2006). Maslow's hierarchy of needs: A framework for achieving human potential in hospice. *Journal of Palliative Medicine, 9*(5), 1120–1127. doi: 10.1089/jpm.2006.9.1120

Zani, Bruna & Cicognani, Elvira. (2006). Sexuality and intimate relationships in adolescence. In Sandy Jackson & Luc Goossens (Eds.), *Handbook of adolescent development* (pp. 200–222). New York, NY: Psychology Press.

Zapf, Jennifer A. & Smith, Linda B. (2007). When do children generalize the plural to novel nouns? *First Language, 27*(1), 53–73. doi: 10.1177/0142723707070286

Zatorre, Robert J. (2013). Predispositions and plasticity in music and speech learning: Neural correlates and implications. *Science, 342*(6158), 585–589. doi: 10.1126/science.1238414

Zavos, Helena M. S.; Gregory, Alice M. & Eley, Thalia C. (2012). Longitudinal genetic analysis of anxiety sensitivity. *Developmental Psychology, 48*(1), 204–212. doi: 10.1037/a0024996

Zeanah, Charles H.; Berlin, Lisa J. & Boris, Neil W. (2011). Practitioner review: Clinical applications of attachment theory and research for infants and young children. *Journal of Child Psychology and Psychiatry, 52*(8), 819–833. doi: 10.1111/j.1469-7610.2011.02399.x

Zehr, Mary Ann. (2011b). Study stings KIPP on attrition rates. *Education Week, 30*(27), 1, 24–25.

Zeiders, Katharine H.; Umaña-Taylor, Adriana J. & Derlan, Chelsea L. (2013). Trajectories of depressive symptoms and self-esteem in Latino youths: Examining the role of gender and perceived discrimination. *Developmental Psychology, 49*(5), 951–963. doi: 10.1037/a0028866

Zeifman, Debra M. (2013). Built to bond: Coevolution, coregulation, and plasticity in parent-infant bonds. In Cindy Hazan & Mary I. Campa (Eds.), *Human bonding: The science of affectional ties* (pp. 41–73). New York, NY: Guilford Press.

Zentall, Shannon R. & Morris, Bradley J. (2010). "Good job, you're so smart": The effects of inconsistency of praise type on young children's motivation. *Journal of Experimental Child Psychology, 107*(2), 155–163. doi: 10.1016/j.jecp.2010.04.015

Zentner, Marcel & Mitura, Klaudia. (2012). Stepping out of the caveman's shadow: Nations' gender gap predicts degree of sex differentiation in mate preferences. *Psychological Science, 23*(10), 1176–1185. doi: 10.1177/0956797612441004

Zhao, Jinxia & Wang, Meifang. (2014). Mothers' academic involvement and children's achievement: Children's theory of intelligence as a mediator. *Learning and Individual Differences, 35*, 130–136. doi: 10.1016/j.lindif.2014.06.006

Zhu, Qi; Song, Yiying; Hu, Siyuan; Li, Xiaobai; Tian, Moqian; Zhen, Zonglei, . . . Liu, Jia. (2010). Heritability of the specific cognitive ability of face perception. *Current Biology, 20*(2), 137–142. doi: 10.1016/j.cub.2009.11.067

Zhu, Weimo; Boiarskaia, Elena A.; Welk, Gregory J. & Meredith, Marilu D. (2010). Physical education and school contextual factors relating to students' achievement and cross-grade differences in aerobic fitness and obesity. *Research Quarterly for Exercise and Sport, 81*(Suppl. 3), S53–S64. doi: 10.5641/027013610X13100547898194

Zhu, Ying; Zhang, Li; Fan, Jin & Han, Shihui. (2007). Neural basis of cultural influence on self-representation. *NeuroImage, 34*(3), 1310–1316. doi: 10.1016/j.neuroimage.2006.08.047

Zhu, Zengrong & Huangfu, Danwei. (2013). Human pluripotent stem cells: An emerging model in developmental biology. *Development, 140*, 705–717. doi: 10.1242/dev.086165

Zieber, Nicole; Kangas, Ashley; Hock, Alyson & Bhatt, Ramesh S. (2014). Infants' perception of emotion from body movements. *Child Development, 85*(2), 675–684. doi: 10.1111/cdev.12134

Zimmer, Carl. (2009). On the origin of sexual reproduction. *Science, 324*(5932), 1254–1256. doi: 10.1126/science.324_1254

Zimmer-Gembeck, Melanie J. & Collins, W. Andrew. (2003). Autonomy development during adolescence. In Gerald R. Adams & Michael D. Berzonsky (Eds.), *Blackwell handbook of adolescence* (pp. 175–204). Malden, MA: Blackwell.

Zimmer-Gembeck, Melanie J. & Ducat, Wendy. (2010). Positive and negative romantic relationship quality: Age, familiarity, attachment and well-being as correlates of couple agreement and projection. *Journal of Adolescence, 33*(6), 879–890. doi: 10.1016/j.adolescence.2010.07.008

Zimmerman, Frederick J. (2014). Where's the beef? A comment on Ferguson and Donnellan (2014). *Developmental Psychology, 50*(1), 138–140. doi: 10.1037/a0035087

Zimmerman, Frederick J.; Christakis, Dimitri A. & Meltzoff, Andrew N. (2007). Associations between media viewing and language development in children under age 2 years. *The Journal of Pediatrics, 151*(4), 364–368. doi: 10.1016/j.jpeds.2007.04.071

Zimmerman, Marc A.; Stoddard, Sarah A.; Eisman, Andria B.; Caldwell, Cleopatra H.; Aiyer, Sophie M. & Miller, Alison. (2013). Adolescent resilience: Promotive factors that inform prevention. *Child Development Perspectives, 7*(4), 215–220. doi: 10.1111/cdep.12042

Zosuls, Kristina M.; Martin, Carol Lynn; Ruble, Diane N.; Miller, Cindy F.; Gaertner, Bridget M.; England, Dawn E. & Hill, Alison P. (2011). "It's not that we hate you": Understanding children's gender attitudes and expectancies about peer relationships. *British Journal of Developmental Psychology, 29*(2), 288–304. doi: 10.1111/j.2044-835X.2010.02023.x

Zucker, Kenneth J.; Cohen-Kettenis, Peggy T.; Drescher, Jack; Meyer-Bahlburg, Heino F. L.; Pfäfflin, Friedemann & Womack, William M. (2013). Memo outlining evidence for change for Gender Identity Disorder in the DSM-5. *Archives of Sexual Behavior, 42*(5), 901–914. doi: 10.1007/s10508-013-0139-4

Name Index

Subject Index

Note: Page numbers followed by f, p, or t indicate features, photographs, or tables respectively.